Law, Business, and Society

Twelfth Edition

Tony McAdams
University of Northern Iowa

Kiren Dosanjh Zucker
California State University, Northridge

Kristofer Neslund
Ashland University

Kari Smoker
State University of New York, The College at Brockport

Mc
Graw
Hill
Education

LAW, BUSINESS, AND SOCIETY, TWELFTH EDITION

Published by McGraw-Hill Education, 2 Penn Plaza, New York, NY 10121. Copyright © 2018 by McGraw-Hill Education. All rights reserved. Printed in the United States of America. Previous editions © 2015, 2012, and 2009. No part of this publication may be reproduced or distributed in any form or by any means, or stored in a database or retrieval system, without the prior written consent of McGraw-Hill Education, including, but not limited to, in any network or other electronic storage or transmission, or broadcast for distance learning.

Some ancillaries, including electronic and print components, may not be available to customers outside the United States.

This book is printed on acid-free paper.

1 2 3 4 5 6 7 8 9 LCR 21 20 19 18 17

ISBN 978-1-259-72188-5
MHID 1-259-72188-4

Executive Portfolio Manager: *Kathleen Klehr*
Product Developers: *Jaroslaw Szymanski; Michael McCormick*
Marketing Manager: *Michelle Williams*
Content Project Managers: *Heather Ervolino; Angela Norris*
Buyer: *Susan K. Culbertson*
Design: *Jessica Cuevas*
Content Licensing Specialist: *DeAnna Dausener*
Cover Image: *©Sokolova23/Shutterstock.com*
Compositor: *Aptara®, Inc.*

All credits appearing on page or at the end of the book are considered to be an extension of the copyright page.

Library of Congress Cataloging-in-Publication Data

Names: McAdams, Tony, author. | Zucker, Kiren Dosanjh, author. | Neslund, Nancy, author. | Neslund, Kristofer, author.
Title: Law, business, and society / Tony McAdams, University of Northern Iowa; Kiren Dosanjh Zucker, California State University, Northridge; Nancy Neslund, University of New Hampshire School of Law; Kristofer Neslund, Ashland University.
Description: Twelfth edition. | New York, NY : McGraw-Hill Education, [2018] | Includes index.
Identifiers: LCCN 2017026377| ISBN 9781259721885 (alk. paper) | ISBN 1259721884 (alk. paper)
Subjects: LCSH: Business enterprises—Law and legislation—United States. | Trade regulation—United States. | Business ethics—United States. | LCGFT: Textbooks.
Classification: LCC KF1355 .M28 2018 | DDC 346.73/065—dc23
LC record available at https://lccn.loc.gov/

2017026377

mheducation.com/highered

About the Authors

Tony McAdams

Tony McAdams is an Emeritus Professor of Management at the University of Northern Iowa. He earned a BA in History from the University of Northern Iowa, a JD from the University of Iowa, and an MBA from Columbia University. Professor McAdams' primary teaching interests include government regulation of business, business and society, and employment law. Professor McAdams' research interests include managerial accountability, business ethics, and employment law. His scholarly articles have appeared in such journals as *The Harvard Business Review*, *The Academy of Management Review*, *The Journal of Business Ethics*, and *The American Business Law Journal*. Professor McAdams received the Iowa Board of Regents Award for Faculty Excellence, the Distinguished Teacher of the Year Award from the student government at the University of Kentucky, and the University of Northern Iowa College of Business Administration Excellence in Teaching Award.

Kiren Dosanjh Zucker

Kiren Dosanjh Zucker, author of Chapters 4, 6, 7, 12, 13, and 14, is a Professor of Accounting at California State University, Northridge (CSUN). She earned a BA in Political Science from Syracuse University and a JD from the University of Michigan. A member of the State Bar of California, she has served on its Committee of Bar Examiners and Committee on Professional Responsibility and Conduct. Her teaching and research interests focus primarily on employment law, pedagogy, and accounting ethics. In 2001, she was selected as a Master Teacher by the Academy of Legal Studies in Business, and in 2004 she received the Outstanding Faculty Award from CSUN's Students with Disabilities Resources Center. In 2004 and 2006, she also received a CSUN University Ambassadors' Polished Apple Award. In 2014, CSUN Accounting students named her the Harvey A. Bookstein Accounting Professor of the Year, and in 2015, she received the Master of Science in Accountancy Program's Outstanding Teaching Award.

Kristofer Neslund

Kristofer Neslund, author of Chapter 9, is Associate Professor of Accounting at Ashland University. He holds a DBA from Kent State University, a JD from Lewis and Clark College, and an LLM in taxation from New York University. He is a CPA and a member of the Oregon bar. Prior to entering academia, he was a tax partner in two law firms, as well as the CFO of a telecommunications company operating in three western states. During the academic year 2004 to 2005, he was a visiting professor in the Master of Professional Accountancy program at UNITEC in New Zealand, and a visiting professor of law at the Europa Universität Viadrina in Germany and La Trobe University in Australia. Dr. Neslund has more recently been a visiting professor of law at the University of New

Hampshire and Roger Williams University. He was selected for a Fulbright Scholarship in Accounting at the University of Iceland for 2015. His research interests are corporate governance, the regulation of the accounting profession, securities regulation, and taxation. He is presently the president of the Tri-State Academy of Legal Studies in Business and president-elect of Region 4 of the Accreditation Council for Business Schools and Programs.

Kari Smoker

Kari Smoker, author of Chapters 16, 17, and 18, is an Associate Professor of Accounting at the State University of New York, The College at Brockport. She earned a BA in Mathematics–Statistics and Economics from the University of Rochester, a JD from The Ohio State University, and a Master's of Taxation from Golden Gate University, School of Taxation. She is also a Certified Fraud Examiner. Prior to entering academia, she worked in public accounting at Arthur Andersen and also as an associate attorney at two law firms. She served as president of the Greater Rochester Association for Women Attorneys and continues to serve as a committee member for the Rochester Business Ethics Foundation. During the academic years 2004 to 2010, she was a visiting professor at St. John Fisher College. She teaches tax law as well as government and nonprofit accounting. In 2009, she received the *Rochester Business Journal*'s Forty under 40 Award, and in 2014 and 2015, she received the Faculty of the Year Award from SUNY Brockport's School of Business Administration and Economics. In 2017, she received the President's Award for Excellence in Teaching at SUNY Brockport.

Preface

Approach

Our primary goal is to provoke student thought. To that end, we place heavy emphasis on analysis. We consider the questions we ask more important than the answers to those questions. We introduce the student to existing policy in the various substantive areas to encourage understanding and retention, as well as careful thought about the desirability of those policies.

Our book takes a strong public policy orientation. Attention in Unit I to political economy and ethics is a necessary foundation on which the student can build a logical understanding of the regulatory process. Thereafter, those business and society themes persist throughout the book. In virtually every chapter, we look beyond the law itself to other social and environmental forces. For example, in the antitrust chapters, economic philosophy is of great importance. Antitrust is explored as a matter of national social policy. We argue that antitrust has a good deal to do with the direction of American life generally. Law is at the heart of the fair employment practices section, but we also present material from management, sociology, history, and popular culture to treat fair employment as an issue of public policy rather than as a series of narrower technical legal disputes. The law is studied in the economic, social, and political context from which it springs. These multidimensional approaches characterize most chapters as we attempt to examine the various topics as a whole and in context. At the same time, the law remains the core of the book.

Broadly, our adjustments for this twelfth edition were designed to refresh the book and achieve increased reader interest, but more specifically this edition is directed to the nation's ongoing debate about how much government we need in our lives, particularly in our business lives. International issues also receive extensive attention, as well as critics of business values and the American legal system. Although the general structure and philosophy of the book are unchanged, we have made significant revisions including many new questions and several new law cases. Law cases are long enough to clearly express the essence of the decision while challenging the reader's intellect.

WHAT'S NEW

Chapter 1 includes discussion of the Wells Fargo scandal, an updated overview of economics and politics in China and Russia, and a brief glimpse at Brexit as well as Martin Shkreli, indicted financier and exploiter of the U.S. pharmaceutical market. Thomas Piketty's highly publicized research examining income inequality and the decline of the middle class is also discussed.

Chapter 2 offers updated discussions of the governmental response to the role of big banks in the Great Recession that resulted in large fines for big banks but few white-collar imprisonments. General Motors' ignition switch failure is examined as a business ethics/

criminal scandal, and a brief case study of the ethical implications of working for a boss who is an authoritarian "jerk" also is provided.

Chapter 3 examines criticism of a "rigged" U.S. tax code permitting tax havens abroad, as well as corporate and family wealth as threats to democracy, along with evidence of an increasing embrace of social responsibility by the business community and millennials. The decision of Dan Price, Gravity Payments CEO, to implement a $70,000 minimum wage for his employees also is discussed.

Chapter 4 poses such questions as whether a Missouri court can assert jurisdiction over a Texas vehicle dealership in a breach of contract claim brought by a Missouri resident who purchased a truck on eBay from it, and whether an employer's discovery request for an employee's cellphone GPS records to defend against a wage claim should be granted. The discussion of whether a party to a lawsuit can be served a summons via Facebook is updated. Whether online legal services such as the smartphone app Shake resolve or make starker the differences in access to justice also is considered. Discussion of the bill "The Fairness in Class Action Litigation Act of 2017" is included.

Chapter 5 looks at the case of Barronelle Stutzman, the Washington floral shop owner who declined to sell flowers for use by her friend in his same-sex marriage, as well as the 2015 *Obergefell* Supreme Court decision affirming a constitutional right to same-sex marriage. The discussion of hate speech is updated to include the fear arising from Donald Trump's rhetoric, as well as a look at the controversial Oregon rock band's name: "The Slants."

Chapter 6 offers an updated look at contractual principles that will engage today's college student. A new Legal Briefcase rules on the issue of whether a liability release signed by a gym member who does not speak or read English is enforceable. A new heading on the Uniform Electronic Transactions Act (UETA) includes a discussion of a 2016 Massachusetts case on whether text messages satisfy the Statute of Frauds, and a "box question" on contract negotiations via text messaging that includes an "emoji-only" reply. A new Internet question asks students to compare the 2016 trial of a Thomas Jefferson School of Law graduate's fraud claim against the law school with fraud claims brought against Trump University. One of the new chapter-end questions considers an Indian Sikh's son's 2016 modern *Hamer v. Sidway* claim. Updated examples include agricultural drones replacing computer sales to illustrate compensatory damages for sales of goods contracts.

Chapter 7, using recent cases arising from secret picture taking and videotaping in gym locker rooms, updates its discussion of invasion of privacy while posing challenging questions requiring students to compare and contrast sets of facts, and consider whether and in what circumstances secretly taking images of another should be a crime. A new Legal Briefcase on negligence asks: should a restaurant serving "sizzling platters" be held liable for injuries suffered by a customer who prayed over the food at his table? The bill the Lawsuit Abuse Reduction Act of 2017 is discussed. The case of the parents of an Aurora, Colorado, movie theater shooting victim who had to pay the legal fees of the gun ammunition sellers they had sued is also offered for discussion. A chapter-end question on initial lawsuits arising from the December 2016 Ghost Ship fire in Oakland, California, in which dozens of people attending an electronic music concert in a warehouse zoned for commercial purposes were killed, asks students to identify defendants and possible claims.

Chapter 8 provides a discussion of the growing federal–state, and state versus state, conflict over marijuana legalization, as well as the Federal Communications Commission's treatment of the Internet as a public utility, thus subjecting it to greater government oversight including net neutrality. Also discussed is whether the "new economy" including ride-sharing services (Uber) and short-term rentals (Airbnb) need more regulation.

Chapter 9 includes a new heading on activist investors, recounting the history of shareholder activism from hostile takeovers in the 1980s to today's campaigns to improve management and board performance, as well as a new heading on major issues faced by boards of directors, including cybersecurity. An updated discussion of securities crowdfunding is also provided. The 2016 U.S. Supreme Court case of *Salman v. United States* on whether the tipper has to receive a personal benefit to be held liable for insider trading is included as a new Legal Briefcase.

Chapter 10 examines critics' arguments for enhanced antitrust enforcement as a remedy for high prices, income and wealth inequality, barriers to new competition, and the distortion of democracy. The application of antitrust law to daily life, including the price of beer, human eggs, and e-books, is discussed, along with athletes' claims against the NCAA. Antitrust law's application to employee "poaching" policies in the Silicon Valley also is included.

Chapter 11 poses challenging questions such as: Are tech giants like Amazon abusive monopolies? Is industry consolidation a threat to the economy? The AB InBev's merger with SABMiller and other proposed mergers, including one among all of the world's leading agrichemical giants, also are highlighted. The Federal Trade Commission's lawsuit blocking the proposed Staples–Office Depot merger also is included.

Chapter 12 updates employment law issues and trends, including an introductory discussion of a case that asks if an employer should be allowed to terminate an employee for using medical marijuana with a state-issued license. The impact of the "gig" or "on-demand" economy and the employment relationship is explored. Along with a new sub-heading on "Online Reputation" of job applicants, the discussion of résumé fraud is updated. The current status of an Obama administration overtime pay rule is offered, as well as updates on the minimum wage. The impact of labor regulations on unpaid internships is explored through a box highlighting the Conde Nast fellowship program. The impact of employer-led "fitness tracker" programs and competitions also is offered for discussion. A new Legal Briefcase asks whether an at-will employee can sue an employer for fraud. The Deepwater Horizon discussion is updated with a video clip from a recent movie inspired by those events. Millennials' possible impact on the enforceability of restrictive covenants also is offered as a point to consider.

Chapter 13 updates the religious accommodation case against Abercrombie & Fitch, and discusses the EEOC's November 2016 Enforcement Guidance on National Origin Discrimination that brings the new glossary term "intersectional discrimination." The debate over the EEOC's systemic enforcement approach is offered with reference to the Texas Roadhouse case, and the 2017–2021 EEOC Strategic Enforcement Plan also is covered. The "gender gap" in workplace opportunities that may have resulted from employers' anti-harassment policies is discussed, and chapter-end questions cover recent high-profile racial harassment and discrimination claims. A disability discrimination claim of a grocery store bagger with Down syndrome who was fired for cursing and insulting a cashier in the presence of customers also is included. A box on high-profile claims of sex discrimination in Silicon Valley offers questions on workplace culture. Competing Executive Orders on sexual orientation and gender identity discrimination protections between the Obama and Trump administrations are included. A new Legal Briefcase offers a fresh look at disparate impact in an appellate decision on a claim brought by prison guards.

Chapter 14 integrates the 2015 NLRB election rule and provides updates that include discussion of recent NLRB cases on social media postings as protected activity, political pins at work, and ethics questions regarding the use of prisoners as laborers. The U.S. Supreme Court's 2014 decision in *Harris v. Quinn* is discussed, and the "right to work" material is updated. An emerging approach to farm labor practices is highlighted.

Chapter 15 includes discussion of the fraud allegations against Trump University, as well as celebrity bankruptcies. The Food and Drug Administration's decision to regulate e-cigarettes also is discussed.

Chapter 16 discusses how globalism, and, alternatively, the recent surge in nationalism, may influence trade and immigration policies. The impact of Brexit on trade agreements is examined. Facebook's efforts to update its global community standards to protect minority groups around the world and its collaborative effort to counter hate speech in Germany are discussed, along with the broader question of whether and to what extent Internet providers have a responsibility to regulate "fake news" posted on their news feeds. The European Union's $14.6 billion tax assessment against Apple also is discussed. Updated cases explore corporations' liability for tortious acts overseas, including a chapter-end question on the aiding and abetting of child slavery in the Ivory Coast.

Chapter 17 includes discussion of the ethical aspects of the water crisis in Flint, Michigan, and the socioeconomic factors that may have made the community more vulnerable to environmental injustice. The Fiat Chrysler and Volkswagen emission scandals also are explored. A discussion of the Paris Agreement reached at the 2015 Paris Climate Change Conference is included, along with a chapter-end question exploring how the 2016 Dakota Access Pipeline controversy highlights the environmental justice issues faced by Native Americans.

Chapter 18 offers an updated discussion of net neutrality and open Internet rules in the United States, as well as of the European Union's new General Data Protection Regulation (effective 2018) and the EU-US Privacy Shield.

OVERVIEW

This text is directed to courses at both the upper-division undergraduate and masters levels in the legal environment of business, government and business, and business and society. Authors of textbooks in these areas often rely on a single discipline (for example, law, economics, or management) as the foundation for their efforts. In this text, we take an interdisciplinary approach, using elements of law, political economy, international business, ethics, social responsibility, and management. This large task necessarily requires certain trade-offs, but we hope the product will more accurately capture the fullness of the business environment.

Our primary goal is to produce an interesting, provocative reading experience. Naturally, accuracy and reasonable comprehensiveness cannot be sacrificed. Our feeling, however, is that a law text can be both intellectually and emotionally engaging without sacrificing substantive ends. To meet our objective, we have presented the bulk of the book in the form of contemporary legal and ethical conflicts emerging from today's news. We have provided scholarly results, surveys, polls, data, anecdotes, and other specific details that lend credibility, immediacy, and interest to the reading experience.

The book is divided into five units, as follows:

Unit I—Business and Society.   We do not begin with the law. Rather, in Chapter 1 (Capitalism and the Role of Government), Chapter 2 (Business Ethics), and Chapter 3 (The Corporation and Public Policy: Expanding Responsibilities), we describe some of the economic and social forces that shape our legal system.

The goals of Unit I are to (a) enhance student awareness of the many societal influences on business; (b) establish the business context from which government regulation arose; and (c) explore the roles of the free market, government intervention, and individual and corporate ethics in shaping business behavior.

The student must understand not merely the law but the law in context. What forces have provoked government intervention in business? What alternatives to our current "mixed economy" might prove healthy? These considerations help the students respond to one of the critical questions of the day: To what extent, if any, should we regulate business?

Unit II—Introduction to Law.   Chapter 4 (The American Legal System) and Chapter 5 (Constitutional Law and the Bill of Rights) survey the foundations of our legal system. Here we set out the "nuts and bolts" of law, combining cases and narrative. Then with Chapter 6 (Contracts) and Chapter 7 (Business Torts and Product Liability), we examine the foundations of business law.

Unit III—Trade Regulation and Antitrust.   Chapter 8 (Government Regulation of Business) raises the book's central policy inquiry: When should the government intervene in business practice? Chapter 9 (Business Organizations and Securities Regulation), Chapter 10 (Antitrust Law—Restraints of Trade), and Chapter 11 (Antitrust Law—Monopolies and Mergers) survey the core of government oversight of business.

Unit IV—Employer–Employee Relations.   Chapter 12 (Employment Law I: Employee Rights), Chapter 13 (Employment Law II: Discrimination), and Chapter 14 (Employment Law III: Labor–Management Relations) are intended not only to survey the law in those areas, but also to introduce some of the sensitive and provocative social issues that have led to today's extensive government intervention in the employment relationship.

Unit V—Selected Topics in Government–Business Relations.   Two of the closing chapters of this book—Chapter 15 (Consumer Protection) and Chapter 17 (Environmental Protection)—emphasize the dramatic expansion of the public's demands for socially responsible conduct in business. Chapter 16 (International Ethics and Law) provides an overview of the legal and ethical issues emerging from global business practice, and Chapter 18 (Internet Law and Ethics) surveys some cyberlaw and ethics problems.

ACCREDITATION

Our text conforms to Association to Advance Collegiate Schools of Business (AACSB) International accreditation standards.

Two chapters are devoted exclusively to ethics, and ethics themes emerge throughout the book. The chapter on employment discrimination should be quite helpful in aiding students' understanding of diversity issues. Ethics and social responsibility are at the heart of the text rather than an afterthought to meet accreditation standards.

Furthermore, as required by the rapidly changing nature of commerce and as recommended by the AACSB, the text devotes extensive attention to legal and ethical issues arising from international business. Various topics throughout the text (for example, comparative economic systems, the Foreign Corrupt Practices Act, and global pollution) afford the student a sense of the worldwide implications of American business practice, and Chapter 16 is entirely devoted to international themes.

KEY FEATURES

Approximately 150 boxed features and ethics vignettes place the law in a practical context and offer many provocative opportunities for discussion.

Privatize Higher Education?

The Anderson School of Management at the University of California at Los Angeles (UCLA) in 2014 entered a three-year agreement with UCLA to substantially privatize its prestigious MBA program. The program will keep most of its income and spend that income on raising its academic profile to better compete with Harvard, Stanford, and the like. Other academic institutions, including the University of Virginia, have been significantly privatized in recent years.

Those opposing Anderson's privatization fear that UCLA's responsibilities for the general welfare may be replaced by the more self-interested goals of those running the MBA program, its donors, and the business community. They argue that a privatized program might be more likely to allow admission to a major donor's child, shape its research agenda to conform to the interests of corporate donors, diminish its attention to community needs, or eventually replace merit-based admission with an auction allowing space to the highest bidders.

Questions
1. *a.* If it is not already, should your college or university become a for-profit institution?
   b. How would your education change?
   c. How would you change?
2. Would our current system of higher education benefit from aggressive private-sector competition or is the current competition among schools sufficient? Explain.

PRACTICING ETHICS | Technology and Loneliness

Since publishing *Bowling Alone,* Robert Putnam has said we need to develop new kinds of connections when old ones die. Electronic links often are considered part of the problem, but he believes they could also be part of the solution. Indeed, a 2008 survey of American adults found 60 percent saying that new technologies had not affected the closeness of their families and a 2011 study found that self-reported feelings of empathy were higher among college students the more time they spent on Facebook. On the other hand, a 2009 Pew report found that social networking users are 26 percent less likely than others to turn to their neighbors for companionship, and a 2016 study of U.K. college students found a negative association between "excessive" Twitter use and "real life" social interaction. MIT professor Sherry Turkle says that we have sacrificed conversation for "mere connection":

> We've become accustomed to a new way of being "along together." Technology-enabled, we are able to be with one

another, and also elsewhere, connected to wherever we want to be.[128]

Questions

1. In your view, is Turkle correct? Explain.

2. How might our ethical standards and performances be affected by excessive reliance on social technology?

Sources: Charles M. Blow, "Friends, Neighbors and Facebook," *The New York Times,* June 11, 2010 [**www.nytimes.com**]; Yamikani Ndasauka et al., "Excessive Use of Twitter Among College Students in the UK," *Computers in Human Behavior* 55, part B (February 2016), p. 963; Donna St. George, "Internet, Cell Phones May Strengthen Family Unit, Study Finds," October 20, 2008, p. A07 [**www.washingtonpost.com**]; and Shirley S. Wang, "Could Those Hours Online Be Making Kids Nicer?" *The Wall Street Journal,* August 16, 2011, p. D1.

Approximately 200 selected websites appear throughout this edition. Each chapter includes at least one Internet Exercise.

 McGraw-Hill Connect® is a highly reliable, easy-to-use homework and learning management solution that utilizes learning science and award-winning adaptive tools to improve student results.

Homework and Adaptive Learning

- Connect's assignments help students contextualize what they've learned through application, so they can better understand the material and think critically.

- Connect will create a personalized study path customized to individual student needs through SmartBook®.

- SmartBook helps students study more efficiently by delivering an interactive reading experience through adaptive highlighting and review.

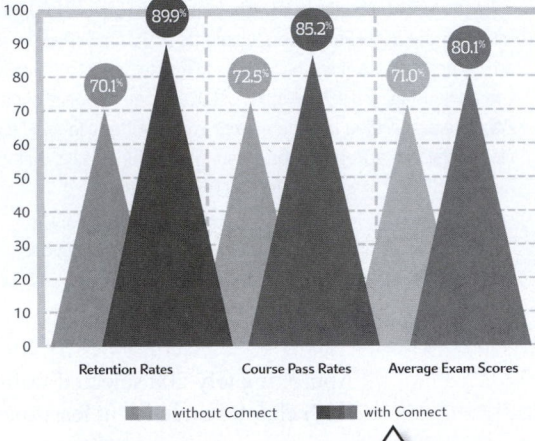

Connect's Impact on Retention Rates, Pass Rates, and Average Exam Scores

without Connect | with Connect

Over **7 billion questions** have been answered, making McGraw-Hill Education products more intelligent, reliable, and precise.

Using **Connect** improves retention rates by **19.8%**, passing rates by **12.7%, and** exam scores by **9.1%.**

73% of instructors who use **Connect** require it; instructor satisfaction **increases** by 28% when **Connect** is required.

Quality Content and Learning Resources

- Connect content is authored by the world's best subject matter experts, and is available to your class through a simple and intuitive interface.

- The Connect eBook makes it easy for students to access their reading material on smartphones and tablets. They can study on the go and don't need internet access to use the eBook as a reference, with full functionality.

- Multimedia content such as videos, simulations, and games drive student engagement and critical thinking skills.

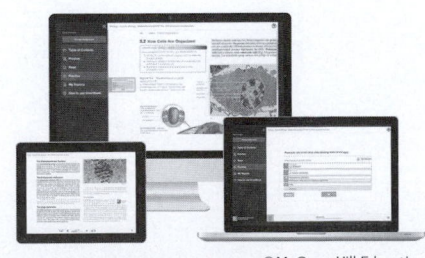

Robust Analytics and Reporting

©Hero Images/Getty Images

- Connect Insight® generates easy-to-read reports on individual students, the class as a whole, and on specific assignments.

- The Connect Insight dashboard delivers data on performance, study behavior, and effort. Instructors can quickly identify students who struggle and focus on material that the class has yet to master.

- Connect automatically grades assignments and quizzes, providing easy-to-read reports on individual and class performance.

Impact on Final Course Grade Distribution

	without Connect	with Connect
A	22.9%	31.0%
B	27.4%	34.3%
C	22.9%	18.7%
D	11.5%	6.1%
F	15.4%	9.9%

More students earn **As** and **Bs** when they use **Connect**.

Trusted Service and Support

- Connect integrates with your LMS to provide single sign-on and automatic syncing of grades. Integration with Blackboard®, D2L®, and Canvas also provides automatic syncing of the course calendar and assignment-level linking.

- Connect offers comprehensive service, support, and training throughout every phase of your implementation.

- If you're looking for some guidance on how to use Connect, or want to learn tips and tricks from super users, you can find tutorials as you work. Our Digital Faculty Consultants and Student Ambassadors offer insight into how to achieve the results you want with Connect.

www.mheducation.com/connect

INSTRUCTOR RESOURCES

Instructor's Manual

A package of supplementary materials is included in the instructor's manual. Those materials include (1) chapter outlines, (2) general advice regarding the goals and purposes of the chapters, (3) summaries of the law cases, and (4) answers for the questions raised in the text.

Test Bank and Quizzes

Instructors can test students using a vast bank of test and quiz questions divided by chapter.

PowerPoints

This edition's revised PowerPoints contain an easy-to-follow lecture outline summarizing key points for every chapter.

You Be the Judge

This interactive product features case videos that showcase courtroom arguments of business law cases. These case videos give students the opportunity to watch profile interviews of the plaintiff and defendant; read background information; hear each case; review the evidence; make their decisions; and then access an actual, unscripted judge's decision and reasoning.

Business Law Newsletter

McGraw-Hill Education's monthly Business Law newsletter, *Proceedings*, is designed specifically with the Business Law educator in mind. *Proceedings* incorporates "hot topics" in business law, video suggestions, an ethical dilemma, teaching tips, and a "chapter key" cross-referencing newsletter topics with the various McGraw-Hill Education business law textbooks. *Proceedings* is delivered via e-mail to business law instructors each month.

Videos

Links to brief videos for classroom use are provided.

Business Law Case Repository

The Case Repository is a collection of cases from previous editions.

ACKNOWLEDGMENTS

Completion of the twelfth edition of this book depended, in significant part, on the hard work of others.

The authors are pleased to acknowledge the contributions of these good people: Heather Ervolino, Content Project Manager; Jaroslaw Szymanski, Product Developer; Kathleen Klehr, Executive Brand Manager; and Tim Vertovec, Managing Director.

The authors also thank the reviewers:

Steve Abraham, *State University of New York*

Wayne Anderson, *Missouri State University*

Teresa Brosnan, *Seattle University*

Nathaniel Gallegos, *Chadron State College*

Eloise Hassell, *University of North Carolina at Greensboro*

Stephanie Joseph, *Winston Salem State University*

Susan O'Sullivan-Gavin, *Rider University*

Kenneth Taurman, *Indiana University Southeast*

SUGGESTIONS

The authors welcome comments and feedback from all readers.

Kiren Dosanjh Zucker

Brief Contents

Contents

UNIT TWO
INTRODUCTION TO LAW   135

Chapter 4
The American Legal System   136

Chapter 5
Constitutional Law and the Bill
of Rights   183

Chapter 9
Business Organizations and Securities Regulation   370

Chapter 10
Antitrust Law—Restraints of Trade   440

Chapter 11
Antitrust Law—Monopolies and Mergers   472

Chapter 14
Employment Law III: Labor–Management Relations   608

Chapter 17
Environmental Protection   745

Chapter 18
Internet Law and Ethics   794

Links to Brief Videos for Classroom Use

The following video links appear in the body of the text in conjunction with the subject matter of the videos.

Chapter 1

Trailer, *Atlas Shrugged* documentary movie [**https://youtu.be/L-cIEcBqgaA**].

Steve Croft, "The Case Against Lehman Brothers," *60 Minutes*, CBS News, April 22, 2012, at [**http://www.cbsnews.com/news/the-case-against-lehman-brothers-23-04-2012/**].

Martin Smith, "The Untouchables," *Frontline*, PBS, January 22, 2013, at [**www.pbs.org/wgbh/pages/frontline/untouchables/**].

Chapter 2

2009 Harvard MBA Ethics Oath, *The Daily Show with John Stewart* [**http://www.cc.com/video-clips/dc3rq6/the-daily-show-with-jon-stewart-mba-ethics-oath**].

Trailer, "The Company Men" [**http://www.youtube.com/watch?v=xa5qg7cB1ZQ**].

Trailer, *Wall Street: Money Never Sleeps*, at [**http://www.youtube.com/watch?v=HcMFA2SHES4**].

Chapter 3

Vermont Senator Bernie Sanders, "A Scandal" (a Senate speech criticizing corporate tax loopholes) [**http://www.youtube.com/watch?v=Sknt-UBRhxo**].

Trailer *Wal-Mart: The Corporation* [**http://www.youtube.com/watch?v=xHrhqtY2khc**]; *The High Cost of Low Price* documentary movie [**http://www.walmartmovie.com**].

Chapter 4

"What Is Mediation?" (a brief overview of mediation and arbitration) [**https://www.youtube.com/watch?v=KLdia39awl0**].

Chapter 5

"1967 ABC News Report on Loving Case" (application of due process and equal protection principles to Virginia antimiscegenation statute) [**http://abcnews.go.com/video/playerIndex?id=3278653**] (upper case I in Index).

Chapter 6

A video of the Pepsi ad that was the basis of the *Leonard v. Pepsico* lawsuit [**http://www.youtube.com/watch?v=ZdackF2H7Qc**].

Chapter 7

Susan Saladoff, "Hot Coffee" documentary movie trailer [**http://hotcoffeethemovie.com/**].

InjuryBoard, "Mr. Fancy Pants" (a video defense of the tort system) [**http://www.youtube.com/watch?v=h85j1vNxd8A**].

Chapter 8

Cato Institute, "There Are Too Many Bureaucrats and They Are Paid Too Much" [**http://www.youtube.com/watch?v=5xzd3puYmiM**].

Video, "IJ's Jeanette Petersen Explains Three Reasons You Can't Get a Cab" [**www.youtube.com/watch?v=Oq-hPuESJng**].

Chapter 9

ChinaForbiddenNews, NTDTV.COM, "Insider Trading 'Rats'" [**http://www.youtube.com/watch?v=IT3FArOeIEo**].

"Billionaire Convicted of Insider Trading," *Boston.com*, May 11, 2011 (Raj Rajaratnam) [**https://youtu.be/sT37Xx2oZXY**].

Chapter 10

The Informant! movie trailer [**http://www.traileraddict.com/trailer/the-informant/trailer**].

Chapter 11

Stephen Colbert, "Mega-Mergers," 2007 [**https://youtu.be/rsCp-1hgfxI**].

Chapter 12

Inland Valley Daily Bulletin and The San Bernardino Sun, "A Special Report on Immigration" ("Smuggler's Gulch") 2005 [**http://lang.dailybulletin.com/socal/beyondborders/video/121805_smugglers_gulch_video.asp**].

Chapter 13

Sheryl Sandberg, "In Her Own Words," discussing her 2013 book: *Lean In: Women, Work, and the Will to Lead* [**http://leanin.org/book/**].

American Civil Liberties Union, "New Video Shows the Need for a Transgender-Inclusive ENDA" [**https://youtu.be/UEPsK_axRqo**].

Chapter 14

Fox News discussion of NLRB–Boeing Conflict [**http://www.youtube.com/watch?v=j_JvA6yKB_M**].

Chapter 15

A Consumer Financial Protection Bureau video explaining the Bureau's mission [**http://www.consumerfinance.gov/the-bureau/**].

2011 ABC News Visit to Consumer Product Safety Commission Testing Lab [**http://abcnews.go.com/GMA/video/consumer-product-safety-commission-test-lab-13827984**].

Chapter 16

2004 John Stossel, *20/20* overview of sweatshop protests followed by Stossel's defense of low-wage jobs [**http://www.youtube.com/watch?v=0VaHmgoB10E**]. (Both large 0 symbols are zeros.)

Chapter 17

2011 Bill McKibben/Stephen Thompson video editorial about the alleged causal relationship between climate change and recent "extreme weather events" in America and around the world [**http://www.grist.org/climate-change/2011-06-11-the-most-powerful-climate-video-youll-see-all-week**].

Chapter 18

Video Essay: "What Is the 'Digital Divide?'" [**http://www.youtube.com/watch?v=fCIB_vXUptY**]. (In CIB, the middle letter is a capital I, as in Iowa.)

Business and Society

CHAPTER ONE

Capitalism and the Role of Government

After completing this chapter, students will be able to fulfill the following learning objectives:

1-1. Describe capitalism and its relationship to individual rights.

1-2. Discuss the theory and practice of privatization.

1-3. Compare and contrast capitalism and collectivism.

1-4. Differentiate between communism and socialism as collectivist philosophies.

1-5. Discuss the current state of capitalism in China and Russia.

1-6. Evaluate arguments regarding government's proper role in the American economy.

1-7. Describe the primary characteristics of a "mixed economy."

1-8. Analyze the impact of capitalism on equality, fairness, and community in American and global society.

1-9. Describe the income and wealth gaps in America.

Part One—Introduction

Are you a capitalist?

Are you a capitalist? If so, what role, if any, should the law play in your business life? How much government does America need? These themes, examining the relationship between government and business in America, are the core of this text. Since the fall of the Soviet Union and the general decline of communist influence, free market reasoning has dominated worldwide economic discourse. Indeed, noted political theorist Francis Fukuyama has argued that capitalism and Western democracy have so thoroughly proven their worth that the capitalism/collectivism debate is over.[1] Democracy and markets, Fukuyama claims, are so clearly triumphant that no new forms of civilization are likely to emerge. Thus, he says, we are at the end of history. Events, however, have challenged Fukuyama's bold thesis. The Great Recession, including the subprime mortgage crisis, the stunning power of the Wall Street banks, and the continuing centrality of governments in economic decision making, have raised doubts about the economic reliability and dominance of capitalism. Likewise, the power of markets has not always produced democracy, as events in China, Russia, and the Middle East have demonstrated. Furthermore, questionable Wall Street behavior, rampant managerial greed, and growing gaps between America's rich and poor have magnified long-standing doubts about the morality of capitalism.

A False Promise?   Renowned French economist Thomas Piketty has recently strengthened the anticapitalist argument by attacking the crucial claim that a healthy market generates a rising economic tide inevitably lifting the welfare of all.[2] Piketty's careful analysis of historical data, while challenged by some, finds that the rate of return on capital investments generally has been several times larger than the rate of general economic growth. Hence, the gap between the rich (investors) and poor (wage earners) likely will continue to expand, thus threatening social justice and democracy itself. Yet Piketty has acknowledged that markets are vital to efficiency and freedom.

American Capitalism Challenged: Economics

To put the concerns of Piketty and other critics in context, we will briefly examine the recent economic turmoil that has increased doubts about the effectiveness and fairness of contemporary American capitalism. More detail will follow in Chapter 2 and occasionally thereafter.

The Great Recession

In late 2008, America's financial markets seemed near collapse. Lending had essentially frozen. A powerful Wall Street bank, Lehman Brothers, went broke, while Bear Stearns and Merrill Lynch, also Wall Street titans, faced failure and were sold. American and global financial markets panicked and appeared unable to correct themselves. Fearing another Great Depression, the George W. Bush and Barack Obama administrations flooded the market with cash, took on much of the debt held by endangered banks, and, through the Troubled Asset Relief Program (TARP), bailed out failing giants such as Goldman Sachs, General Motors, and Chrysler: companies that were deemed "too big to fail." The "ultimate cost" of government expenditures to prop up the endangered economy was recently calculated at over $1.6 trillion, but the study's authors, Alan Blinder and Mark Zandi, estimate that the government's interventions reduced the length of the recession and its job losses by about half and reduced gross domestic product losses from 14 to 4 percent.[3] Critics, however, say the bailouts were illegal extensions of federal power, dramatically increased the federal deficit, expanded the size of the federal government, set the stage for inflation, and encouraged other businesses to believe they would be bailed out if necessary.

Subprime Mortgages

> The nation's housing bubble burst.

The financial community's near collapse was most directly ignited by the subprime mortgage crisis, a situation in which the nation's housing bubble burst and millions of Americans were no longer able to pay their home mortgages. Instead of continuing their sometimes meteoric rise in value, those homes plunged in price and much of the total real estate market essentially imploded. The resulting mountain of bad debt could not be managed by the American financial institutions that were holding it; fear paralyzed the lending markets, and the government felt obliged to step in to prevent a greater financial tragedy.

Greed and inept management certainly were instrumental in the subprime debacle, but mounting evidence[4] suggests that financial fraud (e.g., lenders conspiring with borrowers to overstate borrowers' income in order to qualify for larger loans) played an important role in the collapse. Conservatives, however, place much of the blame on the federal government for its policies encouraging banks to make loans to unqualified low-income buyers.

[For a cynical look at the subprime bubble, see the 2016 Oscar-nominated movie, *The Big Short,* at **https://www.youtube.com/watch?v=LWr8hbUkG9s**]. [For a critical examination of the broader financial meltdown, see the trailer for the 2011 Oscar-winning best documentary, *Inside Job,* at **http://www.youtube.com/watch?v=FzrBurlJUNk**].

Banks Too Big?

> America's biggest banks were deemed "too big to fail."

America's biggest banks were deemed "too big to fail" during the subprime mortgage crisis. Today the five biggest American banks—JPMorgan Chase, Bank of America, Wells Fargo, Citigroup, and U.S. Bancorp—control about 45 percent of America's bank assets, and their stability remains worrisome should the economy falter again. Some political leaders and economic policy experts favor breaking up the biggest banks, but reforms including Federal Reserve rules requiring some banks to increase the amount of capital they hold (thus giving them a bigger cushion in troubled times) has enabled the big banks to pass annual government "stress tests" indicating they may now be better situated to deal with disaster. The 2010 Dodd–Frank Wall Street Reform and Consumer Protection Act (see Chapter 8) also includes provisions designed to reduce the likelihood of big bank failures.

Globalization

Globalization represents the international flowering of capitalism; the power of free markets has been embraced, enthusiastically or reluctantly, almost everywhere on Earth. In a "hyper-connected," "flat" world, we are all linked together in an economic and cultural intimacy scarcely imaginable a few decades back. Largely unanticipated challenges are emerging, however. The turbulence of globalization fosters insecurity, which, in turn, encourages nationalism, tribalism, and religious extremism that tend to rend the world rather than knit it together. In turn, economic ups and downs are unavoidable. On average, profits in international markets are lower than in domestic markets, consumer growth in emerging countries has been slow to develop, political strife threatens many markets, and international cyber theft is rampant.[5] Globalization has elevated living standards for hundreds of millions, but losers have been plentiful. Most notable in America are the millions of high-paying manufacturing jobs that went abroad. Some "reshoring" of those jobs has occurred, but for blue-collar America, globalization has been a mixed blessing. Likewise, Great Britain's 2016 vote to leave the European Union (a decision popularly labeled "Brexit") highlights middle-class anxiety about a dramatically changing world troubled by mass immigration and powerful globalization forces.

American Capitalism Challenged: Morality

Beyond fears about capitalism's economic performance, particularly its instability and harshness, critics point to capitalism's indecencies.

Wall Street Abuses

> Wall Street banks have paid tens of billions in penalties.

Since the financial collapse, Wall Street banks have paid tens of billions of dollars in penalties for their subprime misconduct, currency manipulations, and other wrongs. Nonetheless, no one seems very happy. The bankers feel wronged, the government remains frustrated, and the American people are angered. The U.S. Justice Department says that some 4,000 (mostly low-level) employees have been charged with mortgage fraud alone, but almost all of the Wall Street bosses have escaped jail.[6]

Fairness in Pay

Greed   CEO salaries for the top 350 U.S. corporations (not limited to bankers) averaged $16.3 million in 2014, or about 300 times the pay of the typical worker, a ratio that has risen from 20 to 1 in 1965.[7] Average Wall Street *starting* salaries for recent college graduates are now around $85,000. On the other hand, government rules and difficult market conditions have taken a bit of the sheen off the dominance of the big banks. Average Wall Street bonuses grew only 2 percent in 2014 (to $172,860), and banking royalty Lloyd Blankfein, CEO of Goldman Sachs, and James Gorman, CEO of Morgan Stanley, actually took modest pay cuts in 2016.

Inequality   The CEO–worker pay gap is illustrative of broader income and wealth gaps that continue to grow. We discuss the theme in more detail later, but note here the questionable fairness of an economy that seems, as Piketty charges, to reward the wealthy with economic growth that rather consistently exceeds growth rates for the working class. The ongoing economic recovery has been welcome, but job growth and wage increases (for workers) have lagged profits and revenues (for owners). Were those gaps the product of superior skill and industry alone, fairness might not be an issue, but critics argue that our economic divide seems to be driven, at least in part, by *rent-seeking* behaviors (securing economic gains without creating new wealth or otherwise benefiting society, as in the case of corporate lobbying for government subsidies). A recent study in the respected *Journal of Economic Perspectives* argues that income from rent seeking among the top 1 percent has been "the primary impediment to having growth in living standards for low- and moderate-income households approach the growth rate of economy-wide productivity."[8] To some significant extent, the evidence suggests we are redistributing income and wealth not merely by welfare programs for the poor and elderly, but also through rent seeking by the rich and well-connected who, the critics argue, can lobby the government for favors, move their wealth abroad, avoid taxes by employing armies of accountants and lawyers, engage in monopoly antitrust behaviors, and otherwise manipulate the economy to their advantage.

[For an overview of the Lehman Brothers banking collapse and a critique of the government's regulatory oversight, see Steve Croft, "The Case Against Lehman Brothers," *60 Minutes,* CBS News, April 22, 2012, at **http://www.cbsnews.com/news/the-case-against-lehman-brothers-23-04-2012/].** [For an investigation of "why (few) Wall Street execs have been prosecuted for the financial crisis," see Martin Smith, "The Untouchables," *Frontline,* PBS, January 22, 2013, at **www.pbs.org/wgbh/pages/frontline/untouchables/**].

Questions

1. Thomas Hoenig, a member of the board of directors of the Federal Deposit Insurance Corporation, observed: "[Americans] realize that more must be done to address a threat that remains increasingly a part of our economy: financial institutions that are 'too big to fail.'"[9] Do you agree that our concentrated financial sector is a threat that must be addressed? Explain.

2. Journalist/lecturer Richard Doak laments what he believes to be unfair and excessive pay to executives: "Executive greed has perverted risks, rewards. . . . The American system has been rigged to over-enrich those at the top."[10] What do you think? Is greed the culprit? Has the system been "rigged," or can we continue to count on the market to properly distribute pay? Explain.

American Capitalism Challenged: A Nation in Decline?

The economic and moral challenges to our capitalist system, the rise of China, and the ongoing political dysfunction in Washington, DC, have combined to shake our faith in America's future. When asked in a 2014 *Wall Street Journal*/NBC News poll if "life for our children's generation will be better than it has been for us,"[11] only 21 percent said yes. That pessimism held true regardless of respondents' political preferences, gender, or race, but young people were a bit more optimistic than their elders. Responding to a similar poll, Michael Herdmann, a 54-year-old Ohio retiree, said, "Things have changed a lot. The decks have been stacked against not only the lower class but also the lower middle class."[12] Some critics attribute the nation's problems to fundamental flaws in capitalism and in the American character. Michael Moore's 2009 documentary movie *Capitalism: A Love Story* assails capitalism as "evil."[13] Moore was questioned about his movie:

> *Wall Street Journal:* Why call the movie "Capitalism: A Love Story?" You don't seem to love very much about capitalism. Mr. Moore: It is a love story about the well-to-do. They happen to love their money very much. Now they love our money and they want all our money and our homes. It's about their love.[14]

Wells Fargo fired 5,300 employees.

Wells Fargo   We see some support for Moore's discouraging thesis in the ongoing scandal over phony accounts at Wells Fargo. Under pressure to meet sales goals, Wells Fargo employees opened some two million accounts for customers without their permission. The bank reportedly began receiving employee complaints about the sham accounts as early as 2005.[15] Eventually Wells Fargo fired 5,300 mostly lower-level employees and refunded $2.6 million to customers. It will pay, at this writing, $185 million in fines. CEO John Stumpf resigned in 2016. He was forced to give up $41 million in stock awards, although he left having accumulated tens of millions in salary. Wells Fargo has publicly apologized, but new account openings have plummeted and a number of state and municipal governments have withdrawn from business ties to the bank.[16] Criminal charges seem likely, although the story is unfolding at this writing. [For more, see Chapter 15.]

The scandal may prove to be a perverse blessing. The subprime mortgage collapse and the derivative industry at its heart left most of us puzzled if not bored, but we can understand a straightforward fraud, as Rana Foroohar explained in *Time:*

> Wells' easily grasped misdeeds, and the fallout, come at a pivotal time for the reform-minded. I'm hopeful this scandal . . . represents an opportunity to reconstruct and refresh the narrative around our financial system. Particularly what still needs to be done to make it safer.[17]

Vast Resources

America has been shaken by terrorism, the Great Recession, and political gridlock, but we remain dominant in economic, military, and international affairs. The U.S. ranks third in the world (behind Switzerland and Singapore) in economic competitiveness (a measure of business climate, innovation, strengthen of public institutions, etc.).[18] In advising its clients, Goldman Sachs recently pointed to America's attractiveness to investors, the nation's vast natural resources (especially oil, gas, and arable land), a workforce that is younger and more energetic than those of our chief rivals, and our continuing leadership in innovation.[19] Noted *New York Times* columnist David Brooks says that America is merely in one of its periodic economic pauses, but he is sure that "The gospel of success will recapture the imagination."[20] Brooks summarized our fundamentally commercial nature:

> Walt Whitman got America right in his essay, "Democratic Vistas." He acknowledged the vulgarity of the American success drive. He toted up its moral failings. But in the end he accepted his country's "extreme business energy," its "almost maniacal appetite for wealth." He knew that the country's dreams were all built upon that energy and drive, and eventually the spirit of commercial optimism would always prevail.[21]

Questions

1. Critics argue that the growing economic gap between the wealthy and all other Americans has resulted in a "rigged" economy that unfairly favors the wealthy and the big corporations.
   a. Do you agree? Explain.
   b. Does that economic gap threaten American democracy? Explain.
2. Quoting a fourth-century bishop, Pope Francis in 2015 referred to the unfettered pursuit of money as "the dung of the devil," but soon thereafter he referred to business as "a noble vocation, directed to producing wealth and improving the world." As you study business, do you think you are primarily preparing yourself for an honorable, productive role in life or for the "evil" pursuit of money? Explain.

Purpose: What Do We Hope to Accomplish with This Textbook?

To this point, we have provided a brief reminder of some of the big challenges facing America's capitalist system. The balance of this chapter more carefully examines the philosophical nature of free market capitalism, introduces some alternatives to the free market, and asks where America's political economy is headed. Chapter 1 thereby serves as a foundation for the book's detailed investigation of the following questions:

1. What is the proper ethical/social role of business in American life?
2. How much, if any, government regulation of business is necessary to secure that role?

Markets and Governments

We certainly cannot understand America's system of laws without a firm appreciation for the principles of capitalism from which those laws spring. We have embraced an evolving capitalist, democratic approach to life. Other cultures have placed less faith in the market and more in government planning.

In this chapter we will explore the full economic spectrum, moving from a laissez-faire, free-market approach on the extreme right to a brief reminder of command economy principles on the far left. The bulk of our attention, however, will rest where the world is at this moment. Most nations are practicing varying combinations of markets and rules that we can label *mixed economies.*

The pure free-market approach assumes that we can operate our business system and our society at large free of all but foundational legal mechanisms such as contract and criminal law. The wisdom of the market—our individual judgments, in combination with our individual consciences—would "regulate" American life. Most forms of government including regulatory agencies, consumer protection, environmental rules, occupational licensure, zoning restrictions, antitrust law, and all but the most basic government services would be eliminated.

Should America shrink the size of government? What combination of capitalism and government best serves the needs of America and the world? Substantially open markets have shown themselves to be the stronger vehicle for productivity, efficiency, and personal freedom. Are open markets also the stronger vehicle for improving living conditions for all citizens, for maximizing democracy, for discouraging crime and corruption, and for building strong communities? Are America and the world best served by the speed and efficiency of largely unrestrained markets, or do we still need the "civilizing" influence of government rules?

Law

Once a society settles on some broad political and economic principles, it employs the law as a primary method of governance. So to understand the law—which this text introduces in Chapter 4—we need first to understand its roots in the economic, political, and social preferences of America and the world.

Questions—Part One

1. The John Templeton Foundation asked a number of prominent thinkers the following question: "Does the free market corrode moral character?" Answer that question. [See **www.templeton.org/market**].

2. Do you think higher taxes for the rich would be the best solution for closing the wealth gap in America? Explain.

3. Scholar Robert Skidelsky applauds capitalism for overcoming scarcity, organizing production, and lifting many out of poverty, but he thinks capitalism, at least in rich countries like the United States, has also produced a culture where our main occupation has become the production and consumption of unnecessary goods. He asks whether capitalism can succeed if it continues to produce "more of the same, stimulating jaded appetites with new gadgets, thrills, and excitements? . . . Do we spend the next century wallowing in triviality?"[22] What do you think?

Part Two—Capitalism: Reduce Government?

LO 1-1

Describe capitalism and its relationship to individual rights.

Personal freedom and private property rights, combined with extraordinary human and natural resources, ignited a great American economy. Fraud, monopoly behaviors, and abuse of employees followed, however, and government regulations grew, in part, to curb the power of big business. The proper balance between open markets and government intervention remains perhaps the central public policy debate in American life. The disturbing example of young entrepreneur and pharmaceutical executive Martin Shkreli illustrates both the power and the limitations of the market.

Shkreli   Despite building companies and an estimated $100 million fortune while yet in his early 30s, Shkreli's exploitation of the market has outraged the public and some members of Congress. In 2015, Shkreli's company, Turing Pharmaceuticals, bought the rights to an established toxoplasmosis medication, Daraprim, and soon raised the price from $13.50 to $750 per pill. Shkreli then called a journalist a "moron" for asking why the price was inflated so dramatically. Rejecting charges of greed, Shkreli has said he cares deeply about others, and the price increase was necessary to provide funds for medical research. At this writing, Shkreli has been charged, in an apparently unrelated matter, with securities fraud.

[For a 2016 interview with Shkreli, see "Martin Shkreli on Drug Price Hikes and Playing the World's Villain" at **www.youtube.com/watch?v=2PCb9mnrU1g**].

Ayn Rand and Objectivism   Should we embrace Shkreli's Daraprim example and strive for a purer form of capitalism, largely free of government oversight and moral uncertainty? The controversial philosopher and novelist Ayn Rand (1905–1982) was an uncompromising advocate of capitalist, free-market principles. Rand's philosophy, labelled Objectivism, contends that only free market principles can produce a rational, moral life. Her moral message is summarized in the challenging phrase, "The Virtue of Selfishness," the title of one of her books and an expression of her view that our own happiness is our highest moral purpose. Rational selfishness, that is, maximizing one's own interests through reliance on reason and rejection of sacrifice, is the only path to a just, meaningful life. In every dimension of our lives, we should operate as traders giving value for value. In doing so, all would be free to achieve to their maximum capacity, and all would earn what they deserve; that is, what the market rewards. We would have total responsibility for our own actions and no responsibility for others (with the exception of our children). Rand advocated complete individual freedom so long as we do not violate the rights of others.

Government and Objectivism   To Rand, the purpose of government is to protect individual rights. Therefore, the only necessary components of government are the police, the armed services, and the law courts. Governmental regulation of business would be dramatically reduced or eliminated. Agencies such as the Federal Trade Commission, the Federal Communications Commission, and the Food and Drug Administration would be eliminated. Free market processes along with individual and organizational morality would guide decision making and provide the consumer protection currently afforded by those agencies. Similarly, market forces and charity would replace government in providing social security, education, welfare, and housing. Taxation would be voluntary.

Rand's Influence   Rand's views and her writing style are heavily criticized, but she has been cited as a powerful influence by some of America's leading corporate and political figures. Her books, including *Atlas Shrugged* and *The Fountainhead,* are among the best-selling novels of all time. Indeed, *Atlas Shrugged* is one of the most influential business books in history, and according to a national survey, has been read by over 8 percent of American adults.[23]

[For the trailer of a 2011 documentary treatment of *Atlas Shrugged*, see **https://youtu.be/ L-cIEcBqgaA**].

Big business leaders, who so often are the villains of contemporary American life, are the great heroes of Rand's writing in which she champions selfishness and rejects self-sacrifice. To Rand, big government suppresses individual rights and personal freedom and improperly transfers wealth from the highly productive to those who are less so. Commentator Stephen Moore explained Rand's *Atlas Shrugged* argument that big government threatens the creative and productive power of the market:

> Big business leaders are the great heroes of Rand's writing.

> Politicians invariably respond to crises—that in most cases they themselves created—by spawning new government programs, laws and regulations. These, in turn, generate more havoc and poverty, which inspires the politicians to create more programs . . . and the downward spiral repeats itself until the productive sectors of the economy collapse under the collective weight of taxes and other burdens imposed in the name of fairness, equality and do-goodism.[24]

[See the Center for the Moral Defense of Capitalism at **http://www.moraldefense.com**]. [U.S. Speaker of the House, Paul Ryan, has acknowledged an intellectual and inspirational debt to Ayn Rand. For an explanation, see Jane Mayer, "Ayn Rand Joins the Ticket," *The New Yorker*, August 11, 2012, at **https://youtu.be/L-cIEcBqgaA**].

Questions

1. Mark Zuckerberg and his wife Priscilla Chan in 2015 announced they would donate 99 percent of their worth, about $45 billion, to charitable purposes. Similarly, the Bill

Gates/Warren Buffett Giving Pledge asks wealthy people worldwide to give half or more of their money to philanthropy. German billionaire Peter Kramer objected to the private gifts, encouraged by charitable deductions on donors' taxes, because the donors and their preferences take the place of the collective judgment of the state, which could capture at least a portion of that money through taxes. Thus, wealthy, private Americans, rather than the government, determine what is good for the people. Should that donated money be in the hands of the government rather than the donors? Explain. See Jeff Guo, "Why a German Billionaire Says That Pledges Like Mark Zuckerberg's Are Really Bad,"[25]

2. *a.* Sandy Banks, writing in the *Los Angeles Times:*

> The boys' faces brightened when they got to the front of the line. We're next! They'd been waiting to say it. But their smiles faded when another family was ushered in from the sidelines and slid into "their" Legoland ride. We'd been waylaid by the Premium Play Pass, Legoland's wristband version of the front-of-the-line pass.[26]

Banks asked her readers what they thought of the fairness of paying to jump to the front of the line. Some said it was no different than flying first class or choosing to drive on a toll road. One thought the kids received a good lesson in the competitiveness of capitalism. Legoland, in Carlsbad, California, said they sell only about 65 of the Premium Play wristbands daily, but those who buy them value the time saved.

What do you think of the fairness of paying to jump to the head of the line at amusement parks?

b. Do you think that drivers who pay more should be entitled to drive in a faster lane? Explain.[27]

3. Elementary schools often ban tag, dodge ball, touch football, kickball, and other vigorous games from the playgrounds. One school banned touching altogether. Administrators fear physical injuries, students' reduced self-esteem, and lawsuits. As the *Los Angeles Times* editorialized, "It's hard sometimes to tell whether schools are graduating students or growing orchids."[28] Ayn Rand argued for reduced rules in life, thus relying on the market to address virtually all problems.

a. From Rand's free-market point of view, explain why we should reduce playground rules as much as possible, even at the risk of children being hurt.

b. Would you follow the rules approach or Rand's free-market approach in managing a playground? Explain.

Free Market Solution to the Baby Shortage?

The following ad appeared in the *Stanford Daily* (Stanford University):

> EGG DONOR WANTED $35,000 (PLUS ALL EXPENSES) Ivy League Professor and High-Tech CEO seek one truly exceptional woman who is attractive, athletic, under the age of 29. GPA 3.5+, SAT: 1400+.

Experts estimate that about 10,000 babies annually are born in the United States from "donated" eggs and about $80 million is spent on those eggs. Fees range from a few thousand dollars to $50,000 or more. The U.S. fertility industry is lightly regulated, but most industrial nations have banned paid "donations."

Questions

1. Barnard College president Debora Spar has said, "We are selling children."
    a. Is she correct?
    b. Should we be doing so? Explain.

2. A recent *Washington Post* headline read: "How the Rise of Commercial Surrogacy Is Turning Babies into Commodities."
    a. Does capitalism encourage us to treat people as products?
    b. Are people, in fact, products? Explain.

Sources: Claire Achmad, "How the Rise of Commercial Surrogacy Is Turning Babies into Commodities," *The Washington Post,* December 31, 2014 [**www.washingtonpost.com**]; Jim Hopkins, "Egg-Donor Business Booms on Campus," *USA TODAY,* March 16, 2006, p. 1A; and Tamar Lewin, "Egg Donors Challenge Pay Rates, Saying They Shortchange Women," *The New York Times,* October 16, 2015 [**www.nytimes.com**].

Capitalism in Practice—"Privatization" in America and Abroad

LO 1-2
Discuss the theory and practice of privatization.

Should we sell our struggling postal system to private investors? Should we convert our interstate highway system into tollways, leased or owned by private interests? What about "contracting out" our prison systems, schools, libraries, and parking lots? In general, should we shrink our governments and *privatize* as much of that work as possible in order to increase efficiency, save money, and diminish the role of government in our lives.

Most commonly, privatization follows two patterns: (1) *contracting out,* where government, in effect, turns over a portion of its duties, such as garbage collection, to a private firm; and (2) the sale or lease of public assets, such as an airport, to a private party. Privately operated prisons, now rather common across America, are a primary example of the privatization movement. Of course, privatization also brings worries about job losses, reduced services, reduced responsiveness to consumers, corruption, and so on.

Currently, the most globally visible privatization example, Greece, faces a collapsing economy and an unemployment rate of about 25 percent. Desperate for cash, Greece has been forced by its lenders to begin selling and leasing public property such as land, ports, airports, roads, water utilities, the national lottery, and banks to receive a multibillion-euro bailout. Fraport, a German company, for example, has secured a 40-year lease on a dozen regional Greek airports in exchange for 1.23 billion euros.

Struggling American governments likewise see privatization as a solution for financial distress. Louisiana, for example, has largely privatized its public hospitals, and some 40 states have at least begun to privatize management of their Medicaid programs (low-income health care). State officials say privatization saves millions of dollars while improving medical care, but the initial evidence is mixed.

Citing free-market efficiency and personal freedom while challenging moral conventions, privatization supporters envision major changes to daily life. For example, some doctors and others are arguing for lifting the federal ban on organ sales as a way of addressing the current donor shortage. The resulting increase in supply would save many lives, but others fear the privatized approach would exploit the poor and vulnerable and discourage altruistic donors.[29]

Professor Stephanie Coontz pushes the free-market argument further by challenging the need for the state's permission to marry. For most of Western history, marriage was a private contract, and Coontz wonders if the time has come to let couples, gay or straight, decide entirely on their own if they want to join together to assume the protections and obligations of a committed relationship.[30]

In each of these examples, the underlying idea is that the market can make decisions more efficiently and effectively than government while also maximizing personal freedom. [For a large database supportive of privatization, see **http://reason.org/areas/topic/privatization**].

Space Travel

Trying to save money while emerging from the Great Recession, the U.S. government has retired its shuttle rockets and is encouraging the continuing development of private-sector rockets that are expected to carry on space exploration and travel in cooperation with the government. SpaceX, Orbital ATK, and Sierra Nevada Corporation have contracted with the National Aeronautics and Space Administration to resupply the International Space Station (ISS) in coming years. Some contractors are expected to carry astronauts to the ISS, and NASA has sketched a vision for privatized space stations. Presumably, space will be commercialized with companies hauling space travel customers and exploiting vast mineral resources that may lead to a new "gold rush."

Room for Big Ideas

SpaceX founder Elon Musk (the cocreator of PayPal and the founder of Tesla, the electric car company) is working on a project called a Hyperloop, a vacuum tube with passenger pods that would be capable of moving people from San Francisco to Los Angeles in 30 minutes.

Question

Is a market-based culture of freedom and risk taking necessary to the creation and sustenance of these very big ideas, or is a blend of the market and government more likely to succeed? Explain.

Toll Roads, Parking Meters, and Congestion Pricing

Should users pay fees for access to highways? Private companies are building, maintaining, and operating new toll roads in places such as northern Virginia and suburban San Diego to the Mexican border. Taking the privatization movement a step further, state and local governments are selling or leasing existing roads to private companies. Indiana, for example, leased its 157-mile Indiana East–West Toll Road to an international group for $3.8 billion for 75 years. The new operators can raise tolls each year by 2 percent, the inflation rate, or the increase in GDP; whichever is higher.[31]

Critics worry, however, about declining service, excessive tolls, too much profit for the investors, pricing poorer drivers out of access to the roads, and trading secure government jobs with benefits for low-wage private-sector jobs without benefits.[32] Nonetheless, increasing government revenue problems suggest that transportation privatization will continue. [For labor union opposition to privatization, see **http://www.afscme.org/issues/76.cfm**].

The privatization movement has been extended beyond toll roads to other infrastructure resources. Chicago sold control of its parking garages to Morgan Stanley for $563 million[33] and the city entered a 75-year lease arrangement with private investors who paid about $1.2 billion up front to control 36,000 parking meters and raise rates as much as fourfold.[34] An inspector general's report concludes that the parking meter deal was worth nearly one billion dollars more than Chicago received.[35]

While adding to and upgrading infrastructure through privatization, governments and their agents are also turning to pricing/market mechanisms to reduce demand for that infrastructure. Several cities are experimenting with *congestion pricing* or *surge pricing* that involves making a service more expensive at times of peak demand in order to curb that demand. San Francisco, for example, is rolling out a plan that may raise on-street parking to as much as $18 per hour in high-demand areas during busy hours of the day while lowering prices in less-congested areas and during less frantic hours. Since 2003, London, England, has charged congestion prices to enter the central city. One interesting result is that accidents have declined by about 40 percent, with traffic deaths down about five per year.[36] At least 10 metropolitan areas have in place or are contemplating so-called HOT lanes or Lexus lanes where, for a fee, drivers can move to an express lane with reduced traffic and higher speeds.

Questions

1. Author Joan Didion referred to our highways as America's only communion. Would it be a social/ethical wrong to adopt widespread "congestion fees," privately operated toll roads, and "Lexus lanes" that would permit those with money to avoid the democracy of the highways? Explain.

2. *Governing Magazine* labeled golf courses "perhaps the most non-essential of the non-essential public services."[37] Studies show that payrolls for city-operated golf courses are about 13 percent higher than for privately operated courses.[38] Why do we subsidize golf, and should we continue doing so? Explain.

Schools

Is capitalism the answer? Is capitalism the answer to poor K–12 school performance? The idea was unthinkable a few decades ago, but many policy leaders now view free-market "fixes" as our best hope for education reform. Public school systems are experimenting with market-based approaches such as for-profit web-based classes, open enrollment, charter schools, and vouchers (students "spend" their taxpayer-provided dollars on the school of their choice). The hope is that competition will push all schools to higher achievement levels.

Charter schools, currently permitted by law in 42 states, educate well over two million students in programs largely financed by public funds and managed typically under nonprofit arrangements, although about 10 to 15 percent of the schools are profit-seeking businesses. This experimental revolution, in applying market principles to our national tradition of publicly funded and managed education, is criticized as the "commodification" of an indispensable public good that threatens, the critics say, to leave disadvantaged students even further behind than today's already dismal divide. Indeed, the current evidence is not particularly encouraging. Charter schools, according to scholar Diane Ravitch, perhaps the leading voice in the reform debate, perform on average no better than public schools.[39] On the other hand, clear successes have emerged. One of the more interesting and encouraging examples involves TEP, a New York City charter middle school that pays its teachers $125,000 plus bonuses annually. Although abundant doubts remain, studies show, for example, that 78 percent of the achievement gap between eighth grade Hispanics and whites was erased at TEP.[40] (Are dramatically higher teacher salaries likely to result in significantly improved student performance?)

Privatize Higher Education?

The Anderson School of Management at the University of California at Los Angeles (UCLA) in 2014 entered a three-year agreement with UCLA to substantially privatize its prestigious MBA program. The program will keep most of its income and spend that income on raising its academic profile to better compete with Harvard, Stanford, and the like. Other academic institutions, including the University of Virginia, have been significantly privatized in recent years.

Those opposing Anderson's privatization fear that UCLA's responsibilities for the general welfare may be replaced by the more self-interested goals of those running the MBA program, its donors, and the business community. They argue that a privatized program might be more likely to allow admission to a major donor's child, shape its research agenda to conform to the interests of corporate donors, diminish its attention to community needs, or eventually replace merit-based admission with an auction allowing space to the highest bidders.

Questions

1. *a.* If it is not already, should your college or university become a for-profit institution?
   b. How would your education change?
   c. How would you change?
2. Would our current system of higher education benefit from aggressive private-sector competition or is the current competition among schools sufficient? Explain.

Privatization a Success?

Donald Cohen, president of Public Interest, a group that advocates for "responsible contracting" by government bodies, estimates that $1 trillion of America's $6 trillion in annual government spending at all levels goes to private companies,[41] but now, according to *The Atlantic,* we are experiencing something of a "privatization backlash."[42] Most notably, the federal Justice Department and a number of states—worried about safety, security, and mismanagement—have decided to move away from the use of privatized prisons. Studies examining privatization performance have generated mixed results, but under the right circumstances, privatization can operate in the public interest, particularly in this era of constrained government budgets.

Firefighters Watch a House Burn

Rather than impose a fire tax, Obion County, Tennessee, contracts with local municipal governments to provide fire protection in rural areas. Those firefighters drew national attention in 2010 and 2011 when they allowed two rural family homes to burn to the ground because the families had not paid their $75 annual subscription fee to the city-operated fire department in nearby South Fulton. Apparently, no one was seriously injured in either fire. The homeowner in the 2010 blaze, Gene Cranick, said that he offered to pay the fee on the spot, but the fire department declined and engaged the fire only to the extent necessary to protect the property of a neighbor who had paid the fee.

Questions

1. *a.* Why did the fire department decline Cranick's money at the time of the fire?
   b. Do you think the fire department should have extinguished the fire even though Cranick had not paid? Explain.
2. In 2012, South Fulton decided to respond to all reported fires and bill nonsubscribers $3,500 for the response. Do you think the new policy is an improvement over the original? Explain.
3. Should fire service be privatized across the nation? Explain.

Sources: Jason Hibbs, "Firefighters Watch as Home Burns to the Ground," *WPSD Local 6—News, Sports, Weather*, Paducah, KY, September 30, 2010 [**www.wpsdlocal6.com**]; Timothy W. Martin, "Putting Out Fires for a Fee," *The Wall Street Journal*, March 12, 2012 [**http://online.wsj.com/news/articles/SB10001424052970203961204577269591267553530?mg=reno64-wsj**].

Questions—Part Two

1. From the capitalist viewpoint, why is the private ownership of property necessary to the preservation of freedom?
2. Ayn Rand argued: "Altruism is incompatible with freedom, with capitalism, and with individual rights."
   a. Define altruism.
   b. Explain why Rand rejected altruism.

3. Responding to extreme drought conditions in 2015, California governor Jerry Brown ordered a mandatory 25 percent reduction in water use for most Californians. Commenting on the order, Steve Yuhas, a resident of wealthy San Diego suburb Rancho Santa Fe, reportedly said: "[People] should not be forced to live on property with brown lawns, golf on brown courses or apologize for wanting their gardens to be beautiful. We pay significant property taxes based on where we live. And, no, we're not all equal when it comes to water."[43]
   a. Should the wealthy be able to buy as much water as they wish? Explain.
   b. Explain Yuhas's argument that we're not all equal when it comes to water. See Rob Kuznia, "Rich Californians Balk at Limits: 'We're Not All Equal When It Comes to Water,'" *The Washington Post,* June 13, 2015 [**www.washingtonpost.com**].

4. Assume the federal government removed itself from the purchase and maintenance of its parks.
   a. Left to the private sector, what sorts of parks would develop under the profit incentive?
   b. Would Yellowstone, for example, survive in substantially its present state? Explain.
   c. Make the argument that the federal parks are an unethical, undemocratic expropriation of private resources.

5. Assume the abolition of the federal Food and Drug Administration. How would the free market protect the citizenry from dangerous food and drug products?

6. Puritan leaders felt concern over the morality of merchants who sold goods at prices exceeding the goods' worth. That concern was particularly grave when the goods were scarce or in great demand.
   a. Should our society develop an ethic under which goods are to be sold only "for what they are worth"? Explain.
   b. Can a seller make an accurate determination of worth? Explain.
   c. Does a product's worth differ from the price that product will bring in the marketplace? Explain.
   d. Personalize the inquiry: Assume you seek to sell your Ford car for $10,000. Assume you know of several identical Fords in a similar state of repair that can be purchased for $9,000. Assume you find a buyer at $10,000. Will you unilaterally lower your price or direct the purchaser to the other cars? Explain.
   e. If not, have you acted justly? Explain.

7. Sports columnist Skip Bayless has argued for allowing university sports boosters to bid for the best football recruits: "Boosters should be allowed to entice recruits with whatever they want to offer—cars, signing bonuses, annual salaries, annuities."[44] Do you agree? Explain. See Skip Bayless, "Unleash the Boosters," *ESPN.com*, July 25, 2014 [**www.espn.com**].

8. Gregg Williams, former defensive coordinator for the New Orleans Saints National Football League (NFL) team, was suspended for one year by the league as punishment for his alleged role in establishing a bounty system that paid players for injuring other players. Allegedly many NFL teams had employed similar schemes. Williams has apologized for his "previous actions" and was hired for the 2013/2014 season to be a defensive assistant for the Tennessee Titans. In a free market, rewards for performance

are helpful as an incentive and just as a measure of contribution. Do you think bonuses for injuring opposing players should be permissible in the NFL? Explain.

9. Professor Robert E. Lane argued that the person who is motivated by needs for affiliation, rather than by needs for achievement, does less well in the market. Such a person is not rewarded so well as autonomous, achievement-oriented people.

    a. Is Lane correct? Explain.

    b. Is capitalism, in the long run, destructive of societal welfare in that achievement is better rewarded than affiliation? Explain. See, generally, Robert E. Lane, *The Loss of Happiness in Market Democracies* (New Haven: Yale University Press, 2000).

10. How would poor people be cared for in a free-market society?

11. Critic William Deresiewicz said, "Wall Street is capitalism in its purest form, and capitalism is predicated on bad behavior."[45] Do you agree that capitalism is built on bad behavior? Explain. See William Deresiewicz, "Capitalist and Other Psychopaths," *The New York Times*, May 12, 2012 [**www.nytimes.com**].

12. Using private money, New York City experimented from 2007 to 2010 with a program that paid poorer residents for practicing good life habits such as holding a job ($150 per month), going to the dentist ($100), regular school attendance ($25 to $50 per month), and passing certain examinations ($600). The average family received about $3,000. Would you expect this program to be an effective encouragement to improved life habits? Explain. See Associated Press, "N.Y.C. Pays Poor for Good Habits . . .," *The Des Moines Register,* March 31, 2010, p. 10A.

Part Three—Collectivism: Increase Government?

LO 1-3
Compare and contrast capitalism and collectivism.

The term *collectivism* embraces communism and socialism and associated philosophies on the left side of the political/economic spectrum. Collectivist systems feature economic cooperation and varying degrees of centralized control as contrasted with capitalism's economic individualism and political freedom.

Communism

Although China, Cuba, North Korea, Vietnam, and a few other nations continue to practice communism, the balance of the world has clearly rejected Marxist-Leninist totalitarianism. Indeed, China has rapidly embraced free-market practices within the communist umbrella, a strategy that some label *state capitalism,* as discussed below.

> The communist government remains firmly in charge.

Cuba   The 2016 death of Fidel Castro, communist leader of the 1959 Cuban Revolution, may encourage the decline of communism in Cuba. At this writing, the communist government, under the leadership of Fidel's brother, Raul, remains firmly in charge, but market forces have been emerging in recent years. The Obama administration eased some trade restrictions, United States–Cuban diplomatic ties have recently been restored, tourism in Cuba is booming, and American businesses are striking some deals.

Cubans are now allowed to buy and sell houses and used cars freely. Cubans own cell phones and other electronic devices, some state land is being distributed for private farming, and some private cabs are being licensed. Private-sector jobs such as scooter repair, barber, and produce vendor are emerging. While restaurants, snack bars, and other small shops are springing up, standing in line for government rations, food, banking service, and almost everything else remains a fact of life. Most of the more than 11 million Cubans continue to lead a spare, government-supported existence; much of the nation is in physical decline; and political liberty is nonexistent.

Communist Principles

Despite the decline of communism, we need to briefly remind ourselves of some Marxist fundamentals, among which the core promise of economic justice for all remains a particularly powerful motivator. Lenin, not Marx, created the communist dictatorship in Russia. Lenin and the other communist totalitarians, most notably Stalin in the Soviet Union and Mao in China, did horrific damage. However, Marx, along with Freud and Einstein, is among the thinkers who most profoundly shaped the 20th century. For our purposes, Marx's central message concerns the severe abuses that can accompany unrestrained capitalism. Marx was particularly concerned about the growing imbalance between rich and poor, an issue increasingly familiar to Americans. Moreover, he felt that the pursuit of wealth and self-interest would erode society's moral core. More broadly, Marx built an economic interpretation of history, arguing that "the mode of production in material life determines the general character of the social, political, and spiritual processes of life."[46] [For an introduction to Marxist thought, see **http://www.cla.purdue.edu/English/theory/marxism**].

Communism to Capitalism: A Bumpy Road

People in former communist nations in Eastern Europe, including Romania, Poland, Hungary, the Czech Republic, and Russia, report mixed feelings as they look back on the years following the fall of the Berlin Wall and the end of the Cold War between the former Soviet Union and the Western European/American allies. When dictatorships were replaced by democracy, the initial reaction was euphoria, but in subsequent years some nostalgia for the certainties of communism has emerged. A Czech professor summarized the current feelings of disappointment: "People here admired the freedom and prosperity of the Western world. Now what they see is materialism, corruption, inflation, lawlessness—and they can't find spiritual or material prosperity."[47] High unemployment, poverty, and harsh cuts in public spending have dashed the hopes for post-communist prosperity. Many in Eastern Europe yearn for the comfort of state-provided health care and education and state-subsidized goods and services, but the evidence suggests they tend to forget about the poor quality of those goods and services, state censorship, the absence of freedom, and fear of the state.

Question

1. Do you think capitalism, by its nature, is unfair to ordinary people? Explain.

Sources: Michael J. Jordan, "After the Berlin Wall, Nostalgia for Communism Creeps Back," *The Christian Science Monitor*, November 8, 2009 [**www.csmonitor.com/2009/1109/p11s01-woeu.html**]; and Kurt Biray, "Communist Nostalgia in Eastern Europe: Longing for the Past," *Open Democracy*, November 10, 2015 [**www.opendemocracy.net**].

Socialism

LO 1-4
Differentiate
between
communism and
socialism as
collectivist
philosophies.

Communism appears to have run its course philosophically and pragmatically, but the problems that generated its appeal—poverty, oppression, the rich–poor gap, and so on— remain. Government intervention in the market is often designed to address those problems. The question is: How much government is appropriate? Socialists provide one answer by rejecting communist totalitarianism and embracing democracy while calling for aggressive government intervention to correct economic and social ills. Historically, socialism has often been associated with democratic governments and peaceful change, whereas communism has been characterized by totalitarianism and violent revolution.

Socialists aim to retain the benefits of industrialism while abolishing the social costs often accompanying the free market. The government is likely to be directly involved in regulating growth, inflation, and unemployment. In the contemporary Western world, Austria, Norway, Denmark, Sweden, South Africa, Finland, and France are among the nations where socialist principles have retained a significant presence. Those nations have now embraced free markets, but socialist welfare concerns remain influential.

Socialist Goals

A critical distinction between socialists and capitalists is that the former believe a society's broad directions should be carefully planned rather than left to what some take to be the whimsy of the market. Socialists are convinced, furthermore, that problems of market failure (inadequate information, monopoly, externalities, public goods, and so on—see Chapter 8) mean that the free market is simply incapable of meeting the needs of all segments of society. The socialist agenda includes these elements:[48]

1. **Liberty.** To the capitalist, individual freedom suffers under socialism. To the socialist, the freedoms of capitalism are largely an illusion, accessible only to the prosperous and powerful.

2. **Social welfare.** Socialists reserve much of their concern for the harsh conditions of the lower class—poverty, exploitation, cultural deprivation, and more. Socialists believe that the economy must be directed toward the general interest rather than left free to expand the welfare of successful capitalists. Hence, socialists advocate income supports, free education, free health care, generous sick pay, family planning, and the like to correct the failures of capitalism.

3. **Fulfilling work.** Socialists object to the harshness of working life where a large segment of society is chained to degrading labor.

4. **Community.** Socialists seek a communitarian approach to life where the excessive individualism of capitalism is muted by a concern for the welfare of all.

> All humans are equally meritorious.

5. **Equality.** Class distinctions are anathema to the socialist. All humans are equally meritorious, and distinctions among them are inherently unjust.

6. **Rationality.** Socialists fear the "irrationality" of a society based on competition and unrestrained pursuit of industrial growth.[49]

As explained in the account that follows, poverty and claims of corporate exploitation have allowed socialism to regain a tentative foothold in parts of South America.

Socialism in South America

Deceased Venezuelan president Hugo Chavez hoped to build a "21st century socialism" in South America that would elevate the poor—forgotten by "savage capitalism"—while leading his country and neighbors, including Bolivia, Ecuador, Honduras, and Nicaragua, away from American dominance. He wanted to destroy what he saw as centuries of plundering, humiliation, and discrimination against indigenous people by monied interests, particularly American multinationals. Chavez said that world power is shifting from America:

> The uni-polar world has collapsed. The power of the U.S. empire has collapsed. Everyday, the new poles of world power are becoming stronger. Beijing, Tokyo, Tehran. . . . It's moving toward the East and toward the South.[50]

Chavez nationalized many companies, drove out ExxonMobil and ConocoPhillips, redistributed land, used the world's largest oil reserves to give money to the poor, and dramatically increased state funding for social projects. From 1999 to 2011, Venezuela's poverty rate fell by about 40 percent, and Chavez inspired many Venezuelans to engage in civic life and to feel a new concern for the nation's welfare. Critics, however, say he stifled dissent, took control of almost every government institution, and destroyed the nation's economy.

Post-Chavez Venezuela looks to be a failing state that is abandoning its democratic principles. Oil revenue has plunged, crime is rampant, and food shortages are routine. Current President Nicolas Maduro in early 2016 declared a state of economic emergency and raised fuel prices by 6,000 percent. Officials blocked a referendum designed to replace Maduro and to reform the Chavez "revolution."

Sources: Associated Press, "Chavez Asserts: We'll Bury Capitalism," *The Des Moines Register*, July 19, 2010, p. 10A; Associated Press, "Chavez in China Touts 'New World Order,'" *The Wall Street Journal*, April 8, 2009 [**http:// online.wsj.com**]; Lucas Koerner, "Venezuelan Businessman Replaces Leftist Sociologist as Economy Czar," *venezuelanalysis.com*, February 16, 2016 [**http://venezuelanalysis.com/news/11855**]; and Matt O'Brien, "Venezuela Should Be Rich. Instead It's Becoming a Failed State," *The Washington Post*, May 4, 2016 [**www.washingtonpost.com**].

Coping with Capitalism—China and Russia

China—Economics

LO 1-5
Discuss the current state of capitalism in China and Russia.

Troubled by stock speculation, a slowing economy, and currency (yuan or renminbi) manipulations by its central bank, China's stock market plunged in 2015 and 2016, raising new doubts about the communist leaders' power to assure the well-being of the nation.

China and some other nations practice what is sometimes labeled "state capitalism" in which the government is the dominant economic force as it intervenes in and shapes the market to further the state's political goals. The result has been something of an economic miracle as China has blended its large but shrinking system of state-owned enterprise with the explosive power of the free market (guided by the government) to become the globe's second-ranking economy as measured by gross national product.

China's president Xi Jinping has indicated that his nation of 1.38 billion people must boost market-based competition, but his commitment to the Communist Party seems firm. Facing reduced economic growth (but still reaching 7 to 8 percent annually), rising labor costs, crippling pollution and corruption, and a slower-than-hoped-for transition toward a consumer-driven growth model, China's leadership generally recognizes that adjustments are necessary. Financial reforms, pension and health care plans, rural land reform, and minimum wage rules are all on the table, but entrenched interests make change difficult.

State-owned firms control about 30 percent of the Chinese economy with about 120 giants controlled by the central government and about 150,000 smaller, state-owned companies.[51] Huge sectors of the economy are dominated by government entities, as explained by the *Los Angeles Times:*

> Need a cellphone plan? Choose from the trio of state-owned giants: China Mobile, China Telecom and China Unicom. Looking to fly? You're most likely to take one of the three major state carriers: Air China, China Southern and China Eastern. Upset about gas prices? They're determined by a government duopoly of PetroChina and Sinopec.[52]

China's Economic Future   Having quickly moved more people out of poverty than ever before in history and with a middle class now encompassing more than 10 percent of the population, China's extraordinary progress has changed the nation and the world. Now the economic slowdown, a broad and growing wealth/income gap, and other problems have raised concerns about the future. Perhaps the communist government has achieved the "easy part" of the China turnaround. Will the centralized, authoritarian communist leadership prove to be resourceful enough and flexible enough to cope with the challenges lying in China's economic future?

Law?   From a Western perspective, an underdeveloped ingredient in the Chinese system is the stability, predictability, and fairness that comes with a comprehensive, broadly respected legal system. The Chinese government has made progress in creating a workable legal structure, but a great deal of work remains, particularly in achieving a justice system free of political influence. Dependable, consistent protection of intellectual property; legal and regulatory transparency; and equal treatment for all parties, particularly in the technology sector, are qualities that seem necessary for China's long-term well-being and for the full integration of China's economy into the global trade network.

China—Politics

Freedom   Government repression remains routine in China. The government controls the media, as evidenced by censorship battles between the Chinese government and Internet news sources such as Google and *The New York Times,* and social media sites such as Facebook and Twitter, each of which is blocked to the Chinese public at this writing. China uses its "Great Firewall" of Internet censors to filter search results, particularly those addressing politically sensitive themes such as official corruption, democracy, Tibetan freedom, Taiwan, and the 1989 Tiananmen Square crackdown (during which troops killed hundreds of protesters during pro-democracy demonstrations in Beijing). Determined to maintain order and Communist Party authority, the Chinese government aggressively blocks Internet freedom.

China uses its "Great Firewall" of Internet censors to filter search results.

China has rejected calls to guarantee freedom of speech.

Reforms? Although China has rejected calls to guarantee freedom of speech and move toward democracy, the Communist Party leadership reportedly recognizes the need for gradual change. Curbing corruption in a nation routinely greased by bribes is a major element of President Xi's reform efforts. Bribery, drug use, gambling, and even golf (seen as a millionaires' playground and a convenient breeding ground for insider deals and official graft) are among the government's crackdown targets.

But even as the government attacks corruption and misconduct, it appears to be stifling citizen dissent and cracking down on human rights lawyers. For example, in 2015, President Xi reportedly urged universities to "enhance guidance over thinking and keep a tight grip on leading ideological work in higher education,"[53] and according to the *New York Times,* retired Chinese Major-General Song Fangmin has told colleagues that an internal government directive, Document No. 30, calls for "cleansing Western-inspired liberal ideas from universities and other cultural institutions."[54]

China is a nation in a historic but measured transition. The rule of law is increasingly powerful in Chinese life, as evidenced by a doubling of lawyers in recent years. Still Communist Party bosses use the law as a means of social control; repression remains common; and governance by the rule of law, where no person or political party is above the law, is not yet operative in China.[55] [For the latest Chinese news, see **http://thebeijingnews.net**].

China and America As *New York Times* columnist Thomas Friedman noted, the American and Chinese economies and futures are totally intertwined, with $600 billion in annual bilateral trade, 275,000 Chinese studying in America, and China serving as the largest foreign holder of U.S. debt.[56]

Can the two countries build a comfortable, mutually sustainable economic and political future? The Chinese people mistrust American global intentions and policies and see a new day in the future. According to a 2015 survey, 67 percent of Chinese respondents said their country would replace or already had replaced the United States as the world's dominant power.[57] At the same time, the United States is favorably viewed, at least among the young. They admire America's free-speech tradition, and they are avid consumers of American movies, music, and other popular culture.[58] Perhaps the current American–Chinese geopolitical rivalry is unavoidable, but American fear of Chinese dominance may be inflated, as suggested by civics educator and author Eric Liu:

> America has an enduring competitive advantage over China: America makes Chinese Americans; China does not make American Chinese. China does not want to or know how to take people from around the world, welcome them, and empower them to change the very fabric of their nation's culture.[59]

But Liu, the son of Chinese immigrants, says that America can profit from a "corrective dose" of Chinese values. He argues that Americans suffer from excessive individualism, short-term thinking, and exalting rights over duties, qualities that might be improved by embracing Chinese values of shared responsibility, long-term thinking, humility, and others. Liu says that Chinese culture at its best can bring to America "a better balance between being an individual and being in a community."[60] Do you agree with Liu?

Question

Technology entrepreneur and academic Vivek Wadhwa, in assessing emerging economic trends, asked, "Does China own the future—or does the United States?"[61] Answer Wadhwa's question.

Russia—Economics

Russia's commodity-based economy has struggled in recent years as oil and natural gas prices have plunged worldwide and Western nations have imposed economic sanctions on Russia for its Crimean annexation and its intervention in Ukraine. Government spending was cut by an announced 10 percent in 2016, but some economists believe Russia is gradually stabilizing its economy despite its challenges.

Notwithstanding Russia's struggles, Western visitors to modern Moscow must be hard-pressed to imagine that this energetic, consumption-happy, competitive city was once the global center of communism, the dour capital of the Union of Soviet Socialist Republics, and the home of America's nuclear enemy. After the fall of the USSR and the ideological defeat of communism, Russia developed its own form of state capitalism featuring new reliance on market forces blended with state intervention/direction, including extensive nationalization of industry and comprehensive economic planning. *The Christian Science Monitor* described Moscow's shift toward capitalism:

> The heavy, block buildings of Russia's capital are no longer covered in banners of Lenin, Marx, and Engels. Instead, enormous billboards advertise watches, cars, clothing—items unimaginable in Soviet times. Capitalism has taken hold with a vengeance.[62]

Russia remains something of a developing nation, ranking approximately 10th among the world's economies, although Russia's progress has been significant despite its inefficient reliance on "crony capitalism" (government favors to businesspeople) and widespread corruption. President Vladimir Putin's recent economic plans include a slowdown in the planned privatization of state-owned banks, utilities, oil companies, and other enormous assets. The Russian government controls about 55 percent of the nation's economy,[63] a presence that many economists believe must be reduced if Russia is to encourage foreign investment and achieve a vibrant economic future.

Russia—Politics

Russia exhibits democratic features such as elections and multiple political parties, but in practice President Putin and his allies exert authoritarian dominance on all important matters. Freedom of speech and assembly have been curtailed and honest treatment by the legal system often is missing.

Russia's future economic success is intimately tied, of course, to its political processes. The state needs to win over foreign multinational investors, who fear political tyranny and domestic corruption, but according to *Transparency International,* Russia is the world's most corrupt major economy, ranking 119th out of 167 countries (1 being least corrupt).[64]

> "Russia is remaking itself as the leader of the anti-Western world"

Russia and America   Russian American journalist and author Masha Gessen argues that "Russia is remaking itself as the leader of the anti-Western world."[65] Russian military intervention in Ukraine and Syria has intensified concerns about Russian global intentions. According to a 2015 Gallup Poll, however, the citizens of the 134 nations surveyed most strongly approved of American leadership among the five nations considered world leaders (China, EU, Germany, Russia, United States), while approval of Russian leadership ranked last in that group.[66]

Anti-Americanism is a common sentiment in Russia, a view that seems to be encouraged by the Russian government. Putin and his government defend "traditional values," fending off the "tolerance" and "diversity" of Western nations, and the United States in particular. Gay rights are a matter of special concern in Russia. Recent legislation bans the "propaganda of nontraditional sexual relations" and imposes fines for holding gay pride rallies or providing information about the gay community to minors.[67] The Russian people express strong support for President Putin, but critics question whether state capitalism as practiced in Russia can succeed in the face of political repression, routine corruption, and abuse of the rule of law.[68]

Questions

1. *New York Times* columnist David Brooks wrote recently about Russia's great intellectual and spiritual traditions (think of Tolstoy, Dostoyevsky, and Chekhov, e.g.):

   > The Russian ethos was not bourgeois, economically minded and pragmatic. There were radicals who believed that everything should be seen in materialistic terms. But this was a reaction to the dominant national tendency, which saw problems as primarily spiritual rather than practical, and put matters of the soul at center stage.[69]

   Today, Brooks thinks Russia is a more "normal" country, but its cultural impact has been diminished as grasping for power and money have become dominant motives. In moving toward a more market-based economy, are intellectual and spiritual life doomed in Russia (and all capitalist nations)? Explain. See David Brooks, "The Russia I Miss," *The New York Times,* September 11, 2015 [**www.nytimes.com**].

2. Can China maintain its closed, centrally controlled political system while enjoying the benefits of its somewhat open economic markets? Explain.

Part Four—Middle Ground? A Mixed Economy (The Third Way)

LO 1-6
Evaluate arguments regarding government's proper role in the American economy.

LO 1-7
Describe the primary characteristics of a "mixed economy."

Communism has failed. Socialist principles, to the extent they require central planning, bloated bureaucracies, and restraints on personal freedom, are discredited. The state capitalism of China, Russia, and other nations has little appeal in America and Western Europe and yet America's brand of free-market capitalism lost a great deal of luster in the recent financial collapse. Some left-of-center combination of free-market and welfare-state principles may be the next step. For years, the Nordic states of Sweden, Norway, Denmark, and Finland (Iceland might also be included) have practiced their form of market socialism (or social democracy) with such success that it is labeled a "Third Way" between the harsher extremes of capitalism and communism. Their welfare states have provided generally healthy economic conditions with cradle-to-grave social care for all in a system emphasizing the collective welfare over individual preferences. Finnish journalist Anu Partanen argues appealingly in her book *The Nordic Theory of Everything* (Harper, 2016) that in being spared worries over life's basic necessities, the Nordic people are able to be autonomous and creative.

Sweden

Life expectancy in Sweden as of 2015 was estimated at 81.98 years, as compared with about 78.68 years in the United States.[70] The government provides free or substantially free education, health care, and child care, along with parental leave, unemployment protection, and more. Government incentives promote preferred behaviors. For example, the Swedish government will pay 80 percent of a parent's salary (capped at $65,000) for up to 480 days of paid parental leave from work.

> Sweden provides free or substantially free education, health care, and child care.

Gender Equality

Sweden aggressively encourages gender equality.

Swedish schools strive to eradicate gender stereotypes. At Stockholm's "Egalia" (equality) preschool, for example, the staff avoids using the words "him" or "her" and addresses children as "hen" (an alternative to the male pronoun "han" and the female "hon") or as "friends." Children's books often feature gay couples, single parents, or adopted children and classics like *Cinderella* are shunned. Egalia's methods are controversial, even in Sweden.

Some Swedish theaters identify sexism in movies through the "Bechdel Test," which asks if the film in question has (A) at least two named female characters (B) who talk to each other (C) about something other than men.

Sources: John Tagliabue, "A School's Big Lesson Begins with Dropping Personal Pronouns," *The New York Times,* November 14, 2012, p. A8; and Nick Venable, "Swedish Theaters Judging All Releases for Gender Bias by Posting Bechdel Test Ratings," *Cinemablend,* March 23, 2015 [**www.cinemablend.com**].

Taxes   To pay for its cradle-to-grave welfare benefits, Sweden takes about 43 percent of its national income (gross domestic product—GDP) in taxes, while the United States, in contrast, has one of the developed world's lowest total tax burdens at about 26 percent of GDP.[71] In order to keep its economy healthy, Sweden has followed a policy of a comparatively low corporate tax rate of 22 percent, as compared with a U.S. rate of nearly 40 percent, federal and state combined. With deductions and loopholes included, however, the U.S. effective corporate tax rate is an estimated 29.2 percent, a rate roughly comparable to our competitor nations.[72]

Performance   Sweden's public debt is relatively low and its economic growth rate has been persistently strong. One of the results of that economic strength is a health care system that exceeds its U.S. counterpart on almost all performance measures but costs less than half as much per person (although waiting times for some nonemergency services might be considerably longer in Sweden).[73]

Politics   Worries about high taxes and heavy welfare costs led the Swedes to turn to eight years of center-right political leadership, resulting in a big reduction in business regulations while tens of thousands of the long-term unemployed were pushed back into the labor market. But Sweden in 2014 returned to its traditional center-left leadership as the public grew increasingly restive about a perceived decline in the welfare state.

Why?   One expert attributes the Third Way success to "lavish" spending on research and development as well as higher education.[74] Certainly active government intervention has been successfully combined with free-market principles in Sweden. Recent scholarship by Swedish expert Nima Sanandaji argues, however, that Sweden's prosperity and social justice cannot be attributed to the nation's socialist inclinations. Rather, her research indicates that the Nordic nation's prosperity developed in periods when free-market principles were ascendant. Furthermore, centuries of commitment to healthy values including hard work, egalitarianism, and social cohesion have been crucial to Sweden's success.[75]

We should remember that Sweden is a small, homogeneous nation. Replicating its policies in the United States would be difficult. And the Swedes are, of course, not free from difficulties. Accommodation of Middle East refugees, anger over alleged discrimination, declining school performance, and expanding income inequality are some of the challenges facing the Swedes.

Speeding Ticket

Businessman Reima Kuisla was threatening to leave his homeland in Finland after he was fined about $58,000 for driving at 14 miles over the posted 50 miles per hour speed limit. Kuisla's steep fine was based on his 2013 income of more than $7 million. Finland and the other Nordic nations impose progressive taxation based upon wealth in order to impose an actual penalty on the rich just as a lesser fine punishes those of more modest means. Presumably, Kuisla felt better about Finland after an appeal, which resulted in a reduced fine of about $5,500.

Question

Would you favor penalties in America based on income and wealth? Explain.

Source: Editorial, "Can't Drive 55? If in Finland, You Don't Want to Make $$," *The Des Moines Register*, May 2, 2015, p. 14A.

American Capitalism in Europe?

LO 1-8
Analyze the impact of capitalism on equality, fairness, and community in American and global society.

Does the European Union—ranging broadly from the Scandinavian Third Way to Germany's cooperative but increasingly aggressive capitalism—have a better long-term vision for personal and societal welfare than the United States? Is America's more libertarian "cowboy capitalism" better adapted to the globe's demands than the "coordinated, stakeholder capitalism" characteristic of much of Europe? The evidence is mixed. In building entrepreneurial spirit, personal freedom, and personal wealth and income, the United States is the clear world leader, but the EU's powerful, 500-million-person bloc generates a nominal gross national product somewhat larger than that of the United States. For Europeans, however, quantity seems to be less important than quality. Europeans choose to work less than Americans and, as they see it, enjoy life more. Their economy is less flexible than ours and typically produces fewer jobs, but it is also less harsh. Universal health care, job protection, and strong unemployment benefits are part of the European identity.

Welfare Reform   Europe's warm communal values and practices are inviting, but the aftereffects of the 2008 recession have resulted in a EU unemployment rate of nearly 9.0 percent (as compared with about 5.0 percent in the United States) and the need for Eurozone economic bailouts of nearly bankrupt economies in Ireland, Greece, Spain, and Portugal. Youth (age 15–24) unemployment at about 20 percent for the EU generally[76] and nearly 50 percent in Spain and Greece has produced something approaching a "lost generation"[77] in some countries. In Italy more than 40 percent of 25- to 34-year-olds continue to live at home.[78]

These struggles have also sharpened the divide between the more prosperous northern European nations (Germany's unemployment rate is just over 4.0 percent) and the struggling south (unemployment in Greece exceeds 20 percent).[79] Some nations have instituted austerity policies in the form of higher taxes and sharp cutbacks in government spending. In France, for example, significant government welfare cuts have been implemented. Public spending amounting to more than 50 percent of GDP had produced a protected population with strong family support, low poverty, and generous pensions, but for the present, at least, the French government has concluded that some trimming is necessary.

Germany, on the other hand, has been able to balance a rather generous social safety net (long-term care, vacations, pensions, etc.) with a very robust and highly skilled manufacturing sector, and an effective government to produce job security and a comfortable life. Germany has managed its budget carefully, adopted reforms such as an increased retirement age, and maintained a strong market-based economy to support its social programs.

Brexit/EU Failure?   Struggling to assimilate migrants, fed up with European Union regulatory oversight, and perhaps seeking a renewed sense of Britain as a proud nation state, the British people voted by a narrow margin in 2016 to break from the EU ("Brexit"). At this writing, British authorities must prepare for the exit and establish rules for an independent Britain's economic and political relationship with the EU. Uncertainty about the effect of Brexit is the dominant message of the moment, but both Brexit in Britain and Donald Trump's political movement in America seem, in part, to be messages of deepening unease over globalization, a force that critics blame for blue-collar economic decline while elites thrive.[80]

Will other nations also leave the EU? The Great Recession shook the European Union—so much so that Yale professor Nicholas Sambanis asked in *The New York Times,* "Has 'Europe' Failed?"[81] He argued that the European Union's problems extend beyond economics to its very identity. Can the EU remain united or will its citizens, particularly in the wealthier nations, identify more with their native homeland than with the EU?

Contrasting Values

Obviously, both Europe and America are struggling in this troubled time, but which vision of life seems most promising over the long term? American commentator and social activist Jeremy Rifkin contrasted the American and European "Dreams":[82]

American Dream	vs.	European Dream
Wealth/Individual success	vs.	Quality of life
Growth	vs.	Sustainable development
Property/Civil rights	vs.	Social/Human rights
Live to work	vs.	Work to live
Religiosity/Piety	vs.	Declining faith
Strong military	vs.	Build peace

Rifkin argued that the European strategy is the better one. What do you think? Which of those two lists of values is more comfortable and inspiring for you? Which is more likely to meet the demands of the ongoing global competition and evolution?

Is the Welfare State a Key to Personal Happiness?

Denmark turns out to be the happiest place on Earth, according to the 2016 United Nations/Gallup Poll study of global happiness. The top five countries on the happiness list are European states with strong welfare principles: Denmark (1), Switzerland (2), Iceland (3), Norway (4), and Finland (5). The United States ranks 13th on the list, behind Canada (6) and Sweden (10) and ahead of Germany (16), Mexico (21), United Kingdom (23), Japan (53), Russia (56), and China (83).

What qualities lead to happiness? Broadly, good health, education, freedom, and wealth are associated with happiness, but wealth seems to increase happiness only up to a point. According to a 2010 study, happiness basically peaks at a salary of about $75,000 annually in the United States, and a 2015 study found that the power of money to reduce negative emotions begins to fall off around $70,000 and hits zero around $200,000.

Purpose? So money apparently can help with happiness, but studies show that having money seems to make little difference in building a meaningful life. People from wealthier countries seem to be happier, but people from poorer countries tend to view their lives as being more meaningful. Being more religious, having more children, and achieving stronger social ties may account for that sense of meaning.

Community? Why are the Scandinavian people particularly happy? Simply "hanging out" with friends and family seems to be critical to happiness in Denmark. Ninety-two percent of Danes belong to some kind of social club, and the government encourages these get-togethers by helping to pay for them. Likewise, while Danes value nice things, they are said to be a "post-consumerist" society where consumption is not a high priority. Their extraordinarily high taxes (around 50 percent of income) may also play a role in the happiness quotient in that income is substantially leveled, allowing careers to be chosen more on the basis of interest rather than money and also allowing everyone to "hold his/her head high" regardless of occupational status. Finally, experts point particularly to the Danes' very high quotient of trust, which may be a product of the cradle-to-grave security provided by the government. For example, mothers commonly leave their babies unattended in strollers outside shops and restaurants. Of course, Denmark has the advantage of being a small, homogeneous nation largely free of America's worldwide responsibilities.

Questions

For several decades, the tiny Himalayan nation of Bhutan has sought to measure itself, not by gross domestic product (GDP), but by gross national happiness (GNH), calculated from the nation's "four pillars" of sustainable development, environmental protection, cultural preservation, and good governance, each of equal importance.

1. Would the United States be a better nation if we sought GNH rather than GDP?
2. Would pursuit of GNH produce a winner in today's fierce global competition? Explain.

Sources: John Helliwell, Richard Layard, and Jeffrey Sachs, eds., "World Happiness Report *2016* Update" [**www.worldhappiness.report**]; *Mark Fahey,* "Money Can Buy Happiness, but Only to a Point," *CNBC*, December 14, 2015 [**www.cnbc.com**]; Daisy Grewal, "A Happy Life May Not Be a Meaningful Life," *Scientific American*, February 18, 2014 [**www.scientificamerican.com**]; Rin Hamburgh, "Can Money Buy Happiness?" *The Guardian*, January 7, 2016 [**www.theguardian.com**]; Brook Larmer, "Bhutan's Enlightened Experiment," *National Geographic Magazine*, March 2008 [**http://ngm.nationalgeographic.com/2008/03/bhutan/larmer-text**]; and Bill Weir and Sylvia Johnson, "Denmark: The Happiest Place on Earth," *ABC News*, January 8, 2007 [**http://abcnews.go.com/2020/story?id=40860928page=1**].

Questions—Parts Three and Four

1. Billionaire investor George Soros, in his book *Open Society,* saw "market fundamentalism as a greater threat to open society today than communism."[83] Soros feared contemporary capitalism's extreme commitment to self-interest, which results, he said, in our greatest challenge: "to establish a set of fundamental values."[84]
   a. Explain what Soros meant.
   b. Do you agree with him? Explain.
2. A majority of Americans have faith in the free market. Explain some of the weaknesses in the market. That is, where is the free market likely to fail?
3. Writing in *Dissent,* Joanne Barkan says, "[A]lmost all Swedes view poverty, extreme inequalities of wealth, and the degradation that comes with unemployment as unacceptable."[85]
   a. Do you agree with the Swedes? Explain.
   b. Why are Americans more tolerant of those conditions than are the Swedes?
4. Scholars Daron Acemoglu, James A. Robinson, and Thierry Verdier have argued that the United States would hurt world growth if it adopted the "cuddly capitalism" of Scandinavia. For the United States to maintain its vital role of chief global innovator, Acemoglu and Verdier say that America must maintain an economic system that generously rewards successful innovators, which "implies greater inequality and greater poverty (and a weaker safety net) for a society encouraging innovation."[86] Do you agree? Explain.

5. *a.* Should an American citizen's primary duty be to herself or himself or to all other members of society? Explain.

   b. Should all humans be regarded as of equal value and thus equally worthy of our individual support? Explain.

   c. Can social harmony be achieved in a nation whose citizens fail to regard the state as a "super-family"? Explain.

6. According to a 2014 Pew Research survey examining opinions about the role of government, younger Americans (Millennials) favor bigger government and more services by a 53 to 38 margin, while older Americans (Gen X and Boomers) prefer smaller government and fewer services.[87] How do you account for that difference of views by age?

7. In questioning Oakland Athletics general manager Billy Beane, *The Wall Street Journal* described professional football as "socialist" and baseball as "capitalist":

   > The NFL (National Football League) has been successful as a socialist league, equally divvying up the league's revenue among all the teams. Major league baseball, on the other hand, is a capitalist league, with a clear divide between big-market and small-market teams.[88]

   a. Do you think some of major league baseball's financial rules have to be changed to better balance the playing field?

   b. Is "socialism" or "capitalism" the better system for professional sports? Explain.

8. Pope Francis in 2014 referred to Europe as "elderly and haggard."

   a. List those economic and social conditions in current European life that might have generated the Pope's observation.

   b. Would a more aggressively capitalist Europe be younger and more vibrant? Explain.

Part Five—America's Economic Future: Where Are We Going?

How Much Government? Should we expand our faith in free-market capitalism, or do we need to move our present mixed economy a bit closer to the welfare state model, which itself is under great pressure? Or must a new model emerge? In sum, how much government do we need? To think further about those questions, let's briefly examine some of the key indicators of America's economic and social health.

> Americans have a great deal to be proud of.

Good News Of course, Americans have a great deal to be proud of. We enjoy extraordinary material comfort along with healthy, generally safe lives. As the *Los Angeles Times* reported, since 1980 the percentage of those earning $100,000 or more, in today's dollars, has doubled; the average size of our homes has doubled in the past 50 years to about 2,200 square feet; and the total hours spent working have declined steadily for over 150 years.[89] We are inventive, adventuresome, free, and zealously democratic. Roughly half of all patents are earned by Americans, minorities now hold high-ranking political office, and more women than men are earning college degrees.[90] Much of the world strives to achieve America's blend of entrepreneurial capitalism along with intellectual and pop culture leadership. And we should not forget that capitalist America is among the most generous of global cultures. Indeed, Americans gave a record $358 billion in 2014[91] and polling data ranked the United States first in the world in 2014 and second to Myanmar in 2015 in helping others (donations, volunteering, and aiding strangers).[92]

The American Dream at Risk?

LO 1-9
Describe the income and wealth gaps in America.

America is strong but struggling. Globalization and new technology, in the short run at least, have chipped away at our blue-collar job market. Labor unions have lost much of their power. Our multinational giants seem to be more interested in investing abroad than in America.

The United States remains the world's richest large country, as measured by per capita gross domestic product, but family income has declined or stagnated for years even though overall productivity is generally up. And while individuals with post-college degrees are doing well financially, inflation-adjusted wages for college graduates have been essentially flat for more than a decade.[93] The Great Recession itself explains part of our weak income performance, but the greater long-term problem is that growth in literacy, numeracy, technological skills, and overall educational levels, particularly for young people, has fallen behind our peer nations.

The core of America—the middle class—and the very idea of the American Dream seem at risk. The portion of Americans living in middle-class circumstances declined from 61 percent in 1971 to 50 percent today.[94] Many have moved up, of course, but an increase in those falling to the bottom appears to be the biggest reason for the middle-class shrinkage.[95] Furthermore, middle income growth in other economically advanced countries has exceeded U.S. growth over the past 30 years.[96] Indeed, Canada has now pulled ahead of the United States in middle-class after-tax income.[97]

These discouraging trends were at least temporarily eased in 2015 when American households enjoyed a 5.2 percent increase in income (to an average of $56,516), the biggest jump since 1967.[98] Despite that good news, should we question the top-to-bottom vitality and fairness of our American system? Let's examine some concerns.

Overall Quality of Life

According to a U.N. 2015 report on overall quality of life (based on income, life expectancy, and education), America is doing relatively well, ranking eighth behind Norway (1st) and Australia (2nd).[99] A similar but broader study, the 2015 Social Progress Index, ranked the United States 16th in the world on general quality of life, with Norway and Sweden at the top. America ranks first in freedom of speech and access to advanced education but 30th in personal safety, 30th in life expectancy, and 39th in nutrition and basic medical care.[100]

> America ranks first in freedom of speech.

In general, the United States compares well on standard economic measures and not so well on standard social measures. Our 2015 estimated GDP per capita of $56,300 ranked 19th in the world behind smaller, more specialized economies such as Qatar (1st at $145,000) and Norway (11th at $68,400) and well ahead of our chief industrial rivals such as Germany (29th at $47,400) and Japan (42nd at $38,200).[101]

> The United States leads the world in producing prisoners.

Among the most perplexing areas of U.S. social performance is infant mortality (the probability of dying between birth and age one per 1,000 live births), where infants in 57 nations have a better chance of survival.[102] And even though crime has been declining for a number of years, the United States leads the world in producing prisoners, with nearly seven million in prison, on parole, or on probation.[103]

The United States ranks fifth in the world in total spending for education, but young adult college completion rates have fallen to 14th globally, national K–12 test scores are only middling by international norms, and just half of 3-year-olds are enrolled in preschool (as compared with 90 percent in France, Italy, and Norway).[104] Family structures are changing dramatically. A record 40 percent of households with children under 18 include a mother who is either the sole or primary source of income, with two-thirds of those being single mothers.[105] Marriage itself is in decline, particularly among those who are not well educated.[106] The economically and socially productive institution of marriage with children apparently is becoming a sort of luxury item for growing numbers of middle Americans.

Poverty

The number of Americans in poverty declined in 2015, but 13.5 percent of the population still fell below the official government poverty line ($24,300 for a family of four in 2016).[107] Furthermore, economic insecurity often reaches even those who are working hard:

> While attending high school in the mid-1990s, Derrell Odom worked at KFC, earning $5.50 an hour. That's the equivalent of $8.61 today. After two years of college, two military tours in Iraq and other jobs, he is back working as a cook at an Atlanta location of the fried chicken chain. Two decades after this first stint at KFC, his hourly pay now is only $7.25 an hour.[108]

A 2016 Stanford Center on Poverty and Inequality study ranked the United States 10th of 10 developed countries on measures of poverty and inequality.[109] The result of these difficult economic conditions is that poor people, as commentator Paul Krugman explained, live in a separate America:

> Living in or near poverty has always been a form of exile, of being cut off from the larger society. . . . To be poor in America today, even more than in the past, is to be an outcast in your own country.[110]

Pets or People?

We may not take the best care of our disadvantaged fellow Americans, but we seem to be unstinting in generosity toward our pets. In 2015, Americans spent nearly $61 billion on their pets, a sum that exceeds the gross domestic product of all but about 75 nations.

Question

Would our money for pets be more wisely spent on impoverished children? Explain.

Sources: Amelia Josephson, "The Economics of the Pet Industry," *SmartAsset.com,* December 25, 2015 [**https://smartasset.com**]; and World Bank, "Gross Domestic Product," World Development Indicators database, February 17, 2016 [**http://databank.worldbank.org/data/download/GDP.pdf**].

The Gaps

Extravagant wealth, side-by-side with punishing poverty, is perhaps the greatest disappointment and injustice, from the critics' point of view, in the global advance of capitalist principles.

In recent decades, America's wealth distribution has come to look like a balloon suspended above a very long, narrow string. America's 20 wealthiest people now own more wealth than the entire bottom half of the nation's population (over 150 million people), and the wealthiest 100 households now own about as much wealth as the nation's total African-American population.[111] On a global scale, the 62 richest billionaires own as much wealth as the poorer half of the world's population, about 3.7 billion people.[112] Similarly, the income gap in America has been growing majestically. Fifty years ago, the ratio of CEO to average worker pay, for example, was about 20 to 1; today it is about 300 to 1.[113]

Those gaps in wealth and income raise concerns about fundamental unfairness in American life that might undermine democracy and public health while reducing overall economic strength and social cohesion. Those worries might be diminished if we could be assured that the American Dream of upward mobility is flourishing, but the evidence suggests that mobility has been, at best, unchanged over the past half century.[114] The United States, according to a recent Stanford University study, ranks only eighth among the world's global economic powers in individual ability to move up the economic ladder.[115] Of course, from a free-market perspective, we would argue that the wealth and income gaps are necessary spurs to greater ambition and productivity. [For a discussion of recent research challenging the mainstream findings on income inequality, see Thomas B. Edsall, "What If We're Looking at Inequality the Wrong Way?" *The New York Times,* June 26, 2013, at **http://opinionator.blogs.nytimes.com/**].

PRACTICING ETHICS   Moral Decay in White Working-Class America?

What forces have caused the growing income and wealth gaps in America? Libertarian scholar Charles Murray, in his controversial book *Coming Apart: The State of White America, 1960–2010,* looks at the blue-collar, white working class for some answers. He points to declining moral values in that group as a crucial factor in American inequality and reduced mobility. He provides evidence of an alarming fall in white working-class social capital (neighborliness and civic engagement) prompted by decreasing industry, community, religion, and marriage. Murray does not ignore similar problems in the black working class, but his focus is on white people.

Questions

1. Do you agree with Murray that the erosion of traditional middle-class morals/values helps explain inequality in contemporary America?

2. What other forces might have contributed to increasing inequality in American life?

3. Based on your personal sense of fairness, is a large and growing gap in income and wealth in America an ethical wrong? Explain.

Sources: Charles Murray, *Coming Apart: The State of White America, 1960–2010* (New York: Crown Forum, 2012); and Thomas B. Edsall, "What to Do about 'Coming Apart'," *The New York Times,* February 12, 2012 [**http://campaignstops.blogs.nytimes.com/**].

Community

We see that American capitalism, despite its extraordinary success, is criticized for problems of poverty, inequality, and unfairness. Perhaps the decline of community should join that list. Mounting evidence suggests that our lives are increasingly solitary, distant, and estranged. The market is driven by and rewards individual achievement.

> Spending money on others rather than on oneself produced greater levels of happiness.

Could that struggle for material success be depriving us of the full satisfaction of our shared humanity? A 2013 study found that even trivial exposure to money can trigger unethical intentions and behavior,[116] while a 2008 study demonstrated that spending money on others rather than on oneself produced greater levels of happiness.[117]

Whether a product of capitalist impulses or not, we do have evidence of declining social connections. Only 30 percent of Americans, according to a 2008 study, report a close confidant at work, down from nearly 50 percent in 1985, and American workers report inviting 32 percent of their "close" colleagues to their homes, while Polish and Indian workers report inviting more than double that percentage.[118] More worrisome perhaps are findings from a 2011 study where Americans reported an average of only

> Americans reported only two discussion confidants in their lives.

two discussion confidants in their lives, down from a mean of three in 1985.[119] Current high school students, on the other hand, report modest decreases in loneliness, but they also report having fewer friends and a reduced desire for more friends as compared with teens of the past.[120]

Individualism Up, Morality Down?

Scholars now have access to a giant Google database of 5.2 million books published between 1500 and 2008. They can type in a word and see how frequently it has been used over the years. One study looking at 1960 to 2008 found individualistic words (e.g., self, standout, unique) were used more frequently over those 48 years, whereas communal words (e.g., collective, common good, band together) declined in use. Another study found that general moral terms (e.g., virtue, decency, conscience) and words associated with moral excellence (e.g., honesty, patience, compassion) receded in use over the course of the 20th century.

Questions

1. Do you see a link between increasing attention to individualism and declining attention to morality? Explain.
2. Do you think government can or should do anything about these changing social conditions and the link between them, if it does exist? Explain.

Source: David Brooks, "What Our Words Tell Us," *The New York Times,* May 20, 2013 [www.nytimes.com].

Shrinking Social Capital?

In his now famous book *Bowling Alone,* Robert Putnam meticulously documented the decline of what he labeled "social capital," the community and commitment bonds that seem to emerge in a culture where people regularly interact with one another.[121] Putnam's book explains that virtually every measure of social interaction, from voting to picnics, to playing cards, to church attendance, to membership in social clubs fell significantly from roughly 1975 to 2000. The most vivid example was a decline of 40 percent in league bowling from 1980 to 2000, although the total number of bowlers increased by about 10 percent, thus the notion of "bowling alone." Although social media and other new methods of community engagement are emerging, interpersonal trust may be eroding. Only one-third of Americans say most people can be trusted, down from one-half in 1972.[122] Another recent survey, however, did show increasing trust in neighbors.[123]

An Opportunity Gap and Declining Community?

Putnam's most recent book, *Our Kids: The American Dream in Crisis,*[124] describes the expanding socioeconomic gap between the children of educated parents and the children of parents barely clinging to economic survival. *The Washington Post* summarized some of the crippling consequences of that gap for the disadvantaged children:

> The poor children in "Our Kids" are missing so much more than material wealth. They have few mentors. They're half as likely as wealthy kids to trust their neighbors. The schools they attend offer fewer sports, and they're less likely to participate in after-school activities. Even their parents have smaller social networks.[125]

One of the results of this opportunity divide is that children of the well-off express increasing trust in those around them while that trust has "collapsed" among the less-well-off children.[126]

Questions

1. Is Putnam correct about (a) declining social capital in America and (b) a growing opportunity gap between affluent and less-well-off children? Explain.

2. American Dan Lawton commented on his first trip to Africa:

> In Ghana, I have danced, eaten, and spoken with more strangers in six weeks than I would have in America in six years. And this paradox—that despite its material wealth and technological might America is so standoffish and lonely—has been burning a hole in my head.[127]

   a. Do you agree that Americans are "standoffish and lonely"?
   b. If so, do you have any explanation for that condition?

PRACTICING ETHICS   Technology and Loneliness

Since publishing *Bowling Alone,* Robert Putnam has said we need to develop new kinds of connections when old ones die. Electronic links often are considered part of the problem, but he believes they could also be part of the solution. Indeed, a 2008 survey of American adults found 60 percent saying that new technologies had not affected the closeness of their families and a 2011 study found that self-reported feelings of empathy were higher among college students the more time they spent on Facebook. On the other hand, a 2009 Pew report found that social networking users are 26 percent less likely than others to turn to their neighbors for companionship, and a 2016 study of U.K. college students found a negative association between "excessive" Twitter use and "real life" social interaction. MIT professor Sherry Turkle says that we have sacrificed conversation for "mere connection":

> We've become accustomed to a new way of being "along together." Technology-enabled, we are able to be with one

another, and also elsewhere, connected to wherever we want to be.[128]

Questions

1. In your view, is Turkle correct? Explain.

2. How might our ethical standards and performances be affected by excessive reliance on social technology?

Sources: Charles M. Blow, "Friends, Neighbors and Facebook," *The New York Times,* June 11, 2010 [**www.nytimes.com**]; Yamikani Ndasauka et al., "Excessive Use of Twitter Among College Students in the UK," *Computers in Human Behavior* 55, part B (February 2016), p. 963; Donna St. George, "Internet, Cell Phones May Strengthen Family Unit, Study Finds," October 20, 2008, p. A07 [**www.washingtonpost.com**]; and Shirley S. Wang, "Could Those Hours Online Be Making Kids Nicer?" *The Wall Street Journal,* August 16, 2011, p. D1.

Too Much Capitalism? Or Too Little?

Has America placed too much faith in the market and too little in government? Is the alleged decline in community in some sense a product of capitalism itself? Are poverty, inequality, crime, and the Wall Street collapse inevitable by-products of a "selfish, greedy" market? As a 20-year-old Cuban student and communist organizer argued: "Capitalism is more efficient. . . . But it is not more fair."[129] Even some conservatives are troubled:

> ### Unbridled capitalism is a problem for human beings.

"What I'm concerned about is the idolatry of the market," says conservative intellectual William Bennett, a former education secretary and author of *The Book of Virtues.* He worries particularly that the market for popular music and movies with sexual or violent content has a corrosive effect. "Unbridled capitalism . . . may not be a problem for production and for expansion of the economic pie, but it's a problem for human beings. It's a problem for . . . the realm of values and human relationships."[130]

Can robust capitalism be sustained if it produces not just efficiency and growth but also extreme income and wealth gaps, corruption, and injustice? Can we improve the market through judicious regulation, or should we return to a "purer" form of capitalism with dramatically reduced government? Or must we look for new answers?

A "Remix" Needed?

Following the Great Recession, the government stepped in to bail out a failing economy, but that shift to the left does not signal the sharp decline of markets. According to a 2013 nationwide Marist Poll, 55 percent of Americans favor free enterprise and fear expanded government regulation of business.[131] Perhaps some form of "re-mix" is needed. Journalist Anatole Kaletsky, author of *Capitalism 4.0: The Birth of a New Economy*,[132] reminds us that capitalism is adaptive, reinventing itself through crises.[133] Scholar Robert Skidelsky summarized Kaletsky's view of the evolution of capitalism:

> Laissez-faire Capitalism 1.0, inspired by Adam Smith, lasted from the Napoleonic wars to the First World War, the Russian Revolution and the mass unemployment of the 1930s. Then came the Capitalism 2.0 of John Maynard Keynes, Franklin D. Roosevelt's New Deal and the welfare state, which eventually provoked Capitalism 3.0 in the 1970s in reaction to rising inflation. Capitalism 3.0, a modified return to laissez-faire, has just self-destructed, leaving the door open to Capitalism 4.0.[134]

Kaletsky thinks his Capitalism 4.0 will involve closer government–business relationships with markets operating in a context set to a greater extent by public officials. The business community will need to acknowledge duties beyond profit maximization. Nonetheless, Kaletsky is a strong believer in markets, and he thinks government will need to spend less even as it responds to new responsibilities.

A New World Consensus?

Notwithstanding Kaletsky's hope for a more rational market–government balance, other thinkers say the world is already reshaping itself into two conflicting forms of capitalism.

In his book *The End of the Free Market*,[135] political scientist Ian Bremmer says capitalism may have established its claim as the best economic system, but the world is still in conflict over whether capitalism is the best political/social/economic system. As *New York Times* columnist David Brooks explained in reviewing Bremmer's work, the world now seems to be divided into a pair of general camps. *Democratic capitalism,* in the United States and other nations, respects business as the best wealth creator while employing government to regulate as needed. *State capitalism*, in countries such as China, Russia, and Saudi Arabia, employs market principles to build wealth. The state then controls or guides the distribution of that wealth for its sociopolitical purposes. State capitalism is often criticized for its inefficiency, but some scholars argue that ". . . . new varieties of state capitalism are . . . often performing at least equal to, if not better than, their private counterparts."[136]

Serve All? Former U.S. Secretary of Labor Robert Reich argues that Western capitalism will prevail, but he also says we cannot have a free market without government setting the rules. The real debate, as he sees it, is about whether capitalism can be good for all:

> Capitalism is going to become the universal system of economic organization. The real issue isn't capitalism versus some other "ism." The real issue is whether capitalism is organized for the benefit of the society as a whole or for the benefit of a small group at the top.[137]

Questions—Part Five

1. As you see it, is Western democratic capitalism or state capitalism more likely to prevail over the long term? Explain.

2. Roger Cohen, writing in *The New York Times,* made the interesting point that India, as of 2010, had more cell phones than toilets: 563.7 million people connected to modern communication, but only 366 million had access to modern sanitation. He says this

imbalance could be seen as "skewed development" favoring private goods over public necessities. In India and in America, he sees a kind of schizophrenia where we are increasingly autonomous, wanting to be left alone; our technology connecting us, allowing us to feel no need for government until a crisis, like the recent meltdown, arrives. Then many desperately plead for the government to save us.[138]

  a. Are we giving too much attention to private needs and too little, via government and taxes, to public goods? Explain.

  b. Can we have an autonomous, free-market culture, substantially contemptuous of government, and still maintain a stable, healthy, and fair national and global community? Explain.

3. *a.* Is America deliberately seeking to convert the balance of the globe to American, free-market, democratic values?

  b. Would all nations be well served if they adopted American, free-market, democratic values? Explain.

4. In what ways might American culture be viewed as offensive and threatening to Muslims and others around the globe?

Internet Exercise

The Global Policy Forum provides a broad overview of the globalization movement. Go to the Forum's "Globalization of Law" page [**http://www.globalpolicy.org/globalization/globalization-of-law.html**]. Explain how globalization is changing international legal systems.

Chapter Questions

1. The gravestone of the late baseball great Jackie Robinson is inscribed with this advice: "A life is not important except in the impact it has on other lives." Will your life be meaningful only if you contribute to the well-being of others? Explain.

2. Commenting in *Newsweek*, economist Robert Samuelson said, "The . . . pervasive problem of capitalist economies is that almost no one fully trusts capitalists."[139]

  a. Do you agree? Why?

  b. Do you think free-market capitalism is the best economic system? Explain.

  c. Do you think that multinational companies have more power than national governments? Explain.

3. *a.* In your mature years, do you expect to be as wealthy as your parents, or more so? Explain.

  b. Do you think you deserve to be as wealthy as your parents, or more so, or less so? Explain.

4. According to a 2011 Congressional Budget Office study, the share of government benefits going to the bottom fifth of Americans has declined from 54 percent in 1979 to 36 percent in 2007.[140] According to the conservative Tax Foundation, in 2010, 60 percent of Americans were receiving more in government benefits than they paid in taxes.[141] (Of course, many of those people paid higher taxes in subsequent years.)

  a. Other than aid to those who are poor, disabled, and/or aged, what government benefit programs are you aware of that provide support to working and middle-class Americans?

   b. Do you think it is "fair" that more than half of Americans receive more in government benefits than they pay in taxes? Explain.

   c. Former U.S. Senator Daniel Patrick Moynihan said, ". . . the issue of welfare is not what it costs those who provide it but what it costs those who receive it."[142] What did he mean? Do you agree? Explain. See George Will, "The Harm Incurred by a Mushrooming Welfare State," *The Washington Post*, January 21, 2014 [**www. washingtonpost.com**].

5. *a.* Noted economist Lester Thurow argued that the economic demands of the market are destroying the traditional two-parent, nuclear family. Explain his argument.

   b. Child development authority Benjamin Spock likewise blamed capitalism for the "destruction of the American family," but his reasoning differed from Thurow's:

> The overriding problem is excessive competition and our glorification of it. It may contribute to our rapid technological advancement, but it has done so at a great price. We are taught to be rugged individualists, and we are obsessed with getting ahead. The family gets lost in this intense struggle. In a healthy society, family should come first, community second, and our outside jobs third. In this country, it is the other way around.[143]

Comment.

   c. If Spock was correct, how did we reach this condition?

6. *a.* Scholars Jacob Hacker and Paul Pierson argue in their book *American Amnesia*[144] that a strong government is crucial to American economic growth.[145] Do you agree? Explain.

   b. Hacker and Pierson note that Americans have historically been, on average, the tallest people in the world, but in recent decades Scandinavian and Dutch citizens have passed Americans. Genetics and immigration cannot account for the change. Hacker and Pierson theorize that strong governments in those nations explain their citizen's robust growth. Why might strong government produce taller citizens?

7. We often read that college professors frequently criticize capitalism and support welfare state principles.

   a. Has that been your experience? Explain.

   b. If that assessment is accurate, how do you account for the leftist inclinations among intellectuals?

8. Should we reduce the government's presence throughout our lives? Consider a couple of possibilities.

   a. Facing severe financial problems, the state of Nevada was thinking of expanding legal prostitution from its current rural areas to the gambling centers, Las Vegas and Reno. Do you think legal prostitution managed by the market but subject to reasonable health and safety regulation would be a good policy for your state or any state? Explain.

   b. The bitter, ongoing debate about same-sex marriage raises the question of whether the state's role in marriage should be eliminated. Explain why the state should or should not be involved in regulating marriage. See "Why Do We Need the State's

Permission to Get Married Anyway?" *The Wall Street Journal*, January 14, 2010 [**http://blogs.wsj.com/2010/01/14/why-do-we-need-to-ask-the-state-for-permission-to-get-married-anyway/**].

9. If we are fundamentally selfish, must we embrace capitalism as the most accurate and, therefore, most efficient expression of human nature? Explain.

10. About 57 percent of American college students are female. In 2014, 37.5 percent of women ages 25 to 34 had earned a bachelor's degree, as compared with about 29.5 percent of males of the same age.[146] How do you explain those gaps and what, if anything, do they portend for the future of America?

11. *New York Times* columnist Nicholas Kristof wrote what he called a "blunt" and "politically incorrect truth" about global poverty:

   > It's that if the poorest families spent as much money educating their children as they do on wine, cigarettes and prostitutes, their children's children's prospects would be transformed.[147]

   He told about one Congolese family that is eight months behind on its $6 per month rent and is unable to pay for mosquito netting ($6 each) or the $2.50 per month school tuition for each of their three school-age children. But the parents do spend $10 per month on cell phone expenses, and the father does drink several times weekly at a cost of about $1 per night.[148]

   a. What solutions would you suggest to protect children from the ill-advised financial choices of their fathers and mothers?

   b. Do you think poor parental choices are a significant feature of child suffering in the United States? Explain.

   c. Do you think reduced government in the United States would likely lead to increased personal responsibility? Explain.

12. Commentator Thomas Friedman reflects on the Islamic terrorists' hatred for America:

   > Their constant refrain is that America is a country with wealth and power but "no values." The Islamic terrorists think our wealth and power is unrelated to anything in the soul of this country. . . . Of course, what this view of America completely misses is that American power and wealth flow directly from a deep spiritual source—a spirit of respect for the individual, a spirit of tolerance for differences of faith or politics, a respect for freedom of thought as the necessary foundation for all creativity, and a spirit of unity that encompasses all kinds of differences. Only a society with a deep spiritual energy, that welcomes immigrants and worships freedom, could constantly renew itself and its sources of power and wealth.[149]

   a. Do you agree that the "spiritual source" Friedman cites is the foundation for American success? Explain.

   b. Is America without a meaningful "soul"? Explain.

13. *a.* Make the argument that America's free-market economy is better for children than the welfare-state approach in northern Europe.

   b. Do you think that argument is correct? That is, do you think children are better off in America's free market or in northern Europe's welfare state? Explain.

14. The intellectual Adolph Berle once said, "A day may come when national glory and prestige, perhaps even national safety, are best established by a country's being the most beautiful, the best socially organized, or culturally the most advanced in the world."[150]

    a. Is government intervention necessary to achieving Berle's goal? Explain.

    b. If faced with a choice, would most Americans opt for Berle's model or for a nation preeminent in consumer goods, sports, and general comfort? Explain.

15. Marketing research firm GfK Roper and policy advisor Simon Anholt annually rank the 50 most admired nations globally. The United States ordinarily has ranked at the top of that list in recent years. Their research shows that we can think of countries as being either primarily useful (competent, efficient, smart) or primarily decorative (stylish, sexy, attractive) or both.[151]

    a. List some nations that you take to be primarily useful and some that you believe to be primarily decorative. Which do you prefer?

    b. Do you regard the United States as primarily useful or primarily decorative or both? Explain.

16. Benjamin Barber, writing in *The Atlantic,* saw two possible political futures, which he labeled the "forces of Jihad" and the "forces of McWorld":

    > The first is a retribalization of large swaths of humankind by war and bloodshed . . . culture is pitted against culture, people against people, tribe against tribe—a Jihad in the name of a hundred narrowly conceived faiths against every kind of interdependence. . . . The second is being borne in on us by the onrush of economic and ecological forces that demand integration and uniformity and that mesmerize the world with fast music, fast computers, and fast food—with MTV, Macintosh, and McDonald's pressing nations into one commercially homogeneous global network: One McWorld tied together by technology, ecology, communications, and commerce.[152]

    a. Does either of these scenarios make sense to you? Explain.

    b. Which would you prefer? Explain.

17. Which is more important to you: "freedom to pursue life's goals without state interference" or "state guarantees that nobody is in need."[153] Explain.

18. Hilda Scott wrote a book to which she affixed the provocative title *Does Socialism Liberate Women?*[154]

    a. Answer her question. Explain.

    b. Are minority oppression and oppression of women inevitable by-products of capitalism? Explain.

19. In Wisconsin, members of the Old Order Amish religion declined to formally educate their children beyond the eighth grade. The U.S. Supreme Court held that their First Amendment right to freedom of religion was violated by the Wisconsin compulsory education statute, which required school attendance until the age of 16. Chief Justice Burger explained:

    > They object to the high school, and higher education generally, because the values they teach are in marked variance with Amish values and the Amish way of life; they view

secondary school education as an impermissible exposure of their children to a "worldly" influence in conflict with their beliefs. The high school tends to emphasize intellectual and scientific accomplishments, self-distinction, competitiveness, worldly success, and social life with other students. Amish society emphasizes informal learning-through-doing; a life of "goodness," rather than a life of intellect; wisdom, rather than technical knowledge; community welfare, rather than competition; and separation from, rather than integration with, contemporary worldly society.[155]

a. Have the Amish taken the course we should all follow? Explain.

b. Could we do so? Explain.

20. Distinguished economist Gary Becker argued for a free-market approach to America's immigration difficulties:

In a market economy, the way to deal with excess demand for a product or service is to raise the price. This reduces the demand and stimulates the supply. I suggest that the United States adopt a similar approach to help solve its immigration problems. Under my proposal, anyone willing to pay a specified price could enter the United States immediately.[156]

Comment.

Notes

1. Francis Fukuyama, "Are We at the End of History?" *Fortune*, January 15, 1990, p. 75. See also Fukuyama's 2014 book, *Political Order and Political Decay* (New York: Farrar, Straus and Giroux).

2. For a brief but helpful review of Thomas Piketty's book *Capital in the Twenty-First Century* (Cambridge, MA: Belknap Press, 2014), see Paul Mason, "Thomas Piketty's Capital: Everything You Need to Know about the Surprise Best Seller," *The Guardian,* April 28, 2014 [**www.theguardian.com**].

3. Alan Blinder and Mark Zandi, "The Financial Crisis: Lessons for the Next One," Center on Budget and Policy Futures, October 15, 2015, p. 5 [**www.cbpp.org/research/the-financial-crisis-lessons-for-the-next-one**].

4. Source: Appelbaum, Benjamin, "How Mortgage Fraud Made the Financial Crisis Worse," *The New York Times,* February 12, 2015 [**www.nytimes.com**].

5. See Jeffrey Rothfeder, "The Great Unraveling of Globalization," *The Washington Post,* April 24, 2015 [**www.washingtonpost.com**].

6. James B. Stewart, "In Corporate Crimes, Individual Accountability Is Elusive," *The New York Times,* February 19, 2015 [**www.nytimes.com**].

7. Robert J. Samuelson, "The CEO Backlash," *The Washington Post*, June 21, 2015 [**www.washingtonpost.com**].

8. For a summary of the study, see Kathleen Geier, "An Important New Paper Shows Us What's Driving Economic Inequality—and How We Can Stop It," *The Washington Monthly,* August 11, 2013 [**www.washingtonmonthly.com**].

9. Thomas M. Hoenig, "Too Big to Succeed," *The New York Times,* December 1, 2010 [**www.nytimes.com**].

10. Richard Doak, "Can Capitalism Survive? Sorry, It Already Died," *The Des Moines Register,* June 21, 2009, p. 10OP.

11. Dana Milbank, "Americans' optimism is dying" 2014 *Wall Street Journal*/NBC News poll

12. Andrew Ross Sorkin and Megan Thee-Brenan, "Many Feel the American Dream Is Out of Reach, Poll Shows," *The New York Times*, December 10, 2014 [**www.nytimes.com**].

13. Michael Corkery, "Capitalism, Love and Mr. Moore," Deal Journal, *The Wall Street Journal*, September 23, 2009, p. C3.

14. Ibid.

15. Stacy Cowley, "At Wells Fargo, Complaints about Fraudulent Accounts Since 2005," *The New York Times*, October 11, 2016 [**www.nytimes.com**].

16. Michael Corkery, "Wells Fargo Says Customers Shied Away After Scandal," *The New York Times*, October 14, 2016 [**www.nytimes.com**].

17. Rana Foroohar, "Why the Wells Fargo Scandal Really Matters," *Time*, October 12, 2016 [**http://time.com**].

18. World Economic Forum, "2015–16 Global Competitiveness Index" [**http://reports.weforum.org/global-competitiveness-report-2015-2016**].

19. Robert J. Samuelson, "Is America in Decline?," *The Washington Post*, January 27, 2013 [**www.washingtonpost.com**].

20. David Brooks, "The Commercial Republic," *The New York Times*, March 17, 2009 [**www.nytimes.com**].

21. Ibid.

22. Robert Skidelsky, "Life After Capitalism," *Project Syndicate*, January 19, 2011 [**www.skidelskyr.com/site/article/life-after-capitalism**].

23. "Zogby Poll: *Atlas Shrugged* by Ayn Rand Read by 8.1 Percent," *PRWeb*, October 17, 2007 [**www.prweb.com/releases/1969/12/prweb561836.htm?tag=poll**].

24. Stephen Moore, "*Atlas Shrugged*: From Fiction to Fact in 52 Years," *The Wall Street Journal*, January 9, 2009, p. W11.

25. *The New York Times*, December 2, 2015 [**www.nytimes.com**].

26. Sandy Banks, "When Money Talks to Kids," *latimes.com*, April 17, 2010 [**www.latimes.com**].

27. See "Should Drivers Who Pay More Get a Faster Lane?" *Parade*, October 19, 2008, p. 22.

28. Editorial, "Tag—You're Illegal," *Los Angeles Times*, October 28, 2006 [**www.latimes.com/news/opinion/la-ed-tag28oct28,0,59791.story?coll=la=opinion-leftrail**].

29. Laura Meckler, "Kidney Shortage Inspires a Radical Idea: Organ Sales," *The Wall Street Journal*, November 13, 2007, p. A1.

30. Stephanie Coontz, "Taking Marriage Private," *The New York Times*, November 26, 2006 [**www.nytimes.com/2007/11/26/opinion/26coontz.html**].

31. Brad Plumer, "More States Privatizing Their Infrastructure. Are They Making a Mistake?" *The Washington Post*, March 31, 2012 [**www.washingtonpost.com**].

32. Emily Thornton, "Roads to Riches," *BusinessWeek*, May 7, 2007, p. 50.

33. Ibid.

34. Molly Ball, "The Privatization Backlash," *The Atlantic*, April 23, 2014 [**www.theatlantic.com**].

35. Ibid.

36. Emily Badger, "Charging People More to Drive Saves Lives," *The Washington Post*, March 11, 2015 [**www.washingtonpost.com**].

37. Charles Mahtesian, "Revenue in the Rough," *Governing*, October 1997, pp. 42–44.

38. Editorial, "City-Owned Golf Courses Cannot Be Sacred Cows," *The Waterloo/Cedar Falls Courier,* July 13, 2003, p. C7.

39. Jonathan Kozol, "This Is Only a Test," *The New York Times,* September 26, 2013 [**www.nytimes.com**].

40. Libby Nelson, "This School Paid Teachers $125,000 a Year—and Test Scores Went Up," *Vox,* October 24, 2014 [**www.Vox.com**].

41. Ball, "The Privatization Backlash."

42. Ibid.

43. Rob Kuznia, "Rich Californians Balk at Limits: 'We're Not All Equal When It Comes to Water,'" *The Washington Post,* June 13, 2015 [**www.washingtonpost.com**].

44. Skip Bayless, "Unleash the Boosters," *ESPN.com,* July 25, 2014 [**www.espn.com**].

45. William Deresiewicz, "Capitalist and Other Psychopaths," *The New York Times,* May 12, 2012 [**www.nytimes.com**].

46. Henry Myers, "His Statues Topple, His Shadow Persists: Marx Can't Be Ignored," *The Wall Street Journal,* November 25, 1991, p. A1.

47. Michael J. Jordan, "After the Berlin Wall, Nostalgia for Communism Creeps Back," *Christian Science Monitor,* November 8, 2009 [**www.csmonitor.com**].

48. Elements of this list are drawn from Agnes Heller and Ferenc Feher, "Does Socialism Have a Future?" *Dissent,* Summer 1989, p. 371.

49. Ibid.

50. Associated Press, "Chavez in China Touts 'New World Order,'" *The Wall Street Journal,* April 8, 2009 [**http://online.wsj.com**].

51. David Pierson and Don Lee, "World Bank Tells China to Reform State Sector to Ensure Stability," *latimes.com,* February 27, 2012 [**www.latimes.com/**].

52. Ibid.

53. Chris Buckley and Andrew Jacobs, "Maoists in China, Given New Life, Attack Dissent," *The New York Times,* January 4, 2015 [**www.nytimes.com**].

54. Ibid.

55. Editorial Board, "The Rule of Law Proves Elusive in China," *The Washington Post,* September 28, 2012 [**www.washingtonpost.com/**].

56. Thomas L. Friedman, "What's Up with You?" *The New York Times,* April 15, 2015 [**www.nytimes.com**].

57. Chris Buckley, "Chinese Embrace America's Culture but Not Its Policies," *The New York Times,* September 28, 2015 [**www.nytimes.com**].

58. Ibid.

59. Dana Milbank, "Battle Cry of the White Man," *The Washington Post,* August 5, 2014 [**www.washingtonpost.com**].

60. Ibid.

61. Vivek Wadhwa, "Does China Own the Future—Or Does the U.S.?" *The Washington Post,* December 13, 2012 [**www.washingtonpost.com**].

62. Melanie Stetson Freeman, "In Moscow, Capitalism Now in Full Fashion," *The Christian Science Monitor,* February 21, 2008 [**www.csmonitor.com/2008/0221/p13s01-woeu.html**].

63. Simeon Djankov, "Russia's Economy Under Putin: From Crony Capitalism to State Capitalism," *Policy Brief Number 15-18* (Peterson Institute for International Economics), September 2015 [**www.piie.com**].

64. Transparency International, "Corruption Perceptions Index 2015" [**www.transparency.org/cpi2015/**].

65. Masha Gessen, "Russia Is Remaking Itself as the Leader of the Anti-Western World," *The Washington Post,* March 30, 2014 [**www.washingtonpost.com**].

66. Jon Clifton, "Rating World Leaders: U.S., China, Russia, EU and Germany," Gallup, April 22, 2015 [**www.gallup.com/opinion/gallup/182801/rating-world-leaders-china-russia-germany.aspx**].

67. Associated Press, "Irked with Russia, U.S. Gays Target Vodka and Sochi," *The Moscow Times,* July 31, 2013 [**www.themoscowtimes.com**].

68. Paul Roderick Gregory, "Leading Economist Gives Up on Putin's Russia," *Forbes,* May 30, 2013 [**www.forbes.com**].

69. David Brooks, "The Russia I Miss," *The New York Times,* September 11, 2015 [**www.nytimes.com**].

70. Central Intelligence Agency, *The World Factbook* [**www.cia.gov/library/publications/the-world-factbook/rankorder/2102rank.html**].

71. Organization for Economic Co-Operation and Development, *OECD.stat* [**https://stats.oecd.org/Index.aspx?DataSetCode=REV**].

72. Martin Sullivan, "The Truth about Corporate Tax Rates," *Forbes,* March 25, 2015 [**http://onforb.es/1LX9h6s**].

73. Robert H. Frank, "What Sweden Can Tell Us about Obamacare," *The New York Times,* June 15, 2013 [**www.nytimes.com**].

74. Jeffrey Sachs, "The Social Welfare State, Beyond Ideology," *Scientific American* 295, no. 5 (November 2006), p. 42.

75. Jeff Jacoby, 'No, Bernie Sanders, Scandinavia Is Not a Socialist Utopia," *The Boston Globe,* October 15, 2015 [**www.bostonglobe.com**].

76. "Unemployment Statistics," *Eurostat—Statistics Explained,* January 2016 [**http://ec.europa.eu/statistics-explained/index.php/Unemployment_statistics**].

77. Daniel Bosque Homs, "Spain's 'Lost Generation': Youth Unemployment Hits 57 Percent," *HuffPost World,* May 28, 2013 [**www.huffingtonpost.com**].

78. Alessandra Galloni, "The Nonna State," *The Wall Street Journal,* June 16–17, 2012, p. C1.

79. "EU: Unemployment Rate 2016 by Country," *Statista,* August 2016.

80. Larry Elliott, "Brexit Is a Rejection of Globalisation," *The Guardian,* June 26, 2016 [**www.theguardian.com**].

81. Nicholas Sambanis, "Has 'Europe' Failed?" *The New York Times,* August 26, 2012 [**www.nytimes.com**].

82. Jeremy Rifkin, "Why the European Dream Is Worth Saving," *SpiegelOnline,* July 28, 2005 [**www.spiegel.de/international/0,1518,druck-366940,00.html**].

83. Adrian Karatnycky, quoting George Soros, in "The Merits of the Market, the Perils of 'Market Fundamentalism,'" *The Wall Street Journal,* January 9, 2001, p. A20.

84. Ibid.

85. Joanne Barkan, "Not Yet in Paradise, But . . .," *Dissent,* Spring 1989, pp. 147, 150.

86. Thomas B. Edsall, "Why Can't America Be Sweden?" *The New York Times,* May 29, 2013 [**http://opinionator.blogs.nytimes.com**].

87. Jonathan Chait, "No, America Is Not Turning Libertarian," *New York Magazine,* August 7, 2014 [**http://nymag.com**].

88. Jim Chairusmi, "Winning with Smaller Pockets," *The Wall Street Journal,* October 18, 2004, p. R2.

89. Michael Shermer, "Life Has Never Been So Good for Our Species," *latimes.com,* April 30, 2010 [**www.latimes.com/news/opinion/la-oe-shermer-20100430,0,2676540.story**].

90. David Gergen, "Cheer Up, America," *Parade,* April 11, 2010, p. 26.

91. "Americans' Generosity Has Never Been Like This," *CNNMoney,* June 16, 2015 [**http://money.cnn.com**].

92. Diane Cole, "You'll Never Guess the Most Charitable Nation in the World," *National Public Radio,* November 28, 2015 [**www.npr.org**].

93. David Brooks, "The Temptation of Hillary," *The New York Times,* March 6, 2015, p. A25.

94. Michael A. Fletcher, "Income Inequality Has Squeezed the Middle Class Out of the Majority," *The Washington Post,* December 9, 2015 [**www.washingtonpost.com**].

95. Dionne Searcey and Robert Gebeloff, "Middle Class Shrinks Further as More Fall Out Instead of Climbing Up," *The New York Times,* January 25, 2015 [**www.nytimes.com**].

96. David Leonhardt and Kevin Quealy, "The American Middle Class Is No Longer the World's Richest," *The New York Times,* April 22, 2014 [**www.nytimes.com**].

97. Ibid.

98. Associated Press, "Americans Get a Raise," *The Waterloo-Cedar Falls Courier,* September 14, 2016, p. A4.

99. United Nations, "Human Development Report 2015" [**http://hdr.undp.org/en/2015-report**].

100. Ivana Kottasova, "Forget GDP. These Nations Are Doing Better Than the U.S.," *CNNMoney,* April 9, 2015 [**http://money.cnn.com**].

101. Central Intelligence Agency, "Country Comparison: GDP—Per Capita," *The World Factbook* [**www.cia.gov/library/publications/the-world-factbook/rankorder/2004rank.html**].

102. Central Intelligence Agency, "Country Comparison: Infant Mortality Rate," *The World Factbook* [**www.cia.gov/library/publications/the-world-factbook/rankorder/209/rank.html**].

103. Newt Gingrich, "Our Prison System Is Failing America," *The Des Moines Register,* May 26, 2014, p. 17A.

104. Stephanie Simon, "U.S. Spends Big on Education, but Results Lag Many Nations: OECD," *Reuters,* June 25, 2013 [**www.reuters.com**].

105. Wendy Wang, Kim Parker, and Paul Taylor, "Breadwinner Moms," *Pew Research Social and Demographic Trends,* May 29, 2013 [**www.pewsocialtrends.org**].

106. Kay Hymowitz, W. Bradford Wilcox, and Kelleen Kaye, "The New Unmarried Moms," *The Wall Street Journal,* March 15, 2013 [**http://online.wsj.com**].

107. Lucia Mutikani and Susan Heavey, "U.S. Household Income Posts Record Surge in 2015, Poverty Falls," *Reuters,* September 13, 2016 [**www.reuters.com**].

108. Nelson D. Schwartz, "Low-Income Workers See Biggest Drop in Paychecks," *The New York Times,* September 2, 2015 [**www.nytimes.com**].

109. Stanford Center on Poverty and Inequality, "State of the Union: The Poverty and Inequality Report," *Pathways,* Special Issue 2016 [**http://inequality.stanford.edu/sites/default/files/Pathways-SOTU-2016-2.pdf**].

110. Paul Krugman, "Poverty Is Poison," *The New York Times,* February 18, 2008 [**www.nytimes. com/2008/02/18/opinion/18krugman.html?em**].

111. Chuck Collins and Josh Hoxie, "Billionaire Bonanza: The *Forbes* 400 and the Rest of Us," Institute for Policy Studies, December 1, 2015 [**www.ips-dc.org/billionaire-bonanza**].

112. Larry Elliot, "Richest 62 People as Wealthy as Half of World's Population, Says Oxfam," *The Guardian,* January 18, 2016 [**www.the guardian.com**].

113. Peter Eavis, "S.E.C. Approves Rule on C.E.O. Pay Ratio," *The New York Times,* August 5, 2015 [**www.nytimes.com**].

114. Jim Tankersley, "Economic Mobility Hasn't Changed in a Half-Century in America, Economists Declare," *The Washington Post,* January 22, 2014 [**www.washingtonpost.com**].

115. Regan Pecjak, "Report Ranks U.S. Last on Poverty and Inequality," *Stanford Daily,* February 15, 2016 [**www.stanforddaily.com**].

116. Maryam Kouchaki, Kristin Smith-Crowe, Arthur P. Brief, and Carlos Sousa, "Seeing Green: Mere Exposure to Money Triggers a Business Decision Frame and Unethical Outcomes," *Organizational Behavior and Human Decision Processes* 121, no. 1 (May 2013), p. 53.

117. Elizabeth W. Dunn, Lara B. Aknin, and Michael I. Norton, "Spending Money on Others Promotes Happiness," *Science* 319, no. 5870 (March 21, 2008), p. 1687.

118. Bernie DeGroat, "Do Co-Workers Engage or Estrange after Hours," University of Michigan, *University Record,* February 11, 2008 [**http://www.rcgd.isr.umich.edu/news/Sanchez-Burks. univ.recrd.02.11.08.pdf**].

119. Matthew E. Brashears, "Small Networks and High Isolation? A Reexamination of American Discussion Networks," *Social Networks* 33, no. 4 (October 2011), p. 331.

120. D. Matthew T. Clark, Natalie J. Loxton, and Stephanie J. Tobin, "Declining Loneliness over Time: Evidence from American Colleges and High Schools," *Personality and Social Psychology Bulletin* 41, no. 1 (January 2015), p. 78.

121. Robert Putnam, *Bowling Alone* (New York: Simon & Schuster, 2000).

122. Connie Cass, "In God We Trust Maybe, but Not Each Other," Associated Press, November 30, 2016 [**http://ap-gfkpoll.com/featured/our-latest-poll-findings-24**].

123. Sharon Jayson, "Americans Mostly Trust, Help Neighbors," *USA Today,* December 12, 2012, p. 3A.

124. Robert Putnam, *Our Kids: The American Dream in Crisis* (New York: Simon & Schuster, 2015).

125. Emily Badger, "The Terrible Loneliness of Growing Up Poor in Robert Putnam's America," *The Washington Post*, March 6, 2015 [**www.washingtonpost.com**].

126. David Gergen, Charles Murray, and Robert D. Putnam, "Are We Really Coming Apart?" *Aspen Ideas Festival 2012* [**www.aspenideas.org/session/are-we-really-coming-apart#**].

127. Dan Lawton, "In Ghana, No One Is a Stranger for Long," *The Christian Science Monitor,* November 9, 2009 [**www.csmonitor.com/2009/1109/p18s01-hfes.html**].

128. Sherry Turkle, "The Flight from Conversation," *The New York Times,* April 21, 2012 [**www. nytimes.com**].

129. David Wessel and John Harwood, "Capitalism Is Giddy with Triumph; Is It Possible to Overdo It?" *The Wall Street Journal,* May 14, 1998, p. A1.

130. Associated Press, "A Threat to Castro," *The Des Moines Register,* August 30, 1994, p. 8A.

131. Mark Tapscott, "Majority of Millenials Favor Free Enterprise, Say More Regulation Will Harm Economy, Marist Poll Finds," *San Francisco Examiner,* August 16, 2013 [**www.sfexaminer.com**].

132. Anatole Kaletsky, *Capitalism 4.0: The Birth of a New Economy* (New York: Public Affairs/ Perseus, 2010).

133. Anatole Kaletsky, "Capitalism 4.0," *OECD Observer,* no. 279 (May 2010) [**www.oecdobserver.org**].

134. Robert Skidelsky, "For a New World, New Economics," *New Statesman,* August 30, 2010 [**www.newstatesman.com**].

135. Ian Bremmer, *The End of the Free Market* (New York: Portfolio/Penguin, 2010).

136. Aldo Musacchio, Sergio G. Lazzarini, and Ruth V. Aguilera, "New Varieties of State Capitalism: Strategic and Governance Implications," *Academy of Management Perspectives* 29, no. 1 (2015), p. 115.

137. Mike Konczal, "Robert Reich on Why Capitalism Needs Saving," *Rolling Stone*, October 7, 2015 [**www.rollingstone.com**].

138. Roger Cohen, "Toilets and Cellphones," *The New York Times,* May 24, 2010 [**www.nytimes.com**].

139. Robert Samuelson, "Economics Made Easy," *Newsweek,* November 27, 1989, p. 64.

140. Binyamin Appelbaum and Robert Gebeloff, "Even Critics of Safety Net Increasingly Depend on It," *The New York Times,* February 11, 2012 [**www.nytimes.com**].

141. Brad Plumer, "Who Receives Government Benefits, in Six Charts," *The Washington Post,* September 18, 2012 [**www.washingtonpost.com**].

142. George Will, "The Harm Incurred by a Mushrooming Welfare State," *The Washington Post,* January 21, 2014

143. Carla McClain, "Dr. Spock: Restore the Family," *The Des Moines Register,* November 7, 1993, p. 3E.

144. Jacob Hacker and Paul Peirson, *American Amnesia: How the War on Government Led Us to Forget What Made America Prosper* (New York: Simon & Schuster, 2016).

145. Max Ehrenfreund, "How the Scandinavians Got So Tall," *The Washington Post,* April 8, 2016 [**www.washingtonpost.com**].

146. Nolan Feeney, "Women Are Now More Likely to Have College Degree Than Men," *Time,* October 7, 2015 [**http://time.com**].

147. Nicholas D. Kristof, "Moonshine or the Kids?" *The New York Times,* May 22, 2010 [**http://www.nytimes.com/**].

148. Ibid.

149. Thomas L. Friedman, "Foreign Affairs; Eastern Middle School," *The New York Times,* October 2, 2001 [**www.nytimes.com**].

150. Adolph Berle, *Power* (New York: Harcourt Brace Jovanovich, 1969), pp. 258–59.

151. John Nylander, "Sweden 10th 'Most Admired Country Globally,'" *swedishwire.com,* October 18, 2010 [**www.swedishwisre.com/nordic/6755-sweden-10th-most-admired-country-globally**]. Also see GfK, "USA Regains Position as Top Nation Brand from Germany," press release, November 17, 2015 [**www.gfk.com/en-in/insights/press-release/usa-regains-position-as-top-nation-brand-from-germany-1/**].

152. Benjamin Barber, "Jihad v. McWorld," *The Atlantic* 269, no. 3 (March 1992), p. 53.

153. Roger Cohen, "Incurable American Excess," *The New York Times,* August 6, 2015 [**www.nytimes.com**].

154. Hilda Scott, *Does Socialism Liberate Women?: Experiences from Eastern Europe* (Boston: Beacon Press, 1974).

155. *Wisconsin v. Yoder,* 406 U.S. 205, 210–11 (1972).

156. Gary Becker, "Why Not Let Immigrants Pay for Speedy Entry?" *BusinessWeek,* March 2, 1987, p. 20.

CHAPTER TWO

Business Ethics

After completing this chapter, students will be able to fulfill the following learning objectives:

2-1. Describe some of the ethics issues associated with America's recent banking and finance crisis.

2-2. Discuss America's current moral climate.

2-3. Discuss the leading ethical decision-making theories.

2-4. Distinguish between teleological and deontological ethical systems.

2-5. Distinguish utilitarianism and formalism.

2-6. Describe some of the forces that encourage unethical behavior in the workplace.

2-7. Describe Kohlberg's theory of moral development.

2-8. Explain the general requirements of the Foreign Corrupt Practices Act.

2-9. Discuss some of the risks and rewards of whistle-blowing.

2-10. Explain the general purpose of ethics codes in the workplace.

Part One—Introduction to Ethics

Can we count on self-regulation (ethics) as a useful means of controlling managerial/corporate behavior? More broadly, can we count on the free market as discussed in Chapter 1, along with managerial and corporate ethics, to guide business conduct such that government regulation (law) can be significantly reduced?

This chapter will examine the ethical climate of business and the role of ethics in business decision making. Our goal here is not to teach morality but to sensitize the reader to the vital role honor plays in building a sound career and a responsible life.

PRACTICING ETHICS   Addicted to Money

Sam Polk, a 30-year-old hedge fund trader, recently walked away from his $3.6 million Wall Street bonus convinced that he was addicted to wealth and was pursuing a meaningless life. He had been angry that his bonus wasn't big enough, he described himself as a "giant fireball of greed," and he ruminated on how his colleagues could "buy Micronesia" if they wanted. He did, however, begin to see "the limitations of unlimited wealth" when he asked in a staff meeting if new, hated government regulations were not "better for the system as a whole," a remark that drew scorn from his boss, who said he was concerned only about the effect of the rules on his company.

Polk compared himself to a drug addict and felt what he labeled "withdrawal" when he left Wall Street, but thereafter he married, devoted himself to public service, and says that he is now "much happier."

Questions

1. Polk acknowledged his talent for trading, but in the end he said, "I didn't really do anything." If his sophisticated Wall Street products (credit derivatives) ceased to exist, he felt "the world would hardly change at all."

   a. Was his job meaningless, as he seemed to feel? Explain.

   b. If so, is the market somehow mistaken in the high value it assigns to jobs like his? Explain.

2. *a.* Could you imagine yourself becoming addicted to wealth? Explain.

   b. Is the avid pursuit of wealth too emotionally risky to be a rational act? Explain.

3. The 25 highest-paid hedge fund managers in America collectively earned about $11.62 billion in 2014, which was a "bad year" for them, while the nation's 158,000 kindergarten teachers combined earned about $8.5 billion.

   a. Is that salary imbalance a moral wrong as you see it? Explain.

   b. Is the market mistaken about the relative worth of hedge fund managers and teachers? Explain.

Sources: Sam Polk, "For the Love of Money," *The New York Times*, January 18, 2014 [**www.nytimes.com**]; and Lauren Carroll, "HillaryClinton: Top Hedge Fund Managers Make More Than All Kindergarten Teachers Combined," *PolitiFact*, June 15, 2015 [**www.politifact.com**].

The Financial Crisis: Blame Big Banks?

LO 2-1

Describe some of the ethics issues associated with America's recent banking and finance crisis.

Corporate misconduct has been a staple of the news in this 21st century, but can we legitimately blame banking industry wrongs for the Great Recession (2007–2009; followed by years of slow recovery)? Trillions of dollars were lost when America's subprime mortgage market collapsed, some big financial institutions failed, and the global economy spiraled downward. Mortgage fraud, such as extending loans to clearly unqualified buyers, falsifying documents, and misleading investors, clearly played an important role in the financial meltdown. Other forces, such as inadequate government regulation, government-encouraged easy credit, overextended borrowers, greed, and real estate speculation, also played their part. Of course, no law is broken when lenders merely show poor judgment or borrowers default, but the big banks have paid some $110 billion in mortgage-related government fines (mostly civil, rather than criminal) as penalties for their role in the subprime collapse.[1]

Too Big to Jail?

Wall Street, while struggling at times, seems to be largely recovered from the crisis it helped to generate. Employment levels, pay, and profits are healthy, although not quite at the prerecession levels, as the banks struggle to adjust to extensive new government regulations (see Chapter 8) that have forced some of them to shrink their businesses.[2]

Critics remain frustrated, nonetheless, because criminal prosecutions of banks have been infrequent and only one banking executive has gone to jail as a result of the housing loan crisis. A handful of multinational banks did plead guilty to global currency manipulation charges in 2015 that resulted in $5.7 billion in fines, but as *Rolling Stone*'s Matt Taibbi argues, we have evidence of a two-tiered justice system. After the "greatest crime wave in a generation," Taibbi says, "major systemic offenders walk" while the government puts "the smallest of small fry on the rack for negligible offenses."[3]

Why hasn't the government been more aggressive in jailing bankers and prosecuting banks? Proving *criminal* wrongdoing "beyond a reasonable doubt"—and particularly proving the required intent at the highest levels to commit a crime—are daunting burdens. Thus, the government often turns to *civil* causes of action where proof requirements ("a preponderance of the evidence") are less stringent. Bigger policy considerations, however, have also influenced the government's policy. Former U.S. Attorney General Eric Holder may have revealed the major reason behind the federal government's seeming reluctance to act:

> I am concerned that the size of some of these institutions becomes so large that it does become difficult for us to prosecute them when we are hit with indications that if we do prosecute—if we do bring a criminal charge—it will have a negative impact on the national economy, perhaps even the world economy. . . . I think that is a function of the fact that some of these institutions have become too large.[4]

Holder later said he had been misconstrued and that no bank is too big to prosecute. In any case, the government should move carefully against giants in banking and industry as it learned in the successful prosecution of Arthur Andersen, the venerable public accounting firm. Obstruction of justice charges during the Enron scandal and bankruptcy of the early 2000s put Arthur Andersen out of business and 28,000 jobs were lost. Most of those who lost their jobs had nothing to do with the alleged wrongdoing, and the Andersen conviction was later overturned by the U.S. Supreme Court.

Some Do Go to Jail   Of course, the government sometimes does pursue individuals engaging in Wall Street fraud. Powerful financiers such as Bernie Madoff (Ponzi scheme) and Raj Rajaratnam (insider trading) have been sentenced to long jail terms, and the government in 2015 announced new policies that prioritize prosecuting individuals and pressure corporations to reveal all that is known about wrongdoing by officers and managers.

> "The whole damn industry lost its moral moorings."

Nearly 70 percent of Americans say "most" of those on Wall Street would be willing to break the law to make "a lot of money" if they felt they could get away with it.[5] Additionally, 22 percent of 1,200 U.S. and U.K. finance professionals surveyed in 2015 said they had either directly observed or had firsthand knowledge of wrongdoing in the workplace.[6] Warren Buffet's long-time investments partner, Charlie Munger, was particularly condemnatory in his assessment of Wall Street: "The whole damn industry lost its moral moorings."[7]

A Conscience at Goldman Sachs?

"It makes me ill how callously people still talk about ripping off clients," midlevel Goldman Sachs executive Greg Smith wrote in *The New York Times* as he was resigning from the firm in 2012. Smith's commentary, "Why I Am Leaving Goldman Sachs," claimed that the Goldman Sachs culture had become "toxic," and that the "interests of the client continue to be sidelined in the way the firm operates and thinks about making money." Smith, 33, a Stanford graduate and finalist for a Rhodes scholarship, wrote that he was once proud of Goldman Sachs's culture of teamwork, integrity, humility, and concern for clients, but that spirit, he said, had been lost.

Goldman Sachs says that regular employee feedback contradicts Smith's characterizations. Critics say Smith was angry because he had been denied a promotion and raise prior to his departure. Others simply saw Smith as naive. One Goldman client told *The New York Times* that the company had traded against its clients for years. "Come on, that is what they do and they are good traders, so I do business with them." And a *Bloomberg* editorial satirized Smith's view that the firm was too concerned about making money:

> If you want to dedicate your life to serving humanity, do not go to work for Goldman Sachs. That's not its function, and it never will be. Go to work for Goldman Sachs if you wish to work hard and get paid more than you deserve. . . .[8]

Questions

1. A friend of Smith's characterized his resignation and public condemnation of Goldman Sachs as the "ultimate act of loyalty." What did he mean?
2. *a.* What did Smith mean when he spoke of Goldman Sachs's "culture"?
   b. In seeking a job after graduation, will you be looking for a company whose "culture" matches your values? Explain.
   c. Do you think you would give up the approximately $500,000 per year that Smith reportedly was making because your employer's culture was not consistent with your values? Explain.
3. *a.* *Should* Goldman Sachs's purpose be service to humanity?
   b. Would that approach work in the marketplace? Explain.

Sources: Susanne Craig and Landon Thomas Jr., "Public Rebuke of Culture at Goldman Opens Debate," *The New York Times,* March 14, 2012 [**http://dealbook.nytimes.com**]; Editorial, "Yes, Mr. Smith, Goldman Sachs Is All about Making Money: View," *Bloomberg,* March 14, 2012 [**www.bloomberg.com**]; and Greg Smith, "Why I Am Leaving Goldman Sachs," *The New York Times,* March 14, 2012 [**www.nytimes.com**].

A Pattern of Abuse

His $6,000 shower curtain.

Of course, the subprime mortgage crisis was not the first instance of morally unhinged corporate conduct. We give lengthier attention to corporate crime later in the chapter, but for now we should put the subprime scandal in context by remembering some of the most prominent corporate and white-collar missteps of recent years. The subprime scandal is reminiscent of the savings and loan crisis of the 1980s when $150 billion evaporated, in part because of criminal behavior. The corporate greed of the Enron era (early 2000s) played out on worldwide televisions as some of the great titans of American commerce shuffled off to prison. Tyco International CEO Dennis Kozlowski is infamous for his wife's $2 million Sardinian birthday bash and his $6,000 shower curtain. Kozlowski is currently out of prison on parole after serving over six years on charges of looting nearly $100 million from Tyco. Most breathtaking was Wall Street investment manager Bernard Madoff's colossal Ponzi scheme that stole as much as $65 billion (in paper gains) from his clients before Madoff was caught and sent to prison in 2009 to serve 150 years. [For a comprehensive archive of the Enron story, see **http://archive.wn.com/2007/12/23/1400/enronfiles**].

Of course, we should not condemn the entire American business community based on the misconduct of some. The problems are serious, but former General Electric CEO Jack Welch and his wife, Suzy, remind us that the business community is the source of much of America's greatness:

> Business is a huge source of vitality in the world and a noble enterprise. Thriving, decent companies are everywhere, and they should be celebrated. They create jobs and opportunities, provide revenue for government, and are the foundation of a free and democratic society. . . .[9]

Ethics Survey

We can see that executive wrongdoing has been a significant problem in recent years, but what about questionable employee behavior? Should some commonplace worker practices be considered unethical? The Ethics Officer Association and the Ethical Leadership Group sampled a cross section of workers at large companies nationwide. How would you respond?

1. "Is it wrong to use company e-mail for personal reasons?"
2. "Is it wrong to play computer games on office equipment during the workday?"
3. "Is it OK to take a $100 holiday food basket?"
4. "Due to on-the-job pressure, have you ever abused or lied about sick days?"

Source: "The Wall Street Journal Workplace-Ethics Quiz," *The Wall Street Journal,* October 21, 1999, p. B1.

America's Moral Climate

LO 2-2
Discuss America's current moral climate.

Perhaps more than ever, Americans are questioning the nation's moral health. Spectacular corporate corruption as noted above, steroid use by professional athletes, an economy seemingly permanently tilted toward the rich, government officials paying more attention to reelection than to the general welfare, sexual abuse of children by clerics and teachers, and so on cause us to question our decency as a society. Gallup's 2015 poll of American values and beliefs found 72 percent of respondents saying that our moral values are deteriorating,[10] and a 2015 *Wall Street Journal*/NBC News poll showed that 34 percent of Americans believe "a decline in moral values" is the first or second "most alarming" problem the nation faces (next, at 28 percent, was "terrorist attacks," with the "shrinking middle class" third at 27 percent).[11]

Sociologist David Callahan's book *The Cheating Culture: Why More Americans Are Doing Wrong to Get Ahead* argues that we are a society in moral decline.[12] The result of our winner-take-all ethos, Callahan thinks, is a nation increasingly falling into two groups: a "winning class" who cheated their way to the top and an "anxious class" who fear falling behind if they too do not cheat.[13]

Cheating, in one form or another, does seem to be routine in American life. But we find a glimmer of good news in scholar Dan Ariely's 2012 book *The (Honest) Truth about Dishonesty: How We Lie to Everyone—Especially Ourselves,* which shows, through a series of experiments, that while almost all of us cheat, most of us cheat only a little.[14] Some may take satisfaction in learning that wealthier people cheat more than poorer people, as revealed in a series of experiments conducted in a 2012 study:

> People driving expensive cars were more likely than other motorists to cut off drivers and pedestrians at a four-way-stop intersection in the San Francisco Bay area, . . . researchers observed. Those findings led to a series of experiments that revealed that people of higher socioeconomic status were also more likely to cheat to win a prize, take candy from children and say they would pocket extra change handed to them in error rather than give it back.[15]

This study, which has received some criticism for alleged methodological problems,[16] also found that wealthier people were more likely to condone unethical conduct and to value greed. Similarly, according to another recent study, subjects "primed" to think subconsciously about money were more likely than a control group to demonstrate unethical intentions and to adopt a business decision frame "which led to a greater likelihood of unethical intentions and behavior."[17]

Do you think America is in moral decline? [For the Josephson Institute of Ethics, see **www.josephsoninstitute.org**].

Sex or Cell Phone?

Cell phone practices offer some insight into our values landscape:

- Ten percent of college students in a 2016 study admitted to having used their cell phones while they were also engaged in sex.[18]
- A large 2015 survey found a third of Americans, if forced to choose, would prefer one year without sex rather than one year without their cell phones. Similar results were found in Germany and South Korea, but in Brazil only 25 percent of those surveyed would choose their phone over sex.[19]

College Students

Cheating in college is commonplace,[20] but business students seem to be particularly suspect. A large 2006 survey found 56 percent of graduate students in business admitted to cheating at least once in the previous year, the largest percentage of any discipline surveyed.[21] Among nonbusiness graduate students, 47 percent admitted cheating.[22]

Ninety-five percent of 3,000 undergraduate business students polled in 31 universities admit they cheated in high school or college, although only 1 to 2 percent admit having done so "frequently."[23] Academic ethics expert Donald McCabe's surveys find about 75 percent of college students cheating on either a test or a paper at some point, with business majors, fraternity and sorority members, and male students being among those most likely to cheat.[24]

The cheating evidence is discouraging, but some signs of change should also be noted. High school students who said they had cheated on an examination in the past year declined from 59 percent in 2010 to 51 percent in 2012.[25] Harvard MBA students received a great deal of attention for their voluntary campaign to sign "The MBA Oath," a pledge that Harvard MBAs will act ethically, "serve the greater good," and avoid advancing their own "narrow ambitions" at the expense of others.[26] Now an international oath project pledges higher standards of integrity and service by business leaders. [See **www.theoathproject.org**].

[For a video of *The Daily Show with John Stewart's* treatment of the 2009 Harvard MBA Ethics Oath see **http://www.cc.com/video-clips/dc3rq6/the-daily-show-with-jon-stewart-mba-ethics-oath**]. This clip contains profanity and violent rhetoric.

Questions

1. If you were to sign an ethics oath as a student, do you think your behavior as a student and professional would improve? Explain.

2. Critics accuse business schools of encouraging greed in students. Are they correct? Explain.

3. *New York Times* columnist David Brooks laments the "careerist tide" in higher education:

   > Universities are more professional and glittering than ever, but in some ways there is emptiness deep down. Students are taught how to do things, but many are not forced to reflect on why they should do them or what we are here for. They are given many career options, but they are on their own when it comes to developing criteria to determine which vocation would lead to the fullest life.[27]

   Do you think that your education should have included more attention to why you were taught particular vocational skills, what you are "here for," and guidance in determining the career path most likely to produce, for you, the "fullest life"? Explain.

Changing Values

Contemporary cheating behaviors offer a stark and unflattering contrast to the views of a 1928 Princeton University freshman writing home:

> Father, you suggest that the greatest benefit from college is to be found in . . . habits of intellectual diligence and application. I am nonetheless putting my chief emphasis on the study of right and wrong.[28]

> "We need to stop endlessly repeating, 'you're special.'"

UCLA's annual survey of college first-year students provides evidence of changing values among young people. Responding to the 2015 survey, 81.9 percent of first-year students valued wealth as a goal, but only 46.5 percent sought a "meaningful philosophy of life." That result is a reversal of the 1971 survey when 37 percent of freshmen identified being "very well off financially" as an essential or very important objective, and 73 percent felt the same about "developing a meaningful philosophy of life."[29] The college experience, however, seems to strengthen some important values. A 2010 UCLA study found that students were more likely as juniors than as freshmen to say that "they wanted to develop a meaningful philosophy of life, seek beauty, become a more loving person, and attain inner harmony."[30] And among young adults, careers that have an impact on others seem to be of growing interest.[31]

On the other hand, *The Atlantic* in 2013 reported on a growing body of evidence claiming we are in the midst of a "narcissism epidemic."[32] Using the Narcissistic Personality Inventory, one study of college students nationwide, responding to such statements as "I think I am a special person," concluded that the average college student today is about 30 percent more self-absorbed than the average student in 1982.[33] One of the study leaders, Jean Twenge of San Diego State University, remarked: "We need to stop endlessly repeating 'you're special,' . . . Kids are self-centered enough already."[34] [The UCLA freshmen survey website: **www.heri.ucla.edu/cirpoverview.php**]. [Professor Twenge's website: **www.jeantwenge.com/**].

Questions

1. University of Michigan studies show today's students scoring about 40 percent lower on empathy measures than students of 30 years ago.[35] Do you think you and your college friends are excessively narcissistic and insufficiently empathetic? Explain.

2. Why might empathy be declining among college students? [To measure your own level of empathy and to compare it with the average empathy level of college students, see **http://umichisr.qualtrics.com/SE/?SID=SV_bCvraMmZBCcov52&SVID**].

Too Little Studying = Cheating?

According to the 2011 National Survey of Student Engagement (NSSE), business majors reported spending less time studying than students in any other broad field. Nearly half of senior business majors said they studied fewer than 11 hours per week outside of class. NSSE results for 2015 remained discouraging with 45 percent of senior business majors studying fewer than 11 hours per week, but communications and social services majors reported studying less than business majors. According to the Collegiate Learning Assessment national essay test, business majors in their first two years of college improve their writing and reasoning skills less than any other major.

Questions

1. Can you explain why business majors apparently study less, on average, than students in most or all other majors?

2. Can you explain why business students' writing and reasoning skills apparently increase less than those of any other major during the first two years of college?

3. The evidence, as noted above, indicates that business students cheat more than those majoring in other fields. What relationship, if any, do you see between

student study patterns and student cheating patterns? Put another way, do you think cheating in business schools would decline if students studied more? Explain.

4. Do you think that studying ethics, as you are assigned to do in this chapter and in this book, is likely to materially improve the ethical quality of your professional life following graduation? Explain.

Sources: David Glenn, "Business Educators Struggle to Put Students to Work," *The Chronicle of Higher Education,* April 14, 2011 [**http://chronicle.com/**]; and National Survey of Student Engagement, *Annual Results 2015* [**www.nsse.indiana.edu/html/annual_results.cfm**].

Part Two—Analyzing Ethical Dilemmas

Ethics Theories

LO 2-3
Discuss the leading ethical decision-making theories.

We have looked in a preliminary way at some business ethics issues and at America's moral climate. Now we turn to an overview of the primary philosophical theories employed in examining ethics problems. Ethics, of course, involves judgments as to good and bad, right and wrong, and what ought to be. Business ethics refers to the measurement of business behavior based on standards of right and wrong, rather than relying entirely on principles of accounting and management. (In this discussion, the word *morals* will be used interchangeably with the word *ethics.* Distinctions between the two are not vital for our purposes.)

Finding and following the moral course is not easy for any of us, but the difficulty may be particularly acute for the businessperson. The pressure to produce is intense, and the temptation to cheat may be great. Although the law provides very useful guides for minimum comportment, clear moral answers frequently do not exist. The businessperson facing a difficult decision may, therefore, simply do what he or she takes to be correct at any given moment: do "what my judgment and feelings tell me is right"; "follow my gut."

Existentialism Reliance on personal, subjective judgments to make ethical decisions, however, seems unscientific and risky, even lazy or sloppy. Surely well-developed standards are required? Perhaps, but before turning to those approaches, we will briefly examine *existentialism,* a highly individualized philosophy that explicitly shuns rules and, indeed, all external norms. The individual is free to find his or her own moral course.

Existentialists, including Nobel Prize winner Jean-Paul Sartre, believe standards of conduct cannot be objectively discovered or rationally justified via ethical theory and reasoning. No actions are inherently right or wrong. Thus, each person may reach his or her own choice about ethical principles. Moral decision making—indeed, all decision making—is a solitary act. Personal freedom is the defining characteristic of every person. Each of us is, therefore, fully and exclusively responsible for our own moral decisions.[36] That view finds its roots in the notion that humans are only what we each will ourselves to be. If God does not exist, there can be no general human nature because there is no one to conceive that nature.

| Existence precedes essence. | In Sartre's famous interpretation, existence precedes essence. First humans exist; then we individually define what we are—our essence. |

Therefore, each of us is free, with no rules to turn to for guidance. Just as we all choose our own natures, so must we choose our own ethical precepts. Moral responsibility belongs to each of us individually.

Responsibility

Indian spiritual, political, and civil rights leader Mahatma Gandhi viewed moral responsibility quite differently from Sartre. Gandhi's view: "All humanity is one undivided and indivisible family, and each one of us is responsible for the misdeeds of all the others."[37] Whose view makes more sense to you?

Universal Truths?

Have we then no rules or universal standards by which to distinguish right from wrong? Have we no absolutes? Philosophers seek to provide guidance beyond the uncertainties of ethical relativism. We will survey two ethical perspectives, *teleology* and *deontology,* which form the core of the philosophical approach to ethical analysis. Before proceeding to those theories, we will note the important role of religion in ethics and take a brief look at two additional formulations—libertarianism and virtue ethics—that have been increasingly influential in contemporary moral analysis.

1. **Religion.** Judeo–Christian beliefs, Islam, Confucianism, Buddhism, and other faiths are powerful ethical voices in contemporary life. They often feature efforts such as the Golden Rule to build absolute and universal standards. Scholarly studies indicate that most American managers believe in the Golden Rule and take it to be their most meaningful moral guidepost. From a religious point of view, the deity's laws are absolutes that must shape the whole of one's life, including work. Faith, rather than reason, intuition, or secular knowledge, provides the foundation for a moral life built on religion. [For worldwide coverage of ethics issues, see **www.bbc.co.uk/ethics**].

Spirituality at Work

Many businesses directly practice Christian principles in the workplace. Hobby Lobby, for example, closes its hundreds of stores on Sunday, donates Christian counseling services, and buys holiday ads promoting the Christian faith. The top boss of the family-owned business, David Green, says, "We're Christians and we run our business on Christian principles."[38] Responding to employees' personal and spiritual needs and sometimes fulfilling the religious convictions of the owners, many U.S. companies provide on-the-job chaplains.

We should note, however, that the growing spirituality movement in business often does not explicitly involve religion at all. Rather, managers may see spirituality as an expression of the whole person and a part of the broader search for meaning in life. Business, they think, must acknowledge the soul to maximize performance.

Questions

1. Do you think corporate America must now make room for spirituality and the soul in the workplace to maximize success? Explain.

2. *a.* Must we believe in God to be moral? Explain.
   b. Is religion a force for moral good? Explain.

3. Do you expect your religious beliefs, if any, to influence your postcollege professional decision making? Explain.

Sources: Cathy Lynn Grossman, "Survey: Number of Religious 'Nones' Hits Nearly 20 Percent," *The Des Moines Register,* July 23, 2012, p. 6A; and Bill Keller, "The Conscience of a Corporation," *The New York Times,* February 10, 2013 [**www.nytimes.com**].

2. **Libertarianism.** Contemporary philosopher Robert Nozick (1938–2002) built an ethical theory rooted in personal liberty. For him, morality coincided with the maximization of personal freedom. Justice and fairness, right and wrong are measured not by equality of results (such as wealth) for all, but from ensuring equal opportunity for all to engage in informed choices about their own welfare. Hence, Nozick took essentially a free-market stance toward ethics.

3. **Virtue ethics.** In recent years, an increasing number of philosophers have argued that the key to good ethics lies not in rules, rights, and responsibilities but in the classic notion of character. As Plato and Aristotle argued, our attention should be given to strategies for encouraging desirable character traits such as honesty, fairness, compassion, and generosity. Aristotle believed that virtue could be taught much as any other skill. Virtue ethics applauds the person who is motivated to do the right thing and who cultivates that motivation in daily conduct. A part of the argument is that such persons are more morally reliable than those who simply follow the rules but fail to inspect, strengthen, and preserve their own personal virtues. [For an overview of virtue ethics, see **http://plato.stanford.edu/entries/ethics-virtue/**].

Teleology or Deontology—An Overview

LO 2-4
Distinguish between teleological and deontological ethical systems.

Religion, libertarianism, and virtue provide crucial ethical lessons. Philosophers have further clarified ethical theory by defining two broad analytical systems, *teleology* and *deontology,* that capture much of our current understanding about how to engage in careful ethical analysis.

Teleological ethical systems (often referred to as *consequentialist ethical systems*) are concerned with the consequences—the results—of an act rather than the act itself. A teleological view of life involves ends, goals, and the ultimate good. Duty and obligation are subordinated to the production of results that are good or desirable. For the teleologist/consequentialist, the end is primary and that end or result is the measure of the ethical quality of a decision or act.

To the deontologist, on the other hand, principle is primary and consequence is secondary or even irrelevant. Maximizing right rather than good is the deontological standard. The deontologist might well refuse to lie, as a matter of principle, even if lying would maximize good.

Deontology, derived from the Greek word meaning *duty,* is directed toward what ought to be, toward what is right. Similarly, deontology considers motives. For example, why a crime was committed may be more important than the actual consequences of the crime. Relationships among people are important from a deontological perspective primarily because they create duties. A father may be bound by duty to save his son from a burning building, rather than saving another person who could do more total good for society.

The distinction here is critical. Are we to guide our behavior by rational evaluation of the consequences of our acts, or according to duty and principle—that which ought to be? Let's take a closer look at *utilitarianism,* the principal teleological ethical theory, and *formalism,* the principal deontological ethical theory.

Teleology

LO 2-5
Distinguish
utilitarianism
and formalism.

Utilitarianism   In reaching an ethical decision, good is to be weighed against evil. A decision that maximizes the ratio of good over evil for all those concerned is the ethical course. Jeremy Bentham (1748–1832) and John Stuart Mill (1806–1873) were the chief intellectual forces in the development of utilitarianism. Their views and those of other utilitarian philosophers were not entirely consistent. As a result, at least two branches of utilitarianism have developed. According to *act-utilitarianism,* our moral judgment is to be guided by evaluation of individual acts. The moral path is achieved by performing those acts that generate the greatest good; that is, the greatest overall utility in each particular situation. *Rule-utilitarianism,* on the other hand, involves following those *rules* that generate the greatest good; that is, the greatest overall utility.

Thus, the rule-utilitarian may be forced to shun a particular act that would result in greater immediate good (punishing a guilty person whose constitutional rights have been violated) in favor of upholding a broader rule that results in the greater total good over time (maintaining constitutional principles by freeing the guilty person). In sum, the principle to be followed for the utilitarian, whether examining acts or rules, is the greatest good for the greatest number. [For an extensive database exploring utilitarianism, see **www.hedweb. com/philsoph/utillink.htm**].

Deontology

Formalism   The German philosopher Immanuel Kant (1724–1804) developed perhaps the most persuasive and fully articulated vision of ethics as measured not by consequences (teleology) but by the rightness of rules. Thus, in this formalistic view of ethics, the rightness of an act depends little (or, in Kant's view, not at all) on the results of the act. Rather, Kant advocated ethical decision making based on what is right within the act itself, regardless of the consequences of the act. Moral worth springs from one's decision to discharge one's duty. Thus, the student who refuses to cheat on exams is morally worthy if his or her decision springs from duty or adherence to rules, but morally unworthy if the decision is merely one born of self-interest, such as fear of being caught.

How does a person of goodwill know what is right? Here Kant propounded the *categorical imperative,* the notion that every person should act on only those principles that he or she, as a rational person, would prescribe as universal laws to be applied to the whole of humankind. A moral rule is "categorical" rather than "hypothetical" in that its prescriptive force is independent of its consequences. The rule guides us independent of the ends we seek. Kant believed that every rational creature can act according to his or her categorical imperative because all such persons have "autonomous, self-legislating wills" that permit them to formulate and act on their own systems of rules. To Kant, what is right for one is right for all, and each of us can discover that "right" by exercising our rational faculties.

Questions

1. Fifty-year-old Wesley Autry, waiting with his two young daughters in January 2007 at a New York City subway station, saw a man collapse and fall off the passenger platform into the space between the train rails. The headlight of a train appeared. Mr. Autry immediately jumped on top of the fallen man, holding him down while the train passed over them, inches above Autry's head. Asked later why he jumped to the rescue, Autry said: "I did what I felt was right."[39] What form of ethical reasoning did Autry seem to employ in making his courageous decision?

2. British priest Tim Jones caused a big stir by telling his congregation in 2009 that shoplifting is sometimes morally permissible for desperate people. In a sermon, Jones said that shoplifting can be justified when a person is in real need, is not greedy, and takes only what is necessary to get by. Later Jones said: "The point I'm making is that when we shut down every socially acceptable avenue for people in need, then the only avenue left is the socially unacceptable one."[40]

   a. Was Jones arguing from a teleological/consequentialist or a deontological/formalist point of view? Explain.

   b. Do you agree with Jones? Explain.

3. As Tiger Woods was recovering from, by his standards, a long period of poor performance, Nike released an ad with his picture and the caption "Winning Takes Care of Everything," a remark Woods reportedly made many times in reference to his golf game. Critics attacked Woods and Nike, saying the ad implied that golf victories would cancel out the shortcomings and misconduct of Woods's past, including his failed marriage, repeated infidelities, and what many took to be arrogant, rude behavior.

   a. Is the ad an example of consequentialist or formalist thinking? Explain.

   b. In assessing the moral quality of an individual's life, can we properly weigh exemplary productivity against extensive wrongdoing? Consider cyclist Lance Armstrong, who has acknowledged having cheated by engaging in forbidden doping measures. Can we, nonetheless, consider Armstrong a "good person" in light of the contribution he has made as an advocate for cancer research and as an inspiration to those who suffer from cancer? Explain.

   c. In your view, was Nike wrong to run the "Winning Takes Care of Everything" ad? Explain.

Using Ethical Reasoning: Two Cases

Obviously, ethical theory does not provide magical answers to life's most difficult questions. Those theories are useful, however, in identifying and sorting the issues that lead to better decision making. Apply those theories to the cases that follow, as you think about what kind of boss you aspire to be and how you would treat your employees.

Case One: Boss as "Jerk"

Management trainer and author Mary Donohue claims that tyranical, authoritarian bosses are commonplace: "This is a virus that has spread far and wide." These are managers, she says, who rule over their employees and use fear "as their primary weapon."[41] Georgetown University business professor Christine Porath says that one-quarter of those she surveyed reported they were treated rudely at work at least once per week in 1998, but that portion had risen to over 50 percent by 2011.[42]

While Apple visionary Steve Jobs was celebrated for his remarkable accomplishments, he was often accused of harsh, dictatorial management practices. *Business Insider* lists 16 episodes of "Jobs Being a Huge Jerk," including allegations of lying to his partner Steve Wozniak about the money involved in a deal, firing employees without notice or severance pay, and firing a boss in front of his team.[43] Reports suggest that Jobs was often a good, charming person and boss and that he mellowed somewhat in later years.

Business journalist Jerry Useem recently summarized some of the scholarly evidence about tyrannical bosses in a 2015 *Atlantic* article, "Why It Pays to Be a Jerk."[44] The data are mixed, as would be expected. Stanford business professor Jeffrey Pfeffer says that ". . . all the things we rate negatively"—like immodesty—"are the best predictors of higher salaries or getting chosen for a leadership position."[45] And research at the University of Amsterdam finds that overconfidence and some degree of obnoxiousness can make us seem more powerful and, in fact, can make us more powerful.[46] But other research by Yale professor David Rand shows that being accommodating—being nice—pays off at least in environments where we interact with the same people on a regular basis.[47] In sum, Useem concluded that being a jerk is likely to fail, at least in the long run, if others do not receive spillover benefits, if the boss is dealing with the same people repeatedly, or if the boss lacks the brilliance of someone like Steve Jobs.

Wharton professor Adam Grant has received a great deal of attention recently for his research on whether being nice pays off at work. He divides people into three categories: Takers (who look out for themselves), Givers (who are generous and expect nothing in return), and Matchers (who help others but with the expectation of reciprocal favors). In his study of engineers, salespeople, and medical school students, Grant found that the Givers were over-represented in the bottom 25 percent of their field but also in the top 25 percent. Being too nice can hurt in the short run but pay off in the long run through engendering goodwill in others and through the learning that comes with being generous.[48] Broadly, however, Grant has said: "What I've become convinced of is that nice guys and gals really do finish last."[49] Grant thinks the most effective people are those whom he labels "disagreeable givers." They are not necessarily the nicest people. They are demanding and direct and they push others, but they do so, Grant says, with the interests of others and the organization in mind.[50]

So being an unkind, authoritarian boss may or may not be productive, but is it the right approach? Is being a "jerk" as a boss an ethically defensible posture? Consider the following questions.

Questions

1. Does the boss as "jerk" raise ethical issues? Explain.
2. *a.* Will your personal values require you to be a nice person at work regardless of the consequences?
   b. If so, which of the ethical theories noted above seems to be guiding your behaviors?
   c. If not, would one of the ethical theories justify your other-than-"nice" behaviors? Explain.
   d. Do you think nice men/women finish last? Explain.
3. Do you think the "disagreeable giver" approach to management is ethically defensible? Explain by using the ethics theories examined above.
4. Is the authoritarian, even tyrannical, approach to management ethically justifiable? Explain.

Sources: Olga Khazan, "It Pays to Be Nice," *The Atlantic,* June 23, 2015 [**www.theatlantic.com**]; and Jerry Useem, "Why It Pays to Be a Jerk," *The Atlantic,* June 2015 [**www.theatlantic.com**].

Case Two (Part I): Are Layoffs Unethical? Aaron Feuerstein and Malden Mills

Fabric manufacturer Malden Mills of Lowell, Massachusetts, provided 3,100 high-paid manufacturing jobs in the Boston area when a 1995 fire destroyed most of the plant. The next morning Aaron Feuerstein, CEO of the family-controlled mill, announced that the business would be rebuilt and all employees would retain their jobs. Feuerstein said that keeping all of the workers through the rebuilding process was "the right thing to do and there's a moral imperative to do it, irrespective of the consequences."[51] Apparently, Feuerstein was significantly influenced by his Jewish heritage. In his youth, Feuerstein reportedly memorized in Hebrew the Leviticus passage: "You are not permitted to oppress the workingman because he is poor and needy."

The new plant was designed to expand production of the company's patented and very successful Polartec fabric. Following the fire, makeshift production lines were developed in warehouses and about 85 percent of the employees returned to work, with the remaining 400 workers or so remaining idle but paid. The new plant, machinery, and business losses cost Feuerstein some $300 million, much of which was covered by insurance. Feuerstein was convinced that the big investment would pay in the long run and because he had a highly successful, patent-protected product and because the company was family owned and thus under no immediate pressure to perform, he felt he could afford to do what his long-time family investment in the community and workers seemed to require.

Questions

1. Aaron Feuerstein became something of an overnight national hero by protecting his workers. Feuerstein said, "It was the right thing to do and there's a moral imperative to do it, irrespective of the consequences."
   a. Was Feuerstein employing utilitarian or formalist reasoning? Explain.

b. In your view, was he correct to say that the consequences, in this instance, did not matter? Explain.

2. Commenting on Feuerstein's approach to his employees' needs, Wharton School professor Michael Useem said, "The thinking is: employees can be seen as an ultimate competitive advantage. If you treat them well, they'll pay you back in really hard work later on."[52]

   a. Was Useem expressing formalist or utilitarian reasoning?

   b. In a 1986 pastoral letter, the U.S. Catholic bishops argued that "every economic decision and institution must be judged in light of whether it protects or undermines the dignity of the human person."[53] Does the thinking summarized by Useem undermine that dignity and as such require rejection under either utilitarian or formalist reasoning? Explain.

3. If you were a successful entrepreneur with the flexibility of Aaron Feuerstein, would you operate your business like an extended family? Explain.

Sources: Richard Lorant, Associated Press, "A Mill Owner's Compassion Rescues Thousands of Jobs after Devastating Fire," December 10, 1996, *Chicago Tribune,* p. 8; and Mary McGrory, "Tale of Two Bankruptcies," *Pittsburgh Post-Gazette,* December 22, 2001, p. A15.

[For a film treatment of corporate downsizing/layoffs, see *The Company Men* trailer at **youtube.com/watch?v=Pie66GR63Fc**].

Case Two (Part 2): Are Layoffs Unethical? Aaron Feuerstein, Malden Mills, and Bankruptcy

In November 2001, Malden Mills was forced to enter Chapter 11 bankruptcy proceedings (see Chapter 15) for the purpose of reorganizing its finances under court protection. At the time, Malden Mills was bearing a $140 million debt load. Lenders demanded the bankruptcy action as a condition for extending an additional $20 million to keep the company afloat. In late 2003, Malden Mills emerged from bankruptcy. Creditors controlled the board of directors with Aaron Feuerstein occupying the family's one seat. Malden's precarious financial position was the product of a variety of forces: Customers were lost during the rebuilding after the fire, cheaper fleece substitutes entered the market, the company took on substantial debt in rebuilding and in keeping on its employees following the fire, and the company probably overbuilt following the fire. As a result, the Malden Mills workforce shrunk to 1,200 employees. Then, in 2007, Malden Mills was once again forced into bankruptcy and was purchased by Chrysalis Capital partners, a private-equity firm that renamed the company Polartec LLC. Aaron Feuerstein's association with the company ended with the sale.

Questions

1. *The Wall Street Journal* raised the question, "Are layoffs moral?"[54]

   a. Should we establish a universal, formalist rule forbidding layoffs of all hard-working, competent employees, or should we rely on utilitarian reasoning, libertarian thought, virtue theory, or religious beliefs to answer that question? Explain.

   b. Is morality irrelevant to the question of when layoffs are necessary? Explain.

2. Do you think it would be accurate and fair to say that Feuerstein's ethical choice to protect his employees led to the decline of his business? Explain.

3. Did Feuerstein make an error in judgment in relying on an absolute principle—that is, the immediate protection of his workers at all costs? Explain.

4. How might Feuerstein's workers have benefited by being laid off following the fire?

5. John MacKenzie, in a letter to *The New York Times,* said he had a duty to help Aaron Feuerstein and Malden Mills: "Of course I have an ethical obligation to buy from Malden Mills if I have a choice and if my purchase can make a difference. It would reward Mr. Feuerstein for what he has done and what he is trying to do, and the system needs more of that."[55] Do you have a duty to buy only from the most ethically responsible sellers? Explain.

Source: "Articles about Aaron M. Feuerstein," The New York Times [**topics.nytimes.com/topics/reference/timestopics/people/f/aaron_m_feuerstein/index.html**].

[For another view of the Malden Mills facts, as well as an analysis of the wisdom of Feuerstein's decision, see David W. Gill, "Was Aaron Feuerstein Wrong?," *Ethix,* June 25, 2011 (**ethix.org/2011/06/25/was-aaron-feuerstein-wrong**)].

Part Three—Managerial Misconduct?

Can We Trust Corporate America?

Earlier in this chapter and in Chapter 1 we noted evidence of corporate misconduct. Given the subprime mortgage crisis, a strong sense of wrongdoing on Wall Street, and our ongoing economic problems, we should not be surprised that public attitudes toward big business are not enthusiastic. In Gallup's 2016 poll of confidence in major institutions, only 18 percent of Americans expressed a "great deal" or "quite a lot" of confidence in big business. For some perspective, we should note that Congress ranked last among the 16 institutions mentioned in the Gallup survey with only 6 percent of Americans expressing a great deal or quite a lot of confidence.[56]

In 2015, Gallup asked the American public how it would rate the honesty and ethical standards of people in 21 professions. Several categories of businesspeople, including executives, stockbrokers, advertising practitioners, and car salespeople, ranked near the bottom of that list, with accountants and bankers somewhat more highly regarded.[57]

Still, a 2016 *Fortune* headline suggests an opportunity for improvement: "Business Leaders, the Public Wants to Trust You. Now's Your Chance."[58] *Fortune* pointed to the results of the 2016 Edelman Trust Barometer (a worldwide survey of trust in institutions) that showed trust in business increasing recently. Richard Edelman explained, "Now people have absorbed a truth: business can make money and improve economic and social conditions in a country. This is very new."[59] Georg Kell, founding director of the United Nations Global Compact, says that business for the past 10 years has been undergoing a "silent revolution" from within: "Business has been repositioning its mission to include purpose, community work, and values."[60] That promise for a better business and society relationship is threatened, however, by the great divide in American life between the well-educated, well-to-do, and those struggling at the bottom of our economy. Those at the top, not surprisingly, express much more trust in business and other societal institutions than those at the bottom. Indeed, according to Edelman, the "trust gap" between America's highest and lowest income quartiles is at 31 points, the widest such gap in the world.[61]

We can fairly say that public perceptions of trustworthiness and ethical quality in corporate America are mixed at best, but are those perceptions fair and accurate? We have considerable evidence about unethical behavior in the business community. Drawing on 6,400 responses nationwide, the 2013 National Business Ethics Survey found that 41 percent of workers reported seeing misconduct on the job, most commonly by managers. Nevertheless, the observed misconduct in American workplaces is at its lowest level in 20 years, according to the survey.[62] The Ethics Resource Center, a Virginia-based nonprofit that conducts the survey, theorized that the improved behavior could be attributed to "businesses continuing and growing commitment to strong ethics and compliance programs."[63]

As ethicist Chris MacDonald argues: "Workplaces, while still far from perfect, are less sexist, less racist, and generally more civilized and humane than at any time in history (in considerable part as a response to government oversight and public pressure).[64] [For "The Business Ethics Blog," see **https://businessethicsblog.com**].

Misconduct remains a major problem, nonetheless. A 2015 survey of 1,200 financial professionals in the United States and the United Kingdom (cited earlier in this chapter) found 47 percent of respondents thought it likely that their competitors cheat (up from 39 percent in 2012) and 23 percent thought it likely that their fellow employees cheat (up from 12 percent in 2012). The study's authors at the University of Notre Dame and the law firm Labaton Sucharow conclude: "Nearly seven years after the global financial crisis rocked investors' confidence in the markets and financial services in general, our survey clearly shows that a culture of integrity has failed to take hold."[65]

Now we turn to an examination of what forces may encourage corporate misconduct and its accompanying trust problems.[66]

Why Do Some Managers Cheat?

Moral Development

LO 2-6

Describe some of the forces that encourage unethical behavior in the workplace.

Scholars argue that some individuals are better prepared to make ethical judgments than others. Psychologist Lawrence Kohlberg built and empirically tested a comprehensive theory of moral development in which he claimed that moral judgment, at least as applied to judgments of justice, evolves and improves primarily as a function of age and education.

Kohlberg, via interviews with children as they aged, was able to identify moral development as movement through distinct stages, with the later stages being improvements on the earlier ones. Kohlberg identified six universal stages grouped into three levels:

LO 2-7

Describe Kohlberg's theory of moral development.

1. **Preconventional level:**

    Stage 1: Obey rules to avoid punishment.

    Stage 2: Follow rules only if it is in own interest, but let others do the same. Conform to secure rewards.

2. **Conventional level:**

Stage 3: Conform to meet the expectations of others. Please others. Adhere to stereotypical images.

Stage 4: Doing right is one's duty. Obey the law. Uphold the social order.

3. **Post-conventional or principled level:**

Stage 5: Current laws and values are relative. Laws and duty are obeyed on rational calculations to serve the greatest number.

Stage 6: Follow self-chosen universal ethical principles. In the event of conflicts, principles override laws.[67]

At Level 3 the individual is able to reach independent moral judgments that may or may not conform with conventional societal wisdom. Thus, the Level 2 manager might refrain from sexual harassment because it constitutes a violation of company policy and the law. A manager at Level 3 might reach the same conclusion, but his or her decision would be based on independently defined universal principles of justice.

Kohlberg found that many adults never pass beyond Level 2. Consequently, if Kohlberg was correct, many managers may behave unethically simply because they have not reached the upper stages of moral maturity. Of course, some managers may achieve mature moral judgments but fail to take moral action based on those judgments.

Kohlberg's model is based on extensive longitudinal and cross-cultural studies over more than three decades. For example, one set of Chicago-area boys was interviewed at three-year intervals for 20 years. Thus, the stages of moral growth exhibit "definite empirical characteristics" such that Kohlberg was able to claim that his model had been scientifically validated.[68] Although many critics remain, the evidence, in sum, supports Kohlberg's general proposition. [For a link to an overview of moral development and moral education, see **www.davidsongifted.org/db/Resources_id_11335.aspx**].

Feminine Voice   One of those lines of criticism requires a brief inspection. Kohlberg colleague Carol Gilligan contends that our conceptions of morality are, in substantial part, gender-based.[69] She claims that men typically approach morality as a function of justice, impartiality, and rights (the ethic of justice), whereas women are more likely to build a morality based on care, support, and responsiveness (the ethic of care). Men, she says, tend to take an impersonal, universal view of morality as contrasted with the feminine "voice" that rises more commonly from relationships and concern for the specific needs of others. Gilligan criticizes Kohlberg because his highest stages, 5 and 6, are structured in terms of the male approach to morality while the feminine voice falls at stage 3. Furthermore, Kohlberg's initial experimental subjects were limited to young males. The result, in Gilligan's view, is that women are underscored. Of course, a danger in the ethic of care is that it might be interpreted to restore and legitimize the stereotype of women as care-giving subordinates not deserving of moral autonomy.[70] Subsequent research both challenges[71] and supports[72] Gilligan's view. [For a video outlining Gilligan's theory, see **www.youtube.com/watch?v=HctzZwwueL4**].

Reason or Emotion?

Controlled or automatic? We have seen that Kohlberg and Gilligan (and most moral philosophers) take the position that moral decision making is the controlled product of analysis, deliberation, and experience. In recent years, however, new psychological and neuroscience evidence has supported an alternative theory of morality that involves decision making by emotion or intuition. The emotion/intuition approach claims that moral decision making is an automatic, nonreflective process in which our minds, when confronted with a moral question, instantaneously generate feelings of approval or disapproval.[73] Brain-scanning experiments have provided support for the automatic emotion/intuition hypothesis.[74] Some scientists speculate that controlled moral reasoning may be little more than an after-the-fact method of justifying conclusions already reached automatically via emotions/intuitions.

Moral theorist Marc Hauser extends the emotion/intuition thesis in his book *Moral Minds*.[75] He claims that our brains are biologically endowed with a moral faculty that has evolved over eons and is designed to reach very rapid judgments about right and wrong based on unconscious processes that are involuntary and universal. Thus, when we judge an action to be morally right or wrong, Hauser says we are doing so instinctively, using our inborn moral faculty. Even babies seem to make moral judgments. Experiments show that one-year-old infants, for example, prefer taking one graham cracker from a "good" puppet rather than two from a "bad" puppet, but when the bad puppet offered eight graham crackers, the infants tended to accept that offer over a single cracker from the good puppet.[76]

> Even babies seem to make moral judgments.

The emotion/intuition/ biological theory provides a stern challenge to Kohlberg and to our faith in moral reasoning generally. Psychologist Jonathan Haidt compares the intuitive, moral machinery of the brain with an elephant and conscious moral reasoning with a small rider on the elephant's back.[77] Other scholarly evidence, however, continues to support a very robust role for rational moral decision making,[78] and reasoning may at times override intuitions, as Haidt himself acknowledges.[79] Overall, moral decision making may be the product of a dual process system employing both automatic emotions (produced deep in the brain in its older structures) and controlled reasoning (produced in the newer, frontal lobes of the brain).[80] [For more, see the website **YourMorals.org,** where Haidt and his colleagues invite you to "learn about your own morality, ethics, and/or values, while also contributing to scientific research."].

Moral Identity?

The moral development story does not end with an understanding of moral reasoning and moral emotion. Neither of those forces, according to current research, adequately explains why some among us are moved, after reaching a moral judgment, to take moral action.[81] Early evidence suggests that a critical feature in total moral development, including the will to act, involves what is labeled *moral identity*. In general, moral identity involves the degree to which moral concerns are central to our sense of self. As Professor Sam Hardy explains it, a person might have a stronger sense of moral identity if that identity is centered more on moral virtue than on amoral virtues such as creativity.[82] Some studies find that those with stronger moral identities are more likely to engage in good behaviors such as volunteering or showing respect for members of "out-groups."[83] Remember, however, that the moral identity evidence remains quite tentative.

Organizational Forces

Ethisphere Institute, in its 2016 ranking of the world's most ethical companies, identified 131 (99 of which were American) that met its standards. Ethisphere bases it rankings on what it calls an Ethics Quotient derived from nominees' codes of ethics, regulatory and legal infractions, sustainable investment policies, corporate citizenship, and more.[84] One of the companies honored, 3M, described the importance of a strong ethical culture:

> It takes more than a few company policies to be held as an example of how to do business the right way. . . . What it takes is a strong ethical culture that is so fully intertwined with every-day business practices that doing the right thing is never questioned. . . . [85]

[For the Business Roundtable Institute for Corporate Ethics, see **www.corporate-ethics.org/**]. Pressure to cheat is often cited as a measure of an organization's ethical culture, but according to the 2013 National Business Ethics Survey, only 9 percent of American for-profit workers "perceived pressure to compromise standards in order to do their jobs."[86] Organizational pressure to cheat appears to be declining, but when that pressure emerges, it can disrupt or destroy managers' lives, as suggested by interviews some years ago with 30 young Harvard Business School graduates:

> "[My boss] was not willfully unethical. It was the pressure of the time."

I really feel for people who are middle management, with a wife and four kids, under financial strain. . . . You see it happen all the time, that people are indicted for fraud or larceny. You can empathize with their situation. The world is changing fast. And a lot of people have been blindsided by it—so they've done things that they don't like. I can't say that will never happen to me. It's easy for me as a single person . . . but when you're desperate, you're desperate.

[My boss] was not willfully unethical. It was the pressure of the time. . . . I have no idea what pressures were on him to drive the project. It probably wasn't [his] initiative to fudge the numbers. There may have been a good intention at some point in the organization. But as it got filtered through the organization, it changed. Some executive may have said, "This is an interesting project." Unfortunately this got translated as, "The vice president really wants this project." This sort of thing can happen a lot. Things start on high. As they go down they are filtered, modified. What was a positive comment several levels above becomes "do this or die" several levels down.[87]

The Boss

Top corporate bosses have hit a particularly rough patch in American life. Many have been disgraced by scandals, and some are in jail. Wall Street executives are accused of bringing the economy to near collapse. Although blame is often attributed to a "few bad apples," the 2013 Edelman Trust Barometer found that only 18 percent of respondents worldwide "would trust a business leader to tell the truth in a complex situation."[88] The vital role of the boss in setting and practicing firm ethical standards is evidenced by a 2014 global survey of nearly 2,000 financial professionals, over 60 percent of whom said the tone at the top of the organization is the most important determinant of behavior in the workplace.[89] The Bill Hawkins story that follows illustrates the challenges of ethical leadership.

[For a film treatment of ethical issues in the business community, see the trailer *Wall Street: Money Never Sleeps,* at **http://www.youtube.com/watch?v=HcMFA2SHES4**].

Bill Hawkins: A Tough Decision

Bill Hawkins, CEO at Medtronic (Minneapolis-based medical device maker with over 85,000 employees worldwide), faced a critical ethical decision-making moment in 2007 when he learned that Medtronic's Sprint Fidelis leads might have been malfunctioning at an unacceptably high rate. Leads are very thin wires that connect implanted heart defibrillators to the heart, thus allowing a shock to be delivered from the defibrillator to the heart muscle. Sprint Fidelis leads (Sprint was the brand name for Medtronic's leads and Fidelis was the particular model of lead) were the company's newest, and thinnest, model. Medtronic began receiving reports of fractures in the Sprint Fidelis leads. Those fractures might prevent a needed shock from reaching the heart, or patients might receive random shocks.

Hawkins had been with Medtronic for about five years and had been serving as president and chief operating officer for about two months when he learned in March 2007 that one hospital was reporting problems with the leads. According to Hawkins, Medtronic's internal experts and an independent physician advisory board investigated, and the company concluded that monitoring should continue but the leads should not be removed from the market. In October 2007, when Hawkins had been CEO for two months, he received new data showing that the Fidelis lead's resistance to fracture was 97.7 percent versus 99.1 for the previous model, a statistically insignificant difference, but a gap that would become statistically significant over time if the fracture rates remained constant. Hawkins consulted with other company officers and an independent physician advisory board. Various Medtronic leaders and physicians met for discussion. The next day they met again by teleconference and after 90 minutes of back and forth, the decision was reached to voluntarily recall the Sprint Fidelis.

The leads had been on the market for about 38 months and 268,000 had been implanted. The day the recall was announced, Medtronic had its worst day on the stock market in 23 years with a 12 percent decline, and its market share in the category fell from 51 to 47 percent. By March 2009, Medtronic's physician panel had identified 13 deaths that might have been associated with the lead fractures. Within two years, however, Medtronic had largely recovered from the episode, a software package had been developed that would alert patients that a lead might be fracturing, and a favorable U.S. Supreme Court decision was offering Medtronic substantial shelter from lawsuits.

Hawkins described how Medtronic's culture influenced him and his company:

> Our founder wrote in 1960 that the purpose of our company is to "alleviate pain, restore health, and extend life." I am not being coy when I say that I take this very personally and that our company is strongly influenced by this sense of mission. During the course of our Fidelis discussions, not once did we talk about what might happen to the stock price or market share if we suspended distribution. The conversation was about our responsibility to do the right thing.[90]

Questions

1. Beyond market share and stock market prices, what considerations would have influenced Hawkins's decision?

2. Some critics have said that Hawkins's decision could not be considered difficult because lives were at risk. Do you agree that Hawkins's decision was, in fact, easy? Explain.

Sources: Bill Hawkins, as told to Cait Murphy, "Bill Hawkins: How I Made the Toughest Call of My Career," *CBS MoneyWatch,* October 5, 2009 [**www.cbsnews.com**]; Cait Murphy, "The Price Medtronic Paid," *BNET,* October 5, 2009 [**www.bnet.com**]; and Chris MacDonald, "Can Life-Saving Decisions Really Be 'Tough Calls'?" *The Business Ethics Blog,* October 15, 2009 [**www.businessethics.ca/blog**].

Questions—Part Three

1. *a.* Do you think heroes are important to our character development? Explain.
   b. Do you think we have fewer heroes today than in the past? Explain.
   c. Do you have a hero? Explain.

2. Ethics expert Kirk O. Hanson has identified "six ethical dilemmas every professional faces," including "What Is Worthwhile Work?"[91] In thinking about that question, Hanson mentions a number of considerations, including whether the work contributes to human welfare.
   a. Will you pursue only those forms of work that contribute to human welfare? If you fail to do so, will you commit an ethical wrong? Does all work contribute to human welfare? Explain.
   b. A 2014 Gallup poll of 30,000 college graduates of all ages who had moved into the workforce were asked if they were "deeply interested" in the work they do. The poll found that those who had majored in business were least interested in their work, regardless of the career path they chose, as compared to those who had majored in social sciences/education, science/engineering, or arts and humanities.[92] Do you expect to be "deeply interested" in your future work? If you choose a career in business, do you expect to be disengaged from your work? If you choose a high-paying career that does not interest you, would that decision constitute an ethical wrong? Explain.

3. A 2014 Harvard University study, based on a national survey as well as conversations and observations, asked middle and high school students to rank what was most important to them: "achieving at a high level, happiness (feeling good most of the time), or caring for others." Almost 80 percent of the students selected high achievement or happiness as their first choice. About 80 percent of the students also reported that their parents valued achievement or happiness for their children more than they valued caring for others.[93]
   a. As a college student, which of those qualities do you value most?
   b. Which of those qualities will you/do you most encourage in your children? Explain.

4. Does a corporation have a conscience? Explain. See Kenneth Goodpaster and John B. Matthews Jr., "Can a Corporation Have a Conscience?," *Harvard Business Review,* January–February 1982, p. 136.

5. Kansas City Royals pitcher Gil Meche, 32 years old and troubled by a shoulder injury, decided in 2011 to retire from baseball. The decision would not be considered particularly newsworthy beyond the sports pages except that Meche passed up the $12 million final year of his contract by doing so. Others in similar situations have reported to spring training, gone through the motions, and collected their big paychecks. Meche said, "When I signed my contract, my main goal was to earn it. Once I started to realize I wasn't earning my money, I felt bad." Meche thought he had already earned enough from the Royals: "Making that amount of money from a team that's already given me over $40 million for my life and for my kids, it just wasn't the right thing to do."[94]
   a. Would you do the same as Meche if you were similarly situated? Explain.
   b. Have you ever spurned money for reasons of principal?

c. Why did you do so?

d. Was Meche employing utilitarian or formalist reasoning? Explain. See Tyler Kepner, "Pitcher Spurns $12 Million, to Keep Self-Respect," *The New York Times,* January 26, 2011 [**www.nytimes.com**].

6. Boris Siperstein, then 38, of Austin, Texas, reported biking to meetings for his private-equity firm and estimated that he saved the firm several thousand dollars because he took his folding bike on business trips and used it in place of cabs. Siperstein also slept on the floor of the company's former Manhattan headquarters rather than exceed his personal limit of $200 for a hotel room. David Payne, then 41 and a trainer for a Brooklyn, New York, software firm, often washed his clothing in the bathtub while on the road. He traveled with detergent and used local laundromats, thus saving, he estimated, $30 to $40 off hotel service.[95]

a. Will you impose frugal spending limits on yourself when you are on a company expense account? Explain.

b. Is frugality morally required? Explain.

c. Do employers value frugal employees? Explain.

Part Four—Business Ethics in Practice

Introduction: Corporate/White-Collar Crime

General Motors

Ignition Switch   The deaths of at least 124 people in recent years have been linked to a faulty ignition switch in some General Motors small cars. The switch, if jarred in particular ways, could shut off the engine with the vehicle in motion, resulting in a loss of power steering, airbags, and other systems. GM has acknowledged it was aware of the problem by at least 2005, although some reports had emerged as early as 2001. Various adjustments were made over the years, but the problem persisted and some potential solutions reportedly were rejected on cost grounds. In 2009 GM, struggling with the Great Recession, filed for Chapter 11 bankruptcy and was "bailed out" with a $49.5 billion federal investment that made the government GM's primary owner. In 2014 GM, much improved financially and having paid back the bailout, officially notified the National Highway Traffic Safety Administration of the switch defect and ultimately recalled millions of cars. GM apologized for mishandling the problem; a number of employees, including several executives, were fired/disciplined; a $35 million civil penalty was imposed; a victim compensation fund was established; and civil lawsuits for damages have followed.[96]

Corporate Crime?   Was General Motors guilty of criminal behavior? What about its managers and officers? When does wrongful, unethical behavior become criminal? In 2015 GM agreed to pay $900 million to settle a U.S. Justice Department criminal probe involving fraud and concealing a deadly safety defect. The federal government and General Motors also entered a *deferred prosecution agreement* under which the Justice Department, after three years, will dismiss its criminal charges without additional penalties if GM continues to satisfactorily cooperate with the government. In explaining the deal, prosecutors pointed to GM's "fairly extraordinary" cooperation in the investigation, but victims and critics are outraged. Margie Beskau, whose daughter Amy Rademaker was killed in a 2006 crash, said, "I don't understand how they can basically buy their way out of it. They knew what they were doing, and they kept doing it."[97]

Bosses?   To date, General Motors officers and managers have escaped prosecution by the federal government. Preet Bharara, former U.S. attorney for the Southern District of New York, explained: "There are gaps in the law. It's not a criminal violation to put into the stream of commerce an auto that might harm people."[98] The government takes the position that the law, as currently written, simply does not permit criminal charges against the individuals involved. While penalties certainly are possible under present law, the auto industry and its lobbyists have successfully blunted congressional efforts to enact firmer legislation. Furthermore, criminal convictions ordinarily require proof of some degree of evil intent (*mens rea*—see Chapter 4). In the case of the auto industry, establishing that intent, that guilty mind, is a very challenging standard for prosecutors, who must sift through the complex decision-making processes in giant bureaucracies like General Motors.

We should also note that some legislators, jurists, and others believe Congress has criminalized too much conduct. They argue for firm, consistent *mens rea* standards throughout criminal law so that Americans cannot be prosecuted for behavior they reasonably believe to be lawful.

Jail for Some Bosses

Nine people died and over 700 reportedly were ill from salmonella poisoning that was linked to a Peanut Corporation of America processing plant in Georgia. Prosecutors showed that the plant did not meet federal health standards and that bosses knowingly shipped contaminated peanut butter. The plant was shut down, the company was liquidated, and three defendants received prison terms. The CEO, Stewart Parnell, was sentenced to 28 years in prison for his crimes, including conspiracy, obstruction of justice, and introduction of adulterated food.[99]

Corporations as Crime Victims

While the headlines in recent years have often featured allegations of criminal conduct by corporations, particularly Wall Street banks, we should remember that corporate America itself is the victim of criminals, both employees and outsiders. Cybercrime, bribery, money laundering, fraud, and outright theft harm the bottom line for big corporations.

Thirty-six percent of global respondents and 38 percent of U.S. respondents to PricewaterhouseCoopers' (PwC) 2016 economic crime survey reported that their organizations had suffered economic crime in the previous 24 months.[100] As PwC explained, "Crime continues to forge new paths into business. Regulatory compliance adds stress and burden to responsible organizations. The increasingly complicated landscape challenges the balance between resources and growth."[101] That is, while we might be inclined to call for more rules and closer government oversight to address criminal problems in big business, we must also remember that the cost of complying with those rules and government expectations diverts money from the investments that lead to economic growth.

Is Theft Sometimes OK?

A shopper wrote a letter to the editor explaining how he felt after observing what appeared to be a theft:

> [A]t Wal-Mart I saw a person try to put an item in their jacket. At first I thought this person was a jerk. . . . But after I returned home, I became convinced that it was OK to steal. . . . When I compare the theft of a $15 item to the grand larceny by corporate America, which ran Enron into the ground, which reaps record oil profits, . . . which occupies the seats of government and takes bribes, I now see the act of stealing a small gift . . . as heroic.[102]

Questions

1. What do you think the letter writer meant when he applied the label "heroic" to the apparent theft?
2. Should we be more aggressive in pursuing corporate fraud? Explain.

Source: Greg Wilcox, "It's All Relative," *The Des Moines Register,* December 12, 2005, p. 6A.

Prevention or Enhanced Punishment

Responding to public outrage over Enron, WorldCom, and other stunning and destructive corporate scandals, Congress and the president approved the 2002 Sarbanes–Oxley Act (SOX) to attack corporate crime by publicly traded companies. Among its provisions, the bill

- Establishes an independent board to oversee the accounting profession.
- Requires corporate executives to personally certify the accuracy of their financial reports.
- Creates new crimes and raises penalties.
- Requires publicly traded companies to establish internal control systems designed to assure the accuracy of financial information.
- Requires publicly traded companies to disclose whether they have adopted an ethics code for senior financial management, and if not, why not.

SOX is often criticized as a drain on company resources and an impediment to economic growth, but the evidence to date is mixed. About two-thirds of 460 audit executives and professionals responding to a 2015 Protiviti survey said the hours devoted to compliance increased in 2014.[103] At the same time, about three out of four large company respondents said that SOX requirements had spurred improved financial reporting processes in their organizations. Fewer smaller companies reported similar benefits.[104] A 2014 review of 120 studies of the SOX impact likewise found improved financial reporting quality, but fears that SOX discourages risk taking and thus potential economic growth could neither be confirmed nor denied.[105] A 2009 Securities and Exchange Commission study concluded, however, that the benefits of SOX exceed its costs.[106] Worrisome, perhaps, is the arguable underutilization of SOX as reported by *The Wall Street Journal* in 2012:

> As the Sarbanes–Oxley Act turns 10 years old, the law's biggest hammer—the threat of jail time for corporate executives who knowingly certify inaccurate financial reports—is going largely unused.[107]

Sentencing

Federal sentencing guidelines, issued by the U.S. Sentencing Commission, provide ranges (e.g., 10–12 months' imprisonment) within which judges are advised to impose sentences. The guidelines are designed to provide greater predictability and consistency in punishment. Relying on the crime's "offense level" and the defendant's criminal history, the punishment range for individuals is established for each category of both white-collar and street crime. The Justice Department in 2015 issued a memo to emphasize the importance of holding *individuals* responsible when they are involved in illegal corporate conduct.

Organizational sentencing guidelines are applied to corporate crime. Companies involved in crimes may receive reduced penalties if they have effective compliance programs in place. Companies must develop programs to prevent and detect crime, provide ethics training, and monitor the success of compliance efforts. Responsibility for compliance rests explicitly with the board of directors and top-level executives. Directors and officers complying with the guidelines may receive leniency, while those engaging in aggravating behaviors such as a leadership role in crime may face increased punishment. Of course, the challenges of maintaining close, effective compliance in extended, complex giants such as Walmart and McDonald's are formidable.

Recent Supreme Court decisions have diminished the power of the guidelines by significantly restoring federal judges' authority to deviate from them. Judges who follow the guidelines are presumed to have acted reasonably, but departures from the guidelines are now permissible on a case-by-case basis.

Too Lenient?

Federal judge Sandra Beckwith in Ohio stretched judicial latitude to the maximum in her 2011 sentencing of Michael E. Peppel, former chair and CEO of technology firm MCSi. Peppel pleaded guilty to fraud, resulting in estimated damages of $18 million. The federal sentencing guidelines called for 8 to 10 years of incarceration, but the judge handed down a sentence of seven days in jail and three years of supervised release. The judge had responded to evidence of Peppel's 100 letters of support, strong role in the community, business expertise, five children, and other family needs. On appeal, however, the federal Sixth Circuit Court of Appeals ruled that Judge Beckwith had abused her discretion. The appeals court specifically rejected the reasoning that Peppel's professional skills and capacity to contribute to society justified a lighter sentence. Following the appellate decision, Judge Beckwith sentenced Peppel to two years in prison, three years of court supervision, and a $5 million fine.

Question

Critics of increased government activism regard the free market as the best protection against corporate misconduct. They see SOX, the sentencing guidelines, and aggressive prosecution as government-inflicted drags on the economy. Do you agree? Explain. [For more on white-collar crime, see **www.fbi.gov/investigate/white-collar-crime**].

Sources: United States v. Peppel, 707 F.3d 627 (6th Cir. 2013); and Walter Pavlo, "6th Circuit to Michael Peppel 'You Need More Prison Time,'" *Forbes,* February 18, 2013 [**www.forbes.com**].

Global Bribery

LO 2-8
Explain the general requirements of the Foreign Corrupt Practices Act.

Door-to-door cosmetics giant Avon agreed in 2014 to pay $135 million to settle charges that its China subsidiary had paid about $8 million in bribes to various Chinese officials and that Avon's books failed to properly record those payments.[108] U.S. Attorney Preet Bharara said,

> Avon China was in the door-to-door influence-peddling business, and for years its corporate parent, rather than putting an end to the practice, conspired to cover it up.[109]

Polo-brand clothier Ralph Lauren paid $1.6 million in fines in 2013 to resolve federal bribery charges.[110] Ralph Lauren Corp. reportedly bribed Argentine customs officials with about $600,000 worth of perfume, dresses, and cash from 2004 to 2009 to facilitate passage of company products into the country. Lauren officials say they reported the misconduct as soon as they learned of it.

In many cultures, the payment of bribes—*baksheesh* (Middle East), *huilu* (China), *vzyatku* (Russia), *mordida* (Latin America), or *dash* (Africa)—is accepted as a necessary and, in some cases, a lawful way of doing business. American firms and officers, sometimes willingly and sometimes under great pressure, have engaged in practices that are illegal and unethical in American culture.

The Foreign Corrupt Practices Act (FCPA), the chief federal weapon against bribery abroad, was enacted in 1977 in response to disclosure of widespread bribery by American firms. In brief, the FCPA provides that U.S. nationals and businesses acting anywhere in the world, foreign nationals and companies acting in U.S. territory, and foreign companies listed on a U.S. stock exchange are engaging in criminal conduct if they offer or provide money or anything of value to foreign government officials to obtain or retain business or otherwise secure "any improper advantage." In addition, the FCPA requires rigorous internal accounting controls and careful record keeping to ensure that bribes cannot be concealed via "slush funds" and other devices. Civil and criminal fines can be imposed on both individuals and companies, and individuals can be imprisoned under the FCPA. [For a "series of measures to help organizations prevent, detect and address bribery," see the International Organization for Standardization (ISO) antibribery global standard at **www.iso.org/iso/home/standards/management-standards/iso37001.htm**].

Grease   The act does not forbid "grease" payments to foreign officials or political parties where the purpose of the payments is "to expedite or to secure the performance of a routine governmental action," such as processing papers (like visas), providing police protection, and securing phone service. Likewise a "small gift or token of esteem or gratitude" ordinarily is permissible. And those accused may offer the affirmative defense that the alleged payoff was lawful in the host country or was a normal, reasonable business expenditure directed to specific marketing and contract performance activities. [For the FCPA Blog, see **www.fcpablog.com**].

FCPA Controversy   The FCPA has been controversial from the outset. Some businesspeople see it as a blessing both because it is an honorable attempt at a firm moral stance and because it is often useful for an American businessperson abroad to say, "No, our laws forbid me from doing that." On the other hand, some consider the act damaging to American competitiveness. Indeed, U.S. Assistant Attorney General Leslie Caldwell recently said: "In more than half of all countries it's very difficult to do business without being faced with the potential of a FCPA violation."[111]

Recognizing that corruption is a great risk to the global economy. most industrial countries are now moving toward the zero tolerance view held by the United States. In 2015, China, Mexico, and South Korea adopted new anticorruption reforms. In addition to the FCPA, the United States participates in several other global anticorruption initiatives. [For example, see the OECD Anti-Bribery Convention at **www.oecd.org/corruption/**].

U.S. Corruption   FCPA enforcement actions by the Justice Department and the Securities and Exchange Commission in 2015 totaled 21, down from 26 in 2014, and penalties totaled $140 million in 2015, as opposed to $1.57 billion in 2014.[112] The Justice Department attributed the year-to-year decline to an increased focus on bigger, more complicated cases, including greater attention to the individuals involved in them.

By far the most publicized FCPA news in recent years involves continuing investigations of Walmart's alleged bribes in Mexico that were designed to outflank competitors by winning approval for new store construction, including one near ancient pyramids. The inquiry has been broadened to China, Brazil, and India and seems likely to cost Walmart one to two billion dollars or more in investigation expenses alone.[113] *The Wall Street Journal* has reported that the federal investigation "has found little in the way of major offenses,"[114] but *The New York Times* earlier reported that Walmart was often the aggressor in these alleged deals:

> The *Times*'s examination reveals that Wal-Mart de Mexico was not the reluctant victim of a corrupt culture that insisted on bribes as the cost of doing business. Nor did it pay bribes merely to speed up routine approvals. Rather, Wal-Mart de Mexico was an aggressive and creative corrupter, offering large payoffs to get what the law otherwise prohibited. It used bribes to subvert democratic governance—public votes, open debates, transparent procedures. It used bribes to circumvent regulatory safeguards that protect Mexican citizens from unsafe construction. . . .[115]

> The United States ranked 16th in Transparency International's 2015 Corruption Perceptions Index.

The United States ranked 16th in Transparency International's 2015 Corruption Perceptions Index, which aggregates data provided by experts and business leaders to assess the perceived level of *public sector* corruption around the globe. The countries perceived to be least corrupt were Denmark, Finland, and Sweden. Most of northern and western Europe as well as Canada, the United Kingdom, and Australia were perceived to be less corrupt than the United States. France (23), China (83), and Russia (119) were among the nations ranking lower than the United States.[116]

Bribery Touches Daily Life

Soccer, the "Beautiful Game," is a barely controlled passion for hundreds of millions around the globe. The U.S. Justice Department in 2015 initiated a criminal action against a number of officials in FIFA, soccer's governing body, and several corporate executives.

The charges included racketeering, fraud, and money laundering involving $150 million. The alleged wrongdoing involves kickbacks to FIFA officials from soccer marketing companies and bribes and kickbacks associated with the site selection for the 2010 World Cup and the 2011 FIFA presidential election.[117]

The FCPA applies only to bribes directed to foreign officials and only to those who pay bribes, not recipients, as in the case of the FIFA officials. So the FCPA may not play a role in the FIFA case, but the Justice Department charges refer to a U.S. sportswear company that allegedly secured a late 1990s sportswear contract with the Brazilian Soccer Federation in part by paying millions to a middleman who in turn allegedly paid bribes.[118] *The Wall Street Journal* has reported that the sportswear company in question is believed to be Nike.[119] If so, Nike could be subject to the FCPA rules requiring accurate books and records.

Beyond the FIFA scandal, bribery in many countries touches daily life in much more direct and frustrating ways:

> ### Nikolai can't even count the number of bribes he has paid in his life.

Like many Russians, Nikolai can't even count the number of bribes he has paid in his life. He remembers the big ones, like the $1,000 he paid to avoid mandatory military service or the $1,200 he gave his wife's obstetrician to ensure her a place at one of Moscow's state-run maternity hospitals. But the small ones, like the dozens of $10 to $20 bribes he's handed to traffic police over the years, are instantly forgotten.[120]

Russian President Vladimir Putin in 2016 praised Russia's progress in combating corruption, but he acknowledged that eliminating everyday bribes may be a long time in coming. Bribes are simply part of the cost of doing business, as a Russian trucker explained: "I've left St.

> ### I've left St. Petersburg and I'm en route to Irkutsk.

Petersburg and I'm en route to Irkutsk, 5,000 kilometers away, and if a traffic policeman starts extorting a bribe from me halfway, what am I supposed to do? Turn back?"[121] According to the Associated Press, bribes for that long trip likely would range from about $900 to $1,300.[122]

PRACTICING ETHICS   Bribe the Terrorists?

Banadex, a subsidiary of Cincinnati-based Chiquita Brands International, paid bribes to Colombian rebels over a period of years, including $1.7 million from 1997 to 2004 to the AUC (Autodefensas Unidas de Colombia—now disbanded), a right-wing Colombian terrorist group. Chiquita, one of the world's leading banana producers with operations in 70 nations, learned of the payments in 2000 but allowed them to continue. At the time, terrorists in Colombia were holding Americans for ransom or killing some of them, and years earlier four Chiquita employees had been killed by left-wing guerrillas. The bribes, then lawful under American and Colombian law, were thought necessary to protect employees and company property at Chiquita's Colombian operations.

In 2003, Chiquita allegedly "stumbled across" news that the AUC had in 2001 been designated a "foreign terrorist organization" by the U.S. government, which meant payments thereafter were unlawful, but the payments continued. Chiquita said it was a victim of extortion and that stopping the payments would have endangered its employees. The bribe payments were stopped in 2004, and Chiquita sold its Colombian interests. Chiquita had earned about $50 million in profits from the time AUC was designated a terrorist organization until the period when the payments ceased.

During the period of Chiquita payments to AUC, some 4,000 Colombians were killed in the banana-growing region of Colombia. An Organization of American States investigation concluded that 3,000 Central American rifles and millions of rounds of ammunition reached the terrorists after allegedly being unloaded at a Colombian port by Banadex.

In 2007, Chiquita pleaded guilty to U.S. charges of engaging in transactions with terrorists and paid a $25 million fine. U.S. Justice Department officials concluded their investigation in 2007 by deciding not to bring criminal charges against former Chiquita officials.

Families of Colombians killed or tortured by the terrorists along with human rights groups have filed several civil lawsuits against Chiquita. In 2014, the U.S. 11th Circuit Court of Appeals ruled that those claims could not be litigated in the United States, and the U.S. Supreme Court declined to review that decision. However, in 2016, a federal district court in Florida did rule that the Colombian victims' lawsuits against specific Chiquita executives could go forward.

Questions

1. Chiquita argued that the safety of its employees required payment of the bribes, even after learning of their illegality. What would you have done, had you been in charge? Explain.

2. Should Chiquita's corporate officers have been prosecuted by the U.S. government? Explain.

Sources: Sibylla Brodzinsky, "Chiquita Case Puts Big Firms on Notice," *The Christian Science Monitor,* April 11, 2007 [**www. csmonitor.com/2007/0411/p01s03-woam.html**]; Business & Human Rights Resource Center, "Chiquita Lawsuits (re Colombia)," 2016 [**https://business-humanrights.org/en/chiquita-lawsuits-re-colombia**]; David J. Lynch, "Murder and Payoffs Taint Business in Colombia," *USA TODAY,* October 30, 2007, p. 1B; *Cardona v. Chiquita Brands Int'l,* 760 F.3d 1185 (11th Cir. 2014); and *In re Chiquita Brands International Inc. Alien Tort Statute and Shareholder Derivative Litigation,* 08-MD-01916-KAM, U.S. District Court, Southern District of Florida (2016).

Whistle-Blowing

LO 2-9
Discuss some of the risks and rewards of whistle-blowing.

Whistle-blower Bradley Birkenfeld was awarded a $104 million government payment in 2012 for telling the Internal Revenue Service how his employer, Swiss bank UBS, helped thousands of Americans evade taxes. Birkenfeld's inside information helped the U.S. government crack open Swiss banking secrecy. As a result, at least 33,000 Americans voluntarily disclosed their offshore accounts, resulting in perhaps $5 billion in revenue for the Internal Revenue Service.[123] UBS avoided prosecution by paying $780 million and disclosing useful information to the federal government. Birkenfeld had been sentenced in 2009 to 40 months in prison for fraud in withholding information from federal investigators, but he was released early. Birkenfeld reportedly also told a court that he had smuggled diamonds for a client in a tube of toothpaste.[124] Despite those alleged misdeeds, the government decided to make the big payment to Birkenfeld to avoid discouraging other potential whistle-blowers.[125]

> Whistle-blower Bradley Birkenfeld was awarded $104 million.

Many federal and state statutes include whistle-blower provisions, and the federal False Claims Act rewards those who help stop fraud against the government. Federal false claims recoveries in fiscal year 2015 totaled over $3.5 billion, and whistle-blowers were paid nearly $600 million for their assistance.[126] Whistle-blowers typically are entitled to 10 to 30 percent of the recovery from the wrongdoer. [For an overview of whistle-blower activity and protections, see **www.whistleblowers.org/**; for a law firm representing whistle-blowers as well as some whistle-blower stories, see **www. phillipsandcohen.com/**].

Retaliation

Americans have long deplored "squealing."

James Nordgaard, a hedge fund trader, said his former employer, Paradigm Capital, "embarked on a campaign of retaliation" against him after he blew the whistle on what he says were "trading violations." Nordgaard says he was removed from his trading desk, isolated in a room "with little ventilation," and subsequently demoted.[127]

Federal law provides varying degrees of protection, but whistle-blowers like Nordgaard often pay a high price for exercising their consciences. Americans have long deplored "squealing," and we sometimes ignore violations, partly out of fear of retribution. Among employees who observed workplace misconduct in 2012, 63 percent reported what they saw, and 92 percent of those reports went to someone inside the organization.[128]

Employers sometimes discourage whistle-blowing by requiring employees to sign confidentiality/nondisclosure agreements. Employers have a right to protect confidential information such as trade secrets, but in general, they cannot legally require employees to desist from legitimate whistle-blowing to the government. On the other hand, some critics believe the very high recoveries available to whistle-blowers may turn employees into "entrepreneurs" searching for possible wrongdoing in their companies in order to secure a financial payoff.

Questions

1. Why is the role of "squealer" or whistle-blower so repugnant to many Americans?
2. *a.* How would you feel about a classmate who blew the whistle on you for cheating on an examination?
   b. Would you report cheating by a classmate if it came to your attention? Explain.

Ethics Codes

LO 2-10
Explain the general purpose of ethics codes in the workplace.

Most big companies have voluntarily developed ethics codes. Section 406 of Sarbanes–Oxley specifically requires publicly traded companies to adopt a code of ethics for senior financial officers or to explain why they have not done so. Section 406 defines a code of ethics as written standards that are reasonably designed to deter wrongdoing and to promote such behaviors as honest conduct, full disclosure in reports, compliance with all applicable laws and rules, prompt reporting of violations, and methods for conforming to the code's expectations.

Responding to SOX and other pressures, an increasing number of companies have prepared more detailed codes, displayed them more prominently, required employees to read and sign the codes, and created training methods to more firmly integrate ethical expectations into company decision making. Companies that can show well-developed ethical systems, including codes of conduct and compliance with those codes, may receive more sympathetic treatment from the justice system if criminal problems emerge. [For the Ethics & Compliance Initiative, see **www.ethics.org/**].

Are codes effective in practice? The evidence on that question is mixed, although a 2011 study of 392 international companies found a positive relationship between the quality (topics covered, tone, commitment to corporate values, nonretaliation provisions, etc.) of codes of conduct and ethical performance. Companies that maintained high-quality codes of conduct were found to rank highly in corporate citizenship, sustainability, ethical behavior, and public perception of the firm.[129] Likewise, a 2016 study supports the effectiveness of Sarbanes–Oxley Section 406 in that public companies that developed a meaningful ethics code for their senior financial officers improved the integrity of their financial reporting.[130] [For information on global corporate governance and citizenship, see **www.conference-board.org/**].

Internet Exercise

Can ethics be taught? Many people say no. Experts at the Markkula Center for Applied Ethics at Santa Clara University explored that question. Look for their answer at **http://www.scu.edu/ethics/practicing/decision/canethicsbetaught.html**].

    a. Explain their conclusion.

    b. Do you agree? Explain.

Chapter Questions

1. *Business Ethics* magazine reported the following ethical dilemma submitted by an anonymous reader:

   > Mary had only a few days to earn $1,000 in sales that would allow her to reach the $1 million sales plateau where she would receive a $10,000 bonus allowing her to finance the dream home she had found. The sales climate was tough, but she had one remaining prospect, inner-city Lincoln School, which could make especially good use of new educational materials. Lincoln had no budget for discretionary purchases, but Mary considered "donating" $1,000 to the school in return for which they would make the purchases that would put her over the top. She knew her donation would help disadvantaged students and herself, but her conscience was troubled.[131]

   What should she do? Explain.

2. Psychologists Jean Twenge and W. Keith Campbell say that we are in the midst of a "narcissism epidemic."[132]

   a. Have you observed any evidence that supports their conclusion?

   b. Do you agree with their conclusion? Explain.

3. *a.* Would you say that female undergraduate business students are more ethically inclined than their male counterparts? Explain.

   b. Would you say that religious commitment correlates with a stronger ethical inclination among undergraduate business students? Explain.

4. *a.* In her book *Lying,*[133] Sissela Bok argued that lying by professionals is commonplace. For example, she took the position that prescribing placebos for experimental purposes is a lie and immoral. Do you agree with her position? Explain.

   b. Is the use of an unmarked police car an immoral deception? Explain.

   c. One study estimates that Americans average 200 lies per day if one includes "white lies" and inaccurate excuses. On balance, do you believe Americans approve of lying? Explain.

5. A group of 12 employees at a real estate office in south Florida chipped in $20 each toward the purchase of lottery tickets for a March 2013 Powerball drawing. One employee, Jennifer Maldanado, an administrative assistant who had been working in the office for only two weeks and had not even received her first paycheck yet, declined to join the pool. The group of 12 won $1 million, which came to over $83,000 each. Laurie Finkelstein Reader, the team leader in the office, said that winning was not going to be as much fun for the group without Maldanado, so she texted the other winners, and they all agreed to give a portion (undivulged) of their winnings to Maldanado.[134]

   a. Morally speaking, is sharing winnings more commendable than keeping all for oneself? Explain.

   b. Could this real estate office operate effectively if workers shared their earnings as well as their lottery winnings? Explain.

   c. Morally speaking, would sharing earnings be the more commendable approach to the office's pay policies? Explain.

   d. Most of the office workers who shared with Maldanado were women. Do you think women are more inclined to share than men? If so, are women more worthy of moral approval than are men? Explain.

6. According to a recent study, only 9 percent of those committing major corporate fraud during the years studied were women.[135] Of course, fewer women than men occupy the top corporate positions that offer access to lucrative fraud.

   a. What other reasons might explain why women currently are much less likely to engage in corporate fraud than men?

   b. Do you think corporate crime will decline as more women assume leadership roles? Explain.

7. *The Los Angeles Times* headlined a story: "Getting Brilliant Students to Seek Jobs beyond Wall Street."[136] The article examined the movement at some of the nation's top universities to encourage the brightest graduates to broaden their job search beyond high-paying Wall Street opportunities. An online campaign labeled "Stop the Brain Drain" gathers signatures and pushes for changes in campus recruiting practices. The prestigious Massachusetts Institute of Technology has created an entrepreneurship center to provide support for students seeking work with start-ups and other smaller ventures. Bill Aulet, who heads the center, explained some of his reasoning: "Once it became clear that financial instruments were a big cause of the [financial] crisis, and that's what our incredibly intelligent students were being used for, we thought, 'Boy, can't they be used to do more useful things?'"[137]

   a. Would we be better off as a nation if more of our brighter students shunned Wall Street jobs? Explain.

   b. What will you do? Explain.

8. A pharmacist in Lexington, Kentucky, refused to stock over-the-counter weight reducers. His reasons were (1) the active ingredient was the same as that in nasal decongestants; (2) he feared their side effects, such as high blood pressure; and (3) he felt

weight reduction should be achieved via self-discipline.[138] Assume the pharmacist manages the store for a group of owners who have given him complete authority about the products stocked. Was his decision ethical? Explain.

9. When *Business and Society Review* surveyed the presidents of 500 large U.S. companies, 51 responded with their reactions to hypothetical moral dilemmas. One question was this:

> Assume that you are president of a firm that provides a substantial portion of the market of one of your suppliers. You find out that this supplier discriminates illegally against minorities, although no legal action has been taken. Assume further that this supplier gives you the best price for the material you require, but that the field is competitive. Do you feel that it is proper to use your economic power over this supplier to make them stop discriminating?[139]

Respond to this question.

10. *a.* Do you think taking office supplies home from work for personal use is unethical? Explain.

   b. Are employers committing a serious ethics breach when they monitor their employees' e-mail? Explain.

11. Risperdal, a Johnson & Johnson antipsychotic medicine, provides significant benefits, but it also can cause strokes among the elderly, and it can generate large breasts in boys. Johnson & Johnson reportedly knew about these problems, but it manipulated and hid data about the problems and eventually pleaded guilty to a crime. Johnson & Johnson was expected to pay about $6 billion in penalties for its alleged wrongdoing, but it earned an estimated $18 billion in profits on the drug. The person in charge of marketing Risperdal was subsequently named CEO, a role in which he earned about $25 million in 2014.[140]

   a. Should Johnson & Johnson have been punished in an amount equal to its profits? Explain.

   b. Does corporate crime pay? Explain.

   c. Should managers who participate in serious wrongdoing be denied subsequent promotions? Explain.

12. In general, does the American value system favor "cheaters" who win in life's various competitions over virtuous individuals who "lose" with regularity? Explain.

13. If you were an executive about to hire a new manager, which of the following qualities would you consider most important/least important: verbal skills, honesty/integrity, enthusiasm, appearance, sense of humor? Explain.

14. Noted University of Sydney psychologist Vince Cakic has warned that students are increasingly using drugs to enhance performance on examinations and papers.[141]

   a. Is the use of drugs to enhance school performance unfair/wrong/immoral in your view? Explain.

   b. Would you advocate urine testing as a means of identifying those using brain-boosting drugs in examination situations? Explain.

15. *a.* Rank the following occupations as to your perception of their honesty and ethical standards: clergy, bankers, lawyers, medical doctors, high school teachers, police officers, car salespeople, members of congress, business executives, and accountants.

    b. In general, do you find educated professionals to be more ethical than skilled but generally less-educated laborers? Explain.

    c. Can you justify accepting an occupation that is not at or near the top of your ethical ranking? Explain how your ranking affects your career choices.

16. Can business people successfully guide their conduct by the Golden Rule?

17. Comment on the following quotes from Albert Z. Carr:

    [M]ost bluffing in business might be regarded simply as game strategy—much like bluffing in poker, which does not reflect on the morality of the bluffer.

    I quoted Henry Taylor, the British statesman who pointed out that "falsehood ceases to be falsehood when it is understood on all sides that the truth is not expected to be spoken"—an exact description of bluffing in poker, diplomacy, and business.

    * * * * *

    [T]he ethics of business are game ethics, different from the ethics of religion.

    * * * * *

    An executive's family life can easily be dislocated if he fails to make a sharp distinction between the ethical systems of the home and the office—or if his wife does not grasp that distinction.[142]

18. Is lying a routine ingredient in American sales practice? Explain.

19. Assume you are working as manager of women's clothing in a large department store. You observe the manager of equivalent rank to you in men's clothing performing poorly in that she arrives late for work, she keeps records ineptly, and she is rude to customers. Her work, however, has no direct impact on your department.

    a. Do you have any responsibility either to help her or to report her poor performance? Explain.

    b. If the store as a whole performs poorly, but you have performed well, do you bear any personal responsibility for the store's failure in that you confined your efforts exclusively to your own department even though you witnessed mismanagement in the men's clothing department? Explain.

20. We are often confronted with questions about the boundaries of our personal responsibilities.

    a. How much money, if any, must you give to satisfy your moral responsibility in the event of a famine in a foreign country? Explain.

    b. Would your responsibility be greater if the famine were in America? Explain.

Notes

1. Christina Rexrode and Emily Glazer, "Big Banks Paid $110 Billion in Mortgage-Related Fines. Where Did the Money Go?" *The Wall Street Journal,* March 9, 2016 [**www.wsj.com**].

2. Neil Irwin, "Wall Street Is Back, Almost as Big as Ever," *The New York Times,* May 18, 2015 [**www.nytimes.com**].

3. Hedrick Smith, "'The Divide: American Injustice in the Age of the Wealth Gap' by Matt Taibbi," *The Washington Post,* April 11, 2014 [**www.washingtonpost.com**].

4. "Eric Holder Admits Some Banks Are Just Too Big to Prosecute," *HuffPost Business,* March 6, 2013 [**www.huffingtonpost.com**].

5. Carl Hausman, "Most Doubt the Integrity of Wall Street," *Ethics Newsline,* March 15, 2010 [**www.globalethics.org/newsline**].

6. Labaton Sucharow LLP, "Historic Survey of Financial Services Professionals Reveals Widespread Disregard for Ethics," press release, May 19, 2015 [**www.labaton.com**].

7. Scott Patterson and Susan Pulliam, "Buffett Is Expected to Fire at Will," *The Wall Street Journal,* April 30, 2010, p. C1.

8. Editorial, "Yes, Mr. Smith, Goldman Sachs Is All about Making Money: View," *Bloomberg,* March 14, 2012 [**www.bloomberg.com**]

9. Jack and Suzy Welch, "The Welch Way," *BusinessWeek,* June 12, 2006, p. 100.

10. Justin McCarthy, "Majority in U.S. Still Say Moral Values Getting Worse," *Gallup Poll Social Issues,* June 2, 2015 [**www.gallup.com**].

11. Gerald Seib, "'Decline in Moral Values' Likely to Be Big Topic in 2016 Debate," *The Wall Street Journal,* June 30, 2015 [**www.wsj.com**].

12. David Callahan, *The Cheating Culture: Why More Americans Are Doing Wrong to Get Ahead* (New York: Harcourt, 2004).

13. Eriq Gardner, "Cheat Sheet," *Corporate Counsel,* June 2004, p. 131.

14. For a commentary on Ariely's book, see David Brooks, "The Moral Diet," *The New York Times,* June 7, 2012 [**www.nytimes.com**].

15. Paul Piff et al., "Higher Social Class Predicts Increased Unethical Behavior," *Proceedings of the National Academy of Sciences of the United States of America* 109, no. 11 (March 13, 2012), p. 4086.

16. Chris McDonald, "Social Class and Unethical Behavior," *Canadian Business,* March 1, 2012 [**www.canadianbusiness.com**].

17. Maryam Kouchaki et al., "Seeing Green: Mere Exposure to Money Triggers a Business Decision Frame and Unethical Outcomes," *Organizational Behavior and Human Decision Processes* 121 (2013), p. 53.

18. Fariss Samarrai, "Study: Smartphone Alerts Increase Inattention—And Hyperactivity," *UVA Today,* May 9, 2016 [**www.news.virginia.edu/content/study-smartphone-alerts-increase-inattention-and-hyperactivity**].

19. Rich Miller, "Give Up Sex or Your Mobile Phone? Third of Americans Forgo Sex," *Bloomberg,* January 15, 2015 [**www.bloomberg.com**].

20. Margaret Barthel, "How to Stop Cheating in College," *The Atlantic,* April 20, 2016 [**www.theatlantic.com**].

21. Donald L. McCabe, Kenneth D. Butterfield, and Linda Klebe Trevino, "Academic Dishonesty in Graduate Business Programs: Prevalence, Causes, and Proposed Action," *Academy of Management Learning & Education* 5, no. 3 (2006), p. 294.

22. Ibid.

23. Lee Berton, "Business Students Hope to Cheat and Prosper, New Study Shows," *The Wall Street Journal,* April 25, 1995, p. B1.

24. Susan C. Thomson, "Internet Helps Swell E-Cheating on Campuses," *The Washington Post,* March 14, 2004, p. A08.

25. Cathy Payne, "High School Students Cheating Less, Survey Finds," *USA TODAY,* November 25, 2012 [**www.usatoday.com**].

26. Leslie Wayne, "A Promise to Be Ethical in an Era of Immorality," *The New York Times,* May 30, 2009 [**www.nytimes.com**].

27. David Brooks, "The Big University," *The New York Times,* October 6, 2015 [**www.nytimes.com**].

28. Mary Rourke, "What Happened to America's Moral Climate?" *Los Angeles Times,* April 26, 2001, p. E1.

29. Kevin Eagen et al., "The American Freshman: National Norms Fall 2015," Cooperative Institutional Research Program, UCLA Higher Education Research Institute, 2016 [**www.heri.ucla.edu/monographs/TheAmericanFreshman2015.pdf**].

30. Beckie Supiano, "How Spiritual Traits Enhance Students' Lives—And Maybe Their Grades," *The Chronicle of Higher Education,* November 16, 2010 [**http://chronicle.com**].

31. Emily Smith and Jennifer Aaker, "Millennial Searchers," *The New York Times,* November 30, 2013 [**www.nytimes.com**].

32. Ibid.

33. "The Most-Praised Generation Goes to Work," *The Wall Street Journal,* April 20, 2007, p. W1.

34. Jonah Goldberg, "Our Centers of the Universe," *latimes.com,* August 7, 2007 [**www.latimes.com/news/opinion/la-oe-goldberg7aug07,0,692285.column?coll=la-tot-opinion&track=ntottext**].

35. David Brooks, "The Streamlined Life," *The New York Times,* May 5, 2014 [**www.nytimes.com**].

36. For more about existentialism, see Andrew West, "Sartrean Existentialism and Ethical Decision-Making in Business," *Journal of Business Ethics* 81 (2008), p. 15.

37. Carl Hausman, "Responsibility," *Ethics Newsline,* September 28, 2009 [**www.globalethics.org/newsline/2009/09/28/responsibility**].

38. Mark Oppenheimer, "The Rise of the Corporate Chaplain," *BusinessWeek,* August 23, 2012 [**www.businessweek.com**].

39. Cara Buckley, "Man Is Rescued by Stranger on Subway Tracks," *The New York Times,* January 3, 2007.

40. Associated Press, "British Priest: Shoplifting Is Sometimes OK," *The Waterloo/Cedar Falls Courier,* December 23, 2009, p. 3A.

41. Mary Donohue, "Fighting Back Against the Tyranny of the Manager," *HuffPost Business Canada,* January 23, 2014 [**www.huffingtonpost.ca**].

42. Olga Khazan, "It Pays to Be Nice," *The Atlantic,* June 23, 2015 [**www.theatlantic.com**].

43. Dylan Love, "16 Examples of Steve Jobs Being a Huge Jerk," *Business Insider,* October 25, 2011 [**www.businessinsider.com**].

44. Jerry Useem, "Why It Pays to Be a Jerk," *The Atlantic,* June 2015 [**www.theatlantic.com**].

45. Ibid.

46. Ibid.

47. Khazan, "It Pays to Be Nice."

48. Tessa Berenson, "The Science Behind Why Nice People Finish Last—And How to Fix That," *Time,* September 26, 2015 [**http://time.com**].

49. Jerry Useem, "Why It Pays to Be a Jerk," *The Atlantic,* June 2015 [**www.theatlantic.com**].

50. Ibid.

51. Richard Lorant, Associated Press, "A Mill Owner's Compassion Rescues Thousands of Jobs after Devastating Fire," *Chicago Tribune,* December 10, 1996, p. 8.

52. Richard Lorant, "Rebuilding Corporate Compassion—Oath to Millworkers May Pay Off," *Seattle Times,* December 11, 1996 [**http://community.seattletimes.nwsource.com**].

53. Timothy Schelhardt, "Are Layoffs Moral? One Firm's Answer: You Ask, We'll Sue," *The Wall Street Journal,* August 1, 1996, p. A1.

54. Ibid.

55. John P. MacKenzie, "Lending a Hand If a Company Asks," *The New York Times,* February 3, 2002, Sec. 3, p. 11.

56. Gallup, "Confidence in Institutions," *Gallup Historical Trends,* June 1–5, 2016 [**www.gallup.com**].

57. Gallup, "Honesty/Ethics in Professions," *Gallup Historical Trends,* December 2–6, 2015 [**www.gallup.com**].

58. Geoff Colvin, "Business Leaders, the Public Wants to Trust You. Now's Your Chance," *Fortune,* January 20, 2016 [**http://fortune.com**].

59. Maureen Kline, "Why Business Leaders Need to Earn Trust, and How to Go about Doing It," *Inc.com,* February 18, 2016 [**www.inc.com**].

60. Ibid.

61. Colvin, "Business Leaders, the Public Wants to Trust You."

62. Samuel Rubenfeld, "Employees' Ethical Behavior Is Best in 20 Years," *The Wall Street Journal,* February 4, 2014 [**http://blogs.wsj.com**].

63. Ibid.

64. Chris MacDonald, "The Golden Age of Ethical Business," *The Business Ethics Blog,* March 15, 2010 [**https://businessethicsblog.com**].

65. Ann Tenbrunsel and Jordan Thomas, "The Street, the Bull and the Crisis: A Survey of the U.S. & U.K. Financial Services Industry," Labaton Sucharow, May 2015 [**www.secwhistlebloweradvocate.com/LiteratureRetrieve.aspx?ID=224757**].

66. "Confidence in Institutions," *Gallup Historical Trends,* June 7–10, 2012 [**www.gallup.com/poll/1597/confidence-institutions.aspx**].

67. For an elaboration of Kohlberg's stages, see, for example, W. D. Boyce and L. C. Jensen, *Moral Reasoning* (Lincoln, NE: University of Nebraska Press, 1978), pp. 98–109.

68. Lawrence Kohlberg, "The Cognitive–Development Approach to Moral Education," *Phi Delta Kappan* 56 (June 1975), p. 670.

69. Carol Gilligan, "In a Different Voice: Women's Conceptions of Self and Morality," *Harvard Educational Review* 47, no. 4 (November 1977), p. 481.

70. For an overview of the justice versus care debate, see Grace Clement, *Care, Autonomy, and Justice* (Boulder, CO: Westview Press, 1996).

71. James Weber and David Wasieleski, "Investigating Influences on Managers' Moral Reasoning," *Business & Society* 40, no. 1 (March 2001), pp. 79, 83.

72. Diana Robertson et al., "The Neural Processing of Moral Sensitivity to Issues of Justice and Care," *Neuropsychologia* 45 (2007), pp. 755, 763.

73. For a description of the moral intuition argument, see Jonathan Haidt, "The Emotional Dog and Its Rational Tail: A Social Intuitionist Approach to Moral Judgment," *Psychological Review* 108, no. 4 (2001), p. 814.

74. See Joshua Greene and Jonathan Haidt, "How (and Where) Does Moral Judgment Work?" *Trends in Cognitive Science* 6 (2002), p. 517.

75. Marc Hauser, *Moral Minds* (New York: HarperCollins Publishers, 2006).

76. Ana Swanson, "The Disturbing Thing Scientists Learned When They Bribed Babies with Graham Crackers," *The Washington Post*, April 25, 2016 [**www.washingtonpost.com**].

77. Nicholas Wade, "Is 'Do Unto Others' Written into Our Genes?" *The New York Times*, September 18, 2007 [**www.nytimes.com/2007/09/18/science/18mora.html?**].

78. See, e.g., David Pizarro and Paul Bloom, "The Intelligence of the Moral Intuitions Comment on Haidt," *Psychological Review* 110, no. 1 (2003), p. 193.

79. David Brooks, "The End of Philosophy," *The New York Times*, April 7, 2009 [**www.nytimes.com**].

80. Benedict Carey, "Study Finds Brain Injury Changes Moral Judgment," *The New York Times*, March 21, 2007 [**www.nytimes.com**].

81. Sam A. Hardy, "Identity, Reasoning, and Emotion: An Empirical Comparison of Three Sources of Moral Motivation," *Motivation and Emotion* 30 (2006), p. 207.

82. Ibid.

83. Ruodan Shao, Karl Aquino, and Dan Freeman, "Beyond Moral Reasoning: A Review of Moral Identity Research and Its Implications for Business Ethics," *Business Ethics Quarterly* 18, no. 4 (2008), p. 513.

84. Ethisphere, "Ethisphere Announces the 2016 World's Most Ethical Companies," press release, March 7, 2016 [**https://ethisphere.com**].

85. 3M, "3M Named as a 2016 World's Most Ethical Company," press release, March 7, 2016 [**http://news.3m.com**].

86. Ethics and Compliance Initiative, "National Business Ethics Survey (NBES) 2013," press release, 2013 [**www.ethics.org/research/eci-research/nbes/nbes-reports/nbes-2013**].

87. Joseph L. Badaracco Jr. and Allen P. Webb, "Business Ethics: A View from the Trenches," *California Management Review* 37, no. 2 (Winter 1995), pp. 8, 12.

88. Richard Edelman, "Denial in the Corner Office," *The Conference Board CEO Challenge 2013*, May 9, 2013 [**www.edelman.com/p/6-a-m/denial-in-the-corner-office**].

89. Jo Iwasaki, "Tone at the Top," *Ethical Boardroom*, May 26, 2016 [**http://ethicalboardroom.com**].

90. Bill Hawkins, as told to Cait Murphy, "Bill Hawkins: How I Made the Toughest Call of My Career," *CBS MoneyWatch*, October 5, 2009 [**www.cbsnews.com**].

91. Kirk O. Hanson, "The Six Ethical Dilemmas Every Professional Faces," lecture, Bentley University Verizon Visiting Professorship in Business Ethics, February 3, 2014.

92. Andrew Dugan and Stephanie Kafka, "In U.S., Business Grads Lag Other Majors in Work Interest," *Gallup Poll*, October 2, 2014 [**www.gallup.com**].

93. Executive Summary, "The Children We Mean to Raise: The Real Messages Adults Are Sending about Values," Making Caring Common Project, Harvard Graduate School of Education [**http://mcc.gse.harvard.edu/files/gse-mcc/files/mcc-executive-summary.pdf**].

94. Tyler Kepner, "Pitcher Spurns $12 Million, to Keep Self-Respect," *The New York Times*, January 26, 2011.

95. Lauren Weber, "Expense-Account Tightwads Take the Road Less Expensive," *The Wall Street Journal*, March 30, 2012, p. A1.

96. Tanyu Basu, "Timeline: A History of GM's Ignition Switch Defect," *National Public Radio,* March 31, 2014 [**www.npr.org**].

97. Danielle Ivory and Bill Vlasic, "$900 Million Penalty for G.M.'s Deadly Defect Leaves Many Cold," *The New York Times,* September 17, 2015 [**www.nytimes.com**].

98. Vikas Bajaj, "The Lesson of the General Motors Settlement," *The New York Times,* September 17, 2015 [**www.nytimes.com**].

99. Kevin McCoy, "Peanut Exec in Salmonella Case Gets 28 Years," *USA TODAY,* September 22, 2015 [**www.usatoday.com**].

100. PricewaterhouseCoopers, "Global Economic Crime Survey 2016," [**www.pwc.com**].

101. Ibid.

102. Source: Greg Wilcox, "It's All Relative," *The Des Moines Register,* December 12, 2005, p. 6A.

103. Matthew Heller, "SOX Compliance Getting More Costly," *CFO.com,* May 20, 2015 [**ww2.cfo.com**].

104. "SOX Compliance—Changes Abound Amid Drive for Stability and Long-Term Value," Highlights from Protiviti's 2015 Sarbanes–Oxley Compliance Survey [**www.protiviti.com/en-US/ Documents/Surveys/2015-SOX-Compliance-Survey-Protiviti.pdf**].

105. John C. Coates IV and Suraj Srinivasan, "SOX after Ten Years: A Multidisciplinary Review," *Harvard Law and Economics Discussion Paper No. 758,* January 12, 2014. Available at SSRN: **http://ssrn.com/abstract=2343108**.

106. Lora Bentley, "SEC Study: Benefits of Sarbanes–Oxley Compliance Outweigh Cost," *ITBusinessEdge,* October 16, 2009 [**www.itbusinessedge.com**].

107. Michael Rapoport, "Law's Big Weapon Sits Idle," *The Wall Street Journal,* July 29, 2012 [**http://online.wsj.com**].

108. Richard Cassin, "Avon Pays $135 Million for China FCPA Resolution," *The FCPA Blog,* December 17, 2014 [**www.fcpablog.com**].

109. Ibid.

110. Chad Bray, "Perfume, Dresses and Cash in Ralph Lauren Bribe Scheme," *The Wall Street Journal,* April 22, 2013 [**http://online.wsj.com**].

111. Kara Scannell, "U.S. Redoubles Efforts on Foreign Bribery Cases," *Financial Times,* February 10, 2016 [**www.ft.com**].

112. Jones Day, "FCPA 2015 Year in Review," January 2016 [**www.jonesday.com/fcpa-2015-year-in-review**].

113. "The Anti-Bribery Business," *The Economist,* May 9, 2015 [**www.economist.com**].

114. Aruna Viswanatha and Devlin Barrett, "Wal-Mart Bribery Probe Finds Few Signs of Major Misconduct in Mexico," *The Wall Street Journal,* October 19, 2015 [**www.wsj.com**].

115. David Barstow and Alejandra Xanic von Bertrab, "How Wal-Mart Used Payoffs to Get Its Way in Mexico," *The New York Times,* December 17, 2012 [**www.nytimes.com**].

116. Transparency International, "Corruption Perceptions Index 2015," [**www.transparency.org/ cpi2015**].

117. Michael E. Miller and Fred Barbash, "U.S. Indicts World Soccer Officials in Alleged $150 Million FIFA Bribery Scandal," *The Washington Post,* May 27, 2015 [**www.washingtonpost.com**].

118. "The FIFA-Related Action Is Not an FCPA Enforcement Action—But Could Potentially Lead to Exposure for Certain Companies," *FCPA Professor,* June 1, 2015 [**http://fcpaprofessor. com/the-fifa-related-action-is-not-an-fcpa-enforcement-action-but-could-potentially-lead-to-exposure-for-certain-companies**].

119. Sara Germano and Patricia Kowsmann, "Nike's Bold Push into Soccer Entangled It in FIFA Probe," *The Wall Street Journal,* June 4, 2015 [**www.wsjcom**].

120. Michael Mainville, "Bribery Thrives as Big Business in Putin's Russia," *SFGate.com,* January 2, 2007 [**www.sfgate.com/cgi-bin/article.cgi?file=/c/a/2007/01/02/MNG8QNBCTN1.DTL**].

121. Nataliya Vasilyeva, "Cost of Corruption in Russia: Where Police Are Openly Taking $1,000 Bribes That Are Raising Grocery Bills," *National Post,* April 1, 2016 [**http://news.nationalpost.com**].

122. Ibid.

123. Tom Schoenberg and David Voreacos, "UBS Whistle-Blower Secures $104 Million Award from IRS," *Bloomberg,* September 11, 2012 [**www.bloomberg.com**].

124. David Kocieniewski, "Whistle-Blower Awarded $104 Million by I.R.S.," *The New York Times,* September 11, 2012 [**www.nytimes.com**].

125. Ibid.

126. Department of Justice, "Justice Department Recovers over $3.5 Billion from False Claims Act Cases in Fiscal Year 2015," *Justice News,* December 3, 2015 [**www.justice.gov**].

127. Ben Protess and Nathaniel Popper, "Hazy Future for Thriving S.E.C. Whistle Blower Effort," *The New York Times,* April 23, 2013 [**http://dealbook.nytimes.com**].

128. Dori Meinert, "Minimizing the Risk of Whistle Blower Lawsuits," *HR Magazine,* May 21, 2014 [**www.shrm.org/hr-today/news/hr-magazine/pages/0614-whistle-blower-protections.aspx**].

129. Patrick Erwin, "Corporate Codes of Conduct: The Effects of Code Content and Quality on Ethical Performance," *Journal of Business Ethics* 99 (2011), pp. 535–548.

130. Saurabh Ahluwalia, O. C. Ferrell, and Terri L. Rittenburg, "Sarbanes–Oxley Section 406 Code of Ethics for Senior Financial Officers and Firm Behavior," *Journal of Business Ethics* (July 2016), doi:10.1007/s10551-016-3267-7.

131. Shel Horowitz, "Should Mary Buy Her Own Bonus?" *Business Ethics.* Submitted by Anonymous, August 1, 2007 [**www.business-ethics.com/node/65**].

132. Bill Davidow, "The Internet 'Narcissism Epidemic,'" *The Atlantic,* March 2013 [**www.theatlantic.com**].

133. Sissela Bok, *Lying: Moral Choice in Public and Private Life* (New York: Vintage Books, 1999).

134. Maria Camila Bernal, "Lucky Lady: She Opted Out of Powerball Pool, but Gets a Cut of $1 Million Anyway," *The Miami Herald,* March 26, 2013 [**www.miamiherald.com**].

135. Darrell J. Steffensmeier, Jennifer Schwartz, and Michael Roche, "Gender and Twenty-First-Century Corporate Crime: Female Involvement and the Gender Gap in Enron-Era Corporate Frauds," *American Sociological Review* 78 (June 2013), p. 448.

136. Nathaniel Popper, "Getting Brilliant Students to Seek Jobs beyond Wall Street," *latimes.com,* November 4, 2011 [**www.latimes.com**].

137. Ibid.

138. Reported on WKYT TV, Channel 27, Evening News, Lexington, Kentucky, May 12, 1980.

139. "Business Executives and Moral Dilemmas," *Business and Society Review,* no. 13 (Spring 1975), p. 51.

140. Nicholas Kristof, "When Crime Pays: J&J's Drug Risperdal," *The New York Times,* September 17, 2015 [**www.nytimes.com**].

141. "Students Turn to 'Smart' Drugs to Boost Grades," *The Guardian,* October 1, 2009 [**www.theguardian.com**].

142. Albert Z. Carr, "Is Business Bluffing Ethical?" *Harvard Business Review* 46, no. 1 (January–February 1968), pp. 143–52.

Video icon credit: ©Comstock Images/Alamy

CHAPTER THREE

The Corporation and Public Policy: Expanding Responsibilities

After completing this chapter, students will be able to fulfill the following learning objectives:

3-1. Recognize the interdependent relationship between business and the larger society.

3-2. Discuss whether business should play a more or less active role in politics, education, and other public-sector activities.

3-3. List some of the critics' primary complaints about the alleged abuse of corporate power in contemporary America.

3-4. Discuss concerns about globalization.

3-5. Make a tentative assessment regarding the proper role of business in society.

3-6. Explain the concept of corporate social responsibility.

3-7. Explain the triple bottom line/sustainability approach to corporate citizenship.

3-8. Discuss whether socially responsible business is "good business."

3-9. Contrast the stakeholder and shareholder approaches to corporate social responsibility.

PRACTICING ETHICS   Yvon Chouinard and Patagonia

Outdoor adventurer Yvon Chouinard and his wife, Ellen Pennoyer, in 1972, founded Patagonia, Inc., the sports clothing and outdoor gear retailer. Privately owned, Ventura, California–based Patagonia, with annual revenues exceeding $600 million, is the product of entrepreneurial drive and a corporate culture practicing "green" business and "management by absence."

Chouinard's 2005 memoir, *Let My People Go Surfing,* explains his commitment to a workplace where capitalism, ethics, and fun can coexist. Patagonia minimizes workplace monitoring, surf breaks are encouraged, health care is 100 percent paid for, and everyone takes vacations. Two-month paid leaves are offered to both parents, and Patagonia encourages a "traveling baby program," where babies accompany parents on business trips and the company pays for an accompanying child development teacher. Patagonia is often recognized as one of the best companies to work for in America.

Chouinard was an early advocate of doing business in an environmentally friendly way, including, for example, placing notes in Patagonia catalogs encouraging customers to buy only what they need. Since 1985, Patagonia has donated 1 percent of its annual sales to environmental groups. Chouinard's 2012 book, *The Responsible Company,* details methods for making money while avoiding undue societal damage.

Chouinard threatened to leave Patagonia in 1994 when he learned that the cotton bought by the company often was produced by industrial farming that used toxic chemicals and was having, he felt, a devastating effect on the Earth. That cotton figured in 20 percent of the company's sales, but Patagonia changed over to organic cotton and persuaded others such as Nike and Timberland to begin to do the same. Chouinard said

that Patagonia went a year without making a profit while the company found organic suppliers, overcame bankers' resistance, and contracted with new gins and mills. The bigger point is that the switch was profitable and the right thing to do, an approach often missed by corporate America, he said.

Patagonia clothing is made in China, Thailand, Vietnam, and a number of other countries, along with limited production in the United States. When establishing ties with a new manufacturing partner, Patagonia's Social and Environmental Responsibility team engages in constant audits, visits, and corrective measures to assure a safe, healthy, environmentally sound operation. Patagonia refuses to contract with companies employing workers under the age of 15. All workers must be paid "a legal minimum wage," but Patagonia admits to falling short of its goal of a "living wage" for all those who make its products.

Questions

1. Is Chouinard correct that companies can treat workers well, respect the environment, and still make money? Explain.

2. If he is correct, why aren't all companies following the Patagonia model?

Sources: "Employees Who March to Their Own Music," *BusinessWeek,* December 19, 2005, p. 81; Keith Garber, "Yvon Chouinard: Patagonia Founder Fights for the Environment," *U.S. News & World Report,* October 22, 2009 [**www.usnews.com/news/best-leaders/articles/2009/10/22**]; Hugo Martin, "Outdoor Retailer Patagonia Puts Environment Ahead of Sales Growth," *latimes.com,* May 24, 2012 [**www.latimes.com**]; Brigid Schulte, "A Company That Profits as It Pampers Workers," *The Washington Post,* October 25, 2014 [**www.washingtonpost.com**]; and Brad Wieners, "The Gospel of Yvon," *Men's Journal,* July 2007, p. 51.

Introduction

The Yvon Chouinard/Patagonia story expresses the central mission of this chapter: the examination of the corporation's societal duties, if any, beyond providing the best products and services at the lowest prices. Should the corporate community emulate the Patagonia model by addressing public policy challenges such as environmental decline, employee welfare, product safety, public health, poverty, discrimination, and more? Commentator

Frank Bruni recently argued that corporations, often for reasons of self-interest, are now playing crucial leadership roles in addressing these issues:

> [T]hose efforts, coupled with whatever genuine altruism and civic obligation some corporate leaders feel, have produced compelling recent examples of companies showing greater sensitivity to diversity, social justice and the changing tides of public sentiment than lawmakers often manage to.[1]

Historically, we have counted on government to identify and resolve public policy concerns, but as Bruni explains, businesses increasingly recognize a self-interest (and perhaps a duty) to employ their resources in helping to solve those concerns. In doing so, those businesses may be setting aside short-term profit maximization goals to practice what is often labeled *corporate social responsibility*. That is, they are voluntarily contributing to the general welfare in ways not necessarily required by the market and government.

In this chapter, we explore the business and society relationship in four parts: (1) criticism of corporate America, (2) the emergence of the expectation of corporate social responsibility, (3) the management of social responsibility, and (4) the examination of some specific business and society issues.

Part One—Corporate Power and Corporate Critics

LO 3-1
Recognize the interdependent relationship between business and the larger society.

Critics have long argued that the public interest has not been well served by America's big corporations. We recognize that colossal size and the accompanying economies of scale have been critical to American competitiveness in today's tough global market. At the same time, that very size, the critics say, permits continuing abuse of the American public. (This chapter's examination of corporate America is limited to the critics' objections to corporate conduct. The legal standards governing corporate practice are addressed primarily in Chapter 9.)

By sales revenue, Walmart is the largest company in America (see Table 3.1) and the first service company to hold the top spot. Walmart is, by a wide margin, America's number-one employer with some 2.2 million workers globally, 1.4 million of whom work in the United States.[2]

By some measures of economic might, American corporations tower over most countries of the world. If we compare corporate revenue with gross domestic product (a common approach, but one that somewhat overstates the size of corporations relative to

TABLE 3.1   **America's Largest Corporations**

Corporation	Location	Sales Revenue (in billions)
Walmart Stores	Bentonville, AR	$482.1
ExxonMobil	Irving, TX	246.2
Apple	Cupertino, CA	233.7
Berkshire Hathaway	Omaha, NE	210.8
McKesson	San Francisco, CA	181.2

Source: *Fortune* 500 2016 Annual Ranking of America's Largest Corporations.

countries), Walmart is the 22nd largest economic entity in the world and 44 of the 100 largest economic entities are corporations.[3]

ExxonMobil, number two on the *Fortune* 500 list, is often cited by critics as an example of threatening and sometimes abusive corporate power. In 2012, respected investigative journalist Steve Coll released his book *Private Empire: ExxonMobil and American Power*[4] detailing a company that operates much like a nation, as described by reviewer Adam Hochschild:

> [T]his book isn't so much a story of ExxonMobil's influence over the American government. Rather, it's a picture of a corporation so large and powerful—operating in some 200 nations and territories—that it really has its own foreign policy.[5]

* * *

> . . . ExxonMobil has its own armies. . . . In Chad, its 2,500 security men patrolled the countryside in white radio-equipped S.U.V.'s, watching for guerrillas as the company set up an intelligence operation bigger and better than the local C.I.A. station. In the war-[w]racked Niger Delta, it gave boats to the Nigerian Navy, deployed its own vessels at sea to scout for pirates and "recruited, paid, supplied and managed sections of the Nigerian military and police."[6]

Another reviewer reminds us, however, that Coll's book portrays ExxonMobil as possessing "an honorable if rigid culture that seeks to supply a product . . . that a functioning society actually must have."[7]

Predictably, we have a conflicted view of big corporations. We are grateful for corporate jobs, products, and services, but according to a 2016 Gallup Poll, 63 percent of Americans say too much power is concentrated in a few large companies.[8]

The Corporate State—Economics

LO 3-2
Discuss whether business should play a more or less active role in politics, education, and other public-sector activities.

LO 3-3
List some of the critics' primary complaints about the alleged abuse of corporate power in contemporary America.

Perhaps the most pressing and immediate fear about corporate power is that it threatens America's economy rather than strengthening it. Mounting evidence shows an ongoing shift in the distribution of national income from workers to owners, and economists are increasingly concerned that concentrated power is reducing America's legendary and crucial power to innovate and thereby improve life for all.[9]

One of the critics' concerns about expanding corporate power is the fear that working life may change for the worse. Consulting firm PricewaterhouseCoopers (PwC) recently published its outlook on work in 2022 based on interviews with 500 human resource experts and 10,000 others here and abroad.[10] PwC outlined three "plausible" projections for the 2022 work world. To the critics, the most worrisome of the three involves big-company capitalism, characterized by its extraordinary achievements in efficiency and productivity, but also manifesting some disturbing tendencies, as described by *Yahoo Finance:*

> You probably won't be surprised to hear that big companies could end up so powerful and influential they morph into "mini-states" that fill the void when government is unable to provide essential services. Companies will also use sensors and other gizmos to monitor employees around the clock. And workers will mostly acquiesce to this digital leash, in exchange for job security, decent pay and important benefits.[11]

Another of PwC's other plausible possibilities is an emerging world of "small is beautiful" organizations where big business will be "outflanked" by many small entrepreneurial organizations characterized by advanced, disruptive technology; global networks; and lean, external workforces. A third possibility is a "green" world in which organizations, driven by a strong sense of ethics and duty, drive their organizations according to social responsibility and sustainability goals. Patagonia, as we have seen, is exemplary of green firms. Perhaps most companies will manifest elements of each of the three PwC projections. Which do you expect? Which do you prefer?

Taxes

Commentator Nicholas Kristof argues that the real welfare cheats in America are not poorer citizens, but prosperous corporations that benefit from a "rigged" tax code.[12] Kristof cites a 2016 Oxfam study finding that for each dollar they paid in federal taxes between 2008 and 2014, America's 50 largest companies got $27 in federal loans, loan guarantees, and bailouts.[13] Furthermore, nearly one-fifth of America's profitable, larger companies paid no federal income tax in 2012 (the most recent year for which data are available).[14] Of course, big companies legitimately avoid taxation in some years, but critics say a great deal of tax avoidance, while usually lawful, is unfair. They point particularly to the use of tax havens abroad. One recent study estimates that 20 percent of all American corporate profits are shifted offshore.[15] One highly publicized but relatively infrequent means of escaping U.S. taxes (corporate rate: 35 percent) is what is called an *inversion,* where U.S. companies merge with a firm in a nation like Ireland (corporate rate: 12.5 percent), thereby creating a new corporate parent abroad while keeping the actual working headquarters and most of the business in the United States.[16] Responding to these lawful but highly criticized maneuvers, the U.S. Treasury Department announced new rules in 2016 that will limit but not end inversions.

Many experts argue that we should lower or do away with corporate taxes. America's combined federal and state corporate tax rates are now considered the highest in the world at about 39.2 percent.[17] "Loopholes," however, allow American corporations to pay an actual rate of about 29.2 percent, which is somewhat below average globally, according to a U.S. Treasury Department analysis.[18] Regardless of rates and loopholes, we should remember that many large corporations do pay very significant amounts of taxes. ExxonMobil averaged about $25.2 billion in annual federal income taxes in recent years, ranking it first among American companies in payments.[19]

[See 2016 presidential candidate Senator Bernie Sanders' brief speech criticizing corporate tax loopholes at **http://www.youtube.com/watch?v=Sknt-UBRhxo**].

Question

Corporate managers have a duty to maximize shareholder value. Do managers, therefore, have a duty to employ inversions and all other lawful methods to minimize corporate taxes, or do corporations have a social responsibility to balance shareholder interest in tax reduction with societal interest in tax revenues to address social problems? Explain.

Monopoly and Other Misconduct

To the critics, not merely the tax code but the American economy in total is "rigged," allowing a few big companies to dominate most industries such that meaningful competition cannot enter. Four airlines, for example, control about 80 percent of U.S. flights. The result, the critics claim, is higher prices and poorer service/products. Today's high profits relative to historical norms suggest reduced competition. Airline ticket prices, for example, did not fall meaningfully when fuel prices plummeted.

Many economists, such as Nobel Prize winner Paul Krugman and former Harvard University president Lawrence Summers, are now publicly worrying over dangerous levels of monopoly power in the American economy. Krugman recently argued in *The New York Times* that the federal government, particularly during the Reagan and Bush administrations, largely abandoned its historical role of reining in companies that had become too dominant.[20] The Obama White House signaled its concern by issuing an executive order in 2016 directing all federal agencies to promote competition. From a free-market perspective, of course, those dominant firms have earned their success by serving the market better than have their competitors. (For much more detail about monopoly problems and antitrust law, see Chapters 10 and 11.)

Beyond monopoly problems, complaints about the corporate role in pollution, discrimination, white-collar crime, abuse of workers, and so on remain commonplace. To the corporate critics, many of America's most troublesome and persistent problems are, at least in part, products of corporate misconduct. On the other hand, in a democratic, free-market society such as America's, we all must share some of the blame for our problems. If we are not happy with, for example, Walmart's treatment of its employees, we are free to shop elsewhere. Arguably, then, the role of business in American life merely reflects the values of the American people.

Globalization

LO 3-4
Discuss concerns about globalization.

The Rana Plaza eight-story garment factory collapsed outside Dhaka, Bangladesh, on April 24, 2013. More than 1,100 workers were killed, but perhaps a new global awareness of sweatshop working conditions and careless, if not abusive, international supply chains emerged. A Bangladeshi government report concluded that the building had been constructed with substandard materials and a disregard for building codes. Upper floors were illegally added to the building and large power generators installed on those floors shook the building when they were switched on. On the day of the collapse, factory owners apparently ordered workers to enter the building despite cracks in the walls and other evidence of safety hazards. The collapse was one in a long line of accidents and fires in the Bangladeshi garment industry that provides desperately needed jobs but is caught in a *race to the bottom* to provide the globe's cheapest labor.

> A *race to the bottom* to provide the globe's cheapest labor.

Our tightly interconnected, highly efficient global supply systems have brought millions of jobs, substantial capital, and vital first steps on a path toward prosperity for currently struggling nations such as Bangladesh. But globalization of the garment industry and many others has also brought new challenges, particularly for the wealthy, powerful Western manufacturers who profit spectacularly from cheap labor in less developed nations. Major brands such as Gap, H&M, and Walmart are among the many that are supplied by garment factories in Bangladesh.

Who is responsible, and what should be done? Two apparel groups (a largely European collective including H&M and an American group headed by Walmart and The Gap) and the Bangladesh government have made some progress toward justice. The apparel groups have hired engineers who have inspected many buildings and ordered changes. A small number of nonconforming factories have been excluded from further work for the retailers. The owner of the collapsed building and 40 others, including government inspectors, have been charged with murder. Victims and their families have received compensation of about $65 per month for two years.

Yet the four million Bangladeshi garment workers (mostly women) often continue to work in hazardous conditions. H&M, an aggressive leader in worker safety, found in 2016 that more than half of its top Bangladeshi suppliers have yet to install basic fire protection and 13 percent still have locks on doors that might serve as fire escape routes.[21]

Question

Canada's Loblaw Companies Limited, owner of the Joe Fresh brand, was among the companies whose clothing was produced at the collapsed factory. (Loblaw quickly announced that it would pay compensation to the families of victims.) Ethics expert Chris MacDonald responded to the tragedy by saying, "I'm still shopping at Joe Fresh . . . and with a clear conscience."[22]

Can we all continue to shop for cheap clothing while maintaining a clear conscience? Explain.

Globalization Fears   The garment factory tragedy illustrates the critics' worry that global free trade is merely an opportunity for America's giant corporations to exploit cheap, power-less labor abroad. Further, the *outsourcing* of good, high-paid factory jobs from the United States to less developed nations has wounded the American working class. All have bene-fited from cheaper goods, but real wages for blue-collar workers are almost unchanged over the past 35 years, even as productivity has increased by more than 200 percent.[23]

In general, we can see that critics' concerns about corporate domination of American life also apply to the entire globe. With the triumph of capitalism, the world has come to under-stand that free markets usually are more efficient decision makers than government rules. As a result, national boundaries are receding in importance, technology is shrinking the globe, and multinational companies are treating the world as one big marketing opportunity. Clearly, the universal advance of American corporate interests has produced problems, but enormous gains in global standards of living, literacy, and poverty reduction also have been achieved.

The interesting question for our purposes is whether globalization brings with it new responsibilities for American corporations such as those raised in the wake of the garment factory deaths in Bangladesh. As McDonald's, Apple, and American popular culture cap-ture the attention of the global populace, does that increasing "Americanization" or "West-ernization" bring new corporate duties? For example, does the corporate community bear any responsibility for the ongoing conflict between Western and Muslim values? Histori-cally, governments are expected to address questions of that nature, but as globalization has magnified corporate power, we must wonder whether corporations won't be expected to fulfill expanded and, doubtless, uncomfortable new roles.

Corporations as Psychopaths?

The 2004 movie documentary *The Corporation* argues that the corporation has become the dominant institution in American life, exceeding the influence of both religion and government. One result is that corporations often demonstrate the "traits of the prototypical psychopath." The contemporary corporation is depicted as an "exploitative monster" driven not by the greater good but by its first responsibility to stockholders.

Questions

1. In your view, are corporations more powerful than government, religion, our educational system, and all other American institutions? Explain.
2. According to some polls, nearly three-quarters of Americans think corporations have too much power. Do you agree that corporations are too powerful? Explain.

Source: Jim Keough, "Film Sees Evil in Corporations," *Worchester Telegram & Gazette,* September 29, 2004, p. C5.

[For *The Corporation* homepage, see **www.thecorporation.com**. To view the movie, visit **www.youtube.com/watch?v=xHrhqtY2khc**].

The Corporate State—Politics

We turn now to politics, where, critics argue, big money enables the business community to disproportionately influence the electoral and law-making processes.

Corporate Contributions

PACs   Corporate funds cannot lawfully be given directly to candidates for federal office. However, corporations (as well as labor unions, special interest groups, and others) can lawfully establish political action committees (PACs) to solicit contributions from employees, shareholders, and others. That money is then put in a fund, carefully segregated from general corporate accounts, and disbursed by the PAC in support of a political agenda preferred by the organization. Although PAC contributions are voluntary, corporate employees often feel pressured to participate. Unlike the federal rules, about one-half of the states allow corporations to lawfully donate corporate funds to parties and candidates for state elections.

The **Citizens United** *Case*   The role of conventional PACs in the political process has receded in importance following a momentous U.S. Supreme Court decision in the 2010 *Citizens United* case[24] The Supreme Court's highly controversial 5–4 ruling held that federal laws limiting corporate campaign contributions violated corporate free speech rights. Essentially, the decision allows corporations, labor unions, and some other aggregations to spend unlimited organizational funds for candidates and causes so long as they do not coordinate that spending with parties and/or candidates.

> The Supreme Court's highly controversial 5–4 ruling.

The five "conservative" justices in the *Citizens United* majority, treating dollars as speech, saw political spending limits as a direct denial of liberty guaranteed by the First

Amendment. Corporations and labor unions were viewed by the Court as associations of individuals that should possess the same constitutional rights as the individuals themselves. Previous high court rulings had frequently recognized that First Amendment rights extend to corporations and that corporations are persons for some legal purposes. The four dissenters, from the "liberal" wing of the Court, argued that corporations and unions, in many other ways, are not treated as people and doing so in the case of political contributions could allow those organizations to dominate and further corrupt the political process.

In practice, *Citizens United* and other court decisions opened the door to gushers of personal and corporate money funneled through Independent Expenditure PACs (usually called Super PACs) and nonprofit 501(c)(4) social welfare organizations. Prior to the November 2016 elections, Super PACs had collected nearly $1.6 billion in the election cycle, some from corporations but much of it from a relative handful of individual/family megadonors.[25] Critics now argue that America is more accurately labeled a corporate and family *oligarchy* rather than a democracy. Do you agree?

Big Money Dominance?   Are big-money contributors able to "buy" elections? Has the broadly condemned *Citizens United* decision led to corporate domination of the electoral process? A highly preliminary answer to those questions, based upon early results from the 2016 presidential primary and the 2012 general election, is "no." In the 2016 presidential primaries, the candidates favored by the big PACs frequently fell to the wayside while more successful candidates, Hillary Clinton, Ted Cruz, and especially Bernie Sanders, relied considerably on smaller donors. In 2012, the U.S. Chamber of Commerce spent nearly $24 million backing conservative candidates in the U.S. Senate races, but only two of the Chamber favorites prevailed.[26]

So big money may not consistently buy elections, but it does appear to be reshaping the electoral landscape, as commentator Ezra Klein argued:

> If you step back, then, two things are happening simultaneously among the key interest groups in American politics. Labor is getting weaker. And corporations, in part due to *Citizens United,* are getting much stronger. The electoral effect of that is obvious: It favors Republicans.[27]

Change the Law?   Many Americans believe we should amend the U.S. Constitution to make it clear that money does not constitute speech and that corporations are not entitled to the inalienable rights of persons, including expansive political contributions. In considering these concerns about corporate political spending, we need to remember that labor unions and other groups also have a big monetary voice in the political process. Thus, as *The Wall Street Journal* argues, corporations need to be sure that their voices are heard in the political process:

> [P]oliticians have created a gargantuan state that is so intrusive that businesses have no alternative than to spend money to defend themselves and their shareholders. . . . Liberals want business to disarm unilaterally.[28]

Furthermore, a recent study found that "corporate political efforts generally have positive effects on a firm's market value and its shareholder returns."[29] Arguably, then, corporations, in looking out for shareholder welfare, need to be very active in the political process.

Lobbying

Lobbying (efforts to influence the actions of public officials) is an essential ingredient in big business strategy. Lobbying also often serves the very useful role of efficiently educating busy politicians about the vast array of issues they must address but cannot possibly master without assistance. Lobbying is not confined to the business community. Labor unions, consumer and environmental interest groups, and myriad others battle to have their voices heard. So lobbying serves a valuable role in government. Unfortunately, that role is often thoroughly corrupt.

Part of the blame for the nation's disastrous subprime mortgage crisis, for example, doubtless rests with lenders' ability to exert influence over government decision making. *The Washington Post* reported about former mortgage giant Countrywide Financial Corp.'s practice of making discount loans to former and current members of Congress and to executives at the taxpayer-backed mortgage company, Fannie Mae. While extending those favors, Countrywide was lobbying to block legislation that would have decreased the sale of subprime mortgages. Indeed, when Countrywide employees resisted making loans to Jim Johnson, CEO of Fannie Mae from 1991 to 1998, because he reportedly had a low credit score, Countrywide CEO Angelo Mozillo rejected those concerns saying, "Jim Johnson continues to be a source of many loans for our company and this is just a small token of appreciation for the business that he sends to us."[30]

Lobbying by the Numbers   Total spending on lobbying in Washington, D.C., for 2015 was about $3.22 billion, and more than 11,500 individuals were registered as lobbyists.[31] The biggest spenders continue to be business groups, with the Chamber of Commerce at the top, spending nearly $85 million in 2015 and over $136 million in the 2012 election year.[32]

While the number of lobbyists has actually declined in recent years, they remain so influential in Congress that legislation is often the product of their thinking. Sometimes lobbyists actually write the laws. When the House of Representatives, in 2013, passed a measure that would have rolled back part of the financial reforms in the 2010 Dodd–Frank bill (see Chapter 8), National Public Radio reported that 70 of the 85 lines in the final bill reflected Citigroup (one of the nation's largest banks) recommendations and two Citigroup paragraphs were copied almost word for word.[33] Furthermore, the "revolving door" between Congress and lobbying firms remains robust with more than 340 former members of Congress and nearly 3,700 former government staffers working in lobbying or in a related field, according to a 2011 report.[34]

Democracy Threatened?   Does corporate lobbying disproportionately influence federal policy? The evidence is mixed but worrisome. A Sunlight Foundation study of 200 corporations showed that those firms investing heavily in lobbying enjoyed lower federal tax rates.[35] A recent study of lobbying results concluded that opposing lobbyists and interest groups hold each other in check about 60 percent of the time. Thus, lobbyists, over a four-year period, are successful in influencing policy about 40 percent of the time. The study also concluded that money influenced outcomes only when heavily weighted to one side.[36] According to a 2014 statistical analysis, when economic elites and organized groups representing business interests support a new federal government policy, it has about a 45 percent chance of being approved, but average citizens and even mass-based interest groups have virtually no influence over federal policy.[37] Indeed, the analysts go so far as to say that democracy is threatened by "powerful business organizations and a small number of affluent Americans."[38]

On the other hand, commentator Steven Pearlstein, writing in 2016 in *The Washington Post,* argued that corporate influence on government is as "low as anyone can remember."[39] Corporate lobbying on narrow issues, he acknowledges, remains effective, but corporate influence over big policy issues like immigration and tax reform has declined—particularly as public respect for corporations has fallen with plant closings, layoffs, extravagant executive pay, and scandals like Enron and WorldCom in the early 2000s. One unfortunate result, he argues, is that big business can no longer perform its traditional stabilizing role in Washington. Political extremism and gridlock, therefore, have intensified. [For the Center for Responsive Politics and its extensive database on money in politics, see **http://www. opensecrets.org/**].

The Corporate State—Social Issues and Institutions

As we've seen, the critics believe America's corporate community harms our economic and political lives, but the critics' concerns do not end there. The corporate message, they say, pervades and shapes all dimensions of American life including the education you are participating in as you read these words.

Schools

Higher Education   Big business is accused of turning college campuses into marketing and development opportunities, as *The New York Times* described:

> It's move-in day here at the University of North Carolina and Leila Ismail, stuffed animals in tow, is feeling some freshman angst. A few friendly upperclassmen spring into action. But wait: there is something odd, or at least oddly corporate, about this welcome wagon. These U.N.C. students are all wearing identical T-shirts from American Eagle Outfitters. Turns out three of them are working for that youth clothing chain on this late August morning, as what are known in the trade as "brand ambassadors" or "campus Evangelists"—and they have recruited several dozen friends as a volunteer move-in crew.[40]

As *The Times* observed, "Corporations have been pitching college students for decades on products from cars to credit cards. But what is happening on campuses today is without rival, in terms of commercializing everyday college life."[41]

Many universities (as well as states, cities, businesses, and school districts) enter *"pouring rights"* contracts where Pepsi and Coke, among others, compete for multi-million-dollar deals to secure exclusive on-campus sales rights. At some universities, however, students have raised health, sustainability, and commercialism concerns about those deals. San Francisco State University in 2015 responded to student protests and declined to enter into a soft drink pouring rights contract, thereby forfeiting much-needed dollars.

Thus, higher education, the critics argue, is increasingly viewed as a product to be marketed and consumed on the road to prosperity in the corporate state. Hunter Rawlings, former president of Cornell University, decried that trend:

. . . Genuine education is not a commodity, it is the awakening of a human being.[42]

[The documentary movie *Starving the Beast* examines efforts to treat education as a consumer product and to run universities more like businesses. See the trailer and more at **www.starvingthebeast.net**].

PreK–12 Similar commercial concerns have emerged in the earliest years of education. Private corporations such as EdisonLearning operate a significant number of American public schools. Even some PreK–12 daily lessons are the product of corporate influence. Seeking quality education for their own needs and for the nation, corporations commendably prepare model curricula and lesson plans while donating money and other resources to strengthen PreK–12 school performance. Sometimes, however, those contributions can be unbalanced and self-serving while commercializing the school setting.

A few million children learn daily from Channel One's telecasts, but ads are a part of that learning experience. Google's low-priced Chromebook is a leader in schoolrooms nationwide, but critics are concerned about Google's practice of collecting data from student use of those computers. Domino's developed its Smart Slice pizza with reduced fat and salt for the school market, but the healthier pizza often comes with saturation displays of the Domino's logo on pizza boxes, delivery personnel, delivery trucks, and lunch-line placards.

Questions

The Wall Street Journal talked with critics, including corporate recruiters, who are increasingly skeptical about the value of an undergraduate business degree:

[N]ow faculty members, school administrators and corporate recruiters are questioning the value of a business degree at the undergraduate level. The biggest complaint: The undergraduate degrees focus too much on the nuts and bolts of finance and accounting and don't develop enough critical thinking and problem-solving skills through long essays, in-class debates and other hallmarks of liberal-arts courses.[43]

1. Do you think your business courses should have a stronger liberal arts flavor? Explain.
2. If you are a business major, do you think you chose the wrong field of study? Explain.

Religion

In her book *Brands of Faith*, Professor Mara Einstein argues that religion has become a product and, in consequence, churches and pastors are changing their methods and messages to suit the market, and they are marketing themselves to stand out in the spiritual community.[44] Do you think authentic spiritual life is threatened when religion is treated as a product to be marketed?

> Televangelist Creflo Dollar will receive a $65 million jet.

Churches now routinely employ standard business practices such as advertising, promotional giveaways, and marketing campaigns. Some pastors preach the "prosperity gospel" that material success is a mark of God's favor. Televangelist Creflo Dollar has been assured by the board of directors of his World Changers Church International that he will receive a $65 million luxury jet that he believes is needed to spread his prosperity theology.

> **The megachurches have taken on corporate characteristics.**

Megachurch pastor David Platt questions the commercial direction of contemporary religion in his book *Radical: Taking Back Your Faith from the American Dream*.[45] Platt says the megachurches have taken on corporate characteristics in competing for market share by serving as social centers while offering day care and comfortable entertainment. Platt asks his followers to put a cap on their consumer lives. He believes that our pursuit of the materialist American Dream cannot be reconciled with an authentic spiritual life.[46] Do you think your pursuit of your American Dream conflicts with your spiritual life?

To many, Jesus is a pop-culture icon and thus is the inspiration for a vast array of commercial expressions including T-shirts, license plates, dolls, video games, perfume, golf balls, scripture chocolates, and much more. The marriage of religion and commerce has even reached the business of sports, where "Faith Nights" have become popular promotional devices at professional ball games. [For a review of *Christianity Incorporated: How Big Business Is Buying the Church,* see **http://www.directionjournal.org/article/?1301**].

Questions

1. Do you see any risks to religion in treating it as a product to be marketed and sold? Explain.

2. *a.* Why has religion increasingly become a product in the commercial world?

   b. Is everything a product in some sense?

Culture

Does America possess a cultural life? For decades, the concern was that so-called high culture—classical music, opera, ballet, and the like—would give way to rock and roll, television, and video games. Now that battle is over; Americans (and the world) have clearly voted for *Dancing with the Stars* and *The Voice*.

> **Americans (and the world) have clearly voted for *Dancing with the Stars*.**

Corporate America has been generous in its support for traditional intellectual culture. At the same time, corporate bottom-line concerns appear to the critics to be steadily degrading America's cultural life.

For example, the world-famous visual art extravaganza Art Basel Miami Beach, a financial blessing to artists, is widely criticized for its celebration of money, consumer excess, and sometimes wretched taste. Much of that excess, according to the critics, is attributable to corporate sponsors, as *The New York Times* explained:

> In Miami Beach, at the main fair, the consumer-oriented glitter abounds this week: coffee carts with $20-a-glass Ruinart Champagne; Davidoff cigar rollers; BMW's artist-designed cars; and Takashi Murakami's $70,000-and-up commissioned portraits. One could almost imagine that the Barbara Kruger work on display at L & M gallery—a super-sized sign reading "Greedy" on one line and an unprintable expletive on the next—had an invisible subtitle telling the wealthy V.I.P.'s who had come to shop, "I'm Talking to You—Yeah, You!"[47]

While the recent emergence of some challenging cable television programming is encouraging, popular culture (rock, movies, television, hip hop, and so on) is largely a wasteland, the critics say, debased not merely by a mindless market (that's us), but by corporate greed, indifference to quality, and relentless consolidation.

Are the Corporate Suits Ruining TV?

The *Los Angeles Times* asked: "Are the Corporate Suits Ruining TV?"[48] As the *Times* explained, "Your TV may receive 200 channels, but virtually every one of them is owned by one of six big companies—NBC Universal, Disney, Time Warner, Viacom/Paramount, Sony, and News Corp."[49] Similarly, one 850-station giant, iHeartMedia, dominates and, critics say, diminishes the radio industry by its "McDonald's approach to programming" that makes one station virtually indistinguishable from another regardless of locale.[50]

Perhaps we should applaud corporate America for efficiently providing us with precisely what we want. But do we, particularly at a young age, have the information necessary to steer our cultural lives in healthy, challenging directions? Consider, for example, a recent study confirming what your parents have told you: "[M]usic has, indeed, become both more homogeneous and louder over the decades."[51] The 2012 study found that today's popular music relies largely on the same 10 most popular chords that were the foundation of music in the 1950s. The sound itself has changed, however, in that songs are about nine decibels louder on average, apparently part of a "loudness race" designed to catch our attention over the noise clutter of our lives.[52]

But does it matter that current popular music all sounds pretty much the same? Or that reality TV is a central feature of American daily life? Or that *Sesame Street* must move to HBO in order to secure the finances necessary to carry on? Does it matter that the cutting-edge Austin, Texas–based South by Southwest Music Festival is starting "to feel corporate,"[53] or that "Capitalism's Suffocating Music,"[54] as critics have recently argued?

Sports

I think we've sold out.

Kansas State University head football coach Bill Snyder surprised the sports world in 2014 by publicly and pointedly saying what many privately acknowledge:

> It's changed. I mean college athletics, football in particular, has changed dramatically over the years. I think we've sold out. We're all about dollars and cents.[55]

Snyder's point of view seems indisputable today as college sports programs at the highest level are in an increasingly desperate race for money. Most of that money, of course, is tied to and driven by another enormous industry: television. Former Colorado State University chancellor Michael Martin wryly spoke to the power of the networks by saying, "I think we could end up with two enormous conferences, one called ESPN and one called FOX."[56] Sports commentator Eric Crawford concurred with Martin by saying,

> We're not far away now. We even have a set of sub-conferences: Nike, Adidas, Reebok and Under Armour. College sports today are not about college and, increasingly, they are not about sports. It's all business.[57]

Marketing   Rabid commercialism seems to be the new normal in college sports. Perhaps the University of Alabama's remarkably successful head football coach Nick Saban is untroubled about commercialism concerns as he reportedly walks to his postgame press conference with a bottle of Dasani water (a sponsor) in his hand while a Coca Cola (a sponsor) sets at the podium awaiting him.[58]

Likewise, the University of Maryland expresses no official misgivings about its nearly $33 million, 10-year contract with Under Armour and its president, Kevin Plank, a Maryland graduate.[59] Maryland, *The New York Times* reports, is positioning itself to be the University of Under Armour just as the University of Oregon has described itself as "the University of Nike."[60]

What Have We Lost?   The social significance of athletics' evolution from sport to business is unclear. Profit seeking in collegiate sports is not without its benefits. Thousands of students complete college every year who might otherwise not have done so, funding is provided for many unprofitable sports including women's programs, and sports revenues often support academic programs.

But what have we lost when the innocence and idealism of amateur sports are forfeited in favor of professionalism and profit? Is the pursuit of profit the route to the slow but sure death of honorable, meaningful sports? Or perhaps innocence, idealism, and amateurism are myths or largely forgotten relics of a pretelevision past? Perhaps we are better off when corporate and personal profit—the free market—drives sports.

Children Next?   Business values and practices have spread from professional sports to college athletics, and now are rapidly emerging in youth sports as well. Elite high school teams travel the country to play in special events, more and more games are televised, and in Texas at least $60-million-plus high school football stadiums are popping up around Dallas and Houston. Even Little League baseball, with its multimillion-dollar World Series, may consider the possibility of some kind of payment system for players.[61]

PRACTICING ETHICS   The Sports Business and Compromised Values?

BEER

About 25 percent of the 128 major college football stadiums sell beer at football games, a total that has more than doubled in the past 10 years. West Virginia University reports a net profit of $500,000 to $750,000 per year in stadium-wide beer sales along with a decline in incidents of binge drinking on game days. One of the reasons for the beer-selling trend is that college football attendance has been falling over the past decade.[62]

Questions

1. Do you think universities that sell beer at football games are hypocritical in that those same schools energetically discourage binge drinking by students? Explain.

2. Commenting on selling beer at college football games, a fan experience expert at Aecom, Emily Golembiewski, said: "[I]t's important to keep some of what people love about college and not make it a mini-NFL."[63] Do you agree? Explain.

America's Soul?

LO 3-5

Make a tentative assessment regarding the proper role of business in society.

Critics contend that the power of the business community has become so encompassing that virtually all dimensions of American life have absorbed elements of the business ethic. Values commonly associated with businesspeople (competition, profit-seeking, reliance on technology, faith in growth) have overwhelmed traditional humanist values (cooperation, individual dignity, human rights, meaningful service to society). In the name of wealth, efficiency, and productivity, the warmth, decency, and value of life have been debased. We engage in meaningless work. Objects dominate our existence. We operate as replaceable cogs in a vast, bureaucratic machine. Indeed, we lose ourselves, the critics argue. Charles Reich, former Yale University law professor, addressed the loss of self in his influential book of the Vietnam War era, *The Greening of America:*

> Objects dominate our existence.

> Of all of the forms of impoverishment that can be seen or felt in America, loss of self, or death in life, is surely the most devastating. . . . Beginning with school, if not before, an individual is systematically stripped of his imagination, his creativity, his heritage, his dreams, and his personal uniqueness, in order to style him into a productive unit for a mass, technological society. Instinct, feeling, and spontaneity are repressed by overwhelming forces. As the individual is drawn into the meritocracy, his working life is split from his home life, and both suffer from a lack of wholeness. Eventually, people virtually become their professions, roles, or occupations, and are henceforth strangers to themselves.[64]

> Commentator Ben Stein lamented an increasingly divided America.

Some interesting empirical evidence supports Reich's view that we have become hollow men and women dominated by the demands of big institutions. The Harris Alienation Index measures the degree to which people feel their interests are noticed and addressed by those with power and influence. Survey questions inquire about, for example, feelings of economic inequity (the rich get richer, and the poor get poorer) and feelings of powerlessness (being left out and not counting for much). Responses are combined into an alienation "score." That score stood at a low of 29 in its first year, 1966, and has generally been rising since with a 2015 score of 70, the highest ever.[65]

Actor/commentator Ben Stein, speaking in 2006, lamented an increasingly divided America where the interests of corporations and the wealthy are dominant and the well-being of others is in danger of being forgotten:

> The Saturday before Memorial Day I spoke to a gathering of widows and widowers, parents and children of men and women in uniform who have lost their lives in Iraq and Afghanistan. The person who spoke before me was a beautiful woman named Joanna Wroblewski, whose husband of less than two years—after four years of dating at Rutgers—had been killed in Iraq. She cried as she spoke. . . . She spoke of her devotion to her country and her husband's pride in the flag. . . .
>
> Are we keeping the faith with Joanna Wroblewski? . . . Are we maintaining an America that is not just a financial neighborhood, but also a brotherhood and a sisterhood worth losing your husband for? Is this still a community of the heart, or a looting opportunity? Will there even be a free America for Mrs. Wroblewski's descendants, or will we be a colony of the people [foreign lenders] to whom we have sold our soul?[66]

Questions

1. A recent *Washington Post* headline included the question: "Yosemite, Sponsored by Starbucks?" Facing flat to declining congressional appropriations, the National Park Service is proposing a plan, to be effective at the end of 2016, that would build partnerships with donors, including corporations, in return for naming rights, logo displays, advertising banners on Park Service vehicles, and the like. In response to the proposal, one unidentified Park Service superintendent said: "For me as a federal employee and a taxpayer, I think it is unethical to be advertising for a corporation."[67]

   a. Do you see anything unethical about the Park Service proposal? Explain.

   b. Do you think an increased corporate presence at our national parks will in any way threaten those parks? Explain.

2. The U.S. Chamber of Commerce and its foreign affiliates often work to block anti-smoking laws in other nations. Do you think those efforts are improper? Explain.

3. Facebook founder and CEO Mark Zuckerberg, in 2016, spoke about his ambitions for reaching all of the world's seven billion people through the Internet. Zuckerberg criticized people and nations who oppose a connected world and a global community. He envisioned Facebook as a primary vehicle for world connectivity. Do you see any problems with Mr. Zuckerberg's vision? Explain.

4. A brief analysis of social media advertising techniques employed to promote Ford, Mello Yello, Grey Poupon, and Sephora emphasized the value and power of those ads on Facebook, Twitter, and other social media. The article, entitled "4 Examples of How Corporate America Is Crushing Social Media,"[68] argued that those four products were marketed online by presenting interesting content that readers would be inclined to share with their social networks.

   a. Do those corporate advertising campaigns diminish the quality of your social media experience? Explain.

   b. Do we need a social media "zone" free of corporate advertising messages? Explain.

5. *a.* Do Americans trust the business community? Explain.

   b. Does it matter?

6. In your opinion, which of the following will be the biggest threat to America in the future: big government, big labor, or big business?

7. *a.* Do you think allegiance to the company will become more important than allegiance to the state?

   b. Is that a desirable direction? Raise the pros and cons of the latter question.

Part Two—Corporate Social Responsibility

Introduction

Journalist Daniel Seligman sums up today's widespread criticism of Corporate America:

> A standard view of the American corporation . . . is that it is an efficient deliverer of goods and services, yet also a wellspring of social injustice. Driven by a narrow calculus of profits,

it is oblivious to the common good. And so, the litany goes, it degrades the environment, promotes unsafe products, skimps on workplace safety and . . . lays off workers who have given it years of service.[69]

That perception of business misdeeds or indifference, in conjunction with the growing influence of business values throughout American life, has led in recent decades to the development of the doctrine of *corporate social responsibility* (CSR—sometimes also referred to as *corporate citizenship*). CSR raises this crucial question: Must business decision making include consideration not merely of the welfare of the firm but of society as a whole? For most contemporary readers, the answer is self-evident—of course business bears a social responsibility. Business has enjoyed a central and favored role in American life. As such, it must assume a portion of the burden for the welfare of the total society. Indeed, business people themselves now generally endorse businesses' responsibility to help solve society's problems.

LO 3-6
Explain the concept of corporate social responsibility.

The popular appeal and potential power of CSR are evident, for example, in a 2016 Deloitte survey of nearly 7,700 millennials from 29 countries that found that 73 percent of millennials think business has a positive impact on society, but they would like employers to focus more on people and purpose and less on profits (although they recognize the necessity for long-term financial success).[70] Fifty-eight percent of respondents said that businesses "behave in an ethical manner," and 57 percent believe "their leaders are committed to helping improve society."[71]

Before turning to a more detailed analysis of corporate social responsibility practice, let's think for a moment about how you could direct your forthcoming professional life toward socially responsible, ethically sustainable business practice. *Social enterprise or social entrepreneurship* is a movement in which people launch nonprofits and businesses or take jobs using entrepreneurial and managerial skills for the purpose, in part, of addressing social problems.

Social Enterprise/Social Entrepreneurship

Drew Chafetz, in his mid-twenties and a huge soccer fan, did not turn directly to the job market following college graduation. Rather, in 2006 he co-founded love.futbol [see **www.lovefutbol.org**], an organization to help build safe soccer fields for children in impoverished nations. At this writing in 2016, love.futbol is partnering with ESPN to build community sports facilities in Buenos Aires and Rio de Janeiro.

Others share Chafetz's social welfare goals but are pursuing them from a profit-seeking direction. TOMS, perhaps the best known of the for-profit social enterprises, sells shoes and other consumer products. For each sale, TOMS provides a free pair of shoes, eyewear, or other necessities to people in need around the world.

Some of those committed to social welfare simply seek jobs that allow them to apply their expertise and zeal directly to community causes. Dawn Carpenter gave up her high-paying job at JP Morgan to work for a small District of Columbia community bank whose customers include D.C. Habitat for Humanity and Bread for the City. Carpenter said she "needed to put over two decades of experience to work for my mission."[72] Still others believe they can make socially responsible contributions by taking mainstream, high-paying jobs that, for example, help build power stations in developing nations, improve financing opportunities for inner-city entrepreneurs, or enable affordable medical care. [For an introduction to B Corps—benefit corporations—"for-profit companies certified by the non-profit B Lab to meet rigorous standards of social and environmental performance, accountability, and transparency," see **www.bcorporation.net.** Etsy and Patagonia are among 1,600 certified B corporations in 42 nations.]

Questions

1. *a.* Do you aspire to a social enterprise/social entrepreneurship role in your future professional life?

   b. Should you? Explain.

2. Have your business school courses given sufficient attention to social responsibility issues? Explain.

3. Do consumers care whether companies are socially responsible? Explain.

A New Ideology

The ascendance of the social responsibility doctrine represents a striking ideological shift. Historically, business was expected to concentrate on one goal—the production and distribution of the best products and services at the lowest possible prices. Business was largely exempt from any affirmative duty for the resolution of social problems until the 1950s, when business scholars and critics began to encourage a broader conception of corporate duty. Now in the 21st century, expectations for business in society have been radically altered. Profit-seeking remains central and essential, but for most businesspeople, the sometimes awkward ingredient of social responsibility must be a consideration. [For the Business for Social Responsibility home page, see **www.bsr.org**].

What Is Social Responsibility?

The sweeping notion of corporate social responsibility is not readily reduced to a brief definition, but Davis and Blomstrom some years ago captured the core ingredients: "The idea of social responsibility is that decision makers are obligated to take actions which protect and improve the welfare of society as a whole along with their own interests."[73]

The social role of business can be envisioned as an ideological continuum, corresponding roughly to the familiar American political spectrum of conservative/Republican views on the right, moderates in the middle, and liberal/Democrats on the left. Figure 3.1 depicts that continuum and is best understood by reading "backwards" from right to left. On the right side of the spectrum lies the free-market view holding that *profit maximization* is the best measure of social responsibility. Across the middle (*long-term company interest*) lies a hybrid, blended perspective where profits are the first consideration, but where satisfied workers, customers, and community members are also of importance, within some reasonable limits, to secure the firm's long-term survival. On the left side of the spectrum lies the *triple bottom line/sustainability* movement that calls for a revolutionary re-visioning of corporate goals and practices such that profit maximization is only one of three key measures of success. Triple bottom line advocates specifically call for managerial and accounting practices that respect and measure the firm's *social and environmental*

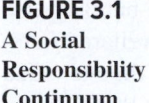

FIGURE 3.1
A Social Responsibility Continuum

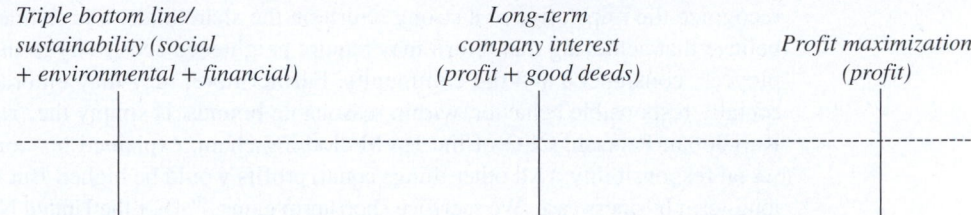

| *Triple bottom line/ sustainability (social + environmental + financial)* | *Long-term company interest (profit + good deeds)* | *Profit maximization (profit)* |

performance just as the firm's *financial* performance is respected and measured. The goal is to ensure the long-term viability (sustainability) of the organization and the total society.

Now let's examine the continuum in a bit more detail. [For the "Global Reporting Initiative" on sustainability practices around the world, see **https://www.globalreporting.org**].

> The only responsible and moral course of behavior is to reap the highest return possible, within the law.

Profit Maximization   Here the dominant concern lies in maximizing shareholders' interests. Those shareholders, after all, are the owners of the firm. They are taking the financial risk. Hence, from a profit maximization point of view, the only responsible and moral course of behavior is to reap the highest return possible, within the law. Nobel prize–winning economist Milton Friedman was the most prominent advocate of the profit maximization view:

> [In a free economy] there is one and only one social responsibility of business—to use its resources and engage in activities designed to increase its profits, so long as it stays within the rules of the game, which is to say, engages in open and free competition, without deception or fraud.[74]

Friedman, employing free-market reasoning, believed the firm that maximizes its profits is necessarily maximizing its contribution to society. Furthermore, he argued that any dilution of the profit-maximizing mode—such as charitable contributions—is a misuse of the stockholders' resources. The individual stockholder, he contended, should dispose of assets according to her or his own wishes. Finally, he asked how managers could be expected to know what the public interest is.

Herbert Stein, former chair of the President's Council of Economic Advisers, shared Friedman's doubts about the idea of social responsibility, but Stein's concerns were of a more pragmatic nature. He argued that business is simply ill suited for solving social problems:

> Efficiency in maximizing the nation's product . . . is not the only objective of life. But it is the one that private corporations are best qualified to serve. I don't want to be a purist about this. I don't object to corporations contributing to the United Givers Fund. . . . But to rely on corporations' responsibility to solve major social problems—other than the problem of how to put our people and other resources to work most efficiently—would be a wasteful diversion from their most important function. Our other objectives can be better served in other ways, by individuals and other institutions.[75]

Long-Term Company Interest   Across the middle ground of our social responsibility continuum lie those firms that believe that a strong bottom line sometimes requires considerations beyond the immediate, short-run, profit-maximizing interests of the firm. In a sense, these managers are merely taking a longer-term view of profit maximization. They recognize the imperative of a strong return on the shareholder's investment, but they also believe that achieving that return may require heightened sensitivity to the welfare of employees, consumers, and the community. Furthermore, they may embrace the view that socially responsible behavior, within reasonable bounds, is simply the "right thing" to do. Karl-Johan Persson, CEO of the H&M clothing chain, explained his company's view of social responsibility: "All other things equal, profits would be higher. But we believe in the long-term business case. We sacrifice short-term gains."[76] [For the United Nations's initiative to encourage responsible corporate citizenship, see **https://www.unglobalcompact.org**].

LO 3-7

Explain the triple bottom line/ sustainability approach to corporate citizenship.

Triple Bottom Line/Sustainability   Managers are being pushed to adopt a bigger, broader conception of social responsibility, an approach that will produce a healthy, enduring global community where our resources are not dangerously depleted or damaged. The triple bottom line calls for attention to the three Ps: people, planet, and profit. Social responsibility expert Steve Rochlin explains:

> The new corporate citizenship challenges executives to find alternatives to zero-sum solutions that often emphasize shareholder value at the cost of social and environmental welfare. Instead, the new corporate citizenship challenges companies to deliver not just financial returns but also environmental and social value—together marking the pillars of what is called a "triple bottom line.". . .[77]

The triple bottom line/sustainability approach employs free-market principles and recognizes the necessity for financial success but also argues that profit along with social and environmental responsibility are of equal importance. According to sustainability advocates, corporations giving close attention to social and economic duties, in addition to the bottom line, have a powerful competitive advantage that will contribute to organizational and societal sustainability.

Building a just, healthy, sustainable future makes a lot of sense, but reasonable people continue to differ about the most effective path to that goal. For many companies, shorter-term profit motives continue to dominate. A 2016 study of supply chain sustainability plans in 50 larger American firms concluded:

> While the survey showed many companies are thinking about and/or prioritizing supply chain optimization, few at this point seem to be embracing sustainability initiatives in a meaningful way. Until regulations force action, many companies likely won't prioritize the resources and funding necessary to make significant change.[78]

Nonetheless, progress is evident. Some big American corporations are appointing sustainability officers and committing themselves to global sustainability projects. For example, Muhtar Kent, Coca-Cola CEO, spoke of his company's close attention to improved practices in water, packaging, energy conservation, and climate. He went on to specifically cite one small but illustrative step forward:

> Preeti Gupti, for example, is a mother of three in rural India. In the town of Agra, about 125 miles south of Delhi, she has a small store in her home, which lacks reliable electrical service. With a solar-powered Coca-Cola cooler, she can now sell cold beverages, stay open later and help her children study after dark. Her income has also increased, creating still more opportunities for her children.[79]

[For a critique of triple bottom line thinking, see **www.businessethics.ca/3bl**].

"Green" Jeans?

Americans' fashion-forward sensibility is sustained by globe-spanning supply chains that consume enormous amounts of water, energy, chemicals, cotton, oil, and other resources while casting off equally enormous amounts of waste and entangling workers in often dangerous, poorly paid jobs. Now the Sustainable Apparel Coalition, which represents about one-third of the global apparel and footwear industries and includes such prominent companies as Adidas, Columbia Sportswear, Levi, and Walmart, is cooperating in a system to measure the apparel industry's environmental, social, and labor impact through its tool called the Higg Index. Companies can enter data about their business practices and the Higg Index system produces a "score card" that allows those companies to compare their sustainability performance with competitors and industry standards.

Question

Think about shopping. Assume you are considering two pairs of jeans of equal style and quality, one with a favorable sustainability score, one without. Assume the jeans without the favorable score are priced at $50. How much more would you be willing to pay for the jeans with a favorable score?

a. Nothing more
b. $1
c. $5
d. $10
e. $25

Explain.

Sources: Tara Savarese, "Measuring the Fashion Supply Chain," *Peacock Plume,* March 24, 2016 [**http:// peacockplume.fr**]; and Tom Zeller, "Clothes Makers Join to Set 'Green Score,'" *The New York Times,* March 1, 2011 [**www.nytimes.com**].

Social Responsibility Pyramid

Professor Archie Carroll proposed another way of visualizing socially responsible business practice, as depicted in Figure 3.2. Socially responsible business practice necessarily begins at the foundation of the pyramid with the duty to make a profit in a lawful fashion; but simultaneously the socially responsible firm moves (up the pyramid) beyond the fundamental demands of economics and law to pursue the ethical course of action. In striving for profitable, lawful, ethical conduct, that company may also choose to engage in discretionary philanthropic (charitable) efforts to build a better community. While the social responsibility pyramid has been criticized and revised, it remains a useful way of thinking about corporations' expanding duties.[80] [ISO, the International Organization for Standardization, has developed a set of guidelines for socially responsible corporate behavior labeled ISO 26000. For an overview of ISO 26000, see **www.iso.org/iso/home/standards/ iso26000.htm**].

FIGURE 3.2

The Social Responsibility (CSR) Pyramid

Source: Archie B. Carroll, "The Pyramid of Corporate Social Responsibility: Toward the Moral Management of Organizational Stakeholders." *Business Horizons* 34, no. 4 (July–August 1991), pp. 39, 42. The Foundation for the School of Business at Indiana University.

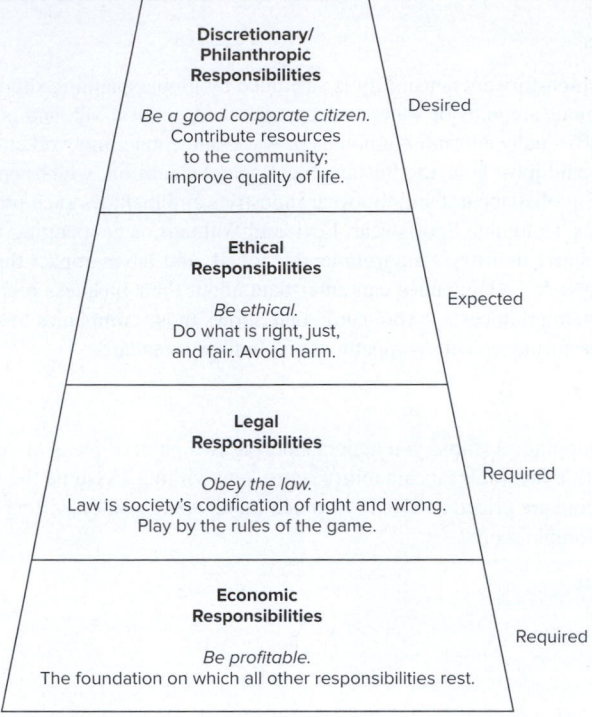

Discretionary/ Philanthropic Responsibilities

Be a good corporate citizen. Contribute resources to the community; improve quality of life.

Desired

Ethical Responsibilities

Be ethical. Do what is right, just, and fair. Avoid harm.

Expected

Legal Responsibilities

Obey the law. Law is society's codification of right and wrong. Play by the rules of the game.

Required

Economic Responsibilities

Be profitable. The foundation on which all other responsibilities rest.

Required

Auto Makers and the Social Responsibility Pyramid

General Motors, Hyundai, Kia, Mitsubishi, Suzuki, Toyota, and Volkswagen, worldwide manufacturing giants, in recent years have committed moral and legal wrongs leading to deaths, environmental despoliation, and enormous economic losses.

General Motors agreed in 2015 to pay $900 million to settle federal criminal charges arising from its failure to disclose an ignition defect (see Chapter 2) that reportedly led to at least 124 deaths. GM employees reportedly were aware of the problem for a decade or more prior to disclosure. Mitsubishi admitted in 2016 that its employees had intentionally inflated fuel mileage test results for some of its models. Hyundai, Kia, and Suzuki have recently made similar admissions. Toyota agreed to pay $1.2 billion in 2014 to settle federal criminal charges that it had failed to disclose information about a defect that caused some of its cars to accelerate suddenly, leading to at least 37 deaths. Volkswagen has set aside $18 billion to cover the costs associated with its scheme to defeat emissions tests. Some of its diesel vehicles were fitted with software permitting cleaner fuel burning during those tests.

In applying Carroll's Social Responsibility Pyramid reasoning, we see that the auto makers compromised their capacity to fulfill their long-term economic responsibilities. Beyond the costs noted above, civil lawsuits, vehicle recalls, product redesigns and other expenses will pile up for years to come. Of course, these companies clearly failed to meet their legal and ethical responsibilities.

Some of the auto makers have rather forthrightly addressed their shortcomings. Toyota president Akio Toyoda acknowledged that quality had been sacrificed for faster growth and profits. Toyoda said, "[S]ome people just got too big-headed and focused too excessively on profit."[81] [For Toyota's Corporate Social Responsibility policy, see **www.toyota-global.com/sustainability/csr/csr/**].

Sources: Danielle Douglas and Michael Fletcher, "Toyota Reaches $1.2 Billion Settlement to End Probe of Accelerator Problems," *The Washington Post,* March 29, 2014 [**www.washingtonpost.com**]; Peter Henning, "Volkswagen's Legal Endgame in Emissions Scandal," *The New York Times,* April 25, 2016 [**www.nytimes.com**]; Danielle Ivory, "G.M. to Pay U.S. $900 Million over Ignition Switch Flaw," *The New York Times,* September 17, 2015 [**www.nytimes.com**]; Norihiko Shirouzu, "Toyoda Rues Excessive Profit Focus," *The Wall Street Journal,* March 2, 2010, p. B3; and Chris Woodyard, "GM Ignition Switch Deaths Hit 124," *USA TODAY,* July 13, 2015 [**www.usatoday.com**].

Corporate Social Responsibility in Practice

Operating in a troubled world, the corporate community is taking an increasingly active role in addressing a very wide range of social problems. Google, a zealous CSR practitioner, topped the Reputation Institute's corporate responsibility rankings in both 2014 and 2015.[82] Google, through its charitable arm Google.org, says that it annually donates $100 million, 200,000 hours, and $1 billion in products.[83]

Beyond philanthropy, many social responsibility advocates, including Google, believe that an entrepreneurial, profit-seeking, capitalist approach is the best route to correcting social problems. By investing in businesses, lobbying for political causes, and directing portions of its employees' time to developing business and technology solutions, Google seeks social welfare through market mechanisms as well as conventional philanthropy. Google's big commitments to environmentalism, for example, benefit both society and the Google bottom line. Google has been carbon neutral since 2007, and its data centers use 50 percent less energy than typical data centers.[84]

Google is only one of many companies that have expanded their CSR efforts to include both giving and building. Many of those companies view social responsibility as workable only if it contributes to the strategic mission of the business and ultimately to the bottom line. Nike, for example, turned aggressively to social responsibility measures as a way of restoring its brand image after criticism for its use of global sweatshop labor. Examples of corporations that practice social responsibility both as a means of "giving back" and as a strategic business practice that can contribute to the bottom line in the long term have become increasingly common:

- After about one year in operation, some 4,000 Starbucks workers are receiving an online education through Arizona State University with all tuition paid by Starbucks.[85]

- CVS announced in 2014 that it would stop selling tobacco products, a decision expected to reduce annual revenues by about $2 billion.[86]

- McDonald's is requiring its pork suppliers to phase out sow gestation crates (metal stalls so small that pigs cannot turn) in favor of more humane arrangements.[87]

- Seattle's six-story Bullitt Center, the "world's greenest building," is running so efficiently after its 2013 opening that it generated 60 percent more electricity (using geothermal wells and solar panels) in 2014 than it used. The $30 million building—featuring composting toilets, bike-only on-site parking, a stairway designed to allow magnificent views of Puget Sound, and no storm water runoff—has also proven to be profitable with a 2015 occupancy rate of 90 percent.[88]

Questions

1. In general, we understand decisions to lay off employees when companies are losing money, but how should we feel about profitable companies that lay off employees? Powerful executive Barry Diller, in 2009, condemned "preemptive" layoffs:

   > The idea of a company that's earning money, not losing money, that's not, let's say, "industrially endangered," to have just cutbacks [sic] so they can earn another $12 million or $20 million or $40 million in a year where no one's counting is really a horrible act when you think about it on every level.[89]

   a. Do you think a socially responsible company that operates at a profit would engage in layoffs? Explain.
   b. Construction, farm, and mining equipment manufacturer Vermeer Corp. suffered a 40 percent drop in revenue in 2009. To cope with the "Great Recession" of that era, Vermeer cut workers' hours, but no one lost their job. Why would Vermeer sacrifice profit to keep workers who could simply have been let go?
   c. Vermeer is privately held by the family that started the company. How might that status affect layoff decisions?

2. Some critics argue that Wall Street's financial collapse in 2008–2009 was, at least in part, a product of male "group think." They claim that men take excessive risks and women are more comprehensive thinkers. Hence, they say the financial community needs more women:

   > Barnard College president Deborah Spar dubbed our predicament [the Wall Street crash] a "one gender crash," and *The New York Times*' Nicholas Kristof wonders if we might all have been better off had it been "Lehman Brothers and Sisters."[90]

   Do finance companies have a social responsibility to hire more women? Explain.

Finding an Employer with a Conscience

Surveys of young people in recent years suggest that employers trying to replace millions of retiring baby boomers may need to demonstrate a social commitment in order to be fully competitive in the hiring market. One of those surveys found that Gen Y workers (born after early 1980s and prior to early 2000s) seek challenging, interesting jobs, but they also seek jobs that make a valuable contribution to the economy or society.

Questions

1. a. Will you insist on a job with a "social purpose"? Explain.
   b. Do all jobs have a social purpose? Explain.

2. Would you expect money to replace social goals in the Gen Y hierarchy as they age? Explain.

3. Do you expect social goals to remain important to young people? Explain.

Source: Charlotte Seager, "Generation Y: Why Young Job Seekers Want More than Money," *The Guardian,* February 2014 [**www.theguardian.com**].

CSR: Two Big Questions

I. Is CSR Good Business?

LO 3-8

Discuss whether socially responsible business is "good business."

The evidence is at least mildly supportive of the idea that the market rewards socially responsible performance. A 2015 meta-analysis of 275 studies found that consideration of social responsibility in stock market portfolios is "neither a weakness nor a strength"[91] and a 2009 meta-analysis found a "positive but small" relationship between corporate social performance and corporate financial performance.[92] In a 2015 survey of 1,025 investors, 55 percent of respondents said profit was their only consideration in making their investment decisions, while 34 percent said they balance profit with a positive social impact. Ten percent said they would accept lesser profits to make a social impact, while 1 percent said they were concerned only with social impact of their investments.[93]

II. Do We Have a Better Alternative? Creating Shared Value

Michael Porter, highly influential Harvard professor and corporate consultant, and others have recently been arguing for moving beyond CSR to a business model labeled *creating shared value* (CSV).[94] They say that CSR has often been treated merely as a necessary expense and a way to improve a firm's reputation, but CSV calls for transcending philanthropy, good citizenship, and sustainability to produce products and services that create both economic and social value. They see creating shared value as a new form of capitalism that enhances economic competitiveness while simultaneously advancing social returns.

Nestlé, for example, strives to create shared value by making nutritious, profitable products while protecting scarce water resources and helping coffee growers secure financing and improve production. Nestlé and other shared-value advocates are identifying those opportunities where social and economic value creation align, thus enabling them to achieve favorable economic and sustainability results for communities while also making money for shareholders. Low-cost cell phones, for example, can be profitable while serving poorer populations.

Questions

1. Construct a list of the arguments for and against social responsibility for business.

2. In a recent commentary, ethicist Chris MacDonald explained the idea that businesses must earn and maintain an unwritten "social license" to operate.[95] That is, businesses must secure the support and goodwill of the community. MacDonald then asked what steps a business can take to maintain its "social license" to operate. Answer MacDonald's question.

Part Three—Managing Corporate Social Responsibility

Stakeholder Approach

LO 3-9
Contrast the stakeholder and shareholder approaches to corporate social responsibility.

A recent *Harvard Business Review* article argues that the principal goal of corporate social responsibility must be "to align a company's social and environmental activities with its business purpose and values."[96] Doubtless a laudable goal, but as a practical matter how can businesses identify and manage their CSR goals while meeting their bottom-line responsibilities? One approach is to employ the *stakeholder model* of social responsibility. Under that model, the corporation identifies all of the groups (stockholders, customers, employees, communities, governments, unions, schools, and the like) that may significantly affect the firm's performance or be affected by it. These are groups with a "stake" in the activities of the corporation. To stakeholder advocates, simply maximizing the interests of the primary stakeholders, that is, the shareholders, would not satisfy the corporation's social duties.

That more expansive view of social responsibility was emphasized in a 2010 discussion among corporate leaders who were thinking about how to restore the public's confidence in business after the financial collapse and scandals of recent years. First among the group's recommendations was "A New Stakeholder Approach":

> Companies should talk less about benefits to shareholders and short-term profits and instead focus on customer needs, investment in workers and sustainability (from ecology to education). We talk too much about benefits we provide to shareholders. We should be talking about benefits provided to our employees, customers and to the public. This will boost public confidence in business.[97]

Manage or Collaborate? Many companies now acknowledge the importance of their stakeholder relationships, but their dominant goal may amount to little more than controlling those relationships, as we often see, for example, in union–management negotiations. An arguably more effective approach to stakeholders involves a collaborative strategy in which stakeholder relationships are regarded as being mutually defined, cooperative, and reciprocal. The firm endeavors to understand and balance the interests and needs of all stakeholders with the view that this collaborative effort results in enhanced firm performance over the long term while building a healthier society.

A. G. Lafley, Procter & Gamble executive chair and two-time former CEO, has thoroughly and personally embraced stakeholder practice. As CEO, making money was Lafley's first job, but he led P&G on a broader mission, partly to ensure the company's continuing success. He came to think of consumers as citizens who often are concerned about P&G's approach to global warming or its animal-testing methods. Lafley, in fact, dealt directly with groups such as Greenpeace and People for the Ethical Treatment of Animals. Lafley also extended his stakeholder engagement to worldwide relief efforts on behalf of P&G. Those are citizenship responsibilities, he said, that go with P&G's big role in the changing global economic and political environment. "At P&G, we believe part of our responsibility is to give back to the communities in which we work, whether it's the safe drinking water program that we've provided to the developing world or Pampers vaccinations for neonatal tetanus," Lafley said.[98]

As Lafley recognized, profit now rests not merely in providing the best product or service at the lowest price, but in understanding and dealing with the complex interplay among the corporation, government, and society. Thus, today's manager is likely to be increasingly involved in identifying and addressing social issues and stakeholder concerns.

Stakeholder Results   Assessing the success of social responsibility efforts is very difficult, but various measurement systems have emerged, including, most prominently, Social Accountability 8000 (SA8000), the first global standard measuring companies' social and environmental records. Social Accountability Accreditation Services in New York City accredits companies that meet the SA8000 standards in the areas of child labor, forced labor, health and safety, freedom of association, discrimination, disciplinary practices, working hours, collective bargaining wages, and management systems. As of 2015, over 3,700 facilities employing over 2 million employees in 69 countries had been certified.[99] [For more, see **http://www.saasaccreditation.org**]. [Also see the Global Reporting Initiative at **www.globalreporting.org**].

Bhopal: A Social Responsibility Failure?

One way of measuring the results of stakeholder activism is to review how the business community responds when wrongs occur. The devastating 1984 explosion and chemical spill at Bhopal, India, was one of the great tragedies in global industrial history. Water entered a methyl isocyanate storage tank at a Union Carbide plant, producing an uncontrollable chemical reaction and a toxic cloud that spread across nearby slums. Up to 3,000 people were killed immediately and between 15,000 and 30,000 in total have perished. Nearly 600,000 people have qualified for compensation as a result of health problems attributed to the leak. Union Carbide reached a settlement in 1989 with the Indian government that absolved the company of liability and sent $470 million to India, including $2,000 for each death and $500 for each survivor. Claims totaled $3 billion, and litigation continues over a quarter of a century later. Union Carbide maintained that the gas release resulted from sabotage.

As of 2014, the hundreds of tons of toxic waste remaining at the site apparently continue to pollute groundwater, kill crops, and cause birth defects, cancer, and more. Local residents have been frustrated by slow responses from both the government and corporations. Indeed, the close relationship between the two is the fundamental problem, according to Satinath Sarangi, a metallurgist and activist. *The New York Times* explained Sarangi's view:

> Union Carbide got off easy in the 1980s because pesticides were a cornerstone of [India's] "green revolution" policy to enhance agricultural productivity, [Sarangi] said. A quarter of a century later, multinationals continue to wield enormous influence over governments that measure progress solely in economic terms. "If you are an ordinary person, you can't depend on your government, judiciary or regulatory bodies to protect you from corporate crime." [Sarangi] said.[100]

Nonetheless, these cataclysmic events can produce a dramatic and positive corporate response, as *The Wall Street Journal* reported about Bhopal:

> The chemical leak . . . spurred a revolution in approaches to safety, pollution, and community relations that have made chemical plants in the United States more accessible and more accountable to their neighbors. New laws forced plants to disclose safety and pollution data. And an army of community activists won new powers.[101] [A 2014 movie, *Bhopal: A Prayer for Rain,* is inspired by the Bhopal chemical disaster.]

Sources: "Asia: Bhopal's Deadly Legacy; India," *The Economist,* November 27, 2004, p. 76; Manjeet Kripalani, "Dow Chemical: Liable for Bhopal?" *BusinessWeek,* June 9, 2008, p. 61; Maddie Oatman, "Photos: Living in the Shadow of the Bhopal Chemical Disaster," *Mother Jones,* June 2, 2014 [**www.motherjones.com**]; and Julien Bouissou, "Why the Bhopal Disaster Site, 28 Years Later, Is Still a Toxic Killer," *Le Monde/Worldcrunch,* October 8, 2012 [**www.worldcrunch.com**].

Shareholder Approach

> The company that maximizes profits necessarily does what is best for society.

As we have seen, stakeholder theory and corporate social performance are increasingly influential in management practice. Nonetheless, many if not most organizations take the approach that shareholders must remain the consuming concerns of management, and that a skilled focus on the bottom line will, incidentally but inevitably, result in the greatest good for society. That is, the company that maximizes profits necessarily does not only what is best for its shareholders but also what is best for society generally. The shareholder/stakeholder debate is well illustrated by the heated competition between massive retailers Walmart and Costco.

Each day Walmart focuses relentlessly on the bottom line and hence on the interests of its shareholders. Costco, on the other hand, has drawn great praise from management scholars for its close attention to worker welfare. Costco workers average about $21 per hour while Walmart pay averages over $13 per hour for full-time employees.[102] Both companies raised minimum wages in 2016 (Walmart to $10 per hour or more and Costco to $13–$13.50), but Walmart also cut some workers' hours, and many Walmart workers still require food stamps and other public assistance. About 88 percent of Costco workers have company-sponsored health insurance, whereas Walmart reports "more than half" of its workers have company plans.[103] Reports vary, but Costco's employee turnover is much lower than Walmart's. Twenty-eight percent of customers, according to a recent survey, view Walmart unfavorably—about five times the negative sentiments felt for Costco.[104]

Facing consumer resistance and other market pressures, Walmart has sought an improved public image and happier employees by making significant sustainability advances, buying more products from American factories, extending benefits to the same-sex partners of its employees, relaxing its dress code, and even agreeing to raise or lower store temperatures across the country. Walmart also points to its success in providing economic opportunities for its massive and often modestly educated workforce, about 57 percent of whom are women and 40 percent minorities.[105] Walmart's big contribution, however, is its extraordinary efficiency that saves billions for American shoppers.

The Bottom Line   Both companies have investment strengths, with Walmart consistently offering favorable dividends while Costco's share prices have soared in recent years. Walmart shares plunged in 2015, and despite an early 2016 surge, remained down by 25 percent from early 2015.[106] Costco has been expanding both domestically and internationally while Walmart in 2016 announced 269 store closings globally along with about 300 openings.[107] Walmart has felt harsh, market-based pressure to respond to social issues and to better integrate its digital and physical store operations, but its shareholder orientation is intact and remains a strategic contrast to Costco's stakeholder approach.

[For a documentary critique of Walmart, see the trailer for *Wal-Mart: The High Cost of Low Price* at **www.bravenewfilms.org/walmartmovie**].

Share More with Employees?

Chobani (Greek yogurt) founder and CEO Hamdi Ulukaya announced in 2016 that he is giving shares totaling about 10 percent of Chobani to his 2,000 employees. The employees can sell their shares in the $3 billion company if it is sold or goes public, or they can sell the shares back to Chobani. Some employees may become millionaires.

Ulukaya is a firm advocate of social responsibility practices. Refugees constitute one-third of his workforce, and he gives 10 percent of Chobani profits to charity. Employees earn more than the minimum wage, and they receive health, 401 (k), and other benefits.

Questions

1. Which management strategy—Walmart's low-cost efficiency, including modest wages, or Ulukaya's stock grants—do you think is more socially responsible? Explain.
2. Can Walmart, a publicly traded company owned by its shareholders, practice the same kind of generosity to employees that Ulukaya is following in distributing shares that are literally his own? Explain.
3. Ulukaya's gift came in the form of a stock grant, but an estimated 10 percent of American workers are part of an Employee Stock Ownership Plan (ESOP) that operates with special tax advantages and allows employees to own part or all of their organization. What advantages to the company and society might come from ESOPs?

Sources: Yuki Noguchi, "Why Chobani Gave Employees a Financial Stake in [sic] Company's Future," *NPR,* April 28, 2016 [**www.npr.org**]; and Stephanie Strom, "At Chobani, Now It's Not Just the Yogurt That's Rich," *The New York Times,* April 26, 2016 [**www.nytimes.com**].

Questions

1. Retired Costco CEO James Sinegal says high employee pay makes for good business. How can that be so?
2. Professor William Beaver writes, "And what of the stakeholder model? Beyond generating some academic interest, perhaps the best that can be said is that although corporations will not be unmindful of their other stakeholders, the latter's concerns will remain a distant second to those holding the share."[108] Will shareholders or other stakeholders dominate corporate thought in the coming years? Explain.

3. Jack Ma, founder and executive chairman of Chinese online commerce giant Alibaba, said: "Putting the shareholders first is capitalism's biggest mistake."[109] Ma puts customers first and employees second.

   a. Why would Ma value customers and employees more than investors?

   b. Do you agree with him? Explain.

Part Four—Social Responsibility Cases

Case One: Guns

Does the gun industry bear any portion of the blame and responsibility for Adam Lanza's decision to murder 20 children and 6 adult staff members at Sandy Hook Elementary School in Newtown, Connecticut, on December 14, 2012? Lanza, who also killed his mother and himself, carried into the school a Bushmaster XM15 assault rifle (an AR-15 variant) along with two handguns. Assault rifles have been used in a number of mass murders, including those in Orlando, Florida, and San Bernardino, California.

Efforts to pass new federal gun control legislation have been unsuccessful, but many scholars and journalists have suggested that the firearms industry should police itself as a means of reducing gun violence. E. J. Dionne, a *Washington Post* columnist, says: "We must call for corporate responsibility, and enforce it by law if it's not forthcoming."[110]

Reduce the number of guns diverted into criminal use.

Police, lawmakers, and others have pressed firearms firms to voluntarily enforce policies in their distribution chains that would reduce the number of guns diverted into criminal use. Cornell University business ethics lecturer Dana Radcliffe argues that the gun industry must do so:

If the gun industry *could* act to reduce significantly the availability of their weapons to criminals, then it is reasonable to think it *should* do so. The commonsense assumption that gun makers have a special responsibility to help combat gun violence was expressed in an affidavit by Robert Hass, a former Smith & Wesson executive. As he put it, "[T]he nature of the product demands that its distribution be handled in such a way as to minimize illegal and unintended use."[111]

Guns are not intrinsically evil.

Congress and President George W. Bush substantially shielded the gun industry from liability in 2005 through the Protection of Lawful Commerce in Arms Act (PLCAA), which immunizes gun manufacturers and sellers from most civil claims (such as negligence and public nuisance) arising from the unlawful misuse of firearms. The gun industry argues that obeying the law, which does not impose a duty to police distributors and dealers, satisfies corporate responsibilities. Furthermore, they remind us that guns are not intrinsically evil, and those who fire guns must bear primary responsibility for the results.

Some Sandy Hook families filed a wrongful death lawsuit against Remington, the parent company of Bushmaster. A Connecticut judge has dismissed the case at this writing on the grounds that the defendants are shielded from liability by the PLCAA. The plaintiffs are expected to appeal by citing an exception in the law when a seller "negligently entrusts" a weapon to a buyer likely to use it in a crime. Remington argues the exception applies to retailers but not manufacturers.

One of the plaintiff families' arguments is that guns like those used by Lanza are intentionally and negligently marketed as military-style weapons and that ads for those weapons deliberately target young men, some of whom may be inclined to violence. One ad, accompanied by a picture of a black rifle, read: "Consider your man card reissued."[112] Another ad read: "Forces of opposition, bow down. You are single-handedly outnumbered."[113] In light of the PLCAA, experts think the plaintiffs' chances of success are "remote."[114]

Case One Questions

1. *a.* What did Robert Hass mean when he said, "[T]he nature of the product demands that its distribution be handled in such a way as to minimize illegal and unintended use"?
   b. Do you agree with Hass? Explain.
   c. Do gun manufacturers have a social responsibility for their products beyond the demands of the market and the law? Explain.

2. Following the Sandy Hook murders, Cerberus Capital Management, a very large private equity firm, conducted a failed auction to sell one of its companies, Freedom Group (now Remington), which makes the Bushmaster rifle that was used in the school shootings. Apparently, the California State Teachers' Retirement System, which had $750 million invested with Cerberus, encouraged the auction. Cerberus then kept Remington and bought out investors that wanted to sell. Cerberus explained its thinking: "As a firm, we are investors, not statesmen or policy makers. Our role is to make investments on behalf of our clients. It is not our role to take positions or attempt to shape or influence the gun policy debate."[115]
   a. Do those decisions represent a shareholder or stakeholder approach to management? Explain.
   b. As you develop your own financial portfolio, should you decline to hold investments in gun companies? Explain.

3. Jackie Barden, mother of one of the Sandy Hook victims, read the gun advertising language noted above and asked herself: "How can it be, in this day and age, that they are advertising like this? This is so irresponsible."[116] Do you think those gun ads are "irresponsible"? Explain.

Case Two: $70,000 Minimum Wage

Her life suddenly got better.

Single mother "Alyssa" now provides stable, improved living conditions for her son, and she is thinking of buying her own house. Her life suddenly got better when Dan Price, the CEO and controlling shareholder at her privately held employer, Gravity Payments, decided in 2015 that he would provide in stages a $70,000 minimum salary by 2017 for his more than 130 employees. Gravity, founded in 2004 by Dan Price and his brother, Lucas, in their Seattle-area dorm room, operates a "more simple" and "more affordable" electronic credit card processing system for small businesses.

Dan Price previously received attention for his shoulder-length hair and resemblance to Brad Pitt, but now his $70,000 decision has given him near-celebrity status. Price says he was motivated by the income and wealth gap (see Chapter 1), and research showing a relationship between employee income and emotional health. Price himself took a pay cut from $1 million to $70,000, although he says his personal wealth is in the $3 million range.

Following the $70,000 decision, Price was criticized for practicing "socialism." Some customers left Gravity because they felt Dan was simply making a political statement and was making their own employer–employee relations harder. Two of Gravity's best employees quit because they felt they were not being rewarded enough relative to all those who had received raises.

The one-year results, however, have been generally positive for Gravity. Revenue and profits are up significantly, employees say they are better able to focus on their jobs, new clients increased by 55 percent, employee turnover declined by 19 percent, employee retirement account contributions are up 130 percent, and 10 employees expect to be parents, up from 0 to 2 in a typical previous year.[117] Of course, the intense publicity probably explains a portion of those gains, and in early 2016 profits fell slightly and customer attrition increased a bit.[118] [For a brief video of Dan Price, see Christine Wang, "$70K CEO: I Wasn't Ready for the Attention," *CNBC.COM,* April 18, 2016 [**www.cnbc.com**].]

Case Two Questions

1. *a.* Should we expect other profitable companies to follow Gravity's generous minimum wage policy? Explain.
   b. Should CEOs diminish their pay, as Dan Price has done, once they are financially comfortable? Explain.
   c. Is the free market the best measure of a "fair" wage for all? Explain.
2. Dan Price wrote in the *Huffington Post:* "My 40-year goal is to create a world where values-based companies suck up all the oxygen and take over the economy. I don't mind if existing companies convert, but I want to send the ones that don't out of business."[119]
   a. Do you admire Price's goal? Explain.
   b. Do you think that "purpose-driven" companies will eventually dominate the American economy? Explain.
3. Do you find anything morally amiss in an American economy that pays poorly for hard-working, but low-skilled, labor? Explain.

Case Three: Restrooms at Target

> Use the restrooms and fitting rooms of their choice.

Target moved to the center of the national debate over restroom privacy when it announced in 2016 that its transgender employees and customers could use the restrooms and fitting rooms of their choice. Soon thereafter, an online customer boycott petition had gathered about 1.2 million signatures. Target CEO Brian Cornell then said the company would not be reversing its policy. He pointed to the growing availability of family restrooms at Target, and he noted the company's long history of embracing diversity and inclusion. Target was among the first, in the mid-1960s, to employ African American models in advertising.[120]

Case Three Questions

1. Do you think Target is taking the socially responsible course of action in allowing restroom/fitting room choice for its transgender employees and customers? Explain.

2. As a business decision, is Target doing the right thing? Explain.

Internet Exercise

1. Visit the Global Policy Forum website at **https://www.globalpolicy.org/** and examine corporate influence on global governance and on U.N. decision making, in particular at under the Corporate Influence button.

2. Using the website of OpenSecrets.org, Center for Responsive Politics, at **http://www. opensecrets.org/** and its Politicians and Elections button, find the latest campaign finance data for your congressperson or one of your senators. While there, you can take a look at the personal financial condition of those same politicians.

Chapter Questions

1. *a.* In general, do you think employers are more concerned with profits or with delivering quality goods and services? Explain.

   b. Which should they be more concerned about? Explain.

   c. Are you most concerned about receiving a quality education or earning a degree? Explain.

2. Scholar Denis Goulet argued that we will find "no facile resolution to the conflict between the values of a just society and the sharply opposing values of successful corporations."[121]

   a. Do you agree that the values of a just society oppose those of successful corporations? Explain.

   b. Can a solution be found? Explain.

3. Greenwashing is a form of "spin" or propaganda in which an organization, typically a corporation, makes environmental ("green") claims that may or may not be true, but that fail to reveal the organization's overall environmental performance. Do you think, for example, that hotels are engaging in deceptive greenwashing when they encourage guests to reuse sheets and towels during their stay if that hotel otherwise does little to reduce its water and energy consumption? Explain.

4. New York University's Stern Center for Business and Human Rights, founded in 2013, was the first such program in a business school. Why should business schools be studying human rights, a topic normally residing in the government/legal domain?

5. A Pennsylvania Chick-fil-A franchise, on its own in 2011, provided food for a local marriage seminar, "The Art of Marriage: Getting to the Heart of God's Design." Chick-fil-A CEO Dan Cathy in 2012 spoke out against gay marriage. Protests followed and today Cathy says he will focus his attention on building his organization. Chick-fil-A Foundation contributions to anti-gay organizations reportedly have ended, although critics object to continued support for the Fellowship of Christian Athletes. Chick-fil-A, a privately held company, is always closed on Sundays, has

given millions to Christian causes, and includes the glorification of God among its corporate purposes.[122]

   a. In your view, is the operation of a privately held business on Christian principles a moral wrong? Explain.

   b. Would you consider it to be a moral wrong if Chick-fil-A continued to actively oppose gay and lesbian marriage? Explain.

   c. Is Chick-fil-A correct in changing its public approach to gay and lesbian matters? Explain.

6. Worried about Junior misbehaving? Here's an answer:

> Call a board meeting. As crazy as it sounds, some Americans are trying to keep tabs on the kids by bringing business strategies into the traditional family meeting. They're hashing out everything from vacations to disputes over toys with techniques that seem right out of a management textbook: mission statements, rotating chairmanships, motivational seminars, even suggestion boxes. The most corporate of clans hire professional meeting facilitators, just to smooth over family squabbles.[123]

   a. List some of the strengths and weaknesses of the business approach to raising children.

   b. Do you regard the business approach in the home as a promising development or another encroachment of business values into life outside of work? Explain.

7. Sam Wong, speaking during his sophomore year at Iowa State University:

> Materialism, like patience, is a virtue. Ever since my parents bought me my first Transformer, almost everyone has tried to convince me that owning a lot of toys wouldn't make me happy. Oh, how wrong they were. Toys make me very, very happy. That's why today I have more of them than ever. I own every Nintendo. I own two CD-R burners. My drum set cost as much as a semester of school. I drive a Miata. What's more, I'm not ashamed to be a consumer. I consider it part of my American heritage, and I'm proud of it.[124]

   a. Do you share Wong's values? Explain.

   b. Is materialism in America's best interests? Explain.

8. Spartanburg, South Carolina, clothing company Alta Gracia's apparel, much of it college-branded, is produced in the Dominican Republic. Its workers are paid a living wage of more than three times the minimum wage. The factory has been remodeled, including ergonomic chairs for workers and bright lighting. Unionization is permitted, and workers are treated with respect. A big concern is whether customers will continue to pay as much for the Alta Gracia clothing as for premium brands like Nike that are similarly priced. [For the Alta Gracia home page, see **www.altagraciaapparel.com**].

   a. Would you forgo the Nike clothing of similar price and quality to support the Alta Gracia brand? Explain.

   b. Do you, as a student, have a responsibility to protest if your college logo appears on sportswear made in low-wage sweatshops? Explain.

   c. Have you ever inquired about the manufacturing source of a product you were considering, or have you declined, as a matter of principle, to buy certain garments or other items because you believe the manufacturer engages in unfair labor practices? Explain.

9. Should American companies refuse to do business in countries that

    a. Do not practice democracy?

    b. Routinely practice discrimination?

    c. Tolerate or even encourage the abuse of children? Explain.

10. In criticizing General Motors many years ago, Ralph Nader is reported to have said,

    > Someday we'll have a legal system that will criminally indict the president of General Motors for these outrageous crimes. But not as long as this country is populated by people who fritter away their citizenship by watching TV, playing bridge and Mah-Jongg, and just generally being slobs.[125]

    a. Is the citizenry generally unconcerned about unethical corporate conduct? Explain.

    b. To the extent that corporations engage in misdeeds, does the fault really lie with the corporate community or with society at large?

11. The forepart of this chapter discusses the very substantial power exercised by America's giant corporations. One South Korean conglomerate, Samsung, accounts for approximately one-fifth of the nation's economy. Samsung, well known for electronics production, also builds roads, operates hotels, and sells insurance, among other activities. Critics say Samsung destroys smaller competitors, fixes prices, and avoids criminal punishment. "You can even say the Samsung chairman is more powerful than the South Korean President," said Woo Suk-hoon, host of a popular economics podcast. "Korean people have come to think of Samsung as invincible and above the law."[126] Of course, Samsung generates hundreds of thousands of jobs and makes the world's best-selling smartphone, the Galaxy.

    a. If not already the case, do you envision a future in which a relatively small number of corporations dominate world economics? Explain.

    b. Would we be better off if that domination were to transpire? Explain.

12. Noting improved wages and working conditions at Walmart, *Des Moines Register* columnist Rekha Basu asked her readers: "Could it finally be time to go back to Wal-Mart—or at least go there with a clear conscience?"[127] Answer Basu's question.

13. Michael Vick, Kobe Bryant, Tiger Woods, and other high-profile athletes have been entangled in very serious legal problems. Disgraced cyclist Lance Armstrong has admitted to persistent cheating. Many major league baseball players have been linked to steroid use. Should you refuse to watch these tarnished athletes and refuse to buy products they endorse? Explain.

14. Make the argument that corporations are not well-suited to be stakeholder-driven "do-gooders" looking out for the general welfare of society.

15. You are the sole owner of a neighborhood drugstore that stocks various brands of toothpaste. Assume that scientific testing has established that one brand is clearly superior to all others in preventing tooth decay.

    a. Would you remove from the shelves all brands except the one judged best in decay prevention? Explain.

    b. What alternative measures could you take?

    c. Should the toothpaste manufacturers be required to reveal all available data regarding the effectiveness of their products? Explain.

16. The Santa Monica, California, City Council in 2013 approved a "Sustainability Bill of Rights" striving for a clearer environment and asserting that corporations do not have special privileges under the law that supersede community rights. The ordinance also requires a report every two years detailing the city's progress toward its Sustainable City Plan. According to councilmember Kevin McKeown, the ordinance shifts power away from the business community in a way that had not previously happened in the environmental movement. He blamed "unrestrained capitalism" for harming the environment.[128] In your view, should all communities adopt a "Sustainability Bill of Rights" confirming the importance of sustainability and asserting the supremacy of community rights over corporate authority? Explain.

17. Tens of millions of dollars are expended annually for alcohol ads in college newspapers and in other youth-oriented publications such as *National Lampoon* and *Rolling Stone*. The beer industry sponsors many campus athletic contests. Brewers have established promotional relationships with rock bands. Is beer and liquor advertising directed to the youth market unethical? Explain.

18. McDonald's announced in 2015 that it would be paying wages at least $1 per hour higher than the local minimum wage. Critics applauded the progress, but they think fast-food companies must do more to advance their employees toward a living wage. A recent study found that raising fast-food wages to $15 per hour would raise prices by about 4 percent. A $3.99 Big Mac would therefore cost $4.16 and an average fast-food meal priced at $7.00 would rise to $7.31.[129]

    a. Would you be willing to pay 4 percent more for your fast food in exchange for $15 per hour wages for workers? Explain.

    b. In your judgment, *should* the fast-food companies raise wages to a minimum of $15 per hour? Explain.

19. Former General Motors vice president John Z. DeLorean wrote in his book *On a Clear Day You Can See General Motors*:

    > It seemed to me then, and still does now, that the system of American business often produces wrong, immoral, and irresponsible decisions, even though the personal morality of the people running the business is often above reproach. The system has a different morality as a group than the people do as individuals, which permits it willfully to produce ineffective or dangerous products, deal dictatorially and often unfairly with suppliers, pay bribes for business, abrogate the rights of employment, or tamper with the democratic process of government through illegal political contributions.[130]

    a. How can the corporate "group" possess values at odds with those of the individual managers?

    b. Is DeLorean merely offering a convenient rationalization for corporate misdeeds? Explain.

    c. Realistically, can one expect to preserve individual values when employed in a corporate group? Explain.

20. Do you agree or disagree with the following statements? Explain.

    a. "Social responsibility is good business only if it is also good public relations and/or preempts government interference."

b. "The social responsibility debate is the result of the attempt of liberal intellectuals to make a moral issue of business behavior."

c. "'Profit' is really a somewhat ineffective measure of business's social effectiveness."

d. "The social responsibility of business is to 'stick to business.'"[131]

Notes

1. Frank Bruni, "The Sunny Side of Greed," *The New York Times,* July 1, 2015 [**www.nytimes.com**].

2. Walmart, "Company Facts" [**http://corporate.walmart.com/newsroom/company-facts**].

3. Tracey Keys and Thomas Malnight, "Corporate Clout: The Influence of the World's Largest 100 Economic Entities" [**http://docslide.us/documents/corporate-clout-the-worlds-100-largest-economic-entities.html**].

4. Steve Coll, *Private Empire: ExxonMobil and American Power* (New York: Penguin Press, 2012).

5. Ibid.

6. Adam Hochschild, "Well-Oiled Machine," *The New York Times,* June 8, 2012 [**www.nytimes.com**].

7. Dwight Garner, "Oil's Dark Heart Pumps Strong," *The New York Times,* April 26, 2012 [**www.nytimes.com**].

8. Rebecca Rifkin, "Majority of Americans Dissatisfied with Corporate Influence," *Gallup Poll,* January 20, 2016 [**www.gallup.com/poll/188747/majority-americans-dissatisfied-corporate-influence.aspx**].

9. Thomas B. Edsall, "The Obama Coalition vs. Corporate America," *The New York Times,* January 9, 2013 [**http://opinionator.blogs.nytimes.com**].

10. PwC, "The Future of Work: A Journey to 2022." [**www.pwc.com/gx/en/issues/talent/future-of-work/journey-to-2022.html**].

11. Rich Newman, "How Your Boss Will Run Your Life in a Few Years," *Yahoo Finance,* August 19, 2014 [**http://finance.yahoo.com/news/how-your-boss-will-run-your-life-in-a-few-years-165905475.html**].

12. Nicholas Kristof, "The Real Welfare Cheats," *The New York Times,* April 14, 2016 [**www.nytimes.com**].

13. Ibid.

14. Alain Sherter, "1 in 5 Big U.S. Companies Pay No Federal Income Tax," *MoneyWatch,* CBS News, April 13, 2016 [**www.cbsnews.com**].

15. Jacques Leslie, "The True Cost of Hidden Money," *The New York Times,* June 15, 2014 [**www.nytimes.com**].

16. Reuven Avi-Yonah, "Why Corporate Taxes Are Good for You," *Politico,* August 28, 2014 [**www.politico.com**].

17. Chris Isidore, "U.S. Corporate Tax Rate: No. 1 in the World," *CNNMoney,* March 27, 2012 [**http://money.cnn.com/**].

18. Ibid.

19. Eric McWhinnie, "Top Five Companies with the Biggest Income Tax Bills," *The CheatSheet,* May 9, 2015 [**www.cheatsheet.com**].

20. Paul Krugman, "Robber Baron Recessions," *The New York Times,* April 18, 2016 [**www.nytimes.com**].

21. Sarah Butler, "Bangladesh Fashion Factory Safety Work Severely Behind Schedule," *The Guardian,* January 28, 2016 [**www.theguardian.com**].

22. Chris MacDonald, "Bangladesh, Joe Fresh and the Burden of Responsibility," *Canadian Business,* April 26, 2013 [**www.canadianbusiness.com**].

23. Jared Bernstein, "The Era of Free Trade Might Be Over. That's a Good Thing," *The New York Times,* March 14, 2016 [**www.nytimes.com**].

24. *Citizens United v. Federal Election Commission,* 130 S. Ct. 876 (2010).

25. Center for Responsive Politics, "Super Pacs," *OpenSecrets.org,* October 31, 2016 [**www.opensecrets.org**].

26. Jia Lynn Yang and Tom Hamburger, "For U.S. Chamber of Commerce, Election Was a Money-Loser," *The Washington Post,* November 7, 2012 [**www.washingtonpost.com**].

27. Ezra Klein, "Wonkbook: Wisconsin Recall Shows Labor Isn't Coming Back. So What's Next?," *The Washington Post,* June 6, 2012 [**www.washingtonpost.com**].

28. "Political Spending Pays," *The Wall Street Journal,* June 20, 2012 [**http://online.wsj.com**].

29. Ibid.

30. Clea Benson and Roxana Tiron, "Countrywide Used a Special VIP Loan Program to Influence Lawmakers, Report Says," *The Washington Post,* July 5, 2012 [**www.washingtonpost.com**].

31. Center for Responsive Politics, "Lobbying Database," *OpenSecrets.org* [**www.opensecrets.org/lobby/index.php**].

32. Center for Responsive Politics, "Top Spenders 2015," *OpenSecrets.org* [**www.opensecrets.org/lobby/top.php?**].

33. Ailsa Chang, "When Lobbyists Literally Write the Bill," *NPR,* November 11, 2013 [**www.npr.org**].

34. Dana Milbank, "Big Business Is Back," *The Washington Post,* January 12, 2011 [**www.washingtonpost.com**].

35. Thomas B. Edsall, "Kill Bill," *The New York Times,* May 22, 2013 [**http://opinionator.blogs.nytimes.com**].

36. John Cassidy, "Is America an Oligarchy?" *New Yorker,* April 18, 2014 [**www.newyorker.com**].

37. Ibid.

38. Ibid.

39. Steven Pearlstein, "How Big Business Lost Washington," *The Washington Post,* September 2, 2016 [**www.washingtonpost.com**].

40. Natasha Singer, "On Campus, It's One Big Commercial," *The New York Times,* September 10, 2011 [**www.nytimes.com**].

41. Ibid.

42. Hunter Rawlings, "Stop Treating College Like a Commodity," *The Des Moines Register,* June 13, 2015 [**www.desmoinesregister.com**].

43. Melissa Korn, "Wealth or Waste? Rethinking the Value of a Business Major," *WSJ.com,* April 5, 2012 [**http://online.wsj.com**].

44. Mara Einstein, *Brands of Faith* (New York: Routledge, 2008).

45. David Platt, *Radical: Taking Back Your Faith from the American Dream* (Colorado Springs: Multnomah Books, 2010).

46. David Brooks, "The Gospel of Wealth," *The New York Times,* September 6, 2010 [**www.nytimes.com**].

47. Patricia Cohen, "An Art World Gathering, Divided by Money," *The New York Times,* December 7, 2012 [**www.nytimes.com**].

48. Marshall Herskovitz, "Are the Corporate Suits Ruining TV?" *latimes.com,* November 7, 2007 [**www.latimes.com/news/opinion/la-oe-herskovitz7nov07,0,5402981.story?coll=la-tot-opinion&track=ntothtml**].

49. Ibid.

50. Jacques Steinberg, "Radio Days," *The New York Times,* April 13, 2008 [**www.nytimes.com**].

51. L. R., "Same Old Song," *The Economist,* July 26, 2012 [**www.economist.com**].

52. Ibid.

53. Jon Pareles, "Big Money Upends a Festival," *The New York Times,* March 16, 2014 [**www.nytimes.com**].

54. Frank Bruni, "Capitalism's Suffocating Music," *The New York Times,* October 21, 2014 [**www.nytimes.com**].

55. Associated Press, "Snyder: 'College Athletics Has Sold Out,'" *Waterloo/Cedar Falls Courier,* August 7, 2014, p. B3.

56. Eric Crawford, "It's Time for Leagues to Pay Up," *Louisville Courier-Journal.com,* October 27, 2011 [**www.courier-journal.com**].

57. Ibid.

58. Joe Drape, "Alabama Is Rolling in Cash, with Tide Lifting All Boats," *The New York Times,* November 5, 2015 [**www.nytimes.com**].

59. Marc Tracy, "Under Armour Seeks to Do for Maryland What Nike Did for Oregon," *The New York Times,* August 26, 2015 [**www.nytimes.com**].

60. Ibid.

61. "Little League Baseball CEO Will Consider Compensating Players," *SI Wire,* August 23, 2014 [**www.si.com**].

62. See Mark Mitchell and Robert Montgomery, "Beer and Ball on Campus? The Issue of In-Stadium Alcohol Sales," *Sport Journal* (2015), p. 1; and Marc Tracy, "Beer Here! Beer Here?," *The New York Times,* October 9, 2015 [**www.nytimes.com**].

63. Tracy, "Beer Here! Beer Here?"

64. Charles Reich, *The Greening of America* (New York: Bantam Books, 1970), pp. 7–8.

65. Allyssa Birth, "Feeling of Alienation among Americans Reaches Highest Point on Record," *The Harris Poll,* January 20, 2015 [**www.theharrispoll.com/politics/Feeling_of_Alienation_Among_Americans_Reaches_Highest_Point_On_Record.html#**].

66. Ben Stein, "A City on a Hill, or a Looting Opportunity," *The New York Times,* July 9, 2006 [**www.nytimes.com**].

67. Joe Davidson, "Park Service and Corporate Advertising, a Dangerous Mix," *The Washington Post,* May 9, 2016 [**www.washingtonpost.com**].

68. Joseph Pickett, "4 Examples of How Corporate America Is Crushing Social Media," *Business 2 Community,* February 8, 2013 [**www.business2community.com**].

69. Daniel Seligman, "Helping the Shareholder Helps the Society," *The Wall Street Journal,* June 21, 1996, p. A12.

70. "The Deloitte Millennial Survey 2016" [**www2.deloitte.com/global/en/pages/about-deloitte/articles/millennialsurvey.html**].

71. Ibid.

72. Thomas Heath, "Capital Buzz: Banker Switches Jobs in Order to Help Others Do Good," *The Washington Post,* June 23, 2013 [**www.washingtonpost.com**].

73. Keith Davis and Robert L. Blomstrom, *Business and Society: Environment and Responsibility,* 3rd ed. (New York: McGraw-Hill, 1975), p. 6.

74. Milton Friedman, *Capitalism and Freedom* (Chicago: University of Chicago Press, 1962), p. 133.

75. Herbert Stein, "Corporate America, Mind Your Own Business," *The Wall Street Journal,* July 15, 1996, p. A10.

76. Robin Givhan, "Can Cheap Clothing Generate Fair Wages? H&M Believes It Can," *The Washington Post,* November 25, 2014 [**www.washingtonpost.com**].

77. Steven A. Rochlin, "The New Corporate Citizenship," *BusinessWeek,* December 13, 2003, p. 66.

78. Yves Leclerc and David South, "Study: Prioritizing Supply Chain Sustainability, but the Real Work Remains Ahead," *Stakeholder Trends and Insights,* February 5, 2016 [**www. sustainablebrands.com**].

79. Muktar Kent, "Toward a Sustainable Future," *Raytheon Lectureship in Business Ethics of Bentley University,* April 5, 2012 [**www.bentley.edu/cbe**].

80. Archie Carroll and others have pointed to some descriptive and theoretical limitations associated with Carroll's social responsibility pyramid; and Carroll has proposed a three-domain approach of economic, legal, and ethical responsibilities arrayed in a Venn framework. The newer model appears to satisfy some of the concerns of Carroll and others about Carroll's pyramid, but for both teaching and research purposes, the pyramid remains a useful construct. For Carroll's newer construct, see Mark S. Schwartz and Archie B. Carroll, "Corporate Social Responsibility: A Three Domain Approach," *Business Ethics Quarterly* 13, no. 4 (October 2003), p. 503. For an example of research employing the Carroll pyramid and a discussion of some of the strengths and weaknesses of the pyramid, see Dane K. Peterson, "The Relationship between Perceptions of Corporate Citizenship and Organizational Commitment," *Business & Society* 43, no. 3 (September 2004), p. 296.

81. Toyota president Akio Toyoda.

82. Max Miceli, "Google Tops Reputation Rankings for Corporate Responsibility," *U.S. News & World Report,* September 17, 2015 [**www.usnews.com**].

83. "A Better World, Faster." [**www.google.org**].

84. "A Better Web. Better for the Environment." [**www.google.com/green/**].

85. Katie Lobosco, "4,000 Starbucks Workers Are Going to College for Free," *CNNMoney,* October 14, 2015 [**http://money.cnn.com**].

86. Editorial Board, "Taking Tobacco Off the Shelves," *The New York Times,* February 6, 2014 [**www.nytimes.com**].

87. Mark Bittman, "OMG: McDonald's Does the Right Thing," *The New York Times Opinionator,* February 13, 2012 [**http://opinionator.blogs.nytimes.com**].

88. Sanjay Bhatt, "Bullitt Center Tops Its Green Goals, Is Making Energy to Spare," *Seattle Times,* March 27, 2015 [**www.seattletimes.com**].

89. Aaron Task, "Mass Layoffs by Profitable Firms a 'Horrible Act,' Diller Says," *Yahoo!* Finance, December 10, 2008 [**http://finance.yahoo.com**].

90. Linda Basch, "More Women in Finance, a More Sustainable Economy," *The Christian Science Monitor,* June 24, 2009 [**www.csmonitor.com/2009/0624/p09s02-coop.html**].

91. Joshua Margolis, Hillary Elfenbein, and James Walsh, "Does It Pay to Be Good . . . and Does It Matter? A Meta-Analysis of the Relationship between Corporate Social and Financial Performance," March 2009. Available at SSRN: [**http://ssrn.com/abstract=1866371**].

92. Ibid.

93. Jae Yang and Alejandro Gonzalez, "Profit vs. Social Impact," *The Des Moines Register,* May 6, 2015, p. 4B.

94. Michael E. Porter and Mark R.Kramer, "Creating Shared Value," *Harvard Business Review* 89, nos. 1–2 (January-February 2011), p. 62.

95. Chris MacDonald, "How Can Business 'Give Back' to Society?" *The Business Ethics Blog,* January 31, 2012 [**https://businessethicsblog.com/2012/01/31/how-can-business-give-back-to-society/**].

96. V. Kasturi Rangan, Lisa Chase, and Sohel Karim, "The Truth about CSR," *Harvard Business Review* 93, no. 1–2 (January–February 2015), p. 40.

97. John Bussey, "CEO Council (A Special Report)—Restoring Confidence in Business: Not Just about Shareholders," *The Wall Street Journal,* November 22, 2010, p. R3.

98. Cedric Rose, "Q&A: A. G. Lafley," *Cincinnati Magazine,* May 1, 2013 [**www.cincinnatimagazine.com**].

99. Social Accountability Accreditation Services, "SA8000 Certified Organisations," December 2015 [**www.saasaccreditation.org/certfacilitieslist**].

100. Mark Magnier, "Anguish Lingers in Bhopal, 25 Years after Chemical Disaster," *latimes.com,* December 3, 2009 [**www.latimes.com/news/nation-and-world/la-fg-india-bhopal3-2009dec03,0,3728767.story**].

101. Susan Warren, "Chemical Companies Keep Lessons of Bhopal Spill Fresh," *The Wall Street Journal,* February 13, 2001, p. B4.

102. Bourree Lam, "What Costco's New Wages Say about the Health of the American Economy," *The Atlantic,* March 5, 2016 [**www.theatlantic.com**].

103. Brad Stone, "Costco CEO Craig Jelinek Leads the Cheapest, Happiest Company in the World," *Bloomberg Businessweek,* June 6, 2013 [**www.businessweek.com**].

104. Timothy Egan, "The Corporate Daddy," *The New York Times,* June 19, 2014 [**www.nytimes.com**].

105. Walmart, "2015 Diversity and Inclusion" [**https://cdn.corporate.walmart.com**].

106. Trey Thoelcke, "Why Wal-Mart Is Still among the Best 2016 Dow Stocks Despite Earnings Miss," *24/7 Wall St.,* February 18, 2016 [**http://247wallst.com**].

107. David Goldman, "Walmart Will Close 269 Stores This Year, Affecting 16,000 Workers," *CNNMoney,* January 15, 2016 [**http://money.cnn.com**].

108. William Beaver, "Is the Stakeholder Model Dead?" *Business Horizons* 42, no. 2 (March–April 1999), p. 8.

109. William Mellor, Lulu Yilun Chen, and Zijing Wu, "Alibaba's Jack Ma Has: $30 Billion, an Odd Relationship with Investors and No Coding Skills," *Bloomberg,* November 9, 2014 [**www.bloomberg.com**].

110. E. J. Dionne, "It's Time to Hold America's Gunmakers Accountable," *The Washington Post,* October 7, 2015 [**www.washingtonpost.com**].

111. Dana Radcliffe, "Gun Makers See No Problem Selling for Self-Defense and Allowing Sales to Criminals," *Huff Post Politics,* June 28, 2013 [**www.huffingtonpost.com**].

112. Lois Beckett, "Families of Sandy Hook Victims Go After 'Untouchable' Gun Manufacturers," *The Guardian,* April 20, 2016 [**www.theguardian.com**].

113. George Zornick, "Gunmaker in the Sandy Hook Case: Sorry, We're Immune," *The Nation,* February 23, 2016 [**www.thenation.com**].

114. Beckett, "Families of Sandy Hook Victims."

115. Andrew Ross Sorkin, "Guns in your 401(k)? The Push to Divest Grows," *The New York Times,* December 7, 2015 [**www.nytimes.com**].

116. Beckett, "Families of Sandy Hook Victims."

117. Paul Davidson, "Does a $70,000 Minimum Wage Work?" *USA TODAY,* May 26, 2016 [**www. usatoday.com**].

118. Ibid.

119. Dan Price, "Purpose—Not Profit—Driven Companies Will Take Over the Economy," *Huffington Post,* November 2, 2015 [**www.huffingtonpost.com**].

120. Travis Andrews, "Target CEO Responds to Nationwide Boycott of the Store over Transgender Bathroom Policy," *The Washington Post,* May 13, 2016 [**www.washingtonpost.com**].

121. Robert Kaiser, "Seminar Explores Judeo-Christian Ethics and Modern Corporations," *Toledo Blade,* April 25, 1980, p. 14.

122. Kim Severson, "A Chicken Chain's Corporate Ethos Is Questioned by Gay Rights Advocates," *The New York Times,* January 29, 2011 [**www.nytimes.com**].

123. Nancy Jeffrey, "Kids, Come to Order," *The Wall Street Journal,* August 10, 2001, p. W1.

124. Sam Wong, "Materialism Makes Me Feel Happy, Not Guilty," *The Des Moines Register,* September 10, 2000, p. 11A.

125. Charles McCarry, *Citizen Nader* (New York: Saturday Review Press, 1972), p. 301.

126. Chico Harlan, "In South Korea, the Republic of Samsung," *The Washington Post,* December 9, 2012 [**http://articles.washingtonpost.com**].

127. Rekha Basu, "Is It Acceptable to Do Business with Wal-Mart?" *Waterloo/Cedar Falls Courier,* June 12, 2015, p. A6.

128. Ashley Archibald, "City Council Passes Environmental Bill of Rights," *Santa Monica Daily Press,* March 14, 2013 [**http://smdp.com**].

129. Sally French, "Raising Fast-Food Hourly Wages to $15 Would Raise Prices by 4%, Study Finds," *MarketWatch,* July 28, 2015 [**www.marketwatch.com**].

130. John Z. DeLorean with J. Patrick Wright, "Bottom-Line Fever at General Motors" (excerpted from *On a Clear Day You Can See General Motors), The Washington Monthly,* January 1980, pp. 26–27.

131. Steven N. Brenner and Earl A. Molander, "Is the Ethics of Business Changing?" *Harvard Business Review* 55, no. 1 (January–February 1977), p. 68.

Introduction to Law

CHAPTER FOUR

The American Legal System

After completing this chapter, students will be able to fulfill the following learning objectives:

4-1. Describe the importance of law to private enterprise.

4-2. Compare and contrast the objectives of law in society.

4-3. Differentiate constitutional law, case law, and statutory law.

4-4. Differentiate the elements of a case brief.

4-5. Distinguish between substantive and procedural law

4-6. Compare and contrast civil and criminal law.

4-7. Describe the elements of the basic court system structure.

4-8. Explain the purposes of subject matter and personal jurisdiction as requirements for a court's power to hear a dispute.

4-9. Describe the typical steps in the civil trial process.

4-10. Distinguish trials and appeals.

4-11. Identify dispute resolution alternatives to trials.

Introduction

Presumably we can agree that some business behavior is bad for society. This text examines what should be done to change that behavior. In the United States, four basic options exist: Let the market "regulate" the behavior; leave the choice to the individual decision maker's own ethical dictates; pass a law; or rely on some combination of the market, ethics, and law. Market regulation was discussed in Chapter 1. Self-regulation through ethics was explored in Chapters 2 and 3. This chapter begins the discussion of the legal regulation of business with a brief outline of the American legal system. We will also look at alternative conflict resolution processes such as negotiation, mediation, and arbitration that do not

LO 4-1
Describe the importance of law to private enterprise.

resort to the court system. We begin by reminding ourselves of the indispensable role of law in supporting business practice.

Law and the Market   Whatever we may think about lawyers, judges, and America's dispute resolution methods, the crucial role of a reliable legal system in fostering and maintaining capitalism is indisputable. The following law review excerpt explains.

READING

The Importance of Law to the Private Enterprise System

Deb Ballam

Nobel economist Frederich von Hayek describes the theoretical importance of law to private enterprise. According to Hayek, law that secures property rights in modern society is a prerequisite to private enterprise. Without the order of law enforcing private property ownership and facilitating the transfer of property rights, business enterprise in a complex, heterogeneous culture is simply infeasible.

The importance of law to the conduct of private enterprise is evident in economic developments in . . . the Republic of China. In moving from state-controlled to private enterprise, [China] faced substantial difficulties arising from the lack of a legal system that would secure property ownership and the contractual transfer of property rights.

. . . China's economy has grown steadily in recent years. Minxin Pei, a political scientist at Princeton University, explains law's contribution to that growth: "Legal reform has become one of the most important institutional changes in China since the late 1970s. . . . Within China, the changing legal institutions have begun to play an increasingly important role in governing economic activities, resolving civil disputes, enforcing law and order, and setting the boundaries between the power of the state and the autonomy of society. . . ."

Of course, the importance of law to private enterprise goes far beyond its initial support as an institutional framework guaranteeing ownership rights. As the market system grows more complex both nationally and internationally, the legal recognition of promise keeping becomes increasingly significant in facilitating business. A condition for emerging economies entering international trade is learning how to keep promises to strangers, and whether enforced through litigation or arbitration, promise keeping in business requires the ordering presence of contract law.

In a democracy, law is important to business for another reason quite separate from its function in establishing ownership rights and facilitating promise keeping necessary to their transfer: It provides the formal expression of democratic social will. That expression implicates private enterprise in a plethora of ways, including regulation of the environment, employment laws, securities regulation, consumer protection statutes, and product liability. As contemporary society becomes increasingly diverse, law grows, not diminishes, in its importance to private enterprise; and in spite of valid concerns about the impact of law on efficiency, future business managers will need to know more, not less, about how law affects business operations. No evidence suggests any other conclusion.

Source: Deb Ballam, quoting from "The Importance of Law to the Private Enterprise System," *The American Legal Studies in Business Task Force Report* by O. Lee Reed. *American Business Law Journal* 36, no. 1 (Fall 1998), p. ix. Reprinted by permission.

Question

As reported by *The Wall Street Journal*, a recent trend among the major oil companies is to shift investment of resources to economically developed countries. This strategy is reflected in Royal Dutch Shell's 2012 Annual Report, which noted Shell's investments in countries with the "necessary infrastructure," such as, among others, Australia, Canada, the United Kingdom, Norway, Germany, Denmark, and the United States. What role might the law play in creating a favorable environment for oil companies' investments?

Sources: Guy Chazan, "Big Oil Heads Back Home," *The Wall Street Journal*, December 5, 2011, p. R1; and Royal Dutch Shell, *2012 Annual Report: Business Overview* [**http://reports.shell.com/annual-report/2012/businessreview/ourbusinesses/businessoverview.php**].

Objectives of the Law

LO 4-2
Compare and contrast the objectives of law in society.

Americans differ dramatically in their views of the role the law should play in contemporary life. For some, the courts and the police primarily act as obstructions to personal freedom and to a fully efficient marketplace. Others seek much more law to ensure that everyone who is in need is cared for and everyone is sheltered from wrongdoers. Although we may argue about the law's precise path in our lives, most of us can agree on some foundational expectations for a fair, efficient legal system. Certainly we expect the law to *maintain order* in our diverse, rapidly changing society. Of course, we rely on law to peacefully, fairly, and intelligently *resolve conflict*. Perhaps less obvious, but no less important, the law serves to *preserve dominant values*. Americans differ about core values, but we have reached a workable accord about our most fundamental beliefs. Some of those, such as freedom of speech, press, and religion, are guaranteed by our Bill of Rights, thus setting a steady foundation for an enduring nation. We can see that the law is a vital force in *guaranteeing freedom*. (But freedom can be confusing: Are you free to smoke wherever you wish, or do I have a right to smoke-free air?)

Justice

Broadly, we count on the law to *achieve and preserve justice.* The pursuit of justice often relies on honorable, efficient government. The World Justice Project's 2013 "Rule of Law Index" ranks governmental quality by such measures as criminal and civil justice, order and security, open government, and limited corruption. Among the 97 countries studied, Sweden ranked particularly well. In most categories, the United States ranked in the bottom half of the 29 high-income nations studied.[1] Perhaps the study is correct in the sense that America still has abundant room for improvement. Nonetheless, Americans can properly be proud of a long struggle to build a more just society for all. Efforts, for example, to curb discrimination; guarantee due process; reduce violence; protect those in need; maintain order and security; build fair, efficient regulatory systems; and respect the rights of all are central practices in an extraordinarily complex and rapidly evolving American culture.

> All legal studies must involve the search for justice.

As you read this chapter, ask yourself repeatedly, "Does this rule (this procedure, this case) contribute to the search for justice?" In the end, all legal studies must involve the search for justice. [For a daily update of legal news, see **www.law.com**].

Question

When a 16-year-old girl was benched on a club volleyball team, denying her a chance to impress varsity coaches and possibly college recruiters, she and her family sued. A father in the Philadelphia suburbs sued his son's high school track coach for $40 million after his son was cut from the team, claiming that his son's chances of obtaining a college scholarship were badly hurt. Such lawsuits are increasing as families turn to the courts to resolve disputes arising from youth sports.

As a matter of justice, should club leagues, school sports programs, and coaches be subjected to such lawsuits? Explain. See Justin Jouvenal, "Teen Volleyball Player Takes Her Dispute to Another Kind of Court," *The Washington Post,* March 31, 2015 [**www.washingtonpost.com/local/crime/teen-volleyball-player-takes-her-dispute-to-another-kind-of-court/2015/03/31/e72fb174-c8f0-11e4-b2a1-bed1aaea2816_story.html?utm_term=.e9edf24ee16f**].

Cyberbullying

Twenty-year-old Rutgers University student Dharun Ravi secretly activated the webcam in his dorm room so that he and a friend could watch his roommate, 18-year-old Tyler Clementi, engage in a romantic encounter with another male. Ravi used texts and Twitter to encourage friends to watch a second planned video that did not occur. Clementi subsequently committed suicide. In March 2012, Ravi was convicted of invasion of privacy and bias intimidation, among other crimes, and sentenced to 30 days in jail, 300 hours of community service, and a fine of $10,000 to be paid to hate crime victims.

The Tyler Clementi Higher Education Anti-Harassment Act, a bill introduced in Congress in 2015, would have required colleges and universities receiving federal student aid funding to have and distribute a policy prohibiting harassment. Prohibited harassment included cyberbullying of enrolled students by other students, faculty, and staff based on, among other things, actual or perceived sexual orientation.

Questions

1. Do you think the Tyler Clementi Higher Education Anti-Harassment Act should have been enacted? Explain.

2. Cosponsors of the bill, New Jersey senator Frank Lautenberg and New Jersey representative Rush D. Holt, pointed to the actions and subsequent firing in 2013 of Mike Rice, head basketball coach at Rutgers University, who was videotaped making slurs regarding sexual orientation to players and engaging in other harassing conduct, as proof of the need for such antibullying legislation. Do you agree? Explain.

3. Although he was not charged with causing Clementi's death, Ravi was facing a possible 10 years in state prison. Do you think Ravi's actual sentence was fair or too light? Explain.

Sources: Mark Trumbull, "Why Dharun Ravi Got 30 Days in Jail in Rutgers Webcam Spying Case," *The Christian Science Monitor*, May 21, 2012 [**http://www.christiansciencemonitor.com**]; Niels Lesniewski and Emily Bazelon, "Make the Punishment Fit the Cyber-Crime," *The New York Times*, March 19, 2012 [**www.nytimes.com**]; "Rutgers Firing Prompts New Look at Anti-Bullying Bill," *Rollcall*, April 3, 2013 [**www.rollcall.com**]; and H.R.482, Tyler Clementi Higher Education Anti-Harassment Act of 2015, 114th Congress (2015–2016) [**http://beta.congress.gov/bill/113th-congress/house-bill/482**].

Primary Sources of Law

LO 4-3
Differentiate constitutional law, case law, and statutory law.

U.S. law is a vast, constantly growing, and mutating body of rules and reason. That law is derived from four primary sources: constitutions, statutes, regulations, and cases (called the *common law* or judge-made law).

Constitutions

These are the supreme expressions of law at both the federal and state levels of government. All other law is subordinate to federal constitutional law. Among other things, constitutions prescribe the general structure of governments and provide protection for individual rights. Chapters 5 and 8 give extensive attention to the U.S. Constitution and the Bill of Rights.

Statutes

These are laws that are adopted by legislative bodies, particularly Congress and the state legislatures. City councils enact statutes that usually are called ***ordinances***. Legislators and the statutes they enact shape the policy direction of U.S. law. Of course, legislators are not free of constraints. Federal legislation cannot conflict with the U.S. Constitution, and state legislation cannot violate either federal law or the constitutions of that state and the nation.

Regulations

Administrative agencies include such bodies as the Federal Trade Commission and the Securities and Exchange Commission at the federal level, and a Public Service Commission (to regulate utilities) and a Human Rights Commission (to address discrimination problems) at the state level. These agencies have the specialized expertise to carry out much of the day-to-day business of government. Among other duties, they produce and oversee regulations that add the details needed to implement the broader mandates provided by federal and state statutes. (For more detail, see Chapter 8.)

Common Law (Also Called Case Law or Judge-Made Law)

Our case law has its roots in the early English king's courts, where rules of law gradually developed out of a series of individual dispute resolutions. That body of law, the common law, was imported to America, where it is has grown and evolved as the courts address the constantly changing legal requirements of our complex society.

The development of English common law and American judicial decisions into a just, ordered package is attributable in large measure to reliance on the doctrine of ***stare decisis*** (let the decision stand). That is, judges endeavor to follow the precedents established by previous decisions. Following precedent, however, is not mandatory. As societal beliefs and practices change, judges are called on not only to interpret precedent, but to create new law as cases reflecting these changes are brought. For example, a U.S. Supreme Court decision approving racially separate but equal education was eventually overruled by a Supreme Court decision mandating integrated schools. Nonetheless, the principle of *stare decisis* is generally adhered to because of its beneficial effect. It offers the wisdom of the past and enhances efficiency by eliminating the need for resolving every case as though it were the first of its kind. *Stare decisis* affords stability and predictability to the law.

The Case Law: Locating and Analyzing

To prepare for the *Nichols* case, which follows, a bit of practical guidance should be useful. The study of law is founded largely on the analysis of judicial opinions. Except for the federal level and a few states, trial court decisions are filed locally for public inspection rather than being published. Appellate (appeals court) opinions, on the other hand, are generally published in volumes called *reports*. State court opinions are found in the reports of that state, and in a regional reporter series published by West Publishing Company that divides the United States into units, such as South Eastern (S.E.) and Pacific (P.).

Within the appropriate reporter, the cases are cited by case name, volume, reporter name, and page number. For example, *Nichols v. Niesen,* 746 N.W.2d 220 (Wis. 2008) means that the opinion will be found in volume 746 of the *North Western Reporter,*

2nd series, at page 220, and that the decision was reached in 2008 by the Wisconsin Supreme Court. Federal court decisions are found in several reporters, including the *Federal Reporter* and the *U.S. Supreme Court Reports.* In practice, of course, those cases can most readily be found via a standard search engine or in online databases such as LexisNexis and Westlaw. [For broad databases of law topics, see **http://www.findlaw.com**, **http://www. yahoo.com/government/law**, or **www.justia.com**].

Briefing the Case

LO 4-4

Differentiate the elements of a case brief.

Most students find the preparation of *case briefs* (outlines or digests) to be helpful in mastering the law. A brief should evolve into the form that best suits the individual student's needs. The following approach should be a useful starting point:

1. Parties   Identify the plaintiff and the defendant at the trial level. At the appeals level, identify the appellant (the party bringing the appeal; Nichols, in this instance) and the appellee (the other party on appeal; Niesen, in this instance).

2. Facts   Summarize only those facts critical to the outcome of the case.

3. Procedure   How did the case reach this court? Who won in the lower court(s)?

4. Issue   Note the central question or questions on which the case turns.

5. Holding   How did the court resolve the issue(s)? Who won?

6. Reasoning   Explain the logic that supported the court's decision.

LEGAL BRIEFCASE

Nichols v. Niesen
746 N.W.2d 220 (Wis. 2008)

Justice N. Patrick Crooks

The court of appeals allowed the claim of Shannon, Lee, Brooke, and Brittney Nichols (the Nichols) to proceed against the Niesens for common-law negligence. The Nichols claimed that the Niesens were social hosts who did not provide any alcoholic beverages to underage guests, but allegedly were aware that minors were on their property consuming alcoholic beverages. After leaving the Niesens' premises, one of these guests allegedly caused injuries while driving intoxicated. The circuit court had granted the Niesens' . . . motion to dismiss the Nichols' complaint, after concluding that the complaint failed to state a claim in common-law negligence. The primary issue upon review is whether a claim for common-law negligence should be permitted against social hosts under these circumstances.

I

On June 5, 2004, the Nichols were in a motor vehicle on County Trunk Highway J in Columbia County, Wisconsin, when that vehicle was struck by another motor vehicle, driven by Beth Carr (Carr), which had crossed the highway's center line. The Nichols alleged that the accident was caused by Carr's "failure to properly manage

and control the vehicle she was operating, due in part to the voluntary ingestion by her of intoxicating beverages." As a result of the accident, Shannon Nichols "suffered very severe personal injuries," and Brittney, Brooke, and Lee Nichols "suffered injuries requiring medical care and treatment."

On the night of June 4, 2004, and into the early morning of June 5, 2004, the Nichols alleged that "a large gathering of underage high school students" congregated and consumed alcohol at the premises controlled by the Niesens. . . . [T]he Nichols alleged that "the Niesens were aware that the minors on their property were consuming alcohol." The Nichols did not allege that the Niesens knew, in advance, that the students would be consuming alcohol. The Nichols contended that the Niesens "had a duty to supervise and monitor the activities on their property" and that they were negligent because they failed to do so.

The Nichols contended that the consumption of alcohol by Carr was a substantial factor in causing the accident. Defendant Michael Shumate (Shumate), "or one or more adult residents of his household[,]" not the Niesens, was alleged to have provided the alcohol that was consumed by Carr on the Niesens' property. There was no allegation that Shumate was at the Niesens' property.

II [OMITTED—ED.]

III

On review, the Nichols claim that the Niesens' conduct was negligent, and that it was reasonably foreseeable that someone drinking on the Niesens' property would cause an accident. . . .

[T]he Niesens argue that knowledge of someone drinking on one's premises does not create a foreseeable risk of harm to others, and that public policy issues preclude liability in cases such as this one. The Niesens argue that the court of appeals created a new basis of liability for social hosts in Wisconsin. They argue that social hosts have never been held liable in Wisconsin solely because they were aware that an underage person had been consuming alcohol. To allow the court of appeals' decision to stand would mean that liability would apply to any social hosts who knew of underage drinking, regardless of where the alcohol was possessed or consumed, which would lead to liability with no sensible stopping point. The Niesens argue that they had limited involvement with the party outside of their alleged knowledge of underage drinking at the party, and, as a result, they should not be held liable. To hold social hosts liable in such circumstances would place an unreasonable burden on social hosts. The Niesens argue that a reasonable person would not foresee that knowledge of some unidentified underage person drinking would create an unreasonable risk to others. Rather, a reasonable person would conclude that any such risk was created by the provider of the alcohol and the underage drinker. The Niesens contend that, because they played no role in procuring or furnishing the alcohol, a negligence analysis should not be applied to their actions in this matter. Finally, the Niesens argue that the legislature, not the judiciary, is the branch of Wisconsin's government that should impose any new liability on social hosts who do not provide alcoholic beverages to underage guests.

Whether the Nichols' complaint states a claim for common-law negligence depends on whether they sufficiently pled facts, which if proven true, would establish all four required elements of an actionable negligence claim. First, the plaintiff must establish "the existence of a duty of care on the part of the defendant. . . ." Second, the plaintiff must establish that the defendant breached that duty of care. Third, the plaintiff must establish "a causal connection between the defendant's breach of the duty of care and the plaintiff's injury. . . ." Fourth, the plaintiff must establish that he or she suffered an actual loss or damage that resulted from the breach.

* * * * *

The court of appeals framed the issue for the first element of the test for common-law negligence as "whether the Niesens owed a duty to refrain from knowingly permitting minors to consume alcohol on their property, thus enabling them, including Carr, to drive away from their property while intoxicated." As a result, the court held that the first factor had been met because "it was reasonably foreseeable that permitting underage high school students to illegally drink alcohol on the Niesens' property would result in harm to some person or something," and because the Nichols had adequately "alleged the Niesens had a duty to refrain from knowingly permitting underage high school students from engaging in illegal alcohol consumption on their property."

[T]he court of appeals also determined that the Nichols had appropriately alleged the second factor of an actionable common-law negligence claim, which is that the Niesens had breached a duty of care that they owed to the Nichols. The court stated, "Because the Nichols' complaint alleges the Niesens knowingly permitted and failed to supervise underage alcohol consumption on their property, it alleges 'a breach of their duty to exercise ordinary care.'" . . .

The court also held that the Nichols had established the third factor of a common-law negligence claim by showing "a causal connection between the defendant's breach of the duty of care and the plaintiff's injury. . . ." That court stated, "The Nichols have sufficiently alleged that the Niesens' permitting underage alcohol consumption on their property was a substantial factor in causing the automobile accident that resulted in their injuries."

The court of appeals further held that the Nichols had appropriately alleged the fourth factor of a common-law negligence claim, that they had suffered an actual loss or damage that resulted from the Niesens' breach. . . .

For purposes of our public policy analysis, we will assume, without deciding, that the court of appeals was correct in holding that the Nichols had stated a common-law negligence claim. [E]ven if a plaintiff adequately establishes all four elements of a common-law negligence claim, Wisconsin courts have "reserved the right to deny the existence of a negligence claim based on public policy reasons. . . ." As a result, "even if all the elements for a claim of negligence are proved, or liability for negligent conduct is assumed by the court, the court nonetheless may preclude liability based on public policy factors." This is so because "negligence and liability are distinct concepts."

In turning to our analysis of the public policy factors that bear on the Nichols' common-law negligence claim against the Niesens, it is instructive to note what is not alleged by the Nichols. The Nichols do not allege that the Niesens provided alcohol to Carr, that the Niesens were aware that Carr (specifically) was consuming alcoholic beverages, that the Niesens knew or should have known that Carr was intoxicated, or that the Niesens knew or should have known that Carr was not able to drive her motor vehicle safely at the time of the accident. We note that there also is no allegation by the Nichols that the Niesens aided, agreed to assist, or attempted to aid Carr or any other person in the procurement or consumption of alcohol on premises under their control. There also are no allegations that the Niesens knew in advance that any underage individuals would be drinking.

* * * * *

If one or more of the public policy "factors so dictates, the court may refuse to impose liability in a case."

The first public policy factor upon which recovery against a negligent tortfeasor may be denied is when "the injury is too remote from the negligence. . . ."

The second public policy factor upon which recovery against a negligent tortfeasor may be denied is when "the injury is too wholly out of proportion to the tortfeasor's culpability. . . ."

The third public policy factor upon which recovery against a negligent tortfeasor may be denied is when "in retrospect it appears too highly extraordinary that the negligence should have brought about the harm. . . ."

The fourth public policy factor upon which recovery against a negligent tortfeasor may be denied is when "allowing recovery would place too unreasonable a burden upon the tortfeasor. . . ."

The fifth public policy factor upon which recovery against a negligent tortfeasor may be denied is when "allowing recovery would be too likely to open the way to fraudulent claims. . . ."

The sixth, and here perhaps the most significant, public policy factor upon which recovery against a negligent tortfeasor may be denied is when "allowing recovery would have no sensible or just stopping point. . . ."

*   *   *   *   *

Here, the Niesens and their insurer argue that there would be no sensible or just stopping point if the court of appeals' decision stands. They claim that the decision of the court of appeals would put tort law on the path of strict liability for anyone who owns property in Wisconsin, and who knows even scant details of an underage person consuming alcohol on the property under his or her control. They argue that the next step, beyond such a proposed expansion in common-law negligence liability, may be to include in the framework of liability not just social hosts but anyone who knows that an underage person was drinking on property that is not even under their control, or to include anyone, not just property owners, who knows that any underage individual has had too much to drink.

We note that there is no allegation by the Nichols here that the Niesens knew Carr was intoxicated, impaired, or unable to safely drive a vehicle. The Niesens argue that they could not have foreseen that people coming onto their property, who already had broken the law before they arrived, would break the law again after leaving. The Niesens could not reasonably have foreseen that an underage guest who they were not specifically aware was intoxicated, and who arrived at the premises under their control with alcohol purchased elsewhere, would cause foreseeable harm to others.

We agree with the Niesens . . . that allowing recovery here would have no sensible or just stopping point.

*   *   *   *   *

If the Nichols' claim were allowed to proceed, the expansion of liability might also include liability for parents who allegedly should have known that drinking would occur on their property while they were absent, based on the proclivities of teenagers in a given area to consume alcohol. Imposing such liability would be only a short step away from imposing strict liability upon property owners for any underage drinking that occurs on property under their control. As Judge David G. Deininger stated in his dissent in the court of appeals, "if liability is permitted to extend to parents and property owners who fail to 'supervise and monitor the activities on their property,'" as the Nichols contend of the Niesens, "then parents or other owners of property occupied by sixteen- to twenty-year-olds" would "be well-advised to never leave home, or if they must, to ensure that all underage persons go elsewhere as well. . . ." As a result, even assuming that the Nichols had pled a viable claim for common-law negligence against the Niesens using the four-factor test, we are satisfied that the Nichols' claim should be barred on public policy considerations, since allowing recovery here would have no sensible or just stopping point.

*   *   *   *   *

Liability has never been applied to conduct like that of the Niesens, and liability has required active, direct and affirmative acts, such as the provision of alcohol. Neither the legislature nor this court has expanded liability to social hosts who have not provided alcohol to minors. The legislature is the appropriate governmental branch to expand liability if it desires to do so. As a result for the reasons stated herein, we reverse the court of appeals, and hold that such an expansion of liability should come from the legislature, if it is to occur at all.

*   *   *   *   *

Questions

1. Explain the Nichols' legal claim.

2. *a.* Who won this case and why?
   b. Do you agree with the court's decision and its reasoning? Explain.

3. LaMarre rode with his wife and their neighbors, the Plummers, in the Plummers' modified golf cart to have dinner at the nearby Fort Mitchell Country Club. As per Mr. Plummer's request, country club staff retrieved and chilled two bottles of champagne from Plummer's locker. During dinner, the couples consumed one of the champagne bottles as well as a bottle of red wine that Plummer retrieved from his locker. The two couples opened the second bottle of champagne in the golf cart after dinner. After making a stop on the way home at another neighbor's house, Mr. Plummer accelerated the golf cart while Mr. LaMarre was trying to take his seat. LaMarre fell and sustained serious injuries. The LaMarres filed a lawsuit against the Plummers and

the Fort Mitchell Country Club. Should the country club be liable for LaMarre's injuries? Explain. See *Fort Mitchell Country Club v. LaMarre,* 394 S.W.3d 897 (Ky. 2012).

4. Nichols, age 26, and Dobler, a minor, were guests at Maldonado's party. Dobler was served alcohol and, while intoxicated, repeatedly hit Nichols with a hammer. Nichols sued Maldanado for negligence in serving alcohol to a minor. The jury found for Nichols. Maldanado appealed. How would you rule on that appeal? Explain. See *Nichols v. Dobler,* 655 N.W.2d 787 (Mich. Ct. App. 2002).

5. Richard Paul Dube suffered serious injuries when the vehicle he was driving was struck head-on by a vehicle being driven in the wrong direction on a Massachusetts highway by Ravindra Bhoge. Bhoge had earlier in the evening consumed a number of drinks with three friends at a bar. Bhoge and his friends met regularly on Fridays after work to drink at local bars. Each person took turns paying the bill, or on some occasions, payment would be equally divided. On the night of the accident, Bhoge drank enough that the trial judge inferred that Bhoge's intoxication would have been apparent. Bhoge's three friends said they saw nothing to indicate that Bhoge was impaired, although Bhoge had left his coat behind in the bar on a particularly cold evening, and he was outside the bar for 45 minutes prior to his departure. Bhoge indicated to his friends that he was "okay" as they all prepared to leave in their vehicles. Dube sued Bhoge's three friends claiming they were social hosts and were negligent in permitting Bhoge to continue drinking. How would you rule on Dube's claim? Explain. See *Dube v. Lanphear & Others,* 868 N.E.2d 619 (2007). [For the National Center for State Courts, see **http://www.ncsconline.org/**].

Classifications of Law

We can divide the law into some categories that will help us better understand the many legal domains and processes.

LO 4-5
Distinguish between substantive and procedural law.

Substantive and Procedural Law

Substantive laws create, define, and regulate legal rights and obligations. Thus, for example, the federal Civil Rights Act of 1964 forbids discrimination in employment and other matters (see Chapter 13).

Procedural law embraces the systems and methods available to enforce the rights specified in the substantive law. So procedural law includes the judicial system and the rules by which it operates. Questions of where to hear a case, what evidence to admit, and which decisions can be appealed fall within the procedural domain. [For a "community built, freely available legal dictionary and encyclopedia," see **http://www.law.cornell.edu/wex**].

Law and Equity

Following the Norman conquest of England in 1066, a system of king's courts was established in which the king's representatives settled disputes. Those representatives were empowered to provide remedies of land, money, or personal property. The king's courts became known as *courts of law*, and the remedies were labeled *remedies of law*. Some litigants, however, sought compensation other than the three provided. They took their pleas to the king.

Typically the chancellor, an aide to the king, would hear these petitions and, guided by the standard of fairness, could grant a remedy (such as an ***injunction*** or ***specific performance***—see the glossary of legal terms in the back of the book) specifically appropriate to the case. The chancellors' decisions accumulated over time such that a new body of remedies—and with it a new court system, known as *courts of equity*—evolved. Both court systems were adopted in the United States following the American Revolution, but today actions at law and equity are typically heard in the same court.

Public Law and Private Law

Public law deals with the relationship between government and the citizens. Constitutional, criminal, and administrative law (relating to such bodies as the Federal Trade Commission) fall in the public law category. **Private law** regulates the legal relationship among individuals. Contracts, agency, and commercial paper are traditional business law topics in the private category.

Civil Law and Criminal Law

LO 4-6
Compare and contrast civil and criminal law.

The legislature or other lawmaking body normally specifies that new legislation is either *civil* or *criminal* or both. Broadly, all legislation not specifically labeled criminal law falls in the civil law category. **Civil law** addresses the legal rights and duties arising among individuals, organizations such as corporations, and governments. Thus, for example, a person might sue a company raising a civil law claim of breach of contract. **Criminal law,** on the other hand, involves wrongs against the general welfare as formulated in specific criminal statutes. Murder and theft are, of course, criminal wrongs because society has forbidden those acts in specific legislative enactments. (For a brief discussion of business and white-collar crime and the federal sentencing guidelines, see Chapter 2.)

Crimes   Crimes are of three kinds. In general, *felonies* are more serious crimes, such as murder, rape, and robbery. They are typically punishable by death or by imprisonment in a federal or state penitentiary for more than one year. In general, *misdemeanors* are less serious crimes, such as petty theft, disorderly conduct, and traffic offenses. They are typically punishable by fine or by imprisonment for no more than one year. *Treason* is the special situation in which one levies war against the United States or gives aid and comfort to its enemies.

Elements of a Crime   In a broad sense, crimes consist of two elements: (1) a wrongful act or omission (*actus reus*) and (2) evil intent (*mens rea*). Thus, an individual who pockets a pen and leaves the store without paying for it may be charged with petty theft. The accused may defend, however, by arguing that he or she merely absentmindedly and unintentionally slipped the pen in a pocket after picking it off the shelf to consider its merits. Intent is a state of mind, so the jury or judge must reach a determination from the objective facts as to what the accused's state of mind must have been.

Criminal Procedure   In general, criminal procedure following an arrest, and an initial appearance before a magistrate (and, in some cases, a preliminary hearing), is structured as follows: For misdemeanor cases, prosecutors typically file what is called an *information,* a formal expression of the charges. The information may be reviewed by a magistrate before issuance. For felony cases, the process begins with the prosecuting officials either filing an information or seeking an *indictment* by bringing their charges before a grand jury of citizens to determine whether the charges have sufficient merit to justify a trial.

After an indictment or information, the individual is brought before the court for *arraignment,* where the charges are read and a plea is entered. If the individual pleads not guilty, he or she will go to trial, where guilt must be established *beyond a reasonable doubt.* In a criminal trial, the burden of proof is on the state. The defendant is, of course, presumed innocent and is entitled to a jury trial, but she or he may choose to have the case decided by the judge alone. If found guilty, the defendant can, among other possibilities, seek a new trial or appeal errors in the prosecution. If found innocent, the defendant may, if necessary, invoke the doctrine of ***double jeopardy,*** under which a person cannot be prosecuted twice in the same tribunal for the same criminal offense. [For an extensive criminal justice database, see **https://www.ncjrs.gov/**].

Miranda **Warnings**

The 1966 *Miranda v. Arizona* U.S. Supreme Court decision provided that a suspect in police custody must be told:

> You have the right to remain silent. Anything you say can and will be used against you in a court of law. You have the right to an attorney. If you cannot afford an attorney, one will be appointed for you.

If warnings are not properly provided, any statements made by the suspect and any evidence derived from those statements cannot subsequently be used in court. The warnings are highly controversial, and the current Supreme Court appears to be inclined to relax the *Miranda* requirements.

Michigan police informed a suspect, Van Thompkins, of his Fifth Amendment rights against self-incrimination, including the right to remain silent. Thompkins said he understood, but he did not say he wanted the questioning to stop or that he wanted a lawyer. Rather, he sat through two hours and 45 minutes of questioning without speaking until an officer asked: "Do you pray to God to forgive you for shooting that boy down?" Thompkins said, "Yes." He did not speak further, and he did not sign a confession. He was later convicted of murder, that verdict being based largely on his one-word reply. The U.S. 6th Circuit Court of Appeals overturned the conviction, ruling that the use of the incriminating answer violated Thompkins's Fifth Amendment rights, as defined and required by *Miranda*.

The case, *Berghuis v. Thompkins,* then reached the U.S. Supreme Court in 2010, where the Court chipped away at the *Miranda* requirements in a 5–4 reversal of the court of appeals ruling. The Court said, "A suspect who has received and understood the *Miranda* warnings and has not invoked his *Miranda* rights waives the right to remain silent by making an uncoerced statement to the police." The Court's decision requires a criminal suspect to explicitly and unambiguously tell the police he or she wants to remain silent. Merely remaining silent had previously been treated as an invocation of the right to remain silent, but the Court's *Thompkins* ruling changed that practice and, in the view of critics, ill advisedly diminished rights previously guaranteed to defendants. The Supreme Court further relaxed the Miranda requirements in two other 2010 decisions (*Florida v. Powell* and *Maryland v. Shatzer*).

However, in 2011, the Court strengthened *Miranda* protection for young people when it ruled that the police must consider the age of a suspect in deciding whether *Miranda* warnings must be issued. In *J.D.B. v. North Carolina,* a 13-year-old Chapel Hill, North Carolina, student confessed to a pair of home break-ins during a half hour of questioning by police officers and school administrators in a middle school conference room. The warnings were not issued and J.D.B. was not permitted to call his grandmother, who was his guardian. The state, however, claimed J.D.B. was not in custody and therefore the warnings were not required. In general, a suspect is considered not to have been in custody if a "reasonable person" under the circumstances would have felt free to leave. The North Carolina courts ruled that J.D.B. was not in custody, but the U.S. Supreme Court held that the police must consider the suspect's age when deciding if custody has been achieved such that the warnings are required. The case was returned to North Carolina to determine whether J.D.B., given his age, was in custody during the questioning.

Questions

1. Do you think Thompkins's response of "yes" to the police inquiry should have been admissible in court against him? Explain.

2. In general, do you think the *Miranda* warnings offer too much protection for criminal suspects? Explain.

Sources: *Berghuis v. Thompkins,* 130 S. Ct. 2250 (2010); *Florida v. Powell,* 130 S. Ct. 1195 (2010); *J.D.B. v. North Carolina,* 564 U.S. 261 (2011); *Maryland v. Shatzer,* 130 S. Ct. 1213 (2010); *Miranda v. Arizona,* 86 S. Ct. 1602 (1966); Jesse J. Holland, "Miranda Warning Rights Trimmed Bit by Bit by High Court," *The Christian Science Monitor,* August 2, 2010 [**www.csmonitor.com**]; and David Savage, "Supreme Court Backs Off Strict Enforcement of Miranda Rights," *latimes.com* [**http://latimes.com/news/la-na-court-miranda-20100602,0,2431552.story**].

PRACTICING ETHICS   "Stand Your Ground" on a Slippery Slope?

In February 2012, Trayvon Martin, a 17-year-old African American male, was shot and killed by 28-year-old George Zimmerman. In the early evening, Martin, wearing a hooded gray sweatshirt, had walked from his relative's townhouse to a nearby convenience store to buy candy and a soft drink; he was unarmed. On his way back, he called his girlfriend to tell her that he was being followed. Zimmerman called 911 from his car to report that he saw someone suspicious in his neighborhood. Although the 911 operator told Zimmerman that he should not follow Martin, Zimmerman apparently got out of his car when Martin began to run. Although it was dark, eyewitness accounts reported seeing two men fighting and then seeing one of them laying on the grass, apparently shot.[2] In July 2013, a jury found Zimmerman not guilty of second-degree murder and manslaughter based on Florida's 2005 stand-your-ground law.[3]

Under Florida's stand-your-ground law, those who "reasonably believe" that force—even deadly force—is necessary to protect against death or great bodily harm may use such force instead of retreating.[4] This expanded right to defend oneself now exists in more than 30 states. A recent study by an economics professor and PhD student at Texas A&M University concluded that stand-your-ground laws do not deter burglary, robbery, or aggravated assault.[5]

Questions

1. In your view, are stand-your-ground laws moral? Explain.

2. Under the castle doctrine, recognized in more than 20 states, generally homeowners may use force—including deadly force—to defend themselves in their own home.

   a. How might the castle doctrine be supported morally?

   b. Fredenberg, an unarmed Montana resident, was shot and killed by Harper, a man who was romantically involved with Fredenberg's wife. Fredenberg had gone to Harper's home to confront him about the affair. Under Montana's castle doctrine, Harper did not face charges.[6] In your view, is this an appropriate application of the castle doctrine? Explain.

Questions—Part One

1. Jonathan Rauch argued that America is making a mistake in allowing what he calls Hidden Law to be replaced by what he calls Bureaucratic Legalism. Hidden Law refers to unwritten social codes, whereas Bureaucratic Legalism refers to state-provided due process for every problem. Thus, universities formerly expected insults and epithets

among students to be resolved via informal modes such as apologies, while today many universities have written codes forbidding offensive or discriminatory verbal conduct. Similarly, four kindergarten students in New Jersey were suspended from school for three days because they were observed "shooting" each other with their fingers serving as guns.

a. Should we leave campus insults and schoolyard finger "shootings" to the Hidden Law? Explain.

b. Can you think of other examples where we have gradually replaced Hidden Law with Bureaucratic Legalism?

c. Rauch argued that the breakdown of one Hidden Law, the rule that a man must marry a woman whom he has impregnated, may be "the most far-reaching social change of our era." Do you agree? Explain. See George Will, "Penalizing These Kids Is Zero Tolerance at a Ridiculous Extreme," *The Des Moines Register,* December 27, 2000, p. 11A.

2. Should we remove criminal penalties from all of the so-called victimless crimes including vagrancy, pornography, and gambling? Should we regulate those practices in any way? Explain.

3. A 19-year-old woman who didn't pay the fare for a 30-mile cab ride was given the choice of spending 30 days in jail or taking a 30-mile walk;[7] she chose to take the walk. One Florida judge has sentenced hundreds of shoplifters to carrying in public a sign that reads: "I stole from this store." Constitutional law expert Jonathan Turley says "creative sentencing" is growing, a trend he disapproves of and regards as a strategy for entertaining the public more than deterring crime.[8]

a. What objections would a defendant's lawyer raise to these public humiliation punishments?

b. Would you impose a "humiliation sentence" if you were the judge? Explain.

Part Two—The Judicial Process

Most disputes are settled without resort to litigation, but when agreement cannot be reached, we can turn to the courts—a highly technical and sophisticated dispute resolution mechanism.

State Court Systems

LO 4-7
Describe the elements of the basic court system structure.

While state court systems vary substantially, a general pattern can be summarized. As shown in Figure 4.1, at the base of the court pyramid in most states is a trial court of general jurisdiction, commonly labeled a *district court* or a *superior court*. Most trials—both civil and criminal—arising out of state law are heard here, but certain classes of cases are reserved to courts of limited subject-matter jurisdiction or to various state administrative agencies (such as the state public utilities commission and the workers' compensation board). Family, small claims, juvenile, and traffic courts are examples of

FIGURE 4.1   State and Federal Court Systems

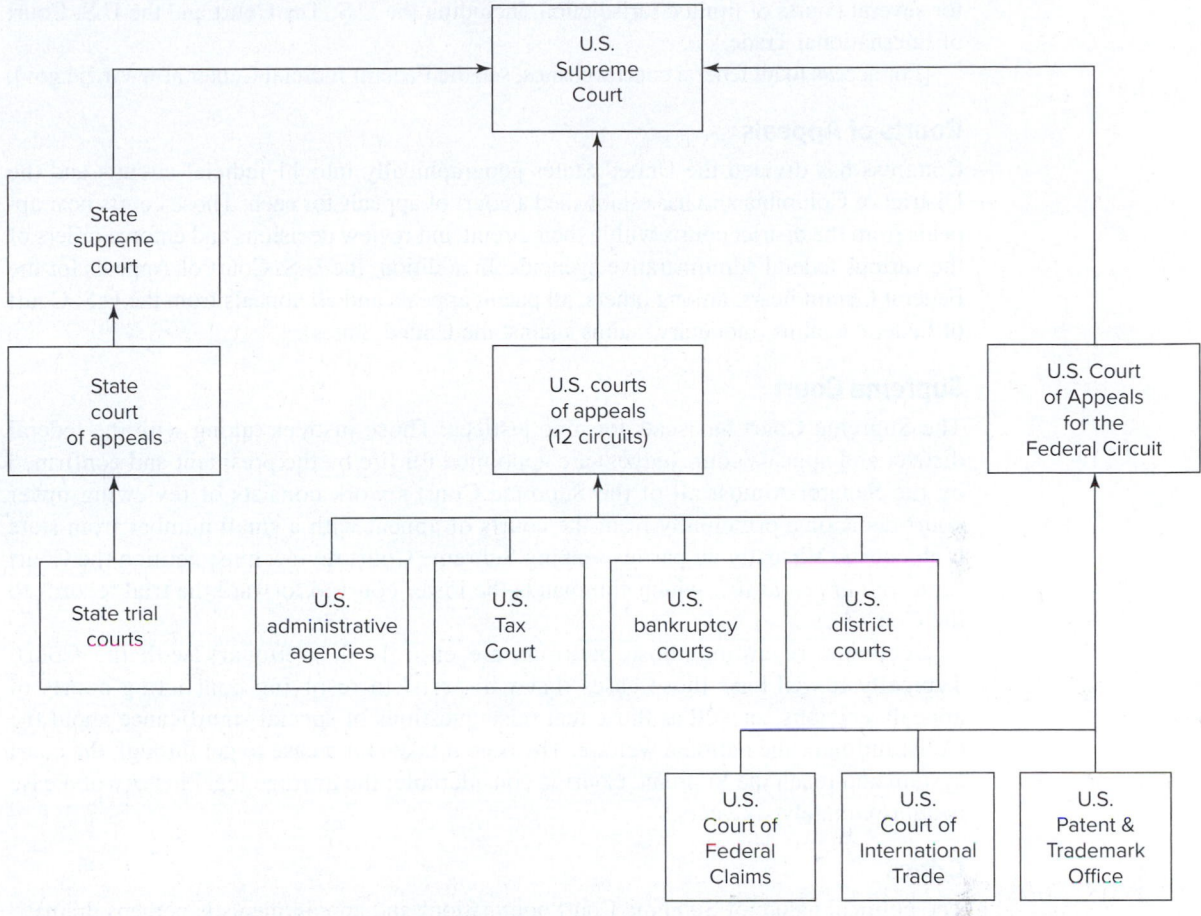

trial courts with limited jurisdiction. At the top of the judicial pyramid in all states is a court of appeals, ordinarily labeled the *supreme court*. A number of states also provide for an intermediate court of appeals located in the hierarchy between the trial courts and the highest appeals court.

Federal Court System

District Courts

The Constitution provides for a Supreme Court and such inferior courts as Congress shall authorize. Pursuant to that authority, Congress has established at least one district court for each state and territory. The 94 district courts serve as the foundation of the federal judicial system. These are trial courts where witnesses are heard and questions of law and fact are resolved. Most federal cases begin in the district courts or in a federal administrative agency (such as the Federal Communications Commission). Congress also has provided for several courts of limited jurisdiction, including the U.S. Tax Court and the U.S. Court of International Trade.

[For access to all federal court websites, see the Federal Judicial Center at **www.fjc.gov**].

Courts of Appeals

Congress has divided the United States geographically into 11 judicial circuits and the District of Columbia and has established a court of appeals for each. Those courts hear appeals from the district courts within their circuit and review decisions and enforce orders of the various federal administrative agencies. In addition, the U.S. Court of Appeals for the Federal Circuit hears, among others, all patent appeals and all appeals from the U.S. Court of Federal Claims (monetary claims against the United States).

Supreme Court

The Supreme Court has seats for nine justices. Those justices (along with the federal district and appeals court judges) are appointed for life by the president and confirmed by the Senate. Almost all of the Supreme Court's work consists of reviewing lower court decisions, principally from the courts of appeal with a small number from state high courts. Virtually all parties seeking Supreme Court review must petition the Court for a *writ of certiorari,* which commands the lower court to forward the trial records to the Court.

Decisions regarding those petitions are entirely discretionary with the Court. Typically it will hear those cases that will assist in resolving conflicting courts of appeal decisions, as well as those that raise questions of special significance about the Constitution or the national welfare. The time it takes for a case to get through the court system and reach the Supreme Court is considerable; the average legal history of a case is approximately six years.[9]

Critics

The political nature of Supreme Court nominations and appointments is perhaps dramatically shown in the U.S. Senate's refusal to hold confirmation hearings for Merrick Garland, President Obama's nominee to fill the late Justice Scalia's seat.[10] Questions of "judicial activism," the liberal/conservative balance on the Supreme Court, the politics of the justices, and the justices' deference to big business interests have made the Court a target for criticism.

> The Roberts Supreme Court has been said to defy political labels.

However, the Supreme Court led by Chief Justice John Roberts ("the Roberts Supreme Court") has been said to defy political labels.[11] The Court has supported fired workers, has expanded antidiscrimination law, and was deadlocked in 2016 in a decision favoring public employee unions.[12]

Ideological Rulings?

We want to believe that the Supreme Court reaches its decisions in a rational, objective fashion relying on the commands of the Constitution and precedent to maintain a consistent, fair, orderly judicial system free of political influence. A study by the Brookings Institution provided "striking evidence of a relationship between the political party of the appointing president and judicial voting patterns."[13] Critics say that those conservative ideological inclinations have led the Roberts Court to at times abandon traditional judicial restraint and decide issues that were broader than required by the case before it.[14]

In 2012, the late Justice Scalia drew criticism for reading aloud his dissenting opinion that criticized President Obama's immigration policy; both conservative and liberal observers voiced concerns that Scalia's political pronouncements undermined the integrity of his opinion.[15]

Of course, public respect for the fairness and the rationality of Supreme Court decisions could be undermined if they come to be viewed as the product of liberal or conservative political/ideological views, rather than dispassionate, lawyerly analysis. Shortly before Justice Scalia read his controversial dissenting opinion described above, a *New York Times* and *CBS News* poll showed that three-quarters of Americans believe the Supreme Court justices' decisions may be influenced by their political views.[16] Declining respect for Supreme Court rulings would undermine the rule of law in America and perhaps threaten democracy itself.[17] [For an overview of the Supreme Court, see **http://www.supremecourt.gov/**].

Jurisdiction

LO 4-8

Explain the purposes of subject matter and personal jurisdiction as requirements for a court's power to hear a dispute.

A plaintiff may not simply proceed to trial at the court of his or her preference. The plaintiff must go to a court with *jurisdiction*—that is, a court with the necessary power and authority to hear the dispute. The court must have jurisdiction over both the subject matter and the persons (or, in some instances, the property) involved in the case.

Subject-Matter Jurisdiction

Subject-matter jurisdiction imposes bounds on the classes of cases a court may hear. The legislation or constitution creating the court will normally specify that court's jurisdictional authority. State courts of *general jurisdiction,* for example, may hear most types of cases, but a criminal court or probate court is limited in the subject matter it may hear.

The outer bounds of federal jurisdiction are specified in the Constitution, and Congress has further particularized those boundaries by statute. Essentially, the federal district courts may hear two types of cases: (1) those involving a federal question and (2) those involving diversity of citizenship and more than $75,000.

Federal question jurisdiction exists in any suit where the plaintiff's claim is based on the U.S. Constitution, a U.S. treaty, or a federal statute. Thus, litigants can bring cases to the federal courts involving, for example, the federal antitrust statutes, federal criminal laws, constitutional issues such as freedom of the press, and federal tax questions. Federal question jurisdiction does not require an amount in controversy exceeding $75,000. Furthermore, federal and state courts have *concurrent jurisdiction* for some federal questions. Thus, some federal question cases are decided in state courts applying federal law. Federal courts also can hear cases involving state laws. Congress has accorded the federal courts exclusive jurisdiction over certain subjects, including federal criminal laws, bankruptcy, and copyrights.

Under *diversity jurisdiction,* federal district courts may hear cases involving more than $75,000 where the plaintiff(s) and the defendant(s) are citizens of different states. (Corporations are treated as citizens both of their state of incorporation and the state in which their principal place of business is located.) Diversity cases also may be heard in state courts, but plaintiffs frequently prefer to bring their actions in federal courts. The quality of the federal judiciary is generally believed to be superior to that of the states, and the federal courts are considered less likely to be influenced by local bias.

Personal Jurisdiction

Judicial authority over the person is known as ***in personam jurisdiction.*** In general, a state court's powers are limited to the bounds of the state. Broadly, state court jurisdiction can be established in three ways. First, when the defendant is a resident of the state, a summons may be served at that residence. Second, if the defendant is not a resident, a summons may be personally served should he or she be physically present in the state. Third, most states have legislated "long-arm" statutes that allow a state or federal court to secure jurisdiction against an out-of-state party where the defendant has committed a tort in the state or where the defendant is conducting business in the state. Hence, in an auto accident in Ohio involving both an Ohio resident and a Kentucky resident, the Ohio resident may sue in Ohio and use the long-arm statute to achieve service of process over the defendant living in Kentucky.

A state court also may acquire jurisdiction via an *in rem action.* In that instance, the defendant may be a nonresident, but his or her property, which must be the subject of the suit, must be located within the state.

The following case involves a dispute about the commercial use of the name of celebrated actor and former California governor Arnold Schwarzenegger.

Arnold Schwarzenegger v. Fred Martin Motor Company

LEGAL BRIEFCASE 374 F.3d 797 (9th Cir. 2004)

Circuit Judge Fletcher

Arnold Schwarzenegger, an internationally known movie star and, currently, the governor of California, appeals the district court's dismissal of his suit against Fred Martin Motor Company ("Fred Martin"), an Ohio car dealership, for lack of personal jurisdiction. Fred Martin had run a series of five full-page color advertisements in the *Akron Beacon Journal,* a locally circulated Ohio newspaper. Each advertisement included a small photograph of Schwarzenegger, portrayed as the "Terminator," without his permission. Schwarzenegger brought suit in California, alleging that these unauthorized uses of his image infringed his right of publicity. We affirm the district court's dismissal for lack of personal jurisdiction.

I. BACKGROUND

Schwarzenegger is a resident of California. When Schwarzenegger brought this suit, he was a private citizen and movie star, best known for his roles as a muscle-bound hero of action films and distinctive Austrian accent. As explained in his complaint, Schwarzenegger was generally cast as the lead character in so-called star-driven films. One of Schwarzenegger's most popular and readily recognizable film roles is that of the title character in "The Terminator" (1984). . . .

Fred Martin is an automobile dealership incorporated under the laws of Ohio and located in Barberton, Ohio, a few miles southwest of Akron. There is no evidence in the record that Fred Martin has any operations or employees in California, has ever advertised in

California, or has ever sold a car to anyone in California. Fred Martin maintains an Internet website that is available for viewing in California and, for that matter, from any Internet cafe in Istanbul, Bangkok, or anywhere else in the world.

In early 2002, Fred Martin engaged defendant Zimmerman & Partners Advertising, Inc. ("Zimmerman") to design and place a full-page color advertisement in the *Akron Beacon Journal,* a local Akron-based newspaper. The advertisement ran in the *Akron Beacon Journal* five times in April 2002. Most of the advertisement consists of small photographs and descriptions of various cars available for purchase or lease from Fred Martin. Just below a large-font promise that Fred Martin "WON'T BE BEAT," the advertisement includes a small, but clearly recognizable photograph of Schwarzenegger as the Terminator. A "bubble quotation," like those found in comic strips, is drawn next to Schwarzenegger's mouth, reading, "Arnold says: 'Terminate EARLY at Fred Martin!'" This part of the advertisement refers to a special offer from Fred Martin to customers, inviting them to close out their current leases before the expected termination date, and to buy or lease a new car from Fred Martin.

Neither Fred Martin nor Zimmerman ever sought or received Schwarzenegger's permission to use his photograph in the advertisement. Schwarzenegger states in his complaint that, had such a request been made, it would have been refused. The advertisement, as far as the record reveals, was never circulated outside of Ohio.

Schwarzenegger brought suit against Fred Martin and Zimmerman in Los Angeles County Superior Court alleging six state law causes of action arising out of the unauthorized use of his image in the advertisement. He claims that the defendants caused him financial harm in that the use of his photograph to endorse Fred Martin "diminishes his hard earned reputation as a major motion picture star, and risks the potential for overexposure of his image to the public, thereby potentially diminishing the compensation he would otherwise garner from his career as a major motion picture star." According to Schwarzenegger's complaint, his compensation as the lead actor in star-driven films was based on his ability to draw crowds to the box office, and his ability to do so depended in part on the scarcity of his image. According to his complaint, if Schwarzenegger's image were to become ubiquitous—in advertisements and on television, for example—the movie-going public would be less likely to spend their money to see his films, and his compensation would diminish accordingly. Therefore, Schwarzenegger maintains, it is vital for him to avoid "oversaturation of his image." According to his complaint, he has steadfastly refused to endorse any products in the United States, despite being offered substantial sums to do so.

Defendants removed the action to federal district court in California, and Fred Martin moved to dismiss the complaint for lack of personal jurisdiction. The district court granted Fred Martin's motion, and Schwarzenegger appealed.

II. PERSONAL JURISDICTION

For a court to exercise personal jurisdiction over a nonresident defendant, that defendant must have at least "minimum contacts" with the relevant forum such that the exercise of jurisdiction "does not offend traditional notions of fair play and substantial justice." *International Shoe Co. v. Washington,* 326 U.S. 310, 316 (1945).

A. General Jurisdiction

Schwarzenegger argues, quite implausibly, that California has general personal jurisdiction over Fred Martin. For general jurisdiction to exist over a nonresident defendant such as Fred Martin, the defendant must engage in "continuous and systematic general business contacts," *Helicopteros Nacionales de Colombia, S.A. v. Hall,* 466 U.S. 408 (1984) that "approximate physical presence" in the forum state. *Bancroft & Masters,* 223 F.3d at 1086. This is an exacting standard, as it should be, because a finding of general jurisdiction permits a defendant to be haled into court in the forum state to answer for any of its activities anywhere in the world.

Schwarzenegger contends that Fred Martin's contacts with California are so extensive that it is subject to general jurisdiction. He points to the following contacts: Fred Martin regularly purchases Asian-made automobiles that are imported by California entities. However, in purchasing these automobiles, Fred Martin dealt directly with representatives in Illinois and New Jersey, but never dealt directly with the California-based importers. Some of Fred Martin's sales contracts with its automobile suppliers include a choice-of-law provision specifying California law. In addition, Fred Martin regularly retains the services of a California-based direct-mail marketing company; has hired a sales training company, incorporated in California, for consulting services; and maintains an Internet website accessible by anyone capable of using the Internet, including people living in California.

These contacts fall well short of the "continuous and systematic" contacts that the Supreme Court and this court have held to constitute sufficient "presence" to warrant general jurisdiction. Schwarzenegger has therefore failed to establish a prima facie case of general jurisdiction.

B. Specific Jurisdiction

Alternatively, Schwarzenegger argues that Fred Martin has sufficient "minimum contacts" with California arising from, or related to, its actions in creating and distributing the advertisement such that the forum may assert specific personal jurisdiction. We have established a three-prong test for analyzing a claim of specific personal jurisdiction:

(1) The nonresident defendant must purposefully direct his activities or consummate some transaction with the forum or resident thereof; or perform some act by which he purposefully avails himself of the privilege of conducting activities in the forum, thereby invoking the benefits and protections of its laws;

(2) the claim must be one which arises out of or relates to the defendant's forum-related activities; and

(3) the exercise of jurisdiction must comport with fair play and substantial justice, i.e., it must be reasonable.

The plaintiff bears the burden of satisfying the first two prongs of the test. If the plaintiff fails to satisfy either of these prongs, personal jurisdiction is not established in the forum state. If the plaintiff succeeds in satisfying both of the first two prongs, the burden then shifts to the defendant to "present a compelling case" that the exercise of jurisdiction would not be reasonable. For the reasons that follow, we hold that Schwarzenegger has failed to satisfy the first prong.

1. Purposeful Availment or Direction Generally
Under the first prong of our three-part specific jurisdiction test, Schwarzenegger must establish that Fred Martin either purposefully availed itself of the privilege of conducting activities in California, or purposefully directed its activities toward California.

* * * * *

A showing that a defendant purposefully availed himself of the privilege of doing business in a forum state typically consists of evidence of the defendant's actions in the forum, such as executing or performing a contract there. By taking such actions, a defendant "purposefully avails itself of the privilege of conducting activities within the forum State, thus invoking the benefits and protections of its laws." *Hanson v. Denckla,* 357 U.S. 235, 253 (1958). In return for these "benefits and protections," a defendant must—as a quid pro quo—"submit to the burdens of litigation in that forum." *Burger King,* 471 U.S. at 476.

A showing that a defendant purposefully directed his conduct toward a forum state, by contrast, usually consists of evidence of the defendant's actions outside the forum state that are directed at the forum, such as the distribution in the forum state of goods originating elsewhere.

2. Purposeful Direction
Schwarzenegger does not point to any conduct by Fred Martin in California related to the advertisement that would be readily susceptible to a purposeful availment analysis. Rather, the conduct of which Schwarzenegger complains—the unauthorized inclusion of the photograph in the advertisement and its distribution in the *Akron Beacon Journal*—took place in Ohio, not California. Fred Martin received no benefit, privilege, or protection from California in connection with the advertisement, and the traditional quid pro quo justification for finding purposeful availment thus does not apply. Therefore, to the extent that Fred Martin's conduct might justify the exercise of personal jurisdiction in California, that conduct must have been purposefully directed at California.

* * * * *

Here, Fred Martin's intentional act—the creation and publication of the advertisement—was expressly aimed at Ohio rather than California. The purpose of the advertisement was to entice Ohioans to buy or lease cars from Fred Martin and, in particular, to "terminate" their current car leases. The advertisement was never circulated in California, and Fred Martin had no reason to believe that any Californians would see it and pay a visit to the dealership. Fred Martin certainly had no reason to believe that a Californian had a current car lease with Fred Martin that could be "terminated" as recommended in the advertisement. It may be true that Fred Martin's intentional act eventually caused harm to Schwarzenegger in California and Fred Martin may have known that Schwarzenegger lived in California. But this does not confer jurisdiction, for Fred Martin's express aim was local. We therefore conclude that the advertisement was not expressly aimed at California.

CONCLUSION

We hold that Schwarzenegger has established neither general nor specific jurisdiction over Fred Martin in California. Schwarzenegger has not shown that Fred Martin has "continuous and systematic general business contacts," *Helicopteros,* 466 U.S. at 416, that "approximate physical presence" in California, *Bancroft & Masters,* 223 F. 3d at 1086, such that it can be sued there for any act it has committed anywhere in the world. Further, while Schwarzenegger has made out a prima facie case that Fred Martin committed intentional acts that may have caused harm to Schwarzenegger in California, he has not made out a prima facie case that Fred Martin expressly aimed its acts at California.

Affirmed.

AFTERWORD

Schwarzenegger's claim was settled out of court in 2004 when the Fred Martin Motor Company issued a written apology and agreed to pay a "substantial" sum to Arnold's All-Stars, an after-school program founded by Schwarzenegger.

Questions

1. Why was Schwarzenegger unable to sue Fred Martin in California?

2. Nicastro injured his hand while using a metal-shearing machine in New Jersey manufactured by J. McIntyre Machinery, a company incorporated and operating in England. Nicastro filed a products liability lawsuit against J. McIntyre Machinery in a New Jersey state court, basing personal jurisdiction in New Jersey on three primary facts: A U.S. distributor agreed to sell the company's machines in the United States; J. McIntyre officials attended trade shows in several other states; and four of the company's machines were located in New Jersey. J. McIntyre Machinery had not advertised in or sent goods to New Jersey.

   a. Build an argument to support the claim of jurisdiction in the New Jersey court.

b. Decide. See *J. McIntyre Machines Ltd. v. Nicastro,* 131 S. Ct. 2780 (2011).

3. Andra, a Missouri resident, used the eBay auction site to purchase a truck from Left Gate, a company based in Texas and a vehicle dealership doing a substantial portion of its sales through eBay with no physical presence or employees in Missouri. Andra agreed to purchase the vehicle using eBay's usual process. After completing the purchase, Andra spoke several times to Left Gate representatives in Texas to discuss delivery of the vehicle, and Left Gate mailed a contract and buyer's guide to him at his Missouri address. The truck was delivered to Andra in Missouri by a third-party transporter. Andra later sued Left Gate, for breach of contract due to vehicle defects, in a Missouri trial court. Does that Missouri court have jurisdiction over Left Gate? Explain. See *Andra v. Left Gate Property Holding, Inc.,* 453 S.W.3d 216 (Mo. 2015).

4. Burger King conducted a franchise, fast-food operation from its Miami, Florida, headquarters. John Rudzewicz and a partner, both residents of Michigan, secured a Burger King franchise in Michigan. Subsequently, the franchisees allegedly fell behind in payments, and Burger King subsequently ordered the franchisees to vacate the premises. They declined to do so, and continued to operate the franchise. Burger King brought suit in a federal district court in Florida. The defendant franchisees argued that the Florida court did not have personal jurisdiction over them because they were Michigan residents and also the claim did not arise in Florida. The court found the defendants to be subject to Florida's "long-arm statute," which extends jurisdiction to "[a]ny person, whether or not a citizen or resident of this state," who "[b]reach[es] a contract in this state by failing to perform acts required by the contract to be performed in this state." The franchise contract provided for governance of the relationship by Florida law. Franchise policy was set in Miami, although daily supervision was managed through various district offices. The case ultimately reached the U.S. Supreme Court.

   a. What constitutional argument would you raise on behalf of the defendant franchisees?

   b. Decide. See *Burger King Corp. v. Rudzewicz,* 471 U.S. 462 (1985).

Venue

Once jurisdictional authority—that is, the power to hear the case—is established, the proper **venue** (geographic location within the court system) comes into question. Ordinarily, a case will be heard by the court geographically closest to the incident or property in question or to where the parties reside. Sometimes one of the parties may seek a *change of venue* based on considerations such as unfavorable pretrial publicity or the pursuit of a more favorable legal climate. The importance of venue is evident in a 2010 decision forcing Los Angeles–based Occidental Petroleum to defend itself in an environmental dispute in California rather than in Peru, where the conflict emerged. Members of the Achuar tribe, indigenous to the Amazon rain forest, brought a class action in Los Angeles against Occidental alleging the oil company dumped millions of gallons of waste water into their rivers and contaminated their land with waste.[18] A California federal district court dismissed the Achuar claim, but the 9th Circuit U.S. Court of Appeals reversed the district court. The appeals court ruled, among other things, that Occidental had failed to demonstrate that Peru was the more convenient forum for the lawsuit.[19] In 2013, the U.S. Supreme Court denied Occidental's petition for review.[20] The Achuar plaintiffs want the case tried in California, in part, because the Peruvian courts have a history of favoring corporate interests in conflicts with natives. The parties settled for an undisclosed amount, with the money to fund community development projects.[21]

> The Achuar tribe, indigenous to the Amazon rain forest, brought a class action in Los Angeles.

Standing to Sue

Not all who wish to bring a claim before a court will be permitted to do so. To receive the court's attention, the litigant must demonstrate *standing to sue*. That is, the person must show that her or his interest in the outcome of the controversy is sufficiently direct and substantial as to justify the court's consideration. The litigant must show that she or he is personally suffering, or will be suffering, injury. Mere interest in the problem at hand is insufficient to grant standing to sue. We all suffer injustices. We all have complaints in life. But have we suffered an injury to a legally protected right or interest? That is the question in the *Mayer* case that arose out of "Spygate," an alleged National Football League cheating scandal.[22]

Mayer v. Bill Belichick; The New England Patriots; National Football League

605 F.3d 223 (3d Cir. 2010), *cert. denied,*
562 U.S. 1271 (2011)

LEGAL BRIEFCASE

FACTS

In an episode popularly known as "Spygate," an employee of the New England Patriots National Football League team was caught videotaping New York Jets' sideline signals, in violation of NFL rules, during a 2007 game with the Jets. The taping was later discovered to have been part of an illicit taping program that reportedly had been ongoing since the 2000 season. The NFL penalized the Patriots and their coach, Bill Belichick. Mayer sued on behalf of himself and a class of Jets season ticketholders claiming the improper conduct violated the contractual expectations and rights of the ticketholders who had paid to observe an honest football game played in conformance with the rules. Mayer lost at trial, where the federal district court ruled that he had failed to demonstrate an actionable injury; that is, he was unable to show the court that the facts he asserted could support a right to relief under the law. Put another way, he did not have standing to sue. Mayer then appealed to the Third Circuit Federal Court of Appeals.

Circuit Judge Cowen

[I–III OMITTED—ED.]

IV

The District Court, while noting that Mayer alleged numerous theories of liability in this case, appropriately turned to the following

dispositive question: namely, whether or not he stated an actionable injury (or, in other words, a legally protected right or interest) arising out of the alleged "dishonest" videotaping program undertaken by the Patriots and the NFL team's head coach.

* * * * *

Initially, we consider how tickets to sporting and other entertainment events have been treated in the past. New Jersey has generally followed a so-called "license" approach[#]. . . .

Although it did not use the specific term "license," the ticket stub provided by the Patriots nevertheless appears consistent with this traditional approach. For example, it unambiguously stated that "[t]his ticket only grants entry into the stadium and a spectator seat for the specified NFL game." The stub further made clear that the Jets and the owners of the stadium retain sole discretion to refuse admission or to eject a ticketholder. . . . Given that Mayer was never barred or expelled from any game at Giants Stadium, much more is needed to establish a cognizable right, interest, or injury. . . .

Mayer possessed either a license or, at best, a contractual right to enter Giants Stadium and to have a seat from which to watch a

---

[#]A license, for our purposes, is generally defined as "[a] permission . . . to commit some act that would otherwise be unlawful; esp., an agreement that it is lawful for the licensee to enter the licensor's land to do some act that would otherwise be illegal, such as hunting game." *Black's Law Dictionary* 1002 (9th ed. 2009).

professional football game. In the clear language of the ticket stub, "[t]his ticket only grants entry into the stadium and a spectator seat for the specified NFL game." Mayer actually was allowed to enter the stadium and witnessed the "specified NFL game[s]" between the Jets and Patriots. He thereby suffered no cognizable injury to a legally protected right or interest.

Accordingly, we need not, and do not decide, whether a ticketholder possesses nothing more than a license to enter and view whatever event, if any, happens to transpire. Here, Mayer undeniably saw *football* games played by two *NFL* teams. This therefore is not a case where, for example, the game or games were canceled, strike replacement players were used, or the professional football teams themselves did something nonsensical or absurd, such as deciding to play basketball.

* * * * *

Furthermore, we do recognize that Mayer alleged that he was the victim, not of mere poor performance by a team or its players, but of a team's ongoing acts of dishonesty or cheating in violation of the express rules of the game. Nevertheless, there are any number of often complicated rules and standards applicable to a variety of sports, including professional football. It appears uncontested that players often commit intentional rule infractions in order to obtain an advantage over the course of the game. . . . Mayer further does not appear to contest the fact that a team is evidently permitted by the rules to engage in a wide variety of arguably "dishonest" conduct to uncover an opponent's signals. For example, a team is apparently free to take advantage of the knowledge that a newly hired player or coach takes with him after leaving his former team, and it may even have personnel on the sidelines who try to pick up the opposing team's signals with the assistance of lip-reading, binoculars, note-taking, and other devices. In addition, even Mayer acknowledged in his amended complaint that "[t]eams are allowed to have a limited number of their own videographers on the sideline during the game."

In fact, the NFL's own commissioner did ultimately take action here. He found that the Patriots and Belichick were guilty of violating the applicable NFL rules, imposed sanctions in the form of fines and the loss of draft picks, and rather harshly characterized the whole episode as a calculated attempt to avoid well-established rules designed to encourage fair play and honest competition. At least in this specific context, it is not the role of judges and juries to be second-guessing the decision taken by a professional sports league purportedly enforcing its *own* rules. . . .

This Court refuses to countenance a course of action that would only further burden already limited judicial resources and force professional sports organizations and related individuals to expend money, time, and resources to defend against such litigation. . . .

In conclusion, this Court will affirm the dismissal of Mayer's amended complaint. Again, it bears repeating that our reasoning here is limited to the unusual and even unique circumstances presented by this appeal. We do not condone the conduct on the part of the Patriots and the team's head coach, and we likewise refrain from assessing whether the NFL's sanctions (and its alleged destruction of the videotapes themselves) were otherwise appropriate. We further recognize that professional football, like other professional sports, is a multi-billion dollar business. In turn, ticketholders and other fans may have legitimate issues with the manner in which they are treated. . . . Significantly, our ruling also does not leave Mayer and other ticketholders without any recourse. Instead, fans could speak out against the Patriots, their coach, and the NFL itself. In fact, they could even go so far as to refuse to purchase tickets or NFL-related merchandise. However, the one thing they *cannot* do is bring a legal action in a court of law.

Affirmed.

Questions

1. *a.* Why did Mayer lose this case?
   b. Do you think he should have won?

2. According to the court, under what circumstances might a plaintiff conceivably have an actionable claim involving a sports event gone wrong?

3. In an antitrust action brought against Apple Inc. regarding iPods, a federal judge questioned whether any of the plaintiffs had actually purchased an iPod. Why would the judge be concerned about that? How might the plaintiffs respond if they did not in fact purchase an iPod? Explain. See Jeff Elder, "Judge Questions Plaintiffs in Apple iPod Case," *The Wall Street Journal*, December 4, 2014 [**www.wsj.com**].

Class Actions

In some instances, multiple plaintiffs may join together to represent themselves and all others who are similarly situated to file a single lawsuit alleging similar harm arising from the same, or substantially the same, wrong. The high cost of litigation, the great uncertainty of victory, and the likelihood of small individual recoveries have made the class action a very useful tool for plaintiffs. Of course, the class action also enhances judicial efficiency by bringing many claims together in one case. The Class Action Fairness Act of 2005 gave federal courts jurisdiction over class actions worth more than $5 million or where plaintiffs are from multiple states.

Several recent U.S. Supreme Court rulings have impacted the viability of the class action in business disputes. For example, a small group of Walmart employees sued the company for sex discrimination on behalf of a nationwide class of 1.5 million female employees; Walmart challenged the class action certification. The Court held that the claims against Walmart did not share enough common elements to tie together the millions of employment decisions affecting women at Walmart. As a matter of company policy, discretion over pay and promotions rested with local managers at the 4,000 or so company stores; without a specific employment practice that tied all of their claims together, the class lacked the necessary commonality.[23] The Supreme Court's decision led to regional class action suits by female Walmart workers. In 2015, a federal appeals court allowed such a lawsuit to proceed, and the Supreme Court denied Wal-Mart's petition for review.[24]

In two 2013 decisions regarding antitrust class actions, the Supreme Court further limited class actions. In *Comcast Corp. v. Behrend,* the Court held that class certification requires proof that damages may be treated as classwide.[25] Further, in *American Express Co. v. Italian Colors Restaurant,* the Court held that a waiver of class arbitration was enforceable even when arbitrating a claim individually would cost far more than the potential recovery.[26]

Class Action Lawyers as "One Night Stands"?

At this writing, a bill, the "Fairness in Class Action Litigation Act of 2017," has been introduced in Congress that would codify *Comcast* in requiring that all class members suffer the same type and scope of injury. Further, it also would make it difficult for securities class actions to be brought using institutional investors, such as a state pension fund, as the lead plaintiff; the lead plaintiff would not be able to retain the law firm that it usually uses to bring the class action.

Question

Professor John C. Coffee of Columbia University Law School has suggested that the bill might "impose a legal regime of 'one night stands' on clients and their counsel." How might this affect individual investors who want to assert a securities-based claim? Who would this bill benefit? Explain.

Sources: Ben Dipietro, "Class Action Lawsuit Changes Could Lead to 'One Night Stands,'" *The Wall Street Journal,* February, 24, 2017 [**http://blogs.wsj.com/riskandcompliance/2017/02/24/the-morning-risk-report-class-action-lawsuit-changes-could-lead-to-one-night-stands/**]; and John C. Coffee, Jr., "How Not to Write a Class Action 'Reform' Bill", *The CLS Blue Sky Blog,* February 21, 2017 [http://clsbluesky.law.columbia.edu/2017/02/21/how-not-to-write-a-class-action-reform-bill/].

The Civil Trial Process

Civil procedure varies by jurisdiction. The following generalizations merely typify the process. (See Figure 4.2.) [For a vast "catalog" of law on the Internet, see **http://catalaw.com**].

FIGURE 4.2   **Stages of a Lawsuit**

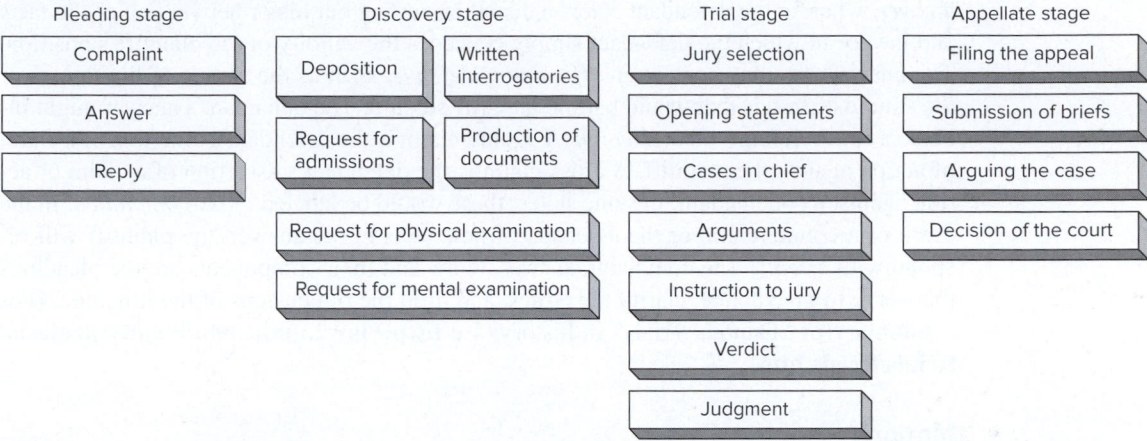

Pleading stage

| Complaint |
| Answer |
| Reply |

Discovery stage

| Deposition | Written interrogatories |
| Request for admissions | Production of documents |

| Request for physical examination |
| Request for mental examination |

Trial stage

| Jury selection |
| Opening statements |
| Cases in chief |
| Arguments |
| Instruction to jury |
| Verdict |
| Judgment |

Appellate stage

| Filing the appeal |
| Submission of briefs |
| Arguing the case |
| Decision of the court |

Pleadings

LO 4-9

Describe the typical steps in the civil trial process.

Pleadings are the documents by which each party sets his or her initial case before the court. A civil action begins when the plaintiff files his or her first pleading, which is labeled a *complaint.* The complaint specifies (1) the parties to the suit, (2) evidence as to the court's jurisdiction in the case, (3) a statement of the facts, and (4) a prayer for relief (a remedy).

The complaint is filed with the clerk of court and a summons is issued, directing the defendant to appear in court to answer the claims alleged against him or her. A sheriff or some other official attempts to personally deliver the summons to the defendant. If personal delivery cannot be achieved, the summons may be left with a responsible party at the defendant's residence. Failing that, other modes of delivery are permissible, including a mailing. Publication of a notice in a newspaper will, in some instances, constitute good service of process. Ordinarily, a copy of the complaint accompanies the summons, so the defendant is apprised of the nature of the claim.

The defendant has several options. He or she may do nothing, but failure to respond may result in a **default judgment** in favor of the plaintiff. The defendant may choose to respond by filing a *demurrer* or a *motion to dismiss,* the essence of which is to argue that even if the plaintiff's recitation of the facts is accurate, a claim on which relief can be granted has not been stated.

Served on Facebook?

The plaintiff in a divorce proceeding asked the court for permission to serve a divorce summons on the defendant, her husband, via Facebook, a social media site. The plaintiff had tried to locate the defendant's current address through the post office, the Department of Motor Vehicles, and even the defendant's prepaid phone bill, but was unsuccessful. The court analyzed whether service by Facebook could be "reasonably calculated" to give the defendant notice of the divorce. The court held that service by Facebook, although nontraditional, was the form of service that would most likely offer the defendant notice and comported most to the due process standards set under the law.

Source: *Baidoo v. Blood-Dzraku,* 48 Misc. 3d 309, 311 (N.Y. Sup. Ct. 2015).

Alternatively, the defendant may file with the court an initial pleading, called an *answer,* wherein the defendant enters a denial by setting out his or her version of the facts and law, or in which the defendant simply concedes the validity of the plaintiff's position. The answer also may contain an *affirmative defense,* such as the statute of limitations or the statute of frauds that would bar the plaintiff's claim. The defendant's answer might include a *counterclaim* or *cross-claim.* A counterclaim is the defendant's assertion of a claim of action against the plaintiff. A cross-claim is the defendant's assertion of a claim of action against a codefendant. In some states, these would be labeled *cross-complaints.* In the event of a counterclaim or the assertion of new facts in the answer, the plaintiff will respond with a *reply.* The complaint, answer, reply, and their components are the pleadings that serve to give notice, clarify the issues, and limit the dimensions of the litigation. [For a summary of "Famous Trials" in history, see **http://law2.umkc.edu/faculty/projects/ftrials/ftrials.htm**].

Motions

As necessary during and after the filing of the pleadings, either party may file motions with the court. For example, a party may move to clarify a pleading or to strike a portion deemed unnecessary. Of special importance is a *motion for a judgment on the pleadings* or a *motion for summary judgment.* In a motion for a judgment on the pleadings, either party simply asks the judge to reach a decision based on the information in the pleadings. The judge will do so only if the defendant's answer constitutes an admission of the accuracy of the plaintiff's claim, or if the plaintiff's claim clearly has no foundation in law.

In a motion for summary judgment, the party filing the motion is claiming that no facts are in dispute. Therefore, the judge may make a ruling about the law without taking the case to trial. In a summary judgment hearing, the court can look beyond the pleadings to hear evidence from affidavits, depositions, and so on. These motions avoid the time and expense of trial.

Discovery

Discovery is the primary information-gathering stage in the pretrial process. That information clarifies the trial issues, promotes pretrial settlements, and helps prevent surprises at the trial, among other things. Discovery may consist of *depositions* (recorded, sworn testimony in preparation for trial), physical and mental examinations, answers to written questions (*interrogatories*), requests for access to documents and property to inspect them prior to trial, and *admissions* (agreement by the parties to stipulated issues of fact or law prior to trial).

The era of electronic communication and storage has added important new expectations and burdens to the discovery process by requiring that litigants exchange all relevant electronically stored information (ESI) during the discovery phase. Individuals and companies must be able to produce ESI from all sources, including e-mail, files, scanned handwritten notes, stored records, voice mail, fax data, instant messages, spreadsheets, videos, PowerPoint presentations, and so on. The following case illustrates both the potential power and limitations of ESI in discovery requests.

Crabtree v. Angie's List

2017 U.S. Dist. LEXIS 12927 (S.D. Ind. January 31, 2017)

LEGAL BRIEFCASE

Magistrate Judge Mark J. Dinsmore

* * * * *

I. BACKGROUND

In this Fair Labor Standards Act ("FLSA") action, Plaintiffs assert they were wrongfully denied overtime compensation during a one-year period in which they worked as Senior Sales Representatives, also known as "Closers." In that position, Plaintiffs finalized sales with service providers for advertising on the Angie's List website and spent a significant portion of their workday on the telephone. Because Defendant did not provide company-issued laptops or cell phones for use outside the office, Plaintiffs often used their personal electronic devices for work purposes.

Plaintiffs believe they spent approximately 10–12 hours per day working for Defendant, but were paid based upon an eight-hour day and 40-hour workweek. Defendant now seeks to obtain GPS and location services data from Plaintiffs' personal cell phones to "construct a detailed and accurate timeline of when Plaintiffs were or were not working." Plaintiffs object, arguing that the request poses significant privacy concerns and that the GPS data will not accurately portray whether Plaintiffs were working at any given time. Plaintiffs further argue that Defendant has alternative, and far less intrusive, means to identify periods of time when Plaintiffs were working.

* * * * *

II. LEGAL STANDARD

A party may seek an order to compel discovery when an opposing party fails to respond to discovery requests or provides evasive or incomplete responses. A party objecting to the discovery request bears the burden of showing why the request is improper.

Federal Rule of Civil Procedure 26(b)(1) defines the scope of discovery as follows:

> Parties may obtain discovery regarding any nonprivileged matter that is relevant to any party's claim or defense and proportional to the needs of the case, considering the importance of the issues at stake in the action, the amount in controversy, the parties' relative access to relevant information, the parties' resources, the importance of the discovery in resolving the issues, and whether the burden or expense of the proposed discovery outweighs its likely benefit.

Rule 26 further provides that the Court may impose additional limitations if a discovery request is cumulative, late, or out of proportion to the needs of the case:

* * * * *

III. DISCUSSION

A. Interrogatory No. 12 and Request for Production No. 19

Defendant initially sought the identification of all equipment used by Plaintiffs as part of their employment with Defendant and requested that Plaintiffs submit for forensic examination all such equipment. Defendant subsequently narrowed its request to the production of GPS and/or location services data between September 2014 and September 2015 from any and all computers, cellular telephones, smartphones, tablets, and other communication devices used by Plaintiffs during work time during their employment with Defendant. Defendant asserts that this data is relevant to establishing how many hours Plaintiffs worked during that yearlong period. For example, Defendant notes that Plaintiffs could remain logged in to their computers on the SalesForce software, but be inactive for up to four hours. Defendant asserts the GPS data would identify whether Plaintiffs left for the day, left for lunch or some other unpaid break during that four-hour window when they were still logged on to SalesForce. Yet if Plaintiffs were permitted, in fact expected, to work outside the office to accommodate clients in different time zones, the fact that Plaintiffs' phones had left the Angie's List building would have no meaningful impact on whether the employees were performing work at that time.

Nevertheless, Defendant cites a number of district court cases purporting to support its theory that other courts have allowed similar production requests. . . . In [citation omitted], plaintiff was permitted to obtain GPS data from trucks used in defendant's business to test the accuracy of the run data previously provided by defendant. Angie's List asserts that the GPS data in conjunction with the SalesForce data would create a more accurate picture of Plaintiffs' work hours. But Defendant is overlooking a clear distinction between its request and [the cases it cites]: Plaintiffs' privacy interests. In [citation omitted], it was plaintiff who sought the GPS data from the device in the defendant employer's *truck*, which presumably tracked location while the truck was being driven during the workday—a much more pointed request than seeking all GPS/location data for 24-hours a day for a one year period from a personal device that would be tracking Plaintiffs' movements well outside of their working time.

. . . In each of the other cases relied upon by Defendant, the courts compelled the production of cell phone *records*—such as the call history—not data as intrusive as GPS data that would track Plaintiffs' locations at every moment of the day for a year. Plaintiffs have already produced cell phone records that are the equivalent of those ordered to be produced in the cases cited by Defendant.

Rule 26 requires the Court to limit discovery if it can be obtained from another source that is more convenient, less burdensome, or less expensive. Additionally, the Advisory Committee Notes to the Federal Rules [of Civil Procedure] advises the courts to act with caution when evaluating requests to inspect a party's electronic devices or systems for ESI, in order to avoid unduly impinging on a party's privacy interests.

* * * * *

Discovery must also be "proportional to the needs of the case." In this FLSA action, the parties will need to establish when Plaintiffs were performing work for Defendant. Plaintiffs assert they have already provided Defendant with cell phone records that would allow Defendant to identify business-related calls. Defendant also has access to data from SalesForce that will show when Plaintiffs were logged into the software as well as data that will show when Plaintiffs were present at Angie's List offices such as badge swipe data and log in data from their work computers. Defendant has not demonstrated that the GPS/location services data from Plaintiffs' electronic devices will be more probative than any of the above data Defendant already has in its possession. Therefore, the Court finds that the forensic examination of Plaintiffs' electronic devices is not proportional to the needs of the case because any benefit the data might provide is outweighed by Plaintiffs' significant privacy and confidentiality interests. Defendant's Motion is DENIED as to Request for Production No. 19.

In response to Interrogatory No. 12, Plaintiffs state they have identified their cell phones by virtue of producing their cell phone records to Defendant. Plaintiffs assert that they have no other personal devices or equipment to identify that was used as part of their employment with Defendant. Consequently, Defendant's Motion is DENIED as to Interrogatory No. 12.

[B–E omitted—ed.]

F. Request for Production No. 27
This request seeks documents such as email messages, social media posts, . . . [or] text messages . . . "prepared, created, obtained, or used by" Plaintiffs from September 2014 to September 2015 that related to absences from or attendance at work. Plaintiffs respond that they did not "keep any diaries, journals, calendars, or appointment books" and have no documents responsive to the requests for those items. Plaintiffs further state that to the extent the request seeks emails, text messages and social media posts, it is a "fishing expedition" not relevant to the claims or defenses in the case.

As Judge Posner has noted, "of course pretrial discovery is a fishing expedition and one can't know what one has caught until one fishes. But Fed. R. Civ. P. 45(c) allows the fish to object." In this instance, the Court shares Plaintiffs' concerns that Defendant casts too wide a net as it does not sufficiently justify the breadth of the request. Defendant argues that it is entitled to discovery if Plaintiffs "took 2-hour lunches, were gone running errands during the day, or remained logged in to SalesForce during periods they were not working." And on this point Defendant is correct. However, Defendant has not shown how emails, text messages or social media posts from this one year time period may be more probative as to these issues than other less intrusive data already within its control, such as the SalesForce data, computer log ins, or badge swipe data. As discussed with regard to the GPS/location services data, the Court has an obligation to guard against intrusive discovery. Defendant's broad request would encompass clearly personal communications such as an email string relating to an upcoming vacation between an employee and his or her spouse, or text messages planning a lunch date. These communications "relate to absences from work" yet have absolutely no relevance to this lawsuit. Additionally, the scope of the information sought by Defendant is plainly not proportional to the needs of this case. Therefore, Defendant's Motion is DENIED as to this request.

* * * * *

V. CONCLUSION
Based on the foregoing, Defendant's *Motion to Compel* is **DENIED**.

Questions
1. Why did the court distinguish between a plaintiff truck driver's request for a defendant employer's truck's GPS records and Angie's List's request for their employees' GPS data? Explain.
2. What other discovery requests might help Angie's List obtain the evidence it was seeking with the GPS data, social media posts, text messages, etc., of the plaintiffs? Explain.
3. Should data from health monitors such as Fitbits or pedometers be discoverable in personal injury actions seeking recovery for pain and suffering? Explain.

Pretrial Conference

Either party may request, and many courts require, a pretrial meeting involving the attorneys, the judge, and occasionally the parties. Usually following discovery, the conference is designed to plan the course of the trial in the interests of efficiency and justice. The participants seek to define the issues and settle the dispute in advance of trial. If no settlement is reached, a trial date is set.

The Judge and Jury

The federal Constitution and most state constitutions provide for the right to a jury trial in a civil case (excepting equity actions). Some states place dollar minimums on that guarantee. At the federal level and in most states, unless one of the parties requests a jury, the judge alone will hear the case and decide all questions of law and fact. If the case is tried before a jury, that body will resolve questions of fact, but all questions of law will be resolved by the judge, who also will instruct the jury as to the law governing the case.

Jurors are selected from a jury pool composed of a cross section of the community. A panel is drawn from that pool. The individuals in that panel are questioned by the judge, by the attorneys, or by all to determine if any individual is prejudiced about the case such that he or she could not reach an objective decision on the merits. The questioning process is called *voir dire.*

From an attorney's point of view, jury selection is often not so much a matter of finding jurors without bias as it is a matter of identifying those jurors who are most likely to reach a decision favorable to one's client. To that end, elaborate mechanisms and strategies have been employed—particularly in criminal trials—to identify desirable jurors. For example, sophisticated, computer-assisted surveys of the trial community have been conducted to develop objective evidence by which to identify jurors who would not admit to racial prejudice but whose "profile" suggests the likelihood of such prejudice.

After questioning, the attorneys may *challenge for cause,* arguing to the judge that the individual cannot exercise the necessary objectivity of judgment. Attorneys are also afforded a limited number of ***peremptory challenges,*** by which the attorney can have a potential juror dismissed without the judge's concurrence and without offering a reason. Peremptory challenges may not be used to reject jurors on the basis of race or gender.

Facebook the Jury Pool?

Social media, such as Facebook, MySpace, and Twitter, can be a valuable source of information to attorneys as they try to shape the composition of juries. Information that might not be revealed in *voir dire* sometimes comes to light online. Jury consultant Amber Yearwood in San Francisco discovered online that a member of a jury pool was highly opinionated and often dispensed medical and sex advice, a personality not well suited to the client's cause. The prospective juror was dismissed.

Source: Ana Campoy and Ashby Jones, "Searching for Details Online, Lawyers Facebook the Jury," *The New York Times,* February 22, 2011, p. A2.

The Trial

The trial begins with opening statements by the attorneys. Each is expected to outline what he or she intends to prove. The plaintiff, bearing the burden of proof, then presents evidence, which may include both testimony and physical evidence, such as documents and photos. Those are called *exhibits.*

The plaintiff's attorney secures testimony from his or her own witnesses via questioning labeled *direct examination*. After the plaintiff's attorney completes direct examination of a witness, the defense attorney may question that witness in a process labeled *cross-examination*. *Redirect* and *recross* may then follow. After all of the plaintiff's witnesses have been questioned, the plaintiff rests his or her case.

At this stage, the defense may make a motion for a **directed verdict,** arguing, in essence, that the plaintiff has offered insufficient evidence to justify relief, so time and expense may be saved by terminating the trial. Understandably, the judge considers the motion in the light most favorable to the plaintiff. Such motions ordinarily fail, and the trial goes forward with the defendant's presentation of evidence.

At the completion of the defendant's case, both parties may be permitted to offer *rebuttal* evidence, and either party may move for a directed verdict. Barring a directed verdict, the case goes forward, with each party making a closing argument. When the trial is by jury, the judge must instruct the jurors as to the law to be applied to the case. The attorneys often submit their views of the proper instructions. In most civil cases, a verdict for the plaintiff must be supported by a *preponderance of the evidence* (more likely than not). After deliberation, the verdict of the jury is rendered, and a judgment is entered by the court. [For a company providing a virtual jury in advance of trial, see **http://www.virtualjury.com**].

Experts

In this highly technological and scientific era, one of the biggest dilemmas facing judges and juries is the weight to give to expert testimony. Very often, in cases such as medical malpractice and product liability (see Chapter 7), the testimony of experts is decisive to the outcome; but that testimony varies wildly in its reliability and credibility. The golfing case that follows investigates the theme of experience as a qualification for expert testimony.

LEGAL BRIEFCASE

Nickles v. Schild
617 N.W.2d 659 (S.D. 2000)

Justice Gilbertson

Larry Nickles, the guardian of Mark Nickles, appeals the trial court's admission of expert testimony.

FACTS

On May 5, 1996, Jay Schild (Schild), Mark Nickles and Schild's younger brother drove to the Human Services Golf Course in Yankton, South Dakota, to play golf. All three boys were minors. Both Nickles and Schild had previously received golf instructions and had been taught some golfing rules.

After playing five holes, Schild and Nickles proceeded to the next tee box. Schild's younger brother was still on the fifth hole green retrieving his ball, which Nickles had knocked a short distance from the green. Schild proceeded to tee up his ball at the front center of the tee box and was preparing to hit his next drive. In the meantime, Nickles moved off the tee box approximately 10 feet and was facing the previous green watching Schild's brother. Schild, who had seen Nickles walk off the tee box, stepped back from his ball and took three practice swings. On the third practice swing, Schild hit Nickles in the head, fracturing his skull and permanently injuring his left eye.

Guardian (*sic*) commenced a personal injury action against Schild for damages sustained as a result of Schild's negligence and failure to exercise reasonable care in swinging his golf club. Schild denied he was negligent and claimed that Nickles was contributory (*sic*) negligent and assumed the risk of his injuries. During trial, Schild called Robert Boldus as an expert witness. Boldus was a former member of the Professional Golfer's (*sic*) Association and golf professional at Fox Run Golf Course in Yankton, South Dakota. Boldus had often given golfing lessons to junior golfers while at Fox Run.

Schild asked Boldus whether "as a golf professional," he had "formed any opinions as to what had happened in this case?" Nickles immediately requested permission to briefly interrogate Boldus for purposes of objecting to his opinion. During this interrogation, the following discussion occurred:

Q: (Nickles's attorney): Mr. Boldus, as a professional golfer, a member of PGA or based upon your experience, have you had any training in evaluating liability or standards of care required in golf liability cases?

A: (Boldus): No, I haven't.

Nickles then objected to the opinion by Boldus regarding standards of care or the ultimate issue. The trial judge overruled Nickles's objection and allowed Boldus to give his opinion:

Q: (Schild's attorney): And could you tell the jury what opinions you have come to?

A: (Boldus): In my opinion it was an accident. But one of the players moved, and when you're in your preshot routine if you move, you back away from the ball six inches to a foot or one step, and then you take your practice swings. My opinion, somehow Mark Nickles had moved in the way of the swing and got hit.

Q: (Schild's attorney): In your opinion did [Schild] violate any standards of care?

A: (Boldus): No.

The jury returned a verdict in favor of Schild. Nickles appealed, raising the following issue:

> Whether the trial court abused its discretion by permitting expert testimony from Boldus.

*   *   *   *   *   *

DECISION

*   *   *   *   *   *

[A]n expert is not limited to testifying only upon those areas in which he or she has received formal training. Rather, when giving an opinion, an expert is allowed to draw upon all the knowledge, skill, or experience that he or she has accumulated.

[W]hile Boldus may not have had any formal classroom "training" in the applicable liability standards, it is clear Boldus was no novice at the game of golf. He was a former member of the PGA and a golf professional at Fox Run Golf Course in Yankton. While at Fox Run, he had often given golf lessons to junior golfers, which included golf etiquette and safety. He had even previously given golf lessons to Nickles. By any of these methods of acquiring the appropriate expertise or combination thereof, he could have qualified himself as an expert to testify as to "what happened."

It is quite clear from the testimony of Boldus and his vitae that he did have an opinion on the standards of care required in golf and the expertise to give such an opinion. The following testimony regarding the standard of care applicable to the game of golf was elicited from Boldus during direct testimony:

Q: When someone has addressed the ball and stepped back and they're doing their practice swings, what is the person's duty when they're doing those practice swings?

A: Well, basically there's nothing stated that says that you have to look around. You should be, when you begin your preshot routine, prior to taking your practice swings you should look and kind of [get] an idea where people are at so they are out of your way so you can take a swing. Once you begin your practice swings I think it's a duty of the other person to stay out of the way.

Q: So once, right before you start your preshot routine is when you have the duty to check what's going around?

A: Yes.

Q: And then as you start your preshot routine then it's the duty of those around you to become aware that that's what you're going to do, to watch?

A: Yes.

*   *   *   *   *

Boldus merely described, in his opinion, "what happened in this case" and that Schild's actions did not violate any standard of care concerning the game of golf. He did not invade the province of the jury as Nickles suggests. Boldus did not testify as to the ultimate issue of negligence. In fact, Boldus did not discuss the issue of liability at all until he was asked upon cross-examination, "but one party is liable, aren't they?" Boldus responded, "I wouldn't—yah—I don't know about liable, but somebody [is responsible for that]."

Nickles' objection as to the qualifications of Boldus goes in part to formal training concerning the issue of ultimate liability. The ultimate liability of one of the parties is not the same as standard of care. One can violate a standard of care and still not be held liable. There could be further potential questions of contributory negligence, assumption of the risk, financial responsibility of a minor and/or his parents, questions of duty to supervise a minor and the like, all of which can have a decisive effect on liability and which clearly are outside the expertise of a golf pro and his knowledge of golf standards of care. Boldus did not testify as to any of these issues; his testimony was limited to describing the standard of care for the game of golf.

Affirmed.

DISSENT

Justice Sabers

I dissent.

I write specially to point out that the majority opinion misses the point—not once, but several times.

Whether Boldus was qualified as an expert witness is immaterial. The point is that under the pretense of being an expert witness, Boldus cannot testify as a fact witness. He was not present at the scene. He does not know what happened. Only fact witnesses can testify "as to what happened?" Therefore, under these circumstances it was totally improper for Boldus to testify to his opinion "as to what happened in this case."

Questions

1. What were Nickles's objections to the expert, Boldus's, testimony?

2. What objection was raised by dissenting Justice Sabers?

3. Do you agree with the expert, Boldus, that once a golfer has properly started the preshot routine, the duty of care shifts to those around the golfer to be aware of what is happening and to keep themselves out of harm's way? Explain.

4. Dodge slipped leaving work and claimed that she suffered knee, ankle, and back injuries. Dodge sued the workplace cleaning service, but she provided no expert testimony to establish that the fall caused the injuries. Rather Dodge provided her own explanation of the fall and resulting injuries. Did the trial court err in admitting Dodge's layperson testimony? Explain. See *Dodge-Farrar v. American Cleaning Services Co.,* 54 P.3d 954 (Idaho Ct. App. 2002).

Posttrial Motions

The losing party may seek a ***judgment notwithstanding the verdict (judgment n.o.v)*** on the grounds that the jury's decision was clearly inconsistent with the law or the evidence. Such motions are rarely granted. The judge is also empowered to enter a judgment n.o.v on his or her own initiative.

Either party also may move for a new trial. The winning party might do so on the grounds that the remedy provided was inferior to that warranted by the evidence. The losing party commonly claims an error of law to support a motion for a new trial. Other possible grounds for a new trial include jury misconduct or new evidence.

Appeals

LO 4-10

Distinguish trials and appeals.

After the judgment is rendered, either party may appeal the decision to a higher court. The winner may do so if he or she feels the remedy is inadequate. Ordinarily, of course, the losing party brings the appeal. As noted, the appealing party is the ***appellant*** or the *petitioner*, while the other party is the ***appellee*** or *respondent*. The appeals court does not try the case again. In theory, at least, its consideration is limited to mistakes of law at the trial level. The appellant will argue, for example, that a jury instruction was erroneous or that the judge erred in failing to grant a motion to strike testimony alleged to have been prejudicial. The appeals court does not hear new evidence. Its decision is based on the trial record, materials filed by the opposing attorneys, and oral arguments.

The appellate court announces its judgment and ordinarily explains that decision in an accompanying document labeled an *opinion*. (Most of the cases in this text are appellate court opinions.) If no error is found, the lower court decision is *affirmed*. In finding prejudicial error, the appellate court may simply ***reverse*** (overrule) the lower court. Or the judgment may be to *reverse and* ***remand,*** wherein the lower court is overruled and the case must be tried again in accordance with the law as articulated in the appeals court opinion.

After the decision of the intermediate appellate court, a further appeal may be sought at the highest court of the jurisdiction. Most of those petitions are denied.

Questions—Part Two

1. What are the purposes and uses of the concept of jurisdiction? Why do we limit the courts to which a claim can be taken?

2. Law cases often read like soap operas, even as they reveal important truths. A woman and man, each married to others, had engaged in a long-term love affair. The woman's husband died, and she pleaded with her paramour to leave his New York home to visit her in Florida. She affirmed her love for the man. They made arrangements to meet in Miami, but on his arrival at the airport, he was served a summons informing him that he was being sued. His Florida "lover" sought $500,000 for money allegedly loaned to him and for seduction inspired by a promise of marriage.

   a. Does the Florida court have proper jurisdiction over him?

   b. What if he had voluntarily come to Florida on vacation? See *Wyman v. Newhouse,* 93 F.2d 313 (2d Cir. 1937).

3. Sea Pines, a privately owned suburban community on Hilton Head Island, South Carolina, was designated a wildlife sanctuary by the state legislature. After study, the state Department of Natural Resources decided to issue permits to allow limited deer hunting on the land to reduce overpopulation. Various environmental groups challenged the issuance of the permits. What defense would you expect the state to offer in court? Explain. See *Sea Pines Association for Protection of Wildlife v. South Carolina Department of Natural Resources,* 550 S.E.2d 287 (S.C. 2001).

Part Three—Criticism and Alternatives

Criticism

To many Americans, our system of justice is neither systematic nor just. With more than 1.2 million lawyers in a population of over 312 million people, critics argue that excessive, unproductive litigation is inevitable.

Too Many Lawyers and Lawsuits?

Many lawsuits are less a search for justice and more a pursuit of big dollars for attorneys, the critics claim. A large law firm sued an energy industry executive for unpaid legal bills, resulting in a counterclaim asserting that the firm overbilled as a matter of practice. During discovery, e-mails between three attorneys at the firm surfaced that included such statements as "That bill shall know no limits." Even though the firm described

> "That bill shall know no limits"

the e-mail exchange as "unfortunate banter" between colleagues, the messages may reflect a larger problem with the approaches that law firms have to billing.[27] A confidential settlement ended the litigation.[28]

Legal critic Philip K. Howard argues that we need fewer lawsuits, fewer rules, and greater personal responsibility. He thinks we feel powerless in the face of rules:

> Ordinary choices–by teachers, doctors, officials, managers, even volunteers—are paralyzed by legal self-consciousness. Did you check the rules? Who will be responsible if there is an accident? . . . We have become a culture of rule followers, trained to frame every solution in terms of existing law or possible legal risk. . . .[29]

Even the late Supreme Court Justice Antonin Scalia argued that we have too many lawyers:

> Lawyers don't dig ditches or build buildings. When a society requires such a large number of its best minds to conduct the unproductive enterprise of the law, something is wrong with the legal system.[30]

Polling results suggest that Americans have deep reservations about our legal system, but they also recognize its indispensable role in maintaining a just society. A recent survey conducted by the American Tort Reform Association, for example, shows that nine of 10 American voters believe lawsuit abuse is a problem, and 60 percent believe that consumers and small businesses are hurt by it.[31] On the other hand, a national poll by the American Association for Justice (formerly the American Trial Lawyers Association) found more concern about corporate abuse than about lawyers and the legal system.[32]

> **Nine of 10 American voters believe lawsuit abuse is a problem.**

The Corporate Perspective

The legal system plays an invaluable role in facilitating and stabilizing commercial practice, but for corporate America, the law is also a source of significant expense and abundant frustration. As one expert explained, dealing with legal responsibilities and problems has become a central ingredient in management practice:

> Only a few decades ago, the law was peripheral to the core activities of doing business. When I became a business lawyer in the late 1950s, for example, our involvement was generally limited to forming a corporation or partnership for a client, providing for the investment capital, doing a lease for an office or factory, and maybe handling a key contract with a CEO or a major supplier. . . . Today the law can affect almost every action a manager takes. It has moved closer to the core activities of conducting business and succeeding in a red-hot, competitive environment. More people now have "rights" they can assert against your company, so you face claims from employees, consumers, competitors, and the government. Consequently, today's manager needs to know something about employment law, discrimination claims, sexual harassment rules, product safety issues, the rules of advertising and competition, antitrust rules, environmental law, the value of intellectual property, and more.[33]

[For a critique of the American legal system, see the U.S. Chamber Institute for Legal Reform (an affiliate of the U.S. Chamber of Commerce) at **http://www.facesoflawsuitabuse. com/**]. [For a critique of the U.S. Chamber Institute for Legal Reform, see the American

Association for Justice's 2011 report "Do as I Say, Not as I Sue" at **https://www.justice.org/sites/default/files/file-uploads/Do_As_I_Say_Not_As_I_Sue_2011.pdf**].

Pants: Abusing the Legal System?

Washington, DC, administrative law judge Roy Pearson attracted the attention of journalists from around the world by suing his neighborhood laundry for $54 million, down from an earlier claim of $67 million, over the alleged loss of the pants belonging to his $1,000 suit. Pearson thought he was entitled to $18,000 per day for each day the pants were missing over a period of nearly four years. Owners Soo and Jin Chung of Custom Cleaners attempted to give Pearson a pair of pants they said were the missing item, but he said the ones offered were not his. Pearson brought claims of mental suffering, inconvenience, discomfort, and fraud (based on the "Satisfaction Guaranteed" sign at Custom Cleaners). Along the way, Pearson had rejected settlement offers that reached $12,000. The Chungs won an easy trial victory with the court concluding that Pearson was unable to prove the pants offered to him were not his and that the "Satisfaction Guaranteed" sign did not require the Chungs to satisfy a customer's unreasonable demands. Pearson was ordered to pay the Chungs' court costs, and the legal fees for the Chungs' defense were covered by contributions. The Chungs' dry cleaner went out of business. Pearson subsequently failed in his bid to be reappointed to his judge's position. He sued for wrongful discharge and lost at the federal district court and then appealed to the federal court of appeals, where he also lost.

Sources: Henri E. Cauvin, "Court Rules for Cleaners in $54 Million Pants Suit," *The Washington Post,* June 26, 2007, p. A01; and "'Pants Judge' Roy Pearson Strikes Out in Court," *The Wall Street Journal,* May 27, 2010 [**http://blogs.wsj.com/law**].

Criticized in America; Embraced Abroad

The United States is not alone in its ongoing debate about whether more or fewer lawyers and lawsuits are needed.

Japan   Historically in Japan, lawsuits have seldom been used to settle disputes, as reflected in its relatively small number of attorneys. With the rise of international mergers, bankruptcy, patents, and other business disputes, Japan became concerned with its lawyer shortage. A government council recommended U.S.-style law schools be established, calling for an increase in the number of lawyers. Although the number of lawyers per capita is still relatively fewer than in the United States, the number of lawyers in Japan nearly doubled between 2000 and 2015. However, the number of lawsuits have not increased and bankruptcy proceedings have decreased, creating an employment problem for lawyers in Japan.[34]

PRACTICING ETHICS   Legal Services at a Click or a Tap?

Subscribers of Rocket Lawyer pay a monthly fee ($39.95 for a "premium plan" and $49.95 for a plan called "accelerate" at this writing)[35] for instant access to pre-prepared documents, law tutorials, and online legal advice from experts at participating firms. Users of Shake, a smartphone app, can get help in creating contracts that others, such as the users' customers, can then sign with a finger touch on their screen.[36] Such innovations have allowed those previously unable to afford an attorney to obtain legal services. The founder of Rocket Lawyer compares the service to a health plan with physicians in the health plan's network.[37] Some view these plans as a way not only to address access to justice, but to create new and needed opportunities for lawyers who face an increasingly poor labor market.[38] The American Bar Association (ABA) has partnered with Rocket Lawyer in a pilot program that allows small businesses in Illinois, Pennsylvania, and California to connect with lawyers who are ABA members to have their business-related legal questions answered for a $4.95 monthly subscription.[39]

Questions

1. How does the online provision of legal services resolve access to justice problems of those who have not been able to afford a lawyer?
2. If a lower-income individual seeks to resolve a conflict with a *Fortune* 500 company by using an online service or legal services app, would that individual be at a disadvantage? Explain.

On the Other Hand—Litigation as a Last Resort

Almost everyone seems to be unhappy about lawyers and lawsuits, but at the same time Americans expect lawyers and the courts to settle disputes; preserve freedom and justice; and correct problems not satisfactorily addressed by the market, legislatures, and regulators. Feeling threatened by abusive bosses, corporate fraud, dangerous drugs, defective products, environmental decline, and so on, Americans count on the justice system to protect our pecuniary interests as well as the personal freedom and democracy we prize. Lawyers and the courts often are the only available weapons to right what we believe to be a wrong. So the frustration many feel about exploding litigation may be attributable to us as much as to greedy lawyers. Furthermore, laws and lawyers are central to economic efficiency. Lawyers devise the rules, processes, and structures that permit capitalism to operate effectively. As we have read, the balance of the world is coming to recognize that law and lawyers are prerequisites to economic stability and progress.

Fewer Trials   A National Center for State Courts study of the state courts in 75 of the most populous counties revealed that from 1992 to 2005, the number of civil trials decreased by more than 50 percent.[40] In 2015, the center reported that contractual disputes dominated courts' civil caseload; tort claims were typically a small portion of state courts' civil caseload; and the number of tort filings seems to have stabilized.[41] Trials often are an inefficient way of resolving disputes, so these numbers may be considered very good news. On the other hand, trials are visible affirmations of the indispensability of justice, and they provide the careful reasoning and precedents that identify impermissible behavior.

> Trials often are an inefficient way of resolving disputes.

PRACTICING ETHICS) Declining Access to Lawyers?

One of the reasons for the declining number of trials, despite increasing disputes, may be difficulty in affording a lawyer in civil suits. *The New York Times* and other publications have reported an increasing number of cases going forward with one of the parties serving as a "do-it-yourself" lawyer.[42] Pursuing a claim in a federal district court costs an average of $15,000, with more complicated cases involving scientific evidence often reaching $100,000.[43] The expense of bringing lawsuits has attracted litigation funders, who invest in business disputes in exchange for a portion of the proceeds received by the party to whom they have given capital.[44] Litigation funders assert that they are helping litigants seek justice from wealthier opponents and not supporting frivolous lawsuits, which would be risky investments.[45] One other possible result is that some litigants appear to be victimized by lawsuit lenders in a lightly regulated industry where interest rates "often exceed 100 percent per year."[46]

A 2012 San Francisco ordinance created a right to civil counsel, similar to what criminal defendants receive. Those living within 200 percent of the federal poverty line and who have a case regarding such key issues as housing, safety, or child custody would be eligible for free legal assistance.[47] Although critics may view such programs as being best left to private legal aid organizations, supporters believe that by providing legal assistance to civil litigants in need, the city will avoid the long-term costs arising from self-represented parties, such as court delays.[48]

Question

While indigent criminal defendants are assured the right to counsel under American law, the same is not assured in civil disputes. Do you think San Francisco's Civil Justice initiative should be followed throughout the United States? Explain.

Reform: Judicial Efficiency

Governments, businesses, lawyers, judges—all are frustrated with the expense and inefficiency of our overburdened judicial system. Some small businesses are now buying legal services insurance or prepaid legal services for a flat monthly fee.

Some cities have taken novel approaches to adjudication such as business courts that hear only commercial claims, thus allowing jurists to become very efficient in handling contract problems, shareholder claims, and the like. Those systems are variations on the small claims courts that have long proven effective in settling minor disputes.

Small Claims Courts

Suppose you move out of your apartment and your landlord refuses to return your $500 damage deposit even though the rooms are spotless. Hiring a lawyer doesn't make good financial sense and is beyond your means anyway, but a **small claims court** may provide an effective solution.

Small claims courts, for the most part, resolve relatively minor disputes, like your landlord–tenant problem. A wide range of problems, such as divorce or bankruptcy, cannot be litigated in small claims courts. Maximum recoveries vary from place to place but typically range from a few thousand dollars up to $7,500 or so. To prepare for a small claims case, the key is developing and presenting to the judge as much credible evidence as possible. If you can present witnesses on your behalf, do so, but if not, clearly written memos expressing what the witnesses would have said may be acceptable to the judge. You need not hire a lawyer, but in most states you may do so if you wish. Should the small claims litigation not work out well for you, an appeal is permitted in many states.[49]

Honda in Small Claims Court

After rejecting a class-action settlement that would have paid Honda Civic hybrid owners $100 to $200 each and offer some rebates on a new Honda purchase, in 2012 Heather Peters sued Honda in small claims court and won $9,867.19 in damages after the judge ruled that Honda misled her into thinking her hybrid could get 50 miles per gallon, when its fuel economy actually dropped from approximately 42 miles per gallon to 30 miles per gallon after a software update. Honda successfully appealed to the Los Angeles County Superior Court. Even though she lost on appeal, Peters prompted other customers to file lawsuits against Honda in small claims courts across the United States, including in New Bedford, Massachusetts; St. Louis, Missouri; and Arlington, Washington.

Sources: Jerry Hirsch, "Honda Loses Civic Hybrid Small Claims Court Lawsuit," *Los Angeles Times,* February 1, 2012 [**www.latimes.com**]; and Jerry Hirsch, "Honda Wins Appeal in Civic Hybrid Mileage Lawsuit," *Los Angeles Times,* May 10, 2012 [**www.latimes.com**].

Alternative Dispute Resolution

LO 4-11
Identify dispute resolution alternatives to trials.

Businesses, in particular, are increasingly looking outside the judicial system for dispute resolution strategies. Dot-com entrepreneurs are developing interesting new online mechanisms for conveniently addressing Internet-based disputes. Networks of human mediators, dispute resolution software, and PayPal dispute resolution are among the online methods of settling problems outside of court.

Cybersettle is an online system for resolving insurance disputes, often of the fender-bender or slip-and-fall variety. The parties log on to Cybersettle and type in their monetary demands or offers. The system works 24 hours a day, seven days a week. The computer compares the bids, round by round. When those numbers come within a predetermined range, the two sides are notified that a settlement has been achieved. If necessary, a telephone facilitator may join the process to help reach the final sum to be paid. Cybersettle has patented its system and says it has settled more than 200,000 transactions and has facilitated over $1.9 billion in settlements. [See **http://www.cybersettle.com/**]. In 2011, New York City comptroller John Liu replaced the city's Cybersettle process to settle small personal injury and property damages claims with an in-house staff of claims adjusters as a more cost-effective alternative.[50] Critics say some Internet legal resources such as **http://www.whocanisue.com/,** a highly advertised website that matches potential clients with lawyers, may degrade the legal profession and serve primarily to generate litigation.[51]

What Is Alternative Dispute Resolution?

Of course, any form of negotiation and settlement would constitute an alternative to litigation, but mediation and arbitration are the most prominent of the substitutes. Given the expense, frustration, and risk of lawsuits, we are seeing increasing imagination in building other alternative dispute resolution (ADR) options including private trials and minitrials. [For many ADR links, see **www.hg.org/adr.html**].

Mediation

Mediation introduces a neutral third party into the resolution process. Ideally, the parties devise their own solution, with the mediator as a facilitator, not a decision maker. Even if the mediator proposes a solution, it will likely be in the nature of a compromise, not a determination of right and wrong. The bottom line is that only the disputing parties can adopt any particular outcome. The mediator may aid the parties in a number of ways, such as opening up communication between them.

Arbitration

In **arbitration** a neutral third party is given the power to determine a binding resolution of the dispute. Depending on the situation, the resolution may be either a compromise solution or a determination of the rights of the parties and a win–lose solution. Even in the latter case, however, arbitration may be quicker and less costly than a trial, and the arbitrator may be an expert in the subject area of the dispute instead of a generalist, as a judge would be. Arbitration is procedurally more formal than mediation, with the presentation of proofs and arguments by the parties, but less formal than court adjudication.

The arbitrator's decision ordinarily is legally binding and final, although an increasing but still small number of arbitration decisions are reaching court.[52]

Private Trials

"Rent-a-Judge"

A number of states now permit mutually agreed-on private trials, sometimes labeled "rent-a-judge." Normally, a third party such as a mediation firm makes the necessary arrangements, including hiring a retired judge and jurors. The proceedings are conducted much as in a courtroom. Because the parties are paying, however, the process normally moves along more rapidly, and the proceeding may be conducted in private. Appeals to the formal judicial system are provided for in some states. Critics question the fairness of the private system and wonder if it will further erode faith in public trials, but the time and money saved can be quite substantial.

Minitrials

In recent years, some corporations have agreed to settle their disputes by holding informal hearings that clarify the facts and the issues that would emerge if the dispute were litigated. In the minitrial, each organization presents its version of the case to a panel of senior executives from each organization. The trial is presided over by a neutral third party, who may be expected to issue a nonbinding opinion as to the likely result were the case to be litigated. The executives then meet to attempt to negotiate a settlement. The neutral third party sometimes facilitates that discussion. Minitrials are voluntary and nonbinding, but if an agreement is reached, the parties can formalize it by entering a settlement contract.

ADR Assessed

Alternative dispute resolution (ADR) mechanisms generally have been sustained in the courts. ADR—particularly arbitration—is often the required dispute-resolution mechanism for employee complaints such as discrimination or harassment. Mandatory arbitration clauses are often included in consumer transactions involving loans, credit cards, cable service, auto warranties, brokerage accounts, insurance, and more. Ordinarily, ADR costs less and is resolved more quickly than litigation. ADR is less formal and less adversarial than the judicial process. Furthermore, the parties have more control over the proceedings in that they can choose the facilitator, they can choose when and where the dispute will be heard, and they can keep the dispute private if they wish. Despite those strengths, alternative dispute resolution has some limitations when compared with litigation.

A recent study of nearly 4,000 employee arbitration cases found an employee win rate of only 21.4 percent, a lower result than in litigation. In arbitration cases won by employees, the median recovery was $36,500 and the mean was $109,858, both of which are substantially lower than awards reported from litigation. On the other hand, arbitration, on average, was both quicker and less expensive than litigation.[53]

A 2011 U.S. Supreme Court decision makes arbitration less functional for consumers by allowing businesses to continue their commonplace practice of requiring arbitration of disputes but forbidding class action arbitration (and litigation), thus compelling consumers to individually arbitrate alleged wrongdoing. In that case, Vincent and Liza Concepcion complained that AT&T Mobility charged them $30.22 in sales tax and other fees for what was advertised as a "free" phone. They sought class-action status for themselves and others, but the 5–4 Supreme Court ruling denied that possibility and left the Concepcions and others similarly aggrieved to file individual claims for very small amounts of money.[54] The case that follows examines whether a mandatory arbitration clause in a travel agency contract to climb Mount Kilimanjaro was unconscionable under California law.

> AT&T Mobility charged them $30.22 for a "free" phone.

LEGAL BRIEFCASE

Lhotka v. Geographic Expeditions

181 Cal. App. 4th 816 (Cal. Ct. App. 1st Dist. 2010), *petition for review denied,* 2010 Cal. LEXIS 3320 (April 14, 2010)[55]

Judge Siggins

Geographic Expeditions, Inc. (GeoEx), appeals from an order denying its motion to compel arbitration of a wrongful death action brought by the survivors of one of its clients who died on a Mount Kilimanjaro hiking expedition. . . .

BACKGROUND

Jason Lhotka was 37 years old when he died of an altitude-related illness while on a GeoEx expedition up Mount Kilimanjaro with his mother, plaintiff Sandra Menefee. GeoEx's limitation of liability and release form, which both Lhotka and Menefee signed as a requirement of participating in the expedition, provided that each of them released GeoEx from all liability in connection with the trek and waived any claims for liability "to the maximum extent permitted by law." The release also required that the parties would submit any disputes between themselves first to mediation and then to binding arbitration. It reads: "I understand that all Trip Applications are subject to acceptance by GeoEx in San Francisco, California, USA. I agree that in the unlikely event a dispute of any kind arises between me and GeoEx, the following conditions will apply: (a) the dispute will be submitted to a neutral third-party mediator in San Francisco, California, with both parties splitting equally the cost of such mediator. If the dispute cannot be resolved through mediation, then (b) the dispute will be submitted for binding arbitration to the American Arbitration Association in San Francisco, California; (c) the dispute will be governed by California law; and (d) the maximum amount of recovery to which I will be entitled under any and all circumstances will be the sum of the land and air cost of my trip with GeoEx. I agree that this is a fair and reasonable limitation on the damages, of any sort whatsoever, that I may suffer. I agree to fully indemnify GeoEx for all of its costs (including attorneys' fees) if I commence an action or claim against GeoEx based upon claims I have previously released or waived by signing this release." Menefee paid $16,831 for herself and Lhotka to go on the trip.

A letter from GeoEx president James Sano that accompanied the limitation of liability and release explained that the form was mandatory and that, on this point, "our lawyers, insurance carriers and medical consultants give us no discretion. A signed, unmodified release form is required before any traveler may join one of our trips. Ultimately, we believe that you should choose your travel company based on its track record, not what you are asked to sign. . . . My review of other travel companies' release forms suggests that our forms are not a whole lot different from theirs."

After her son's death, Menefee sued GeoEx for wrongful death and alleged various theories of liability including fraud, gross negligence and recklessness, and intentional infliction of emotional distress. GeoEx moved to compel arbitration.

The trial court found the arbitration provision was unconscionable and on that basis denied the motion.

*   *   *   *   *

This appeal timely followed.

DISCUSSION

The question . . . posed here [is] whether the agreement to arbitrate is unconscionable and, therefore, unenforceable.

*   *   *   *   *

[I omitted—ed.]

II. *Unconscionability*

(1) We turn first to GeoEx's contention that the court erred when it found the arbitration agreement unconscionable. . . . "[U]nconscionability has generally been recognized to include an absence of meaningful choice on the part of one of the parties together with contract terms which are unreasonably favorable to the other party. Phrased another way, unconscionability has both a 'procedural' and a 'substantive' element." The procedural element requires oppression or surprise. Oppression occurs where a contract involves lack of negotiation and meaningful choice, surprise where the allegedly unconscionable provision is hidden within a prolix printed form. The

substantive element concerns whether a contractual provision reallocates risks in an objectively unreasonable or unexpected manner. Under this approach, both the procedural and substantive elements must be met before a contract or term will be deemed unconscionable. Both, however, need not be present to the same degree. A sliding scale is applied so that 'the more substantively oppressive the contract term, the less evidence of procedural unconscionability is required to come to the conclusion that the term is unenforceable, and vice versa.'" . . .

A. Procedural Unconscionability

. . . GeoEx led plaintiffs to understand not only that its terms and conditions were nonnegotiable, but that plaintiffs would encounter the same requirements with any other travel company. This is a sufficient basis for us to conclude plaintiffs lacked bargaining power.

GeoEx also contends its terms were not oppressive . . . because Menefee and Lhotka could have simply decided not to trek up Mount Kilimanjaro. It argues that contracts for recreational activities can *never* be unconscionably oppressive because, unlike agreements for necessities such as medical care or employment, a consumer of recreational activities *always* has the option of foregoing [sic] the activity. . . .

(2) While the nonessential nature of recreational activities is a factor to be taken into account in assessing whether a contract is oppressive, it is not necessarily the dispositive factor. . . .

*   *   *   *   *

(3) Here, certainly, plaintiffs could have chosen not to sign on with the expedition. That option, like any availability of market alternatives, is relevant to the existence, and degree, of oppression. . . . But we must also consider the other circumstances surrounding the execution of the agreement. . . . GeoEx presented its terms as both nonnegotiable and *no different than what plaintiffs would find with any other provider*. Under these circumstances, plaintiffs made a sufficient showing to establish at least a minimal level of oppression to justify a finding of procedural unconscionability.

B. Substantive Unconscionability

With the "sliding scale" rule firmly in mind, we address whether the substantive unconscionability of the GeoEx contract warrants the trial court's ruling. . . .

*   *   *   *   *

The arbitration provision in GeoEx's release is . . . one-sided. . . . It guaranteed that plaintiffs could not possibly obtain anything approaching full recompense for their harm by limiting any recovery they could obtain to the amount they paid GeoEx for their trip. In addition to a limit on their recovery, plaintiffs, residents of Colorado, were required to mediate and arbitrate in San Francisco—all but guaranteeing both that GeoEx would never be out more than the amount plaintiffs had paid for their trip, and that any recovery plaintiffs might obtain would be devoured by the expense they incur in pursing their remedy. The release also required plaintiffs to indemnify GeoEx for its costs and attorney fees for defending any claims covered by the release of liability form. Notably, there is no reciprocal limitation on damages or indemnification obligations imposed on GeoEx. Rather than providing a neutral forum for dispute resolution, GeoEx's arbitration scheme provides a potent disincentive for an aggrieved client to pursue any claim, in any forum—and may well guarantee that GeoEx wins even if it loses. Absent reasonable justification for this arrangement—and none is apparent—we agree with the trial court that the arbitration clause is so one-sided as to be substantively unconscionable.

* * * * *

Affirmed.

Questions

1. Why was the Lhotka/Geographic Expeditions agreement to arbitrate ruled unconscionable?

2. Differentiate procedural and substantive unconscionability.

3. Kalliope and David Valchine entered court-ordered mediation to try to resolve the problems that had led them to seek a divorce.

Lawyers represented both Kalliope and David at mediation. The mediation led to a marital settlement agreement between Kalliope and David. One month later, Kalliope sought to set aside the agreement, arguing that she had been coerced by her husband, her husband's attorney, and the mediator. Kalliope testified that the mediator threatened to report her to the judge for being uncooperative in refusing to sign a reasonable settlement offer. She claimed that the mediator also told her that she could sign the agreement and then object to its provisions at the final hearing. See *Kalliope Vitakis-Valchine v. David L. Valchine*, 793 So. 2d 1094 (Fla. App. 4th Dist. 2001); *Vitakis v. Valchine*, 34 So. 3d 17 (Fla. App. 4th Dist. 2010).

Should the settlement be set aside? Explain.

4. Is an arbitration clause as a condition of employment a fair method of alternate dispute resolution, if entered knowingly and voluntarily? Explain.

5. In an effort to reduce legal expenses, some major banks and other businesses follow policies providing that all customer complaints will be subject to arbitration. Is mandatory arbitration fair to consumers? Explain.

Internet Exercise

Go to the "2012 Lawsuit Climate Study" of the U.S. Chamber of Commerce Institute for Legal Reform (ILR) at **http://www.instituteforlegalreform.com/states/** and click on your state. Scroll down to "All Results" for your state and select articles to read opinions on legal issues facing your state. For a critique of the ILR's Lawsuit Climate Study, go to **http://www.justice.org/cps/rde/xchg/justice/hs.xsl/11932.htm.**

Chapter Questions

1. Economist Stephen Magee argues that one way to strengthen the American economy would be to close the law schools:

   Every time you turn out one law school graduate, you've got a 40-year problem on your hands, he says. These guys run around and generate a lot of spurious conflict. They're like heat-seeking missiles.[56]

   Comment.

2. The National Registry of Exonerations, a joint project of the University of Michigan Law School and Professor Samuel Gross of the University of Michigan Law School, shows that from January 1989 through January 2014, 1,304 convicted individuals were exonerated.[57] In 2013, 87 exonerations were recorded; of these, 15 had pleaded guilty, 40 had been convicted of murder, and 18 had been convicted of rape or sexual assault.[58]

   a. The U.S. prison population has been estimated at approximately 2 million, generally viewed as the highest number of incarcerations in the world. In your opinion, what may the number of exonerations recorded in the National Registry of Exonerations compared to the U.S. prison population show about the U.S. criminal justice system? Explain.

b. Trends of the National Registry of Exonerations show both an increase in the number of those exonerated who had pleaded guilty, as well as an increase in the investigations by law enforcement into possible false convictions. What conclusions might be drawn from these trends? Explain.

3. The 17-year-old employee of an auto repair shop in Iowa was severely injured when a tire he was inflating on a customer's trailer exploded. The tire manufacturer is located in China but sold thousands of tires in Iowa through an American distributor. The injured employee's mother brought a product-liability claim on behalf of her son against the Chinese tire manufacturer in an Iowa state court. Can the court exercise jurisdiction over the Chinese tire manufacturer? Explain. See *Book v. Doublestar Dongfeng Tyre Co.*, 860 N.W.2d 576 (Iowa 2015).

4. Dubuque, Iowa's City Council and mayor in 2011 enacted a parental responsibility ordinance providing: "A failure by a parent to exercise reasonable control over the parent's minor which causes the minor to commit an unlawful act is a violation. . . ." The ordinance is directed to derelict parents whose negligence or indifference facilitates criminal behavior by children and leads to big investments of police time in simply locating parents. A violation initially results in a warning, with increasing fines (or parenting classes) for violations thereafter. The city's plan is to provide resources to aid parents who are in violation of the ordinance. The city has indicated that "reasonable control" means doing what the average person would do.[59]
   a. What objections would you raise to this ordinance?
   b. Do you think a parent would violate the reasonable control standard if his or her child failed to come home from the movies by the hour agreed on, but the parent then made an effort to find the child? Explain.
   c. Is the ordinance a good idea in your judgment? Explain.

5. In 2013, Megan Thode, a former graduate student, sought $1.3 million in damages from Lehigh University for receiving a C+ in a class in which a B or above was needed to enroll in the next required course toward her goal of becoming a licensed professional counselor. Thode's complaint was based on claims of breach of contract and sexual discrimination. The trial judge ruled for the defendant, Lehigh University.[60]
   a. If you were the trial judge, what information would you expect to be presented at trial? Explain.
   b. What could be the impact of Thode's lawsuit on student–professor relations and grading in college? Explain.

6. The California Medical Injury Compensation Reform Act (MICRA) of 1975 capped non-economic damages such as pain and suffering at $250,000; as of this writing, the cap has never been adjusted for inflation, with a 2015 California appellate court concluding that raising the MICRA cap was a legislative matter. Such award caps have been criticized as limiting those injured from seeking legal redress, as most attorneys representing plaintiffs in medical malpractice actions work on contingency. Further, plaintiffs with permanent injuries will be able to collect no more for their pain and suffering than those who will recover fully.[61]

   A 2014 California ballot measure that would have raised the MICRA cap to $1.1 million was defeated. What are the advantages and disadvantages of limiting damages in medical malpractice suits? Explain.

7. According to Warren Avis, founder of Avis Rent-a-Car,

   > We've reached a point in this country where, in many instances, power has become more important than justice—not a matter of who is right, but of who has the most money, time, and the largest battery of lawyers to drag a case through the courts.[62]

   a. Should the rich be entitled to better legal representation, just as they have access to better food, better medical care, better education, and so on? Explain.
   b. Should we employ a nationwide legal services program sufficient to guarantee competent legal aid to all? Explain.

8. Peremptory challenges may not constitutionally be used to exclude a potential juror from a trial on racial or gender grounds.
   a. Must a criminal jury reflect the ethnic or racial diversity of the community? Explain. See *Powers v. Ohio,* 111 S. Ct. 1364 (1991).
   b. Could potential jurors lawfully be rejected on the basis of their place of residence? Explain. See *United States v. Bishop,* 959 F.2d 820 (9th Cir. 1992).

9. Former workers and families of former workers of Mercedes-Benz Argentina (MBA), a subsidiary of the German corporation Daimler AG, brought a claim under the Alien Tort Claims Act and the Torture Victims Protection Act alleging that MBA had assisted the Argentine government in violating human rights in Argentina. The lawsuit against Daimler AG was brought in California. The plaintiffs argued that Daimler AG was liable for the acts of its MBA subsidiary because another of its subsidiaries, Mercedes-Benz USA, operated in California. Does the California court have jurisdiction over Daimler AG in this case? Explain. See *Daimler AG v. Bauman,* 134 S. Ct. 746 (2014).

10. In 1982, a security guard was murdered during a robbery of a south Chicago McDonald's. Alton Logan was sentenced to life in prison for that murder. At the same time, two Chicago public defenders, Dale Coventry and Jamie Kunz, were representing Andrew Wilson, who was accused of murdering two police officers. Based on a tip, Coventry and Kunz suspected that Wilson was the actual murderer in the McDonald's case. They questioned Wilson, who admitted that he, not Logan, was the murderer. Because of their duties under the attorney–client privilege, Coventry and Kunz felt they could not reveal what they knew. Logan, therefore, went to prison an innocent man, they believed. The public defenders decided to write the story in a notarized affidavit and lock it in a box in case something should happen that would allow them to reveal what they knew. When Wilson died in prison of natural causes in 2008, Coventry and Kunz revealed their client's confession. After 26 years, Logan was released from prison. He was granted a certificate of innocence; in 2013, the city of Chicago agreed to pay Logan $10.25 million.[63]
    a. Why does the legal profession expect lawyers to keep secret their clients' confidential communications?
    b. Had you been Coventry and Kunz, would you have revealed what you knew in order to immediately secure justice for Logan? Explain.

11. On July 5, 1884, four sailors were cast away from their ship in a storm 1,600 miles from the Cape of Good Hope. Their lifeboat contained neither water nor much food. On the 20th day of their ordeal, Dudley and Stevens, without the assistance or agreement of

Brooks, cut the throat of the fourth sailor, a 17- or 18-year-old boy. They had not eaten since day 12. Water had been available only occasionally. At the time of the death, the men were probably about 1,000 miles from land. Prior to his death, the boy was lying helplessly in the bottom of the boat. The three surviving sailors ate the boy's remains for four days, at which point they were rescued by a passing boat. They were in a seriously weakened condition.

    a. Were Dudley and Stevens guilty of murder? Explain.

    b. Should Brooks have been charged with a crime for eating the boy's flesh? Explain. See *The Queen v. Dudley and Stephens,* 14 Queen's Bench Division 273 (1884).

12. Tompkins was a citizen of Pennsylvania. While walking on a railroad footpath in that state, he was struck by an object protruding from a passing freight train owned by the Erie Railroad Company, a New York corporation. Tompkins, by virtue of diversity of citizenship, filed a negligence suit against Erie in a New York federal court. Erie argued for the application of Pennsylvania common law, in which case Tompkins would have been treated as a trespasser. Tompkins argued that the absence of a Pennsylvania statute addressing the topic meant that federal common law had to be applied to the case. Should the federal court apply the relevant Pennsylvania state law, or should the court be free to exercise its independent judgment about what the common law of the state is or should be? See *Erie Railroad v. Tompkins,* 304 U.S. 64 (1938).

13. In July 2011, two high-speed trains collided near Wenzhou, China. Shortly after, law offices in Wenzhou were notified by the local judicial bureau and lawyers' association to "immediately report" requests for legal assistance and told not to respond "without authorization."[64]

    In your view, would China benefit from a Western-style approach to litigation? Explain.

14. Boschetto, a California resident, bought a 1964 Ford Galaxie 500XL advertised on eBay from Hansing, a Wisconsin resident. Hansing said the car was in excellent condition, including an "R code" classification. After delivery to California, Boschetto discovered many problems, including the fact that the car was not an "R code." The parties could not reach an out-of-court settlement, so Boschetto sued. Hansing moved for dismissal of the claim on the grounds of lack of personal jurisdiction. Does the fact that the transaction was conducted via eBay satisfy the jurisdictional requirement? Explain. See *Boschetto v. Hansing*, 539 F.3d 1011 (9th Cir. 2008), *cert. denied,* 129 S. Ct. 1318 (2009).

15. University of Chicago law professor Richard Epstein pointed out how quickly Americans turn to legal remedies rather than relying on informal social customs (negotiation, neighborhood groups, simply accepting small losses and disturbances rather than fighting about them) to resolve conflicts. In your view, why are social customs often ineffective in settling disputes in this country? Explain.

16. Judicial reform advocates often argue that the United States should adopt the English rule providing that the losing party in a lawsuit must pay the reasonable litigation expenses of the winner.

    a. In brief, what are the strengths and weaknesses of the English rule?

    b. Would you favor it? Explain. See "Loser Pays, Everyone Wins," *The Wall Street Journal,* December 15, 2010 [**http://online.wsj.com/**].

17. Plaintiff Jonathan Gold was hired to work at defendant Deutsche Bank after completing his MBA degree at New York University. Before beginning employment, Gold signed various documents, including Form U-4 that the National Association of Securities Dealers (NASD) required all registered representatives to sign. Form U-4 provided for arbitration for all employment disputes. Gold was fired after working about one year. He then filed suit claiming sexual harassment based on his sexual orientation. Deutsche Bank moved to compel arbitration. Gold resisted arbitration, arguing, among other things, that Form U-4 was too difficult to understand and that it raised questions in his mind. Gold also showed that Deutsche Bank had certified that it provided Gold with the relevant NASD rules when it had not. Was Gold required to submit his claim to arbitration? Explain. See *Gold v. Deutsche Aktiengesellschaft,* 365 F.3d 144 (2d Cir. 2004), *cert. denied,* 543 U.S. 874 (2004).

Notes

1. Mark David Agrast et al., *The World Justice Project: Rule of Law Index 2012–2013* [**http://worldjusticeproject.org/sites/default/files/WJP_Index_Report_2012.pdf**].

2. Tina Susman, "Last Phone Call May Provide Clues in Florida Teen's Shooting Death," *Los Angeles Times,* March 20, 2012 [**http://www.latimes.com**].

3. Lizette Alvarez and Cara Buckley, "Zimmerman Is Acquitted in Trayvon Martin Killing," *The New York Times,* July 13, 2013 [**www.nytimes.com**].

4. Robert Leider, "Understanding 'Stand Your Ground,'" *The Wall Street Journal,* April 18, 2012, p. A17.

5. Joe Palazzolo, "Study Says 'Stand Your Ground' Laws Increase Homicides," *The Wall Street Journal Law Blog,* June 11, 2012 [**http://blogs.wsj.com/law**].

6. Jack Healy, "Unarmed and Gunned Down by Homeowner in His Castle," *The New York Times,* October 23, 2012 [**www.nytimes.com**].

7. Avianne Tan, "Walk 30 Miles or Do Jail Time, Judge Tells Ohio Teen Who Didn't Pay Cab Fare," *ABC News,* June 2, 2015 [**http://abcnews.go.com/US/walk-30-miles-jail-time-judge-tells-ohio/story?id=31473002**].

8. *Orlando Sentinel,* "More U.S. Judges Impose Creative Punishments," *The Des Moines Register,* October 29, 2010, p. 10A.

9. Brent Kendall, "Why Supreme Court Cases Are Marathons," *The Wall Street Journal,* December 1, 2014 [**http:www.wsj.com**].

10. Jeffrey Toobin, "Merrick Garland and the Politics of the Supreme Court," *The New Yorker,* March 28, 2016 [**www.newyorker.com/magazine/2016/03/28/merrick-garland-and-the-politics-of-the-supreme-court**].

11. Richard Wolf, "At 10, the Roberts Court Defies Labels," *USA TODAY,* October 4, 2015 p. 1B.

12. David G. Savage, "Justices Have Been Siding with Workers, Underdogs," *latimes.com,* March 13, 2011 [**http://latimes.com/news/nationworld/nation/la-na-court-unanimous-20110313,0,4601488.story**]; and Robert Savage, "Justices Deadlock on Public-Employee-Union Case; Calif. Teachers Must Pay Dues," *Los Angeles Times,* March 29, 2016 [**www.washingtonpost.com/politics/courts_law/supreme-court-deadlocks-over-public-employee-union-case-calif-teachers-must-pay-dues/2016/03/29/b99faa30-f5b7-11e5-9804-537defcc3cf6_story.html?utm_term=.70e125deec71**].

13. John C. Henry, "Do You Know Who Works Here? They Can Change Your Life," *AARP.org/Bulletin,* November 2010, p. 26.

14. Editorial, "Our Constitutional Court," *The New York Times,* November 22, 2010 [**www.nytimes.com**].

15. Ethan Bronner, "A Dissent by Scalia Is Criticized as Political," *The New York Times,* June 27, 2012 [**www.nytimes.com**].

16. Adam Litpak and Allison Kopicki, "Approval Rating for Justices Hits Just 44% in New Poll," *The New York Times,* June 7, 2012 [**www.nytimes.com**].

17. Lincoln Caplan, "A Judge's Warning about the Legitimacy of the Supreme Court," *The New York Times,* September 26, 2010 [**www.nytimes.com**].

18. Editorial, "Case Against Oxy Hits Home," *latimes.com,* December 10, 2010 [**www.latimes.com/news/opinion/opinionla/la-ed-peru-20101210,0,2576676.story**].

19. *Carijano v. Occidental Petroleum,* 626 F.3d 1137 (9th Cir. 2010).

20. *Occidental Petroleum v. Carijano,* 133 S. Ct. 1996 (2013).

21. Associated Press, "Occidental Petroleum Settles Peru Pollution Case," *Los Angeles Times,* March 5, 2015 [**www.latimes.com**].

22. For an archive of "Spygate" articles, see "Spygate," *The New York Times,* July 12, 2011 [**http://topics.nytimes.com**].

23. *Wal-Mart Stores v. Dukes,* 564 U.S. 338 (2011).

24. *Phipps v. Wal-Mart,* 792 F.3d 637 (6th Cir. 2015), *cert. denied,* 136 S. Ct. 1163 (2016).

25. 133 S. Ct. 1426 (2013).

26. 133 S. Ct. 2304 (2013).

27. Steven J. Harper, "The Tyranny of the Billable Hour," *The New York Times,* March 28, 2013 [**www.newyorktimes.com**].

28. Peter Latiman, "Settling Fee Dispute, Law Firm Denounces 'Email Humor,'" *DealBook,* April 17, 2013 [**http://dealbook.nytimes.com**].

29. Philip K. Howard, "How Modern Law Makes Us Powerless," *The Wall Street Journal,* January 26, 2009 [**http://online.wsj.com**].

30. Lyric Wallwork Winik, "Are There Too Many Lawyers?" *Parade,* September 14, 2008, p. 9.

31. Luce Research, "Americans Speak on Lawsuit Abuse: Results of a National Survey," *American Tort Reform Association,* August 2012, p. 2 [**http://atra.org/sites/default/files/documents/ATRA%20SOL%20Voter%20Survey%20Summary%20FINAL.pdf**].

32. John O'Brien, "Poll: Voters Not Worried about Tort Reform," *LegalNewsline.com,* July 12, 2007 [**www.legalnewsline.com/news/197868-poll-voters-not-worried-about-tort-reform**].

33. Milton Bordwin, "Your Company and the Law," *Management Review,* January 2000, p. 58.

34. Majirox News, "Too Many Lawyers in Japan, Says Ministry of Internal Affairs," *Majirroxnews.com,* April 23, 2012 [**www.majirrox.news.com**]; and Mitsuru Obe, "Japanese Lawyers' Problem: Too Few Cases," *The Wall Street Journal,* April 3, 2016 [**www.wsj.com/articles/japanese-lawyers-problem-too-few-cases-1459671069**].

35. Rocket Lawyer website [**www.rocketlawyer.com/plans-pricing.rl#**].

36. Shan Li, "Technology Is Bringing Legal Advice and Documents to the Masses," *Los Angeles Times,* February 17, 2014 [**www.latimes.com**].

37. Ibid.

38. Ibid.

39. American Bar Association, "ABA, Rocket Lawyer Launch Test of Legal Services for Small Businesses in 3 States," *American Bar Association News,* October 1, 2015 [**www.americanbar.org/news/abanews/aba-news-archives/2015/10/aba_rocket_lawyerl.html**].

40. "Civil Bench and Jury Trials in State Courts, 2005," U.S. Department of Justice, Bureau of Justice Statistics [**www.bjs.gov**].

41. Court Statistics Project, National Center for State Courts, "Examining the Work of State Courts: An Overview of 2015 State Court Caseloads" [**www.courtstatistics.org/~/media/microsites/files/csp/ewsc%202015.ashx**].

42. John T. Broderick Jr. and Ronald M. George, "A Nation of Do-It-Yourself Lawyers," *The New York Times,* January 2, 2010 [**www.nytimes.com**].

43. Binyamin Appelbaum, "Investors Put Money on Lawsuits to Get Payouts," *The New York Times,* November 14, 2010 [**www.nytimes.com**].

44. Jennifer Smith, "Lawsuit Investors Gain in U.S.," *The Wall Street Journal,* January 13, 2014, p. B7.

45. Ibid.

46. Binyamin Appelbaum, "Lawsuit Loans Add New Risk for the Injured," *The New York Times,* January 16, 2011 [**www.nytimes.com**].

47. Mike Rosen, "Testing Civil Gideon," *California Lawyer,* June 2012 [**www.callawyer.com**].

48. Ibid.

49. This paragraph is derived from "Small Claims Court FAQ," NOLO [**www.nolo.com**].

50. Vanessa O'Connell, "At GE, Robo-Lawyers," *The Wall Street Journal,* October 10, 2011 [**http://online.wsj.com**].

51. Missy Diaz, "Lawyers Are Divided over WhoCanISue.com," *latimes.com,* October 11, 2009 [**www.latimes.com**].

52. "Arbitration: Increasingly, It's Not Over until the Vacatur Motion Fails," *The Wall Street Journal,* February 14, 2011 [**http://blogs.wsj.com**].

53. Alexander J. S. Colvin, "An Empirical Study of Employment Arbitration: Case Outcomes and Processes," *Journal of Empirical Legal Studies* 8, Issue 1 (March 2011), p. 1.

54. *AT&T Mobility v. Vincent Concepcion,* 131 S. Ct. 1740 (2011).

55. See related proceedings: *Geographic Expeditions, Inc. v. Lhotka,* 2010 U.S. LEXIS 6305 (October 4, 2010), *cert. denied.*

56. "An Economist Out to Be Sued," *Los Angeles Times,* October 8, 1990, p. D1.

57. "Known Exonerations in the United States as of January 1, 2014," National Registry on Exonerations, University of Michigan Law School and Center on Wrongful Convictions, Northwestern University, February 4, 2014 [**www.law.umich.edu/special/exoneration/Documents/Exonerations_in_2013_Report.pdf**].

58. Ibid.

59. Dubuque, Iowa, Ordinance No. 28-11, March 21, 2011; and Andy Piper, "Police: Ordinance Will ID Derelict Parents," *Dubuque Telegraph Herald,* March 23, 2011 [**www.thonline.com/article.cfm?id=315715**].

60. Carolyn Foster Segal, "The Curious Case of Megan Thode," *Inside Higher Ed,* February 19, 2013 [**www.insidehighered.com**].

61. Nora Freeman Engstrom and Robert L. Rabin, "Limiting Damages Limits Justice," *Los Angeles Times,* August 13, 2013, p. A11; and *Chan v. Curran,* 237 Cal. App. 4th 601 (Cal. Ct. App. 1st Dist. 2015).

62. Warren Avis, "Court before Justice," *The New York Times,* July 21, 1978, p. 25.

63. Associated Press, "Illinois Man Imprisoned for 26 Years Declared Innocent," *Springfield State Journal-Register,* April 17, 2009 [**www.sj-r.com**]; Fran Speilman, "Chicago to Pay $10.25 Million in Another Burge Case," *Chicago Sun-Times,* January 14, 2013 [**www.suntimes.com**]; and "26-Year Secret Kept Innocent Man in Prison," *60 Minutes,* March 8, 2008 [**http://truthinjustice.org/alton-logan.htm**].

64. Yu Hua, "In China, the Grievances Keep Coming," *The New York Times,* January 1, 2012 [**www.nytimes.com**].

Video icon credit: ©Comstock Images/Alamy

CHAPTER FIVE

Constitutional Law and the Bill of Rights

After completing this chapter, students will be able to fulfill the following learning objectives:

5-1. Recognize the purposes of the U.S. Constitution.

5-2. Describe the separation of powers under the U.S. Constitution.

5-3. Describe the powerful role the Bill of Rights plays in protecting personal freedoms.

5-4. Identify the freedoms protected under the First Amendment.

5-5. Discuss the differences between First Amendment protections of commercial speech versus political speech.

5-6. Describe some of the issues arising under the Fourth Amendment "search and seizure" rules.

5-7.   Explain the "exclusionary rule."

5-8. Describe the law of the Fifth Amendment "Takings Clause" and the property rights controversy associated with it.

5-9. Compare and contrast substantive due process and procedural due process.

5-10. Identify some examples of the impact of the Equal Protection Clause on business and society.

> *We the People of the United States, in Order to form a more perfect Union, establish Justice, insure domestic Tranquility, provide for the common defence, promote the general Welfare, and secure the Blessings of Liberty to ourselves and our Posterity, do ordain and establish this Constitution for the United States of America.*

The Preamble to the U.S. Constitution is inspiring in its expression of the founders' idealistic goals for America. In reading the Preamble, we should reflect on the dream of America and the Constitution's role in molding and protecting an entirely new image of a nation. That we continue to be guided, some 230 years later, by the Constitution's rather few words is testimony to the brilliance and wisdom of its creators and to Americans' determination to build a free, democratic, just society. The U.S. Constitution is a remarkable document, so powerful in its ideas and images that it has helped shape the entire world. (See the Constitution in Appendix A at the back of this text.)

Creating a Constitution—The United States

You may recall that the Constitution grew out of the 1778 Articles of Confederation. The Revolutionary War had basically bankrupted the colonies. Currency was largely worthless. The 13 new states fought over economic resources, interstate disputes were routine, and the federal union that emerged under the Articles of Confederation had little real authority. As a result of this turmoil, and in an effort to strengthen the Articles, the Constitutional Convention convened in Philadelphia on May 25, 1787.

In the hot Philadelphia summer, with windows and curtains closed to assure secrecy (as a means of encouraging open debate), the often chubby and usually heavily clothed delegates sweated their way toward a new government. All 55 delegates, our Founding Fathers, were white males, and most of them were wealthy landowners, but they were also immensely talented with a wide range of interests and experiences.

> All 55 delegates, our Founding Fathers, were white males.

The delegates agreed that a stronger central government was needed, but they were split on how far that notion should go. Virginia, led by the brilliant James Madison, favored a dominant central government with greatly diminished state authority. Alexander Hamilton (now the subject of an acclaimed Broadway musical) wanted to go further yet by, among other things, instituting the presidency as a lifetime office. On the other hand, several states, led by New Jersey, wanted to retain strong states' rights. After weeks of debate, a middle ground began to emerge that led toward our current balance of power between big states and small states and between all of the states and the federal government. In the end, the delegates reached consensus on a Constitution that guaranteed the revolutionary notion of rule by the people.

On September 17, 1787, the great document, one of the most influential expressions in human history, was formally signed. Following bitter disputes in some states, the Constitution was ratified and the new government haltingly moved forward under the leadership of George Washington and John Adams.[1] [For links to national constitutions around the globe, see **confinder.richmond.edu**].

A Right to Bear Arms

Addressing one of the most contentious questions in American constitutional history, the U.S. Supreme Court, in its 2008 *District of Columbia v. Heller* decision, ruled 5–4 that the Second Amendment guarantees individual Americans a fundamental, but not unlimited, right to bear arms.[2] The Supreme Court's four conservative justices, joined by the more moderate Justice Kennedy, ruled that individuals have a constitutional right to keep loaded arms for self-defense, at least in the home. The majority view was based on its reading of the historical record associated with the Second Amendment, while the four dissenting, liberal justices argued that the Second Amendment guaranteed only a collective right to bear arms in a militia.

The decision struck down a District of Columbia law that effectively banned handgun possession. Security guard Dick Heller applied for and was denied a permit for a handgun in his home located in a dangerous Washington, D.C., neighborhood. He sued the District arguing that the gun ban violated his individual rights under the Second Amendment.

The Court's *Heller* ruling did preserve the constitutionality of "reasonable" gun regulations. Justice Scalia, writing for the majority, said nothing in the ruling should "cast doubt on long-standing prohibitions on the possession of firearms by felons or the mentally ill, or laws forbidding the carrying of firearms in sensitive places such as schools and government buildings, or laws imposing conditions and qualifications on the commercial sale of arms." "Dangerous and unusual" weapons also could be banned.

In its 2010 *McDonald v. Chicago* decision,[3] the Supreme Court extended its *Heller* reasoning, which had applied only to federal jurisdictions, to the states and cities in throwing out a Chicago handgun restraint. More than one thousand Second Amendment challenges to gun regulations have been raised, but according to *The New York Times,* 93 percent of those decisions have upheld the gun regulations.[4] Gun rights challenges failed, for example, in 2016 when the Supreme Court declined to review lower court decisions upholding New York and Connecticut laws banning semiautomatic assault weapons and high-capacity magazines. A national law barring assault weapons like the one used in the Orlando, Florida, murders and others expired in 2004, and Congress has subsequently rejected national gun restrictions.

According to a 2013 Rasmussen Poll, 74 percent of Americans support the right to own a gun.[5] Nearly two-thirds of Americans, according to a 2016 poll,[6] said they wanted the next president to push for stricter gun laws, but a 2014 Pew study found that more Americans, for the first time, said protecting gun rights is more important than rules controlling gun ownership.[7]

Questions

1. As you interpret the Second Amendment, did the Supreme Court reach a *correct* decision in the *Heller* case? Explain.

2. The United States, with the highest rate of private gun ownership among developed nations, likewise leads in gun deaths with about 30 homicides per one million people, while Switzerland, with the next highest rate, has 7.7 homicides per million people.[8] As a matter of public policy, did the Supreme Court reach a *wise* decision in the *Heller* case? Explain.

3. "When May I Shoot a Student?" was a Boise State University professor's satirical query of the Idaho state legislature just prior to its decision to permit guns on Idaho campuses.[9] Eight states specifically permit the concealed carrying of weapons on campus by students. What are your thoughts about students and faculty members carrying guns on your campus?

Structure and Purpose

LO 5-1
Recognize the purposes of the U.S. Constitution.

The Preamble identifies certain goals for our society, such as unity (among the various states), justice, domestic tranquility (peace), defense from outsiders, increasing general welfare, and liberty. Article I creates Congress and enumerates its powers. Article I, Section 8, Clause 3 is particularly important because it gives Congress the power to regulate commerce (the Commerce Clause). Article II sets up the executive branch, headed by the president, while Article III establishes the court system. Articles IV and VI, as well as the

14th Amendment, address the relationship between the federal government and the states. Article VI provides in Clause 2 (the Supremacy Clause) that federal law takes precedence over state law. Article V provides for amendments to the Constitution. The first 10 amendments, known as the Bill of Rights, were ratified by the states and put into effect in 1791. The remaining 17 amendments (11 through 27) were adopted at various times from 1798 through 1992.

From this review we can see that the Constitution serves a number of broad roles:

1. It establishes a national government.
2. It controls the relationship between the national government and the government of the states.
3. It defines and preserves personal liberty.
4. It contains provisions to enable the government to perpetuate itself.[10]

Government Power and Constitutional Restraints

The Constitution was designed to protect the citizenry from the government. The Constitution does not protect citizens from purely private concentrations of power, such as large corporations. In fact, corporations themselves are often entitled to the protections of the Constitution. (Remember the *Citizens United* discussion in Chapter 3.) The Constitution divides governmental power between the federal and state governments. Congressional power is formally limited to certain *enumerated (specified) powers* (Article I, Section 8), such as the authority to regulate commerce. The 10th Amendment provides that all power not expressly accorded to the federal government in the Constitution resides in the states or the people. Certain constitutional checks or restraints, including the Bill of Rights, limit how far Congress can reach even within its enumerated powers. In practice, however, those enumerated powers have been expansively interpreted, giving Congress extensive authority in American life. Furthermore, in the landmark 1819 Supreme Court decision *McCulloch v. Maryland,*[11] the U.S. Supreme Court interpreted the Necessary and Proper Clause (Article I, Section 8) to afford Congress the implied powers necessary to execute the enumerated powers, thus permitting a workable national government. The *McCulloch* Court also ruled that the Constitution's Supremacy Clause (Article VI—"This Constitution and the Laws of the United States . . . shall be the Supreme Law of the Land.") nullifies state action that conflicts with federal law. Thus, in one sweeping decision, the Supreme Court dramatically expanded the power of Congress and certified the federal government's superior authority relative to the states.

Too Much Government?

Has that federal power and regulation gone too far? The Affordable Care Act (Obamacare) along with measures to combat the "Great Recession," to deal with the subprime mortgage crisis, and to reform banking practices (see Chapter 8) outraged millions of Americans. The Tea Party movement emerged in 2009, and a heated national debate ensued about the appropriate balance between individual rights as expressed in the free market versus an interventionist federal government designed to correct market failures and protect those least able to care for themselves. Donald Trump's 2016 presidential victory along with Republican Party congressional and state government dominance may signal widespread voter frustration either with the size of government or with its effectiveness, or both.

The "Tea Party" movement emerged.

Separation of Powers

LO 5-2

Describe the separation of powers under the U.S. Constitution.

As a further means of controlling the power of government, the Constitution sets up the three federal branches and provides mechanisms for these to act as checks and balances on each other. Specialized areas of authority are reserved by the Constitution to the president, Congress, and the courts. The president, among other things, executes laws, makes treaties, and commands the armed forces; the Supreme Court and the inferior courts exert judicial review; and Congress alone has the power to legislate. President Obama was harshly criticized for some of his executive orders that, for example, sought to shield millions of undocumented immigrants from deportation, a maneuver that his critics saw as unconstitutional legislation by the executive branch.

The role of the judiciary has been a matter of particular controversy in recent years. The historic 1803 *Marbury v. Madison* decision[12] was the first time the Supreme Court had declared an act of Congress unconstitutional, and the decision also established the principle of judicial review; that is, the power of the courts to consider and, if necessary, invalidate congressional and executive branch decisions. Although neither of those powers was expressly provided for in the Constitution, the Court considered them to be implicit in the legal structure created by the Constitution. Critics today argue that the *Marbury* reasoning has been stretched too far and that, in effect, courts have been making law, rather than merely interpreting it. Those critics say that federal and state judicial decisions finding a "constitutional right" to, for example, abortion or same-sex marriage have reduced the authority of our directly elected legislators and placed too much power in the hands of appointed jurists. Of course, an aggressive judiciary has played a crucial role in the advancement of justice and the protection of personal freedom. [For the National Constitution Center, see **www.constitutioncenter.org**].

Questions

1. As noted, the Constitution does not expressly authorize judicial review. Should we, therefore, assume that the framers of the Constitution did not intend to afford that power to the courts?
2. In your view, do the courts have too much power in our lives? Explain.

Federalism

The U.S. government is built on *federalism* principles; that is, the Constitution provides for shared power among national, state, and local governments. A primary role of the Constitution is to balance central federal authority with dispersed state power. The American Civil War, driven as it was by slavery, was also provoked, in part, by differing conceptions of federalism. Southerners held the view, labeled *states' rights,* that each state was entitled to make its own policy decisions about crucial matters such as slavery, while Northerners favored a strong central government. That constitutional divide over federalism persists today. Many "conservative" Americans distrust big government and favor bringing power closer to the people. They think the federal government has often exercised authority beyond its express constitutional powers. "Liberals," on the other hand, tend to fear local biases and favor a more unified national approach to issues such as regulation of business, educational policy, medical care, and civil rights.

The Constitution and the New Federalism

Over the course of American history and especially during the Depression era, federal power has grown and state authority has receded, but Republican presidents Nixon and Reagan, in particular, took policy steps to revive state authority. Similarly, after decades of interpreting the Constitution in a flexible, expansive manner that accorded great power to the federal government, the Supreme Court in the mid-1990s revisited the federal–state relationship with some decisions curbing federal authority. No major federal initiative was struck down, but the Court signaled legislators and lower courts to look more closely at the federal–state balance of power.

These new federalism views expressed themselves in a landmark 2013 U.S. Supreme Court decision, *Shelby County v. Holder,*[13] that challenged the constitutionality of the federal Voting Rights Act of 1965, which, among other things, subjected nine mostly southern states and selected counties in other states to federal supervision of their election processes because of a long history of discrimination against minorities in voting practices. Those states often gerrymandered election districts and imposed "voter integrity" rules (e.g., literacy tests, character standards, and onerous identification requirements) that officially were designed to assure honesty in elections, but often had sought to exclude minorities from voting.

> A long history of discrimination in voting practices.

Under the 1965 act, any change to voting rules in the covered states required "pre-clearance" from the federal government. Shelby County, Alabama, challenged the Voting Rights Act, claiming, in brief, that in reauthorizing the act in 2006, Congress exceeded its constitutional authority and, in so doing, violated state and local rights. By a 5–4 vote, divided on familiar conservative–liberal grounds, the Supreme Court ruled for Shelby County, saying that the Voting Rights Act's Section 4(b) that determined which jurisdictions' voting practices were tainted by discrimination and thus required pre-clearance, was based on 40-year-old discrimination data and thus did not necessarily speak to current conditions.

The Supreme Court acknowledged the effectiveness of the act in reducing voting discrimination but said that discriminatory practices and the states that use them have changed and Congress must keep the law up to date. The act and its supporting data can, of course, be revisited, but given Congress's current fractures, analysts do not expect quick action. Texas and a number of other states rushed to enforce or enact new restrictions on voting following the *Shelby County* decision. The Texas law, ostensibly designed to prevent fraud, required presentation of a driver's license, a passport, or another approved form of photo identification prior to voting. The act was challenged in court on the grounds that its requirements were too burdensome and too expensive for those lacking a driver's license. In 2016, the federal Fifth Circuit Court of Appeals ruled that the Texas law violated the Voting Rights Act,[14] and Texas agreed to modify its law for the November 2016 election. Fifteen states have recently enacted tighter voter fraud laws, even though in-person voter fraud is quite rare. Six of those state laws, at this writing, have either been blocked or softened by court order.

Immigration policy presents a conflict much like voting rights. Comprehensive, uniform federal immigration control is often at odds with state rules that address the specific needs and political preferences of those individual states. Do we need a consistent national immigration policy or should we allow more room for state-by-state preferences?

On the other side of the coin, when a state like California, known for its aggressive rules on workplace safety, consumer protection, and environmental quality, imposes new restrictions, the business community may fight back in Washington, D.C. Rather than working with an inefficient patchwork of rules differing from state to state, the business community may seek comprehensive federal laws applying to all the states, thus preempting California's particular measures.

Nullification

Conservative activists, Republican lawmakers, and others, in recent years, have reasserted the historical constitutional law theory of *nullification* to attack what they take to be a broad pattern of unconstitutional usurpation of power by the federal government. Nullification advocates are furious over the imposition of national laws and court orders governing highly volatile issues like gun control, abortion, same-sex marriage, and Obamacare.

Each state, according to nullification theory, can, by its own judgment, invalidate (nullify) federal laws it takes to be unconstitutional. Thus, if Arizona, for example, believes federal immigration rules to be unconstitutional, it can, according to nullification proponents, declare the federal law unconstitutional and forbid its enforcement in Arizona by the federal government. Nullification theory is rooted in the 10th Amendment (see Appendix A) and in the reasoning that the states preceded and created the federal government that exists only by the will of the states. Each state, therefore, can make its own decisions about which federal laws are constitutional in that state.

Nullification has become a powerful expression of states' rights and of resentment toward the federal government. No federal court decision, however, has ever validated nullification, the Supreme Court unanimously rejected a form of it in at least one instance, and it appears to conflict with the Supremacy Clause of the Constitution (see Chapter 8).

Questions

1. Constitutional law aside, do you think the federal government has asserted too much authority over issues such as same-sex marriage, abortion, marijuana laws, and gun control? Explain.

2. Would the nation be improved if each state could more nearly make its own laws about those matters? Explain.

For a brief history of nullification, see Robert A. Levy, "The Limits of Nullification," *The New York Times,* September 3, 2013 [**www.nytimes.com**].

Sources: Cooper v. Aaron, 358 U.S. 1, 18–19 (1958); and Ryan Card, "Can States 'Just Say No' to Federal Health Care Reform?," *Brigham Young University Law Review* 2010, no. 5 (2010), pp. 1795, 1808.

The Constitution, the Bill of Rights, and Business

LO 5-3
Describe the powerful role the Bill of Rights plays in protecting personal freedoms.

The Constitution and, in particular, the Commerce Clause profoundly shape the practice of American business. Indeed, in some important ways, the Constitution is a commercial document reflecting the economic interests of the framers. We will defer further discussion of the Commerce Clause and the Supremacy Clause until Chapter 8. In this chapter, we will devote our attention primarily to the Bill of Rights, which serves to limit the powers of the federal government and the states. When we think of the Bill of Rights, corporations ordinarily do not come to mind. Extensive litigation in recent years, however, serves notice that the relationship between the corporate "person" and the fundamental freedoms is both important and unclear.

The Bill of Rights protects our personal freedoms (speech, religion, and more) from encroachment by the federal government. Furthermore, the Supreme Court has ruled that the Due Process Clause of the 14th Amendment, which is directed at the states, absorbs or incorporates those fundamental freedoms and protects them against intrusion by state governments. [For the "Guide to Law Online," prepared by the U.S. Law Library of Congress, see **www.loc.gov/law/help/guide.php**].

The First Amendment

LO 5-4
Identify the freedoms protected under the First Amendment.

Congress shall make no law respecting an establishment of religion, or prohibiting the free exercise thereof; or abridging the freedom of speech, or the press, or the right of the people peaceably to assemble, and to petition the Government for a redress of grievances.

These few words constitute one of the most powerful and noble utterances in history. Much of the magnificence that we often associate with America is embodied in the protections of the First Amendment. Surely we must feel some sense of wonder that our nearly 324 million citizens continue to rely on that sentence as a cornerstone of American life. Notwithstanding the importance of the First Amendment, a 2015 nationwide survey found that one-third of Americans cannot name even one of its crucial protections.[15] [For First Amendment news and commentary, see **www.newseuminstitute.org/first-amendment-center/**].

1. Freedom of Religion

The First Amendment forbids (1) the establishment of an official state religion (the Establishment Clause) and (2) undue state interference with religious practice (the Free Exercise Clause). Government may neither encourage nor discourage the practice of religion generally, nor may it give preference to one religion over another. Broadly, the idea of the First Amendment is to maintain a separation between church and state. The precise boundary of that separation, however, has become one of the more contentious social issues in contemporary life.

Religious Freedom Laws

Barronelle Stutzman, owner of Arlene's Flowers in Richland, Washington, declined to design custom floral arrangements for long-time customer and friend Robert Ingersoll, who was buying the flowers for his wedding to Curt Freed. Stutzman said that her Southern Baptist religious beliefs precluded her from involvement in the same-sex marriage:

> Rob was asking me to choose between my affection for him and my commitment to Christ, ... As deeply fond as I am of Rob, my relationship with Jesus is everything to me.

The state of Washington sued Arlene's Flowers, and the trial court ruled that Stutzman had violated Washington's consumer protection laws, which forbid sexual orientation discrimination. The state's Supreme Court affirmed the trial court's judgment.

Was Ms. Stutzman practicing unlawful discrimination or lawfully following her religious conscience? Over the years, at least 21 states have passed "religious freedom" laws, often designed to prevent government from interfering with religious practices such as Muslim women wearing veils or Amish riding in buggies.

Recently, however, religious freedom laws appear to be directed at the conflict between religious beliefs and laws forbidding discrimination against the LGBTQ community. That conflict was inflamed by the U.S. Supreme Court's 2015 *Obergefell* ruling that denial of marriage rights to same-sex couples is unconstitutional. In response, the state of Mississippi passed a bill in 2016 forbidding government agencies from acting against state employees, individuals, organizations, and private entities that deny services based on religious objections. Thus, state employees could lawfully refuse to issue same-sex marriage licenses, and private companies and religious groups could deny a lengthy list of services (weddings, for example) to LGBTQ people. (Unlike the Mississippi statute, most state religious freedom laws do not extend to the denial of private-sector services.)

A federal judge has ruled, at this writing, that the Mississippi statute violates the constitutional protections of religious neutrality and equal protection under the law, but an appeal is expected. A number of lawsuits have emerged from this religion–discrimination conflict, but thus far, according to religious freedom expert Professor Douglas Laycock, religious freedom claimants, including, for example, a New Mexico wedding photographer, "have lost all of those cases."[16]

No federal law directly forbids discrimination based on sexual orientation or gender identity, and only about half of the states do so. Thus, LGBTQ rights are at risk in many states, but Americans of religious faith believe their constitutionally protected rights may likewise be compromised.

The Supreme Court shed some light on this dilemma in 2014 in the *Hobby Lobby* case, where the Court, by a 5–4 vote, ruled in favor of the family owned corporation's right, on religious grounds, to exclude certain contraceptives from its employee health plan despite federal law requiring employers to provide that coverage. The Court ruled that the 1993 federal Religious Freedom Restoration Act (RFRA) protected the company from the government mandate. RFRA provides that the government cannot "substantially burden a person's exercise of religion" unless it is furthering a "compelling government interest" and acting in the "least restrictive" way possible. Thus, for the first time, RFRA was extended to a corporation, but remember that Hobby Lobby is privately owned by a family with strong, demonstrable religious convictions.

Sources: Camila Domonoske, "Here's Why Mississippi's 'Religious Freedom' Bill Is So Controversial," *NPR,* April 1, 2016 [**www.npr.org**]; Warren Richey, "A Florist Caught Between Faith and Financial Ruin," *The Christian Science Monitor,* July 12, 2016 [**www.csmonitor.com**]; *Barber v. Bryant,* 2016 U.S. Dist. LEXIS 86120 (June 30, 2016); *Burwell v. Hobby Lobby,* 134 S. Ct. 2751 (2014); *Obergefell v. Hodges,* 135 S. Ct. 2584 (2015); and S*tate of Washington v. Arlene's Flowers,* 2017 Wash. LEXIS 216 (Wash. 2017).

Prayer, the Pledge, and Currency

Prayer in legislative settings has been routine and lawful for many years, but the U.S. Supreme Court clarified and expanded constitutional protection for that practice in a 2014 decision, *Town of Greece, New York v. Galloway.*[17] The Greece city council opened its meetings with prayers offered by a rotating group of clergy who were dominantly Christian and who sometimes invoked Jesus Christ in their remarks. Greece was sued on the grounds the prayers were an unconstitutional establishment of religion, amounting to government-sponsored worship. The Supreme Court, however, by a 5–4 margin, said ceremonial prayers at all levels of government are constitutional so long as they do not require participation and do not "denigrate nonbelievers or religious minorities, threaten damnation or preach conversion."[18]

Federal courts have reached similar conclusions about other official, but ceremonial, references to religion. In two Ninth Circuit cases, an atheist, Michael Newdow, said official

| Godless Communists. |

references to God amount to an endorsement of religion, thus violating the First Amendment Establishment Clause. Newdow argued that the phrase "Under God" was placed in the Pledge of Allegiance for religious purposes. Indeed, the Pledge was amended in 1954 to include the words "Under God," and some members of Congress, at the time, said it was needed to distinguish the United States from "Godless Communists."[19] The Ninth Circuit panel, however, saw the voluntary Pledge as an expression of American ideals rather than as a religious endorsement.[20] In a separate case, Newdow challenged the phrase "In God We Trust" on currency, but another Ninth Circuit panel ruled the phrase is simply patriotic and ceremonial and has nothing to do with the establishment of religion.[21]

God and Student Organizations

The University of California Hastings College of the Law refused to recognize a student organization, the Christian Legal Society (CLS). Hastings said the group's faith-based rules discriminated against gays, lesbians, and others who do not share the group's religious beliefs. The organization's rules required members to pledge they would not engage in a "sexually immoral lifestyle," including "all acts of sexual conduct outside God's design for marriage between one man and one woman." Thus, to Hastings officials, the pledge represented discrimination based on religion and sexual orientation, whereas CLS members regarded it as an expression of faith. CLS challenged Hastings's policy as a violation of the member students' First Amendment rights to freedom of religion, speech, and association. The U.S. Supreme Court, by a 5–4 margin, ruled in 2010 that the students' constitutional rights were not violated in that the university policy was a reasonable, viewpoint-neutral condition on access to student recognition in a public university. The majority reasoned that Hastings was concerned about the group's exclusionary conduct rather than its religious beliefs. That is, all student groups must be open to all students. Dissenting justices said the decision supported suppression of unpopular and politically incorrect speech.[22]

Notwithstanding the *CLS* ruling, at least eight states, including Kansas in 2016, have passed legislation allowing public college and university religious organizations to lawfully restrict membership to students who share the groups' religious beliefs.[23] The constitutionality of those statutes is untested, at this writing.

Veils and French Values

France, in 2011, began enforcing its new law forbidding, with some exceptions, the wearing of a garment in public that hides the wearer's face. The law was promoted as a matter of security and of cultural assimilation, while it was assailed as an affront to the Muslim faith and a political move designed to appeal to voters worried about threats to traditional European values and culture. Only an estimated 2,000 women of the five million French Muslims are believed to wear burqas or niqabs covering the face. Some fines have been imposed, but, in general, enforcement has not been aggressive.

The law was challenged in court as a violation of religious and expressive freedom, but it was upheld in 2014 by the European Court of Human Rights.

Sources: "European Court Upholds French Full Veil Ban," *BBC,* July 1, 2014 [**www.bbc.com**]; Steven Erlanger and Elvire Camus, "In a Ban, a Measure of European Tolerance," *The New York Times,* September 1, 2012 [**www. nytimes.com**]; and Robert Marquand, "Face Veil Ban: Will France Take a Hard Line?" *The Christian Science Monitor,* April 11, 2011 [**www.csmonitor.com**].

2. Freedom of Speech

Hustler Magazine publisher Larry Flynt: "If the First Amendment will protect a scumbag like me, then it will protect all of you. Because I am the worst."[24] [For a bawdy, provocative view of freedom of speech, see the 1996 movie *The People vs. Larry Flynt,* starring Woody Harrelson, Courtney Love, and Edward Norton.]

Freedom of speech arguably is the primary guarantor of the American approach to life. Not only is it indispensable to democracy and personal dignity, but Americans believe that the free expression of ideas is the most likely path to the best ideas. We believe in a marketplace of ideas just as we believe in a marketplace of goods.

> We cannot freely yell "Fire" in a crowded theater.

Freedom of speech is not absolute. We cannot freely make slanderous statements about others, publicly utter obscenities at will, speak "fighting words" that are likely to produce a clear and present danger of violence, or yell "Fire" in a crowded theater.

At the same time, in general, the state cannot tell us what we can say; that is, the state cannot, for the most part, regulate the *content* of our speech. On the other hand, the state does have greater authority to regulate the *context* of that speech; that is, the state may be able to restrict where, when, and how we say certain things if that regulation is necessary to preserve compelling state interests. We have broad free speech rights in so-called *public forums* such as downtown business districts, parks, college campuses, and public plazas. Even in those places, however, the state may need to impose reasonable time and manner regulations. Thus, although the Ku Klux Klan can express hatred for black people (the content of the message), the state may restrict where, when, and how those expressions are made (the context of the message) if necessary for the public safety. [For freedom of speech links, see **http://gjs.net/freetalk.htm**].

What Is Expression?

Expression is not limited to oral and written utterances. Freedom of speech clearly extends to messages not communicated with words. Dancing, flag burning, cross burning, artistic production, and disrobing, for example, may all be forms of protected expression. In *Tinker v. Des Moines School District,* one of the leading free speech cases in American history, the U.S. Supreme Court found First Amendment protection for the wearing of a black armband to a high school as a protest against the Vietnam War where no evidence of disruption was presented.[25]

Political contributions, as we saw in our Chapter 3 discussion of the *Citizens United* case, are also a form of protected expression. The Supreme Court expanded that protection in the 2014 *McCutcheon* case, which struck down, as a violation of freedom of expression, a portion of a 1971 federal law that limited the aggregate amount of money a donor can give to all candidates or party committees.[26] Some contribution limits remain, but critics believe the decision undermines democratic principles by further expanding the political influence of wealthy individuals and organizations.

Congress may constitutionally regulate political contributions to curb corruption, but according to the Supreme Court in *Citizens United,* independent expenditures, even when made by corporations, do not promote corruption or the appearance of corruption. National polls, however, show that the American public both perceives a great deal of corruption involving campaign contributions and supports limits on campaign donations.[27]

Free Speech Analysis

How do we decide when the government has violated speech rights? The courts have taken numerous approaches to that question. We will look briefly at cases involving content and context issues as well as the *balancing test,* where the judges must try to weigh the interests of the state against the expressive rights of the individual.

Content: Vile Words   One of the most controversial Supreme Court cases of recent years involved the Topeka, Kansas, Westboro Baptist Church and its practice of protesting at the funerals of American soldiers killed in service. Pastor Fred W. Phelps and his small congregation, most of whom are family members, contend that battlefield deaths are God's punishment for America's sins, including homosexuality. The funeral protests include signs displaying messages such as "Thank God for dead soldiers" and "God Hates Fags." Pastor Phelps and his family picketed the 2006 funeral of Matthew Snyder, a Marine who had been killed in Iraq. Snyder's father sued Phelps and Westboro and won a $10.9 million damage award (reduced by the judge to $5 million) based on his claims of invasion of privacy and intentional infliction of emotional distress. That decision was reversed on appeal, and the case reached the U.S. Supreme Court in 2011, where the church's First Amendment freedom of expression argument prevailed by an 8–1 margin.[28] The quiet, nonviolent Westboro protests addressed matters of public importance on a public street at a distance from the funeral (approximately 1,000 feet) specified by authorities.

> God's punishment for America's sins.

Thus, the Court's unpopular decision affirmed the long-standing position that the government ordinarily cannot restrict speech based on its content, however tasteless or valueless. As lawyer and commentator Adam Cohen said about the Westboro expression: "We defend it not because these ideas are particularly worthy of being protected, but because all ideas, even the most loathsome, are."[29] Recent federal legislation requires demonstrators to be at least 300 feet from military funerals from two hours before until two hours after the ceremonies.

Context: Panhandling   Noting safety concerns about panhandlers in roadway median strips, the Portland, Maine, City Council passed an ordinance making it illegal to stand, sit, or stay on a median except to cross a road. When challenged, the ordinance was struck down in 2015 on First Amendment grounds not, the federal First Circuit Court of Appeals concluded, because of the content of the message (begging) but because of its context (where the speech takes place).[30] The court went on to find that the means employed to protect public safety in Portland were broader than necessary and thus too intrusive on expression.

In general, some restraints on panhandling *in the street* or on *aggressive* panhandling might well be permissible. The content of the message (begging) may not be restricted, but for compelling reasons, authorities might lawfully shift the time, place, or manner (the context) of the expression.

Balancing Interests: Speech at School   Joseph Frederick was across the street from his school with many other students watching, with school permission, an Olympic torch parade when Frederick, a Juneau, Alaska, high school senior, and

| "Bong Hits 4 Jesus." |

some friends unfurled a large banner reading "Bong Hits 4 Jesus." The banner was a prank designed to attract attention from television cameras. The school principal, Deborah Morse, told Frederick to lower the banner. He refused, and he was suspended from school. Frederick sued, and the case reached the U.S. Supreme Court. In balancing Frederick's free speech interests versus the school's educational and safety duties, does the First Amendment protect Frederick? [See *Deborah Morse v. Joseph Frederick,* 127 S. Ct. 2618 (2007); and Mark W. Cordes, "Making Sense of High School Speech after *Morse v. Frederick,*" *William & Mary Bill of Rights Journal* 17, no. 3 (2009), p. 657.]

Public Sector Workers Off the Job? On the Job?

Remember that the Constitution and Bill of Rights protect us from the government but not from, for example, our corporate employer. On the other hand, the First Amendment does

| Derogatory comments such as "frightfully dim" and "utterly loathsome." |

generally shield *public-sector* workers' *off-the-job* expressions when speaking as citizens about matters of public concern.

Nonetheless, employer restrictions necessary to effective operation of a government enterprise may be permissible, as illustrated by the 2012 dismissal of Natalie Munroe, a Pennsylvania high school English teacher. Munroe created a blog, intended for her friends but not password protected, to which she posted over 80 messages. Most of Munroe's blog comments addressed personal matters, but in several instances she included derogatory comments about her students, such as "frightfully dim" and "utterly loathsome," and she said parents were "breeding a disgusting brood of insolent, unappreciative, selfish brats." Upon learning of the comments, parents and students were furious; later, after poor performance reviews, Munroe was fired. Munroe sought to sue the school claiming she was retaliated against for exercising her free speech rights. A panel of the federal Third Circuit Court of Appeals, however, ruled that she could not sue, finding that the school's interest in avoiding educational disruptions outweighed her expressive interests.[31]

Government employees' free speech rights are substantially limited *on the job.* Los Angeles Deputy District Attorney Richard Ceballos lost his job in a whistle-blowing episode. Ceballos sued and in 2006 the U.S. Supreme Court ruled that government employees who speak out "pursuant to their official duties" are speaking as employees, not as citizens, and therefore are not protected by the First Amendment regardless of the content of their message. The Court pointed to the government's need for efficiency and order in its workplace.[32]

Politically Correct Speech/Hate Speech

We are largely free of government restraints on what we can say, but should it always be so? Is free speech sometimes too hurtful to be tolerated? Are some remarks so inflammatory and insensitive that they actually depreciate discourse?

> Charles Barkley: "[T]urn off your damn television. I am not going to change."

Donald Trump's 2016 presidential campaign capitalized on public frustration with so-called politically correct speech; that is, the practice of avoiding language or behavior that might offend a particular group, especially with respect to race, gender, and sexual orientation. Charles Barkley, basketball commentator and former NBA star, challenged speech limits, as he often does, by remarks about overweight women in San Antonio, Texas: "That's a gold mine for Weight Watchers. . . . Victoria is definitely a secret [in San Antonio] . . . they can't wear no Victoria's Secret down there." Barkley later refused to apologize and said, ". . . [T]urn off your damn television. I am not going to change."[33]

Disputes about offensive language often arise in university life where the law requires policies to curb and punish civil rights violations, including racial and sexual harassment. Shouldn't we be troubled, for example, when a UCLA fraternity has a Kanye West–themed, "blackface" party? Or are we being too sensitive when students at Emory University feel threatened by "Trump 2016" campaign messages written in chalk across campus? Professors now issue "trigger warnings" that some class material might trouble students. Some recent editions of the Mark Twain novels *Adventures of Huckleberry Finn* and *Tom Sawyer* have been published with the "N-word" being replaced by the word "slave" in an effort to avoid disturbing readers. These practices have led to allegations of "The Coddling of the American Mind."[34]

At least in public spaces, racist, sexist, hurtful speech that does not constitute a direct threat to an individual or that is not likely to provoke an imminent breach of the peace ordinarily is protected by the First Amendment. Balancing the value of free speech against the decency of curbing empty, hurtful, inflammatory remarks is difficult, however. Many universities have responded with campus speech codes designed to stop hate speech, harassment, bullying, and other offensive conduct. Those codes are accused, of course, of mandating politically correct speech.

Speech codes often suffer from a First Amendment problem of *overbreadth* (forbidding what should be protected speech along with speech that can rightfully be prohibited) and a Fifth Amendment due process of law problem of *vagueness* (a lack of clarity about what speech is and is not forbidden). A number of university speech codes have been invalidated as violations of First Amendment rights.[35]

Yale   Complaints of a hostile sexual environment and intimidation of female students caused Yale University in 2011 to impose a five-year ban on all campus activities for a prestigious fraternity that counts both Bush presidents among its alumni. One of the complaints involved the fraternity's pledges chanting, "No means yes! Yes means anal!" outside a women's dormitory area. Other, more individualized and more threatening concerns were also raised. Following a federal investigation, Yale agreed to change its harassment policy and reached a settlement that did not involve disciplinary action.[36]

Maricopa CCC   Recently, a Maricopa County Community College (Arizona) math instructor won a Ninth Circuit U.S. Court of Appeals decision involving his right to send racially charged e-mails over the school district–maintained server to all employees with an e-mail address. Professor Walter Kehowski sent three messages declaring, for example,

His right to send racially charged e-mails.	"It's time to acknowledge and celebrate the superiority of Western Civilization." On his university-maintained website, he said, "[T]he only immigration reform imperative is preservation of White majority (*sic*)."

A group of Hispanic employees then sued the school district, claiming that it had failed to properly respond to Kehowski's remarks, thus allowing the creation of a hostile work environment. The court of appeals, however, ruled that the e-mails addressed matters of public concern and were protected by the First Amendment and thus could not constitute illegal harassment. The court did note that some workplace harassment, such as racial insults or sexual advances toward particular individuals, may be prohibited because it lacks the expressive quality of speech directed toward a larger audience.[37]

"Be Happy, Not Gay"

Following a day designated to show support for gays and lesbians at her high school in Naperville, Illinois, student Heidi Zamecnik wore a T-shirt to school displaying the expression "Be Happy, Not Gay." The school's dean forbade the expression at the school. Another student, Alexander Nuxoll, unsuccessfully sought to wear a similar shirt. Both students objected to homosexuality on religious grounds. The two students subsequently sued the school for infringing their free speech rights. The Seventh Circuit U.S. Circuit Court of Appeals reasoned that the forbidden expression did not constitute "fighting words" or some other recognized First Amendment exception and ruled that the students had a right to wear the shirts and express their opinions.

Judge Richard Posner said:

> [A] school that permits advocacy of the rights of homosexual students cannot be allowed to stifle criticism of homosexuality. The school argued (and still argues) that banning "Be Happy, Not Gay" was just a matter of protecting the "rights" of the students against whom derogatory comments are directed. But people in our society do not have a legal right to prevent criticism of their beliefs or even their way of life.

Source: *Zamecnik and Nuxoll v. Indian Prairie School District,* 636 F.3d 874 (7th Cir. 2011).

Ole Miss   Colleges and universities have sometimes been accorded considerable latitude in regulating campus speech. The Fifth Circuit Court of Appeals, for example, upheld the right of the University of Mississippi to ban flags, including the Confederate flag, at campus events.[38] Specifically banning only the Confederate flag presumably would not have met with the Court's approval.

George Mason   Many First Amendment scholars believe the correct antidote to hate speech is simply more speech; that is, they place their faith in the marketplace of ideas rather than in rules, however well intended. The decision that follows demonstrates the First Amendment's role in resolving claims of racism, sexism, and general insensitivity springing from a George Mason University fraternity's "ugly woman contest." [For a vigorous critique of campus "political correctness," see the Foundation for Individual Rights in Education at **www.thefire.org/**].

IOTA XI Chapter v. George Mason University   993 F.2d 386 (4th Cir. 1993)

Senior Circuit Judge Sprouse

George Mason University appeals from a summary judgment granted by the district court to the IOTA XI Chapter of Sigma Chi Fraternity in its action for declaratory judgment and an injunction seeking to nullify sanctions imposed on it by the University because it conducted an "ugly woman contest" with racist and sexist overtones.

I

Sigma Chi has for two years held an annual "Derby Days" event, planned and conducted both as entertainment and as a source of funds for donations to charity. The "ugly woman contest," held on April 4, 1991, was one of the "Derby Days" events. The Fraternity staged the contest in the cafeteria of the student union. As part of the contest, eighteen Fraternity members were assigned to one of six sorority teams cooperating in events. The involved Fraternity members appeared in the contest dressed as caricatures of different types of women, including one member dressed as an offensive caricature of a black woman. He was painted black and wore stringy, black hair decorated with curlers, and his outfit was stuffed with pillows to exaggerate a woman's breasts and buttocks. He spoke in slang to parody African-Americans.

There is no direct evidence in the record concerning the subjective intent of the Fraternity members who conducted the contest. The Fraternity, which later apologized to the University officials for the presentation, conceded during the litigation that the contest was sophomoric and offensive.

Following the contest, a number of students protested to the University that the skit had been objectionably sexist and racist. Two hundred forty-seven students, many of them members of the foreign or minority student body, executed a petition, which stated, "[W]e are condemning the racist and sexist implications of this event in which male members dressed as women. One man in particular wore a black face, portraying a negative stereotype of black women."

Dean for Student Services Kenneth Bumgarner discussed the situation with representatives of the objecting students [and] student representatives of Sigma Chi. [The University decided to impose sanctions on Sigma Chi including] suspension from [most] activities for the rest of the 1991 spring semester and a two-year prohibition. . . .

On June 5, 1991, Sigma Chi brought this action against the University and Dean Bumgarner. It requested declaratory judgment and injunctive relief to nullify the sanctions as violative of the First and Fourteenth Amendments. Sigma Chi moved for summary judgment on its First Amendment claims on June 28, 1991.

. . . University President George W. Johnson . . . presented the "mission statement" of the University:

* * * * *

(3) George Mason University is committed to promoting a culturally and racially diverse student body. . . . Education here is not limited to the classroom.

(4) We are committed to teaching the values of equal opportunity and equal treatment, respect for diversity, and individual dignity.

(5) Our mission also includes achieving the goals set forth in our affirmative action plan, a plan incorporating affirmative steps designed to attract and retain minorities to this campus.

* * * * *

(7) George Mason University is a state institution of higher education and a recipient of federal funds.

* * * * *

The district court granted summary judgment to Sigma Chi on its First Amendment claim, 773 F. Supp. 792 (E.D. Va. 1991).

II [OMITTED—ED.]

III

We initially face the task of deciding whether Sigma Chi's "ugly woman contest" is sufficiently expressive to entitle it to First Amendment protection.

* * * * *

A

First Amendment principles governing live entertainment are relatively clear: Short of obscenity, it is generally protected. As the Supreme Court announced in *Schad v. Borough of Mount Ephraim,* 452 U.S. 61 (1981), "[e]ntertainment, as well as political and ideological speech, is protected; motion pictures, programs broadcast by radio and television, and live entertainment . . . fall within the First Amendment guarantee." Expression devoid of "ideas" but with entertainment value may also be protected because "[t]he line between the informing and the entertaining is too elusive." *Winters v. New York,* 333 U.S. 507, 510 (1948).

* * * * *

Even crude street skits come within the First Amendment's reach. In . . . *Schacht v. United States,* 398 U.S. 58, 61–62 (1970), . . . Justice Black [declared] that an actor participating in even a crude performance enjoys the constitutional right to freedom of speech.

Bearing on this dichotomy between low- and high-grade entertainment are the Supreme Court's holdings relating to nude dancing. See *Barnes v. Glen Theatre, Inc.,* 111 S. Ct. 2456, 2460 (1991).

[I]n *Barnes,* the Supreme Court conceded that nude dancing is expressive conduct entitled to First Amendment protection.

*   *   *   *   *

. . . [I]t appears that the low quality of entertainment does not necessarily weigh in the First Amendment inquiry. It would seem, therefore, that the Fraternity's skit, even as low-grade entertainment, was inherently expressive and thus entitled to First Amendment protection.

B

The University nevertheless contends that discovery will demonstrate that the contest does not merit characterization as a skit but only as mindless fraternity fun, devoid of any artistic expression. It argues further that entitlement to First Amendment protection exists only if the production was intended to convey a message likely to be understood by a particular audience. . . .

As indicated, we feel that the First Amendment protects the Fraternity's skit because it is inherently expressive entertainment. Even if this were not true, however, the skit, in our view, qualifies as expressive conduct under the test articulated in *Texas v. Johnson,* 491 U.S. 397 (1989). It is true that the *Johnson* test for determining the expressiveness of conduct requires "'[a]n intent to convey a particularized message'" and a great likelihood "'that the message would be understood by those who viewed it.'"

*   *   *   *   *

[T]he affidavits establish that the punishment was meted out to the Fraternity because its boorish message had interfered with the described University mission. It is manifest from these circumstances that the University officials thought the Fraternity intended to convey a message. The Fraternity members' apology and post-conduct contriteness suggest that they held the same view.

*   *   *   *   *

As to the second prong of the *Johnson* test, there was a great likelihood that at least some of the audience viewing the skit would understand the Fraternity's message of satire and humor. Some students paid to attend the performance and were entertained. . . .

*   *   *   *   *

. . . [W]e are persuaded that the Fraternity's "ugly woman contest" satisfies the *Johnson* test for expressive conduct.

IV

If this were not a sufficient response to the University's argument, the principles relating to content and viewpoint discrimination recently emphasized in *R.A.V. v. City of St. Paul,* 112 S. Ct. 2538 (1992), provide a definitive answer. Although the Court in St. Paul reviewed the constitutional effect of a city "hate speech" ordinance, and we review the constitutionality of sanctions imposed for violating University policy, *St. Paul's* rationale applies here with equal force. Noting that St. Paul's city ordinance prohibited displays of symbols that "arouse[d] anger, alarm, or resentment in others on the basis of race, color, creed, religion, or gender," but did not prohibit displays of symbols which would advance ideas of racial or religious equality, Justice Scalia stated, "The First Amendment does not permit St. Paul to impose special prohibitions on those speakers who express views on disfavored subjects."

As evidenced by their affidavits, University officials sanctioned Sigma Chi for the message conveyed by the "ugly woman contest" because it ran counter to the views the University sought to communicate to its students and the community. The mischief was the University's punishment of those who scoffed at its goals of racial integration and gender neutrality, while permitting, even encouraging, conduct that would further the viewpoint expressed in the University's goals and probably be embraced by a majority of society as well. "The First Amendment generally prevents government from proscribing . . . expressive conduct because of disapproval of the ideas expressed."

The University, however, urges us to weigh Sigma Chi's conduct against the substantial interests inherent in educational endeavors. We agree wholeheartedly that it is the University officials' responsibility, even their obligation, to achieve the goals they have set. On the other hand, a public university has many constitutionally permissible means to protect female and minority students. We must emphasize, as have other courts, that "the manner of [its action] cannot consist of selective limitations upon speech." The University should have accomplished its goals in some fashion other than silencing speech on the basis of its viewpoint.

Affirmed.

Questions

1. Is speech that consists merely of entertainment without benefit of meaningful ideas protected by the First Amendment? Explain.

2. Explain the court's conclusion that the fraternity skit met the *Texas v. Johnson* test of "an intent to convey a particularized message" and a great likelihood "that the message would be understood by those who viewed it."

3. *a.* Should racist/sexist remarks be forbidden in college classrooms?

   b. The Stanford University speech code was ruled unconstitutional and the superior court judge in that case said, among other things, that the code was "overbroad."[39] What did he mean?

   c. Do we give too much attention to freedom of speech at the expense of community civility? Explain.

4. For an extra fee, Texas will issue specialty auto license plates, but state law allows rejection of the request if "the design might be offensive to any member of the public." The Sons of Confederate Veterans (TSCV) asked the Texas Department of Motor Vehicles Board to issue a specialty license plate displaying a Confederate battle flag, but the request was denied citing the

"offensive to any member of the public" standard. TSCV sued, and the case reached the U.S. Supreme Court. See *Walker v. Sons of Confederate Veterans*, 135 S. Ct. 2239 (2015).

a. Is a specialty plate private speech or government speech? Explain.

b. Were TSCV's First Amendment rights violated? Explain.

5. The U.S. Supreme Court and lower federal courts have repeatedly ruled that burning the American flag is speech protected by the First Amendment. Congress often considers a flag protection amendment to the Constitution to make flag burning illegal. Would you favor that amendment? Explain.

Commercial Speech

LO 5-5

Discuss the differences between First Amendment protections of commercial speech versus political speech.

Governments often want to regulate commercial expressions ranging from advertisements and billboards to real estate "for sale" signs and circulars placed on car windshields. Does the First Amendment protect those messages from government intervention in the same manner that it protects political speech? In 1942, the U.S. Supreme Court ruled that *commercial speech* was not entitled to First Amendment protection.[40] Subsequently the Court changed its stance and extended First Amendment rights to commercial speech, but those rights were much more limited than for political speech. In more recent years, the Court has been gradually expanding protection for commercial speech.

Corporate Political Speech Should corporations enjoy full First Amendment rights? Can we properly think of corporate political expressions as commercial speech? Or is commercial speech limited to those expressions that propose a commercial transaction? Experts differ on these questions, but their importance is evident if we think again about the 2010 *Citizens United* decision allowing corporations to spend more freely on elections (discussed previously in Chapter 3).[41] In the late 1970s, Justices William Rehnquist and Byron White had described corporations as "creatures of the law" possessed of wealth-creation powers but not entitled to the rights possessed by voters. By contrast, the *Citizens United* majority described corporations as "associations of citizens" deserving of free speech rights in the manner of individuals.[42] Justice Scalia said: "[T]o exclude or impede corporate speech is to muzzle the principal agents of the modern economy. We should celebrate rather than condemn the addition of this speech to the public debate."[43] This shift in constitutional interpretation reflects, according to a *Los Angeles Times* analysis, the President Ronald Reagan–era efforts to reduce government regulation of business. All five justices in the *Citizens United* majority were either appointed to the Court by Reagan or worked as young lawyers in the Reagan administration.[44] Hence, shifting political views sometimes influence the course of judge-made law. Do you think a corporation should be regarded as a person for First Amendment purposes?

The Slants and the Redskins

The Slants play rock/dance music, and the Washington Redskins play football in the National Football League. Both have been struggling to protect their names. The federal Lanham Act prohibits the registration of "disparaging" trademarks. The U.S. Patent and Trademark Office (PTO), considering the name an ethnic slur against Asians, refused to allow The Slants (a Portland, Oregon, band composed of Asian Americans) to trademark and thus strengthen protection of the commercial, artistic, and expressive value of its name. The band's leader, Simon Tam, sued claiming the trademark denial was an unconstitutional restriction of free speech rights. Tam sought to "take ownership" of anti-Asian stereotypes and transform them to statements of pride. Tam's lawsuit reached the United States Supreme Court which unanimously ruled in 2017 that the disparagement clause of the Lanham Act violates the First Amendment's free speech clause. The court reasoned that the public expression of ideas may not be prohibited merely because those ideas are offensive to some.

The PTO canceled the Redskins' trademark in 2014 on the grounds that it disparaged Native Americans. The Redskins disputed the PTO finding in court. Days after the Slants decision was handed down both the federal Justice Department and the Native American litigants dropped their challenge to the Redskins' trademark acknowledging that the Slants decision had resolved the legal question in the Redskins favor.

Historically, the PTO has canceled numerous other trademark names such as "Marriage Is for Fags," but it has approved marks such as "Asian Efficiency."

Questions

1. Why did the Supreme Court find that the provision forbidding registration of "disparaging trademarks" violated The Slants's First Amendment rights? Do you agree with the court? Explain.

2. In your view, should the Redskins continue to use their nickname? Explain.

Sources: Matal v. *Tam*, 2017 U.S. LEXIS 3872 and Joe Coscarelli, "Why the Slants Took a Fight Over Their Band Name to the Supreme Court, *New York Times*, June 19, 2017 [**www.nytimes.com**], Josh Gerstein, "Feds Give Up Fight Against Redskins Trademark," *Politico*, June 28, 2017 [**www.politico.com**].

Commercial Speech on Campus The *Virginia Tech* decision below examines the constitutionality of government regulations restricting beer advertising in college newspapers as measured by the commercial free speech test articulated in the Supreme Court's important *Central Hudson* decision.[45]

LEGAL BRIEFCASE

Educational Media Company at Virginia Tech v. Insley
731 F.3d 291 (4th Cir. 2013)

Judge Thacker

The Virginia Alcoholic Beverage Control Board (the "ABC") prohibits college student newspapers from printing alcohol advertisements. Appellants Educational Media and the Cavalier Daily are non-profit corporations that own student newspapers at Virginia Polytechnic Institute and State University and the University of Virginia, respectively. . . .

The district court granted summary judgment in favor of the ABC, concluding that the challenged regulation is a constitutionally appropriate restriction of commercial speech given Virginia's substantial interest in combating underage and abusive drinking on college campuses. . . .

I.

Virginia precludes college student newspapers from printing alcohol advertisements. The challenged regulation provides:

> Advertisements of alcoholic beverages are not allowed in college student publications unless in reference to a dining establishment, except as provided below. A "college student publication" is defined as any college or university publication that is prepared, edited or published primarily by students at such institution, is sanctioned as a curricular or extra-curricular activity by such institution and which is distributed or intended to be distributed primarily to persons under 21 years of age.

* * * * *

A.

The ABC asserts that the purpose of the challenged regulation is to combat underage and abusive college drinking. During discovery, each party proffered expert testimony. . . . Specifically, the ABC offered a declaration of Dr. Henry Saffer, an economics professor at Kean University in New Jersey. Dr. Saffer testified that, while the vast majority of studies found that alcohol advertising bans do not, in fact, reduce the overall market demand for alcohol, those studies are inapplicable here. Notably, Dr. Saffer contends that, while most scholars assume that a prohibition on alcohol advertising in one forum simply pushes alcohol advertising to other forums, according to him, (sic) this assumption only holds true where a reasonable substitute for the regulated forum exists. Dr. Saffer testified that this assumption does not hold true in the context of college student newspapers, because "[a] college newspaper is a very targeted, specific kind of media," and there is "nothing else that can replace that kind of targeted media that's specifically oriented towards and reaches college students." According to Dr. Saffer's reasoning, in the unique instance of college newspapers, alcohol advertising bans actually do have a significant effect on market demand despite the vast majority of studies that show otherwise outside of this particular context.

In contrast, the College Newspapers offered the testimony of Dr. Jon P. Nelson, an economics professor at Pennsylvania State University. Based on his research, Dr. Nelson testified that "[a]dvertising bans, partial or comprehensive, do not reduce the demand for alcohol." Rather, he explains, "[i]n a 'mature market,' such as alcohol beverages, the primary effect of advertising is to create and maintain brand loyalty[,]" as opposed to expanding overall market demand. He also notes that college students are continually exposed to alcohol advertisements in a variety of forums—including television, radio, and the internet—which "will totally offset any possible temperance effect of the ABC regulation."

. . . Dr. Nelson noted that Dr. Saffer did not present any specific evidence in support of his proposition that targeted advertising bans in college student publications actually achieve the desired goal, that is, reduced drinking. Moreover, Dr. Saffer conceded that, in addition to the lack of empirical support for selective bans on alcohol advertising in college student publications, other methods of combating alcohol consumption on college campuses have been proven more effective. Specifically, as the district court noted, "Dr. Saffer also admits that increased taxation has been shown to reduce underage consumption in a more effective manner than advertising bans and that counter-advertising has effectively reduced levels of alcohol consumption."

The College Newspapers also established . . . that a majority of their readers are over the age of 21.

* * * * *

B.

[T]he district court granted summary judgment in favor of ABC.

* * * * *

II. [OMITTED—ED.]

III.

A.

While commercial speech is protected by the First Amendment, there is a "commonsense distinction" between commercial speech and other varieties of speech. [*Central Hudson Gas & Electric Corp. v. Public Service Commission of New York,* 447 U.S. 557, 562 (1980).] Thus, "[t]he Constitution . . . accords a lesser protection to commercial speech than to other constitutionally guaranteed expression. . . ." [*Id.* at 562–63.] The parties agree that the challenged regulation impacts only commercial speech.

* * * * *

B.

Next, we consider whether the challenged regulation violates *Central Hudson* as applied to the College Newspapers. Under *Central Hudson,* a regulation of commercial speech will be upheld if (1) the regulated speech concerns lawful activity and is not misleading; (2) the regulation is supported by a substantial government interest; (3) the regulation directly advances that interest; and (4) the regulation is not more extensive than necessary to serve the government's interest. . . . We address each of the four *Central Hudson* prongs in turn.

1. LAWFUL ACTIVITY

All parties are in agreement that the first prong of *Central Hudson,* i.e. whether the regulated speech concerns lawful activity and is not misleading, is satisfied. Specifically, the challenged regulation regulates lawful activity, as alcohol advertisements—even those that reach a partially underage audience—concern the lawful activity of alcohol consumption. Additionally, the ABC has not presented any evidence that the advertisements implicated by this regulation are misleading. Thus, this prong is clearly satisfied.

2. SUBSTANTIAL GOVERNMENT INTEREST

"Next, we ask whether the asserted governmental interest is substantial." [*Id.* at 566.] As with the first prong, the parties are in agreement that Virginia's stated interest in combating underage and abusive drinking on college campuses represents a substantial governmental interest. Accordingly, the second *Central Hudson* prong is satisfied.

3. DIRECT AND MATERIAL ADVANCEMENT

a. Under *Central Hudson*'s third prong, the ABC must prove that the challenged regulation directly advances the government's asserted interest. "This burden is not satisfied by mere speculation or conjecture; rather, a governmental body seeking to sustain a restriction on commercial speech must demonstrate that the harms it recites are real and that its restriction will in fact alleviate them to a material degree.' [*Edenfield v. Fane,* 507 U.S. 761, 770–71 (1993).]

* * * * *

In [*Educational Media Co. et al. v. Swecker,* 602 F.3d 583 (4th Cir. 2010)], we concluded that the challenged regulation satisfies the third prong because, given the general correlation between advertising of a product and demand for that product, it follows that a decrease in alcohol advertising on college campuses will necessarily result in a decrease in alcohol consumption by college students. Additionally, we concluded that the efficacy of the regulation was further substantiated by the fact that "alcohol advertisers *want* to advertise in college student publications. It is counterintuitive for alcohol vendors to spend their money on advertisements . . . if they believed that these ads would not increase demand by college students." [*Id.* at 590.]

b. . . . We agree [with *Swecker*'s analysis].

* * * * *

4. REGULATION MORE EXTENSIVE THAN NECESSARY

. . . Under this prong of *Central Hudson,* the party defending the regulation "must demonstrate narrow tailoring of the challenged regulation to the asserted interest—a fit that is not necessarily perfect, but reasonable; that represents not necessarily the single best disposition but one whose scope is in proportion to the interest served." [*Greater New Orleans Broadcasting Association, Inc. v. United States,* 527 U.S. 173, 188 (1999).]

The ABC argues that the challenged regulation does not fail under this fourth prong because it is "reasonably tailored" to the stated aim of reducing underage and abusive alcohol consumption. Specifically, the ABC notes that the challenged regulation does not prohibit all alcohol advertisements and is but one facet of its multifaceted approach to combat the problem of underage drinking. Given the dual purpose of the regulation to combat both underage and abusive drinking, the district court agreed. Specifically, the district court held that, while the challenged regulation did have the effect of preventing the dissemination of truthful information to legal adults, this was not unduly out-of-proportion to the second half of the government's stated aim: reducing abusive alcohol consumption by college students who are 21 years of age or older.

We disagree. Instead, we conclude that . . . the challenged regulation fails under the fourth *Central Hudson* prong because it prohibits large numbers of adults who are 21 years of age or older from receiving truthful information about a product that they are legally allowed to consume.

* * * * *

[A] majority of the College Newspapers' readers are age 21 or older. Specifically, roughly 60% of [Virginia Tech's] *Collegiate Times*'s readership is age 21 or older and the [University of Virginia's] *Cavalier Daily* reaches approximately 10,000 students, nearly 64% of whom are age 21 or older. Thus, the College Newspapers have a protected interest in printing non-misleading alcohol advertisements, just as a majority of the College Newspapers' readers have

a protected interest in receiving that information. Accordingly, the challenged regulation is unconstitutionally overbroad.

* * * * *

[T]he portion of the challenged regulation seeking to prevent the dissemination of alcohol advertisements to readers age 21 or older . . . attempts to keep would-be drinkers in the dark based on what the ABC perceives to be their own good. Therefore, the district court erred in concluding that the challenged regulation is appropriately tailored to achieve its objective of reducing abusive college drinking.

IV.

Because a regulation of commercial speech must satisfy all four *Central Hudson* prongs in order to survive, . . . and the regulation in question here does not satisfy the fourth prong, the challenged regulation violates the First Amendment as applied to the College Newspapers.

Reversed.

DISSENT

Judge Shedd

* * * * *

This comprehensive plan adopted by Virginia only minimally impacts commercial speech by attempting to limit advertising aimed at a targeted market which includes a substantial percentage of readers for whom use of the product is illegal. Virginia's approach does not prohibit all advertising of alcohol which will reach this audience; it is a minor limitation on such advertising in college newspapers as part of a comprehensive plan to address a very serious problem.

* * * * *

Questions

1. *a.* Why did the court rule for the two college newspapers?
   b. What did the court mean in saying the alcohol advertising regulation is unconstitutionally overbroad?

2. *a.* Do you think the elimination of alcohol ads in college newspapers would be effective in reducing underage student alcohol consumption and alcohol abuse? Explain.
   b. Do you favor limits on alcohol ads in college newspapers? Explain.
   c. Do you favor higher alcohol taxes as a means of reducing underage alcohol consumption and alcohol abuse? Explain.

3. In online fantasy sports leagues, fans "draft" current professional players in baseball, football, etc. to create their own teams that then compete based on the actual performance of those players. A Missouri company, C.B.C. Distribution and Marketing, Inc., operated a for-profit online league. In 2005, Major League Baseball changed its licensing policies and

declined to allow C.B.C. a license to continue using the names and statistics of major league baseball players. C.B.C. then sued, claiming it had a First Amendment right to use the information, while M.L.B. argued that the information was protected by the intellectual property/publicity rights of the players. Decide the case. Explain. See *C.B.C. Distribution and Marketing, Inc. v. Major League Baseball Advanced Media,* 505 F.3d 818 (8th Cir. 2007), *cert. denied sub nom. Major League Baseball v. C.B.C. Distribution & Marketing,* 553 U.S. 1090 (2008).

4. Two Rhode Island statutes prohibited all price advertising on liquor in the state, except for in-store price tags and signs that were not visible on the street. The state sought to reduce alcohol consumption. Two licensed liquor dealers challenged the statutes' constitutionality. See *44 Liquormart, Inc. v. Rhode Island,* 116 S. Ct. 1495 (1996).
   a. How would you rule on that challenge? Explain.
   b. Why would the elimination of price advertising arguably contribute to reduced alcohol consumption?

The Fourth Amendment

LO 5-6

Describe some of the issues arising under the Fourth Amendment "search and seizure" rules.

Search and Seizure Case   David L. Riley was pulled over by the San Diego police because of an expired automobile registration. Guns were found in the car, Riley was arrested, and a warrantless search of his smartphone revealed information associating him with a gang shooting. Riley was later convicted of attempted murder. Riley sought to suppress all of the evidence secured through the cell phone search and that claim, along with a companion case, *United States v. Wurie,*[46] involving a flip phone search, reached the U.S. Supreme Court. The Court's 2014 unanimous rulings in *Riley v. California*[47] and in *Wurie* held that a warrant is required to search a cell phone, absent emergencies or a threat to officers.

Officer safety and prevention of evidence destruction have historically been cited as justifications for warrantless searches incident to arrests, but the *Riley* Court said those concerns do not apply to cell phone searches. Furthermore, the routine role of cell phones in everyday life and their immense storage capacity make them a repository of many aspects of phone owners' lives. Such a search might be even more damaging than a warrantless search of an individual's home, the Court reasoned. The Court acknowledged the additional burden the decision places on law enforcement.

Search and Seizure Law   The authorities are under great pressure to cope with America's crime and terrorism problems. They must do so, however, within the confines of the Constitution, which is designed to protect us all—including criminals and terrorists—from the power of an unfair, overreaching government. The Fourth Amendment provides that

> The right of the people to be secure in their persons, houses, papers, and effects, against unreasonable searches and seizures, shall not be violated, and no Warrants shall issue, but upon probable cause. . . .

Two crucial inquiries in search and seizure cases are whether a search has, in fact, occurred (as in the *Riley* case) and whether the search violated the subject's reasonable expectation of privacy (which is much more likely in one's home than on the street, for example).

In general, a *search warrant* issued by a judge is necessary to comply with the Constitution in making a search. A warrantless search is permissible, however, if reasonable, as in association with an arrest or where probable cause exists to believe a crime has been committed, but circumstances make securing a warrant impracticable. Under the *plain view* doctrine, law enforcement officers can lawfully seize evidence of a crime (such as weapons or drugs) without a warrant if that evidence is in plain view during a lawful observation. An example would be during a vehicle stop where an officer sees a weapon on the seat in the vehicle.

Did a Search Occur?   Antoine Jones, a nightclub owner, was suspected of being associated with an illegal narcotics operation. Police lacked a valid warrant but nonetheless put a GPS tracker on Jones's Jeep and followed his movements for four weeks. Jones was arrested in 2005 and in a 2008 trial, a jury found him guilty of intent to distribute cocaine, for which he was sentenced to life in prison. On appeal, Jones argued that his conviction should be overturned because the warrantless use of the GPS tracker violated his Fourth Amendment right to be protected from unreasonable search and seizure. His case reached the U.S. Supreme Court, which unanimously ruled that installing a GPS device is, indeed, a *search* in constitutional law terms.[48] The Court did not resolve the question of whether a search warrant is required in such situations. Future decisions will address that crucial question as the Court tries to achieve a coherent line of reasoning in applying the centuries-old Fourth Amendment to the complex new world of high technology.

How Far Can the Search Go?   For nearly 30 years, police officers have commonly understood that lawfully arresting an occupant of a vehicle confers the right to search the passenger compartment of that vehicle. In a 2009 decision, *Arizona v. Gant*,[49] the U.S. Supreme Court significantly diminished that authority by ruling that such searches are permissible in only two circumstances: when the individual being arrested is close enough to the vehicle to reach in for a weapon or evidence and when the officer can reasonably believe that the vehicle contains evidence relevant to the crime of arrest. Thus, arrests for routine traffic stops ordinarily would not justify vehicle searches, while such searches are more likely to be permissible incident to arrests for more serious crimes.[50]

Drug-Sniffing Dog

The Miami-Dade Police Department received a tip that the residence of Joelis Jardines was being used to grow marijuana. A drug-sniffing dog was taken to the door of the home. The dog signaled the presence of marijuana, a search warrant was obtained, and a search discovered marijuana growing in the house. Jardines was arrested.

Question

Did the use of the drug-sniffing dog render the search unconstitutional? Explain.

Source: Florida v. Jardines, 133 S. Ct. 1409 (2013).

LO 5-7
Explain the "exclusionary rule."

Exlusionary Rule   Perhaps the most controversial dimension of Fourth Amendment interpretation is the *exclusionary rule,* which provides that, as a matter of due process, evidence secured in violation of the Fourth Amendment may not be used against a defendant at trial. As ultimately applied to all courts by the 1961 U.S. Supreme Court decision in *Mapp v. Ohio,*[51] we can see that the exclusionary rule, while a very effective device for discouraging illegal searches, seizures, and arrests, also from time to time has the effect of freeing wrongdoers.

The Supreme Court has developed several exceptions to the exclusionary rule, including in its 2016 ruling in *Utah v. Strieff,*[52] where South Salt Lake City police officer Douglas

> Fackrell arrested Strieff and found methamphetamine.

Fackrell stopped Edward Strieff as he exited a house that was being observed for drug activity following an anonymous tip. Officer Fackrell detained Strieff, secured Strieff's identification, and called a police dispatcher, who told Fackrell that Strieff had an outstanding arrest warrant for a minor traffic violation. With that information, Fackrell arrested Strieff, searched him, and found methamphetamine and drug paraphernalia. Strieff claimed that the drug evidence was inadmissible under the exclusionary rule since Fackrell's investigatory stop did not provide reasonable suspicion of criminal conduct. Strieff's claim reached the U.S. Supreme Court, which agreed that the initial stop was illegal, but ruled 5–3 that Strieff could lawfully be searched after Fackrell learned of the outstanding warrant. The discovery of the valid arrest warrant, the majority reasoned, broke the connection between the unconstitutional stop and the evidence seized incident to the lawful arrest. Justice Sonia Sotomayor, expressing particular concern for the treatment of minorities by the police, issued an angry dissent:

> . . . [T]his case tells everyone, white and black, guilty and innocent, that an officer can verify your legal status at any time. It says that your body is subject to invasion while courts excuse the violation of your rights. It implies that you are not a citizen of a democracy but the subject of a carceral state, just waiting to be cataloged. . . .[53]

Privacy

Hidden cameras, government surveillance, phone records, Internet exposure of personal matters, medical records, academic records, school lockers, bodily searches, and many more dimensions of our lives raise privacy concerns. Although the word *privacy* does not appear in the Constitution, courts have cited the Fourth Amendment and other constitutional provisions to firmly establish a right to privacy. Interpreting the bounds of that protection, however, is complex.

Drug testing and the disturbing photographic practice of "upskirting" are among the many situations where privacy concerns have been litigated. Drug testing clearly is a search for Fourth Amendment purposes, but when is it an unconstitutional intrusion on privacy?

Testing Students   In 1998, the school board in rural Tecumseh, Oklahoma, instituted a mandatory random urinalysis drug-testing program for all students participating in competitive extracurricular activities. The tests checked for illegal drugs but not for alcohol. Test results were not turned over to the police. An honor student, Lindsay Earls, challenged the program as a violation of her Fourth Amendment rights. A U.S. court of appeals agreed with her, ruling that school officials needed to provide evidence of an "identifiable drug abuse problem."[54] The U.S. Supreme Court, however, reversed that decision and held by a 5–4 margin that the school's interest in addressing drug problems outweighed students' privacy rights.[55] The Court reasoned that those participating in extracurricular activities are subjected to many rules and restrictions that diminish their expectation of privacy, and the Court said the program is a health and safety measure rather than an assault on personal privacy. Some state supreme courts, however, have ruled that school drug testing violates state constitutional law,[56] but even middle schools in at least eight states are now requiring drug testing for students participating in activities ranging from athletics to scrapbooking.[57]

Testing Welfare Applicants   At least 10 states require welfare applicants through the federal government's Temporary Assistance for Needy Families (TANF) to be screened and perhaps tested for drug abuse. Some states apply testing requirements to all applicants, while others limit testing to individuals who are reasonably suspected of illegal drug-related activity.

Florida's warrantless, suspicionless drug-testing requirement for all welfare applicants was ruled unconstitutional in 2014.[58] A three-judge panel of the federal 11th Circuit Court of Appeals said Florida failed to show that TANF applicants differed from the general population in their drug behaviors such that the state had reason to subject them to testing. Florida had failed, the court said, to show a "substantial need" (such as safety concerns) that would justify testing all welfare applicants rather than limiting testing to particularized situations of individualized suspicion.

Of course, testing proponents argue that substantial need does exist. They point to unfairness in using tax dollars to subsidize drug use, and they argue that the state has a duty to discourage drug use and, in particular, to protect children. Florida data, however, showed that only 2.6 percent of those tested were found to have used narcotics, so the program actually cost more to administer than it saved.[59]

Voyeurism and the Surveillance Society   Georgia, Massachusetts, Michigan, Texas, and Washington courts, among others in recent years, have overturned criminal convictions involving the practice of "upskirting" and similar photographic intrusions on privacy. In the Washington case, for example, Richard Sorrells and Sean Glas were found guilty of violating a state voyeurism statute for taking pictures up the skirts of some women who were working and shopping in a public mall. On appeal, their convictions were overturned because the voyeurism law did not apply, the Washington State Supreme Court unanimously ruled, to actions in public places.[60] The women had no "reasonable expectation of privacy" in the shopping mall, so their privacy could not have been invaded. A federal law, the Video Voyeurism Prevention Act (limited to federal jurisdiction/property), and a number of state laws have expanded protection against photographic voyeurism, but those laws will, of course, be subject to constitutional scrutiny, particularly on First Amendment grounds, because photographs are a form of expression. [For an overview of privacy issues, see **http://epic.org/**].

Questions

1. More than 13 million people are admitted to American jails each year. Albert Florence was mistakenly arrested for failing to pay a traffic fine that, in fact, he had paid. After arrest, he was subjected to a pair of strip searches involving showering with a delousing

agent, officers lifting his genitals, officers looking in his body openings, and more. Does the Constitution allow authorities to strip search those admitted to jail for minor violations? Explain. See *Florence v. Board of Chosen Freeholders,* 132 S. Ct. 1510 (2012).

2. Alonzo King was arrested in 2009 on an assault charge and, without first obtaining a search warrant, police swabbed the inside of his cheek for a DNA sample. Several months later his DNA was matched with a 2003 rape case. He was then convicted of that rape. He appealed his conviction arguing that he was a victim of an unreasonable search in violation of his Fourth Amendment rights. Maryland law allowed the sampling in cases where the suspect had been arrested, but not yet convicted, of serious crimes including burglaries, rape, and murder. Is DNA collection simply a part of the normal criminal booking process, much like fingerprinting, and thus a minimal intrusion on privacy? Explain.

3. A Connecticut resident, Paul DeFusco, was convicted of drug trafficking based on evidence found in his home. The police conducted the home search with a warrant secured on the basis of an informant's information as well as evidence (some short cut straws, glassine baggies, and prescription bottles) turned up in sifting through DeFusco's garbage. See *State of Connecticut v. Paul DeFusco,* 620 A.2d 746 (Conn. 1993).
   a. Can the police lawfully search an individual's garbage once it has been placed at the curb for disposal?
   b. Explain the central issue in this case.

4. Tucson, Arizona, police, cruising in an area associated with the Crips street gang, stopped a car because its insurance coverage had been suspended. Johnson, a backseat passenger, was wearing the blue colors associated with the Crips and Officer Trevizo saw that Johnson had a police scanner in his pocket. Trevizo questioned Johnson, learning that he was from a town frequented by the Crips gang, that he had recently been in prison, and that he had no identification with him. Trevizo asked Johnson to exit the car. He did so. Trevizo conducted a pat-down search and felt a gun. Johnson struggled, but he was arrested, and a further search revealed marijuana. Johnson was charged with unlawful possession of a gun, possession of marijuana, and resisting arrest. In court, Johnson challenged the legality of the search saying it had nothing to do with the traffic stop. Did the pat-down violate the Fourth Amendment's prohibition on unreasonable searches and seizures? Explain. See *Arizona v. Johnson,* 555 U.S. 323 (2009).

Business Searches

Government tries to protect us from business hazards including pollution, defective products, and unsafe workplaces as well as business crimes such as fraud and bribery. To do so, government agents often want to enter company buildings, observe working conditions, and examine company books. We know our homes are generally protected from searches in the absence of a warrant. Excepting urgent circumstances such as terrorism concerns, can the same be said for a place of business? The Supreme Court has answered that question:

> The Warrant Clause of the Fourth Amendment protects commercial buildings as well as private homes. To hold otherwise would belie the origin of that Amendment, and the American colonial experience. . . . "[T]he Fourth Amendment's commands grew in large measure out of the colonists' experience with the writs of assistance . . . [that] granted sweeping power to

customs officials and other agents of the king to search at large for smuggled goods." Against this background, it is untenable that the ban on warrantless searches was not intended to shield places of business as well as of residence.[61]

The Fifth Amendment

LO 5-8
Describe the law of the Fifth Amendment "Takings Clause" and the property rights controversy associated with it.

Takings—Eminent Domain

The Fifth Amendment prohibits the taking of private property for *public use* without *just compensation* for the owner. In cases where owners do not want to sell, governments often use the power of *eminent domain* to take private real property for public uses such as building highways, bike trails, and parks, while providing just compensation.

Takings can also involve personal property. A 1937 federal law allows the government to require raisin growers to set aside a portion of their crops for the government. Farmers then share in the proceeds if the government later sells the reserve raisins. The purpose of the set-aside is to restrict supply in order to maintain stable raisin prices for farmers. Marvin Horne, a California raisin farmer/handler, did not want to set aside any of his raisins, and he challenged the rule as an unlawful taking. The U.S. Supreme Court in 2015 agreed with Horne, ruling that the government must pay just compensation for taking personal property just as for real property.[62]

Now what about the situation where the property claimed by the government is to be used for a *private* purpose? Communities across America, hungry for an improved tax base and more jobs, have made the practice routine, but are they violating the Fifth Amendment rights of the property owners? The following 5–4 Supreme Court decision involves a challenge to a New London, Connecticut, plan to clear a portion of the city to make way for a private-sector office/research park along with a waterfront hotel, conference center, residences, a marina, and a river walk. Small businesses and residences were to make room for bigger, more successful private ventures providing a stronger tax base for New London.

LEGAL BRIEFCASE

Kelo v. City of New London, Connecticut
545 U.S. 469 (2005)

Justice Stevens

In 2000 the city of New London approved a development plan that, in the words of the Supreme Court of Connecticut, was "projected to create in excess of 1,000 jobs, to increase tax and other revenues, and to revitalize an economically distressed city, including its downtown and waterfront areas" (843 A.2d 500, 507 [2004]). In assembling the land needed for this project, the city's development agent has purchased property from willing sellers and proposes to use the power of eminent domain to acquire the remainder of the property from unwilling owners in exchange for just compensation. The question presented is whether the city's proposed disposition of this property qualifies as a "public use" within the meaning of the Takings Clause of the Fifth Amendment to the Constitution.

I

The city of New London (hereinafter City) sits at the junction of the Thames River and the Long Island Sound in southeastern Connecticut. Decades of economic decline led a state agency in 1990 to designate the City a "distressed municipality." In 1996 the Federal Government closed the Naval Undersea Warfare Center, which had been located in the Fort Trumbull area of the City and had employed over 1,500 people. In 1998 the City's unemployment rate was nearly double that of the State, and its population of just under 24,000 residents was at its lowest since 1920.

These conditions prompted state and local officials to target New London, and particularly its Fort Trumbull area, for economic revitalization. To this end, respondent New London Development Corporation (NLDC), a private nonprofit entity established some years earlier to assist the City in planning economic development, was reactivated. In January 1998 the State authorized a $5.35 million bond issue to support the NLDC's planning activities and a $10 million bond issue toward the creation of a Fort Trumbull State Park. In February the pharmaceutical company Pfizer Inc. announced that it would build a $300 million research facility on a site immediately adjacent to Fort Trumbull; local planners hoped that Pfizer would draw new business to the area. Upon obtaining state-level approval, the NLDC finalized an integrated development plan focused on 90 acres of the Fort Trumbull area.

The Fort Trumbull area is situated on a peninsula that juts into the Thames River. The area comprises approximately 115 privately owned properties, as well as the 32 acres of land formerly occupied by the naval facility (Trumbull State Park now occupies 18 of those 32 acres). The development plan encompasses seven parcels. Parcel 1 is designated for a waterfront conference hotel at the center of a "small urban village" that will include restaurants and shopping. . . . Parcel 2 will be the site of approximately 80 new residences organized into an urban neighborhood and linked by public walkway to the remainder of the development, including the state park. This parcel also includes space reserved for a new U.S. Coast Guard Museum. Parcel 3, which is located immediately north of the Pfizer facility, will contain at least 90,000 square feet of research and development office space. Parcel 4A is a 2.4-acre site that will be used either to support the adjacent state park, by providing parking or retail services for visitors, or to support the nearby marina. Parcel 4B will include a renovated marina, as well as the final stretch of the riverwalk. Parcels 5, 6, and 7 will provide land for office and retail space, parking, and water-dependent commercial uses.

* * * * *

The city council approved the plan in January 2000 and designated the NLDC as its development agent in charge of implementation. The city council also authorized the NLDC to purchase property or to acquire property by exercising eminent domain in the City's name. The NLDC successfully negotiated the purchase of most of the real estate in the 90-acre area, but its negotiations with petitioners failed. As a consequence, in November 2000 the NLDC initiated the condemnation proceedings that gave rise to this case.

II

Petitioner Susette Kelo has lived in the Fort Trumbull area since 1997. She has made extensive improvements to her house, which she prizes for its water view. Petitioner Wilhelmina Dery was born in her Fort Trumbull house in 1918 and has lived there her entire life. Her husband Charles has lived in the house since they married some 60 years ago. In all, the nine petitioners own 15 properties in Fort Trumbull. . . . There is no allegation that any of these properties is blighted or otherwise in poor condition; rather, they were condemned only because they happen to be located in the development area.

In December 2000 petitioners brought this action in the New London Superior Court. They claimed, among other things, that the taking of their properties would violate the "public use" restriction in the Fifth Amendment. After a seven-day bench trial, the Superior Court granted a permanent restraining order prohibiting the taking of the properties located in parcel 4A (park or marina support). It, however, denied petitioners relief as to the properties located in parcel 3 (office space).

After the Superior Court ruled, both sides took appeals to the Supreme Court of Connecticut. That court held that all of the City's proposed takings were valid.

* * * * *

III

Two polar propositions are perfectly clear. On the one hand, it has long been accepted that the sovereign may not take the property of A for the sole purpose of transferring it to another private party B, even though A is paid just compensation. On the other hand, it is equally clear that a State may transfer property from one private party to another if future "use by the public" is the purpose of the taking; the condemnation of land for a railroad is a familiar example. Neither of these propositions, however, determines the disposition of this case.

As for the first proposition, the City would no doubt be forbidden from taking petitioners' land for the purpose of conferring a private benefit on a particular party. Nor would the City be allowed to take property under the mere pretext of a public purpose, when its actual purpose was to bestow a private benefit. The takings before us, however, would be executed pursuant to a "carefully considered" development plan. The trial judge and all the members of the Supreme Court of Connecticut agreed that there was no evidence of an illegitimate purpose in this case.

* * * * *

On the other hand, this is not a case in which the City is planning to open the condemned land—at least not in its entirety—to use by the general public. Nor will the private lessees of the land in any sense be required to operate like common carriers, making their services available to all comers. But although such a projected use would be sufficient to satisfy the public use requirement, this "Court long ago rejected any literal requirement that condemned property be put into use for the general public." Indeed, while many state courts in the mid-19th century endorsed "use by the public" as the proper definition of public use, that narrow view steadily eroded over time. Not only was the "use by the public" test difficult to administer (e.g., what proportion of the public need have access to the property? at what price?), but it proved to be impractical given the diverse and always evolving needs of society. Accordingly, when this Court began applying the Fifth Amendment to the States at the close of the 19th century, it embraced the broader and more natural interpretation of public use as "public purpose."

*   *   *   *   *

The disposition of this case therefore turns on the question whether the City's development plan serves a "public purpose." Without exception, our cases have defined that concept broadly, reflecting our long-standing policy of deference to legislative judgments in this field.

In *Berman v. Parker,* this Court upheld a redevelopment plan targeting a blighted area of Washington, D.C., in which most of the housing for the area's 5,000 inhabitants was beyond repair. Under the plan, the area would be condemned and part of it utilized for the construction of streets, schools, and other public facilities. The remainder of the land would be leased or sold to private parties for the purpose of redevelopment, including the construction of low-cost housing.

*   *   *   *   *

IV

Those who govern the City were not confronted with the need to remove blight in the Fort Trumbull area, but their determination that the area was sufficiently distressed to justify a program of economic rejuvenation is entitled to our deference. The City has carefully formulated an economic development plan that it believes will provide appreciable benefits to the community, including—but by no means limited to—new jobs and increased tax revenue. . . . Given the comprehensive character of the plan, the thorough deliberation that preceded its adoption, and the limited scope of our review, it is appropriate for us to resolve the challenges of the individual owners, not on a piecemeal basis, but rather in light of the entire plan. Because that plan unquestionably serves a public purpose, the takings challenged here satisfy the public use requirement of the Fifth amendment.

To avoid this result, petitioners urge us to adopt a new bright-line rule that economic development does not qualify as a public use. Putting aside the unpersuasive suggestion that the City's plan will provide only purely economic benefits, neither precedent nor logic supports petitioners' proposal. Promoting economic development is a traditional and long accepted function of government.

*   *   *   *   *

In affirming the City's authority to take petitioners' properties, we do not minimize the hardship that condemnations may entail, notwithstanding the payment of just compensation. We emphasize that nothing in our opinion precludes any State from placing further restrictions on its exercise of the takings power. Indeed, many States already impose "public use" requirements that are stricter than the federal baseline.

*   *   *   *   *

Affirmed.

AFTERWORD—PROPERTY RIGHTS REVOLUTION?

The *Kelo* decision was an angry disappointment for property rights advocates. A government taking of Americans' long-time homes, even for just compensation, is a powerful and frightening image. Susette Kelo eventually settled with New London, vacated her home, and received $442,000. Her "little pink house" was disassembled and moved to another lot, where it stands as something of a national symbol for property rights.

Clearly, however, governments need, and have long exercised, substantial authority to take property for economic development. Of course, government planning sometimes does not work out as expected, and the Pfizer development appears to be one of those failures. In 2009, Pfizer announced it was abandoning the Fort Trumbull office complex as a cost-saving measure. Fourteen hundred jobs were departing. The hotels, stores, and condominiums planned for the lots taken from Kelo and her neighbors have yet to materialize.

Kelo produced one of the angriest backlashes to any Supreme Court decision in history. At least 44 states have passed legislation or amended their constitutions to limit eminent domain, but the effectiveness of those measures is unclear. Some of them still allow takings involving "blighted" property, an exception readily subject to abuse, from the critics' point of view. [For property rights analysis and updates and more on the *Kelo* story, see **www.ij.org**].

Questions

1. What reasoning was offered by Justice Stevens to support the majority view that the New London development complied with due process requirements?

2. *a.* What was the issue, the central question, in this case and how did the majority answer that question?

   b. How would you expect the dissent to answer that question?

3. From the dissenting point of view, what harm is likely to emerge from this decision?

4. Marilyn and James Nollan applied for a permit to replace their beachfront home with a larger structure. The California Coastal Commission agreed on the condition that the Nollans grant an easement on their beach that would allow the public to cross that property and thus facilitate movement between the public beaches that lay on both sides of the Nollan beach. The Nollans sued, claiming a violation of the Takings Clause. Decide. Explain. See *Nollan v. California Coastal Commission,* 483 U.S. 825 (1987).

5. Tina Bennis sued when Wayne County (Detroit), Michigan, authorities took the car she jointly owned with her husband after police arrested him for receiving oral sex from a prostitute while parked in the car. A 1925 antinuisance law permitted the seizure, but Tina Bennis claimed it amounted to an unconstitutional taking because she was an innocent half owner of the 1977 Pontiac for which the couple had paid $600. Bennis's claim eventually reached the U.S. Supreme Court. Decide the case. Explain. See *Bennis v. Michigan,* 116 S. Ct. 994 (1996).

Takings—Regulatory

We have seen how the law treats situations where the government uses its power of eminent domain to condemn property for either public or private use and pays just compensation. What happens when the government does not take the property but rather *regulates* it in a manner that deprives that property of some or all of its economic usefulness? For example, without providing just compensation, can a state lawfully limit the amount a landlord can charge for rent in an effort to preserve low-income housing? Can the state forbid billboards in order to enhance roadside beauty?

These *regulatory takings,* whether temporary or permanent, normally do not require government compensation because doing so would severely impair the state's ability to govern in an orderly manner. Nonetheless, in recent years the courts have been more aggressive about requiring just compensation for some regulatory takings. Three broad classes of such takings have emerged in court decisions.

1. Total Takings If a governmental body acts in a way that permanently takes all of the economic value of a property or permanently physically invades the property, the taking requires just compensation unless (1) the government is preventing a nuisance or (2) the regulation was permissible under property law at the time of the purchase of the property. When the South Carolina Coastal Commission passed erosion rules having the effect of preventing David Lucas from building any permanent structure on his $975,000 beachfront lots, Lucas sued, claiming a Fifth Amendment violation. The U.S. Supreme Court agreed with Lucas and held that a taking requiring just compensation had occurred because the state had deprived Lucas of *all* economically beneficial use of the property, and the property did not fall in one of the two exceptions.[63]

> The South Carolina Coastal Commission passed erosion rules having the effect of preventing David Lucas from building any permanent structure on his $975,000 beachfront lots.

2. Exaction/Mitigation A second class of regulatory takings involves situations where the government allows land development only if the owner dedicates some property interest (called an *exaction*) or money (called a *mitigation* or *impact fee*) to the government. Thus, if you are developing land for housing, the city government might require that you devote a portion of that land to parks or pay a fee to help with community recreation needs. The Supreme Court dealt with just such a case in *Dolan v. City of Tigard*.[64] Florence Dolan, owner of a plumbing and electrical supply store in Tigard, Oregon, applied for a city permit to nearly double the size of her store and to pave her parking lot. Concerned with increased traffic and water runoff due to the proposed expansion, the city granted the permit, subject to a pair of conditions: (1) Dolan was to dedicate the portion of her property that lay within the 100-year floodplain to the city to improve drainage for the creek that ran along her property and (2) she was to dedicate an additional 15-foot strip of her land adjacent to the floodplain for use as a bicycle path/walkway to relieve traffic congestion. Dolan sued and eventually the U.S. Supreme Court ruled that government can compel a dedication of private property to public use where it can establish two factors: (1) a nexus or relationship between the government's legitimate purpose (flood and traffic control in *Dolan*) and the condition imposed (the land Dolan was to dedicate to public purposes) and (2) a "rough proportionality" between the burden imposed (the land given over to public use) and the impact of the development (increased water runoff and increased traffic).[65] The Supreme Court ruled that Tigard had failed to meet those standards, and Dolan won the case.

A 2013 U.S. Supreme Court decision stretched the *Dolan* reasoning and strengthened property rights. Coy Koontz Sr. wanted to build on his wetlands property, but the local water management district, consistent with Florida law, denied permission. Koontz was unwilling to either turn over part of his property for public purposes or pay for improvements on other public land as a way of "offsetting" the environmental damage that would have accompanied the development. Koontz sued. The Court, by a 5–4 vote, said the water management district's requirements constituted a taking and were subject to *Dolan*.[66]

3. Partial Takings   Government may take part of a piece of property in order to expand a road, install a bike path, or establish a buffer zone, for example. These are neither total takings nor exactions, but rather fall into a case-by-case analysis that, very briefly, considers the importance of the government's goals and the extent of the burden on the property owner.

Zoning in the Sixth Century

Government restraints on property development are not merely a modern imposition, as we learn from the following description of a zoning law in the Byzantine Empire:

> Next came the first zoning law for the beach. Coastal vistas were so cherished, and the competition for them so keen, that by the sixth century the Emperor Justinian the Great was compelled to pass an ordinance barring construction within 100 feet of the shore to protect sea views.

Source: Lena Lencek and Gideon Bosker, *The Beach: The History of Paradise on Earth* (New York: Penguin Group, 1998), p. 31.

The 14th Amendment

LO 5-9

Compare and contrast substantive due process and procedural due process.

Due Process

The Due Process Clauses of both the Fifth Amendment (applying to the federal government) and the 14th Amendment (applying to the states) provide that the government may not deprive citizens of life, liberty, or property without due process of law.

Substantive Due Process

Laws that arbitrarily and unfairly infringe on fundamental personal rights and liberties such as privacy, voting, and the various freedoms specified in the Bill of Rights may be challenged on due process grounds. Basically, the purpose of the law must be so compelling as to outweigh the intrusion on personal liberty or the law will be struck down. For example, the U.S. Supreme Court ruled that a Connecticut statute forbidding the use of contraceptives violated the constitutional right to privacy.[67] By judicial interpretation, the 14th Amendment Due Process Clause "absorbs" the fundamental liberties of the *federal* Constitution and prohibits *state* laws (in this case, the Connecticut contraceptive ban) that abridge those fundamental liberties such as privacy.

Procedural Due Process

Basically, procedural due process means that the government must provide a fair procedure including *notice* and a *fair hearing* before taking an action affecting a citizen's life, liberty, or property. A fair hearing might require, among others, the right to present evidence, the right to a decision maker free of bias, and the right to appeal. The precise nature of procedural due process depends, however, on the situation. A murder trial requires meticulous attention to procedural fairness; an administrative hearing to appeal a public university decision to expel a student for disciplinary reasons, while required to meet minimal constitutional standards, can be more forgiving in its procedural niceties.

Due Process: Void for Vagueness

A statute may violate due process rights if it is so vaguely written that the ordinary person cannot understand it. The *Skilling* case that follows involves a *void for vagueness* claim arising from the infamous Enron fraud scandal that caused the former Houston, Texas, energy giant—then the seventh largest company in America—to collapse into bankruptcy in 2001.

> Skilling allegedly pumped up Enron's share prices.

Enron founder Ken Lay (now deceased), chief executive officer Jeffrey Skilling, and chief accounting officer Richard Causey were among those indicted for various crimes in association with Enron's spectacular rise from its founding in 1985 to its collapse fewer than 20 years later. Among other alleged wrongs, Skilling was convicted of depriving the corporation and the public of his "honest services" by deceiving the investors about Enron's finances. Skilling allegedly pumped up Enron's share prices by failing to reveal the company's true financial condition. His appeal reached the Supreme Court in 2010, where he claimed that pretrial publicity and Enron's financial damage to Houston poisoned the jury pool and denied him his Sixth Amendment right to trial by an impartial jury. That claim was rejected by the Supreme Court, but Skilling also argued that the language of the "honest services" federal statute used to convict him was so vague that he was deprived of his due process rights.

Justice Ginsburg

[I AND II OMITTED—ED.]

III

We next consider whether Skilling's conspiracy conviction was premised on an improper theory of honest-services wire fraud. The honest-services statute, Section 1346, Skilling maintains, is unconstitutionally vague. . . .

A

To place Skilling's constitutional challenge in context, we first review the origin and subsequent application of the honest-services doctrine.

1

Enacted in 1872, the original mail-fraud provision, the predecessor of the modern-day mail- and wire-fraud laws, proscribed, without further elaboration, use of the mails to advance "any scheme or artifice to defraud." See *McNally v. United States,* 483 U.S. 350, 356, 107 S. Ct. 2875, 97 L. Ed. 2d 292 (1987). In 1909, Congress amended the statute to prohibit, as it does today, "any scheme or artifice to defraud, *or for obtaining money or property by means of false or fraudulent pretenses, representations, or promises.*" Section 1341 (emphasis added). Emphasizing Congress' disjunctive phrasing, the Courts of Appeals, one after the other, interpreted the term "scheme or artifice to defraud" to include deprivations not only of money or property, but also of intangible rights.

* * * * *

2

In 1987, this Court, in *McNally v. United States,* stopped the development of the intangible-rights doctrine in its tracks. *McNally* involved a state officer who, in selecting Kentucky's insurance agent, arranged to procure a share of the agent's commissions via kickbacks paid to companies the official partially controlled. The prosecutor did not charge that, "in the absence of the alleged scheme[,] the Commonwealth would have paid a lower premium or secured better insurance." Instead, the prosecutor maintained that the kickback scheme "defraud[ed] the citizens and government of Kentucky of their right to have the Commonwealth's affairs conducted honestly."

We held that the scheme did not qualify as mail fraud. "Rather than constru[ing] the statute in a manner that leaves its outer boundaries ambiguous and involves the Federal Government in setting standards of disclosure and good government for local and state officials," we read the statute "as limited in scope to the protection of property rights." "If Congress desires to go further," we stated, "it must speak more clearly."

3

Congress responded swiftly. The following year, it enacted a new statute "specifically to cover one of the 'intangible rights' that lower courts had protected . . . prior to *McNally:* 'the intangible right of honest services.'" In full, the honest-services statute stated:

> For the purposes of th[e] chapter [of the United States Code that prohibits, *inter alia,* mail fraud, Section 1341, and wire fraud, Section 1343], the term "scheme or artifice to defraud" includes a scheme or artifice to deprive another of the intangible right of honest services.

B

Congress, Skilling charges, reacted quickly but not clearly: He asserts that Section 1346 is unconstitutionally vague. To satisfy due process, "a penal statute [must] define the criminal offense [1] with sufficient definiteness that ordinary people can understand what conduct is prohibited and [2] in a manner that does not encourage arbitrary and discriminatory enforcement." *Kolender v. Lawson,* 461 U.S. 352, 357, 103 S. Ct. 1855, 75 L. Ed. 2d 903 (1983). The void-for-vagueness doctrine embraces these requirements.

According to Skilling, Section 1346 meets neither of the two due process essentials. First, the phrase "the intangible right of honest services," he contends, does not adequately define what behavior it bars. Second, he alleges, Section 1346's "standardless sweep allows policemen, prosecutors, and juries to pursue their personal predilections," thereby "facilitat[ing] opportunistic and arbitrary prosecutions."

In urging invalidation of Section 1346, Skilling swims against our case law's current, which requires us, if we can, to construe, not condemn, Congress' enactments.

* * * * *

There is no doubt that Congress intended Section 1346 to refer to and incorporate the honest-services doctrine recognized in Court of Appeals' decisions before *McNally* derailed the intangible-rights theory of fraud. . . . Congress enacted Section 1346 on the heels *of McNally* and drafted the statute using that decision's terminology.

* * * * *

Satisfied that Congress, by enacting Section 1346, "meant to reinstate the body of pre-*McNally* honest-services law," we have surveyed that case law. In parsing the Courts of Appeals decisions, we acknowledge that Skilling's vagueness challenge has force, for honest-services decisions preceding *McNally* were not models of clarity or consistency.

* * * * *

Although some applications of the pre-*McNally* honest-services doctrine occasioned disagreement among the Courts of Appeals, these cases do not cloud the doctrine's solid core: The "vast majority" of the honest-services cases involved offenders who, in violation of a fiduciary duty, participated in bribery or kickback schemes.

* * * * *

In view of this history, there is no doubt that Congress intended Section 1346 to reach *at least* bribes and kickbacks. Reading the statute to proscribe a wider range of offensive conduct, we acknowledge, would raise the due process concerns underlying the vagueness doctrine. To preserve the statute without transgressing constitutional limitations, we now hold that Section 1346 criminalizes *only* the bribe-and-kickback core of the pre-*McNally* case law.

* * * * *

Interpreted to encompass only bribery and kickback schemes, Section 1346 is not unconstitutionally vague. Recall that the void-for-vagueness doctrine addresses concerns about (1) fair notice and (2) arbitrary and discriminatory prosecutions. . . .

As to fair notice, "whatever the school of thought concerning the scope and meaning of" Section 1346, it has always been "as plain as a pikestaff that" bribes and kickbacks constitute honest-services fraud, *Williams v. United States,* 341 U.S. 97, 101, 71 S. Ct. 576, 95 L. Ed. 774 (1951). . . .

As to arbitrary prosecutions, we perceive no significant risk that the honest-services statute, as we interpret it today, will be stretched out of shape. Its prohibition on bribes and kickbacks draws content not only from the pre-*McNally* case law, but also from federal statutes proscribing—and defining—similar crimes.

* * * * *

C

It remains to determine whether Skilling's conduct violated Section 1346. Skilling's honest-services prosecution, the Government concedes, was not "prototypical." The Government charged Skilling with conspiring to defraud Enron's shareholders by misrepresenting the company's fiscal health, thereby artificially inflating its stock price. It was the Government's theory at trial that Skilling "profited from the fraudulent scheme . . . through the receipt of salary and bonuses, . . . and through the sale of approximately $200 million in Enron stock, which netted him $89 million."

The Government did not, at any time, allege that Skilling solicited or accepted side payments from a third party in exchange for making these misrepresentations. ("[T]he indictment does not allege, and the government's evidence did not show, that [Skilling] engaged in bribery.") It is therefore clear that, as we read Section 1346, Skilling did not commit honest-services fraud.

* * * * *

Affirmed in part. Vacated in part. Remanded.

AFTERWORD

The Supreme Court returned Skilling's case to the federal Fifth Circuit Court of Appeals where, in 2011, the Skilling saga appeared to be nearing its conclusion. The Fifth Circuit upheld Skilling's conviction finding the honest-services error was "harmless" in that ample evidence unrelated to the honest-services charge supported Skilling's conviction on 19 counts of securities fraud, conspiracy, insider trading, and making false representations.[68] At this writing, Skilling is serving his sentence in a Colorado prison, but an agreement was reached to reduce his 24-year sentence by 10 years because of a mistake in interpreting the federal sentencing guidelines. Skilling also agreed to give up about $42 million, all of which will go to Enron fraud victims. The case now seems to be at an end, and Skilling may depart prison as early as 2017.

Questions

1. Why did the Court conclude that Skilling did not commit honest-services fraud?

2. Why did the Court conclude that the honest-services statute was unconstitutional?

3. How did the Court correct the unconstitutional infirmity in the honest-services statute?

4. Christopher Keating, a physics professor at the University of South Dakota, was involved in an ongoing conflict with a coworker, and Keating sent an inflammatory e-mail to his department head. Keating's contract with the university was not renewed because the e-mail violated a university policy requiring civil behavior:

   > Faculty members are responsible for discharging their instructional, scholarly and service duties civilly, constructively and in an informed manner. They must treat their colleagues, staff, students and visitors with respect, and they must comport themselves at all times, even when expressing disagreement or when engaging in pedagogical exercises, in ways that will preserve and strengthen the willingness to cooperate and to give or to accept instruction, guidance or assistance.

   Keating sued the university claiming, among other things, that the university's "civility policy" was impermissibly vague in violation of the Due Process Clause of the Fourteenth Amendment. How would you rule on that void-for-vagueness claim? Explain. See *Keating v. University of South Dakota,* 569 F. App'x 469 (8th Cir. 2014).

Equal Protection

LO 5-10

Identify some examples of the impact of the Equal Protection Clause on business and society.

The 14th Amendment provides that no state shall "deny to any person within its jurisdiction the equal protection of the laws." The Due Process Clause of the Fifth Amendment has been interpreted to provide that same protection against the power of the federal government. Fundamentally, these laws forbid a government from treating one person (including a corporation) differently from another without a rational basis for doing so. Most notably, the Equal Protection and Due Process Clauses have played an enormous role in attacking discrimination (see Chapter 13), but they can also significantly influence routine business practice in many ways. For example, can we lawfully impose higher taxes on a gambling casino than we impose on the sale of groceries? Or can we require the oil industry to follow more rigorous environmental standards than we expect of coal mines? In general, the answer to these questions is yes, but only if the legislation can pass the rational basis test. If not, such legislation would be unconstitutional and unenforceable.

[The U.S. Supreme Court, in *Loving v. Virginia,*[69] employed due process and equal protection principles to declare unconstitutional Virginia's antimiscegenation statute, thus ending race-based restrictions on marriage in the United States. For the 2016 *Loving* feature movie trailer, see **https://www.youtube.com/watch?v=zRXuCY7tRgk**].

How Many Renters?

Trying to reduce the flow of university students into certain portions of Ames, Iowa, home of Iowa State University, the city passed a zoning ordinance that permitted only single-family residences in specified areas. Under the ordinance, "family" was defined as any number of related persons or no more than three unrelated persons. The Ames Rental Property Association challenged the constitutionality of the ordinance.

Questions

1. Describe the constitutional claim raised by the plaintiffs.
2. Criticize the Ames standards for achieving its housing goals.
3. Decide the case. Explain.

Source: Ames Rental Property Association v. City of Ames, 736 N.W.2d 255 (Iowa 2007).

Same-Sex Marriage: Equal Rights?

In *Obergefell v. Hodges,* the U.S. Supreme Court in 2015 ruled by a 5–4 margin that the right to marry is guaranteed to same-sex couples by the Due Process and Equal Protection Clauses of the 14th Amendment.[70]

> Marriage is one of our fundamental liberties.

Citing well-established precedent, the Court majority affirmed that marriage is one of our fundamental liberties. Those liberties include choices at the core of individual dignity and autonomy and as such are protected by the Due Process Clause. Among those choices is the decision to marry. Marriage protects the sanctity of the two-person unions at the core of American life, it safeguards children and families, and it protects the social order. Because all of those principles apply equally to both opposite-sex and same-sex unions, the denial of marriage rights to same-sex couples abridges due process of law and equal protection under the law.

The decision requires all states to issue marriage licenses to same-sex couples and to recognize the legitimacy of same-sex marriages validly performed in other states. By its ruling, the Court changed American life and reminded all of the Constitution's expectation of equality before the law.

The dissenting justices argued that the Constitution simply does not address the same-sex marriage dispute and is a matter, therefore, that should be left to each state legislature. The majority view, on the other hand, treats the Constitution as a living document that should change with society.

In his dissent, Chief Justice Roberts noted that only 11 states and the District of Columbia had affirmed same-sex marriage democratically through voting booths and legislatures, and he argued that the decision denied same-sex marriage supporters the opportunity to achieve "true acceptance" of their view by persuading others of the justice of their cause. Of course, Supreme Court rulings serve to educate the public and in almost all instances (excepting most notably the *Roe v. Wade*[71] abortion decision), controversial decisions such as those involving school integration and the right to contraception have been broadly accepted by the public. The religious freedom laws noted earlier in this chapter reflect, however, stern initial resistance by some to the *Obergefell* decision.

PRACTICING ETHICS   Same-Sex Marriage: How Should We Feel?

Nearly two dozen nations, mostly in the Americas and Europe, permit same-sex marriages. According to the Pew Research Center, Americans in 2001 opposed same-sex marriage by a margin of 57 percent to 35 percent; in 2016 Americans supported same-sex marriage by a 55 to 37 percent margin. Those numbers represent extraordinarily rapid changes in views of gay and lesbian marriage. Those who remain in opposition to same-sex marriage are often troubled on moral and religious grounds. Consider some questions that examine those concerns:

1. What issues should one consider in deciding whether gay and lesbian marriages are morally defensible?

2. Because the American people, according to polling data, support gay and lesbian marriage, can we then consider it a morally defensible practice? Explain.

3. If scholarly studies ultimately demonstrate that homosexuality and lesbianism are substantially commanded by genetic characteristics, would we be morally required to accept same-sex marriage? Explain.

Source: Pew Research Center, "Changing Attitudes on Gay Marriage," May 12, 2016 [**www.pewforum.org**].

Stop-and-Frisk

The New York City police department practices a "stop-and-frisk" policy by which a police officer can stop and question those whom the officer reasonably believes to have committed, be committing, or be about to commit a felony or serious misdemeanor. Those stopped can be frisked for weapons if the officer reasonably believes he or she is in danger of physical injury.

The stop-and-frisk police practice is constitutionally permissible if conducted properly, but in a 2013 class-action lawsuit, *Floyd v. City of New York,* federal district court judge Shira Scheindlin ruled that stop-and-frisk, as practiced in recent years in New York City, was an impermissible violation of citizens' Fourth Amendment (search and seizure) and 14th Amendment (equal protection) rights. The judge ruled that police had routinely stopped innocent people without reasonable suspicion and that the police had been engaging in racial profiling. About 83 percent of the 4.4 million stops between 2004 and 2012 had involved blacks and Hispanics, two demographics that make up slightly more than 50 percent of the city population. The city argued that the racial pattern of the stops reflected the disproportionate share of crimes committed by young minority men, but the judge rejected that reasoning, saying that comparison would be valid only if those stopped were criminals, but 88 percent of those stopped were released with no finding of a justification for the stops.

Judge Scheindlin did not order a halt to stop-and-frisk, which is an important law enforcement tool if properly employed. She did, however, appoint a monitor to ensure police compliance with remedies including new training practices and the use of body-worn cameras by some officers. From a peak of 685,000 stops in 2011, the total fell to about 24,000 in 2015. As stops declined, major crime rates in total continued to fall, but in 2015 homicides, rapes, and robberies increased.

Question

Judge Scheindlin said, "It is impermissible to subject all members of a racially defined group to heightened police enforcement because some members of that group are criminals." Would you agree with Judge Scheindlin if homicides, rapes, and robberies continue to climb? Explain.

Sources: Joseph Goldstein, "Judge Rejects New York's Stop-and-Frisk Policy," *The New York Times,* August 12, 2013 [**www.nytimes.com**]; *Floyd v. City of New York*, 959 F. Supp. 2d 540 (S.D.N.Y. 2013); Lia Eustachewich and Bob Fredericks, "Stop-and-Frisks Plunge, but Cops Struggle to Comply with Record-Keeping Rules: NYPD Mointor," *New York Post,* February 16, 2016 [**http://nypost.com**]; and Pervaiz Shallwani and Mark Morales, "NYC Officials Tout New Low in Crime, but Homicide, Rape, Robbery Rose," *The Wall Street Journal,* January 4, 2016 [**www.wsj.com**].

Internet Exercise

Civil asset forfeiture is a particularly controversial but generally lawful police practice involving state and federal law enforcement authorities seizing property and cash from individuals who often are simply *suspected* of committing a crime. Read stories of civil asset forfeitures at **www.aclunc.org/articles/read-stories-civil-asset-forfeiture-victims.** Then see Merrill Matthews, "Civil Asset Forfeiture and the Constitution," *IPI Ideas,* no. 70, February 18, 2016 [**www.ipi.org/ipi_issues/detail/civil-asset-forfeiture-and-the-constitution**]. Explain the constitutional challenges that might be raised against civil asset forfeitures.

Chapter Questions

1. Danny Birchfield drove into a ditch in North Dakota. Responding officers believed he was intoxicated. He failed field sobriety tests and was arrested. In violation of North Dakota law, he refused to take a chemical test. Birchfield challenged the state statute that criminalized his refusal to take a chemical test. He argued that the statute violated the Fourth Amendment search-and-seizure provision because the officers did not have probable cause that would have supported a search warrant. Are warrantless breath

tests incident to arrest constitutionally permissible? What about warrantless blood tests? Explain. See *Birchfield v. North Dakota,* 136 S. Ct. 2160 (2016).

2. Bradley Johnson, a high school mathematics teacher, posted on his classroom walls large banners with familiar phrases such as "In God We Trust," "One Nation Under God," and "God Shed His Grace on Thee." School officials told him he needed to put the phrases in context (e.g., put the entire Declaration of Independence on the wall) or remove them. He did the latter and sued the school district for violating his First Amendment free speech and religious expression rights. In part, he defended his banners by pointing to displays in other classrooms that included Tibetan prayer flags, a Dalai Lama poster, and more. Decide Johnson's lawsuit. See *Johnson v. Poway Unified School District,* 658 F.3d 954 (9th Cir. 2011), *cert. denied,* 132 S. Ct. 1807 (2012).

3. Members of the Ku Klux Klan were distributing gun rights leaflets in Desloge, Missouri, when informed by a police officer that they were violating a city ordinance that prohibited "stand[ing] in or enter[ing] upon a roadway for the purpose of soliciting rides, employment, business or charitable contributions from, or distribut[ing] anything to, the occupant of any vehicle." The officer had observed Klan members stepping into the street to give leaflets to passing drivers. The Klan sued Desloge claiming the ordinance violated Klan members' First Amendment rights. How would you rule on that case? Explain. See *Traditionalist American Knights of the Ku Klux Klan v. City of Desloge, Missouri,* 775 F.3d 969 (8th Cir. 2014).

4. The Georgia Outdoor Advertising Control Act, in essence, prohibited any off-premises outdoor advertising of commercial establishments where nudity was exhibited. Cafe Erotica lawfully provided food and adult entertainment, including nude dancing, and advertised those services on billboards. Cafe Erotica challenged the constitutionality of the Advertising Control Act. Decide. Explain. See *Georgia v. Cafe Erotica,* 507 S.E.2d 732 (Ga. 1998).

5. Early in the morning hours, McNeeley was stopped by Missouri police for speeding and erratic driving. McNeeley was required to take a blood test after he had refused a breath test with a portable machine. His blood alcohol content was about twice the legal limit. He was charged with driving while intoxicated. Was the warrantless blood test an unreasonable search? Explain. See *Missouri v. McNeely,* 133 S. Ct. 1552 (2013).

6. Police officer Hughes, from Council Bluffs, Iowa, saw Sorick, 28 years of age, riding his bicycle at 12:35 a.m. without lights in violation of a city ordinance. Hughes stopped Sorick, asked if he was carrying a weapon, and then frisked him, at which time he felt what he believed to be a baggie containing a hard substance. Hughes asked Sorick what the substance was, and Sorick said it was marijuana. Hughes issued a citation for possession of marijuana. Sorick was found guilty at trial but appealed, claiming the frisk was an unreasonable search. Hughes testified that he searched Sorick because Hughes feared for his safety. The episode was late at night, the street was not lit, Sorick was in close proximity to Hughes, and people in that neighborhood were known to have weapons. Was the search lawful? Explain. See *Iowa v. Sorick,* 810 N.W.2d 896 (Iowa Ct. App. 2012).

7. James D. Harmon Jr. owns an apartment building on West 76th Street near Central Park in New York City. Three of his apartments are subject to rent control, a long-time

city program designed to maintain affordable housing in the very expensive Manhattan market. The rent-stabilized tenants were paying rent at 59 percent below market rates, according to Harmon.

a. Harmon called rent control "privatized welfare." Explain what he meant.

b. Harmon challenged the rent restriction. What constitutional law claim(s) was(were) raised by Harmon?

c. Who won the case? Explain. See *Harmon v. Markus,* 412 F. App'x 420 (2011), *cert. denied sub nom. Harmon v. Kimmel,* 132 S. Ct. 1991 (2012).

8. An Erie, Pennsylvania, public indecency ordinance prohibited knowingly or intentionally appearing in public in a "state of nudity." Pap's A.M., the owner of Kandyland, an Erie establishment featuring totally nude dancers, challenged the constitutionality of the ordinance.

a. Explain the nature of that constitutional challenge.

b. Decide the case. Explain. See *City of Erie v. Pap's A.M.,* 529 U.S. 277 (2000).

9. An individual and a group applied to the Chicago Park District for permits to hold rallies advocating the legalization of marijuana. The Park District, a municipal agency, required a permit to conduct a public assembly, parade, or other event involving more than 50 individuals. Applications for permits had to be processed within 28 days, and denials had to be clearly explained. Denials could be appealed to the general superintendent and then to the courts. The Park District denied some of the permits for pro-marijuana rallies. Those denied filed suit, claiming the Park District permit rules were unconstitutional.

a. What constitutional challenge was raised by the plaintiffs?

b. Decide the case. Explain. See *Thomas and Windy City Hemp Development Board v. Chicago Park District,* 534 U.S. 316 (2002).

10. Former U.S. Supreme Court Justice Antonin Scalia was asked if the judicial system had "gone off in error" by applying the equal protection requirements of the 14th Amendment to sex discrimination and sexual orientation discrimination. Scalia responded, "Yes, yes. . . . Certainly the Constitution does not require discrimination on the basis of sex. The only issue is whether it prohibits it. It doesn't. . . ."[72]

a. Explain why Scalia believed the 14th Amendment does not forbid discrimination based on sex and sexual orientation.

b. Do you agree with Scalia? Explain.

11. Lancaster, California, located about 45 miles from Los Angeles, was trying to build its local economy but was tripped up by the U.S. Constitution. Costco, a big-box retailer, wanted to expand into next-door space leased to 99 Cents Only Stores. Costco told the city it would move to Palmdale if it could not expand. Lancaster tried to buy 99 Cents' lease, but the company refused. Lancaster then used its power of eminent domain to condemn the 99 Cents property for the purpose of making it available to Costco. The city noted that blight might follow if Costco left, and the city contrasted 99 Cents' under $40,000 per year in sales taxes generated with Costco's more than $400,000. 99 Cents then sued the city seeking an order blocking the effort to take the 99 Cents property.

a. How would you have ruled on the case when it was tried in 2001? Explain.

b. Would the result be any different today after the Supreme Court's 2005 decision in the *Kelo* (New London, Connecticut) case? Explain. See *99 Cents Only Stores v.*

Lancaster Redevelopment Agency, 237 F. Supp. 2d 1123 (C.D. Cal. 2001), *appeal dismissed,* 60 F. App'x 123 (9th Cir. 2003).

12. Long Island, New York, resident Stephanie Fuller was secretly videotaped by her landlord, who had installed a video camera in the smoke detector above her bed. Fuller's landlord was found guilty of trespassing and was fined $1,500 and sentenced to 280 hours of community service.

    a. Why was the landlord not charged with a more serious felony offense?

    b. After Fuller's experience, New York enacted a criminal unlawful surveillance statute; the statute includes language forbidding secret surveillance in places where the victim has "a reasonable expectation of privacy." What legal significance attaches to that language?

13. Former North Carolina State University basketball stars Tom Gugliotta and Chris Corchiani were ejected from North Carolina State's arena during a 2012 game with Florida State University. Referee Karl Hess asked a police officer to eject the two men, who were seated immediately behind the scorer's table. Hess said he requested the ejections because excessive demonstration by the two men incited the crowd. Both men said they had not used inappropriate language. The Atlantic Coast Conference reprimanded Hess for not following conference protocol in the incident. Home game management officials, rather than a security officer, should have been involved in ejecting the fans. Does the First Amendment protect speech uttered at sporting events? Explain.

14. Milwaukee prostitutes, who had been arrested on multiple occasions, sued to block the city from enforcing a court-ordered injunction that permanently enjoined them from engaging in certain specified activities in certain specified areas of the city. They were prohibited from "engaging in beckoning to stop, or engaging male or female passersby in conversation, or stopping or attempting to stop motor vehicle operators by hailing, waving of arms or any other bodily gesture, or yelling in a loud voice" and other such activities. The women challenged the order on constitutional grounds.

    a. Explain the nature of that constitutional challenge.

    b. Decide the case. Explain. See *City of Milwaukee v. Burnette,* 637 N.W.2d 447 (Wis. Ct. App. 2001), *petition for rev. denied,* 638 N.W.2d 590 (Wis. 2001).

15. Jennifer O'Brien, a tenured teacher in the Paterson, New Jersey, schools with an unblemished performance record, was assigned to teach first grade in a school populated primarily by minority students. After a time, O'Brien concluded that several students in the class had behavioral problems that were disturbing the learning environment. Some students were hitting each other, one struck O'Brien, and another stole money from O'Brien and other students. O'Brien felt administrators had not responded adequately to her complaints, and she posted on her own Facebook page after school hours: "I'm not a teacher—I'm a warden for future criminals." Parents and others were outraged. Protests followed. O'Brien said her remarks were not a commentary on race or ethnicity but were legitimate concerns about the behavior of some students. O'Brien was dismissed from her teaching position. She sued claiming her actions, among other things, were protected by the First Amendment. Decide the case. Explain. See *In the Matter of the Tenure Hearing of Jennifer O'Brien, State Operated School*

District of the City of Paterson, Passaic County, 2013 N.J. Super. Unpub. LEXIS 28 (N.J. Super. Ct. App. Div. January 11, 2013).

16. Paul Palmer submitted three shirts to his Waxahachie, Texas, school for approval under the school's dress code. Two of the shirts said "John Edwards for President" and one said "Freedom of Speech" on the front and had the text of the First Amendment on the back. The shirts were rejected as violations of the school's dress code that did not allow shirts with printed messages except for those related to the school and those smaller than two inches by two inches. Political messages were permitted on pins, buttons, bumper stickers, and the like. The dress code was designed to curb gang problems, reduce distractions, encourage professional dress, and maintain a safer, more orderly learning environment. Palmer sued the school claiming a violation of his First Amendment freedom of speech rights. Decide that case. Explain. See *Palmer v. Waxahachie Independent School District,* 579 F.3d 502 (5th Cir. 2009), *cert. denied,* 130 S. Ct. 1055 (2010).

17. The sons of a murder victim brought a wrongful death/negligence action against a magazine, *Soldier of Fortune,* alleging that it had published an ad creating an unreasonable risk of violent crime. A former police officer had placed the ad offering his services as a bodyguard under the heading "Gun for Hire." The ad resulted in the officer being hired to kill the plaintiffs' father. The ad included the phrases "professional mercenary" and "very private" and a statement indicating that "all jobs" would be considered, but it also included a list of legitimate jobs that involved the use of a gun. The plaintiffs won the negligence action and were awarded a $4.3 million judgment. *Soldier of Fortune* appealed on First Amendment grounds. Decide. See *Braun v. Soldier of Fortune Magazine, Inc.,* 968 F.2d 1110 (11th Cir. 1992), *cert. denied,* 113 S. Ct. 1028 (1993).

18. The Madisonian idea of the First Amendment was to protect serious political discourse. Now the First Amendment often protects hate speech and commercial babble. In a 1996 book review and commentary, lawyer Paul Reidinger raised the concern that we may have "too much" free speech. Reidinger said, "The question these days is not whether government threatens free speech, but whether free speech threatens us. . . . [T]here is a tidal wave of fetid speech washing over the American landscape." Has the marketplace of ideas failed? See Paul Reidinger, "Weighing Cost of Free Speech," *ABA Journal* 82 (January 1996), p. 88.

Notes

1. Portions of this history of the U.S. Constitution rely on Gordon Lloyd, "Introduction to the Constitutional Convention" [**http://teachingamericanhistory.org/convention/intro.html**].

2. 554 U.S. 570 (2008).

3. 130 S. Ct. 3020 (2010).

4. Editorial Board, "An Opening for States to Restrict Guns," *The New York Times,* December 9, 2015 [**www.nytimes.com**].

5. "74% Think Americans Have Constitutional Right to Own a Gun," *Rasmussen Reports,* January 9, 2013 [**www.rasmussenreports.com**].

6. Megan Cassella, "Majority of Americans Support Next President Pushing Tighter Gun Laws: Poll," *Reuters,* January 13, 2016 [**www.reuters.com**].

7. Pew Research Center, *Growing Public Support for Gun Rights,* December 10, 2014 [**www.people-press.org**].

8. Ibid.

9. Greg Hampikian, "When May I Shoot a Student?" *The New York Times,* February 27, 2014 [**www.nytimes.com**].

10. Jerre Williams, *Constitutional Analysis in a Nutshell* (St. Paul: West, 1979), p. 33.

11. 17 U.S. 316 (1819).

12. 5 U.S. (1 Cranch) 137 (1803).

13. 133 S. Ct. 2612 (2013).

14. *Veasey v. Abbott,* 815 F.3d 958 (5th Cir. 2016).

15. Editorial, "Importance of Rights Grows; So Does Ignorance," *The Des Moines Register,* July 5, 2015, p. 1 OP.

16. Remesh Ponnuru, "Tim Cook Needs to Do Some Homework," *BloombergView,* March 30, 2015 [**www.bloombergview.com**].

17. 134 S. Ct. 1811 (2014).

18. Ibid.

19. Terence Chea, "'Under God' in Pledge of Allegiance Upheld by Court," *Huffington Post,* March 12, 2010 [**www.huffingtonpost.com**].

20. *Newdow v. Rio Linda Union School District,* 597 F.3d 1007 (9th Cir. 2010).

21. *Newdow v. Lefevre,* 598 F.3d 638 (9th Cir. 2010), *cert. denied,* 131 S. Ct. 1612 (2011).

22. *Christian Legal Society v. Leo P. Martinez,* 130 S. Ct. 2971 (2010).

23. Associated Press, "New Kansas Law Lets Campus Religious Groups Restrict Members," *Business Insider,* March 28, 2016 [**www.businessinsider.com**].

24. Cheryl Lavin, "The Redemption of Larry Flynt," *Chicago Tribune,* December 27, 1996 [**http://articles.chicagotribune.com/**].

25. 393 U.S. 503 (1969).

26. *McCutcheon v. Federal Election Commission,* 134 S. Ct. 1434 (2014).

27. Megan Thee-Brenan, "Polls Show Broad Support for Campaign Spending Caps," *The New York Times,* April 2, 2014 [**www.nytimes.com**].

28. *Snyder v. Phelps,* 131 S. Ct. 1207 (2011).

29. Adam Cohen, "Why Spewing Hate at Funerals Is Still Free Speech," *Time,* September 29, 2010 [**www.time.com**].

30. *Cutting v. City of Portland, Maine,* 802 F.3d 79 (1st Cir. 2015).

31. *Munroe v. Central Bucks School District,* 805 F.3d 454 (3rd Cir. 2015).

32. *Garcetti v. Ceballos,* 126 S. Ct. 1951 (2006).

33. Nick Sanchez, "Charles Barkley: San Antonio Women Won't Get Apology from Me," *Newsmax,* May 14, 2014 [**www.newsmax.com**].

34. Greg Lukianoff and Jonathan Haidt, "The Coddling of the American Mind," *The Atlantic,* September 2015 [**www.theatlantic.com**].

35. Erica Goldberg, "Universities' Compliance with Speech Code Decisions Leaves Much to Be Desired," September 24, 2009, *Foundation for Individual Rights in Education—The Torch* [**http://thefire.org/article/11121.html**].

36. David Ariosto and Leigh Remizowski, "Yale Settles Sexual Harassment Complaint," *CNN.com* [**www.cnn.com**].

37. *Rodriguez v. Maricopa County Community College,* 605 F.3d 703 (9th Cir. 2010).

38. *Barrett v. University of Mississippi,* 232 F.3d 208 (5th Cir. 2000), *cert. denied,* 531 U.S. 1052 (2000).

39. *Corry v. Stanford University,* Case No. 740309 (Cal. Super. Ct. February 27, 1995).

40. *Valentine v. Chrestensen,* 316 U.S. 52 (1942).

41. *Citizens United v. Federal Election Commission,* 130 S. Ct. 876 (2010).

42. David G. Savage, "Corporate Free-Speech Ruling Speaks of Shift in Supreme Court," *Los Angeles Times,* February 9, 2010 [**www.latimes.com**].

43. *Citizens United,* 130 S. Ct. at 929.

44. Savage, "Corporate Free-Speech."

45. *Central Hudson Gas & Electric Corp. v. Public Service Commission,* 447 U.S. 557 (1980).

46. 134 S. Ct. 2473 (2014).

47. 134 S. Ct. 2473 (2014).

48. *United States v. Jones,* 132 S. Ct. 945 (2012).

49. 129 S. Ct. 1710 (2009).

50. This paragraph is derived in part from Adam Liptak, "Supreme Court Cuts Back Officers' Searches of Vehicles," *The New York Times,* April 22, 2009 [**www.nytimes.com**].

51. 367 U.S. 643 (1961).

52. 136 S. Ct. 2056 (2016).

53. *Id.* at 2070–71 (Sotomayor, J., dissenting).

54. *Earls v. Board of Education,* 242 F.3d 1264 (10th Cir. 2001).

55. *Board of Education of Pottawatomie County v. Earls,* 122 S. Ct. 2559 (2002).

56. Floralynn Einesman, "Drug Testing Students in California—Does It Violate the State Constitution?" *San Diego Law Review* 47 (Summer 2010), p. 681.

57. Mary Pilon, "Middle Schools Add a Team Rule: Get a Drug Test," *The New York Times,* September 22, 2012 [**www.nytimes.com**].

58. *Lebron v. Secretary of the Florida Department of Children and Families,* 772 F.3d 1352 (11th Cir. 2014).

59. Frances Robles, "Florida Law on Drug Tests for Welfare Is Struck Down," *The New York Times,* December 31, 2013 [**www.nytimes.com**].

60. *State of Washington v. Glas,* 54 P.3d 147 (Wash. 2002).

61. *Marshall v. Barlow's,* 436 U.S. 307 (1978).

62. *Horne v. Department of Agriculture,* 135 S. Ct. 2419 (2015).

63. *Lucas v. South Carolina Coastal Commission,* 112 S. Ct. 2886 (1992).

64. 114 S. Ct. 2309 (1994).

65. Frank A. Vickory and Barry A. Diskin, "Advances in Private Property Protection Rights: The States in the Vanguard," *American Business Law Journal* 34, no. 4 (Summer 1997), p. 561.

66. *Koontz v. St. Johns River Water,* 133 S. Ct. 2586 (2013).

67. *Griswold v. Connecticut,* 381 U.S. 479 (1965).

68. *United States v. Skilling,* 638 F.3d 480 (5th Cir. 2011).

69. 388 U.S. 1 (1967).

70. 135 S. Ct. 2584 (2015).

71. 410 U.S. 959 (1973).

72. "The Originalist," *California Lawyer,* January 2011 [**www.callawyer.com/story.cfm?eid =913358&evid=1**].

Video icon credit: ©Comstock Images/Alamy

CHAPTER SIX

Contracts

After completing this chapter, students will be able to fulfill the following learning objectives:

6-1. Explain the importance of contracts to a capitalist, free-market system.

6-2. Determine whether the Uniform Commercial Code or common law governs a contract dispute.

6-3. Identify the elements of a legally enforceable contract.

6-4. Classify a contract as bilateral or unilateral, express or implied, executory or executed.

6-5. Distinguish between valid, unenforceable, void, and voidable contracts.

6-6. Describe the elements of a valid offer.

6-7. Describe the elements of a valid acceptance.

6-8. Explain the significance of consideration as an element of a legally enforceable contract.

6-9. Compare and contrast the rights and duties arising in contractual assignment and delegation.

6-10. Compare and contrast different types of third-party beneficiaries to a contract.

6-11. Explain how a contract may be discharged.

6-12. Describe the remedies available for breach of contract.

Preface: The Role of Contracts in a Complex Society

LO 6-1
Explain the importance of contracts to a capitalist, free-market system.

A free-market system cannot operate effectively and fairly without a reliable foundation in contract law. At the practical level, all buyers and sellers must be confident that the deal they are about to make will be completed as specified, or that they will have a remedy available if it is not completed. Otherwise, the legal risk in making deals would act as a drag on the commercial process, reducing certainty and depreciating the extraordinary efficiency of the free market. At the philosophical level, the fundamental point of a contract is personal freedom. Contract law gives each of us a reliable mechanism for freely expressing our preferences in life. From buying a tube of toothpaste, a car, or a house, to paying tuition, to accepting an employment offer, to franchising a business, to borrowing millions of dollars, to adopting a child, and so on, the direction and value of our lives are shaped and protected to a significant degree by our contractual choices. To a considerable extent, we define ourselves by the contractual choices we make, and contract law protects those choices. The indispensable role of contract law is revealed in the remarkable Facebook story that follows.

Sharing Facebook?

Mark Zuckerberg, Facebook CEO, developed the fabulously successful social network while still a student at Harvard. However, prior to Facebook becoming a publicly traded company in 2012, Zuckerberg's ownership was challenged twice. In 2011, entrepreneur Paul Ceglia claimed that he and Zuckerberg entered into a contract in 2003 that entitled Ceglia to a 50 percent share in Facebook. In 2012, Ceglia pleaded not guilty to federal charges of mail and wire fraud for forging evidence in his lawsuit. In 2013, Ceglia's lawsuit was dismissed after a federal judge found "clear and convincing evidence" that the contract on which Ceglia had based his complaint was forged. In yet another twist, in 2014, Facebook and Zuckerberg brought a malicious prosecution lawsuit against Ceglia's lawyers, which they continue to pursue at this writing.

The battle between Zuckerberg and his college business partners, twins Cameron and Tyler Winklevoss, over the rights to the Facebook idea was the subject of the 2010 movie *The Social Network*. The twins claimed Zuckerberg stole their social networking idea. Zuckerberg denied that accusation, but the parties reached a settlement of about $65 million in 2008. The twins sued, however, to have the settlement overturned on the grounds that Facebook had not provided accurate valuation information during the settlement process. A court of appeals panel in 2011 rejected the twins' request; the Winkelvoss twins later dropped their U.S. Supreme Court appeal of that decision.

In 2015, the Winklevoss twins won a motion for summary judgment in a breach of contract claim brought by Boston software developer Wayne Chang seeking a share of the Winklevoss–Zuckerberg settlement based on a partnership he claims to have entered with the twins during their Harvard years to create and operate a social networking site named ConnectU.

Sources: Sara Randazzo, "Facebook Keeps Pushing Fraud Claims against DLA Piper, Milberg," *The Wall Street Journal Law Blog,* January 29, 2016 [**blog.wsj.com/law**]; Brandon Gee, "Winklevoss Twins Prevail on Summary Judgment in Facebook Suit," *Massachusetts Lawyers Weekly,* January 13, 2015 [**http://masslawyer-sweekly.com**]; Jonathan Stempel and Nate Raymond, "Judge Recommends Ceglia Case vs. Facebook Be Dismissed," *Reuters.com,* March 26, 2013 [**www.reuters.com**]; Bob Van Voris, "Facebook Says Ceglia Fraud Is Proven by 'Authentic Contract' Sent in 2004," *Bloomberg Technology,* August 18, 2011 [**www.bloomberg.com**]; Galen Moore, "Boston Entrepreneur Chang Seeks Half of Winklevoss' Facebook Settlement," *Boston Business Journal,* June 23, 2011 [**www.bizjournals.com**]; Bob Van Voris, "Facebook Claimant Says He Owns 50%, Has E-Mails as Proof," *Bloomberg Businessweek,* April 12, 2011 [**www.businessweek.com**]; "Boston Developer Wants Cut of Winklevoss Twins' $65-Million Facebook Settlement," *Los Angeles Times,* May 12, 2011 [**http://latimesblogs.latimes.com/technology/2011/05/boston-developer-wants-cut-of-winklevoss-twins-65-million-facebook-settlement.html**]; and Henry Blodget, "Analyzing the Facebook Contract: Is Mark Zuckerberg Screwed?" *Business Insider,* July 23, 2010 [**www.businessinsider.com**].

Part One—Building a Binding Contract

Introduction

Have you breached a contract?

We make promises routinely in our lives. Some of those create binding contracts; some do not. You promise, for example, to meet a friend after class, but you break your promise. Could your friend sue you in court for breach of contract? Doubtless your answer is "no" and, barring unusual circumstances, you would be correct. But why? This raises the central question in this chapter: Under what circumstances do promises become enforceable contracts? For the most part, the answer to that question has been provided by court decisions (the common law) accumulating over the many centuries of evolving contract law stretching from the ancient Middle East to England and across the Atlantic to America. Those centuries of decisions have provided a substantially fair, consistent, and predictable body of contract law, particularly in a time when the parties normally dealt with each other face-to-face, often as acquaintances. As business transactions became more complicated, the parties more and more distant from each other, and the comparative power between individuals and corporations evermore unbalanced, the need for government intervention increased. State legislatures began to impose new rules on what had been purely private transactions. Look, for example, at state and federal regulation of employment contracts/relationships governing working conditions such as hours of work, safety on the job, break time, and more (as explained in detail in Chapter 12). State laws and court decisions resulted, to some extent, in a confusing, inefficient patchwork of laws that didn't conform to the reality of complex, contemporary business practice. As a result, the Uniform Commercial Code, a body of rules on commercial law across the United States, was developed and then adopted by state legislatures.

The Uniform Commercial Code

LO 6-2

Determine whether the Uniform Commercial Code or common law governs a contract dispute.

The National Conference of Commissioners on Uniform State Laws (NCCUSL) and the American Law Institute (ALI) developed, for state-by-state approval, the Uniform Commercial Code (UCC), a body of rules designed to render commercial law consistent across the 50 states. The UCC has been adopted in 49 states, and Louisiana has adopted portions of it. With a set of uniform, predictable rules, business can be practiced with confidence and minimal legal confusion.

The UCC is divided into a series of articles addressing the multitude of potential issues that arise in complex commercial practice. For our purposes the most important of those articles is Number 2, Sales, which governs all transactions involving the *sale of goods*. Section 2-105 of the UCC defines goods as tangible, movable things, such as cars, clothing, and appliances. Real estate, stocks, bonds, money, and so forth are not covered. Nor are contracts for services governed by the UCC. Of course, many transactions involve both goods and services. Characteristically, in determining whether the UCC applies, the courts have asked whether the dominant purpose of the contract is to provide a service or to sell a good. [For a complete version of Article 2, see **https://www.law.cornell.edu/ucc**].

The first question, then, in contract disputes is whether the UCC or the common law governs the situation. Throughout this chapter, you should remember that the UCC is always controlling (1) if the transaction is addressed by the UCC—that is, it involves a contract for the sale of goods—and (2) if a UCC rule applies to the issue in question. On the other hand, the judge-made, common law of contracts continues to govern transactions (1) not involving the sale of goods or (2) involving the sale of goods but where no specific UCC provision applies. Increasingly, in non-UCC cases, courts analogize to UCC reasoning in arriving at their judgments; that is, the common law is borrowing or absorbing UCC principles. This chapter, while focusing primarily on the common law of contracts, will introduce the role of the sales article in the practice of business. Article 2A of the UCC governs **leases** of goods. In essence, Article 2A mimics the sales article except that it governs leases of goods rather than sales. Because of space constraints, Article 2A will not receive further attention in this text.

What Is a Contract?

LO 6-3
Identify the elements of a legally enforceable contract.

Legally enforceable contracts must exhibit all of the following features:

1. **Agreement.** A meeting of the minds of the parties based on an offer by one and an acceptance by the other. The determination as to whether the parties have actually reached agreement is based on the *objective* evidence (the parties' acts, words, and so on) as a "reasonable person" would interpret it rather than on an effort to ascertain the subjective or personal intent of the parties.

2. **Consideration.** The bargained-for legal value that one party agrees to pay or provide to secure the promise of another.

3. **Capacity.** The parties must have the legal ability to enter the contract; that is, they must be sane, sober, and of legal age.

4. **Genuineness of assent.** The parties must knowingly agree to the same thing. Their minds must meet as shown by the objective evidence. If that meeting does not occur because of, for example, mistake or fraud, or the like, a contract does not exist because the parties' assent was not real.

5. **Legality of purpose.** The object of the contract must not violate the law or public policy.

Contracts embracing these five features are enforceable by law; therefore, they are distinguishable from unenforceable promises. As explained later, some contracts must also be in writing to be enforceable.

Classification of Contracts

LO 6-4
Classify a contract as bilateral or unilateral, express or implied, executory or executed.

LO 6-5
Distinguish between valid, unenforceable, void, and voidable contracts.

Contracts fall into a series of sometimes overlapping categories. These categories reveal the rather well-ordered logic of our contract system (see Figure 6.1).

Contract Formation

1. **Bilateral and unilateral contracts.** A *bilateral contract* emerges from a situation in which *both* parties make promises. A *unilateral contract* ordinarily involves a situation in which one party makes a promise and the other *acts* in response to that promise. For example, as you establish your new restaurant, you promise a college friend that if he completes his degree, you will hire him. He can accept your promise—or offer—by the act of completing college.

2. **Express and implied contracts.** When parties overtly and explicitly manifest their intention to enter an agreement, either in writing or orally, the result (if other requirements are fulfilled) is an express contract. For example, in managing the accounting department at an insurance firm, you sign a form contract with a local computer store ordering a new computer. In turn, the supplier's signature on the form creates an express, bilateral agreement.

FIGURE 6.1
Classification
of Contracts

Contract Formation

1. Bilateral/unilateral
   a. Bilateral contract—a promise for a promise.
   b. Unilateral contract—a promise for an act.
2. Express/implied
   a. Express contract—explicitly stated in writing or orally.
   b. Implied-in-fact contract—inferred from the conduct of the parties.
   c. Quasi-contract—implied contract created by a court to prevent unjust enrichment.

Contract performance

1. Executory contract—not yet fully performed.
2. Executed contract—fully performed by all parties.

Contract enforceability

1. Valid contract—includes all of the necessary ingredients of a binding contract.
2. Unenforceable contract—contract exists, but a legal defense prevents enforcement.
3. Void contract—no enforceable contract at all.
4. Voidable contract—one party has the option of either enforcing or voiding the contract.

If, on the other hand, you ask your local computer service to repair a computer that is not working properly and one of the service's technicians does so, you have probably entered an *implied-in-fact contract.* A court would infer a promise by you to pay a reasonable price in return for the service's promise to make a commercially reasonable effort to repair the computer. The contract is inferred on the basis of the facts—that is, by the behavior of the parties.

Suppose in managing the accounting department at the insurance firm, you receive a premium payment for a policy that was not issued by your company, but rather by your rival firm. In these circumstances, it would be unfair for you to be able to keep the unearned money; therefore, the courts construct an implied-in-law or **quasi-contract** permitting the actual insurer to collect the money. This unusual situation in which the court infers the existence of a contract is employed only when necessary to prevent *unjust enrichment* (as would have been the case if you were to collect an insurance premium without having issued a policy).

Contract Performance

1. **Executory contracts.** A contract is labeled *executory* until all parties fully perform.

2. **Executed contracts.** When all parties have completed their performances, the contract is *executed.*

Contract Enforceability

1. **Valid contracts.** A valid contract meets all of the established legal requirements and thus is enforceable in court.

2. **Unenforceable contracts.** An unenforceable contract meets the basic contractual requirements but remains faulty because it fails to fulfill some other legal requirement. For example, an oral contract may be unenforceable if it falls in one of those categories of contracts, such as the sale of land, that must be in writing (see the **Statute of Frauds** later in this chapter).

3. **Void contracts.** A void contract is, in fact, no contract at all because a critical legal requirement is missing; usually it is either an agreement to accomplish an illegal purpose (such as to commit a crime) or an agreement involving an incompetent party (such as an individual judged by a court to be insane). In either case, what is otherwise an enforceable contract is in fact void.

4. **Voidable contracts.** A voidable contract is enforceable but can be canceled by one or more of the parties. The most common voidable contracts are those entered by minors who have the option, under the law, of either disaffirming or fulfilling most contracts, which will be explained later.

With this Ring . . . ?

Christopher and Melissa had been living together for four years when Christopher proposed marriage to Melissa, buying her an engagement ring worth $10,000. After continuing to live together with their child and Melissa's other child, Melissa discovered that Christopher had cheated on her; Christopher then asked Melissa to move out with the children. Melissa had already quit her job to be a full-time mother, having assumed that Christopher would support the family as her husband. Melissa sued Christopher for "breach of promise to marry" among other claims. Christopher argued that his relationship with Melissa was illegal, making the promise to marry unenforceable. Further, he asserted he had only given Melissa a ring but had never said the words "will you marry me?" to her. Who should win, and why? Consider these questions further as you learn about contracts in this chapter.

Source: Neetzan Zimmerman, "Georgia Man Ordered to Pay Ex $50K for 'Breach of Promise to Marry,'" *Gawker.com,* December 6, 2013 [**gawker.com**].

The Agreement: Offer

LO 6-6
Describe the elements of a valid offer.

Characteristically, an offer consists of a promise to do something or to refrain from doing something in the future. A valid offer must include all of these elements:

1. Present *intent* to enter a contract.
2. Reasonable *definiteness* in the terms of the offer.
3. *Communication* of the offer to the offeree.

Intent

Assume that you are the purchasing manager for a trucking firm, and you need a small used van to do some local light hauling. Because time is of the essence, you decide to bypass the normal bidding process and go directly to the local dealers to make a quick purchase. At the first lot you find a suitable van. In discussing it, the sales manager says, "Well, we don't usually do this, but since you've been such a good customer, I'll tell you, we paid $10,000 for this one so I guess we are gonna need about $11,000 to deal with you." You say, "Fine. That's reasonable. I'll take it." The manager then says, "Now wait a minute, I was just talking off the top of my head. I'll have to punch up the numbers to be sure."

Do you have a deal at that point? The core question is whether the sales manager made an *offer.* Normally, language of that kind has been treated by the courts as preliminary negotiation lacking the necessary *intent* to constitute an offer. Of course, if no offer exists, you cannot accept, and no contract can emerge absent further negotiation.

Gambling

In 2006, Troy Blackford, a Des Moines, Iowa, truck driver, won $9,387 gambling at Prairie Meadows casino. Blackford tried to collect the winnings, but his request was denied by the casino. Officials said that he had been banned from the casino since 1996, and the ban had not been lifted. (In the 1996 episode, Blackford had punched a slot machine and was belligerent with casino security.) Blackford sued the casino.

Questions

1. What was the central issue in the case? Explain.
2. Decide the case. Explain.

Source: Blackford v. Prairie Meadows Racetrack & Casino, 778 N.W.2d 184 (Iowa 2010).

> Suppose you were responding to an ad that said, "2012 full-size Ford cargo van, $20,000." Is that ad language an offer such that you can accept by promising to pay $20,000?

Advertisements   The question of intent sometimes arises with advertisements. In buying the van for your business, suppose you were responding to an ad that said, "2012 full-size Ford cargo van, $20,000." Is that ad language an offer such that you can accept by promising to pay $20,000? Ordinarily, ads do not constitute offers, but rather are treated by the courts as *invitations to deal.* Were an ad actually treated as an offer, it would put the seller in the commercially impracticable position of being required to provide the advertised product at the advertised price to everyone who sought it, regardless of available supply. Presumably, that open-ended duty was not the seller's intent when issuing the ad. It follows then that the buyer, in responding to an ad, is technically making an offer, with the seller free to accept or decline.

On the other hand, courts have held that some ads do manifest a present intent to make an offer. The key terms in those ads must be highly specific and complete, leaving nothing open for negotiation.

A Jet Fighter from Pepsi?

A 1995 Pepsico promotion offered merchandise in exchange for points earned by buying Pepsi-Cola. The television ad showed a teenager modeling some of the available merchandise. A Pepsi T-shirt was displayed for 75 points and a leather jacket for 1450 points. At the end of the ad, a U.S. Marine Corps Harrier "jump jet" landed outside a school, and from the cockpit, the boy said, "Sure beats the bus." The ad then stated that the jet was 7 million points. John D. R. Leonard, at the time a 21-year-old business student in Seattle, Washington, joined five investors in writing a check to Pepsi for $700,008.50 and demanded the 7 million

Pepsi points. Pepsi returned the check and said it had no intention of giving Leonard the $24 million jet. Leonard sued. Who wins? Explain.

Source: Leonard v. Pepsico, 210 F.3d 88 (2d Cir. 2000).

View the video of the ad at **https://www.youtube.com/watch?v=ZdackF2H7Qc.**

Definiteness

Suppose your friend Ken has completed a management training program for a "big box" retailer. In Ken's first assignment as an assistant manager, his boss, Jane, asks him to seek bids and make the other arrangements (subject to her approval) to resurface the store's large asphalt parking lot. Ken secures bids, and the lowest bidder offers to complete the work "later this summer" for $120,000. Ken briefly explains the offer to Jane, who tells Ken to take care of all the details. Ken is busy with other matters and puts off the parking lot project for a couple of weeks. When Ken gets back to the lowest bidder, he is told: "Sorry, man, we hadn't heard from you, and we got another deal." Can that contractor be held to his initial offer?

One of the requirements of a binding offer is that all of its critical terms must be sufficiently clear so that a court can determine both the intentions of the parties and their duties. In the asphalt case, many critical details—precisely when the work would be done, what surfacing material would be used, and how thickly it should be poured—had not been established. Consequently, no offer existed. In a contract for the sale of goods, UCC Section 2-204 relaxes the definiteness standard by allowing a contract to be recognized even with "one or more terms" missing if (1) "the parties have intended to make a contract" and (2) "there is a reasonably certain basis for giving an appropriate remedy." Under the UCC, the courts can actually fill in missing terms in a sale of goods contract, such as by specifying a reasonable price. However, because asphalt resurfacing is a service contract, the UCC would not provide Ken any relief for failing to follow up with the lowest bidder. The following case involving Mariah Carey, the pop music star, demonstrates some of the problems that can arise when an understanding is indefinite.

Vian v. Carey   1993 U.S. Dist. Lexis 5460
(S.D.N.Y. April 26, 1993)

Judge Mukasey

Defendant Mariah Carey is a famous, successful and apparently wealthy entertainer. Plaintiff Joseph Vian was her stepfather before she achieved stardom, but at the start of this litigation was in the process of becoming divorced from defendant's mother. He claims defendant agreed orally that he would have a license to market singing dolls in her likeness. . . . Plaintiff claims that he and Carey had an oral contract for him to receive a license to market "Mariah dolls." These dolls would be statuettes of the singer and would play her most popular songs. Plaintiff claims that the contract was in consideration of his financial and emotional support of defendant, including picking her up from late-night recording sessions, providing her with the use of a car, paying for dental care, allowing her to use his boat for business meetings and rehearsals, and giving her various items, including unused wedding gifts from his marriage to her mother, to help furnish her apartment.

The alleged basis of the oral contract is that on at least three occasions, twice in the family car and once on Vian's boat, Vian told Carey, "Don't forget the Mariah dolls," and "I get the Mariah dolls." According to Vian, on one occasion Carey responded "okay" and on other occasions she merely smiled and nodded. Although Carey admits Vian mentioned the dolls two or three times, she testified that she thought it was a joke. For 30 years plaintiff has been in the business of designing, producing, and marketing gift and novelty items. Although it is not clear from the evidence the parties have submitted, it will be assumed that the alleged contract was formed after defendant turned 18. Under New York law, an oral agreement can form a binding contract. . . . In determining whether a contract exists, what matters are the parties' expressed intentions, the words and deeds that constitute objective signs in a given set of circumstances.

Therefore, the issue is whether the objective circumstances indicate that the parties intended to form a contract. Without such an intent, neither a contract nor a preliminary agreement to negotiate in good faith can exist. In making such a determination, a court may look at "whether the terms of the contract have been finally resolved." In addition, a court may consider "the context of the negotiations." Plaintiff has adduced no evidence that defendant ever intended by a nod of her head or the expression "okay" to enter into a complex commercial licensing agreement involving dolls in her likeness playing her copyrighted songs. The context in which this contract between an 18-year-old girl and her stepfather allegedly was made was an informal family setting, either in the car or on plaintiff's boat, while others were present. Vian's own version of events leads to the conclusion that there was no reason for Carey to think Vian was entirely serious, let alone that he intended to bind her to an agreement at that time. He admits he never told her he was serious. The objective circumstances do not indicate that Carey intended to form a contract with plaintiff. Although plaintiff's five-page memorandum of law fails to raise the possibility, plaintiff

also has not shown that Carey intended to be bound to negotiate with plaintiff at some later date over the licensing of "Mariah dolls."

There can be no meeting of the minds, required for the formation of a contract, where essential material terms are missing. Thus, even if the parties both believe themselves to be bound, there is no contract when "the terms of the agreement are so vague and indefinite that there is no basis or standard for deciding whether the agreement had been kept or broken, or to fashion a remedy, and no means by which such terms may be made certain."

. . . The word "license" was not even used. As defendant points out, no price or royalty term was mentioned, nor was the duration or geographic scope of the license, nor was Carey's right to approve the dolls. Plaintiff admits he would not have gone ahead without defendant's approval, thus conceding the materiality of that term.

* * * * *

In sum, plaintiff has not raised a triable issue of fact as to the existence of a contract. Defendant's motion for summary judgment is granted.

Questions

1. Why did the court find for Carey?

2. As noted in the text, in UCC cases judges fill in contract terms where the parties clearly intended a deal. Should the court here fill in the missing terms to provide the necessary definiteness? Explain.

3. In 1961, Duke Ellington entered a copyright agreement with Mills Music, now EMI Music. Under this contract, the music publisher, defined to include "any other affiliate," agreed to pay Duke Ellington and named members of his family "fifty percent of the net revenue actually received" from foreign publication of the copyrighted music. In 2014, the New York Court of Appeals ruled on a breach of contract action brought by Ellington's grandson that claimed EMI had breached the contract by diluting the family's share of royalties in subcontracting foreign publication rights to others whose fees were deducted from the amount, then divided equally between EMI and Ellington family members. Had EMI breached the contract? Decide. Explain. *Ellington v. EMI Music, Inc.*,997 N.Y.S.2d 339 (N.Y. 2014).

Communication

As explained, an effective offer must be the product of a present intent, it must be definite, and it must be communicated to the offeree. Communication of an offer expresses the offeror's intent to make that offer. Suppose a friend tells you that your neighbor has offered to sell his classic jukebox for $10,000. You call your neighbor and say, "I accept. I'll be right over with the $10,000." Do you have a deal? No. The owner did not communicate the offer to you. The fact that it was not communicated to you may suggest that your neighbor does not want to sell or does not want to sell to you.

Duration of an Offer   Communication of an offer affords the offeree the opportunity to create a contract by accepting that offer, but how long does that opportunity last? Here are some general rules:

1. The offeror may revoke the offer anytime prior to acceptance. (Some exceptions are explained later.) Normally, revocation is effective on receipt by the offeree. Under common law the offeror has the right to revoke at any time prior to acceptance, even if he or she expressly promised to keep the offer open for a specified period.
2. The offer may specify that it is open for an express period (such as 10 days).
3. Where a time limit is not specified in the offer, it will be presumed to be open for a reasonable period.
4. An offer expires if rejected or on receipt of a counteroffer.

Irrevocable Offers

Some kinds of offers may not be revoked. We will note three of them.

1. **Option contracts.** When an offeror promises to keep an offer open for a specified period and, in return, the offeree pays consideration (usually money), the parties have created an option contract, which is a separate agreement and is enforceable by its terms. For example, a friend has offered to sell to you his customized car that you have long cherished, but you want to think about it for a few days. You might enter an option contract with your friend under which you pay $100 for the seller's promise to keep the offer open for seven days. You are under no obligation to buy the car, but the seller is under a binding obligation not to withdraw the offer or sell to another during the seven days.
2. **Firm offers.** Under the UCC, if the owner of that customized car is a dealer (a merchant) and he made a written, signed offer to sell that car (a good) to you, indicating that his offer would remain open for seven days, he is bound to that promise whether you paid consideration for it or not. That situation is labeled a firm offer under UCC Section 2-205, which also provides that if such offers do not mention a time, then they will be kept open for a reasonable period, not exceeding three months.
3. **Offers for unilateral contracts.** A problem sometimes arises when the offeror attempts to revoke a unilateral offer after the offeree has begun to perform. For example, your neighbor invites you to rake her leaves for $10, and then, when you are virtually done, she yells from the doorway, "Oh, sorry, I changed my mind. You go home now." Historically, the offeror (the neighbor, in this case) was free to revoke at any time, but the modern position holds that the offeror normally cannot revoke if the offeree (you) has commenced performance. If that performance is then completed (you ignore your neighbor's admonition to go home, and you finish the raking), the offeror (your neighbor) is bound to perform fully by paying the $10.

The Agreement: Acceptance

LO 6-7
Describe the elements of a valid acceptance.

Suppose you are in training with a large real estate firm and your boss has authorized you to enter negotiations to buy a parcel of farmland that the company hopes to develop for housing. After preliminary discussions, you extend a written offer to the property owner indicating, among other terms, that the company is willing to pay $10,000 per acre for a

10-acre parcel. Assume the owner responds by writing, "I accept your offer at $10,000 per acre, but I need to keep the two-acre homesite." The offeree has used the word *accept*, but does the response constitute a legally binding *acceptance*?

The general rule is that an effective acceptance must be a mirror image of the offer; that is, ordinarily its terms must be the same as those in the offer. Here, by changing the offer's terms, the offeree has issued a *counteroffer* that extinguishes the original offer.

Communication of Acceptance

An offer may be accepted only by the offeree—that is, the person to whom the offer was directed. Because unilateral offers are accepted by performance, no communication of acceptance beyond that performance ordinarily is necessary. In the case of a bilateral contract (a promise for a promise), acceptance is not effective until communicated.

Broadly, acceptance can be accomplished by a "yes" communicated face-to-face, by a nod of the head or some other appropriate signal, by phone, or by other unwritten means, unless the law of the state requires writing in that particular kind of transaction.

Mailbox Rule   Confusion sometimes arises when the parties are not dealing face-to-face. In general, acceptance is effective upon dispatch by whatever mode of communication has been explicitly or implicitly authorized by the offeror. This well-settled position is labeled the *mailbox rule* and means, among other things, that an acceptance is effective when sent even if never received. [For one professor's review of the mailbox rule and related rules, see **http://www.tomwbell.com/teaching/KMailbox.pdf**].

Authorization   The offeror controls the acceptance process and may specify an exclusive manner in which an acceptance must be communicated. If so, a contract is not created if the acceptance is communicated in anything other than the stipulated fashion. Traditionally, if the offeror did not give an *express authorization* to a means of communication, an acceptance by the same or faster means than that used by the offeror was implied. *Implied authorization* might also arise from such factors as prior dealings between the parties and custom in their industry.

Modern View   Under the UCC, the rules of acceptance have relaxed a bit. If no specific instructions for acceptance are included in the offer, the offeree is free to accept in any reasonable manner within a reasonable period, and acceptance is effective upon dispatch. Even when the means chosen are "unreasonable," acceptance is effective on dispatch under UCC 1-201(38) if it is actually received in a timely manner.

Consideration

LO 6-8
Explain the significance of consideration as an element of a legally enforceable contract.

Earlier we identified the five key ingredients in an enforceable contract: agreement, consideration, capacity, genuineness of assent, and legality of purpose. Having examined the agreement (offer/acceptance) process, we turn now to consideration. As noted earlier, consideration is the bargained-for legal value that one party agrees to pay or provide to secure the promise of another. It is what the promisor demands and receives in exchange for his or her promise. Consideration distinguishes an enforceable contract from an unenforceable gratuitous promise. An enforceable contract requires that the *promisee* suffer a *legal detriment;*

that is, the promisee must give up something of value (an act or a promise) or must refrain from doing an act otherwise allowed in order to enforce the promise offered by the **promisor.** Each party, then, must pay a "price" for a contract to be enforceable. In sum, consideration consists of a detriment to the promisee that is bargained for by the promisor.

The classic case that follows explores the idea of consideration and demonstrates that consideration can have legal value without involving monetary loss to the promisee.

LEGAL BRIEFCASE

Hamer v. Sidway
27 N.E. 256 (N.Y. 1891)

FACTS

In 1869 William E. Story Sr. promised his nephew, W.E. Story II, that he would pay the nephew $5,000 upon his 21st birthday if the nephew would refrain from drinking liquor, using tobacco, swearing, and playing cards or billiards for money until he reached that 21st birthday. The nephew agreed and performed his promise, but the uncle died in 1887 without paying the money, and the administrator of the estate, Sidway, declined to pay the $5,000 plus interest. The nephew had assigned (sold) his rights to the money to Louisa Hamer, who sued W.E. Story Sr.'s estate. Hamer, the plaintiff, won at the trial level, lost on appeal, and then appealed to the New York Court of Appeals.

*   *   *   *   *

Judge Parker

When the nephew arrived at the age of 21 years and on the 31st day of January 1875, he wrote to his uncle informing him that he had performed his part of the agreement and had thereby become entitled to the sum of $5,000. The uncle received the letter and a few days later and on the sixth of February, he wrote and mailed to his nephew the following letter:

> Buffalo, February 6, 1875
> W.E. Story, Jr.
> Dear Nephew:
> Your letter of the 31st came to hand all right, saying that you had lived up to the promise made to me several years ago. I have no doubt but you have, for which you shall have five thousand dollars as I promised you. I had the money in the bank the day you was 21 years old that I intend for you, and you shall have the money certain. Now, Willie I do not intend to interfere with this money in any way till I think you are capable of taking care of it and the sooner that time comes the better it will please me. I would hate very much to have you start out in some adventure that you thought all right and lose this money in one year. The

first five thousand dollars that I got together cost me a heap of hard work. You would hardly believe me when I tell you that to obtain this I shoved a jackplane many a day, butchered three or four years, then came to this city, and after three months' perseverance I obtained a situation in a grocery store. I opened this store early, closed late, slept in the fourth story of the building in a room 30 by 40 feet and not a human being in the building but myself. All this I done to live as cheap as I could to save something. I don't want you to take up with this kind of fare. I was here in the cholera season '49 and '52 and the deaths averaged 80 to 125 daily and plenty of smallpox. I wanted to go home, but Mr. Fisk, the gentleman I was working for, told me if I left then, after it got healthy he probably would not want me. I stayed. All the money I have saved I know just how I got it. It did not come to me in any mysterious way, and the reason I speak of this is that money got in this way stops longer with a fellow that gets it with hard knocks than it does when he finds it. Willie, you are 21 and you have many a thing to learn yet. This money you have earned much easier than I did besides acquiring good habits at the same time and you are quite welcome to the money; hope you will make good use of it. I was 10 long years getting this together after I was your age. Now, hoping this will be satisfactory, I stop . . .
> Truly Yours,
> W.E. STORY
> P.S.—You can consider this money on interest.

The nephew received the letter and thereafter consented that the money should remain with his uncle in accordance with the terms and conditions of the letter. The uncle died on the 29th day of January 1887, without having paid over to his nephew any portion of the said $5,000 and interest.

*   *   *   *   *

The defendant contends that the contract was without consideration to support it, and, therefore, invalid. He asserts that the promisee by refraining from the use of liquor and tobacco was not harmed but benefited; that that which he did was best for him to do independently of his uncle's promise, and insists that it follows that unless the promisor was benefited, the contract was without consideration. A contention, which if well founded, would seem to leave open for controversy in many cases whether that which the promisee did or omitted to do was, in fact, of such benefit to him as to leave no consideration to support the enforcement of the promisor's agreement. Such a rule could not be tolerated, and is without foundation in the law.

* * * * *

"In general a waiver of any legal right at the request of another party is a sufficient consideration for a promise" (Parsons on Contracts).

Pollock, in his work on contracts, says, "Consideration means not so much that one party is profiting as that the other abandons some legal right in the present or limits his legal freedom of action in the future as an inducement for the promise of the first."

Now, applying this rule to the facts before us, the promisee used tobacco, occasionally drank liquor, and had a legal right to do so. That right he abandoned for a period of years upon the strength of the promise of the testator that for such forbearance he would give him $5,000. We need not speculate on the effort which may have been required to give up the use of those stimulants. It is sufficient that he restricted his lawful freedom of action within certain prescribed limits upon the faith of his uncle's agreement, and now having fully performed the conditions imposed, it is of no moment whether such performance actually proved a benefit to the promisor, and the court will not inquire into it, but were it a proper subject of inquiry, we see nothing in this record that would permit a determination that the uncle was not benefited in a legal sense.

* * * * *

Reversed.

Questions

1. *a.* What detriment, if any, was sustained by the nephew?
   b. What benefit, if any, was secured by the uncle?
   c. As a matter of law, do we need to inquire into the uncle's benefit? Explain.

2. Lampley began work as an at-will (can be dismissed or can quit at any time) employee of Celebrity Homes in Denver, Colorado, in May 1975. On July 29, 1975, Celebrity announced a profit-sharing plan for all employees if the company reached its goals for the fiscal year, April 1, 1975, to March 31, 1976. Lampley was dismissed in January 1976. Celebrity distributed its profits in May 1976. Lampley sued when she did not receive a share of the profits. Celebrity argued that its promise to share its profits was a gratuity, unsupported by consideration. Decide. Explain. See *Lampley v. Celebrity Homes*, 594 P.2d 605 (Colo. Ct. App. 1979).

3. An accident in the early 1960s rendered Hoffman paraplegic. At Hoffman's invitation, Thomas lived with and provided extensive physical care for Hoffman until Hoffman's death in 2004. Thomas did not pay rent and Hoffman paid for Thomas's food, provided her with a car and cell phone, and made occasional cash payments to Thomas. While never married, the couple exchanged rings in 2002 and Thomas testified that she felt they "lived as man and wife." Thomas filed suit seeking $44,625 for services rendered to Hoffman. According to the trial court, her claim was based on the theories of "express or implied contract of employment" or "unjust enrichment." Thomas lost at the trial level. How would you rule on appeal? Explain. See *In re Estate of Hoffman*, 2006 Iowa App. LEXIS 473 (May 24, 2006). [For a detailed analysis of *Hamer v. Sidway*, see **http://www.lawnix.com/cases/hamer-sidway.html**].

Adequacy of Consideration

With certain exceptions, the courts do not, as Judge Parker indicated in the *Hamer* case, inquire into the economic value of the consideration in question. Legal sufficiency depends not on the value of the consideration but on whether the promisee suffered a detriment in some way. To hold otherwise would put the courts in the place of the market in deciding the value of transactions. We are all free to make both good and bad bargains.

On the other hand, the courts will rule that consideration is found wanting in situations of pretense or sham where the parties have clearly agreed on token or nominal consideration in an effort to present the transaction as a contract rather than a gift. Likewise, an extreme inadequacy of consideration will sometimes cause the court to question a contract on the grounds of *fraud, duress,* or *unconscionability* (all are discussed later in this chapter). In these instances, the agreements would be unenforceable because of a failure of consideration. These cases are uncommon, however, and the courts rarely inquire into the adequacy of consideration.

Appearance of Consideration

Some agreements appear to be accompanied by consideration, but, in fact, that appearance may turn out to be an illusion. Hence, if one agrees to perform a preexisting duty, consideration would be found wanting. For example, if you were to pay your neighbor $50 to keep his dog on a leash when outdoors and a city ordinance already requires dogs to be on a leash when outdoors, your promise would be unenforceable because your neighbor already had a preexisting duty under the law to keep his dog on a leash. Performance of a preexisting legal duty does not constitute consideration because no legal detriment or benefit has arisen.

Similarly, preexisting duties sometimes arise from contracts. Suppose you hire a contractor to resurface the parking lot at your accounting firm's office. You agree on a price of $12,000. With a portion of the work completed, the contractor asks you to amend the agreement to add $2,000 because the project is requiring more time than anticipated. You agree. The work is completed. Could you then legally refuse to pay the additional $2,000? The answer is yes because the contractor failed to provide consideration for the modification of your service contract. He was under a preexisting duty to finish the contract; hence, he did not sustain a legal detriment in the modified agreement. Note, however, that under UCC section 2-209(1), which applies to sales of goods, "an agreement modifying a contract within this Article needs no consideration to be binding."

Suppose you are a realtor and learn from your neighbor that your friend Ames wants to sell his house. You find a buyer for the house and make all of the necessary arrangements for the sale out of regard for your friendship with Ames. Then when the transaction is complete, Ames says, "Well, this has been great of you, but I don't feel right about it. When I get my check for the sale, I'll pay you $2,000 for your hard work. I really appreciate it." What if Ames does not then pay the $2,000? Do you have recourse? No. This is a situation of ***past consideration,*** where the performance—arranging the sale of your friend's house—was not bargained for and was not given in exchange for the promise and thus cannot constitute consideration. In effect, the performance was a gift. Of course, past consideration is really not consideration at all. In some states, courts enforce promises to pay for benefits already received where doing so amounts to a moral obligation that must be enforced to prevent injustice.

Substitutes for Consideration

When necessary to achieve justice, the courts sometimes conclude that a contract exists even though consideration is clearly lacking. Moral obligation and ***quasi-contract*** (discussed earlier) are two such instances, but the most prominent of these substitutes for consideration is found in the doctrine of ***promissory estoppel,*** in which the promisor is "stopped" from denying the existence of a contract where the promisee has detrimentally relied on that promise. Promissory estoppel requires the following:

1. A promise on which the promisor should expect the promisee to rely.
2. The promisee did justifiably rely on the promise.
3. Injustice can be avoided only by enforcing the promise.

Consider the following. You have been a part-time employee of a small fast-food chain restaurant while attending college. Upon graduation, you tell the manager of the restaurant that you think you could handle your own franchise. He says you need to get more experience and advises you to take a full-time position with the company. You do so. Everything goes well, and when you next approach the manager, he says, "If you can come up with the $50,000 and a good location, we will get you in a franchise right away. But you've gotta move on this. Maybe you better quit your job with us and concentrate on this thing." You take his advice and quit your job. You raise the $50,000 and find a vacant building to rent in a good location for a franchise. You show the building to the manager, and he agrees that it looks like a favorable location and one that can easily be converted to the company's needs. He says, "Looks like you have everything in place. If you can come up with $50,000 more we will make this thing happen." You refuse and decide to bring suit against the fast-food chain for breach of contract. The chain defends by saying that you did not provide consideration for its promise. No formal financing arrangement was ever agreed to, and you had not committed yourself to any franchising obligations. Under these circumstances, you may well prevail using a promissory estoppel claim. In brief, you would argue that you had changed your position in reliance on the franchisor's promises and that relief is necessary to prevent injustice. [For a similar case, see *Hoffman v. Red Owl Stores,* 133 N.W.2d 267 (Wis. 1965).]

Capacity

Having examined two of the required ingredients in an enforceable contract, agreement and consideration, we turn now to a third: capacity to contract. To enter a binding agreement, one must have the legal ability to do so; that is, one's mental condition and maturity must be such that the agreement was entered with understanding and in recognition of one's own interests. The three primary areas of concern are intoxication, mental impairment, and minority (infancy/youthfulness), with minority being much the more common area of dispute.

> The three primary areas of concern are intoxication, mental impairment, and minority.

Intoxication

Assume you have been drinking to celebrate your 21st birthday. You enter a contract with a friend to sell him your autographed Willie Mays baseball card for $200. You receive the money and turn over the card. Later, when sober, you regret the deal. Will a court nullify that contract on the grounds of your intoxication? That decision depends on whether you were sufficiently intoxicated that you did not understand the nature and purpose of the contract. If the objective evidence suggests that you did not understand the transaction, the contract would be considered voidable, in which case you could probably disaffirm the contract and demand the return of the card, although courts are often not sympathetic with people who attempt to escape contracts made while intoxicated. In most states, if you recovered the card, you would be required to return the $200 to your friend.

If, on recovering your sobriety, your friend argued that the contract was invalid because of your intoxication, and he demanded the return of his $200 in exchange for the card, you could then *ratify* (affirm) the contract and hold him to it. If the contract had been for one of life's *necessaries* (such as food, shelter, clothing, medical care, or tools of one's trade), you would have been liable for the reasonable value of that necessary.

Mental Incompetence

In most cases, an agreement involving a mentally incompetent person is either *void* or *voidable*. The transaction would be void—that is, no contract would exist—where the impaired party had been *adjudged* insane. If the impaired party was unable to understand the purpose and effect of the contract but had not been legally adjudged insane, the contract would be voidable (void in some states) at the option of the impaired party. The competent party cannot void the contract, and the impaired party would have to pay the reasonable value of any necessaries received under the contract.

Minority

Minors may complete their contracts if they wish, but they also have an absolute right to rescind most of those contracts. They may rescind until they reach adulthood and for a reasonable time thereafter. (Many states have enacted statutes forbidding minors from disaffirming some classes of contracts such as those for marriage, student loans, and life insurance.) The minor has a right of recovery for everything given up in meeting the terms of the contract. Similarly, the minor must return everything that remains in her or his possession that was received from the contract. In many states, if nothing of the bargained-for consideration remains or if its value has been depreciated, the minor has no duty to replace it but can still recover whatever she or he put into the contract. If not disaffirmed in a reasonable time after the minor reaches the age of majority, the contract is considered to be ratified, and the minor is bound to its terms. The minor is also liable for the reasonable value (not necessarily the contract price) of necessaries purchased from an adult. That is, a minor must pay the adult the reasonable value of contracted-for items such as food, clothing, shelter, medical care, basic education, and tools of the minor's trade.

Despite the flexibility accorded to minors entering contracts, the adults who are parties to those contracts are bound to them and do not have the power to disaffirm. Hence, adults put themselves at risk when they choose to bargain with minors. As noted, in many states a minor need not make restitution if the consideration is lost, destroyed, or depreciated. On the other hand, the case that follows illustrates the growing view that minors do have some monetary obligation after disaffirming a contract.

> Minors may complete their contracts if they wish, but they also have an absolute right to rescind most of those contracts.

LEGAL BRIEFCASE

Dodson v. Shrader
824 S.W.2d 545 (Tenn. 1992)

Justice O'Brien

In early April of 1987, Joseph Eugene Dodson, then 16 years of age, purchased a used 1984 pickup truck from Burns and Mary Shrader. The Shraders owned and operated Shrader's Auto Sales in Columbia, Tennessee. Dodson paid $4,900 in cash for the truck, using money he borrowed from his girlfriend's grandmother. At the time of the purchase there was no inquiry by the Shraders, and no misrepresentation by Dodson, concerning his minority. However, Shrader did testify that at the time he believed Dodson to be 18 or 19 years of age.

In December 1987, nine months after the date of purchase, the truck began to develop mechanical problems. A mechanic diagnosed the problem as a burnt valve, but could not be certain without inspecting the valves inside the engine. Dodson did not want, or did not have the money, to effect these repairs. He continued to drive the truck despite the mechanical problems. One month later, in January, the truck's engine "blew up" and the truck became inoperable.

Dodson parked the vehicle in the front yard at his parents' home, where he lived. He contacted the Shraders to rescind the purchase of the truck and requested a full refund. The Shraders refused to accept the tender of the truck or to give Dodson the refund requested.

Dodson then [sued] to rescind the contract and recover the amount paid for the truck. Before the circuit court could hear the case, the truck, while parked in Dodson's front yard, was struck on the left front fender by a hit-and-run driver. At the time of the circuit court trial, according to Shrader, the truck was worth only $500 due to the damage to the engine and the left front fender.

The case was heard in the circuit court in November 1988. The trial judge, based on previous common-law decisions, and under the doctrine of stare decisis, reluctantly granted the rescission. The Shraders were ordered, upon tender and delivery of the truck, to reimburse the $4,900 purchase price to Dodson. The Shraders appealed.

[T]he rule in Tennessee is in accord with the majority rule on the issue among our sister states. This rule is based on the underlying purpose of the "infancy doctrine," which is to protect minors from their lack of judgment and "from squandering their wealth through improvident contracts with crafty adults who would take advantage of them in the marketplace."

There is, however, a modern trend among the states, either by judicial action or by statute, in the approach to the problem of balancing the rights of minors against those of innocent merchants. As a result, two minority rules have developed that allow the other party to a contract with a minor to refund less than the full consideration paid in the event of rescission.

The first of these minority rules is called the "Benefit Rule." The rule holds that, upon rescission, recovery of the full purchase price is subject to a deduction for the minor's use of the merchandise. This rule recognizes that the traditional rule in regard to necessaries has been extended so far as to hold an infant bound by his contracts, where he failed to restore what he has received under them to the extent of the benefit actually derived by him from what he has received from the other party to the transaction.

The other minority rule holds that the minor's recovery of the full purchase price is subject to a deduction for the minor's "use" of the consideration he or she received under the contract, or for the "depreciation" or "deterioration" of the consideration in his or her possession.

We are impressed by the statement made by the Court of Appeals of Ohio:

> At a time when we see young persons between 18 and 21 years of age demanding and assuming more responsibilities in their daily lives, when we see such persons emancipated, married, and raising families; when we see such persons charged with the responsibility for committing crimes; when we see such persons being sued in tort claims for acts of negligence; when we see such persons subject to military service; when we see such persons engaged in business and acting in almost all other respects as an adult, it seems timely to reexamine the case law pertaining to contractual rights and responsibilities of infants to see if the law as pronounced and applied by the courts should be redefined.

* * * * *

We state the rule to be followed hereafter, in reference to a contract of a minor, to be where the minor has not been over-reached in any way, and there has been no undue influence, and the contract is a fair and reasonable one, and the minor has actually paid money on the purchase price, and taken and used the article purchased; that he ought not be permitted to recover the amount actually paid, without allowing the vendor of the goods reasonable compensation for the use of, depreciation, and willful or negligent damage to the article purchased, while in his hands. If there has been any fraud or imposition on the part of the seller or if the contract is unfair, or any unfair advantage has been taken of the minor inducing him to make the purchase, then the rule does not apply. Whether there has been such an overreaching on the part of the seller, and the fair market value of the property returned, would always, in any case, be a question for the trier of fact. . . .

This rule is best adapted to modern conditions under which minors are permitted to, and do in fact, transact a great deal of business for themselves, long before they have reached the age of legal majority. Many young people work and earn money and collect it and spend it oftentimes without any oversight or restriction. The law does not question their right to buy if they have the money to pay for their purchases. It seems intolerably burdensome for everyone concerned if merchants and businesspeople cannot deal with them safely, in a fair and reasonable way.

* * * * *

We note that in this case, some nine months after the date of purchase, the truck purchased by the plaintiff began to develop mechanical problems. Plaintiff was informed of the probable nature of the difficulty, which apparently involved internal problems in the engine. He continued to drive the vehicle until the engine "blew up" and the truck became inoperable. Whether or not this involved gross negligence or intentional conduct on his part is a matter for determination at the trial level. It is not possible to determine from this record whether a counterclaim for tortious damage to the vehicle was asserted. After the first tender of the vehicle was made by plaintiff, and refused by the defendant, the truck was damaged by a hit-and-run driver while parked on plaintiff's property. The amount of that damage and the liability for that amount between the purchaser and the vendor, as well as the fair market value of the vehicle at the time of tender, are also an issue for the jury.

[Reversed and remanded.]

Questions

1. What was the issue in this case?
2. Distinguish the two minority rules that are summarized in this case.
3. To achieve justice in contract cases involving a minor and an adult, what would you want to know about the adult's behavior toward the minor?

4. White, a 17-year-old high school sophomore, operated a trucking business, including hiring drivers, securing jobs, and so forth. He lived with his parents and received his food, clothing, and shelter from them. Valencia operated a garage and repaired White's equipment until they had a disagreement over replacement of a motor. White then disaffirmed his contract with Valencia and refused to pay what he owed. At trial the jury found that White had caused the damage to the motor, but the court held that White could disaffirm the contract and required Valencia to refund any money paid to White under the contract. Valencia appealed.

   a. Is the fact that White was in business for himself in any way relevant to the outcome of this case? Explain.

   b. Decide the case. Explain. See *Valencia v. White*, 654 P.2d 287 (Ariz. Ct. App. 1982).

Genuineness of Assent

Sometimes parties appear to have concluded a binding contract, but the courts will allow them to escape that obligation because they had not, in fact, achieved an agreement. They had achieved the appearance of agreement, but not the reality. That situation arises when the contract is the product of misrepresentation, fraud, duress, undue influence, or mistake. Ordinarily, such agreements are voidable and may be rescinded by the innocent party because of the absence of genuine assent, the fourth of five ingredients in a binding contract.

Misrepresentation and Fraud

An innocent untruth is a misrepresentation. Intentional untruths constitute fraud. In either case, a party to a contract who has been deceived may rescind the deal, and restitution may be secured if benefits were extended to the party issuing the untruth. The test for fraud is as follows:

1. Misrepresentation of a material fact.
2. The misrepresentation was intentional.
3. The injured party justifiably relied on the misrepresentation.
4. Injury resulted.

Note that the test requires a misrepresented fact. In general, misrepresented opinions are not grounds for action, but many courts are now recognizing exceptions to that rule, especially when the innocent party has relied on opinion coming from an expert.

> **You are selling a house that allegedly is "haunted."**

If you are selling a house that allegedly is "haunted," does your failure to reveal the ghostly presence constitute a misrepresentation? The *Stambovsky* case that follows addresses that unusual question.

Stambovsky v. Ackley et al.
169 A.D.2d 254 (N.Y. App. Div. 1991)

Justice Rubin

Plaintiff, to his horror, discovered that the house he had recently contracted to purchase was widely reputed to be possessed by poltergeists, reportedly seen by defendant seller and members of her family on numerous occasions over the last nine years. Plaintiff promptly commenced this action seeking rescission of the contract of sale.

The unusual facts of this case clearly warrant a grant of equitable relief to the buyer who, as a resident of New York City, cannot be expected to have any familiarity with the folklore of the Village of Nyack. Not being a "local," plaintiff could not readily learn that the home he had contracted to purchase is haunted. Whether the source of the spectral apparitions seen by defendant seller are parapsychic or psychogenic, having reported their presence in both a national publication (*Readers' Digest*) and the local press (in 1977 and 1982, respectively), defendant is estopped to deny their existence and, as a matter of law, the house is haunted. More to the point, however, no divination is required to conclude that it is defendant's promotional efforts in publicizing her close encounters with these spirits which fostered the home's reputation in the community. In 1989, the house was included in [a] five-home walking tour of Nyack and described in a November 27th newspaper article as "a riverfront Victorian (with ghost)." The impact of the reputation thus created goes to the very essence of the bargain between the parties, greatly impairing both the value of the property and its potential for resale.

While I agree that the real estate broker, as agent for the seller, is under no duty to disclose to a potential buyer the phantasmal reputation of the premises and that, in his pursuit of a legal remedy for fraudulent misrepresentation against the seller, plaintiff hasn't a ghost of a chance, I am nevertheless moved by the spirit of equity to allow the buyer to seek rescission of the contract of sale and recovery of his down payment. New York law fails to recognize any remedy for damages incurred as a result of the seller's mere silence, applying instead the strict rule of caveat emptor. Therefore, the theoretical basis for granting relief, even under the extraordinary facts of this case, is elusive if not ephemeral.

From the perspective of a person in the position of plaintiff herein, a very practical problem arises with respect to the discovery of a paranormal phenomenon: "Who you gonna' call?" as a title song to the movie "Ghostbusters" asks. Applying the strict rule of caveat emptor to a contract involving a house possessed by poltergeists conjures up visions of a psychic or medium routinely accompanying the structural engineer and Terminix man on an inspection of every home subject to a contract of sale. It portends that the

prudent attorney will establish an escrow account lest the subject of the transaction come back to haunt him and his client—or pray that his malpractice insurance coverage extends to supernatural disasters. In the interest of avoiding such untenable consequences, the notion that a haunting is a condition which can and should be ascertained upon reasonable inspection of the premises is a hobgoblin which should be exorcised from the body of legal precedent and laid quietly to rest.

It has been suggested by a leading authority that the ancient rule which holds that mere nondisclosure does not constitute actionable misrepresentation "finds proper application in cases where the fact undisclosed is patent, or the plaintiff has equal opportunities for obtaining information which he may be expected to utilize, or the defendant has no reason to think that he is acting under any misapprehension" (Prosser, Torts Section 106, at 696 [4th ed 1971]). However, with respect to transactions in real estate, New York adheres to the doctrine of caveat emptor and imposes no duty upon the vendor to disclose any information concerning the premises unless there is a confidential or fiduciary relationship between the parties or some conduct on the part of the seller which constitutes "active concealment." Normally, some affirmative misrepresentation or partial disclosure is required to impose upon the seller a duty to communicate undisclosed conditions affecting the premises.

Common law is not moribund. . . . Where fairness and common sense dictate that an exception should be created, the evolution of the law should not be stifled by rigid application of a legal maxim.

The doctrine of caveat emptor requires that a buyer act prudently to assess the fitness and value of his purchase and operates to bar the purchaser who fails to exercise due care from seeking the equitable remedy of rescission. For the purposes of the instant motion to dismiss the action . . . plaintiff is entitled to every favorable inference which may reasonably be drawn from the pleadings, specifically, in this instance, that he met his obligation to conduct an inspection of the premises and a search of available public records with respect to title. It should be apparent, however, that the most meticulous inspection and the search would not reveal the presence of poltergeists at the premises or unearth the property's ghoulish reputation in the community. Therefore, there is no sound policy reason to deny plaintiff relief for failing to discover a state of affairs which the most prudent purchaser would not be expected to even contemplate.

* * * * *

Where a condition which has been created by the seller materially impairs the value of the contract and is peculiarly within the knowledge of the seller or unlikely to be discovered by a prudent purchaser exercising due care with respect to the subject transaction, nondisclosure constitutes a basis for rescission as a matter of equity. Any other outcome places upon the buyer not merely the obligation to exercise care in his purchase but rather to be omniscient with respect to any fact which may affect the bargain. No practical purpose is served by imposing such a burden upon a purchaser. To the contrary, it encourages predatory business practice. . . .

* * * * *

In the case at bar, defendant seller deliberately fostered the public belief that her home was possessed. Having undertaken to inform the public-at-large, to whom she has no legal relationship, about the supernatural occurrences on her property, she may be said to owe no less a duty to her contract vendee. . . . Where, as here, the seller not only takes unfair advantage of the buyer's ignorance but has created and perpetuated a condition about which he is unlikely to even inquire, enforcement of the contract (in whole or in part) is offensive to the court's sense of equity. Application of the remedy of rescission, within the bounds of the narrow exception to the doctrine of caveat emptor set forth herein, is entirely appropriate to relieve the unwitting purchaser from the consequences of a most unnatural bargain.

Accordingly, the judgment of the Supreme Court, New York County (Edward H. Lehner, J.), entered April 9, 1990, which dismissed the complaint should be modified and the first cause of action seeking rescission of the contract reinstated.

DISSENT

Justice Smith (dissenting).
I would affirm the dismissal of the complaint. . . .

* * * * *

"It is settled law in New York State that the seller of real property is under no duty to speak when the parties deal at arm's length. The mere silence of the seller, without some act or conduct which deceived the purchaser, does not amount to a concealment that is actionable as a fraud. . . ."

The parties herein were represented by counsel and dealt at arm's length. . . . There is no allegation that defendants, by some specific act, other than the failure to speak, deceived the plaintiff. . . .

Finally, if the doctrine of caveat emptor is to be discarded, it should be for a reason more substantive than a poltergeist. The

existence of a poltergeist is no more binding upon the defendants than it is upon this court.

Based upon the foregoing, the [lower] court properly dismissed the complaint.

Questions

1. a. According to the court, did the defendant seller engage in a fraudulent misrepresentation in failing to disclose the "ghostly" condition of her house?

    b. The plaintiff won this case on equitable/fairness grounds. Explain the court's reasoning.

    c. Do you agree with the court's equity/fairness reasoning? Explain.

    d. Did the real estate agent engage in fraud for failing to disclose the house's haunted reputation? Explain.

2. a. What did the court mean by the phrase "caveat emptor"?

    b. Why did the court find for the plaintiff buyer, even though "caveat emptor" seemed to be the controlling law in this situation?

    c. Would the buyer have been successful in a misrepresentation claim if the seller had said: "This house is so peaceful. We never have any disturbances."?

    d. The defendant seller had fostered the belief that her house was haunted. Did that promotional effort by the defendant influence the court's decision making? Explain.

3. Explain dissenting Justice Smith's objection to the majority's ruling.

4. In 2007, soon after moving from California into the home she had bought in Pennsylvania, Janet Milliken learned that previous occupants, Konstantinos Koumboulis and his wife, died in an apparent murder/suicide after Koumboulis allegedly shot his wife and himself in the house. The sellers, Kathleen and Joseph Jacono, had later bought the home in a real estate auction. Milliken filed a complaint against the Jaconos and the real estate firms involved in her purchase of the house, alleging fraud and misrepresentation for failure to disclose the murder/suicide. Milliken stated in her opening brief that after she and her family had moved into the home, various paranormal events had occurred. How should the court rule? Explain. See *Milliken v. Jacono*, 60 A.3d 133 (Pa. 2012).

Toy Yoda

Former Hooters waitress Jodee Berry sued Gulf Coast Wings, corporate owner of the Hooters restaurant where she had worked, for not awarding a new Toyota as a prize for her victory in an April 2001 sales contest. Berry alleged that her manager told the waitresses in the Florida Hooters that the server selling the most beer would be entered in a drawing (involving other Hooters locations) to win a new Toyota. At one point during the contest, the manager allegedly said he did not know whether the winner would receive a Toyota car, truck, or van but knew that the winner would be required to pay registration fees. At the close of the contest, the manager told Berry that she had won. He blindfolded her and took her to the restaurant parking lot. He laughed when Berry found not the car she expected, but a doll based on the *Star Wars* movie character Yoda (a toy Yoda). Berry did not laugh, but sued instead. The case was settled out of court. The terms of that settlement were not disclosed, but Berry's lawyer did say that she would be able to afford whatever Toyota she wanted.

Questions

1. What contract-based causes of action did Berry bring in this case?
2. Defend the Hooters restaurant owner, Gulf Coast Wings.
3. Make the argument that the Hooters manager never actually made an offer to the waitresses.
4. If an offer was made, how did Berry accept that offer?
5. Make the argument that the offer and acceptance, if they existed, were not supported by consideration.

Sources: Berry v. Gulf Coast Wings, Inc., Case No. 03-2001-2642-J (Fla. 14th Cir. Ct. July 24, 2001); and Keith A. Rowley, "You Asked for It, You Got It . . . Toy Yoda: Practical Jokes, Prizes, and Contract Law," *Nevada Law Journal* 3 (Spring 2003), pp. 526–559.

Duress

Sometimes genuine assent is not secured and a contract may be rescinded because one of the parties is forced to agree. Fear lies at the heart of a duress claim. The party seeking to escape the contract must establish that a wrongful act was threatened or had occurred, causing the party to enter the contract out of fear of harm such that free will was precluded. Increasingly, courts are also setting aside contracts on the grounds of economic duress. For example, suppose you know that one of your regular customers depends on your timely delivery of steel to his factory and that he cannot expeditiously find an alternative supply. Therefore, you tell your customer that delivery will be delayed until he agrees to pay a higher price for the steel. If he agrees, the resulting contract probably could be rescinded on the grounds of economic duress.

Undue Influence

Under some circumstances, the first party to an apparent contract can escape its terms by demonstrating that the second party so dominated her will that she (the first party) did not act independently. These claims are most common in cases involving those who are old or infirm and who lose their independence of thought and action to the undue influence of a caregiver or adviser.

Mistake

Most of us, on taking a new job, operate at least for a time in fear that we will make a mistake. Assume you are new to your job as an assistant manager at a custodial company, and

> **You inadvertently submit a final price of $50,000 rather than $500,000. What happens?**

are preparing the company's bid for a general maintenance contract for a large office building. In preparing the bid, you inadvertently submit a final price of $50,000 rather than $500,000. What happens? Do you lose your job?

In some cases, mistakes involving critical facts can be grounds for rescinding contracts. A ***mutual mistake*** is one in which both parties to the contract are in error about some critical fact. With exceptions, either party can rescind those contracts because genuine assent was not achieved. Your erroneous bid, however, is a ***unilateral mistake;*** that is, only one party to the contract made an error. The general rule is that those contracts cannot be rescinded. Nevertheless, if you are able to show that the other party to the contract knew or should have known about your mistake, many courts would allow you to rescind. Certainly you would make that argument in this instance because the $50,000 bid presumably is dramatically out of line with the other bids and at odds with reasonable business expectations about the value of the contract. In cases where an error is made in drafting a contract, and both parties are unaware of the error (a mutual mistake), the courts will reform the contract rather than void it. That is, the contract will be rewritten to reflect what the parties actually intended.

Flying for Free?

For about two hours in 2013, the Delta Airlines website advertised $6.90 round-trip flights to Hawaii. Some travelers wait for such mistaken fares, learning of them through airfare websites or social media, and quickly purchase their tickets before the obvious error is corrected. Delta honored the $6.90 airfare for purchased tickets. In 2015, the U.S. Department of Transportation (DOT) issued a temporary rule that in cases of mistaken fares, it would not enforce a requirement prohibiting airlines from raising an airline ticket price after purchase. The airlines would be obligated to reimburse the out-of-pocket expenses of those who had already purchased their tickets under the mistaken fare, however.

Questions

1. Is purchasing an airline ticket for an obviously incorrect, low fare unethical? Why or why not?

2. As a matter of contract law, what is an argument in support of the DOT's temporary rule?

Sources: Mary Forgione, "Airlines Don't Have to Honor 'Mistake' Fares, U.S. Agency Rules," *Los Angeles Times,* May 12, 2015 [**www.latimes.com**]; and Christopher Elliott, "Airlines May Be Off Hook for Mistake Fares," *USA Today,* May 31, 2015 [**www.usatoday.com**].

Legality of Purpose

Having examined agreement, consideration, capacity, and genuineness of assent, we turn now to the final requirement for the creation of a binding contract: legality of purpose. *Illegality* refers to bargains to commit a crime or a tort (such as a deal with a coworker to embezzle funds from one's employer); more broadly, illegality involves bargains that are forbidden by statute or violate public policy. We can identify three general categories of illegal agreements: (1) contracts that violate statutes, (2) contracts that are unconscionable, and (3) contracts that violate public policy. In general, the effect of an illegal contract is that it cannot be enforced, and the courts will not provide a remedy if its terms are unfulfilled. With exceptions, the parties to illegal deals are left where the courts find them.

1. ***Contracts violating statutes.*** As noted, a contract to commit a crime or a tort is illegal and unenforceable. The states have also specified certain other agreements that are illegal. Those provisions vary from state to state, but they commonly include antigambling laws, laws forbidding the conduct of certain kinds of business on Sundays (***blue laws***), laws forbidding ***usury,*** and laws forbidding the practice of certain professions (law, real estate, hair care) without a license.

Modern Family **Contract Feud**

On July 24, 2012, cast members of the popular and Emmy Award–winning television comedy *Modern Family* filed a breach of contract lawsuit against producer 20th Century Fox, seeking to have their current contracts declared null and void under California law prohibiting enforcement of a personal service contract after seven years. Shortly after the lawsuit was filed, Fox agreed to enter into new agreements with the cast members, who then dropped the lawsuit. If the lawsuit had gone to trial, what issues would have to be decided? Who would have won? Explain.

Sources: California Labor Code Sec. 2855; and Joe Flint, "Cast of *Modern Family* Strikes New Deal," *Los Angeles Times,* July 27, 2012 [**www.latimes.com**].

---

2. ***Unconscionable contracts.*** Certain agreements are so thoroughly one-sided that fairness precludes enforcing them. Problems of unconscionability often arise in situations in which the bargaining power of one of the parties is much superior to that of the other—where one can, in effect, "twist the arm" or otherwise take advantage of the other. Both the common law of contracts and UCC Section 2-302 give the courts the power to modify or refuse to enforce such deals.

> Certain agreements are so thoroughly one-sided that fairness precludes enforcing them.

3. ***Public policy.*** The courts may decline to enforce certain otherwise binding contracts because to do so would not be in the best interest of the public. For example, an agreement between the local convenience stores to charge $5.00 for a gallon of gasoline would be a restraint of trade (price-fixing) and as such would be contrary to public policy and to antitrust laws (see Chapter 10) and thus would be unenforceable. Similarly, suppose as a condition of being hired for a job you must sign an agreement providing that you will not leave your employer to work for one of your employer's competitors. These *noncompete* clauses (see Chapter 12) are common and may be fully lawful depending largely on whether the time and geographic restrictions imposed are reasonable. If unreasonable, the courts will either not enforce the clause or will alter it to achieve a fair result.

Another commonplace public policy concern arises from the ***exculpatory clause,*** *limited liability clause*, or ***release.*** If you participate in any potentially hazardous activity such as attending a professional hockey game, whitewater rafting, joining a school field trip, or entering an amusement park, you may be required to agree to release others of any liability for harm that might befall you. If you own or manage a potentially hazardous enterprise such as a water slide, bungee tower, or even a health spa, you may try to protect yourself from litigation should a customer be hurt by including a release in the customer agreement. Often, such agreements are enforceable in the manner of any other contractual provision, but sometimes they are not. Many factors can influence that decision, including how sweeping the exculpation is, whether it was knowingly entered, and the relative bargaining power of the parties. The case that follows analyzes the enforceability of a liability release signed by a woman who did not speak or read English at the time she joined a gym.

LEGAL BRIEFCASE

Jimenez v. 24 Hour Fitness USA, Inc.
188 Cal. Rptr. 3d 228 (Cal. App. 4th Dist. 2015)

Justice Murray

Plaintiffs Etelvina and Pedro Jimenez appeal from summary judgment in favor of defendant 24 Hour Fitness USA, Inc. (24 Hour), in plaintiffs' negligence action stemming from a catastrophic injury sustained by Etelvina while using a treadmill at 24 Hour. Plaintiffs asserted that 24 Hour was grossly negligent in setting up the treadmill in a manner that violated the manufacturer's safety instructions. 24 Hour moved for summary judgment, contending that it was not liable as a matter of law because Etelvina signed a liability release when she joined the gym. The trial court agreed and granted summary judgment.

On appeal, plaintiffs contend that the trial court erred in granting summary judgment in 24 Hour's favor because (1) the liability release is not enforceable against plaintiffs' claim of gross negligence; [and] (2) the release was obtained by fraud and misrepresentation . . . we agree. . . . Accordingly, we reverse.

FACTUAL AND PROCEDURAL BACKGROUND

Undisputed Facts

Plaintiffs filed a complaint against 24 Hour stating causes of action for premises liability, general negligence, and loss of consortium. The action arose out of injuries Etelvina sustained on January 16, 2011, while exercising at a 24 Hour facility in Sacramento, California. Etelvina's expert opined that she fell backwards off of a moving treadmill and sustained severe head injuries when she hit her head on the exposed steel foot of a leg exercise machine that 24 Hour placed approximately three feet 10 inches behind the treadmill.

24 Hour filed an answer to the complaint generally denying the allegations and claiming several affirmative defenses, including the defense that plaintiffs' claims were barred by a liability release.

At the time of her injuries, Etelvina was a member of 24 Hour. She joined 24 Hour approximately two years before the day she sustained her injury, and thereafter, she used the facilities regularly several times per week. On the day she joined, she was directed to the membership manager, Justin Wilbourn. She was then required to sign a membership agreement. However, Etelvina could not read or speak English, and Wilbourn did not speak Spanish. Wilbourn knew Etelvina did not read or speak English. Nevertheless, he did not call a Spanish-speaking employee to help him translate. Instead, he pointed to his computer screen to a figure, $24.99, indicating the membership fee, and made pumping motions with his arms like he was exercising. Etelvina understood the numbers, which are identical in Spanish, and she understood Wilbourn's physical gestures to mean that if she paid that amount, she could use the facility. She could not read anything else. Wilbourn then pointed to the lines in the agreement for Etelvina to sign.

The membership agreement contained a liability release provision, which provided: "Using the 24 Hour USA, Inc. (24 Hour) facilities involves the risk of injury to you or your guest, whether you or someone else causes it. Specific risks vary from one activity to another and the risks range from minor injuries to major injuries, such as catastrophic injuries including death. **In consideration of your participation in the activities offered by 24 Hour,** *you understand and voluntarily accept this risk and agree that 24 Hour,* **its officers, directors, employees, volunteers, agents and independent contractors** *will not be liable for any injury,* **including, without limitation, personal, bodily, or mental injury, economic loss or any damage to you, your spouse, guests, unborn child, or relatives resulting from the negligence of 24 Hour or anyone on 24 Hour's behalf or anyone using the facilities** *whether related to exercise or not.* . . . By signing below, you acknowledge and agree that you have read the foregoing and know of the nature of the activities at 24 Hour and you agree to all the terms on *pages 1 through 4* of this agreement and acknowledge that you have received a copy of it and the membership policies."

Wilbourn did not point out the release to Etelvina or make any other indications about the scope of the agreement aside from his gestures mimicking exercise and the fee. Etelvina believed she signed an agreement only to pay the monthly fee of $24.99.

* * * * *

In his deposition, Wilbourn, the membership manager for 24 Hour, said that he did not remember meeting Etelvina, although he identified himself as the employee who assisted her based on his signature on her membership agreement. Wilbourn testified that typically, when he encountered a potential customer who only spoke Spanish, his habit and custom was to have a Spanish-speaking employee handle the signup for that potential customer.

* * * * *

[A]nalysis

* * * * *

Generally, a person who signs an instrument may not avoid the impact of its terms on the ground that she failed to read it before signing. However, a release is invalid when it is procured by misrepresentation, overreaching, deception, or fraud. In cases providing the opportunity for overreaching, the releasee has a duty to act in good faith and the releaser must have a full understanding of his legal rights. Furthermore, it is the province of the jury to determine whether the circumstances afforded the opportunity for overreaching, whether the releasee engaged in overreaching and whether the releaser was misled. . . .

Here, if a jury were to be persuaded that Wilbourn made misrepresentations to Etelvina about the contents of the agreement by making nonverbal gestures indicating that what she was signing related *only* to being allowed to exercise if she paid the price on the computer screen, it would be entitled to find that Etelvina's signature on

the release was produced by misrepresentation and that the release is not enforceable against her. . . .

* * * * *

A recent Ninth Circuit case applying California law, *Doe v. Gangland Productions, Inc.,* 730 F.3d 946 (9th Cir. 2013), is also instructive. There, the plaintiff sued two production companies for broadcasting a television documentary without concealing his identity. . . . [T]he defendants contended that the plaintiff's claims were barred because he signed a release consenting to disclosure of his real identity in the broadcast and waiving all claims for liability. . . . In a declaration, the plaintiff stated that he was dyslexic, illiterate, and that he informed the Gangland producer who asked him to sign the release that he had "'extreme difficulty reading.'" The plaintiff also stated that "when he was provided the alleged release, [the producer] told him it was 'just a receipt' for his $300 payment for the interview. Because of these representations, [the plaintiff] did not ask his girlfriend to read out loud the document before he signed it." The court reasoned that the plaintiff "made a sufficient showing of fraud in the execution of the release, which, if true, would render the release void."

In reaching its conclusion, the court in *Gangland* cited *Mairo v. Yellow Cab Co.* (1929) 208 Cal. 350. In *Mairo,* the California Supreme Court reviewed a directed verdict in the defendant's favor, where the trial court concluded that the plaintiff had waived his rights by executing several releases. The plaintiff was an illiterate Russian immigrant who understood little spoken English. He was injured after being hit by the defendant's taxicab and during the course of his medical treatment, the defendant had him sign several releases in exchange for the payment of his medical treatment. The plaintiff asserted that the defendant misrepresented the true contents of the releases and that he believed they were merely a permit to operate on him and receipts. The court held that if the true nature of the releases was "misrepresented to [the plaintiff] so that he did not know what he was really signing, they are, of course, void. But under the conflicting evidence here it is impossible to tell whether such was the fact. This also was an issue which should have gone to the jury and it was, therefore, erroneous for the trial court to direct said verdict for defendant."

* * * * *

. . . 24 Hour contends that these nonverbal communications cannot, as a matter of law, amount to *affirmative* misrepresentations because Etelvina "could not reasonably have relied upon anything Mr. Wilbourn said" since he spoke a different language. 24 Hour's argument implies that nonverbal communications cannot be misrepresentative or induce reasonable reliance. We reject this argument. While it may be less reasonable for a plaintiff to rely on nonverbal communications in a case where the parties speak the same language, in this case, gesturing was virtually the *only* form of communication between Wilbourn and Etelvina. It is undisputed that Etelvina did not speak English and Wilbourn did not speak

Spanish. Further, Wilbourn knew Etelvina did not speak or read English. And he knew that Etelvina did not read the contract, including the terms setting forth the release, even though, as the membership manager, he must have known that the release says, "By signing below, you acknowledge and agree that *you have read* the foregoing . . ." provisions of the release. (Italics added.) Under these circumstances, already ripe for misrepresentation and overreaching, Wilbourn's gestures and pointing may very well have misrepresented the nature of the document Etelvina signed. This is an inherently factual question for a jury to decide.

*   *   *   *   *

DISPOSITION

Accordingly, we reverse the trial court's ruling . . . .

Questions

1. What are the similarities between *Jimenez* and *Gangland*? What are the differences? Explain the relevance of *Gangland* to the *Jimenez* court.

2. If you were on the jury having to decide the factual questions identified by this court, how would you decide? Explain.

3. What could 24 Hour Fitness do to ensure that its liability release is enforceable in such situations?

4. Ning Yan went to Vital Power Fitness Center to use a one-week complimentary pass. On each visit he signed in on a sheet that contained a standard exculpatory clause including this language: "I also understand that Vital Power Fitness Center assumes no responsibility for any injuries and/or sicknesses incurred to me. . . ." On February 18, 1999, Yan fell from a treadmill and sustained a severe head injury. He later died from that injury. No one witnessed the fall. Yan's estate claims he struck his head against a window ledge because the treadmill was placed too close to the window. If he did strike the window ledge, who would likely win this case? What questions might *Jimenez* raise about this case? Explain. See *Xu v. Gay,* 668 N.W.2d 166 (Mich. Ct. App. 2003).

PRACTICING ETHICS   2010 Gulf Oil Disaster: BP Contracts Unfair/Unconscionable?

In May 2010, British Petroleum (BP) oil company was in the midst of frantic efforts to stop the oil flowing into the Gulf of Mexico from its doomed Macondo 252 well while also trying to clean up the immense quantity that escaped after the explosion of the Deepwater Horizon drilling vessel. "Several hundred" shrimpers, oyster harvesters, and others making their living from the Gulf signed contracts with BP to work as paid volunteers in the cleanup process. Among the provisions in those contracts were promises by the volunteers not to file legal claims against the oil company should they sustain damages of any kind in the cleanup process. The provisions, which many of those signing may not have fully understood, included promises not to sue in case of accident or injury and not to talk to anyone about the disaster or cleanup without BP approval. Those provisions also required a 30-day notice before pursuing legal claims against BP, even in the event of an emergency. Reportedly, BP also expected workers to add the oil giant to their personal insurance policies so that worker injuries or damages would fall to each worker's insurance rather than to BP. Commercial fisherman and United Commercial Fisherman's Association president George Barisich filed suit to block enforcement of the restrictive promises and U.S. District Judge Helen Berrigan ruled the offending provisions were overbroad and "unconscionable" and declared them null and void. BP and the Fisherman's Association soon reached an agreement removing the waiver language and agreeing not to enforce those provisions in contracts already signed. BP officials said the provisions were a "mistake," and they ordered the provisions removed as soon as they learned about them.

Questions

1. *a.* Were BP's protective provisions "wrong" as a matter of ethical business practice? Explain.

   b. If you were a boss or lawyer at BP, would you have included those protective provisions? Explain.

2. *a.* If you were a boss and you knew you could compel an employee to accept a pay cut in order to enhance an already healthy bottom line, would you do so? Explain.

   b. In your personal life, do you think you have made agreements with friends that were "one-sided" and "unconscionable" because of your possession of superior leverage of some kind?

   c. If so, were you "wrong" to do so? Explain.

Sources: Sabrina Canfield, "Judge Enjoins BP's Unconscionable Contract with Fishermen-Volunteers," *Courthouse News Service,* May 4, 2010 [**www.courthousenews.com**]; and Brendan Kirby, "Full Report: BP Backs Away from Controversial Oil Spill Settlement Language," May 5, 2010 [**http://blog.al.com**].

Part Two—Interpreting and Enforcing Contracts

We have examined the five ingredients in a binding contract: agreement, consideration, capacity, genuineness of assent, and legality of purpose. Having established those conditions, a contract may have been created, but the door to contract problems has not been closed. Contracts sometimes must fulfill writing formalities to be enforceable. Third parties may have claims against some contracts. And what happens when a party to a contract does not perform as called for by the agreement?

In Writing?

> In most cases, oral contracts are fully enforceable.

Certainly a common belief is that agreements must be in writing to be enforceable; but in most cases, oral contracts are fully enforceable. The exceptions, however, are important. Oral contracts are subject to misunderstanding or to being forgotten, and fraudulent claims can readily arise from oral understandings. Consequently, our states have drawn on the English *Statute of Frauds* in specifying that the following kinds of contracts, in most cases, must be in writing to be enforceable:

1. **Collateral contract.** Assume you have just graduated from college and you want to get started in a small printing business. You secure a bank loan on the condition that you find a creditworthy third party as a guarantor for the loan. Jacobs, a family friend, agrees with the bank to pay the debt if you fail to do so. Jacobs' promise to pay the debt must be in writing to be enforceable.

2. **The sale of land.** Broadly, land is interpreted to include the surface itself, that which is in the soil (minerals) or permanently attached to it (buildings), and growing crops when accompanying the transfer of land. Thus, if a building was permanently attached to a lot you seek for the aforementioned printing business, that building would need to be included in the written contract, but if you contracted to have a building constructed on your lot, you would not need (at least for the purposes of the Statute of Frauds) to execute a written agreement with the building contractor because you would not be contracting for an interest in land. A long-term lease (normally more than one year) for that land and building would, in most states, need to be in writing. All of these principles simply reflect the special role of land in our view of wealth and freedom.

3. **Promises that cannot be performed within one year.** This requirement springs from a concern about faulty memories, deaths, and other impediments to the satisfactory conclusion of long-term contracts. The courts have interpreted this provision narrowly, in effect saying that such a contract need not be in writing if it is *possible,* according to its terms, to perform it within one year from the day of its creation. It follows then that a contract for an indefinite period (such as an employment contract "for the balance of the employee's life") need not be in writing to be enforceable. (It is possible that the employee will die within one year.)

4. **Contracts for the sale of goods at a price of $500 or more.** With exceptions, under both the English-derived Statute of Frauds and UCC Section 2-201, contracts for the sale of goods (having a value of $500 or more under the UCC) must be in writing to be

enforceable. Under the UCC, informal writing will suffice so long as it indicates that a contract was made, it contains a quantity term, and it was signed "by the party against whom enforcement is sought." Section 2-201 provides exceptions for certain transactions of $500 or more in goods in which a contract will be enforceable even though not in writing.

5. **Contracts in consideration of marriage.** The mutual exchange of marriage promises need not be in writing, but any contract that uses marriage as the consideration to support the contract must be in writing to be enforceable. Such contracts would include, for example, prenuptial agreements that are entered prior to marriage and serve the purpose, among others, of specifying how the couple's property will be divided in the event of a divorce. Those contracts must be in writing to be enforceable.

6. **Executor/administrator's promise.** When an individual dies, a representative is appointed to oversee the estate. A promise by that executor/administrator to pay the estate's debts must be in writing if the payment will be made from the executor/administrator's personal funds. Thus, where the executor of an estate contracts with an auctioneer to dispose of the decedent's personal property, the executor's promise to pay the auctioneer must be in writing if the funds are to come from the executor's personal resources; the promise need not be in writing if the payment is to come from the estate.

Electronic Transactions and Statute of Frauds   The Uniform Electronic Transactions Act (UETA), widely adopted by state legislatures, gives electronic records and signatures the same legal power as paper documents and manually signed "wet signatures."[1]

Courts have held that e-mail exchanges, and the typed name of the sender at the bottom of an e-mail message, may satisfy the Statute of Frauds writing requirement.[2] [See *Whinfield v. Capitas Distributors,* 111 F. Supp. 3d 177 (D. Conn. 2015); *Williamson v. Bank of N.Y. Mellon,* 947 F. Supp. 2d (N.D. Texas 2013). However, the parties to the e-mail exchange must have intended to enter into an agreement in this manner.[3] Text messaging has created a new issue under the UETA. A Massachusetts court recently ruled that a text message from a real estate broker accepting an offer to buy a client's commercial building was binding on the seller.[4]

Contract Emoji?

Suppose you are the president of your school's Business Students Club and are negotiating via text message with Dani, a t-shirt manufacturer, for the purchase of 75 t-shirts emblazoned with the club's logo. You had asked Dani how much the t-shirts will cost and received a reply: "$15 each." You then text back Dani: "How about $10 each for the 75 t-shirts?" and receive a text reply from Dani with an emoji of a "thumbs up," which signals approval.

Questions

1. Is there an enforceable contract for the sale of the t-shirts at $10 each? What questions would you need answered before deciding? Explain.

2. Consider which emojis might be used in negotiating a contract through text messages. What problems might arise? Discuss.

Failure to Comply A fully performed oral contract, even though not in compliance with the Statute of Frauds, will not be rescinded by the courts. However, incomplete oral contracts that fail to comply with the statute are unenforceable. If a party to an unenforceable oral contract has provided partial performance in reliance on the contract, the courts will ordinarily provide compensation under quasi-contract principles for the reasonable value of that performance. [For more on the Statute of Frauds, see **www.expertlaw.com/library/business/statute_of_frauds.html**].

The Parol Evidence Rule

Suppose you are the purchasing manager for a large manufacturer. You entered a written contract for 50 new personal computers. During negotiations, the seller said it would "throw in" 10 new printers if it got the computer order, but you failed to include a provision for the printers in the contract. Is your boss about to have a fit? Perhaps, because you probably will not be able to introduce evidence of that oral understanding to alter the terms of the written contract. In general, whenever a contract has been reduced to writing with the intent that the writing represents a complete and final integration of the parties' intentions, none of the parties can introduce parol evidence (oral or written words outside the "four corners" of the agreement) to add to, change, or contradict that contract when that evidence was expressed/created at the time of or prior to the writing. The written agreement is presumed to be the best evidence of the parties' intentions at the time they entered the contract. (The parol evidence rule under UCC Section 2-202 is essentially the same as the common-law provisions discussed here.)

Exceptions Parol evidence may be admissible under the following exceptional circumstances:

1. To add missing terms to an incomplete written contract.
2. To explain ambiguities in a written contract.
3. To prove circumstances that would invalidate a written contract; that is, to establish one of the grounds of mistake, fraud, illegality, and so forth explained earlier in this chapter.

Contract's Terms: Paper versus Website?

Fadal Machining Centers, a machine and machine parts manufacturer, sued Compumachine, one of its distributors, for breach of contract. Under the distributorship agreement, a hard copy of which was attached to Fadal's complaint, any legal action arising out of the contract would be heard in a California federal district court. The agreement also stated that Fadal could establish the terms of sale on occasion. Each of the 15 allegedly unpaid invoices referred to Fadal's website for the terms and conditions of sale. The terms found on the website, under the label "Contract" in large bold type, included an arbitration clause and a statement that they would prevail over any other agreement. Should Fadal's claim be heard in the California federal district court, or be submitted to arbitration? Decide and explain.

Source: See *Fadal v. Compumachine,* 461 F. App'x 630 (9th Cir. 2011).

Third Parties

LO 6-9
Compare and
contrast the
rights and duties
arising in contrac-
tual assignment
and delegation.

We turn now to the rights and duties of those who are not parties to a contract but hold legally recognizable interests in that contract. Those interests arise when (1) contract rights
are assigned to others, (2) contract duties are delegated to others, or (3) contracts have
third-party beneficiary provisions.

Assignment of Rights

Ordinarily, a party to a contract is free to transfer her or his rights under the contract to a
third party. Thus, if Ames owes Jones $500 for work performed, Jones can assign that right
to Smith, who can now assert her right to collect against Ames. That transfer of rights is
labeled an assignment (see Figure 6.2). Jones, the party making the transfer, is the assignor; Smith, the one receiving the right, is the assignee; and Ames, the party who must
perform, is the obligor. Ames, the obligor, must now perform the contract for the benefit of
the assignee; that is, Ames must pay the $500 to Smith. The completed assignment then
extinguishes the assignor's rights under the contract.

FIGURE 6.2
**Assignment of
Rights.**

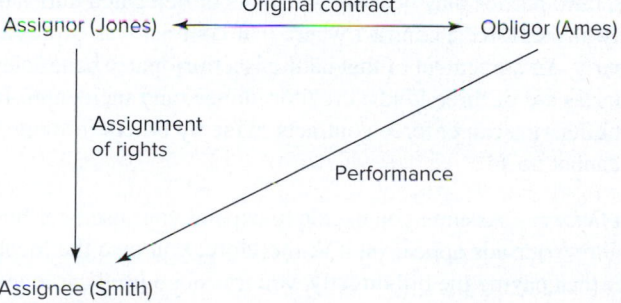

Some contracts are not assignable without consent of the obligor. That would be the case
where the obligor's duties are materially altered by the assignment. For example, if you
have a contract to serve as a personal fitness trainer for a busy chief executive officer, your
contract could not be assigned without your consent to another CEO, or movie star, or the
like because the highly personal and specific obligations under the contract would necessarily be materially altered with a different client.

Delegation of Duties

The parties to a contract may also delegate their duties under the contract to one or more
third parties. Assume Allen has secured a contract to install windows in Boyd's new office
building (see Figure 6.3). Allen could delegate that duty to another contractor, Harms
(although Allen would more commonly simply enter a subcontracting arrangement without
actually transferring the underlying contract). A delegation of duty leaves Harms, the delegatee (the one to whom the duty is delegated), primarily responsible for performance; but
Allen, the obligor/delegator (the one who made the delegation), remains secondarily liable
in case Harms, the delegatee, fails to fulfill the duty to Boyd, the obligee (the one to whom

FIGURE 6.3
Delegation of
Duties.

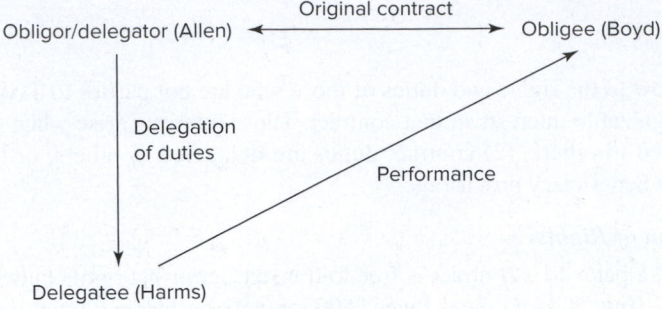

the duty is owed under both the original contract and the delegation). As with the assignment of rights, some contractual duties, particularly those of a personal service nature,
cannot be delegated without consent.

Third-Party Beneficiary Contracts

LO 6-10

Compare and
contrast different
types of third-
party beneficia-
ries to a contract.

Normally, those not a party to a contract have no rights under that contract. As we have
seen, however, third parties may be assigned rights or delegated duties under a contract. A
third party may also enforce a contract where that contract was expressly intended to benefit the third party. An agreement of that nature is a third-party beneficiary contract. Third-
party beneficiaries are of three kinds: creditor, donee, and incidental. In general, creditor
and donee beneficiaries can enforce contracts made by others for their benefit; incidental
beneficiaries cannot do so.

Creditor Beneficiary   Assume you decide to expand your used-car business by advertising on television. Your ads appear on TV; therefore, you owe the local television station
$2,000. Rather than paying the bill directly, you transfer a used car to your friend Gleason,
with the understanding that he will pay off your bill with the television station. Thus, the
station becomes the creditor beneficiary of the contract between you and Gleason, and the
station can sue Gleason for that money if necessary while you remain secondarily responsible for the payment.

Donee Beneficiary   When the promisee's primary purpose in entering a contract is to
make a gift to another, that third party is a donee beneficiary of the contract. The most
common of these situations involves an ordinary life insurance policy for which the owner
(the promisee) pays premiums to the life insurance company (the promisor), which is
obliged to pay benefits to the third party upon the death of the promisee/policy owner. If
necessary, the third-party beneficiary can sue the insurance company for payment.

Incidental Beneficiary   Often a third party receives benefit from a contract although
conferring that benefit was not the contracting parties' primary purpose or intent. For example, assume a General Motors car dealer enters into a contract to buy land adjacent to
your used-car lot for the purpose of opening a large dealership. You would benefit immensely from the spillover effect of the large, adjacent dealership. In such a situation, you
would be an incidental beneficiary of the land sale contract because that contract was not

intended for your benefit. If the landowner or the GM dealer failed to perform, you, as an incidental beneficiary, would have no legal rights against either of them.

The case that follows involves a third-party claim by Gill Plumbing against its subcontractor, Jimenez. The dispute arose out of a dormitory construction contract where the general contractor, Gilbane Building, had hired Gill to do the dormitory plumbing and Gill, in turn, had hired Jimenez to install some portion of that plumbing.

LEGAL BRIEFCASE

Jimenez v. Gilbane Building Company et al.
693 S.E.2d 126 (Ga. Ct. App. 2010)

Judge Adams

. . . The background facts are that Gilbane Building Company was the general contractor for the construction of a new dormitory at Georgia Southern University. Gilbane hired Gill Plumbing as the plumbing contractor, and Gill Plumbing, in turn, hired Jose Alfredo Jimenez to perform plumbing installation work. The building was completed in July 2005, but in October, after the dormitory was occupied by students, a pipe failed causing extensive water damage to the dormitory and to some students' personal belongings. Gilbane was forced to hire Belfor USA Group, Inc., to perform remediation and repair work. Belfor's $990,060.63 bill for the services has not been paid.

Belfor filed this action against Gilbane, Gilbane filed a third-party action against Gill Plumbing, and Gill Plumbing filed a fourth-party action against Jimenez. The parties have since been realigned. Currently, both Belfor and Gilbane have claims against Gill Plumbing, and Gill Plumbing has a third-party claim against Jimenez for the costs of the remediation and repair.

In its third-party claim, Gill Plumbing asserts that it had a written agreement with Jimenez that included an indemnity agreement, and that the damages to the dormitory resulted from negligent work performed by Jimenez. Jimenez denied that he entered into a valid and enforceable contract or an indemnity agreement with Gill Plumbing and denied the negligence. The trial court granted Gill's motion for partial summary judgment against Jimenez, finding that he was liable "for indemnification to Gill Plumbing" "in the amount, if any, of damages proven to have resulted from Mr. Jimenez's defective work." Jimenez appeals this ruling and contends that "no contract existed between Mr. Jimenez and the Appellee as a matter of law" or, at least, that there are material issues of fact regarding the contract and the indemnity agreement.

Summary judgment is proper when there is no genuine issue of material fact and the movant is entitled to judgment as a matter of law. . . .

There is no question that the parties had an oral agreement. The issue before us is whether there was an enforceable written agreement and, if so, what were the terms of that agreement. The undisputed facts show that Jimenez was hired by Gill Plumbing to perform plumbing services in the "Eagle Village" construction project at Georgia Southern University, that he performed plumbing services, and that he has been paid for the work in the amount of $167,000.

Jimenez has never worked for any company other than Gill Plumbing and the two have worked together for at least 15 years. On September 15, 2004, Jimenez signed two documents, which, Gill Plumbing contends, constitute the parties' entire written agreement; Jimenez has signed other documents for Gill Plumbing in the past. The first document is contained on one page, it is dated September 15, 2004, and it has Jimenez's typewritten name and his signature. The main body of the document is as follows:

LABOR CONTRACT
Project: Eagle Village.

Item 1	Slab	50,100.00
Item 2	Rough	66,800.00
Item 3	Set Out	50,100.00

— Weekly billing to be submitted in draw format. All work must be approved by Larry Pollett.

— Weekly safety meetings must be attended. Sub required to attend all jobsite agenda and safety meetings.

— Subs required to comply with all general contractor regulations and jobsite regulations.

— All Subs required to provide certificate of insurance with adequate coverages per limits set by general contractor.

— Subs are required to honor subcontractor Warranty for labor & installation free of all defects for a period of (1) year from date of substantial completion.

— *Subs agree & abide by all terms in the attached Exhibit "A" for insurance & indemnity.*

Total Contract Amount $167,000.00

(Emphasis supplied.) Jimenez's signature appears below the following words, which are written on the side of the above chart:

Sub-Labor

Affidavit

I certify the work for which above payment is requested has been completed according to the plans and specifications and in compliance with the terms of our contract and all labor and material bills applicable to this job have been paid to date and that Federal income, social security, and unemployment taxes have been withheld and will be paid when due on all employees employed by me on this job.

_____/s/_____ CONTRACTOR

Notably, this first document does not name Gill Plumbing anywhere, and the "affidavit" is written in the past tense, as if the project had already been completed, but as of the date on the document, Jimenez's work at Eagle Village had not begun. The second document—"Exhibit A"—is two pages long, and it begins as follows:

INSURANCE AND INDEMNITY SUBCONTRACTOR AGREEMENT

The Work performed by the Subcontractor shall be at the risk of the Subcontractor exclusively. To the fullest extent permitted by law, Subcontractor shall indemnify, defend (at Subcontractor's sole expense) and hold harmless Contractor, the Owner (if different from Contractor), affiliated companies of Contractor, . . . from and against any and all claims for . . . damage to property . . . which arise or are in any way connected with the Work performed, Materials furnished, or Services provided under this Agreement by Subcontractor or its agents. . . .

The exhibit goes on to require the "Subcontractor" to obtain commercial general liability insurance in the amount of $1,000,000, and to meet other related requirements. The exhibit is signed by Jimenez on the second page over the word "Subcontractor," but it is not dated. Also, the document does not include Gill Plumbing's name anywhere. Finally, Jimenez never performed any work at Eagle Village that could be called "Set Out" as stated on page one of the document.

Jimenez contends the three-page document is not an enforceable agreement because it does not state who the other party is or mention Gill Plumbing's name; it does not include a promise by Gill Plumbing, or anyone else, to pay him; it does not specify the location or address where the work is to be performed; it leaves several terms undefined; it does not specify the time for performance; it does not direct Jimenez to perform any work at all; and although it mentions additional documents, none are attached or defined. He argues the "sub-labor affidavit" found on page one of the document is written in the past tense, suggesting that the work was already completed when, in fact, it had not begun as of the only date indicated on the document. He also complains that the indemnification provision fails to identify who should be indemnified and that it fails to define the terms "subcontractor," "contractor," or "owner." Finally, Jimenez contends he cannot read or communicate well in English and he did not know what he signed.

In Georgia,

The first requirement of the law relative to contracts is that there must be a meeting of the minds of the parties, and mutuality, and in order for the contract to be valid the agreement must ordinarily be expressed plainly and explicitly enough to show what the parties agreed upon. A contract cannot be enforced in any form of action if its terms are incomplete or incomprehensible.

Bagwell-Hughes, Inc. v. McConnell, 224 Ga. 659, 661–662 (164 SE2d 229) (1968). But "[a]n objection of indefiniteness may be obviated by performance on the part of one party and the acceptance of the performance by the other." *Aukerman v. Witmer*, 256 Ga. App. 211, 216 (1) (568 SE2d 123) (2002). Nevertheless, performance as a cure has its limits:

Performance does not cure the deficiencies in an agreement that is so vague, indefinite, and uncertain "as to make it impossible for courts to determine what, if anything, was agreed upon, therefore rendering it impossible to determine whether there had been performance."

Razavi v. Shackelford, 260 Ga. App. 603, 605 (1) (580 SE2d 253) (2003).

Here, the attendant and surrounding circumstances show that Jimenez entered into an agreement with Gill Plumbing, that he performed work, and that he was paid by Gill Plumbing. The three-page document shows that the work was to be performed on the "Eagle Village" project; it stated the amount to be paid for each phase of the work, and the total equaled the amount that Jimenez was paid for the work. And Jimenez attended weekly safety meetings. Thus, there is some evidence of performance consistent with the three-page document. But there is also evidence of performance that is inconsistent with the three-page document. Jimenez did not perform some of the work listed in the document, and the document suggests that the work had already been completed when the document was signed.

In addition, the document is ambiguous at best, and the rules of construction do not resolve the ambiguity. Jimenez is identified as the "subcontractor" in the indemnification agreement, which provides that he is to identify the "contractor" and others. Yet, the first page of the three page document identifies Jimenez as the "contractor," suggesting that he should indemnify himself. And there are two contractors who are parties to the lawsuit and other contractors on the entire project. . .

. . . Here, among other problems, it is impossible to tell from the terms of the written document who Jimenez may have promised to indemnify, and that fact has not been made sufficiently clear by either the rules of construction or any performance under the agreement.

The trial court erred by granting partial summary judgment in favor of Gill Plumbing on the purported indemnification agreement. Jury issues remain on the terms of the parties' agreement. . . .

Judgment reversed.

Questions

1. Explain what the trial court meant in finding that Jimenez was liable "for indemnification to Gill Plumbing" "in the amount, if any, of damages proven to have resulted from Mr. Jimenez's defective work."

2. Why did the court conclude that Gill did not have an enforceable agreement with Jimenez?

3. Why did the appeals court overturn the trial court's summary judgment?

Discharge

LO 6-11
Explain how a contract may be discharged.

At some point, obligations under a contract come to an end. When that moment arrives, we say the duties of the contracting parties have been discharged. In this section, we examine some of the methods of contract discharge. Discharge can occur in many ways, but the most important of these are (1) conditions, (2) performance or breach, (3) lawful excuses, (4) agreement, and (5) by operation of law.

Discharge by Conditions

Sometimes a contract is useful to one or more of the contracting parties only if some future event occurs or fails to occur. Under those circumstances, the parties may write into the contract a clause providing that performance is required only if the specified condition occurs or fails to occur. Otherwise, the duty to perform is discharged. Those conditions take three forms: conditions precedent, conditions subsequent, and conditions concurrent.

Conditions Precedent   A conditions precedent clause specifies that an event must occur before the parties to the contract are obliged to perform. Assume you are attempting to establish a business booking rock-and-roll acts for performances.

> You sign a deal with the rock group Passion Pit.

You sign a deal with the rock group Passion Pit, providing for a performance "contingent upon obtaining satisfactory lease arrangements for the university field house within 14 days." If you are unable to achieve an acceptable lease, both parties are discharged from performance requirements under the contract.

Conditions Subsequent   A conditions subsequent clause excuses performance if a future event transpires. Thus, in the Passion Pit example, the band might include a clause providing that the agreement will be null and void if any member of the band is ill or otherwise unable to perform on the contracted evening. Hence, in a contract with a condition subsequent, the parties have bound themselves to perform unless a specified event occurs;

whereas in a contract with a condition precedent, the parties have no binding duties until the specified event occurs.

Conditions Concurrent Here the contract simply specifies that the parties are to perform their duties at the same time. Each performance is dependent on the other. So if Passion Pit performs as contracted, you have a simultaneous duty to pay for the band's performance. Your duty to pay is conditioned on Passion Pit's performance and vice versa.

Express or Implied Conditions Another way of classifying the aforementioned conditions is to treat them either as express or implied. Express conditions are those explicitly agreed to by the parties, as in the situation where you, a concert promoter, expressly conditioned performance on your ability to secure the university field house for the concert. Express conditions are often prefaced by words such as *when*, *if*, *provided*, and so forth.

Implied-in-fact conditions are not explicitly stated in the contract but are derived by the court from the conduct of the parties and the circumstances surrounding the bargain. Suppose you contract to remove snow from your neighbor's driveway during the winter. An implied-in-fact condition of your neighbor's duty to pay would be that you would complete the work within a reasonable period.

Implied-in-law conditions (also called ***constructive conditions***) are those that, although not expressly provided for in the contract or not able to be reasonably inferred from the facts, the court imposes on the contract to avoid unfairness. Hence, if you contracted to put a new roof on your neighbor's house, but your written contract did not include a date for payment, the court might imply a contract clause providing that your neighbor need not pay you until the job is complete.

Discharge by Performance or by Breach of Contract

Complete performance is, of course, the normal way of discharging a contract. Failure to fully perform without a lawful excuse for that failure results in a breach of contract. The consequences of both full performance and breach of contract can be described in four parts.

Complete Performance—No Breach of Contract Here we find the most common method of discharge—the situation in which the parties simply do precisely what the contract calls for: pay $500, provide a particular product, present the deed for a piece of land, and so on. When fully performed, a contract has been ***executed.***

Substantial Performance—Nonmaterial Breach of Contract In some cases, complete performance is not achieved because of minor deviations from the agreed-on performance. Most notably in construction contracts and in many personal or professional service contracts, the courts have recognized the doctrine of substantial performance. For example, assume a contractor painted a house as agreed, except that he replaced the Benjamin Moore paint called for in the contract with a Sherwin-Williams paint of comparable quality. Assuming the variation has not materially altered the end product and assuming that the variation was not the result of bad faith, the court will enforce the contract as written but require a deduction for any damages sustained as a consequence of the imperfect performance.

Unacceptable Performance—Material Breach of Contract   When a party falls beneath substantial performance and does not have a lawful excuse for that failure, a material breach of contract has occurred. No clear line separates substantial performance (a nonmaterial breach) from unacceptable performance (a material breach). Such decisions must be made case by case. We can say that material breaches are those that fall short of what the nonbreaching party should reasonably expect—that is, full performance in some cases and substantial performance in others. A material breach discharges the nonbreaching party's duties and permits that party to sue for damages or rescind the contract and seek restitution.

Duke University Breached Its Contract with a Student?

Andrew Giuliani (son of former New York mayor Rudy Giuliani) was recruited by Coach Rod Myers to play golf at Duke University. Coach Myers allegedly said that Giuliani would be given "life-time access" to Duke's "state-of-the-art" training facilities when he became a Duke alum, and that he would be able to compete for the opportunity to play against the best golfers in the NCAA. Giuliani said those promises and others were instrumental in his decision to attend Duke. Giuliani alleged that Duke "promised to provide [Mr. Giuliani] with various educational services, lodging, and a right of access to the Athletic Department's Varsity program and facilities." Coach Myers unexpectedly passed away in the spring of 2007 and Coach O. D. Vincent took over. Vincent decided to cut the squad in half and announced that he was canceling Giuliani's golf eligibility. Vincent pointed to several incidents of alleged bad behavior by Giuliani. Vincent then presented Giuliani with a written agreement setting out the steps that would have allowed Giuliani to rejoin the team. Giuliani refused to sign the agreement. Giuliani then filed a breach of contract suit against Duke University and Vincent.

Questions

1. Giuliani claimed that his contractual right to play golf at Duke was based on (a) Coach Myers's oral statements and (b) Duke's Student-Athlete Handbook, the Duke Student Bulletin, the Duke Athletic Policy Manual, and the NCAA Division I Manual. Giuliani lost the case. Why did the court reject Giuliani's contract claims?
2. Could you successfully sue your university for breach of contract if you were dismissed from school because of low grades? Explain. See, for example, *Bissessur v. The Indiana University Board of Trustees,* 581 F.3d 599 (7th Cir. 2009).

Source: Giuliani v. Duke University, 2010 U.S. Dist. LEXIS 32691 (M.D.N.C. March 30, 2010).

Advance Refusal to Perform—Anticipatory Breach of Contract   Sometimes one of the parties, before performance is due, indicates by word or deed that she or he will not perform. Normally an anticipatory breach (also called anticipatory repudiation) is the equivalent of a material breach, discharging the nonbreaching party from any further obligations and allowing the nonbreaching party to sue for damages, if any.

When Has a Breach of Contract Occurred? When Should the Law Intervene in a Contract?

The Legal Briefcase that follows raises many claims, including breach of contract, but it also serves as an interesting test of the role of law. Should sports fans be able to secure a remedy through contract law when an event merely does not meet their expectations? The idea seems preposterous and another instance of abuse of the legal system, but consider the facts.

> Tyson spit out his mouthpiece and bit both of Holyfield's ears.

The case deals with ex-convict and former heavyweight boxing champion Mike Tyson and his famous 1997 bout with then-champion Evander Holyfield, a fight ended by disqualification in the third round when Tyson bit both of Holyfield's ears. Incensed pay-per-view customers joined in a class action seeking their money back ($50–$60 each) claiming they were "ripped off" or "scammed" by Tyson. They sued Tyson, fight promoters, and fight telecasters. A lower court dismissed the complaint for failure to state a cause of action. The plaintiffs appealed.

LEGAL BRIEFCASE

Castillo v. Tyson
701 N.Y.S.2d 423 (N.Y. App. Div. 2000)

Judge Ramos

Plaintiffs claim that they were entitled to view a "legitimate heavyweight title fight" fought "in accordance with the applicable rules and regulations" of the governing boxing commission—that is, a fight that was to end either in an actual or technical knockout or by decision of the judges after 12 rounds—and that they are entitled to their money back because the fight ended in a disqualification. Many legal theories are invoked in support of this claim—breach of contract, breach of implied covenant of good faith and fair dealing, unjust enrichment, breach of express and implied warranties, tortious interference with contractual relations, "wantonness," fraud, negligent representation—none of which have merit. Plaintiffs are not in contractual privity with any of the defendants, and their claim that they are third-party beneficiaries of one or more of the contracts that defendants entered into among themselves was aptly rejected by the motion court as "contrived." Nothing in these contracts can be understood as promising a fight that did not end in a disqualification. The rules of the governing commission provide for disqualification, and it is a possibility that a fight fan can reasonably expect. Plaintiffs could not reasonably rule out such a possibility by the boxer's and promoters' public statements predicting a "sensational victory" and "the biggest fight of all time," and assuming other representations were made promising or implying a "legitimate fight," there can be no breach of warranty claim absent privity of contract between plaintiffs and defendants and also because defendants provided only a service. Nor is a claim of fraud supported by plaintiffs' allegations that the boxer's former trainer predicted that the boxer would get himself disqualified if he failed to achieve an early knockout and that the boxer came out without his mouthpiece in the beginning of the round that he was disqualified. Plaintiffs' claim for unjust enrichment was properly dismissed by the motion court on the ground that plaintiffs received what they paid for, namely, "the right to view whatever event transpired." We have considered plaintiffs' other arguments . . . and find them unpersuasive.

Affirmed.

Questions

1. Why did the court reject the plaintiffs' breach of contract claim?

2. What is unjust enrichment, and why was that claim denied by the court?

3. Defects discovered in the Michelin tires to be used by 14 of the 20 teams in a Formula One race at the Indianapolis Speedway caused those teams to withdraw prior to the start, leaving only six cars running in the race. The race was completed, but fans sued for breach of contract claiming the race was not what they had purchased tickets to see and that the race advertising had indicated that 20 cars would be racing. Decide the case. Explain. See *Bowers v. Federation Internationale de L'Automobile*, 489 F.3d 316 (7th Cir. 2007).

4. Pelullo promoted boxers and boxing matches through his company, Banner Productions. In 1999 Echols signed an agreement with Banner giving Echols a $30,000 bonus and giving Banner "the sole and exclusive right to secure all professional boxing bouts" for Echols. Banner was to provide no fewer than three bouts per year, and Echols was to be paid not less than a specified minimum amount for each fight, but the payments could be lowered or the whole agreement canceled, at Banner's option, if Echols lost a fight. Echols lost a championship bout, and Banner said it would thereafter negotiate each purse on a bout-by-bout basis. Echols continued to fight for Banner, but various disputes over purses arose, and Echols sued. Among other claims, Echols argued that the agreement was unenforceable for indefiniteness. Decide that claim. Explain. See *Echols v. Pelullo,* 377 F.3d 272 (3d Cir. 2004).

Discharge by Lawful Excuses (for Nonperformance)

Sometimes contracts are discharged lawfully even in the event of nonperformance. This can occur when performance is either impossible or impractical.

Impossibility   After agreement is reached but performance is not yet due, circumstances may be so altered that performance is a *legal impossibility.* In such situations nonperformance is excused. Impossibility here refers not simply to extreme difficulty but to objective impossibility; that is, the contracted-for performance cannot be accomplished by anyone. Notable examples of such situations are a personal service contract where the promisor has died or is incapacitated by illness, a contract where the subject of the agreement was rendered illegal by a change in the law subsequent to the agreement but prior to its performance, or a contract where an ingredient essential to performance has been destroyed and no reasonable substitutes are available. [For more on impossibility of performance, see **www.west.net/~smith/imposbl.htm**].

Commercial Impracticability   Akin to the doctrine of impossibility is the situation in which duties are discharged because of unforeseen events that render performance exorbitantly expensive or thoroughly impractical. Commercial impracticability is specifically provided for in UCC Section 2-615, which reads: "Delay in delivery or nondelivery in whole or in part by a seller . . . is not a breach of his duty under a contract for sale if performance as agreed has been made impracticable by the occurrence of a contingency the nonoccurrence of which was a basic assumption on which the contract was made. . . ."

The UCC's commercial impracticability standard is more easily established than the impossibility doctrine of the common law, but note that only exceptional and unforeseeable events fall within the impracticability excuse for nonperformance. Mere changes in market conditions do not give rise to commercial impracticability. Historically, the commercial impracticability doctrine had been applied only to transactions involving the sale of goods, but now we see courts increasingly willing to apply it to other kinds of contracts as well.

Discharge by Agreement

A contractual discharge is sometimes achieved by a new agreement arrived at after entering the original contract. These agreements take a variety of forms, but one—*accord and satisfaction*—will serve here to illustrate the general category. Parties reach an accord when they agree to a performance different from the one provided for in their contract. Performance of the accord is called satisfaction, at which point the original contract is discharged. A binding accord and satisfaction must spring from a genuine dispute between the parties, and it must include consideration as well as all of the other ingredients in a binding contract.

Discharge by Operation of Law

Under some circumstances, contractual duties are discharged by the legal system itself. For example, the contractual responsibilities of a debtor may be discharged by a bankruptcy decree. Additionally, each state has a *statute of limitations* that specifies the time within which a performing party can initiate a lawsuit against a nonperforming party. For the UCC statute of limitations for sales of goods contracts, see UCC Section 2-725.

Remedies

LO 6-12
Describe the remedies available for breach of contract.

We have looked at the elements of a binding contract and at those circumstances that discharge a party's duties under a contract. Now our concern is with what happens when one of the parties does not fulfill his or her contractual duties—that is, when the contract is breached. Remedies are provided in both law and in **equity** (see Glossary and Chapter 4).

Remedies in Law

In general, a *breach of contract* allows the nonbreaching party to sue for money damages. The general goal of remedies law is to put the parties in the position they would have occupied had the contract been fulfilled. Normally, the best available substitute for actual performance is monetary damages.

Compensatory Damages   In brief, the plaintiff in a breach of contract action is entitled to recover a sum equal to the actual damages suffered. The plaintiff is compensated for her losses by receiving a sum designed to "make her whole," to put her where she would have been had the contract not been breached.

Sale of Goods A breach involving a sale of goods contract is governed by the UCC. Typically, the measure of *compensatory damages* would be the difference between the contract price and the market price of the goods at the time and place the goods were to be delivered (see UCC Sections 2-708 and 2-713). Suppose you are working for a newly established drone manufacturer, and you have contracted with an agricultural company to deliver 1,000 fixed-wing agricultural drones at $1,500 each, although the current market price is $1,600. If you fail to make that delivery, damages could be assessed in the amount of $100,000 ($100 × 1,000), which is the additional amount the agricultural company would need to pay to make a substitute purchase.

Consequential Damages   The victim of a breach may be able to recover not just the direct losses from the breach but also any indirect losses that were incurred as a consequence of that breach. Such consequential damages are recoverable only if they were foreseen or were reasonably foreseeable by the breaching party. For example, if

> The grand opening of your new bar and the band fails to appear.

you contract for a well-known local band to play for the grand opening of your new bar and dance club and the band fails to appear, you may be able to recover damages for any lost profits that you can attribute to the band's absence. Those lost profits are a reasonably foreseeable *consequence* of the breach. Of course, you will have some difficulty in specifying the profits lost and in proving that the loss was attributable to the band's failure to perform.

Not a Fan?

Construction worker Brent Loveland showed up at the home of Oklahoma State University football coach Mike Gundy to begin work on a trim installation—wearing a University of Oklahoma Sooners baseball T-shirt. He was fired from the job that day. Loveland sued Gundy and his wife, Kristen, alleging, among other things, breach of contract. Loveland's lawsuit sought the $80,600 that he was allegedly to be paid for the 13-week job, and the potential income of over $30,000 he lost because he turned down other jobs owing to his commitment to work on the Gundy home.

Questions

1. What are the issues in this case?
2. Decide.

Sources: Zac Ellis, "Report: Lawsuit Against Oklahoma State Coach Will Move Forward," *Sports Illustrated Campus Union,* June 5, 2013 [**http://college-football.si.com**]; and Gina Mizell, "Oklahoma State Football: Lawsuit Against Mike Gundy Dismissed," August 7, 2013 [**http://newsok.com**].

Incidental Damages   The costs incurred by the nonbreaching party in arranging a substitute performance or otherwise reducing the damages sustained because of the breach are recoverable as incidental damages. They would include such items as phone calls and transportation expenses.

Nominal Damages   In some cases of breach, the court will award only an insignificant sum, perhaps $1.00 (plus court costs), because the nonbreaching party has suffered no actual damages. The point of nominal damages is to illustrate the wrongfulness of the breach.

Punitive Damages   Sometimes when the breaching party's conduct is particularly reprehensible, the court will penalize that wrongful behavior by awarding punitive damages to the injured party. The idea is to deter such conduct in the future. Normally, punitive damages cannot be awarded in breach of contract cases except when provided for by statute or when the breach is accompanied by a tort such as fraud (as where one buys a defective car having reasonably relied on the falsehoods of a salesperson).

Rescission and Restitution   In some instances, including a material breach, mistake, fraud, undue influence, and duress, the wronged party may rescind (undo) the contract. The effect of a contract rescission is to return the parties to the positions they occupied before they entered the agreement. Generally, both parties must then make restitution to each other by returning whatever goods, property, and so forth were transferred under the contract or an equivalent amount of money.

Mitigation   Obviously the law should penalize a breaching party, as we have discussed, but you may be surprised to learn that the law also imposes expectations on the victim (the nonbreaching party). Specifically, the nonbreaching party is required to take reasonable steps toward mitigation—that is, to minimize her or his damages. What happens, for example, if you are wrongfully dismissed in breach of contract from your first job after college? You are expected to mitigate your damages by seeking another job. You need not take an inferior job, nor must you disturb your life by moving to another state or community, but you must take reasonable measures to minimize your claim against your former employer.

Liquidated Damages   We have reviewed both the legal penalties for breach and the duty to mitigate damages. The law also offers the opportunity to provide some control over the penalty for breach by including in the contract a liquidated damages clause. Here you and the other party to the contract agree in advance about the measure of damages should either of you default on your duties. That clause is fully enforceable so long as it is not designed to be a penalty but rather a good faith effort to assess in advance an accurate measure of damages. A valid liquidated damages clause limits the nonbreaching party to recovery of the amount provided for in that clause.

Remedies in Equity

Where justice cannot be achieved via money damages alone, the courts will sometimes impose equitable remedies. The chief forms of equitable remedy in contract cases are specific performance, injunction, reformation, and quasi-contract.

Specific Performance   In unusual circumstances, the court may order the breaching party to remedy its wrong by performing its obligations precisely as provided for in the contract. Normally that specific performance is required only where the subject matter of the contract is unique and thus cannot be adequately compensated with money. Examples of such subject matter might include a particular piece of land, an art work, or a family heirloom. By contrast, specific performance would not be available in contracts involving conventional personal property such as a television or a car unless those items were unique (such as a one-of-a-kind Rolls Royce).

Normally the courts will not grant a specific performance remedy in personal service contracts (such as an agreement by a cosmetic surgeon to perform a face-lift). If the surgeon refused to perform, specific performance probably would not be ordered. The quality of the surgery likely would not be equal to what had been bargained for; courts do not want to be in the position of supervising the completion of contracts, and as a matter of public policy, we do not want to put parties, in this case, the surgeon, in a position that amounts to involuntary servitude.

Injunction   An injunction is a court order that may either require or forbid a party to perform a specified act. Injunctions are granted only under exceptional circumstances. Perhaps the most common of those are the noncompetition agreements. For example, you take a computer programming job that will afford you access to company secrets. To protect itself, the company expects you to sign an agreement specifying that you will not take employment with a competing firm for one year after departure from your employer. If you should quit and seek to work for a competitor within one year, your former employer might be able to secure an injunction preventing you from doing so until the year has passed.

Reformation   Reformation is an equitable remedy that permits the court to rewrite the contract where it imperfectly expressed the parties' true intentions. Typically, such situations involve a mutual mistake or fraud. Thus, if the parties sign a contract to sell a lot in a housing development, but the contract is written with an incorrect street address for the lot, an equity court could simply correct the error in the contract.

Quasi-Contract   What happens if one party has conferred a benefit on another, but a contract has not been created because of a failure of consideration, the application of the Statute of Frauds, or something of the sort? As mentioned earlier, to prevent unjust enrichment, the court might then imply a contract as a matter of law. For example, assume a lawn service mistakenly trims your shrubs and you watch them do so, knowing that they are supposed to be caring for your neighbor's lawn. You have not entered a contract with the lawn service, but a court might well require you to pay the reasonable value of trimming your shrubs. To do otherwise would unjustly enrich you.

PRACTICING ETHICS   Bloggers Work for Free?

The Huffington Post, the blog aggregator and opinion site, was sued in a class action in 2011 on the grounds that it had failed to pay the more than 9,000 bloggers who had provided content for the blog over a period of years. In submitting copy to *The Huffington Post,* bloggers knew they would not be paid, but presumably they valued the professional/political/personal exposure afforded by publication. The lawsuit, however, claimed the agreement to provide content without compensation had resulted in unjust enrichment for Huffington. AOL purchased *The Huffington Post* earlier in 2011 for $315 million; the bloggers sought approximately a third of the purchase price, asserting their contributions had made *The Huffington Post* that valuable an acquisition. In 2012, a federal judge dismissed the lawsuit, concluding that the bloggers had not expected money in return for their contributions to *The Huffington Post.*

Questions

1. The law aside, does *The Huffington Post* have a moral duty to compensate the bloggers who knowingly gave away their content when that content subsequently proved to be instrumental in building Huffington into a valuable property? Explain.

2. Do you feel a duty to pay others when you are the beneficiary of "unjust enrichment?" Explain.

Sources: Chad Bray, "*Huffington Post* Wins Dispute with Unpaid Bloggers," *The Wall Street Journal Law Blog,* March 30, 2012 [**http://blogs.wsj.com/law/2012/03/30/huffington-post-wins-dispute-with-unpaid-bloggers/**]; and Stephanie Francis Ward, "Huffington Post Bloggers Sue, Seeking Payment for Writing," *ABA Journal,* April 12, 2011 [**www.abajournal.com/news/article/huffpo_bloggers_sue_seeking_payment_for_writing/**].

Internet Exercise   Go to the *ContractsProf Blog* [**http://lawprofessors.typepad.com/contractsprof_blog/**] for June 2, 2016. Read about the "playbook" used to recruit students to the Trump Entrepreneur Initiative, also referred to as Trump "University." Do a broader Internet search to identify and find the status on lawsuits against this now-defunct business operation alleging fraud. Compare these to the claim against Thomas Jefferson School of Law discussed in the June 2, 2016, blog post.

**Chapter
Questions**

1. Wardle made a standard real estate offer to buy a house owned by Kessler. The offer contained a "time is of the essence" clause specifying that the deal had to be completed on or before 11 A.M. on September 26, 1997. Owen then submitted a backup purchase offer for the same price as offered by Wardle. Wardle's completed contract was not delivered to Kessler until approximately 11:20 A.M. on September 26, so Kessler sold to Owen. Wardle then sued Kessler. Decide. Explain. See *Owen v. Kessler,* 778 N.E.2d 953 (Mass. App. Ct. 2002).

2. In a 2013 televised interview with Oprah Winfrey, Lance Armstrong admitted to taking performance-enhancing drugs during his cycling career. Afterward, Armstrong faced several lawsuits, including one from SCA Promotions, seeking to recover approximately $12 million in bonuses it had paid Armstrong for several Tour de France victories. SCA, already suspecting Armstrong of taking performance-enhancing drugs in the 2004 Tour de France, had tried to withhold payment of his bonus for winning that race. Armstrong had sued, and the parties entered into a settlement agreement under which Armstrong received the bonus money—under the terms of that agreement, an award that "no party may challenge, appeal or attempt to set aside." How should this case be decided? Explain.

3. Allen M. Campbell Co. sought a contract to build houses for the U.S. Navy. Approximately one-half hour before the housing bids were due, Virginia Metal Industries quoted Campbell Co. a price of $193,121 to supply the necessary doors and frames. Campbell, using the Virginia Metal quote, entered a bid and won the contract. Virginia Metal refused to supply the necessary doors, and Campbell had to secure an alternative source of supply at a price $45,562 higher than Virginia Metal's quote. Campbell sued. Explain Campbell's claim. Defend Virginia Metal. Decide. See *Allen M. Campbell Co. Inc. v. Virginia Metal Industries,* 708 F.2d 930 (4th Cir. 1983).

4. Jesse Dimmick, trying to escape police questioning in a murder investigation, burst into Jared and Lindsay Rowley's Kansas home with a knife. After gaining his trust by feeding him and watching a movie with him, the Rowleys were able to escape when Dimmick fell asleep. Police entered the house and arrested Dimmick, who was accidentally shot in the process. The Rowleys sued Dimmick for damages; Dimmick countersued for breach of contract, seeking $160,000 to cover hospital bills and $75,000 for pain and suffering. Dimmick said the Rowleys had broken their promise to keep him hidden from authorities in return for cash. What defenses could the Rowleys raise to this claim? Explain. See **http://cjonline.com/news/2011-11-28/dimmick-sues-couple-he-kidnapped.**

5. The 2009 motion picture *The Merry Gentleman* was considered a commercial failure despite some critical acclaim. The film's producers sued Michael Keaton, the film's lead actor and director, and Keaton's "loan-out company" that he uses for professional contracting, seeking $5.5 million in damages for breach of contract. The plaintiffs alleged that Keaton had, among other things, failed to timely prepare the first cut of the film, communicated directly with Sundance Film Festival threatening to boycott the festival if it did not accept his director's cut instead of the producers' preferred cut, failed to cooperate with the producers during the post-production process, and failed to promote the film. If you were on the jury, what questions would you want answered?

Explain. *Merry Gentleman, LLC v. George & Leona Prods.,* 76 F. Supp. 3d 756 (N.D. Ill. 2014).

6. Sherwood agreed to purchase a cow, Rose 2d of Aberlone, from Walker at a price of 5½ cents per pound (about $80). The parties believed the cow to be barren. Sherwood came to Walker's farm to collect the cow, but at that point it was obvious that Rose was pregnant. Walker refused to give over the cow, which was then worth $750 to $1,000. Sherwood sued. Should he get the cow? Explain. See *Sherwood v. Walker,* 33 N.W. 919 (Mich. 1887).

7. Weaver leased a service station from American Oil. The lease included a clause providing that Weaver would hold American Oil harmless for any negligence by American on the premises. Weaver and an employee were burned when an American Oil employee accidentally sprayed gasoline while at Weaver's station. Weaver had one and one-half years of high school education. The trial record provides no evidence that Weaver read the lease, that American's agent asked him to read it, or that Weaver's attention was drawn to the "hold harmless" clause. The clause was in fine print and contained no title heading. Is the contract enforceable against Weaver? Explain. See *Weaver v. American Oil Co.,* 276 N.E.2d 144 (Ind. 1971).

8. Republic Bank acquired medical equipment through a lease default and contracted Tetra Financial Services to facilitate sale of the equipment. Mark, a Tetra employee, was assigned to the task. West Penn, a large hospital system in the Pittsburgh, Pennsylvania, area, expressed an interest in purchasing the equipment and had one of its contract negotiators, Michele, handle it.

    Michele sent Mark an e-mail on February 26, stating:

    > We are interested in the 64-slice scanner, CT workstation, ultrasound, and ultrasound table.

    > Our offer is as follows:

    > Scanner: $600,000

    > CT workstation: $50,000

    > Ultrasound and ultrasound table: $26,500

    On March 13, Mark sent Michele an e-mail stating:

    > Michele: I met with the bank president this morning and he gave me approval to sell West Penn the 64-slice scanner, CT workstation, and ultrasound unit with table for the total amount offered below [referring to Michele's February 26 e-mail]. There is still some question regarding the cooler unit being moved to your location or left in place and a replacement provided for you. We can discuss that issue.

    > Please let me know if you work through a purchase order system or if we need to put together a sales agreement.

    Is there a contract between Republic Bank and West Penn for the purchase of the medical equipment? Decide. Explain. See *Republic Bank v. Allegheny Health,* 475 F. App'x 692 (10th Cir. 2010).

9. In 1994, California raisin grape grower Sardul Sihota allegedly promised his son Paul that if he pursued his education, continued to work on the family's ranches, and

married an Indian Sikh girl, then he and Paul's stepmother, Jitendra, would take care of him financially. Paul graduated from college in 1994. Sardul and Jitendra arranged Paul's 1996 marriage to Rajneet, an Indian Sikh girl. Paul continued to work on the famiy's ranches until 1999. The couple lived on the Elkhorn Ranch owned by Sardul until 2012, during which time they did not pay rent. When Sardul had to sell the Temperance Ranch in which Paul had an interest, Paul alleged that Sardul promised to put the Elkhorn Ranch in Paul's name when he was able to do so financially. Sardul denied making such a promise. Paul and Rajneet sued Sardul and Jitendra for breach of contract and fraud. Decide. Explain. See Myanna Delllinger, "A Modern 'Hamer v. Sidway'-like Case with an International Twist," *ContractsProf Blog,* June 23, 2016 [**http://lawprofessors.typepad.com/contractsprof_blog/**]; *Sihota v. Sihota* (unpublished opinion, Cal. App. 5th Dist. 2016).

10. The Wongs bought a hillside home in San Carlos, California, for $2.35 million from the Stolers. Several months after they moved in, the Wongs discovered that they were connected to a private sewer system and were not directly serviced by the city's public system. Believing they had been deceived, they sued the Stolers and the real estate agents who brokered the sale alleging several causes of action, including rescission. After the Wongs settled their dispute with the real estate agents for $200,000, a court trial was held on the rescission claim only. Although the court found that the Stolers, with reckless disregard, made negligent misrepresentations to the Wongs, it declined to effectuate a rescission of the contract. Instead, it ordered the Stolers to be, for a limited time, indemnifiers to the Wongs for sewer maintenance and repair costs exceeding the $200,000 they obtained in their settlement with the agents. The Wongs appealed. Decide. Explain. *Wong v. Stoler,* 237 Cal. App. 4th 1375 (Cal. App. 1st Dist. 2015).

11. Preference Personnel, a North Dakota corporation, entered a contract with Peterson to help him find employment in the tax law field. The contract provided that the employer would pay the placement fee, unless Peterson voluntarily quit within 9 days, in which case he would be responsible for the fee, which was 20 percent of one year's salary. Peterson was placed in a job with an annual salary of $60,000, but he quit after one month. Peterson refused to pay the fee, and Preference sued for breach of contract. The lower court found that Peterson breached the contract, but at the time of the contract, Preference Personnel's state-required license to operate had been allowed to lapse. The court, therefore, dismissed the Preference claim, ruling that the agreement was unenforceable as a matter of public policy. Preference appealed. Rule on that appeal. Explain. See *Preference Personnel, Inc. v. Peterson,* 710 N.W.2d 383 (N.D. 2006).

12. Panera, the bakery/café chain, had a clause in its lease that prevented the White City Shopping Center in Shrewsbury, Massachusetts, from renting space to another sandwich shop: "Landlord agrees not to enter into a lease, . . . for a bakery or restaurant reasonably expected to have annual sales of *sandwiches* (emphasis added) greater than ten percent (10%) of its total sales. . . . " Panera asked a Massachusetts Superior Court to block the shopping center from leasing space to a Qdoba Mexican Grill on the grounds that a lease with the Grill would violate the terms of the Panera lease. How should the court rule? Explain. See *White City Shopping Center, LP v. PR Restaurants, LLC*, 2006 Mass. Super. LEXIS 544 (October 31, 2006).

Notes

1. Uniform Electronic Transactions Act (National Conference of Commissioners on Uniform State Laws 1999) [**www.uniformlaws.org/shared/docs/electronic%20transactions/ueta_final_99.pdf**].

2. See *Whinfield v. Capitas Distributors,* 111 F. Supp. 3d 177 (D. Conn. 2015); *Williamson v. Bank of N.Y. Mellon,* 947 F. Supp. 2d (N.D. Texas 2013).

3. *Waddle v. Elrod,* 367 S.W.3d 217 (Tenn. 2012).

4. *St. John's Holdings v. Two Electronics,* 2016 Mass. LCR LEXIS 166 (Mass. 2016).

CHAPTER SEVEN

Business Torts and Product Liability

After completing this chapter, students will be able to fulfill the following learning objectives:

7-1. Compare and contrast the three fundamental kinds of torts: intentional, negligent, and strict liability.

7-2. Describe selected intentional torts against persons including battery, assault, fraud, invasion of privacy, intentional infliction of emotional distress, and defamation.

7-3. Describe selected intentional torts against property such as trespass and nuisance.

7-4. Identify selected intentional tort defenses.

7-5. Discuss the impact of product liability on business practice.

7-6. Identify the requirements of a successful negligence claim.

7-7. Differentiate between types of negligence claims emerging from defective products.

7-8. Analyze whether negligence defenses may be successfully asserted in a negligence claim.

7-9. Compare and contrast claims based on express warranties and implied warranties.

7-10. Identify the elements of the strict liability cause of action.

7-11. Identify the defenses available in strict liability cases.

7-12. Evaluate arguments for and against tort reform.

PRACTICING ETHICS   Trampled to Death

Despite his 6'5," 270-pound frame, Jdimytai Damour, 34, was no match for the unruly crowd of an estimated 2,000 Black Friday, 2008, shoppers at a Long Island, New York, Walmart. The crowd, some of whom had been waiting for many hours, pushed against the double glass doors. Damour, a worker of one week hired through a temporary agency, and 6 to 10 other Walmart employees pushed back from the inside, but at 4:55 AM the doors bowed in and the shoppers surged through, crushing Damour to his death and injuring others. Damour had no experience with crowd control and reportedly had not been trained for that purpose. Crowd control barriers were not employed and security personnel reportedly were inside the store rather than being outside to monitor and manage the crowd. Police had been on the scene for 30 minutes at 3 AM, but the crowd of 400 at the time was orderly and the police left. Walmart argued that it had taken appropriate and sufficient safety measures, but authorities subsequently questioned those measures and compared them unfavorably with other retailers' approaches.

Without admitting guilt, Walmart avoided criminal charges by agreeing to pay $400,000 into a victims' compensation fund, along with $1.5 million to local social services causes. Walmart also agreed to build improved holiday crowd management plans for all of its New York stores. (Changes also were to be implemented nationwide on a store-by-store basis.) The federal Occupational Safety and Health Administration (OSHA; see Chapter 12) imposed a $7,000 fine for failing to maintain a safe workplace; Walmart lost its appeal of the OSHA fine. Damour's family sued Nassau County officials and Walmart. To avoid criminal prosecution in Nassau County, Walmart agreed to improve its Black Friday crowd control, donate approximately $1.2 million to local community programs, and create a $400,000 victims' compensation fund.

Questions

1. *a.* Who bears the blame for Damour's death? Explain.
    b. How do we decide where blame lies?
2. *a.* Were the shoppers guilty of criminal behavior? Explain.
    b. Immoral behavior? Explain.
3. Did Walmart fail to fulfill its responsibilities to its employees and customers? Explain.
4. Do you think the OSHA fine and Walmart's donations to community programs, a victims' compensation fund, and improved crowd control plans achieved justice? Explain.

Sources: Steve Greenhouse, "Judge Upholds $7,000 Fine in Trampling at Walmart," *The New York Times,* March 25, 2011 [**www.nytimes.com**]; "Walmart Settles Trampling Case," *The New York Times,* May 6, 2009 [**www.nytimes.com**]; Associated Press, "Wal-Mart Worker Trampled to Death Lacked Training, Attorney Says," Fox News.com, December 1, 2008; Robert D. McFadden and Angela Macropoulos, "Wal-Mart Employee Trampled to Death," *The New York Times,* November 29, 2008; and Associated Press, "Wal-Mart Fights $7,000 Fine in Black Friday Death," *USA TODAY,* July 8, 2010.

Part One—Torts: An Introduction

We have looked at the Walmart Black Friday story as an ethics dilemma. Now we turn to the law that resolves personal injury claims like those asserted against Walmart. From the Damour family's point of view, Walmart's Black Friday promotion and the subsequent crowd stampede involved both torts and crimes. *Torts* are civil wrongs not arising from contracts. Torts involve breaches of duty to particular persons causing loss or injury, while *crimes* are regarded as public wrongs breaching duties to society as a whole (although, of course, they are most commonly directed at a specific person or persons). Crimes are prosecuted by the state; tort actions are initiated by individuals. Criminal law punishes wrongdoers, but the point of tort law is to make whole an injured party. At the same time, many acts can be treated either as a civil wrong (a tort) or as a crime, or both. For example, a physical attack on another can, of course, lead to criminal charges, but it also can produce civil tort claims, most commonly *assault* and *battery.*

The injured party in a tort litigation can seek ***compensatory damages*** to make up for the harm suffered. Those damages may consist of medical expenses, lost income, and pain and suffering, among other possibilities. In some cases, ***punitive damages*** may be awarded to punish the wrongdoer and to discourage others from similar behavior.

Tort Categories

LO 7-1
Compare and contrast the three fundamental kinds of torts: intentional, negligent, and strict liability.

Fundamentally, there are three kinds of torts: (1) intentional, (2) negligent, and (3) strict liability. ***Intentional torts*** involve voluntary acts that harm a protected interest. Intent is established by showing the defendant meant to do the act that caused the harm. The plaintiff need not show that the harm itself was intended. The defendant would be liable for all reasonably foreseeable injuries from that intentional act.

To explain, if you run an advertisement defaming a fast-food competitor by saying its food processing does not meet government standards, but you cannot prove the truth of your allegations, you will probably be guilty of the intentional tort of ***injurious falsehood*** (product disparagement).

Negligence involves situations in which harm is caused accidentally. Intent is absent, but because of one party's carelessness, another has suffered injury. Thus, if one of your employees is making a delivery for the printing business you are managing, and carelessly runs a red light, striking another car, the employee appears to be guilty of negligent conduct for which both she and your firm may be subject to civil damages. Furthermore, you and/or your firm might bear responsibility if, for example, you hired her knowing that she had been a careless driver in the past.

A detailed discussion of negligence law follows in Part Two of this chapter, but for the moment, we should notice that negligence concerns are ubiquitous in our lives, ranging from traffic accidents, to inadequate snow clearance from our sidewalks, to failure to keep dangerous kitchen utensils away from children, to ill-timed golf shots, and on and on. Negligence ordinarily is the core claim for those suffering a personal injury caused by the carelessness of another. Broadly, negligence litigation involves an analysis of when that alleged carelessness amounts to a breach of the "duty of due care." For example, can an injured party properly bring a negligence claim against homeowners when parts of their dismantled but not yet stowed away trampoline blow into the nearby road, causing a passing driver to crash? The Iowa Supreme Court said "yes" because the homeowners had a duty to exercise reasonable care to see that obstructions did not reach the roadway and they breached that duty by creating a foreseeable risk in dismantling the trampoline but failing to secure the parts over the passage of several weeks' time. [For the court's complete negligence analysis, see *Thompson v. Kaczinski,* 774 N.W.2d 829 (Iowa 2009).]

Strict liability is, in essence, a no-fault concept where an individual or organization is responsible for harm without proof of carelessness. Strict liability expands the reach of the law beyond instances where carelessness (negligence) must be established to situations where there is actual proof of the breach of the duty of due care; that is, proof of negligence is not required because the risks inherent in that situation are so great. Strict liability is limited to "unreasonably dangerous" products and practices about which we have decided, as a matter of social policy, that responsibility for injury will automatically attach without establishing blame. Thus, if a product is (1) defective and (2) unreasonably dangerous and someone is hurt, strict (absolute) liability may attach even though fault is not established. Strict liability is explained in the *Gallagher* case below and in greater detail in Part Two of this chapter.

Tort Law

LO 7-2
Describe selected intentional torts against persons including battery, assault, fraud, invasion of privacy, intentional infliction of emotional distress, and defamation.

Selected Intentional Torts Against Persons

Suppose you are a warehouse manager for a plumbing supply business, and a subordinate does a poor job with some work, which in turn brings your boss down on you. In your frustration, you call the subordinate into your office, where you chastise him and then light up a cigar and casually but pointedly blow smoke in his face. Could he file a tort claim against you for your insulting behavior? Let's look at the law in this area. (Of course, many states forbid workplace smoking.)

Battery

Intentionally touching another in a harmful or offensive way without legal justification or the consent of that person is a **battery.** Merely touching another's clothing or touching an occupied car may constitute a battery. Our concern here is with civil wrongs, but perhaps the most interesting recent battery allegation involves a criminal claim. Believing his student, Krista Bowman, was web surfing in class, Professor Frank J. Rybicki of Valdosta State University (Georgia) reportedly asked her to be attentive. Rybicki apparently believed Bowman continued to surf. Bowman claims that Rybicki then closed the laptop on her fingers, injuring one or more of them. Bowman filed a criminal battery charge against Rybicki, who was arrested, but later found not guilty by a jury. [For more details, see Scott Jaschik, "Not Guilty, and Not Long Employed," *Inside Higher Education,* August 25, 2011, at **www.insidehighered.com/news/2011/08/25/jury_rejects_charges_against_professor_in_case_of_student_laptop**].

> Krista Bowman was web surfing in class. Bowman claims Professor Rybicki closed the laptop on her fingers.

Assault

Intentionally causing another to reasonably believe that he or she is about to be the victim of a battery is an ***assault.*** The battery need not occur and the victim need not be frightened, but an assault nonetheless transpires if the victim reasonably anticipated a substantially imminent battery. Thus, raising one's hand as if to strike another even though the blow never transpires constitutes the tort of assault if the victim reasonably thought herself to be in immediate danger.

False Imprisonment

If you have anticipated a career in retailing, you may have given thought to the problem of shoplifters and strategies for preserving your inventory without yourself violating customers' rights. The statutory and common (judge-made) law of most states now protects store managers and owners from ***false imprisonment*** claims if they justifiably detain a suspected shoplifter for a reasonable period and in a reasonable manner. Broadly, false imprisonment occurs when someone is intentionally confined against his or her will; that is, his or her freedom of movement is restricted. That restriction might include being shut in a room, being bound, being threatened, and so on. Even a moment could conceivably constitute imprisonment, although simply sending a customer, for example, through a more distant store exit ordinarily would not meet the test.

Nine Hours on Grounded Plane: False Imprisonment?

Catherine Ray and her husband were flying from Oakland, California, to Dallas, Texas, when the American Airlines plane was rerouted to Austin, Texas, because of bad weather in Dallas. Their flight landed in Austin around noon, refueled, and began to depart, but the weather problems had then closed the Dallas airport. After an hour on the ground, a bus took some passengers to the terminal, but Ray and her husband chose not to deplane because, as Ray later testified, the pilot said the flight would likely resume in about an hour and anyone who left the plane "would be on their own." Ray therefore believed that departing passengers would need to fund their further transportation, which the Rays could not afford. Approximately three hours later, another bus arrived and passengers were told that the bus offered their last chance for departure. The Rays decided to remain on the plane despite apparently deteriorating conditions on the plane, including little food and drink, agitated passengers, and some nonfunctioning lavatories. Subsequently, the pilot announced he could no longer fly because he had reached his maximum duty hours. Lightning in Austin delayed ground crew work, but after another three hours, at 9 PM, the plane was taken to a gate, where Ray and all other passengers deplaned. Some time after deplaning, food and lodging vouchers were provided. Ray and her husband decided to spend the night in the terminal. They flew from Austin the following morning. Ray subsequently filed a civil action for false imprisonment, among other claims. How would you rule on that claim? Explain.

Source: Catherine Ray v. American Airlines, 609 F.3d 917 (8th Cir. 2010).

Fraud

Intentional misrepresentations of facts, sometimes identified by the formal title of *deceit,* can lead to tort claims. We discuss *fraud* in the contracts (Chapter 6) and consumer protection (Chapter 15) chapters. For now, simply note the general test for fraud:

1. A material fact was misrepresented.
2. The misrepresentation was intentional.
3. The injured party justifiably relied on the misrepresentation.
4. Injury resulted.

Father of the Child?

Peters told Dier that he was the father of her baby. Dier paid child support. Through paternity tests, however, he learned he was not the father. Can Dier sue Peters for fraud? What additional facts might you need to know before making a decision? Explain.

Source: See Dier v. Peters, 815 N.W.2d 1 (Iowa 2012).

Defamation

Uttering an untruth about another may constitute a tort. **Slander** is the spoken form of the tort of **defamation. Libel** is defamation in print or some other tangible form such as a picture, movie, or video. Most courts also treat defamatory radio and television statements as forms of libel. The basic test for establishing defamation includes

1. A false statement.
2. Harm to the victim's reputation.
3. Publication of the statement. (The statement must reach someone other than the one being defamed.)

The law's interest here is in protecting reputations. Any living person or any organization can be the victim of defamation, although *public figures* such as politicians or actors face the additional burden of proving **malice** if they are to be successful in a defamation claim. Malice generally requires a showing of actual knowledge of the falsehood or reckless disregard for the truth. Libel or slander about a company's products or property often is treated as the tort of injurious falsehood, which is discussed below.

A one-star review on Yelp led to a lawsuit against the reviewer. In 2011, after contractor Christopher Dietz completed plumbing, painting, and other work on her Fairfax, Virginia, home, Jane Perez posted a scathing review of Dietz's contracting firm on the online review

> A one-star review on Yelp led to a lawsuit against the reviewer.

site Yelp. Perez claimed that her house had been damaged, that she was billed for work not done, and that jewelry had disappeared from her home. Dietz rebutted online that Perez had stolen his goods and services by not paying him and did not allow him to pick up valuable items from her house. Claiming Perez's negative reviews on Yelp as well as on Angie's List (another online review site) caused him to lose business and suffer personally, Dietz filed a defamation lawsuit against Perez seeking $750,000 in damages. At trial, the jury decided that both Dietz and Perez had defamed each other, but neither was awarded damages.[1]

In general, a claim of slander requires a showing of actual harm, such as job loss. Some statements, however, are so inherently damaging that actual injury need not be shown. Those statements are labeled **slander per se** and include allegations of serious sexual misconduct, commission of a serious crime, professional incompetence, or having a loathsome disease. Similarly, libel, leaving a more permanent stain, generally does not require a showing of actual harm.

Truth acts as a complete defense to a defamation claim. Hence, if we tell the truth about others, we cannot be guilty of the tort of defamation, regardless of our evil intentions. Furthermore, many statements are protected because of the circumstances in which they are made. We label these protections either absolute or qualified privileges. An **absolute privilege** to defame includes, for example, remarks by government officials in the course of their duties or by participants in a trial. A **qualified privilege** to defame protects, most notably, former employers providing references for a job applicant. In that instance, the reference will not be treated as defamatory, even though false, unless it was motivated by malice. [For an overview of online defamation law for bloggers, see **www.eff.org/issues/bloggers/legal/liability/defamation**].

Invasion of Privacy

A key ingredient in personal freedom is the right to be left alone. Our courts recognize a right of recovery in tort law when we are the victims of some kind of unconscionable exposure of our private lives. *Invasion of privacy* takes four forms:

1. **Misappropriation of a person's name or likeness.** When an individual's name or image is wrongfully used without permission for commercial purposes (called a *misappropriation*), that person probably has a cause of action for invasion of privacy. Typically, this tort involves a company's use of a celebrity's name or picture to imply that he or she has endorsed a product even though no such approval was secured. A celebrity's name or likeness also may be wrongfully used in the product itself, such as in a video game. In 2013, a federal appeals court ruled that Ryan Hart, former Rutgers University quarterback, could sue Electronic Arts (EA), maker of a college football video game, for allegedly misappropriating his likeness through animation.[2] EA soon settled with Hart and other college athletes with similar claims. Although the settlement's terms are confidential, EA announced it would not release that video game in 2014.[3]

> College athletes claimed EA's college football video game featured their animated likenesses.

2. **Intrusion.** An intentional invasion of a person's solitude is labeled an *intrusion* if it would be highly offensive to a reasonable person. Physical intrusions such as opening an employee's mail or more subtle strategies such as an electronic probe of an employee's bank account are examples of tortious intrusion.

3. **Public disclosure of private facts.** We believe that certain elements of one's life, such as debt payment practices or sexual preferences, are, with rare exceptions, no one else's business. If the disclosure would be highly offensive to a reasonable person, and the subject of the disclosure is not a matter of public importance, the tort of *public disclosure of private facts* might be invoked. In these cases, the truth may not constitute a complete defense.

4. **False light.** When claims are published about another that have the effect of casting the victim in a *false light* in the public mind, a tort claim may emerge. False light claims involve injury to one's mental or emotional well-being rather than one's reputation. Again, the claim would need to be highly offensive to the reasonable person. The courts have struggled to differentiate defamation and false light claims, and we will not pursue the distinction further here.

Locker Rooms

After working out with her husband at the Life Time Fitness gym where they were members late one evening, a pregnant woman took a shower in a private, lockable room in the family locker room. When her husband entered the family locker room to check on her, he discovered an employee crouched in front of one of the private rooms, holding what appeared to be a smartphone under a small gap below the locked door the woman was showering behind. The husband confronted the employee, who claimed that he was "just looking at her feet." The husband informed the front desk. However, the police were not called and the employee, who was later terminated, was allowed to leave with his cellphone.

The couple sued the gym and the former employee, who the gym allegedly refused to identify, alleging, among other things, invasion of privacy and intentional infliction of emotional distress against the employee.

In a second case, Dani Mathers, a former Playboy model, was charged with criminal invasion of privacy after secretly taking a photo of an elderly woman as she changed in the women's locker room at an LA Fitness gym, which she then posted on Twitter with a second photo of herself in mock horror with the caption: "If I can't unsee this, neither can you." Mathers later said she did not intend to post the picture publicly, and knew that "body shaming" is wrong, and pleaded not guilty. LA Fitness banned Mathers permanently from any of its gyms, condemning her actions. The woman photographed came forward and cooperated with the criminal investigation. At this writing, the victim has not brought a civil action based on the incident.

Questions

1. What are the similarities in these two cases? What are the differences? Explain.

2. What tort claims might the woman who was the subject of Dani Mathers' tweet bring against Mathers? Explain.

3. Some states have made taking secret images of another a felony. Should invasion of privacy rise to a crime? Under what circumstances? Explain.

Source: Eric Stomgren, "Lawsuit: Life Time Fitness Employee Allegedly Videotapes Pregnant Woman in Gym Shower," *Club Industry,* March 28, 2016 [**http://clubindustry.com/lifetime-fitness/lawsuit-life-time-fitness-employee-allegedly-videotapes-pregnant-woman-gym-shower**]; and Richard Winton, "Former Playboy Playmate Pleads Not Guilty in Body Shaming Case," *Los Angeles Times,* November 28, 2016 [**www.latimes.com/local/lanow/la-me-ln-playmate-body-shaming-charge-20161128-story.html**].

Intentional Infliction of Emotional Distress

Employment terminations (firings), drug tests, and sexual harassment cases have become particularly fertile grounds for emotional distress claims, although it should be understood that the courts have demanded compelling evidence of *outrageous conduct causing severe emotional pain*. Thus, Mahmoud Abdul-Malik, a ramp agent for AirTran at the Atlanta, Georgia, airport, was unsuccessful in his intentional infliction of emotional distress claim against his employer after he was fired for allegedly threatening to blow up the house of another employee. Abdul-Malik claimed that his distress from being fired caused him to lose sleep and gain weight, but the Georgia Court of Appeals ruled, among other things, that those problems did not rise to the level of severity needed for a successful claim. [For the full case, see *Abdul-Malik v. Airtran Airways,* 678 S.E.2d 555 (2009), *cert denied,* 2009 Ga. LEXIS 711 (Ga. November 2, 2009).]

Selected Intentional Torts Against Property

LO 7-3
Describe selected intentional torts against property such as trespass and nuisance.

We will briefly examine four prominent tort claims arising from wrongs to property.

*Trespass to **real property*** (land and immovable objects attached to it) occurs with the intentional entry onto the land of another without consent. *Trespass to **personal property*** (movable property; all property other than real property) involves an intentional interference with a person's right to enjoy his or her personal property—for example, the manager of a parking lot refuses for a day to return a car to its owner in the mistaken belief that the owner has not paid his monthly bill.

More serious and extensive interference with personal property may be labeled a *conversion.* For example, if the parking lot company kept the car for months, and it suffered damage during the impoundment, a conversion probably occurred.

Injurious falsehood, sometimes called *trade libel,* is a form of defamation that is directed against the property of a person. Thus, falsely claiming that a competitor's product is defective or harmful might constitute injurious falsehood. As with defamation, the statement must be false and it must be published. Damages must result. Often malice/intent also must be shown.

Nuisance is the situation in which enjoyment of one's land is impaired because of some tortious interference. That interference often takes the form of light, noise, smell, or vibration. Here, the owner is not deprived of the land and the land has not been physically invaded, but the full enjoyment of the land cannot be achieved because of the interference. The case that follows involves the owner of a historic Baltimore, Maryland, home who raises both strict liability and nuisance claims in a dispute over alleged damage to her home from nearby pile driving. [For the Jurist Torts Guide, see **http://jurist.law.pitt.edu/sg_torts.htm**].

LEGAL BRIEFCASE

Michela Gallagher v. H.V. Pierhomes, LLC et al.

957 A.2d 628 (Md. Ct. Spec. App. 2008)

Judge Rubin

THE PROCEEDINGS BELOW

On June 14, 2005, Gallagher sued HV Pierhomes LLC and HV Development & Contracting Co. The initial complaint contained claims for negligence, strict liability, and public and private nuisance. On December 21, 2005, Gallagher filed an amended complaint, which abandoned the negligence claim. All of Gallagher's claims for relief arose out of the pile driving operations conducted by the defendants on the site of the former Key Highway Shipyard. Gallagher contended that vibrations from the pile driving damaged her home, located at 423 East Hamburg Street in Baltimore. Key Highway; a row of mixed use properties; Covington Street; a retaining wall; and a solid earthen wall, on which Gallagher's house rests, separate Gallagher's house from the pile driving site.

The Key Highway Shipyard, formerly owned by the Bethlehem Steel Corporation, was used to repair naval (sic) ships during World War II and through the Vietnam War. A shipyard of some sort has operated at this location from the beginning of the 20th century until 1982, when Bethlehem Steel closed the facility.

The defendants demolished the original shipyard piers, which were built 40 to 50 years ago and constructed new piers in the same location, by driving piles into the Baltimore Inner Harbor. The

defendants built 58 townhomes on these new piers. Pile driving was the only method of constructing the new townhomes in this particular location because the U.S. Army Corps of Engineers would not allow the Inner Harbor to be "back filled." The pile driving of which Gallagher complained occurred periodically between September 2003 and October 2004.

The plaintiff's home was constructed shortly before the War of 1812. She testified that no pile driving was conducted in the area during the years she lived in the house, beginning in 1997, until the defendants' activities commenced in September 2003. Previously, pile driving was used to build the Seagirt Marine Terminal, the Dundalk Marine Terminal, as well as the Pratt and Light Street Pavilions, which are located across from the plaintiff's residence in the Inner Harbor.

Before the defendants began their project, permits were received from the U.S. Army Corps of Engineers, the Maryland Department of the Environment, and the City of Baltimore. The permitting process took approximately two years. Pile driving on the site began only after geotechnical studies were conducted by engineering firms. During the course of actual pile driving, two permanent seismic stations and five mobile geophones were placed in the surrounding neighborhood to ensure that vibrations were monitored and did not exceed the limits established by the engineers. During the course of the defendants' activities, there was only a single recorded vibration that exceeded the limits.

The case proceeded to trial on December 15, 2006. The plaintiff testified that she heard and felt vibrations from the pile driving in her home. She further testified that cracks began to develop in her plaster walls and in other portions of her home soon after the pile driving began and that no cracks occurred once the pile driving was completed. She was not aware of any other residents in the area who made claims or filed lawsuits for damage to their homes as a result of the vibrations caused by the defendants' pile driving. No evidence of any other claims or suits on account of pile driving vibrations was presented at trial.

* * * * *

On December 21, 2006, the jury returned a verdict in Gallagher's favor. The jury found that: (1) pile driving caused damage to Gallagher's home, and HV Pierpont and HV Development were responsible for the pile driving; (2) the pile driving created a public nuisance; (3) the pile driving created a private nuisance; and (4) Gallagher suffered damages in the amount of $55,189.14.

After the jury's verdict was announced, the defendants renewed their motions for judgment. . . . By Order entered on August 20, 2007, the circuit court granted the defendants' motion for judgment notwithstanding the verdict [the judge overruled the jury—ed.] on all claims. Gallagher [appealed].

* * * * *

STRICT LIABILITY IN MARYLAND

* * * * *

[The Restatement of Torts,] Section 519, sets forth the general principle upon which courts have held defendants to be liable regardless of fault: "One who carries on an abnormally dangerous activity is subject to liability for harm to the person, land or chattels of another resulting from the activity, although he has exercised the utmost care to prevent the harm."

* * * * *

In summary, Maryland recognizes strict liability, [and] adopts the definition of abnormally dangerous activity as set forth in Section 519 of the Restatement (Second) of Torts (1977). In many, but not all cases, the "thrust of the doctrine is that the activity be abnormally dangerous in relation to the area where it occurs."

STRICT LIABILITY IN PILE DRIVING CASES

The circuit court acknowledged that "whether pile driving is an abnormally dangerous activity has yet to be determined by the Maryland Court of Appeals." The circuit court nevertheless concluded, after applying sections 519 and 520 to the facts of the case, that the Court of Appeals would hold that the pile driving activity in this case would not warrant the application of strict liability.

In the 1984 revision of Dean Prosser's landmark treatise, Professor Page Keaton observed that varying formulations of strict liability have been applied by some courts to hold that pile driving is an abnormally or unreasonably dangerous activity warranting liability without fault. The reasoning of these decisions, as well as the results, is far from uniform. Some courts consider pile driving to be no different than blasting, and therefore dangerous enough to warrant strict liability regardless of the place in which it occurs. Others have taken a more fact-based approach, considering the activity in conjunction with the locale and the type of harm that resulted.

For example, in *Caporale v. C.W. Blakeslee & Sons, Inc.*, 149 Conn. 79, 175 A.2d 561 (1961), the Supreme Court of Connecticut held that pile driving activity during the construction of the Connecticut turnpike in 1958 and 1959, in close proximity to the plaintiff's business premises, warranted the application of strict liability. The Connecticut court analogized pile driving to blasting and aligned itself with those courts that imposed strict liability not only for flying debris but also for the vibrations caused by the explosive force of the blast. The Connecticut court noted, but declined to follow, a line of New York decisions, illustrated by *Fagan v. Pathe Industries, Inc.*, 274 A.D. 703, 86 N.Y.S.2d 859, 863–64 (App. Div., 1st Dept. 1949), that rejected strict liability for pile driving where the damage was caused only by vibrations.

* * * * *

STRICT LIABILITY IN THIS CASE

* * * * *

The appellant argues that pile driving should be considered abnormally dangerous simply because it produces uncontrollable vibrations, similar to blasting. She also asserts that pile driving created an abnormal risk to persons, such as Gallagher, who have historic homes, and that damage resulting from the inevitable emission of vibration cannot be eliminated through the exercise of due care. Although some courts have adopted this view, others have declined to impose strict liability for vibrations resulting from blasting (as opposed to flying debris).

The circuit court, after reviewing the evidence presented at trial, concluded that the defendants' pile driving in the Inner Harbor did not involve a high degree of risk of harm to the person, land or chattels of another, ... We agree. Comment g to section 520 states: "The harm threatened must be major in degree, and sufficiently serious in its possible consequence to justify holding the defendant strictly liable for subjecting others to an unusual risk." The risk of harm proven in this case, relatively minor damage to a 200-year-old home from the vibrations of the pile driving, simply is not a high degree of risk which requires the application of strict liability. . . .

[A] plaintiff must show that the defendants' pile driving was likely to produce significant harm, not simply that she suffered some harm as a result of the pile driving activity.

After considering the factors of section 520 of the Restatement, we agree with the circuit court's conclusion that the pile driving in this case was not an abnormally dangerous activity.

NUISANCE

Gallagher also contends that the defendants' conduct interfered with the use and enjoyment of her land, amounting to a public and private nuisance. The circuit court disagreed, concluding that Gallagher's evidence of a private or public nuisance was insufficient as a matter of law.

Under Maryland law, to sustain a private nuisance claim "there must be a substantial interference with the plaintiff's reasonable use and enjoyment of its property." *Exxon Corp. v. Yarema,* 69 Md. App. 124, 151, 516 A.2d 990 (1986), *cert. denied,* 309 Md. 47, 522 A.2d 392 (1987). In *Yarema,* we held that the defendants' "contamination of ground water imposed crippling restrictions not only on the contaminated land but on all the property adjacent to the land." A private nuisance requires the interference to be "substantial and unreasonable and such as would be offensive or inconvenient to the normal person."

Nothing of that order occurred in this case. The defendants' activity was reasonable in time, place, manner, and duration and did not substantially interfere with Gallagher's use and enjoyment of her land. . . . Residents of Baltimore City must accept the occasional annoyance and discomforts incidental to city life.

The elements of a public nuisance were discussed by the Court of Appeals in *Tadjer v. Montgomery County*. Quoting Dean Prosser, the Court of Appeals said: "To be considered public, the nuisance must affect an interest common to the general public, rather than peculiar to one individual, or several."

* * * * *

The circuit court concluded that the evidence produced at trial was insufficient to prove a public nuisance under these standards. We agree.

Affirmed.

Questions

1. *a.* The plaintiff, Gallagher, brought three causes of action in her amended complaint. List them.

   b. Why do you think the jury ruled in favor of Gallagher?

   c. Why did Gallagher lose at the trial level even though the jury had ruled in her favor?

   d. Explain why the appeals court upheld the judgment against Gallagher.

   e. Who do you think should have won this case? Explain.

2. Rattigan and Horvitz owned a house and prime oceanfront lot in Beverley Farms, Massachusetts. The house was rented during the summer months. Wile owned an adjacent undeveloped oceanfront lot. The only land access to Wile's lot was through the Rattigan/Horvitz lot. Rattigan and Horvitz successfully challenged Wile's application for a building permit and, thereafter, Wile began a series of retaliatory acts, including putting several portable toilets on his lot immediately adjacent to the Horvitz swimming pool; landing his helicopter on his vacant lot; placing debris such as a rusted crane bucket, broken cement, and the bed of a pickup truck on his property; and holding parties (not attended by Wile) for 150 to 200 guests from the local youth shelter. Some of these tactics by Wile were sporadic rather than persistent. Were Rattigan and Horvitz the victims of a nuisance? Explain. See *Rattigan v. Wile,* 841 N.E.2d 680 (Mass. 2006).

Selected Intentional Tort Defenses

LO 7-4

Identify selected intentional tort defenses.

Let's take a brief look at a few of the more significant defenses to the intentional torts that we have been examining.

Consent

Clearly, if you consent to the use of your picture in an advertising campaign and you subsequently feel that your public image has been harmed, you will have difficulty in pursuing a tort claim. Of course, if you gave permission under mistake, fraud, or duress, your consent was not meaningful.

Mistake

As store security manager, you are radioed by a clerk to "stop the guy in the New York Yankees cap" on suspicion of shoplifting. After stopping someone fitting that description, you later discover that someone else, also wearing a Yankees cap, was the actual suspect.

If the store is sued for false imprisonment, can it successfully raise a mistake defense? Unless protected under state law, probably not. Having acted intentionally, you and, by extension, your employer probably will bear responsibility. Of course, false imprisonment does not occur unless the detention was unreasonable.

On the other hand, mistake can be a good defense, particularly in instances in which events happen rapidly. Say, for example, a store's security personnel broke up what looked like an assault and battery in the mall parking lot, only to discover that the incident was merely horsing around by the parties. A mistake defense might be appropriate here.

Necessity

In what we would broadly label emergency situations, one may intentionally commit a tort and yet be excused. A case of public necessity might involve, for example, a person breaking into an unoccupied building late at night because he saw a fire burning inside. An example of a private necessity is when a defendant intrudes on the property of another to save himself only; he might thereafter raise a necessity defense against the tort claim of trespass.

Self-Defense

Suppose your career has taken you into retail management, and you have now decided to buy your own hardware store. You encounter the ups and downs that characterize entrepreneurial life, but you become particularly frustrated by the theft and vandalism that seem so much a part of small business. Finally, in an effort to stop the breaking, entering, and minor theft that has troubled your business, you build a trap in your store. You take up a few floorboards in a rear entryway where vandals have broken in, and you pound nails (points facing up) into those boards. Then you cover the nail points with some soft felt so they are not visible; but when stepped on, the nails will pierce the felt and stab the feet of any intruder. Suppose your trap works, and an intruder is injured. Suppose the intruder then sues you for his injury. Could you cite self-defense of your property as an excuse? What if a police officer stepped on a nail responding to an alarm at your business? The *Katko* case that follows looks at the self-defense theme.

LEGAL BRIEFCASE

Katko v. Briney
183 N.W.2d 657 (Iowa 1971)

FACTS

The Brineys, defendants/appellants in this case, owned an unoccupied farmhouse. During the period from 1957 to 1967, trespassers broke into the house, broke windows, and stole some items. The Brineys boarded windows and erected "no trespassing" signs on the land. On June 11, 1967, the Brineys attached a 20-gauge, loaded shotgun to a bed in the house, pointing the barrel toward the bedroom door. They attached a wire to the trigger and the bedroom doorknob so that the gun would fire if the door were opened. At first, Mr. Briney directed the gun so that it would hit an intruder in the stomach, but agreed with Mrs. Briney's suggestion to lower the barrel so that it would strike an intruder's legs. The gun could not be seen from the outside, and no warning about it was posted.

Katko, the plaintiff/appellee, worked in an Eddyville, Iowa, gas station. He and a friend, McDonough, had found antiques—old bottles and fruit jars—on their first trip to the Briney house, which Katko considered to be abandoned. On their second trip, they entered the house through a window. Katko opened the bedroom door and was shot in the right leg. Much of that leg, including part of the tibia, was blown away. Katko was hospitalized for 40 days. His leg was in a cast for approximately one year, and he was required to wear a brace for an additional year. His leg was permanently shortened by the trauma.

Katko sued the Brineys and secured a jury verdict of $30,000. The Brineys appealed to the Iowa Supreme Court.

* * * * *

Chief Justice Moore

The primary issue presented here is whether an owner may protect personal property in an unoccupied, boarded-up farmhouse against trespassers and thieves by a spring gun capable of inflicting death or serious injury.

We are not here concerned with a man's right to protect his home and members of his family. Defendant's home was several miles from the scene of the incident to which we refer.

* * * * *

Plaintiff testified he knew he had no right to break and enter the house with intent to steal bottles and fruit jars therefrom. He further testified he had entered a plea of guilty to larceny in the nighttime of property of less than $20 value from a private building. He stated he had been fined $50 and costs and paroled during good behavior from a 60-day jail sentence. Other than minor traffic charges this was plaintiff's first brush with the law. . . .

The main thrust of the defendants' defense in the trial court and on this appeal is that "the law permits use of a spring gun in a dwelling or warehouse for the purpose of preventing the unlawful entry of a burglar or thief." . . .

In the statement of issues the trial court stated plaintiff and his companion committed a felony when they broke and entered defendant's house. In instruction 2 the court referred to the early case history of the use of spring guns and stated under the law their use was prohibited except to prevent the commission of felonies of violence and where human life is in danger. The instruction included a statement that breaking and entering is not a felony of violence.

Instruction 5 stated, "You are hereby instructed that one may use reasonable force in the protection of his property, but such right is subject to the qualification that one may not use such means of force as will take human life or inflict great bodily injury. Such is the rule even though the injured party is a trespasser and is in violation of the law himself."

Instruction 6 stated, "An owner of premises is prohibited from willfully or intentionally injuring a trespasser by means of force that either takes life or inflicts great bodily injury; and therefore a person owning a premise is prohibited from setting out 'spring guns' and like dangerous devices which will likely take life or inflict great bodily injury, for the purpose of harming trespassers. The fact that the trespasser may be acting in violation of the law does not change the rule. The only time when such conduct of setting a 'spring gun' or a like dangerous device is justified would be when the trespasser was committing a felony of violence or a felony punishable by death, or where the trespasser was endangering human life by his act." . . .

The overwhelming weight of authority, both textbook and case law, supports the trial court's statement of the applicable principles of law.

Prosser on Torts, Third Edition, pages 116–18, states,

[T]he law has always placed a higher value upon human safety than upon mere rights in property; it is the accepted rule that there is no privilege to use any force calculated to cause death or serious bodily injury to repel the threat to land or chattels, unless there is also such a threat to the defendant's personal safety as to justify a self-defense . . . spring guns and other man-killing devices are not justifiable against a mere trespasser, or even a petty thief. They are privileged only against those upon whom the landowner, if he were present in person, would be free to inflict injury of the same kind.

* * * * *

In *Hooker v. Miller,* 37 Iowa 613, we held defendant vineyard owner liable for damages resulting from a spring gun shot although plaintiff was a trespasser and there to steal grapes. At pages 614, 615, this statement is made: "This court has held that a mere trespass against property other than a dwelling is not a sufficient justification to authorize the use of a deadly weapon by the owner in its defense; and that if death results in such a case it will be murder, though the killing be actually necessary to prevent the trespass. . . ."

In Wisconsin, Oregon, and England the use of spring guns and similar devices is specifically made unlawful by statute.

* * * * *

Affirmed.

Questions

1. Why did the Iowa Supreme Court rule in favor of the criminal intruder, Katko?

2. What classes of people other than intruders are of concern to the courts in cases like *Katko*?

3. Did the Iowa Supreme Court reach a just verdict? Explain.

4. A businessman in Cordele, Georgia, troubled by small thefts from a cigarette machine in front of his store, allegedly booby-trapped the machine after hours with dynamite. A teenager then died when tampering with the machine. What legal action should be taken? Resolve.

Part Two—Product Liability

Introduction

We have examined intentional torts against both persons and property. Now we turn to tort and contract claims arising from products.

How does the law handle the situation where a wheel falls off a car, or a lighter explodes in a consumer's face? Product liability lawsuits deal with cases where buyers, users, and in some cases bystanders are injured or killed by defective products. Those harmed may have causes of action in torts (negligence or strict liability) or contracts (breach of warranty). If so, the manufacturers, distributors, and sellers of that product must then defend themselves against often enormously expensive claims. Part Two of this chapter explains product liability law and raises some of the public policy considerations that have caused critics to call for legal reforms to reduce the burden of product liability lawsuits. [For a product liability overview, see **http://topics.law.cornell.edu/wex/Products_liability**].

LO 7-5
Discuss the impact of product liability on business practice.

Product Liability and Business Practice   When Blitz USA, manufacturer of the familiar red plastic gasoline cans, filed for bankruptcy and shut its Oklahoma factory, *The Wall Street Journal* described Blitz and its employees as the "latest victims" of trial lawyers after spending millions on product liability lawsuits, which, in turn, increased its product liability insurance costs.[4] Plaintiffs in these lawsuits sought damages for serious burn injuries and deaths suffered when Blitz gas cans exploded after gasoline vapors outside the can were ignited. The claims alleged that these "flashback" explosions could have been prevented had "flame arrester" shields been installed in the cans.[5]

Why did Blitz not add the flame arrester to its plastic gasoline cans? Predictably, the answers to that question offered by trial lawyers and Blitz executives vary greatly. According to lawyers responding to *The Wall Street Journal* editorial, these shields were included in Blitz's metal gasoline cans but were removed from their plastic containers, and arguably cost less than $1.00 per can.[6] A lawyer representing plaintiffs against Blitz contended that the company dropped plans to add the arresters to their plastic cans as a money-saving maneuver shortly before being acquired by a private equity firm.[7] Blitz asserted that adding a flame arrester would not have been effective. This defense was successful in a Texas case involving a man who died in an explosion when he poured gasoline from a Blitz can onto a fire; however, a federal judge subsequently ruled that internal documents later uncovered might have eliminated that defense if it had been presented at trial.[8] For example, in 2005, Blitz's then-CEO, Rocky Flick, wrote a 2005 memo, entitled "My Wish List," in which he indicates his desire that Blitz cans would soon include a "device to eliminate flashback from a flame source."[9] Blitz was ordered to pay sanctions and to give the court's opinion and order to each plaintiff who had sued Blitz in the previous two years.[10] Flick countered that Blitz executives believed the flame arresters, if installed, would cause other safety problems, such as creating a false sense of security when pouring gas on an open flame.[11]

Whether you believe that corporate greed or trial lawyers were to blame, Blitz's closure offers a cautionary tale on the importance of anticipating litigation expenses as a part of business strategy. [For a general database on defective products, see **http://consumerlawpage.com/resource/defect.shtml**].

Justice for Auto Consumers

As discussed in Chapter 2, GM faced civil and criminal liability for its defective ignition switches. On the same day as it reached a settlement with the federal government, GM also settled nearly 1,400 civil claims for personal injury and wrongful death arising from the defective ignition switch, with other claims remaining in a consolidated lawsuit in federal court. As we have seen in this chapter, product liability law can sometimes be devastating to a company or industry. As harsh as the consequences may be, the law is often the only recourse for those wronged by defective products, and it is one of the most effective methods of curbing dangerous business practices.

Toyota has faced allegations of causing injuries and deaths due to product defects, including sudden acceleration. The plaintiffs also argued that Toyota failed to disclose what it knew about the acceleration problem, and that Toyota was negligent in failing to install a brake-override system that would automatically release the throttle if the brake is depressed.

In 2013, Toyota settled a class-action lawsuit for financial losses for $1.6 billion. In 2014, Toyota entered into a $1.2 billion settlement with the federal government under which Toyota stated that it had deceived consumers about Toyota vehicles' sudden acceleration.

Questions

1. Could the market alone protect us satisfactorily from dangerous products, or do you think the threat of very costly lawsuits is necessary to force American manufacturers to be fully responsible in monitoring the safety of the products they build? Explain.

2. After a recall of its airbags that affected vehicles made by multiple automakers, Takata, an auto parts supplier, admitted to knowingly deceiving automakers in selling the defective airbags. What questions would you have for those automakers? Explain.

Sources: Jacklyn Trop, "Toyota Seeks a Settlement for Sudden Acceleration Cases," *The New York Times,* December 13, 2013 [**www.nytimes.com**]; Ken Bensinger and Ralph Vartabedian, "Toyota Kept Sudden Acceleration Issue Silent, Lawsuit Says," *latimes.com,* October 29, 2010 [**http://latimes.com/business/la-fi-toyota-suit-20101029,0,5864831.story**]; Ken Bensinger and Ralph Vartabedian, "Toyota Sudden-Acceleration Lawsuits Focus on Lack of Brake Override," *latimes.com,* January 3, 2011 [**http://latimes.com/business/la-fi-toyota-legal-20110104,0,867993.story**]; Mike Ramsey, "U.S. Ends Toyota Probe," *The Wall Street Journal,* February 25, 2011, p. B2; Danielle Douglas and Michael A. Fletcher, "Toyota Reaches $1.2 Billion Settlement to End Probe of Accelerator Problems," *The Washington Post,* March 19, 2014 [**www.washingtonpost.com/business/economy/toyota-reaches-12-billion-settlement-to-end-criminal-probe/2014/03/19/5738a3c4-af69-11e3-9627-c65021d6d572_story.html?utm_term=.1a8c2b797763**]; Jeff Plunges, "What's Happening with the Takata Airbag Recall?" *Consumer Reports,* March 1, 2017 [**www.consumerreports.org/airbags/what-is-happening-with-takata-airbag-recall**]; and Mike Spector, "GM Settles Ignition Switch Lawsuits," *The Wall Street Journal,* September 17, 2015 [**www.wsj.com/articles/gm-settles-ignition-switch-lawsuits-1442499604**].

Negligence

The three major product liability causes of action are negligence, breach of warranty, and strict liability. In dangerously simplified terms, negligence is a breach of the duty of due care. A negligent act is the failure to do what a reasonable person would do or doing what a reasonable person would not do. Thus, a producer or distributor has a duty to exercise reasonable care in the entire stream of events associated with the development and sale of a product. In designing, manufacturing, testing, repairing, and warning of potential dangers, those in the chain of production and distribution must meet the standard of the reasonably prudent person. Failure to do so constitutes negligence. Some decisions also extend potential liability to situations in which a product is being put to an unintended but reasonably foreseeable *misuse*.

Historically, consumers dealt face-to-face with producers and could bring breach of contract claims if injured by a defective product. However, the development in the modern era of multilayered production and distribution systems eliminated that contractual relationship between producer and consumer, making it difficult for consumers to sue producers. Then, in a famous 1916 decision (*McPherson v. Buick Motor Co.*),[12] the New York high court ruled that a consumer could bring a negligence claim against the manufacturer of a defective automobile even though the consumer did not purchase the car directly from that manufacturer. That view has since been broadly adopted, thus permitting victims of negligence to bring actions against all careless parties in the chain of production and distribution.

Donald Trump Owes a Duty?

In 1996, Mark Merrill entered a clinic for compulsive gamblers and wrote to Trump Indiana, a casino in Gary, Indiana, asking that he be evicted if he ever entered to gamble. Merrill's name appeared on Trump Indiana's casino "eviction list." Nonetheless, Merrill later gambled at the casino, suffering substantial losses. In December 1998 and January 1999, Merrill robbed banks, apparently to cover his gambling losses. He was convicted of bank robbery, but while in prison he filed suit claiming Trump Indiana was negligent in failing to keep him from gambling at the casino. Rule on Merrill's negligence claim. Explain. The four-part negligence test that follows will help you resolve Merrill's claim.

Source: Mark Merrill v. Trump Indiana, Inc., 320 F.3d 729 (7th Cir. 2003).

Negligence Test

LO 7-6
Identify the requirements of a successful negligence claim.

To establish a successful negligence claim, the plaintiff must meet each of the following requirements:

1. **Duty.** The plaintiff must establish that the defendant owed a duty of due care to the plaintiff. In general, the standard applied is that of the fictitious reasonable man or woman. That *reasonable person* acts prudently, sensibly, and responsibly. The standard of reasonableness depends, of course, on the circumstances of the situation.

2. **Breach of duty.** The plaintiff must demonstrate that the defendant breached the duty of due care by engaging in conduct that did not conform to the reasonable person standard. Breach of the duty of due care may result from either the commission of a careless act or the omission of a reasonable, prudent act. Would a reasonable man or woman discharge a firearm in a public park? Would a reasonable person foresee that failure to illuminate one's front entry steps might lead to a broken bone? More formally, we might think of reasonable behavior as decision making that weighs the costs and benefits of acting or not acting. The reasonable person "takes precautions against harms when doing so costs less than the discounted value of the harms risked."[13]

3. **Causation**
   a. **Actual cause.** Did the defendant's breach of the duty of due care in fact cause the harm in question? Commonly, the "but for" test is applied to determine cause in fact. For example, but for the defendant's failure to stop at the red light, the plaintiff pedestrian would not have been struck down in the crosswalk.
   b. **Proximate cause.** The plaintiff must establish that the defendant's actions were the *proximate cause* of the injury. As a matter of policy, is the defendant's conduct sufficiently connected to the plaintiff's injury as to justify imposing liability? Many injuries arise from a series of events—some of them wildly improbable. Did the defendant's negligence lead directly to the plaintiff's harm, or did some intervening act break the causal link between the defendant's negligence and the harm? For example, the community's allegedly negligent maintenance resulted in a blocked road, forcing the plaintiff to detour. While on the detour route, the plaintiff's vehicle was struck by a plane that fell from the sky when attempting to land at a nearby airport. Was the community's negligence the proximate cause of the plaintiff's injury?[14]

4. **Injury.** The plaintiff must have sustained injury, and, due to problems of proof, that injury often must be physical. [For a tort law library, see **www.findlaw.com/01topics/22tort**].

The case that follows asks whether a bowling alley is liable for a patron's injuries resulting from an altercation on its premises.

LEGAL BRIEFCASE

Hoyt v. Gutterz Bowl & Lounge
829 N.W.2d 772 (Iowa 2013)

Justice Hecht

Defendant-appellee Gutterz Bowl & Lounge (Gutterz) is a bowling alley and tavern located in Guthrie Center, Iowa. On March 20, 2009, Curtis Hoyt and several members of his construction crew finished work and went to Gutterz for refreshments. Curtis Knapp was also a customer at Gutterz that afternoon. Hoyt soon came to believe that Knapp was scowling at him. Hoyt and Knapp had formerly been friendly, but tension had arisen between them as a result of Hoyt's alleged mistreatment of the sister of Knapp's friend.

* * * * *

[T]he staff of Gutterz had [no] knowledge of this history between Hoyt and Knapp.

After consuming a few beers, Hoyt and coworker Chris Brittain approached and verbally confronted Knapp. Knapp did not respond and continued to scowl at Hoyt. The waitress serving Hoyt and Brittain observed their behavior with concern and threatened to discontinue serving them unless they calmed down. Hoyt and Brittain ignored the waitress's warning, and thus she requested and secured

permission from Gutterz's owner, Rodney Atkinson, to discontinue serving them. Atkinson, who had been preparing food in the kitchen, went to the bar area to assess the situation. Hoyt and Brittain complained to Atkinson that they were no longer being served and continued to taunt Knapp.

Shortly thereafter, Atkinson grew concerned that an altercation might occur. He requested that Hoyt and Brittain leave.

* * * * *

Hoyt finished his beer and exited the tavern. As Hoyt walked through the parking lot toward his vehicle, [Knapp] . . . struck him in the back of the head, knocking him unconscious. Hoyt suffered several injuries including a compound fracture of his ankle. Knapp admitted to police who later arrived on the scene that he had struck Hoyt, but claimed he had done so in self-defense.

* * * * *

Hoyt filed this action alleging that Knapp and Gutterz were liable for the injuries he sustained when Knapp assaulted him. Gutterz moved for summary judgment, alleging Gutterz owed Hoyt no duty of reasonable care, there was no evidence of a breach of any duty, and the assault by Knapp and Hoyt's injury were not foreseeable. The district court granted Gutterz's motion for summary judgment and dismissed Gutterz from the lawsuit.

* * * * *

The court of appeals reversed the district court's summary judgment ruling.

* * * * *

III. DISCUSSION

Hoyt contends the district court erred in concluding as a matter of law that Gutterz did not breach a duty of reasonable care under these circumstances. Further, Hoyt contends, the district court erred in its consideration of foreseeability of injury to Hoyt in making its summary judgment ruling.

* * * * *

A. Duty

[T]he determination of whether a duty is owed under particular circumstances is a matter of law for the court's determination.

* * * * *

Traditionally . . . a property owner "is ordinarily under no duty to exercise any care until he knows or has reason to know that the acts of the third person are occurring, or are about to occur."

* * * * *

That general proposition was subject to the caveat that a duty would be imposed in scenarios where the property owner knew or had reason to know of a likelihood of third party conduct that could endanger visitors or where the place or character of the business was such that the property owner should reasonably anticipate careless or criminal conduct by third parties.

* * * * *

Recently . . . we examined a scenario in which the trampoline of a landowner had been blown by high winds into a nearby roadway, obstructing the travel of and causing injury to a driver. . . . We questioned and then rejected an assessment of foreseeability of risk in determining whether the landowner owed the driver a duty.

* * * * *

Instead . . . no-duty rulings should be limited to exceptional cases in which "an articulated countervailing principle or policy warrants denying or limiting liability in a particular class of cases."

* * * * *

Removing foreseeability from the duty analysis, we must consider whether some principle or strong policy consideration justifies exempting Gutterz, or the class of tavern owners in general, from the duty to exercise reasonable care. . . . [W]e cannot discern . . . any such considerations compelling exemption of tavern owners from the duty.

* * * * *

Accordingly, we conclude Gutterz owed Hoyt a duty of reasonable care under the circumstances presented here. We now turn to the question of whether Hoyt raised a genuine issue of material fact regarding the alleged breach of this duty.

B. Reasonable Care

* * * * *

While taverns are not insurers of patrons' safety against third-person criminal attacks, various jurisdictions have explained taverns must make reasonable efforts to maintain order and supervise and control patrons.

* * * * *

That a tavern may create a physical environment where instances of misconduct are likely to take place raises converging questions of reasonable care and the appropriate scope of liability for the defendant. . . . In a tavern, for example, the environment may foreseeably bring about the misconduct of a third party, resulting in injury to a plaintiff. While the foreseeability of misconduct raises an issue of the appropriate level of care, it also raises the issue of whether the harm suffered by the plaintiff is within the range of risks that may make the defendant's conduct negligent in failing to exercise that care.

* * * * *

Here, the district court found that Gutterz exercised reasonable care as a matter of law, based largely on the notion that the information available to Gutterz at the time failed to suggest any possibility of harm to Hoyt.

* * * * *

[W]e disagree that the record established as a matter of law that an injury to Hoyt was unforeseeable. Gutterz's duty of reasonable care applied . . . to risks arising from Hoyt's conduct, as well as those created by a third party's conduct, whether innocent, negligent, or intentional.

* * * * *

[B]ars are business venues in which alcohol-fueled disturbances causing injury and even death are known to occur.

* * * * *

Given the . . . general tenor of bar behavior, and Atkinson's own testimony regarding concern about a physical altercation, we conclude that a reasonable person might find the risk of harm to Hoyt foreseeable. Accordingly, that Hoyt may have initiated the conflict cannot serve as the basis for summary judgment that Gutterz acted reasonably under the circumstances.

* * * * *

Hoyt contends that Gutterz could have exercised reasonable care by any of the following: (1) calling the police when the conflict developed, (2) escorting Hoyt to his vehicle in the parking lot, or (3) verifying that Knapp was not lying in wait in the parking lot. Gutterz contends that it did escort Hoyt to his vehicle, and that its precautions here were reasonable as a matter of law. . . . [R]esolution of the factual dispute is best left to the fact finder. . . .

* * * * *

[Reversed]

DISSENT

WATERMAN, Justice, joined by Cady, C. J., and Mansfield, J.

I respectfully dissent. . . . Uncontroverted facts establish the defendant acted reasonably as a matter of law.

There is no evidence or claim that prior fights or third-party criminal acts showed a need for a bouncer or other security at Gutterz. Bars are not insurers strictly liable for injuries on their premises inflicted by others.

* * * * *

Having kicked out the troublemakers—Hoyt and his companion—what else should Gutterz have done? How was the bar negligent? The majority concludes a jury could find Gutterz negligent for failing to call the police. But, no crime had (yet) been committed, and Hoyt exited the bar when told to leave. Knapp was not threatening anyone or misbehaving in any way. At that point, why call the police? From Gutterz's standpoint, the incident had been defused by Hoyt's departure. The majority also argues Atkinson should have done more to ensure Hoyt left the parking lot safely. This theory assumes Atkinson reasonably should have foreseen *Knapp* would attack Hoyt. Knapp had not so much as even raised his voice.

* * * * *

I would affirm the district court's summary judgment in favor of Gutterz.

Questions

1. Why did the Iowa Supreme Court conclude that Gutterz owed a duty of reasonable care to Hoyt? According to the court, when would a landowner not owe a duty of reasonable care to a plaintiff? Describe a scenario in which a landowner would not owe such a duty to an injured party.

2. Why should Hoyt, who initiated the conflict with Knapp in the Gutterz bar area, be able to recover from Gutterz for his resulting injuries? Explain.

3. Both the majority and dissenting opinions offer that taverns are not ensurers of safety of their patrons against injury caused by third parties. On what point does the dissenting opinion disagree with the majority? Do you agree with the majority or dissenting opinion? Explain.

4. Spuds, a restaurant in a college town that does not serve alcohol but is located near several other establishments that do, advertised itself on Facebook as a place to go after a night of drinking. For example, one post read: "Don't forget to come get some Spuds after dollar drinks tonight. We are open until 3 AM!" One late night during Homecoming weekend, a man visiting Spuds was subjected to abusive conduct by other Spuds patrons, and was physically assaulted two doors down from Spuds, suffering a traumatic brain injury and permanent damage to his right eye. He sued Spuds for his injuries. Should Spuds be held liable? Decide. Explain. See *Paynton v. Spuds,* 2014 U.S. Dist. LEXIS 92988 (E.D. Pa. July 9, 2014).

5. Johnny Burnett, described by his mother, Sheila Watters, as a devoted "Dungeons & Dragons" player, killed himself. (The record did not disclose his age at the time of death.) Watters blamed the death on her son's absorption in the game. She claimed that "he lost control of his own independent will and was driven to self-destruction."

   "Dungeons & Dragons" is an adventure game set in an imaginary ancient world; the players assume the roles of various characters as suggested by illustrated booklets. The play is orchestrated by a player labeled the "Dungeon Master." The outcome of the play is determined by using dice in conjunction with tables provided with the game. The game's materials do not mention suicide or guns. More than 1 million copies of the game have been sold, many to schools, where it is used as a learning tool.

   In federal district court, Watters brought a wrongful death claim against TSR, the manufacturer of "Dungeons & Dragons." The plaintiff's complaint alleged that TSR violated its duty of care in two ways: It disseminated "Dungeons & Dragons" literature to "mentally fragile persons" and it failed to warn that the "possible consequences" of playing the game might include "loss of control of the mental processes." Decide. Explain. See *Watters v. TSR, Inc.,* 904 F.2d 378 (6th Cir. 1990).

6. Plaintiff was seven months pregnant and the mother of 17-month-old James. She was standing on the sidewalk, and James was in the street. A truck being negligently driven bore down on the boy, running him over. The shock caused the mother to miscarry and suffer actual physical and emotional injury. She brought suit against the driver for harm to herself and the infant child.
   a. What is the issue in this case?
   b. Decide the case. Explain. See *Amaya v. Home Ice, Fuel & Supply Co.,* 379 P.2d 513 (Cal. 1963). But also see *Dillon v. Legg,* 441 P.2d 912 (Cal. 1968).

7. Is a fireworks manufacturer liable for harm to children who ignited an explosive that had failed to detonate in the town public display the previous day? Explain.

8. An individual took his car to Quality Pontiac in Albuquerque, New Mexico, for repairs and was told to leave the car unlocked with the keys in the ignition. The lot was fenced, but the gate

was unlocked. Billy Garcia entered the car lot at 9 PM, apparently looking in the cars for something to steal. Garcia stole the individual's car. The next day at approximately 11 AM, a deputy sheriff observed Garcia driving quickly through a school zone and pursued him, engaging his sirens and emergency lights. Garcia sped the car up to 90 miles an hour and collided with Herrera's car, killing one occupant and seriously injuring the other; Herrera and others sued Quality Pontiac. The complaint included an affidavit of a sociologist asserting that Albuquerque's car theft rate was the second highest in the United States and that a significant portion of cars stolen had been left unlocked and with keys in the ignition. Further, stolen cars were highly likely to be involved in joy riding, and nearly 17 percent of stolen cars were involved in accidents shortly after the theft. Should Quality Pontiac be held liable? Explain. See *Herrera et al. v. Quality Pontiac,* 73 P.3d 181 (N.M. 2003).

Classes of Negligence Claims

LO 7-7

Differentiate between types of negligence claims emerging from defective products.

Negligence claims emerging from defective products fall into three categories of analysis: (1) manufacturing defects, (2) design defects, and (3) inadequate warnings.

Manufacturing Defects

McDonald's sells a billion cups of coffee each year, in part because its coffee is extremely hot—180 to 190 degrees—which is exactly what its customers prefer and which, McDonald's believes, produces tastier coffee than the 140 to 145 degrees normally achieved at home. In 1992, then 79-year-old Stella Liebeck ordered coffee at an Albuquerque, New Mexico, McDonald's drive-through. Her grandson, who was driving, pulled forward and stopped so that Liebeck could add cream and sugar to her coffee. The dashboard of the car was slanted so that the coffee could not be set on it. Liebeck, therefore, placed the coffee between her legs, and while trying to get the top off the container, she spilled the coffee on her lap, resulting in third-degree burns. She was hospitalized, required skin grafts, and was disabled for two years. She sought a settlement with McDonald's, but according to her family, McDonald's offered only $800.[15] Liebeck sued, accusing McDonald's of gross negligence for selling coffee that was "unreasonably dangerous" and "defectively manufactured."[16]

Liebeck was awarded $200,000 in compensatory and $2.7 million in punitive damages. The jury found Liebeck 20 percent responsible for her own injury, thus reducing her compensatory award to $160,000. The judge subsequently reduced the punitive award to $480,000. The parties then settled out of court for an undisclosed amount. According to news reports, the jury awarded Liebeck $2.7 million in punitive damages because of what it perceived to be McDonald's callous attitude toward the accident and because of the more than 700 previous coffee-burn claims that had been filed against McDonald's. A McDonald's human factors engineer testified that the number of hot coffee burns was "statistically insignificant" when compared with the billions of cups sold by McDonald's annually.[17] [For the "actual facts" on the Liebeck/McDonald's episode, see **www.lectlaw.com/files/cur78.htm**].

> The number of hot coffee burns was "statistically insignificant."

[For the *Hot Coffee* trailer, see **http://hotcoffeethemovie.com**].

A British High Court justice, however, viewed the hot coffee situation quite differently:

Persons generally expect tea or coffee purchased to be consumed on the premises to be hot. . . . They accordingly know that care must be taken to avoid such spills.[18]

The case that follows involves an injury from hot food.

Jimenez v. Applebee's

2015 N.J. Super. Unpub. LEXIS 430

(N.J. Super. Ct. App. Div. March 4, 2015)

LEGAL BRIEFCASE

PER CURIAM

Plaintiff Hiram Jimenez appeals from an order entered by the Law Division on December 6, 2013, granting summary judgment in favor of defendants. We affirm.

This appeal arises from the following facts. On March 4, 2010, plaintiff met his brother Rafael at an Applebee's Neighborhood Grill ("Applebee's") in Westampton, New Jersey. After they were seated in a booth, plaintiff and his brother ordered their meals. Plaintiff ordered a steak fajita. He spoke with Rafael until a waitress brought the food to their table. According to plaintiff, his meal was served in a "sizzling skillet," which the waitress placed "right in front of [him]."

Plaintiff described the dish as "real dark," smoking, sizzling and "real hot." According to plaintiff, the waitress did not say anything when she served the food, other than to "enjoy your meal." After the waitress walked away, Rafael "reached over and said let's have prayer." Plaintiff bowed his head "[c]lose to the table." Plaintiff said he heard a loud, sizzling noise, followed by "a pop noise," and then felt a burning sensation in his left eye and on his face.

Plaintiff panicked, knocked his plate onto his lap and caused his prescription eyeglasses to fall from his face. Plaintiff said he tried to push away from the table with his right arm. He used his left arm to brush the food from his lap. He soon felt that he had "pulled" something in his right arm. He stopped applying pressure to the table, "let [his] [right] hand go because [he] felt pain," and "banged" his elbow on the table.

Rafael called for help and the restaurant's employees came to assist. A manager eventually provided Rafael with an incident report form. The description of the incident contained on the report is as follows: "[H]ot food order[] burned me after grease popped causing several burns to face, neck, and arms." According to plaintiff's deposition testimony, the alleged burns left no scarring.

Plaintiff thereafter filed a complaint in the trial court against defendants, alleging that defendants owned, possessed, controlled, managed, operated or supervised Applebee's. Plaintiff alleged that, on March 4, 2010, while a business invitee at Applebee's, he was injured solely as a result of defendants' negligence when he came in contact with a dangerous and hazardous condition, specifically, "a plate of hot food." Plaintiff claimed he sustained serious and permanent personal injuries for which he sought damages. Defendants filed an answer denying liability and demanding judgment dismissing the complaint.

After the completion of discovery, defendants filed a motion for summary judgment. Defendants argued that, even if plaintiff established the existence of a dangerous or hazardous condition, they were entitled to judgment as a matter of law because the condition was open, obvious and easily understood. Defendants further argued that they were entitled to summary judgment because plaintiff had not established that his damages were proximately caused by their acts or omissions. Plaintiff opposed the motion.

The motion judge . . . determined that defendants had a duty to provide their patrons with reasonably safe premises, but had no duty to warn against a danger that is open and obvious. The judge found that defendants did not breach any duty owed to plaintiff.

The judge noted that there was no dispute as to the fact that plaintiff had been served a platter of food which was sizzling, or that plaintiff opted to place his face close to the food. The judge determined that plaintiff was injured because of the actions plaintiff took with regard to a hazard that was "open and obvious." The judge concluded that defendants were entitled to summary judgment.

* * * * *

On appeal, plaintiff argues that: (1) the trial court erred by finding as a matter of law that defendants did not owe him a duty; (2) the trial court erroneously assumed that plaintiff placed his face within inches of the sizzling platter and issues involving the manner in which the subject incident occurred should have been reserved for the jury; and (3) the court made an erroneous finding as to the existence and extent of plaintiff's comparative negligence which was an issue for the jury.

The trial court may grant summary judgment when there are no genuine issues of material fact, and the moving party is entitled to judgment as a matter of law. . . .

Plaintiff argues that the motion judge erred by finding that defendants owed no duty to warn defendant of the danger posed by the sizzling plate of food that had been served to him.

There are three elements to a cause of action for negligence: "(1) a duty of care owed by defendant to plaintiff; (2) a breach of that duty by defendant; and (3) an injury to plaintiff proximately caused by defendant's breach." . . .

A business owner owes its invitees "a duty of reasonable or due care to provide a safe environment for doing that which is within the scope of the invitation." "Th[is] duty of due care requires a business owner to discover and eliminate dangerous conditions, to maintain the premises in safe condition, and to avoid creating conditions that would render the premises unsafe."

Here, plaintiff does not allege that there was any dangerous condition on defendants' premises. He claims, however, that the "sizzling fajita platter" created a danger to him, and argues that the motion judge erred by finding that defendants owed him no duty to warn him of the danger.

In determining whether a person owes another a duty of reasonable care, the court considers "the foreseeability of the risk of injury." The determination of whether such a duty exists also "'involves identifying, weighing, and balancing several factors—the relationship of the parties, the nature of the attendant risk, the opportunity and ability to exercise care, and the public interest in the proposed solution.'"

Here, the risk of injury was foreseeable since the plate of food, as described by plaintiff, was sizzling, smoking and "real hot." The relationship of the parties was that of business owner and invitee. Moreover, once the platter was served, defendants had no control over it, and plaintiff had the opportunity and ability to act to protect himself from any danger that it posed, since the danger was open and obvious. We conclude that, balancing these factors, imposition of a duty upon defendants to warn plaintiff of the danger presented by the sizzling hot platter is not required as a matter of fairness and sound policy.

The decision in *Tighe v. Peterson,* 175 N.J. 240 (2002), supports this conclusion. There, the plaintiff injured himself while diving in the sloped bottom of the shallow end of the defendants' in-ground swimming pool. The plaintiff was the defendants' brother-in-law and he had used the defendants' pool about twenty times before the accident. The plaintiff acknowledged that he was aware of where the shallow and deep sections of the pool were situated.

The Supreme Court noted that a social host has a duty to warn a guest "of a known dangerous condition on the premises except when the guest is aware of the condition or by reasonable use of the facilities would observe it." The Court held that the defendants did not have to warn the plaintiff "where the shallow part of the pool was situated and where the shallow end began its slope downward toward the deepest portion of" the pool.

The Court stated that, "[i]t defies notions of reasonableness to regard plaintiff as being unaware of the slope of the pool bottom, or to conclude he could not reasonably have detected it from his use of the pool that day and on the many occasions before." There also was no evidence that the defendants "encouraged a dangerous use of th[e] pool." Under the circumstances, the defendants had no duty to warn the plaintiff.

* * * * *

Although . . . *Tighe* . . . involved the duty that a social host owes to a guest, the principles set forth in [that case] also appl[ies] to determining whether, under the circumstances presented, a business owner owes a duty to warn a patron of a dangerous condition that is open and obvious. Here, the danger posed by a plate of sizzling hot food was self-evident. Therefore, we conclude that the motion judge correctly determined that defendants had no duty to warn plaintiff that the food was sizzling hot and should be approached with due care.

* * * * *

Here, the motion judge determined that plaintiff's negligence claim failed as a matter of law because defendant owed plaintiff no duty to warn him regarding the self-evident danger posed by the sizzling plate of food. In view of that determination, the judge had no reason to make any decision as to plaintiff's comparative negligence.

* * * * *

We conclude that the motion judge correctly determined that there was no genuine issue of material fact and defendants were entitled to judgment as a matter of law.
Affirmed.

Questions

1. Why did the appellate court affirm the trial court's decision to grant Applebee's summary judgment? Explain.

2. The appellate court used a state supreme court decision regarding social hosts' liability as precedent. Why did the appellate court view that case as relevant to a restaurant's liability to its customer? Explain.

3. Hollister was badly burned when her shirt came into contact with a burner as she leaned over her electric stove. She sued the store where she bought the shirt, claiming that it was defectively designed. How is this case different from *Jimenez v. Applebee's?* How is it similar? Explain. See *Hollister v. Dayton-Hudson,* 188 F.3d 414 (6th Cir. 1999).

4. Sutton bought a McDonald's fried chicken sandwich at a truck stop. When he bit into the sandwich, Sutton said, "the grease from the inside of the chicken sandwich spread out all over my bottom lip, my top lip, down onto my chin." Sutton immediately dropped the sandwich. His wife dabbed his face with ice as blisters formed on his lips. Sutton reported the incident to a pair of McDonald's employees, one of whom reportedly said, "This is what happens to the sandwiches when they aren't drained completely." Sutton's lips continued to bother him. He went to a doctor, who provided lip balm and told Sutton to avoid excessive exposure to sunlight. Sutton thereafter sued McDonald's and the local franchise owner for negligence, among other claims. How is this case different from *Jimenez v. Applebee's?* How is it similar? Should McDonald's and the franchise owner be held liable for Sutton's injuries? Decide. Explain. See *Sutton v. Roth,* 361 F. App'x 543 (4th Cir. 2010) (unpublished op).

Res Ipsa

As we see with the McDonald's and Applebee's cases, allegedly improper manufacturing of products often generates negligence claims. However, the extremely complex process of producing, distributing, and using a product sometimes so obscures the root of the injury in question that proof of fault is nearly impossible to establish. In those circumstances, many courts have adopted the doctrine of ***res ipsa loquitur*** (the thing speaks for itself), which in some cases permits the court to infer the defendant's negligence even though that negligence cannot be proved—that is, the facts suggest that the plaintiff's injury must have resulted from the defendant's negligence, but the circumstances are such that the plaintiff is unable to prove negligence. A showing of res ipsa loquitur requires that (1) the injury was caused by an instrumentality under the control of the defendant, (2) the accident ordinarily would not happen absent the defendant's negligence, and (3) there is no evidence of other causes for the accident.[19]

Design Defects

From Cessna's single-engine airplanes to five-gallon buckets (which may hold liquid sufficient to drown a child) to automobile seat belts and on across the spectrum of American products, manufacturers must think about designing products to anticipate and avoid consumer injury. Two principal lines of analysis have emerged in these cases: (1) The ***risk–utility test*** holds that a product is negligently designed if the benefits of a product's design are outweighed by the risks that accompany that design. (2) The *consumer expectations test* imposes on the manufacturer a duty to design its products so that they are safe not only for their intended use but also for any reasonably foreseeable use.

The *Restatement of the Law Third, Torts: Products Liability,* which is published by the American Law Institute (ALI), a group of legal experts, does not constitute law but represents those experts' best judgment about what the law should be. The ALI has recommended to the courts a design defect standard that supports the balancing/risk–utility model and gives much less attention to consumer expectations. Furthermore, a product would be considered defective in design only if its foreseeable risks could have been reduced or avoided by a reasonable alternative design and if failure to include that design makes the product not reasonably safe. That is, plaintiffs would need to show that some better design was available and was not incorporated in the product in question.[20]

Warnings

Warnings seem to be everywhere in our lives. Some of them seem downright silly—so much so that the Foundation for Fair Civil Justice [**www.foundationforfairciviljustice.org/**] hosts a "Wacky Warning Labels" contest. Leading recent entries included these:

> "Remove child before folding"—on a child car safety seat!
> "Harmful if swallowed"—a warning on a brass fishing lure with a three-pronged hook.[21]

Even though the use of warnings can be abused, we should remember that they help protect us from foreseeable dangers. For example, in 2007, the federal Consumer Product Safety Commission (see Chapter 15) ordered warnings on all new generators and generator packaging after recording 220 deaths from generator-related carbon monoxide poisoning over three years.[22]

A product may be considered defective because of inadequate warnings when reasonable warnings would have reduced or avoided the foreseeable risks and the failure to warn resulted in a product that was not reasonably safe. Courts also might consider the feasibility of an effective warning and the probable seriousness of the injury. The case that follows raises a failure-to-warn product liability claim.

LEGAL BRIEFCASE

White v. Victor Automotive Products   2010 Mich. App. LEXIS 914
(May 18, 2010) (unpublished op.)

Per Curiam (Judges Michael J. Kelly and Douglas B. Shapiro)

I. Summary of Facts and Proceedings

Plaintiff's decedent, Craig White, purchased a muffler repair kit manufactured and marketed by defendants. The kit included a metal patch to be placed over the hole in the muffler, a strip of "bandage" to be wrapped around the patch and the muffler to hold the patch in place, and mechanic's wire to wrap around and secure the bandage. The packaging described the product as a "Muffler and Tail Pipe Repair Kit" and stated, "Just wrap it on for instant repair." The instructions included with the kit, however, directed the user to "start the engine and run at idle for at least 10 minutes" after applying the "bandage." The instructions provided with the kit read in total:

INSTRUCTIONS:

1. Allow exhaust system and muffler to cool to a touch.
2. Clean surface of muffler or pipe to be repaired with sand paper, steel wool, or wire brush.
3. Cover holes with included metal heat shield, or by using metal or tin can.
4. Open foil packet containing bandage.
5. Wrap bandage completely around damaged area, overlapping each wrapping at least 3/4 inch. Note: Large repairs may require more than one bandage to adequately cover repair.
6. Secure bandage with mechanic's wire enclosed.
7. Start engine and run at idle for at least 10 minutes.
8. Bandage will cure with heat from exhaust system.

WARNING: Always wear safety classes and cloth or leather gloves when working on exhaust systems. Rust and debris can injure eyes and skin. Flush eyes thoroughly with water if contacted—for skin use soap and water. Never work on vehicle suspended in air NOT supported by adequate jack stands.
IF SWALLOWED, DRINK WATER AND GET IMMEDIATE MEDICAL ATTENTION. [Emphasis in original.]

White attempted to perform the muffler repair on April 29, 2005. According to the testimony of White's wife and son, when they left the house at about 11:00 A.M., White was in the driveway, working on the muffler. When they returned at about 2:15 P.M., they found White dead in the garage with the car up on a floor jack, the motor running and the garage door closed.[1] Tools were under the car and the bandage was found wrapped around the muffler. White was found near the exit to the garage. The police report stated in pertinent part:

> In the garage I observed the Buick to be elevated on a jack stand. Underneath the Buick I observed a small, rolling platform, that is used to enable a subject to crawl underneath a vehicle and assist with mobility while working on the vehicle. I further observed an activated utility light as well as several tools and accessories lying on the floor. On the rear trunk area of the Buick, I observed an empty package that contained a muffler repair kit. By looking at the picture on the muffler repair kit, and observing the muffler underneath the Buick, it was apparent that the victim had in fact used the kit as its contents were on the muffler.
>
> When Detective Steinaway arrived, I assisted in his investigation. During the investigation, I collected the empty package from the Buick to be placed as evidence at LCSD. While reading instructions listed on the back of the package, *it appeared as though the victim went step by step with the*

---

[1] The reason why White moved from the driveway into his garage remains unknown.

directions. The final instruction on these directions was to turn on the automobile and allow it to run for approximately ten minutes, which would in turn allow the bonding agent applied to the muffler to heat up and activate properly. This could be a possible explanation for why the vehicle's ignition was activated and running. *While reading the warning label on the package listed directly below the instructions, it did not advise of the dangers of carbon monoxide.* [Emphasis added.]

An autopsy confirmed that White died of asphyxiation from carbon monoxide.

Plaintiff's complaint alleged two violations of the duty to warn. First, plaintiff alleged that "Defendants breached their duty of care . . . in failing to include an instruction with the product that vehicles should not be run in an enclosed space or must be moved outside before starting the engine as directed [in the instructions]." Second, that "Defendant's breached their duty of care . . . in failing to warn of the dangers of carbon monoxide poisoning."

* * * * *

After a hearing, the trial court granted summary disposition to defendants, concluding:

> [I]t's clear that the material risk of death due to carbon monoxide poisoning as a result of running a car in an enclosed garage would be obvious to the reasonably prudent user of a muffler repair kit. I don't think you can really argue that much about it. . . . I think it would be obvious and that would be to the general public, and it would be especially obvious to someone who used motors. Granted he may have been an . . . outboard engine mechanic, but nevertheless, it seems to me that he was in a position especially to know this even more than an average citizen. But nevertheless, to a reasonably prudent person it would be obvious this was a highly dangerous thing. I think it is common knowledge that it's a dangerous thing and—especially when you look at so many other options he would have had, like just open the garage door, might have been a lot better.

Plaintiff now appeals.

* * * * *

A. REASONABLY PRUDENT PRODUCT USER

[T]he first issue is whether a reasonable juror could find that the material risk of remaining in a closed garage with a running automobile while the muffler bandage cures is or should be "obvious to a reasonably prudent product user." . . .

* * * * *

Given the lack of an obvious risk of harm contained within the product's appearance or function, defendants argue that no reasonable person could fail to know that remaining present while running a car in a closed garage while the muffler bandage cured carried with it a risk of material harm. For reasonable minds not to differ on the issue, it would have to be obvious that the exhaust contained carbon monoxide or other injurious chemicals and that exposure for a period long enough for the muffler bandage to cure created a material risk of harm.

A fact finder may ultimately conclude that defendants are correct that a reasonably prudent person would be aware that automobile exhaust contains carbon monoxide or other injurious chemicals and that exposure for a period long enough for the muffler bandage to cure creates a material risk of harm. However, defendants have not provided any *evidence* from which such a conclusion may be drawn. . . .

* * * * *

At the time of the motion, plaintiff had proffered several articles and data that significant numbers of people, as many as 100 per year die, from accidental carbon monoxide poisoning in Michigan in a manner that supports plaintiff's claim that the danger of exposure to automobile exhaust is not necessarily "obvious to a reasonably prudent user." Plaintiff also presented an expert affidavit in this regard. Finally, plaintiff submitted warnings from devices that create carbon monoxide exhaust. . . .

* * * * *

In contrast to plaintiff's presentation, the defense did not proffer *any* evidence supporting its contention that a reasonable person would know that carbon monoxide is present in automobile exhaust or that an exposure long enough for the muffler bandage to cure presents a material risk of harm.

* * * * *

Defendants provided no evidence in the present case that a reasonable person would know that an exposure to automobile exhaust in a garage for the time needed to cure the muffler repair presented a risk of material harm. Indeed, the only evidence in the record at this time is the data provided by plaintiff that significant numbers of people die from accidental carbon monoxide poisoning and the affidavit from plaintiff's expert supporting plaintiff's claim that the danger was not obvious. Under these circumstances, defendants were not entitled to summary disposition on the question of whether the risk of material harm from carbon monoxide inhalation from running an automobile long enough to cure this muffler product is or should be obvious to a reasonably prudent product user.

B. PERSONS IN THE SAME OR SIMILAR POSITION

* * * * *

We take no position on whether a reasonably prudent user knows that automobile exhaust contains carbon monoxide nor that a [*sic*] exposure long enough to cure the muffler bandage can cause material harm. . . . Rather, we hold that there was insufficient evidence in the record as it presently exists to make that determination as a matter of law. . . .
Reversed and remanded.

Judge Kirsten F. Kelly, Dissenting

I disagree with my colleagues' conclusion that the trial court's grant of summary disposition in this matter was premature. . . . [R]unning the engine of a car in a small, enclosed space, such as a garage, is an obvious material risk to a reasonably prudent product user and would be especially obvious to a person like decedent whose employment involved servicing and repairing engines. I would affirm the trial court.

* * * * *

Questions

1. Do you agree with the lower court that the risk of carbon monoxide poisoning from running a car in an enclosed garage would be obvious to the reasonably prudent user? Explain.

2. Why did the plaintiff win this case on appeal?

3. Michigan law bars liability in these situations if the risk "is or should be a matter of common knowledge to persons in the same or similar positions." Craig White had some, unspecified experience in servicing and repairing marine engines. He had also served as an "engine dynamo technician" and a "marine technician." Is that background, in and of itself, sufficient to establish that the carbon monoxide risk was a matter of "common knowledge" to White? Explain.

4. Bresnahan, age 50 and 5'8" tall, was driving her Chrysler LeBaron, equipped with a driver's side air bag, at between 25 and 30 miles per hour. She was seated less than one foot from the air bag cover. Bresnahan was distracted by police lights and rear-ended a Jaguar, triggering the LeBaron air bag, which broke Bresnahan's arm and caused various abrasions. The vehicle did not include a warning about the danger of sitting too close to the air bag. Was the vehicle defective because of the absence of a warning? Explain. See *Bresnahan v. Chrysler Corp.*, 65 Cal. App. 4th 1149 (1998).

5. Laaperi installed a smoke detector in his bedroom, properly connecting it to his home's electrical system. Six months later, Laaperi's house burned and three of his children were killed. A short circuit, which caused the fire, also deprived the A.C.-powered smoke detector of electricity. Thus, the detector did not sound a warning. Laaperi then claimed that Sears, Roebuck, where he purchased the detector, was guilty of negligence for failing to warn him that a fire might disable his smoke detector such that no warning would issue. How would you rule in this case? See *Laaperi v. Sears, Roebuck & Co.*, 787 F.2d 726 (1st Cir. 1986).

Negligence Defenses: Introduction

Even if the plaintiff has established all of the necessary ingredients in a negligence claim, the defendant may still prevail by asserting a good defense. The two most prominent legal defenses in these cases are (1) comparative or contributory negligence and (2) assumption of the risk.

> Oscar Whitlock unsuccessfully attempted a flip at 10 PM in the dark.

A trampoline at the Beta Theta Pi fraternity house at the University of Denver led to a broken neck and paralysis when a 20-year-old fraternity member, Oscar Whitlock, unsuccessfully attempted a flip at 10 PM in the dark. Whitlock had extensive experience with trampolines. The day of the accident, he had slept until 2 PM after drinking that morning until 2 AM. The trampoline was located in front of the house on university land that was leased by the fraternity. The trampoline had been used over a 10-year period by students and community members. A number of injuries had resulted. The university kept its own trampoline under lock and key because of safety concerns.

At trial the jury found the university 72 percent at fault, with the remainder of the blame lying with the plaintiff/student. He recovered 72 percent of $7,300,000 ($5,256,000). On appeal the judgment was upheld but the dissent argued that the university had no duty to warn against obvious risks, saying that "no reasonable person could conclude that the plaintiff was not at least as negligent as the defendant." Hence the dissent was saying, in effect, that the plaintiff had assumed the risk and, in any case, was himself arguably more negligent than the university.[23]

The Colorado State Supreme Court then reviewed the appeals court decision and reversed on the grounds that the university did not maintain a "special relationship" with the plaintiff that would have justified imposing a duty of due care on the university to ensure safe use of the trampoline.[24]

Questions

Assume you own an amusement park.

1. Would the dissent's reasoning in the *Whitlock* court of appeals decision apply to the trampoline in your amusement park business? Explain.
2. Would a warning and close supervision protect you from liability under the court of appeals decision? Explain.
3. Would you have the duty of due care for your customers that the Colorado Supreme Court said the University of Denver did not have for Whitlock? Explain.

Negligence Defenses: Rules

LO 7-8

Analyze whether negligence defenses may be successfully asserted in a negligence claim.

Let's look more closely at the central defenses in negligence cases.

Comparative Negligence

Most states have adopted comparative negligence as a defense, an approach that involves weighing the relative negligence of the parties. Though the formula varies from state to state, typically the plaintiff's recovery is reduced by a percentage equal to the percentage of the plaintiff's fault in the case. Assume a plaintiff sustained $10,000 in injuries in an accident. If the plaintiff's own negligence is found to be 20 percent responsible for the injuries, then the plaintiff's recovery will be reduced to $8,000. In many states, however, when the plaintiff is more than 50 percent at fault, she or he will be barred from recovery.

Contributory Negligence

Rather than employing the comparative negligence doctrine, a few states continue to follow the historic rule that any contribution by the plaintiff to his or her own harm constitutes a complete bar to recovery. This is called contributory negligence. If the plaintiff is found to have contributed in any way to his or her injury, even if that contribution is minuscule, he or she is unable to recover.

Assumption of Risk

A plaintiff who willingly enters a dangerous situation and is injured, in many states, will be barred from recovery. For example, if a driver sees that the road ahead is flooded, he probably will not be compensated for the injuries sustained when he loses control as he attempts to drive through the water. His recovery is barred even though the road was flooded owing to operator error in opening a floodgate. The requirements for use of the assumption of risk defense are (1) knowledge of the risk and (2) voluntary assumption of the risk. Assumption of the risk and contributory negligence are distinguishable in that the former is based on consent whereas the latter is rooted in carelessness. Increasingly, states that have adopted the comparative negligence doctrine do not treat assumption of the risk as a complete bar to recovery, but rather as a factor in negligence balancing.

Do Cheerleaders Assume the Risk of Injury?

Underlying the assumption of the risk doctrine is one of the central philosophical themes in this book: To what extent should the law/government shield us from life's risks? Departing for a moment from product liability considerations, how should the law resolve disputes arising from potentially hazardous recreational activities entered freely? Gabriella Ballou, then a 9th grader and experienced cheerleader, allegedly improperly performed the "prep cradle twist," causing her head to miss the safety mat and strike the floor. An expert witness testified that the stunt was inadequately supervised, among other problems. Should Ballou be able to recover for injuries she sustained in high school cheerleading tryouts, or should she be deemed to have assumed the risks attendant to that activity?

Source: Ballou v. Ravena-Coeymans-Selkirk School District, 72 A.D.3d 1323 (N.Y. App. Div. 2010).

Warranties

LO 7-9
Compare and contrast claims based on express warranties and implied warranties.

As explained previously, negligence claims often are difficult to prove. For that reason and others, a wronged consumer may wish to bring a breach of warranty claim in addition to or in place of a negligence action. A warranty is simply a contractually based guarantee. If the product does not conform to the standards of the warranty, the contract is violated (breached), and the wronged party is entitled to recovery. [For the text of the Uniform Commercial Code, Article II, Sales, see **www.law.cornell.edu/ucc**.]

Express Warranties

An express warranty exists if a seller of goods states a fact or makes a promise regarding the character or quality of the goods. (Some lease arrangements are also covered by warranty law, but we will limit our discussion to the sale of goods.) Warranties are governed primarily by the Uniform Commercial Code. The UCC is designed to codify and standardize the law of commercial practice.

UCC 2-313. Express Warranties by Affirmation, Promise, Description, Sample

1. Express warranties by the seller are created as follows:
   a. Any affirmation of fact or promise made by the seller to the buyer which relates to the goods and becomes part of the basis of the bargain creates an express warranty that the goods shall conform to the affirmation or promise.
   b. Any description of the goods which is made part of the basis of the bargain creates an express warranty that the goods shall conform to the description.
   c. Any sample or model which is made part of the basis of the bargain creates an express warranty that the whole of the goods shall conform to the sample or model.

The UCC 2-313 standard is straightforward: The seller who seeks to enhance the attractiveness of her product by offering representations as to the nature or quality of the product must fulfill those representations or fall in breach of contract and pay damages. [At this writing, the various state legislatures are considering changes to the UCC.]

Puffing

Perhaps the area of greatest confusion in determining the existence and coverage of an express warranty is distinguishing a seller's promise from a mere expression of opinion. The latter, often referred to as sales talk or puffing, does not create an express warranty. The UCC requires an affirmation of fact or promise. Hence, a statement of opinion is not covered by the code. For example, the sales clerk who says, "This is the best TV around," would not be guaranteeing that the television in question is the best available. The salesperson is expressing a view. We, as consumers, seem to be quite patient with sellers' exaggerations. If, on the other hand, the clerk said, "This TV is rated at 1080 pixels," when in fact it offered only 768 pixels, a breach of warranty action might ultimately be in order. The reasonable expectations test is to be applied in such situations. An expression of opinion coming from an expert may well create an express warranty because the buyer should reasonably be able to rely on the expert's affirmations. That would particularly be the case if the buyer is not knowledgeable about the product.

Implied Warranties

When a seller enters a contract for the sale of goods, an implied warranty arises by operation of law. That is, an implied warranty automatically attaches to the sale of goods unless the warranty is disclaimed (disavowed) by the seller.

Two types of implied warranties are provided:

UCC 2-314. Implied Warranty: Merchantability; Usage of Trade

(1) Unless excluded or modified (Section 2-316), a warranty that the goods shall be merchantable is implied in a contract for their sale if the seller is a merchant with respect to goods of that kind. Under this section the serving for value of food or drink to be consumed either on the premises or elsewhere is a sale.

UCC 2-315. Implied Warranty: Fitness for Particular Purpose

Where the seller at the time of contracting has reason to know any particular purpose for which the goods are required and that the buyer is relying on the seller's skill or judgment to select or furnish suitable goods, there is unless excluded or modified under the next section an implied warranty that the goods shall be fit for such purpose.

The implied warranty of merchantability is a powerful tool for the wronged consumer. If the seller is a merchant regularly selling goods of the kind in question, the warranty of merchantability automatically accompanies the sale unless the warranty is excluded via a disclaimer (explained below). The warranty arises even if the seller made no certification as to the nature or quality of the goods. UCC 2-314 enshrines the consumer's reasonable expectation that only safe goods of at least ordinary quality will appear on the market.

The implied warranty of fitness for a particular purpose likewise arises by operation of law, but only when the seller (merchant or not) knows (or has reason to know) that the goods are to be used for a specific purpose, and the seller further knows that the buyer is relying on the seller's judgment. If those conditions obtain, the warranty exists automatically unless disclaimed. For example, Chris Snapp engages an audio products clerk in a discussion regarding the proper sound system for Chris's classic Austin Healey 3000 sports car. Chris explains the joy he expects to receive in driving his car along the winding Kentucky roads with the convertible top down and his songs booming. Unfortunately, the audio system selected on the clerk's advice proves insufficiently powerful to be heard clearly above the rushing wind. Should Chris recover for breach of the implied warranty of fitness for a particular purpose? Merchantability?

Disclaimers

Express warranties may be disclaimed (excluded) or modified only with great difficulty. In any contract displaying both an express warranty and language disclaiming that warranty (for example, sold "as is" or "with all faults"), the warranty will remain effective unless the warranty and the disclaimer can reasonably be read as consistent.

Implied warranties may be excluded or modified by following either of the two patterns explained in UCC Section 2-316(2) and (3)(a).

2. Subject to subsection (3), to exclude or modify the implied warranty of merchantability or any part of it the language must mention merchantability and in case of a writing must be conspicuous, and to exclude or modify any implied warranty of fitness the exclusion must be by a writing and conspicuous. . . .
3. Notwithstanding subsection (2)
   a. unless the circumstances indicate otherwise, all implied warranties are excluded by expressions like "as is", "with all faults" or other language which in common understanding calls the buyer's attention to the exclusion of warranties and makes plain that there is no implied warranty[.]

Finally, when a buyer, before entering a contract, inspects the goods (or a sample thereof) or declines to inspect, no implied warranty exists with regard to defects that should have been apparent on inspection. See UCC Section 2-316(3)(b).

Magnuson–Moss Warranty Act

The federal Magnuson–Moss Warranty Act extended and clarified UCC warranty rules. Congress found that warranties were often vague, deceptive, or simply incomprehensible to the average purchaser. The act, administered by the FTC, applies only to consumer products and only to written warranties. It does not require offering an express written warranty, but where such a warranty is offered and the cost of the goods is more than $10, the warranty must be labeled full or limited. A full warranty requires free repair of any defect. If repair is not achieved within a reasonable time, the buyer may elect either a refund or replacement without charge. If a limited warranty is offered, the limitation must be conspicuously displayed.

If a warranty is offered on goods costing more than $15, the warrantor must "fully and conspicuously disclose in simple and readily understandable language the terms and conditions of the warranty."

The effect of the Magnuson–Moss Act has not been entirely consistent with Congress's hopes. In practice, many sellers have either offered limited warranties or eliminated them entirely.

In many states, implied warranty law has been incorporated within broader product liability actions, reflecting an emerging preference for treating personal injury and property damages as torts rather than contract-based (warranty) claims. The *Hodges* case that follows, however, finds the Kansas Supreme Court examining a breach of warranty claim under conventional contracts reasoning. Notice that the Kansas court struggles, as other courts have, in determining when the warranty of merchantability should apply to used goods.

LEGAL BRIEFCASE

Hodges v. Johnson
199 P.3d 1251 (Kan. 2009)

Justice Davis

FACTS

Jim Johnson owns a car dealership in Saline County that sells high-end, used vehicles. In January 2005, Johnson sold Dr. Merle Hodges and Melissa Hodges a 1995 Mercedes S320 with 135,945 miles for $17,020 (the sales price of $ 15,900 plus tax). Johnson had been driving the Mercedes as his personal vehicle for roughly 2 years before the sale. Johnson testified before the district court in this case that he told the Hodges when they purchased the Mercedes that it was a nice car in good condition. Dr. Hodges testified that Johnson said the car "was just pretty much a perfect car" and that Johnson "loved driving it."

At the time the Hodgeses bought the Mercedes from Johnson, there was no discussion about the operation of the air conditioning, heating, or other components of the vehicle. Both Dr. Hodges and Johnson testified that they had no reason to believe that the air conditioner did not work when the Mercedes was sold to the Hodgeses.

In February 2005, about a month after he had bought the car from Johnson, Dr. Hodges noticed that the vent in the Mercedes did not circulate cool air and that the car emitted a strange smell. In March of the same year, the Hodgeses noticed that the Mercedes' air conditioning did not work and contacted the Hodgeses' mechanic, Virgil Anderson. Anderson added Freon to the air conditioner. About a month later, the air conditioner again was not working; Anderson added more Freon. The Hodgeses contacted Johnson to notify him of the air conditioning problem, and Johnson told them that some older vehicles may need a yearly boost of Freon to work properly.

In May 2005, the air conditioner failed a third time. After checking the air conditioning system for leaks, Anderson informed the Hodgeses that the Mercedes' evaporator, condenser, and compressor

needed to be replaced. Anderson explained that these repairs would cost approximately $3,000 to $ 4,000.

At some time around May 2005, a mechanic who worked for Anderson told the Hodgeses that Johnson had requested that the mechanic put a product called Super Seal into the Mercedes' air conditioner in May 2003 (when he was using the car as his personal vehicle). The mechanic explained that the use of Super Seal complicated the current repair of the air conditioner and that the mechanic personally would not recommend Super Seal or apply it unless requested.

Johnson testified that he did not recall any problems with the Mercedes' air conditioner after the mechanics added Super Seal in May 2003, though he could not recall whether additional Freon was added during that time. Johnson further testified that the air conditioning problem in 2003 only involved the car's evaporator.

Anderson identified the condenser as the main problem with the Mercedes' air conditioner in 2005. Anderson testified during the pendency of this case that he could not determine whether the problem with the Mercedes' air conditioner existed at the time that the Hodgeses bought the car from Johnson or occurred at some time later.

The Hodgeses asked Johnson to pay to repair the air conditioning unit in the Mercedes. Johnson refused.

Shortly thereafter, the Hodgeses filed an action in small claims court against Johnson, alleging he caused them damages of $3,474—Anderson's estimate of the repair costs. The small claims court found in favor of the Hodgeses and awarded them $3,474 damages, plus $56 in costs and interest.

Johnson appealed to the district court. [T]he district court also found in favor of the Hodgeses, noting that "while [Johnson] may not have known of the failure of the air conditioning unit[,] . . . there is an implied warranty of merchantability," and Johnson "is responsible to the plaintiffs to provide a car that is merchantable." The court therefore entered a judgment in favor of the Hodges for $3,474, together with costs of $56 plus interest. The court found that attorney fees were not warranted because Johnson's actions did not rise "to a level of misrepresentation."

[Both parties appealed] to the Court of Appeals. . . . The Court of Appeals reversed . . . and held as a matter of law that the implied warranty of merchantability on a used vehicle extends only to "the operation of major components that are necessary for the vehicle to operate, such as the engine and transmission." The court further held that "it is the responsibility of the buyer to ensure that the components incidental to operation are in working condition."

* * * * *

This court granted the Hodgeses' petition for review.

IMPLIED WARRANTY OF MERCHANTABILITY

Kansas' implied warranty of merchantability is contained in K.S.A. 84-2-314, which states that "a warranty that the goods shall be merchantable is implied in a contract for their sale if the seller is a merchant with respect to goods of that kind." K.S.A. 84-2-314(1). The statute further states that in order for goods to be "merchantable," they must be "at least such as . . . are fit for the ordinary purposes for which such goods are used." K.S.A. 84-2-314(2)(c).

* * * * *

ANALYSIS

The comments to K.S.A. 84-2-314 make clear that this implied warranty of merchantability applies by operation of law to "all sales by merchants" and "arises from the fact of the sale." K.S.A. 84-2-314, Kansas Comment 1. Applying this standard to the facts before us, it is clear that the transaction in this case—the sale of the Mercedes by Johnson to the Hodgeses—fits within the implied warranty. There is no dispute that Johnson is a merchant dealing in the sale of used vehicles or that the Mercedes is a "good" within the meaning of the statute. Thus, when Johnson sold the Mercedes to the Hodgeses, he implicitly warranted that the Mercedes would be "merchantable."

* * * * *

The Court of Appeals majority recognized that the sale of the Mercedes triggered the implied warranty but concluded as a matter of law under K.S.A. 84-2-314(2) that the vehicle's air conditioner was not covered by the warranty because the air conditioner did not affect the vehicle's merchantability. To reach this conclusion, the majority employed a three-part syllogism: First, for goods to be merchantable under the statute, they must be "fit for the ordinary purposes for which such goods are used." K.S.A. 84-2-314(2)(c). Second, the majority concluded that the primary purpose for which used vehicles are used is transportation; thus only the major components of a vehicle that bear upon its ability to effectively transport

people from one location to another affect the vehicle's merchantability. Finally, the majority interpreted our past cases involving the warranty of merchantability in the sale of used vehicles to suggest that the warranty may not apply "unless a major component or several components are defective, causing the vehicle to become virtually inoperable." [*Hodges,*] 39 Kan. App. 2d at 225.

Applying this syllogism, the Court of Appeals majority determined that the air conditioner was not a major component of the Mercedes and thus did not impair the primary purpose for which used cars vehicles are employed:

"An air conditioner is not a major component of a car that is 10 years old with over 135,000 miles on it, and does not fall within the implied warranty of merchantability. We find no implied warranty of merchantability, considering the age of the car, the high mileage, and the fact that the Hodges provided no proof that the air conditioner did not work when they purchased the vehicle." *Hodges,* 39 Kan. App. 2d at 225.

This conclusion is not supported by the case law. Although it may be that the implied warranty of merchantability does not extend to some components of a used vehicle in a particular transaction, this is a case-by-case determination in most cases—not a question of law. . . .

The Court of Appeals majority's approach is similarly unsupported by the statutes. K.S.A. 84-2-314(2)(c) defines merchantable goods as goods that are "fit for the ordinary *purposes* for which such goods are used." (Emphasis added.) The Court of Appeals interpreted this provision to mean that a used vehicle must be fit for the *primary* purpose of transportation. This interpretation is inconsistent with the plain language of K.S.A. 84-2-314(2)(c), which clearly contemplates goods that may be put to more than one use. Although there can be little doubt that the *primary* purpose of a vehicle is transportation, the Court of Appeals' opinion ignores the reality that a buyer may purchase a particular vehicle for a number of other purposes—among which may be safety, fuel economy, utility, or *comfort* in traveling to and from various destinations.

Contrary to the Court of Appeals' conclusion, the extent of a merchant's obligation under the implied warranty of merchantability depends on the circumstances of a transaction. . . . The determination as to whether the implied warranty has been breached turns on a number of factors, including "[t]he buyer's knowledge that the goods are used, the extent of their prior use, and whether the goods are significantly discounted." [*International Petroleum Services,*] 230 Kan. at 457.

The broad range of used goods that may be covered by the implied warranty of merchantability underscores the wisdom of this court's previous recognition that a "late model, low mileage car, sold at a premium price, is expected to be in far better condition and to last longer than an old, high mileage, 'rough' car that is sold for little above its scrap value." *Dale,* 234 Kan. at 844. In this case, we have a 1995 Mercedes S320 with 135,945 miles selling for $17,020 in 2005. Johnson related to the buyer that it was a nice car in good condition; Dr. Hodges testified that he was told the car "was pretty much a perfect car." In short, this vehicle falls somewhere between the extremes of a "late model, low mileage car, sold at a premium price" and "an old, high mileage, 'rough' car . . . sold for little above its scrap value." 234 Kan. at 844.

. . . The question remaining to be resolved is not the existence of this warranty, but rather the *extent of the seller's obligation* under the warranty. Because this case does not involve either extreme on the spectrum of used vehicles, the resolution of this question is not a question of law, but rather a factual determination. . . .

After hearing the evidence in this case, the district court determined that the Hodgeses were entitled to judgment against Johnson for the sum of $3,474, together with costs of $56 and interest, and thus affirmed the award of the small claims court. . . .

To demonstrate a breach of the implied warranty of merchantability, a plaintiff must show that the purchased goods were defective, that the defect was present when the goods left the seller's control, and that the defect caused the injury sustained by the plaintiff. The circumstantial evidence in this case is sufficient to establish that the defect in the air conditioner existed at the time of sale. In 2003, 2 years before the Hodgeses purchased the vehicle, the Mercedes' air conditioner failed while Johnson was using it as his personal vehicle. Johnson insisted that his mechanic, against the mechanic's advice, use a product called Super Seal to fix the problem. The Hodgeses discovered that the air conditioner was again defective as soon as the weather became warm enough to require climate control. The use of the Super Seal, the strong odor emanating from the vehicle's ventilation system immediately after the sale, and the complete breakdown of the air conditioner when the buyer first attempted to use it all tend to establish that it was defective at the time of sale. While Johnson may not have known that the Mercedes' air conditioner was defective when he sold the vehicle to the Hodgeses, there is no requirement that a buyer establish that the seller knew of a defective component at the time of sale to trigger the implied warranty.

With regard to damages, there is no question that the complete failure of the air conditioner's operation led to the buyer replacing it. As this court has concluded:

". . . As concerns used or secondhand goods it is generally understood that the measure of damages is the cost of repair when repair is possible." *International Petroleum Services,* 230 Kan. at 460.

* * * * *

We find that there is substantial competent evidence to support the district court's conclusion that the implied warranty of merchantability in this transaction was not limited to only the Mercedes' major components affecting transportation, but rather extended at a minimum to the vehicle's air conditioning unit. We also find that there was substantial competent evidence to demonstrate that the air conditioning unit was defective at the time of sale and that the required repairs would cost $3,474. Accordingly, we reverse the Court of Appeals' reversal of the district court's judgment in favor of the Hodgeses and affirm the district court's decision.

* * * * *

Questions

1. *a.* Why did the court of appeals rule for Johnson, the car dealer?
   b. Why did the Kansas Supreme Court reverse the court of appeals' judgment that the vehicle's air conditioner was not covered by a warranty?
   c. What test did the Kansas Supreme Court employ to determine whether the implied warranty of merchantability had been breached?
   d. How would the Kansas Supreme Court determine when a used car would be protected by the implied warranty of merchantability?

2. In buying a new motor home, Leavitt told the dealer that he wanted to have plenty of power and braking capacity for driving in the mountains. He was assured by the dealer on both counts. He brought the motor home and found it unsatisfactory for mountain use. After many warranty repairs, he sued for breach of warranty.
   a. What warranty was breached, according to Leavitt?
   b. Decide the case. Explain. See *Leavitt v. Monaco Coach,* 616 N.W.2d 175 (Mich. Ct. App. 2000).

3. Priebe bought a used car without a warranty (sold as is). The seller, Autobarn, told Priebe that the car had not been in any accidents. After driving the car more than 30,000 miles, Priebe crashed the car. Priebe sued Autobarn claiming the car was dangerous to drive because of a previous, undisclosed accident. Priebe did not show that Autobarn had knowledge of the previous accident, nor did Priebe show that the value of the car was reduced by the previous accident. Priebe sued for breach of warranty. Decide. Explain. See *Priebe v. Autobarn,* 240 F.3d 584 (7th Cir. 2001).

4. Douglas Kolarik alleged that he used several imported, pimento-stuffed green olives in a salad. In eating the salad, he bit down on an olive pit and fractured a tooth. The olive jar label included the words "minced pimento stuffed." The defendants are importers and wholesalers of Spanish olives that reach the defendants in barrels and are then inspected for general appearance, pH, and acid level and then washed and placed in glass jars suitable for distribution for the purpose of retail sales.
   a. What legal claim would be expected from the plaintiff based on the "minced pimento stuffed" language?
   b. Decide that claim. Explain. See *Kolarik v. Cory International,* 721 N.W.2d 159 (Iowa 2006).

Skoal and Copenhagen

Bobby Hill of Canton, North Carolina, began chewing tobacco at age 13. He died in 2003 at age 42. U.S. Smokeless Tobacco Co., makers of Skoal and Copenhagen, agreed in 2010 to pay Hill's family $5 million to settle the relatives' wrongful death claim. Apparently, the settlement was the first of its kind involving smokeless tobacco.

Source: Associated Press, "First Lawsuit Won on Chewing Tobacco," *The Des Moines Register,* December 8, 2010, p. 7A.

Strict Liability

Sometimes things happen that businesses can neither prevent nor even explain and yet liability may attach. For example, imagine you are operating a clothing store. A customer enters and decides to try on a pair of slacks. You show her to the dressing room. Soon after, you hear a scream from the room. As it turns out, your customer has been bitten by a spider. Not surprisingly, she thinks the blame lies with your store. She sues, but her negligence and breach of warranty claims are rejected by the court. (Can you explain why she loses?) Finally, she raises a strict liability in tort argument, but the court denies that claim also. Read the overview of strict liability that follows and think about why the court denied her claim. See *Flippo v. Mode O'Day Frock Shops of Hollywood,* 449 S.W.2d 692 (Ark. 1970).

> Your customer has been bitten by a spider.

Strict Liability: Overview

LO 7-10

Identify the elements of the strict liability cause of action.

Negligence and warranty claims are helpful to the harmed consumer. However, rapid changes in the nature of commercial practice, as well as an increasing societal concern for consumer protection, led the legal community to gradually embrace yet another cause of action. Strict liability in tort offers the prospect of holding all of those in the chain of distribution liable for damages from a defective product, rather than imposing the entire burden on the injured consumer. Manufacturers and sellers are best positioned to prevent the distribution of defective products, and they are best able to bear the cost of injury by spreading the loss via pricing policies and insurance coverage.

Strict liability as an independent tort emerged in 1963 in the famous California case of *Greenman v. Yuba Power Products, Inc.*[25] In the ensuing 40 years, most states have adopted strict liability in concept. The essence of the strict liability notion is expressed in Section 402A of the *Restatement (Second) of Torts.* In brief, Section 402A imposes liability where a product is sold in a defective condition, unreasonably dangerous to the user. Here is the Section 402A text:

§ 402A Special Liability of Seller of Product for Physical Harm to User or Consumer

1. One who sells any product in a defective condition, unreasonably dangerous to the user or consumer or to his property, is subject to liability for physical harm thereby caused to the ultimate user or consumer, or to his property, if
   a. the seller is engaged in the business of selling such a product, and,
   b. it is expected to and does reach the user or consumer without substantial change in the condition in which it is sold.

2. The rule stated in Subsection (1) applies although
   a. the seller has exercised all possible care in the preparation and sale of his product, and
   b. the user or consumer has not bought the product from or entered into any contractual relation with the seller.

Thus, we see that strict liability does not require proof of negligence on the part of the defendant. Strict liability law focuses on the condition of the product, rather than the conduct of the parties. Therefore, a seller who is free of actual fault may, nonetheless, be liable for injuries caused by a defective and unreasonably dangerous product. The Aim N Flame lighter case that follows considers the conditions under which a strict liability claim may be raised.

LEGAL BRIEFCASE

Calles v. Scripto-Tokai
864 N.E.2d 249 (Ill. 2007)

Justice Burke

On March 31, 1998, plaintiff Susan Calles resided with her four daughters, Amanda, age 11, Victoria, age 5, and Jenna and Jillian, age 3. At some point that night, Calles left her home with Victoria to get videos for Amanda. When she left, the twins were in bed and Amanda was watching television. Calles returned to find fire trucks and emergency vehicles around her home. It was subsequently determined by a fire investigator, Robert Finn, that Jenna had started a fire using an Aim N Flame utility lighter Calles had purchased approximately one week earlier. The Aim N Flame was ignited by pulling a trigger after an "ON/OFF" switch was slid to the "on" position. As a result of the fire, Jillian suffered smoke inhalation. She was hospitalized and died on April 21.

Calles filed suit against Tokai, designer and manufacturer of the Aim N Flame, and Scripto-Tokai, distributor (collectively Scripto), alleging that the Aim N Flame was defectively designed and unreasonably dangerous because it did not contain a child-resistant safety device. According to the complaint, a safety device was available, inexpensive, and would have reduced the risk that children could ignite the lighter. Calles' claims sounded in strict liability.

Thereafter, Scripto filed a motion for summary judgment. . . . In her deposition, Calles admitted she was aware of the risks and dangers presented by lighters in the hands of children, and, for this reason, she stored the Aim N Flames on the top shelf of her kitchen cabinet. Calles further admitted that the Aim N Flame operated as intended and expected.

In opposition to Scripto's motion for summary judgment, Calles offered affidavits from several experts. . . . All of [the] experts opined that the Aim N Flame was defective and unreasonably dangerous because it lacked a child-resistant design. They also opined that a technologically and economically feasible alternative design, which included a child-resistant safety device, existed at the time the Aim N Flame was manufactured. Several of the experts averred that Scripto was aware of the desirability of a child-safety device because it knew children could operate the Aim N Flame. Further, according to these experts, Scripto owned the technology to make the Aim N Flame child resistant in 1994 and 1995.

With respect to the cost of an alternative design, . . . the Consumer Product Safety Commission, the regulatory body for lighters, estimated the increased cost of adding a safety device to the lighter would be $ 0.40 per unit. However [one of Calles' experts estimated], the cost would have been negligible.

Calles also offered evidence of the dangerousness of lighters in the hands of children and Scripto's awareness of such dangers. . . . Scripto admitted they had been named as defendants in 25 lawsuits filed between 1996 and 2000 for injuries that occurred between 1992 and 1999 under circumstances similar to this case.

The trial court granted summary judgment in favor of Scripto. . . .

On appeal, the appellate court . . . reversed [the trial court's summary judgment in favor of Scripto . . .].

STRICT LIABILITY

[T]his court adopted the strict liability doctrine set forth in section 402A of the Second Restatement of Torts. Under this doctrine, strict liability is imposed upon a seller of "any product in a defective condition unreasonably dangerous to the user or consumer or to his property." The test outlined in section 402A for determining whether a product is "unreasonably dangerous" is known as the consumer-expectation test. This test provides that a product is "unreasonably dangerous" when it is "dangerous to an extent beyond that which would be contemplated by the ordinary consumer who purchases it, with the ordinary knowledge common to the community as to its characteristics."

*　*　*　*　*

An ordinary consumer would expect that a child could obtain possession of the Aim N Flame and attempt to use it. Thus, a child is a reasonably foreseeable user. Likewise, an ordinary consumer would appreciate the consequences that would naturally flow when a child obtains possession of a lighter. . . .

Under the facts of this case, the Aim N Flame performed as an ordinary consumer would expect—it produced a flame when used in a reasonably foreseeable manner, i.e., by a child. This leads to the inescapable conclusion that the ordinary consumer's expectations were fulfilled. . . . Thus, as a matter of law, no fact finder could conclude that the Aim N Flame was unreasonably dangerous under the consumer-expectation test. Therefore, Calles cannot prevail under this theory.

This does not end our analysis, however. Though the Aim N Flame satisfies the consumer-expectation test, it may, nonetheless, be deemed unreasonably dangerous under the risk-utility test.

RISK-UTILITY TEST

Under the risk-utility test, a plaintiff may prevail in a strict liability design-defect case if he or she demonstrates that the magnitude of the danger outweighs the utility of the product, as designed. . . .

*　*　*　*　*

Under the risk-utility test, a court may take into consideration numerous factors. In past decisions, this court has held that a plaintiff may prove a design defect by presenting evidence of "the availability and feasibility of alternate designs at the time of its manufacture, or that the design used did not conform with the design standards of the industry. . . ."

*　*　*　*　*

. . . Calles presented specific and detailed evidence as to the likelihood of injury and the seriousness of injury from lighters which do not have child-safety devices.

Factors which would favor Scripto and a finding that the product is not unreasonably dangerous are the utility of the Aim N Flame and the user's awareness of the dangers. As to the utility of the Aim

N Flame, it is both useful and desirable to society as a whole—it serves as an inexpensive alternative source of fire. . . . With respect to the user's awareness of the dangers, there is no question, based on Calles' deposition testimony, that it was obvious to her that the lighter could come into the hands of a child and the dangers and risks that situation would pose.

In connection with the remaining relevant factors, we find that these neither weigh for nor against a finding of unreasonably dangerous. Calles claims that a substitute product was available, but the only evidence she relies upon is the fact Bic introduced a child-resistant utility lighter in March 1998, the very same month of the incident here. This is insufficient to demonstrate that a substitute product was available at the time of the manufacture of the Aim N Flame.

Calles offered expert affidavits regarding the availability and feasibility of an alternative design, including product impairment and cost factors, along with industry standards. Each expert opined that a feasible alternative design existed. . . .

*　*　*　*　*

There is nothing in our record showing Scripto provided any amount as to the increase in cost of incorporating a safety device. Apparently . . . an internal Scripto memorandum estimated the cost increase would be $0.03 per unit. In light of the foregoing, we conclude that the question of whether there was a feasible alternative design available cannot be determined on the basis of the record as it currently stands.

Lastly, with respect to the user's ability to avoid the danger, Calles testified she put the Aim N Flames on the top shelf of her kitchen cabinet. However, she also acknowledged she could have left them on the counter. . . .

Based on a review of the foregoing factors, reasonable persons could differ on the weight to be given the relevant factors and thus could differ on whether the risks of the Aim N Flame outweigh its utility. Therefore, reasonable persons could differ as to whether the Aim N Flame is unreasonably dangerous, and we cannot say that Scripto was entitled to judgment as a matter of law. As such, we affirm the appellate court's decision reversing the trial court's decision granting summary judgment in favor of Scripto on the strict liability claims.

*　*　*　*　*

Questions

1. *a.* Explain the plaintiff Calles's claim that the Aim N Flame lighter was defective and unreasonably dangerous.

   b. Explain the court's resolution of Calles's claim.

2. What evidence must a plaintiff provide to maintain a successful defective design product liability claim?

3. Is the manufacturer excused from liability if the product's danger is obvious or if the product is used in an unintended but foreseeable fashion?

4. In a case similar to *Calles* [*Griggs v. Bic Corp.*, 981 F.2d 1429 (3d Cir. 1992)], the court, employing a negligence analysis, found that the central question was whether the foreseeable risk was unreasonable. The court noted that residential fires started by children playing with lighters are estimated to take an average of 120 lives each year, and total damages amount to $300–$375 million or 60–75 cents per lighter sold.

   a. Is the foreseeable risk unreasonable, in your judgment?

   b. How did you reach your conclusion?

   c. In your view, are the parents the responsible parties in these episodes? Explain.

5. Alison Nowak, a 14-year-old girl, tried to spray her hair with Aqua Net. Because the spray valve on the recently purchased aerosol can would not work properly, she punctured the can with an opener. She was standing in her kitchen near a gas stove at the time, and the cloud of spray that gushed from the can ignited. She was severely burned. Nowak sued Faberge, the maker of the spray, on strict liability grounds. Although the back of the can contained the warnings "Do not puncture" and "Do not use near fire or flame," the jury determined that Faberge had not adequately warned of the fire hazard and awarded her $1.5 million. Faberge appealed. Decide. Explain. See *Nowak v. Faberge USA Inc.*, 32 F.3d 755 (3d Cir. 1994).

Strict Liability: Coverage

All of those engaged in the preparation and distribution of a defective product may be liable for any harm caused by the defect, regardless of proof of actual fault. Furthermore, the courts have extended strict liability coverage to reach injured bystanders. Coverage generally extends to both personal injuries and property damage, but in some states the latter is excluded. Some states limit strict liability recovery to new goods, and some have limited liability to a designated period (for example, 15 years) after the manufacture or sale of the product.

Furthermore, the *Restatement of the Law Third, Torts* recommends applying strict liability claims to manufacturing defects but not to design and warning defect cases. Thus, in effect, the latest *Restatement* recommends applying the reasonableness, fault-based analysis explained earlier in the negligence material to all defective design and failure-to-warn cases. Of course, the courts may choose to stick with the current expansive use of the strict liability doctrine.

Strict Liability: Defenses

LO 7-11
Identify the defenses available in strict liability cases.

Assumption of risk and *product misuse* are both good defenses and, if factually supported, in many states can act as a complete bar to strict liability recovery. Assumption of the risk involves the plaintiff's decision to proceed to use the product despite obvious dangers associated with that use. Thus, if a pilot decided to fly knowing that the plane's wing flaps were not operating properly, she may well have assumed the risk if she subsequently crashed. When the product is used improperly, or its directions are ignored, or it is used in an unforeseeable way, the defendant would raise the misuse defense. Suppose you find yourself late for class and you decide to save time by drying your tennis shoes in your microwave or ironing your clothes after you have put them on your body. If the microwave blows up or you burn yourself with the iron, not only have you had a very bad day, you probably would not be able to sue successfully for damages because you likely would be found to have misused the products. Some courts, however, hold those in the chain of

> Drying your tennis shoes in your microwave

distribution liable for foreseeable misuses. Because strict liability is a no-fault theory, contributory negligence ordinarily is not a recognized defense. [For the "evolution" of product liability laws, see **www.productliabilitylawyer.com/evolutionOfProductLiability.cfm**].

Video Games and *The Basketball Diaries*

Michael Carneal, a 14-year-old high school freshman in Paducah, Kentucky, brought a .22-caliber pistol and five shotguns to Heath High School, where he shot and killed three students and wounded a number of others. Carneal regularly played violent video games such as *Doom and Quake,* and viewed violent Internet sites. He also watched violent movies including *The Basketball Diaries,* in which a high school student dreams of killing his teacher and other students. The parents of the victims sued several video game, movie production, and Internet content providers raising negligence and strict liability claims. Who should win that case? Explain.

Source: James v. Meow Media, 300 F.3d 683 (6th Cir. 2002), cert. denied, 537 U.S. 1159 (2003).

Part Three—Product Liability and Public Policy

LO 7-12
Evaluate arguments for and against tort reform.

Giant tort awards involving products such as asbestos and breast implants have bankrupted businesses. When we hear about a $4 million punitive damage award against a BMW dealer that sold a physician a car as new but that had actually been repainted, we may wonder if the justice system has lost its bearings, and whether product liability has gone too far.[26] We may not understand that these large awards are almost always dramatically reduced, as in the BMW case.[27] Furthermore, awards in big class action cases often come in the form of product coupons or gifts to charity.[28] For example, exploding tires on Ford Explorers resulted in a 2008 class action settlement for 1,647 eligible claimants of $500 toward the purchase of a new Explorer and $300 toward the purchase of another Ford vehicle.[29] Legislation such as The Protection of Lawful Commerce in Arms Act, which shields gun manufacturers and dealers from negligence liability when their products are used in illegal activities, also limits the risk of litigation. Nonetheless, the threat of tort litigation significantly affects business decision making and, in some instances, actually prevents products from reaching the market.

Because of those problems, many critics, particularly in the business community and among free-market advocates, have argued for *tort reform*. They want to change the legal system in ways that would reduce the heavy costs of personal injury claims. The proposed reforms vary widely, but common prescriptions include limiting class actions, reducing or eliminating punitive damages, curbing attorneys' fees, penalizing frivolous lawsuits, and imposing "loser pays" rules, requiring the losing party in a civil lawsuit to pay the other party's legal fees and related costs.

Are big tort judgments harming the American economy and distorting justice, or are lawsuits Americans' only effective protection against callous corporations? Consider some of the evidence.

For Tort Reform   Consultants Towers Watson estimated that 2010 tort costs (not limited to product liability) for the United States totaled $264.6 billion: a sum amounting to a "tort tax" of $857 per year for every American.[30] As a result, critics say, American businesses must struggle with rising costs, innovation is reduced, and new jobs are less plentiful. Critics are particularly frustrated that much of the tort money goes to lawyers rather than to the injured plaintiffs. A number of states have imposed caps on punitive damages while, as noted in Chapter 5, the U.S. Supreme Court has handed down several decisions curbing punitives. [For further criticism of tort claims and our legal system generally, see **overlawyered.com** or **www.legalreform-now.org/**. For a critique of the 2009 Towers Watson (formerly Towers Perrin) report, see J. Robert Hunter and Joanne Doroshow, "Towers Perrin: 'Grade F' for Fantastically Inflated 'Tort Cost' Report," **www.consumerfed.org/elements/www.consumerfed.org/file/Insurance%20Report%20Towers%20 Perrin%202010(1).pdf**].

> A "tort tax" of $857 per year for every American.

In February 2017, the House Judiciary Committee approved the Lawsuit Abuse Reduction Act (LARA), which would impose mandatory penalties on those who bring frivolous lawsuits. LARA has been considered in previous years, but at this writing, its supporters are more hopeful of its passage.[31]

Against Tort Reform   Can we rely on the market and managerial ethics to protect us from dangerous products? Some point to the long-running battle over Toyota's sudden acceleration problems as evidence that the market alone does not adequately protect consumers from dangerous products.[32] Nearly a decade passed by before Toyota and the federal government began to aggressively examine the several thousand sudden acceleration claims.[33] Improvements in products such as air bags, seat belts, tires, tobacco products, antidepressants, and many more may have been encouraged by product liability litigation.[34]

More broadly, those opposing tort reform say that the tort burden simply is not of the magnitude suggested by the critics. Lawsuits, consuming less than 2 percent of spending, constitute a modest part of the cost of doing business; product liability claims are a small fraction of the total legal landscape; and studies show that insurance costs do not decline appreciably when damages are capped.[35] Furthermore, only about 3 percent of tort cases ever make it to trial; those cases that are settled before judgment often involve reasonable sums of money[36] and punitive damages are awarded in only about 3.3 percent of tort cases won by plaintiffs.[37] Even ardent defenders of tort practice often agree, however, that the system needs to be improved so that lawyers do not gobble up so much of the money themselves and so that the system produces a more consistent, predictable form of justice.[38]

Aurora victim's parents owe the ammunition suppliers

The parents of Jessica Ghawi, who was shot and killed by James Holmes when he opened gunfire in an Aurora, Colorado movie theatre, sued the ammunition sellers, Lucky Gunner and The Sportsman's Guide, who sold Holmes the ammunition online, asking for an injunction to prevent the defendants from selling ammunition to dangerous individuals through the Internet. A federal judge dismissed the lawsuit and, under a Colorado gun shield law, ordered the parents to pay over $200,000 to the defendants.

Question

What is the impact of the Colorado law, which only applies to lawsuits against gun manufacturers? What impact might LARA have if passed? Explain.

Source: Sandy Phillips and Lonnie Phillips, "We Lost Our Daughter to a Mass Shooter and Now Owe $203,000 to His Ammo Dealer, *The Huffington Post,* September 25, 2015 [**www.huffingtonpost.com/lonnie-and-sandy-phillips/lucky-gunner-lawsuit_b_8197804.html**].

Big Case: Lead Paint?

A helpful way to look at tort reform is to consider one of the massive claims that have emerged periodically as plaintiffs attempt to prove themselves wronged by a defective product or wrongful conduct. Tobacco smokers, Ford Explorer drivers, Vioxx users, and victims of gun violence are among those who have made headlines pursuing alleged corporate wrongdoers. Lead paint, banned since 1978, often produces developmental difficulties, including IQ deficiencies, learning disabilities, hyperactivity, and impaired hearing, when ingested or inhaled by children. Ordinarily, lead paint is troublesome only when it is reduced to flakes or dust, commonly in buildings that have not been properly maintained. While the potential for exposure to lead has declined dramatically in recent years, an estimated several hundred thousand young children, often living in old, inner-city housing, have been victims:

> Crawling across the wooden floor of his mother's Brooklyn (New York) apartment, Jaylin paused to lick his chubby hand, swallowing flecks of toxic paint. The boy's mother had no idea the poison lurked within the cracks of the baseboard.[39]

Should paint manufacturers be responsible for the harm caused by paint applied decades back by willing consumers before anyone fully understood the long-term hazards? What about owners and landlords who failed to properly maintain painted surfaces? Even if we can establish responsibility, how do we apportion damages when we cannot identify the specific producers of the paint in question? Or should we expect the paint manufacturers to share the damages burden according to the percentage each holds in the market (a product liability claim labeled *market share liability*)?

Lead paint lawsuits have been pursued in a number of states. In most cases, the plaintiffs have been states and municipalities that have sued paint manufacturers or landlords/property owners for creating a *public nuisance* (a significant interference with a right common to the general public such as the public health, public safety, or public peace). Market share liability claims also have been raised in some instances, but most claims under both theories of recovery have been rejected in court. For example, a unanimous Rhode Island Supreme Court in 2008 overturned a jury verdict against three paint companies when the court concluded that "however grave the problem of lead poisoning is in Rhode Island, public nuisance law simply does not provide a remedy for this harm."[40] Lawsuits continued, however, and in 2009, a Mississippi jury ruled that the Sherwin-Williams paint company was liable for illnesses suffered by a young boy who had eaten paint chips. The jury awarded $7 million in damages, but Sherwin-Williams successfully appealed that verdict.[41] Nevertheless, in 2014, the Mississippi Supreme Court reversed a trial court's grant of summary judgment to Sherwin-Williams in another case brought by five adults who, as minor children, attended a local Head Start program to which Sherwin-Williams sold paint used on its playground equipment, causing injury to the plaintiffs.[42]

> A young boy who had eaten paint chips.

Fast Food = "Fat" Lawsuits?

Fortune magazine's February 2003 issue asked "Is Fat the Next Tobacco?" *Fortune* and many other publications suggested that fast-food companies might soon be buried in lawsuits like those attacking the tobacco industry. Although the prospect of blaming McDonald's, Wendy's, and others for obese people's health problems caused dismay, those lawsuits, for the most part, have not materialized. Most of the handful of cases filed have been unsuccessful, and those that did gain some traction were based in mislabeling and consumer fraud. Furthermore, at least 24 states have passed "cheeseburger bills," providing some protection for fast-food companies facing obesity lawsuits. However, in vetoing the Minnesota state legislature's Personal Responsibility in Food Consumption Act, Minnesota governor Mark Dayton observed that although he supported the bill's intent, he believed the bill would create too broad an exemption from liability for food manufacturers and sellers.

Sources: Jennifer Pomeranz and Lainie Rutkow, "Efforts to Immunize Food Manufacturers from Obesity-Related Lawsuits: A Challenge for Public Health," *Corporations and Health Watch,* August 17, 2011 [**http://corporation-sandhealth.org/2011/08/17/efforts-to-immunize-food-manufacturers-from-obesity-related-lawsuits-a-challenge-for-public-health**]; and Lianne S. Pinchuk, "Are Fast-Food Lawsuits Likely to Be the Next 'Big Tobacco'?" *The National Law Journal,* February 28, 2007.

Too Much Law?

Perhaps we rely too much on the law. Clearly, legal intervention often is necessary to achieve justice. At the same time, that intervention sometimes can be inefficient and unproductive. As we conclude this chapter, give some thought to the cases you have read. On balance, do you think legal intervention was necessary in those situations, or would our society be stronger if we resolved more of those problems through private arrangements such as arbitration, as we discussed in Chapter 4, or risk assignment provisions included in contracts when we buy a new product?

[For the American Tort Reform Association, see **www.atra.org**].

Internet Exercise

Go to the American Tort Reform Association's website: **http://www.atra.org/.**

1. Go to "How States Perform" and click on a state to find its tort reforms. Review what type of reforms have passed in that state.

2. Select one of the state's reforms and read the statement on the purpose of that reform, and whether it was upheld as constitutional.

Chapter Questions

1. Cotillo, a power lifter with 10 years' experience, attempted to lift 530 pounds during an American Powerlifting Association–sponsored meet, organized by Duncan, the faculty sponsor of the local high school's weightlifting club, and Taylor, the APA president. Lifters were allowed to use spotters of their own choice or those provided by the meet. Cotillo used those provided by the meet, who were high school students with weightlifting experience. As Cotillo attempted the lift, Duncan was positioned "in the middle," and a student was on each side of the bar. Cotillo dropped the weight, shattering his jaw and causing other injuries. The spotters were in the proper positions to provide assistance, but they could not do so quickly enough to prevent injury. Cotillo then sued Duncan, the APA, and the APA Board, claiming, among other things, that the spotters were improperly trained. The spotters had received some instruction prior to the meet, but the record was unclear as to whether the training was improper or inadequate.

    a. What was Cotillo's cause of action?

    b. Defend Duncan et al.

    c. Decide the case. Explain. See *American Powerlifting Association v. Cotillo,* 934 A.2d 27 (Md. Ct. Spec. App. 2007).

2. Stopczynski, age 17, had used her neighbor's pool "hundreds of times." Stopczynski and her neighbor's nephew, a 34-year-old male, went to the pool. Stopczynski was noticed floating face down in the pool. She had broken her neck, apparently from diving into the four-foot-deep, above-ground pool. She died a few hours later. The pool originally had stickers around the edge that said "no diving," but that edge had been replaced and the stickers were gone. Stopczynski's mother sued the property owner, Woodcox, for negligence. Decide the case. Explain. See *Stopczynski v. Woodcox,* 258 Mich. App. 226 (2003).

3. After drinking alcoholic beverages at The Depot Sports Bar and Grill from 2:30 pm to approximately 10:30 pm, Dion died in a single-car wreck. During his time at The Depot, Dion was visibly intoxicated and a Depot employee asked for Dion's car keys, but Dion refused. Dion's widow brought a wrongful death action against The Depot, claiming that the conduct of The Depot's employees proximately caused Dion's death. Decide. Explain. See *Dion v. Y.S.G. Enterprises, Inc. d/b/a The Depot Sports Bar & Grill,* 296 Ga. 185 (2014).

4. Thomas Woeste died as a result of contracting a bacteria after eating about one dozen raw oysters at the Washington Platform Saloon & Restaurant. The bacteria, *Vibrio vulnificus,* are naturally occurring in oysters harvested in warm waters. Most people are unaffected by the bacteria, but those with weakened immune systems like Woeste

can be susceptible to illness or death. Washington Platform's menu contained the following warning:

> There may be risks associated when consuming shell fish. . . . If you suffer from chronic illness of the liver, stomach or blood . . . or if you have other immune disorders, you should eat these products fully cooked.

Woeste ordered and ate the oysters without opening the menu and reading the warning. A civil lawsuit was filed against Washington Platform alleging that the restaurant was both negligent and strictly liable for failure to adequately warn. Decide that case. Explain. See *Woeste v. Washington Platform Saloon & Restaurant,* 836 N.E.2d 52 (Ohio Ct. App. 2005).

5. In playgrounds, tall swings and slides along with sliding poles have typically been replaced by safer but less thrilling playground devices. U.S. playground safety standards, widely adopted in the 1990s, called for new safety surfaces to cushion falls, with the result that the swings became very costly. Thus, government rules and the threat of lawsuits have made playgrounds safer while reshaping childhood fun. Are we better off? See Gregg Toppo, "The Great American Swing Set Is Teetering," *USA Today,* March 19, 2006 [**www.usatoday.com/news/nation/2006-03-19-swing-sets_x.htm**].

6. Sandage loaded a car on a transport trailer. The car door could not be fully opened because of a support bar on the trailer. He suffered a back injury when he squeezed out of the car. The trailer had been modified to add several feet to its length, and support poles, including the one in question, had been added. Sandage sued the company that modified the trailer. Sandage sued in strict liability and negligence. Decide the case. Explain. See *Sandage v. Bankhead Enterprises, Inc.,* 177 F.3d 670 (8th Cir. 1999).

7. In 1995, a young Oklahoma couple shot and paralyzed a store clerk, Patsy Byers. The young couple had repeatedly viewed Oliver Stone's 1994 movie *Natural Born Killers,* which is about a young couple who go on a killing spree. The Byers family sued Stone and the Warner Brothers movie studio, the film distributor. Should a filmmaker and studio be liable for the alleged copycat behavior of those viewing a movie? Explain.

8. A deputy sheriff drove his marked police cruiser through a Burger King drive-through in Vancouver, Washington. After ordering his hamburger, he decided to check his food. When he pulled into a nearby parking lot and lifted the bun, he found what looked like spit on the meat patty. DNA testing later confirmed that the substance was spit belonging to an employee at the Burger King. The deputy sheriff brought a product liability and negligence lawsuit against Burger King and its franchisee, alleging that he suffered emotional distress as a result of the incident, including vomiting and sleeplessness. Should contaminated food be the basis for such a lawsuit? Decide. Explain. See *Bylsma v. Burger King,* 293 P.3d 1168 (Wash. 2013).

9. Doherty, a franchisee/owner of about 80 Applebee's restaurants, said in a newspaper interview that he treats employees "with dignity and respect" and offers "a great opportunity for them to have a good job." Previously, Michael Murray had represented his daughter, Erin Duby, a former Applebee's employee, in an arbitration claim alleging that she was sexually harassed by Applebee's managers and other employees. Murray

rejected a settlement offer arising out of the arbitration process. Murray then posted an online response to Doherty's interview by saying that "women . . . are routinely sexually harassed and that this behavior is condoned by high-level management at Doherty Enterprises right up to the top." He warned that "any reader who has a daughter, wife, etc. working for Doherty are [*sic*] more than likely being subjected to similar treatment." Doherty then sued Murray on defamation grounds. Was Doherty a victim of defamation? Decide. Explain. See Mary Pat Gallagher, "Applebee's Restaurateur . . . Over Internet Post Charging Harassment," *Corporate Counsel,* May 20, 2009.

10. After being told that Yonaty was gay or bisexual, Mincolla relayed the rumor to Koffman, a longtime friend of Yonaty's girlfriend, hoping the girlfriend would learn of the rumor. The girlfriend was told; Yonaty believed that caused the termination of their romantic relationship. Yonaty, who is not gay, sued Mincolla and Koffman for slander and intentional infliction of emotional distress. Decide the case. Explain. See *Yonaty v. Mincolla,* 97 A.D.3d 141 (N.Y. 2012).

11. A passenger ran after a train as it was leaving a station. Two railroad employees boosted the passenger aboard, but as they did so a package carried by the passenger fell beneath the wheels of the train and exploded. The package, unbeknownst to the employees, contained fireworks. The force of that explosion caused a scale many feet away to topple over, injuring the plaintiff, Palsgraf. Palsgraf sued the railroad on negligence grounds.

    a. Defend the railroad.

    b. Decide. Explain. See *Palsgraf v. Long Island R.R.,* 162 N.E. 99 (N.Y. 1928).

12. On September 8, 2009, Coomer went to the Kansas City Royals baseball game with his father. Instead of sitting in their ticketed seats, Coomer and his father sat in open seats six rows behind the third base dugout, to be closer to the game. Between the third and fourth innings, the Royals had a promotional event called the "Hotdog Launch," which it had held at home games for several years. The Royals mascot launched 20 to 30 hotdogs at the fans, either by throwing or firing through an air gun. The hotdogs shot out of the air gun were wrapped in bubble wrap and the ones thrown by hand were typically wrapped in foil. As the mascot prepared to throw hotdogs from behind his back in Coomer's direction, Coomer looked over at the scoreboard just before something hit him in the face. The impact caused a detached retina and other eye problems, leading to two surgeries. Coomer brought a personal injury lawsuit against the Kansas City Royals.

    a. How might the baseball team defend itself? Explain.

    b. Decide the case. Explain. See *Coomer v. Kansas City Royals,* 2013 Mo. App. LEXIS 46 (January 15, 2013).

13. In a 1993 shooting rampage at a San Francisco high-rise office building, Ferri killed eight people and wounded six before killing himself. Ferri used three guns, two of which were manufactured by Navegar. Survivors and representatives of the deceased sued Navegar under a common law negligence theory. Specifically, they alleged that Navegar was negligent in marketing this particular gun to the general civilian public, rather than restricting its sales to police and military units, given that this gun served

"no legitimate sporting or self-defense purpose." The trial court granted summary judgment to Navegar based on a California statute that provided, in a product liability action, no firearm shall be deemed defective in design on the basis that the benefits do not outweigh the risk of injury posed. The appellate court agreed, finding that "this is a products liability action based on negligence." A strong dissent was filed in the case, pointing out that plaintiffs did not plead their case under product liability for defective design. Rather, plaintiffs' claim was that under general negligence law Navegar had negligently marketed this particular gun to an inappropriate group and that it was the marketing, not the design of the product, to which they were objecting. The 2005 Protection of Lawful Commerce in Arms Act, under which the lawsuit brought against the ammunition sellers by the parents of a mass shooting victim, highlighted in this chapter, was dismissed, substantially shields firearms manufacturers and dealers from civil claims when guns are used in violent crimes. In your opinion, should gun manufacturers be held civilly liable for the criminal use of their products? *Marilyn Merrill v. Navegar,* 28 P.3d 116 (Cal. 2001). Explain.

14. Jennifer Strange, a 28-year-old mother of three living in Sacramento, California, entered a 2007 KDND-FM radio contest to drink as much water as possible without urinating. The prize was a Nintendo Wii game console. She drank nearly 2 gallons in three hours. She commented on her pain to the disc jockeys (DJs); one DJ commented she looked like she was pregnant. Listeners called in to warn of the dangers of water intoxication. The DJs replied, "We are aware of that," and later said the contestants had signed a release so "we're not responsible." During the show, the DJs jokingly discussed the risks. "Maybe we should have researched this before," one DJ added.[43] Apparently, these warnings were not shared with the contestants.[44] Strange finished second in the contest, called in sick to work, and died a few hours later. The Strange family sued the radio station's owners and its parent company for wrongful death.[45] Did the radio station cause Strange's death? Explain.

15. Joseph Birdsong and Bruce Waggoner both purchased iPods manufactured by Apple, Inc. Their iPods came equipped with detachable earbuds. Birdsong and Waggoner sued Apple for, among other claims, breach of implied warranty of merchantability, alleging the iPod is defective because of an unreasonable risk of hearing loss created by the supplied earbuds, which are designed to be placed in consumers' ears. Birdsong and Waggoner did not allege they or other consumers had suffered hearing loss. Apple includes a warning with each iPod regarding the risk of permanent hearing loss. Decide. Explain. See *Birdsong v. Apple, Inc.,* 590 F.3d 955 (9th Cir. 2009).

16. In December 2016, 36 people died in a fire during an electronic music concert at the Ghost Ship in Oakland, California, a warehouse that was zoned for commercial use but was used by its leaseholder as an art collective, concert venue, and residential space with tenants. Former tenants described the Ghost Ship as an internal maze with wood stairs and "do-it-yourself" electrical wiring. At this writing, the families of two of the Ghost Ship victims have filed lawsuits.

   a. Create a list of possible defendants and identify the business torts that might be brought against each. Explain.

   b. If you were a juror in a resulting civil trial, what questions would you have? Explain.

c. What defenses might be raised? Explain. See Richard Winton, "Lawyers for Ghost Ship Manager Say They Fear He Will Be Charged to Hide Government Negligence," *Los Angeles Times,* December 20, 2016 [**www.latimes.com/local/lanow/ la-me-ghost-ship-owner-20161227-story.html**]; and Daniel Kreps, "Families of Oakland Ghost Ship Fire Victims File First Lawsuits," *Rolling Stone,* December 28, 2016 [**www.rollingstone.com/music/news/families-of-oakland-ghost-ship-fire-victims-file-lawsuits-w457997**].

Notes

1. Justin Jouvenal, "In Defamation Lawsuit over Yelp Reviews, Neither Side Wins Damages," *The Washington Post,* January 31, 2014 [**www.washingtonpost.com**].

2. *Hart v. Electronic Arts,* 717 F.3d 141 (3d Cir. 2013).

3. Steve Berkowitz, "EA Drops Football in '14, Settles Cases as NCAA Fights," *USA TODAY,* September 26, 2013 [**www.usatoday.com**].

4. "The Tort Bar Burns On," *The Wall Street Journal,* July 23, 2012, p. A12.

5. Clifford Krauss, "A Factory's Closing Focuses Attention on Tort Reform," *The New York Times,* October 4, 2012 [**www.nytimes.com**].

6. "Letters to the Editor: Tort Suits Exist to Punish Bad Behavior, Help Victims," *The Wall Street Journal,* July 31, 2012, p. A12.

7. Krauss, "A Factory's Closing."

8. Ibid.

9. Ibid.

10. Ibid. See *Green v. Blitz USA,* 2011 U.S. Dist. LEXIS 20353 (E.D. Tex. March 1, 2011).

11. Krauss, "A Factory's Closing."

12. 111 N.E. 1050 (N.Y. 1916).

13. Heidi Hurd, "The Deontology of Negligence," *Boston University Law Review* 76 (April 1996), p. 249.

14. *Doss v. Town of Big Stone Gap,* 134 S.E. 563 (Va. 1926).

15. Aric Press, Ginny Carrol, and Steven Waldman, "Are Lawyers Burning America?" *Newsweek,* March 20, 1995, p. 30.

16. Ibid., p. 34.

17. Kevin Cane, "And Now, the Rest of the Story . . . About the McDonald's Coffee Lawsuit," *Houston Lawyer* 45 (July/August 2007), p. 24.

18. Anthony Ramirez, "Hot Coffee Justice," *National Post,* April 11, 2002, p. FP15.

19. *Pat Stalter v. Coca-Cola Bottling Company of Arkansas and Geyer Springs Food City, Inc.,* 669 S.W.2d 460 (Ark. 1984).

20. For another judicial examination of risk–utility and the Restatement 3d, see *Mikolajczyk v. Ford Motor Co.,* 901 N.E.2d 329 (Ill. 2008).

21. Foundation for Fair Civil Justice, "13th Annual Wacky Warning Labels Contest Winners Selected on National Television," press release, July 12, 2010 [**www.wackywarninglabelstv.com**].

22. "Generator Danger Warning," Consumer Product Safety Commission, January 2007 [**www. cpsc.gov/generator.html**].

23. *Whitlock v. University of Denver,* 712 P.2d 1072 (Colo. Ct. App. 1985).

24. *University of Denver v. Whitlock,* 744 P.2d 54 (Colo. 1987).

25. 27 Cal. Rptr. 697, 377 P.2d 897 (Cal. 1963).

26. *BMW v. Gore,* 517 U.S. 559 (1996).

27. Associated Press, "Huge Awards Aside, Few Companies Forced to Write Big Checks," *The Waterloo/Cedar Falls Courier,* October 12, 1997, p. C5.

28. Dionne Searcey, "Toyota Owners May Reap Little," *The Wall Street Journal,* May 20, 2010, p. B1.

29. Ibid.

30. Towers Watson, "2011 Update on U.S. Tort Cost Trends," January 2012 [**www.towerswatson. com/en-US/Insights/IC-Types/Survey-Research-Results/2012/01/2011-Update-on-US-Tort-Cost-Trends**].

31. Melissa Busch, "Business Groups Hopeful Legislation Targeting Frivolous Lawsuits Will Pass," *Legal NewsLine,* February 14, 2017 [**http://legalnewsline.com**].

32. Mark Robinson and Kevin Calcagnie, "Why We Need Trial Lawyers," *The Wall Street Journal,* February 24, 2010, p. A17.

33. Ibid.

34. Ibid.

35. Dan Zegart, "Tort Reform Advocates Play Fast and Loose with Facts," *The Seattle Post-Intelligencer,* November 21, 2004, p. F1.

36. Lou Dobbs, "Tort Reform Important to U.S. Future," *CNN,* January 6, 2005 [**http://articles. cnn.com**].

37. "Department of Justice Study Disproves Tort 'Reform' Myths," *Public Citizen* [**www.citizen.org**].

38. Zegart, "Tort Reform Advocates Play Fast and Loose with Facts."

39. Tina Moore and Benjamin Lesser, "How City Is Poisoning Kids," *New York Daily News,* January 14, 2007, p. 5.

40. Jeremy Singer-Vine and Joseph Pereira, "Court Scraps Key Lead-Paint Verdict," *The Wall Street Journal,* July 2, 2008, p. B1.

41. *Sherwin-Williams v. Gaines,* 75 So. 3d 41 (Miss. 2011).

42. *Banks v. Sherwin-Williams,* 134 So. 3d 706 (Miss. 2014).

43. "Too Much of Water Hast Thou," *Harper's Magazine,* May 2007 [**http://harpers.org/ archive/2007/05/too-much-of-water-hast-thou**].

44. Bruce Maiman, "Who to Blame in a Sacramento Mom's Death from Wii Water-Drinking Contest," *The Examiner.com,* November 1, 2009 [**www.examiner.com/article/who-to-blame-a-sacramento-mom-s-death-from-wii-water-drinking-contest**].

45. Martha Neil, "Jury Says Radio Station Must Pay $16.6 Million in Woman's Water Intoxication Death," *ABA Journal,* October 30, 2009 [**www.abajournal.com/mobile/article/jury_says_ radio_station_must_pay_16.6m_in_womans_water_intoxication_death**].

Trade Regulation and Antitrust

CHAPTER EIGHT

Government Regulation of Business

After completing this chapter, students will be able to fulfill the following learning objectives:

8-1. Explain some of the considerations involved in deciding to impose government regulations on business practice.

8-2. Describe the concept of market failure.

8-3. Explain the roles of the police power, the Supremacy Clause, the preemption doctrine, and the Commerce Clause in regulating business practice.

8-4. Explain when the federal government has exceeded its authority in regulating commerce.

8-5. Describe some of the ways in which state and local regulations affect business practice.

8-6. List some of the federal agencies that regulate business practice.

8-7. Identify the three broad categories of federal regulatory agencies' authority.

8-8. Compare and contrast the federal agencies' executive, legislative, and judicial roles.

8-9. Describe the executive, congressional, and judicial controls placed on agency conduct to maintain appropriate "checks and balances."

8-10. Analyze the Federal Communications Commission (FCC) role in regulating indecency in broadcasting.

8-11. Evaluate criticisms of the federal regulatory process.

Part One—An Introduction

PRACTICING ETHICS   Regulate Video Games?

Americans were shocked and searching for answers when Adam Lanza, 20, shot and killed 20 children, six Sandy Hook Elementary School staff members, his mother, and himself in Newtown, Connecticut, on December 14, 2012. Lanza reportedly was "enthralled" by violent video games, including one called *School Shooting,* although the state's official investigation of the shooting was unable to establish a motive for his behavior.

Even though video games are subject to an industrywide rating system, a number of states have also legislated restrictions on minors' access to violent video games. California, for example, approved a 2005 law forbidding the sale or rental of violent video games to minors. The video game industry sued to block the law; that challenge reached the U.S. Supreme Court in 2011, where the California law was struck down as a violation of free speech rights.[1] The Court ruled that the statute was a content-based restraint on speech requiring California to establish a compelling reason for the law; a standard the state could not satisfy. Studies linking violent video games and harm to children, the Court concluded, have not established a clear causal relationship between the two. The majority further reasoned that video games are like books, plays, and other forms of protected expression. Video games, they said, communicate ideas and even social messages. While the state has the power to protect children, that power does not extend to restricting the ideas children can receive. Some justices pointed specifically to the vagueness of the law that left uncertainty about which games would have been restricted by the law.

Scholarly Evidence?

While the Supreme Court concluded that California failed to show a sufficient link between violent video games and damage to children, some recent evidence is disquieting. A 2015 American Psychological Association task force reviewed more than 150 studies and concluded that playing violent video games is linked to increased aggression and decreased prosocial behavior in children. The evidence was insufficient, however, to reach a conclusion about a link between playing violent games and engaging criminal violence or delinquency. Other factors such as depression and trouble at home also influenced aggression.[2] [For the Entertainment Software Rating Board, see **www.esrb.org/index-js.jsp**].

Questions

1. In your judgment, are violent and sexually explicit videos harmful to children?

2. Ethics expert Chris MacDonald said that the video game industry should not be proud of selling "gory games" to kids. He has argued that video games are "fertile terrain for industry self-regulation. . . ." "Such a move toward social responsibility might go some distance toward proving that the video game industry is worthy of the constitutional protections it enjoys."[3]

   a. In your judgment, has the video game industry breached its social responsibility to American consumers? Explain.

   b. Would a video retailer have an ethical responsibility to decline to sell violent or sexually explicit videos if evidence revealed that those videos often reach children? Explain.

3. a. Will the free market and industry ethics satisfactorily protect society from any harm that may emerge from video game playing or is legal intervention necessary? Explain.

   b. Should the First Amendment protect video games from government oversight? Explain.

4. a. Do we need to protect children from video games, whether violent or not? Explain.

   b. If so, would government intervention be the most effective way of offering that protection? Explain.

5. Journalist Daniel Akst: "Part of the fun of video games is the chance to inhabit an exciting fictional world. So do people who play these games feel free to behave immorally toward the characters on screen?"[4] Answer Akst's question.

How Much Government?

This chapter and all those that follow are directed to our central question: How much government do we need? In the first three chapters, we looked at the role of the free market and ethics as "regulators" of business behavior. In Chapters 4 through 7 we introduced the foundations of the American legal system. Now we turn to the role the law plays in supplementing the market and ethics/social responsibility. The alleged link between video game use and social problems, including violence, is one relatively small example of an enormous array of disputes about the optimal balance between unconstrained business practice and government intervention in the market. America's public policy concerns are many: ongoing financial struggles, wealth and income inequality, health care reform, immigration, and climate change, for example. Do we need more rules to address these problems or does the market in combination with corporate ethics/social responsibility provide the most efficient, effective response? How do we decide when a new rule is needed?

Why Regulation?

LO 8-1

Explain some of the considerations involved in deciding to impose government regulations on business practice.

LO 8-2

Describe the concept of market failure.

Market Failure

In theory, government intervention in a free enterprise economy would be justified only when the market is unable to serve the public interest—that is, in instances of market failure. Market failure is attributed to certain inherent imperfections in the market itself.

1. Imperfect Information

Reasoned decisions require adequate information. Because we cannot have perfect information and often will not have adequate information, governments sometimes impose regulations either to improve the available information or to diminish the unfavorable effect of inadequate information. Hence, we have, for example, mandates for labeling consumer goods, licensure requirements for many occupations, and health standards for the processing and sale of goods.

Are Markets Rational? Can we make rational, efficient decisions in the absence of good information? Research demonstrates that we often face situations of *asymmetric information* where some parties to a transaction simply know more than the other parties to that transaction, with the result that optimal efficiency cannot be achieved. Beyond information deficiencies, the standard view of market rationality is questioned in other ways. Recent research in behavioral economics suggests that we often altruistically pursue social goals rather than simply maximizing our economic interests, as would be expected. The rational market model is likewise challenged by recent studies finding that risk taking by male financial traders increases as testosterone and cortisol levels climb, thus threatening market stability and supporting the view that financial decisions may be less rational than we have long believed.[5] Our free market system assumes rational decision making, but we might more accurately recognize that we operate with limited or *bounded rationality*. Hence, government intervention might be appropriate in some cases.

2. Monopoly

Of course, the government intervenes to thwart anticompetitive behaviors (monopoly) throughout the marketplace. (That process is addressed in Chapters 10 and 11.) We are concerned that the efficiency and fairness advantages of an open market will be compromised by large, powerful players and by conspiracies among competitors. The government plays the role of referee in creating and enforcing rules that curb anticompetitive conduct such as price-fixing and abuse of market dominance that undercut the virtues of the free market.

3. Externalities

When all the costs and benefits of a good or service are not fully internalized or absorbed by producers or consumers, those costs or benefits fall elsewhere as what economists have labeled *externalities*, *neighborhood effects*, or *spillovers*. Pollution is a characteristic example of a *negative externality*. The environment is used without charge as an ingredient in the production process (commonly as a receptacle for waste). Consequently, the product is underpriced. The producer and consumer do not pay the full social cost of the product, so those remaining costs are thrust on parties external to the transaction. Government regulation is then considered necessary to place the full cost on those who generated it, which in turn is expected to result in less wasteful use of resources.

Positive externalities are those in which a decision maker does not receive the full benefit of a decision because a portion of those benefits "spill over" on to third parties (often society at large) who were not direct participants in the decision. An example of a positive externality is a business firm that landscapes its grounds and develops a sculpture garden that benefits the firm but also benefits the neighborhood. Positive externalities ordinarily are not regulated. [See the work of Nobel Prize–winning economist Ronald Coase for the view that, under certain conditions, solutions for negative externalities and other market failures could be more efficiently and effectively resolved through private negotiations than through government intervention.]

Burgers and Negative Externalities

Food journalist Mark Bittman recently argued that burger chains would have to raise prices significantly or go out of business if they were forced to pay the full cost of producing burgers. He estimated the cost of burger production's negative externalities—such as carbon emissions from raising cows, obesity, and other health risks—at 68 cents to $2.90 per burger.

Source: *Mark Bittman,* "The True Cost of a Burger," *The New York Times*, July 15, 2014 [**www.nytimes.com**].

---

4. Public Goods

Some goods and services cannot be provided through the pricing system because we have no method for excluding those who choose not to pay. For such *public goods*, the added cost of benefiting one person is zero or nearly so, and, in any case, no one can effectively be denied the benefits of the activity. National defense, insect eradication, street lighting, and pollution control are examples of this phenomenon. Presumably, most individuals would refuse to voluntarily pay for what others would receive free. Thus, in the absence of government regulations, public goods would not be produced in adequate quantities.

Regulatory Life Cycle?

These market failures and other forces, to be explained later, sometimes lead to government intervention such as the Clean Air Act (see Chapter 17) or the Occupational Safety and Health Act (see Chapter 12). Looking at the historical record, law school dean Joseph Tomain argued that a rather predictable pattern or life cycle typically emerges when the government decides to regulate an industry. Stage One in Tomain's life cycle is the free market itself, the period when government regulation is absent from the market in question. In Stage Two, a market failure is identified, suggesting the need for government intervention. In Stage Three, government regulation is imposed in the form of a rule (such as a minimum drinking age). In Stage Four, regulatory failure occurs because, in brief, we believe the benefits of the rule in question no longer exceed its costs. In Stage Five, the government may respond with regulatory reform to correct the failure, or it may move to Stage Six, where the regulation in question is simply eliminated. The market, thus fully deregulated, has returned to Stage One (the free market) and the regulatory life cycle is complete.[6]

Tomain's regulatory cycle is illustrated by the experience of the American airline industry. Historically, the government had specified routes and fares. Then the airlines were deregulated in 1978. Following deregulation, low-cost carriers entered the market; some carriers could not compete and went out of business, but air travel became much more broadly available to the general public. Now traveler advocate Charles Leocha argues that some re-regulation could benefit consumers:

> Airlines should be held to their schedules. In Europe, all are punished for delays in service and consumers are compensated. . . . Egregiously outrageous fees such as $200 to $450 for cancellation of flights should be limited to a reasonable amount. . . . The Department of Transportation should require that airlines disclose all . . . fees so consumers are able to comparison shop on more than just airfare alone. . . .[7]

Tight states?

America is substantially fractured. Our Red State–Blue State political divide is only one expression of our cultural separations. Research from psychologists Jesse Harrington and Michele Gelfand helps explain America's great divide. Their work concludes that America is split among "tight" and "loose" states; the former have "many strongly enforced rules and little tolerance for deviance" and the latter have "few strongly enforced rules and greater tolerance for deviance." Citizens in "tight" states value order and structure, while those in "loose" states value change and new experiences. The "tightest" states include Mississippi, Alabama, Texas, and Oklahoma (all Red states) and the loosest include California, Oregon, and Massachusetts (all Blue states).

Harrington and Gelfand help explain the divide by pointing to the greater challenges faced by the "tight" states: ecological, territorial, and historical threats; natural disasters; higher populations densities; and higher health risks.

As you read this chapter, think about "tight" states versus "loose" states as a partial explanation for our national conflict over how much government intervention (rules) we need in our lives.

Question

Do you think of yourself as "tight" or "loose," and how does that attitude affect your view of the wisdom of government rules?

Source: Jesse Harrington and Michele Gelfand, "Tightness and Looseness: A New Way to Understand Differences Across the 50 United States," *Scientific American*, July 2, 2014 [**www.scientificamerican.com**].

Philosophy and Politics

Correction of market failure is a powerful motivation for government regulation of business, but an alternative or perhaps supplemental explanation lies in the political process. Three general arguments have emerged.

1. One view is that regulation is necessary for the protection and general welfare of the public. We find the government engaging in regulatory efforts designed to achieve a more equitable distribution of income and wealth (such as Social Security and the minimum wage). Many believe government intervention in the market is necessary to stabilize the economy, thus curbing the problems of recession, inflation, and unemployment. Affirmative action programs seek to compensate for racism and sexism. We even find the government protecting us from ourselves, both for our benefit and for the well-being of the larger society (consider seat belt requirements).

2. Another view is that regulation is developed at the request of industry and is operated primarily for the benefit of industry. Here the various subsidies and tax advantages afforded to business might be cited. In numerous instances, government regulation has been effective in reducing or entirely eliminating the entry of competitors. Government regulation has also permitted legalized price-fixing in some industries. Of course, it may be that regulation is often initiated primarily for the public welfare, but industry eventually "captures" the regulatory process and ensures its continuation for the benefit of the industry. On the other hand, some corporations seek government standards so they can do what is best for society without being undercut by their less socially responsible competitors.

3. Finally, bureaucrats who perform government regulation are themselves a powerful force in maintaining and expanding that regulation.

Bring Back Danger?

We often count on government rules to shelter us from dangers the market seems unable to handle. Hence, we created the federal Food and Drug Administration (FDA) to protect us from dangerous food, drugs, and medical devices (see Chapter 15). But sometimes rules cause harm. Indeed, safety may not always be in our best interest. Some critics argue that boys, in particular, need a certain amount of danger in their lives. Brothers Conn and

Hal Iggulden wrote *The Dangerous Book for Boys* as a manual of activities for boys.[8] Their book describes how to make a bow and arrow, hunt and cook a rabbit, build a tree house, set a trip wire, and so on. They point to that bygone era when every boy had a jackknife.

Journalist Hanna Rosin agrees with the Igguldens:

> In the past generation, the rising preoccupation with children's safety has transformed childhood, stripping it of independence, risk-taking, and discovery. What's been gained is unclear: rates of injury have remained fairly steady since the 1970s, and abduction by strangers was as rare then as it is now. . . .[9]

Questions

1. Do you agree with the Iggulden brothers and Rosin that we should allow boys to experience a certain amount of danger in their lives? Explain

2. How about girls? [See Andrea Buchanan and Miriam Peskowitz, *The Daring Book for Girls* (New York: HarperCollins, 2007).]

The Constitutional Foundation of Business Regulation

LO 8-3

Explain the roles of the police power, the Supremacy Clause, the preemption doctrine, and the Commerce Clause in regulating business practice.

The Commerce Clause of the U.S. Constitution broadly specifies the power accorded to the federal government to regulate business activity. Article I, Section 8 of the Constitution provides that "The Congress shall have the Power . . . To regulate Commerce with foreign Nations, and among the several States, and with the Indian Tribes." State authority to regulate commerce resides in the *police power* specified by the Constitution. Police power refers to the right of the state governments to promote the public health, safety, morals, and general welfare by regulating persons and property within each state's jurisdiction. The states have, in turn, delegated portions of the police power to local government units.

Commerce Clause Examined

The Commerce Clause, as interpreted by the judiciary, affords Congress exclusive jurisdiction over *foreign commerce*. States and localities, nevertheless, sometimes seek in various ways to regulate foreign commerce. A state may try, for example, to impose a tax on foreign goods that compete with those locally grown or manufactured. Such efforts are unconstitutional violations of the Commerce Clause and thus are unenforceable.

Federal authority over "commerce among the several states," that is, *interstate commerce*, affords the federal government very broad power to regulate commercial activities across the United States and was designed to create an open, effectively borderless market throughout the nation, wherein goods would move freely among the states, unimpeded by state and local tariffs and duties. The Constitution does not, however, expressly forbid state regulation of interstate commerce. As with foreign commerce, the states and localities pass laws to influence interstate commerce, often to favor local economic interests. The judiciary has aggressively curbed those efforts, and in the process, the reach of the federal government has been dramatically expanded. Even purely *intrastate* activities can be regulated by the federal government if they have a substantial effect on interstate commerce. In the 1942 case *Wickard v. Filburn*,[10] the U.S. Supreme Court, in interpreting a federal statute regulating the production and sale of wheat, found that one farmer's production of 23 acres of homegrown and largely home-consumed wheat, in combination with other similarly situated farmers growing and consuming wheat locally, could substantially affect the interstate wheat market by reducing demand for that wheat among those such as Wickard, who grew it locally. Thus, a local product could be subject to federal regulation. In 2005, the Supreme Court affirmed the *Wickard* reasoning in an interesting California case, *Gonzalez v. Raich*,[11] involving the federal government's constitutional authority to regulate the use of medical marijuana.

Raich   In 1996, California decriminalized the doctor-approved medical use of marijuana. The federal Controlled Substances Act (CSA), on the other hand, forbids the use, cultivation, or possession of marijuana for any purpose. A Californian, Angel Raich, who, under a doctor's prescription, used marijuana for pain control, challenged the application of the CSA against California medical marijuana users. The heart of her claim was that the Commerce Clause does not give the federal government the authority to regulate the noncommercial cultivation and personal, medical use of marijuana that does not cross state lines. She won at the U.S. Court of Appeals for the Ninth Circuit, but the U.S. Supreme Court, by a 6–3 vote, ruled against Raich. Addressing the central question, the Court reasoned that the wholly *intrastate* use of marijuana had a substantial effect on *interstate* commerce in marijuana and thus was subject to federal regulation, as the Court had ruled decades earlier in *Wickard*. Personal consumption of marijuana, even for medical purposes, has the potential to displace demand for marijuana in the illegal interstate market, thus substantially affecting interstate commerce.

> Angel Raich used marijuana for pain control.

Too Much Federal Power?

LO 8-4
Explain when the federal government has exceeded its authority in regulating commerce.

Dissenting in *Raich*, Supreme Court Justice Thomas warned:

> If Congress can regulate this under the Commerce Clause, then it can regulate virtually anything—and the federal government is no longer one of limited and enumerated powers.[12]

Lopez   Perhaps seeking to demonstrate that the Constitution does not accord unlimited power to the federal government, the Supreme Court has occasionally issued decisions expressly restraining that Commerce Clause authority. In the 1995 *United States v. Lopez* case,[13] the Supreme Court clearly spoke for states' rights. In 1990 the federal government approved the Gun-Free School Zones Act, which forbade "any individual knowingly to possess a firearm at a place that [he] knows . . . is a school zone."[14] Congress claimed that gun possession in school zones would increase violence, retard learning, and discourage travel, thus affecting commerce. Lopez, a 12th-grade San Antonio, Texas, student, carried an unloaded, concealed gun into his high school and was charged with violating the act. His case reached the Supreme Court, where he claimed and the Court agreed that Congress did not have the constitutional authority to regulate the matter. By a 5–4 vote, the Court held that the possession of a gun at a school is not an economic activity that could, even if repeated elsewhere, have a substantial effect on interstate commerce.

> A 12th-grade San Antonio, Texas student carried an unloaded, concealed gun into his high school.

Brzonkala Strengthening its *Lopez* reasoning, the U.S. Supreme Court in the 2000 *Brzonkala* case[15] ruled by a 5–4 vote that Congress exceeded its Commerce Clause authority in approving some portions of the federal Violence Against Women Act (VAWA). The law allowed women who had been victims of gender-based violence to sue in federal court even though the crimes did not directly involve more than one state. In debating VAWA, Congress held hearings and developed a record on the aggregate economic impact of violence against women, including driving up medical costs and discouraging women from traveling and from holding jobs, but the Supreme Court said Congress did not have the power to regulate noneconomic violent crime because it does not have a substantial effect on interstate commerce. To rule otherwise, the Court said, might "obliterate" the constitutional distinction between federal and state/local authority.

The case involved a woman, Brzonkala, who claimed she was raped by two football players, Morrison and Crawford, when all three were students at Virginia Polytechnic Institute:

> Brzonkala alleges that soon after she met Morrison and Crawford, the two defendants pinned her down on a bed in her dormitory and forcibly raped her. Afterward, Morrison told Brzonkala, "You better not have any f* *ing diseases." And, subsequently, Morrison announced publicly in the dormitory's dining hall, "I like to get girls drunk and f* * * the s* * * out of them."[16]

After Brzonkala complained to the university, Morrison was found guilty of abusive conduct by the VPI judicial committee and was suspended for one year, but that punishment was subsequently lifted. Brzonkala then sued for civil damages in federal court under the VAWA. As explained above, Brzonkala eventually lost, however, when the Supreme Court invalidated the portions of the VAWA that she was relying on by ruling that the acts of violence the VAWA was aimed at did not have a substantial effect on interstate commerce. [For the federal Violence Against Women Action Center, see **www.ovw.usdoj .gov/**].

> Brzonkala claimed she was raped by two football players.

Obamacare In June 2012, the U.S. Supreme Court, by a 5–4 vote, upheld the constitutionality of the Affordable Care Act (Obamacare), but the decision raised further doubts about the federal government's Commerce Clause power.[17] The core of the Supreme Court review involved what is called the "individual mandate": a requirement in the bill forcing most Americans to maintain "minimum essential" health insurance. The mandate was challenged on the grounds that it violated the Commerce Clause by attempting to regulate *inactivity* (commanding action from those who are not buying health insurance) rather than regulating already-existing interstate activity. The Court, by a 5–4 margin, ruled that the individual mandate was, indeed, a violation of the Commerce Clause. The Court reasoned that construing the Commerce Clause to allow Congress to regulate inactivity would open up potentially expansive new territory to congressional intervention.

Nonetheless, the case turned out to be a victory for Obamacare. The Court, once again by a 5–4 margin, ultimately upheld the constitutionality of the individual mandate on the grounds that it constituted a *tax* on those who do not have health insurance. In as much as Congress clearly has the constitutional authority to "lay and collect Taxes" (Article I, Section 8, Clause 1—see the Constitution in Appendix A at the back of this text), the Court ruled that Obamacare's individual mandate is constitutionally permissible. At this writing,

President Trump and Republican congressional leaders have indicated their intent to replace (or perhaps amend) Obamacare.

Public Accommodations   The classic decision that follows illustrates the importance of Commerce Clause reasoning. In this case, Congress used its economic authority under the Commerce Clause to open public accommodations (hotels, restaurants, and the like) to all persons, thus reshaping American social and racial practices.

LEGAL BRIEFCASE

Heart of Atlanta Motel v. United States   379 U.S. 241 (1964)

Justice Clark

This is a declaratory judgment action, attacking the constitutionality of Title II of the Civil Rights Act of 1964. [The lower court found for the United States.]

1. THE FACTUAL BACKGROUND AND CONTENTIONS OF THE PARTIES

. . . Appellant owns and operates the Heart of Atlanta Motel, which has 216 rooms available to transient guests. The motel is located on Courtland Street, two blocks from downtown Peachtree Street. It is readily accessible to interstate highways 75 and 85 and state highways 23 and 41. Appellant solicits patronage from outside the State of Georgia through various national advertising media, including magazines of national circulation; it maintains over 50 billboards and highway signs within the state, soliciting patronage for the motel; it accepts convention trade from outside Georgia, and approximately 75 percent of its registered guests are from out of state. Prior to passage of the act the motel had followed a practice of refusing to rent rooms to Negroes, and it alleged that it intended to continue to do so. In an effort to perpetuate that policy this suit was filed.

The appellant contends that Congress in passing this act exceeded its power to regulate commerce under [Article I] of the Constitution of the United States. . . .

The appellees counter that the unavailability to Negroes of adequate accommodations interferes significantly with interstate travel, and that Congress, under the Commerce Clause, has power to remove such obstructions and restraints. . . .

[A]ppellees proved the refusal of the motel to accept Negro transients after the passage of the act. The district court sustained the constitutionality of the sections of the act under attack and issued a permanent injunction. . . . It restrained the appellant from "[r]efusing to accept Negroes as guests in the motel by reason of their race or color" and from "[m]aking any distinction whatever upon the basis of race or color in the availability of the goods, services, facilities, privileges, advantages, or accommodations offered or made available to the guests of the motel, or to the general public, within or upon any of the premises of the Heart of Atlanta Motel, Inc."

2. THE HISTORY OF THE ACT

. . . The act as finally adopted was most comprehensive, undertaking to prevent through peaceful and voluntary settlement discrimination in voting, as well as in places of accommodation and public facilities, federally secured programs, and in employment. Since Title II is the only portion under attack here, we confine our consideration to those public accommodation provisions.

3. TITLE II OF THE ACT

This Title is divided into seven sections beginning with Section 201(a), which provides,

> All persons shall be entitled to the full and equal enjoyment of the goods, services, facilities, privileges, advantages, and accommodations of any place of public accommodation, as defined in this section, without discrimination or segregation on the ground of race, color, religion, or national origin.

4. APPLICATION OF TITLE II TO HEART OF ATLANTA MOTEL

It is admitted that the operation of the motel brings it within the provisions of Section 201(a) of the act and that appellant refused to provide lodging for transient Negroes because of their race or color and that it intends to continue that policy unless restrained.

The sole question posed is, therefore, the constitutionality of the Civil Rights Act of 1964 as applied to these facts. . . .

[Part 5 omitted—ed.]

6. THE BASIS OF CONGRESSIONAL ACTION

While the act as adopted carried no congressional findings, the record of its passage through each house is replete with evidence of the burdens that discrimination by race or color places upon interstate commerce. . . . This testimony included the fact that our people have become increasingly mobile with millions of people of all races traveling from state to state; that Negroes in particular have been the subject of discrimination in transient accommodations, having to travel great distances to secure the same; that often they have been unable to obtain accommodations and have had to call upon friends to put them up overnight; and that these conditions have become so acute as to require the listing of available lodging for Negroes in a special guidebook which was itself "dramatic testimony to the difficulties" Negroes encounter in travel. These exclusionary practices were found to be nationwide, the Under Secretary of Commerce testifying that there is "no question that this discrimination in the North still exists to a large degree" and in the West and Midwest as well. This testimony indicated a qualitative as well as quantitative effect on interstate travel by Negroes. The former was the obvious impairment of the Negro traveler's pleasure and convenience that resulted when he continually was uncertain of finding lodging. As for the latter, there was evidence that this uncertainty stemming from racial discrimination had the effect of discouraging travel on the part of a substantial portion of the Negro community. This was the conclusion not only of the Under Secretary of Commerce but also of the Administrator of the Federal Aviation Agency, who wrote the Chairman of the Senate Commerce Committee that it was his "belief that air commerce is adversely affected by the denial to a substantial segment of the traveling public of adequate and desegregated public accommodations." We shall not burden this opinion with further details since the voluminous testimony presents overwhelming evidence that discrimination by hotels and motels impedes interstate travel.

7. THE POWER OF CONGRESS OVER INTERSTATE TRAVEL

The power of Congress to deal with these obstructions depends on the meaning of the Commerce Clause.

* * * * *

In short, the determinative test of the exercise of power by the Congress under the Commerce Clause is simply whether the activity sought to be regulated is "commerce which concerns more States than one" and has a real and substantial relation to the national interest. Let us now turn to this facet of the problem.

* * * * *

The same interest in protecting interstate commerce which led Congress to deal with segregation in interstate carriers and the white-slave traffic has prompted it to extend the exercise of its power to gambling, to criminal enterprises, to deceptive practices in the sale of products, to fraudulent security transactions, and to racial discrimination by owners and managers of terminal restaurants. . . .

That Congress was legislating against moral wrongs in many of these areas rendered its enactments no less valid. In framing Title II of this act Congress was also dealing with what it considered a moral problem. But that fact does not detract from the overwhelming evidence of the disruptive effect the racial discrimination has had on commercial intercourse. It was this burden which empowered Congress to enact appropriate legislation, and, given this basis for the exercise of its power, Congress was not restricted by the fact that the particular obstruction to interstate commerce with which it was dealing was also deemed a moral and social wrong.

It is said that the operation of the motel here is of a purely local character. But, assuming this to be true, "[i]f it is interstate commerce that feels the pinch, it does not matter how local the operation which applies the squeeze."

* * * * *

Thus the power of Congress to promote interstate commerce also includes the power to regulate the local incidents thereof, including local activities in both the states of origin and destination, which might have a substantial and harmful effect upon that commerce. One need only examine the evidence which we have discussed above to see that Congress may—as it has—prohibit racial discrimination by motels serving travelers, however "local" their operations may appear.

* * * * *

The only questions are (1) whether Congress had a rational basis for finding that racial discrimination by motels affected commerce, and (2) if it had such a basis, whether the means it selected to eliminate that evil are reasonable and appropriate. If they are, appellant has no "right" to select its guests as it sees fit, free from governmental regulation.

* * * * *

It is doubtful if in the long run appellant will suffer economic loss as a result of the act. Experience is to the contrary where discrimination is completely obliterated as to all public accommodations. But whether this be true or not is of no consequence since this Court has specifically held that the fact that a "member of the class which is regulated may suffer economic losses not shared by others . . . has never been a barrier" to such legislation. . . .

We, therefore, conclude that the action of the Congress in the adoption of the act as applied here to a motel which concededly serves interstate travelers is within the power granted it by the Commerce Clause of the Constitution, as interpreted by this Court for 140 years. . . .

Affirmed.

Questions

1. In your judgment, does the Commerce Clause afford the federal government the authority to regulate a local business like the Heart of Atlanta Motel? Explain.

2. Should the federal government regulate local business to further the cause of racial equity? Explain.

3. What arguments were offered by the government to establish that the Heart of Atlanta racial policy affected interstate commerce? Are you persuaded by those arguments? Explain.

4. What test did the Court articulate to determine when Congress has the power to pass legislation based on the Commerce Clause?

5. Ollie's Barbecue, a neighborhood restaurant in Birmingham, Alabama, discriminated against black customers. McClung brought suit to test the application of the public accommodations section of the Civil Rights Act of 1964 to his restaurant.

In the suit, the government offered no evidence to show that the restaurant ever had served interstate customers or that it was likely to do so. Decide the case. See *Katzenbach v. McClung*, 379 U.S. 294 (1964).

6. Juan Paul Robertson was charged with various narcotics offenses and with violating the federal Racketeer Influenced and Corrupt Organizations Act (RICO) by investing the proceeds from his unlawful activities in an Alaskan gold mine. He paid for some mining equipment in Los Angeles and had it shipped to Alaska. He hired seven out-of-state employees to work in the Alaskan mine. Most of the resulting gold was sold in Alaska, although Robertson transported $30,000 in gold out of the state. He was convicted on the RICO charge but appealed, claiming that the gold mine was not engaged in or affecting interstate commerce. Was Robertson's gold mine engaged in or affecting interstate commerce? Explain. See *United States v. Juan Paul Robertson*, 115 S. Ct. 1732 (1995).

Supremacy Clause

State or local law sometimes conflicts with federal law. As noted in Chapter 5, such situations are resolved by the Supremacy Clause of the Constitution (Article VI, paragraph 2), which provides that "This Constitution, and the Laws of the United States . . . shall be the Supreme Law of the Land." In the event of an irreconcilable conflict between federal and state law, the Supremacy Clause, as interpreted by the courts, provides that federal law will *preempt* (supersede) state or local law, rendering it unconstitutional.

As explained in Chapter 5, ours is a federalist form of government wherein we divide authority among federal, state, and local units of government. Conflicts are inevitable, but each level of government brings strengths to the process. State rules benefit from being enacted by bodies very close to the people themselves. On the other hand, optimal efficiency, especially for the business community, often demands one uniform federal rule rather than a patchwork of 50 state rules.[18]

In general, Supreme Court decisions have affirmed the federal government's regulatory authority even when faced with conflicting state rules. Were it not so, we would have great difficulty in achieving a unified national policy on any issue. Recent Supreme Court preemption decisions have been split, some allowing state law to stand despite conflicts with federal law, others being struck down.[19]

Marijuana: Federal Preemption?   Colorado and Washington legalized recreational marijuana use, but under the federal Controlled Substances Act (CSA), marijuana possession remains a criminal wrong. The Obama administration decided against aggressively enforcing federal marijuana law in those two states, but state attorneys general in Nebraska and Oklahoma filed suit arguing that the Colorado marijuana law impermissibly conflicted with the CSA and was preempted by it. Nebraska and Oklahoma claimed that Colorado's marijuana policy was increasing drug

> Nebraska and Oklahoma claimed that Colorado's marijuana policy was increasing drug trafficking.

trafficking into their states, causing law enforcement and social challenges. Thus, we see that the states themselves often prefer uniform federal regulation under the Supremacy Clause. Because the case involved a dispute between states, it was taken directly to the U.S. Supreme Court, but in 2016 the Court declined to hear the case.[20] At this writing, Nebraska and Oklahoma have sought to join another challenge to Colorado's marijuana laws that is being heard by the U.S. 10th Circuit Court of Appeals.

Also at this writing, recreational marijuana use is lawful in eight states, while 28 states permit medical use of marijuana. Do you think the federal government should begin to more actively enforce federal laws criminalizing marijuana use even where state law permits that use?

Our Guns: Feds Must Stay Out

Gary Marbut of Missoula, Montana, hoped to manufacture .22-caliber rifles he called Montana Buckaroos. He wanted to produce and sell the guns exclusively in Montana from materials originating in Montana. He argued that Buckaroos could not be subject to federal regulation if made and sold only on an intrastate basis. Marbut (and others) brought suit seeking a court order affirming the right in Montana to manufacture and sell guns free of federal regulation. Marbut lost at the federal district court.

On appeal, the federal Ninth Circuit Court ruled that the guns, even if initially sold only in Montana, would, in the aggregate, affect the national firearms market and thus were subject to the federal government's gun rules, which preempted the Montana law. The Supreme Court in 2014 declined to review the case. Other states have laws much like Montana's.

Sources: Tim Murphy, "Gun Enthusiasts' Hot New Idea: You Can't Regulate Guns We Make In-State," *Mother Jones*, February 1, 2013 [**www.motherjones.com**]; and *Montana Shooting Sports Association v. Holder*, 727 F.3d 975 (9th Cir. 2013), cert. denied, 134 S. Ct. 955 (2014) and *Montana v. Holder*, 134 S. Ct. 1335 (2014).

Part Two—State and Local Regulation of Interstate Commerce

As noted, the states via their constitutional police power have the authority to regulate commerce within their jurisdictions for the purpose of maintaining public health, safety, and morals. We have seen, however, that the U.S. Constitution's Commerce Clause accords the federal government broad authority over commerce. As explained, the federal government has exclusive authority over foreign commerce. Purely intrastate commerce, having no significant effect on interstate commerce, is within the exclusive regulatory jurisdiction of the states and localities. Of course, purely intrastate commerce is uncommon. The confusion arises in the middle ground of interstate commerce where regulation by the federal government or state governments or both may be permissible. Although federal government regulation of interstate commerce is pervasive, it is not exclusive, especially in matters involving the states' police powers.

Our concern in this section is with commerce that is clearly interstate in nature but is, nonetheless, subjected to state and/or local regulation. The issue is whether that regulation is unconstitutional because it (1) *discriminates* against interstate commerce or (2) *unduly burdens* interstate commerce such that the burden imposed clearly exceeds the local benefits.

In the *Granholm* case that follows, we see elements of the continuing conflict between federal and state control of interstate commerce, especially in matters of health and safety (police power). At the commercial level, the case is about another classic conflict: free trade versus protectionism. Can states lawfully protect their local wineries from out-of-state competition? The lower courts were divided on the question of whether the Commerce Clause of the federal constitution is violated when a state permits in-state wineries to ship directly to in-state customers while not permitting out-of-state wineries to do the same. Historically, only a few states had allowed wineries to ship directly to customers, but gradually about half of the states allowed direct shipments, resulting in a confusing situation where some states allowed all shipments, some permitted in-state shipments only, and some forbade all shipments. In its 5–4 *Granholm* decision, the central question facing the Supreme Court was the conflict between the requirements of the Commerce Clause versus the requirements of the Twenty-First Amendment to the U.S. Constitution. That amendment ended Prohibition in 1933 and gave the states broad authority to regulate the sale of alcohol.

> Can states lawfully protect their local wineries from out-of-state competition?

LEGAL BRIEFCASE

Granholm v. Heald
544 U.S. 460 (2005)

Justice Kennedy

These consolidated cases present challenges to state laws regulating the sale of wine from out-of-state wineries to consumers in Michigan and New York. The details and mechanics of the two regulatory schemes differ, but the object and effect of the laws are the same: to allow in-state wineries to sell wine directly to consumers in that state but to prohibit out-of-state wineries from doing so, or, at the least, to make direct sales impractical from an economic standpoint. It is evident that the object and design of the Michigan and New York statutes is to grant in-state wineries a competitive advantage over wineries located beyond the states' borders.

*   *   *   *   *

I

Like many other states, Michigan and New York regulate the sale and importation of alcoholic beverages, including wine, through a three-tier distribution system. Separate licenses are required for producers, wholesalers, and retailers. . . . We have held previously that states can mandate a three-tier distribution scheme in the exercise of their authority under the Twenty-First Amendment.

As relevant to today's cases, though, the three-tier system is, in broad terms and with refinements to be discussed, mandated by Michigan and New York only for sales from out-of-state wineries. In-state wineries, by contrast, can obtain a license for direct sales to consumers. The differential treatment between in-state and out-of-state wineries constitutes explicit discrimination against interstate commerce.

This discrimination substantially limits the direct sale of wine to consumers. . . . From 1994 to 1999, consumer spending on direct wine shipments doubled, reaching $500 million per year, or 3 percent of all wine sales. . . . [T]he number of small wineries in the United States has significantly increased. At the same time, the wholesale market has consolidated. . . . The increasing winery-to-wholesaler ratio means that many small wineries do not produce enough wine or have sufficient consumer demand for their wine to make it economical for wholesalers to carry their products. This has led many small wineries to rely on direct shipping to reach new markets. Technological improvements, in particular the ability of wineries to sell wine over the Internet, have helped make direct shipments an attractive sales channel.

Approximately 26 states allow some direct shipping of wine, with various restrictions. Thirteen of these states have reciprocity laws, which allow direct shipment from wineries outside the state, provided the state of origin affords similar nondiscriminatory treatment. In many parts of the country, however, state laws that prohibit or severely restrict direct shipments deprive consumers of access to the direct market.

The wine producers in the cases before us are small wineries that rely on direct consumer sales as an important part of their businesses. Domaine Alfred, one of the plaintiffs in the Michigan suit, is a small winery located in San Luis Obispo, California. . . . Domaine Alfred has received requests for its wine from Michigan consumers but cannot fill the orders because of the state's direct shipment ban. . . .

Similarly, Juanita Swedenburg and David Lucas, two of the plaintiffs in the New York suit, operate small wineries in Virginia (the Swedenburg Estate Vineyard) and California (the Lucas Winery). Some of their customers are tourists from other states, who purchase wine while visiting the wineries. If these customers wish to obtain Swedenburg or Lucas wines after they return home, they will be unable to do so if they reside in a state with restrictive direct shipment laws. . . .

A

We first address the background of the suit challenging the Michigan direct shipment law. Most alcoholic beverages in Michigan are distributed through the state's three-tier system. Producers or distillers of alcoholic beverages, whether located in state or out of state, generally may sell only to licensed in-state wholesalers. Wholesalers, in turn, may sell only to in-state retailers. Licensed retailers are the final link in the chain, selling alcoholic beverages to consumers at retail locations and, subject to certain restrictions, through home delivery.

Under Michigan law, wine producers, as a general matter, must distribute their wine through wholesalers. There is, however, an exception for Michigan's approximately 40 in-state wineries, which are eligible for "wine maker" licenses that allow direct shipment to in-state consumers. The cost of the license varies with the size of the winery. For a small winery, the license is $25. Out-of-state wineries can apply for a $300 "outside seller of wine" license, but this license only allows them to sell to in-state wholesalers.

* * * * *

B

New York's licensing scheme is somewhat different. It channels most wine sales through the three-tier system, but it too makes exceptions for in-state wineries. As in Michigan, the result is to allow local wineries to make direct sales to consumers in New York on terms not available to out-of-state wineries. Wineries that produce only from New York grapes can apply for a license that allows direct shipment to in-state consumers. These licensees are authorized to deliver the wines of other wineries as well, but only if the wine is made from grapes "at least seventy-five percent the volume of which were grown in New York state." An out-of-state winery may

ship directly to New York consumers only if it becomes a licensed New York winery, which requires the establishment of "a branch factory, office, or storeroom within the state of New York."

* * * * *

C

We consolidated these cases and granted certiorari on the following question: "Does a state's regulatory scheme that permits in-state wineries directly to ship alcohol to consumers but restricts the ability of out-of-state wineries to do so violate the Commerce Clause in light of Section 2 of the Twenty-First Amendment?"

II

A

Time and again this Court has held that, in all but the narrowest circumstances, state laws violate the Commerce Clause if they mandate "differential treatment of in-state and out-of-state economic interests that benefits the former and burdens the latter." This rule is essential to the foundations of the Union. The mere fact of nonresidence should not foreclose a producer in one state from access to markets in other States. States may not enact laws that burden out-of-state producers or shippers simply to give a competitive advantage to in-state businesses. This mandate "reflects a central concern of the Framers that was an immediate reason for calling the Constitutional Convention: the conviction that in order to succeed, the new Union would have to avoid the tendencies toward economic Balkanization that had plagued relations among the Colonies and later among the States under the Articles of Confederation."

* * * * *

B

The discriminatory character of the Michigan system is obvious. Michigan allows in-state wineries to ship directly to consumers, subject only to a licensing requirement. Out-of-state wineries, whether licensed or not, face a complete ban on direct shipment. The differential treatment requires all out-of-state wine, but not all in-state wine, to pass through an in-state wholesaler and retailer before reaching consumers. These two extra layers of overhead increase the cost of out-of-state wines to Michigan consumers. The cost differential, and in some cases the inability to secure a wholesaler for small shipments, can effectively bar small wineries from the Michigan market.

* * * * *

The New York scheme grants in-state wineries access to the state's consumers on preferential terms. . . . In-state producers, with the applicable licenses, can ship directly to consumers from their wineries. Out-of-state wineries must open a branch office and warehouse in New York, additional steps that drive up the cost of their wine.

* * * * *

We have no difficulty concluding that New York, like Michigan, discriminates against interstate commerce through its direct shipping laws.

III

State laws that discriminate against interstate commerce face "a virtually per se rule of invalidity." The Michigan and New York laws by their own terms violate this proscription. The two states, however, contend their statutes are saved by Section 2 of the Twenty-First Amendment, which provides,

> The Transportation or importation into any State, Territory, or possession of the United States for delivery or use therein of intoxicating liquors, in violation of the laws thereof, is hereby prohibited.

*   *   *   *   *

State policies are protected under the Twenty-First Amendment when they treat liquor produced out of state the same as its domestic equivalent. The instant cases, in contrast, involve straightforward attempts to discriminate in favor of local producers. The discrimination is contrary to the Commerce Clause and is not saved by the Twenty-First Amendment.

IV

We still must consider whether either state regime "advances a legitimate local purpose that cannot be adequately served by reasonable nondiscriminatory alternatives." The states offer two primary justifications for restricting direct shipments from out-of-state wineries: keeping alcohol out of the hands of minors and facilitating tax collection.

The states claim that allowing direct shipment from out-of-state wineries undermines their ability to police underage drinking. Minors, the states argue, have easy access to credit cards and the Internet and are likely to take advantage of direct wine shipments as a means of obtaining alcohol illegally.

The states provide little evidence that the purchase of wine over the Internet by minors is a problem. Indeed, there is some evidence to the contrary. A recent study by the staff of the FTC found that the 26 states currently allowing direct shipments report no problems with minors' increased access to wine.

*   *   *   *   *

Even were we to credit the states' largely unsupported claim that direct shipping of wine increases the risk of underage drinking, this would not justify regulations limiting only out-of-state direct shipments. As the wineries point out, minors are just as likely to order wine from in-state producers as from out-of-state ones. Michigan, for example, already allows its licensed retailers (over 7,000 of them) to deliver alcohol directly to consumers. . . .

The states' tax collection justification is also insufficient.

*   *   *   *   *

Michigan and New York benefit from provisions of federal law that supply incentives for wineries to comply with state regulations. The Tax and Trade Bureau has authority to revoke a winery's federal license if it violates state law. Without a federal license, a winery cannot operate in any state. . . .

These federal remedies, when combined with state licensing regimes, adequately protect states from lost tax revenue.

*   *   *   *   *

V

If a state chooses to allow direct shipment of wine, it must do so on evenhanded terms. Without demonstrating the need for discrimination, New York and Michigan have enacted regulations that disadvantage out-of-state wine producers. Under our Commerce Clause jurisprudence, these regulations [are unconstitutional].

*   *   *   *   *

Afterword

Over 40 states and the District of Columbia now allow wineries to ship directly to residents, although those shipments are often limited to just a few cases or to small wineries, and the *Granholm* decision applied only to wineries; thus retailers, in most states, still cannot ship directly to consumers. The alcohol industry continues to resist an open market, preferring instead the three-tier producer, wholesaler, retailer distribution system that has been in place for decades, in part, to restrict access by minors and to encourage a broader selection of products while affirming states' rights. Despite *Granholm,* a maze of state rules continues to discourage online wine sales. Only about 5 percent of U.S. retail wine sales are achieved by direct shipment to consumers.[21]

Questions

1. *a.* Why did the *Granholm* court strike down the New York and Michigan laws?
   b. What legal and practical justifications were presented by New York and Michigan in defense of their laws?

2. *a.* What choice faced the states affected by this decision?
   b. What practical effect has this decision likely had on the wine industry?

3. In 1988, Oneida and Herkimer counties in upstate New York created a Solid Waste Management Authority and enacted a "flow control ordinance" requiring that all waste generated within their borders was to be delivered to the Authority's newly created waste-processing facilities. In 1995, six waste haulers and a trade association sued the Authority and the counties claiming that the flow control ordinance and associated regulations violated the Commerce Clause by discriminating against interstate commerce. The plaintiffs provided evidence that they could dispose of the waste much less expensively at out-of-state facilities. How would you rule in this case? Explain.

See *United Haulers Association, Inc. v. Oneida-Herkimer Solid Waste Management Authority,* 127 S. Ct 1786 (2007).

4. North Dakota rules required those bringing liquor into the state to file a monthly report, and out-of-state distillers selling to federal enclaves (military bases, in this instance) were required to label each item indicating that it was for consumption only within the enclave. The United States challenged those rules after sellers said they would discontinue dealing with the military bases or they would raise their prices to meet the cost of dealing with the two rules.

a. What were the constitutional foundations of the federal government's challenge?

b. What were the state's reasons for adopting the rules?

c. Decide. Explain. See *North Dakota v. United States,* 495 U.S. 423 (1990).

5. Premium Standard Farms, a large Missouri hog-raising operation, was pumping manure through a two-mile-long pipe into Iowa to be spread on a farm whose operator sought the manure for fertilizer. Iowa citizens objected and asked Attorney General Tom Miller to act. Could the Iowa attorney general stop the pumping? Explain.

Summary of State and Local Regulation

LO 8-5

Describe some of the ways in which state and local regulations affect business practice.

The federal government receives greater attention, but state and local rules have an enormous impact on business practice. The states are primarily responsible for regulating the insurance industry and are heavily involved in regulating banking, securities, and liquor sales. Many businesses and professions—from psychology to funeral preparation to barbering to the practice of medicine—require a license from the state. Public utilities (gas, electricity, sewage disposal) are the subject of extensive regulation governing entry, rates, customer service, and virtually all of the companies' activities. All states have some form of public service commission charged with regulating utilities in the public interest. Many states seek to directly enhance competition via antitrust legislation. Many states have passed laws forbidding usury, false advertising, stock fraud, and other practices harmful to the consumer. [For the Council of State Governments and updates on state law, see **www.csg.org**].

Big Soda Tax/Ban

Seeking revenue and responding to health concerns, Philadelphia in 2016 approved a 1.5-cents-per-ounce tax on sugar-added and artificially sweetened soft drinks. Berkeley, California, voters approved a one-cent-per-fluid-ounce sugary drink tax in 2015, and one year later, at least in lower-income neighborhoods, a study found that consumption had declined by about 20 percent, a large decline that might not be sustained over time.[22]

Trying a different route, the New York City Board of Health in 2012 approved a ban on the sale of sugary drinks in containers over 16 ounces in restaurants, stadiums, theaters, and other establishments regulated by the city health department. The rule did not forbid refills. The soda ban was quickly struck down by the New York state courts. A local state court judge determined the rule wasn't founded in fact and was riddled with loopholes and exceptions, making it unlawfully "arbitrary and capricious." The judge also found that the board of health "trespassed" on the legislative powers of the New York City Council, thus "eviscerating" the constitutional separation of powers doctrine.[23]

Questions

1. Would you approve of a nationwide soda ban or tax? Explain. See Michael Grynbaum, "New York's Ban on Big Sodas Is Rejected by Final Court," *The New York Times,* June 27, 2014 [**www.nytimes.com**].

2. *a. New Republic* senior editor Timothy Noah: "[E]ven as liberals and conservatives profess to hate the idea of government paternalism, both practice it." Provide some examples of government restrictions on individual choices as favored by liberals and as favored by conservatives.

   b. Do you support these restraints? Explain. See Timothy Noah, "Nanny Dearest," *The New Republic*, June 8, 2012 [**www.tnr.com**].

3. Professor David B. Agus asks: "[W]hen does regulating a person's habits in the name of good health become our moral and social duty?" Answer his question. See David B. Agus, "The 2,000-Year-Old Wonder Drug," *The New York Times*, December 11, 2012 [**www.nytimes.com/**].

Licensure   Local regulation is much less economically significant than state regulation. Local government intervention in business typically involves various licensure requirements. For example, businesses like bars and theaters are often required to obtain a local permit to operate. More broadly, more than 1,000 of America's occupations (medicine, law, building construction, electrical work, and so on) can be practiced only by those who have secured licensure from federal, state, and/or local authorities. Today nearly 30 percent of workers need a license, as compared with under 10 percent in the 1970s.[24]

Licensure is designed to protect the public from unsafe, unhealthful, and substandard goods and services, but critics contend that licensure often blocks entry by competitors and that the benefits of licensure are exceeded by its costs in increased prices, decreased services, and administrative overhead. Do we need to license tour guides in Washington, D.C., and historic Savannah, Georgia? Should teeth-whitening services in Alabama be limited to dentists? Do Louisiana consumers need to be protected from unlicensed florists?

Regulate Coffins?   Benedictine monks at St. Joseph Abbey outside New Orleans recently challenged a state licensure rule when they were ordered by the Louisiana State Board of Embalmers and Funeral Directors to close their business of building and selling caskets. The funeral industry cited a Louisiana regulation making it a crime for anyone other than state-licensed funeral directors to sell coffins in Louisiana. The monks sued and won when the U.S. Fifth Circuit Court of Appeals held that the funeral directors did not provide a rational basis for the challenged rule. Judge Patrick Higginbotham wrote that the rule "adds nothing to protect consumers and puts them at a greater risk of abuse including exploitative prices."[25] Other courts have upheld state regulatory policy in similar cases, but the state funeral directors' petition for review to the U.S. Supreme Court was rejected, and the monks can continue their work.

More Rules for Uber and Lyft?

Ride-sharing services Uber and Lyft left Austin, Texas, in 2016 rather than comply with a city ordinance mandating fingerprint-based criminal background checks for their drivers. They argue their own vetting is adequate, and they object to the added cost as well as delays in driver acquisition caused by the Austin rule. The market responded quickly with six smaller competitors agreeing to Austin's terms.

Similarly, ride-sharing services are often criticized for not meeting the insurance and licensure rules imposed on cabs. Cities in the United States and around the world are trying to accommodate these new, disruptive, often cheaper, and more consumer-friendly services while preserving closely regulated, job-providing, politically connected taxi services. California, for example, approved rules in 2016 setting basic safety, insurance, and reporting requirements.

Taxi deregulation in the 1970s and 80s, according to critics, led to higher rates, poorer service, traffic congestion, environmental pollution, and safety worries. Re-regulation followed rather quickly.

Questions

Catherine Rampell, opinion writer for *The Washington Post*, has speculated that the ride-sharing wars will not, in the end, result in a victory for consumers.

1. What social and environmental costs accompany ride-sharing services?

2. If the ride-sharing industry "wins" the taxi war, how might consumers lose? See Catherine Rampell, "Who Will Win the Ride-Sharing War? Probably Not Consumers," *The Washington Post*, October 2, 2014 [**www.washingtonpost.com**].

Sources: Paul Stephen Dempsey, "Taxi Industry Regulation, Deregulation & Re-Regulation: The Paradox of Market Failure," *Transportation Law Journal* 24, no. 1 (Summer 1996), p. 73; Catherine Rampell, "Uber Continues to Flout Laws and Brawl with Cities," *The Washington Post*, July 16, 2015 [**www.washingtonpost.com**]; and Reuters, "Why Uber and Lyft Rivals Are Flocking to Austin, Texas," *Fortune*, June 21, 2016 [**www.fortune.com**].

 For a brief, free-market, libertarian view of taxi regulation, see the video *IJ's Jeanette Petersen Explains Three Reasons You Can't Get a Cab*, at **www.youtube.com/watch?v=Oq-hPuESJng.**

Rules and Community Welfare   Most of us would say, in the abstract, that we need less government in our lives, but when we are the victims of problems that the market is ill-suited to resolve, those rules become much more attractive. The case that follows shows how Tampa, Florida, tried to apply its rules to the age-old problem of adult entertainment businesses but with what was at the time a new twist—product distribution by the Internet rather than face-to-face.

LEGAL BRIEFCASE

Voyeur Dorm v. City of Tampa
265 F.3d 1232 (11th Cir. 2001), *cert. denied,* 122 S. Ct. 1172 (2002)

Circuit Judge Dubina

This appeal arises from Voyeur Dorm L.C.'s alleged violation of Tampa's City Code based on the district court's characterization of Voyeur Dorm as an adult entertainment facility.

BACKGROUND

Voyeur Dorm operates an Internet-based Web site that provides a 24-hour-a-day Internet transmission portraying the lives of the residents of 2312 West Farwell Drive, Tampa, Florida. Throughout its existence, Voyeur Dorm has employed 25 to 30 different women, most of whom entered into a contract that specifies, among other things, that they are "employees," on a "stage and filming location," with "no reasonable expectation of privacy," for "entertainment purposes." Subscribers to "voyeurdorm.com" pay a subscription fee of $34.95 a month to watch the women employed at the premises and pay an added fee of $16.00 per month to "chat" with the women. From August 1998 to June 2000, Voyeur Dorm generated subscriptions and sales totaling $3,166,551.35.

In 1998 Voyeur Dorm learned that local law enforcement agencies had initiated an investigation into its business. In response, counsel for Voyeur Dorm sent a letter to Tampa's zoning coordinator requesting her interpretation of the city code as it applied to the activities occurring at 2312 West Farwell Drive. In February of 1999, Tampa's zoning coordinator, Gloria Moreda, replied to counsel's request and issued her interpretation of the city code:

* * * * *

It is my determination that the use occurring at 2312 W. Farwell Dr., is an adult use. Section 27-523 defines adult entertainment as "Any premises, except those businesses otherwise defined in this chapter, on which is offered to members of the public or any person, for a consideration, entertainment featuring or in any way including specified sexual activities, as defined in this section, or entertainment featuring the displaying or depicting of specified anatomical areas, as defined in this section; 'entertainment' as used in this definition shall include, but not be limited to, books, magazines, films, newspapers, photographs, paintings, drawings, sketches or other publications or graphic media, filmed or live plays, dances or other performances distinguished by their display or depiction of specified anatomical areas or specified anatomical activities, as defined in this section."

Please be aware that the property is zoned RS-60 Residential Single Family, and an adult use business is not permitted use. You should advise your client to cease operation at that location.

Thereafter, in April of 1999, Dan and Sharon Gold Marshlack [owners of the property located at 2312 W. Farwell] appealed the zoning coordinator's decision to Tampa's Variance Review Board. On or about July 13, 1999, the Variance Review Board conducted a hearing. At the hearing, Voyeur Dorm's counsel conceded the following: that five women live in the house; that there are cameras in the corners of all the rooms of the house; that for a fee a person can join a membership to a Web site wherein a member can view the women 24 hours a day, seven days a week; that a member, at times, can see someone disrobed; that the women receive free room and board; that the women are part of a business enterprise; and that the women are paid. At the conclusion of the hearing, the Variance Review Board unanimously upheld the zoning coordinator's determination that the use occurring at 2312 West Farwell Drive was an adult use. Subsequently, Mr. and Mrs. Marshlack filed an appeal from the decision of the Variance Review Board to the

City Council. The Tampa City Council . . . unanimously affirmed the decision of the Variance Review Board.

Voyeur Dorm filed this action in the middle district of Florida. The City of Tampa and Voyeur Dorm then filed cross-motions for summary judgment. The district court granted Tampa's motion for summary judgment, from which Voyeur Dorm now appeals.

ISSUE

1. Whether the district court properly determined that the alleged activities occurring at 2312 West Farwell Drive constitute a public offering of adult entertainment as contemplated by Tampa's zoning restrictions.

[Issues 2. and 3. are omitted—ed.]

DISCUSSION

The threshold inquiry is whether section 27-523 of Tampa's city code applies to the alleged activities occurring at 2312 West Farwell Drive. Because of the way we answer that inquiry, it will not be necessary for us to analyze the thorny constitutional issues presented in this case.

* * * * *

Tampa argues that Voyeur Dorm is an adult use business pursuant to the express and unambiguous language of Section 27-523 and, as such, cannot operate in a residential neighborhood. In that regard, Tampa points out that members of the public pay to watch women employed on the premises; that the employment agreement refers to the premises as "a stage and filming location;" that certain anatomical areas and sexual activities are displayed for entertainment; and that the entertainers are paid accordingly. Most importantly, Tampa asserts that nothing in the city code limits its applicability to premises where the adult entertainment is actually consumed.

In accord with Tampa's arguments, the district court specifically determined that the "plain and unambiguous language of the city code . . . does not expressly state a requirement that the members of the public paying consideration be on the premises viewing the adult entertainment." While the public does not congregate to a specific edifice or location in order to enjoy the entertainment provided by Voyeur Dorm, the district court found 2312 West Farwell Drive to be "a premises on which is offered to members of the public for consideration entertainment featuring specified sexual activities within the plain meaning of the city code."

Moreover, the district court relied on Supreme Court and Eleventh Circuit precedent that trumpets a city's entitlement to protect and improve the quality of residential neighborhoods. *Sammy's of Mobile, Ltd. v. City of Mobile* (noting that it is well established that the regulation of public health, safety, and morals is a valid and substantial state interest); *Corn v. City of Lauderdale Lakes* (noting that the "Supreme Court has held [that] restrictions may be imposed to protect 'family values, youth values, and the blessings of quiet seclusion'").

In opposition, Voyeur Dorm argues that it is not an adult use business. Specifically, Voyeur Dorm contends that section 27-523 applies to locations or premises wherein adult entertainment is actually offered to the public. Because the public does not, indeed cannot, physically attend 2312 West Farwell Drive to enjoy the adult entertainment, 2312 West Farwell Drive does not fall within the purview of Tampa's zoning ordinance.

The residence of 2312 West Farwell Drive provides no "offering [of adult entertainment] to members of the public." The offering occurs when the videotaped images are dispersed over the Internet and into the public eye for consumption. The city code cannot be applied to a location that does not, itself, offer adult entertainment to the public.

* * * * *

It does not follow, then, that a zoning ordinance designed to restrict facilities that offer adult entertainment can be applied to a particular location that does not, at that location, offer adult entertainment. Moreover, the case law relied upon by Tampa and the district court concerns adult entertainment in which customers physically attend the premises wherein the entertainment is performed. Here, the audience or consumers of the adult entertainment do not go to 2312 West Farwell Drive or congregate anywhere else in Tampa to enjoy the entertainment. Indeed, the public offering occurs over the Internet in "virtual space." While the district court read Section 27-523 in a literal sense, finding no requirement that the paying public be on the premises, we hold that section 27-523 does not apply to a residence at which there is no public offering of adult entertainment.

* * * * *

Reversed.

Questions

1. *a.* Why did the court rule against Tampa?
    b. Make the argument, as the lower court did, that the Tampa statute does apply to Voyeur Dorm.
    c. Why was Tampa concerned about Voyeur Dorm operating in a residential neighborhood?
    d. Does Tampa have any additional legal grounds for challenging Voyeur Dorm? Explain.

2. The city government in Cedar Falls, Iowa, home of the University of Northern Iowa, declined to renew the liquor license of a local bar after 58 of 100 "bar checks" over a period of nearly two years found minors drinking illegally. One hundred seventy-four alcohol-related tickets were issued over that period.[26]
    a. Could the free market satisfactorily protect the public from the various risks associated with excessive drinking by college-age students, or are rules necessary?
    b. Would you vote to renew this bar's liquor license? Explain.

3. Two Dallas, Texas, ordinances were challenged in court. One gave the police very broad authority to deny licenses to "adult" businesses such as bookstores. The other, which was directed at prostitution, barred motel owners from renting rooms for fewer than 10 hours.
    a. What challenges would you raise against these ordinances?
    b. How would you rule? Explain. See *FW/PBS Inc. v. City of Dallas,* 493 U.S. 215 (1990).

4. The Los Angeles municipal code prohibits some types of new billboards and restricts the size, placement, and illumination of others. The Los Angeles code seeks to "promote public safety and welfare" by "providing reasonable protection to the visual environment" and by ensuring that billboards do not "interfere with traffic safety or otherwise endanger public safety." One provision of the code specifically forbids new "Freeway Facing Signs" located within 2,000 feet of and "viewed primarily from" a freeway or an on-ramp/off-ramp. Another forbids, with exceptions, new "supergraphics," large-format signs projected onto or hung from building walls. The Los Angeles rules allow new signs in some portions of the city while banning them in others.
    a. The billboard rules were challenged on constitutional grounds. Explain those grounds and rule on the constitutionality of the rules. See *World Wide Rush v. City of Los Angeles,* 606 F.3d 676 (9th Cir. 2010).
    b. Should Los Angeles simply allow the market to determine where billboards are placed? Explain.

5. Tattoo and body piercing statutes sometimes require liability insurance, licensing, training, and health inspections, and parents are to accompany minors. Does each of those requirements seem appropriate to you? Explain.

6. *a.* Can we rely on the market to protect teens from excessive tanning? Explain.
    b. Has the market failed? Explain.

Questions—Parts One and Two

1. Matthew Hale, a law school graduate, was denied a license to practice law in Illinois because Hale was an avowed racist and the leader of a white supremacist group. A state panel assessed the character and general fitness of all those who had passed the bar exam and graduated from law school and decided that Hale's active racism disqualified him. Illinois was one of 32 states with character and fitness standards. Hale appealed on

First Amendment grounds, among others. Should Hale have been excluded from the practice of law, or should the market decide his fitness? Explain. See *Hale v. Committee on Character and Fitness for the State of Illinois*, 335 F.3d 678 (7th Cir. 2003).

2. The National Association of Home Builders announced in 2016 that the cost of compliance with rules for home building had increased by 30 percent over the previous five years. State and local governments commonly require builders to comply with construction codes, buy storm-water discharge permits, and pay impact fees (for water, sewer, roads, parks, schools, police, fire, and sometimes open space and affordable housing, for example). Regulations account for $85,000 of the cost of the average new single-family home, according to the Association. One result, the Association argued, is that builders are now much less likely to build homes for the lower-cost, entry-level market.[27]

   a. In general, do you think we should cut back on the public services paid for, in part, by impact fees in order to reduce the cost of housing? Explain.

   b. Some Georgia jurisdictions imposed tree-planting requirements that reportedly raised costs per lot by $7,500 to $15,000. How would you vote on a rule requiring tree planting on all new home lots in your local area? Explain.

3. Notwithstanding the rather robust deregulation efforts in recent decades, the larger trend in the United States over the past 50 years, and particularly since the financial crisis of recent years, has been increased government regulation of business. How do you explain that trend?

4. As a safety measure, Arizona enacted a statute that limited the length of passenger trains to 14 cars and freight trains to 70 cars. Trains of those lengths and greater were common throughout the United States. The Southern Pacific Railroad challenged the Arizona statute.

   a. What was the legal foundation of the Southern Pacific claim?

   b. Decide the case. Explain. See *Southern Pacific Railroad v. Arizona*, 325 U.S. 761 (1945).

5. The Florida legislature in 2014 adopted a new law governing parasailing, previously a largely unregulated commercial recreational activity. The new rules, among other things, require insurance for operators, require an on-board observer, and allow operation only when winds do not exceed 20 miles per hour.

   In 2012, a Connecticut woman dropped from her harness to her death while parasailing near Pompano Beach, Florida. Such deaths are unusual, with an estimated several dozen worldwide in the past 30 years, but Florida has seen four in recent years.

   a. How would you argue that parasailing deaths often constitute a market failure?

   b. Would you vote for a parasailing rule, or would you leave parasailing safety to the market? Explain.

Part Three—Administrative Agencies and the Regulatory Process

Introduction to Administrative Agencies[28]

Suppose you start a small, relatively simple business, perhaps a restaurant. You quickly come to realize that the government is going to be your partner in that business. Taxes, wages, hours, sanitation, safety, advertising, zoning—at every turn a government rule shapes the conduct of your business. In many cases, those rules are created and enforced by administrative agencies, a powerful subset of government little understood by the public but immensely influential in every corner of American life.

The Federal Agencies

LO 8-6
List some of the federal agencies that regulate business practice.

Federal law defines an *agency* as any government unit other than the legislature and the courts. Thus, the *administrative law* governing those agencies technically addresses the entire executive branch of government. Our attention, however, will be directed to the prominent regulatory agencies (Federal Trade Commission, Federal Communications Commission, Securities and Exchange Commission, and the like) rather than the various executive departments (Agriculture, Defense, and so on) and nonregulatory welfare agencies (Social Security Administration and Veterans Administration). We will focus on the federal level, but administrative law principles are generally applicable to the conduct of state and local governments. At the state level, public utility commissions and the various state licensure boards for law, medicine, architecture, and the like are examples of administrative agencies. At the local level, one might cite planning and zoning boards and property tax assessment appeals boards. [For an online guide to federal government information and services, see **www.usa.gov**].

History

Congress established the Interstate Commerce Commission (ICC), the first federal regulatory agency, in 1887 for the purpose of regulating railroad routes and rates. The Food and Drug Administration (FDA—1907) and the Federal Trade Commission (FTC—1914) followed, but federal regulation became pervasive only in response to the Great Depression of the 1930s. Congress created the Securities and Exchange Commission (SEC—1934), the Federal Communications Commission (FCC—1934), the Civil Aeronautics Board (CAB—1940; abolished 1985), and the National Labor Relations Board (NLRB—1935), among others, as a response to the widely shared belief that the stock market crash and the Depression were evidence of the failure of the free market.

The next major burst of regulatory activity arrived in the 1960s and 1970s when Congress created such agencies as the Equal Employment Opportunity Commission (EEOC—1965), the Environmental Protection Agency (EPA—1970), the Occupational Safety and Health Administration (OSHA—1970), and the Consumer Product Safety Commission (CPSC—1972).

Note that most of the early agencies were designed to achieve economic goals by exerting substantial control over entire industries such as transportation or communications. Then with the arrival of the prosperity and social turbulence of the 1960s and 1970s, Congress built an array of new agencies directed not to economic issues but to social reform in such areas as discrimination, the environment, job safety, and product safety.

The free-market enthusiasm of the 1980s, led by President Ronald Reagan, resulted in strenuous efforts to deregulate the economy and reduce the influence of the federal agencies and the government generally. Now, in the early 21st century, we have been in a period of general respect for the free market, but current problems in the finance industry, particularly in home mortgages, have resulted in aggressive new rules, as explained below.

Creating the Agencies

Broadly, federal agencies are of two kinds: executive and independent. The cabinet-level departments (Defense, Education, Energy, et al.) are considered executive agencies and within them are smaller units, also labeled executive agencies. Our primary interest is in the independent agencies (FTC, FCC, and SEC). Congress created those agencies via statutes labeled *enabling legislation* and accorded them substantial authority to regulate a specified segment of American life. The FTC, for example, is empowered by its enabling legislation to pursue unfair trade practices. The president has direct authority over the executive agencies, while the independent agencies are intended to operate with less fear of interference. In practice, of course, the president and Congress have substantial influence on all the agencies.

In creating an agency, Congress delegates a portion of its authority to that body. Congress acknowledges the existence of a problem and recognizes that it is not the appropriate body to address the specific elements of that problem—hence, the agency. The president, ordinarily with the advice and consent of the Senate, appoints the administrator or the several commissioners who direct each agency's affairs. Commissioners are appointed in staggered terms, typically of seven years' duration. The appointment of commissioners for most of the independent agencies must reflect an approximate political balance between the two major parties.

In effect, Congress has created a fourth branch of government. Possessing neither the time nor the expertise to handle issues arising from nuclear power, product safety, racial discrimination, labor unions, and much more, Congress wisely established "mini governments" supported by the necessary technical resources and day-to-day authority to address those complicated problems.

Agency Duties

LO 8-7

Identify the three broad categories of federal regulatory agencies' authority.

The authority of the federal regulatory agencies falls broadly into three categories.

1. **Control of Supply.** Some agencies control entry into certain economic activities. The Federal Communications Commission grants radio and television licenses. The Food and Drug Administration (see Chapter 15) decides which drugs may enter the American market. The Securities and Exchange Commission (see Chapter 9) acts as a gatekeeper, preventing the entry of new securities into the marketplace until certain standards are met. The general concern is that the market alone cannot adequately protect the public interest.

2. **Control of Rates.** Historically, those federal agencies charged with regulating utilities and carriers (Federal Energy Regulatory Commission, ICC, and CAB) set the prices to be charged for the services offered within their jurisdictions, but the deregulation movement resulted in the elimination of the CAB and the ICC and a general decline in agency rate-setting. The federal government decided to reduce or eliminate its authority in decisions such as the price of airline tickets, cable TV rates, and long-distance telephone rates.

3. **Control of Conduct.** Federal agencies may compel or restrict business conduct.

    a. Information. Agencies commonly compel companies to disclose consumer information that would otherwise remain private. Warning labels, for example, may be mandated.

b. *Standards.* Where simply requiring information is deemed inadequate for the public needs, the government may establish minimum standards that the private sector must meet. Thus, the Federal Aviation Administration created 624 pages of new rules seeking to bring order to the exploding interest in commercial use of unmanned aircraft systems (drones) for activities like real estate photography and site inspections. The rules, effective in 2016, allow small drones weighing less than 55 pounds to fly during daylight hours under 400 feet and in sight of the operator. Operators must pass a certification test. Hobbyist drone operators have similar flight guidelines, but licensure is not required.

Some package delivery, as advocated by Amazon and others, may emerge under the new rules, but use of autonomous drones for mass delivery is not yet permitted. Package delivery by autonomous drones is emerging in a few nations.

c. *Product banishments.* In rare circumstances, products can be banned from the market. The Food and Drug Administration in 2004 banned the sale of weight loss products containing ephedra (ma huang) with the active ingredient ephedrine. The ban and associated publicity have been useful in that serious ephedra poisonings through 2013 had declined by more than 98 percent.[29]

Questions

1. The phrase "government regulation" embraces many functions. Define it.

2. Is the federal regulatory process limited in its goals to the correction of market failures? Should it be so limited? Explain.

3. According to *The Washington Post*, self-described "drone slayer" William Merideth of Kentucky saw a drone hovering over his land, so he "grabbed his Benelli M1 Super 90 shotgun, took aim and unleashed three rounds of birdshot." The $1,500 drone was downed and its owner, hobbyist John Boggs, who was taking pictures of the scenery, has filed suit claiming Merideth had no right to shoot down the drone because the U.S. government controls all airspace. Merideth and witnesses say the drone was flying below the treeline.
   a. Do you think Boggs was trespassing?
   b. How do you feel about widespread drone use, including package delivery to housing units? See Andrea Peterson and Matt McFarland, "You May Be Powerless to Stop a Drone from Hovering over Your Own Yard," *The Washington Post,* January 13, 2016 [**www.washingtonpost.com**].

Operating the Agencies

LO 8-8
Compare and contrast the federal agencies' executive, legislative, and judicial roles.

As we have noted, the administrative agencies act as mini governments, performing quasi-executive, quasi-legislative (rule-making), and quasi-judicial (adjudicatory) roles broadly involving control of supply, rates, and conduct in large segments of American life. Agency action is guided generally by the Administrative Procedure Act (APA), which provides a framework for agency rule-making and details broad standards for judicial review of agency decisions. Let's look at how those agencies practice their business.

Executive Functions

A big part of the agencies' executive duties is the protection of the public by ensuring compliance with laws and regulations. Most agencies, therefore, spend a great deal of time conducting inspections and investigations and collecting information. Agencies enter into contracts, lease federal lands, register securities offerings, award grants, resolve tax disputes, settle workers' compensation claims, administer government benefits to the citizenry, and much more. Supervisory duties, including active and close attention to the banking industry, are a further illustration of agency executive duties.

Legislative Functions

The agencies create *rules* that, in effect, are laws. These rules provide the details necessary to carry out the intentions of the enabling legislation. In day-to-day business practice, the rules are likely to be much more important than the original congressional legislation. The Occupational Safety and Health Act, for example, calls for a safe and healthful workplace, but the rules necessary for interpreting and enforcing that general mandate come, not from Congress, but from the Occupational Safety and Health Administration (OSHA).

Rules   Agencies enact three types of rules: (1) Procedural rules delineate the agency's internal operating structure and methods. (2) Interpretive rules offer the agency's view of the meaning of those statutes for which the agency has administrative responsibility. Internal Revenue Service regulations are an example of interpretive rules. (3) Legislative rules are policy expressions having the effect of law. The agency is exercising the law-making function delegated to it by the legislature. The National Highway Traffic Safety Administration, for example, recently issued a rule requiring all new vehicles under 10,000 pounds to have rear visibility technology (typically, backup cameras) by 2018.

Questions

Once all vehicles have rear-view systems (expected by 2054), NHTSA expects 58 to 69 lives to be saved annually. Valuing a life at $6.1 million, the rule is expected to cost between $11.8 million and $19.7 million per life saved.[30]

1. Do you agree with the backup camera requirement? Explain.
2. How much is your life worth? Explain.
3. Should the value of lives be a consideration in federal rules and spending decisions? Explain.

The Rule-Making Process

The Administrative Procedure Act provides for both *informal* (often called "notice and comment") and *formal* rule-making processes for legislative rules. Under both approaches, the process begins with the publication of a Notice of Proposed Rule Making in the *Federal Register* (a daily publication of all federal rules, regulations, and orders). Thereafter, in the case of informal rule-making, the agency must permit written comments on the proposal and may hold open hearings. To enhance participation in the rule-making process, the federal government provides an online portal where the public can comment on proposed rules [see **www.regulations.gov**]. Having received public comments, the agency either discontinues the process or prepares the final rule.

In the case of formal rule-making, after providing notice, the agency must hold a public hearing conducted with most of the procedural safeguards of a trial, where all interested parties may call witnesses, challenge the agency evidence, and so on.

Hybrid Rule-Making   Although not specifically provided for in the APA, agency rule-making now is often achieved by a compromise (hybrid) process that combines elements of formal and informal rule-making. Hybrid rule-making is informal rule-making with additions in the form of some trial elements (more oral testimony and hearings) that have the effect of providing a more detailed record without all of the procedural requirements of formal rule-making.

Whether by formal, informal, or hybrid procedures, final agency rules are published in the *Federal Register* and later compiled in the *Code of Federal Regulations*. [To search the *Federal Register*, see **www.federalregister.gov**].

Challenging an Agency Rule

Suppose you are clever enough to devise an Internet challenger to Facebook or Instagram. Should you be able to access the Internet through Internet service providers (ISPs) at the same prices and the same level of quality as the established giants? Doubtless our initial thought is: "Of course, everybody should be treated the same." After all, fast, affordable Internet access is increasingly central to commercial success and to conducting daily life. But in a free market, shouldn't the Internet service providers, including the giants like AT&T, Comcast, and Verizon, charge whatever best suits their interests? Or should the government intervene to be sure that barriers to entry for new Internet-based products will be as low as possible?

> Of course, everybody should be treated the same.

Net Neutrality   To address those issues, the Federal Communications Commission (FCC) has recently implemented new rules requiring *net neutrality*, meaning ISPs should treat all legal data the same. Those rules are particularly directed at a trio of problems: *blocking*, where an ISP denies access to lawful content and services; *throttling*, where an ISP deliberately slows down delivery of some content; and *paid prioritization*, where an ISP provides "fast lanes" for content providers like Netflix and YouTube that may pay more for that speed. Those big-content providers would then pass on the higher costs to consumers while some Internet services might be available only at slower speeds and some content might be entirely blocked by the ISP.

The broadband industry challenged the new rules in court, but in 2016 a panel of the U.S. Court of Appeals for the District of Columbia ruled 2–1 in favor of the FCC approach.[31] By re-classifying the Internet as a public utility (from an information service provider), the FCC argued that it could regulate the ISPs in much the same manner as it has regulated telephone service for decades. The court of appeals agreed, and it upheld both the reclassification and the FCC's rules implementing net neutrality.

The FCC now intends to employ its new rules to assure open, fair access to the Internet for all on both fixed and mobile networks. Critics, however, say the net neutrality policy will slow innovation and discourage network infrastructure investment. An appeal to the Supreme Court may be filed, and President Trump appears to be opposed to net neutrality. [For a "source of regulatory news, analysis, and opinion," see *RegBlog* at **www.law.upenn.edu/blogs/regblog**].

Judicial Processes

Although informal procedures such as settlements are preferred, agencies commonly must turn to judicial proceedings to enforce agency rules. The National Labor Relations Board may hold a hearing to determine if an employee was wrongfully dismissed for engaging in protected union activities. The Federal Communications Commission may decide whether to remove a radio license because of a failure to serve the public interest. The Federal Trade Commission may judge whether a particular ad is misleading.

Rule-Making or Adjudication?   Many issues facing agencies could properly be resolved either by rule-making or by adjudication. Rule-making ordinarily involves standards to be applied to the future conduct of a class of unspecified parties. An adjudication, on the other hand, characteristically addresses specific parties involved in a specific present or past dispute. The rule-making/adjudication decision is discretionary with the agency (subject to judicial review) and is based on the nature of the issue and fairness to the parties. Regardless, the agencies are, in effect, "making law" either by passing a rule that has authority much like a law or by setting a judicial-like precedent in the case of an adjudication.

Administrative Hearing   After an agency investigation, a violation of a statute and/or rule may be alleged. Affected parties are notified. An effort is made to reach a settlement via a *consent order*, in which the party being investigated agrees to steps suitable to the agency but makes no admission of guilt (thus, retarding the likelihood of subsequent civil liability).

Administrative Law Judge   Failing a settlement, the parties proceed much as in a civil trial. Ordinarily the case is heard by an *administrative law judge* (ALJ). Parties have the right to present their cases, hire counsel, cross-examine, file motions, raise objections, and so on. They do not have the right to a jury trial, however. The ALJ decides all questions of law and fact and then issues a decision (*order*). In general, that decision is final unless appealed to the agency/commission. After exhausting opportunities for review within the agency, appeal may be taken to the federal court system.

PRACTICING ETHICS   Revolving Doors, Regulatory Capture, and Iron Triangles?

Rohit Bansal moved in 2014 from his government job at the New York Federal Reserve Bank to Wall Street mega-bank Goldman Sachs, which is regulated by the Federal Reserve. Bansal reportedly had been coached by Goldman Sachs executive Joseph Jiampietro about how to get the new job with Goldman Sachs. Then, after making the move, Bansal allegedly obtained leaked Federal Reserve documents and passed them to Jiampietro. When the leaks were discovered, Bansal was fired by Goldman Sachs. He pleaded guilty to misdemeanor criminal charges and was permanently banned from the bank-

ing industry. Goldman Sachs was fined over $86 million. Jiampietro was fired by Goldman Sachs. He denies all of the allegations against him.[32]

Bansal's story illustrates the danger in the "revolving doors" between government and industry. Regulators, like Bansal, often leave government to work for the industry they formerly regulated, and regulators often come from the very industry they are hired to regulate. A recent Sunlight Foundation study of federal lobbying calculated that 44 percent of all active contract lobbyists in 2012 had previous government experience, up from 18 percent in 1998.[33] Troublesome as these government/industry ties may seem, we should remember that we need close associations between government agencies and the industries being regulated. Each benefits from the expertise of the other. Further, federal conflict of interest laws do impose some restrictions on private-sector work following government service.

The revolving doors encourage *regulatory capture,* a form of government failure that can occur when regulators are too cozy with the industry being regulated or when industry representatives have the interest and resources to offer detailed advice on agency business while the public voice, being much less focused, is seldom or never heard by the agency.

Political scientists argue that regulatory capture of both agencies and congressional committees sometimes produces a stable, nearly impregnable, *iron triangle.* Powerful interest groups (often businesses like Goldman Sachs) occupy one corner of the triangle, congressional committees are at another corner, and agency bureaucrats (like Bansal) occupy the third. In the resulting alliance, each group cultivates its own welfare by providing political support (from interest groups to members of Congress), by writing favorable laws (from Congress to interest groups), and by agency enforcement of those laws in ways favorable to the interest groups and Congress. The likely result is diminished attention to the public good.

Controlling the Agencies

LO 8-9
Describe the executive, congressional, and judicial controls placed on agency conduct to maintain appropriate "checks and balances."

Although agency influence in business practice and in American life generally is enormous, none of these agencies and their thousands of employees is directly accountable to the people, and all of them operate under necessarily broad grants of power. What is to keep them from abusing their discretion or from being "captured" by special interests? Just as with our constitutional system generally, certain checks and balances constrain agency conduct while allowing the latitude necessary to achieve effectiveness.

Executive Constraints

As noted, the president appoints the top administrators for the various agencies, thus significantly influencing the conservative or liberal slant of the agency. Furthermore, the president obviously has great influence in the budget process.

Recent presidents have strengthened executive oversight of agency action by requiring *cost–benefit analyses* for new rules (President Clinton) and commanding agencies to cite a specific *market failure* before issuing a new rule (President George W. Bush). President Obama maintained the cost–benefit expectation, and he introduced a new initiative to get rid of what he labeled "dumb" rules. President Obama ordered all federal agencies to eliminate outdated rules that "stifle job creation and make our economy less competitive," and he asked Congress for authority to consolidate a number of federal agencies.[34] [For an OMB "watchdog," see **www.ombwatch.org/**].

Congressional Constraints

Congress creates and can dissolve the agencies. Congress controls agency budgets and thus can encourage or discourage particular agency action. Broadly, Congress oversees agency action, and agencies often negotiate with Congress before undertaking major initiatives. Congress can directly intervene by amending the enabling legislation or by passing laws that require agencies to take specific directions. The difficulty in balancing congressional and agency authority is well illustrated by an important 2001 Supreme Court decision involving the federal Clean Air Act (CAA). The case, *Whitman v. American Trucking*

Associations, Inc.,[35] raised the question of whether Congress had improperly delegated its authority to the Environmental Protection Agency and whether the EPA must take the cost of implementing clean air regulations into consideration when developing new rules. A unanimous Supreme Court ruled that Congress had built into the CAA constitutionally sufficient limitations on agency action, and the Court ruled that Congress clearly did not require the EPA to conduct cost–benefit analyses before establishing new rules. Thus, the Court concluded that Congress can constitutionally offer agencies broad authority in carrying out Congress's general intentions.

Judicial Review

Agency rules and orders are often challenged in court. Historically, however, the courts have taken a rather narrow approach to judicial review. The jurists, being generalists in the field of law, have been reluctant to overrule the judgment of specialists, and very crowded judicial calendars act as a natural brake on activist judicial review. For those reasons, judges readily sustain agency judgments where reasonable. Of course, the courts overrule the agencies when appropriate.

Not surprisingly, judicial review of agency decisions raises a variety of technical issues of law. Cases turn on questions like these:

1. Does the legislature's delegation of authority meet constitutional requirements?
2. Has the agency exceeded the authority granted by the enabling legislation?
3. Are the agency's findings of fact supported by substantial evidence in the record as a whole?
4. Was the agency's decision "arbitrary and capricious" (a standard provided for in the Administrative Procedure Act and discussed in the *FCC v. Fox* case below)?

While these issues are technically important, their detailed exploration is not necessary for our purposes. The case that follows will be our only consideration of the formalities of judicial review. This 8–0 U.S. Supreme Court ruling examines the question of when the government should regulate distasteful expression over the airwaves.

Federal Communications Commission v. Fox Television Stations and Federal Communications Commission v. ABC   132 S. Ct. 2307 (2012)

LEGAL BRIEFCASE

[Three episodes of alleged indecency on network television are at issue in this case. First, at the 2002 Billboard Music Awards, televised by Fox, Cher made the following unscripted remark: "I've also had my critics for the last 40 years saying that I was on my way out every year. So f*** 'em." Second, during the Fox telecast of the 2003 Billboard Music Awards, Nicole Richie made the following unscripted remark: "Have you ever tried to get cow s*** out of a Prada purse? It's not so f***ing simple." Third, ABC's February 25, 2003, telecast of *NYPD Blue* displayed the nude buttocks of an adult female character for about seven seconds and the side of her breast for a moment, as she was preparing for a shower. A child portraying her boyfriend's son entered the bathroom during the scene.

Then in 2004 the Federal Communications Commission sanctioned NBC for the following remark by Bono, who won an award at the 2003 Golden Globe show: "This is really, really, f***ing brilliant. Really, really great." The FCC found use of the F-word actionably indecent. Reversing prior rulings, the Commission ruled that even fleeting expletives, like the single use of the F-word by Bono, were actionable. The isolated and apparently impromptu nature of the remark did not excuse its indecency.

Applying its new policy to the Cher, Richie, and *NYPD Blue* cases, the FCC then ruled that Fox and ABC had violated the Commission's indecency standards by televising fleeting expletives and fleeting nudity. The case *(Fox I)* then went to the U.S. Second Circuit Court of Appeals, which overturned the Commission ruling saying it was "arbitrary and capricious" in that the FCC made a 180-degree turn regarding fleeting expletives without providing a reasoned explanation. *Fox I* then went to the U.S. Supreme Court in 2009, where the Court of Appeals ruling was reversed, with the Court saying that a change in FCC policy must be announced, but detailed justifications are not required as a matter of law.

Fox I then returned to the Second Circuit Court of Appeals, which struck down the Commission's entire indecency policy, finding it unconstitutionally vague because it failed to give broadcasters sufficient notice of what would be considered indecent. The Supreme Court then agreed to review the cases again in the *Fox II* opinion that follows.]

Justice Kennedy

*   *   *   *   *

I

A

Title 18 U.S.C. § 1464 provides that "[w]hoever utters any obscene, indecent, or profane language by means of radio communication shall be fined . . . or imprisoned not more than two years, or both." The Federal Communications Commission (Commission) has been instructed by Congress to enforce § 1464 between the hours of 6 am and 10 pm.

This Court first reviewed the Commission's indecency policy in *FCC v. Pacifica Foundation,* 438 U.S. 726 (1978). In *Pacifica,* the Commission determined that George Carlin's "Filthy Words" monologue was indecent. It contained "language that describes, in terms patently offensive as measured by contemporary community

standards for the broadcast medium, sexual or excretory activities and organs, at times of the day when there is a reasonable risk that children may be in the audience." *Id.,* at 732. This Court upheld the Commission's ruling.

*   *   *   *   *

In 2001, the Commission . . . [in describing] what it considered patently offensive, . . . explained that three factors had proved significant:

> "(1) [T]he explicitness or graphic nature of the description or depiction of sexual or excretory organs or activities; (2) whether the material dwells on or repeats at length descriptions of sexual or excretory organs or activities; (3) whether the material appears to pander or is used to titillate, or whether the material appears to have been presented for its shock value."

As regards the second of these factors, the Commission explained that "[r]epetition of and persistent focus on sexual or excretory material have been cited consistently as factors that exacerbate the potential offensiveness of broadcasts. In contrast, where sexual or excretory references have been made once or have been passing or fleeting in nature, this characteristic has tended to weigh against a finding of indecency."

*   *   *   *   *

B

It was against this regulatory background that the three incidents of alleged indecency at issue here took place.

*   *   *   *   *

II

A fundamental principle in our legal system is that laws which regulate persons or entities must give fair notice of conduct that is forbidden or required. . . . This requirement of clarity in regulation is essential to the protections provided by the Due Process Clause of the Fifth Amendment. . . . It requires the invalidation of laws that are impermissibly vague. . . .

Even when speech is not at issue, the void for vagueness doctrine addresses at least two connected but discrete due process concerns: first, that regulated parties should know what is required of them so they may act accordingly; second, precision and guidance are necessary so that those enforcing the law do not act in an arbitrary or discriminatory way. When speech is involved, rigorous adherence to those requirements is necessary to ensure that ambiguity does not chill protected speech.

These concerns are implicated here because . . . the broadcasters claim they did not have, and do not have, sufficient notice of what is proscribed. . . . Under the 2001 Guidelines in force when the broadcasts occurred, a key consideration was "'whether the material dwell[ed] on or repeat[ed] at length'" the offending description or depiction. [*Fox Television Stations v. FCC,* 613 F.3d 317

(2d Cir. 2010) at 322.] In the 2004 *Golden Globes* Order, issued after the broadcasts, the Commission changed course and held that fleeting expletives could be a statutory violation. [*Fox I—FCC v. Fox TV Stations,* 556 U.S. 502 (2009) at 512.] In the challenged orders now under review the Commission applied the new principle promulgated in the *Golden Globes* Order and determined fleeting expletives and a brief moment of indecency were actionably indecent. This regulatory history, however, makes it apparent that the Commission policy in place at the time of the broadcasts gave no notice to Fox or ABC that a fleeting expletive or a brief shot of nudity could be actionably indecent; yet Fox and ABC were found to be in violation. The Commission's lack of notice to Fox and ABC that its interpretation had changed so the fleeting moments of indecency contained in their broadcasts were a violation of § 1464 as interpreted and enforced by the agency "fail[ed] to provide a person of ordinary intelligence fair notice of what is prohibited." [*United States v. Williams,* 553 U.S. 285 (2008) at 304.]

* * * * *

The Commission failed to give Fox or ABC fair notice prior to the broadcasts in question that fleeting expletives and momentary nudity could be found actionably indecent.

Therefore, the Commission's standards as applied to these broadcasts were vague, and the Commission's orders must be set aside.

* * * * *

The judgments of the United States Court of Appeals for the Second Circuit are vacated, and the cases are remanded. . . .

Questions

1. *a.* Following the *Fox I* Supreme Court decision in 2009, the case went back down to the Second Circuit Court of Appeals, which ruled that the entire FCC indecency policy was unconstitutional. What constitutional infirmity did the Second Circuit cite in striking down the indecency policy? Explain.

    b. Did the Supreme Court in *Fox II* agree with the Second Circuit Court of Appeals that the FCC indecency policy was unconstitutional in its entirety? Explain.

2. When would an agency ruling be considered "arbitrary or capricious"?

3. Balancing First Amendment considerations (not addressed by the Supreme Court in the *Fox II* case) with concerns about the social effects of indecent language and behavior, what policy do you personally think the FCC should follow in regulating "fleeting expletives" like those uttered on television by Cher and Nicole Richie? Explain.

4. In commenting on the ongoing indecency debate, *The New York Times* argued: "The Supreme Court . . . should end all government regulations on the content of broadcasts. Technological change has undermined any justification for limiting the First Amendment rights of broadcast media outlets but not others."[36]

    Explain what the *Times* meant about technology eliminating the need for government oversight of broadcasting content.

The FCC and Indecency Today

LO 8-10

Analyze the Federal Communications Commission (FCC) role in regulating indecency in broadcasting.

A six pm newscast in 2012 on Roanoke, Virginia's WDBJ TV included a story about a former adult film star who had joined a local volunteer rescue squad. Station staff obtained a sexually explicit video clip for broadcast but accidentally failed to edit out an image of an erect penis that occupied 1.7 percent of the screen at the edge for 2.7 seconds. After receiving complaints, the FCC proposed a $325,000 fine, the largest allowable under the law. WDBJ is challenging the proposed fine at this writing.

Changing Attitudes?   So the FCC remains vigilant, especially in sensational cases like the Roanoke episode, but we seem to be in a period of some uncertainty about government oversight of broadcast obscenity and indecency. Janet Jackson's right breast was momentarily bared during the halftime show of the 2004 Super Bowl, a "wardrobe malfunction" that led to a $550,000 FCC fine levied against CBS television. That fine, however, was thrown out by a 2011 Third Circuit Court of Appeals decision calling the FCC action "arbitrary and capricious" in that it was an unexplained departure from the agency's longtime tolerance of fleeting indecency.[37] The Supreme Court declined to review that decision[38] and the eight-year exposed breast saga came to whimpering end. Of course, *Fox I* and *Fox II* have clarified the law so that future such moments might be subject to government penalties, but public complaints to the FCC about obscenity and indecency plummeted from 1.4 million in 2004 to 1,003 in 2014.[39]

Now the f-bomb makes fairly regular appearances on basic cable television, and premium cable channels like HBO and Showtime, not being accountable to advertisers, are somewhat unfiltered in their words and images. Cable television is not subject to FCC oversight, but even on FCC-regulated broadcast television, we see some scripted bleeping and rather common use of the b-word, for example. At the same time, broadcast networks must continue to be mindful of viewer and advertiser concerns as well as possible FCC objections.[40]

Safe Harbor   As noted in *Fox II,* FCC rules forbid indecent materials on conventional broadcast services between 6 pm and 10 pm—hours when children are likely to be in the audience. The 10 pm to 6 am slot, on the other hand, offers a "safe harbor" for indecent programming, but broadcast channels, even at late hours, remain restrained about pushing indecency boundaries.

Free Speech   The Supreme Court likely will need to revisit the First Amendment issues that were avoided in *Fox I* and *Fox II*. Many parents and other critics favor sterner broadcast oversight, as exemplified in the fleeting expletives/nudity situations, whereas the broadcast industry and civil liberties advocates prefer generous room for expression along with aggressive defense of First Amendment free speech standards.

The threat of stiff penalties along with the FCC's broadly drawn indecency standards have caused some stations to refrain from broadcasting shows with profanity, such as the acclaimed movie *Saving Private Ryan*. Critics worry that FCC rules, designed to protect viewers—particularly children—may have a "chilling effect" on the free flow of ideas that is so vital to the nation's political, cultural, and economic health. So we seem to be witnessing an increasingly delicate balance between freedom and censure that reflects society's split on matters of indecency. [For continuing analysis of broadcast law, see **www.broadcastlawblog.com**].

> Stations refrain from broadcasting shows such as *Saving Private Ryan*.

Dirty Words

Comedian George Carlin's 1972 album *Class Clown* was added in 2016 to the Library of Congress National Recording Registry for landmark aural contributions. The album includes Carlin's famous "Seven Dirty Words" monologue (mentioned above in *Fox II*), which examines and satirizes America's discomfort with "indecent" language.

Questions—Part Three

1. The Parents Television Council filed 36 indecency complaints with the FCC alleging that popular television shows, including *Friends* and *The Simpsons,* contained indecent scenes that either were sexually explicit or used indecent or profane language. How would you vote on the following scenes?

a. In the *Gilmore Girls,* one character says to another, "You're a dick."

b. In *The Simpsons,* students carry picket signs with the phrases "What would Jesus glue?" and "Don't cut off my pianissimo."

2. Sports betting, other than the "fantasy football" variety, is illegal in the United States, with the exception of four states. A federal court of appeals in 2016 blocked a New Jersey plan to legalize sports betting in that state.[41] Writing in *The New York Times* in 2014, National Basketball Association commissioner Adam Silver called on Congress to adopt a "federal framework that allows states to authorize betting on professional sports, subject to strict regulatory requirements and technological safeguards." He said the regulations should include mechanisms to exclude problem gamblers, education about responsible gambling, reporting of unusual betting-line movements, technology to ensure betting is available only where legal, licensing for betting operators, and minimum-age verification for gamblers. Professional and amateur sports associations have long opposed gambling on their games and most still do so.

a. Why would Silver now be advocating federal legalization of professional sports betting?

b. Do you agree with him? Explain. See Adam Silver, "Legalize and Regulate Sports Betting," *The New York Times,* November 13, 2014 [**www.nytimes.com**].

3. Cable television operators use signal scrambling to ensure that only paying customers have access to some programming. Congress was concerned that some sexually explicit cable programming, even though scrambled, might reach children via signal "bleeding." Section 505 of the Telecommunications Act of 1996 required cable operators to fully block sexually oriented channels or to "time channel"—that is, transmit only in hours when children are unlikely to be viewing. Most cable operators adopted the latter approach, with the result that for two-thirds of the day no viewers in the operators' service areas could receive the sexually explicit programming. Section 504 of the Telecommunications Act required cable operators to block undesired channels at individual households on request. A supplier of sexually oriented programming challenged Section 505 on First Amendment grounds. Decide the case. Explain. See *United States v. Playboy Entertainment Group,* 529 U.S. 803 (2000).

Part Four—The Federal Regulatory Process Evaluated

> Conservative activists have angrily, sometimes violently, resisted what they see as an overreaching government.

Free-market advocates want to sharply reduce government, while free-market skeptics favor an activist government engaged in preventing and correcting market failure. Federal authority continues to grow, and conservative activists have angrily, sometimes violently, resisted what they see as an overreaching government intruding in matters such as education and energy policy better left to local communities and the market.

Bailing Out the American Economy

The 2007–2009 Great Recession, ignited by irresponsible subprime mortgage lending, brought millions of job losses, the complete collapse of the housing market, the bankruptcy or near bankruptcy of some of America's biggest banks and other businesses, and a worldwide financial contraction.

Experts differ dramatically in their explanations for the collapse. Free-market advocates tend to blame the subprime problems on government intervention, especially easy credit policies that allowed many more Americans to buy homes. Many of those buyers, unfortunately, were not well qualified to make their payments. Critics of the free market, on the other hand, say that deregulation was a big factor in the collapse. For 30 years prior to the meltdown, the government gradually diminished its oversight of the banking industry in an effort to allow the market a greater voice and to strengthen American banks' competitiveness in the global market.

Government (Taxpayers) to the Rescue Departing dramatically from America's free-market heritage, the George W. Bush and Barack Obama administrations employed aggressive financial bailouts and fiscal stimulus policies to help steady the collapsing economy. In Chapter 1, we noted a $1.6 trillion estimate of government expenditures, but other estimates are higher. *Fortune* magazine concluded that taxpayer money has been repaid with a slight profit likely from bailout-related income, but that conclusion depends on how we look at the numbers.[42]

As noted in Chapter 1, economists Alan Blinder and Mark Zandi estimate that the length of the Recession would have doubled in the absence of government intervention, unemployment that reached 10 percent would have climbed to a disastrous 16 percent, and the gross domestic product decline of about 4 percent would have ballooned to 14 percent.[43]

Legendary investor Warren Buffet has applauded the federal government's decision to intervene in the financial markets. Buffet noted the economic meltdown the nation faced, the giant banks that were teetering, the major industrial companies that were running out of money, and the millions of Americans whose prosperity was at risk. The threat was enormous, as Buffet saw it, and he judged the government to have provided the proper remedy.[44]

Nonetheless, the enormous government intervention in the market continues to be criticized as a Wall Street bailout, an abandonment of free-market principles, and an unwarranted expansion of government authority. Critics claim the economy likely would have moved out of recession by 2009 on its own. More broadly, their argument is that progressive economic theory is mistaken; government spending simply cannot stimulate the economy and as much money as possible should be left in taxpayer pockets for spending and investment.[45] [For a detailed investigation of the government's efforts to repair the recession-shattered economy, see the PBS video *Money, Power and Wall Street* at **www.pbs.org/wgbh/frontline/film/money-power-wall-street**].

Financial Reform
Dodd–Frank Concluding that the financial markets needed more effective and thorough oversight in light of the nation's near crash, Congress and President Obama in 2010 approved the Dodd–Frank Wall Street Reform and Consumer Protection Act to improve America's financial regulatory structure. Dodd–Frank is primarily directed to large financial institutions, including a few very large "nonbanks" like insurance companies. Smaller, community banks are exempt from some of its provisions. As perhaps its chief goal, the law is designed to prevent the financial collapse of giant banks and businesses that are so

big ("too big to fail") that some form of government bailout would be necessary. Toward that objective, a 15-member Financial Stability Oversight Council headed by the Secretary of the Treasury monitors the health of the entire U.S. financial system. Big financial companies are required to maintain larger capital holdings in order to reduce risky lending, provide funds for emergencies, and make enormous size less attractive. They also must create and update "living wills" to provide for their own quick and orderly shutdown in the event of financial failure.

The act also reforms mortgage lending practices in an effort to ensure that borrowers actually have the wherewithal to repay. The enormous bill (more than 2,300 pages) has many more provisions, including the creation of the Consumer Financial Protection Bureau (see Chapter 15), other mortgage reforms, increased oversight of derivatives and hedge funds, new rules for credit rating agencies, a larger shareholder voice in executive pay decisions, and limits (under the so-called Volcker Rule) on the amount of a bank's own assets that can be used for some risky forms of proprietary trading (investing the firm's own money rather than that of its clients).

At this writing, more than six years after the enactment of Dodd–Frank, about 70 percent of its provisions have been implemented. Federal regulators are slowly creating new rules, but lobbyists for the banking industry and philosophical opposition from free-market politicians are challenging those rules and restraining funding. Beyond damage to the banks themselves, critics believe Dodd–Frank threatens overall economic growth. Small businesses and consumers may face rising borrowing costs and fewer services. Congressional Republicans and President Trump, at this writing, are expected to pursue changes in Dodd–Frank, including reductions in small bank regulations and perhaps exemptions from some regulations for big banks that maintain very large capital reserves.

Banking Stability   Notwithstanding those complaints about excessive government, many political leaders and economists believe Dodd–Frank does not do enough to address its central concern: the stability of the American banking system. Six giant firms—JPMorgan Chase, Bank of America, Wells Fargo, Citigroup, Goldman Sachs, and Morgan Stanley—hold about $9.7 trillion in assets, equal to over 63 percent of all U.S. bank assets.[46]

Top banking regulators announced in 2016 that five of the nation's largest banks, including JPMorgan Chase and Bank of America, were still "too big to fail" and did not have credible plans for winding themselves down in a crisis. At the same time, government regulatory pressure clearly has been successful in shrinking the big banks and in curbing their most risky practices. Citigroup, for example, has sold 60 businesses and reduced its assets by about $700 million in recent years.[47]

In summary, the Dodd–Frank goal of ending too big to fail and freeing taxpayers from the risk of future bailouts has not yet been attained, but progress is evident. Liberals continue to see the big banks as the product of unrestrained capitalism and excessive lobbying power, whereas many conservatives also oppose the big banks because they see them as the product of big government cronyism and government safety nets. Of course, the banking industry and many experts believe big banks are necessary to achieve big deals in a global economy, and they fear that China might well replace the United States as the world's financial leader if the big banks are downsized. And we should remind ourselves that many of the financial problems leading to the Great Recession came from smaller, less-publicized financial firms.

Too Much Government?

LO 8-11
Evaluate criticisms of the federal regulatory process.

Until the 2008 subprime mortgage crisis and recession, the United States had been in a period, since the late 1970s, of *deregulation,* during which great efforts were made to reduce the role of government in big portions of American life. Once tightly controlled industries, including energy, transportation, and telecommunications, were substantially returned to market forces. The results often included lower prices and increased innovation. Republicans and Democrats alike generally embraced the idea that greater efficiency, competitiveness, and freedom would accompany reduced government oversight. Government authority remained enormous, however, and regulation persisted or increased in areas such as workplace safety, the environment, equal opportunity, and consumer protection where the market did not seem to be performing well.

Now, as we have seen, the threat of a banking collapse and economic chaos for America and the world generated a resurgence in federal economic intervention. Obamacare, Dodd–Frank, and very aggressive Federal Reserve and Treasury Department policies have highlighted the crucial but divisive question of just how much government we need in our lives. At this writing, the sweeping Republican Party victories in the 2016 general election are expected to bring renewed challenges to "big government" and to specific regulatory regimes such as some elements of environmental protection law. Are we excessively regulated or insufficiently regulated? Or are government regulations simply ineffective? Consider the following evidence.

I. Excessive Regulation

In brief, the excessive regulation argument is that government rules reduce business efficiency, kill jobs, discourage innovation, impose very high compliance costs, and curb freedom while expanding the government bureaucracy and the taxes/borrowing that fund it.

A recent survey of Midwestern business owners found that the volume of government regulations was the third biggest concern facing their businesses (behind taxes and employee health benefits).[48] The conservative American Action Forum projected that regulatory compliance costs for new 2016 federal rules would total about $200 billion and more than 100 million paperwork hours.[49]

[For a Cato Institute video, *There Are Too Many Bureaucrats and They Are Paid Too Much,* see **www.youtube.com/watch?v=5xzd3puYmiM**].

Small businesses, crucial job creators, particularly struggle to bear the costs of new government rules. Even employee protection laws such as Obamacare, the minimum wage, and overtime pay can sink struggling small businesses. More broadly, a 2016 report from the conservative Mercatus Center estimated that federal regulations from 1980 to 2012 reduced the size of the American economy by about 25 percent ($4 trillion, or nearly $13,000 per American).[50] Of course, estimates on the cost of regulation vary dramatically, and regulations often bring significant benefits along with their costs. [For an array of conservative analyses of tax issues, see **www.atr.org**]. [For more detailed criticisms of the federal regulatory process, see **www.heritage.org**, **http://cei.org**, or **www.cato.org/pubs/regulation**].

Unnecessary Reports

Congress and President Obama in 2014 approved the Government Reports Elimination Act, which removed 53 unnecessary reports from federal employees' workloads. One of the eliminated reports called for Homeland Security to annually detail illegal imports of products made with dog or cat fur.

Source: "President Signs Sen. Warner's Bipartisan Initiative to Eliminate Unnecessary Federal Reports," *Senator Mark R. Warner E-Newsletter,* December 1, 2014 [**www.warner.senate.gov/public/index.cfm/bloghome?sr=31&label=Govt%20Performance**].

II. Insufficient Regulation

Advocates of increased regulation point to the many successes of government intervention: a vast highway network, legal equality for minorities and women, cleaner air, safer workplaces, greatly diminished child labor, enhanced auto safety, and so on.

> **Does government intervention pay off?**

Does government intervention pay off? Free-market advocates say "no" in many instances, but some powerful numbers and respected opinions say "yes." The federal Office of Management and Budget's 2015 assessment of the "Benefits and Costs of Federal Regulations" found that the estimated annual benefits of major federal rules reviewed by the OMB for which cost–benefit data were available from 2004 to 2014 totaled between $261 billion and $981 billion, whereas the estimated costs were between $68 billion and $103 billion, reported in 2010 dollars.[51]

Does regulation actually harm economic growth in America? Considerable evidence suggests that fear is not convincing. A federal Bureau of Labor Statistics survey of extended mass layoffs, for example, found only 3,300 layoffs nationwide in 2012 that employers attributed to government regulation or intervention.[52] A *Washington Post* overview of economists' judgments as to the effect of regulations on job loss found generally that those effects were "minimal."[53] More broadly, the World Bank's 2016 "ease of doing business" report placed the United States seventh highest in the world, well ahead of most of our primary competitors.[54]

III. Ineffective Regulation

Just as the market can fail, so can the regulatory system. The sources of that regulatory failure are multiple (bureaucratic inefficiency, for example), but one specific problem is highlighted in a recent series of Government Accountability Office (GAO) reports detailing duplication of tasks in the federal government. According to the 2011 report, 15 different agencies oversee food safety, 80 programs address economic development, 82 programs improve teacher quality, 56 help people understand finances, and so on.[55] Happily, the 2016 report found that about 75 percent of its recommendations for improvement had been fully or partially implemented, at a savings of about $125 billion.[56]

Government Too Slow?

From the fatal ignition switches on several General Motors models (see Chapter 2) to Jeep fuel tank fires, unintended acceleration in Toyotas, and air bag ruptures in Hondas, the National Highway Traffic Safety Administration (NHTSA), according to a *New York Times* investigation, was "slow to identify problems, tentative to act and reluctant to employ its full legal powers against companies."[57] Federal regulators at NHTSA admitted in 2016 that they had failed to fulfill their automobile safety duties satisfactorily.[58] NHTSA has committed to more aggressive auto safety oversight, but budget limitations often constrain its activities.

The Winner: The (Carefully) Mixed Economy?

Economist and columnist Sebastian Mallaby argues that we should embrace a role for both the market and government in our mixed economy and recognize that the American people will continue to demand more and more from the government (security from criminals and terrorists, clean air, safe food, good schools, and so on).[59] Indeed, he argues that those public goods in our prosperous society probably matter more than private pleasures such as smartphones and exotic vacations. As a result, government will likely be under great pressure to spend more, but we should also "be ruthless about making government and markets more efficient."[60]

Historian John Steele Gordon makes the point that regulation has made America more stable and richer:

Capitalism without regulation and regulators is inherently unstable, Gordon claims, "as people will usually put their short-term interests ahead of the interests of the system as a whole, and either chaos or plutocracy will result. . . . The country since the New Deal has been a far richer, far more economically secure, far more just society."[61]

Indeed, as economist and legal scholar Neil Buchanan has explained, some measure of government is necessary for capitalism to thrive:

The government stands in the background of every transaction, and whether the parties to the transaction know it or not (and whether they like government or hate it), their wealth and prosperity could not exist were it not for a government providing a legal framework that allows capitalism to exist and function.[62]

We cannot forget, however, that excessive regulation can kill jobs, kill prosperity, and kill ambition, so a delicate negotiation between market and government is necessary, as columnist *New York Times* Nicholas Kristof explains:

Critics are right that regulators are sometimes too zealous and bureaucratic. Sometimes regulations do curb profits and undermine jobs. But, on the whole, we need regulations to guard against human nature. The truth is that bad things usually aren't done by evil people, but rather by essentially decent people who go to work and get so wrapped up in the "business case" they sometimes lose their moral compass.[63]

So while freedom and prosperity require a strong free market, a healthy, just society seems to require some significant, but appropriately measured role for government. Scholar Cass Sunstein makes an argument for a government that relies to a considerable extent on "soft interventions" that preserve freedom while nudging us in desirable directions. His recent, national survey of Americans found, for example, 87 percent approval of federal rules requiring calorie labels at chain restaurants, 85 percent approval of aggressive public education about distracted driving, 82 percent approval of public education about obesity, and 75 percent approval of federal government–sponsored public education to discourage sexual orientation discrimination.[64]

God Up; Government Down

How much government do we need in our lives? Our answers to this important question apparently depend, in part, on our view of God. The Baylor (University) Religion Survey, conducted by the Gallup Poll in 2011, found that people who strongly believe "God has a plan for me" were much more likely to also believe that "the government does too much." Sociologist Paul Froese, coauthor of the study, says the strong believers see the invisible hand of the free market as God at work. Those who do not believe in God or who believe God to be more removed from daily affairs tend to be more supportive of government.

Sources: Cathy Lynn Grossman, "Baylor Religion Survey Reveals Many See God Steering Economy," *USA TODAY*, September 20, 2011 [**http://usatoday.com**]; and G. Jeffrey MacDonald, "Does Government Do Too Much? That Could Depend on Your View of God," *The Christian Science Monitor*, September 23, 2011 [**www.csmonitor.com/**].

Young People?

What does the future hold for big government in America? Must the market and government work together for success in tomorrow's America? *The New York Times* in 2013 took an interesting look at those questions by interviewing young people in the Montana college town of Missoula, a majority of whom see government as a constructive force:

> "Young people absolutely believe that there's a role for government," said Matt Singer, a founder of Forward Montana. "At the same time, this is not a generation of socialists. They are highly entrepreneurial, and know that some of what it takes to create an environment where they can do their own exciting, creative things is having basic systems that work."[65]

According to a Pew Research Center survey, under-30 voters are "the only age group in which a majority said the government should do more to fix problems."[66] What role do you see for government in your life? Do you think big government is an impediment to your happy, prosperous future? Or do you view government as a natural, necessary ally of the market?

Global Regulation

We should remember that regulation in the United States remains modest relative to the balance of the globe. Even though the cost of regulation in the United States is great, government rules are, in fact, less burdensome in America than in most nations.

The Washington Post in 2013 reported the critics' view that France is "drowning in rules and regulations,"[67] and *The New York Times* in 2012 applied the word *abysmal* to Greece's climate for doing business while citing a McKinsey & Company study that found start-ups in Greece facing "immense amounts of red tape, complex administrative and tax systems and procedural disincentives."[68] The global trend, however, seems to be toward more sensible rules. The World Bank's *Doing Business 2016* report found that significant progress has been made in the last 10 years in improving business regulatory practices around the globe.[69]

We should also understand that regulation, particularly in the banking sector, is an increasingly cooperative, international process recognizing the value of cutting global red tape while also acknowledging the necessity of firm rules to maintain a healthy global economy and prevent future financial crises.

Basel III

The big industrial nations expect to fully phase in by 2019 regulatory measures (labeled Basel III) to promote global financial stability. At the center of those rules are increased capital reserve standards designed to both discourage risk taking and assure capital availability if a crisis occurs. At this writing, the United States is implementing its compliance with Basel III. Big banks around the world have made progress in building their capital reserves, but objections to Basel III have mounted, implementation has been slow, the "too big to fail" problem clearly remains unsolved, and, of course, holding capital in reserve is expensive.

Two Concluding Cases

We close this chapter about government rules by asking if we should have more of them.

Case I. Sharing Economy: Airbnb

At this writing in 2016, cities across the country, including San Francisco, Seattle, Los Angeles, and Chicago, are deciding whether Airbnb, Vacation Rentals by Owner, and other online, short-term room/home rental services should be regulated. As we saw earlier in this chapter, the ride-hailing portion of the sharing economy (Uber and Lyft, among others) is likewise facing regulatory pressure. Governments do not want to discourage a vibrant, growing, efficient new source of economic vitality, supplementary income, and community service. Problems have emerged, however, that the market may not be able to resolve.

Questions

1. What problems are causing communities to begin imposing rules on Airbnb and other short-term rental housing facilitators?
2. Do you think government is wise to regulate this industry? Explain.

Case II. Cell Phones: A Deadly Distraction?

According to a national survey, 20 percent of drivers 18–20 said texting does not affect their driving and 30 percent of those 21–34 said the same.[70] The National Safety Council attributes about one-quarter of car accidents to cell phones.[71] The National Highway Traffic Safety Administration reported that 3,179 people died in distraction-related crashes in 2014.[72] Research at the University of Utah found that cell phone conversation is a much more dangerous distraction than passenger conversation.[73]

No state forbids all cell phone use while driving, but 46 ban text messaging for all drivers, and 14 states forbid all drivers from using handheld cell phones while driving.[74] Are these restraints effective? The four states without blanket bans on texting while driving have a 17 percent higher average rate of texting than drivers in other states.[75] Of course, the real problem may be distractions of all kinds, but survey results find 96 percent of Americans agree that texting should not be permitted while driving.[76]

Questions

1. Mike Hashimoto, assistant editorial page editor at the *Dallas Morning News*:

   > I get as mad as the next person at the minivan driver cruising along 5 mph below the speed limit in the left lane, basically causing everyone else with someplace to be to dodge around him/her in a slightly dangerous way. That doesn't mean we need another annoying law in the long-running series of laws intended to remove all risk from our daily lives. . . . A cell phone ban might make us feel better, but at best, it would have the same practical effect as banning Big Macs while driving, shaving while driving, reading a map while driving or reaching into the back seat for your kid while driving. . . .[77]

   a. Would you favor government rules forbidding all cell phone use while driving? Explain.
   b. What about text messaging, grooming, eating, and so on? Explain.

2. Technology companies are rapidly bringing powerful information technology to car dashboards. Government regulators argue that those products are slowing their efforts to reduce hazards from distracted driving. According to National Transportation Safety Board chair Deborah Hersman:

   > If the technology producers focused more on what is safe than what sells, we'd see highway fatalities go down.[78]

   Do you agree that technology companies are irresponsibly putting profit before safety in developing ever more advanced, and doubtless distracting, technology in cars? Explain.

3. Distinguished economist Herbert Stein, perhaps best known as father of celebrity Ben Stein, said that we are desperate for cell phone conversations to ward off our loneliness:

   > It is the way of keeping contact with someone, anyone who will reassure you that you are not alone. You may think you are checking on your portfolio but deep down you are checking on your own existence.[79]

   a. Are you dependent on your cell phone?
   b. If so, should the government discourage that use by, for example, imposing higher taxes on cell phone purchases? Explain.

Guy Davenport: "The telephone is God's gift to the bore."

Source: Interview by John Jeremiah Sullivan, *The Paris Review,* Fall 2002.

Internet Exercise

Should the U.S. government impose new rules requiring all bicyclists to wear helmets? New Zealand has enforced a national mandatory all-age bicycle helmet law since 1994. To help with your recommendation for the United States, consider the evidence from the New Zealand experience at **http://en.wikipedia.org/wiki/Bicycle_helmets_in_New_Zealand.**

Chapter Questions

1. According to a 2014 Health Policy Institute study, about 15 percent of Americans surveyed said they could not afford dental care when needed.[80] The average dentist in 2013 earned, after expenses, about $181,000 (as compared with about $175,000 for family doctors). A *Washington Post* 2015 commentary argued that dentists may be overpaid, in part because they are protected from competition by law in most states. Minnesota, however, is now licensing "dental therapists," who are not dentists but are allowed to clean, fill, and pull teeth when under the "general supervision" of a dentist. One study found that dentists' income was reduced by 16 percent where hygienists were allowed to offer independent care. Do you think we should allow market forces to drive down the cost of dental care by permitting less expensive dental personnel, if appropriately trained, to do some of the work of dentists? Explain. See Max Ehrenfreund, "Why Dentists Are So Darn Rich," *The Washington Post,* July 29, 2015 [**www.washingtonpost.com**].

2. Regulatory critics often advocate a free-market approach to cable television, in part because it is a "nonessential activity."

   a. Should the government be involved in regulating only those products and services that we cannot do without? Explain.

   b. Do you trust the free market? The government? Both? Neither? Explain.

   c. Do you think government oversight is necessary to reduce the risk of a future banking crisis such as the one we faced in recent years? Explain.

3. Delaware and New Jersey offer legal, online casino gambling and Nevada offers poker online. Other states may follow. The federal government has considered legislation ranging from a complete ban to a moratorium to a uniform, national policy that would allow poker but forbid other forms of online gambling.

   a. List some of the pros and cons of allowing and regulating Internet gambling.

   b. Would you favor that direction? Explain.

4. The Heritage Foundation's 2016 global Index of Economic Freedom generally demonstrates that the nations most successful in increasing their economic freedom (by reducing taxes and so forth) enjoy, according to the editors of the study, higher incomes and higher overall well-being.[81] When the Index was first published in 1995, the United States ranked fifth in the world, but it fell to eleventh in the 2016 study. Hong Kong ranked first in 2016, with Canada sixth and the United Kingdom tenth.[82]

   a. What is economic freedom?

   b. The Heritage Foundation lists 10 factors, including, for example, business freedom, in its list of ingredients in measuring economic freedom. In addition to business freedom, what other factors would you include in a list designed to measure a nation's level of overall economic freedom?

c. How does economic freedom help an economy grow?

5. Former Secretary of Labor Robert Reich: "The era of big government may be over, but the era of regulation through litigation has just begun."[83] Explain what Reich meant.

6. In recent years, the National Collegiate Athletic Association (NCAA), the primary governing body for college athletics, has been debating proposals to deregulate some oversight practices. Effective August 2016, for example, college football coaches (among several other sports) were free to send unlimited text messages to prospects. Coaches can also "indicate approval" (re-tweet, like, or share) of recruits' social media posts.

Many coaches oppose relaxed recruiting rules. Northwestern University head football coach Pat Fitzgerald actually favored greater regulation:

> The term that makes the hair stand up on the back of my neck is "deregulate." The question we should be asking is how can we re-regulate, get up to the 21st century and make best practices in recruiting for all those involved.[84]

a. Broadly, do you think NCAA rules governing sports recruiting should be deregulated or "re-regulated" toward best practices, as suggested by Coach Fitzgerald?

b. In raising children of high school age, would you favor a parental approach involving heavy reliance on rules, or would you prefer a more deregulated, free-market approach? Explain.

7. Although frustrating and imperfect, government regulation often leads to better lives. We notice, for example, that seat belt use in 2012 reached a record high with 86 percent of motorists buckled up, as compared with 58 percent in 1994,[85] and we know that smoking bans have directly and quickly led to reductions in heart attacks and other ailments.[86] "Fracking" technology necessary to our current natural gas drilling boom was significantly propelled by more than $100 million in government subsidies and much more in tax breaks.[87] Given those successes and many others, do we need more aggressive government intervention in America's endangered family life? At first glance, most Americans would probably say "no," but a 2012 University of Virginia (UVA) study argued that government intervention is needed to restore the institution of marriage among the 60 percent of our population that does not have a college education. In the 1980s, about 13 percent of American children were born outside of marriage; now that number is about 44 percent. The UVA study estimates the cost to taxpayers at over $100 billion annually when stable families do not develop.[88] The study suggests, among other things, various tax and welfare policy changes to encourage marriage.

Is marriage a private and personal affair that should be left free of further government intervention? Explain. [For more information, see **stateofourunions.org**].

8. The expense of government regulation is not limited to the direct cost of administering the various agencies. Explain and offer examples of the other expenses produced by regulation.

9. To the extent the federal government achieves deregulation, what substitutes will citizens find for protection from dangers previously regulated?

10. Pulitzer Prize–winning author and presidential adviser Arthur Schlesinger:

    > The assault on the national government is represented as a disinterested movement to "return" power to the people. But the withdrawal of the national government does not transfer power to the people. It transfers power to the historical rival of the national government and the prime cause of its enlargement—the great corporate interests.[89]

    a. Using 19th- and 20th-century American economic history, explain Schlesinger's claim that corporate interests are the primary cause of big government.
    b. Do you agree with Schlesinger that we continue to need big government to counteract corporate interests and achieve fairness for all in American life? Explain.

11. Make the argument that increasing government rules and jobs leads to decreasing private-sector businesses and jobs.

12. One authority estimates that obesity contributes to the deaths of 100,000 Americans annually.[90] A strategy for reducing the health risks of obesity is to impose a tax on high-calorie junk foods such as soda, donuts, and potato chips. Maine, for example, imposed a 5.5 percent snack tax as a means of closing a budget gap, but that state's adult obesity rate doubled during the 10 years the tax was in place.[91] Two-thirds of the states already impose a tax (averaging 5.2 percent) on soft drinks, but for a 5-foot-10, 279-pound person, the average weight loss associated with the tax has been about 3 ounces.[92]

    a. What objections would you raise to increased taxes on junk food.
    b. Would you support a significant tax, say, 25 percent, on junk food? Explain.
    c. Would subsidies to lower the price of healthy food be a more effective strategy than taxes on unhealthy food? Explain.

13. Section 706 of the federal Telecommunications Act of 1996 requires the Federal Communications Commission to "accelerate deployment" of high-speed Internet access to all Americans by "removing barriers to infrastructure investment and by promoting competition in the telecommunications market." Public utility customers in Chattanooga, Tennessee, and Wilson, North Carolina, enjoy high-speed Internet access. People outside those communities want the high-speed services expanded to them, but state law forbids that access, thus limiting service to large private-sector providers such as Comcast and Time Warner Cable. The Federal Communications Commission (FCC) issued an order preempting the state laws in Tennessee and North Carolina, thus allowing the public utilities to expand their service.

    a. Can the FCC lawfully preempt state law in this situation? Explain.
    b. Should the FCC be able to preempt state law in this situation? Explain. See *State of Tennessee, State of North Carolina v. Federal Communications Commission*, 832 F.3d 597 (6th Cir. 2016).

14. Joseph Stiglitz, the chief White House economist at the time, argued in 1996 that "a huge economic literature" supports his view that "appropriately circumscribed government programs can lead to a higher-growth economy."[93] How can government programs stimulate the economy rather than act as a drag on it?

15. A major issue facing the Federal Aviation Administration is congestion in the airways caused by too many planes seeking to take off or land at peak times at high-demand airports. How might we solve that problem while maintaining reasonable service?

16. In calculating the costs and benefits of a new rule, make the argument that added regulation normally slows the economy and leads to increased deaths.

17. *a.* In general, do you trust our government in Washington, D.C.? Explain.
    b. More specifically, do you trust the federal agencies we have been discussing in this chapter, including, for example, the Food and Drug Administration, the Environmental Protection Agency, and the Internal Revenue Service? Explain.

18. A bipartisan coalition labeled "Mayors Against Illegal Guns" released a 2010 study finding that 43,000 of the guns confiscated at crime scenes in 2009 came from out-of-state gun dealers. Georgia, Virginia, West Virginia, Alabama, Mississippi, and Alaska were among the largest gun exporters. States with strong restrictions export guns at only about one-seventh the rate of those with lax rules. Between 11 and 12 thousand Americans annually are murdered by guns.[94] Commenting in *The New York Times,* columnist Nicholas Kristof said:

    > To protect the public, we regulate cars and toys, medicines and mutual funds. So, simply as a public health matter, shouldn't we take steps to reduce the toll from our domestic arms industry?[95]

    Do you think firmer gun regulations are needed? Explain.

Notes

1. *Brown v. Entertainment Merchants Association,* 564 U.S. 789 (2011).
2. American Psychological Association, "APA Review Confirms Link Between Playing Violent Video Games and Aggression," press release, August 13, 2015 [**www.apa.org/news/press/releases/2015/08/violent-video-games.aspx**].
3. Chris McDonald, "In Praise of Self-Regulation," *Canadian Business,* July 14, 2011 [**www.canadianbusiness.com**].
4. Daniel Akst, "In Playing Video Games, Morality Rules," *The Wall Street Journal,* October 9, 2012 [**http://blogs.wsj.com**].
5. See, e.g., Carlos Cueva et al., "Cortisol and Testosterone Increase Financial Risk Taking and May Destablilize Markets," *Scientific Reports* 5, no. 11206 (2015), doi:10.1038/srep11206.
6. Joseph P. Tomain, "American Regulatory Policy: Have We Found the 'Third Way'?" *Kansas Law Review* 48 (May 2000), p. 829.
7. Charles Leocha, "For Airlines, the Free Market Doesn't Need to Be Unfettered," *The New York Times,* May 25, 2016 [**www.nytimes.com**].
8. Conn Iggulden and Hal Iggulden, *The Dangerous Book for Boys* (New York: HarperCollins, 2007).
9. Hanna Rosin, "Hey! Parents, Leave Those Kids Alone," *The Atlantic,* April 2014, p. 75.
10. 317 U.S. 111 (1942).
11. 545 U.S. 1 (2005).
12. *Id.* at 57–58 (Thomas, J., dissenting).
13. 115 S. Ct. 1624 (1995).
14. 18 U.S.C. § 922(q)(1)(A).
15. *Brzonkala v. Morrison and United States v. Morrison,* 529 U.S. 598 (2000).
16. *Brzonkala v. Virginia Polytechnic Institute,* 169 F.3d 820, 827 (4th Cir. 1999).
17. *National Federation of Independent Business v. Sebelius,* 132 S. Ct. 2566 (2012).

18. John F. Cooney, "Federalism Spring: Evolution of the Federal-State Balance of Power," *Bloomberg Law Reports—Administrative Law,* no. 4 (2009).

19. See, e.g., *Williamson v. Mazda Motor of America, Inc.,* 131 S. Ct. 1131 (2011) [state tort suit not preempted]; *Bruesewitz v. Wyeth LLC,* 131 S. Ct. 1068 (2011) [state tort suit preempted]; and *Gobeille v. Liberty Mutual Insurance Co.,* 136 S. Ct. 936 (2016) [Employee Retirement Income Security Act (ERISA) preempts a Vermont statute requiring health insurers to report data about health care claims].

20. *Nebraska and Oklahoma v. Colorado,* 136 S. Ct. 1034 (2016).

21. Greg Bensinger, "Wine: The Web's Final Frontier," *The Wall Street Journal,* October 27, 2012, p. B3.

22. Dan Charles, "Berkeley's Soda Tax Appears to Cut Consumption of Sugary Drinks," *The Salt: NPR,* August 23, 2016 [**www.npr.org**].

23. Bianca Nunes, "NYC 'Soda Ban' Overturned: An Analysis of the Opinion," *Reg Blog,* April 2, 2013 [**www.law.upenn.edu/blogs/regblog/2013/04/02-nunes-nyc-soda-ban-overturned.html**].

24. Morris Kleiner, "States' Overzealous Licensing Laws Lead to 'Why'?" *The Des Moines Register,* July 20, 2014, p. 1OP.

25. See *St. Joseph Abbey v. Castille,* 712 F.3d 215 (5th Cir. 2013).

26. Jennifer Jacobs, "Judge Backs City's Refusal to Renew Bar's License," *The Waterloo/Cedar Falls Courier,* November 22, 1998, p. C3.

27. Chris Kirkham, "Home Builders Say They Are Squeezed by Rising Compliance Costs," *The Wall Street Journal,* May 7, 2016 [**www.wsj.com**].

28. The organizational structure of the introductory administrative law materials owes a great deal to the suggestions of Professor Cynthia Srstka, Augustana College (South Dakota).

29. Michele Zell-Kanter and Meghan A. Quigley, "Reduction in Ephedra Poisonings after FDA Ban," *New England Journal of Medicine* 372 (May 28, 2015), p. 2172.

30. Pete Bigelow, "After Years of Delays, NHTSA Issues Backup Camera Rules," *Autoblog,* March 31, 2014 [**www.autoblog.com**].

31. *U.S. Telecom Association v. FCC,* 825 F.3d 674 (D.C. Cir. 2016).

32. Renae Merle, "How a Goldman Sachs Executive Allegedly Stole Government Data to Woo Clients," *The Washington Post,* August 4, 2016 [**www.washingtonpost.com**].

33. Lee Drutman and Alexander Furnas, "How Revolving Door Lobbyists Are Taking Over K Street," *Sunlight Foundation Blog,* January 22, 2014 [**http://sunlightfoundation.com/blog**].

34. Lori Montgomery, "Obama Orders All Fed Agencies to Review Regulations," *The Washington Post,* January 18, 2011 [**www.washingtonpost.com**].

35. 531 U.S. 457 (2001).

36. Editorial, "Free Speech for Broadcasters," *The New York Times,* July 16, 2010 [**www.nytimes.com**].

37. *CBS v. Federal Communications Commission,* 663 F.3d 122 (3rd Cir. 2011).

38. *Federal Communications Commission v. CBS Corporation,* 132 S. Ct. 2677 (2012).

39. James Shiffer, "FCC Still on Hunt for Indecent and Profane on TV," *Minneapolis Star Tribune,* October 19, 2015 [**www.startribune.com**].

40. Bethonie Butler, "Is There Anything You Can't Say on TV Anymore? It's Complicated," *The Washington Post,* March 29, 2016 [**www.washingtonpost.com**].

41. *National Collegiate Athletic Association v. Governor of the State of New Jersey,* 832 F.3d 389 (3rd Cir. 2016).

42. Allan Sloan, "Surprise! The Big Bad Bailout Is Paying Off," *Fortune,* July 8, 2011 [**http://fortune.com**].

43. Alan Blinder and Mark Zandi, "The Financial Crisis: Lessons for the Next One," Center on Budget and Policy Priorities *Policy Futures,* October 15, 2015 [**www.cbpp.org/research/economy/the-financial-crisis-lessons-for-the-next-one**].

44. Warren E. Buffett, "Pretty Good for Government Work," *The New York Times,* November 16, 2010 [**www.nytimes.com/**].

45. Brian Riedl, "Why Government Spending Does Not Stimulate Economic Growth: Answering the Critics," Heritage Foundation *Backgrounder #2354,* January 5, 2010 [**www.heritage.org/research/reports/2010/01/why-government-spending-does-not-stimulate-economic-growth-answering-the-critics**].

46. Editorial Board, "Talk about Breaking Up Big Banks Ignores Reforms Made Since the Recession," *The Washington Post,* February 3, 2016 [**www.washingtonpost.com**].

47. Nathaniel Popper and Michael Corkery, "Shrunken Citigroup Illustrates a Trend in Big U.S. Banks," *The New York Times,* April 15, 2016 [**www.nytimes.com**].

48. Stuart Shapiro, "Are There Too Many Regulations?" *The Hill,* September 29, 2014 [**www.thehill.com**].

49. Sam Batkins, "A Few Costs and a Lot of Paperwork," *Week in Regulation,* July 25, 2016 [**www.americanactionforum.org/week-in-regulation/costs-lot-paperwork/#**].

50. Mark J. Perry and Thomas A. Hemphill, "Regulations Are a Really Big Drag on US Growth," *Investor's Business Daily,* May 16, 2016 [**www.investors.com**].

51. Office of Management and Budget, "2015 Report to Congress on the Benefits and Costs of Federal Regulations and Agency Compliance with the Unfunded Mandates Reform Act," [**www.whitehouse.gov/sites/default/files/omb/inforeg/2015_cb/2015-cost-benefit-report.pdf**].

52. Robert Weissman, "The Administrative State: An Examination of Federal Rulemaking," *Written Testimony before the Senate Committee on Homeland Security and Government Affairs,* April 20, 2016 [**http://Testimony-Weissman-2016-04-20-REVISED(1).pdf**].

53. Jia Lynn Yang, "Does Government Regulation Really Kill Jobs? Economists Say Overall Effect Minimal," *The Washington Post,* November 13, 2011 [**www.washingtonpost.com**].

54. World Bank Group, *Doing Business 2016,* p. 5 [**www.doingbusiness.org/~/media/GIAWB/Doing%20Business/Documents/Annual-Reports/English/DB16-Full-Report.pdf**].

55. Damian Paletta, "Billions in Bloat Uncovered in Beltway," *The Wall Street Journal,* March 1, 2011, p. A1.

56. Stephen Dinan, "GAO Urges Feds to Crack Down on Bad Spending, Increase Efficiency," *Washington Times,* April 13, 2016 [**www.washingtontimes.com**].

57. Hilary Stout, Danielle Ivory, and Rebecca Ruiz, "Regulator Slow to Respond to Deadly Vehicle Defects," *The New York Times,* September 14, 2014 [**www.nytimes.com**].

58. Ashley Halsey III, "Federal Regulators Admit They Bungled Investigation of Deadly Auto Ignition," *The Washington Post,* June 5, 2015 [**www.washingtonpost.com**].

59. Sebastian Mallaby, "Capitalism: The Remix," *Washingtonpost.com,* December 4, 2008, p. A21.

60. Ibid.

61. John Steele Gordon, *An Empire of Wealth: The Epic History of American Economic Power* (New York: Harper Collins, 2004), quoted in Wayne E. Yang, "The Wealth of America Is Wealth," *The Christian Science Monitor,* December 7, 2004 [**www.csmonitor.com/2004/1207/p15s02-bogn.html**].

62. Neil H. Buchanan, "The Ebola Crisis Highlights the Dangerous Consequences of Habitually Demonizing the Government," Justia *Verdict,* October 9, 2014 [**https://verdict.justia.com**].

63. Nicholas Kristof, "Job Crushing or Lifesaving?," *The New York Times,* April 30, 2014 [**www.nytimes.com**].

64. Cass R. Sunstein, "When America Says Yes to Government," *The New York Times,* June 19, 2015 [**www.nytimes.com**].

65. Sheryl Gay Stolberg, "Young, Liberal and Open to Big Government," *The New York Times,* February 11, 2013 [**www.nytimes.com**].

66. Ibid.

67. Edward Cody, "France Drowning in Rules and Regulations, Critics Say," *The Washington Post,* April 16, 2013 [**www.washingtonpost.com**].

68. Suzanne Daley, "A Tale of Greek Enterprise and Olive Oil, Smothered in Red Tape," *The New York Times,* March 18, 2012 [**www.nytimes.com**].

69. World Bank Group, "Business Reform Summaries," *Doing Business 2016* [**www.doingbusiness. org/reforms**].

70. National Safety Council, "Learn, Share and Help End this Deadly Epidemic," *Distracted Driving Research Studies,* 2016 [**www.nsc.org/learn/NSC-Initiatives/Pages/distracted-driving-research-studies.aspx**].

71. Gabriel Kratsas, "Phones Behind 1 in 4 Auto Crashes," *The Des Moines Register,* March 29, 2014 [**www.desmoinesregister.com**].

72. "Distracted Driving: Facts and Statistics," National Highway Traffic Safety Administration [**www.distraction.gov/stats-research-laws/facts-and-statistics.html**].

73. "Chatty Driving: Phones vs. Passengers," *Well Blog, The New York Times,* December 1, 2008 [**http://well.blogs.nytimes.com/2008/**].

74. Denise Lavoie, "Why Cops Are Losing Battle Against Texting Drivers," *Los Angeles Daily News,* September 3, 2016 [**www.dailynews.com**].

75. "Texting Road Risk," USA Snapshots, *The Des Moines Register,* April 13, 2016, p. 1B.

76. Jenny Guarino, "Survey Reveals Public Open to Ban on Hand-Held Cell Phone Use and Texting," *Special Report, Bureau of Transportation Statistics,* January 2013 [**www.rita.dot.gov/bts/sites/rita.dot.gov.bts/files/bts_sr_distracted_driving.pdf**].

77. Nicole Stockdale, "Time to Ban Cell Phones while Driving? (Ed Board Sounds Off)," *Dallas Morning Star,* July 22, 2009 [**http://dallasmorningviewblog.dallasnews.com**].

78. Angela Greiling Keane, "Gadgets Share Blame for Distracted Driving, NTSB Chief Says," *The Washington Post,* March 27, 2012 [**www.washingtonpost.com**].

79. James Gleick, *The Acceleration of Just about Everything* (New York: Vintage Books, 1999), p. 89.

80. Thomas Wall, Kamyar Nasseh, and Marko Vujicic, "Most Important Barriers to Dental Care Are Financial, Not Supply Related," Health Policy Institute *Research Brief,* October 2014 [**www.ada.org/~/media/ADA/Science%20and%20Research/HPI/Files/HPIBrief_1014_2.ashx**].

81. The Heritage Foundation, "2016 Index of Economic Freedom" [**www.heritage.org/index/about**].

82. Ibid.

83. Robert Reich, "Regulation Is Out, Litigation Is In," *USA TODAY,* February 11, 1999, p. 15A.

84. Stewart Mandel, "Recruiting Deregulation Fiasco Underscores Deeper NCAA Disconnect," *SI.com,* April 30, 2013 [**www.si.com**].

85. John Bacon, "Seat Belt Use Reaches Record: 86% of All Motorists in USA," *USA TODAY,* November 15, 2012, p. 2A.

86. Liz Szabo, "Smoking Bans Cut Number of Heart Attacks, Strokes," *USA TODAY,* October 30, 2012, p. 4A.

87. Associated Press, "Shale Gas Supporters Give Credit to Government-Backed Research," *The Waterloo/Cedar Falls Courier,* September 24, 2012, p. A6.

88. Kathleen Parker, "Un-Hitched Middle Class a Problem," *The Waterloo/Cedar Falls Courier,* December 18, 2012, p. A5.

89. Arthur Schlesinger Jr., "In Defense of Government," *The Wall Street Journal,* June 7, 1995, p. A14.

90. Karen Kaplan, "Calls to Tax Junk Food Gain Ground," *latimes.com,* August 23, 2009 [**www.latimes.com**].

91. Ibid.

92. Ibid.

93. Bob Davis, "In Presidential Race, the Key Question Is, 'What Causes Growth?'" *The Wall Street Journal,* September 27, 1996, p. A1.

94. CDC/National Center for Health Statistics, "Assault or Homicide," July 6, 2016 [**www.cdc.gov/nchs/fastats/homicide.htm**].

95. Nicholas D. Kristof, "Why Not Regulate Guns as Seriously as Toys?" *The New York Times,* January 12, 2011 [**www.nytimes.com**].

Business Organizations and Securities Regulation

After completing this chapter, students will be able to fulfill the following learning objectives:

9-1. Describe the nature, advantages, and disadvantages of corporations, general partnerships, sole proprietorships, and limited liability companies.

9-2. Explain the business judgment rule.

9-3. Explain the relationship between limited liability and the doctrine of "piercing the corporate veil."

9-4. Describe equity and debt capital.

9-5. Explain how corporations are governed and discuss the challenges facing modern boards of directors, including determining the appropriate level of executive compensation.

9-6. Define the term *initial public offering* (IPO) and explain the securities registration process.

9-7. Compare the regulatory roles of the 1933 and 1934 federal securities acts.

9-8. Identify when a "material misrepresentation" has occurred.

9-9. Explain the due diligence defense.

9-10. Describe the fraud-on-the-market theory of reliance and explain its importance.

9-11. Define insider trading and identify when it has occurred.

9-12. Describe the tender offer process and some defenses against it.

Introduction

This chapter provides an introduction to some of the fundamental laws governing business—the types and characteristics of available business forms, key corporate governance issues, and business access to capital.

First, we need to recognize the overlapping coverage of state and federal business regulation. State law governs most issues—such as the creation of business entities, the powers and duties of management, and capital structure. The owners of a corporation are called *stockholders* or *shareholders* because the ownership interests are called shares of *stock*. The fundamental legal duties corporations, corporate boards, and officers owe to their shareholders are defined by the state of incorporation. More than one million businesses have incorporated in Delaware (despite having a population of only about 950,000—the sixth smallest state), including over half of the publicly traded companies and two-thirds of the Fortune 500.[1] Thus, when state corporate law is discussed, Delaware often drives the discussion. Part One of this chapter will discuss the key characteristics of the most common business forms.

Delaware: Race to the Bottom or to the Top?

Delaware generates over a quarter of its total revenue from taxes related to corporate domicile, each corporation paying up to $180,000 annually.[2] During 2014 and 2015, 85 percent of all IPOs were by entities incorporated in that state.[3] Delaware's success in attracting corporations is alternatively described as the fruits of a "race to the top" or a "race to the bottom." In 2015, the U.S. Chamber Institute for Legal Reform's *Lawsuit Climate Survey* ranked Delaware's legal system the best in the country for business for the 10th consecutive time.[4] Corporate management appreciates the business-friendly Court of Chancery. In June 2013, that body upheld a bylaw restricting shareholder lawsuits to Delaware courts. Many believe such bylaws give management the "home-field advantage" by depriving those states that are more sympathetic to shareholders of jurisdiction[5]—part of the race to the bottom that favors the interests of entrenched management over those of shareholders, employees, the environment, or the community.

The first decade of the 21st century was scarred by two systemic failures involving corporate actors and the capital markets. The first is commonly referenced by the 2001 collapse of Enron (although it was not the largest corporate failure of that era—just the most spectacular). The second was the financial crisis that struck in the fall of 2008 (often referenced by the collapse of Lehman Brothers). Contributing to both disasters were failures of corporate governance. Congress responded each time with significant legislation imposing additional requirements on *publicly held corporations* (corporations with publicly traded shares): the *Sarbanes–Oxley Act of 2002* (SOX) and the *Dodd–Frank Act of 2010* (see Chapter 8). Part Two of this chapter will discuss governance issues specific to such corporations.

Part Three will take a closer look at how businesses are financed beyond the resources of the founders. Although state law plays a role here, federal law dominates. Triggered by the 1929 stock market crash and the extended failure of the capital markets and banking system during the Great Depression, the federal government, largely under its interstate commerce powers, created the Securities and Exchange Commission (SEC) to regulate the national securities markets. Part Three of this chapter will focus on this regulation.

Part One—Business Entities and Their Defining Characteristics

LO 9-1
Describe the nature, advantages, and disadvantages of corporations, general partnerships, sole proprietorships, and limited liability companies.

One of the most significant business decisions is the choice of form in which to conduct an enterprise. Among other things, this decision will affect the legal relationships among the owners, between them and the entity, and between them and various third parties. It also will affect the access to outside capital and the tax treatment accorded business profits and losses. Part One of this chapter outlines the principal business forms. It also examines a few lesser-used forms and discusses important new forms. It ends with a brief consideration of the circumstances that might favor one form over another.

The three traditional business forms are *corporations, general partnerships,* and *sole proprietorships*. Partnerships and sole proprietorships are default forms. Thus, if an individual starts a business and takes no active steps to house it within a legally recognized entity, the business form will, by default, be a sole proprietorship. Strictly speaking, a sole proprietorship is not a business entity—the law treats the business and the individual as the same legal person. If two or more persons join together to start a business and take no active steps to create an entity, the law will, again by default, classify the business form as a general partnership. The only way to establish a business as a corporation, or indeed as any of the other forms discussed in this part, is for its founders to take deliberate steps, specified by state law, to create the entity.

One such other entity is the *limited liability company* (LLC). LLCs are often referred to as a *hybrid form* because they are specifically designed to combine certain desired corporate characteristics with those of general partnerships. Another hybrid form is the *subchapter S corporation* (also called an *S corporation*). For state corporate law purposes, it is a corporation like any other; but for income tax purposes, the legal entity is largely ignored and virtually all of the entity's tax consequences flow through to the tax returns of the shareholders. This is similar, but not identical, to the way the tax consequences of a partnership flow through to the tax returns of the partners.

According to the latest data available, and if we set aside the 23 million businesses operated as sole proprietorships, more businesses are housed in these two hybrid entities, LLCs (2.2 million) and S corporations (4.2 million)—total 6.4 million—than in traditional corporations (1.6 million) and partnerships (1 million)—total 2.6 million. In terms of revenues, however, corporations ($23 trillion) and partnerships ($1.7 trillion)—total $24.7 trillion—overwhelm the hybrids in significance to the economy: S corporations ($6.6 trillion) and LLCs ($3 trillion)—$9.6 trillion combined.[6]

Each of these forms will be evaluated using the following criteria:

Formation and nontax costs: The method of, and costs related to, bringing the form into existence.

Management structure: The degree to which control of the form is exercised in a hierarchical structure.

Limited liability: The extent to which owners are personally liable for the form's obligations.

Transferability of ownership interests: Whether the law restricts form owners from freely transferring their interests.

Duration of existence: The events, including those impacting the owners personally, that will end the form's existence.

Taxes: The way the choice of form affects the income tax treatment of the business and its owners.

Capital structure: The impact of form selection on the ability to access additional capital.

[For a table summarizing the key characteristics of each business form, see **www.bizfilings.com/learning/comparison.htm**].

Corporations

Although only 5 percent of all businesses are conducted as traditional corporations (often referred to as *C corporations*), they account for 62 percent of all business revenue. C and S corporations combined represent 18 percent of all businesses and account for 80 percent of all business revenue.[7] There are good reasons for corporate financial dominance, which will become evident in the discussion below.

Throughout this topic, we must keep in mind two very different corporate realities: the publicly held corporation and the *closely held corporation* (a corporation with relatively few shareholders, the stock of which has no readily available market).

Corporate Constitutional Rights?

Under state law corporations are legal persons.[8] This raises the question of whether they have constitutionally protected rights. Over the years the Supreme Court has held that sometimes they do[9] and sometimes they do not.[10] As discussed in Chapter 1, the issue arose again in *Citizens United v. Federal Election Commission*, in which the Court, over a strong dissent, enunciated a wide-reaching principle that "the Government may not suppress political speech on the basis of the speaker's corporate identity."[11] Justice Stevens, with three others, dissented:

> The real issue [is] how, not if, [Citizens United] may finance its electioneering. Citizens United is a wealthy nonprofit corporation that runs a political action committee (PAC) with millions of dollars in assets. Under [the campaign finance restriction being challenged] it could have used those assets to televise and promote *Hillary: The Movie* [a negative portrayal of the 2008 presidential candidate] wherever and whenever it wanted to . . . other than the 30 days before the last primary election. Neither Citizens United's nor any other corporation's speech has been "banned." . . . In the context of election to public office, the distinction between corporate and human speakers is significant. Although they make enormous contributions to our society, corporations are not actually members of it. They cannot vote or run for office[.] The financial resources, legal structure, and . . . orientation of corporations raise legitimate concerns about their role in the electoral process.[12]

More recently, in *Burwell v. Hobby Lobby Stores, Inc.*, the Court in another five-to-four ruling held that the portions of the Affordable Care Act of 2010 mandating the corporation's

---

provision of certain contraception benefits "substantially burden the exercise of religion."[13] The family that owned the company had strong religious convictions against certain approaches to contraception. The full implications are difficult to predict. For example, Justice Ginsburg asked in her dissent: "Would the exemption the Court [grants] extend to . . . religiously grounded objections to blood transfusions (Jehovah's Witnesses) . . . antidepressants (Scientologists) . . . and vaccinations (Christian Scientists . . .)?"[14]

Questions

1. When a corporation funds political speech, for whom is it speaking? Consider these possibilities from the *Citizens United* majority and dissenting opinions:

   a. "[W]ealthy individuals and unincorporated associations can spend unlimited amounts on independent expenditures. Yet certain disfavored associations of citizens—those that have taken on the corporate form—are penalized for engaging in the same political speech." *Citizens United*, 130 S. Ct. at 908 (majority opinion).

   b. "It is an interesting question 'who' is even speaking when a business corporation places an advertisement that endorses or attacks a particular candidate. Presumably it is not the customers or employees, who typically have no say in such matters. It cannot realistically be said to be the shareholders, who tend to be far removed from the day-to-day decisions of the firm and whose political preferences may be opaque to management. Perhaps the officers or directors of the corporation have the best claim to be the ones speaking, except their fiduciary duties generally prohibit them from using corporate funds for personal ends." *Citizens United*, 130 S. Ct. at 972 (Stevens, J., dissenting).

2. A large fast-food chain owned by evangelical Christians adopts a policy that homosexuals will not be served. Would those denied service have a cause of action based on *Hobby Lobby*? Consider the baker who was fined $135,000 for refusing to supply a wedding cake to a homosexual couple. *In the Matter of Melissa and Aaron Klein, dba Sweetcakes by Melissa* (July 2, 2015), Final Order Nos. 44-14 & 45-14.

Formation and Nontax Costs

To create a corporation, an *incorporator* files *articles of incorporation* with the state. A modest fee is typically charged. The articles have mandatory elements, such as the corporation's name, the person designated to receive certain communications (for example, subpoenas), and a description of the stock to be issued. Discretionary content like voting rules also may appear.

Once the articles are filed, the corporation comes into existence. An *organizational meeting* will be held at which the initial members of the *board of directors* are appointed. The board will then meet to undertake the corporation's initial business. Among other things, it will appoint officers and adopt *bylaws*. Bylaws contain key policies and procedures, such as the percentage of shareholders that must approve major corporate actions like mergers. The issuance of stock will be authorized in exchange for contributions of capital, property, or services. [For a large library of business forms like bylaws, see **www. lectlaw.com/formb.htm**].

At least annually, the board of directors and shareholders must hold meetings, and the corporation will have to make brief filings with the state to keep its records up-to-date, usually accompanied by a small fee. [To see how Delaware computes this fee, see **www. corp.delaware.gov/fee.shtml**].

Corporations and general partnerships are separate accounting entities from their owners and therefore must establish an accounting system. The cost generally reflects the scale and sophistication of the operation, not the decision to do business in corporate versus partnership form.

Selection and Protection of Corporate Name, Trademarks, and Domains

The articles of incorporation identify the desired name for the about-to-exist corporation. States require the name to be distinguishable from those already registered. Other matters that should be considered include:

Trademark/tradename issues—Will someone sue to stop the use of the chosen mark or name? Check with the U.S. Patent & Trademark Office database. It may be wise to protect the desired names or marks by registering them with that agency. [For more, see **www.uspto.gov/trademarks/process/index.jsp**].

Domain name—Do an Internet search on the selected corporate name. Is the name still available as a domain name? If yes, register it with a registrar accredited by the Internet Corporation for Assigned Names and Numbers (ICANN). If not, what name is available that will be effective for customers and others trying to find you? [For a list of registrars, see **https://www.icann.org/registrar-reports/accredited-list.html**].

Doing business in other states—If business will be conducted in other states, the corporation must register as a foreign corporation. The business name databases for those states should be checked.

Source: Kermit Pattison, "How to Register a Start-Up," *The New York Times*, March 31, 2010.

Management Structure

One strength of the corporate form, an attribute that has allowed it to become the Western world's most effective engine of economic growth, is its ability to separate ownership from management. Shareholders contribute the capital that allows the business to be established. In exchange they receive stock, each share of which represents an ownership unit. Annually the shareholders meet to elect a board of directors. All corporate powers are exercised by, or under the authority of, the board on behalf of the shareholders. Boards do not operate the business on a day-to-day basis; they are policy and oversight bodies. To actually run the company, boards appoint *officers*, often a CEO (chief executive officer), secretary, CFO (chief financial officer), and possibly vice presidents. Officers are employees of the corporation, and they hire the other employees needed to operate the business. This hierarchy is referred to as *centralized management*. Keep in mind that a small corporation will likely have the same formal structure, but its operational dynamics may be quite different if, as is common, some of the shareholders are also *directors* and/or officers—perhaps even holding multiple executive positions.

Both directors and officers have *fiduciary duties* to the corporation. A *fiduciary* is a person who acts on behalf of another (*beneficiary*) and is required to do so with great integrity. (Another fiduciary relationship is parent to minor child.) The *duty of loyalty* requires a fiduciary to act in the best interests of the beneficiary. This prohibits, for example, directors from authorizing the corporation to lease real estate from the board chairman unless the rental terms are consistent with the market. Directors and officers also owe the corporation a *duty of due care*, which requires that they act in good faith toward the corporation and in the manner a reasonably prudent person would employ under the same circumstances.

Business Judgment Rule

LO 9-2

Explain the business judgment rule.

What happens if the board or CEO makes a decision that causes the stock value to decline significantly? Has the duty of due care been breached? The judicial system has developed the *business judgment rule* to help make that determination. A good statement of the rule, which is explored in the *Wrigley* case below, is

The rule posits a powerful presumption . . . that a decision made by a loyal and informed board will not be overturned . . . unless it cannot be "attributed to any rational business purpose." [The] shareholder . . . challenging a board decision [can] rebut the . . . presumption [by] providing evidence that directors [or officers] breached . . . their fiduciary duty[.] If a shareholder . . . fails to meet this . . . burden, the . . . rule attaches to protect [the] officers and directors and the decisions they make, and our courts will not second-guess these business judgments.[15]

LEGAL BRIEFCASE

Shlensky v. Wrigley
237 N.E.2d 776 (Ill. App. Ct. 1968)

FACTS

Shlensky, a minority stockholder of the Chicago Cubs (a professional baseball team), sued the directors on the grounds of mismanagement and negligence because of their refusal to install lights at Wrigley Field, then the only major league stadium without them. One of the directors, Wrigley (80 percent owner), objected to lights because of his opinion that "baseball is a 'daytime sport' and that the installation of lights and night baseball games would have a deteriorating effect upon the surrounding neighborhood." The other directors deferred to Wrigley.

The Cubs were losing money. Shlensky attributed those losses to poor attendance and argued that without lights the losses would continue. His evidence was that the Chicago White Sox night games drew better than the Cubs' day games. Shlensky sought damages and an order requiring lights and night games. He lost at trial and appealed.

Justice Sullivan

* * * * *

[D]efendants argue that the courts will not step in and interfere with the honest business judgment of the directors unless there is a showing of fraud, illegality, or conflict of interest.

The court in *Wheeler v. The Pullman Iron & Steel Co.* said:

It is . . . fundamental in the law of corporations that the majority of its stockholders shall control the policy of the corporation[.] Everyone purchasing [stock] impliedly agrees that he will be bound by the [lawful acts of] a majority of the shareholders, or [of their corporate agents duly chosen,] and courts . . . will not undertake to control the policy or business methods of a corporation, although it may be seen that a wiser policy might be adopted and the business more successful if other methods were pursued.

* * * * *

Plaintiff . . . argues that the directors are acting for reasons unrelated to the . . . welfare of the Cubs. However, we are not satisfied that the motives assigned to . . . Wrigley [and] the other directors . . . are contrary to the best interests of the corporation[.] For example[,] the effect on the surrounding neighborhood might well be considered by a director who was considering the patrons who would or would not attend the games if the park were in a poor neighborhood. Furthermore, the long-run interest [in the] property value at Wrigley Field might demand all efforts to keep the neighborhood from deteriorating. [W]e do not mean to say . . . that the decision of the directors was a correct one. That is beyond our jurisdiction and ability. We are merely saying that the decision is one properly before the directors and the motives alleged . . . showed no fraud, illegality, or conflict of interest in their making of that decision.

While all . . . courts do not insist that one or more of [these] three elements must be present for a stockholder's derivative action [described later in this chapter—ed.] to lie, nevertheless we feel that unless the conduct of the defendants at least borders on one of [them], the courts should not interfere[.]

* * * * *

Finally, we do not agree . . . that failure to follow . . . the other major league clubs in scheduling night games constituted negligence. [It] cannot be said that directors, even those of corporations that are losing money, must follow the lead of [others] in the field. Directors are elected for their business . . . judgment and the courts cannot require them to forgo their judgment because of the decisions of directors of other companies.

Affirmed.

AFTERWORD—DUTY OF DUE CARE

Some states now require proof of *intentional misconduct* or *recklessness* to establish a breach of the duty of due care.

Questions

1. What was the issue in this case?
2. The Cubs added lights in 1988. How could the board be meeting its duty of due care both in the 1960s by not installing lights and in the 1980s by doing so?

Liability of Directors, Officers, Employees

Wrigley was a **shareholder derivative suit,** which is initiated when the corporation is being harmed and neither the board nor the senior executives will take action to protect it. Self-dealing by directors and officers is often involved. The suit is brought by a minority shareholder, but any recovery inures to the corporation.

These cases are extremely difficult to win in light of the business judgment rule. Nevertheless, many such suits are filed in the wake of a disaster befalling a publicly held corporation. The Gulf of Mexico oil spill of more than 100 million gallons (often referred to as *Deepwater Horizon*) has already resulted in BP's spending $12 billion to settle 300,000 private claims[16] and another $31 billion in fines and penalties. In 2016, BP estimated the total cost of the disaster at $62 billion.[17] Plaintiffs have asserted that the BP board and executives "recklessly disregarded accidents and safety warnings for years" in violation of their fiduciary duties. As another example, many lawsuits have been filed by shareholders against directors and officers of financial services companies that played key roles in the 2008 financial crisis.

Regulators and prosecutors have been criticized for demonstrating little zeal for attempting to punish officers or directors personally responsible for corporate misconduct. Attempts to hold such individuals accountable have often thus fallen upon the shareholders. In a chilling development, in May 2014, the Delaware Supreme Court held that a company may adopt, without shareholder approval, a bylaw that requires an investor-plaintiff to pay the corporation's legal fees should its lawsuit not prevail. One expert characterized this development as "a nuclear weapon against shareholders," bolstering Delaware's reputation as a jurisdiction tilted in favor of entrenched corporate interests. In addition to the risk of losing, plaintiffs now face the possibility of liability for the often enormous costs of defense. Some believe this will deter bringing meritorious actions related to corporate fraud, misrepresentation, and breach of fiduciary duties. In the decision's aftermath, a number of companies (including Alibaba) have adopted such a bylaw. On the other hand, critics have pointed out that 95 percent of all acquisitions are challenged in court and that plaintiffs have "shopped" for sympathetic forums 54 percent of the time. Since Delaware permitted the jurisdictional bylaw, that figure has dropped to 23 percent. Asymmetrically, however, companies are waiving the bylaw when litigating in another jurisdiction would promote a more favorable outcome for them.[18]

When an employee or director commits a tort or crime while conducting corporate business, both the actor and the corporation are liable for the consequences. The legal doctrine that makes an employer liable for an employee's acts is ***respondeat superior***. (For more, see Chapter 12.)

Because officers and directors are ultimately responsible for corporate acts and because corporations are frequently sued, these persons face a high risk of becoming involved in costly litigation. Most corporations therefore ***indemnify*** (directly pay the costs of, or reimburse the costs incurred by) these individuals for the expenses of defense. Many states permit indemnification even where the matter involves a breach of fiduciary duty. Delaware, for example, permits indemnification for breaches of the duty of due care, although not for breaches of the duty of loyalty or for intentional misconduct or knowing violation of the law.[19] When the SEC resolved its civil suit for securities fraud against Angelo Mozilo, the CEO of Countrywide Financial (the nation's largest mortgage lender before the 2008 housing market collapse), Bank of America (which had acquired Countrywide) paid $45 million of Mozilo's $67.5 settlement.[20]

Limited Liability

LO 9-3

Explain the relationship between limited liability and the doctrine of "piercing the corporate veil."

To a lawyer, there are two types of persons: natural and artificial. Natural persons are people. Artificial persons, like corporations, are created by law; they have a separate legal existence. Corporations can own property, be sued, take on debts, and otherwise act as legal entities. As discussed earlier, they even have limited constitutional rights. One of the great advantages of the corporate form is that the owners are generally not responsible for the entity's obligations. Should the corporation find that its liabilities overwhelm its assets, its creditors cannot reach the personal assets of the shareholders. Shareholder liability is restricted to the loss of their investment, which is the essence of *limited liability*—perhaps the most cherished characteristic of the corporate form. For closely held corporations, however, this feature is often severely constrained because lenders are well aware of limited liability and usually require the principal shareholders to guarantee the corporation's debts. Still, limited liability will exist for other obligations, such as tort claims.

Closely held corporations also face the loss of limited liability under the doctrine of ***piercing the corporate veil***, which is explored in the *Wolfe* case that follows. It usually has two elements: (1) misuse of the corporate form and (2) an unjust result if limited liability is allowed to stand.

Charles E. Wolfe v. United States
612 F. Supp. 605 (D. Mont. 1985),
aff'd, 798 F.2d 1241 (9th Cir. 1986)

Judge Battin

* * * * *

Charles E. Wolfe was the sole shareholder and president of [a corporation] which leased tractor-trailers. Wolfe also operated [a trucking business] as a proprietorship[.]

[T]he corporation incurred a $114,472.91 federal tax bill[.] Wolfe paid the taxes . . . after the Internal Revenue Service [initiated collection action against him personally]. The Service contends [that] the corporation was the alter ego of Mr. Wolfe, thus justifying the piercing of the corporate veil.

* * * * *

As a general rule, a corporation is treated as a legal entity, separate and distinct from its shareholders[, who] enjoy limited liability.

When the corporate entity is abused, however, the protection of limited liability may be lost. In such cases, courts may exercise their equitable powers to pierce the corporate veil[.]

* * * * *

The facts . . . present the classic case of a shareholder so pervasively dominating corporate affairs that the shareholder and the corporation no longer have separate identities[.] Mr. Wolfe was the sole shareholder[,] a director and the president of the corporation.

Mr. Wolfe made all the corporate decisions without consulting the other directors. The corporation did not even have a bank account. All the corporation's banking transactions were done through the proprietorship's bank account[.] The corporation and the proprietorship were housed in the same office. The corporation's employee was paid by the proprietorship. Some of the corporation's equipment was purchased on the proprietorship's credit. [Other corporate] purchases were paid for on a proprietorship bank account. When the corporation received payment from third parties, the money was deposited into the proprietorship's bank account. Even Mr. Wolfe could not distinguish between the corporation and the proprietorship[.]

It is clear that the corporation and the proprietorship were operated as a single instrumentality under the sole control of Mr. Wolfe. Therefore, it was proper for the Service to look to Wolfe's personal assets to satisfy the taxes of his alter ego corporation.

[Held for the United States.]

Questions

1. Which person owed the taxes?
2. How was the corporate form misused?
3. What injustice would have resulted if Wolfe had not been required to pay?

Transferability of Ownership Interests

Federal securities laws impose broad restrictions on the transfer of a publicly traded corporation's stock, as will be seen in Part Three of this chapter. Beyond these (and analogous state) laws, no statutory restrictions are generally imposed on stock transfers. It is not uncommon, however, for stock dispositions to be restricted by contract. For example, an employment contract might require that stock granted to an employee be sold back to the corporation when the employee leaves.

A common contractual restriction in closely held corporations is a ***buy-sell agreement***, which, at a minimum, forces a shareholder to offer the stock to be sold to the corporation or other shareholders before selling it to a third party. [For more on buy-sell agreements, see **http://smallbusiness.findlaw.com/incorporation-and-legal-structures/faq-regarding-buy-sell-agreements.html**].

Duration of Existence

In general, a corporation has indefinite duration. Nothing that transpires in the lives of the stockholders automatically affects the corporation's existence.

The termination of a corporation can occur voluntarily or involuntarily. Voluntary termination requires a vote by the shareholders, who might do so, for example, if business prospects are no longer favorable. Upon termination the corporation is **liquidated**, which involves first satisfying all creditors and second distributing any remaining assets to the shareholders. **Articles of dissolution** are then filed, officially ending the corporation's existence.

Involuntary terminations are caused by the action of a court or of the state corporation regulator. A court might end a closely held corporation's existence if, for example, there is an irreconcilable deadlock among the shareholders. Common reasons for the state to terminate a corporation are the failure to pay annual fees and make required annual filings.

Taxes

> "Taxes are what we pay for civilized society."

As Justice Oliver Wendell Holmes said: "Taxes are what we pay for civilized society."[21] But Judge Learned Hand said: "[T]here is nothing sinister in so arranging one's affairs as to keep taxes as low as possible."[22]

Taxation transfers about 35 percent of the United States' economic output to the government.[23] Virtually everyone wants to minimize tax payments, hopefully by legal **tax avoidance** (careful planning within the law), not by illegal **tax evasion** (engaging in fraudulent conduct).

Because a corporation is a separate legal entity, it is subject to taxation in its own right. This leads to what many would say is the corporation's greatest disadvantage: **double taxation**. In the United States, a corporation pays tax on its income. When it later distributes its after-tax income to its shareholders as **dividends,** the shareholders are taxed on that amount as well; hence, "double taxation." Note, however, that dividends are not mandatory. They are paid only if the board declares them, which it is generally never required to do and which it legally cannot do if the corporation's solvency (measured in cash flow and/or net worth terms) is insufficient.

To illustrate, assume a corporation is subject to income taxes at the rate of 35 percent[24] and its shareholders all face a rate of 33 percent on income in general, but a lower rate on dividends of 15 percent. On an income of $10 million, the corporation would pay $3.5 million in taxes, leaving only $6.5 million for distribution as dividends. If that entire amount were distributed, the shareholders would pay $975,000 in taxes. Thus, of the $10 million corporate income, only $5.525 million can actually be spent by the owners—an effective tax rate of about 45 percent. Had it been possible to own the business in a form that was not subject to taxation in its own right, the total income taxes would have been $3.3 million, leaving $6.7 million available for the owners to spend—21 percent more.[25]

However, the assertion that corporations are necessarily disadvantageous because of double-taxation is misleading. There are a variety of circumstances in which employing the corporate form yields clear tax advantages, especially for smaller closely held corporations. For example, corporations are the only form of business that comprehensively permits tax-deductible fringe benefits. [For more on fringe benefits, see **https://www.irs.gov/pub/irs-pdf/p15.pdf**].

Capital Structure

LO 9-4
Describe equity
and debt capital.

Businesses need access to *capital* to finance their activities. Capital is of two types: debt and equity—two ends of a spectrum with a boundary that can be challenging to identify. The providers of both debt and equity capital hold claims against the corporation's assets. However, creditors' claims (priority claims) are always satisfied before equity holders' claims (residual claims).

Equity capital (stock) has a long-term horizon. Although any given shareholder may intend to hold the stock for only a short period, the stock itself is generally expected to exist for the full life of the corporation. Three property rights are associated with stock ownership: the rights to participate in earnings (that is, dividends), receive assets upon liquidation, and control (through voting). There are two principal classes of stock: preferred and common. Where only one class exists, it is **common stock**. Common stockholders typically share all three property rights in proportion to their holdings; but recently a dual-class structure has begun to appear, particularly in the high-tech industry, as noted in the following text box.

Dual-Class Common Stock Undermines Control

During the first seven months of 2015, 14 percent of the initial public offerings (IPOs) in the United States featured a dual-class structure, up from 1 percent in 2005. In such a structure, the common shares owned before the IPO are granted vastly disproportionate voting power, which allows the pre-IPO owners to retain control. This technique gained notoriety in the 2004 Google IPO.[26] Facebook followed suit in 2012, as did Alibaba in 2014. Such arrangements were rampant in the United States until the late 1920s, when a Harvard professor led a campaign to stop a practice that "disenfranchise[s] public investors." They began to reappear during the corporate raider era of the 1980s, but subsided until 2004. Alibaba had intended to list on the Hong Kong exchange, but it prohibits ownership structures in which voting power is disproportionate to common stock holdings. The SEC permits dual-class stock only at the IPO stage; a corporation may not adopt such an arrangement after the company has gone public. Fearing the loss of IPO business, exchanges throughout the world are now considering permitting the technique.[27]

> Institutional investors own 70 percent of all publicly traded stock.

Preferred stock was created largely for institutional investors such as pension funds to fill the gap on the risk-return spectrum between long-term debt and common stock; in 2016, institutional investors owned 70 percent of all publicly traded stock.[28] Finance professionals find it advantageous to have many different ways to combine risk and return. Preferred stock is associated with "preferences" related to distributions. Preferred stockholders are paid their required annual dividend in full before any dividends are distributed to common stockholders. Upon the corporation's liquidation, after the creditors are satisfied, the preferred shareholders receive the next round of distributions, up to their stock's *redemption value*—typically a few percent over its par value. Common shareholders receive whatever remains.

The cost of these two preferences is the loss of the right to participate in control. Having no vote, preferred stockholders cannot elect directors to protect their interests. To help ensure that its owners regularly receive dividends, most preferred stock is *cumulative*. This means that if a preferred stock dividend is missed, then before the common stockholders get any dividends, the preferred stock *arrearage* (all dividends not paid in any prior year) must be made up.

Because preferred stockholders never get more than their required dividends and, upon liquidation, a little more than the purchase price, all corporate growth inures to the common stockholders. If both you and Bill Gates had invested $1 million in Microsoft at the outset, you taking all the preferred stock and Gates taking all the common stock, your stock would still be worth about $1 million, whereas Gates's stock would be worth tens of billions.

Debt capital may be short or long term. Companies that provide motherboards to Dell are a source of short-term debt capital. They expect to be paid fairly quickly, but not at the moment of delivery. They have extended Dell a very short-term form of debt capital. The long-term debt of a closely held corporation is likely to come from a commercial lender that takes a security interest in specified corporate property. This is much like an individual who obtains a mortgage from a bank secured by the home purchased with the borrowed funds. Large corporations have another alternative for obtaining long-term debt capital. Just as a publicly held corporation may sell its stock to the public, it also may sell the public units of debt, called ***bonds***. A pension plan that holds Dell's 30-year bonds is providing long-term debt capital to the company.

Debt capital specifies an interest rate (or a formula for computing the rate) to be paid on the principal borrowed. Principal and interest are required to be paid in set amounts, usually over a defined term.

Corporations carefully manage their ***capital structures*** (the balance between debt and equity). If the debt/equity ratio is too high, the corporation may be exposed to severe risk because debt obligations must be timely paid without regard to how profitable business operations are. Further, the capital structure must be managed to ensure that ***debt covenants*** are not breached. A debt covenant is a term in the lending contract that makes the debt essentially immediately payable should the condition specified cease to be satisfied (such as exceeding a specified debt/equity ratio). On the other hand, if the debt/equity ratio is too low, opportunities for *positive financial leverage* (employing borrowed funds at a rate of return that exceeds the interest rate) may be forfeited. Executives also understand that interest is tax deductible, whereas dividends are not. This encourages the use of debt capital.

If one compares the characteristics of debt capital with those of common stock, it can readily be seen that preferred stock does indeed bridge the gap. Increasingly, preferred stock is being issued with more debt-like characteristics, posing serious debt-versus-equity classification problems for accountants auditing financial statements, tax authorities, and bankruptcy courts.

Questions

1. *a.* What characteristics of the corporate form make it particularly desirable as a business entity?

   b. Particularly undesirable?

   c. Do S corporations share those characteristics?

2. What are the two ends of the capital spectrum? Where does preferred stock fit into this continuum?

3. *a.* What property rights are associated with common stock?

   b. Does preferred stock carry the same rights?

General Partnerships

A general partnership is the default form for any business with two or more owners.

This section discusses traditional *general partnerships*. A *partnership* is two or more persons (*partners*) who carry on a business as co-owners. Recall that this is the default form for any business with two or more owners that does not specifically act to create a separate entity. Whereas corporate ownership interests are called stock or shares, the equity interest of a partner is called a *partnership interest*.

Partnerships are *mutual agencies*. Every partner is an agent of the partnership with the capacity to bind it when acting within the scope of the partnership's business. Knowledge held by any partner is deemed held by the partnership. As an agent, each partner is entitled to reimbursement for costs personally incurred in furtherance of the partnership's business. Every partner has the right to examine all partnership records and to demand a formal determination by a court of the value of the partner's equity interest (an *accounting*).

Although partnerships originated under the common law, all states except Louisiana have adopted the Uniform Partnership Act (UPA), originally developed by the National Conference of Commissioners on Uniform State Laws (NCCUSL) in 1914. The NCCUSL adopted a revised version of UPA in 1994 (RUPA), which to date has been adopted by 39 states, the District of Columbia, and the Virgin Islands. Pennsylvania introduced RUPA in 2016. Except as noted, the discussion below is based on the provisions of RUPA.

> **What Is the Law in Your State?**
>
> There are significant differences between UPA and RUPA. Which is the law in your state? You can find out at **http://www.uniformlaws.org/Act.aspx?title=Partnership%20Act%20(1997)%20(Last%20Amended%202013)**.

Formation and Nontax Costs

If persons intend to go into business together and take no steps to establish a different form, they will automatically create a general partnership. Mere co-ownership of property, however, does not create a partnership. The co-owners must intend to join in the sharing of risks and rewards via the active conduct of business.

As will be seen below, the partnership relationship carries substantial risks for the partners. One might therefore expect the contract that creates and governs the partnership, the *partnership agreement,* to very precisely specify the terms of that relationship. This is sometimes true when the partnership agreement is written. However, the vast majority are oral agreements; if disagreements arise, the partners may find it very difficult to establish conclusively what the original intentions were. This will not be helped by the fact that when important disputes arise, the partners often discover that their interests have become adverse and that the elation shared at formation has been displaced by anger and a sense of betrayal.

So if the problems associated with a lack of clarity can be substantial, why are partnership agreements often oral and, even if written, often vague? The answer relates in part to the fact that to draft a quality partnership agreement, a host of touchy, even unpleasant issues must be concretely addressed. The drafter must ask, "How should the profit-sharing arrangement change if a partner becomes ill or fails to meet expectations?" and, "If the partnership does not work out, how will the relationship be unwound? Who will make sure all the creditors have been paid?" Soon-to-be partners often shy away from tough questions like these; there may be a feeling that asking them will sour the high spirits in which so many partnerships are born.

Partnership agreements also tend to be expensive to draft because (1) there are many opportunities for customization, (2) state law provides only a general framework, and (3) the personal risks of being a partner are so significant. Partnership accounting systems can be among the most costly due to the need to track the customized economic arrangements established under the partnership agreement. However, the partnership form generally requires few, if any, annually recurring events such as state filings or owner meetings.

Management Structure

By default, management in a general partnership is not centralized. Absent an agreement to the contrary, each partner has an equal right to participate in control, regardless of the size of the partner's ownership interest. As the number of partners grows, this can make governance unwieldy. In response, some partnerships create a centralized management structure by adding provisions to the partnership agreement by which the partners yield many of their management rights to a subset of partners (perhaps to only one—a *managing partner*).

Partners owe each other the fiduciary duties of loyalty, due care, confidentiality, and sharing information. The *Veale* case below explores some of these.

LEGAL BRIEFCASE

Veale v. Rose
657 S.W.2d 834 (Tex. Ct. App. 1983)

FACTS

Rose was a partner in an accounting firm. The partnership agreement permitted partners to pursue other business interests so long as doing so did not conflict with the partnership practice. Rose performed accounting work for Right Away Foods and Payne, taking the compensation personally. Rose's partners claimed he owed them a share in that he had competed with the firm in violation of the partnership agreement. The jury held for Rose. The partners appealed.

Chief Justice Nye

* * * * *

The partnership agreement . . . provided in part:

> Except with the express approval of the other partners as to each specific instance, no partner shall perform any public accounting services . . . other than . . . on behalf of this partnership.

Partners . . . occupy a fiduciary relationship . . . which requires of them the utmost degree of good faith and honesty in dealing with one another[.]

It is undisputed that . . . Rose rendered accounting services for Right Away Foods for which he . . . received payment personally. [The] partnership did not share in the proceeds[.] . . . The preponderance of all the evidence clearly establishes that Rose . . . performed accounting services . . . in competition with the partnership. The [jury] was in error.

. . . Rose also admitted that he performed accounting services for [Payne] for which he . . . received payment personally. [His] testimony that he performed the services, in effect, after hours, or in addition to his duties to the partnership, is of no value in light of the obligations imposed by the partnership agreement[.]

[Reversed and remanded.]

Questions

1. *a.* Why was Rose's work for Right Away Foods considered a violation of the partnership agreement?
   b. Why did Rose's "after-hours" argument fail?
2. Could Rose operate a car wash without violating the partnership agreement?

Limited Liability

> Partners are personally liable for all partnership obligations should it default.

A general partnership does not offer limited liability. The general partners are personally liable for the partnership's obligations should it default. This is widely viewed as the greatest disadvantage of the general partnership form.

Under RUPA, general partners are *jointly and severally liable* for both contract obligations and torts.[29] If a partnership is found liable, the victorious claimant must first exhaust the partnership's assets, but then can proceed to collect the remainder from any or all of the partners.[30] If one partner pays the debt, that partner is entitled to recoup an appropriate share from the other partners pursuant to the *right of contribution*.

Under the doctrine of *respondeat superior* mentioned previously, the partnership, and therefore the partners, are liable for the torts committed by partnership employees and for the unintentional torts committed by partners. For example, an individual injured by the negligent driving of an employee who was traveling on partnership business can sue and recover from the partnership (and then from the partners if partnership assets are insufficient).

Under some circumstances, partners may be jointly and severally liable for crimes committed by employees, but they ordinarily will not be liable for crimes committed by partners (unless they participated in or authorized the crime).

Transferability of Ownership Interests

Because partnerships are mutual agencies, involve fiduciary relationships, and do not offer limited liability, without an express agreement to the contrary, the law does not allow a partner to substitute a third party for itself without the unanimous consent of the other partners. A partnership interest can be assigned to a third party, but the *assignment* entitles the *assignee* only to the distribution rights of the assigning partner (*assignor*). The assignee has no right to participate in control and does not have the status of partner.

Duration of Existence

Under UPA, a partnership automatically ceases upon the death, incapacity, bankruptcy, expulsion, or withdrawal of any partner. Thus, events in the private lives of the partners can seriously impact the venture. To minimize the harm from such an automatic *dissolution*, it is common to include a provision in the partnership agreement allowing a new, successor partnership to be formed immediately by the remaining partners. The ex-partner's partnership interest would be valued and paid out.

Under RUPA, the only event listed above that will automatically dissolve a partnership is the withdrawal of a partner holding more than 50 percent of the partnership interests. The remaining events will result in the *disassociation* of the affected partner, but will not dissolve the partnership nor require the formation of a new partnership by the remaining partners. The power of any partner to withdraw cannot be removed by the partnership agreement, but the right to exercise that power can be circumscribed; and a wrongfully withdrawing partner can be required to compensate the partnership for any resulting damages. The remaining partners have a statutory right to continue the business as if no dissolution had occurred.[31]

Taxes

The greatest advantage of the partnership form is the extraordinary range of economic relationships that can be crafted. Whereas a 10 percent shareholder is simply entitled to 10 percent of whatever distributions are made by the corporation, a partnership agreement can detach percentage ownership from the stream of distributions and tax consequences. To illustrate, assume L contributes land to a real estate development partnership, K contributes knowledge as the general contractor, and C contributes the cash necessary to undertake the venture. It would be acceptable to allocate the partnership cash flow as follows: C gets all of the net cash flow until C's initial cash contribution has been recouped, then L gets all of the net cash flow until the value of L's contributed land has been received, then K gets a specified amount of the net cash flow, after which all three share the remaining net cash flows equally. Note, however, that with this great flexibility comes an obligation to precisely adhere to very complex tax rules, which significantly increases the cost of operating in the partnership form.

Double taxation does not apply to partnerships because the tax law does not treat them as separate entities. The partnership's income is taxed only once—on the tax returns of the partners pursuant to the allocations specified in the partnership agreement. There is a downside risk, however: partners must pay tax annually on their share of partnership income whether or not anything has actually been distributed to them. For this reason, it is not uncommon for partnership agreements to require distributions equal to the partners' expected tax liabilities.

There are two important negative tax consequences of a partnership. First, fringe benefits provided to partners are generally not tax-deductible (fringes provided to employees are). Second, a partner's share of the partnership's business income is generally subject to the self-employment tax (at an effective rate of about 13 percent on the first approximately $120,000 of earnings).

Capital Structure

The sole source of equity is the partners themselves, although new partners can be added to infuse additional equity capital. Debt capital can be raised based on the creditworthiness of the individual partners, as well as by offering partnership assets to lenders as collateral.

Question

What characteristics of the general partnership form make it particularly desirable as a business entity? Particularly undesirable?

Limited Liability Companies—Increasingly the Entity of Choice

Today, a very popular business form is the ***limited liability company*** (LLC). After 1958, the S corporation could be used to combine limited liability with the elimination of double taxation. It was not attractive to many, however, because of its one-class-of-stock limitation, the low number of permitted shareholders, and the requirement that all economic and tax consequences be shared pro rata according to stock ownership. The desire for a limited-liability form with the flexibility of a partnership led to the LLC, which is one of the most common forms of business.

Although a uniform act for LLCs was established by the NCCUSL in 1994, only nine states adopted it. In 2006 a revised act was promulgated, which has been adopted by 16 jurisdictions, with three having introduced legislation. Thus, there is still considerable variation in LLC law from state to state. The general outline of LLC characteristics is provided below.

To create an LLC, the owners, called ***members***, file ***articles of organization*** with the state. The ownership units are called ***members' interests***. An ***operating agreement***, which can be oral but is most likely written, will be prepared that sets forth information similar to that found in well-drafted partnership agreements. Minor annual filings and fees are generally required, but statutes do not impose annual member meetings. The cost of setting up an accounting system will be essentially the same as for a general partnership because LLCs have the same economic and tax flexibility.

The management structure of LLCs is variable: the operating agreement generally specifies whether it will be centrally managed (manager-managed, often by one or two of the members) or member-managed (similar to a general partnership).

LLCs are hybrids. As to limited liability and the duration of existence, they closely resemble corporations. With regard to tax treatment and the opportunity for economic customization, they closely resemble general partnerships. It is still an open question whether the limited liability of LLC members can be "pierced," as is the case with corporations. But some states have spoken. Minnesota's LLC statute expressly provides for piercing the veil of LLCs.[32] In 2002, the Wyoming Supreme Court held: "We can discern no reason . . . to treat LLCs differently than we treat corporations. If the members and officers of an LLC fail to treat it as a separate entity, they should not enjoy immunity from individual liability for the LLC's acts that cause damage to third parties."[33]

Sole Proprietorships

Sole proprietorships, business ventures undertaken by a single individual, are not actually entities—they have no legal existence distinct from their owners. Nonetheless, the same characteristics used to evaluate other forms can be applied to them. A sole proprietorship comes into existence simply upon the proprietor's decision to pursue a venture. Thus, it is the default form for single-owner enterprises. This largely explains why 72 percent of all businesses are sole proprietorships, although they generate less than 4 percent of all business revenue—averaging a little over $55,000. No legal filings or fees are required to establish a sole proprietorship. Because there is only one owner, centralization of management exists automatically. Like a general partner, the owner is personally liable for all business obligations.

A proprietor may dispose of the proprietorship freely, but this can be accomplished only through the transfer of the individual assets that comprise the business, not by a transfer of the "business" in its own right. Further, the lack of a separate legal entity generally results in the termination of a sole proprietorship if the owner dies. In the case of incapacity, only the holder of a durable power of attorney, a custodian, or a guardian has the legal power to continue operations. This impractical arrangement tends to destroy the business's value in short order.

A sole proprietorship is not a taxable entity. All of its revenues and expenses appear on the tax return of the proprietor. Like partnerships, all business income is subject to self-employment tax. The capital structure issues for a sole proprietorship are similar to those of a partnership—without a change in business form, new equity can only come from the proprietor. Any lending will be based on the proprietor's creditworthiness and the property that can be offered as security.

Other Hybrid Forms

Limited Liability Partnerships

At the same time LLCs were being conceived, the great multinational accounting firms were reeling from another episode in which the quality of their audits proved less than advertised—the savings and loan "debacle" of the 1980s. Over $1.6 billion in settlements (a staggering sum for that era) was paid out and these firms feared extinction if professional liability damages could not be constrained. Efforts to obtain tort reform that would limit such liability failed, so a new approach was sought—the *limited liability partnership* (LLP). The enabling statute was first enacted in Texas in 1991 at the instigation of a number of its major law firms, which also sought relief from professional liability.[34]

All states now have some form of LLP. In spite of the similarity of name and its creation in the shadow of LLCs, its closest analogue is the general partnership, not the LLC. For example, its governing law is included as Article 10 of RUPA. To bring an LLP into existence, a document called a *statement of qualification* in RUPA is filed with the state. Minor annual filings and fees are required. LLPs (and their partners) are taxed like a general partnership and, in all other characteristics except for limited liability (discussed next), most closely resemble general partnerships.

As originally conceived, an LLP partner's limited liability extended only to the negligence of other partners. Partners retained full liability for all other partnership obligations. However, RUPA now provides full limited liability "whether arising in contract, tort, or otherwise" to all partners.[35]

Limited Partnerships

Limited partnerships have existed for a considerable time and were extremely popular until the advent of LLCs. They have two classes of owners: general partners and limited partners. ***General partners*** have the same legal benefits and burdens as the partners of a general partnership. They (often only one) are the only managers. ***Limited partners*** invest in the entity but do not participate in control (except with respect to matters like dissolution). In exchange for having very little control, they receive limited liability. Although unlimited liability is generally cited as the principal disadvantage of general partner status, in practice most general partners are corporations (or LLCs) with minimal capital investment. Thus, unlimited liability is little threat unless grounds for piercing the veil exist.

Forty-nine states have adopted the Uniform Limited Partnership Act (ULPA) in one of its three versions. The latest, ULPA (2001), has been adopted in 19 states and the District of Columbia, with other states having introduced legislation. Limited partnerships come into existence only upon filing a ***certificate of limited partnership***. Minor annual filings and fees are required. The law of limited partnerships provides that those events involving limited partners that would terminate a general partnership under UPA have minimal impact on the entity's existence. Limited partnerships are generally taxed like general partnerships. Importantly, the income of a limited partner is not subject to self-employment tax.

Limited Liability Limited Partnerships

State legislation establishing limited liability limited partnerships (LLLPs) is generally directed at facilitating the acquisition of limited liability for the general partners of preexisting limited partnerships. In some cases, reorganization of an existing limited partnership would entail expensive or challenging hurdles. Under ULPA (2001), an LLLP is created simply by stating that the limited partnership is an LLLP in the certificate of limited partnership.[36]

International Hybrids

Dozens of other business forms exist throughout the world. For the most part, these forms are intended to achieve various combinations of the characteristics just discussed. Using these criteria, managers operating in a multinational environment should be able to evaluate form-of-business decisions under a variety of regimes.

Social Businesses on the Horizon?

The concept of "*social business*" comes from Dr. Muhammad Yunus, an economist and winner of the 2006 Nobel Peace Prize. It occupies a unique place on the continuum running from for-profit to not-for-profit organizations. A social business is distinguished from a for-profit business in that it is formed primarily to further a specific positive social objective, rather than to seek profit-maximization. Profits are applied to the achievement of its stated social objective. Regular reporting includes both financial statements and the identification of concrete progress toward social goal attainment. A social business is distinct from a nonprofit enterprise in at least two key respects: (1) it is intended to be an economically self-sustaining enterprise (which means that it must adhere to commercially reasonable business practices) and (2) its start-up capital must be returned to its investors (although without interest). For such businesses to become a reality, another new form was required. Thirty-one states have adopted "benefit corporation" statutes and another seven are considering doing so. In such corporations the directors' fiduciary duties require the elevation of nonfinancial interests. [For more, see **http://benefitcorp.net/policymakers/state-by-state-status**].

In July 2006 the nonprofit B Lab was created. "Its vision is that one day all companies compete not only to be the best in the world, but the Best for the World® and as a result society will enjoy a more shared and durable prosperity." Companies embracing this view can apply for the status "Certified B Corporation," which requires committing to a "Declaration of Interdependence." Among other things, the company must "create[] benefit for all stakeholders, not just shareholders"; conduct its affairs "as if people and place matter[]"; ensure its activities "do no harm and benefit all"; and acknowledge that "we are . . . responsible for each other and future generations." [For more, see **https://www.bcorporation. net/what-are-b-corps**].

In April 2015, Etsy became the second Certified B Corporation to go public. In part, this is "an experiment in corporate governance, a test of whether Wall Street will embrace a company that puts doing social and environmental good on the same pedestal with, if not ahead of, maximizing profits."[37]

Circumstances Favoring a Specific Business Form

Before the expansion in the availability of the various hybrid forms discussed, some states required certain activities to be carried on in general partnership form, most notably the licensed professions. The primary concern was that these professionals should not be able to escape personal liability for malpractice by incorporating their practices. As noted above, all states now offer an alternative to the general partnership for these professions.

Today, selection of a particular form is driven by market realities, as well as by the founders' preferences for the characteristics previously discussed. Some of those market realities will now be addressed.

One consideration in the selection of an appropriate form is the total capital needed by the enterprise. Large businesses need billions of dollars. Only access to global capital markets (like the New York Stock Exchange) can fulfill this need. With few exceptions, the only form that has met with success in these markets is the C corporation.

Use of Noncorporate Limited Liability Entities

It is not rare to find someone with a great idea but with insufficient resources to take the idea to market. Some investors, such as *venture capitalists*, seek out such persons. They will usually insist that the venture have limited liability, as would be true with a corporation or an LLC. [For more on venture capitalists, see **www.nvca.org**].

Similarly, *franchisors* normally demand that *franchisees* operate their franchises in a business form with limited liability. A *franchise* is the right to exploit the franchisor's intangible assets (such as trade names and business systems) and to partake of the franchisor's marketing, purchasing, and other services. The key advantages to the franchisee are a proven product or service, turnkey implementation, and access to support. The franchisor gains by earning fees and by achieving accelerated market penetration using the capital of others (franchisees). Unfortunately, franchisor fraud and oppression are not unusual, so careful investigation by potential franchisees is essential. Premium franchises can be expensive. [For an extensive listing of franchise opportunities and their minimum cash requirements, see **www.franchisedirect.com**].

With the availability of LLCs, LLPs, and S corporations, under most circumstances the disadvantages of the general partnership form are so severe that one is usually well advised to avoid it.

Questions—Part One

1. Why are corporations the dominant form of business based on revenues in the United States?
2. *a.* Why are sole proprietorships problematic if a proprietor dies or becomes disabled?
   b. Do partnerships experience similar problems?
3. *a.* What characteristics of an LLC cause it to be the fastest-growing business form in the United States?
   b. What are its advantages over a corporation? Are there any disadvantages?
4. Do corporations have constitutional rights?
5. Why is the business judgment rule needed?
6. What is the primary difference between a benefits corporation and a:
   a. For-profit corporation?
   b. Nonprofit corporation?

Part Two—Corporate Governance in Public Corporations

Public corporations have thousands of shareholders, the vast majority of whom do not plan to spend their time intimately involved in the company's business. They wish to entrust their resources to the stewardship of the corporation's management and return to their personal affairs. To ensure the corporation is acting to further their interests, the shareholders elect a board of directors. The boards of publicly held corporations generally have both inside and outside directors. **Inside directors** are senior executives. **Outside directors** are not employed by the company. Boards govern by meeting at regular intervals to monitor the corporation's activities, establish policies, hire and replace senior executives, and make major decisions such as whether to pursue a merger.

> Enron called the world's attention to extraordinary failings in corporate governance.

The foregoing is the textbook description of *corporate governance*. What has become painfully evident from both the accounting scandals of the Enron era and the 2008 collapse of the financial system is that reality can be quite different. Enron called the world's attention to extraordinary failings in corporate governance, but its demise was not an isolated event. Disturbingly, the pre-Enron collapse of numerous companies failed to alert the markets and regulators, and many more implosions followed, at least two of which were actually larger (WorldCom and Parmalat). The 2008 financial crisis made clear that the flaws in corporate governance persisted. The report of the Financial Crisis Inquiry Commission (the body charged by Congress to determine the causes of the so-called Great Recession) identified serious issues. The majority report stated: "We conclude dramatic failures of corporate governance and risk management at many systemically important financial institutions were a key cause of this crisis."[38] In the words of Carl Icahn, "The entirely preventable financial catastrophe . . . has many culprits: reckless executives who gambled with their company's futures, feckless regulators and somnambulant boards of directors."[39]

This part of the chapter will consider corporate governance issues, including the reforms adopted in the wake of the Enron era and the 2008 financial crisis. Several rising corporate governance issues also will be identified.

The Management Pyramid

Corporations have centralized management. At the apex of the pyramid is the board of directors. Immediately below is the chief executive officer (CEO). In the next layer are the other top executives, such as the chief financial officer (CFO) and chief operating officer (COO). This classic management pyramid further expands through layers of middle management, finally coming to the base comprised of rank-and-file employees. The light shed on the boardroom by various government investigations and shareholder lawsuits during the Enron era revealed that the pyramid had become inverted at the top. Far too frequently, boards simply abdicated responsibility to their CEOs, who often held the ultimate power because of their strong influence over the board nomination process and board compensation, and their control over the information provided to the board. Directorships can be lucrative. In 2015, the median S&P 500 outside director compensation was $225,000. The average was $326,000. In an attempt to align directors' interests with those of the investors, the primary form of compensation is stock options. As to the work required to earn these sums, the typical director averages five hours per week of service, although members of certain committees (like the audit committee) can find their jobs expanding to nearly full time.[40] Far too few directors have been willing to challenge CEO actions out of fear of forfeiting such substantial compensation. In addition, many conflicts of interest have been discovered. At Enron, for example, some directors were personal friends of senior managers, others were academics whose institutions were receiving large contributions from the company or its officers, and another was the former senior government official who was responsible for exempting Enron from the regulation of its principal line of business (dealing in energy derivatives).

The federal legislation passed after Enron, the Sarbanes–Oxley Act of 2002 (SOX), attempted to address some of these governance issues. To limit the CEO's control of audit information reaching the board, it requires a board audit committee consisting exclusively of ***independent directors***—outside directors without conflicts of interest—at least one of whom must be a financial expert. SOX gives the audit committee direct responsibility for hiring the auditing firm and setting its compensation. It further prohibits the auditor from also rendering many types of consulting services in order to promote independence. To limit the CEO's control over board membership, SOX requires a nominating committee also composed solely of independent directors.

Even after SOX there were serious concerns about who truly sits at the top of the pyramid. The CEO still controls much of the information that reaches the board. Shortly before the financial crisis, *The Wall Street Journal* published a special report headlined "Why CEOs Need to Be Honest with Their Boards: Too Often Chief Executives Sugarcoat the Truth. That's More Dangerous Than Ever."[41] Many still wonder whether boards are active in setting policies and making major decisions or are simply following the CEO's lead. Such concerns seem plausible. For example, immediately after Lehman Brothers' CEO announced a $3.9 billion third-quarter loss in 2008 (the prelude for the company's implosion not long thereafter), he said: "I must say the board's been wonderfully supportive."[42]

One logical response to this problem would be to require that the positions of board chair and CEO be held by different individuals. "No one can reasonably expect a person to oversee himself or herself[.] . . . The CEO works for the board, not the other way around; the continuation of combined roles inhibits the board in exercising its responsibilities because it creates an insurmountable imbalance of power."[43] At the time the Great Recession unfolded in 2008, both positions were more often than not held by a single person in *Fortune* 500 companies.[44] The Dodd–Frank Act of 2010, enacted in response to the financial crisis, now requires corporations to disclose the reasons for choosing the same person for both positions, but does not prohibit the practice.

Question

What should the board's role be? Consider the following two opinions:

> [B]oards [are] supposed to monitor risks, provide judgment and supervise managers on behalf of shareholders.[45]
>
> Most boards meet one or two days a month and are composed of individuals who also hold demanding full-time jobs. Given those circumstances, it's absurd to believe that board members, even the most experienced and best-intentioned of them, will uncover systemic flaws or acts of malfeasance[.] That's what regulators, outside accountants, and internal controls are for—to help boards ferret out excessive risk and wrongdoing.[46]

The Shareholder-Rights Movement

Although shareholders own the corporation, control rests with the board. As noted in the discussion of the business judgment rule, state law significantly restricts the shareholders' ability to control management, other than indirectly through the annual election of the board.

> The notion that shareholders can exercise control is doubtful.

The notion that shareholders can actually exercise control through the board election process is doubtful. As stated above, shareholders do not select the candidates for board positions; a committee of the existing board does. Could a dissatisfied shareholder offer a different slate of directors for the shareholders to vote on? In theory, yes; in practice, **proxy fights** are difficult and expensive.

Management annually solicits proxies from its shareholders. A **proxy** is written permission to vote a shareholder's stock on an issue such as the election of directors. Management's solicitation is done in conjunction with its required notification to shareholders of the annual meeting and the cost is thus borne by the corporation. Shareholders wanting to propose alternative candidates have to be prepared to bear the entire cost themselves. State law gives shareholders the right of access to shareholder lists maintained by the company, but a shareholder will often have to sue, at a substantial cost in time and money, to force the corporation to comply. If successful, the shareholders involved must then incur heavy costs to develop the solicitation materials for SEC review.

It is no surprise, then, that proxy fights are rare. Most shareholders who disagree with management's decisions simply sell their shares and invest elsewhere. From society's and the shareholders' points of view, the management of publicly held corporations proceeds largely unchecked, unless securities law violations (discussed in Part Three of this chapter) are involved. One commentator refers to this as "the myth that boards [are] accountable to shareholders."[47]

In recent years, various proposals to give shareholders more input have gained ground, largely through the efforts of institutional investors and independent activists. Institutional investors, such as pension funds and mutual funds, have significant influence in the capital markets. When the largest public pension in the United States, the California Public Employees' Retirement System (CALPERS), contacts the C-suite at a company in which it holds a significant amount of stock, management is likely to listen.

Collusion Among Institutional Investors?

A widely held view is that the rise of the institutional investor has improved the securities markets because their size makes it cost-effective to take an active role in holding companies accountable. In 2016, however, a study found a correlation between institutional investors holding meaningful minority investments in multiple companies within the same industry (a common feature of mutual funds) and a decline in competition and an increase in prices. The Justice Department's antitrust division has commenced an investigation grounded on possible collusion. The theory: it is in the best interests of these institutional investors for there to be less competition within the industry. Less competition translates into increased prices, in turn driving increased profits across the industry. One expert offers a contrary explanation: "Institutional investors . . . fulfill the conventional wisdom that shareholders do not do enough to challenge" corporate management. Because managements within the industry believe their competition-restricting activities will not be contested by investors who actually have the capacity to exert influence, there is no incentive not to increase prices, regardless of the detriment to the public.[48]

Director Elections

One shareholder reform that has gained ground involves the number of votes required to elect a director. Many states, including Delaware, allow directors to be elected by just a plurality of the votes cast. If the only names before the shareholders are those on management's slate, management's nominees will generally win even if a substantial number of shareholders withhold their votes in protest. In 2006, only 16 percent of firms in the S&P 500 had any form of majority vote rule. Within 18 months, the number was 60 percent. Unfortunately, the impact is not as great as might first appear. In most cases where management has agreed to a majority vote rule, it has not agreed to reject automatically a candidate who has commanded only a plurality, but only to review whether or not to seat such a candidate.[49]

Broker Voting

Another concern is broker voting. Many individual shareholders do not hold their shares but leave them on account with their broker. Past practice was that, unless the account owner specifically directed otherwise, the broker could vote the shares, which typically occurred in a pro-management fashion. That practice was reversed by the Dodd–Frank Act. Brokers are prohibited from voting shares unless specifically authorized by the shareholder. Counterintuitively, the likely consequence will be that fewer shares will be voted, shifting even greater influence to the large institutional shareholders who do vote, as well as to the shares management controls directly or via proxy.

Proxy Access

One of the most controversial issues in recent years has been proxy access. As previously discussed, although it is possible for dissatisfied shareholders to wage a proxy fight, it is usually not feasible to do so. A cost-effective solution would be to require management to include shareholder nominees on the company's ballot sent to shareholders in advance of the annual meeting. In 2010, the SEC issued a new rule permitting shareholder groups (owning at least 3 percent of a company's stock for at least three years) to submit nominees for inclusion in the company's ballot; however, in 2011 a federal court struck down the regulation on procedural grounds. Nonetheless, pressure from a broad array of institutional investors has led at least 15 companies, including Citigroup, Bank of America, and General Electric, to voluntarily agree to the "three percent rule."[50]

Activist Investors

Shareholder activism originated in the 1980s. One form, associated with the so-called corporate raider, involved engaging in a **hostile takeover** (acquiring control of a company in the face of strong management resistance), often by encouraging other shareholders to join forces. If successful, the company would be broken up, sometimes even liquidated, because the total value of the corporation's individual components exceeded the current market value of the entity as a whole. The process was illustrated in the 1991 movie *Other Peoples' Money*. Another form was "going private," in which the hostile takeover was accomplished by offering the current shareholders a price far above current market value (a **tender offer**, discussed in Part Three of this chapter). The acquisition was funded by "junk bonds" collateralized only with the acquired stock (less pejoratively called a "leveraged buyout"). The bonds were characterized as "junk" because they were enormously risky, a result of the fact that the debt represented the vast majority of the corporation's value (debt-to-equity ratios of up to 80 percent were observed).[51] In each case, the key objective was to enjoy a gain in a relatively short amount of time, from either dismantling the company or dramatically altering its operations so as to significantly increase its profitability and hence market value. The 1993 movie *Barbarians at the Gate* portrayed the leveraged buyout of RJR Nabisco. Because of their tactics and intense focus on quick profits, these activists came to be thought of as a "blight"—"the cult of short-term shareholder value gone mad."[52]

> Activists are good because plenty of companies suffer from rotten management.

Modern shareholder activism is primarily driven by disappointment in current management's performance in developing value over a number of years. Even where the target is broken up into separate companies, as with steel and bearing producer Timken in 2014,[53] the objective is to unlock intermediate- and long-term value. In sharp contrast to the SEC's views during the 1980s, in 2015 the SEC chair said that shareholder activism "can be compatible with the kind of engagement that I hope companies and shareholders can foster."[54] According to *The Economist*, "One reason [activists are a force for good] is that plenty of companies suffer from rotten management. . . . [Activists] often seek to improve [the performance of] firms' boards."[55]

Nonetheless, activist "attacks" (often called "campaigns" by those sympathetic to the activist's goals) are dreaded by management, and for good reason. Major companies have been forced to oust their CEOs (Procter & Gamble, Microsoft), break up (Motorola, eBay, Yahoo), and return enormous amounts of cash to shareholders (Apple has so far distributed $90 billion). The CEO of a major Silicon Valley corporation said: "We think about an attack all the time."[56] Despite this statement, recent surveys found that 46 percent of corporate boards are entirely unprepared for a campaign and 90 percent have had no training in how to deal with an attack.[57] Yet activism has reached unprecedented levels, with 344 campaigns being launched against publicly held companies in 2014–2015. One in seven S&P 500 companies experienced an attack between 2011 and 2015.[58]

Most recently to appear are the *reluctavists* (reluctant activists): "long-suffering shareholders . . . who have reached a point where they see opportunities for value that the company isn't pursuing after years of underperformance." Reluctavists launched 49 campaigns against publicly held corporations in 2015 (36 in 2014, 15 in 2011).[59]

Major Issues Currently Confronting Boards of Directors

LO 9-5

Explain how corporations are governed and discuss the challenges facing modern boards of directors, including determining the appropriate level of executive compensation.

Cybersecurity

During the first half of 2015 alone, 45 billion corporate data records were stolen by hackers (245 million per day).[60] Only 14 percent of directors believe they have a solid understanding of the risk and only 19 percent believe they are overseeing the risk well.[61] When it comes to a cyber attack, the issue is no longer "if," but "when." Unnervingly, many boards have expressed concerns that an attack has already occurred but has not yet been detected—concerns that have proven prescient. In December 2016, Yahoo! reported the discovery of the world's largest (thus far) data breach—one that occurred in August 2013. The records of over one billion users were compromised. Full copies were sold on the "dark web" for $300,000. The problem is expected to get much worse, the most calamitous occurrence being the loss of the corporation's "'crown jewels'—the critical information that, if compromised, would undermine [the entity's] ability to continue[.]"[62]

Bribery

Becoming the subject of a bribery investigation can lead to extraordinary reputational damage and enormous cost. Boards are, as a result, increasingly devoting attention to detecting bribery and creating an environment in which such behavior is discouraged.

Since 1977, the Foreign Corrupt Practices Act (FCPA) has made it illegal for a U.S. company to ***bribe*** a foreign official to violate local law in order to obtain or maintain business, or to secure an improper advantage. It also prohibits false accounting for payments (for example, entering a bribe on the books as a "consulting fee"). Note that it is not illegal to bribe a foreign official to do a ministerial act that is not in violation of local law (for example, bribing a corrupt foreign government clerk to actually issue the construction permits to which a company is lawfully entitled). While originally enforcing the FCPA only tepidly, Department of Justice action has been vigorous since the late 1990s.

The Organization for Economic Cooperation and Development studied 400 bribery cases over 15 recent years.[63] Contrary to widely held views, bribes were not made primarily by rogue employees. Fifty-three percent were authorized by senior management—12 percent by the CEO. The size of the bribe as compared to the total transaction amount varied considerably—for example, 21 percent for extractive industries, 16 percent for manufacturing, and 4 percent for construction. In 40 percent of the cases, the penalties exceeded the total profit generated from the transaction. Forty-seven percent of the bribes were accomplished through an intermediary (for example, a party purporting to act as a consultant, lawyer, or accountant); 35 percent were accomplished through a chain of entities housed in secrecy jurisdictions (discussed later) like the Cayman Islands. In 31 percent of the cases, the bribery was discovered internally and voluntarily disclosed to the public (leading to greatly reduced sanctions); whistle-blowers were responsible for one-sixth of the detections.

Siemens (a German engineering company) paid $2.4 billion in 2008 under the antibribery provisions, an amount that does not include the staggering $1.25 billion paid in accounting and legal fees.[64] In March 2016, Japan's Olympus, the largest distributor of endoscopes in the United States, agreed to pay $646 million related to bribery in Latin American and kickbacks in New Jersey. In November 2016, JPMorgan Chase settled an FCPA case for $264 million. It admitted hiring 200 often-unqualified children of elite Chinese decision makers, many of whom did little actual work, in exchange for a "directly attributable linkage to business opportunity." There were blatant internal communications, such as: "How do you get the best quid pro quo from the relationship upon confirmation of the offer?" followed by: "The client has communicated clearly the quid pro quo for this hire." In December 2016, Israel's Teva, the world's largest maker of generic drugs, agreed to pay $519 million to settle bribery charges involving Mexican, Russian, and Ukrainian government officials. The largest corruption fine in history was imposed on Brazil's Odebrecht, also in December 2016, as discussed in the text box below.

Odebrecht SA—Largest Corruption Fine in History

On December 21, 2016, Odebrecht SA, a Brazilian company and Latin America's largest construction firm operating in 27 countries, admitted violating the FCPA and agreed to the largest anticorruption fine in history—$4.5 billion. Odebrecht built the Miami International Airport and was a major contractor for the 2014 World Cup and 2016 Rio Olympics. Over two decades it paid $800 million in bribes to government officials in 12 countries related to more than 100 projects in order to reap $3.34 billion in illegal profits. The largest bribes occurred in Brazil ($349 million), Venezuela ($98 million), and the Dominican Republic ($92 million). In Venezuela, an $8 billion hydropower project is five years behind schedule and has no projected completion date; an eight-mile bridge "remains a line of barren concrete columns a decade after the start of construction." The company's former CEO has been sentenced to 19 years in prison and 77 other insiders have entered criminal plea bargains. Odebrecht's petrochemical subsidiary, Braskem SA, has agreed to an additional $1 billion in fines.

So rampant and extensive were its corrupt payouts that it established a department, the "Division of Structured Operations" with a separate communication system, to manage the bribery. This unit arranged for "deliveries of cash-stuffed suitcases to secret locations" in addition to wire transfers. It used banks in secrecy jurisdictions like Antigua to hide transactions. "In one case . . . Odebrecht bought the local branch of a bank, allowing other members of the conspiracy, including politicians from multiple countries, to open accounts and receive transfers without arousing attention." Upon becoming aware of the investigation, Odebrecht directed its employees to "conceal or destroy evidence" and "delete records that might reveal illegal activities."

The company issued a statement that provides insight into the environment in which such corruption flourishes: "[We apologize for our] participation in illicit actions. . . . It does not matter that we gave in to external pressure. Nor is it relevant that there are behaviors [in international dealings] that the private and public sectors must resist[.] What matters is that we acknowledge our involvement. We were complicit and did not fight these practices, as we should have."[65]

Questions

1. What does this incident suggest about the integrity of many international business environments?
2. Odebrecht has been described as "brazen." Does this characterization sound correct?
3. Following these events, Odebrecht's credit rating plummeted, its revenues declined precipitously, and its workforce shrank from 250,000 to 140,000. Should boards of directors be concerned about whether their executives and employees are engaged in activities that violate the Foreign Corrupt Practices Act?

[For a complete listing of all antibribery actions, go to **https://www.justice.gov/criminal-fraud/related-enforcement-actions**].

Disclosures

Political Spending

Investors have always had some interest in the amounts corporations spend on political activities; but with the dramatic increase pursuant to the 2010 Supreme Court decision in *Citizens United,*[66] many large investors are increasingly pressing for detailed disclosures. They want to be able to determine whether the spending is properly aligned with the company's stated strategy. They want to know that the spending is, in the words of the official who manages the New York City pension funds, not simply to promote "the personal political preferences of a particular executive with access to the corporate purse strings." More than 100 shareholder resolutions to provide such disclosures are expected by the end of 2016. About half the S&P 500 companies offer voluntary disclosure, but it is limited and inconsistent. The SEC proposed a rule in 2012 that would require clear disclosures; despite the majority support found in the 1,200,000 comment letters, no rule followed. Under pressure from politicians, in 2013 the SEC chair assured Congress that no rule would be forthcoming; in the federal budget enacted in December 2015, the SEC was prohibited from expending its resources on such a rule.[67]

To understand the impact of the *Citizens United* decision, consider the following statistics. In the 2014 federal elections, interest groups benefiting from the decision outspent the candidates in 80 percent of the competitive races.[68] Through 2015, $1.5 billion of unlimited contributions were made, including $500 million from secret donors. In the 2012 presidential and other national elections, the top 100 donors each contributed an average of $4.7 million, with one couple contributing $90 million (including $30 million for the exclusive benefit of one presidential candidate). As for the 2016 election season, the Koch brothers (worth over $80 billion) indicated that they spent $750 million. By October 2015, 158 families had contributed $176 million—half of the total amount raised by the presidential candidates. Fifty of these families were on the *Fortune* 400 list of the wealthiest Americans. Both political parties benefit. For example, four billionaires gave $36 million to Republican presidential candidate Ted Cruz. Three billionaires gave $3 million to Democratic candidate Hillary Clinton.[69] The problem is considerably worse at the state and local levels, where amounts made available by *Citizens United* that would be deemed trivial in the national context are sufficient to "totally swamp" elections. Judges have become particularly vulnerable. In 2015, the Supreme Court decided *Williams-Yulee v. Florida State Bar*.[70] It upheld a narrow rule prohibiting candidates for judgeships from personally soliciting funds, but it continued to allow judges to create campaign committees to raise money. Justice Ginsburg said in her partial concurrence: "In recent years . . . issue-oriented organizations and political action committees have spent millions of dollars opposing the reelection of judges whose decisions do not toe a party line or are alleged to be out of step with public opinion."[71] More broadly, the well-known conservative Seventh Circuit Judge Richard Posner said in a National Public Radio interview: "Our political system is pervasively corrupt due to our Supreme Court taking away campaign-contribution restrictions [in *Citizens United*] on the basis of the First Amendment."[72]

The public cares about this issue. A 2015 *New York Times*/CBS news poll found that 85 percent want the campaign finance system fundamentally changed. A Bloomberg News poll the same year discovered that 78 percent want *Citizens United* overturned. Corporate boards cannot ignore the reputational risks associated with failing to be transparent about political spending.[73]

Climate Change

Both reputational and serious financial risks are implicated when it comes to corporate disclosure of climate-change risks. Large investors are increasingly pressing for more relevant information. In 2015 more than 50 shareholder proposals were submitted on this matter. A larger number were expected by the end of 2016.[74] In 2015 billionaire former New York City mayor Michael Bloomberg, who led the G20 Financial Stability Board's Task Force on Climate-Related Financial Disclosure, said: "It's critical that industries and investors understand the risks posed by climate change, but currently there is too little transparency about those risks." Also in 2015 Robert Rubin, the former chair of Goldman Sachs and former secretary of the treasury, said: "Investors should demand that companies disclose the impact that climate change could have on their business and assets[.] . . . I believe that such disclosures should be . . . mandated by the SEC, not just requested by investors." The International Monetary Fund published a report in 2016 that included a broader perspective: "[I]ncreased disclosure of firms' carbon footprints . . . and appropriate stress testing for climate risks will help ensure financial stability during the transition to a low-carbon economy."[75]

Since 2010 climate-risk disclosures have purportedly been mandatory pursuant to interpretive guidance issued by the SEC. Initial enforcement was meaningful, with 49 comment letters being sent to companies in 2010 and 2011. But only three were issued in 2012 and none thereafter. The SEC has come under significant criticism from investors, environmentalists, and politicians who believe enforcement is no longer being taken seriously.[76] In April 2015 a coalition of 62 large investors (including CALPERS) sent a letter to the SEC chair raising concerns about inadequate climate-risk disclosures by oil and gas companies because of their enhanced vulnerability. Concurrently, the heads of New York State and City pension funds asked the SEC to "consider enforcement and other actions to bring disclosures by companies in the fossil fuel industry into compliance with SEC . . . guidance." In October that year, 35 members of Congress sent the SEC chair a letter raising concerns about the "level of scrutiny the SEC is utilizing to robustly . . . enforce" its guidance on climate-risk disclosure.[77]

> Climate-risk disclosures are too often little more than vague generalizations.

Because of the SEC's disinclination to enforce the 2010 guidance, actual climate-risk disclosures are far too often little more than vague generalizations of little value to investors.[78] Indeed, "most mainstream investors and asset managers say that [the disclosed information] plays no role in their investment decisions."[79]

Some companies assert that the impact of climate change is too difficult to quantify to provide a reliable estimate for investors. But many believe that large businesses routinely perform significant internal analyses that guide their climate-risk mitigation decisions. Peabody Energy, the world's largest private coal company, was successfully sued by the New York Attorney General for misleading investors by not disclosing its own sophisticated analyses, which demonstrated material future adverse financial impacts associated with the increased regulation of its core product.[80] That company's stock fell from approximately $1,000 in 2011 to $4 at the beginning of 2016 as a result of the slump in coal prices related to the increasing environmental concerns about using coal, increased regulation of that use, and the decline in energy prices in general.[81]

A major legal battle is underway at this writing involving the climate-risk disclosures of ExxonMobil. In November 2015, the New York Attorney General began a sweeping investigation of the company, asserting, among other things, that it is misleading investors about the impacts climate change will have on its business in the years ahead. A core component of the case is that, as purportedly demonstrated by company documents from as early as the 1970s, ExxonMobil knew from its own research of the ultimate adverse financial consequences of the continued use of its core product, but it failed at all times to disclose the information investors need to make sound judgments.[82] According to *Politico*,[83] ExxonMobil is facing "the biggest existential threat . . . in decades." National politicians from both political parties have joined the fray,[84] and ExxonMobil is fighting back with the strong support of the industry.[85] It could be years before this highly charged matter resolves.

Clearly, boards must manage climate-change risk in order to avoid potentially substantial reputational and financial harm.

Taxes

In its "2016 Directors' Alert," international accounting and consulting firm Deloitte said:

> The global reset around tax is a significant business issue[.] Corporate tax affairs are very much in the spotlight, not just for tax authorities but also for investors, other stakeholders, some politicians [and] the media[.] Multinational organizations have been attracting a lot of critical public scrutiny[,] with concerns expressed that they are not paying their "fair share" of tax in all of the jurisdictions in which they operate. Business leaders have been called before government commissions in different countries . . . to defend their tax strategies. Investors and other stakeholders have raised concerns about the reputational risks created by this negative publicity[.] . . . Tax is an important issue for directors.[86]

There are at least three major dimensions to the current risks confronting boards of directors with respect to taxation: inversions, "parking" untaxed profits overseas, and profit-shifting.

Inversions An ***inversion*** occurs when, while not changing the headquarters location, the situs of principal operations, or any other significant economic characteristic, a U.S. company merely shifts its legal domicile to a ***tax haven*** (a nation that imposes little or no tax), which is sometimes also a ***secrecy jurisdiction*** (a nation that permits the anonymous ownership of entities and that refuses to cooperate with other countries' investigations). Ireland is a tax haven, as is the Cayman Islands (which is also a secrecy jurisdiction). In substance, nothing changes, but the total taxes paid to the United States decline dramatically. The primary pro-inversion argument is that the United States has the highest marginal corporate income tax rate (35 percent) of any major economy. This is often compared against the average European rate of 24 percent,[87] but this is highly misleading. In 2014, the average effective federal corporate income tax rate was only 19.4 percent, far lower than the 35 percent statutory rate. The lower effective rate was achieved through a variety of opportunities for tax savings provided in the tax law. When state and local taxes are included, the total effective rate for U.S. companies is 25.7 percent, well below the average OECD rate of 34.1 percent.[88] Despite these facts, the 35 percent rate makes for good headlines when pressing for large reductions in corporate income taxes. Nonetheless, it is true that there are nations in Europe, Asia, and the Caribbean that offer exceptionally low corporate tax rates (such as Ireland's 12.5 percent[89]) to entice businesses to change domicile. This dysfunctional race-to-the-bottom tax competition is impossible for the United States to win because, to achieve victory, it would need to commit to a zero percent tax rate.

If not addressed, corporate inversions could cost the United States as much as $40 billion between 2016 and 2025.[90] Over 50 major companies have inverted since 1982, with more than 20 since 2012.[91] Despite statutory and regulatory changes in 2004, 2012, and 2014, major corporations have continued their attempts to invert.[92] The most recent anti-inversion measure was announced in April 2016. The new rules were, to a significant extent, the result of public outrage from the announced inversion of the large U.S. pharmaceutical company Pfizer (involving the Irish company Allergan). Pfizer's projected tax savings were $35 billion. The record-setting $160 billion merger was abandoned after the new rules were promulgated.[93] Allergan stock declined 21 percent immediately thereafter.[94]

Parking As a result of both express policy and rules put in place that have had tremendous adverse unintended consequences, U.S. companies have "parked" $2.1 trillion of untaxed profits in tax havens. Ten companies alone (including Apple, Microsoft, Oracle, Citigroup, JPMorgan Chase, Goldman Sachs, and Bank of America) have $540 billion overseas, which, if made subject to immediate taxation, would generate $162 billion for the Treasury.[95] A 2015 study of the *Fortune* 500 found that 72 percent (358) had at least 7,622 subsidiaries located in tax havens. Just 30 employed 1,225 subsidiaries to avoid taxation on $1.4 billion of profits. Pfizer (discussed above) used 151 subsidiaries to keep $74 billion offshore. Apple held the largest amount overseas—$181 billion, which would result in $59 billion in taxes if the off-shore scheme was unwound. The two most popular tax havens were Bermuda and the Cayman Islands. The profits alleged to have been earned by U.S. multinationals in those countries represented an absurd 1,643 percent and 1,600 percent, respectively, of their GDPs.[96]

Profit-Shifting The two primary means by which corporations shift profits out of the United States and into low- or no-tax jurisdictions are earnings-stripping and intangible asset transfers. In an *earnings-stripping* arrangement, a U.S. company borrows money from an affiliated company situated in a tax haven, paying the highest interest rate that can be plausibly asserted. The interest is treated as an expense in the United States (leading to a large reduction in taxes) and is treated as income in the tax haven (but little or no tax is paid in the haven). In an *intangible asset transfer*, a U.S. company purports to sell its most crucial intangibles at fair market value to an affiliated company in a tax haven like Ireland, the Netherlands, or Luxembourg. The affiliate charges the maximum arguable royalty for the use of the intangibles, resulting in an impact similar to earnings-stripping. These intangibles, which were developed in the United States, are widely believed to have been sold at a price far below their true value. The schemes are frequently given odd monikers that hint of something not quite legitimate, like "a double Irish with a Dutch sandwich" (because the tax avoidance mechanism requires the involvement of entities in both Ireland and the Netherlands). In July 2016, the Internal Revenue Service sued Facebook to force the disclosure of documents related to the transfer of key intangible assets to an Irish subsidiary, asserting that the asset valuations were unreasonably low.[97]

> Apple sought the Holy Grail of tax avoidance—stateless income.

Many companies have suffered great reputational and financial damage because of their use of these tax arrangements, including McDonald's,[98] Google,[99] Starbucks, and Fiat.[100] Apple is becoming the poster child for using the international tax system to defeat U.S. taxation. Senator Carl Levin, chair of the Permanent Subcommittee on Investigations, said, "Apple sought the Holy Grail of tax avoidance," referring to the company's claim of **stateless income**—income that is purportedly beyond the reach of taxation by any country in the world.[101] In 2009 to 2011 alone, Apple paid essentially no tax on $38 billion of income.[102] The result was an effective tax rate of only 1.8 percent.[103] Apple CEO Tim Cook was summoned to appear before Congress in 2013 to defend the company's tax strategies,[104] and in April 2016 he felt it necessary to make a "personal appeal" to the European Union urging it to cease investigating Apple's tax arrangements. Nonetheless, the EU recently ordered Ireland to collect almost $15 billion in back taxes from the company.[105]

Boards must seriously consider the trade-offs between tax savings and reputational damage and chart a course that keeps their companies out of the critical spotlight while maintaining global competitiveness through tax cost management. Massive disclosures of tax avoidance schemes, most recently those known as the "Panama Papers," are increasing the risk associated with using offshore tax schemes. The leak of 11.5 million files (a record-breaking 2.6 GB of data) revealed the use of over 200,000 offshore entities to facilitate tax avoidance and evasion by individuals (including heads of governments) and companies.[106] Further such leaks seem virtually certain.

Nontraditional Financial Metrics

As will be discussed further in Part Three of this chapter, one of the primary purposes of the securities laws is to ensure that market participants have all the information they need to make sound investment decisions. When it comes to information about income, assets, and liabilities, companies must use a set of measurement and disclosure rules known as **generally accepted accounting principles** (GAAP). These rules are established by the Financial Accounting Standards Board, a private-sector organization whose promulgations have force-of-law status pursuant to authority delegated by the SEC. Disclosing material information in financial statements that was not prepared in accordance with GAAP subjects the company to potentially draconian liability for losses sustained in the market, as well as to civil and criminal penalties. A corporation fails to adhere to GAAP at its peril.

Nonetheless, the disclosure of non-GAAP financial metrics is common. About 90 percent of the S&P 500 made such disclosures in 2015.[107] This does not violate the securities laws so long as the disclosures are neither misleading nor more prominent than the GAAP disclosures. GAAP figures commonly include such things as one-time occurrences; for example, a major litigation loss in a product liability suit. Management often asserts that eliminating such items makes non-GAAP measures useful supplements to GAAP information, helping readers better perceive the company's actual operating performance and financial position.

In response to non-GAAP metrics that grossly distorted reality during the Enron era of the early 2000s, the SEC issued corrective regulations in 2003. A belief that inappropriate non-GAAP measures were still being used led to a revision of those regulations in 2010. In the years since, the SEC has grown increasingly concerned by the opportunistic manner in which non-GAAP disclosures are being prepared. In June 2016, SEC Chair Mary Jo White said: "I have . . . significant concerns about companies taking this flexibility [to make reasonable adjustments to GAAP metrics] beyond what is allowed by our rules." She enumerated the primary concerns: "In too many cases, the non-GAAP information, which is meant to supplement the GAAP information, has become the key message[,] effectively supplanting the GAAP presentation. . . . [Companies are excluding] normal, recurring cash operating expenses; [are] individually tailor[ing] non-GAAP revenues; [are failing to make adjustments with] consistency; [and are] cherry-picking [only the favorable items for inclusion]."[108] These comments were made shortly after the SEC issued new guidance to help eliminate these problems in May 2016.

The difference between GAAP and non-GAAP measures is significant. Over the period 2012 to 2015, GAAP income measures were essentially flat, but non-GAAP measures showed income increasing 14 percent.[109] In an analysis of 380 large U.S. companies, non-GAAP measures showed income rising 7 percent; GAAP income measures fell 11 percent. For 8 percent of the companies, non-GAAP metrics converted GAAP losses to profits.[110] As part of an accelerating trend, in the fourth quarter of 2015, non-GAAP income was 29 percent higher than GAAP income—the largest difference since the beginning of the 2008 Great Recession. In virtually all of the cases, non-GAAP income exceeded GAAP income.[111]

Boards of directors, and especially audit committees, are being warned by a frustrated SEC and are increasingly under the spotlight from the financial media about the employment of metrics that exaggerate the positives and downplay the negatives. SEC Chief Accountant James Schnurr, the agency's chief enforcement officer, said in March 2016: "The proliferation of non-GAAP reporting measures [and their] reporting by analysts [to the public] should warrant increased focus by management and the audit committee. [T]he focus should . . . include probing questions on why . . . the non-GAAP measure is an appropriate way to measure . . . performance[. C]ompanies should ensure that the measure[s are] prepared [under] oversight[.]."[112]

Board Independence

As discussed earlier in this part, good corporate governance requires an independent board of directors. The majority of large U.S. companies assert that their boards are independent.[113] However, there are three primary concerns. First, despite efforts to preclude CEOs from selecting board members via direct or indirect control over the nominating process, there are still concerns that CEOs are able to handpick purportedly independent directors who, in fact, have strong allegiance to the chief executive. Apple under Steve Jobs is a case in point. The successor CEO, Tim Cook, said he wanted to free the Apple board from CEO dominance. Although an arguably independent director was named board nominating committee chair, the chair's actual independence has been called into question. Observers believe Cook can still exert great influence over the selection of board candidates.[114]

Second, although a person might be a genuinely independent director at the outset, long association with the company could shift the director's mindset more toward that of an insider. Critics are increasingly concerned about the tenure of independent directors. Internationally, a relationship in excess of 12 years is generally considered to impair independence. Yet in 24 percent of the largest U.S. companies, most independent board members have been in place for at least 10 years. Among the S&P 500, about one-sixth of the independent directors have held their seats for at least 15 years. Only 13 companies have time limits for directorships and two-thirds expressly elect not to specify maximum tenures. If the international 12-year rule were applied, 30 percent of U.S. companies would no longer have a majority of independent directors.[115]

Finally, relationships between purportedly independent directors and the company, and relationships among the independent directors themselves, can impair independence. Highly interconnected, assertedly "independent" board members were common during the Enron era. SOX was expected to improve the quality of corporate governance by largely precluding such relationships. The changes, however, have not been effective. Instead of a substantive rule that requires asking the fundamental question: "Are there factors that might cause [a reasonable person] to conclude that this director is not independent?,"[116] bright-line rules have been implemented, such as having not been employed by the company for the last three years.[117] As a result, relationships that would clearly put a reasonable person on notice that independence is threatened pass muster. To illustrate, John Hennessy, the president of Stanford University, is considered an independent director of Google despite the fact that over the past 12 years, the company has donated or paid in licensing fees $25 million to the school. Andrew McKenna is held out to be an independent director of McDonald's even though his family-owned business has sold $71 million of goods to the company. Carnival director Randall Weisenburger is treated as independent even though his company has received $34 million for advertising services. And Bank of America directors Charles Gilford and Thomas May are considered independent even though the former is on the board compensation committee of the company that employs the latter as CEO.[118]

Activist shareholders, proxy-advising firms, and the financial media are increasingly calling boards to account for their failure to insist on genuine board independence.

Executive Compensation

> CEO compensation is not an award for achievement. It is frequently a warm personal gesture by the CEOs to themselves.

Executive compensation has long been an issue for shareholders. The 20th-century American economist John Kenneth Galbraith observed that "[t]he salary of the chief executive of a large corporation is not a market award for achievement. It is frequently in the nature of a warm personal gesture by the individual to himself."[119] In 2016, the highest-paid CEO was Expedia's Dara Khosrowshahi ($95 million). That year Yahoo! chief operating officer Henrique de Castro received compensation of $40 million despite the company's rapid decline in performance; and after 14 months he was terminated, triggering a $60 million severance package.[120] In the late 1970s, public company CEOs earned 30 to 40 times the average worker's income; by 2015, they earned 373 times that amount. The ratios for the chief executives of Discovery, Chipotle, and Starbucks were 2282, 1500, and 994, respectively.[121] The Dodd–Frank Act is scheduled to require the ratio to be disclosed annually beginning in 2017,[122] but the Trump administration is expected to overturn the rule.[123]

Median CEO perquisites in the *Fortune* 100 increased 22 percent in 2016 to $127,000, but this figure obscures some extraordinary benefits. For example, John Tyson, chairman of Tyson Foods, enjoyed aircraft privileges valued at $820,000. Amazon CEO Jeff Bezos received security services worth $1.5 million. Comcast CFO Michael Cavanaugh was awarded $11.8 million in retirement plan contributions.[124]

The public is concerned about executive compensation. Only 16 percent of American workers believe the ratio of CEO-to-average-worker pay is appropriate, even though they underestimate CEO compensation by a factor of 10. Sixty-two percent think such compensation should be capped, with 49 percent favoring direct government action.[125] Even institutional investors feel there is a problem, with 21 percent believing there is no link between CEO pay and corporate performance.[126] Research suggests that excessive executive compensation reduces the typical company's value by 4 percent.[127]

Directors hold a starkly different opinion. They attribute 40 percent of company performance to the CEO, 87 percent believing CEO pay is properly aligned with accomplishment. Ninety-seven percent oppose any government intervention in executive compensation.[128] CEO pay continues to ratchet up over time, in large part because individual boards decide to pay above-average amounts to signal a belief that the recipients are above average in caliber and will achieve above-average results.[129] Another factor in CEO compensation inflation is whether the board chair is an insider. A 2016 study of the S&P 500 found a 40 percent average differential in pay: $15.6 million with an insider chair and $11 million with an independent outsider chair.[130]

In response to public outcry, since 2011 the Dodd–Frank Act has mandated a ***say-on-pay***, which requires companies to put a separate, but nonbinding, resolution before the shareholders to approve senior executive compensation.[131] But it has had little impact. A mere 2 percent of companies lost say-on-pay votes in 2015, the same proportion as in 2014.[132] Only 40 percent of institutional investors believe such votes have any influence on executive compensation.[133] For example, Oracle investors voted against pay packages four consecutive times to no avail.[134] However, votes seem to be impactful only when the company has performed very poorly and the CEO is paid very well (the driving force typically being proxy advisor recommendations against shareholder pay package approval).[135] BP provides an example. It finally agreed to discuss pay packages with shareholders before adopting them after 60 percent voted against the board's executive compensation proposal. That proposal included $20 million for the CEO, despite the company's loss of $6.5 billion, its elimination of thousands of jobs, and its freeze on employee pay in the wake of the *Deepwater Horizon* disaster.[136]

> By 2015, CEOs of large public corporations earned 373 times average worker income.

PRACTICING ETHICS — Excessive Executive Compensation?

An interesting shareholder derivative suit alleging a violation of the duty of due care arose out of CEO Michael Eisner's hiring, and subsequent firing, of Michael Ovitz from his position as president of The Walt Disney Co. The suit alleged that Eisner and the Disney board had violated their duty of due care both in initially hiring Ovitz (who had no previous experience as an executive of a public company in the entertainment industry) and in granting him a no-fault termination clause. The consequence of invoking the no-fault clause was that, after barely one year, Ovitz received $38 million in cash, as well as three million stock options. Significantly, the maximum salary Ovitz could have earned actually working was $11 million annually. Following a three-month trial, the Delaware judge wrote, "For the future, many lessons of what not to do can be learned from defendants' conduct here. Nevertheless, I conclude that . . . the defendants did not act in bad faith, and were at most ordinarily negligent, in connection with the hiring of Ovitz[.] In accordance with the business judgment rule, . . . ordinary negligence is insufficient to constitute a violation of the fiduciary duty of [due] care."

Question

Apart from the legality, is it ethical for a board to agree to an executive severance package that will pay out even if the executive is terminated for poor performance?

Source: Jane Sasseen, "A Better Look at the Boss's Pay," *BusinessWeek*, February 26, 2007, p. 44.

Questions—Part Two

1. Why have corporate governance concerns arisen since the early 2000s with respect to the relationship between the board and the CEO? Do you believe there are still grounds for continuing concern?
2. Evaluate the opinion that board accountability to shareholders is a myth.
3. What are the major concerns of present-day boards of directors?
4. Is the Foreign Corrupt Practices Act needed?
5. Explain the growing demand for climate-change disclosure.
6. Why are some shareholders concerned about corporate political spending?
7. Describe the current controversy over the international taxation of corporations?
8. How are corporations potentially materially misleading the market with non-GAAP disclosures?
9. Why might it make sense to have only independent outside directors determine the compensation of senior executives?

Part Three—Regulation of the Securities Markets

Introduction

> Vast sums have been lost in companies with incompetent or corrupt management.

To amass the resources needed to pursue sizable business opportunities, particularly global ventures, a large number of investors must be convinced to entrust their wealth to third-party managers. History shows that this trust has often been misplaced, vast sums having been lost in companies with incompetent or corrupt management. As a result, the federal government has undertaken to promote the reliability of the U.S. securities markets through regulation. The backbone of this regulation grew out of the stock market crash of 1929 and the Great Depression that followed. As mentioned previously in this chapter, significant additional regulation has followed the corporate failures of the Enron era and the Great Recession of 2008, regulation to which this chapter now turns.

Initial Public Offerings

LO 9-6

Define the term *initial public offering* (IPO) and explain the securities registration process.

LO 9-7

Compare the regulatory roles of the 1933 and 1934 federal securities acts.

When a corporation wants to sell a new security (whether debt or equity) through the public capital markets, if the corporation (*issuer*) and any of the persons to whom the security is offered (*offerees*) are domiciled in different states (*interstate offering*), federal law governs the sale. If the corporation and all offerees are domiciled in the same state (*intrastate offering*), state law (considered later) applies. If a company has not previously sold equity securities to the public, the issuance is referred to as an *initial public offering* (IPO) or, more colloquially, *going public*. For example, on June 17, 2015, Fitbit went public at $20 a share. The share's price immediately jumped 50 percent to $30.40.[137] The price peaked at $47.60 on July 31, 2015. As of this writing, Fitbit stock is trading at less than $7.50. Conversely, if a private investor seeks to purchase all of the publicly held equity securities of a corporation, that company is said to be *going private*.

In this context, the term *security* embraces not only stocks and bonds but also the much-broader *investment contract*. The *Howey* case that follows defines the term.

FACTS

The Howey Company owned large tracts of citrus acreage in Florida. Each prospective customer was offered both a land sales contract and a service contract by which Howey maintained the groves and marketed the produce. Purchases were usually narrow strips arranged so an acre consisted of a row of 48 trees. These tracts were not separately fenced and the purchaser had no right of entry and no right to specific fruit. All the produce was pooled. The purchasers were mostly non-residents of Florida and were predominantly professionals. They were attracted by the expectation of substantial profits.

Justice Murphy

* * * * *

It is admitted that the mails and instrumentalities of interstate commerce are used in the sale of the land and service contracts and that no registration statement . . . has ever been filed with the [Securities and Exchange Commission].

[The Securities Act of 1933] defines the term "security" to include the commonly known [instruments like stocks and bonds]. The definition also includes [the term] "investment contract"[.] The legal issue [is] whether the land sales contract . . . and the service contract together constitute an "investment contract" within the meaning of [the Act]. An affirmative answer brings into operation the registration requirements[.]

By including an investment contract within the scope of . . . the Securities Act, Congress was using a term the meaning of which had been crystallized by prior judicial interpretation. It is therefore reasonable to attach that meaning to the term as used by Congress, especially since such a definition is consistent with the statutory

aims. In other words, an investment contract for purposes of the Securities Act means a contract, transaction or scheme whereby a person invests his money in a common enterprise and is led to expect profits solely from the efforts of the promoter or a third party[.]

The transactions in this case clearly involve investment contracts as so defined. The respondent [is] offering an opportunity to contribute money and to share in the profits of a large citrus fruit enterprise managed [by respondent, who is] offering this opportunity to persons who reside in distant localities and who lack the equipment and experience requisite to the cultivation, harvesting and marketing of the citrus products[.]

[Respondent's] failure to abide by the statutory and administrative rules in making such offerings cannot be sanctioned under the Act[.]

Questions

1. Would an investment in Microsoft stock satisfy the definition of "investment contract"?

2. Why do you think Congress added the term "investment contract" to the definition of "security"?

AFTERWORD

Following the *Howey* case, courts have looked more closely at the final criterion, that the investor "is led to expect profits *primarily* from the efforts" of others [emphasis added], and have generally taken a practical view of the requirement. The goal has been to distinguish circumstances in which investors will be primarily passive from those in which there is a reasonable expectation of significant investor control.[138] Thus, membership units in an LLC may or may not qualify as investment contracts, depending on the surrounding facts.[139]

1933 Act

The federal law governing initial securities offerings is the *Securities Act of 1933* (1933 Act), which is administered by the **Securities and Exchange Commission** (SEC). The 1933 Act seeks to (1) ensure full disclosure of all material facts about the investment opportunity to offerees before they invest and (2) eliminate fraudulent conduct in the markets. Thus, a securities offering that passes muster under the federal securities law has not been approved by the government as a good investment. [For more on the SEC, see **www.sec.gov**].

> The 1933 Act seeks to ensure full disclosure and eliminate fraud.

To promote full disclosure, the 1933 Act forbids any interstate offering of a new security until a *registration statement* has been filed with, and approved by, the SEC. The registration statement has two parts: (1) the prospectus and (2) the supplemental information. The *prospectus* is the major component and is delivered to offerees to satisfy the requirement for pre-investment disclosure. There are three main sections in a prospectus. One contains general information about the company: the industry in which it operates, the quality of its products and services and of its management, its business plan, and so on. Another section contains a risk assessment of the business model, local operating conditions (such as political instability), and similar information. For example, and as discussed in Part Two, in 2010 the SEC began requiring companies to disclose the risks of global climate change, such as whether any new law or treaty limiting carbon dioxide emissions might increase operating costs.[140]

The third portion of the prospectus is the ***audited financial statements***. An investor's goal is to make money. Investors want to know how well the corporation under consideration has accomplished this in the past so they can estimate its future economic potential. A corporation's ability to make a profit is shown on its ***income statement,*** which presents the company's revenues, gains, expenses, and losses on an annual basis.

Because the income statement seeks to measure economic income, it employs accrual accounting. Revenues are recognized when earned (not when cash is received) and expenses are recognized in the period during which the related revenue is reported (regardless of when those expenses are paid). Because the income statement focuses only on economic income, a ***statement of cash flows*** reconciling the beginning and ending cash balances is also presented. Proper cash management is crucial both to a company's day-to-day functioning and to its ability to seize opportunities and cope with adversities.

The ***balance sheet*** presents the business's assets (economic resources), liabilities (claims against those assets held by nonowners), and equity (residual claims against the assets held by owners after all liabilities have been satisfied). Although balance sheets have numerous deficiencies (such as the use of historical cost rather than current value to measure assets), they attempt to describe the corporation's financial position as of a particular date, such as the end of the year presented in the income statement.

Technically, the financial statements are prepared by the corporation's management. To give comfort to investors that management has prepared these statements properly and honestly, independent ***certified public accountants*** (CPAs) are engaged to audit them. Audits must be performed in accordance with ***generally accepted auditing standards*** (GAAS). GAAS are intended to ensure that the procedures used to investigate the financial statements are thorough. The objective of the investigation is to determine whether the financial statements are not ***materially misleading*** in accordance with ***generally accepted accounting principles*** (GAAP). GAAP provides the rules for how revenues, gains, expenses, losses, assets, liabilities, and equity are measured and disclosed. One might paraphrase an audit: independent experts (CPAs) are supposed to "look hard" (GAAS) and decide whether the financial statements prepared by management accurately measure the income, cash flow, and financial position of the corporation (GAAP).

The ***supplemental information*** portion (the second part) of the registration statement, which is not distributed to offerees, describes such matters as how much it is costing to "float" the offering and what major contracts exist with unions, suppliers, and customers.

The SEC vigorously enforces the 1933 Act's prescribed relationship between ***solicitation*** (offering to sell) or sales of a security and the registration process. There are three stages. During the ***prefiling period*** (before the registration statement has been filed with the SEC), no solicitation or sales are permitted. During the ***waiting period*** (after the registration statement has been filed, but before it has been approved by the SEC), no sales are permitted but a limited amount of solicitation is allowed. A ***tombstone ad*** (so called because of its shape and borders) may be published in forums like *The Wall Street Journal* to make the market aware of the anticipated issuance. A **red herring prospectus** (name taken from the prominent red ink cautionary statement required on its first page)—the draft prospectus included with the filed registration statement—may be distributed. Once the SEC approves the registration statement, the ***post-effective period*** begins. Solicitation is permitted and sales may be consummated, but only if the offerees have first received the final prospectus.

Some companies do ***shelf registrations*** that allow them to issue securities in portions over a two-year period under a single registration statement. This allows them to float the securities when market conditions are most favorable rather than issuing them all shortly after the registration statement becomes effective.

Typically not wanting to sell the securities themselves, issuers employ an ***underwriter***. A *best-efforts underwriter* acts as the issuer's sales agent, does not take title to the securities, and earns its profit from sales commissions. A *firm-commitment underwriter* purchases the securities from the issuer at a discount, intending to profit by reselling them. Institutional investors and ***dealers*** typically purchase new offerings—the former for investment, the latter for resale to retail investors.

Private Placement General Solicitation Ban Lifted

In July 2013, the SEC reversed a long-standing prohibition on the solicitation of unregistered securities. ***Private placements***, which comprise over 40 percent of all securities issuances, can now be advertised to anyone, although only accredited investors (discussed later) can make purchases. Any means of solicitation, including the Internet, is permitted. Advocates assert that the new rule promotes the ability of start-ups and small businesses to raise capital without first having to go through the onerous registration process. Critics counter that allowing speculative start-ups and high-risk hedge funds to solicit investments through mass marketing undermines the integrity of the market.[141]

PRACTICING ETHICS   Credit-Rating Agencies—Another Cause for Concern?

Corporations may use the securities markets to raise debt capital by selling bonds. Bonds are "securities" and thus are governed by the federal securities laws. To issue new bonds, a corporation will usually seek to have them rated by a credit-rating agency such as Moody's, Standard & Poor's, or Fitch. Without such a rating, it may be hard to sell a sufficient number of, or to obtain the best price for, its bonds. Most of these agencies' revenues come from fees paid by issuers seeking to have their debt rated. This raises potential conflicts of interest—on one hand, the agencies are in business to produce credible, independent evaluations of issuers and bonds, but on the other, they have to compete with other agencies for issuers' business.

These conflicts played a major role in the 2008 financial crisis—not from the ratings of corporate bonds, but from the ratings of mortgage-backed securities (investment vehicles based on the performance of a pool of mortgages). According to the Financial Crisis Inquiry Report, "Failures in credit rating and securitization transformed bad mortgages into toxic financial assets."[142] Congressional hearings uncovered internal e-mails containing such statements as "sold our soul to the devil for revenue" (Moody's) and "let's hope we are all wealthy and retired by the time this house of cards falters" (Standard & Poor's). In January 2015, Standard & Poor's announced a $1.44 billion settlement related to multiple transgressions.[143]

Unfortunately, the government has so far accomplished very little in terms of new regulation.[144]

Question

A bondholder would be concerned about whether a corporation has purchased a favorable bond rating. Should a shareholder also be worried?

Exemptions

Neither *exempt securities* nor *exempt transactions* require full registration with the SEC. The most common exempt securities are those issued by governments, charities, and financial institutions like banks and insurance companies. Thus, they have little application to most businesses.

Depending on the exempt transaction involved, the presale disclosures and filings with the SEC range from none to something only slightly less than a full registration statement. Most exemptions prohibit general solicitation.

Some exempt transactions were created statutorily as an accommodation to small issuers to lessen the financial burden of raising capital. For example, all intrastate offerings are exempt transactions. There is an exemption for purely private offerings, but it can sometimes be problematic determining whether a particular offering will be considered private or public. Thus, small issuers are more likely to rely on one of the regulatory exemptions created by the SEC. Rules 504 (which exempts certain transactions with an aggregate offering amount of $1 million or less) and 505 (which exempts certain transactions with an aggregate offering amount of up to $5 million) are little used. The workhorse is Rule 506, for which there is no amount limitation, but which can involve only *accredited investors* and up to 35 *sophisticated investors*. Accredited investors include financial institutions, directors and officers of the issuer, and individuals with annual net income of at least $200,000 and/or net worth of at least $1,000,000 (excluding the personal residence). Such persons are presumed to understand, and be able to withstand the risk associated with, securities investments. A sophisticated investor is one who has sufficient knowledge and experience in financial matters to be able to evaluate the merits and risks of an investment (or a person advised by a party with such expertise).

Note that even when exemptions reduce or eliminate registration under the 1933 Act, the law's sweeping antifraud provisions (discussed later) still apply.

Securities Crowdfunding Emerges

Securities crowdfunding is the use of the Internet to raise capital, with each contributor investing a comparatively small amount. Until recently, crowdfunding has been limited to no-interest loans and donations because, if a return is provided (for example, dividends or interest), the securities laws require the investment's registration with the SEC.[145]

Securities crowdfunding was authorized by Title III of the 2012 JOBS Act through a new registration exemption. Companies are allowed to raise up to $1 million annually by selling stock via the Internet using "intermediaries" (SEC-regulated third parties that manage the process). Individuals are limited in the amount they can invest each year. For example, those whose annual income and net worth are both less than $100,000 will be permitted to invest not more than 5 percent of the greater of those amounts (but not more than $2,000). Companies must disclose information about their business, their officers and directors, and how they will use the money. Audited financial statements are required if the amount to be raised exceeds $500,000. Nonetheless, the disclosure requirements are substantially less than those applicable to conventional IPOs.[146]

The crowdfunding rules are controversial. Many are concerned about hucksters defrauding naïve and financially unsophisticated investors. Others complain of the burdensome transaction and compliance costs. For example, simply raising $100,000 can cost $18,000; and over five years, $1 million of funding could cost $300,000.[147]

It took the SEC three years to authorize securities crowdfunding. Frustration led 31 states and the District of Columbia to enact their own statutes. Few, however, took advantage of these opportunities.[148] It remains to be seen whether federally authorized securities crowdfunding will be a viable option for "democratizing" the capital markets.

The SEC finalized the rules for securities crowdfunding in October 2015, which went "live" on May 16, 2016.

Although the media "hype" surrounding the 2012 enactment of the JOBS Act was principally directed at the above securities crowdfunding provisions (Title III), many believed it should have been focused on Title IV's authorization of so-called *Regulation A+* mini-IPOs, which went into effect on June 19, 2015.[149] Regulation A+'s predecessor, Regulation A, was limited to $5 million annually and was so inefficient a mechanism for raising capital that only about 25 companies per year used it.[150] Regulation A+ raises the annual limit to $50 million, permits individuals who are not accredited investors—99 percent of the population—to participate (up to the greater of 10 percent of their income or net worth), and imposes fewer initial barriers and ongoing disclosure obligations than a traditional IPO.[151] It costs $50–100,000 to engage in, and takes two to three months to gain SEC approval for, a Regulation A+ issuance.[152]

Despite great expectations, however, successful Regulation A+ offerings have been sparse. In the first year, only 45 received SEC approval, and the great majority of these did not succeed. To some extent this was the result of the market becoming familiarized with the new approach to raising capital. But other factors had an impact. Some offerors set the minimum-raise amount too high. Most failed to appreciate the magnitude of the marketing effort required to interest a sufficient number of investors. Some underestimated the cost and time of producing the required financial information. And many discovered that initial expressions of investor interest failed to ripen to actual financial commitments. "There has been some level of 'magical thinking[.' Offerors] perceived [a] pent-up demand for investment in startup and tech companies . . . and that investors 'would come out of the woodwork.'"[153]

The Secondary Securities Markets

Once a security is issued, it can be sold repeatedly. Such sales may be accomplished on a *physical exchange,* such as the New York Stock Exchange (NYSE), where agents of buyers and sellers deal directly with each other. Others may be made on an *over-the-counter market*, where trades occur electronically over a computer network linking dealers across the nation. An example is NASDAQ, the National Association of Securities Dealers Automatic Quotation system. [To learn more, see **https://nyse.nyx.com/** and **www.nasdaq.com**].

The federal law that governs post-issuance securities trades is the *Securities Exchange Act of 1934* (1934 Act), which also created the SEC. Its purposes are the same as those of its 1933 counterpart: (1) to ensure full disclosure of all material information so investors can make sound decisions and (2) to prevent fraudulent conduct in the markets. A company is generally subject to the 1934 Act's reporting requirements if it has publicly traded securities and has both more than $10 million in assets and more than 500 nonaccredited shareholders.[154]

To promote full disclosure, the SEC requires issuers to submit a variety of reports. Annually, each must file a *Form 10-K,* which includes information very similar to that found in a 1933 Act registration statement, including audited financial statements. To increase the timeliness of disclosures, the SEC requires additional reports, such as the quarterly *Form 10-Q* and *Form 8-K*. The former is a culled-down version of Form 10-K, particularly distinguished by the fact that the included financial statements are not audited. The latter is required whenever a material event occurs, such as a change in control, a major asset acquisition or disposition, bankruptcy, a change in auditor, or the resignation of the director.[155] [To retrieve filings for specific corporations, see **www.sec.gov/edgar.shtml**].

All corporate communications are subject to regulatory standards. Regulation FD requires companies to disseminate material information in a way that rapidly reaches the general public and gives no one an advantage. In April 2013, the SEC approved the use of social media such as Twitter and Facebook for such dissemination, as long as the company has previously advised the public what social media outlets it will use.[156]

Under the 1934 Act, the SEC has the power to *suspend trading* in any security "when it serves the public interest and will protect investors." Thus, the SEC may suspend trading if it suspects price manipulation or has serious questions about a company's assets or operations.[157] The market price of a security is typically devastated by a suspension, which provides a strong incentive for corporations to avoid misconduct.

Brokers and Online Trading

When individuals want to buy or sell securities, they may do so through an intermediary—a *broker*. In addition to facilitating trades, brokers may provide advisory services and assess the suitability of investments for a particular investor. That is, they make recommendations and trades that take into account the investor's needs, financial situation, investment objectives, and risk tolerance.

> An 80-year-old woman with Alzheimer's disease entrusted $500,000 to a broker.

Occasionally brokers face charges of *churning*—repeatedly and unnecessarily engaging in trades to generate commissions. In one case, an 80-year-old woman with Alzheimer's disease entrusted $500,000 to a broker. Fourteen months later, the account was worth only $15,000. The broker had engaged in over 300 trades and charged the account $94,000 in fees. Further, the broker had purchased only high-tech stocks (versus a balanced, conservative portfolio more appropriate to her situation).[158]

One impact of the Internet has been the bypassing of full-service securities brokers by discount brokers offering *online trading*. In response, most major full-service brokers have added online-trading services, which can be less expensive but also tend to leave investors without professional guidance.

One type of online trading is *day trading*. Day traders rarely hold any security more than a few hours, earning profits by exploiting minor price volatility, not inherent value. Only about 10 percent of day traders are successful.[159] The SEC has expressed great concern about advertising suggesting that day trading is easy and certain to be profitable. It cautions that tips and analyses are frequently false.[160] Nonetheless, the market has moved inexorably toward global, 24-hour-a-day, electronic trading.

Violating Federal Securities Laws

LO 9-8

Identify when a "material misrepresentation" has occurred.

The consequences of noncompliance with the securities laws are potentially staggering. They include compensatory damages for losses suffered, as well as civil and criminal penalties. Some of the provisions most commonly violated by corporations and their directors and executives are discussed below.

False or Misleading Statements—1933 Act

LO 9-9

Explain the due diligence defense.

Perhaps the greatest deterrent to misconduct in the securities laws is the civil liability that can be imposed on wrongdoers by harmed investors. The 1933 Act's Section 11 establishes this liability with respect to false or misleading registration statements. The *Omnicare* case below explores whether opinions expressed by a company can rise to the status of sanctionable misrepresentations.

Omnicare, Inc. v. Laborers District Council Construction Industry Pension Fund

LEGAL BRIEFCASE   135 S. Ct. 1318 (2015)

FACTS

Omnicare, the nation's largest provider of pharmacy services to nursing homes, filed a registration statement containing several sentences of which the following is representative: "We believe our contract arrangements with . . . pharmaceutical suppliers . . . are in compliance with applicable . . . laws." Those contracts called for rebates, which were ultimately determined illegal, resulting in losses to the company. The pension fund purchased stock in the IPO and later sued, alleging that the company's opinion statement about legal compliance gave rise to liability under § 11 of the 1933 Act.

Justice Kagan

*   *   *   *   *

The Securities Act of 1933 protects investors by ensuring that companies . . . make a "full and fair disclosure of information" relevant to a public offering. The linchpin of the Act is its registration requirement. . . .

Section 11 . . . promotes compliance with these disclosure provisions by . . . provid[ing]:

"[If] any part of the registration statement . . . contained an untrue statement of a material fact or omitted to state a material fact required to be stated therein or necessary to make the statements therein not misleading, any person acquiring [the] security . . . [may] sue."

*   *   *   *   *

[The pension fund asserts] that a statement of opinion that is ultimately found incorrect—even if believed at the time made—may count as an "untrue statement of a material fact." . . . [It claims that the] issuer's statement that "we believe we are following the law" conveys that "we in fact are following the law"—which is "materially false," no matter what the issuer thinks, if instead it is violating an anti-kickback statute.

[T]hat argument wrongly conflates facts and opinions. A fact is "a thing done or existing" or "[a]n actual happening." An opinion is "a belief[,] a view," or a "sentiment which the mind forms of persons or things." . . . [A] statement of fact expresses certainty about a thing, whereas a statement of opinion . . . does not. . . . [Congress] incorporated . . . that distinction in § 11's first part by exposing issuers to liability not for "untrue statement[s]" full stop (which would have included ones of opinion), but only for "untrue statement[s] of . . . *fact*."

*   *   *   *   *

[E]very [opinion] statement explicitly affirms one fact: that the speaker actually holds the stated belief. . . . "I believe our marketing practices are lawful" . . . would falsely describe [the speaker's] state of mind if she thought her company was breaking the law. In such cases, § 11's first part would subject the issuer to liability[.] . . . [T]he Funds do not contest that Omnicare's opinion was honestly held.

*   *   *   *   *

[T]he Funds also rely on § 11's omissions provision, alleging that Omnicare "omitted to state facts necessary" to make its opinion on legal compliance "not misleading." . . . [W]hether a statement is "misleading" depends on the perspective of a reasonable investor[.] . . .

A reasonable person understands . . . the difference . . . between a statement of fact and one of opinion. She recognizes the import of words like "I think" or "I believe," and grasps that they convey some lack of certainty as to the statement's content. . . . [T]he investor thus distinguishes between the sentences "we believe X is true" and "X is true." . . .

But . . . a reasonable investor may . . . understand an opinion statement to convey facts . . . about the speaker's basis for holding that view. . . . Consider [the] opinion . . . : "We believe our conduct is lawful." . . . In the context of the securities market, an investor, though recognizing that legal opinions can prove wrong in the end, still likely expects such an assertion to rest on some meaningful legal inquiry—rather than, say, on mere intuition[.] . . . Similarly, if the issuer made the statement in the face of its lawyers' contrary advice, or with knowledge that the Federal Government was taking the opposite view, the investor again has cause to complain: He expects not just that the issuer believes the opinion . . . , but that it fairly aligns with the information in the issuer's possession at the time. Thus, if a registration statement omits material facts about the issuer's inquiry into or knowledge concerning a statement of opinion, and if those facts conflict with what a reasonable investor would take from the statement itself, then § 11's omissions clause creates liability.

An opinion statement, however, is not necessarily misleading when an issuer knows, but fails to disclose, some fact cutting the other way. Reasonable investors understand that opinions sometimes rest on a weighing of competing facts; indeed, the presence of such facts is one reason why an issuer may frame a statement as an opinion, thus conveying uncertainty. . . .

* * * * *

[W]hether an omission makes an expression of opinion misleading always depends on context. Registration statements [are] filed with the SEC as a legal prerequisite for selling securities to the public. Investors do not, and are right not to, expect opinions contained in those statements to reflect baseless, off-the-cuff judgments, of the kind that an individual might communicate in daily life. At the same time, an investor reads each statement within such a document . . . in light of all its surrounding text, including hedges, disclaimers, and apparently conflicting information. . . . [Section] 11 creates liability only for the omission of material facts that cannot be squared with such a fair reading. . . .

* * * * *

[Remanded.]

Questions

1. Describe the pension fund's argument as to why Omnicare incurred Section 11 liability because of
   a. What it said.
   b. What it did not say.
2. How did the Court respond to each of the pension fund's arguments?

Virtually anyone with a significant role in preparing the registration statement can be sued (the issuer, its directors, its underwriters, and its accountants and other experts). The liability can be vast—essentially, all damages sustained by investors while the misleading registration statements were outstanding. No proof of actual plaintiff reliance on the content of the registration statement is required. Auditors and investment bankers, because of their "deep pockets," are often at the top of the list of defendants. Accounting firms have paid hundreds of millions of dollars to settle securities fraud suits.

The principal defense in a Section 11 action is *due diligence*, which every defendant other than the issuer can raise. The defendant must show that, based on a reasonable investigation, he or she reasonably believed that the registration statement was not misleading. What constitutes "reasonable" is generally determined by reference to the conduct expected of a prudent person in the management of his or her own property.

However, the due diligence standard for experts (like accountants and lawyers) is much higher. Their inquiries must rise to the standards expected of professionals, not merely of prudent businesspersons. Thus, at an absolute minimum, the accounting firm that audits the financial statements included in the registration statement must design its audit to comport with GAAS and must evaluate the financial statement content by reference to GAAP. Lawyers, actuaries, appraisers, and other experts whose work has a material impact on the registration statement must follow analogous rules established by their professional associations and regulators. The *BarChris* case, below, explores the due diligence defense.

FACTS

Bowling as a leisure activity and sport grew rapidly in the 1950s. BarChris built alleys. Its revenues grew from $800,000 in 1956 to $9,165,000 in 1960. By 1962 overbuilding caused construction to halt. BarChris ran into serious financial problems. It filed a registration statement (effective May 1961) for new bonds to raise cash, and the bonds were issued. Circumstances were grave when the registration statement became effective. BarChris filed for bankruptcy in October 1962.

BarChris' financial statements dated December 31, 1960, were included in the prospectus. They were audited by Peat Marwick (predecessor to KPMG) and contained material errors. Revenues and current assets were overstated and contingent liabilities were understated.

The prospectus overstated the demand for alley construction. It misrepresented how the proceeds would be used (a large portion would actually go to pay overdue debts and retire loans from officers). It failed to note that, because of defaults, BarChris had repossessed and was now operating several alleys. Escott and other bondholders sued under Section 11 of the 1933 Act, alleging the prospectus was materially misleading. All defendants but BarChris raised the due diligence defense.

Judge Mclean

I turn now to the question of whether defendants have proved their due diligence defenses. The position of each defendant will be separately considered.

Russo

Russo was, to all intents and purposes, the chief executive officer of BarChris. He was a member of the executive committee. He was familiar with all aspects of the business[. He] knew all the relevant facts. He could not have believed that there were no untrue statements or material omissions in the prospectus. Russo has no due diligence defenses.

Vitolo and Pugliese

They were the founders[.] Vitolo was president and Pugliese was vice president. Despite their titles, their [control] over BarChris's affairs [was far less] than Russo's. [They are] each men of limited education. It is not hard to believe that for them the prospectus was difficult reading, if indeed they read it at all. But [the] liability of a director who signs a registration statement does not depend upon whether or not he read it or, if he did, whether or not he understood what he was reading.

And in any case, Vitolo and Pugliese were not as naive as they claim to be. They were members of BarChris's executive committee[.] They must have known what was going on. Certainly they knew of the inadequacy of cash[.] They knew of their own large advances to the company which remained unpaid. They knew that they had agreed not to deposit their checks until the financing proceeds were received. They knew and intended that part of the proceeds were to be used to pay their own loans.

All in all, [their situation] is not significantly different . . . from Russo's. They could not have believed that the registration statement was wholly true and that no material facts had been omitted[.] They have not proved their due diligence defenses.

* * * * *

Trilling

[Trilling was . . . a CPA and former member of Peat Marwick. He was BarChris's] controller. He signed the registration statement in that capacity, although he was not a director[.]

Trilling may well have been unaware of several of the inaccuracies in the prospectus. But he must have known of some of them[.] I cannot find that Trilling believed the entire prospectus to be true.

But even if he did, he still did not establish his due diligence defenses. He . . . failed to prove, as to the [nonaudited] parts of the prospectus . . . , that he made a reasonable investigation which afforded him a reasonable ground to believe that it was true. As far as appears, he made no investigation[.] This would have been well enough but for the fact that he signed the registration statement. As a signer, he could not avoid responsibility[. He has not proved] his due diligence defenses.

Birnbaum

Birnbaum was a young lawyer [employed as in-house counsel. He was] secretary and a director[.] He signed the later amendments [to the registration statement], thereby becoming responsible for the accuracy of the prospectus[.]

. . . He did not participate in the management of the company. As house counsel, he attended to legal matters of a routine nature[.]

One of Birnbaum's more important duties . . . was to keep the corporate minutes[.] This necessarily informed him to a considerable extent about the company's affairs[.]

It seems probable that Birnbaum did not know of many of the inaccuracies in the prospectus. He must, however, have appreciated some of them. In any case, he made no investigation[. He] was entitled to rely upon Peat Marwick for the 1960 figures[.] But he was not entitled to rely upon [anyone else] for the other portions of the prospectus. As a lawyer, he should have known his obligations[.] Having failed to make such an investigation, he did not have reasonable ground to believe that all these statements were true. Birnbaum has not established his due diligence defenses except as to the audited 1960 figures.

Auslander

Auslander was an "outside" director[.] He was chairman . . . of Valley Stream National Bank. [He became a director shortly before the sale of the bonds. He signed the registration statement.]

. . . As to the [financial statements], Auslander knew that Peat Marwick had audited [them, so he] believed them to be correct[.] He had no reasonable ground to believe otherwise.

As to the [non-audited portions of the prospectus], however, Auslander is in a different position[. He] made no investigation of the accuracy of the prospectus. He relied on the assurance of Vitolo and Russo[.]

It is true that Auslander became a director on the eve of the financing. He had little opportunity to familiarize himself with the company's affairs[.]

Section 11 imposes liability . . . upon a director, no matter how new he is. He is presumed to know his responsibility when he becomes a director. He can escape liability only by using that reasonable care to investigate the facts which a prudent man would employ in the management of his own property. In my opinion, a prudent man would not act in an important matter . . . in sole reliance upon representations of persons who are comparative strangers[.] To say that such minimal conduct measures up to the statutory standard would, to all intents and purposes, absolve new directors from responsibility merely because they are new. This is not a sensible construction of Section 11[.]

Auslander has not established his due diligence defense [except as to the financial statements].

* * * * *

Grant

. . . [Grant's] law firm was counsel to BarChris in matters pertaining to the registration of securities. Grant drafted the registration statement[.] As the director most directly concerned with writing [it] and assuring its accuracy, more was required of him in the way of reasonable investigation than could fairly be expected of a director who had no connection with this work[.]

. . . I find that Grant honestly believed that the registration statement was true and that no material facts had been omitted from it.

In this belief he was mistaken, and the fact is that for all his work, he never discovered any of the errors or omissions which . . . could have been detected without an audit. The question is whether, despite his failure to detect them, Grant made a reasonable effort to that end.

. . . BarChris's affairs had changed for the worse[.] Grant never discovered this. He accepted the assurances of [others] that any change which might have occurred had been for the better[.]

It is claimed that a lawyer is entitled to rely on the statements of his client[.] This is too broad a generalization. It is all a matter of degree. To require an audit would obviously be unreasonable. On the other hand, to require a check of matters easily verifiable is not unreasonable. Even honest clients can make mistakes. The statute imposes liability for untrue statements regardless of whether they are intentionally untrue[.]

. . . Grant knew that minutes of certain meetings of the BarChris executive committee held in 1961 had not been written up[.] Grant did not insist that the minutes be written up, nor did he look at Kircher's notes[.]

. . . He knew that BarChris was short of cash, but he had no idea how short. He did not know that BarChris was withholding delivery of checks already drawn and signed because there was not enough money in the bank to pay them. He did not know that the officers of the company intended to use immediately approximately one-third of the financing proceeds in a manner not disclosed in the prospectus, including approximately $1,000,000 in paying old debts[.]

Grant was entitled to rely on Peat Marwick for the 1960 figures. [But as to the rest of the prospectus, Grant] was obliged to make a reasonable investigation. I am forced to find that he did not make one[.] Grant has not established his due diligence defenses except as to the audited 1960 figures.

* * * * *

Peat Marwick

. . . The part of the registration statement . . . made upon the authority of Peat Marwick as an expert was . . . the 1960 [audited financial statements]. But because the statute requires the court to determine Peat Marwick's belief, and the grounds thereof, "at the time . . . the registration statement became effective," . . . the matter must be viewed as of May 16, 1961[.]

The 1960 Audit

[The audit] was in general charge of a member of the firm, Cummings[.] Most of the actual work was performed by a senior accountant, Berardi, [who was about thirty]. He was not yet a C.P.A. He had no previous experience with the bowling industry. This was his first job as a senior accountant[.]

* * * * *

The S-1 Review

The purpose of reviewing events subsequent to the date of a certified balance sheet, [an S-1 review,] is to ascertain whether any material change has occurred in the company's financial position which should be disclosed in order to prevent the . . . figures from being misleading. The scope of such a review [is not] a complete audit.

Peat Marwick prepared a written program [which] conformed to generally accepted auditing standards[.]

Berardi made the S-1 review in May 1961. He devoted a little over two days to it[.] He did not discover any of the errors or omissions[.] The question is whether, despite his failure to find out anything, his investigation was reasonable within the meaning of the statute.

What Berardi did was to look at a . . . trial balance as of March 31, 1961[,] compare it with the audited December 31, 1960[,] figures, discuss with Trilling certain unfavorable developments[,] and read certain minutes. He did not examine any [other] "important financial records." . . .

In substance, what Berardi did is [he] asked questions, he got answers which he considered satisfactory, and he did nothing to verify them[.]

Berardi had no conception of how tight the cash position was. He did not discover that BarChris was holding up checks in substantial amounts because there was no money in the bank to cover them. He did not know of . . . the officers' loans. Since he never read the prospectus, he was not even aware that there had ever been any problem about loans from officers.

* * * * *

There had been a material change for the worse in BarChris's financial position. That change was sufficiently serious so that the failure to disclose it made the 1960 figures misleading. Berardi did not discover it. As far as results were concerned, his S-1 review was useless.

Accountants should not be held to a standard higher than that recognized in their profession. I do not do so here. Berardi's review did not come up to that standard. He did not take some of the steps which Peat Marwick's written program prescribed. He did not spend an adequate amount of time on a task of this magnitude. Most important of all, he was too easily satisfied with glib answers to his inquiries.

. . . [T]here were enough danger signals in the materials which he did examine to require some further investigation on his part. Generally accepted accounting standards required such further investigation under these circumstances. It is not always sufficient merely to ask questions.

Here again, the burden of proof is on Peat Marwick. I find that that burden has not been satisfied. I conclude that Peat Marwick has not established its due diligence defense.

Questions

1. *a.* Why were so many defendants not held responsible for the misleading audited financial statements?
    b. Which defendants were not successful raising the due diligence defense with respect to these financial statements? Why were they denied the defense?

2. Does being "new" make any difference in terms of directoral liability for a signed registration statement?

3. What would you do differently in the future if you were Peat Marwick?

False or Misleading Statements Post-Issuance—1934 Act

LO 9-10
Describe the fraud-on-the-market theory of reliance and explain its importance.

Section 18 of the 1934 Act, relating to false or misleading statements in any filing required to maintain the registration of a security, is similar to the 1933 Act's Section 11. However, the only defense offered by Section 18 is that the defendant acted in good faith, without knowledge of the false or misleading nature of the statement. Further, unlike Section 11, where reliance by the plaintiff on the false or misleading statements is presumed, under Section 18 the plaintiff must prove he or she relied on the statements.

Fraud

> Bernard Madoff was sentenced to 150 years in prison.

Under the 1933 Act's Section 17(a) and the 1934 Act's Section 10(b) and its related Rule 10b-5, it is illegal, in connection with the sale or purchase of any security, to employ any scheme or to engage in any practice that defrauds another person participating in the financial markets. These provisions intentionally cast a "broad net" and can reach such Ponzi schemes as the one run by Bernard Madoff, who in 2009 was sentenced to 150 years in prison for perpetrating a $50 billion fraud. In essence he promised very lucrative rates of return to investors, which returns were paid out of new funds collected from an ever-increasing pool of investors. When the economy turns down, such schemes collapse, revealing just how widespread the phenomenon is. More than 150 Ponzi schemes imploded in 2009, compared with about 40 in 2008.[161]

> Merrill Lynch settled a
> suit for $475 million.

Fraudulent acts can be committed by corporate wrongdoers as well. Making misleading statements about material facts or failing to state material facts in required SEC disclosure documents or in other company communications can be fraudulent, providing powerful grounds for damage suits by harmed investors. Large companies have paid substantial settlements in lawsuits arising from the 2008 financial collapse. For example, in 2009, Merrill Lynch paid $475 million to settle a suit with investors who alleged that it had understated its subprime debt exposure. In 2013, JPMorgan Chase agreed to pay $4.5 billion to settle charges that it misled investors in complicated deals involving pooled mortgages.[162]

Actual reliance on the issuer's material misstatement is an element of a Section 10(b) action. Bringing forward direct evidence of reliance on fraudulent statements can be difficult, so the ***fraud-on-the-market theory*** has evolved. It is the subject of the *Basic Inc.* case below.

LEGAL BRIEFCASE

Basic Inc. v. Levinson et al.
485 U.S. 224 (1988)

FACTS

Prior to December 20, 1978, Basic Inc. was a publicly traded company primarily engaged in the business of manufacturing related to the steel industry. As early as 1965, Combustion Engineering, a company in the same industry, expressed some interest in acquiring Basic, but was deterred from pursuing this inclination because of antitrust concerns. Beginning in 1976 Combustion had meetings with Basic concerning the possibility of a merger. During 1977 and 1978 Basic made three public statements denying merger negotiations. On December 19, 1978, Basic's board endorsed the merger.

Respondents were former Basic shareholders who had sold their stock after Basic's first public denial in 1977 but before the December 1978 announcement. They asserted that the defendants issued three false or misleading public statements in violation of Section 10(b) and of Rule 10b-5, and further that they were injured by selling Basic shares at artificially depressed prices in a market affected by petitioners' misleading statements and in reliance thereon.

Rule 10b-5 provides that it "shall be unlawful [t]o make any untrue statement of a material fact or to omit to state a material fact necessary . . . to make the statements made . . . not misleading . . . in connection with the purchase or sale of any security."

Justice Blackmun

* * * * *

. . . [T]o fulfill the materiality requirement "there must be a substantial likelihood that the disclosure of the omitted fact would have been viewed by the reasonable investor as having significantly altered the 'total mix' of information made available." . . .

* * * * *

We turn to the question of reliance and the fraud-on-the-market theory. Succinctly put:

> The fraud on the market theory is based on the hypothesis that, in an open and developed securities market, the price of a company's stock is determined by the available material information regarding the company and its business[.] Misleading statements will therefore defraud purchasers . . . even if [they] do not directly rely on the misstatements[.] The causal connection between the defendants' fraud and the plaintiffs' purchase . . . is no less significant than in a case of direct reliance on misrepresentations.

* * * * *

Reliance provides the requisite causal connection between a defendant's misrepresentation and a plaintiff's injury. There is, however, more than one way to demonstrate the causal connection[.]

The modern securities markets, literally involving millions of shares changing hands daily, differ from the face-to-face transactions contemplated by early fraud cases, and our understanding of Rule 10b-5's reliance requirement must encompass these differences.

With the presence of a market, the market is interposed between seller and buyer and, ideally, transmits information to the investor in the processed form of a market price. Thus the market is performing a substantial part of the valuation process performed by the investor in a face-to-face transaction. The market is acting as the unpaid agent of the investor, informing him that given all the information available to it, the value of the stock is worth the market price.

* * * * *

Presumptions typically serve to assist courts in managing circumstances in which direct proof . . . is rendered difficult. The courts below accepted a presumption, created by the fraud-on-the-market theory and subject to rebuttal by petitioners, that persons who had traded Basic shares had done so in reliance on the integrity of the price set by the market, but because of petitioners' material misrepresentations that price had been fraudulently depressed. Requiring a plaintiff to show . . . how he would have acted if omitted material information had been disclosed . . . or if the misrepresentation had not been made . . . would place an unnecessarily unrealistic evidentiary burden on the Rule 10b-5 plaintiff who has traded on an impersonal market.

. . . The presumption of reliance employed in this case is consistent with [the] congressional policy embodied in the 1934 Act. In drafting that Act, Congress expressly relied on the premise that securities markets are affected by information, and enacted legislation to facilitate an investor's reliance on the integrity of those markets[.]

. . . Recent empirical studies . . . confirm Congress' premise that the market price . . . on well-developed markets reflects all publicly available information, and, hence, any material misrepresentations[.] Because most publicly available information is reflected in market price, an investor's reliance on any public material misrepresentations, therefore, may be presumed for purposes of a Rule 10b-5 action.

* * * * *

Any showing that severs the link between the alleged misrepresentation and [the] decision to trade will be sufficient to rebut the presumption of reliance. For example, . . . if, despite petitioners' allegedly fraudulent attempt to manipulate market price, news of the merger discussions credibly entered the market and dissipated the effects of the misstatements, those who traded Basic shares after the corrective statements would have no direct or indirect connection with the fraud[.]

. . . It is not inappropriate to apply a presumption of reliance supported by the fraud-on-the-market theory. That presumption, however, is rebuttable.

[Remanded.]

Questions

1. When is an item of undisclosed information about a company "material" for Rule 10b-5 purposes?

2. Is reliance on a misrepresentation essential in a Rule 10b-5 action?

3. *a.* Why would it be difficult for a plaintiff to demonstrate actual reliance on a material omission?

   b. What solution did the courts create to deal with this problem?

AFTERWORD

As noted by the Court in *Basic Inc.*, investors who trade with knowledge of alleged misrepresentations will not be allowed to use the fraud-on-the-market theory. Those investors have not relied on the market price as an accurate reflection of all material information.[163] In its 2014 decision in *Halliburton v. Erica P. John Fund*,[164] the Supreme Court rejected the defendant's argument that the efficient-markets hypothesis on which Basics Inc. is grounded had been substantially discredited by the financial crisis and various studies. The Court noted that Basic Inc. recognized that markets are only imperfectly efficient and "based the presumption on the fairly modest premise that 'market professionals generally consider most publicly announced material statements about companies, [which] affect[s] stock . . . prices.'"[165]

Insider Trading

LO 9-11
Define insider trading and identify when it has occurred.

Classical *insider trading* occurs when an "insider" breaches a fiduciary duty to shareholders by buying or selling a security while in possession of material, nonpublic information. An *insider* is often a director, officer, or employee of an issuer, but also could be someone who only temporarily has a confidential relationship with an issuer, such as an accountant or attorney. The prohibition against trading on undisclosed inside information is based on Section 10(b), which prohibits the use of any manipulative or deceptive device in connection with the purchase or sale of a security.

In recent years prosecution of insider-trading violations has increased substantially. Publicized incidents have run from the intricate and clandestine to the inept and ridiculous:

- Billionaire Galleon Group hedge fund manager Raj Rajaratnam was convicted in 2011 of reaping $65 million in ill-gotten gains by tapping into contacts at top-tier American businesses to secure information not publicly known.[166]
- Former Goldman Sachs director Rajat Gupta was convicted in 2012 for leaking inside information to Rajaratnam.[167]
- In 2013, hedge fund SAC Capital Advisors pleaded guilty to criminal insider trading and agreed to pay a record $1.8 billion penalty. The founder, Steven Cohen, paid $135 million.[168]
- A partner at Ernst & Young developed a relationship with a woman he found through a website for those in search of extramarital affairs. She testified against him as part of a plea bargain and he was convicted of insider trading. In another case, a KPMG partner was convicted of giving a friend tips about the firm's clients. Despite claiming that he just wanted to help the friend through business difficulties, the former CPA took $60,000 in "gifts."[169]
- A respected business school professor, a popular lecturer at Wall Street firms, passed inside information to another business professor.[170]
- An executive secretary at Walt Disney and her boyfriend were charged with insider trading after sending 33 letters to investment firms offering to sell Disney's quarterly earnings reports before they were publicly released. An e-mail stated, "I was thinking $20,000 is a fair compensation but you are free to make an offer." Multiple firms receiving the offer reported it to the SEC.[171]
- In December 2016, Xu Xiang, the man dubbed the Carl Icahn of China, pleaded guilty to insider trading. He employed over 100 false accounts to conceal his activities.[172]

The *Texas Gulf Sulphur* case below expresses the rule for those possessing inside information—either disclose the information or refrain from trading until the information is public.

LEGAL BRIEFCASE — SEC v. Texas Gulf Sulphur Co.
401 F.2d 833 (2d Cir. 1968)

FACTS

In November 1963, TGS drilled a "discovery hole" in Canada that revealed possibly one of the largest ore strikes in history. Insiders began buying TGS stock at around $18. Further testing confirmed the magnitude of the strike. Rumors began to circulate. On April 12, 1964, when the stock had passed $30 and the best estimate was eight million tons, TGS issued a press release naysaying the rumors. On April 16 a Canadian mining journal story put the tonnage at 10 million. The same day a Canadian government official estimated it at 25 million and the stock passed $36. By May 15 it exceeded $58. The SEC brought an insider-trading suit.

Judge Waterman

* * * * *

[Rule 10b-5] is based . . . on the justifiable expectation . . . that all investors trading on impersonal exchanges have relatively equal access to material information[.] The essence of the Rule is that anyone who, trading for his own account, [has access] to information intended to be available only for a corporate purpose . . . may not take "advantage of such . . . knowing it is unavailable to those with whom he is dealing," i.e., the investing public. Insiders . . . are, of course[,] precluded from so unfairly dealing, but the Rule is also applicable to one possessing the information who may not be strictly termed an "insider." . . . [A]nyone in possession of material inside information must either disclose it to the investing public [or] abstain from trading in or recommending the securities [while it] remains undisclosed[.]

An insider's duty to disclose [or] abstain . . . arises only in "those situations . . . which are reasonably certain to have a substantial effect on the market price [if] disclosed." . . . [W]hether facts are material [will depend] upon a balancing of both the indicated probability that the event will occur and the anticipated magnitude of the event[. Here,] knowledge of the possibility, which surely was more than marginal, of the existence of a mine of the vast magnitude indicated by the remarkably rich drill core . . . would certainly have been an important fact to a reasonable . . . investor in deciding whether he should buy, sell, or hold[.] . . . [A] major factor in determining whether the . . . discovery was a material fact is the importance attached to the drilling results by those who knew about it. [T]he timing . . . of their stock purchases . . . virtually compels the inference that the insiders were influenced by the drilling results[.]

* * * * *

We hold, therefore, that all transactions in TGS stock . . . by individuals apprised of the drilling results . . . were made in violation of Rule 10b-5[.]

* * * * *

Coates, who placed orders . . . immediately after the official announcement . . . , [contends that his] purchases were not proscribed purchases for the news had already been . . . disclosed. We disagree. . . . The reading of [the announcement] . . . is merely the first step in the process of dissemination required for compliance with the regulatory objective of providing all investors with an equal opportunity to make informed investment judgments[. A]t the minimum Coates should have waited until the news could reasonably have been expected to appear over the media of widest circulation, the Dow Jones broad tape, rather than hastening to insure an advantage to himself[.]

Questions

1. If you possess undisclosed inside information, what are your options for trading in the company's stock?

2. How soon after disclosure can an insider trade in the stock?

AFTERWORD

As stated by the *Texas Gulf Sulphur* court, the rule prohibits persons who have access to information that was available to them only for a corporate purpose from trading in corporate securities with those who do not have that information. This is the *classical* theory of insider trading. Officers and employees, for example, have a fiduciary duty not to use their principal's—that is, their employer's—information for personal gain.

Tipping

The insider concept has been extended to include *tippees*. In some cases, the *tipper* (the insider or an "upstream" tippee) intends to improperly convey the inside information to a third party and hopes to derive personal benefit from so doing. In such a case, both the tipper and the tippee are liable. In other cases, the tippee is deemed to "misappropriate" the inside information from the inadvertent tipper, knowing that it was confidential. This would occur, for example, if a psychiatrist learned material inside information during a session with a senior corporate executive and traded on that information. Here, the tippee, but not the tipper, would be liable. In the *O'Hagan* case, below, the Supreme Court approved the *misappropriation theory*.

LEGAL BRIEFCASE

United States v. O'Hagan
521 U.S. 642 (1997)

FACTS

O'Hagan was a partner in a law firm. In July 1988 Grand Metropolitan retained the firm to represent it in a tender offer for Pillsbury stock. O'Hagan did no work on this matter. In August O'Hagan began purchasing Pillsbury stock and stock options. When the tender offer was announced, O'Hagan sold his options and stock, making a profit of $4.3 million. He used the profits to conceal his previous embezzlement of unrelated client trust funds.

The SEC investigated. O'Hagan was convicted of securities fraud. The Eighth Circuit reversed, rejecting liability under the "misappropriation theory." The Supreme Court granted certiorari.

Section 10(b) proscribes (1) using any deceptive device (2) in connection with the purchase or sale of securities. It does not confine its coverage to deception of a purchaser or seller; rather, it reaches any deceptive device used "in connection with the purchase or sale of any security."

Justice Ginsburg

* * * * *

Under the . . . "classical theory" of insider trading . . . , Section 10(b) and Rule 10b-5 are violated when [an] insider trades in the securities of his corporation on the basis of material, nonpublic information. Trading on such information qualifies as a "deceptive device" . . . because "a relationship of trust [exists] between the shareholders [and the] insiders who have obtained confidential information by reason of their position with [the] corporation." That relationship . . . "gives rise to a duty to disclose [or to abstain from trading.]" The classical theory applies not only to officers, directors, and other permanent insiders . . . , but also to attorneys, accountants, consultants, and others who temporarily become fiduciaries of a corporation.

The "misappropriation theory" holds that a person commits fraud "in connection with" a securities transaction . . . when he misappropriates confidential information for securities trading purposes, in breach of a duty owed to the source of the information. Under this theory, a fiduciary's undisclosed, self-serving use of a principal's information to purchase or sell securities, in breach of a duty of loyalty and confidentiality, defrauds the principal of the exclusive use of that information. In lieu of premising liability on a fiduciary relationship between company insider and purchaser or seller of the company's stock, the misappropriation theory premises liability on a fiduciary-turned-trader's deception of those who entrusted him with access to confidential information.

The two theories are complementary, each addressing efforts to capitalize on nonpublic information through the purchase or sale of securities[.]

In this case, the indictment alleged that O'Hagan, in breach of a duty of trust . . . he owed to his law firm . . . and to its client . . . , traded on the basis of nonpublic information regarding the client's tender offer[.] This conduct, the Government charged, constituted a fraudulent device in connection with the purchase and sale of securities[.]

We agree[.] We observe, first, that misappropriators . . . deal in deception. A fiduciary who "[pretends] loyalty to the principal while secretly converting the principal's information for personal gain" . . . defrauds the principal.

* * * * *

We turn next to the Section 10(b) requirement that the misappropriator's deceptive use of information be "in connection with the purchase or sale of [a] security." This element is satisfied because the fiduciary's fraud is consummated, not when the fiduciary gains the confidential information, but when, without disclosure to his principal, he uses the information to purchase or sell securities[.]

* * * * *

The misappropriation theory [is] well-tuned to an animating purpose of the [1934] Act: to insure honest securities markets and thereby promote investor confidence. Although informational disparity is inevitable in the securities markets, [an] investor's informational disadvantage vis-a-vis a misappropriator . . . stems from contrivance, not luck; it is a disadvantage that cannot be overcome with research or skill[.]

[Reversed and remanded.]

Questions

1. Are both insider-trading theories needed to fulfill the 1934 Act's desire to keep the markets "honest"?

2. Both insider-trading theories depend heavily on fiduciary relationships. Contrast the parties in the fiduciary relationships under the "classical" and "misappropriation" theories.

3. Would it have made any difference if O'Hagan had established with his broker, long before this trading, a portfolio diversification plan such that, pursuant to the plan, the identical trading would have occurred?

Does the tipper (the original insider or an upstream tippee) have to receive a personal benefit for liability to attach to the disclosure of confidential information? And if so, of what kind? The *Salman* case, below, considers this issue.

FACTS

Maher was a Citigroup investment banker with extensive access to sensitive client information. Maher's brother, Michael, kept pestering him for information he could use to trade while the public was unaware. Maher provided such information. Unknown to him, Michael was also passing the information to Salman, Michael's friend and Maher's brother-in-law, who reaped profits of $1.5 million. Salman knew the information came from Maher. He was convicted of insider trading and sentenced to 36 months in prison and $730,000 in restitution.

On appeal to the Ninth Circuit, Salman asserted that he could not be found guilty of insider trading because Maher had received no personal benefit in the form of "a pecuniary or similarly valuable nature," as was held necessary by the Second Circuit, interpreting *Dirks v. SEC*, 463 U.S. 646 (1983), in *United States v. Newman*, 773 F.3d 438 (2014), a decision rendered while the Ninth Circuit case was pending.

Justice Alito

Section 10(b) [and] Rule 10b–5 prohibit undisclosed trading on inside corporate information by individuals who are under a duty of trust and confidence that prohibits them from secretly using such information for their personal advantage. . . . [S]ee United States v. O'Hagan[.] . . .

These persons also may not tip inside information to others for trading. The tippee acquires the tipper's duty to disclose or abstain from trading if the tippee knows the information was disclosed in breach of the tipper's duty[.] In *Dirks* . . . this Court explained that a tippee's liability for trading on inside information hinges on whether the tipper breached a fiduciary duty by disclosing the information. A tipper breaches such a fiduciary duty . . . when the tipper discloses the inside information for a personal benefit. [A] jury can infer a personal benefit . . . where the tipper receives something of value in exchange for the tip or "makes a gift of confidential information to a trading relative or friend."

* * * * *

Pointing to *Newman*, Salman argued that his conviction should be reversed [by the Ninth Circuit because] there was no evidence that Maher received anything of "a pecuniary or similarly valuable nature" in exchange [for the information.] The Ninth Circuit disagreed[.] . . .

We granted certiorari to resolve the tension between the Second Circuit's *Newman* decision and the Ninth Circuit's decision in this case.

* * * * *

In *Dirks*, we explained that . . . "[t]he test . . . is whether the insider personally will benefit, directly or indirectly, from his disclosure." . . . In determining whether a tipper derived a personal benefit, we instructed courts to "focus on . . . whether the insider receives a direct or indirect personal benefit from the disclosure, such as a pecuniary gain or a reputational benefit that will translate into future earnings." This personal benefit can . . . be inferred [from facts and circumstances] such as "a relationship between the insider and the recipient that suggests a *quid pro quo* from the latter, or an intention to benefit the particular recipient." In particular, we held that [insider trading occurs] "*when an insider makes a gift of confidential information to a trading relative or friend*." In such cases, "[t]he tip and trade resemble trading by the insider followed by a gift of the profits to the recipient." . . .

. . . Maher would have breached his duty had he personally traded on the information [and] then given the proceeds as a gift to his brother. . . . But Maher . . . achieved the same result by disclosing the information to Michael, and allowing him to trade on it. . . .

To the extent the Second Circuit held that the tipper must . . . receive something of a "pecuniary or similarly valuable nature" in exchange for [the information, that] is inconsistent with *Dirks*.

* * * * *

[T]he Ninth Circuit's judgment is affirmed. . . .

Question

Identify a range of circumstances in which a tipper would be viewed as having received sufficient personal benefit to make the tippee liable for insider trading.

Short-Swing Profits

Closely related to insider trading is liability for ***short-swing profits***. An insider-trading case requires proof that the insider had material inside information and traded to exploit it. A short-swing profit case conclusively presumes that the insider had such information and did so unlawfully trade on it any time the insider engages in any purchase and sale, or sale and purchase, of an equity security of the insider's corporation if both transactions occur within a six-month period. The insider's actual motive is irrelevant.

Securities Law Enforcement Actions

> **short-swing profits**
> Any profits made by an insider through sale of company stock within six months of acquisition. Insider trading is conclusively presumed.

> The SEC brings civil securities actions; the Justice Department brings criminal actions.

Most of the securities law violations just discussed can be enforced against the violators by harmed private parties seeking damages and by the government seeking penalties. The SEC brings civil enforcement actions; the Justice Department brings criminal enforcement actions. All three suits can be brought against the same defendant for the same violation.

Private Enforcement

In civil damage cases, harmed plaintiffs typically join together in a class-action lawsuit (see Chapter 4). Since the 1990s, actions taken by Congress, and more recently decisions of the Supreme Court, have combined to make the bringing of, and prevailing in, such suits much more difficult. Some history may be illuminating.

As noted in Part One of this chapter, as a consequence of the savings and loan debacle of the 1980s, major accounting firms paid out over $1.6 billion in class-action damages. Responding to these payouts, accounting firms and others began intense lobbying to curtail such suits. Among other things, they argued that law firms specializing in plaintiffs' securities actions selected and groomed "professional plaintiffs" to bring damage suits in which the allegations of wrongdoing were primarily supported by a significant drop in the market price of the securities. Then after filing a complaint, it was argued, plaintiffs could proceed to discovery and undertake "fishing expeditions" until sufficient facts were accumulated to motivate defendants to settle rather than endure litigation.

Some evidence of long-standing systemic abuse by plaintiffs' lawyers was revealed in September 2007 when William Lerach, a former partner of the law firm of Milberg Weiss, pleaded guilty to conspiracy. The allegations were that he and other lawyers in the firm had paid illegal kickbacks to individuals to serve as named plaintiffs in securities actions. This often allowed the firm to be the first to file suit, which in turn resulted in Milberg Weiss more frequently representing the lead plaintiff in class-action cases. The firm would then receive a larger share of any legal fees awarded.[173] On April 2, 2008, Melyvn Weiss, the senior securities law partner at Milberg Weiss, pleaded guilty to similar charges. He was sentenced to 30 months in prison and fined $10 million.

The lobbying against runaway securities class-action suits paid off. In December 1995, Congress enacted the Private Securities Litigation Reform Act (1995 Act). The 1995 Act eliminated joint and several liability for accountants and underwriters whose deep pockets have historically attracted plaintiffs' lawyers. It also increased plaintiffs' procedural hurdles in bringing suit. No fraudulent conduct can be presumed from the simple fact that a security's price dropped precipitously. Plaintiffs in their complaints must state with particularity both the facts that constitute the alleged violation and the facts evidencing defendant's intention "to deceive, manipulate, or defraud."[174]

In early 2008, the Supreme Court reduced the exposure of some noncorporate defendants to claims of *aiding and abetting* securities fraud. In instances in which plaintiffs allege damage based on fraudulent representations by the corporation, third parties who may have aided the fraudulent conduct but whose deceptive acts were not communicated to the public are not liable to private plaintiffs.[175] As discussed below, only the government can bring such lawsuits. [For more on securities class-action lawsuits, see **http://securities.stanford.edu**].

Government Enforcement

The government can bring suits for aiding and abetting securities fraud against third parties. The Dodd–Frank Act expanded the government's reach in such cases to any third party who, knowingly or recklessly, substantially assists the primary wrongdoer.

Whereas private parties sue to recover damages suffered from the wrongdoing, the SEC enforces the law by imposing *civil* penalties up to $750,000 for individuals and $15 million for corporations, as well as forcing defendants to give up ill-gotten gains, called *disgorgement*. The SEC may impose a penalty of up to 300 percent of the profit gained or loss avoided by insider trading. In addition to imposing monetary penalties, the SEC can issue *cease-and-desist orders,* obtain *injunctions* against persons committing securities fraud, and prohibit violators in the future from serving as officers or directors of publicly traded companies. Since establishing its Center for Risk and Quantitative Analytics in 2013 to help identify and investigate misconduct, investigations have increased dramatically. Enforcement actions are expected to increase with the 2016 creation of a comprehensive database (the "consolidated audit trail") that monitors all U.S. securities transactions. It will be able to track up to 120 million trading events daily.[176]

The Department of Justice seeks *criminal* sanctions for *willful* (knowing and deliberate) violations of the 1933 and 1934 Acts, with fines of up to $25 million and imprisonment for up to 20 years. As with criminal statutes in general, the principal problem for prosecutors is convincing a jury of the defendants' guilt beyond a reasonable doubt. As a result, civil penalties are often substituted for criminal prosecutions.

For decades the SEC has permitted parties to settle without admitting guilt. In June 2013, Chair Mary Jo White announced that those committing serious securities law violations would now be required to admit culpability as a prerequisite to settlement. JPMorgan Chase was among the first to confront this policy when, in September 2013, it was forced to admit that it had violated the securities laws by permitting an "'egregious' breakdown" in control and governance.[177]

The SEC instituted a whistle-blower program in 2011. In 2016, 4,218 tips were submitted, a 40 percent increase over the first year. Thirty-seven whistle-blowers have so far received awards totaling $136 million for helping the SEC impose $900 million in financial sanctions against companies violating the securities laws. A study released in 2016 showed a significant reduction in the tendency to engage in accounting fraud or abusive tax avoidance by firms that had been the subject of a whistle-blower complaint.

> A senator demanded a list of federal agency managers who retaliated against whistle-blowers.

Unfortunately, whistle-blowers often suffer after coming forward, experiencing employer retaliation and being ostracized by their industry. The SEC is increasingly enforcing a rule that prohibits any company from taking "any action to impede an individual from communicating directly with the Commission staff about a possible securities law violation, including . . . a confidentiality agreement[.]" In 2016, Bank of America paid a $415 million fine related to charges that included imposing such confidentiality provisions. As of this writing, the most recent case involved SandRidge Energy Inc., which agreed to pay $1.4 million to settle charges that it engaged in similar behavior. The lack of whistle-blower protection extends to the U.S. government itself. In December 2016, Senator Claire McCaskill demanded a list of federal agency senior managers who retaliated against whistle-blowing employees. Of particular concern were seven substantiated retaliation cases against Transportation Security Administration employees who disclosed senior management failings or misconduct.[178] [For more on the SEC's whistle-blower program, see **https://www.sec.gov/whistleblower**].

Tender Offers

LO 9-12

Describe the tender offer process and some defenses against it.

There are several ways to acquire control of a corporation. Where mergers or direct acquisitions fail, a **tender offer** (also called a *takeover*) can be attempted. Alternatively, the person seeking to acquire control can mount a **proxy fight**, as discussed in Part Two of this chapter, by nominating an alternative slate of directors and then soliciting shareholders for their annual proxies in preference to returning proxies to current management.

In a tender offer, the offeror announces to the public that it wishes to acquire a specific number of shares (typically the number needed to gain control). It identifies where stockholders who want to participate must tender (that is, deliver) their shares. It also specifies the opening bid price. If fewer than the desired number of shares are tendered, the tender offeror can either walk away or increase the offering price. Every tendering shareholder receives the highest price if the offer is successful. The shares are returned if the offer fails.

When faced with a tender offer, the target corporation's management realizes that a successful offer will likely result in its dismissal because the offeror will want to put its own management in place. Often the target's management will not be eager to leave. It will resist, which accounts for the term **hostile takeover**. Management has a problem, however, because it has a duty to act exclusively in the shareholders' best interests and the tender offer may well be in their best interests. To avoid liability, management will generally try to style its resistance as "safeguarding the stockholders."

Management can resist in various ways. It could launch its own tender offer (that is, *go private*). Or it could start using corporate cash to buy back shares in the market, driving up the price to discourage the tender offeror. Here management has to worry that it could be sanctioned for violating Section 9 of the 1934 Act, which prohibits price manipulation. However, there is a safe harbor: each day management is permitted to purchase up to 25 percent of the security's average daily trading volume.

Another resistance tactic is **greenmail**, in which the target's management uses corporate cash to buy the tender offeror's current stake at a significant premium to ensure the latter "goes away." Changes in the federal tax law have discouraged this technique.

Management sometimes puts takeover defenses in place by arranging "disasters" if a tender offer is attempted. Two notorious tactics are the crown jewel and poison pill defenses. In general, the **crown jewel defense** involves the target company selling its most attractive assets (its "crown jewels"). Management arranges for a friendly third party to purchase them at a reasonable price should a tender offer be launched, thus making the target less appealing to the hostile bidder. At the same time, management is protected because the third party will continue to make these assets available on "friendly" terms should the tender offer fail. The ***poison pill defense*** takes a variety of forms. One strategy gives current shareholders a tender offer–triggered right to buy additional stock at a discount, thus diluting the hostile bidder's shares. The trigger is commonly the acquisition by the bidder of 10 to 15 percent of the outstanding common stock.

If all else fails, the target's senior management may find comfort in the ***golden parachutes*** (generous severance pay packages) they may have negotiated to protect themselves in the event of a successful takeover bid. The Dodd–Frank Act now requires a shareholder vote on such arrangements.

State Securities Regulation

After the enactment of the 1933 Act, the United States operated under a dual regulatory environment for securities. Both the state and federal governments were entitled to regulate the issuance of new securities and their subsequent purchases and sales. In 1996, the lack of regulatory uniformity among the states led Congress to enact the *National Securities Markets Improvement Act*, preempting state registration requirements for securities traded on national markets. Then, in 1998, Congress mandated that securities fraud claims related to national-market securities be litigated only in federal court applying only federal law. As a result, state securities regulation, known as ***blue sky laws***, now has only a shadow of its former significance, being primarily applicable only to intrastate offerings. [For more on state securities regulation, see **www.nasaa.org/about-us/our-role**].

International Securities Regulation

Critics claim the United States is losing its place as the world's leading financial center, citing such evidence as the percentage of large IPOs being listed outside the United States. Aggressive regulation in America is often blamed for driving those IPOs abroad.

American securities regulation is the world's strongest, but whether that will continue to be true and whether it is responsible for the growth in foreign securities markets is not clear. Other factors undoubtedly contribute to the shift, such as the natural maturation of international markets, the speed of overall economic growth elsewhere in the world, and the concomitant rise in wealth, especially in Europe and Asia.[179] "Because companies want to list in the fastest-rising markets, many are staying in their home countries, which have often outperformed the United States in recent years."[180] Stringent regulation in the United States is not necessarily a net disincentive for securities registration. Foreign securities with dual listings in the United States and elsewhere appear to enjoy an advantage in the price they command.[181] Finally, as the securities markets in other countries mature, their regulation often models U.S. policies.

> Nothing equivalent to the SEC exists in Europe.

Nothing equivalent to the SEC exists in Europe. In the wake of the 2008 financial crisis, however, the European Union may be moving closer to such a body. In 2010, the EU finance ministers endorsed the creation of a supervisory structure for European securities markets, the European Securities and Markets Authority (ESMA). It began its work on January 1, 2011. One role it may eventually be called to play is the regulation of audit firms.[182] [For more on ESMA, see **www.esma.europa.eu**; for more on international securities regulation generally, see **www.iosco.org/about**].

Questions—Part Three

1. What is meant by going public? By going private?
2. Contrast instrastate and interstate offerings.
3. What is a security?
4. *a.* What information is contained in a registration statement under the 1933 Act?

   b. What role in the registration process is played by the prospectus?

   c. Describe the three primary financial statements. Why are they audited?
5. Explain the general purposes of the Securities Act of 1933 and the Securities Exchange Act of 1934.
6. Contrast exempt securities and exempt transactions.
7. Describe the recent developments in securities crowdfunding.
8. What is meant by "Regulation A+"? Why might it be of more significance than securities crowdfunding?
9. What triggers liability under Section 11 of the 1933 Act? Can an opinion result in a violation?
10. What is the primary defense in a Section 11 action? Contrast the defense's requirements as between a director, officer, or employee versus an outside expert like an accountant, lawyer, or appraiser.
11. *a.* Under Rule 10b-5, is investor reliance on the issuer's misrepresentation required?

    b. Why was the fraud-on-the-market theory developed?

    c. What is the importance of *Halliburton v. Erica P. John Fund*?
12. Assume a midlevel manager learns that his corporation is on the verge of bankruptcy because of about-to-be-publicly disclosed improprieties. He calls his lawyer to ask about his personal exposure. After advising him, the lawyer immediately sells all of her holdings in that stock. Later that day, the news breaks and the stock price tumbles 60 percent. Does anyone have insider trading liability? If so, in what amount?
13. If a corporate officer knowingly omits material adverse information from a corporate communication, by whom might he or she be sued?

Internet Exercise	Using the Frequently Asked Questions segment of **www.securitieslaw.com** answer the following questions:

1. What duties are owed by stockbrokers and brokerage firms to customers?
2. How does a customer know when he or she has been defrauded?

147. SEC Regulation CF, 80 Fed. Reg. 71388 (Nov. 16, 2015) (amending C.F.R. Parts 200, 227, 232, 239, 240, 249, 269, and 274); Yin Wilczek, "High Costs of SEC Approach Would Stymie Successive Crowdfunding, Commentators Warn," *Bloomberg Law*, February 7, 2014 [**http:// about.bloomberglaw.com/law-reports/high-costs-of-sec-approach-would-stymie-success- of-crowdfunding-commenters-warn**].

148. Clark, "State Lawmakers Are Getting on the Crowdfunding Bandwagon."

149. "Raising Capital Using a Regulation A+ Mini-IPO," SeedInvest [**www.seedinvest.com/blog/ jobs-act/raising-capital-reg-a-mini-ipo**].

150. "Regulation A+: Not Everyone Can Invest in Your Startup," *Forbes*, June 19, 2015.

151. Kiran Lingam, "The Reg A+ Bombshell: $50M Unaccredited Equity Crowdfunding Title IV Takes Center Stage," *Crowdfund Insider*, March 25, 2015 [**https://crowdfundingtimes.word- press.com/2015/03/26/the-reg-a-bombshell-50m-unaccredited-equity-crowdfunding-title- iv-takes-center-stage**].

152. "Raising Capital Using a Regulation A+ Mini-IPO."

153. Ruth Simon, "Few Small Businesses Take Advantage of Mini-IPOs," *The Wall Street Journal*, July 6, 2016.

154. "Small Business and the SEC," U.S. Securities and Exchange Commission [**www.sec.gov/info/ smallbus/qasbsec.htm**].

155. These forms can be found at **www.sec.gov/about/forms/form10-k.pdf**, **www.sec.gov/about/ forms/form10-q.pdf**, and **www.sec.gov/about/forms/form8-k.pdf**.

156. Jessica Holzer and Greg Bensinger, "SEC Embraces Social Media," *The Wall Street Journal*, April 2, 2013.

157. "Fast Answers: Trading Suspensions," U.S. Securities and Exchange Commission, June 7, 2011 [**www.sec.gov/answers/tradingsuspension.htm**].

158. *Department of Enforcement v. Hennion & Walsh, Inc.*, Disciplinary Proceeding No. C9B040013 (NASD January 10, 2005) [**www.finra.org/sites/default/files/OHODecision/ p013658.pdf**].

159. Jaime Holguin, "The Return of the Day Trader," *CBS Evening News*, September 30, 2002 [**www.cbsnews.com/stories/2002/09/30/eveningnews/main523766.shtml**].

160. "Day Trading: Your Dollars at Risk," U.S. Securities and Exchange Commission, April 20, 2005 [**www.sec.gov/investor/pubs/daytips.htm**].

161. Associated Press, "Meltdown Left Ponzi Schemes in Ashes," *The Des Moines Register*, December 29, 2009.

162. Dan Campbell, "Wells Fargo to Pay $85M Fine," *Star Tribune*, July 20, 2011; and Dan Fitzpat- rick and Julie Steinberg, "J.P. Morgan Reaches $4.5 Billion Settlement with Investors," *The Wall Street Journal*, November 15, 2013.

163. *Stark Trading v. Falconbridge Ltd.*, 552 F.3d 358 (7th Cir. 2009).

164. 134 S. Ct. 2398 (2014).

165. *Id.* at 2410.

166. Michael Rothfeld and Chad Bray, "Galleon Founder Convicted on All Counts in Insider- Trading Trial," *The Wall Street Journal*, May 11, 2011.

167. Peter Lattman, "Ex-Goldman Director to Serve Two Years in Prison on Insider Trading Case," *The New York Times*, October 24, 2012.

168. Michael Rothfeld, "SAC Agrees to Plead Guilty in Insider-Trading Settlement," *The Wall Street Journal*, November 4, 2013; and Rob Copeland, "Steven Cohen, SAC Reach $135 Million Insider-Trading Settlement," *The Wall Street Journal*, November 30, 2016.

169. "Insider Affair: An SEC Trial of the Heart," *The Wall Street Journal*, July 29, 2009; and Tamara Audi, "Former KPMG Partner Scott London Gets 14 Months for Insider Trading," *The Wall Street Journal*, April 24, 2014.

170. Louise Story, "Charges of Insider Trading for a Wall Street Luminary," *The New York Times*, May 30, 2008.

171. Ethan Smith, "Disney Drama as Stock Plot Is Foiled," *The Wall Street Journal*, May 27, 2010.

172. Keith Bradsher, "Top Chinese Financier Pleads Guilty to Insider Trading," *The New York Times*, December 6, 2016.

173. Barry Meier, "Lawyer Pleads Guilty in Kickback Case," *The New York Times*, September 19, 2007.

174. *Tellabs, Inc. v. Makor Issues & Rights, Ltd.*, 127 S. Ct. 2499 (2007).

175. *Stoneridge Investment Partners LLC v. Scientific-Atlanta, Inc.*, 128 S. Ct. 761 (2008).

176. Rebekah Mintzer, "Big Data and Analytics Use 'Transformative' for SEC, White Says," *Corporate Counsel*, November 23, 2016 [**www.corpcounsel.com/resources/id=1202773189270/ Big-Data-and-Analytics-Use-Transformative-for-SEC-White-Says?mcode=12026191583 80&curindex=1&slreturn=20161122181059**].

177. Jean Eaglesham, "A Historic Admission from J. P. Morgan," *The Wall Street Journal*, September 19, 2013.

178. Andrew Ackerman, "Regulators Rap Firms Using Severance to Silence Whistleblowers," *The Wall Street Journal*, December 20, 2016; Gretchen Morgenson, "Whistle-Blowers Spur Companies to Change Their Ways," *The New York Times*, December 16, 2016; and Ron Nixon, "Senator Looks to Expand Protections for Whistle-Blowers," *The New York Times*, December 22, 2016.

179. Edgar Ortega and Elizabeth Hester, "IPO Fees in Europe Catch Wall Street for First Time Since WWII," *Bloomberg*, May 29, 2007.

180. Walter Hamilton, "Stock Rules Irk NYC as Wall Street Parties On," *The Los Angeles Times*, April 23, 2007.

181. John C. Coffee, "Law and the Market: The Impact of Enforcement," *Columbia Law and Economics Working Paper No. 304*, March 7, 2007 [**http://ssrn.com/abstract=967482**].

182. Stephen Fidler, "Plans Grow for European Audit Cop," *The Wall Street Journal*, October 12, 2010.

Video icon credit: ©Comstock Images/Alamy

CHAPTER TEN

Antitrust Law—Restraints of Trade

After completing this chapter, students will be able to fulfill the following learning objectives:

10-1. Recognize the primary goals of antitrust law.

10-2. Describe the key antitrust statutes.

10-3. Explain the meaning of "horizontal restraints of trade."

10-4. Analyze when an unlawful price-fixing arrangement has been created.

10-5. Identify a group boycott.

10-6. Define resale price maintenance.

10-7. Explain the requirements for establishing an unlawful tying arrangement.

10-8. Describe the commercial advantages and disadvantages of exclusive dealing.

10-9. Contrast price discrimination and predatory pricing.

10-10. Explain how predatory pricing may be proven.

Antitrust is a word that is only dimly recognizable to most of us, but antitrust law touches all corners of our lives and significantly shapes our economic and social practices, reaching even collegiate athletics, as described below.

Ed O'Bannon, former UCLA and NBA basketball star, led a group of current and former Division I college football (FBS) and men's basketball players seeking a share of National Collegiate Athletic Association (NCAA) income from television broadcasts as well as royalties from use of the players' names, images, and likenesses. O'Bannon and the other plaintiffs in 2009 alleged that the NCAA and its member schools violated the federal Sherman Act, an antitrust statute that forbids unreasonable restraints of trade (explained below). The plaintiffs partially prevailed when a federal district court and a panel of the federal 9th Circuit Court of Appeals ruled that NCAA limits on *education-related* scholarship payouts constituted a restraint of trade, but the 9th Circuit panel also ruled that colleges need not pay athletes cash sums beyond actual educational expenses. In that 2015 ruling, the 9th Circuit embraced, to some degree, the NCAA view that preservation of amateurism is an important goal and one that requires limits on athletic scholarships. The U.S. Supreme Court in 2016 declined to review the case, but at least one other significant challenge to NCAA amateurism rules is currently pending in the courts.

Questions

1. Are O'Bannon and other present and former NCAA athletes being unfairly denied a bigger share of the income they help generate in order to preserve amateurism? Explain.

2. Should college athletes be free to "sell" their services to the highest bidder among America's colleges and universities? Explain.

3. Joseph Agnew and Patrick Courtney earned college football scholarships but were injured early in their college careers. Consistent with NCAA rules, both players had received one-year scholarships with the possibility of renewal. Neither Agnew nor Courtney received scholarship renewals following their injuries. Both players sued the NCAA claiming its rules forbidding multiyear scholarships and imposing caps on the number of scholarships given per team prevented them from securing scholarships that would have covered their full college experience.

   a. Explain why the two plaintiffs thought they had been wronged by the NCAA rules.

   b. Do you agree with the two plaintiffs? Explain. See *Agnew v. National Collegiate Athletic Association*, 683 F.3d 328 (7th Cir. 2012).

Source: *O'Bannon v. National Collegiate Athletic Association*, 802 F.3d 1049 (9th Cir. 2015), cert. denied, 137 S. Ct. 277 (2016).

Part One—The Foundations of Antitrust Law

Antitrust—Early Goals

LO 10-1
Recognize the primary goals of antitrust law.

Antitrust, perhaps more than any other branch of the law, is a product of changing political and economic tides. Historically, antitrust law sought to allow every American, at least in theory, the opportunity to reach the top. More specifically, antitrust advocates were concerned about the following issues:

1. **The preservation of competition.** Antitrust law was designed to provide free, open markets resulting in enhanced efficiency and increased consumer welfare. The belief was (and generally continues to be) that competition would generate the best products and services at the lowest possible prices.

2. **The preservation of democracy.** Many businesses in competition meant that none of them could corner economic, political, or social power.

3. **The preservation of small businesses, or, more generally, the preservation of the American Dream.** Antitrust was designed to preserve the opportunity for ordinary Americans to compete with the giants.

4. **An expression of political radicalism.** At least for a segment of society, antitrust laws were meant to be tools for reshaping America to meet the needs of all people, thus counteracting, to some degree, the power of big business. [For professors' analyses of recent antitrust developments, see **http://lawprofessors.typepad.com/antitrustprof_blog**].

Antitrust: Increase Government Intervention?

As we discussed in Chapters 1 to 3, critics argue that big business has too much authority in American life. That concentration of power, they claim, has led to dramatic income and wealth inequality and reduced upward economic mobility while generating higher consumer prices, barriers to new competition, and even distortion of the democratic process. If the critics are correct, what can be done? In Chapter 1 we thought about the power of the free market to correct itself and in Chapters 2 and 3, we looked at ethics and social responsibility as preventatives and remedies for corporate abuse. Then, in Chapter 8, we suggested the importance of government intervention in correcting market failure, one form of which is monopoly conduct. Antitrust law, as we will examine in this chapter and in Chapter 11, is the government's primary tool for addressing monopoly market failure and thus assuring the benefits of a competitive economy.

Interest in antitrust seems to be climbing. Respected commentators, legislators, and other experts are questioning whether the federal government needs to be more aggressive in enforcing the antitrust laws. They are particularly troubled by the seemingly relentless consolidation that has led to dominance in most lines of commerce by only a few firms, a subject we address in Chapter 11. Journalist Harold Meyerson, for example, suggested that a "new trust-busting movement" might be necessary.[1] The respected British magazine *The Economist* said: "America needs a giant dose of competition,"[2] and economist/journalist Robert Samuelson questioned whether we have a "competition deficit."[3]

Campaigning in 2008 for his first term, Democrat Barack Obama promised to "reinvigorate antitrust enforcement," following what critics considered a rather passive antitrust policy during Republican George W. Bush's presidency. Obama's goal was realized to some extent: The Antitrust Division of the U.S. Department of Justice imposed a record $3.6 billion in criminal fines and penalties during fiscal year 2015.[4] In 2016, President Obama issued an executive order instructing all executive agencies to develop systems to detect and report anticompetitive behaviors such as price-fixing, and the Justice Department announced a policy shift toward strengthened detection and prosecution of individuals involved in antitrust wrongs. So we have seen some enhanced antitrust attention (often the case with Democratic administrations), but critics remain unsatisfied. They maintain that American welfare hinges, in part, on meaningful antitrust enforcement. At this writing, President Trump's antitrust enforcement stance is unclear.

Antitrust Enforcement and Statutes

LO 10-2

Describe the key antitrust statutes.

The Justice Department and the Federal Trade Commission, the federal agencies responsible for antitrust enforcement, bring relatively few antitrust actions, but a government victory sends a powerful message to the business community about the risks of anticompetitive behavior. The government prefers to avoid litigation, and most cases are settled before going to court. Furthermore, the Justice Department practices leniency, sometimes allowing cooperative defendants to avoid criminal prosecution.

> A government victory sends a powerful message to the business community.

Private parties also may sue under the antitrust laws. However, segments of the economy that are already closely regulated by the government, such as the securities industry, can sometimes successfully claim they are immune from the antitrust laws. [For the Justice Department Antitrust Division, see **www.usdoj.gov/atr**].

Sherman Antitrust Act, 1890

Section 1 of the Sherman Antitrust Act (Sherman Act) forbids restraints of trade, and Section 2 forbids monopolization, attempts to monopolize, and conspiracies to monopolize. Two types of enforcement options are available to the federal government:

1. **Violation of the Sherman Act opens participants to criminal penalties.** The maximum corporate fine is $100 million per violation, while individuals may be fined as much as $1 million and/or imprisoned for up to 10 years.
2. **Injunctive relief is provided under civil law.** The government or a private party may secure a court order preventing continuing violations of the act and affording appropriate relief (such as dissolution or divestiture). Those harmed by a violation of the Sherman Act also may bring a civil action seeking three times the actual damages sustained (treble damages).

Clayton Act, 1914

The Clayton Act forbids price discrimination, exclusive dealing, tying arrangements, requirements contracts, mergers restraining commerce or tending to create a monopoly, and interlocking directorates. Civil enforcement of the Clayton Act is similar to that of the Sherman Act: injured parties may sue for injunctive relief and treble damages. In general, criminal law remedies are not available under the Clayton Act. [For links to antitrust sites worldwide, see **www.justice.gov/atr/contact/otheratr.html**].

Federal Trade Commission Act

The Federal Trade Commission Act created the Federal Trade Commission (FTC), a powerful, independent agency designed to devote its full attention to the elimination of anticompetitive practices in American commerce. The FTC proceeds under the Sherman Act, the Clayton Act, and Section 5 of the FTC Act itself, which declares that "unfair methods of competition" and "unfair or deceptive acts or practices in or affecting commerce" are unlawful. The FTC's primary enforcement device is the cease and desist order, but it also may impose fines. [For the FTC Guide to Antitrust Laws, see **www.ftc.gov/bc/antitrust/index.shtm**].

Federal Antitrust Law and Other Regulatory Systems

State Law

Most states, through legislation and judicial decisions, have developed their own antitrust laws. Some states have recently become more attentive to antitrust enforcement, as illustrated by their resistance to the U.S. Supreme Court's controversial *Leegin* decision set out later in this chapter.

Patents, Copyrights, and Trademarks

Each of these devices offers limited, government-granted, government-shielded market strength, thus serving to protect and encourage commercial creativity and product development. The patent, copyright, or trademark holder is held to the terms of its government-granted privilege, restricting the privilege from growing into an unlawful monopoly.

Law of Other Nations

Chapter 11 introduces the practical and ideological significance of international antitrust issues in this era of globalization. [For an antitrust database, see **www.antitrustinstitute.org**].

Part Two—Horizontal Restraints

LO 10-3

Explain the meaning of "horizontal restraints of trade."

When competitors collude, conspire, or agree among themselves in ways that unreasonably harm competition, they are engaging in an unlawful *horizontal restraint of trade*. Instead of competing to drive prices down and quality up, competitors may be fixing prices, restricting output, dividing territories, and the like. Horizontal restraints are governed by Section 1 of the Sherman Act, which forbids contracts, combinations, or conspiracies in *restraint of trade*.

Rule of Reason   In the 1911 *Standard Oil*[5] decision, the U.S. Supreme Court articulated the *rule of reason*, which essentially provides that the Sherman Act forbids only *unreasonable* restraints of trade. After proof of the defendants' agreement or conspiracy that has caused anticompetitive effects, the courts would then balance the pro- and anticompetitive effects of that restraint of trade to determine whether it unreasonably harms competition.

Per Se   Some antitrust violations, such as horizontal price-fixing, are so injurious to competition that their mere existence ordinarily constitutes unlawful conduct. Plaintiffs must prove that the violation in question occurred, but they need not prove that the violation caused, or is likely to cause, competitive harm. These *per se* violations are simply unlawful on their face. We turn now to an examination of specific categories of horizontal restraints of trade.

Horizontal Territorial and Customer Restraints

Principal Legislation: Sherman Act, Section 1

> Sherman Act, Section 1. Every contract, combination in the form of trust or otherwise, or conspiracy, in restraint of trade or commerce, among the several states, or with foreign nations, is declared to be illegal. . . .

Assume two big companies dominate the wholesale food market in their small state. Could they lawfully agree between themselves to divide their state geographically with one supplying the eastern half while the other supplies only the western half? Or could they lawfully allocate their customers such that, for example, one supplies all small-town grocers while the other restricts itself to grocers in the few major cities? Suppliers might want to eliminate that competition among themselves, but such arrangements ordinarily are *per se* violations of the Sherman Act because they attempt to nullify the powerful benefits of competition. [For an antitrust overview, see **http://topics.law.cornell.edu/wex/antitrust**].

Horizontal Price-Fixing

LO 10-4

Analyze when an unlawful price-fixing arrangement has been created.

Principal Legislation: Sherman Act, Section 1

Competitors cannot lawfully agree on prices. That principle is simple and fundamental to an efficient, fair marketplace. Establishing the presence of an unlawful price-fixing arrangement, on the other hand, ordinarily is anything but simple.

Proof

Proof of a contract, combination, or conspiracy is a threshold requirement for proving price-fixing and all other Sherman Act Section 1 violations. Evidence of collusion arises in a variety of ways. For example, LaQuinta Inns entered an agreement in 2010 with the Connecticut Attorney General to stop its "call around" practice. Reportedly, motel managers identified their primary local competition and called them frequently to give and receive information about occupancy rates and room charges, a practice that is widespread in the motel industry. The concern is that the frequent exchange of information, in effect, constitutes collusion to fix prices among the competitors. LaQuinta agreed to desist from its call-around practices throughout the United States.[6] Broadly, a showing of cooperative action amounting to an agreement may be developed by any of the following four methods of proof:

1. **Agreement with direct evidence.** In the easiest case, the government/plaintiff can produce direct evidence such as writings or testimony from participants proving the existence of collusion.
2. **Agreement without direct evidence.** Here, the defendants have directly but covertly agreed, so circumstantial evidence such as company behavior must be used to draw an inference of collusion.
3. **Agreement based on a tacit understanding.** In this situation, no direct exchange of assurances has occurred, but the parties employ tactics that act as surrogates for direct assurances and thus "tell" each other that they are, in fact, in agreement.
4. **Agreement based on mutual observation.** These defendants have simply observed each others' pricing behavior over time; therefore, they are able to anticipate each others' future conduct and act accordingly without any direct collusion but with results similar to those that would have followed from a direct agreement.[7]

Poaching Employees

"If you hire a single one of these people that means war." According to court records, that was the response of Apple founder Steve Jobs (now deceased) when in 2005 Google wanted to hire some Apple engineers. In 2015, a federal court in California approved a $415 million settlement of an antitrust class action claiming several Silicon Valley tech firms, including Apple and Google, had conspired to suppress job opportunities and wages by, among other practices, agreeing not to "poach" each other's employees. Similarly, eBay agreed in 2014 to settle Justice Department charges that it violated antitrust law by agreeing with Intuit to refrain from recruiting each other's employees. At this writing, baseball scouts and a Duke University radiology professor have filed lawsuits claiming they too are victims of anticompetitive agreements between their employers and their employers' competitors that reduce employment mobility and artificially constrain wages.

Questions

1. Why might high-tech companies be particularly concerned about employee poaching?
2. What antitrust claims might be raised against a high-tech company that poaches employees?
3. What damages would the plaintiffs in these claims allege?

Sources: John F. Allgood, "Federal Court Approves $415 Million Settlement of Employee Antitrust Claims Against California Technology Employers," *LEXOLOGY,* September 4, 2015 [**www.lexology.com**]; "U.S. Judge Approves DOJ Settlement with eBay over Tech Hiring," *Reuters,* September 2, 2014 [**www.reuters.com**]; and Mark C. Katz, "Competition Law Considerations for H.R. Professionals," *LEXOLOGY,* March 23, 2016 [**www.lexology.com**].

Parallel Conduct

An unlawful conspiracy is distinct from independent but parallel business behavior by competitors. So-called *conscious parallelism* is fully lawful because the competitors have not agreed either explicitly or implicitly to follow the same course of action. Rather, their business judgment has led each to independently follow parallel paths. On the other hand, a conspiracy can sometimes be established by proof that the parallel behavior in question was not arrived at independently, but rather was the product of a preceding agreement, either explicit or tacit.[8]

Aggressive Enforcement

Both government intervention advocates and free-market champions agree that price-fixing cripples the market. Therefore, government intervention, at the federal and state levels, and damage claims by wronged consumers are sometimes essential to maintain effective competition. Antitrust law, including price-fixing prohibitions, is designed to protect the consumer from a variety of commercial arrangements—some well-intentioned, some meant as a way to cheat—that nullify the favorable effects of competition. Consider some prominent examples that follow.

- Visa, MasterCard, and their associated banks (including, e.g., Bank of America and JPMorgan Chase) are accused of engaging in a price-fixing cartel to set arbitrarily high interchange or "swipe" fees that merchants pay to card-issuing banks and credit card companies for processing card transactions. (American Express and Discover were not involved in this lawsuit.) The parties settled for $7.25 billion, but in 2016 a federal appeals court overturned the settlement. Further negotiations are expected.

- The federal Justice Department reportedly is investigating whether America's big airlines have been colluding to keep airfares high by, among other practices, limiting the number of routes and the number of affordable seats. Critics accuse airlines of "signaling" to each other to restrain capacity and keep prices high. Air executives reportedly emphasized the importance of "capacity discipline" at their 2015 International Air Transport Association meeting. The airlines, on the other hand, point to many flying options for consumers, and some experts say climbing ticket prices, fewer flights, and denser seating are simply a function of the mergers in the industry that have reduced industry leaders from nine to four. (Those mergers were approved by the Justice Department.)[9]

- Price-fixing behavior can touch our lives in surprising ways. A group of women reached an agreement in 2016 with the American Society for Reproductive Medicine to settle claims that the group's published guidelines on human egg donor prices constituted price-fixing. The price guidelines were not mandates, but they were widely followed. The fertility association said the guidelines were needed to prevent coercion and exploitation, but the plaintiff women said they amounted to horizontal price-fixing. The women received financial settlements, and the pricing language was to be removed from the association's guidelines.[10] (Remember that settlements often do not constitute admissions of wrongdoing.)

- Ending nine years of litigation over alleged conspiracies to fix corn syrup prices, Archer Daniels Midland, A. E. Staley, and others agreed in 2004 to pay $531 million to settle a class action against them.[11] [For a movie account of former ADM executive Mark Whitacre's decision to blow the whistle on the alleged conspiracy, see *The Informant!* starring Matt Damon. The trailer is available at **www.traileraddict.com/trailer/the-informant/trailer**].

These are only a few of the many examples in recent years of alleged price-fixing conspiracies in America and around the world. The effect of these arrangements, when unlawful, is to harm competition and raise prices. Antitrust expert John M. Connor has estimated that cartels "typically push prices up at least 20 percent and sometimes much more."[12]

PRACTICING ETHICS Antitrust Law and the Price of Beer

College students spend about $5.5 billion on alcohol annually, most of that on beer. That total exceeds what students spend on books, soda, coffee, juice, and milk combined. Could antitrust law affect the consumption, or at least the price, of beer? Perhaps. A group of consumers in Madison, Wisconsin, home of the University of Wisconsin, sued some local bars and the Madison-Dane County Tavern League, Inc., for price-fixing. The plaintiffs claimed that the defendant bars had agreed to fix prices by adopting a "voluntary ban on drink specials." The plaintiffs pointed to a September 2002 press release from the "Downtown Tavern Working Group" announcing that drink specials would not be offered after 8 pm on Friday and Saturday nights for "at least a year."

The defendants said the new policy was a self-imposed effort to curb binge drinking, especially by students, and that the policy was a response to pressure from the city and the University of Wisconsin. Further, the defendants said that the press release did not reflect an agreement of any kind and thus could not violate the law because all bar owners remained free to do as they wished. Eventually, the Wisconsin Supreme Court held that the policy was immune from the antitrust laws because the city effectively compelled the arrangement. Given the state legislature's broad grant of regulatory authority over alcohol to municipalities, the court concluded that the legislature must have intended the defendant taverns' actions to be exempt (immune from scrutiny) from the antitrust laws.

Questions

1. The legality of this arrangement aside, *should* bar owners be free to reach an agreement eliminating drink specials?
2. Is the Madison dispute too trivial and frivolous to justify court time? Explain.
3. Will the market satisfactorily protect youthful drinkers and society? Explain.
4. *a.* How would you expect the Supreme Court decision to affect the consumption of beer in Madison?

   b. Explain how a "voluntary ban on drink specials" might constitute price-fixing.

Sources: *Eichenseer v. Madison-Dane County Tavern League,* 748 N.W.2d 154 (Wis. 2008); and "Frequently Asked Questions about College Binge Drinking," AlcoholPolicyMD.com [**www.alcoholpolicymd.com/alcohol_and_health/faqs.htm**].

Real Estate Sales Commissions

The following case examines alleged horizontal price-fixing by Kentucky Realtors.

Circuit Judge Norris

Class representatives Christopher and Mystic Burnette appeal three rulings by the district court that resulted in judgment for defendant real estate firms, all of which operate in Kentucky. The fourth amended complaint alleged that defendants violated Section 1 of the Sherman Antitrust Act by participating in a horizontal conspiracy to fix the commissions charged in Kentucky real estate transactions at an anti-competitive rate. The certified class consists of people who sold residential real estate in Kentucky from October 11, 2001, to October 11, 2005, and used the services of defendants. Plaintiffs contend the district court erred by granting summary judgment to defendants.

Plaintiffs filed suit in October 2005. The crux of the allegation brought by plaintiffs is that defendants violated the Sherman Act by conspiring to charge a supra-competitive real estate broker commission of 6% and thereby injured sellers of residential property.

* * * * *

To become a real estate agent in Kentucky, an individual must be licensed by the Commonwealth's Real Estate Commission ("KREC"). Agents typically join local realtors' boards, such as the Greater Louisville Association of Realtors, the Lexington-Bluegrass Association of Realtors, and the Kentucky Association of Realtors ("KAR").

In 1991, the KREC passed a regulation (the "Rebate Ban") that prohibited licensed real estate brokers in Kentucky from offering any item or thing of value, including rebates, to induce clients to retain their services. The United States Department of Justice filed suit in 2005 against the KREC alleging that the Rebate Ban violated Section 1 of the Sherman Act. That suit was settled and the Rebate Ban was abolished.

This action was filed shortly thereafter. The complaint alleges that defendants "combined, conspired and agreed to fix, maintain and inflate real estate broker commissions and associated fees and refuse to compete on the basis of price." Specifically, defendants "have charged a real estate broker commission of 6%, have described this 6% fee as the 'standard' or 'typical' fee, and have habitually refused to negotiate a lower fee." According to the complaint, this collusion resulted in sellers being forced to pay artificially inflated commissions.

* * * * *

Evidence of Conspiracy

An antitrust conspiracy can be established by either direct or circumstantial evidence.

a. Direct Evidence

The district court turned first to the public hearing that was held before the KREC on November 28, 2000. Plaintiffs maintain that the transcript of this hearing represents direct evidence of illegal collusion. The purpose of the hearing was ostensibly to share a survey of inducement laws in other states and to invite comments on the possible repeal of the KREC Rebate Ban. At the hearing, Ray Rector of Rector-Hayden expressed the opinion that the consumer pays for inducements in the form of higher fees or a decreased level of service. Jerry McMahan spoke at greater length and supported maintaining commissions. Doug Myers of Semonin echoed these sentiments: "I'd like to see our competition based on our professional performance, not upon our brokerage fees. . . ." Broker Barbara Campbell, whose agency charged only a 4.5% commission, contended that her clients were contacted by brokers who would tell them that other realtors "would not show my clients' homes to their buyers so long as they continue to do business with Campbell Realty." Another broker, Steven Gavin, reported harassment for offering only 2% to the buyer's broker.

The district court assessed this evidence and concluded that it did not constitute "direct evidence that Defendants conspired to fix real estate commissions at a supra-competitive 6%." The court observed that it had reviewed the transcript of the KREC meeting and found that plaintiffs have taken remarks made by individual realtors "out of context and construed them in a highly-strained manner."

We agree with this assessment. Like the district court, we view Jerry McMahan's statements at the hearing as ambiguous at best and they therefore do not establish direct evidence of a conspiracy. McMahan was highlighting the fact that his "full-service" firm offered more to its clients than his Internet rivals and thereby justified its higher commission rate. Also absent in the record is any comment by McMahan suggesting that brokers negotiate among themselves their respective commission rates. With respect to those who spoke about having undergone harassment for offering lower rates, the district court observed that these speakers are not parties to this action, nor did they implicate defendants.

* * * * *

b. Circumstantial Evidence

Evidence of "conscious parallelism," . . . can support . . . a claim based upon circumstantial evidence. . . . This court has set out the following considerations, sometimes referred to as "plus factors," in determining when circumstantial evidence amounts to a finding of concerted action: 1) whether defendants' actions, if taken independently, would be contrary to their economic interests; 2) product uniformity; 3) whether the defendants have been uniform in their actions; 4) whether the defendants have exchanged or have had the opportunity to exchange information relative to the alleged conspiracy; and 5) whether the defendants have a common motive to conspire or have engaged in a large number of communications.

The district court then reviewed evidence of parallel pricing behavior and the plus factors. It found them to be insufficient to withstand summary judgment. In reaching this conclusion, the court relied upon these conclusions:

- "Plaintiffs' evidence of parallel pricing shows merely that each Defendant had a policy of charging a minimum commission of 6% and that each Defendant occasionally deviated from its respective policy for various reasons."

- "The prevalence of the 6% rate, then, is just as consistent with independent pricing decisions. The existence of a conspiracy cannot be inferred solely on the basis that Defendants tended to charge the same amount for their services."

- "The Sixth Circuit has unequivocally proclaimed that 'setting cooperative sales-commission rates is not price fixing: it has no relation to the amount charged to clients for an agent's service.' Thus, even if it was necessary for a listing broker to offer a 3% buyer's broker commission to the cooperating broker as an incentive, the listing broker is free to charge his client 4%, 5%, 10%, or even 3% plus a flat fee. . . ."

* * * * * *

- ". . . [C]harging a standard commission rate across the board and retaining increasing profits from the sale of higher priced homes is consistent with rational business judgment and not probative of an illegal agreement to fix commissions."

- ". . . [M]ere awareness of competitors' commissions does not support an inference that Defendants agreed to conspire."

* * * * * *

- With respect to Jerry McMahan's comment at the 2000 KREC meeting that "the most unprofessional thing we can do in this business is cut our commissions," the court stated: ". . . A plausible inference is that Mr. McMahan thought full service brokers should not compete with the Internet brokers by offering inducements in the form of rebates, but should compete with the Internet brokers by making their services worth what they charge—whatever that may be."

- "Plaintiffs have presented no evidence of any parallel change or impact on Defendants' pricing decisions after any alleged communication or invitation that was made at the KREC public hearing or any other meeting between Defendants."

* * * * * *

Having reviewed this evidence, which it characterized as circumstantial, the court held that "[p]laintiffs have not presented sufficient evidence to meet the stringent summary judgment standard in antitrust cases."

. . . [W]e agree with its conclusion that the circumstantial evidence is insufficient. [T]he evidence does not, as it must, eliminate a finding that the same actions are "equally consistent with independent conduct." . . .

* * * * * *

The judgment of the district court is affirmed.

Questions

1. *a.* Who are the alleged conspirators in this price-fixing dispute, and how did they allegedly fix prices?

   b. Who won this case at the federal district court (the lower court), and why did that court rule as it did?

   c. In general, is parallel pricing a lawful behavior? Explain.

2. *a.* Why did the federal district court and the 6th Circuit Court of Appeals require a showing of "plus factors" to demonstrate that the Realtors had engaged in price-fixing?

   b. Why was the KREC Rebate Ban challenged by the U.S. Justice Department?

3. Why did the defendant real estate firms win this case?

4. Assume two drugstores, located across the street from each other and each involved in interstate commerce, agree to exchange a monthly list of prices charged for all nonprescription medications. Is that arrangement lawful in the absence of any further cooperation? Explain.

5. The "Three Tenors"—Luciano Pavarotti, Placido Domingo, and Jose Carreras—recorded a 1990 World Cup concert, distributed by Polygram, and a 1994 World Cup concert, distributed by Warner. Polygram and Warner subsequently agreed to jointly distribute and share profits from the 1998 World Cup Three Tenors concert. The 1998 recording apparently was less "new and exciting" than had been hoped. Concerned that sales of the earlier recordings would drain interest from the 1998 recording, Polygram and Warner agreed to cease all discounting and advertising of the two earlier recordings for several weeks surrounding the release of the 1998 album. In 2001, the Federal Trade Commission issued complaints against Polygram and Warner. Those complaints eventually reached the District of Columbia Federal Circuit Court of Appeals, where Polygram and Warner defended themselves by arguing that the agreement was good for competition in that it increased the joint venture's profitability from new recordings and it eliminated free riding by each company (for the 1990 and 1994 recordings) on the joint venture's 1998 marketing.

   a. What antitrust violation was alleged by the Federal Trade Commission?

   b. What is free riding, and why is it a problem?

   c. Decide the case. Explain. See *Polygram v. Federal Trade Commission*, 416 F.3d 29 (D.C. Cir. 2005).

6. Assume that 10 real estate firms operate in the city of Gotham. Further assume that each charges a 7 percent commission on all residential sales.

   a. Does that uniformity of prices in and of itself constitute price-fixing? Explain.

   b. Assume we have evidence that the firms agreed to set the 7 percent level. What defense would be raised against a price-fixing charge?

   c. Would that defense succeed? Explain. See *McLain v. Real Estate Board of New Orleans, Inc.*, 444 U.S. 232 (1980).

Refusal to Deal/Group Boycotts

LO 10-5
Identify a group
boycott.

Principal Legislation: Sherman Act, Section 1

In America we are free to enter into business relationships with whomever we prefer, correct? Generally, yes; but antitrust problems sometimes emerge. When does a *refusal to deal* with another raise antitrust issues? The clearest problem is a *horizontal group boycott* where competitors agree not to deal with a supplier, customer, or another competitor. Ford and GM, for example, presumably could not jointly refuse to buy tires from Bridgestone. Such arrangements so thoroughly subvert the market that they ordinarily are *per se* violations of the Sherman Act Section I and thus do not require a detailed evaluation of competitive harm and benefits, although a showing of market power by those in the group may be required. A unilateral (individual) refusal to deal by a buyer or a seller sometimes raises antitrust concerns if the firm refusing to deal is a monopolist and harm to competition can be proven,[13] but the Supreme Court has severely restricted the use of the "unilateral refusal" doctrine.[14]

> A jury found a distributor-led conspiracy.

A continuing conflict in the steel industry illustrates "refusal to deal" reasoning. Two steel industry salespeople founded a new steel distributor, MM Steel, after leaving their sales jobs with two other steel distributors, American Alloy (AA) and Chapel. Apparently upset that their former salespeople had established a new competitor, AA and Chapel allegedly agreed to pressure steel manufacturers JSW, Nucor, and SSAB not to sell to MM. MM then sued the distributors and manufacturers alleging an illegal group boycott. SSAB settled before trial, but the balance of the litigation continued.[15] A jury found a distributor-led conspiracy, and the Fifth Circuit Court of Appeals upheld that finding.[16] At this writing, the defendants have asked the Supreme Court to review the case.[17] [For a trade regulation blog, see **http://traderegulation.blogspot.com/**].

Clarett Boycotted by NFL?

Antitrust shapes all dimensions of our lives, as football running back Maurice Clarett learned when he tried to enter the 2004 National Football League draft. Clarett, as a freshman, led Ohio State University to an undefeated season in 2002. Clarett was ineligible for college football in his sophomore year because of allegations that he accepted improper benefits and lied about doing so. Clarett then tried to enter the NFL draft but was barred by a league rule providing that players must have been out of high school for three seasons. Clarett sued the NFL, claiming its eligibility rules violated federal antitrust laws by, in effect, allowing competing teams to agree among themselves to boycott certain players (including Clarett). Clarett won at the federal district court level, but he lost on appeal when the court ruled that the eligibility rule is exempt from the antitrust laws. The NFL eligibility rule is the product of a collective bargaining agreement between the league and the players' union, the National Football League Players Association. Antitrust promotes competition while unions restrict it in various ways, but in balancing those competing interests, Congress and the courts have long granted unions certain exemptions from antitrust laws. The Supreme Court subsequently declined to review Clarett's case.

In 2010, Clarett was released from prison, where he had served a three-and-one-half-year sentence for aggravated robbery and carrying a concealed weapon. Following his release, Clarett played football with the Omaha Nighthawks and published a book about his life. At this writing, he is a public speaker and entrepreneur, and he was featured in an ESPN *30 for 30* episode, "The Youngstown Boys."

Questions

1. Should Clarett and future football players be free to sell their services on the open market?

2. Is the NFL correct to encourage players to stay in college and mature before entering professional football? Explain.

3. Congressman Steve Cohen, Democrat of Tennessee, wrote a letter in 2009 to the National Basketball Association and the NBA players union asking them to repeal the rule requiring players to be 19 years old and one year removed from high school before they are eligible for the NBA. The rule is part of the collective-bargaining agreement between the league and the players. Cohen labeled the law "a vestige of slavery."
   a. What do you think Cohen meant by his "vestige of slavery" remark?
   b. Does the rule constitute an unlawful restraint of trade? Explain.
   c. Do you agree that the rule should be repealed? Explain.

Sources: Clarett v. National Football League, 369 F.3d 124 (2d Cir. 2004); and Pete Thamel, "Congressman Asks N.B.A. and Union to Rescind Age Minimum for Players," *The New York Times,* June 4, 2009 [**www.nytimes.com**].

Questions

1. Baptist Eye Institute (BEI), a group of nonspecialized ophthalmologists in Jacksonville, Florida, controlling approximately 15 percent of the referral market, sent nearly all of its retina cases to the Florida Retina Institute. Is BEI engaging in an unlawful group boycott against plaintiff Retina Associates, a retina care provider in competition with the Florida Retina Institute? Explain. See *Retina Associates P.A. v. Southern Baptist Hospital of Florida Inc.,* 105 F.3d 1376 (11th Cir. 1997).

2. Discon, a telephone salvage company, sold services to MECo, a subsidiary of NYNEX, a phone company for the New York/New England area. MECo switched from Discon to AT&T Technologies, a Discon competitor, and paid a higher price to AT&T than it had paid to Discon. Discon claimed that the buyer and NYNEX then received a rebate from AT&T at the end of the year. Discon argued that NYNEX was able to pass on its higher costs to its customers because NYNEX was a part of a regulated phone market. Discon claimed that NYNEX, its subsidiaries, and AT&T were engaging in a group boycott in violation of the Sherman Act in order to drive Discon out of the market. Decide. Explain. See *NYNEX Corp. v. Discon, Inc.,* 119 S. Ct. 493 (1998).

Part Three—Vertical Restraints

We have been studying unfair trade practices by competitors—that is, horizontal restraints of trade. Now we turn to antitrust violations on the vertical axis—that is, restraints involving agreements between two or more members of a supply chain (such as a manufacturer and a retailer of that manufacturer's products). *Horizontal restraints* are those arising from an agreement among the *competitors* themselves, while *vertical restraints* ordinarily are those imposed by *suppliers* on their *buyers*. Horizontal restraints often are *per se* unlawful while vertical restraints, in general, are to be resolved under the rule of reason. Horizontal restraints eliminate competition, thereby undermining the power of the market, while vertical restraints may either be harmful or beneficial to competition.

E-Books: Apple Fixing Prices?

[The following price-fixing case involving Apple's e-book marketing practices illustrates some of the principles of horizontal price-fixing, as discussed above, along with elements of vertical price-fixing (resale price maintenance) discussed below.]

The Kindle e-book reader was introduced by Amazon in 2007, followed by Barnes & Noble's Nook reader (2009) and Apple's iPad (2010). Amazon priced many of its e-book best sellers at a very attractive $9.99 (often below its cost) to increase demand for the Kindle, to solidify its market position, and to encourage broader shopping at Amazon. By some measures, Amazon's share of digital book sales peaked as high as 90 percent of the market. Book publishers, including HarperCollins and Penguin, apparently fearing Amazon's power in the e-book market, allegedly entered negotiations among themselves and with Apple to change e-book pricing from Amazon's "wholesale" model (where Amazon itself set e-book retail prices) to an "agency" model (where the publishers set the retail price of books [e.g., $14.99] and the retailers, including Apple and Barnes & Noble, kept a 30 percent share). Having achieved an agreement with Apple, the publishers allegedly were able to compel Amazon to accept the same terms. Thereafter, Amazon's e-book market share reportedly fell to about 60 percent.

In 2012, the Justice Department and about 30 states filed a civil complaint against Apple and five book publishers claiming that the defendant publishers had conspired among themselves and with Apple to fix prices in violation of the Sherman Act. The publishers denied misconduct but reached a settlement agreeing to pay $170 million to consumers. In their defense, the publishers and Apple claimed they acted independently in implementing agency pricing, and Apple argued that its entry strengthened competition.

Relying principally on horizontal price-fixing reasoning, a federal judge in 2013 found Apple guilty of colluding with the publishers to fix prices. The judge ordered Apple to modify its contracts and submit to oversight. Apple lost on appeal, and a request for Supreme Court review was denied. Apple must pay a $450 million settlement, mostly in credits to some 23 million consumers who overpaid.

Amazon has maintained its dominant position in the e-book market, but e-book sales are slipping and physical bookstores are enjoying a considerable resurgence. Is Amazon a monopolist? We will discuss that topic in Chapter 11.

Sources: Alexandra Alter, "The Plot Twist: E-Book Sales Slip, and Print Is Far from Dead," *The New York Times*, September 22, 2015 [**www.nytimes.com**]; Thomas Catan, Jeffrey A. Trachtenberg, and Chad Bray, "U.S. Alleges E-Book Scheme," *The Wall Street Journal*, April 12, 2012, p. A1; and *United States v. Apple*, 791 F.3d 290 (2d Cir. 2015), *cert. denied, Apple v. United States*, 136 S. Ct. 1376 (2016).

Resale Price Maintenance

LO 10-6
Define resale price
maintenance.

Principal Legislation: Sherman Act, Section 1; Federal Trade Commission Act, Section 5

Manufacturers and distributors often seek to specify the price at which their customers may resell their products, a policy we might think of as vertical price-fixing but that is formally called *resale price maintenance*. Having sold its product, why should a manufacturer or distributor seek to influence the price at which the product is resold? We note five primary reasons: (1) establishing a minimum price to enhance the product's reputation, (2) helping retailers make a profit sufficient to provide customer service, (3) preventing discount stores from pricing beneath full-price retail outlets, (4) preventing *free riding*, and (5) reducing *showrooming*—where consumers educate themselves about products in brick-and-mortar stores, such as Target, and then buy online after making instant price comparisons.

A *unilateral* specification of a resale price, with nothing more involved, has long been permissible. Under the Supreme Court's 1919 *Colgate*[18] decision, sellers can lawfully engage in resale price maintenance if they do nothing more than announce prices at which their products are to be resold and unilaterally refuse to deal with anyone who does not adhere to those prices. On the other hand, an agreement between a seller and a buyer dictating the price at which the buyer may resell the product was, for decades, a *per se* violation of the law. Then, in 1997, the Supreme Court ruled that agreements specifying *maximum* resale prices would no longer be considered *per se* violations and must be evaluated under the rule of reason.[19] In the 2007 *Leegin* case that follows, the Supreme Court overturned a nearly 100-year-old precedent in the *Dr. Miles* case[20] to rule that agreements specifying *minimum* resale prices also must be analyzed under the rule of reason; that is, those agreements are no longer *per se* violations of the law. Rather, they must be considered on a case-by-case basis weighing their pro- and anticompetitive effects.

LEGAL BRIEFCASE

Leegin Creative Leather Products, Inc. v. PSKS, dba Kay's Kloset   127 S. Ct. 2705 (2007)

Justice Kennedy

I

Petitioner, Leegin Creative Leather Products, Inc. (Leegin), designs, manufactures, and distributes leather goods and accessories. In 1991, Leegin began to sell belts under the brand name "Brighton." The Brighton brand has now expanded into a variety of women's fashion accessories. It is sold across the United States in over 5,000 retail establishments, for the most part independent, small boutiques and specialty stores. . . . Leegin asserts that, at least for its products, small retailers treat customers better, provide customers more services, and make their shopping experience more satisfactory than do larger, often impersonal retailers. [Leegin's president Jerry] Kohl explained: "[W]e want the consumers to get a different experience than they get in Sam's Club or in Wal-Mart. And you can't get that kind of experience or support or customer service from a store like Wal-Mart."

Respondent PSKS, Inc., operates Kay's Kloset, a women's apparel store in Lewisville, Texas. Kay's Kloset buys from about 75 different manufacturers and at one time sold the Brighton brand. It first started purchasing Brighton goods from Leegin in 1995. Once it began selling the brand, the store promoted Brighton. For example, it ran Brighton advertisements and had Brighton days in the store. Kay's Kloset became the destination retailer in the area to buy Brighton products. Brighton was the store's most important brand and once accounted for 40 to 50 percent of its profits.

In 1997, Leegin instituted the "Brighton retail pricing and Promotion Policy." Following the policy, Leegin refused to sell to retailers that discounted Brighton goods below suggested prices. . . . In the letter to retailers establishing the policy, Leegin stated:

> In this age of mega stores like Macy's, Bloomingdales, May Co. and others, consumers are perplexed by promises of product quality and support of product which we believe is lacking in these large stores. Consumers are further confused by the ever popular sale, sale, sale, etc.
>
> We, at Leegin, choose to break away from the pack by selling [at] specialty stores; specialty stores that can offer the customer great quality merchandise, superb service, and support the Brighton product 365 days a year on a consistent basis. . . .

Leegin adopted the policy to give its retailers sufficient margins to provide customers the service central to its distribution strategy. It also expressed concern that discounting harmed Brighton's brand image and reputation.

* * * * *

In December 2002, Leegin discovered Kay's Kloset had been marking down Brighton's entire line by 20 percent. Kay's Kloset contended it placed Brighton products on sale to compete with nearby retailers who also were undercutting Leegin's suggested prices. Leegin, nonetheless, requested that Kay's Kloset cease discounting. Its request refused, Leegin stopped selling to the store. The loss of the Brighton brand had a considerable negative impact on the store's revenue from sales.

PSKS sued Leegin in the United States District Court for the Eastern District of Texas. It alleged, among other claims, that Leegin had violated the antitrust laws by "enter[ing] into agreements with retailers to charge only those prices fixed by Leegin."

* * * * *

The jury agreed with PSKS and awarded it $1.2 million.

* * * * *

The Court of Appeals for the Fifth Circuit affirmed. We granted certiorari to determine whether vertical minimum resale price maintenance agreements should continue to be treated as *per se* unlawful.

* * * * *

II

Resort to *per se* rules is confined to restraints . . . "that would always or almost always tend to restrict competition and decrease output." *Business Electronics*, 485 U.S. at 723. . . .

As a consequence, the *per se* rule is appropriate only after courts have had considerable experience with the type of restraint at issue, and only if courts can predict with confidence that it would be invalidated in all or almost all instances under the rule of reason. . . .

III

The Court has interpreted *Dr. Miles Medical Co. v. John D. Park & Sons Co.*, 220 U.S. 373 (1911), as establishing a *per se* rule against a vertical agreement between a manufacturer and its distributor to set minimum resale prices. . . .

The reasons upon which *Dr. Miles* relied do not justify a *per se* rule. As a consequence, it is necessary to examine . . . the economic effects of vertical agreements to fix minimum resale prices, and to determine whether the *per se* rule is nonetheless appropriate.

A

Though each side of the debate can find sources to support its position, it suffices to say here that economics literature is replete with procompetitive justifications for a manufacturer's use of resale price maintenance.

* * * * *

The justifications for vertical price restraints are similar to those for other vertical restraints. Minimum resale price maintenance can stimulate interbrand competition—the competition among manufacturers selling different brands of the same type of product—by reducing intrabrand competition—the competition among retailers selling the same brand. The promotion of interbrand competition is important because "the primary purpose of the antitrust laws is to protect [this type of] competition." *Khan*, 522 U.S. at 15. . . .

Absent vertical price restraints, the retail services that enhance interbrand competition might be under provided. This is because discounting retailers can free ride on retailers who furnish services and then capture some of the increased demand those services generate.

Resale price maintenance, in addition, can increase interbrand competition by facilitating market entry for new firms and brands. "[N]ew manufacturers and manufacturers entering new markets can use the restrictions in order to induce competent and aggressive retailers to make the kind of investment of capital and labor that is often required in the distribution of products unknown to the consumer." *GTE Sylvania*, 433 U.S. at 55. . . .

Resale price maintenance can also increase interbrand competition by encouraging retailer services that would not be provided even absent free riding. It may be difficult and inefficient for a manufacturer to make and enforce a contract with a retailer specifying the different services the retailer must perform. Offering the retailer a guaranteed margin and threatening termination if it does not live up to expectations may be the most efficient way to expand the manufacturer's market share by inducing the retailer's performance and allowing it to use its own initiative and experience in providing valuable services.

* * * * *

B

While vertical agreements setting minimum resale prices can have procompetitive justifications, they may have anticompetitive effects in other cases; and unlawful price fixing, designed solely to obtain monopoly profits, is an ever-present temptation. Resale price maintenance may, for example, facilitate a manufacturer cartel. An unlawful cartel will seek to discover if some manufacturers are undercutting the cartel's fixed prices. Resale price maintenance could assist the cartel in identifying price-cutting manufacturers who benefit from the lower prices they offer. Resale price maintenance, furthermore, could discourage a manufacturer from cutting prices to retailers with the concomitant benefit of cheaper prices to consumers.

Vertical price restraints also "might be used to organize cartels at the retailer level." *Business Electronics*, at 725–726. A group of retailers might collude to fix prices to consumers and then compel a manufacturer to aid the unlawful arrangement with resale price maintenance.

A horizontal cartel among competing manufacturers or competing retailers that decreases output or reduces competition in order to increase price is, and ought to be, *per se* unlawful. To the extent a vertical agreement setting minimum resale prices is entered upon to facilitate either type of cartel, it, too, would need to be held unlawful under the rule of reason.

* * * * *

A manufacturer with market power . . . might use resale price maintenance to give retailers an incentive not to sell the products of smaller rivals or new entrants. As should be evident, the potential anticompetitive consequences of vertical price restraints must not be ignored or underestimated.

C

Notwithstanding the risk of unlawful conduct, it cannot be stated with any degree of confidence that resale price maintenance "always or almost always tend[s] to restrict competition and decrease output." Vertical agreements establishing minimum resale prices can have either procompetitive or anticompetitive effects, depending upon the circumstances in which they are formed.

Respondent contends, nonetheless, that . . . the *per se* rule is justified because a vertical price restraint can lead to higher prices for the manufacturer's goods. . . . Respondent is mistaken in relying on pricing effects absent a further showing of anticompetitive conduct. . . . For, as has been indicated already, the antitrust laws are designed primarily to protect interbrand competition, from which lower prices can later result. . . .

Respondent's argument, furthermore, overlooks that, in general, the interests of manufacturers and consumers are aligned with respect to retailer profit margins. . . . A manufacturer has no incentive to overcompensate retailers with unjustified margins. The retailers, not the manufacturer, gain from higher retail prices. The manufacturer often loses; interbrand competition reduces its competitiveness and market share because consumers will "substitute a different brand of the same product." See *Business Electronics*, at 725. . . .

Resale price maintenance, it is true, does have economic dangers. If the rule of reason were to apply to vertical price restraints, courts would have to be diligent in eliminating their anticompetitive uses from the market. This is a realistic objective. . . .

As a final matter, that a dominant manufacturer or retailer can abuse resale price maintenance for anticompetitive purposes may not be a serious concern unless the relevant entity has market power. If a retailer lacks market power, manufacturers likely can sell their goods through rival retailers.

* * * * *

For all of the foregoing reasons, we think that were the Court considering the issue as an original matter, the rule of reason, not a *per se* rule of unlawfulness, would be the appropriate standard to judge vertical price restraints.

* * * * *

Reversed.

Questions

1. *a.* What potential procompetitive considerations were cited by the court in supporting a rule of reason approach to resale price maintenance?
   b. What potential anticompetitive considerations were cited by the court?

2. Could we fairly conclude from the *Leegin* decision that resale price maintenance agreements are now "*per se* legal"? Explain.

3. Explain why the Court said the seller's market power is an important consideration in assessing the legality of a resale price-maintenance agreement.

Leegin *in Practice (the Law)*   The *Leegin* ruling seems to affirm the Supreme Court's current preference for free-market principles and reduced judicial intervention in business practice. Accordingly, more competition and better service should follow, but critics think the decision simply allows manufacturers to pressure and cut out discounters with the result that consumers will pay higher prices. Of course, if anticompetitive behavior emerges, it still can be attacked under the rule of reason, and some states continue to treat resale price maintenance as a *per se* violation of law. Similarly, the European Union generally forbids resale price maintenance, unless clear efficiencies are identified.

Leegin *in Practice (the Business Response)*   Many manufacturers practice resale price maintenance. Consider contact lenses. Forty million Americans wear them, and they spend about $4 billion annually on those lenses.[21] Ninety-seven percent of lens manufacturing is controlled by four companies: Alcon, Bausch & Lomb, Cooper Vision, and Johnson & Johnson.[22] To protect optometrists' lens sales from being undercut by discounters like Costco and 1-800-CONTACTS, those manufacturers allegedly have worked jointly to impose price floors on the retail sale of lenses. In response, the state of Utah (home to 1-800-CONTACTS) passed a law in 2015 forbidding any practice that "has the effect of fixing or otherwise controlling the price that a contact lens retailer charges or advertises."[23] At this writing, the Utah statute has survived two court challenges, but others may follow. Johnson & Johnson says it has discontinued its minimum pricing policy. Nationwide, more than 50 class action lawsuits have been filed alleging price-fixing by the lens manufacturers.

Question

Is the *Leegin* decision good or bad for consumers? Explain.

Vertical Territorial and Customer Restraints

Principal Legislation: Sherman Act, Section 1; Federal Trade Commission Act, Section 5

In addition to price restraints, manufacturers commonly impose nonprice restraints, including where and to whom their product may be resold. Those restrictions typically afford an exclusive sales territory to a distributor. Similarly, manufacturers may prevent distributors from selling to some classes of customers (for example, a distributor might be forbidden to sell to an unfranchised retailer). Of course, such arrangements necessarily retard or eliminate *intrabrand* competition. Because price and service competition among dealers in the same brand ordinarily benefits the consumer, the courts have frequently struck down such arrangements. Still, those territorial and customer allocations also have merits. The *GTE Sylvania* case[24] enunciated those virtues and established the position that vertical restrictions are to be judged case by case, balancing interbrand and intrabrand competitive effects while recognizing that interbrand competition is the primary concern of antitrust law. Thus, the rule of reason is to be applied to vertical territorial and customer restraints.

Tying Arrangements

LO 10-7
Explain the requirements for establishing an unlawful tying arrangement.

Principal Legislation: Clayton Act, Section 3; Sherman Act, Sections 1 and 2; Federal Trade Commission Act, Section 5

Clayton Act, Section 3. That it shall be unlawful for any person engaged in commerce, in the course of such commerce, to lease or make a sale or contract for sale of goods . . . or other commodities . . . or fix a price charged therefore, or discount from or rebate upon, such price, on the condition, agreement, or understanding that the lessee or purchaser thereof shall not use or deal in the goods . . . or other commodities of a competitor or competitors of the lessor or seller, where the effect of such lease, sale, or contract for sale or such condition, agreement, or understanding may be to substantially lessen competition or tend to create a monopoly in any line of commerce.

Tying arrangements (sometimes called *bundling*) are another form of nonprice vertical restraint. Typically, tying arrangements permit a customer to buy or lease a desired product (the tying product) only if the customer also buys or leases another, less desirable product (the tied product).

McDonald's does not violate antitrust law when it bundles a hamburger, fries, and soft drink as a "meal" in part because customers are also allowed to buy the three products separately. What about when a firm like Google, with market dominance, requires smartphone manufacturers wanting to use Google's free, "open" Android operating system to accept a bundle that includes Google search, Gmail, and Google Maps if they want to offer any Google services on their phones? Those smartphone manufacturers, like Samsung and Motorola, are free to include their own services and apps on their phones, but if they want any Google services, they must accept the Google package, which comes preinstalled.[25] At this writing, the U.S. Federal Trade Commission and the European Union antitrust authorities are investigating whether these tying packages unfairly advantage Google services over competing services/apps.

Russia's antitrust authority has fined Google about $6.75 million for requiring mobile device makers using the Android operating system to install Google services, including search, on their devices if they also want access to Google Play (app store). [See Chapter 11 for a discussion of Microsoft's historic antitrust battle over its alleged practice of tying its Internet Explorer browser (the tied product) to its dominant Windows operating system (the tying product).]

The Law   Tying arrangements raise two primary antitrust concerns: (1) A party who already enjoys market power over the tying product is able to extend that power into the tied product market and (2) competitors in the tied product market are foreclosed from equal access to that market.

The basic tying violation test is as follows:

1. The existence of separate products. That is, there are two products present rather than two components of one product, or two entirely separate products that happen to be elements in a single transaction.

2. A requirement that the purchase of one of the products (the tying product) is conditioned on the purchase of another product (the tied product).

3. Market power in the tying product.

4. Substantial impact on commerce in the tied product market. (Some courts require a substantial anticompetitive effect in the tied product market.)

Proof of all four of those elements establishes *per se* illegality. When all four elements cannot be satisfied, the analysis may proceed on a rule of reason basis, weighing pro- and anticompetitive considerations. Critics argue that tying arrangements often enhance consumer welfare and, as such, the *per se* approach should be overturned, as in the *Leegin* case.

Cable/Satellite TV Bundling

Consumers often are frustrated because their cable and satellite television services ordinarily come in packages of channels rather than in an "a la carte" menu where the subscriber can choose preferred individual channels. In a recent California case, a group of consumers sued several television networks and cable and satellite distributors, including NBC, Fox, and Time Warner Cable, claiming, among other things, that the defendants engaged in Sherman Act violations. The defendant television networks sold television programming to the defendant cable distribution companies in bundles rather than on a per channel basis. The distributors, in turn, sold to consumers in those prepackaged bundles or on a "tier" basis. The plaintiff consumers claimed the practice of offering subscriptions only in bundles was unlawful under the Sherman Act.

Questions

1. Explain the nature of the alleged Sherman Act violation.

2. Who won the case? Explain.

Source: Brantley et al. v. NBC Universal, Inc. et al., 675 F.3d 1192 (9th Cir. 2012), *cert. denied*, 133 S. Ct. 573 (2012).

Franchise Tying?

The following case examines tying allegations in the context of Shell and Texaco gas station franchises. The case turns in part on market definition, a topic that we address more thoroughly in Chapter 11. In brief, in order to establish market power in the tying product, the market itself must be defined. In doing so, we consider the geographic market (where the product is sold in commercially significant quantities) and the product market (those products that are interchangeable and thus compete, one with the other).

Rick-Mik Enterprises, Inc. v. Equilon Enterprises, LLC
532 F.3d 963 (9th Cir. 2008)

Judge King

Equilon Enterprises, LLC ("Equilon") does business as Shell Oil Products. Equilon's standard franchise agreement requires its franchisees, Shell and Texaco gasoline stations, to use Equilon to process credit-card transactions. In addition to payment for sales of petroleum products, Equilon allegedly gets (1) transaction fees associated with the processing, or (2) some kind of unspecified "kickback" from unidentified banks that process the transactions, or both. Rick-Mik Enterprises, Inc., Mike M. Madani, and Alfred Buczkowski (collectively "Rick-Mik") are Equilon franchisees who—on behalf of themselves and other, similarly situated Equilon franchisees—allege that Equilon violated antitrust laws by illegally tying two distinct products (the franchises and the credit-card processing services). Rick-Mik contends franchisees could pay lower transaction fees from others for credit-card processing. . . .

The district court dismissed the antitrust and related state-law counts. . . .

DISCUSSION
Tying Claim
a. The market power allegations are flawed.
The alleged tying product here is gasoline franchises. Rick-Mik has a contract for an Equilon franchise to sell Shell branded gasoline and diesel. The alleged tied-product is credit-card processing services. Rick-Mik alleges it cannot get a franchise without the "tied" credit-card processing services.

Rick-Mik's complaint does not allege that Equilon has market power in the relevant market, which is the market for the tying product—gasoline franchises. Indeed, other than stating that "[Equilon] rank[s] number one in the industry in branded gasoline stations," there are no specific allegations at all as to the franchise market. The complaint alleges nothing about, for example, what percentage of gasoline franchises are Equilon's (Shell/Texaco) as compared to other franchises like Chevron, Mobil, Marathon Oil, or Union 76. There are no factual allegations as to the percentage of gasoline retail sales that are made through *non-franchise* outlets. There are no factual allegations regarding the amount of power or control that Equilon has over prospective franchisees. There are no factual allegations regarding the relative difficulty of a franchisee to switch franchise brands.

If Equilon lacks market power in the gasoline-franchise market, there can be no cognizable tying claim. For, in that case, Equilon has no power to force, exploit, or coerce a franchisee to purchase a tied-product such as credit card processing (if the processing is a distinct product for tying purposes) or to affect competition in the tied-product market. Such an arrangement would not raise antitrust concerns.

* * * * *

Rick-Mik argues that it alleged sufficient facts to *infer* that Equilon has sufficient economic power in the gasoline-franchise market, which has significant barriers to entry. It points to statistics indicating Equilon is an important player in the petroleum industry. According to . . . the complaint: (1) Equilon sells petroleum products to approximately 9,000 Shell and Texaco-branded retail outlets; (2) it ranks first in the industry in branded gasoline stations; (3) at 13 percent of the market, it ranks first in total gallons of gasoline sold in the United States; (4) it has annual gross revenues of approximately $24 billion; (5) it is number one or two in gasoline market share in 17 states; (6) it has four refineries, refining approximately 753,000 barrels of petroleum products per day and owns a 50 percent interest in Motiva's three refineries, refining approximately 865,000 barrels of petroleum products per day; (7) it owns an interest in approximately 10,000 miles of pipeline used to transport its petroleum products throughout the United States; and (8) it serves, on average, more than six million customers per day and sells approximately 19 billion gallons of gasoline per year, most of which is purchased by customers' credit or debit cards issued by thousands of banks, banking associations and financial institutions throughout the United States.

All of those allegations, however, relate to the *retail* gasoline market—a market where Rick-Mik is a seller—not the relevant market for franchises where it is a buyer. Further, the statistics alleged in the complaint do not distinguish between franchise-based sales and other potential types of sales (e.g., sales by directly owned outlets or sales to other distributors). Thus, the complaint fails to allege market power in the relevant market.

Nor is Rick-Mik's complaint saved by the allegation that "Shell and Texaco-branded gasolines are protected by various trademarks, copyrights and patents providing Equilon sufficient economic power over Plaintiffs in connection with its tying products to appreciably restrain competition in the tied-product market." . . . Because intellectual property rights are no longer presumed to confer market power, *see Illinois Toolworks Inc.*, 547 U.S. at 42–43, Rick-Mik's conclusory allegation that Equilon's intellectual property rights nonetheless do confer market power, unaccompanied by supporting facts, is insufficient.

Finally, the complaint's allegation of a contractual franchise relationship also fails to plead market power. A tying claim generally requires that the defendant's economic power be derived from the market, not from a contractual relationship that the plaintiff has entered into voluntarily. *See, e.g., Queen City Pizza, Inc.*, 124 F.3d at 443 ("where the defendant's 'power' to 'force' plaintiffs to purchase the alleged tying product stems not from the market, but from plaintiffs' contractual agreement to purchase the tying product, no claim will lie.")

* * * * *

b. Credit-card processing is not a distinct product.
There is another fatal flaw in Rick-Mik's complaint. Equilon's franchises are not a separate and distinct product from the credit-card processing services that are part of the franchise.

Franchises, almost by definition, necessarily consist of "bundled" and related products or services—not separate products.

* * * * *

With franchises, "the proper inquiry is . . . whether [the allegedly tied-products] are integral components of the business method being franchised. Where the challenged aggregation is an essential ingredient of the franchised system's formula for success, there is but a single product and no tie in exists as a matter of law." *Principe v. McDonald's Corp.*, 631 F.2d 303, 309 (4th Cir. 1980).

Here, Equilon's credit card services are an essential part of its franchise. Its agreement authorizes Equilon to use credit card proceeds to pay off a franchisee's account (i.e., money the franchisee owes Equilon for the gasoline Equilon delivers to the franchisee). The agreement also authorizes Equilon to charge or refund unauthorized transactions to the franchisee, helping secure the integrity of point-of-sale transactions.

* * * * *

Equilon points to the many other areas which are part and parcel of a franchise: signs, advertising, marketing, appearance, as well as methods of delivery and payment. Similarly, the method of receiving and processing credit transactions is an integral part of the franchise's operation. The franchise and the method of processing credit transactions are not separate products, but part of a single product (the franchise).

* * * * *

With franchises, the franchisee knows the contractual limitations and duties before entering into the contract. A complaint about such contractual obligations is not an antitrust matter.

* * * * *

Affirmed.

Questions

1. *a.* Identify the tying and tied products in the *Rik-Mik* case.
   b. Explain how Rik-Mik attempted to establish that Equilon had market power in the tying product.
2. How does Rik-Mik claim to have been harmed by the alleged tying arrangement?
3. Why did the court reason that a franchising contract ordinarily cannot, by itself, be the basis for an antitrust claim?
4. Who won this case and why?
5. When *Late Night with David Letterman* was an NBC show, the network, for some time, reportedly required those wanting to advertise on *Late Night* (then generally favored by a younger audience) to also buy spots on another talk show, the *Tonight Show with Johnny Carson* (then generally favored by an older audience).
   a. Does that packaging constitute a tying arrangement?
   b. Was it lawful? Explain.
6. Chrysler included the price of a sound system in the base price of its cars. Chrysler's share of the auto market was 10 to 12 percent. Chrysler did not reveal the "subprice" for the sound systems. Independent audio dealers objected on antitrust grounds. Explain their claim. Decide. See *Town Sound and Custom Tops, Inc. v. Chrysler Motor Corp.*, 959 F.2d 468 (3d Cir. 1992), *cert. denied*, 113 S. Ct. 196 (1992).

Exclusive Dealing and Requirements Contracts

LO 10-8
Describe the commercial advantages and disadvantages of exclusive dealing.

Principal Legislation: Clayton Act, Section 3; Sherman Act, Section 1

An *exclusive dealing contract* is an agreement in which a buyer commits itself to deal only with a specific seller, thereby cutting competing sellers out of that share of the market. A *requirements contract* is one in which a seller agrees to supply all of a buyer's needs, or a buyer agrees to purchase all of a seller's output, or both. Exclusive dealing and requirements contracts typically are lawful, but antitrust problems can arise depending on harm to competition. By its nature, an exclusive deal results in *market foreclosure*; that is, competitors are denied a source of supply or a market for sale. Thus, antitrust issues can emerge depending ordinarily on the market shares controlled by the parties. In general, however, manufacturers, distributors, and retailers have broad latitude in negotiating exclusive deals. We want businesses to produce and distribute their products in the manner they consider most efficient.

Movies

The U.S. Justice Department, at this writing, is investigating whether the handful of big chains that now dominate the movie market have made potentially anticompetitive agreements with the movie studios to receive exclusive first-run rights to some movies, thus shutting out smaller competitors. That practice is labeled "clearance," and it has been a part of industry practice for many years. The three biggest chains, Regal, AMC, and Cinemark, control about 42 percent of American movie screens.[26]

American Needle

> The National Football League was accused of restraint of trade.

In 2010, exclusive dealing concerns reached the U.S. Supreme Court when the National Football League was accused of restraint of trade for giving Reebok in 2000 an exclusive 10-year right to produce and market nearly all NFL-trademarked headware. The plaintiff, American Needle, a Downers Grove, Illinois, apparel manufacturer, was cut out of the premium cap market by the NFL decision. The NFL won at both the trial and federal court of appeals levels with both courts ruling that the NFL is a single entity (one business rather than a collection of competing teams/businesses) and thus could not have conspired as the Sherman Act requires. The U.S. Supreme Court, however, reversed the lower courts in 2010 by a 9–0 margin, saying that each of the teams is independently owned and managed and each proceeds as a separate, competing economic enterprise pursuing separate economic interests.[27]

The NFL and American Needle then settled the case in 2015, thus precluding further insight into the question of whether the NFL is able to "overcharge" for apparel. A class action was likewise settled in California for $4.75 million, where the NFL and Reebok reached an agreement with consumers who claimed that the exclusive Reebok licensing deal violated federal and California antitrust laws.

Condoms

Church & Dwight Co. (C & D) manufactures and distributes Trojan and other brand-name latex condoms. C & D controls about 75 percent of the U.S. retail condom market. The number-two seller has about 14 percent and number three sells just under 10 percent. Mayer Labs, with less than 1 percent of the market, raised antitrust claims against C & D. Mayer alleged that C & D had unlawful exclusive dealing arrangements with some retail chains, including 7-Eleven, and Mayer also argued that a C & D program granting kickbacks/rebates to retailers based on the amount of shelf space devoted to C & D products constituted a form of semi-exclusive dealing in that it put a ceiling or quota on the amount of shelf space competitors could secure.

The U.S. District Court for the Northern District of California ruled for C & D in 2012 finding, broadly, that Mayer had failed to show that C & D's marketing strategies had foreclosed competition. Despite C & D's large market share, the court reasoned that Mayer failed to show that C & D had market power because no evidence was presented of restricted output, supra-competitive prices, or barriers to entry. Further, the alleged exclusive dealing arrangements were of short duration, and they were voluntary. Finally, other channels of distribution were available to competitors. Thus, competition was not impaired.

Source: *Church & Dwight v. Mayer Laboratories*, 868 F. Supp. 2d 876 (N.D. Cal. 2012).

Price Discrimination

LO 10-9

Contrast price discrimination and predatory pricing.

Principal Legislation: Clayton Act, Section 2, as amended by the Robinson–Patman Act [For the statutory language, see **http://assembler.law.cornell.edu/uscode/15/13.html**].

Price discrimination involves selling substantially identical goods (not services) at reasonably contemporaneous times to different purchasers at different prices, where the effect is to harm competition. A seller may resist a claim under the Robinson–Patman Act by establishing one of the following defenses: (1) The price differential is attributable to cost savings. (In practice, the cost savings defense has been difficult to establish.) (2) The price differential is attributable to a good faith effort to meet the equally low price of a competitor. (3) Certain transactions are exempt from the act. Of special note are price changes made in response to changing markets. Thus, prices may lawfully be adjusted for seasonal goods or perishables.

> A coalition of independent video stores sued Blockbuster Video.

Some years ago, a coalition of independent video stores sued Blockbuster Video claiming that the 9,000-store video rental behemoth and the movie studios had conspired to drive the small stores out of business. Blockbuster allegedly received more favorable pricing and service (price discrimination) than the smaller independents. That litigation failed, and that failure teaches a powerful lesson about faith in the market and caution in applying antitrust remedies. If Blockbuster was using its enormous size to crush its competitors, in part through price discrimination practices with the movie studios, the market solved the problem. New technology emerged, and Blockbuster's customers left. The giant company declared bankruptcy in 2010, its business having shifted to Netflix and others. At this writing, about 50 Blockbuster stores still operate independently.

The video store case is among a number in recent years pitting independent operators (such as neighborhood bookstores and local pharmacies) against chains (such as Barnes &

Noble and big hospitals) where the independents claim that suppliers charge their giant rivals lower prices than those charged to the small stores. These complaints reflect the philosophical battle over the role of antitrust law in a rapidly changing global market. Should we use antitrust to protect small businesses, thus supporting neighborhoods, small towns, and a historic way of life in America? Or should we accept the dictates of the market, where the efficiency of giants like Walmart brings low prices and high quality to all?

Free-market advocates condemn price discrimination law as an attack on common, consumer-friendly pricing practices that often result in reduced prices. Why, the critics ask, would we assault those who engage in vigorous price competition? Indeed, *The Wall Street Journal* recently labeled the Robinson–Patman Act "a powerful law" that is "losing a lot of its punch."[28] From 2006 through 2010, plaintiffs (often small businesses) won just 4 percent of the Robinson–Patman cases brought in the federal courts, down from 35 percent in the years 1982 to 1993.[29] Furthermore, the federal government seldom brings a Robinson–Patman action. Nonetheless, as the following case illustrates, smaller businesses often do turn to Robinson–Patman in their ongoing struggle against what they believe to be the unfair competition of "giants."

Drug Mart Pharmacy Corp. v. American Home Products

LEGAL BRIEFCASE

2012 U.S. Dist. LEXIS 115882 (E.D.N.Y.)

U.S. Magistrate Judge Gold

[P]laintiffs are a number of individually owned retail pharmacies. Plaintiffs allege that defendants, five manufacturers of brand name prescription drugs ("BNPDs"), offered discounts and rebates to plaintiffs' competitors but not to plaintiffs, and that this constitutes price discrimination in violation of the Robinson-Patman Act.

BACKGROUND

In 2007, Senior United States District Judge I. Leo Glasser granted defendants' motion for summary judgment ". . . on the ground that plaintiffs have failed to show they are entitled to damages."

* * * * *

After Judge Glasser dismissed the claims of the designated parties, approximately 3,700 individual retail pharmacy plaintiffs remained. Confronted with Judge Glasser's decision, these remaining plaintiffs devised a plan to gather evidence in discovery that might show "that specific plaintiff pharmacies lost sales of BNPDs manufactured by defendants to any specific favored purchaser." Pursuant to this plan, which came to be known as the "matching process," plaintiffs compiled lists of specific BNPD customers who no longer

purchased drugs from them, and then searched the databases of non-party favored purchasers (and one favored purchaser who is a party) to see whether those same individuals were obtaining the same BNPDs from those favored purchasers.

* * * * *

[O]nly approximately 3% (5,147 of 164,501) of the potential lost customers plaintiffs culled from their own records could be "matched" to a customer who subsequently filled the same prescriptions with one or more favored purchasers.

* * * * *

The de minimis nature of these results is further illustrated when they are broken down and analyzed by defendant. According to defendants, when examined in this manner, the results are that approximately 88% of plaintiffs' claims against particular defendants are based on five or fewer lost customers per year. . . . Even Klein's Pharmacy, the plaintiff with the highest number of lost transactions identified by the matching process, lost a total of only 2,521 transactions, or approximately 252 transactions per year. This amounts to only slightly more than 1% of the total BNPD transactions conducted by an average retail pharmacy during any one year (252/22,000).

In short, no matter how analyzed, the matching process identified only a de minimis number of lost customers and transactions.

* * * * *

DISCUSSION

. . . I now consider whether plaintiffs' evidence, revealing as it does that plaintiffs lost only a trivial number of customers and sales to favored purchasers, is nevertheless sufficient to support a Robinson-Patman Act claim. . . .

The Robinson-Patman Act

* * * * *

In enacting Robinson-Patman, "Congress sought to target the perceived harm to competition occasioned by powerful buyers, rather than sellers; specifically, Congress responded to the advent of large chainstores, enterprises with the clout to obtain lower prices for goods than smaller buyers could demand." *Volvo*, 546 U.S. at 175. The purpose of the Act is to prohibit "price discrimination only to the extent that it threatens to injure competition." *Brooke Grp. Ltd. v. Brown & Williamson Tobacco Corp.*, 509 U.S. 209, 220, (1993).

* * * * *

1. Competitive Injury

The Robinson-Patman Act prohibits price discrimination only "where the effect of such discrimination may be substantially to lessen competition." 15 U.S.C. § 13(a).

* * * * *

[A]fter reviewing all of the pertinent authorities, . . . I conclude that a Robinson-Patman claim requires a showing of substantial competitive injury and that the de minimis sales identified by the matching process are insufficient to establish such an injury. . . .

2. Antitrust Injury

* * * * *

Price discrimination does not entitle a disfavored purchaser to "automatic damages." *J. Truett Payne Co. v. Chrysler Motors Corp.*, 451 U.S. 557, 561 (1981). . . . [P]laintiffs here . . . have been unable to "match up their losses" with gains to the favored purchasers. Plaintiffs have identified less than 3% of their total lost customers as having purchased BNPDs from favored purchasers, undermining any inference that price advantages enjoyed by favored purchaser caused plaintiffs' injury.

* * * * *

Because they are essentially unable to match up a significant number of the customers they lost with those the favored purchasers gained, plaintiffs have failed to demonstrate antitrust injury. . . .

CONCLUSION

For all these reasons, defendants' motion for summary judgment is granted.

[This district court decision was upheld on appeal at *Cash & Henderson Drugs v. Johnson & Johnson*, 799 F.3d 202 (2d Cir. 2015)—ed.]

Questions

1. Why did the retail pharmacies lose this case?

2. *a.* In your opinion, have small pharmacies and small businesses generally lost significant revenue over the years to retail giants such as Walmart and Costco? Explain.
   b. If so, does that loss constitute an antitrust wrong that should be remedied by law? Explain.

3. In what sense does the Robinson–Patman Act arguably reduce efficiency, thus harming consumer welfare?

4. Texaco sold gasoline at its retail tank wagon prices to Hasbrouck, an independent Texaco retailer, but granted discounts to distributors Gull and Dompier. Dompier also sold at the retail level. Gull and Dompier both delivered their gas directly to retailers and did not maintain substantial storage facilities. During the period in question, sales at the stations supplied by the two distributors grew dramatically, while Hasbrouck's sales declined. Hasbrouck filed suit against Texaco, claiming that the distributor discount constituted a Robinson–Patman violation. Texaco defended, saying the discount reflected the services the distributors performed for Texaco, and that the arrangement did not harm competition. Decide. Explain. See *Texaco v. Ricky Hasbrouck*, 496 U.S. 543 (1990).

5. Utah Pie produced frozen pies in its Salt Lake City plant. Utah's competitors, Carnation, Pet, and Continental, sometimes sold pies in Salt Lake City at prices beneath those charged in other markets. Indeed, Continental's prices in Salt Lake City were beneath its direct costs plus overhead. Pet sold to Safeway using Safeway's private label at a price lower than that at which the same pies were sold under the Pet label. Pet employed an industrial spy to infiltrate Utah Pie and gather information. Utah Pie claimed that Carnation, Pet, and Continental were in violation of Robinson–Patman. Decide. Explain. See *Utah Pie Co. v. Continental Baking Co.*, 386 U.S. 685 (1967).

Predatory Pricing

Principal Legislation: Sherman Act, Section 2

Can a giant legally reduce its prices below operating costs until a competing discounter drops out of the market and then raise those prices to supracompetitive levels? In 2009, the European Commission fined Intel $1.45 billion for *predatory pricing* and other alleged misconduct. Essentially, Intel was accused of reducing prices for its chips by unlawfully paying rebates/discounts to computer manufacturers and retailers to persuade them not to use rival chips. Among other arguments, Intel claims the rebates had the desirable effect of saving money for consumers, but critics say consumer choice was reduced by discouraging deals with Intel rivals, resulting in higher prices and potentially reduced quality in the long term. Intel also agreed in 2009 to pay Advanced Micro Devices (AMD), a smaller, rival chipmaker, $1.25 billion to settle AMD's allegations of predatory pricing (among other claims).[30]

Predatory pricing charges under European precedents have some reasonable probability of success, but in the United States they are very difficult to win. The U.S. Justice Department claimed that American Airlines engaged in predatory pricing in attempting to monopolize air travel at the Dallas–Fort Worth Airport from 1995 to 1997. Justice argued that American Airlines lowered its prices to drive out seven discount carriers in the expectation that it could then recover its losses by charging monopoly prices. A federal court of appeals, however, ruled for American Airlines, holding that the government was unable to prove that American had priced its flights below cost (as measured by some appropriate formulation, such as average variable cost).[31] Thus, the government had failed to satisfy the standard U.S. two-part test for establishing predatory pricing:

- Pricing below cost.
- A "dangerous probability" of recouping the losses suffered from the below-cost pricing.[32]

The *American Airlines* decision could be seen as a great victory for consumers in that it supports the right to cut prices as low as possible. But consider *BusinessWeek*'s description of American's pricing practices:

> . . . Between Dallas and Kansas City, for instance, American's average one-way ticket was $108 before low-cost start-up Vanguard Airlines Inc. entered the market in early 1995. That prompted American to cut fares to $80 and almost double the number of daily flights to 14. When Vanguard gave up in December 1995, American jacked up prices to $147 and scaled back the number of flights. Justice lawyers even had memos from American execs plotting the upstart's demise.[33]

Antitrust Confronts Intellectual Property

When Google, Pfizer, Monsanto, Adobe, or any other technology innovator, big or small, introduces a new product, we probably take for granted the resulting boost in the quality of our lifestyle, the jobs created, and the promise of additional advances in the future. More and more, however, our social and economic welfare is dependent on those technological breakthroughs. As former U.S. Secretary of Labor, Robert Reich, has noted: "Now information and ideas are the most valuable forms of property."[34] In order to encourage and protect *intellectual property* innovations, the law provides *patents* and *copyrights* as shields to preserve the innovator's rights. (For additional patent and copyright materials, refer to the index in the back of this text.) Preserving those rights, however, can lead to antitrust abuse because a patent or copyright may confer market power. The federal government and legal experts, therefore, are giving attention to the increasing conflicts between antitrust law and intellectual property rights. Antitrust law, designed for smokestack industries, must now be applied to our contemporary, knowledge-based economy.

We believe patent and copyright laws encourage innovation and protect creators' legitimate property interests, but we also believe in free access to knowledge as something of a personal right and as a necessary precondition to continued progress and prosperity. We need the stimulus of antitrust-protected competition to lower prices and maximize consumer welfare, but we also need the shelter of intellectual property rights to encourage innovation and investment. If we do not use patents and copyrights (and sometimes trademarks) to protect intellectual property, will creative efforts be diminished? In providing intellectual property protection, however, do we open the door to abusive behaviors, as Robert Reich has argued:

> The law gives 20 years of patent protection to inventions that are "new and useful," as decided by the Patent and Trademark Office. But the winners are big enough to game the system. They make small improvements warranting new patents, effectively making their intellectual property semi-permanent. They also lay claim to whole terrains of potential innovation including ideas barely on drawing boards and flood the system with so many applications that lone inventors have to wait years. The White House intellectual property adviser Colleen V. Chien noted in 2012 that Google and Apple were spending more money acquiring patents (not to mention litigating them) than on doing research and development.[35]

The U.S. Supreme Court has ruled that patents do not automatically confer market power; rather, that power must be proven.[36] Further, a patent-related antitrust violation does not occur unless some anticompetitive conduct—monopoly, exclusive dealing, tying arrangement, etc.—is identified.[37]

Recent Cases Apple sued Samsung claiming that Samsung copied iPhone design elements (rectangular shape with rounded corners, black translucent front screen, and on-screen icons) in violation of certain Apple design patents. Apple prevailed in the lower courts, and Samsung was ordered to pay $399 million in damages. In late 2016, however, a unanimous Supreme Court reversed that damages award reasoning that damages could be based on the profits attributable to a part or parts of the product rather than the whole product, as the lower court had ruled.[38] Thus, a ruling that a company copied a portion of a competitor's product doesn't automatically mean that all of the profits from that product belong to the competitor. The case was sent back to the Federal Circuit Court of Appeals to decide how much Apple's design patents should be worth.

In total, the case is a victory for Apple and patent rights in the sense that Samsung apparently will pay damages for copying, but Samsung interpreted the Supreme Court ruling as a victory for creativity, innovation, and fair competition.

The Federal Trade Commission addressed patent/antitrust conflicts in its 2013 settlement with Google, which agreed to license, under reasonable terms, essential patents to its competitors, such as Apple. The settlement came after a lengthy FTC investigation of Google's patent practices and its alleged dominance, particularly in the search engine market. (For more on Google as an alleged monopolist, see Chapter 11.)

Internet Exercise

Using the "Frequently Asked Questions" on the "Small Business Notes" web page [**www.smallbusinessnotes.com/managing-your-business/frequently-asked-questions.html**], answer these questions:

1. The gasoline stations in my area have increased their prices the same amount and at the same time. Is that price-fixing?
2. I operate two stores that sell recorded music. My business is being ruined by giant discount store chains that sell their products for less than my wholesale cost. I thought there were laws against price discrimination, but I can't afford the legal fees to fight the big corporations. Can you help?

Chapter Questions

1. After reading this chapter, what is your judgment about the antitrust system?
   a. Does it work? Explain.
   b. How might it be altered?
   c. Could we place more reliance on the market? Explain.
   d. Do the statutes and case law, as a body, seem to form a rational package? Explain.
   e. Should antitrust policy focus exclusively on economic considerations or should social welfare goals (such as maintenance of full employment and the dispersal of political power) assume greater importance? Explain.
2. In recent years, Amazon, Walmart, Target, and others have been dramatically discounting some bestselling books, sometimes selling popular hardcover titles at under $10. In Europe's major publishing markets other than the United Kingdom, most new books, both print and online, must be sold at the price specified by the publisher; that is, discount pricing is forbidden by law.
   a. Why would Europeans accept antidiscounting laws that keep new book prices high?
   b. How would you expect the antidiscounting laws to affect the prices of used books?
   c. Germany, with a population of over 82 million, has about 5,000 bookstores while the United States, with a population of about 325 million, has about 11,000 bookstores. Is America's literary culture threatened by allowing giant retailers to aggressively discount? Explain.
3. Subway sandwich shops required all franchisees to employ a computerized point-of-sale (POS) system. The only approved system was provided by an unrelated company, RBS. Vendors of a competing POS system sued Subway's parent, Doctor's Associates, alleging, among other things, an unlawful tying arrangement.
   a. Describe the alleged tie.

    b. Defend Doctor's Associates (Subway).

    c. Explain what the plaintiffs would need to demonstrate in order to prevail. See *Subsolutions, Inc. v. Doctor's Associates, Inc.*, 62 F. Supp. 2d 616 (D. Conn. 1999) and 436 F. Supp. 2d 348 (D. Conn. 2006).

4. In *Continental T.V., Inc. v. GTE Sylvania, Inc.*, 433 U.S. 36 (1977), the U.S. Supreme Court took the position that interbrand, rather than intrabrand, agreements must be the primary concern of antitrust law.

    a. Why did the Court take that view?

    b. In your opinion, is the Court correct? Explain.

    c. Explain the "free-rider" problem that frequently concerns the courts in cases involving vertical territorial restraints, among others.

5. Could Whirlpool, the appliance manufacturer, lawfully refuse to deal with any purchaser that sells the products of a competitor such as General Electric? Explain.

6. Pool Corporation, the largest wholesale distributor of swimming pool supplies in the United States and the only distributor with a nationwide distribution system, was accused in 2011 by the Federal Trade Commission of abusing its market power by pressuring its product manufacturers to refrain from selling to those seeking to enter the market as pool supply distributors (and thus competitors of Pool Corporation). The FTC found that manufacturers representing about 70 percent of all pool product sales declined to sell to new entrants. The FTC calculated that Pool Corporation accounted for 30 to 50 percent of most pool supply manufacturers' sales, making it by a wide margin the largest customer of those manufacturers. Pool Corporation settled the FTC charges.

    a. What antitrust violation(s) were alleged by the FTC?

    b. How would you rule on those alleged violations? Explain.

7. Tanaka played soccer at the University of Southern California (USC), a member of the PAC 10 Conference. She became unhappy, asked if she could transfer, and was told that she could. She decided to go to another PAC 10 school, UCLA. USC, unhappy with that choice, invoked an NCAA rule limiting transfers within a conference. The rule required her to sit out one year and to lose one year of eligibility. She sued USC and the NCAA on restraint of trade grounds.

    a. Explain her claim.

    b. Decide the case. Explain your decision. See *Tanaka v. University of Southern California*, 252 F.3d 1059 (9th Cir. 2001).

8. Assume two fertilizer dealerships, Grow Quick and Fertile Fields, hold 70 percent and 30 percent, respectively, of the fertilizer business in the farm community of What Cheer, Iowa. Assume the owner of Fertile Fields learns via inquiry, hearsay, and the like of Grow Quick's price quotes. Then, each growing season, the Fertile Fields owner sets her prices exactly equal to those of her competitor. Is that practice unlawful? Explain.

9. Given functionally identical competing products, why is identical pricing virtually inevitable—at least over the long run?

10. In 1968, Business Electronics Corporation (BEC) became the exclusive retailer in the Houston, Texas, area of electronic calculators manufactured by Sharp Electronics

Corporation. In 1972, Sharp appointed Hartwell as a second retailer in the Houston area. Sharp published a list of suggested minimum retail prices, but its written dealership agreements with BEC and Hartwell did not obligate either to observe them or to charge any other specific price. BEC's retail prices were often below Sharp's suggested retail prices and generally below Hartwell's retail prices, even though Hartwell too sometimes priced below Sharp's suggested retail prices. Hartwell complained to Sharp on a number of occasions about BEC's prices. In 1973, Hartwell gave Sharp the ultimatum that Hartwell would terminate his dealership unless Sharp ended its relationship with BEC within 30 days. Sharp terminated BEC's dealership. BEC filed suit alleging that Sharp and Hartwell had unlawfully conspired to terminate BEC and that the conspiracy was illegal *per se* under the Sherman Act, Section 1. Decide the case. Explain. See *Business Electronics Corporation v. Sharp Electronics Corporation*, 485 U.S. 717 (1988).

11. Some antitrust experts argue the government should expect a firm possessing market power to reduce that power as quickly as possible. Others maintain that the government should be patient with short-term market power. Explain those two points of view.

12. Adidas contracts with NCAA schools and their coaches to promote its products. An NCAA rule limits the amount of advertising that may appear on uniforms and equipment. Adidas complained that those restrictions on promotional rights "artificially limit the price and quality options available to apparel manufacturers as consumers of promotional space, force manufacturers to pay additional amounts for billboard space or other advertising, decrease the selection of apparel offered to the end consumer, increase the price of the apparel for end consumers, and financially benefit the NCAA." Adidas sued the NCAA on antitrust grounds.

    a. What antitrust violations were cited by Adidas?

    b. Decide the case. Explain. See *Adidas v. NCAA*, 64 F. Supp. 2d 1097 (D. Kan. 1999).

13. A board-certified anesthesiologist was denied admission to the Jefferson Parish Hospital staff because the hospital had an exclusive services contract with a firm of anesthesiologists. The contract required all surgery patients at the hospital to use that firm for their anesthesiology work. Seventy percent of the patients in the parish were served by hospitals other than Jefferson. The anesthesiologist who was denied admission sued the hospital, claiming the contract was unlawful.

    a. What antitrust violation was raised by the plaintiff?

    b. Decide. Explain. See *Jefferson Parish Hospital District No. 2 v. Hyde*, 466 U.S. 2 (1984).

14. *The Wall Street Journal*: "Teddy Roosevelt busted Standard Oil. The Obama Administration? It's making the world safe from rapacious piano teachers."[39] The Federal Trade Commission alleged that the 22,000-member Music Teachers National Association (MTNA) implemented an ethics code that forbade members from actively recruiting each others' students, and that some MTNA affiliates prohibited members from charging lesson fees lower than the community average or offering free lessons or scholarships. In 2013, the MTNA agreed to change its code and to sever relations with nonconforming affiliates.

a. What antitrust harm was the government seeking to stem?

b. Was the FTC misusing its power in pursuing the music teachers? Explain.

15. Until 2009, McWane produced 100 percent of America's domestically manufactured ductile iron pipe fittings (used to connect municipal water pipes). Star entered the market and captured a 10 percent share. McWane then announced its "Full Support Program," stipulating that its customers must buy their full requirements from McWane or those customers might not receive rebates and their shipments might be delayed by 12 weeks. The Federal Trade Commission charged that the Full Support Program violated antitrust laws.

a. What antitrust violation was alleged by the FTC?

b. Was the FTC correct? Explain. See *McWane v. FTC*, 783 F.3d 814 (11th Cir. 2015), cert. denied, 136 S. Ct. 1452 (2016).

Notes

1. Harold Meyerson, "We Need a New Trust-Busting Movement in America," *The Washington Post*, November 11, 2015 [**www.washingtonpost.com**].

2. "Too Much of a Good Thing," *The Economist*, March 26, 2016 [**www.economist.com**].

3. Robert J. Samuelson, "Do We Have a Competition Deficit?" *The Washington Post*, April 19, 2016 [**www.washingtonpost.com**].

4. Lee Van Voorhis and Roxanne Busey, "U.S. Trends in Antitrust Enforcement of Cartels and Mergers in a Global Environment," *LEXOLOGY*, January 25, 2016 [**www.lexology.com**].

5. *Standard Oil Co. of New Jersey v. United States*, 221 U.S. 1 (1911).

6. Alexander McIntyre Jr., "Halt to 'Call-Arounds' Puts La Quinta in Spotlight," *LEXOLOGY*, May 27, 2010 [**www.lexology.com**].

7. This analysis is drawn from William Kovacic, "The Identification and Proof of Horizontal Agreements under the Antitrust Laws," *Antitrust Bulletin* 38, no. 1 (Spring 1993), p. 5.

8. *Bell Atlantic Corp. v. Twombly*, 127 S. Ct. 1955 (2007).

9. Drew Harwell, Ashley Halsey III, and Thad Moore, "Justice Dept. Investigating Potential Airline Price Collusion," *The Washington Post*, July 1, 2015 [**www.washingtonpost.com**].

10. Jacob Gershman, "Fertility Industry Group Settles Lawsuit over Egg Donor Price Caps," *The Wall Street Journal*, February 3, 2016 [**http://blogs.wsj.com**].

11. Bill Myers, "$100 Million Accord in Price-Fix Lawsuit," *Chicago Daily Law Bulletin*, July 29, 2004.

12. Michael Orey, "Price Fixing, the Perpetual Sequel," *Bloomberg Businessweek*, September 28, 2009 [**www.businessweek.com**].

13. The analysis in this paragraph relies considerably on Donald M. Falk, "Antitrust and Refusals to Deal after *Nynex v. Discon*," *Practical Lawyer* 46, no. 3 (2000), p. 25.

14. See, e.g., Herbert J. Hovenkamp, "Unilateral Refusals to Deal, Vertical Integration, and the Essential Facility Doctrine," July 1, 2008, *U. of Iowa Legal Studies Research Paper* No. 08-31. Available at SSRN: **http://ssrn.com/abstract=1144675**.

15. This summary of the *JSW Steel* facts is largely drawn from Sidley Austin, LLP, "Fifth Circuit Holds That a Manufacturer Pressured by Its Two Largest Distributors Not to Deal with a Third Distributor Is Per Se Liable for Antitrust Conspiracy," *Sidley Update*, December 10, 2015 [**www.sidley.com**].

16. *MM Steel v. JSW Steel (USA)*, 806 F.3d 835 (5th Cir. 2015).

17. Michelle Casady, "JWS Steel Takes $156M Damages Fight to High Court," *Law 360*, June 10, 2016 [**www.law360.com**].

18. *United States v. Colgate & Co.*, 250 U.S. 300 (1919).

19. *State Oil Co. v. Khan*, 118 S. Ct. 275 (1997).

20. *Dr. Miles Medical Co. v. John D. Park & Sons Co.*, 220 U.S. 373 (1911).

21. "Price of Contact Lenses at Issue in Court Case," *PBS NewsHour*, August 30, 2015 [**www.pbs.org**].

22. "54 Class Action Lawsuits Accuse Contact Lens Makers of Price Fixing," *Market Scope*, October 23, 2015 [**https://market-scope.com**].

23. Chris Morran, "Court Allows Utah to Ban Price-Fixing of Contact Lenses," *Consumerist*, June 15, 2015 [**https://consumerist.com**].

24. *Continental T.V., Inc. v. GTE Sylvania, Inc.*, 433 U.S. 36 (1977).

25. This paragraph relies upon Conor Dougherty, "F.T.C. Is Said to Investigate Claims That Google Used Android to Promote Its Products," *The New York Times*, September 25, 2015 [**www.nytimes.com**].

26. Brooks Barnes, "Antitrust Scrutiny for 3 Big U.S. Theater Chains," *The New York Times*, June 2, 2015 [**www.nytimes.com**].

27. *American Needle v. National Football League*, 130 S. Ct. 2201 (2010).

28. Robert J. Toth, "A Powerful Law Has Been Losing a Lot of Its Punch," *The Wall Street Journal*, May 21, 2012, p. R2.

29. Ibid.

30. Steve Lohr and James Kanter, "A.M.D.-Intel Settlement Won't End Their Woes," *The New York Times*, November 13, 2009 [**www.nytimes.com**].

31. *United States v. AMR Corp.*, 335 F.3d 1109 (10th Cir. 2003).

32. *Brooke Group Ltd. v. Brown & Williamson Tobacco Corp.*, 509 U.S. 209 (1993).

33. Dan Carney, "Predatory Pricing: Cleared for Takeoff," *BusinessWeek*, May 14, 2001, p. 50.

34. Robert Reich, "Is Big Tech Too Powerful? Ask Google," *The New York Times*, September 18, 2015 [**www.nytimes.com**].

35. Ibid.

36. *Illinois Tool Works v. Independent Ink*, 547 U.S. 28 (2006).

37. *Verizon Communications Inc. v. Law Offices of Curtis V. Trinko, LLP*, 540 U.S. 398, 407 (2004).

38. *Samsung Electronics Co. v. Apple, Inc.*, 137 S. Ct. 429 (2016).

39. Kimberley A. Strassel, "Strassel: Piano Sonata in FTC Minor," *The Wall Street Journal*, November 28, 2013 [**www.wsj.com**].

Antitrust Law—Monopolies and Mergers

After completing this chapter, students will be able to fulfill the following learning objectives:

11-1.   Identify critics' antitrust concerns about big tech companies.

11-2.   Explain how Microsoft violated U.S. antitrust laws.

11-3.   Analyze when a monopoly has been created.

11-4.   Identify the potential benefits and hazards of mergers.

11-5.   Distinguish between horizontal and vertical mergers.

11-6.   Explain premerger notification requirements.

11-7.   Describe remedies for mergers determined to be anticompetitive.

11-8.   Analyze when a horizontal merger is anticompetitive.

11-9.   Analyze when a vertical merger creates anticompetitive "market foreclosure."

11-10. Contrast antitrust enforcement in the United States and the European Union (EU).

Introduction—Google, Microsoft, and Monopoly

LO 11-1
Identify critics' antitrust concerns about big tech companies.

Corporate goliaths like Google, Microsoft, Exxon, and Walmart, products of American ingenuity, are crucial to national prosperity and to international competitiveness. At the same time, those giants can threaten societal welfare. Monopoly law addresses those threats. Single firms sometimes dominate an industry (monopoly), and more commonly in the contemporary American economy, a few big firms share that dominance (oligopoly), as journalist David Dayen explained in 2016:

> . . .[T]hink about everything you buy and every service you pay for, and how they come from concentrated suppliers. We have four airlines serving 80 percent of all passengers. We have four cable and Internet companies providing most of the nation's cell-companies (only three if two proposed mergers go through this year), and a handful of producers selling every major consumer product. Even when you think you have a choice, like in the array of online travel-booking sites, two companies (Expedia and Priceline) own all the subsidiaries.[1]

This economic concentration can be efficient and a near necessity for international competition, but it can also lead to higher prices, poorer service, suppressed employee wages, economic inequality, reduced start-up opportunities, abuse of political power, and other problems. As *The Economist* observed in 2016: "Profits are too high. America needs a giant dose of competition. . . . [H]igh profits can be a sign of sickness. They can signal the existence of firms more adept at siphoning wealth off than creating it afresh, such as those that exploit monopolies."[2]

With these economic concentration concerns in mind, we turn now to the analysis of the challenges posed by monopolies.

Is Google Too Big?

Jeffrey Katz, NexTag CEO and Google competitor, thinks so:

> Google . . . is the most popular search engine in the world, controlling 82 percent of the global search market and 98 percent of the mobile search market. Its annual revenue is larger than the economies of the world's 28 poorest countries combined. And its closest competitor, Bing, is so far behind . . . that Google has become, effectively, a monopoly.

In the United States, Google handles about two-thirds of all web searches. Nonetheless, the Federal Trade Commission (FTC) ended a 19-month investigation of Google by announcing in early 2013 that it would not pursue litigation against the giant. Rather, Google agreed, among other things, to allow competitors fair, reasonable access to essential patents held by Google. No action was taken, however, regarding the critics' biggest concern: Google's alleged "search bias," in which critics contend that Google's search results are "rigged" to favor its own commercial interests. The FTC unanimously concluded that Google's search practices were not anticompetitive in that they were designed primarily to improve the quality of the product delivered to consumers.

The FTC's resolution of the Google investigation has been harshly criticized, but supporters note that dissatisfied consumers have a number of choices in the search market. This story is not over, however. *Politico* reported in 2016 that the FTC is once again asking questions about whether Google is abusing its search market dominance.

Perhaps most threatening to Google are European Union charges that, among other things, Google manipulates general search results to favor its own comparison shopping services. Thus, consumers cannot be confident they are receiving the most relevant results when looking online for goods and services. Google disputes these charges, and some critics argue that the European Union's antitrust moves are simply an economic attack on American dominance in the tech industry.

Sources: Jeffrey Katz, "Google's Monopoly and Internet Freedom," *The Wall Street Journal,* June 8, 2012, p. A15; Nancy Scola, "Sources: Feds Taking Second Look at Google Search," *Politico,* May 11, 2016 [**www.politco.com**]; and Mark Scott, "E.U. Charges Dispute Google's Claims That Android Is Open to All," *The New York Times,* April 20, 2016 [**www.nytimes.com**].

LO 11-2

Explain how Microsoft violated U.S. antitrust laws.

Microsoft a Monopolist?   Through its relatively brief history, has Microsoft been an outsized, predatory lawbreaker, an amazing force for technological progress, or both? The U.S. Justice Department, 18 states, and the District of Columbia went to trial against Microsoft in 1998, claiming not that the software giant was too big, but that it

An epic legal struggle followed, with major elements of the American justice system challenging one of the world's richest men, Bill Gates.

had violated various antitrust laws in gaining and maintaining its market dominance. An epic legal struggle followed, with major elements of the American justice system challenging one of the world's richest men, Bill Gates.

A federal district court in 2000 and later a federal court of appeals ruled that Microsoft had violated federal antitrust laws by maintaining its 95 percent share of the Intel-compatible PC operating systems market through anticompetitive means (basically using its Windows monopoly power to coerce customers to buy other Microsoft products such as its browser, Internet Explorer).[3] The district court judge ordered Microsoft split into two companies as a remedy for its antitrust wrongs, but the court of appeals threw out that order. Thereafter, the case was settled out of court with Microsoft agreeing, among other things, to not retaliate unfairly against other software and computer makers, to disclose some software code, and to be temporarily monitored by a federal judge.

The settlement, though somewhat of a victory for Microsoft, might also be regarded as a victory for common sense in allowing Microsoft to go forward with its remarkable work. The decision places considerable faith in the market, as it probably should in America, but the case also represents a powerful affirmation of the government's authority to attack monopoly behavior no matter how prominent the wrongdoer.

Settlements   As it turns out, the federal antitrust charges were only the beginning of Microsoft's battles. Settlements with Novell, Sun Microsystems, and others cost Microsoft billions. European Union antitrust enforcers pursued Microsoft for a decade before settling their claims in 2009. The EU argument, much like the concerns in the United States, was that Microsoft's market dominance allowed it to effectively force its Windows operating system users to also use its Internet Explorer browser. The settlement required Microsoft to provide a pop-up screen that would allow European customers to choose among several browsers other than Explorer, thus likely building the market share of rival browsers. Just as the 2009 settlement appeared to have resolved Microsoft's European problems, the European Commission announced in 2013 that it had fined Microsoft over $730 million for breaking the terms of that settlement. Microsoft apologized for what it said was a technical problem that had temporarily denied about 15 million users the promised choice of browsers. Because 25 percent of the global market for many products resides in the European Union, all big companies now think carefully about how their practices will be received by EU regulators even if those practices are not of concern in the United States.

Whether we must employ antitrust to attack great concentrations of power.

The Microsoft battle obliges us to think about what we want America to be and what role the law should play in securing that ideal. Crucially for our purposes, we should ask whether the market and ethics are sufficient to preserve genuine democracy along with social and economic justice, or whether we must employ antitrust law to attack those great concentrations of power that sometimes threaten our core values. Journalist Alan Murray was rather cynical about the Microsoft lesson:

The Microsoft saga serves as a reminder of an important truth: Capitalists, for the most part, don't care much for capitalism. Their goal is to make money. And if they can do it without messy competition, so much the better.[4]

Questions

1. *a.* Do you see increasing concentrations of wealth and power as threats to America's long-term welfare? Explain.
   b. If that concentration is a concern, is antitrust law the best remedy?
2. Does the *Microsoft* case stand simply for the view that bigness is bad? Explain.
3. Critics have argued that technology is eliminating the imperfections of the market, making antitrust law enforcement obsolete in this high-tech era.
   a. Explain that argument.
   b. Now build the argument that high-tech industries may actually be especially susceptible to antitrust problems because of the need to maintain equipment compatibility.

Part One—Monopoly

eBay-owned ticketing service StubHub in 2015 sued Ticketmaster and the Golden State Warriors National Basketball Association team for monopoly practices. StubHub alleged that the team had threatened to cancel season ticket holders' subscriptions if they tried to resell any of their tickets on StubHub instead of Ticketmaster, the team's exclusive ticketing agent. According to StubHub's lawsuit, Ticketmaster and the Warriors monopolized the team's ticket sales and engaged in an unlawful tying arrangement by controlling both first-time and secondary ticket sales. A federal judge dismissed the lawsuit in 2015. Ticketmaster and other ticketing services commonly maintain exclusive ticketing arrangements in the NBA and elsewhere in American life. In a reassuring free-market response, StubHub challenged Ticketmaster in 2016 by introducing its own combined first-time and secondary ticketing platform for its role as the official ticketing partner of the Philadelphia 76ers NBA team. StubHub ticket buyers reportedly will be able to resell their unneeded tickets wherever they wish.

Monopoly Legislation   How do we know when an organization is an unlawful monopolist? Federal laws define the general parameters.

Principal Monopoly Legislation: Sherman Act, Section 2

> Every person who shall monopolize, or attempt to monopolize, or combine or conspire with any other person or persons, to monopolize any part of the trade or commerce among the several States, or with foreign nations, shall be deemed guilty of a felony punishable by a fine.

Section 5 of the Federal Trade Commission Act also applies to antitrust cases, although the wisdom of that use is disputed.

Monopoly Defined   From an economic viewpoint, a monopoly is a situation in which one firm holds the power to control prices and/or exclude competition in a particular market.

The general legal test for monopolization is

1. The possession of monopoly power in the relevant market and
2. The willful acquisition or maintenance of that power, as distinguished from growth or development as a consequence of a superior product, business acumen, or historic accident.[5]

Thus, the critical inquiries are the percentage of the market held by the alleged monopolist and the behavior that produced and maintained or expanded that market share. Antitrust law does not punish efficient companies that legitimately earn and maintain large market shares.

Indeed, high market concentration often promotes competition, whereas a fragmented market of many small firms may produce higher prices. (Imagine a retail food market of many corner grocery stores and no supermarkets.) Nonetheless, the federal government continues to rely strongly on market concentration data (structure) in combination with evidence of actual behavior (conduct) to identify anticompetitive situations. Market share alone is highly unlikely to lead to antitrust action, but a high market share acquired and/ or maintained via abusive conduct (as alleged in *Microsoft*) may be challenged. [For the American Bar Association Antitrust section, see **www.americanbar.org/groups/ antitrust_law.html**].

Oligopoly   A few firms sharing monopoly power constitute an oligopoly. As we mentioned earlier, oligopolistic markets are common in American life, and they have emerged in some global markets as well. A 2009 *New York Times* headline read: "Rising Beer Prices Hint at Oligopoly."[6]

As *The New York Times* noted, we fear that oligopoly conditions will lead to higher prices (along with reduced quality and innovation). In industries such as telecommunications (telecom), food processing, credit ratings, and book publishing, we find enormous American and international markets dominated by a handful of companies. Of course, oligopolies often produce significant efficiencies, and they may leave market space for smaller competitors, including startups. But in many cases, we worry that oligopolies threaten consumer welfare. We see, for example, that only four railroads (Burlington Northern Santa Fe, CSX, Norfolk Southern, and Union Pacific) control approximately 90 percent of the rail freight market. Not coincidentally, railroads enjoy government-granted exemptions from many antitrust rules, although a rather obscure federal agency, the Surface Transportation Board, oversees the rail industry.

Amazon, Apple, Google: Monopolies?

U.S. Senator Elizabeth Warren (D-Mass.) in 2016 attacked the three technology companies of Amazon, Apple, and Google as examples of concentrated corporate power that can undermine competition. Pointing specifically to Amazon, journalist Franklin Foer says it threatens our future by holding "intolerable economic and cultural sway." Amazon, he says, brings us low prices and great service in the short term by its ruthless destruction of rivals:

> . . . Amazon has a record of shredding young businesses, like Zappos and Diapers.com, just as they begin to pose a competitive challenge. It uses its riches to undercut

opponents on price—Amazon was prepared to lose $100 million in three months in its quest to harm Diapers.com—then once it has exhausted the resources of its foes, it buys them and walks away even stronger.

In counterpoint, analyst Tim Worstall, writing in *Forbes*, says that we should worry less about monopolies in the tech area because of their fleeting nature: "No one actually gets a monopoly for long enough to be able to fleece consumers through having that monopoly."

Questions

1. In your view, does the government, through antitrust law, have a useful, meaningful role to play in regulating high-tech companies such as Amazon, Apple, and Google? Explain.

2. Will the market automatically correct, in rather rapid fashion, any monopolistic conditions that may develop in the high-tech arena? Explain.

Sources: Franklin Foer, "Amazon Must Be Stopped," *New Republic,* October 9, 2014 [**https://newrepublic.com**]; Mario Trujillo, "Warren Targets Amazon, Apple, Google in Anti-Monopoly Speech," *The Hill,* June 29, 2016 [**http://the hill.com**]; and Tim Worstall, "Google, Microsoft, Apple, Facebook: Please, Will the Regulators Stop Worrying About Monopolies," *Forbes,* September 29, 2014 [**www.forbes.com**].

Monopolization Analysis

LO 11-3
Analyze when a monopoly has been created.

Although the case law is not a model of clarity, a rather straightforward framework for monopoly analysis has emerged:

1. Define the relevant *product market*.
2. Define the relevant *geographic market*.
3. Compute the defendant's *market power*.
4. Assess the defendant's *intent* (predatory or coercive conduct).
5. Raise any available *defenses*.

1. Product Market

Here the court seeks, effectively, to draw a circle that encompasses categories of goods in which the defendant's products or services compete and that excludes those not in the same competitive arena. The fundamental test is *interchangeability* as determined primarily by the price, use, and quality of the product in question.

An analysis of *cross-elasticity of demand* is a key ingredient in defining the product market. Assume that two products, X and Y, appear to be competitors. Assume that the price of X doubled and Y's sales volume was unchanged. What does that tell us about whether X and Y are, in fact, in the same product market?

Defining the product market is really the process we all go through in routine purchasing decisions. Assume you feel a rather undefined hunger for salty snack food. You go to the nearby convenience store. Many options confront you, but for simplicity, let's confine them to chips, nuts, and popcorn. Each of those food types is, of course, composed of variations. As you sort through the choices—corn chips, cheese curls, peanuts, potato chips, and so on—you employ the criteria of price, use, and quality in focusing your decision. In so doing, you are defining the product market for "salty snack food." Products closely matched in price, use, and quality are interchangeable, and thus are competitors in the same product market. But, for example, an imported salty cheese at $10 per quarter pound presumably is not in the same product market as salted sunflower seeds.

Expressed as a matter of elasticity, the critical question becomes something like the following: If the price of potato chips, for example, falls by 10 percent, does the sales volume of salted nuts likewise fall? If so, we have a preliminary indication that potato chips and salted nuts may lie in the same product market and thus may be competitors.

2. Geographic Market

Once the product market has been defined, we still must determine where the product can be purchased. The judicial decisions to date offer no definitive explanation of the geographic market concept. A working definition might be "any section of the country where the product is sold in commercially significant quantities." From an economic perspective, the geographic market can be defined by elasticity. If prices rise or supplies are reduced within the geographic area in question (New England, for example) and demand remains steady, will products from other areas enter the market in a quantity sufficient to affect price and/or supply? If so, the geographic market must be broadened to embrace those new sources of supply. If not, the geographic market is not larger than the area in question (New England). Perhaps a better approach is to read the cases and recognize that each geographic market must simply be identified in terms of its unique economic properties.

3. Market Power (Market Share)

Does the market share held by the defendant threaten competition? How large that share must be to raise monopoly concerns depends on a variety of considerations including how fragmented or concentrated the market is. *The Harvard Law Review*, however, notes some approximate boundaries:

> Market share above 70 percent typically suffices to support an inference of monopoly power. Conversely, courts have rarely found monopoly power when a firm's market share is below 50 percent, leaving some uncertainty as to market shares between 50 and 70 percent.[7]

Market share alone, however, does not establish monopoly power. Barriers to entry, economies of scale, the strength of the competition, trends in the market, and pricing patterns all help to determine whether the market remains competitive despite a single firm's large share. (Why are the courts interested in barriers to entry?)

4. Intent (Predatory or Coercive Conduct)

Assuming a threatening market share is established, the next requirement is proof of an intent to monopolize. Remember that a monopoly finding requires a showing of both market power (*structure*) and willful acquisition or maintenance of that power (*conduct*). Antitrust law is not designed to attack legitimately earned market power. Rather, the concern lies with those holding monopoly power that was acquired or maintained wrongfully. Thus, a showing of deliberate predatory, coercive, or unfair conduct (such as collusion leading to price-fixing) will normally suffice to establish the requisite intent.

Conduct   Intel, the dominant microchip maker with 80 to 90 percent of the microprocessor market, reached a 2010 settlement of Federal Trade Commission charges that it used unfair tactics to earn and maintain that market share. Basically, Intel was accused of providing discriminatory rebates to Dell, IBM, HP, and others in return for those purchasers' agreement not to buy central processing unit chips from Intel's rival, Advanced Micro Devices (AMD). Intel was also accused of designing its chips so that competing processors could not run efficiently with them. The FTC settlement prohibited those rebate and design practices. [Why might discounts constitute an antitrust violation? Can you defend Intel against those charges? See Edward Wyatt and Ashlee Vance, "Intel Settles with F.T.C. on Antitrust," *The New York Times*, August 4, 2010 (**www.nytimes.com**); and Stephen Labaton, "Intel Facing Antitrust Investigation," *The New York Times*, June 7, 2008 (**www.nytimes.com**).]

5. Defenses

Assuming an anticompetitive monopoly is established in steps 1–4, the defendant may yet prevail if the evidence demonstrates that the monopoly was innocently acquired via "superior skill, foresight, or industry," making the monopoly earned. Sometimes a monopoly may be "thrust upon" the monopolist because the competition failed or because of "natural monopoly" conditions where the market will support only one firm or where large economies of scale exist, such as for electricity suppliers.

Attempted Monopolization

The Sherman Act forbids attempts to monopolize as well as anticompetitive monopoly itself. In the 1993 *Spectrum Sports* decision,[8] the Supreme Court set out a three-part test for attempted monopolization: (1) the defendant has engaged in predatory or anticompetitive conduct with (2) a specific intent to monopolize and (3) a dangerous probability of achieving monopoly power (by which the Court was insisting on evidence of some "realistic" likelihood that monopoly would actually follow).

Is Bob Marley a Product Market?

Music producer Rock River released remixed Bob Marley and the Wailers recordings in 2006. Universal Music Group claimed exclusive rights to those recordings and sent "cease and desist" orders to music distributors (Amazon, iTunes, etc.), who immediately discontinued sale of the Rock River remix. Rock River then sued Universal, alleging attempted monopoly of the reggae genre of sound recordings in the United States, among other claims. Rock River alleged that Universal "accounted for 81 percent of the reggae sound recordings sold, and Bob Marley recordings accounted for 76 percent of the total reggae recordings sold."

Questions

1. Is reggae music, in your judgment, an identifiable product market? Explain.
2. Universal claimed there were no significant barriers to entry in the alleged reggae music market. Explain why the absence of barriers to entry would be a significant consideration in resolving the case.
3. Assuming Universal's share of the alleged product market was correctly calculated by Rock River, who will win this lawsuit? Explain.

Source: Rock River Communications v. Universal Music Group, 2011 U.S. Dist. LEXIS 46023 (C.D. Cal., W. Div. April 27, 2011), *aff'd in part and reversed in part,* 745 F.3d 343 (9th Cir. 2014).

Monopoly Case I

The case that follows is a private antitrust action involving a claim by Christy Sports, a Utah ski rental company, that Deer Valley Resort Company (DVRC), a ski resort developer/operator, had monopoly power over Deer Valley Resort's ski rental business and that DVRC abused that power to harm Christy Sports.

LEGAL BRIEFCASE

Christy Sports v. Deer Valley Resort Company
555 F.3d 1188 (10th Cir. 2009)

Circuit Judge McConnell

When the Deer Valley Resort Company ("DVRC") was developing its world-renowned ski resort in the Wasatch Mountains, it sold parcels of land within the resort village to third parties, while reserving the right of approval over the conduct of certain ancillary businesses on the property, including ski rentals. For about fifteen years, DVRC granted permission to Cole Sports and plaintiff-appellant Christy Sports to rent skis in competition with its own ski rental outlet. More recently, however, DVRC revoked that permission, presumably in order to gain more business for its own newly opened mid-mountain ski rental store. The question is whether this revocation violated the antitrust laws.

I. BACKGROUND

Deer Valley is one of three resorts in the vicinity of Park City, Utah. Many—indeed, "the vast majority," according to the Complaint—of Deer Valley's patrons are destination skiers who fly into Salt Lake City and then take a forty-five minute bus or shuttle ride to the resort. The resort itself is divided into two areas: the base area, located at the bottom of the mountain, and the ritzier mid-mountain village, located halfway up the slope. DVRC has always been the sole provider of ski rentals at the base area, but at the mid-mountain village, Christy and Cole Sports have operated rental facilities; DVRC itself opened a mid-mountain ski rental facility in 2005.

Originally, DVRC owned all the property at the mid-mountain village, but over the years it has sold parcels to third parties. In 1990, DVRC sold one such parcel to S.Y. and Betty Kimball, subject to a restrictive covenant that prohibited use of the property for either ski rental or real estate sales office purposes without DVRC's express written consent. The Kimballs built a commercial building and leased space in it to Christy's corporate predecessor, Bulrich Corporation. The lease expressly prohibited both the rental of skis and

the operation of a real estate office. The next year, though, DVRC gave Bulrich permission to rent skis in return for 15% of the rental revenue. When Bulrich merged with another company in 1994 and formed Christy Sports, LLC, Christy continued to operate the rental business. According to the complaint, Christy stopped paying DVRC 15% of its rental revenue in 1995, though the reason for this change is unknown. Christy rented skis at the Deer Valley mid-mountain village with no objection from DVRC until 2005. During that time, DVRC was the sole purveyor of rental skis at the base area but did not have a ski rental operation at mid-mountain.

DVRC opened a mid-mountain ski rental outlet in 2005. In August of that year, the resort notified Christy that, beginning the following year's ski season, the restrictive covenant would be enforced and Christy would no longer be allowed to rent skis. Christy believes that DVRC issued the same message to Cole's, leaving DVRC as the only rental ski provider at Deer Valley, with the exception of a small operation at the Stein Eriksen Lodge, which serves its own lodgers. This leaves that majority of skiers who fly into Salt Lake City and then shuttle to Deer Valley with few choices: they can carry unwieldy ski equipment onto the plane, take a shuttle into Park City and hunt for cheaper ski rentals in town, or rent from the more conveniently located DVRC location. Christy predicts, not improbably, that most consumers will choose the third option.

Christy argues that DVRC's decision to begin enforcing its restrictive covenant is an attempt to monopolize the market of ski rentals available to destination skiers in Deer Valley, or, alternatively, to the destination skiers in the mid-mountain village itself. It alleges that by eliminating its competitors, DVRC will be able to increase prices and reduce output, thus harming consumers. The complaint states that the number of skis available for rental mid-mountain will decline by 620 pairs, and the price will increase by at least twenty-two to thirty-two percent.

The district court dismissed Christy's antitrust complaints.

II. ANALYSIS

* * * * *

Christy has alleged that DVRC violated Section 2 of the Sherman Act by either actual or attempted monopolization. . . . Under both types of Section 2 claims Christy must plead both power in a relevant market and anticompetitive conduct. The relevant market, according to Christy's complaint, is the market for ski rentals to destination skiers in Deer Valley in general or, even more narrowly, the market for ski rentals in the mid-mountain village. The alleged anticompetitive conduct is the enforcement of the restrictive covenant.

A great many pages in the briefs are devoted to whether the defined market set forth in the complaint—destination skiers at Deer Valley, or alternatively at Deer Valley's mid-mountain village—is too small to constitute a market for antitrust purposes, in light of the proximity of a number of ski rental outlets in Park City, just down the road. For purposes of analyzing the complaint, however, we find it not implausible that destination skiers who arrive at the resort by bus or shuttle will find it sufficiently inconvenient to travel into town to rent skis that a successful monopolist over ski rental at Deer Valley could charge supracompetitive prices. The question, we believe, is not whether DVRC might be able to raise prices and reduce output by becoming the only purveyor of rental skis at the resort, but whether such a market is legally cognizable under the antitrust laws and whether the decision of a resort owner to reserve to itself the right to provide ancillary services counts as anticompetitive conduct.

* * * * *

We begin our analysis with DVRC's original decision to impose the restrictive covenant.

A. IMPOSITION OF THE RESTRICTIVE COVENANT

We agree with the defendant that the creator of a resort has no obligation under the antitrust laws to allow competitive suppliers of ancillary services on its property. A theme park, for example, does not have to permit third parties to open restaurants, hotels, gift shops, or other facilities within the park; it can reserve to itself the right to conduct such businesses and receive revenues from them. Accordingly, if it sells land within the resort to third parties, the antitrust laws do not bar the resort owner from imposing a covenant against use of the property for competitive businesses. This is so even if food, rooms, gifts, or other ancillary goods and services would be cheaper and more plentiful if the resort owner allowed competition in these businesses.

This conclusion can be reached either by reference to the proper definition of a market or by reference to the absence of anticompetitive conduct. Some courts, faced with cases of this sort, have found the market definition implausible. The Seventh Circuit took this approach in *Elliott* v. *United Center,* 126 F.3d 1003 (7th Cir. 1997), when

a peanut vendor challenged a sports arena's decision to ban outside food and thereby monopolize the market for food concessions within the arena. The court rejected that market definition as implausible, saying:

> The logic of [the] argument would mean that exclusive restaurants could no longer require customers to purchase their wines only at the establishment, because the restaurant would be "monopolizing" the sale of wine within its interior. Movie theaters, which traditionally (and notoriously) earn a substantial portion of their revenue from the sale of candies, popcorn, and soda, would be required by the antitrust laws to allow patrons to bring their own food.

* * * * *

Although discussion of sports arenas . . . seems to suggest that Christy's shortcomings lie with its alleged geographic market, the actual problem lies with its product market. In these cases the two are difficult to disentangle because the product (rental skis . . .) is intimately related to the location. Consumers do not travel to Deer Valley for rental skis. . . . The true product in these cases is the overall experience. Deer Valley offers a cluster of products that combine to create a destination ski experience; rental skis are only one small component. . . .

The complaint alleges nothing to suggest that destination skiers are choosing their ski resort based on the price of rental skis, separate and apart from the cluster of services associated with the destination-ski experience. To define one small component of the overall product as the relevant product market is simply implausible.

Alternatively, one could say that the monopolization claim would fail because the alleged conduct is not anticompetitive. Even if a firm has monopoly power in a relevant market, a plaintiff must also show "the willful acquisition or maintenance of that power as distinguished from growth or development as a consequence of a superior product, business acumen, or historic accident." *Grinnell Corp.,* 384 U.S. at 570–71. Deer Valley is not required to invite competitors onto its property to rent skis to its patrons, even if a failure to do so would mean it is the sole supplier of rental skis at the ski area.

The Supreme Court has recognized the economic value of allowing businesses to decide with whom they will deal, as it recently re-emphasized: "[A]s a general matter, the Sherman Act 'does not restrict the long recognized right of [a] trader or manufacturer engaged in an entirely private business, freely to exercise his own independent discretion as to parties with whom he will deal.'" *Verizon Commc'ns, Inc.* v. *Law Offices of Curtis V. Trinko, LLP,* 540 U.S. 398, 408 (2004). In *Trinko,* the Court acknowledged that in rare circumstances a refusal to cooperate with competitors might constitute a Section 2 violation, but that "such exceptions, because of the uncertain virtue of forced sharing and the difficulty of identifying and remedying anticompetitive conduct by a single firm," should be few.

Syufy always treated moviegoers fairly: The movie tickets, popcorn, nuts, and the Seven-Ups cost about the same in Las Vegas as in other, comparable markets. While it is theoretically possible to have a middleman who is a monopolist upstream but not downstream, this is a somewhat counterintuitive scenario. Why, if he truly had significant market power, would Raymond Syufy have chosen to take advantage of the big movie distributors while giving a fair shake to ordinary people? And why do the distributors, the alleged victims of the monopolization scheme, think that Raymond Syufy is the best thing that ever happened to the Las Vegas movie market?

*   *   *   *   *

There is universal agreement that monopoly power is the power to exclude competition or control prices. . . .

1. Power to Exclude Competition

It is true, of course, that when Syufy acquired Mann's, Plitt's, and Cragin's theaters he temporarily diminished the number of competitors in the Las Vegas first-run film market. But this does not necessarily indicate foul play; many legitimate market arrangements diminish the number of competitors. . . . If there are no significant barriers to entry, however, eliminating competitors will not enable the survivors to reap a monopoly profit; any attempt to raise prices above the competitive level will lure into the market new competitors able and willing to offer their commercial goods or personal services for less. . . .

*   *   *   *   *

The district court . . . found that there were no barriers to entry in the Las Vegas movie market. . . . Our review of the record discloses that the district court's finding is amply supported by the record.

*   *   *   *   *

Immediately after Syufy bought out the last of his three competitors in October 1984, he was riding high, having captured 100 percent of the first-run film market in Las Vegas. But this utopia proved to be only a mirage. That same month, a major movie distributor, Orion, stopped doing business with Syufy, sending all of its first-run films to Roberts Company, a dark-horse competitor previously relegated to the second-run market. Roberts Company took this as an invitation to step into the major league and, against all odds, began giving Syufy serious competition in the first-run market. Fighting fire with fire, Roberts opened three multiplexes within a 13-month period, each having six or more screens. By December 1986, Roberts was operating 28 screens, trading places with Syufy, who had only 23. At the same time, Roberts was displaying a healthy portion of all first-run films. In fact, Roberts got exclusive exhibition rights to many of its films, meaning that Syufy could not show them at all.

By the end of 1987, Roberts was showing a larger percentage of first-run films than was the Redrock multiplex at the time Syufy

bought it. Roberts then sold its theaters to United Artists, the largest theater chain in the country, and Syufy continued losing ground. It all boils down to this: Syufy's acquisitions did not short-circuit the operation of the natural market forces; Las Vegas's first-run film market was more competitive when this case came to trial than before Syufy bought out Mann, Plitt, and Cragin.

The Justice Department correctly points out that Syufy still has a large market share, but attributes far too much importance to this fact. In evaluating monopoly power, it is not market share that counts, but the ability to maintain market share. . . . Syufy seems unable to do this. In 1985 Syufy managed to lock up exclusive exhibition rights to 91 percent of all the first-run films in Las Vegas. By the first quarter of 1988, that percentage had fallen to 39 percent; United Artists had exclusive rights to another 25 percent, with the remaining 36 percent being played on both Syufy and UA screens.

Syufy's share of box office receipts also dropped off, albeit less precipitously. In 1985 Syufy raked in 93 percent of the gross box office from first-run films in Las Vegas. By the first quarter of 1988, that figure had fallen to 75 percent. The government insists that 75 percent is still a large number, and we are hard-pressed to disagree, but that's not the point.

*   *   *   *   *

The numbers reveal that Roberts/UA has steadily been eating away at Syufy's market share: In two and a half years, Syufy's percentage of exclusive exhibition rights dropped 52 percent and its percentage of box office receipts dropped 18 percent. During the same period, Roberts/UA's newly opened theaters evolved from absolute beginners, barely staying alive, into a big business.

*   *   *   *   *

2. Power to Control Prices

The crux of the Justice Department's case is that Syufy, top gun in the Las Vegas movie market, had the power to push around Hollywood's biggest players, dictating to them what prices they could charge for their movies. The district court found otherwise. This finding too has substantial support in the record.

Perhaps the most telling evidence of Syufy's inability to set prices came from movie distributors, Syufy's supposed victims. At the trial, distributors uniformly proclaimed their satisfaction with the way the Las Vegas first-run film market operates; none complained about the license fees paid by Syufy. . . . Particularly damaging to the government's case was the testimony of the former head of distribution for MGM/UA that his company "never had any difficulty . . . in acquiring the terms that we thought were reasonable," . . . explaining that the license fees Syufy paid "were comparable or better than any place in the United States. And in most cases better." . . .

The documentary evidence bears out this testimony. Syufy has at all times paid license fees far in excess of the national average, even higher than those paid by exhibitors in Los Angeles, the Mecca of

Moviedom. In fact, Syufy paid a higher percentage of his gross receipts to distributors in 1987 and 1988 than he did during the intensely competitive period just before he acquired Cragin's Redrock.

While successful, Syufy is in no position to put the squeeze on distributors. . . .

* * * * *

It is a tribute to the state of competition in America that the Antitrust Division of the Department of Justice has found no worthier target than this paper tiger on which to expend limited taxpayer resources. Yet we cannot help but wonder whether bringing a lawsuit like this, and pursuing it doggedly through 27 months of pretrial proceedings, about two weeks of trial, and now the full distance on appeal, really serves the interests of free competition.

Affirmed.

Questions

1. At one point, Syufy held 100 percent of the first-run market. Why was Syufy not a monopolist?

2. Is this decision rooted more in structural (market share) or conduct (e.g., predatory pricing) considerations? Explain.

3. What role did the issue of Syufy's intent to monopolize play in this case? Explain.

4. Assume we have historical data showing that when the price of rolled steel has increased, the sales volume of rolled aluminum has remained constant. What, if anything, does that fact tell us about the product market for rolled steel?

5. Define the product market for championship boxing matches. See *United States v. International Boxing Club of New York, Inc.,* 358 U.S. 242 (1959).

6. Adidas provided cash, sporting goods, and the like to universities in exchange for various promotional rights, including the team's or coach's agreement to wear Adidas clothing in athletic activities. National Collegiate Athletic Association (NCAA) rules limited the amount of advertising that could appear on a uniform being used in competition. Adidas sued the NCAA claiming, among other things, that the advertising restrictions constituted an attempted monopoly by the NCAA. In pursuing its monopoly claim, Adidas defined the relevant market as "the market for the sale of NCAA Promotional Rights." The NCAA responded by saying that a market consisting solely of the sale of promotional rights by NCAA member institutions (colleges and universities) on athletic apparel used in intercollegiate activity was not a plausible relevant market.

    a. Define the relevant product market from the NCAA point of view.

    b. How did the court decide where the product market actually lies? See *Adidas America, Inc. v. NCAA,* 64 F. Supp. 2d 1097 (1999).

PRACTICING ETHICS   Break Up the Biggest Banks?

Sanford Weill is one of the most famous names in banking history and the architect of one of the biggest financial mergers, the 1998 combination of Citicorp and Travelers Group. By 2006 Weill had relinquished his Citicorp duties, and his colossal bank took government bailout funds during the recent financial crisis. Weill spoke to that crisis in 2012:

> What we should probably do is go split up investment banking from banking, have banks be deposit-takers, have banks make commercial loans and real estate loans, have banks do something that's not going to risk the taxpayer dollars, that's not too big to fail.

Weill's 1998 merger strategy apparently had failed his bank and arguably threatened the welfare of the nation. Weill was therefore reduced to calling for a return to something like the 1933 Glass–Steagall Act (separating commercial and investment banking), which Congress repealed in 1999, much to the satisfaction of many on Wall Street.

Questions

1. Do you believe the Wall Street banking industry operates by different ethical rules from those practiced by your hometown bankers? Explain.

2. Does the extraordinary size of the big banks (the five biggest: Bank of America, Citigroup, Goldman Sachs, JPMorgan Chase, Wells Fargo), of itself, lead to wrongful practices in those banks? Put another way, is bigness bad?

Source: Roben Farzad, "Sandy Weill's Untimely Second Thoughts," *Bloomberg Businessweek,* July 25, 2012 [**www.businessweek.com**].

Questions—Part One

1. *a.* The *Harvard Law Review* argued, "In the New Economy (information technology) . . . there will inevitably be an increasing number of markets with only a few dominant players."[9] Why would that be so?

   b. Are we mistaken in pursuing Microsoft and other "new economy" giants with "old economy" antitrust principles? Explain.

2. Worldwide Basketball Sports Tours promoted early-season, NCAA-certified basketball tournaments. The National Collegiate Athletic Association's Two in Four Rule limited college basketball teams to "not more than one certified basketball event in one academic year, and not more than two certified basketball events every four years." The promoters sued the NCAA on antitrust grounds, claiming the Two in Four rule hampered their ability to make money. The NCAA argued that the limit on games was academically motivated.

   a. Does antitrust law apply to Division I collegiate basketball? Explain.

   b. Define the product market in this case. See *Worldwide Basketball & Sports Tours, Inc. v. NCAA*, 388 F.3d 955 (6th Cir. 2004), *cert. denied*, 126 S. Ct. 334 (2005).

3. *a.* A traditional concern about monopolies is that a lack of competition discourages efficiency and innovation. Argue that monopolies may actually encourage innovation.

   b. Even if monopolies do not discourage invention, we have firm economic grounds for opposing monopolies. Explain.

4. Real estate developer Ernest Coleman built an apartment complex in Stilwell, Oklahoma (population 2,700), and ordered electric service from an out-of-town utility, Ozark Electric. Stilwell officials said they would deny him city water and sewer service if he did not buy his electricity from the city-owned utility service. Because he could not buy water or sewer service elsewhere, Coleman decided to switch to Stilwell's utility. In 1996, the federal Justice Department sued Stilwell. Explain the federal government's complaint and decide the case. See Bryan Gruley, "Little Town Becomes First Municipality Sued by U.S. for Antitrust," *The Wall Street Journal*, June 3, 1996, p. A1.

5. Historically, perhaps the most important interpretation of the Sherman Act's proscription of monopolization was Judge Learned Hand's opinion in the *Alcoa* case. After finding that Alcoa controlled 90 percent of the aluminum ingot market, Hand had to determine whether Alcoa possessed a general intent to monopolize. Hand concluded that Alcoa's market dominance could have resulted only from a "persistent determination" to maintain control:

   > It was not inevitable that it should always anticipate increases in the demand for ingots and be prepared to supply them. Nothing compelled it to keep doubling and redoubling its capacity before others entered the field. It insists that it never excluded competitors; but we can think of no more effective exclusion than progressively to embrace each new opportunity as it opened, and to face every newcomer with new capacity already geared into a great organization.[10]

   Comment on Judge Hand's remarks.

6. Several smaller airlines sued two giants, United and American, claiming that the two violated the Sherman Act through their computerized reservation systems (CRSs). The heart of the plaintiffs' position was that United and American were monopolists who

violated the law by denying other airlines reasonable access to their CRSs. American and United had the largest CRSs, but other airlines also maintained CRSs. Neither had blocked any other airline's access to its CRS, but they had charged fees (in American's case, $1.75 per booking to the airline that secured a passenger through American's CRS). United and American each controlled about 12 to 14 percent of the total air transportation market. According to the court, the plaintiffs were "unhappy" about United's and American's ability to extract booking fees from them for the use of the CRSs. The U.S. Ninth Circuit Court of Appeals ruled for the defendants, and the Supreme Court declined to review this case.

a. Explain why the plaintiffs felt wronged by American and United.

b. Explain the defendants' argument that they could not successfully charge "excessive" prices for the use of the CRSs. See *Alaska Airlines v. United Airlines*, 948 F.2d 536 (9th Cir. 1991), *cert. denied*, 112 S. Ct. 1603 (1992).

Part Two—Mergers

LO 11-4
Identify the potential benefits and hazards of mergers.

LO 11-5
Distinguish between horizontal and vertical mergers.

Will the price of beer go up now that Anheuser-Busch InBev (Belgium), the world's largest brewer, and SABMiller (United Kingdom) have completed their 2016 merger? The combined company will hold 27 percent of worldwide beer sales.[11] That merger is one of many; 2015 was the biggest merger year ever.[12] Virtually all major sectors of American industry have become highly concentrated, as journalist David Dayen detailed in early 2016:

> . . . We have four airlines serving 80 percent of all passengers. We have four cable and Internet companies providing most of the nation's cellphone and television service. We have four big commercial banks, five big insurance companies (only three if two proposed mergers go through this year), and a handful of producers selling every major consumer product. Even when you think you have a choice, like in the array of online travel-booking sites, two companies (Expedia and Priceline) own all the subsidiaries.[13]

Food At this moment, proposed mergers between Bayer (Germany) and Monsanto (America), Dow Chemical and DuPont (both American), and China National Chemical (China) and Syngenta (Switzerland) would create three global giants dominating the crucial agrichemical/seed industry. Proponents say the mergers will enhance innovation, but farmers worry these moves will drive up their production costs. Should American regulators block the plans of Monsanto, Dow, and DuPont? If so, could those firms (already giants in their own right) compete with ChemChina/Syngenta? Will new competitors emerge to hold the power of the big firms in check? That is, will the market do its job, as theorized?

Telecommunications (Telecom) What about AT&T's proposed $85.4 billion acquisition of Time Warner, the owner of HBO, CNN, TNT, and Warners Brothers film studio? If that deal goes forward, will AT&T treat its newly acquired entertainment content more favorably than that of its rivals? Is the merger necessary, as AT&T argues, to advance the "revolution" in the television industry driven by the convergence of distribution and content and by consumers' desire for multiplatform (e.g., mobile) viewing?

Other telecom providers like Verizon and Comcast (see below) have recently acquired content providers. So, are other content providers such as AMC Networks (*Walking Dead* producer) and Discovery Communications (Discovery Channel and Animal Planet) likely to be bought? Are we in the midst of a domino-style reshaping of the telecommunications/entertainment market?

These are the kinds of concerns that animate merger enforcement law in the United States, but we must remember that American companies are competing in a demanding international market and mergers often bring efficiencies, such as economies of scale, that ultimately benefit consumers.

Failing Companies   Sometimes mergers and the risk of rising consumer prices may be necessary to save failing companies, as was claimed by supporters of the recent US Airways and American Airlines deal. Sterne Agee analyst Jeff Kauffman advised that the bankrupt American could not stand alone:

> We believe that the stand-alone plan would have left [American] with a disadvantaged infrastructure, too small to compete effectively with carriers 40 percent larger for business travel, and too large to be a niche carrier and compete with carriers smaller and more nimble.[14]

Thus, some mergers may be considered a business necessity, but not infrequently they are much better for shareholders than for consumers. A 2016 study of recent manufacturing mergers found a general increase in market power and prices with little evidence of improved efficiency or productivity.[15] *The New York Times* in 2010 cited a study finding higher prices in oil after Pennzoil acquired Quaker State, in tampons after Procter & Gamble bought Tambrands, in cereal after General Mills acquired Chex brands, and in Scotch whisky after the merger of Guinness and Grand Metropolitan.[16] A 2014 PricewaterhouseCoopers study, on the other hand, found that airline mergers have benefited the industry and helped keep fares low, but other experts see a longer-term increase in airfares.[17]

Why?   Technological change, efficiency enhancement, and piles of available cash are important motivators for merger activity, but the big drivers often are growth opportunities and cost cutting. Many companies have extracted maximum value from their own products, making growth possible only by purchasing new lines, and cost savings have become essential in fierce global competition.

Merger Virtues

Mergers often have clearly beneficial effects. Some of the potential virtues of mergers include

1. Mergers permit the replacement of inefficient management, and the threat of replacement disciplines managers to be more productive.
2. Mergers may permit stronger competition with previously larger rivals.
3. Mergers may improve credit access.
4. Mergers may produce efficiencies including economies of scale.
5. Mergers frequently offer a pool of liquid assets for use in expansion and in innovation.
6. Very often, mergers offer tax advantages.
7. Growth by merger is often less expensive than internal growth.
8. Mergers help satisfy the personal ambitions and needs of management.[18]

PRACTICING ETHICS · Mergers That Abuse Customers?

In 2011, the federal government approved, with restrictions, a merger giving Comcast, the cable TV giant, a controlling interest in the NBC television network. Among other concerns, critics feared the merger would allow Comcast to arbitrarily favor NBC channels over those of competitors. Then, in 2013, Comcast announced it was buying the remaining 49 percent of NBCUniversal. From the inception of the merger discussions, one of the parties most concerned was the Santa Monica, California–based Tennis Channel, which feared Comcast would favor its own sports channels (Golf Channel and NBC Sports Network) over the Tennis Channel and other independents.

The Tennis Channel filed a complaint with the Federal Communications Commission alleging that Comcast was violating the law by providing favorable placement for the Golf Channel and NBC Sports Network while leaving the Tennis Channel on a little-watched sports tier. Comcast said the channel placements reflected market realities and a long-term contract signed when the Tennis Channel was a start-up. In 2012, the FCC ruled for the Tennis Channel, finding that Comcast was violating federal antidiscrimination carriage rules, but the U.S. Court of Appeals for the D.C. Circuit, in two reviews, ruled for Comcast, largely on the grounds that the factual record was insufficient to sustain the Tennis Channel's claim.

Questions

1. Do you think Comcast has a responsibility to treat the independent Tennis Channel the same as its own affiliate sports networks, including the Golf Channel and NBC Sports Network? Explain.

2. If you were running a business, would you treat all of your customers the same, regardless of their contributions to your bottom line? Explain.

3. In your view, should the government require Comcast to treat the Tennis Channel as well as it treats its own sports channels? Explain.

Sources: Michael Hiltzik, "Tennis Channel Gets No Love from Comcast," *latimes.com*, November 9, 2011 [**latimes.com/sports/ la-fi-hiltzik-20111109,0,2769562.column**]; Alina Selyukh, "Court Grills FCC, Tennis Channel in Comcast Discrimination Suit," *Reuters,* February 25, 2013 [**www.reuters.com**]; *Comcast Cable v. Federal Communications Commission,* 717 F.3d 982 (D.C. Cir. 2013), *cert. denied sub nom. Tennis Channel v. Comcast Cable,* 134 S. Ct. 1287 (2014); and *Tennis Channel v. Federal Communications Commission,* 827 F.3d 137 (D.C. Cir. 2016).

> ## "Mergers Fail More Often Than Marriages."

Merger Problems

Many studies show that mergers often fail in that they do not add value to the merging companies. Experts generally estimate the merger failure rate, measured in various ways, at between 50 and 80 percent. As *CNN.com* described it, "Mergers Fail More Often Than Marriages."[19] In addition to those frequent financial failures, other merger hazards should be noted:

1. Too much power is being concentrated in too few hands.
2. A particular merger, although not threatening in and of itself, may trigger a merger movement among industry competitors.
3. Higher market concentration may lead to higher prices.
4. Innovation may be harmed.
5. Some companies are so large that they can significantly shape political affairs.
6. Some companies may have become so large that we cannot allow them to fail.[20]

When Should the Government Intervene? The federal government, through the Justice Department and the Federal Trade Commission, has recently been rather aggressive in its merger oversight. Big deals in cable, office supply, and oil drilling have been blocked by antitrust regulators. The government's opposition can be appealed to the courts. Usually, however, the government works out settlements with the merging parties. As noted above, the federal government recently approved Anheuser-Busch InBev's (ABI) $107 billion merger with SABMiller. ABI, itself the product of a merger between American icon Anheuser-Busch and Belgian/Brazilian InBev, earned government approval for its merger by agreeing that SABMiller would sell MillerCoors. Thus, America's two biggest brewers remain competitors, and ABI's U.S. market share remains at about 44 percent.[21]

Crucially, ABI also agreed to refrain from curbing beer distribution by smaller rivals. ABI is precluded, for example, from encouraging beer distributors to drop ABI's competitors, and ABI is required to get government approval before buying smaller breweries. Of course, small craft breweries have been exploding in numbers, but one of the emerging issues in the beer industry is that the many "craft" brands of beer available to consumers often, in fact, are controlled by one of the giants. Thus, the future of the beer market depends to a considerable extent on the government's willingness to carefully police its agreements with ABI. Northeastern University economics professor John Kwoka's studies of past mergers found that federal enforcement is "not demonstrably effective." Kwoka explained that the federal agencies tend not to follow up thoroughly. Of course, they were not designed to do so.[22]

ABI and many experts argue that its mergers are simply part of a much larger global pattern of consolidation necessary to operate efficiently. Indeed, after InBev acquired Anheuser-Busch, the new organization reportedly cut costs by several billion dollars and instituted tighter organizational controls.

Merger Law: Overview

Mergers are addressed by the Sherman Act, Section 1; but the Clayton Act, Section 7, offers the primary legislative oversight:

> That no person engaged in commerce shall acquire the whole or any part of the stock or the assets of another person engaged also in commerce where the effect of such acquisition may be substantially to lessen competition, or to tend to create a monopoly.

Technically, a merger involves the union of two or more enterprises wherein the property of all is transferred to the one remaining firm. Antitrust law, however, reaches all those situations in which previously independent business entities are united—whether by acquisition of stock, purchase of physical assets, creation of holding companies, consolidation, or merger.

Mergers fall, somewhat awkwardly, into three categories:

1. A horizontal merger involves firms that are in direct competition and occupy the same product and geographic markets. A merger of two vodka producers in the same geographic market would clearly fall in the horizontal category. Would the merger of a vodka producer and a gin producer constitute a horizontal merger?

2. A vertical merger involves two or more firms at different levels of the same channel of distribution, such as a furniture manufacturer and a fabric supplier.

3. A conglomerate merger involves firms dealing in unrelated products. Thus, the conglomerate category embraces all mergers that are neither horizontal nor vertical. An

example of such a merger would be the acquisition of a pet food manufacturer by a book publisher. (Conglomerate mergers currently receive little attention from the government, and we will not examine them further.)

LO 11-6
Explain premerger notification requirements.

Premerger Notification   Under the Hart–Scott–Rodino Antitrust Improvements Act (HSR), mergers and acquisitions must be reported to the Federal Trade Commission and the Justice Department if those deals exceed certain dollar thresholds that change annually in accord with the gross national product. [For more HSR threshold details, see **www.ftc.gov/bc/hsr/index.shtm**]. The parties are barred from closing the merger until 30 days after they have made the required HSR filing unless the waiting period is shortened (as it often is) or lengthened by the FTC or the Justice Department. The merging firms are required to provide documentation about the merger's impact on competition. The waiting period gives the government time and information by which to determine whether the merger should be challenged.

LO 11-7
Describe remedies for mergers determined to be anticompetitive.

Remedies   After the HSR review, the government may decide that the merger is not threatening, and it will be allowed to proceed. The government may, on the other hand, conclude that the merger is anticompetitive. If the parties persist with a disfavored merger, the government can file suit. The preferred action, as noted above, is to work out a settlement. One of the parties might sell some of its assets, as we saw in the ABI and SABMiller settlement, or a party might agree to forgo business in some geographic segment of the market for a time. Rental car stalwart Hertz, in 2012, secured FTC approval for its $2.3 billion acquisition of Dollar Thrifty (parent of the Dollar and Thrifty car rental brands) only after agreeing to sell both its Advantage car rental business and 29 existing Dollar Thrifty on-airport locations. The FTC feared reduced competition at 72 airports nationwide.

In cases where negotiation fails and the government decides to sue, it can ask the court for a remedy, such as an order stopping the merger or an order requiring divestiture of certain assets. Government litigation is infrequent, but the resulting message to the business community is powerful. Furthermore, private parties commonly use the antitrust laws to sue for treble damages when they believe a merger has harmed them unlawfully. The threat of those private actions as well as government oversight helps maintain a marketplace where consumers are offered the benefits of vigorous competition including lower prices, improved quality, and innovation. [For recent developments in antitrust law, see *Antitrust Today* at **www.constantinecannon.com/antitrusttoday.com**].

[For a humorous treatment of mergers, see Stephen Colbert's 2007 video segment, "Mega-Mergers," at **https://youtu.be/rsCp-1hgfxI**].

Horizontal Analysis

LO 11-8
Analyze when a horizontal merger is anticompetitive.

Horizontal mergers raise anticompetitive risks because direct rivals seek to join together. Horizontal merger analysis ordinarily follows the FTC/Justice Department merger guidelines, which focus on a pair of concerns:

1. **Coordinated effects/collusion.** Will the merger facilitate cooperation so that the merging parties and their competitors might fix prices, reduce output, reduce quality, or

otherwise coordinate their activities rather than competing against each other? Broadly, the government takes the position that fewer firms and thus greater market concentration increase the likelihood of collusion—a position the courts often, but not always, embrace.

2. **Unilateral effects.** Will the merger allow the newly merged firm to unilaterally raise prices, restrict output, or control innovation? Normally, unilateral effects arise where competing products significantly restrained each other prior to the merger. By removing a rival, a merger could allow the newly merged entity to exercise market power and thereby harm consumers.

Market Power

Broadly, the guidelines are designed to identify mergers that may result in market power, defined as the ability of a seller "profitably to maintain prices above competitive levels for a significant period of time." The guidelines set out a five-step methodology for analyzing horizontal mergers:

1. Market definition.
2. Measurement of market concentration.
3. Identification of likely anticompetitive effects.
4. Likelihood of future entrants to the market.
5. Appraisal of efficiencies and other possible defenses.

Market

The market is defined as the smallest product and geographic market in which a monopolist could raise prices a small but significant and nontransitory amount (usually set at 5 percent above current prices).

Market Concentration

The Herfindahl–Hirschman Index (HHI) is employed to measure market concentration. Notwithstanding the formidable title, the index is computed quite easily. The market share of each firm is squared and the results are summed. Thus, if five companies each had 20 percent of a market, the index for that market would be 2,000. The HHI is useful because it measures both concentration and dispersion of market share between big and small firms. If there are 10 firms, each with 10 percent of the market, the resulting HHI is 1,000. The larger the HHI, the more concentrated the market. In general, a postmerger HHI below 1,500 would reflect an unconcentrated market, while a postmerger concentration of between 1,500 and 2,500 would be considered mildly concentrated and more than 2,500, a highly concentrated market. The greater the HHI and the greater the increase in the HHI, the more likely the government will be concerned about the merger. Thus, the aforementioned American Airlines and U.S. Airways merger with an HHI of 1,269 among the top four carriers in the national market (American after the merger—20 percent, Southwest—18 percent, United Continental—17 percent, and Delta—16 percent) would be classified as "unconcentrated."[23]

The guidelines provide that the potential for competitive concern also depends on the analysis of additional factors, such as a change in the number of competitors along with adverse effects and ease of entry, as explained below. Broadly, the government's guidelines reject the older notion of market size *alone* as a threat to the welfare of the economy.

Adverse Effects

The basic point here is the government's worry that the merger may permit monopoly behavior in the merged firm's market.

Ease of Entry

If new competitors can readily enter the post-merger market, the existing firms will be forced to charge competitive prices and otherwise conform to the discipline of the market.

Defenses

An otherwise unacceptable merger may be saved by certain defenses. The *failing company doctrine* permits a merger to preserve the assets of a firm that would otherwise be lost to the market. *Efficiencies* include such desirable economic results as economies of scale or reduced transportation costs as a result of the merger.

Guideline Changes

In 2010, the Justice Department and the Federal Trade Commission announced revisions to the Horizontal Merger Guidelines that bring the guidelines more in line with actual government practice. Much of the analysis will continue as outlined above, but a key revision involves a reduced role for market definition/market share and increased attention to likely adverse competitive effects. The new reasoning is that the analysis will begin in identifying practical, real-world competitive harm (such as customer injury, reduced innovation, or reduced product variety), at which point market definition and the balance of the analysis outlined above would be influential. This approach may, therefore, allow the government greater flexibility in proving competition problems even if high market shares cannot be established. Ongoing antitrust decisions, including the *Staples/Office Depot* case later in this chapter, will indicate how closely the courts actually follow the new guidance.

Horizontal Merger Blocked

The Justice Department in 2011 successfully challenged a proposed horizontal merger between tax preparers H&R Block and TaxACT. Judge Beryl Howell at the District Court for the District of Columbia agreed with the Justice Department that the relevant product market was digital do-it-yourself (DDIY) tax preparation products (thus excluding assisted and manual tax preparation) with the three largest firms controlling 90 percent of the market (Intuit—62.2 percent, HRB—15.6 percent, and TaxACT—12.8 percent) and the remaining 10 percent split among a number of smaller firms. The merger would have increased the HHI in the DDIY market by 400 points to 4,691. The court concluded that H&R Block had failed to show that collusion would not result in what would have become a highly concentrated post-merger market.

Judge Howell also considered various company documents; in one H&R Block allegedly said the merger would allow it to "regain control of industry pricing and avoid further price erosion." When looking at anticompetitive effects from the proposed merger, the court reasoned that TaxACT's "impressive history of innovation and competition in the DDIY market" had been important in constraining prices, a role that would have disappeared had the merger been consummated. Given these considerations and insufficient evidence that dramatic efficiencies would accompany the merger, Judge Howell ruled for the government. H&R Block did not appeal.

Sources: King & Spaulding, "DOJ Antitrust Division Wins Major Victory in H&R Block Case," *Client Alert,* November 17, 2011 [**www.kslaw.com**]; Michael H. Pryor, "What the H&R Block Merger Opinion Can Tell Us about the AT&T/T-Mobile Merger Case," *LEXOLOGY,* November 16, 2011 [**www.lexology.com**]; and *United States of America v. H&R Block, Inc.,* 833 F. Supp. 2d 36 (D.D.C. 2011).

Vertical Analysis

LO 11-9

Analyze when a vertical merger creates anticompetitive "market foreclosure."

A vertical merger typically involves an alliance between a supplier and a purchaser. The primary resulting threat to competition is labeled *market foreclosure*. As illustrated in Figure 11.1, a vertical merger may deny a source of supply to a purchaser or an outlet for sale to a seller, thus potentially threatening competition in violation of the Clayton Act. The government would then look closely at that foreclosure to determine whether it actually has an anticompetitive effect. In addition to foreclosing sources of supply or outlets for sale, the government may be concerned about other anticompetitive effects such as raising rivals' costs, facilitating collusion, and raising barriers to entry.

FIGURE 11.1
Vertical Merger.

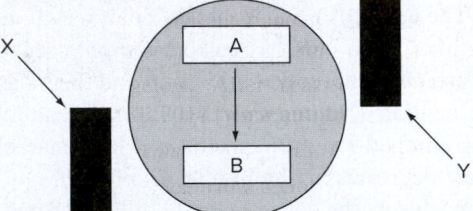

A supplies B. A and B merge. X (A's competitor) had traditionally sold to B, and Y (B's competitor) had traditionally purchased from A. Is the merger lawful? How do we decide?

Vertical Merger Challenge Vertical mergers often do not raise competitive risks, and they can produce important efficiencies, so government challenges have been uncommon.

> Ticketmaster–Live Nation merger.

Conditions that raise the market foreclosure concerns illustrated above, however, may lead to government intervention. That was the case with the 2010 Ticketmaster–Live Nation merger that created a vertically integrated giant with a significant presence up and down the entertainment industry "value chain," including artist management, concert touring, concert venues, and ticketing. The merger also raised horizontal concerns in the ticketing business.

Ticketmaster, the nation's largest ticketing company, owned a controlling share in Front Line Management, whose 200-plus clients included the Eagles and Miley Cyrus. Live

Nation, the country's largest concert promoter, also owned or managed 135 major concert venues around the world, was the world's largest artist-management company, and operated related businesses including product merchandising and online fan clubs. Live Nation was also a recent entrant to the ticketing business.

The merger partners and the Justice Department agreed to a settlement, allowing the creation of the newly merged company—to be called Live Nation Entertainment (LNE). Addressing vertical concerns, LNE agreed to Justice Department monitoring to ensure, for example, that it did not abuse its market power by requiring concert venues wanting access to Ticketmaster's monopoly ticketing services to book only LNE-promoted acts, thus foreclosing other promoters from doing business with those venues. Addressing horizontal concerns, Ticketmaster agreed to divest one of its ticketing divisions while licensing its ticketing software to a competitor, thus effectively allowing the creation of two new competitors for Ticketmaster.[24]

Horizontal Merger Case

In the following case, a federal district court judge reviewed the Federal Trade Commission's request for an order blocking the proposed merger of Staples and Office Depot. The FTC had blocked a previous merger effort by the two firms in 1997.

Federal Trade Commission v. Staples, Inc. and Office Depot, Inc.

LEGAL BRIEFCASE 190 F. Supp. 3d 100 (D.D.C. 2016)

Judge Sullivan

I. INTRODUCTION

* * * * *

Subsequent to Defendants' announcement in February 2015 of their intent to merge, the FTC began an approximate year-long investigation into the $6.3 billion merger and its likely effects on competition. On December 7, 2015, by a unanimous vote, the FTC Commissioners found reason to believe that the proposed merger would substantially reduce competition in violation of Section 7 of the Clayton Act and Section 5 of the FTC Act. That same day, Plaintiffs commenced this action seeking a preliminary injunction to enjoin the proposed merger.

* * * * *

II. BACKGROUND
A. Overview
. . . To sustain employees' use of pens, Post-it notes and paperclips, large companies purchase more than two billion dollars of office

supplies from Defendants annually. Companies that purchase office supplies for their own use operate in what the industry refers to as the B-to-B space. B-to-B customers prefer to work with one vendor that can meet all of the companies' office supply needs. . . .

To establish a primary vendor relationship, companies in the B-to-B space request proposals from national suppliers like Staples and Office Depot. The request for proposal (RFP) process typically results in a multi-year contract with a primary vendor that guarantees prices for specific items, includes an upfront lump-sum rebate, and a host of other services. Because the office supplies consumed by larger companies are voluminous, such companies typically pay only half the price for basic supplies as compared to the average retail consumer.

B. Defendants Staples and Office Depot
Established as big-box retail stores in the 1980s, Defendants are the primary B-to-B office supply vendors in the United States today. Plaintiffs allege that Defendants sell and distribute upwards of seventy-nine percent of office supplies in the B-to-B space. Since the 2013 merger of Office Depot and Office Max, Defendants

consistently engage in head-to-head competition with each other for B-to-B contracts.

. . . Staples is the largest office supplier of consumable office supplies to large B-to-B customers in the United States. . . .

Office Depot is the second largest office supplier of consumable office supplies to large B-to-B customers in the United States. . . . [T]his case focuses on large B-to-B customers, defined by Plaintiffs as those that spend $500,000 or more per year on office supplies. Approximately 1200 corporations in the United States are included in this alleged relevant market.

C. [Omitted—ed.]

D. Regional and Local Vendors

Regional and local office supply vendors exist throughout the country. However, they typically do not bid for large B-to-B contracts.

* * * * *

E. Amazon Business

Amazon.com Inc.'s effort to compete in the office supply industry, including the B-to-B space, is Amazon Business. . . . Although in its infancy, Amazon's vision is for Amazon Business to be the "preferred marketplace for all professional, business and institutional customers worldwide." . . .

III. [Omitted—ed.]

IV. DISCUSSION

* * * * *

A. Legal Principles Considered When Defining a Relevant Market

* * * * *

a. Consumable office supplies as cluster market

Cluster markets allow items that are not substitutes for each other to be clustered together in one antitrust market. . . . Here plaintiffs allege that items such as pens, file folders, Post-it notes, binder clips, and paper for copiers and printers are included in this cluster market. Although a pen is not a functional substitute for a paperclip, it is possible to cluster consumable office supplies into one market for analytical convenience. Defining the market as a cluster market is justified in this case because "market shares and competitive conditions are likely to be similar for the distribution of pens to large customers and the distribution of binder clips to large customers."

* * * * *

B. Application of Relevant Legal Principles to Plaintiffs' Market Definition

. . . Plaintiffs argue that the relevant market is a cluster market of "consumable office supplies" which consists of "an assortment of office supplies, such as pens, paper clips, notepads and copy paper, that are used and replenished frequently." Plaintiffs' alleged relevant market is also a targeted market, limited to B-to-B customers, specifically large B-to-B customers who spend $500,000 or more on office supplies annually.

Defendants, on the other hand, argue that Plaintiffs' alleged market definition is wrong because it is a "gerrymandered and artificially narrow product market limited to *some,* but not all, consumable office supplies sold to only the most powerful companies in the world." In particular, Defendants insist that ink and toner must be included in a proper definition of the relevant product market. Defendants also argue that no evidence supports finding sales to large B-to-B customers as a distinct market.

1. *Brown Shoe* "Practical Indicia"

The *Brown Shoe* practical indicia support Plaintiffs' definition of the relevant product market . . . because there is: (a) industry or public recognition of the market as a separate economic entity; (b) B-to-B customers demand distinct prices and demonstrate a high sensitivity to price changes; and (c) B-to-B customers require specialized vendors that offer value-added services, including: (i) sophisticated information technology (IT) services; (ii) high quality customer service; and (iii) expedited delivery. . . .

2. Expert Testimony of Dr. Carl Shapiro and the Hypothetical Monopolist Test

. . . The parties agree that the main test used by economists to determine a product market is the hypothetical monopolist test. (HMT). This test queries whether a hypothetical monopolist who has control over the products in an alleged market could profitably raise prices on those products. . . .

Dr. Shapiro . . . points out that Staples and Office Depot's head-to-head competition "tells us that a *monopoly* provider of consumable office supplies would charge significantly more to large customers than Staples and Office Depot today charge these same customers." Dr. Shapiro also highlights the record evidence that demonstrates Defendants compete "fiercely" for business in the large B-to-B space. Dr. Shapiro concludes that such competition implies that "the elimination of competition would lead to a significant price increase to large customers. . . ."

* * * * *

C. Defendants' Arguments in Opposition to Plaintiffs' Alleged Market

Defendants make two primary arguments in response to Plaintiffs' alleged market. First, Defendants . . . argue that exclusion of ink and toner, as well as "beyond office supplies" or "BOSS" products from the alleged market, is error. Second, defendants argue that no evidence supports Plaintiffs' contention that large B-to-B customers should be treated as a separate market.

1. Exclusion of ink, toner and BOSS from alleged market is proper

*   *   *   *   *

a. Defendants' argument for inclusion of ink and toner fails because they are not subject to the same competitive conditions as general office supplies

*   *   *   *   *

Competition for the sale of ink and toner has increased due to the "recent and rapid" rise of Managed Print Services (MPS). MPS vendors like Xerox, Hewlett-Packard, Lexmark, and Ricoh provide a bundle of services that includes sale of ink and toner in addition to service and maintenance of printers and copiers. There is ample record evidence to show that ink, toner, and other adjacent BOSS items are properly excluded from the relevant market because they are subject to distinct competitive conditions. For example, some large companies are shifting all of their ink and toner business to an MPS. . . . Other large companies are disaggregating ink and toner purchases between their primary vendor and an MPS. . . .

*   *   *   *   *

2. Antitrust laws exist to protect competition, not a particular set of consumers

Defendants' second primary argument in opposition to Plaintiffs' proposed relevant market is that "there is no evidence to support Plaintiffs' claim that large B-to-B should be treated as a separate market."

*   *   *   *   *

[T]he nature of how large B-to-B customers operate, including the services they demand, supports a finding that they are a targeted customer market for procurement of consumable office supplies. There is overwhelming evidence in this case that large B-to-B customers constitute a market that Defendants could target for price increases if they are allowed to merge. Significantly, Defendants themselves used the proposed merger to pressure B-to-B customers to lock in prices based on the expectation that they would lose negotiating leverage if the merger were approved. . . .

D. [Omitted—ed.]

E. Analysis of the Plaintiffs' Arguments Relating to Probable Effects on Competition Based on Market Share Calculations

Having concluded that Plaintiffs have carried their burden of establishing that the sale and distribution of consumable office supplies to large B-to-B customers in the United States is the relevant market, the Court now turns to an analysis of the likely effects of the proposed merger on competition within the relevant market. . . .

1. Concentration in the *sale* and distribution of consumable office supplies to large B-to-B customers

Dr. Shapiro estimated Defendants' market shares by using data collected from *Fortune* 100 companies [about their spending on

consumable office supplies—ed.]. . . . Defendants' market share of the *Fortune* 100 sample as a whole is striking: Staples captures 47.3 percent and Office Depot captures 31.6 percent, for a total of 79 percent market share. The pre-merger HHI is already highly concentrated in this market, resting at 3,270. . . . If allowed to merge, the HHI would increase nearly 3,000 points, from 3,270 to 6,265. This market structure would constitute one dominant firm with a competitive fringe. Staples' proposed acquisition of Office Depot is therefore presumptively illegal because the HHI increases more than 200 points and the post-merger HHI is greater than 2,500. . . .

F. [Omitted—ed.]

G. Conclusion Regarding Plaintiffs' Market Share Analysis

Plaintiffs have met their burden of showing that the merger would result in "undue concentration" in the relevant market of the sale and distribution of consumable office supplies to large B-to-B customers in the United States. . . .

H. Plaintiffs' Evidence of Additional Harm

Sole reliance on HHI calculations cannot guarantee litigation victories. . . . The bid data . . . shows that Defendants win large B-to-B customer bids more frequently than other bidders. . . . Defendants' own documents created in the ordinary course of their business show that Defendants view themselves as the most viable office supply vendors for large businesses in the United States. . . . Large B-to-B customers view Defendants as their best option for nationwide sale and delivery of consumable office supplies. . . .

This additional evidence strengthens Plaintiffs' claim that harm will result in the form of loss of competition if Staples is permitted to acquire Office Depot.

I. Defendants' Response to Plaintiffs' *Prima Facie* Case

Defendants' sole argument in response to Plaintiffs' *prima facie* case is that the merger will not have anti-competitive effects because Amazon Business, as well as the existing patchwork of local and regional office supply companies, will expand and provide large B-to-B customers with competitive alternatives to the merged entity. . . . The relevant time frame for consideration in this forward looking exercise is two to three years.

*   *   *   *   *

. . . Plaintiffs point to a long list of what they view as Amazon Business' deficiencies, including, but not limited to: (1) lack of RFP experience; (2) no commitment to guaranteed pricing; (3) lack of ability to control third-party price and delivery; (4) inability to provide customer-specific pricing; (5) a lack of dedicated customer service agents dedicated to the B-to-B space; (6) no desktop delivery; (7) no proven ability to provide detailed utilization and invoice reports; and (8) lack of product variety and breadth. Although Amazon Business may successfully address some of these alleged weaknesses in the short term, the evidence . . . does not support the conclusion that Amazon Business will be in a position to restore competition lost by the proposed merger within three years.

* * * * *

V. CONCLUSION

As Judge Mehta observed in *Sysco,* "There can be little doubt that the acquisition of the second largest firm in the market by the largest firm in the market will tend to harm competition in that market." The Court concludes that Plaintiffs have met their burden of showing . . . that Staples' acquisition of Office Depot would lessen competition in the sale and distribution of consumable office supplies in the large B-to-B market in the United States. . . .

. . . Plaintiffs' Motion for Preliminary Injunction is GRANTED.

Questions

1. *a.* What was the court's definition of the market?
   b. How did the court arrive at that definition?
   c. Why were ink, toner, and BOSS excluded from that market?

2. *a.* What evidence supported the FTC's claim that the merger would lead to anticompetitive effects?
   b. In weighing the Federal Trade Commission and Staples/Office Depot arguments, why did the court come down on the side of the government?

3. Do you think consumers will benefit from this decision? Explain.

4. Three firms controlled the $1 billion U.S. baby food market (Gerber—65 percent, Heinz—17.4 percent, and Beech-Nut—15.4 percent). Gerber was sold in over 90 percent of American supermarkets, and it had greater brand loyalty than any other product sold in the United States. Heinz was sold in 40 percent of the supermarkets and Beech-Nut in 45 percent. The baby food HHI was 4,775, which would increase by 510 HHI points if Heinz and Beech-Nut were to merge. Heinz and Beech-Nut agreed to merge. The Federal Trade Commission opposed the merger.
   a. What other facts would you want to know to decide the legality of this proposed merger?
   b. Defend the merger.
   c. Decide. Explain. See *Federal Trade Commission v. H. J. Heinz Co.,* 246 F.3d 708 (D.C. Cir. 2001).

5. In 1958, Pabst Brewing Company acquired Blatz Brewing Company. Pabst was America's 10th largest brewer, while Blatz was the 18th largest. After the merger, Pabst had 4.49 percent of the nationwide beer market and was the fifth-largest brewer. In the regional market of Wisconsin, Michigan, and Illinois, the merger gave Pabst 11.32 percent of the sales. After the merger, Pabst led beer sales in Wisconsin with 23.95 percent of that statewide market. The beer market was becoming increasingly concentrated, with the total number of brewers declining from 206 to 162 during the years 1957 to 1961. In *United States v. Pabst Brewing Co.,* 384 U.S. 546 (1966), the Supreme Court found the merger violated the Clayton Act, Section 7. The Court did not choose among the three geographic market configurations, saying that the crucial inquiry is whether a merger may substantially lessen competition anywhere in the United States. Thus, the Court held that, under these facts, a 4.49 percent share of the market was too large.

Respected scholar and jurist Richard Posner labeled the *Pabst* decision an "atrocity" and the product of a "fit of nonsense" on the part of the Supreme Court.[25] What economic arguments would support Posner's colorful complaint?

Part Three—American Antitrust Laws and the International Market

LO 11-10
Contrast antitrust enforcement in the United States and the European Union (EU).

America's commercial market embraces the entire globe. Antitrust questions can become extremely complex in transactions involving multiple companies in multiple nations where those transactions are potentially governed by both U.S. and foreign antitrust laws. U.S. antitrust laws apply, of course, to foreign firms doing business here, but in addition the Sherman, Clayton, and FTC acts, among others, are all potentially applicable to business abroad that directly affects America regardless of the participants' nationality.

Extraterritoriality

The U.S. Justice Department claims authority to apply American antitrust law abroad, including the power to sue foreign firms that violate U.S. antitrust laws even when the anticompetitive actions take place overseas (extraterritorial application). America does not, however, claim unlimited antitrust reach. The 1982 Foreign Trade Antitrust Improvements Act (FTAIA) basically excludes all foreign conduct from the extraterritorial reach of the Sherman Act except conduct "involving" (1) "import commerce" and (2) nonimport commerce that has a "direct, substantial and reasonably foreseeable effect" on domestic commerce or American exporters. Claims arising from foreign commerce not falling within those two exceptions would have to be litigated in other nations. The precise meaning of "import commerce," "direct effect," and other terms is being sorted out in court at this writing, with confusion likely to persist for years.

International Antitrust Enforcement

Most antitrust enforcement occurs in the United States and the European Union, but other nations, China, in particular, are taking a more aggressive stance, usually by employing laws that largely mimic those of the United States or the European Union.

European Union Antitrust Enforcement   In general, American and European Union antitrust policies are compatible and are the product of constant consultation. Nonetheless, EU regulators have demonstrated they are willing to part ways with America if market conditions require. As we saw in Chapter 10, the European Union has taken a more aggressive stance toward Google's alleged anticompetitive behaviors than has been the case in the United States. Certainly the EU regulators are not timid about blocking American business activities in Europe. UPS, for example, announced in 2013 that it would drop its bid to acquire competing Dutch delivery company TNT Express when it became clear that the European Commission would raise antitrust concerns. On the other hand, FedEx received EU permission to acquire TNT, a deal that was completed in 2016. FedEx's European operations are much smaller than those of UPS.

Given the European Union's powerful economic role, the antitrust decisions of EU regulators necessarily influence business practices worldwide. [For access to EU antitrust law, see **http://ec.europa.eu/competiton/index_en.html**].

Other Nations   The number of nations with competition laws soared from 40 in 1995 to more than 125 in 2009,[26] and we are seeing the beginning of a worldwide convergence of those laws led by the United States, China, and the European Union.[27] China created its Anti-Monopoly Law in 2008. Responding to complaints about inconsistent and unpredictable antitrust enforcement, Chinese antitrust authorities, in 2014, committed to due process improvements in its antitrust practices. China agreed to treat foreign and domestic firms the same, to allow foreign companies to have legal counsel during investigative proceedings, and to publish the results of its investigations.

China's official position is that aggressive antitrust enforcement is necessary to protect consumers from price gouging and other abuses, but foreign companies suspect China is using its strengthened regulations to pursue multinationals and thereby protect and promote Chinese companies. Microsoft, for example, has been the subject of antitrust investigations in China since 2014.

Internet Exercise

"What Do the Antitrust Laws Do for the Consumer?" For an answer, see the U.S. Department of Justice, Antitrust Division, brochure, "Antitrust Enforcement and the Consumer" [**www.justice.gov/atr/public/div_stats/antitrust-enfor-consumer.pdf**].

Chapter Questions

1. The Chicago Skyway, a toll bridge connecting Chicago and Indiana, was owned and operated by the City of Chicago. Chicago earned $52 million in tolls beyond the amount needed to meet bond payments and to maintain the Skyway. The excess was used to pay for other transportation expenses. Skyway tolls were higher than those of other area highways. Endsley, a bridge user, joined others in a class action against Chicago claiming that the city's control of the Skyway provided monopoly power in high-speed limited access travel between Indiana and Chicago and that the city was abusing that power by collecting excessive fees. Chicago demonstrated that at least two alternative, if less desirable, routes were in competition with the Skyway. Was Chicago a monopolist? Explain. See *Endsley v. City of Chicago*, 230 F.3d 276 (7th Cir. 2000), *cert. denied*, 532 U.S. 972 (2001).

2. Major League Soccer (MLS) was the exclusive Division I professional soccer league in the United States, as recognized by the U.S. Soccer Federation (USSF), the national soccer governing body. MLS owned all of the league's 12 teams, set all schedules, negotiated all stadium leases, controlled all intellectual property rights, and controlled all player contracts. Partial control over some teams was transferred by MLS to certain investors. The investors did not hire their own players. Each employment contract was between the player and the league. MLS assigned the players in a manner designed to maintain competitive balance. MLS had been preceded in U.S. professional soccer by the North American Soccer League, which had failed financially. A group of players sued the MLS on antitrust grounds.

   a. What were the players' antitrust claims?

   b. Decide those claims. Explain. See *Fraser v. Major League Soccer*, 284 F.3d 47 (1st Cir. 2002).

3. Poplar Bluff is a city of 17,000 people in southeastern Missouri. Sikeston and Cape Girardeau, Missouri, both towns with populations of over 40,000, are 40 and 60 miles away from Poplar Bluff. Tenet Healthcare owned Lucy Lee Hospital in Poplar Bluff and proposed to buy Doctors' Regional Medical Center, also in Poplar Bluff. Both hospitals were profitable, but both were underutilized and had trouble attracting specialists. The Federal Trade Commission filed suit to block the acquisition. The key question involved definition of the geographic market. The FTC proposed a relevant geographic market that essentially matched the service area: a 50-mile radius of downtown Poplar Bluff. Ninety percent of the two hospitals' patients came from that area. Four other hospitals were in that area. The merged hospital would have had 84 percent of the patients in that geographic market. Tenet argued that the geographic market should have encompassed a 65-mile radius from downtown Poplar Bluff. That area included 16 hospitals. How should the court of appeals have defined the geographic market? See *FTC v. Tenet Health Care Corp.*, 186 F.3d 1045 (8th Cir. 1999).

4. In 2011, the U.S. Justice Department sent a letter to the National Collegiate Athletic Association raising antitrust questions about the Bowl Championship Series (BCS),

which is used to determine a national college football champion. The letter asked why the BCS schools had not established a playoff system. Pressure from critics and the promise of huge payouts then pushed the BCS to establish a four-team playoff system that commenced in 2014. In your judgment, should federal antitrust law be applied to the Bowl Championship Series? Explain.

5. Lina Khan, writing in *Politico*, argued that the federal government should be concerned about threats to competition from online "platform monopolies" such as Amazon, Facebook, and Google.[28] Khan says those online giants are like the "railroads of the Internet economy" connecting buyers and sellers in an online marketplace. Khan says the online companies can use their market power, as the railroads did historically, to squeeze the suppliers and sellers that depend upon them. Explain her concern.

6. Critics worry that increasing mergers, especially those involving media firms, threaten democracy.
    a. Explain that argument.
    b. Do you agree? Explain.

7. In 1986 distinguished economist William Shepherd argued,

    > It may not be too late to turn back from this road to serfdom by reviving the case for antitrust, but the odds aren't favorable. More probably, antitrust will continue to sink.[29]

    a. What did Shepherd mean about "this road to serfdom?"
    b. In reading this chapter, do you think antitrust has been revived? Explain.
    c. Is bigness bad, or is it necessary in today's global economy? Explain.

8. Whole Foods, the natural foods chain, in 2007 acquired its chief competitor, Wild Oats Market. Whole Foods had about 12 percent of the natural foods market, and Wild Oats held about 3 percent. Whole Foods had 197 stores and added 110 by purchasing Wild Oats. About 72 percent of Wild Oats' sales were in markets where the two overlapped. Whole Foods argued that the merger was necessary to allow it to compete effectively with big chains such as Safeway and Walmart.

    Prior to the purchase, Whole Foods co-founder and CEO John Mackey allegedly said the proposed merger would end "forever or almost forever" the possibility of a big grocery chain buying an existing natural foods chain to compete with Whole Foods. Mackey also allegedly said that buying Wild Oats would prevent "nasty price wars."

    The Federal Trade Commission challenged the Whole Foods purchase of Wild Oats.
    a. What was the primary issue facing the federal courts that reviewed the FTC challenge?
    b. Decide the case. Explain. See *Federal Trade Commission v. Whole Foods Market*, 502 F. Supp. 2d 1 (D.D.C. 2007); *Federal Trade Commission v. Whole Foods Market*, 533 F.3d 869 (D.C. Cir. 2008); and David Kesmodel and Jonathan Eig, "A Grocer's Brash Style Takes Unhealthy Turn," *The Wall Street Journal*, July 20, 2007, p. A1.

9. Is the influence of big business so persuasive that it nullifies the effective enforcement of the antitrust laws? Explain.

10. Antitrust authorities must address a critical and empirically difficult policy problem: Does seller concentration in a market ordinarily result in increased prices? That is, in

a particular market, are fewer firms with larger shares likely to produce higher prices than would be the case with a more fragmented market? Free-market theorists are generally untroubled by concentration. What do you think? Explain.

11. Is a monopolist required to deal with its competitors? That question was the core of a 2004 Supreme Court decision in *Verizon Communications v. Law Offices of Curtis V. Trinko*.[30] The Trinko law firm bought its local phone service from AT&T. Trinko brought a class action claiming Verizon maintained a monopoly by exclusionary practices. Trinko contended that local phone services had difficulty connecting with the giant regional Bell operating companies' (Verizon, Qwest, BellSouth, and SBC) local exchange facilities, thus harming competition and consumers. The Telecommunications Act of 1996 specifically requires the regional Bell companies to provide the local phone services with fair, reasonable access. The Supreme Court, however, ruled in favor of Verizon and concluded that antitrust liability in these telephone situations would apply only where a telephone monopolist discontinues a voluntary business relationship with a competitor for the purpose of destroying that competitor. Explain why the Supreme Court decided that Verizon, a telephone monopolist, had no duty to deal with those telephone competitors with whom it had not previously dealt. See Matthew Cantor, "Is 'Trinko' the Last Word on a Telephone Monopolist's Duty to Deal?" *New York Law Journal* 96 (May 19, 2004), p. 4.

12. In the period 1917 to 1919, DuPont acquired 23 percent of the stock in the then-fledgling General Motors Corporation. By 1947, DuPont supplied 68 percent of GM's automotive finish needs and 38 percent of its fabric needs. In 1955, General Motors ranked first in sales and second in assets among all U.S. industrial corporations, while accounting for approximately two-fifths of the nation's annual automobile sales. In 1949, the Justice Department challenged Dupont's 1917–19 acquisitions of GM stock.

    a. Why did the government challenge DuPont's acquisition?

    b. May an acquisition be properly challenged 30 years after the fact, as in *DuPont*? Explain.

    c. Given your general understanding of finishes and fabrics, how would you defend DuPont?

    d. Decide. Explain. See *United States v. E.I. DuPont de Nemours & Co.*, 353 U.S. 586 (1957).

13. How can a merger benefit society?

14. Which economic considerations support the view that unilateral growth is preferable to growth by merger?

15. Excel, a division of Cargill, was the second-largest firm in the beef-packing market. It sought to acquire Spencer Pack, a division of Land-O-Lakes and the third-largest beef packer. After the acquisition, Excel would have remained second ranked in the business, but its market share would have been only slightly smaller than that of the leader, IBP. Monfort, the nation's fifth-largest beef packer, sought an injunction to block the acquisition, claiming a violation of Clayton Section 7. In effect, Monfort claimed the merger would result in a dangerous concentration of economic power in the beef-packing market, with the result that Excel would pay more for cattle and charge less for its processed beef, thus placing its competitors in a destructive and

illegal price–cost squeeze. Monfort claimed Excel's initial losses in this arrangement would be covered by its wealthy parent, Cargill. Then, when the competition was driven from the market, Monfort claimed, Excel would raise its processed beef prices to supracompetitive levels. Among other defenses, Excel averred that the heavy losses Monfort claimed were merely the product of intense competition, a condition that would not constitute a violation of the antitrust laws. The district court found for Monfort, and the appeals court, considering the cost–price squeeze a form of predatory pricing, affirmed. Excel appealed to the Supreme Court. Decide. Explain. See *Cargill, Inc. v. Monfort of Colorado, Inc.*, 479 U.S. 104 (1986).

Notes

1. David Dayen, "The Most Important 2016 Issue You Don't Know About," *The New Republic,* March 11, 2016 [**www.newrepublic.com**].

2. "Too Much of a Good Thing," *The Economist,* May 26, 2016 [**www.economist.com**].

3. See *United States v. Microsoft Corporatio*n, 87 F. Supp. 2d 30 (D.D.C. 2000); and *Microsoft v. United States,* 253 F.3d 34 (D.C. Cir. 2001), *cert. denied,* 122 S. Ct. 350 (2001).

4. Alan Murray, "Microsoft Foe Quits Antitrust Crusade—with Check in Hand," *The Wall Street Journal,* December 7, 2004, p. A4.

5. *United States v. Grinnell,* 384 U.S. 563, 570–71 (1966).

6. Aliza Rosenbaum, Rob Cox, and Pierre Briancon, "Rising Beer Prices Hint at Oligopoly," *The New York Times,* August 27, 2009 [**www.nytimes.com**].

7. Note, "Antitrust and the Information Age: Section 2 Monopolization Analyses in the New Economy," *Harvard Law Review* 114, no. 5 (March 2001), p. 1623.

8. *Spectrum Sports, Inc. v. Shirley McQuillan,* 506 U.S. 447 (1993).

9. Note, "Antitrust and the Information Age," pp. 1623, 1645.

10. *United States v. Aluminum Co. of America,* 148 F.2d 416 (2d Cir. 1945).

11 Chad Bray, "Shareholders Approve SABMiller Takeover by Anheuser-Busch InBev," *The New York Times,* September 28, 2016 [**www.nytimes.com**].

12. "The Most Important 2016 Issue You Don't Know About."

13. Ibid.

14. Justin Bachman, "The American–US Airways Deal: You're Going to Pay More," *Bloomberg Businessweek,* February 12, 2013 [**www.businessweek.com**].

15. Bruce Blonigen and Justin Pierce, "Evidence for the Effects of Mergers on Market Power and Efficiency," *Finance and Economics Discussion Series 2016-082* (Washington: Board of Governors of the Federal Reserve System, 2016) [**https://doi.org/10.17016/FEDS.2016.082**].

16. Editorial, "Big Food," *The New York Times*, January 25, 2010 [**http://nytimes.com**].

17. Hugo Martin, "Airline Mergers Benefit Carriers and Help Keep Fares Low, Study Says," *Los Angeles Times,* January 26, 2014 [**www.latimes.com**].

18. How do mergers affect consumer prices? See Orley Ashenfelter and Daniel Hosken, "The Effect of Mergers on Consumers Prices: Evidence from Five Selected Case Studies," *Economist's View,* April 23, 2008 [**economistsview.typepad.com/economistsview/2008/04/the-effect-of-m.html**].

19. Kevin Voigt, "Mergers Fail More Often Than Marriages," *CNN.com/world business,* May 22, 2009 [**http://edition.cnn.com/2009/BUSINESS/05/21/merger.marriage/index.html**].

20. See Michael J. Mandel, "All These Mergers Are Great, But . . . ," *BusinessWeek,* October 18, 1999, p. 48; and Jeffrey Garten, "Megamergers Are a Clear and Present Danger," *BusinessWeek*, January 25, 1999, p. 28.

21. Haley Edwards, "The Bubbling Concern over Two Beer Giants' Blockbuster Merger," *Time,* July 26, 2016 [**http://time.com**].

22. Ibid.

23. Scott D. Thompson, "Clear Skies Seen Ahead for the American Airlines/U.S. Airways Merger," *LEXOLOGY,* February 22, 2013 [**www.lexology.com**].

24. This paragraph relies in part on Alan J. Meese and Barak D. Richman, "A Careful Examination of the Live Nation–Ticketmaster Merger," *SSRN Electronic Journal,* November 2009. Available at SSRN: **https://ssrn.com/abstract=1542626**.

25. Richard Posner, *Antitrust Law* (Chicago: The University of Chicago Press, 1976), p. 130.

26. Howard W. Fogt Jr., Alan D. Rutenberg, Max Lin, and Wen (Jo) Xu, "Evolving Convergence: Antitrust/Competition Law and Policy/Procedure in the United States, European Union, and China," *LEXOLOGY*, December 9, 2009 [**www.lexology.com**].

27. Ibid.

28. Lina Kahn, "How to Reboot the FTC," *Politico,* April 13, 2016 [**www.politco.com**].

29. William G. Shepherd, "Bust the Reagan Trustbusters," *Fortune,* August 4, 1986, pp. 225, 227.

30. 540 U.S. 398 (2004).

Employer–Employee Relations

CHAPTER TWELVE

Employment Law I: Employee Rights

After completing this chapter, students will be able to fulfill the following learning objectives:

12-1. Distinguish between an employee and an independent contractor.

12-2. Identify potential legal challenges an employer faces in the hiring process.

12-3. Describe employers' liability under the doctrine of *respondeat superior*.

12-4. Analyze claims of negligent hiring, supervision, and retention.

12-5. Explain employees' rights under the Fair Labor Standards Act.

12-6. Describe the role of the Occupational Safety and Health Administration (OSHA) in protecting employees' health and safety at work.

12-7. Describe the benefits, coverage, and requirements for bringing a successful claim under workers' compensation law.

12-8. Discuss workplace drug testing and the legal challenges it faces.

12-9. Describe the Family and Medical Leave Act (FMLA).

12-10. Distinguish between defined benefit and defined contribution pension plans.

12-11. Analyze whether a dismissed at-will employee may bring a claim of wrongful discharge.

12-12. Recognize the purpose and requirements of the employment eligibility verification form (I-9).

Introduction

Brandon Coats is a quadriplegic who has been confined to a wheelchair since he was a teenager. In 2009, he registered for and obtained a Colorado state-issued license to use medical marijuana to treat painful muscle spasms. Coats consumed medical marijuana at home, after work, and in accordance with his license and Colorado state law.

Between 2007 and 2010, Coats worked for Dish Network (Dish) as a telephone customer service representative. In 2010, Coats tested positive for tetrahydrocannabinol (THC), a component of medical marijuana, during a random drug test. Coats informed Dish that he was a registered medical marijuana patient and planned to continue using medical marijuana. Dish fired Coats for violating the company's drug policy.

Coats then filed a wrongful termination claim against Dish under a Colorado state law that generally prohibits employers from terminating employees based on their "lawful activities" conducted off the employer's premises during nonworking hours. Coats argued that his outside-of-work medical marijuana use is "lawful" under Colorado's state law allowing his medical marijuana use. Dish argued that using marijuana, even for medical purposes, was not "lawful" because it violated the federal Controlled Substances Act.

Questions

1. Should an employer be allowed to terminate an employee for using medical marijuana with a state-issued license? Explain.

2. Why would an employer prohibit employees from using marijuana at their home after work? Should employers be allowed to enforce such a policy? Explain. See *Coats v. Dish Network*, 2015 CO 44 (Colo. 2015).

Managing Lawsuits   Managers traditionally have balanced multiple responsibilities, but in recent years the law has added complex, sometimes daunting expectations. Addressing and mitigating the risk of employment-related lawsuits has become an important consideration in management decision making. As union strength has declined (see Chapter 14), government regulations and court decisions have arguably broadened employee rights. These increased legal protections, a volatile economy, downsized workplaces, weakened employer–employee loyalty, and other forces have contributed to higher levels of employee litigation.[1]

Part One—The Employment Relationship

Job Classification   Employment-related legal rights and responsibilities depend on the type of relationship the employer decides to build with the worker. The traditional, stable model of long-term direct employer–employee relationships now is often replaced with new, flexible, nontraditional staffing arrangements including outsourcing and employee leasing, along with the use of freelancers and temporary agencies. These *contingent workers*, along with *independent contractors*, who are increasingly relied on to perform both shorter-term, nonrecurring jobs as well as those traditionally held by full- or part-time company employees, permit employers to rapidly and inexpensively inflate or shrink their workforces as needed. This trend has impacted the typical relationship between a company and its workers and is reflected in the rise of the "on-demand" or "gig" economy.

WHERE DO YOU WORK?

In designing a popular video game, about 70 of the 81 employees of a San Diego video game creator worked with 40 to 50 workers from its worldwide network of independent contractors. A large retailer's shipping containers are unloaded by workers provided by a trucking company, which in turn contracts with a temporary staffing agency. Companies are able to control costs and promote efficiency by outsourcing work ranging from manual labor and customer service to software testing, or "renting" high-skilled workers with needed expertise. On the other hand, the use of temporary workers has created a "parallel workforce" that is vulnerable to pay inequality as they perform the same tasks as employees for notably different compensation. Lack of traditional employment protections add to job instability. Additionally, the intangible rewards of long-term employment relationships, such as upward mobility through promotions from lower- to higher-skilled positions, may be lost as jobs that could have been "stepping stones" for outstanding employees are outsourced.

Sources: Lauren Weber, "For Videogame Makers, Hiring Is a Last Resort," *The Wall Street Journal*, April 11, 2017, p. A1; and Lauren Weber, "The End of Employees," *The Wall Street Journal*, February 2, 2017 [**www.wsj.com/ articles/the-end-of-employees-1486050443**].

LO 12-1
Distinguish between an employee and an independent contractor.

Employee or Independent Contractor? A key question underlying the legal issues discussed in this chapter is whether the worker in question is an employee or an independent contractor: one who enters a contractual rather than employment relationship with an organization in order to perform a specific task. Degree of control is the dominant test in determining whether a worker is an employee or independent contractor. Where an employer controls or has the right or ability to control the worker's performance, the worker is likely to be considered an employee. CBS used the distinction between "independent contractor" and "employee" to successfully appeal the FCC's fine after Justin Timberlake and Janet Jackson appeared to cooperatively expose Ms. Jackson's breast at the end of their 2004 Super Bowl halftime show performance that CBS broadcast. CBS argued that the performers were independent contractors, not employees, and, therefore, CBS could not be held liable for actions taken outside their control.[2] The U.S. Supreme Court declined to review the federal appellate court's decision to throw out the FCC's fine.[3]

What other advantages might a business gain from hiring an independent contractor rather than an employee? A business that hires an independent contractor generally is not required to comply with a wide range of employment and labor law standards that would apply were the worker an employee. Thus, a business must provide, for example, unemployment insurance to its employees, but generally would not need to do so for independent contractors. Furthermore, employers generally are not liable for employment discrimination claims by independent contractors or for most torts committed by independent contractors in the course of work. While employers are responsible for payroll taxes such as FICA and federal and state unemployment insurance, as well as for withholding income tax from their employees, these tax obligations of a business do not extend to its independent contractors.

Classification Problems Employers anxious to reduce financial and legal burdens sometimes improperly classify workers as independent contractors rather than employees. In 2015, Homejoy, a cleaning-service startup, went out of business after facing several lawsuits from its cleaners who claimed they had been misclassified as independent contractors instead of employees, while on-demand ride services Uber and Lyft faced similar challenges, with an Uber driver being found to be an employee by a California Labor Commissioner.[4] The Internal Revenue Service (IRS) has a Voluntary Classification Settlement Program under which employers who meet certain criteria are able to reclassify workers as employees for employment tax purposes with partial relief from federal employment taxes.[5] [For IRS guidance on determining whether a worker is an employee or independent contractor, see **https://www.irs.gov/businesses/small-businesses-self-employed/independent-contractor-self-employed-or-employee**].

LO 12-2

Identify potential legal challenges an employer faces in the hiring process.

Selection and Hiring   An array of potential legal problems have arisen from the increasingly complex process of choosing and employing new workers.

- *Résumé Fraud.* Scott Thompson, former Yahoo CEO, left the company after revelations that he had falsely claimed to hold a computer science degree; he graduated with an accounting degree from a college that apparently did not have a computer science program at the time.[6] Manhattan College men's basketball coach Steve Masiello apparently lost an opportunity to coach at University of South Florida after it was discovered that his biography on Manhattan's website wrongly stated that he had graduated from the University of Kentucky; he had attended that institution but had not yet received a degree.[7] A 2015 survey of more than 2,500 hiring managers revealed that 56 percent had uncovered a lie on a résumé, including exaggeration of job responsibilities and skills. About a quarter of the respondents had found applicants claiming to be currently with an employer for which they had never worked.[8]

- *Background Checks.* Although concerns ranging from résumé fraud to employee theft and workplace violence may have led to background checks becoming an expected part of the hiring process, a 2012 survey conducted by the Society for Human Resource Management (SHRM) showed a decrease in the number of employers who check applicants' credit history and criminal backgrounds compared to 2010. Less than half of employers run credit checks on applicants for at least some positions, compared to 60 percent in 2010, while the percentage of employers *not* checking criminal backgrounds doubled from 7 percent to 14 percent.[9] Using credit checks in hiring arguably helps protect an employer against fraud and employee theft because applicants who have not handled their personal finances responsibly might be more likely to engage in such misconduct. However, questions about the validity and unintended impact of this practice have been raised in recent years. Not only has the connection between a bad credit report and poor job performance been disputed, but as discussed in Chapter 13, concerns have arisen that credit checks can create a discriminatory impact on certain groups' ability to gain employment.[10] Several states have passed legislation limiting the use of credit checks. The Illinois Employee Credit Privacy Act, for example, generally prohibits employers from using an employee's or applicant's credit history in making employment decisions such as hiring.[11]

The U.S. Equal Employment Opportunity Commission (EEOC)'s enforcement guidance on the use of criminal background checks does not ban employers from using this tool to screen applicants or current employees, although employers should not use it unless the conviction is relevant to the position for which the applicants are being considered. The EEOC noted that an arrest alone does not establish criminal conduct and therefore cannot be used in hiring; however, the conduct underlying the arrest could be considered by an employer in making an employment decision. [For the full text of the EEOC Enforcement Guidance on the Consideration of Arrest and Conviction Records in Employment Decisions, see **www.eeoc.gov/laws/guidance/arrest_conviction.cfm**].

> Employers using social media in the hiring process want to see whether candidates present themselves professionally.

- **Online Reputation.** Employers are increasingly searching the online reputation of job applicants. A 2014 survey revealed that over 40 percent of employers browse applicants' social media profiles; over half of these employers reported passing on applicants based on what they found.[12] As discussed further in this chapter, concern for privacy over this practice has led to state legislation preventing employers from requiring social media passwords as part of the application process.

- **Inappropriate Questions.** According to a recent survey, approximately one-third of employers did not know that they should not ask applicants about their marital status or age in an interview.[13] Furthermore, such questions as "How old are you?" and "Are you married?" also expose employers to potential liability for discrimination (see Chapter 13). But what about the enormous array of awkward, intrusive, but nondiscriminatory interview questions that might leave the candidate feeling uncomfortable if not wronged? For example: "What would you do if I gave you an elephant?" has questionable relevance in a job interview.[14]

- **Restrictive Covenants.** Chris Botticella, a former executive with Bimbo Bakeries, which operates under popular brand names such as Thomas' and Entenmann's, was unable to start work for Hostess, Inc., because of the confidentiality agreement and other restrictive covenants he had signed with Bimbo. Information such as recipes and business strategies to which Botticella had access would likely be shared with Hostess.[15] To address problems like these, employers sometimes require employees to sign agreements providing they will not compete with their employer, solicit its customers or employees, pass trade secrets to others, and so on, for a specified period of time. Such agreements are not limited to upper management,[16] and generally are fully enforceable if reasonable in their requirements. California law, however, prohibits noncompetition agreements in employment, with narrow statutory exceptions.[17] Even if such an agreement is enforceable, employers who take such actions as hiring a private investigator to determine whether a former employee is in breach could face liability for intrusion (see Chapter 7).[18]

The Upside of Losing Employees

A 2016 LinkedIn survey showed that millennials will typically work for about four different employers in their first decade after college. While the resources spent to replace talent may be significant, employers may actually gain a competitive edge in recruitment as a result of losing employees to more prestigious job placements. A 2017 study examining law firm hiring found that law firm associates will look favorably on law firms with increased departure rates when those leaving were going to high-status law firms. These findings might apply to other industries such as technology.

Questions

1. How might millennials impact employers' use of restrictive covenants?
2. How might the enforceability of restrictive covenants be impacted by millennials?

Source: Vanessa Furhmans, "The Case for Saying Goodbye," *The Wall Street Journal*, April 19, 2017, p. B7.

- *Arbitration.* New employees are often expected to sign agreements specifying that disputes with the employer will be settled by arbitration (see Chapter 4) rather than by litigation. A study of 21 major corporations' employment contracts found that 93 percent contained mandatory arbitration clauses.[19] Employers like arbitration because it can be cheaper, faster, and less adversarial than a trial. Employees, on the other hand, argue that arbitration is stacked in favor of corporate interests and amounts to a denial of the fundamental right of access to the legal system. Employment arbitration agreements have been supported by U.S. Supreme Court decisions upholding the enforceability of legitimate, equitable employment arbitration agreements.[20] In one case, the Court vacated a state supreme court ruling that the arbitration clause in an employer's restrictive covenant was void under state limitations on enforcement of noncompetition agreements in employment; the U.S Supreme Court held that whether the restrictive covenant was enforceable was for the arbitrator to decide.[21] However, the U.S. Equal Employment Opportunity Commission (see Chapter 13) still retains authority to file discrimination lawsuits on behalf of employees regardless of an arbitration agreement.[22]

> **You decide to fire an employee.**

- *References.* As a manager, you decide to fire an employee, Brown, because of what you believe to be convincing evidence that he had sexually harassed a coworker. Brown applies for a new job, and that employer seeks your evaluation of Brown's work. What should you do? If you tell what you know, you and your employer fear Brown might sue you for *defamation* (*slander* when spoken; *libel* when written). If you fail to say what you know, you fear you might be sued for *misrepresentation* or *negligent referral* if Brown is hired and commits further harassment on his new job. Because of those risks, employers often limit their references to purely factual details such as the date of hire, date of departure, and job title.

Broadly, a successful defamation suit requires the following conditions:

1. A false statement.
2. The statement must be "published" to a third party.
3. The employer must be responsible for the publication.
4. The plaintiff's reputation must be harmed.

Truth is a complete defense in defamation cases, and managers who offer factual, honest professional judgments are unlikely to face such claims. Further, many state courts provide the protection of a *qualified privilege*. Under this privilege, legitimate business communications, with some exceptions, are shielded from liability. Similarly, a number of states have enacted legislation providing employers with immunity from liability for good faith employment references.

Part Two—Liability

Once hired, what happens when employees make mistakes or engage in misconduct on the job that hurts others? Must the employer bear the loss in these situations? Job classification is an important first question in determining company liability for workers' job-related injuries, harm to others, and crimes. An enterprise ordinarily will not be liable for the acts of its independent contractors. Employers, on the other hand, often bear legal responsibility for employees' accidents or wrongs. That liability may spring from the doctrine of **respondeat superior** (let the master answer), a form of *vicarious liability* (sometimes called *imputed liability*).

LO 12-3
Describe employers' liability under the doctrine of *respondeat superior.*

Scope of Employment   Employer liability for employee injuries, accidents, or wrongs is largely dependent on whether the employee was on the job at the time of the incident in question. Employers will be held liable under *respondeat superior*/vicarious liability reasoning for harm to third parties caused by the intentional or negligent acts of their employees when those acts occur within the *scope of employment* (on the job). A finding of employer liability, of course, does not excuse the employee from her personal liability, but the *respondeat superior* reasoning does have the potential effect of opening the employer's deeper pockets to the plaintiff. The following questions ordinarily determine whether the harm occurred in the scope of employment:

1. Was the employee subject to the employer's supervision?
2. Was the employee motivated, at least in part, by a desire to serve the employer's business interests?
3. Did the problem arise substantially within normal working hours and in a work location?
4. Was the act in question of the general kind the employee had been hired to perform?

> The City was held liable for a sexual assault committed by a police officer.

In *Mary M. v. City of Los Angeles*,[23] the city was held liable under the doctrine of *respondeat superior* for a sexual assault committed by a police officer. At 2:30 am on October 3, 1981, Sergeant Leigh Schroyer was on duty, in uniform, carrying a gun, and patrolling in his marked police car. He stopped Mary M. for erratic driving. She pleaded not to be arrested. He ordered her to enter his patrol car and took her to her home. He entered her home and said that he expected "payment" for not arresting her. He raped her and was subsequently sentenced to a term in state prison.

Mary M. sued the City of Los Angeles. The general inquiry was whether Schroyer was acting within the scope of his employment during the rape episode. The jury found for Mary M. and awarded $150,000 in damages. The court of appeals reversed, saying that Schroyer was not acting within the scope of his employment. The case went to the California Supreme Court. The city argued that Schroyer was acting on behalf of his own interests rather than those of the city, and that the city had not authorized his conduct. Therefore, Schroyer could not have been acting within the scope of employment. However, the court said that the correct question was not whether the rape was authorized but whether it happened in the course of a series of acts that were authorized. The court reversed, saying that a jury could find the city vicariously liable (imputed to the principal from the agent) given the unique authority of police officers in our society.

Questions

1. Jean was carrying groceries out of the grocery store Hy-Vee when she was struck and injured by a bicycle driven by Lewis, a 16-year-old Hy-Vee employee. Lewis was hurrying

home to get a belt to complete his required Hy-Vee work uniform. He had received permission from his supervisor to return home for that purpose; Lewis had neither clocked in nor started his shift. Jean sued Hy-Vee for her resulting injuries.

a. What is Jean's claim?

b. Decide the case. Explain. See *Jean v. Hy Vee, Inc.*, 825 N.W.2d 327 (Iowa Ct. App. 2012).

2. Ahern, a chef at the Heathwood Nursing and Rehabilitation Center in Chestnut Hill, Massachusetts, left work and went to the South Pacific Chinese Restaurant, where he met his supervisor, Pacitti, to socialize and discuss work-related matters. Ahern purchased two drinks and consumed at least one drink and one-half of the other before leaving to go home. On his way home, Ahern's vehicle struck Lev as he was crossing a street, causing severe and debilitating injuries. Ahern was arrested and eventually convicted of operating a motor vehicle while under the influence of intoxicating liquor. Lev sued Heathwood's owner and operator, Beverly Enterprises, alleging that Beverly was vicariously liable for Ahern's negligence based on their employment relationship.

a. What was the central issue in this case?

b. Decide the case. Explain. See *Lev v. Beverly Enterprises*, 457 Mass. 234 (2010).

3. What policy justifications support the imposition of liability on an employer for the wrongs of an employee operating within the scope of employment?

A Side Order of Pistol-Whipping?

Harris placed his order with a cashier at a Kentucky Fried Chicken (KFC) restaurant in Philadelphia, Pennsylvania, but hesitated in selecting his side orders that were part of the meal he had selected. Another KFC employee, Henry, told Harris to "hurry up." Harris replied, "I am not dealing with you." Henry then asked Harris: "Do you want the [expletive] chicken or not?" Taken aback, Harris further hesitated; Henry pulled out a gun. Harris put up his hands and asked if Henry was "going to shoot [him] over a bucket of chicken?" While another employee yelled at Henry, Harris tried to escape, but Henry followed and pistol-whipped Harris before he could leave the restaurant, causing him injuries. Harris sued KFC for negligently failing to conduct a criminal background check. In rejecting the claim, the federal district court noted that KFC was not legally required to conduct a criminal background check, and that Henry's criminal history only would have revealed two prior convictions for nonviolent crimes over five years old.

Questions

1. Do you agree with the court's ruling? Explain.

2. How else might KFC have prevented this situation? Explain. See *Harris v. KFC*, 2012 U.S. Dist. LEXIS 84668 (E.D. Pa. June 18, 2012).

Hiring/Retention/Training/Supervision

LO 12-4

Analyze claims of negligent hiring, supervision, and retention.

Negligence

In addition to vicarious liability for employees' actions, employers may be directly liable for negligence in hiring an employee or retaining an employee who subsequently causes harm to a third party, or for careless training or supervision. Typically, the employer is liable on negligence grounds for hiring or retaining an employee whom the employer knew or should have known to be dangerous, incompetent, dishonest, or the like where that characteristic was directly related to the injury suffered by the plaintiff. Note that under negligence liability, an employer may be liable for acts *outside* the scope of employment. The case that follows examines the law of negligent hiring, supervision, and retention.

LEGAL BRIEFCASE

Yunker v. Honeywell, Inc.
496 N.W.2d 419 (Minn. Ct. App. 1993)

Judge Lansing

FACTS

Honeywell employed Randy Landin from 1977 to 1979 and from 1984 to 1988. From 1979 to 1984 Landin was imprisoned for the strangulation death of Nancy Miller, a Honeywell coemployee. On his release from prison, Landin reapplied at Honeywell. Honeywell rehired Landin as a custodian in Honeywell's General Offices facility in South Minneapolis in August 1984. Because of workplace confrontations Landin was twice transferred, first to the Golden Valley facility in August 1986, and then to the St. Louis Park facility in August 1987.

Kathleen Nesser was assigned to Landin's maintenance crew in April 1988. Landin and Nesser became friends and spent time together away from work. When Landin expressed a romantic interest, Nesser stopped spending time with Landin. Landin began to harass and threaten Nesser both at work and at home. At the end of June, Landin's behavior prompted Nesser to seek help from her supervisor and to request a transfer out of the St. Louis Park facility.

On July 1, 1988, Nesser found a death threat scratched on her locker door. Landin did not come to work on or after July 1, and Honeywell accepted his formal resignation on July 11, 1988. On July 19, approximately six hours after her Honeywell shift ended, Landin killed Nesser in her driveway with a close-range shotgun blast. Landin was convicted of first-degree murder and sentenced to life imprisonment.

Jean Yunker, as trustee for the heirs and next-of-kin of Kathleen Nesser, brought this wrongful death action based on theories of negligent hiring, retention, and supervision of a dangerous employee. Honeywell moved for summary judgment and, for purposes of the motion, stipulated that it failed to exercise reasonable care in the hiring and supervision of Landin. The trial court concluded that Honeywell owed no legal duty to Nesser and granted summary judgment for Honeywell.

ISSUE

Did Honeywell have a duty to Kathleen Nesser to exercise reasonable care in hiring, retaining, or supervising Randy Landin?

ANALYSIS

In determining that Honeywell did not have a legal duty to Kathleen Nesser arising from its employment of Randy Landin, the district court analyzed Honeywell's duty as limited by its ability to control and protect its employees while they are involved in the employer's business or at the employer's place of business. Additionally, the court concluded that Honeywell could not have reasonably foreseen Landin's killing Nesser.

Incorporating a "scope of employment" limitation into an employer's duty borrows from the doctrine of *respondeat superior*. However, of the three theories advanced for recovery, only negligent supervision derives from the *respondeat superior* doctrine, which relies on connection to the employer's premises or chattels. We agree that negligent supervision is not a viable theory of recovery because Landin was neither on Honeywell's premises nor using Honeywell's chattels when he shot Nesser.

The remaining theories, negligent hiring and negligent retention, are based on direct, not vicarious, liability. Negligent hiring and negligent retention do not rely on the scope of employment but address risks created by exposing members of the public to a potentially dangerous individual. These theories of recovery impose liability for an employee's intentional tort, an action almost invariably outside the scope of employment, when the employer knew or should have known that the employee was violent or aggressive and might engage in injurious conduct.

I

Minnesota first explicitly recognized a cause of action based on negligent hiring in *Ponticas* in 1983. *Ponticas* involved the employment of an apartment manager who sexually assaulted a tenant. The Supreme Court upheld a jury verdict finding the apartment operators negligent in failing to make a reasonable investigation into the resident manager's background before providing him with a passkey. The court defined negligent hiring as

> predicated on the negligence of an employer in placing a person with known propensities, or propensities which should have been discovered by reasonable investigation, in an employment position in which, *because of the circumstances of the employment*, it should have been foreseeable that the hired individual posed a threat of injury to others.

Honeywell argues that under *Ponticas* it is not liable for negligent hiring because, unlike providing a dangerous resident manager with a passkey, Landin's employment did not enable him to commit the act of violence against Nesser. This argument has merit, and we note that a number of jurisdictions have expressly defined the scope of an employer's duty of reasonable care in hiring as largely dependent on the type of responsibilities associated with the particular job. See *Connes* [v. *Molalla Transp. Sys.*], 831 P.2d [1316,] 1321 [Colo. 1992] (employer's duty in hiring is dependent on anticipated degree of contact between employee and other persons in performing employment duties).

Ponticas rejected the view that employers are required to investigate a prospective employee's criminal background in every job in which the individual has regular contact with the public. Instead, liability is determined by the totality of the circumstances surrounding the hiring and whether the employer exercised reasonable care. The court instructed that

> the scope of the investigation is directly related to the severity of the risk third parties are subjected to by an incompetent employee. Although only slight care might suffice in the hiring of a yardman, a worker on a production line, or other types of employment where the employee would not constitute a high risk of injury to third persons, * * * when the prospective

employee is to be furnished a passkey permitting admittance to living quarters of tenants, the employer has the duty to use reasonable care to investigate his competency and reliability prior to employment.

Applying these principles, we conclude that Honeywell did not owe a duty to Nesser at the time of Landin's hire. Landin was employed as a maintenance worker whose job responsibilities entailed no exposure to the general public and required only limited contact with coemployees. Unlike the caretaker in *Ponticas*, Landin's duties did not involve inherent dangers to others, and unlike the tenant in *Ponticas*, Nesser was not a reasonably foreseeable victim at the time Landin was hired.

To reverse the district court's determination on duty as it relates to hiring would extend *Ponticas* and essentially hold that ex-felons are inherently dangerous and that any harmful acts they commit against persons encountered through employment will automatically be considered foreseeable. Such a rule would deter employers from hiring workers with a criminal record and "offend our civilized concept that society must make a reasonable effort to rehabilitate those who have erred so they can be assimilated into the community."

Honeywell did not breach a legal duty to Nesser by hiring Landin because the specific nature of his employment did not create a foreseeable risk of harm, and public policy supports a limitation on this cause of action. The district court correctly determined that Honeywell is not liable to Nesser under a theory of negligent hiring.

II

In recognizing the tort of negligent hiring, *Ponticas* extended established Minnesota case law permitting recovery under theories of negligent retention. . . .

*   *   *   *   *

. . . The difference between negligent hiring and negligent retention focuses on when the employer was on notice that an employee posed a threat and failed to take steps to ensure the safety of third parties. The Florida appellate court has provided a useful definition:

> Negligent hiring occurs when, prior to the time the employee is actually hired, the employer knew or should have known of the employee's unfitness, and the issue of liability primarily focuses upon the adequacy of the employer's pre-employment investigation into the employee's background. Negligent retention, on the other hand, occurs when, during the course of employment, the employer becomes aware or should have become aware of problems with an employee that indicated his unfitness, and the employer fails to take further action such as investigating, discharge, or reassignment.

. . . The record contains evidence of a number of episodes in Landin's postimprisonment employment at Honeywell that demonstrate a propensity for abuse and violence toward coemployees.

While at the Golden Valley facility, Landin sexually harassed female employees and challenged a male coworker to fight. After his transfer to St. Louis Park, Landin threatened to kill a coworker during an angry confrontation following a minor car accident. In another employment incident, Landin was hostile and abusive toward a female coworker after problems developed in their friendship. Landin's specific focus on Nesser was demonstrated by several workplace outbursts occurring at the end of June, and on July 1 the words "one more day and you're dead" were scratched on her locker door.

Landin's troubled work history and the escalation of abusive behavior during the summer of 1988 relate directly to the foreseeability prong of duty. The facts . . . show that it was foreseeable that Landin could act violently against a coemployee and against Nesser in particular.

This foreseeability gives rise to a duty of care to Nesser that is not outweighed by policy considerations of employment opportunity. An ex-felon's "opportunity for gainful employment may spell the difference between recidivism and rehabilitation," but it cannot predominate over the need to maintain a safe workplace when specific actions point to future violence.

Our holding is narrow and limited only to the recognition of a legal duty owed to Nesser arising out of Honeywell's continued employment of Landin. It is important to emphasize that in reversing the summary judgment on negligent retention, we do not reach the remaining significant questions of whether Honeywell breached that duty by failing to terminate or discipline Landin, or whether such a breach was a proximate cause of Nesser's death. These are issues generally decided by a jury after a full presentation of facts.

* * * * *

DECISION

We affirm the entry of summary judgment on the theories of negligent hiring and supervision, but reverse the summary judgment on the issue of negligent retention.

AFTERWORD

Published reports indicate the *Yunker* case was settled out of court soon after this decision was handed down.

Questions

1. What did the court mean when it said that "negligent hiring and negligent retention are based on direct, not vicarious, liability"?

2. Why did the court reject the negligent supervision claim?

3. Why did the court reject the negligent hiring claim?

4. Why did the court allow the negligent retention issue to go to trial?

5. Gary Weimerskirch, assistant manager at Main Lanes Bowling Alley, walked in on David Coakley, a mechanic at the bowling alley, and Coakley's girlfriend as they were getting dressed, apparently having just engaged in sexual relations. Coakley then told Weimerskirch that he quit and he began to collect his belongings from the work area. Suddenly, Coakley then grabbed a two-by-four plank, ran toward Weimerskirch, and struck him on the head with it. Coakley's criminal record included drug- and alcohol-related offenses, along with one misdemeanor assault. However, his employer did not have any knowledge of this criminal record. Furthermore, Coakley had not acted violently at work previously.

   a. What causes of action might Weimerskirch bring against the bowling alley?

   b. Decide the case. Explain. See *Weimerskirch v. Coakley et al.*, 2008 Ohio 1681 (Ohio Ct. App. April 8, 2008).

Part Three—Fair Labor Standards Act

LO 12-5

Explain employees' rights under the Fair Labor Standards Act.

A note was passed to President Franklin D. Roosevelt in 1936 from a young girl:

> I wish you could do something to help us girls. We have been working in a sewing factory . . . getting our minimum pay of $11 a week. Today, the 200 of us girls have been cut down to $4 and $5 and $6 a week.[24]

Roosevelt reportedly remarked that something needed to be done about child labor. The Depression and its tragic suffering, even of those working hard, shattered many Americans' faith in the free market and led to government intervention, including, in 1938, the Fair Labor Standards Act (FLSA), which is directed toward these major objectives:

1. The establishment of a minimum wage that provides at least the foundation for a modest standard of living for employees.

2. A flexible ceiling on hours worked weekly, the purpose of which is to increase the number of employed Americans.

3. Child labor protection.

4. Equal pay for equal work regardless of gender. (See Chapter 13.)

[For the U.S. Department of Labor home page, see **www.dol.gov**].

Minimum Wage   The federal minimum wage is currently $7.25 per hour, but in 2017, the minimum wage in 19 states increased, some through voter ballots.[25] Critics of a federally mandated minimum wage argue that the government should not interfere in the marketplace and that increases in minimum wages threaten not only job growth but the livelihoods of many small business owners. Supporters of minimum wage increases point to recent studies concluding that raising the minimum wage does not lead to the loss of low-paying jobs.[26] More than 130 municipalities, many where living costs are particularly high, have adopted their own "living wage" requirements.[27] However, as a recent National Low Income Housing Coalition study shows, minimum-wage workers across the United States cannot afford a one- or two-bedroom apartment at fair market rent.[28]

Question

Why might business leaders advocate for raising the federal minimum wage? The group Business for a Fair Minimum Wage, which includes business owners and executives from a range of industries, advocates for raising the federal minimum wage to at least $12 by 2020. [See **https://www.businessforafairminimumwage.org/**].

Overtime   Most workers covered under FLSA must receive overtime pay of at least 1½ times their regular pay rate for hours worked over 40 hours per week. However, FLSA also recognizes exemptions for certain occupations, such as managers, outside salespersons, administrators, and professionals with advanced degrees; these workers are referred to as "exempt" employees. *Misclassification* of "nonexempt" employees who have overtime rights under FLSA is a common basis for wage-and-hour claims against employers, which have led to high-profile settlements. For example, Walmart vision center managers and asset-protection coordinators who were once considered exempt but then reclassified as nonexempt received $4.8 million in back wages and damages.[29] Levi-Strauss was ordered to pay over $1 million in overtime back wages to misclassified workers, including assistant store managers who were incorrectly treated as exempt, given the actual nature of their work.[30] However, a 2012 U.S. Supreme Court decision held that pharmaceutical sales representatives were not entitled to overtime pay.[31]

Overtime claims often involve disputes over whether the employee was actually working, rather than being engaged in a noncompensable activity. These *off-the-clock* claims in which employers are accused of not giving employees recorded credit for all of the time they have worked sometimes spring from advancing technology. A recent poll showed that more than half of employed adults check work messages at least once a day over the weekend, before or after work during the week, and even when they are home sick.[32]

In 2016, a federal judge ordered an injunction on the enforcement of an Obama administration overtime pay rule that would have allowed full-time salaried employees earning up to $47,476 per year to receive overtime pay for time worked over 40 hours per week. The salary threshhold is currently $23,600 per year. The rule would have allowed over 4 million additional workers to be eligible for overtime pay.[33]

Student Interns   In a tough job market, unpaid internships become more attractive to job seekers and employers alike. To address potentially abusive situations in which employers seek "free labor," the U.S. Department of Labor in 2010 issued a test for unpaid internships to determine whether the interns are either employees with wage rights or trainees who are receiving an educational opportunity for their sole benefit and thus excluded from FLSA protection. Generally, the more an internship focuses on an academic or classroom experience rather than the host's operations, the more likely it need not be a paid position. If, on the other hand, interns are assisting with the employer's daily operations such as clerical work, then they have a right to minimum wage and overtime. [For the six criteria of the U.S. Department of Labor's test for unpaid internships, see **www.dol.gov/whd/regs/compliance/whdfs71.pdf**].

Turning the Page on Internships: Conde Nast Paid Fellowships

In 2013, three months after being sued by former interns claiming they were unfairly compensated for their work, publishing conglomerate Conde Nast announced it was ending its internship programs. It later settled the former interns' lawsuit for $5.8 million. In 2015, Conde Nast announced it would offer six-month, full-time paid editorial fellowships.

Questions

1. What are the benefits to college students and recent graduates of the U.S. Department of Labor's student internship rules? What are the drawbacks? Explain.

2. If you were an undergraduate majoring in journalism, what obstacles would there be to participating in Conde Nast's editorial fellowship program? Would you be more likely to participate in an unpaid internship program at another publisher? Explain.

Sources: Erika Adams, "Conde Nast Replacing Internships with Paid Fellowships," *Racked.com*, May 19, 2015 [**www.racked.com/2015/5/19/8621611/conde-nast-editorial-fellowships**]; and "Conde Nast Launches Fellowshp Program to Replace Internships," *News & Tech.com*, June 1, 2015 [**www.newsandtech.com/dateline/article_276e0046-0885-11e5-b892-b7b839e58812.html**].

Questions

1. Answer this person's question: "I work as a pharmacist in a large discount retail store. My employer classifies me as exempt under FLSA. Like other pharmacists, I agree to work a specific number of base hours per week which determines my specific rate of pay. However, the employer has changed my base hours so frequently lately that I am effectively being treated as an hourly employee. There have been weeks I have worked more than 40 hours a week. Do I have a right to overtime?"[34]

2. Answer this person's question: "Before I resigned as a sewing manager for a small manufacturing company, where I supervised several employees and received an hourly

wage, I regularly arrived at the factory 15 to 45 minutes before the start of my 5:00 am shift, spending most of that time doing such tasks as reviewing employee schedules, gathering and distributing fabric to my subordinates' workstations, cleaning work area, etc.—but without pay. Does my former employer owe me overtime pay?"[35]

Part Four—Health and Safety at Work

> He was simply doing his job and making his way through his shift so he could get back home to his family.

Deepwater Horizon   "I am here to describe the profound impact my brother's death, while working on a rig engaged in deepwater drilling, has had on our family," Chris Jones told the U.S. House Committee on Natural Resources in March 2011. He was testifying as the surviving brother of Gordon Jones, one of 11 workers killed in the 2010 oil well explosion in the Gulf of Mexico. "[Gordon] was tragically killed aboard the Deepwater Horizon while earning his living as a mud engineer for MI SWACO, a contractor for BP [British Petroleum]. Gordon had nothing to do with this disaster. He was simply doing his job and making his way through his shift so he could get back home to his family. Instead, he never saw his family again. We can thank poor, and likely grossly negligent, decisions by many people and companies for that."[36] In 2012, BP agreed to plead guilty and pay $4.5 billion to settle criminal charges. Manslaughter charges against individual supervisors stemming from the fatal 2010 explosion were dropped in 2015.[37]

For a preview of the 2016 movie *Deepwater Horizon*, see https://www.youtube.com/ watch?v=8yASbM8M2vg.

Fifteen Die in 2005 Refinery Blast   The 2010 Gulf of Mexico oil well explosion echoed the 2005 disaster at the BP oil refinery in Texas City, Texas. Workers were doing their day's work by restarting a unit that had been down for repair when a gasoline overflow exploded, injuring 170 and killing 15. BP attributed the 2005 disaster primarily to operator error and six employees were fired, but government investigators concluded that management authorized the restart knowing that three key pieces of equipment were not working properly:

> These things do not have to happen. They are preventable. They are predictable, and people do not have to die because they're earning a living.[38]

In August 2010, BP agreed to pay $50.6 million in fines for failing to fix safety hazards at the Texas City refinery after the 2005 explosion.[39]

Deaths, Illnesses, and Injuries   Some workplaces are unacceptably risky, but America has achieved considerable progress in building safety on the job. Workplace fatalities that totaled 6,632 in 1995 fell to 4,386 in 2015, continuing a generally decreasing trend.[40]

Nonfatal injuries and illnesses also have declined from 3.9 per 100 workers in 2008 to 1.6 in 2015.[41] The overall job safety improvement should be viewed in the context of the U.S. labor shift away from such industries as manufacturing to service roles.

OSHA

LO 12-6
Describe the role of the Occupational Safety and Health Administration (OSHA) in protecting employees' health and safety at work.

A federal agency, the Occupational Safety and Health Administration (OSHA), is responsible for ensuring safe workplaces. The 1970 Occupational Safety and Health Act imposes a *general duty* on most employers to provide a workplace free of "recognized hazards causing or likely to cause death or serious physical harm to employees." Employers have an absolute duty to remove any serious and preventable workplace hazards that are generally recognized in the industry and are known to the employer or should be known to the employer. That general duty is then supplemented with numerous specific *standards*. [For the OSHA home page, see **www.osha.gov**].

Standards

OSHA, under the U.S. Department of Labor, promulgates and enforces health and safety standards that identify and seek to correct specific workplace hazards and problems. These can range from exposure to cancer-causing agents (such as the chemical benzene) to the surprisingly commonplace problem of one worker restarting a machine while another is servicing it. For example, under a long-fought-for OSHA standard made effective in 2008, employers must pay for all OSHA-mandated personal protective equipment (safety-specific eyewear, skin creams, clothing, etc.).[42] In 2012, culminating a rule-making process that began in 2006, OSHA issued a revised Hazard Communication Standard to align with an international system adopted by the United Nations in 2002.[43]

More New Standards?

The protracted development of OSHA regulations typifies the ongoing ideological and practical conflict over imposing additional safety rules in American workplaces. Some of the competing considerations are illustrated by disputes over ergonomics and workplace violence.

Ergonomics   Repetitive motion and overexertion injuries, such as carpal tunnel syndrome and back strains, account for about one-third of workplace injuries.[44] Employers often try to address these problems with ergonomics, "the science of fitting the job to the worker"[45] (for example, changing the height of a workstation). After years of work, OSHA issued ergonomics standards in 2000, but Congress repealed those rules in 2001 after business complaints about the costs of implementation. OSHA now employs a system of voluntary ergonomics guidelines, but critics consider them weak and vague. OSHA also can apply its general duty authority to address repetitive motion and overexertion. Experts now believe the carpal tunnel fears about keyboarding may have been exaggerated, although many blue-collar, assembly-line workers certainly are at risk. [For advice on measures to reduce repetitive stress problems for students, see **http://ergo.human.cornell.edu/**].

Violence   "Going postal" became an unfortunate but recognizable shorthand expression for violence in the workplace. Workplace shootings have made for sadly familiar headlines, with no particular job site immune from such tragedy.

> "Going postal."

Should OSHA create specific duties for employers regarding workplace violence? Would those rules be effective? Or will the market and naturally evolving workplace conditions provide the most effective and efficient protection?

Responses to these questions might be informed by legislation enacted in more than 20 states prohibiting employers from banning firearms in parking areas, and employers' reactions to these laws. Concerned with maintaining workplace safety, employers have focused on spotting and protecting against employees' aggression through trainings and increased security when, for example, terminating an employee.[46]

Variances

Employers may seek both permanent and temporary *variances* (exceptions) from OSHA standards. A permanent variance may be granted only if the workplace will be as safe as if the standard were enforced. A temporary variance permits additional time to put in place the necessary compliance measures. Employees have a right to a hearing to contest variances.

OSHA Information Requirements

Right to Know

OSHA has adopted an employee *hazard communication standard* to protect employees from the dangers associated with chemicals and other toxins in the workplace. Chemical manufacturers and importers must develop *material safety data sheets* (MSDS) for all chemicals. Employers must then label all chemical containers so that employees will know about the chemical and its dangers, and employers must educate employees about chemical hazards and how to deal with them.

Records

As a general rule, businesses must maintain records listing and summarizing work-related injuries, illnesses, and deaths. A summary of those records must be posted at the job. Notice of any OSHA citations of imminent dangers on the job also must be posted at the job site. In 2014, OSHA reformed and simplified the record-keeping process. Some smaller companies, especially those engaging in nonhazardous activities, do not need to meet the record-keeping requirements.

Does an employee's injury suffered in a go-cart race held as part of an off-site team-building event need to be reported? According to a 2009 letter from OSHA responding to this inquiry, an injury in those circumstances is work-related, and therefore reportable, even if the employee had the option to return to work or take a half-day vacation instead of participating in the go-cart race that followed a mandatory off-site meeting.[47] A 2012 federal appellate decision suggested that requiring record keeping of all workplace injuries may be more efficient than analyzing whether such an injury is work-related.[48]

Enforcement

OSHA's most publicized enforcement mechanism is the unannounced on-site inspection. Inspections arise at the initiative of the agency itself or at the request of employees or their representatives. The inspections must be conducted in a reasonable manner during working hours or other reasonable times, and ordinarily they must not be announced in advance. Employers can demand a warrant prior to inspection. With proper justification, warrants can easily be secured from a federal magistrate. Employer and employee representatives may accompany the inspector.

To enhance efficiency, OSHA practices a targeted, site-specific inspection plan designed to identify and monitor the workplaces most likely to have safety and health problems. However, an employer can become exempt from such inspections under OSHA's Voluntary Protection Program (VPP), a program that has drawn criticism.[49]

Citations

Citations may be issued if violations are discovered during the inspection process. Immediate, serious threats can be restrained with a court order. Following a citation, the employer may ask to meet with an area OSHA official to discuss the problem. Often a settlement emerges from these meetings. Failing a settlement, the employer can appeal to the independent OSHA Review Commission and thereafter to the federal court of appeals. Violations may lead to fines and/or imprisonment. For example, OSHA cited and fined Excel, a company packing Hershey's chocolates, $283,000 for failing to report dozens of serious injuries to its workers, including students on an international exchange program.[50]

Enforcement versus Compliance? The business community criticizes OSHA for unfairly increasing the cost of production by imposing inflexible and overzealous expectations. Labor organizations and job safety advocates, on the other hand, have criticized OSHA as a timid, faltering safety shield.

The Severe Violator Enforcement Program (SVEP) was part of the Obama administration's efforts to enforce OSHA regulations. SVEP concentrates on employers who have demonstrated indifference to their safety obligations by engaging in willful, repeated, or "failure to abate" violations. SVEP uses mandatory follow-up inspections, press releases, and increased fines, among other tools, to send a clear message that such conduct will be rigorously addressed by OSHA.[51] OSHA makes public its list of severe violators. [For the current SVEP logs, see **https://www.osha.gov/dep/**]. However, legal experts at this writing have predicted that the Trump administration may emphasize compliance assistance over enforcement by emphasizing the Voluntary Protection Program over SVEP.[52]

But the critics' question remains: Is the market the best vehicle for achieving job safety?

Workers' Compensation

LO 12-7
Describe the benefits, coverage, and requirements for bringing a successful claim under workers' compensation law.

Korey Stringer, a 27-year-old Pro Bowl tackle, died of heatstroke complications on August 1, 2001, after going through a preseason Minnesota Vikings workout.[53] Normally, when an employee is injured or dies on the job, the employee or the estate may not sue for damages. Rather, recovery is limited to the fixed sum provided for by the workers' compensation statute, regardless of fault. Stringer's family, however, filed a wrongful death suit seeking to hold the Vikings and various individuals responsible for gross negligence and other wrongs in responding to Stringer's heatstroke. The Vikings argued that the Stringer suit was barred by the state workers' compensation law. Minnesota is one of a number of states, however, that recognize an exception to workers' compensation exclusivity provisions in

> Korey Stringer, a 27-year-old Pro Bowl tackle, died of heatstroke complications.

cases of *gross negligence* by the defendants.[54] The Stringers' case reached the Minnesota Supreme Court, where the 4–2 majority ruled on technical grounds against the family's gross negligence claim, thus limiting their remedy to workers' compensation, a sum much beneath Stringer's projected commercial worth.[55]

Early in the 20th century, the states began enacting workers' compensation laws to provide an administrative remedy for those, like Stringer, who are injured or killed on the job. Previously, employers' superior financial resources and various technical legal defenses meant that employees often could not successfully sue to recover damages for their on-the-job injuries. All states now provide some form of workers' compensation not requiring a lawsuit. Instead, workers or their families apply for compensation based on illness, injury, or death. Typically, the system is governed by a state board or commission. Most decisions are routine and based on the completed application. Often a claims examiner will verify the nature and severity of the injury. Although workers' compensation is generally the exclusive remedy for workplace injury or death caused by employers' negligence, many states recognize an exception for intentional torts. An exception based on gross negligence, however, is rare.

In most states, employers are compelled to participate in workers' compensation, depending on state law, either by purchasing insurance privately, by contributing to a state-managed fund, or by being self-insured (paying claims directly from their own funds). Firms with good safety records are rewarded with lower premium payments.

No Joke?

Matthew Simms worked as a server in the Manassas, Virginia, location of a national chain restaurant. During his work shift, Simms walked into the kitchen to enter an order into a computer and to print a check for a customer. Three other employees in the kitchen who were his friends started throwing ice at him, apparently as a joke. As Simms lifted his hand to block the ice, he felt his left shoulder dislocate. Simms was taken to a hospital for treatment of his injury. As a result of the injury, Simms allegedly was unable to use his shoulder in daily activities or work for a period of time. Should Simms receive workers' compensation for his injuries? Explain.

Source: Simms v. Ruby Tuesdays, Inc., 281 Va. 114, 704 S.E.2d 359 (Va. 2011).

Benefits

Medical and rehabilitation expenses along with partial income replacement are provided according to state law. The amount of the income award is normally a percentage of the worker's salary either for a specified period or indefinitely, depending on the severity of the injury. Injury benefits normally amount to one-half to two-thirds of regular wages. Death benefits ordinarily are tied to the wages of the deceased.

Coverage

Certain employment classifications such as agriculture may be excluded from workers' compensation, but about 90 percent of the labor force is covered. Most on-the-job injuries are covered, but those that are self-inflicted (including starting a fight) and others such as those springing from alcohol or drug use may not be.

Legal Requirements

In general, injuries, illnesses, and deaths are compensable where the harm (1) *arose out of the employment* and (2) *occurred in the course of employment* (explained next in *Wait*). Proof of employer negligence is not required, and the traditional defenses such as contributory negligence are not available to the employer. Thus, workers' compensation provides a form of no-fault protection in the workplace. Workers give up the right to sue, and employers participate in an insurance system that recognizes the inevitability of workplace harm.

Although workers' compensation recovery is the exclusive remedy for workplace injury, illness, or death, some jurisdictions allow litigation in cases of intentional torts and/or gross negligence, as noted earlier. [For the Workers' Compensation Research Institute, see **www.wcrinet.org**].

Litigation

Notwithstanding its no-fault character, workers' compensation has generated many lawsuits. Consider the example of David Gross, a 16-year-old employee at KFC, who was injured when he placed water in a pressurized deep fryer to clean it. KFC's employee handbook explicitly instructed against such an action, as did a warning label on the fryer. Furthermore, immediately preceding the incident, Gross's supervisor and two coworkers admonished him to not do it. The employer fired Gross for violating an important workplace safety rule. The Ohio Supreme Court initially terminated his workers' compensation benefits using the "voluntary abandonment" doctrine, under which workers' compensation benefits may be terminated because the loss of income is not due to the injury itself. However, the court then reconsidered and ordered reinstatement of Gross's benefits.[56] The *Wait* case that follows raises some current issues regarding workers' compensation for the telecommuting employee.

LEGAL BRIEFCASE

Wait v. Travelers Indemnity Company of Illinois
240 S.W.3d 220 (Tenn. 2007)

Chief Justice Barker

I. FACTUAL BACKGROUND

From October 1998 until September 3, 2004, the plaintiff, Kristina Wait, worked as Senior Director of Health Initiative and Strategic Planning for the American Cancer Society ("ACS"). Because of the lack of office space at its Nashville, Tennessee facilities, the ACS allowed the plaintiff to work from her East Nashville home. The plaintiff converted a spare bedroom of her home into an office, and the ACS furnished the necessary office equipment, including a printer, a facsimile machine, a dedicated business telephone line, and a budget to purchase office supplies. In all respects, the plaintiff's home office functioned as her work place. Not only did the plaintiff perform her daily work for the ACS at her home office, the plaintiff's supervisor and co-workers attended meetings at the office in her house. There is no evidence in the record with respect to any designated hours or conditions of the plaintiff's employment, nature of her work space, or other work rules. Significantly, the plaintiff's work for the ACS did not require her to open her house to the public. In fact, during working hours the plaintiff locked the outside doors of her home and activated an alarm system for her protection. Unfortunately, however, on September 3, 2004, the plaintiff opened her door to a neighbor, Nathaniel Sawyers ("Sawyers"), who brutally assaulted and severely injured the plaintiff.

The plaintiff met Sawyers in May or early June of 2004 at a neighborhood cookout she attended with her husband. Thereafter, Sawyers, who lived approximately one block from the plaintiff's home, came to the plaintiff's home for a short social visit on a *weekend* day in late June. The plaintiff and her husband spoke with Sawyers for approximately five minutes, and then Sawyers left. In August, Sawyers came to the plaintiff's home on a weekday for a social visit; however, the plaintiff was preparing to leave her home office for a job-related television interview. The plaintiff told Sawyers that she was going to a business meeting. When Sawyers replied that he was on his way to a job interview in Nashville, the plaintiff allowed Sawyers to ride with her to his job interview.

On September 3, 2004, the plaintiff was working alone at her home office. Around noon, the plaintiff was in her kitchen preparing her lunch when Sawyers knocked on her door. The plaintiff answered and invited Sawyers into the house, and he stayed for a short time and then left. However, a moment later, Sawyers returned, telling the plaintiff that he had left his keys in her kitchen. When the plaintiff turned away from the door, Sawyers followed her inside and brutally assaulted the plaintiff without provocation or explanation, beating the plaintiff until she lost consciousness. As a result of this assault, the plaintiff suffered severe injuries, including head trauma, a severed ear, several broken bones, stab wounds, strangulation injuries, and permanent nerve damage to the left side of her body.

On December 12, 2005, the plaintiff filed a complaint seeking workers' compensation benefits from Travelers Indemnity Company of Illinois, the insurer of the ACS. (The plaintiff did not name the ACS as a defendant.) The plaintiff alleged that she was entitled to workers' compensation benefits for the injuries she sustained in the assault because the assault arose out of and occurred in the course of her employment with the ACS. The defendant . . . [denied] that the injuries arose out of or occurred in the course of the plaintiff's employment.

Following discovery, the defendant filed a motion for summary judgment, which the chancery court granted. The chancery court concluded that the plaintiff's injuries did not arise out of or occur in the course of her employment with the ACS. Additionally, the chancery court noted that Sawyers "was not [at the plaintiff's home office] on any kind of business with the [ACS], nor was he really there on any kind of business with the [p]laintiff."

The plaintiff appealed. We accepted review.

* * * * *

(II OMITTED—ED.)

III. ANALYSIS
A. The Workers' Compensation Act and Telecommuting

The Workers' Compensation Act ("Act"), codified at Tennessee Code Annotated sections 50-6-101 to -801 (2005), is a legislatively created quid pro quo system where an injured worker forfeits any potential common law rights for recovery against his or her employer in return for a system that provides compensation completely independent of any fault on the part of the employer. The Act should be liberally construed in favor of compensation and any doubts should be resolved in the employee's favor. However, this liberal construction requirement does not authorize courts to amend, alter, or extend its provisions beyond its obvious meaning.

* * * * *

This case requires us to apply the Act to a new and growing trend in the labor and employment market: telecommuting. An employee telecommutes when he or she takes advantage of electronic mail, internet, facsimile machines and other technological advancements to work from home or a place other than the traditional work site. In 2006, approximately thirty-four million American workers telecommuted to some degree.

* * * * *

Not surprisingly, however, this innovative working arrangement has resulted in an issue of first impression: whether the injuries a telecommuter sustains as a result of an assault at her home arise out of and occur in the course of her employment.

B. Did the plaintiff's injuries occur in the course of her employment?

It is well settled in Tennessee, and in many other jurisdictions, that for an injury to be compensable under the Act, it must both "arise out of" and occur "in the course of" employment. Although both of these statutory requirements seek to ensure a connection between the employment and the injuries for which benefits are being sought, they are not synonymous. As such, the "arising out of" requirement refers to cause or origin; whereas, "in the course of" denotes the time, place, and circumstances of the injury. Furthermore, we have consistently abstained from adopting any particular judicial test, doctrine, formula, or label that purports to "clearly define the line between accidents and injuries which arise out of and in the course of employment [and] those which do not[.]"

* * * * *

In this case, we will consider the second requirement first. An injury occurs in the course of employment "when it takes place within the period of the employment, at a place where the employee reasonably may be, and while the employee is fulfilling work duties or engaged in doing something incidental thereto."

Generally, injuries sustained during personal breaks are compensable.

* * * * *

[T]he defendant here argues that the plaintiff's injuries are not compensable because the plaintiff was not "fulfilling a work duty" in admitting Sawyers into her kitchen. It is true that the plaintiff suffered her injuries while preparing her lunch in the kitchen of her home; however, the plaintiff's work site was located within her home. Under these circumstances, the plaintiff's kitchen was comparable to the kitchens and break rooms that employers routinely provide at traditional work sites. Moreover, the ACS was aware of and implicitly approved of the plaintiff's work site. Her supervisor and co-workers had attended meetings at the plaintiff's home office. It is reasonable to conclude that the ACS realized that the plaintiff would take personal breaks during the course of her working day. . . .

Thus, after careful review, we conclude that the injuries the plaintiff sustained while on her lunch break, occurred during the course of the plaintiff's employment. The plaintiff was assaulted at a place where her employer could reasonably expect her to be. The ACS permitted the plaintiff to work from home for approximately four years. The plaintiff's supervisor and co-workers regularly came to her home office for meetings. The record does not suggest that the ACS restricted the plaintiff's activities during working hours or prohibited her from taking personal breaks. The facts do not show that the plaintiff was engaging in any prohibited conduct or was violating any company policy by preparing lunch in her kitchen. It is reasonable to conclude that the ACS would have anticipated that the plaintiff would take a lunch break at her home just as employees do at traditional work sites. Importantly, Sawyer's initial visit was very brief and spontaneous. Unless instructed otherwise by the employer, an employee working from a home office who answers a knock at her door and briefly admits an acquaintance into her home does not necessarily depart so far from her work duties so as to remove her from the course of her employment. This is not to say, however, that situations may never arise where more prolonged or planned social visits might well remove the employee from the course of the employment.

In arguing that the plaintiff's injury did not occur "in the course of" her employment, the defendant maintains that the plaintiff's decision to admit Sawyers into her home was not a work duty. However, this argument misses the mark on this requirement because the Act does not explicitly state that the employee's actions must benefit the employer; it only requires that the injuries occur in "the course of" the employment. Because the plaintiff was engaged in a permissible personal break incidental to her employment, we reject the defendant's narrow interpretation of the Act. The question is not whether the plaintiff's injuries occurred while she was performing a duty owed to the ACS, but rather whether the time, place, and circumstances demonstrate that the injuries occurred while the plaintiff was engaged in an activity incidental to her employment. Accordingly, we hold that the plaintiff suffered her injuries during the course of her employment and disagree with the chancery court's conclusion on this important point.

C. Did the plaintiff's injuries arise out of her employment?

Even though the plaintiff's injuries occurred "in the course of" her employment, we nevertheless hold that they did not "arise out of" her job duties with the ACS. The phrase "arising out of" requires that a causal connection exist between the employment conditions and the resulting injury. With respect to whether an assault arises out of employment, we have previously delineated assaults into three general classifications:

> (1) assaults with an "inherent connection" to employment such as disputes over performance, pay or termination; (2) assaults stemming from "inherently private" disputes imported into the employment setting from the claimant's domestic or private life and not exacerbated by the employment; and (3) assaults resulting from a "neutral force" such as random assaults on employees by individuals outside the employment relationship.

When an assault has an "inherent connection" to the employment it is compensable. On the other hand, assaults originating from "inherently private" disputes and imported into the work place are not compensable. However, whether "neutral assaults" are compensable turns on the "facts and circumstances of the employment."

The assault in this case is best described as a "neutral assault." In granting the defendant's motion for summary judgment, the chancery court commented: "[T]here's certainly not any evidence that this person who committed the assault was part of the working employment relationship and was not there on any kind of business related to the [ACS] or really any business with the employee." We agree with the chancery court's conclusions. A "neutral force" assault is one that is "neither personal to the claimant nor distinctly associated with the employment."

The categories focus on what catalyst spurred the assault, i.e., was it a dispute arising from a work-related duty, was it a dispute arising from a personal matter, or was it unexplained or irrational? An assault that is spurred by neither a catalyst inherently connected to the employment nor stemming from an inherently private dispute is most aptly labeled as a "neutral force" assault. Here, the undisputed facts clearly show that the assault had neither an inherent connection with the employment, nor did it stem from a personal dispute between Sawyers and the plaintiff. Therefore, we must focus our attention on the facts and circumstances of the plaintiff's employment and its relationship to the injuries sustained by the plaintiff.

Generally, for an injury to "arise out of" employment, it must emanate from a peculiar danger or risk inherent to the nature of the employment. However, in limited circumstances, where the employment involves "indiscriminate exposure to the general public," the "street risk" doctrine may supply the required causal connection between the employment and the injury.

* * * * *

[T]his Court held that the "street risk" doctrine satisfied the causal connection requirement where the employee was assaulted by unknown assailants as he removed paperwork from his employer's van while it was parked at his residence. We carefully limited application of the street risk doctrine to "workers whose employment exposes them to the hazards of the street, or who are assaulted under circumstances that fairly suggest they were singled out for attack because of their association with their employer. . . ."

Unlike our previous cases in which the facts supported application of the "street risk" doctrine to provide the necessary causal connection, the facts here do not establish that the plaintiff's employment exposed her to a street hazard or that she was singled out for her association with her employer. There is nothing to indicate that she was targeted because of her association with her employer or that she was charged with safeguarding her employer's property. Additionally, the plaintiff was not advancing the interests of the ACS when she allowed Sawyers into her kitchen, and her employment with the ACS did not impose any duty upon the plaintiff to admit Sawyers to her home.

The plaintiff argues that had it not been for her employment arrangement, she would not have been at home to suffer these attacks. However, we have never held that any and every assault which occurs at the work site arises out of employment. Additionally, although Sawyers knew from a previous visit that the plaintiff was home during the day, there is nothing in the record which indicates that there was a causal connection between the plaintiff's employment and the assault.

* * * * *

Affirmed.

Questions

1. The Tennessee Supreme Court in *Wait* (and most courts in workers' compensation cases) required a two-part showing that the injury must "arise out of" and "in the course of" employment.
   a. Explain those two standards.
   b. Must an employee be engaged in an activity that benefits the employer in order to be "in the course of employment"? Explain.
   c. Why did the court conclude that Wait's injuries did not arise out of her employment?

2. Why did the court conclude that the "street risk" doctrine did not apply to Wait's injuries?

3. Fernandez, an exotic dancer, left her job drunk and was seriously injured in a crash while riding as a passenger in a car driven by another dancer. The crash came within one hour of leaving work. Her intoxication led to her decision to ride with her intoxicated coworker. Fernandez sought workers' compensation. She claimed that her employer, Bottoms Up Lounge in Council Bluffs, Iowa, required her to socialize with male customers when not dancing and to generate at least two drinks per hour from customers. Dancers were not required to drink, but most dancers consumed six to eight drinks per night or more. Did Fernandez's injury arise out of and in the course of employment so that she can recover workers' compensation? Explain. See *2800 Corp. v. Fernandez*, 528 N.W.2d 124 (Iowa 1995).

4. Joseph Smyth, a college mathematics instructor, was killed while driving his personal auto home from work. At the time, Smyth had student papers with him, which he intended to grade that evening. He often worked at home. Many faculty members took work home in the evenings. However, the college did not require that practice. Indeed, the college neither encouraged nor discouraged working at home.

   The widely adopted "going and coming rule" provides that employees injured while commuting to and from work, in general, are not covered by workers' compensation.
   a. Should Smyth (and other teachers) be exempted from the going and coming rule, thus permitting recovery by Smyth's family? Explain. See *Santa Rosa Junior College v. Workers' Compensation Appeals Board and Joann Smyth*, 708 P.2d 673 (Cal. 1985).
   b. Would you reach a different conclusion had a student been accompanying Smyth? Explain.

5. Casimer Gacioch worked at a Stroh Brewery. The company provided free beer at work. When he began work in 1947, he drank only three to four beers on the weekend. He was fired in 1974, by which time he was drinking 12 bottles of beer daily. After Gacioch's death, his wife sought workers' compensation benefits. The evidence indicated that Gacioch had a predisposition to alcoholism but was not an alcoholic at the time he was hired. How would you rule on the widow's workers' compensation claim? Explain. See *Gacioch v. Stroh Brewery*, 466 N.W.2d 303 (Mich. Ct. App. 1991).

Part Five—Employee Privacy

Will you have to give up that butterfly tattoo?

Privacy on the Job?   More than half of Americans between 18 and 25 have done at least one of the following: gotten a tattoo, dyed their hair an untraditional color, or had a body piercing other than on their ear lobe. Fewer than a quarter of those between 40 and 64 have done any of these.[57] Will you have to give up that butterfly tattoo on your ankle when you move on to the "real world" of professional employment? Typically, employers have dress codes requiring a neat, clean appearance. Other employers might have specific requirements, such as covering tattoos during work hours.[58]

Employer oversight extends well beyond appearance policies. Drug tests, integrity tests, personality tests, surveillance, and, as seen earlier in this chapter, searches for applicants' online reputations are routine personnel practices in many firms. Employers have an interest in these strategies not only to hire better employees and improve productivity but to protect coworkers, reduce insurance claims, and shield consumers from poor products and service. On the other hand, job applicants and employees resist parking their personal identity and privacy at the office door.

Privacy off the Job?   A growing number of employers offer incentives such as financial rewards or prizes to employees who try to get healthier. These wellness programs may reward employees for taking part in a fitness assessment or weight-loss program, or attaining certain health metrics such as an ideal blood pressure or cholesterol level. Penalties also can be exacted in the form of higher health care premiums or an actual payment.[59] Although supporters praise such programs as benefitting employees who otherwise might not have the incentive or opportunity to improve their health, critics wonder whether these programs are sufficiently regulated to avoid, for example, discrimination against the elderly and individuals with disabilities, especially if tied to health-insurance benefits.[60] Further, critics question whether such programs overstep boundaries in the employment relationship, intruding into employees' rights to make their own health-related choices.

Pacing Yourself at Work: Fitness Trackers and Wellness Programs

Fitness trackers, which are typically in the form of slim bracelets worn on the wrist, keep track of physical activity, sleep, and other health-related information. A 2016 survey of 1,000 employers showed nearly a third offered their employees these devices, and approximately another quarter of those surveyed were considering doing so. Employers have set up voluntary competitions based on the number of steps logged; one company made a corporate donation to the winning office's favorite charity, and gave $100 to the individual employee logging the most steps.

Question

Why might an employer offer employees fitness trackers and then create a voluntary competition? What concerns might such competitions raise?

Sources: Lisa Schencker, "Would You Wear a Fitbit for Work?" *Chicago Tribune*, November 11, 2016 [**www.chicagotribune.com/business/ct-wearables-wellness-programs-1113-biz-20161111-story.html**]; and David Curry, "Fitbit Teams up with Target to Get Employees Moving, Thanks to HIPAA Compliance," *Digital Trends*, September 17, 2015 [**www.digitaltrends.com/wearables/fitbit-hipaa-compliance**].

> Robert Barbee was fired for dating Melanie Tomita.

And what about office romance? Robert Barbee, former national sales manager for Household Automotive Finance, sued HAF after he was fired for dating Melanie Tomita, an HAF salesperson. They worked in different locations, and he did not directly supervise her. He claimed that the dismissal violated his right to privacy, but a California appeals court ruled for HAF in part on the grounds that the company needed to prevent conflicts of interest, sexual harassment claims, and the appearance of favoritism.[61] Although relatively few office romance cases have reached the courts, most employers appear comfortable in restricting office romance to some degree, such as prohibiting relationships between a supervisor and subordinate or requiring employees who are dating to inform their supervisor.[62]

Monitoring

The City of Ontario, California, Police Department issued pagers to its police officers for business purposes. The city paid for a text messaging plan, but officers who exceeded the allotted messaging quota were required to pay overage charges. While at work, Sargeant Jeff Quon sent personal, sometimes sexually explicit, text messages on his police department–issued pager to both his then-wife and a coworker with whom he was romantically involved. Noticing a frequency in overage charges, the police department audited the content of police officers' texts to determine whether the overage charges were the result of work-related messages that might show the need to upgrade the text-messaging plan. Although a workplace policy stated that employees had no expectation of privacy in using Internet or e-mail provided them at work, it did not address the pagers given to the police officers. As a result of the audit, Quon was disciplined for misusing the pager.

The question facing the Supreme Court in 2010 was whether the police department's review of Sargeant Quon's text messages violated his Fourth Amendment right to privacy. Acknowledging that "workplace norms" regarding technology are evolving, in 2010 the U.S. Supreme Court held in *City of Ontario v. Quon* that even assuming Quon had a reasonable expectation of privacy in his text messages, the police department's review of the text messages did not violate Quon's Fourth Amendment rights. Ontario had a legitimate reason for the search, and the search was not excessive in scope.[63]

Employers' rights to monitor electronic messages may be defined on a case-by-case basis. A former employee had sent e-mails to her attorney regarding a possible workplace discrimination claim using a company laptop computer and her personal, password-protected e-mail account rather than her business e-mail address. After she resigned and sued, her former employer hired a computer expert who retrieved the e-mails between her and her attorney, which were then reviewed by the company's attorney. Holding that the employee had a reasonable expectation of privacy in those e-mails, the New Jersey Supreme Court also acknowledged that although employers can establish rules regarding use of workplace computers and discipline employees accordingly, this power did not include the right to read privileged communications between an employee and her attorney.[64]

The Law

In general, employers can lawfully monitor workers' attendance, performance, e-mail, use of the Internet, and so on, but uncertainty remains. Having a clear, written workplace policy regarding the use and monitoring of workplace technology is a good employment practice.

The primary federal legislation, the 1986 Electronic Communications Privacy Act, prohibits private individuals and organizations from intercepting wire, oral, or electronic communications. The act provides for two exceptions, however: (1) prior consent by one of the parties to the communication and (2) employer monitoring in the "ordinary course of business" by telephone or other device furnished by a provider of wire or electronic communication service. Thus, workplace monitoring of phone calls (except for purely private conversations), workplace computers, voice mail, e-mail, and Internet use are all likely to be considered lawful at this point if approached in a reasonable manner.

As discussed previously in this chapter, job applicants face the possibility that their prospective employers might be researching their online reputations. Should the employer be allowed to require job applicants to disclose their passwords to their Facebook and other social media accounts? At this writing, 25 states have enacted legislation prohibiting an employer from requesting or requiring an employee or applicant to disclose a user name or password for a personal social media account.[65]

Requesting access to employees' social media accounts, even in the absence of legislation, still creates potential liability for the employer, as illustrated in a 2009 case involving a restaurant employee's invitation-only group on MySpace.com for coworkers to "vent" about work. Posts included sexual comments about the employer's managers and customers as well as references to illegal drug use. When one member showed the MySpace profile to a manager, she was later asked by another manager to share the password to access the profile. The employer terminated the profile's creator as well as another one of the invited coworkers, who sued for, among other claims, invasion of privacy. Given that a jury could reasonably find that the invited member of the MySpace group was coerced into providing the password, making the employer's access unauthorized, a federal district court upheld the jury's verdict against the employer.[66]

"BYOD" to Work

While some employers provide employees with a cell phone or tablet for work use, others may encourage use of employees' own personal devices, known as "bring your own device (BYOD)." According to a 2013 survey, approximately one-fifth of employers may perform "remote wipes" of employees' devices such as cell phones during or after employment as a means of securing data. This practice results in employees losing photos, contact lists, and other personal data. Employees who are asked to BYOD face the dilemma of either risking the loss of personal information when a cell phone is erased or appearing to be not committed to their jobs for refusing to use a personal device to stay electronically connected to work.

Question

How may an employer limit liability for invasion of privacy claims arising from remote wipes of employees' personal cell phones? Explain.

Source: Lauren Weber, "BYOD? Leaving a Job Can Mean Losing Pictures of Grandma," *The Wall Street Journal*, January 21, 2014 [**http://online.wsj.com/news/articles/SB10001424052702304027204579335033824665964**].

Koeppel v. Speirs

2010 Iowa App. LEXIS 25 (Iowa Ct. App. January 22, 2010) (unpublished op.)

LEGAL BRIEFCASE

EISENHAUER, P. J.

I. BACKGROUND FACTS AND PROCEEDINGS

[Sara] Koeppel and Deanna Miller were the only employees of Speirs, an insurance agent. A small (4' × 7') bathroom with a sink and toilet is located in the office. On December 27, 2005, Koeppel discovered a digital surveillance camera hidden inside the office bathroom. After contacting the Waterloo Police Department, a search warrant was obtained and officers located the camera in the bathroom. The camera was positioned to view the toilet and surrounding area. When confronted by police, Speirs produced the receiver and monitor for the camera from a locked drawer in his desk.

When questioned about the presence of the camera, Speirs admitted he had placed it in the bathroom on December 26, 2005, and stated he did so because he suspected one of his employees was abusing drugs while at work and was concerned she would embezzle money. Speirs claimed he was unable to get a signal from the camera when it was in the bathroom. At the time the officers arrived, the surveillance system was not set up to receive images from the camera. However, setup could be completed by plugging the equipment found in Speirs's desk drawer into an electrical outlet.

After connecting the equipment, the officers tested it and found it did not work. Speirs told the officers the camera battery was likely dead. After changing the battery at Speirs's suggestion, a fuzzy picture of the toilet seat and bathroom wall was visible. The image would cut in and out every few seconds. Videotapes located in Speirs's office were blank.

Speirs purchased the camera on November 26, 2005. Miller told the police, when interviewed on December 28, she saw the camera in the bathroom on November 28, 2005. Speirs, in another proceeding, testified he used the camera to monitor Miller at her desk on December 10, 2005, and in seven or ten viewings, he observed no wrongdoing.

Koeppel [sued] Speirs, alleging . . . invasion of privacy. . . .

Speirs then filed a motion for summary judgment . . . claiming there was no actual intrusion upon Koeppel's privacy because there is no evidence he viewed her in the restroom. Koeppel [argued] Speirs's act of placing the camera in the bathroom with the intent to view her was an invasion of her privacy. She also argued there was sufficient evidence for the jury to find the camera was operational. . . . [T]he district court entered its ruling, granting Speirs's motion. The court agreed Speirs intended to view Koeppel while she was in the bathroom, but concluded Koeppel could only be liable for an actual intrusion on her privacy, not an attempted intrusion. Finding no evidence Speirs viewed Koeppel in the bathroom, the court dismissed the claim.

On November 25, 2008, Koeppel appealed. . . .

* * * * *

III. INVASION OF PRIVACY

Koeppel first contends the court erred in granting summary judgment on her invasion of privacy claim. She contends Speirs's act of placing a camera in the bathroom with the intent to view her is sufficient to support a cause of action for invasion of privacy. In the alternative, she contends there is a question of fact as to whether there was an actual intrusion into her privacy.

Iowa has adopted the tort of invasion of privacy, as set forth in the Restatement (Second) of Torts (1977), which provides the right to privacy can be invaded by "unreasonable intrusion upon the seclusion of another." Under this theory,

> [o]ne who *intentionally intrudes*, physically or otherwise, upon the solitude or seclusion of another or his private affairs or concerns, is subject to liability to the other for invasion of privacy, if the intrusion would be *highly offensive to a reasonable person*.

To recover under this theory, Koeppel must show Speirs intentionally intruded upon her seclusion, and that a reasonable person would find the intrusion "highly offensive."

There is no question viewing or recording Koeppel while in the bathroom would be considered "highly offensive" by any reasonable person. There also can be no dispute a bathroom is a place where one enjoys seclusion. Nor is it debatable that Speirs acted intentionally in placing a recording device in the bathroom. The question presented in this case is whether there is enough evidence to create a question of fact as to whether there was an intrusion on Koeppel's privacy.

The district court concluded an actual invasion of privacy must occur for the cause of action to stand and found no facts supported an actual invasion. Koeppel argues intent to intrude on privacy is enough to maintain a cause of action. She cites *In re Marriage of Tigges* and two cases outside this jurisdiction in support of her argument.

In the case of *Tigges*, our supreme court addressed the question of unreasonable intrusion upon the seclusion of another where a husband secretly videotaped his wife in their bedroom. [*In re Marriage of*] *Tigges*, 758 N.W.2d [824,] 825 [(Iowa 2008)]. The husband argued there was no invasion of privacy because the video captured nothing "private" or "sexual" in nature. *Id.* at 829. In rejecting this claim, our supreme court stated:

> The wrongfulness of the conduct springs not from the specific nature of the recorded activities, but instead from the fact that Cathy's activities were recorded without her knowledge and consent at a time and place and under circumstances in which she had a reasonable expectation of privacy.

Id. at 830. We disagree with Koeppel's assertion that *Tigges* supports the proposition that the focus of invasion of privacy claims are on the intent of the perpetrator; as our supreme court states, it's the fact the victim was *recorded* without her knowledge and consent that results in the intrusion. *See id.*

* * * * *

. . . Koeppel cites *Harkey v. Abate* . . . . In that case, the plaintiffs brought an invasion of privacy suit after using a roller-skating rink restroom with see-through panels installed in the ceiling, which permitted surreptitious observation from above. The Michigan Court of Appeals stated:

In our opinion, the installation of the hidden viewing devices alone constitutes an interference with that privacy which a reasonable person would find highly offensive. And though the absence of proof that the devices were utilized is relevant to the question of damages, it is not fatal to plaintiff's case.

Although this case does not support Koeppel's argument that mere intent to intrude on privacy is enough, it provides guidance in establishing the proof necessary to survive summary judgment on an invasion-of-privacy claim.

* * * * *

In its summary judgment ruling, the trial court . . . cites *Brazinski v. Amoco Petroleum Additives Co.*, where a female business invitee brought an invasion-of-privacy claim after learning the defendant had a television camera trained on the entrance of a locker room for its female employees. The court . . . concluded the plaintiff's claim could not stand because she was unable to show she had been in the locker room during the period the surveillance was being conducted. The case is distinguishable from Koeppel's case, however, because as a business invitee, the plaintiff in *Brazinski* was not presumed to have used the locker room as the defendant's female employees did. . . . Unlike *Brazinski*, there is no doubt in the present case that Koeppel used the office bathroom.

* * * * *

From the foregoing cases, we conclude to succeed on her claim, Koeppel must show the surveillance camera was capable of functioning while in the bathroom. Speirs claims it was not, that he was unable to receive any signal from the camera in the bathroom. Other evidence shows when a new battery was in the camera, a picture of the bathroom was visible on the monitor in Speirs's office, albeit not a clear and consistent one. The images obtained from the bathroom need not have been of high quality to establish an invasion of privacy, nor did the camera need to be pointed at the toilet—it is sufficient that the seclusion of the bathroom, a private area, was intruded upon. There is also evidence the camera was in the bathroom earlier in November.

. . . Accordingly, we reverse the district court ruling granting summary judgment in favor of Speirs on this claim.

* * * * *

Questions

1. At trial, how could Speirs be found liable for invasion of privacy if the bathroom camera was not operating? Explain.

2. The court in *Koeppel* cited an additional case involving the following facts: The director of a nonprofit residential facility for neglected and abused children learned that someone was accessing pornographic websites late at night from a facility office computer located in an enclosed office. The two employees

stationed in that office performed clerical work during normal business hours and were not suspected. Without telling them, the director installed a hidden camera in the office, trained on the computer in question. The camera did not operate during the day. After discovering the camera, the employees sued for invasion of privacy.

a. How might this case support the court's decision in *Koeppel?*

b. Decide. Explain. See *Hernandez v. Hillsides*, 47 Cal. 4th 272 (Cal. 2010).

3. Young was the pastor of Ft. Caroline United Methodist Church in Florida. Young was provided with a private office and a computer in that office. The computer was not networked to any other computers. Young and the church administrator had keys to the office. No one was permitted in the office without Young's permission, and the church administrator was not permitted to log on to the computer unless Young was present.

The church administrator received notice from the church's Internet service provider that spam was linked to the church's Internet address. The administrator ran a "spybot" program on the church computers and found questionable web addresses. The church's district supervisor and bishop were contacted and permission was given to involve police officials. Officers came to the church; the administrator unlocked Young's office and signed "consent to search" forms for the office and the computer. Officers searched the office and computer and found proscribed images and websites.

Young subsequently filed a trial court motion to suppress the evidence gained from the office and computer search. The trial judge granted that motion, ruling that the search violated Young's Fourth Amendment right to be free of unreasonable searches and seizures. The state appealed. Rule on that appeal. See *State v. Young*, 974 So. 2d 601 (Fla. Dist. Ct. App. 2008).

Drug Testing

Mary Wheeler decided that she had to institute an employee drug-testing program for her Chagrin Falls, Ohio, landscaping company. One job applicant at Wheeler's company told the interviewer that he would have no problem with the drug test. Then according to Wheeler: "While filling out his paperwork, the interviewer asked the applicant for a driver's license. The applicant reached into his pocket, and by accident pulled out a small bag of cocaine."[67] That episode certainly confirmed Wheeler's judgment that workplace drug tests were necessary for her company, and the data support Wheeler's fears. According to a federal government study, nearly one out of five workers between the ages of 18 and 25 used illicit drugs in the past month, along with 1 out of 10 between the ages of 26 and 34.[68] One employee high on marijuana dropped his forklift five feet off a loading dock and employees at another job built a meth lab in the back of a truck.[69]

In an effort to address those workplace drug problems, employers provide information about illicit drug abuse, have written policies regarding drug use in the workplace, and offer employee assistance programs (EAPs).[70] Furthermore, as a 2010 Society for Human Resource Management (SHRM) poll revealed, 55 percent of employers use drug testing in hiring employees, whereas 80 percent of employers conduct "reasonable suspicion" workplace drug testing.[71]

Drug-Free Workplace

The Drug-Free Workplace Act of 1988 applies to employers who have contracts of $100,000 or more with the federal government or who receive aid from the government. Those employers are required to develop an antidrug policy for employees. They must provide drug-free awareness programs for employees and must acquaint employees with available assistance for those with drug problems, while also warning them of the penalties that accompany violation of the policy. The act requires employees to adhere to the company policy and to inform the company within five days if they are convicted of or plead no contest to a drug-related offense in the workplace. [For more information on the Federal Drug-Free Workplace Program, see **www.workplace.samhsa.gov**].

Drug Testing in Law and Practice

LO 12-8
Discuss workplace drug testing and the legal challenges it faces.

Drug testing is regulated primarily by state law, so generalizations are difficult. Broadly, we can say, however, that private-sector drug testing, properly conducted, ordinarily is lawful in the following five situations:

1. *Preemployment testing.* State and local law may impose some restrictions.
2. *In association with periodic physical examinations.* Advance notice is often required.
3. *For cause.* An employer has probable cause or reasonable suspicion.
4. *Postaccident testing* where drug use is suspected.
5. *Follow-up testing* for those returning from drug (or alcohol) rehabilitation.

Random testing, on the other hand, sometimes produces significant legal issues. A number of states forbid random drug testing or limit it to safety-sensitive situations. The U.S. Supreme Court has upheld such testing for public-sector employees where public safety is involved and for those having access to particularly sensitive information.[72] The legality of drug testing often reduces to a balancing test where the employee's right to privacy is balanced against the employer's business needs. Where safety and security are involved and when notice is provided, the courts are more supportive of testing. Particularly intrusive or careless testing often tilts that balance toward employees. Beyond the balancing test, a number of other legal considerations influence employer drug-testing practices, particularly in public-sector jobs:

1. **U.S. Constitution.** As explained in Chapter 5, the Fourth Amendment to the U.S. Constitution forbids unreasonable searches and seizures. Thus, government employers ordinarily cannot conduct a search without individualized suspicion—that is, without probable cause. Certain exceptions, however, have been recognized in cases involving such issues as safety, national security, and athletic participation. Remember that the U.S. Constitution protects citizens from the government, not from private-sector employers (with limited exceptions).
2. **State constitutions.** Many state constitutions offer privacy protection, but court decisions, to date, have generally not extended those protections to private-sector employers. On the other hand, certain states, such as California and Massachusetts, explicitly offer constitutional protection to private-sector employees.
3. **Federal statutes.** Drug testing could violate Title VII of the Civil Rights Act of 1964 or the Americans with Disabilities Act (see Chapter 13) if the testing fails to treat all individuals equally. The ADA protects *recovering* drug addicts and those erroneously believed to be drug abusers, but not employees or applicants who are currently abusing drugs.

4. **State and local statutes.** Historically, most state and local drug-testing legislation placed limits on that testing, but in recent years, fears about drug use in the workplace and often intense business community lobbying have, in some cases, relaxed those testing restraints.

5. **Common law claims.** Some of the more prominent judge-made (common law) claims that might provide a challenge to drug testing include invasion of privacy, defamation (dissemination of erroneous information about an employee), negligence (in testing or in selecting a test provider), intentional infliction of emotional distress, and wrongful discharge (discussed later in this chapter).

Part Six—Employee Benefits and Income Maintenance

In recent years, employee benefits have been the subject of political debate and legislative action, and the object of employers' reactions to an uncertain economy.[73] The 2010 Patient Protection and Affordable Care Act (ACA; colloquially labeled Obamacare), which became effective in 2014, raised concerns that employers' decisions to provide health insurance coverage will be negatively impacted. However, surveys throw into question the actual impact of the ACA on employers' practices of providing health insurance. While a March 2017 congressional vote to repeal the ACA failed, at this writing it is unclear whether another such legislative effort will be made by ACA opponents. Meanwhile, in 2013, the Department of Labor required employers to provide notice to employees of health care options available under the ACA through health insurance exchanges.[74]

Notably, the number of Americans without health insurance has dropped in recent years. This increase in coverage has been attributed to government programs.[75]

Under the ACA, employers with 50 or more employees that do not provide affordable health insurance coverage for their employees will face penalties. Those with fewer than 50 employees that do not provide health insurance will not face a penalty but are eligible for tax credits. Critics argue that this amounts to a mandate for larger employers to provide health insurance for their employees in order to avoid paying penalties, or, contrarily, to provide an incentive for employers for whom health care costs outweigh the penalties. A 2015 survey by the International Foundation of Employee Benefit Plans found that although more than a third of employers believed that the ACA costs would increase 5 percent or more in 2016, over half of employers planned to continue their health care coverage in 2016.[76] A 3 to 4 percent increase in costs is typically anticipated.[77] These numbers could be viewed either as a sign that some employers will opt out of health insurance or as evidence that most employers will still offer health care plans under the ACA. In 2012, the U.S. Supreme Court rejected a constitutional challenge to the ACA, holding that the individual penalties under the ACA could be deemed as a tax, which Congress has the power to levy.[78] [For more information on the ACA, see **https://www.healthcare.gov**].

The federal Consolidated Budget Reconciliation Act (COBRA) requires employers with 20 or more employees to permit departing employees to retain group health coverage at their own expense for up to 18 months as long as they are not terminated for gross misconduct.

Unfortunately, COBRA policies are often too expensive for workers who have lost their jobs. The American Recovery and Reinvestment Act of 2009 provides health benefit premium reductions for those who were involuntarily unemployed within a particular time frame.[79]

Along with health care, another pressing social issue affecting the workplace is the care of children and elderly parents: 29 percent of adults in the United States are caregivers to an elderly parent or child with special needs. They provide care an average of 20 hours per week. Approximately three-fourths of these caregivers work outside the home while caregiving, and an increasing number of them report having to make workplace accommodations.[80]

Family Leave

LO 12-9
Describe the Family and Medical Leave Act (FMLA).

The Family and Medical Leave Act (FMLA) entitles eligible employees of covered employers to take job-protected, *unpaid* leave for certain family-related or medical reasons. Eligible employees are entitled to 12 weeks of FMLA leave in a 12-month period for the birth, adoption, or foster care placement of a child; to care for a child, spouse, or parent who has a serious medical condition; or for the employee's own serious medical condition. Employees taking leave are entitled to reinstatement to the same or equivalent job. Employers with 50 or more employees are covered by FMLA. The 2008 National Defense Authorization Act (NDAA) amended FMLA to provide military family leave to eligible employees to care for their spouse, child, or parent who is undergoing medical treatment for a serious injury or illness incurred in the line of duty or for "qualifying exigencies" including child care and counseling arising from their spouse's, child's, or parent's call to active duty status from the military reserves.[81] In its 2015 final rule defining "spouse" under the FMLA, the Department of Labor included same-sex spouses who got married in a state recognizing same-sex marriage, even if the couple does not reside in that state.[82]

Although most worksites are not covered by the FMLA, over half of American employees are eligible for its protections, reflecting the FMLA's coverage of larger workplaces.[83] Lost wages often make FMLA leave unattractive; however, approximately two-thirds of employees taking FMLA leave receive either full or partial pay, typically by using paid vacation leave, sick leave, or other forms of paid time off.[84] Employers in California, New Jersey, and Rhode Island must provide paid family and medical leave; all three states fund these programs through employee-paid payroll taxes.[85] The State of Washington passed such legislation but, at this writing, has indefinitely postponed its implementation.[86] [For more on the FMLA, see **www.dol.gov/whd/fmla/**].

Work Abroad?

Of the 38 countries represented in a recent study, the United States stood alone as a nation not mandating paid leave for new mothers. In comparison, Estonia offers about 2 years of paid leave, and Hungary and Lithuania offer 1½ years or more of fully paid leave. The median amount of fully paid time off available to a mother for the birth of a child is about 5 to 6 months. In most countries providing paid leave, the government pays the bill.

Source: Gretchen Livingston, "Among 38 Nations, the U.S. Is the Outlier When It Comes to Paid Parental Leave," Pew Research Center, December 12, 2013 [**www.pewresearch.org/fact-tank/2013/12/12/among-38-nations-u-s-is-the-holdout-when-it-comes-to-offering-paid-parental-leave/**].

Unemployment Compensation

The tragedy of the Great Depression, when up to 25 percent of the workforce was unemployed, led in 1935 to the passage of the Social Security Act, one portion of which provided for an unemployment insurance program. Today, all 50 states and the federal government are engaged in a cooperative system that helps protect the temporarily jobless. The system is financed through a payroll tax paid by employers.

The actual state tax rate for each employer varies, depending on the employer's *experience ratings*—the number of layoffs in its workforce. Thus, employers have an incentive to retain employees.

Rules vary by state, but in general, employees qualify for unemployment benefits by reaching a specified total of annual wages. Those losing their jobs must apply to a state agency for unemployment compensation, which varies by state. Benefits may be collected up to a specified maximum period, usually 26 weeks. During that time, those collecting compensation must be ready to work and must make an effort to find suitable work. Workers who quit or who are fired for *misconduct* are ineligible for unemployment compensation. The episodes that follow illustrate the improbable cases where compensation has been denied:

- The Swiss Valley Farms dairy worker who led her coworkers in an after-hours swim in the cheese vat (filled with water at the time).[87]
- The on-patrol police officer who was charged with having sex with a woman multiple times, sometimes in parking lots.[88]
- The 25-year-old Sheraton hotel worker who used her employer's computer to write a 300-page manuscript describing her successful efforts to avoid doing any work.[89]

On a sobering note, 1.8 million adults and 620,000 children would have fallen below the poverty line in 2012 without unemployment insurance.[90]

WARN

The Worker Adjustment and Retraining Notification Act (WARN) requires firms with 100 or more employees to provide 60 days' notice if they lay off one-third or more of their workers at any site employing at least 150 workers, drop 500 employees at any site, or close a plant employing at least 50 workers. A General Accounting Office study concluded, however, that the law had been ineffectual, with half of plant closings not covered by the law. [See **http://www.gao.gov/new.items/d031003.pdf**].

Pensions

LO 12-10
Distinguish between defined benefit and defined contribution pension plans.

A recent survey revealed that although Americans have recovered some of their confidence about retirement that were at record lows in recent years, nearly a quarter of American workers are not at all confident in their ability to retire.[91] Confidence was strongly correlated with participation in retirement plans.[92]

Broadly, pensions take two forms: *defined benefit plans* and *defined contribution plans*. Defined benefit plans are of the traditional form providing specified monthly payments

> Nearly a quarter of American workers are not at all confident in their ability to retire.

upon retirement. Although many workers have lost those pensions in recent years, some 40 million Americans remain protected by defined benefit plans.[93] Defined contribution plans, such as the popular 401(k), specify in advance the "match" the employer will provide to go with the employee's own contributions. The employee is offered a menu of investment options for that retirement money, but no promises are made about the amount that will be paid upon retirement. Defined contribution plans are now much more common than defined benefit plans. Defined contribution plans can be attractive to employees because the money *vests* (the point at which the employee has a nonforfeitable right to the funds) quickly and follows the employee who changes jobs. From the employer's point of view, the defined contribution plans are less expensive to manage, and they shift the risk from employer to employee.

Various hybrid pension plans also have been developed. A particularly prominent hybrid, a *cash balance plan*, is a defined benefit plan that acts somewhat like a defined contribution plan. The employer makes regular, defined contributions and guarantees a benefit amount to employees based on an established formula, but the benefits are maintained in individual accounts and are expressed in terms of an accumulated lump sum, a cash balance, rather than as a periodic payment during retirement. All of the investment risk in cash balance plans remains with the employer.[94] [See **www.401khelpcenter.com** and **www.ebri.org** for large databases on 401(k) and other retirement topics.]

Pension Law   The federal Employee Retirement Income Security Act (ERISA) regulates pension funds to help ensure their long-term financial security by reducing fraud and mismanagement. ERISA requires that fund managers keep detailed records, engage in prudent investments, and provide an annual report that has been certified by qualified, impartial third parties. ERISA also establishes strict vesting rights to ensure that employees actually receive the pensions to which they are entitled. Employer contributions typically vest after three years or in a six-year, graduated system. The Pension Benefit Guaranty Corporation (PBGC), funded by company contributions, was created as an element of ERISA to insure defined benefit plans so that vested persons will be paid up to a specified maximum if their plan cannot meet its obligations. Defined contribution arrangements are not covered by the PBGC.

Fears that companies were not sufficiently funding their traditional pension plans led to provisions in the federal Pension Protection Act of 2006 requiring companies to more adequately fund those plans. However, recent studies found pension funds are seriously underfunded, with less than three-quarters of the money needed to meet their obligations.[95]

Now millions of Americans depend on their own investment wisdom and the reliability of their 401(k) plan for their retirement security. In 2012, the Department of Labor issued disclosure guidelines designed to assist employees in managing and investing their 401(k) plans.[96] In 2008, the U.S. Supreme Court strengthened that oversight a bit by finding that retirement account holders can sue if the administrator of their plan fails to follow their investment instructions. On the other hand, in 2010 the Court extended the deference given to plan administrators' discretion to include a plan administrator whose first attempt at interpreting the plan had already been ruled unreasonable.[97]

In 2011, the Court reviewed a district court's ruling in an ERISA class action brought by Cigna employees alleging their employer deceived them in statements made about its pension plan. The lower court had determined the employer had modified the plan's terms under which benefits should be calculated through affirmative misstatements to employees. In a decision hailed by both federal regulators and employers, the Court vacated the district court's ruling, finding that plan participants can sue to enforce but not modify a plan's terms, but also sending the case back to the lower court to determine whether a remedy could be found under another ERISA provision. On remand, the district court ordered enforcement of a reformed plan.[98]

> ### Will you need to work longer than your parents?

The Future? Employer-provided pension and health care benefits for retirees increasingly are at risk. As expenses, including pensions and health care, continue to rise, can American companies compete successfully with lower-cost foreign competition? Will the social constructions of "the good life" and the "golden years" be altered, and how? Will you need to work years longer than your parents?

Part Seven—Termination: Protection from Wrongful Discharge

Catherine Wagenseller, an Arizona nurse; her boss, Kay Smith; and some coworkers joined a Colorado River rafting trip where Wagenseller declined to participate in a "Moon River" skit in which the group allegedly "mooned" the audience. Likewise, Wagenseller did not

> ### Wagenseller declined to participate in a "Moon River" skit.

join Smith in the heavy drinking, "grouping up," public urination, and similar behaviors that allegedly marked the trip. Despite favorable job evaluations preceding the trip, Wagenseller's relationship with Smith deteriorated following the trip, and eventually she was terminated. Wagenseller, an at-will employee, sued, claiming that she was wrongfully discharged. An *at-will employee*, by definition, is not under contract for a definite period of time, and as such can be fired at any time. Wagenseller, however, argued that Arizona should adopt the *public policy exception* to the at-will doctrine. She claimed that she was fired because she refused to engage in behaviors that might have violated the Arizona indecent exposure statute. The state Supreme Court agreed with Wagenseller by finding in the statute a public policy favoring privacy and decency. The case was returned to the trial level, giving Wagenseller the opportunity to prove that her refusal to violate state public policy by engaging in public indecency led to her dismissal.[99]

The *Wagenseller* decision is an exception to the long-standing American rule that at-will employees can be fired for good reasons, bad reasons, or no reason at all. Of course, the employee is likewise free to quit at any time. Furthermore, both employer and employee freely entered the bargain understanding its terms, and thus the court should, in general, enforce those terms. Critics, however, argue that the doctrine ignores the historic inequality of bargaining power between employers and employees. In recent decades, the at-will rule has been softened in most states by legislative and judicially imposed limitations. Statutory exceptions to the at-will rule include our labor laws protecting union workers (see Chapter 14) and the equal employment opportunity laws that forbid the dismissal of an employee for discriminatory reasons (see Chapter 13).

Judicial Limitations on At-Will Principles

LO 12-11
Analyze whether a dismissed at-will employee may bring a claim of wrongful discharge.

An increasing number of court decisions provide grounds for dismissed at-will employees to claim that they have been *wrongfully discharged*. Those judicial decisions were often provoked by transparently unjust dismissals including, for example, whistle-blowers who exposed their employers' misdeeds and employees who declined to commit perjury on behalf of their employers. Those judicial limitations to the at-will doctrine fall into three categories: (1) express or implied contracts, (2) an implied covenant of good faith and fair dealing, and (3) the tort of violating an established public policy, as in *Wagenseller*. Additional tort claims may substitute for or supplement wrongful discharge claims.

1. **Express or implied employment contracts.** A number of states have adopted a contractual protection for at-will employees arising, typically, either from the employee handbook or from the employer's conduct and oral representations. For example, an employee handbook might contain a policy expecting employees to arrive on time to start their shift, and describing the progressive discipline tardy employees will face—such as an oral warning the first time they are late, a written warning for a second late arrival, and other discipline up to dismissal for continued incidents. This policy creates a contract that employees will not be terminated the first, or even second, time they arrive late to work. Similarly, oral assurances of continued employment or an employer's practice of providing mentorship to rehabilitate employees' poor performance rather than firing them may create contracts that protect at-will employees from termination.

2. **Implied covenant of good faith and fair dealing.** A few state courts have held that neither party to a contract may act in bad faith to deprive the other of the benefits of the contract. For example, Bruce Rubenstein gave up his job with Arbor Mortgage to take an at-will position with Huntington Mortgage with the understanding that he would be manager of a new branch office to be opened in central New Jersey. After a few weeks, however, Huntington decided on a downsizing strategy under which the new branch would not be opened. Rubenstein was offered a job as a Huntington loan originator, but he declined. He sued Huntington asserting, among other things, that Huntington had breached the covenant of good faith and fair dealing. Reubenstein believed that Huntington knew of the possibility of downsizing before hiring him. The court agreed that Rubenstein may have had a viable claim for breach of the implied covenant of good faith and fair dealing if the facts, at trial, proved to be as Rubenstein alleged.[100]

3. **Public policy.** Most states have now adopted some form of "public policy" exception to at-will employment, under which a dismissal is wrongful if it results from employee conduct that is consistent with a public good or the public interest as expressed in legislation, constitutional protections, and the like. These exceptions are established case by case, and may differ from state to state. In addition to reporting an employer's illegal activity, commonly known as "whistle-blowing," or refusing to commit an illegal act such as perjury, the exception often protects, for example, employees fired for pursuing a lawful claim against their employer (e.g., workers' compensation or wage claims) as well as those fired for fulfilling a civic responsibility such as jury duty.

Only Funny until Someone Quits: The Firing Contest

The owner of a chain of QC Mart convenience stores in Bettendorf, Iowa, offered a $10 cash prize to workers who could predict which of them would be the next to be fired. A memo distributed to all employees asked them to write down and seal in an envelope the name of the coworker they thought would be fired next. The owner explained that secret shoppers would visit the store to see which cashiers were committing such offenses as wearing a hat, talking on a cell phone, and not wearing a QC Mart shirt. Once a firing occurred, the contest would begin again. After receiving the memo, QC Mart cashier Misty Shelsky, along with her store manager and a few other employees, quit. When Shelsky applied for unemployment benefits, the owner challenged the claim, asserting that she had left the job voluntarily. As defined by the Department of Labor, a constructive discharge (treated as a termination) occurs when a worker's resignation may be found not to be voluntary because the employer has created a hostile or intolerable work environment or has applied other forms of pressure or coercion that forced the employee to quit or resign. Should Shelsky be viewed as a terminated employee? Decide. Explain.

Sources: Clark Kauffman, "Firing Contest by Boss Leads Employees to Quit," *The Des Moines Register*, October 2, 2011, p. 1B; and U.S. Department of Labor, "WARN Advisor Glossary: Constructive Discharge" [**www.dol.gov/elaws/eta/warn/glossaryall.asp#Constructive_Discharge**].

Additional Torts   Dismissed employees are increasingly turning to a variety of tort actions often labeled "tag-along torts"—seeking compensatory and punitive damages to enhance their potential financial recovery. Potential tort claims arising from termination include defamation, intentional infliction of emotional distress, interference with contract, and invasion of privacy. The following case addresses whether at-will employees may bring an action for fraud based on their employer's alleged inducement to join a unit being sold off.

Sawyer v. E. I. Du Pont de Nemours & Co.

LEGAL BRIEFCASE   430 S.W.3d 396 (Tex. 2014)

Justice Nathan L. Hecht

[A question] certified to us by the United States Court of Appeals for the Fifth Circuit ask[s] whether, under Texas law, at-will employees and employees . . . can sue their corporate employer for fraudulently inducing them to move to a wholly owned subsidiary. We conclude that while an employee can sue an employer for fraud in some situations, in the context in which the certified [question] arise[s], the answer . . . is no.

I

The factual background . . . may be summarized as follows.

In February 2002, E. I. du Pont de Nemours and Company announced plans to spin off part of its operations, including its Terathane Products Unit in La Porte, into a wholly owned subsidiary, DuPont Textiles and Interiors ("DTI"). Most of the Unit employees were covered by a collective bargaining agreement ("CBA"), which gave them the right to transfer to other DuPont jobs rather than move to the new DTI subsidiary. DTI's employees were to be covered by an identical CBA and would continue to receive the same pay and benefits they had at DuPont. But the Unit employees, who had worked for DuPont many years, were afraid DuPont would sell DTI, and that such a sale would adversely affect their compensation and retirement packages. DuPont wanted the Unit employees to go to DTI to avoid significant training expenses—both for transferring employees in their new DuPont jobs and for their DTI replacements—and layoffs of people displaced by more senior transferring employees.

DuPont and the union agreed that the Unit employees would be given a deadline to decide whether to move to DTI, and the fate of those who decided to stay would be subject to further bargaining. DuPont allegedly assured the Unit employees, to persuade them to move to DTI, that DuPont would keep DTI, even though, unbeknownst to the employees, DuPont had already discussed selling DTI with a potential buyer, Koch Industries. Effective February 1, 2003, almost all of the Unit employees moved to DTI. A few weeks later, on April 14, DuPont announced it was negotiating a sale of DTI to Koch. The sale was finalized on May 1, 2004. Koch subsequently reduced the former DuPont employees' compensation and retirement benefits.

In November 2006, 63 of the former DuPont employees ("the Employees") sued DuPont for fraudulently inducing them to terminate their employment and accept employment with DTI by misrepresenting that DTI would not be sold. The Employees claim over $23 million in damages. DuPont contends that the Employees were all at will and therefore cannot sue for fraud. The 59 Employees covered by DuPont's CBA argue that they were not at will because the CBA prohibited discharge except for "just cause." DuPont responds, in part, that because the CBA could be terminated on 60 days' notice, the CBA's requirement of "just cause" for discharge did not modify the at-will status of covered employees.

The Fifth Circuit asks:

1. Under Texas law, may at-will employees bring fraud claims against their employers for loss of their employment?

*   *   *   *   *

II

*   *   *   *   *

"For well over a century, the general rule in this State, as in most American jurisdictions, has been that absent a specific agreement to the contrary, employment may be terminated by the employer or the employee at will, for good cause, bad cause, or no cause at all." The Legislature has created a few narrow exceptions, prohibiting, for example, discharge based on certain forms of discrimination or in retaliation for engaging in certain protected conduct. But Texas courts have created only one: prohibiting an employee from being discharged for refusing to perform an illegal act. Otherwise, "[t]he courts of Texas have steadfastly refused to vary from [the general rule]."

Thus, we have repeatedly refused to recognize common-law whistleblower liability. We have refused to impose on employers a duty to exercise ordinary care in investigating employee misconduct because such a duty "would significantly damage the at-will employment relationship that Texas has so carefully guarded." And we have refused to impose a duty of good faith and fair dealing on employers, noting that it would "completely alter the nature of the at-will employment relationship."

We have not determined whether an at-will employee can sue his employer for fraud, but the courts of appeals have dealt with the issue and have almost all held that a fraud claim cannot be based on illusory promises of continued at-will employment. . . .

This does not mean that at-will employees can never sue for fraud. Recovery of expenses incurred in reliance on a fraudulent promise of prospective employment has been allowed because neither the injury nor the recovery depends on continued employment. The distinction is similar to one we have drawn in determining whether an at-will employee's contract with his employer is valid. "At-will employment does not preclude employers and employees from forming subsequent contracts, 'so long as neither party relies on continued employment as consideration for the contract.'" An employer and employee may agree, for example, to arbitrate their disputes, or for reasonable restrictions on post-discharge competition, as long as other consideration is given. But if the employer or employee can avoid performance of a promise by exercising a right to terminate the at-will relationship, which each is perfectly free to do with or without reason at any time, the promise is illusory and cannot support an enforceable agreement.

Such an illusory promise can no more support an action for fraud than one for breach of contract. To recover for fraud, one must prove justifiable reliance on a material misrepresentation. A representation dependent on continued at-will employment cannot be material because employment can terminate at any time. Nor can one justifiably rely on the continuation of employment that can be terminated at will. "I will if I want to" is not fraud. And no one can claim recovery of damages for the loss of an employment relationship he had no right to continue.

To allow a promise that is contingent on continued at-will employment to be enforced in a suit for fraud would mock the refusal of enforcement in a suit for breach of contract, making the non-existence of a contract action largely irrelevant, and would significantly impair the at-will rule. An employee who could not show consideration for an enforceable contract could simply sue for fraud and recover not only the same actual damages but punitive damages as well.

. . . Although common-law fraud is certainly not new, allowing it to be asserted to alter or conflict with at-will employment would be. For all these reasons, we answer the Fifth Circuit's question: an at-will employee cannot bring an action for fraud that is dependent on continued employment.

*   *   *   *   *

Questions

1. Why did the plaintiffs lose their fraud claim? Explain.

2. Did the court bar all fraud claims that might be brought by at-will employees against their former employers after their employment is terminated? Explain.

3. In 2004, Touchstone Television Productions hired Nicollette Sheridan to play Edie Britt in the television series *Desperate Housewives*. Touchstone's agreement with Sheridan gave it the exclusive option to renew her services on an annual basis for up to an additional six seasons; Touchstone exercised this option for seasons 2 through 5. In February 2009, Touchstone informed the actress that it would not exercise its option for season 6 and that Edie Britt would be killed in a car accident during season 5. Sheridan alleged that Touchstone's decision was motivated by her complaint regarding a September 2008 incident in which Marc Cherry, the show's creator, allegedly hit her, amounting to a wrongful termination in breach of public policy. Decide. Explain. *Touchstone Television Productions v. Sheridan*, 208 Cal. App. 4th 676 (2012).

4. IBP operated a large hog-processing plant in Storm Lake, Iowa. IBP prohibited possession of "look-alike drugs" on company property. An employee, Michael Huegerich, was randomly and lawfully inspected as he was entering the plant. The inspection revealed an asthma medication, Maxalert, which was identical in appearance to an illegal street drug, "speed." Maxalert contained the stimulant ephedrine. The pills actually belonged to his girlfriend and were in his possession by accident. Huegerich was terminated for possessing a look-alike drug in violation of company policy. Huegerich admitted that he was generally aware of IBP drug policies, but because he was a transfer from another IBP division, he had not gone through the company orientation program where new employees were advised of the policy against look-alike drugs. About six months after his dismissal, two IBP employees told Huegerich that they had heard he was fired for possessing speed. Huegerich then sued IBP for, among other claims, wrongful discharge and defamation. At trial, Huegerich provided no evidence as to how, when, and from whom the IBP employees had heard that he was terminated for possession of speed. The district court found for Huegerich in the amount of $24,000 on the wrongful discharge claim and $20,000 on the defamation claim. The court said that IBP was guilty of negligent discharge in failing to inform Huegerich about its drug policy. IBP appealed to the Iowa Supreme Court. Iowa law recognizes the doctrine of at-will employment with "narrow" exceptions for public policy violations and where a contract is created by an employer's handbook. Decide. Explain. See *Huegerich v. IBP*, 547 N.W.2d 216 (Iowa 1996).

5. Freeman, a television anchorperson employed by KSN, gave birth to her second child. On the day she returned from the hospital, she was notified that she had been dismissed. Six weeks later, she became unable to lactate. She sued KSN for wrongful discharge, tortious interference with contract, and negligent infliction of emotional distress. Decide. Explain. See *Freeman v. Medevac Midamerica of Kansas, Inc.*, 719 F. Supp. 995 (D. Kan. 1989).

PRACTICING ETHICS   Hearing the Whistle Blow?

Kevin Lamson was a sales manager for an Oregon car dealership, Crater Lake Motors. Crater Lake hired Real Performance Marketing Company (RPM) to conduct a five-day sales promotion at the dealership. During the first few days of the sales event, Lamson observed or was informed of a number of activities that he considered to be unethical and possibly unlawful, such as misrepresenting the event as a bank sale and including various insurance and service agreements in the sales contract without the knowledge of the customer. Lamson complained to the Crater Lake Motors General Manager, Shevlin, who told him to "just go home." The next week, Lamson again expressed his concerns at a Crater Lake Motors meeting.

About a month later, Shevlin criticized Lamson's attitude and recent performance, stating that Lamson "wasn't getting the job done." Shevlin also told Lamson of another planned RPM sales event and asked if Lamson intended to quit. Lamson replied that he did not intend to quit but that it seemed like Shevlin did not want him to work at Crater Lake Motors anymore. Shevlin replied that he did not want the Lamson he had seen recently.

Lamson later complained to the Crater Lake Motors owner, Coleman, about RPM. Coleman told Lamson that working at the second RPM event was mandatory and that failure to attend could result in dismissal. Lamson told Coleman that he could not participate because doing so would condone unethical behavior. Coleman said the agreement with RPM had been amended to explicitly forbid misrepresentations. Lamson did not attend the second RPM event and was fired. Lamson then sued Crater Lake Motors for wrongful discharge.

Questions

1. Was Crater Lake Motors wrong to hire RPM?
2. Was Lamson wrong to refuse to work at the second RPM event?

3. Did Lamson have a duty to complain about the conduct he had observed during the first RPM event?
4. Was Crater Lake wrong to terminate Lamson?
5. Who won the wrongful termination lawsuit?

Source: *Lamson v. Crater Lake Motors*, 346 Or. 628 (2009).

Part Eight—Immigration

Immigration is a vital fuel for America's economic and cultural growth, but immigration is also a source of deep political and public policy divisions. President Trump's 2016 campaign was energized at least in part by tapping into frustration with federal immigration policy. This tension might have been reflected in a 2010 Arizona measure requiring police officers to determine the immigration status of anyone lawfully stopped, detained, or arrested whom they suspected might be in the United States illegally.[101] A Pew poll showed that 59 percent of Americans approved of the 2010 Arizona measure.[102] While striking down other provisions of the law, including one making it a crime for immigrants without work permits to seek employment, the U.S. Supreme Court allowed the controversial section regarding immigration status checks by police to stand.[103]

In 2011, Alabama enacted a law that encompassed many of the 2010 Arizona provisions but was more broadly restrictive in that it, for example, required public schools to check the immigration status of their students and made it a crime for landlords to knowingly rent to, harbor, or transport a known unauthorized ("illegal") immigrant. After the U.S. Supreme Court's ruling on the Arizona legislation, a federal appellate court blocked the Alabama law; the Supreme Court declined to hear Alabama's appeal.[104] The outcomes of these cases underscore that federal immigration policy supersedes state efforts on this issue under the U.S. Constitution's Supremacy Clause (see Chapters 5 and 8).

According to a 2017 Pew Research Center report, while some jobs such as sewing machine operators are more likely to be filled by immigrants rather than U.S-born workers, no specific industry has more immigrant than native-born U.S. employees.[105] Approximately 1 million immigrants are admitted to the United States each year, with most being family members of citizens.[106] Immigrants totaled approximately 17.1 percent of the workforce in 2014.[107] About 5 percent of the total workforce entered illegally.[108] Nearly a third of U.S. immigrants age 25 or older have a bachelor's degree.[109] Without immigrants adding to the U.S. workforce that is faced with an aging population and low birthrates, it has been estimated that the working-age population in the United States would fall by almost 8 million by 2035.[110] However, concerns about the negative impact that large immigrant populations, both legally and illegally entering the United States, may have on low-income Americans have been raised.[111]

LO 12-12
Recognize the purpose and requirements of the employment eligibility verification form (I-9).

American Immigration Law in the Workplace   Businesses in the United States have used the H-1B visa program to bring foreign workers to the United States to fill positions requiring highly skilled, technical expertise in specialized fields such as science, engineering, or computer programming. In seeking an H-1B visa, an employer must affirm to the U.S. Department of Labor that the hiring will not harm wages and working conditions of employees in similar jobs. The number of H-1B visas available annually is limited to 85,000 workers, 20,000 of which are reserved for advanced degree holders, and is typically in high demand; however, for the first time since 2014, the number of H-1B visa applications in 2017 fell below 200,000.[112] In April 2017, President Trump signed an executive order calling for several government agencies to examine changes needed in the H-1B program.[113]

In hiring those already in the United States, federal immigration law, including the 1986 Immigration Reform and Control Act, requires employers to verify that each new hire is a U.S. citizen, a permanent resident, or a foreign national with permission to work in this country. To meet this requirement, employers must complete an employment eligibility verification form (I-9) for each new employee. New employees must present documents establishing the employee's identity and eligibility to work in the United States. The employer must examine the documents and complete the I-9 if the documents appear legitimate. Of course, employers cannot knowingly hire illegal immigrants, but neither can they discriminate against legal immigrants because of national origin and similar factors. [For links to the I-9 form and other immigration information, see **www.uscis.gov/portal/site/uscis**].

Enforcement   Enforcement of immigration laws focuses on two issues: hiring of illegal immigrants and employers' illegal discrimination against applicants based on citizenship status or national origin. Critics charge that these policies create a conflict for employers: on the one hand, employers must be sure to verify applicants' ability to work in the United States, but on the other hand, they must take care not to place extra burdens on applicants because they are of a particular national origin, or are U.S. permanent residents as opposed to U.S. citizens.[114] For example, under a settlement reached with the U.S. Department of Justice, a California company, American Education and Travel Services Inc., agreed to pay $10,000 in back pay and compensatory damages to a lawful permanent resident who was denied a residential counselor position because he was not a U.S. citizen or native English speaker.[115] At the same time, the Obama administration's use of immigration audits, rather than Bush-era workplace raids, led to illegal immigrants being fired. In 2011, for example, fast-food chain Chipotle fired hundreds of illegal immigrants as a result of an audit by U.S. Immigration and Customs Enforcement.[116]

E-Verify is a free online system run by the federal government that determines an employee's eligibility to work in the United States, comparing information reported on an employee's Form I-9 with federal records. Since 2009, the federal government mandates certain federal contractors to use the program. In 2014, the U.S. Citizenship and Immigration Services (USCIS) reported that 500,000 companies were enrolled in E-Verify.[117] However, critics note that E-Verify does not address whether the identity provided is authentic, which could encourage identity theft to help illegal workers clear this employment hurdle.[118] [For overviews of many of the employment law topics in this chapter, see **http://topics.law.cornell.edu/wex/category/employment_law**].

Internet Exercise

Visit the Privacy Rights Clearinghouse at **https://www.privacyrights.org/consumer-guides/workplace-privacy-and-employee-monitoring**.

Think of an employer you have worked for or an employer in the career you plan to enter. After consulting the guidelines on mobile devices, GPS tracking, and social media monitoring, create employee policies addressing each of these issues for that employer.

Chapter Questions

1. In general, employers are forced to bear (or at least share) the legal burden for their employees' negligent conduct on the job.
   a. Why do we force employers to bear that responsibility?
   b. Should we do so? Explain.

2. Abplanalp, a five-year employee of Com-Co Insurance, signed an employment agreement including a restrictive covenant providing that, should he leave Com-Co, he would not use Com-Co customer lists or solicit business from Com-Co clients for three years. Abplanalp moved to Service Insurance, where he sold insurance to some friends and relatives. He did not sell to any other persons whom he came to know while working for Com-Co. Abplanalp was sued by Com-Co for violating the restrictive covenant. Decide. Explain. See *Com-Co Insurance Agency v. Service Insurance Agency*, 748 N.E.2d 298 (Ill. App. Ct. 2001).

3. Two female music students at Boston University (BU) individually brought concerns about their male professor, a renowned musician, to the attention of administrators in the BU College of Fine Arts. One student withdrew from BU apparently as a result of the professor's conduct, but later met with a BU College of Fine Arts administrator, with whom she shared text messages she had received from the professor while a student at BU. The administrator replied that she should have asked the professor to stop sending those messages. The second student was referred by another professor to a different college administrator, who informed the student that the professor's behavior constituted sexual harassment but blamed it on the professor's "personality" and did not remove him as her instructor. The students filed a lawsuit that included claims against BU for negligent hiring, supervision, training, and retention. What questions might you have before deciding on these claims? Explain. See *Shyr v. Boston University*, 2017 U.S. Dist. LEXIS 37161 (D. Mass. March 13, 2017).

4. A group of Fargo, North Dakota, nurses were paid a subminimum wage for their "on-call" time. When on call, the nurses were required to be able to report to their hospital within 20 minutes, they were required to provide a phone number where they could be reached, and they were not to consume alcohol or drugs. After being called, nurses returned to regular pay. In three years, 36 of the 135 nurses who sued had been called in more than once. The nurses sued the hospital for violating the Fair Labor Standards Act's minimum wage provision. Decide. Explain. See *Reimer v. Champion Healthcare Corp.*, 258 F.3d 720 (8th Cir. 2001).

5. Simons, an engineer at the CIA, downloaded child pornography on his workplace computer. The computer was to be used only for work. The pornography was discovered by a search of employee computers. Simons was then convicted of receiving and possessing child pornography. Simons appealed on Fourth Amendment grounds.

Decide. Explain. See *United States v. Simons*, 206 F.3d 392 (4th Cir. 2000), *cert. denied*, 122 S. Ct. 292 (2001).

6. Guz, a longtime Bechtel employee, was dismissed during what Bechtel said was a business slump. Bechtel's personnel policy included a provision saying employees "may be terminated at the option of Bechtel." Guz sued for wrongful dismissal claiming, among other things, that Bechtel breached an implied contract to be terminated only for good cause and that Bechtel breached the implied covenant of good faith and fair dealing. A lower court concluded that Guz's promotions, raises, favorable performance reviews, together with Bechtel's progressive discipline policy and Bechtel officials' statements of company practices supported Guz's position. Bechtel appealed. Decide. Explain. See *Guz v. Bechtel National Inc.*, 8 P.3d 1089 (Cal. 2000).

7. Hershey Company Retail Sales Representatives (RSRs) were classified as exempt under the Fair Labor Standards Act (FLSA), and Hershey never paid hourly compensation to RSRs for any overtime they worked. While the RSRs received bonuses based on performance, they were not eligible to receive sales commissions. RSRs are part of teams that help sell Hershey products to retail outlets of various sizes from Walmart to independently owned shops. In a wage and hour claim seeking overtime compensation, RSRs contended that they are primarily responsible for merchandising tasks such as delivering and setting up product displays, tagging products, and stocking shelves. Hershey defended that RSRs' job duties include selling products directly to retailers, meeting with their key decision makers to increase sales, and only occasionally assisting with merchandising at their stores. Are the RSRs nonexempt employees with rights to overtime compensation under FLSA? Decide. Explain. See *Campanelli v. Hershey Co.*, 765 F. Supp. 2d 1185 (N.D. Cal. 2011).

8. Rodrigues was fired in 2006 by The Scotts Company, the lawn care giant, because a required drug test revealed nicotine in his urine. Company policy forbade employee smoking both on and off the job. Scotts announced in 2005 that it would no longer hire smokers, and it gave its employees one year to comply with the new policy, which was designed to improve employee wellness and reduce company health care costs. Rodrigues was a pack-a-day smoker when he was hired. He was aware of the no-smoking policy, and he had been warned to quit when a supervisor saw a pack of cigarettes on the dashboard of his car. Was Rodrigues wrongfully terminated? What questions would you have before deciding? Explain. See Sacha Pfieffer, "Off-the-Job Smoker Sues over Firing," *The Boston Globe*, November 30, 2006 [**www.boston.com**].

9. Safeway in Denver hosted a picnic for its employees. Safeway bought a 40-pound gas tank to use with a grill that was designed for a 20-pound tank. A label on the grill warned against that use. The grill failed to operate properly and a manager asked Lewis to try to fix it. When Lewis did so, a "ball of fire" erupted and Lewis was badly burned. The Occupational Safety and Health Administration then issued a citation against Safeway. Safeway appealed to the courts.

   a. Defend Safeway.

   b. Decide the case. Explain. See *Safeway, Inc. v. Occupational Safety & Health Rev. Comm.*, 382 F.3d 1189 (10th Cir. 2004).

10. Lloyd was a Drake University security guard on duty at the university's annual street-painting event. A student informed Lloyd of an apparent altercation between a football player, Joseph, and a woman, Kane, the nature of which was later disputed. Seeing Joseph holding Kane in the air with her feet kicking, Lloyd ordered Joseph to release Kane twice before Joseph put Kane down and lunged angrily toward Lloyd, who then used pepper spray on Joseph and hit him on the leg with a baton. Lloyd's actions were the subject of student complaints and local media coverage, and demands from activist groups for an investigation. During the investigation, Lloyd was given a desk job and assured that he would not lose his job. However, Drake fired Lloyd. Lloyd sued for wrongful termination. Decide. Explain. See *Lloyd v. Drake University*, 686 N.W.2d 225 (Iowa 2004).

11. In 2009, Mitchell was employed at-will as an anesthesia technician at the University of Kentucky (UK) Chandler Medical Center, while also attending the university as a graduate student. He had a valid license to carry a concealed deadly weapon under Kentucky law. On April 22, 2009, several of Mitchell's coworkers were under the impression that he had a firearm in his employee locker, and they reported this to hospital administration. Hospital administrators contacted the UK police department. When questioned, Mitchell denied having a firearm in his locker. Police and hospital administrators searched Mitchell's locker with his permission but found no weapons. Mitchell informed the police officers that he had a concealed carry license and admitted that he kept a firearm in his vehicle, which was parked on campus. Campus police escorted Mitchell to his car, where he showed them the semiautomatic pistol he had stored in his vehicle. On April 29, 2009, the university terminated Mitchell's employment for violation of its policy prohibiting possession of a deadly weapon on university property or while conducting university business. Mitchell filed suit, alleging termination in violation of public policy. Decide. Explain. See *Mitchell v. University of Kentucky*, 366 S.W.3d 895 (Ky. 2012).

12. A reader sent the following story to a newspaper question and answer forum:

    > I was fired recently by my employer, an architecture firm, immediately after serving for one month on a federal grand jury. From the moment I informed my boss . . . I was harassed . . . and told I was not putting the company first. I was told to get out of my jury service, "or else." . . . I was fired exactly one week after my service ended.[119]

    Was the dismissal of this at-will employee lawful? Explain.

13. Whigham was employed as the Director of Creative Solutions at a marketing, advertising, and public relations company that sought to cultivate an enjoyable work atmosphere. Whigham proposed the idea of a company kickball game to his superior, who instructed him to proceed. Whigham then made the arrangements for a facility rental, the T-shirts, drinks, and snacks with the company funds he was authorized to use. He promoted the event, which took place on a Friday at 3:00 pm, using the company intranet. Roughly half of the company's employees were in attendance. Whigham was seriously injured in the game, and he filed a claim for workers' compensation. The Workers' Compensation Commissioner denied the claim, and Whigham appealed. Decide. Explain. See *Whigham v. Jackson Dawson Communications*, 410 S.C. 131 (2014).

14. Dancers at Club Orleans in Topeka, Kansas, who earned only tips without a regular wage, were subject to house rules that prohibited illicit or illegal conduct and regulated interaction among the dancers and between the dancers and customers. Violations of the rules could result in the dancer being fined or terminated. The rules also set minimum tips for various types of dances, which were enforced. The dancers were allowed to schedule their own shifts. One of the dancers filed an unemployment benefits claim against Milano's, the company that owned Club Orleans. Is the dancer an employee or an independent contractor? Decide. Explain. See *Milano's v. Kansas Department of Labor*, 296 Kan. 497 (2013).

15. Diana Vail, who received medical treatment for migraine headaches, worked at Raybestos, a car parts manufacturer. Raybestos had been giving Vail intermittent leave under FMLA for her migrane headaches since April 2004. From May to September 2005, Vail's requests for FMLA leave due to migraine headaches became more frequent, often falling on weekdays when her husband's mowing company was busiest. Growing suspicious that Vail's requests were not genuine, Raybestos monitored Vail's activities by hiring an off-duty police officer to conduct video surveillance. The officer reported that Vail mowed the lawns of a cemetery, her husband's client, on a day when Vail called prior to her shift to request leave. Vail was subsequently terminated based on her performance of physical labor while on FMLA.

    a. Did Vail's termination violate FMLA? Explain.

    b. Did the employer's surveillance of Vail interfere with her rights under FMLA? Explain. See *Vail v. Raybestos*, 533 F.3d 904 (7th Cir. 2008).

    c. An employee who had been on FMLA leave for incapacitating back pain posted photos to her Facebook page (as did her friend) showing her drinking and dancing over a period of at least eight hours at a local festival. Several of the employees' coworkers who were her Facebook friends told management what they had seen on the employee's page; the employee was fired as a result. The employee sued the employer for retaliation and interference with her FMLA rights. Decide. Explain. See *Jaszczyszyn v. Advantage Health Physician Network*, 504 F. App'x 440 (6th Cir. 2012) (unpublished op.).

16. An employee of Triple B Cleaning in Texas requested personal protective equipment while performing dry cleaning duties. Triple B denied the request. The employee notified the media, and after a reporter contacted the employee's supervisor, the employee was demoted and assigned menial tasks. Following the airing of the employee's complaint by local news, the employee was terminated.

    After being terminated, the employee filed a whistle-blower complaint alleging that Triple B acted in retaliation for contacting the media about unsafe working conditions. OSHA investigated the complaint and determined that Triple B Cleaning's decision to terminate the employee was in violation of the whistle-blower provisions of the Occupational Safety and Health Act.

    The company entered into a consent judgment under which it paid the employee $30,000 for lost wages, agreed to an injunction prohibiting future discrimination, and posted a notice advising its employees of their rights under OSHA's whistle-blower protection provision.

    a. What public policy—or policies—are at issue in this situation?

    b. Did Triple B act ethically? Did the employee act ethically? Explain.

 c. In OSHA's press release regarding the settlement, OSHA Regional Administrator Dean McDaniel stated: "Employees should be free to exercise their rights under the law without fear of retaliation by their employers . . ." What consequences might be expected to accompany the fear of retaliation employees often feel when exercising their rights?

 See OSHA, "U.S. Department of Labor Settles Whistleblower Case Against Commercial and Industrial Steam Cleaning Company in Houston," regional news release, April 6, 2009 [**www.osha.gov/pls/oshaweb/owadisp.show_document? p_table=NEWS_RELEASES&p_id=17720**].

Notes

1. Johnathan D. Glater, "Layoffs Herald a Heyday for Employee Lawsuits," *The New York Times*, January 30, 2009 [**www.nytimes.com/2009/01/31/business/economy/31employ.html**].

2. *CBS v. FCC*, 535 F.3d 167 (3d Cir. 2008).

3. *FCC v. CBS*, 132 S. Ct. 2677 (2012), *cert. denied*.

4. Ellen Huet, "Cleaning Startup Homejoy Shuts Down, Citing Worker Misclassification Lawsuits," *Forbes*, July 17, 2015 [**www.forbes.com/sites/ellenhuet/2015/07/17/cleaning-startup-homejoy-shuts-down-citing-worker-misclassification-lawsuits/#231f7fca78be**]; and James Surowiecki, "Gigs with Benefits," *The New Yorker*, July 6 & 13, 2015 [**www.newyorker.com/magazine/2015/07/06/gigs-with-benefits**].

5. "Voluntary Classification Settlement Program," *Internal Revenue Service*, December 3, 2013 [**www.irs.gov/Businesses/Small-Businesses-&-Self-Employed/Voluntary-Classification-Settlement-Program**].

6. James B. Stewart, "In the Undoing of a CEO, a Puzzle," *The New York Times*, May 18, 2012 [**www.nytimes.com**].

7. Zach Schonbrun and Matt Krupnick, "Manhattan Coach Is Denied South Florida Job after Résumé Check," *The New York Times*, March 26, 2014 [**www.newyorktimes.com**].

8. Martha C. White, "You Won't Believe How Many People Lie on Their Resumes," *Time*, August 13, 2015 [**http://time.com/money/3995981/how-many-people-lie-resumes**].

9. Society for Human Resource Management, "SHRM Finds Fewer Employers Using Background Checks in Hiring," press release, July 19, 2012 [**www.shrm.org/about/pressroom/PressReleases/Pages/BackgroundChecks.aspx**].

10. Sara Murray, "Credit Checks on Job Seekers by Employers Attract Scrutiny," *The Wall Street Journal*, October 21, 2010, p. A5.

11. Chris Dettro, "New Law Bars Most Credit Checks in Hiring," *The State Journal-Register*, January 1, 2011 [**www.sj-r.com/top-stories/x1733657992/New-law-bars-most-credit-checks-in-hiring**].

12. "Number of Employers Passing on Applicants Due to Social Media Posts Continues to Rise, According to New CareerBuilder Survey," *Careerbuilder.com*, June 26, 2014 [**www.careerbuilder.com/share/aboutus/pressreleasesdetail.aspx?sd=6%2f26%2f2014&id=pr829&ed=12%2f31%2f2014**].

13. "1 in 5 Employers Unknowingly Asked an Illegal Question in an Interview, Careerbuilder Finds," *Careerbuilder.com*, April 9, 2015 [**www.careerbuilder.com/share/aboutus/pressreleasesdetail.aspx?sd=4%2f9%2f2015&id=pr877&ed=12%2f31%2f2015**].

14. Ann Howard and Johanna Johnson, White Paper: "If You Were a Tree, What Kind Would You Be?" Development Dimensions International, 2007 [**http://citeseerx.ist.psu.edu/viewdoc/download?doi=10.1.1.368.1170&rep=rep1&type=pdf**].

15. *Bimbo Bakeries v. Botticella*, 613 F.3d 102 (3d Cir. 2010).

16. Kris Maher, "The Jungle," *The Wall Street Journal*, June 8, 2004, p. B4.

17. *Edwards v. Arthur Andersen*, 44 Cal. 4th 937 (Cal. 2008).

18. *Lawlor v. North American Corp. of Illinois*, 983 N.E.2d 414 (Ill. 2012).

19. Amalia D. Kessler, "Stuck in Arbitration," *The New York Times*, March 6, 2012 [**www.nytimes.com**].

20. *Circuit City Stores, Inc. v. Adams*, 532 U.S. 105 (2001).

21. *Nitro-Lift Technologies v. Howard*, 133 S. Ct. 500 (2012).

22. *Equal Employment Opportunity Commission v. Waffle House*, 534 U.S. 279 (2002).

23. 54 Cal. 3d 202, 814 P.2d 1341 (Cal. 1991).

24. Jenny B. Davis, "Still Working after All These Years," *ABA Journal*, October 2001, p. 67.

25. Amanda Hoover, "Minimum Wage for 4 Million Workers Will Go Up in 19 States in 2017," *Business Insider*, December 30, 2016 [**www.businessinsider.com/minimum-wage-for-4-million-workers-will-go-up-in-19-states-in-2017-2016-12**].

26. Arindrajit Dube, T. William Lester, and Michael Reich, "Minimum Wage Effects across State Borders: Estimates Using Contiguous Counties," *The Review of Economics and Statistics*, September 25, 2010.

27. National Employment Law Project, "Living Wage and Minimum Wage," [**www.nelp.org/index.php/content/content_issues/category/living_wage_and_minimum_wage**].

28. Andrew Khouri, "Low-Wage Workers Can't Afford Rent," *Los Angeles Times*, March 25, 2014, p. B2.

29. Ylan Q. Mui, "Wal-Mart to Pay $4.8 Million in Back Wages," *The Washington Post*, May 1, 2012 [**www.washington.post.com**].

30. U.S. Department of Labor, Wage and Hour Division, "Levi Strauss Agrees to Pay More Than $1 Million in Overtime Back Wages to Nearly 600 Employees Following US Labor Department Investigation," press release, March 29, 2011 [**www.dol.gov/opa/media/press/whd/WHD20110379.htm**].

31. *Christopher v. SmithKline Beecham Corp.*, 132 S. Ct. 2156 (2012).

32. American Psychological Association, "Americans Stay Connected to Work on Weekends, Vacation and Even When Out Sick," press release, September 4, 2013 [**www.apa.org/news/press/releases/2013/09/connected-work.aspx**].

33. Jonnelle Marte, "Judge Halts Rule That Would Have Expanded Overtime Pay to Millions of Workers," *The Washington Post*, November 22, 2016 [**www.washingtonpost.com/news/get-there/wp/2016/11/22/judge-halts-federal-rule-that-would-have-expanded-overtime-pay-to-millions-of-workers/?utm_term=.3765f4c06701**].

34. *Archuleta v. Wal-Mart Stores*, 543 F.3d 1226 (10th Cir. 2008).

35. *Kellar v. Summit Seating Inc.*, 664 F.3d 169 (7th Cir. 2011).

36. Testimony before the House Committee on Natural Resources, U.S. House of Representatives, March 16, 2011, The Effect of—A Brother's Statement. Testimony of Christopher K. Jones [**http://naturalresources.house.gov/UploadedFiles/C.JonesTestimony03.16.11.pdf** at p. 2].

37. Janet McConnaughey and Michael Kunzelman, Associated Press, "Manslaughter charges dropped against 2 BP supervisors over 11 rig worker deaths," *US News & World Report*, December 2, 2015 [**www.usnews.com**].

38. Associated Press, "Federal Probe of Fatal Texas Plant Explosion Cites Oversight," *The Waterloo/Cedar Falls Courier*, March 21, 2007, p. B4.

39. Melanie Trottman, "BP to Pay $50.6 Million Fine in Texas Refinery Case," *The Wall Street Journal*, August 12, 2010 [**www.wsj.com**].

40. U.S. Department of Labor, Bureau of Labor Statistics, "Census of Fatal Occupational Injuries Summary, 2012," Economic News Release, August 22, 2013 [**www.bls.gov/news.release/cfoi.nr0.htm**].

41. U.S. Department of Labor, Bureau of Labor Statistics, "Workplace Injury and Illness Summary. 2012," news release, November 7, 2013 [**www.bls.gov/news.release/osh.nr0.htm**].

42. Employer Payment for Personal Protective Equipment, Final Rule, 29 C.F.R. Parts 1910, 1915, 1917, et al.

43. U.S. Department of Labor, "US Department of Labor's OSHA Revises Hazard Communication Standard," news release, March 20, 2012 [**www.osha.gov/pls/oshaweb/owadisp.show_document?p_table=NEWS_RELEASES&p_id=22038**].

44. OSHA, "Prevention of Musculoskeletal Disorders in the Workplace," [**https://www.osha.gov/SLTC/ergonomics/index.html**].

45. Robert J. Grossman, "Making Ergonomics," *HR Magazine*, April 2000, p. 36.

46. Sara Murray, "Guns in the Parking Lot: A Delicate Workplace Issue," *The Wall Street Journal*, October 15, 2013 [**http://online.wsj.com/news/articles/SB100014240527023039839045790955532026750354**].

47. OSHA Letter of Interpretation on Standard 1904, 1904.5(b)(1), February 24, 2009 [**www.osha.gov/pls/oshaweb/owadisp.show_document?p_table=INTERPRETATIONS&p_id=27415**].

48. *Caterpillar Logistics v. Solis*, 674 F.3d 705 (7th Cir. 2012).

49. Roy Maurer, "OSHA's Oversight of Model-Workplace Program Criticized," *Society for Human Resource Management*, December 30, 2013 [**www.shrm.org/hrdisciplines/safetysecurity/articles/Pages/OSHA-Oversight-VPP-Criticized.aspx**].

50. Julia Preston, "Hershey's Packer Is Fined over Its Safety Violations," *The New York Times*, February 21, 2012 [**www.nytimes.com**].

51. OSHA Instruction, Severe Violators Enforcement Program (SVEP) [**www.osha.gov/dep/svep-directive.pdf**].

52. Tom Musick, "OSHA under Trump: A Closer Look," *Safety and Health*, January 29, 2017 [**www.safetyandhealthmagazine.com**].

53. Associated Press, "Stringer's Widow Settles Lawsuit with NFL," *The New York Times*, January 26, 2009 [**www.nytimes.com/2009/01/27/sports/football/27stringerbox.html?ref=koreystringer**]. Kelci Stringer settled her claim against the NFL. Before her lawsuit against football equipment maker Riddell for her husband's death was settled, the federal district court ruled that Riddell had a duty to warn a football player of the risk of heat exhaustion. *Stringer v. NFL*, 749 F. Supp. 2d 680 (S.D. Ohio 2010); and Associated Press, "Lawsuit over Stringer's Death Settled," June 2, 2014 [**www.foxsports.com/nfl/story/Lawsuit-in-Minnesota-Vikings-Korey-Stringer-death-settled-080811**].

54. *Stringer v. Minnesota Vikings*, 705 N.W. 2d 746 (Minn. S. Ct. 2005).

55. Id.

56. *State ex rel. Gross v. Industrial Commission of Ohio*, 115 Ohio St. 3d 249 (2007).

57. Pew Research Center for the People and the Press, "A Portrait of 'Generation Next,'" January 9, 2007, p. 21 [**http://people-press.org/files/legacy-pdf/300.pdf**].

58. See, e.g., Crisis Collection Management's dress code [**www.crisiscollections.com/about/eh/cpa**].

59. Jen Wieczner, "Your Company Wants to Make You Healthy," *The Wall Street Journal*, April 8, 2013 [**http://online.wsj.com/news/articles/SB10001424127887323393304578360252284151 378**].

60. Rachel Emma Silverman, "Suit Claims Wellness Rules Risk Privacy," *The Wall Street Journal*, October 26, 2016, p. A2.

61. *Robert Barbee v. Household Automotive Finance*, 113 Cal. App. 4th 525 (2003).

62. Sue Shellenbarger, "For Office Romance, the Secret's Out," *The Wall Street Journal*, February 10, 2010, p. D1.

63. *City of Ontario v. Quon*, 130 S. Ct. 2619, 177 L. Ed. 2d 216, 227 (2010).

64. *Stengart v. Loving Care Agency, Inc.*, 201 N.J. 300, 308, 990 A.2d 650 (2010).

65. National Conference of State Legislatures, "State Social Media Privacy Laws," January 11, 2017 [**www.ncsl.org/research/telecommunications-and-information-technology/state-laws-prohibiting-access-to-social-media-usernames-and-passwords.aspx**].

66. *Pietrylo v. Hillstone Restaurant Group*, 2009 U.S. Dist. LEXIS 88702 (D.N.J. September 25, 2009) (unpublished op.).

67. Dalia Fahmy, "Aiming for a Drug-Free Workplace," *The New York Times*, May 10, 2007, sec. C, p. 6.

68. U.S. Department of Health and Human Services, Substance Abuse and Mental Health Services Administration (SAMHSA), "Worker Substance Abuse and Workplace Policies and Programs," 2007 [**http://oas.samhsa.gov/work2k7/toc**].

69. George Lenard, "Employers Falling Off Drug Testing Bandwagon," February 28, 2005 [**www.employmentblawg.com/2005**].

70. SAMHSA, "Worker Substance Abuse and Workplace Policies and Programs."

71. "Background Checking: Drug Testing," SHRM Poll, January 22, 2010 [**www.shrm.org/Research/SurveyFindings/Articles/Pages/BackgroundCheckDrugTesting.aspx**].

72. *National Treasury Employees Union v. Von Raab*, 109 S. Ct 1384 (1989).

73. Society for Human Resource Management, "2013 Employee Benefits: An Overview of Employee Benefits Offerings in the U.S." [**www.shrm.org/research/surveyfindings/articles/documents/13-0245%202013_empbenefits_fnl.pdf**].

74. U.S. Department of Labor, *Technical Release 2013-02*, May 8, 2013 [**www.dol.gov/agencies/ebsa/employers-and-advisers/guidance/technical-releases/13-02**].

75. Robert Pear, "Percentage of Americans Lacking Health Coverage Falls Again," *The New York Times*, September 17, 2013 [**www.nytimes.com/2013/09/18/us/percentage-of-americans-lacking-health-coverage-falls-again.html?_r=0**].

76. International Foundation of Employee Benefit Plans, "2013 Employer-Sponsored Health Care: ACA's Impact," May 16, 2013 [**www.ifebp.org/bookstore/aca-2015/Pages/default.aspx**].

77. Ibid.

78. *National Federation of Independent Business v. Sebelius*, 132 S. Ct. 2566 (2012).

79. U.S. Department of Labor Fact Sheet, "COBRA Premium Reduction," April 26, 2010 [**www.dol.gov/ebsa/newsroom/fscobrapremiumreduction.html**].

80. National Alliance of Caregiving and AARP, "Caregiving in the U.S. 2009" [**www.aarp.org/relationships/caregiving/info-12-2009/caregiving_09.html**].

81. U.S. Department of Labor, "Military Family Leave Provisions of the FMLA: Frequently Asked Questions and Answers" [**www.dol.gov/whd/fmla/finalrule/MilitaryFAQs.pdf**].

82. U.S. Department of Labor, "Final Rule to Revise the Definition of 'Spouse' Under the FMLA," February 25, 2015 [**www.dol.gov/whd/fmla/spouse**].

83. Abt Associates, "Family and Medical Leave in 2012: Technical Report," September 7, 2012 [**www.dol.gov/asp/evaluation/fmla/FMLA-2012-Technical-Report.pdf**].

84. Ibid.

85. National Conference of State Legislatures, "State Family Medical Leave and Parental Leave Laws," December 2013 [**www.ncsl.org/research/labor-and-employment/state-family-and-medical-leave-laws.aspx**].

86. Ibid.

87. Patt Johnson, "Getting the Boot," *The Des Moines Register*, May 4, 2003, p. 1D.

88. Zachary Malinowski, "Unemployment Benefits Denied for Fired Cranston Cop," *The Providence Journal* blog, *www.projo.com*, July 26, 2010 [**http://newsblog.projo.com/2010/07/unemployment-benefits-denied-f.html**].

89. Clark Kauffman, "Diary of a Goof-Off: No Work, No Pay," *The Des Moines Register*, January 19, 2007, p. 1A.

90. Joint Economic Committee, U.S. Congress, "The Economic Case for Continuing Federal Unemployment Insurance," January 2014 [**www.jec.senate.gov/public/?a=Files.Serve&File_id=cf231ec5-d46e-471e-bac7-63c8bb79fb9c**].

91. Employee Benefit Research Institute, "EBRI's 2014 Retirement Confidence Survey: Confidence Rebounds—for Those with Retirement Plans," March 18, 2014 [**www.ebri.org/pdf/surveys/rcs/2014/PR1066.RCS.18Mar14.pdf**].

92. Ibid.

93. Mark Trumbull, "Reform Erodes the Future of US Pensions," *The Christian Science Monitor*, August 18, 2006 [**www.csmonitor.com/2006/0818/p02s02-usec.html**].

94. U.S. Department of Labor, "Fact Sheet: Cash Balance Pension Plans," May 2003 [**www.dol.gov/ebsa/newsroom/fscashbalanceplans.html**].

95. Marc Lifsher, "Pension Funds Seriously Underfunded," *Los Angeles Times*, July 17, 2012 [**http://articles.latimes.com/2012/jul/17/business/la-fi-pension-shortfalls-20120718**].

96. U.S. Department of Labor, "Final Rule to Improve Transparency of Fees and Expenses to Workers in 401(k)-Type Retirement Plans," February 2012 [**www.dol.gov/ebsa/newsroom/fsparticipantfeerule.html**].

97. *LaRue v. DeWolff, Boberg & Associates, Inc.*, 128 S. Ct. 1020 (2008); and *Conkright v. Frommert*, 130 S. Ct. 1640 (2010).

98. *Cigna Corp. v. Amara*, 131 S. Ct. 1866 (2011); and *Amara v. Cigna Corp.*, 925 F. Supp. 2d 242 (D. Conn. 2012).

99. *Wagenseller v. Scottsdale Memorial Hospital*, 710 P.2d 1025 (Ariz. 1985).

100. *Rubenstein v. Huntington Mortgage Company*, N.J. Sup. Ct., App. Div. (1997). For a journalistic account of the case, see Pitney, Hardin, Kipp, and Szuch, "Employers Must Be Cautious about Failing to Disclose Business Plans That Will Affect the Jobs of New Hires," *New Jersey Employment Law Letter*, September 1997.

101. Arizona State Senate, "Fact Sheet for SB 1070," January 15, 2010 [**www.azleg.gov/legtext/49leg/2r/summary/s.1070pshs.doc.htm**].

102. Pew Research Center for the People and the Press, "Public Supports Arizona Immigration Law," May 12, 2010 [**http://pewresearch.org/pubs/1591/public-support-arizona-immigration-law-poll**].

103. *Arizona v. United States*, 132 S. Ct. 2492 (2012).

104. David G. Savage, "Supreme Court Won't Revive Alabama Immigration Law," April 29, 2013 [**http://articles.latimes.com/2013/apr/29/nation/la-na-court-immigration-20130430**].

105. Drew Desilver, "Immigrants Don't Make up a Majority of Workers in Any U.S. Industry," *Pew Research Center*, March 16, 2017 [**www.pewresearch.org/fact-tank/2017/03/16/immigrants-dont-make-up-a-majority-of-workers-in-any-u-s-industry**].

106. Don Lee, "Trump's Immigration Plan Faces Obstacles," *Los Angeles Times*, March 20, 2017, p. A1.

107. Desilver, "Immigrants Don't Make up a Majority of Workers in Any U.S. Industry."

108. Ibid.

109. Lee, "Trump's Immigration Plan Faces Obstacles."

110. Ibid.

111. Lawrence Harrison, "The US Should Think Long and Hard about the High Numbers of Latino Immigrants," *The Christian Science Monitor,* May 28, 2009 [**www.csmonitor.com**].

112. Sara Ashley O'Brien, "H-1B Visa Applications Decline for First Time in 5 Years," *Money.CNN.com*, April 17, 2017 [**http://money.cnn.com/2017/04/17/technology/h-1b-visa-applications/index.html**].

113. Glenn Thrush, Nick Wingfield, and Vindu Goel, "Trump Signs Order That Could Lead to Curbs on Foreign Workers," April 18, 2017 [**www.nytimes.com/2017/04/18/us/politics/executive-order-hire-buy-american-h1b-visa-trump.html?_r=0**].

114. Miriam Jordan, "Policing Illegal Hires Puts Some Employers in a Bind," *The Wall Street Journal*, July 15, 2010, p. A5.

115. U.S. Department of Justice, "Justice Department Resolves Citizenship Status Discrimination Charge against California Employer," press release, March 8, 2011 [**www.justice.gov/opa/pr/2011/March/11-crt-294.html**].

116. Jeffrey S. Passel, D'vera Cohn, and Ana Gonzalez-Barrera, "Population Decline of Unauthorized Immigrants Stalls, May Have Reversed," *Pew Research Hispanic Trends Project*, September 23, 2013 [**www.pewhispanic.org/2013/09/23/population-decline-of-unauthorized-immigrants-stalls-may-have-reversed**].

117. U.S. Citizenship and Immigration Services, "Half a Million Companies Now Participate in E-Verify," January 23, 2014 [**www.uscis.gov/news/news-releases/half-million-companies-now-participate-e-verify-0**].

118. Bruce A. Morrison and Paul Donnelly, "A Simple Way to Keep Illegal Immigrants from Getting Jobs," *The Washington Post*, May 1, 2010, p. A15.

119. *The Washington Post*, "The Boss Can't Fire You for Doing Your Civic Duty," *The Waterloo/Cedar Falls Courier,* May 26, 1999, p. C8.

CHAPTER THIRTEEN

Employment Law II: Discrimination

After completing this chapter, students will be able to fulfill the following learning objectives:

13-1. Discuss the purpose and history of legal protections against employment discrimination.

13-2. Compare and contrast the protections offered under the federal statutes prohibiting employment discrimination: Title VII of the Civil Rights Act of 1964, the Equal Pay Act, the Americans with Disabilities Act, and the Age Discrimination in Employment Act.

13-3. Explain the role of the Equal Employment Opportunity Commission (EEOC) in enforcing federal statutes prohibiting employment discrimination.

13-4. Identify remedies available to victims of unlawful employment discrimination.

13-5. Distinguish the primary forms of employment discrimination analysis: disparate treatment and disparate impact.

13-6. Identify when unlawful sexual harassment has occurred.

13-7. Identify when employers are liable for unlawful sexual harassment.

13-8. Describe protections against retaliation offered under the federal statutes prohibiting employment discrimination.

13-9. Discuss the purposes and development of affirmative action.

13-10. Describe the concept of reasonable accommodation as applied to religious- and disability-based discrimination claims.

13-11. Discuss the current status of protections against sexual orientation discrimination in the workplace.

Introduction

Prior to the 2015 Supreme Court decision of *EEOC v. Abercrombie & Fitch Stores, Inc.,*[1] Abercrombie & Fitch (A & F), the clothing retailer, had been accused of maintaining a virtually all-white image by discriminating in recruiting, hiring, and promoting women and minorities. A & F settled a nationwide class-action lawsuit in 2005 that claimed A & F disproportionately assigned minority employees to stockrooms and other jobs out of the public eye, while white employees were conspicuously on display as a means of projecting the company's "clean-cut, classic" image. Along with paying a monetary settlement, A & F was required to promote diversity in its workforce. A & F also agreed to manifest a more diverse image in its marketing materials such as store posters.[2]

The 2015 Supreme Court decision focused on A &F's refusal to hire based on the applicant's hijab. The Supreme Court reversed a federal appellate court's ruling that A & F's "Look Policy" was necessary to maintain its "classic East Coast collegiate style of clothing."[3]

Questions

1. A & F defenders have argued that the clothier has the right to promote an image of its choice as a means of making a profit.

    a. The law aside, is A & F simply wrong to project an image that, however it is labeled, may be described as a "white image" if, indeed, it does so? Explain.

    b. Would it be wrong for a store promoting a "hip hop" image to refuse to hire an applicant because she wears a hijab? How about if that store refused to hire a white applicant based on race? Explain.

    a. What if a store selling hunting and fishing gear refused to hire African American applicants for cashier and sales associate positions—would that be wrong? Explain.

2. A college student decided not to apply for a job at A & F because she didn't feel "appropriate" for the job after she observed all of the store's "tall, skinny white girls." The college student stated that, in the long run, hiring only employees with that particular look will "hurt A & F."[4]

    a. Do you think the market would have "punished" A & F, even if the law had not intervened? Explain.

Continuing Discrimination   The ethical issues raised by Abercrombie & Fitch's hiring and staffing practices highlight the challenges of enforcing legal protections against employment discrimination, often referred to as Equal Employment Opportunity (EEO) laws.

Employers compare, distinguish, and choose among applicants and employees based on many factors. However, EEO laws forbid those considerations that would undermine equal employment opportunity. Prohibited factors, also called "protected categories" or "protected classes," include an applicant's or employee's race, color, and gender, among other characteristics. Generally, EEO laws protect all employees and are not restricted to certain groups such as women or racial minorities.

Do we still need EEO laws in the United States? Consider a recent study in which black and white men applied for the same entry-level jobs with nearly identical résumés. Some of the white men were instructed to tell the employer that they had felony drug convictions. Who would receive the employer's call— the white ex-convict or the black with no criminal record? Most likely, the study found, the white applicant with the criminal record

> Most likely, the white applicant would be preferred.

would be preferred over the black applicant with no criminal record.[5] As diversity grows in the United States, EEO laws may serve to support and sustain a more inclusive and, ultimately, more productive workplace.[6]

Millennials

The 2015 U.S. Census data revealed that nearly 38 percent of Americans reported their race and ethnicity as "minority"; that is, something other than non-Hispanic white. Further, the "Millennials" are the most diverse generation in history. A recent MTV poll of 14- to 24-year-olds found that most millennials believe their generation is "post-racial" and that racism will become less of an issue as they get older.

Source: Josh Sanburn, "U.S. Steps Closer to a Future Where Minorities Are the Majority," *Time,* June 25, 2015 [**http://time.com**]; and Jamelle Bouie, "Why Do Millennials Not Understand Racism?" *Slate,* May 2014 [**www.slate.com**].

Part One—Employment Discrimination: The Foundation in Law

LO 13-1
Discuss the purpose and history of legal protections against employment discrimination.

LO 13-2
Compare and contrast the protections offered under the federal statutes prohibiting employment discrimination: Title VII of the Civil Rights Act of 1964, the Equal Pay Act, the Americans with Disabilities Act, and the Age Discrimination in Employment Act.

History

In the Reconstruction Era following the Civil War, Congress passed the Civil Rights Act of 1866 to provide the newly freed black slaves with the same right to make and enforce contracts as was enjoyed by white citizens. This law still exists today, with updated language emphasizing its protection against racial discrimination. The Civil Rights Act of 1866 has been interpreted to forbid discrimination on the basis of race in employment, which is essentially a contractual relationship.

However, this legal protection did not prevent discriminatory practices in housing, education, business, and employment. In 1941, A. Philip Randolph, president of the predominantly black Brotherhood of Sleeping Car Porters, organized black leaders who threatened a massive march in Washington, DC, protesting employment discrimination. In response, President Franklin Roosevelt issued Executive Order 8802, which created a Fair Employment Practice Committee. Congress limited the committee's budget, but Roosevelt's action was a striking step for the federal government in addressing racial discrimination.

The next big step toward racial equality was the landmark *Brown v. Board of Education*[7] decision in 1954, in which the Supreme Court forbade "separate but equal" schools. Following *Brown,* citizens engaged in sit-ins, freedom rides, boycotts, and the like to press claims for racial equality. It was a turbulent, sometimes violent, era, but those activities were critical ingredients in subsequent advances for the black population. With the passage of the 1964 Civil Rights Act, the campaign against discrimination solidified as one of the most energetic and influential social movements in American history.[8] The Civil Rights Act of 1964 changed American life by forbidding discrimination in education, housing, public accommodation, and, perhaps most importantly, employment. [For the National Civil Rights Museum, see **www.civilrightsmuseum.org**].

Civil Rights Act of 1964

Reflecting the increased diversity of the U.S. workforce, in which women had gone beyond traditional roles and where immigrants from around the world could be found, Title VII of the Civil Rights Act of 1964 (Title VII) marked a new era in employment practices. Title VII forbids discrimination in employment on the basis of race, color, religion, sex, or national origin. Relying on its authority to regulate commerce, Congress applied Title VII to private-sector employers with 15 or more employees, employment agencies, labor unions with 15 or more members as well as those operating a hiring hall, state and local governments, and most of the federal government. Private clubs are exempt from Title VII, and religious organizations may discriminate in employment on the basis of religion. Broadly, Title VII forbids discrimination in hiring, firing, and all aspects of the employment relationship.

Other Legislation and Orders

Title VII is the core of EEO laws in the United States. Other federal statutes, such as the Americans with Disabilities Act of 1990 (ADA) and its 2008 amendments (ADAAA), and the Age Discrimination in Employment Act of 1967 (ADEA), have established additional protected categories. The Equal Pay Act of 1963 and the Civil Rights Act of 1991 address particular issues in employment discrimination. For example, the Civil Rights Act of 1991 provides that U.S. citizens working abroad for American-owned or American-controlled companies are protected from discrimination under Title VII and the ADA unless such protection would require the employer to violate the laws of its host nation. Later in this chapter, these federal laws will be discussed further.

The Constitution

As explained in Chapter 5, the federal Constitution, among other purposes, protects us from wrongful government action. The Fourteenth Amendment to the Constitution provides that no state shall deny to any person life, liberty, or property without *due process of law* or deny him or her the *equal protection of the laws*. Thus, citizens are protected from discrimination via state government action. Similarly, the Supreme Court has interpreted the Due Process Clause of the Fifth Amendment ("nor shall any person . . . be deprived of life, liberty, or property, without due process of law") to forbid discrimination by the federal government.

Stopping Discrimination through Corporate Pledges

In 2014, then-President Obama secured voluntary pledges from 300 U.S. companies, including Walt Disney, Apple, Gap, and eBay, to not discriminate against applicants who are currently unemployed. In seeking employment, those who are jobless, particularly those who have been unemployed for a significant period of time, often face discrimination based on their employment status. Legislative attempts to ban such discriminatory practices have met with limited success and offer narrow protections against express exclusions of the unemployed in help-wanted ads.

Questions

1. What are the advantages of the corporate pledge approach to protecting against emerging areas of discrimination not addressed through statutory protections? Explain.

2. Assume that a job applicant at one of the U.S. companies that had pledged not to discriminate against the unemployed was rejected because she has been jobless for over two years. Would the applicant have any recourse? Explain.

Sources: Ben Leubsdorf, "Obama Tries New Tack for Long-Term Jobless," *The Wall Street Journal,* January 28, 2014 [**http://online.wsj.com/news/articles/SB10001424052702303277704579347082417660564**]; and Kathleen Hennessey, "CEOs Pledge Not to Discriminate Against Long-Term Unemployed," *Los Angeles Times,* January 31, 2014 [**http://articles.latimes.com/2014/jan/31/business/la-fi-obama-jobs-20140201**].

Employment Discrimination Enforcement

EEOC and State Fair Employment Practice Agencies

LO 13-3

Explain the role of the Equal Employment Opportunity Commission (EEOC) in enforcing federal statutes prohibiting employment discrimination.

The Equal Employment Opportunity Commission (EEOC), an independent federal agency, has the authority to issue regulations and guidelines as well as to receive, initiate, and investigate charges of discrimination against employers covered by federal antidiscrimination statutes such as Title VII. [See the Equal Employment Opportunity Commission's website at **www/eeoc.gov**].

State fair employment practices legislation often mirrors or expands the antidiscrimination protections found in federal statutes such as Title VII. State fair employment practice agencies may serve the same function as the EEOC in enforcing these laws. [For an example, see California Department of Fair Employment and Housing's website at **www. dfeh.ca.gov**]. Municipal ordinances may also address employment discrimination, enforced by a particular branch of the city's government. [For the San Francisco Human Rights Commission, see **http://sf-hrc.org/**].

Litigation

The first step in lawsuits claiming employment discrimination is not taken in a courthouse. A victim of employment discrimination, usually referred to as the "charging party," will file a complaint within a limited period of time with either the EEOC or, where applicable, the local or state fair employment practices agency.

What if the allegedly discriminatory act is ongoing rather than an incident occurring on a certain date—at what moment does the clock start ticking on the victim's time to file an EEOC complaint? After 19 years as a Goodyear employee, Lily Ledbetter discovered that her wages were much lower than those of her male coworkers. She filed an EEOC complaint alleging gender discrimination and later won a jury verdict for back pay and punitive damages. In 2007, the U.S. Supreme Court held in *Ledbetter v. Goodyear Tire & Rubber Co.* that Ledbetter's claim should have been brought within 180 days of the first paycheck at issue.[9] Congress reacted to *Ledbetter* by passing The Lily Ledbetter Fair Pay Act of 2009, signed into law by President Obama in the first days of his administration. Under this statute, each paycheck issued by an employer engaged in pay discrimination is a discriminatory act, meaning that the clock resets on potential discrimination claim each time the affected employee is paid, with a two-year cap on back-pay damages.[10]

Typically, the EEOC will refer the charging party and employer to its free mediation program. If mediation does not resolve the complaint, then the EEOC will investigate. If the investigation reveals that there is reasonable cause to believe that discrimination has occurred, the EEOC will invite the parties to engage in conciliation to resolve the matter. If conciliation fails, the EEOC either files a civil suit on behalf of the charging party or issues a "right to sue" letter. The "right to sue" letter allows the party who filed the EEOC complaint to file a lawsuit, but also removes the EEOC from the matter. A 2015 Supreme Court decision allows for judicial review of whether the EEOC satisfied its statutory obligation to attempt conciliation before it filed a lawsuit; however, this review is limited to whether the EEOC informed the employer about the discrimination complaint and whether the EEOC tried to engage the employer in "some form of discussion."[11]

Many potential employment discrimination lawsuits no longer reach the judicial system because they are resolved in arbitration. Many businesses are now including binding arbitration agreements in job offers, requiring job seekers, as a condition of employment, to waive the right to trial and turn any grievance over to arbitration. A series of U.S. Supreme Court decisions has firmly established the enforceability of those agreements when the arbitration process provided for is legitimate and fair. The Court also has ruled, however, that the EEOC retains its right to sue on behalf of an employee even if the worker has signed away his or her own rights.[12]

Despite headline-grabbing settlements in discrimination cases, a recent American Bar Foundation (ABF) study found that discrimination lawsuits rarely make it to trial and usually end with a modest settlement. If these cases go to court, the plaintiffs have only a one-in-three chance of winning.[13] Another ABF study found that although plaintiffs begin the process optimistically, they rarely get a final ruling based on the substantive merits of a case, causing them to view employment litigation as favoring defendant-employers. On the other hand, defendant-employers view the process as unfair because the employee has the power to initiate what they view as a "meritless" suit requiring their response.[14]

Remedies

LO 13-4

Identify remedies available to victims of unlawful employment discrimination.

Recognizing the gravity and nature of injuries caused by intentional discrimination in the workplace, Congress expanded the remedies available for such injury under Title VII and the Americans with Disabilities Act (ADA) to include compensatory damages as well as punitive damages in some cases. Compensatory damages may be sought to redress, for example, emotional pain and suffering, but combined compensatory and punitive damages are capped at $50,000 to $300,000, depending on the size of the employer's workforce. Damages are not capped for front pay (awarded for future earnings) or in cases of intentional discrimination based on race. The EEOC often negotiates consent decrees that may require employers to adopt new procedures to correct wrongful practices. [For the Civil Rights Division of the U.S. Justice Department, see **www.justice. gov/crt/**].

EEOC's Systemic Enforcement

Under its Strategic Plan for FY 2012–2016, the EEOC made "systemic enforcement" a priority. At the same time, a federal appellate court restricted the EEOC's systemic enforcement efforts by ruling that the EEOC would have to determine the individuals in a class action against an employer before litigation, not during discovery (see Chapter 4). The employer should then have the opportunity to resolve the matter through the EEOC's conciliation process. The EEOC continues to seek plaintiffs to join its age discrimination claim against Texas Roadhouse, a restaurant chain serving "dinner only," which alleges that managers were instructed to hire younger workers. Texas Roadhouse asserts that the company has spent millions defending against the EEOC's efforts. The EEOC defends its action as a strategic use of its limited resources to provide relief not just for one person, but for those "coming down the pipeline." The one older worker, a hostess in the White Marsh, Maryland, Texas Roadhouse who is the general manager's mother, said she believed those her age would prefer daytime work, so don't apply for jobs there.

Questions

1. Should the EEOC be able to investigate and bring an enforcement action against an employer suspected of a systemic pattern of discrimination without a specific individual complaint? Explain.

2. Do you agree with the appellate court that the EEOC should be required to always identify individual victims of a potentially discriminatory employment practice prior to bringing a class-action lawsuit against the employer? How might this impact enforcement of antidiscrimination laws? Explain.

Sources: EEOC v. CRST Van Expedited, 670 F.3d 897 (8th Cir. 2012); Lydia DePillis, "The Government's Anti-Discrimination Watchdog Is Getting More Aggressive—and Employers Are Fighting Back," *The Washington Post*, November 13, 2015; and EEOC, Texas Roadhouse Litigation [**https://www.eeoc.gov/eeoc/litigation/texas_roadhouse.cfm**].

Part Two—"Types of Discrimination"

There are three basic types of illegal employment discrimination: disparate treatment, disparate impact, and harassment. In addition, Title VII and other anti-employment discrimination statutes prohibit *retaliation* for opposing an employment practice reasonably believed to be discriminatory, or for participating in a claim of employment discrimination. Plaintiffs may raise claims of more than one type of employment discrimination, as well as retaliation, against an employer.

Disparate Treatment and Disparate Impact

Title VII of the 1964 Civil Rights Act provides two primary theories of recovery for individuals: disparate treatment and disparate impact (sometimes labeled *adverse impact*). A disparate treatment claim addresses *intentional* discrimination by an employer who has

LO 13-5

Distinguish the primary forms of employment discrimination analysis: disparate treatment and disparate impact.

purposefully treated an employee or applicant less favorably because of his or her race, color, religion, national origin, gender, or membership in a group under another protected category. Disparate impact claims arise from "unintentional" discrimination where an employment practice appearing to be neutral has the effect of adversely impacting a particular group under a protected category more than it impacts other groups.

As we turn now to a close look at disparate treatment and disparate impact analysis, keep in mind the various constitutional, statutory, and executive order protections just outlined.

Disparate Treatment

Employees or applicants making claims of disparate treatment must prove their employers' intent to discriminate with either direct or indirect evidence. For example, a company president's remarks that "women were simply 'not tough enough' to supervise collections and that it was a 'man's job'" (even if tempered by his statement that "I felt that a woman was not competent enough to do this job, but I think maybe you're showing me that you can do it") may constitute *direct evidence* of intentional sex discrimination, as a federal court of appeals found.[15] A warehouse company seeking truck loaders might send a letter to an employment agency stating: "Women would not be welcome as applicants for this physically taxing job." That letter could be used as direct evidence of the employer's intent to treat female applicants adversely compared with male applicants. More often, however, disparate treatment claims rely on *indirect evidence* in accord with the following test, using an applicant's rejection as an example:

1. **Plaintiff's (employee's) *prima facie* case** (sufficient to be presumed true unless proven otherwise) is confirmed by proving each of the following ingredients:
   a. Plaintiff belongs to a protected class.
   b. Plaintiff applied for a job for which the defendant was seeking applicants.
   c. Plaintiff was qualified for the job.
   d. Plaintiff was denied the job.
   e. The position remained open, and the employer continued to seek applicants.
2. **Defendant's (employer's) case.** If the plaintiff builds a successful *prima facie* case, the defendant must "articulate some *legitimate, nondiscriminatory reason* for the employee's rejection" (e.g., greater work experience). However, the defendant need not prove that its decision not to hire the plaintiff was, in fact, based on that legitimate, nondiscriminatory reason. The defendant simply must raise a legitimate issue of fact disputing the plaintiff's discrimination claim.
3. **Plaintiff's response.** Assuming the defendant was successful in presenting a legitimate, nondiscriminatory reason for its action, the plaintiff must show that the reason offered by the defendant was false and thus was merely a *pretext* to hide discrimination. [For an overview of disparate treatment analysis, see **www.hr-guide.com/data/ G701.htm**].

Questions

Matthews, an African American woman, applied for a job as Economic Support Specialist in Waukesha County, Wisconsin. She was not hired. The applicants were separated into four groups based on their prior job experience; individuals with job experience that was most directly related to the open position were placed in Group 1, and only individuals in Group 1 were interviewed. The person hired was from that group. Matthews had been placed in Group 4. Matthews brought a Title VII disparate treatment claim alleging she was not hired because of her race.

1. If you were Matthews' attorney, how would you argue Matthews' case? What evidence would you want to present? Explain. See *Matthews v. Waukesha County,* 759 F.3d 821 (7th Cir. 2014).

2. Stalter, an African American, was fired for theft after working at a Walmart loading dock for four months. While eating a handful of taco chips from an open bag on the countertop in the break room, a coworker entered the room, took the bag from Stalter, and placed it in her locker. Stalter later apologized to her and offered to buy a new bag. She said the incident was "no big deal" and told him to "forget about it." Management then investigated, concluded Stalter had stolen the chips, and fired him. Stalter sued, claiming his termination was race based. What questions would you have if you were on the jury? Explain. See *Stalter v. Wal-Mart Stores,* 195 F.3d 285 (7th Cir. 1999).

Spousal Discrimination?

Craig Holcomb, a white male and assistant coach for the Iona College men's basketball team, married an African American woman. While the team enjoyed a successful record for several years, its lackluster performance and player misconduct between 2001 and 2004 led to changes in the Iona basketball program, including the dismissal of Holcomb and an African American assistant coach. Another white assistant coach, who was not engaged in an interracial relationship, was not fired. Holcomb brought a Title VII claim asserting that he had been discharged because his wife is African American. Holcomb alleged that Iona College's athletic director had made several racist and derogatory remarks about African Americans on the basketball team and had derided Holcomb's decision to marry his wife, whom he referred to as "Aunt Jemima." How would you rule on this case? Explain.

Source: Holcomb v. Iona College, 521 F.3d 130 (2d Cir. 2008).

Disparate Impact

Disparate impact analysis involves situations in which employers use legitimate employment standards that, despite their apparent neutrality, impose a heavier burden on a protected class than on other employees. For example, a preemployment test, offered with the best of intentions and constructed to be a fair measurement device, may disproportionately exclude members of a protected class and thus be unacceptable (barring an effective defense). Alternatively, an employer surreptitiously seeking to discriminate may establish an apparently neutral, superficially valid employment test that has the effect of achieving the employer's discrimination goal. For example, a tavern might require its bouncer to be at least 6 feet 2 inches tall. Generally, height is not a protected class. However, the tavern's requirement will likely disproportionately exclude women. Was this the tavern's intent? Most likely it was not, but disparate impact does not require a showing of intent to discriminate.

The Test

Disparate impact analysis requires the following:

1. The plaintiff/employee must identify the *specific employment practice or policy* (such as test score, skill, or height) that caused the alleged disparate impact on the protected class.

2. The plaintiff must prove (often with statistical evidence) that the protected class is suffering an *adverse or disproportionate impact* caused by the employment practice or policy in question. The statistical analysis to establish a disparate impact (against black job applicants, for example) must be based on a comparison of the racial composition of the group of persons actually holding the jobs in question versus the racial composition of the *job-qualified* population in the relevant labor market.

3. Assuming a *prima facie* case is established in steps 1 and 2, the plaintiff/employee wins unless the defendant/employer demonstrates that the employment practice/policy is (a) *job related* and (b) *consistent with business necessity*. In the bouncer example above, the tavern would have to demonstrate that the height and weight requirements were related to the job in accordance with the needs of taverns.

4. If the defendant/employer succeeds in demonstrating job relatedness and business necessity, the employer wins unless the plaintiff/employee demonstrates that *an alternative, less discriminatory business practice is available and that the employer refuses to adopt it.*

The following classic case examines disparate impact analysis.

LEGAL BRIEFCASE

Griggs v. Duke Power Co.
401 U.S. 424 (1971)

Chief Justice Burger

We granted the writ in this case to resolve the question whether an employer is prohibited by the Civil Rights Act of 1964, Title VII, from requiring a high school education or passing of a standardized general intelligence test as a condition of employment in or transfer to jobs when (a) neither standard is shown to be significantly related to successful job performance, (b) both requirements operate to disqualify Negroes at a substantially higher rate than white applicants, and (c) the jobs in question formerly had been filled only by white employees as part of a longstanding practice of giving preference to whites.

Congress provided, in Title VII of the Civil Rights Act of 1964, for class actions for enforcement of provisions of the Act and this proceeding was brought by a group of incumbent Negro employees against Duke Power Company. . . .

The district court found that prior to July 2, 1965, the effective date of the Civil Rights Act of 1964, the company openly discriminated on the basis of race in the hiring and assigning of employees at its Dan River plant. The plant was organized into five operating departments: (1) Labor, (2) Coal Handling, (3) Operations, (4) Maintenance, and (5) Laboratory and Test. Negroes were employed only in the Labor Department where the highest-paying jobs paid less than the lowest-paying jobs in the other four "operating" departments in which only whites were employed. Promotions were normally made within each department on the basis of job seniority. Transferees into a department usually began in the lowest position.

In 1955 the company instituted a policy of requiring a high school education for initial assignment to any department except Labor, and for transfer from the Coal Handling to any "inside" department (Operations, Maintenance, or Laboratory). When the company abandoned its policy of restricting Negroes to the Labor Department in 1965, completion of high school also was made a prerequisite to transfer from Labor to any other department. From the time the high school requirement was instituted to the time of trial, however, white employees hired before the time of the high school education requirement continued to perform satisfactorily and achieve promotions in the "operating" departments. Findings on this score are not challenged.

The company added a further requirement for new employees on July 2, 1965, the date on which Title VII became effective. To qualify for placement in any but the Labor Department it became necessary to register satisfactory scores on two professionally prepared aptitude tests, as well as to have a high school education. Completion of high school alone continued to render employees eligible for transfer to the four desirable departments from which Negroes had been excluded if the incumbent had been employed prior to the time of the new requirement. In September 1965 the company began to permit incumbent employees who lacked a high school education to qualify for transfer from Labor or Coal Handling to an "inside" job by passing two tests—the Wonderlic Personnel Test, which purports to measure general intelligence, and the Bennett Mechanical Comprehension Test. Neither was directed or intended to measure the ability to learn to perform a particular job or category of jobs. The requisite scores used for both initial hiring and transfer approximated the national median for high school graduates.

The District Court had found that while the company previously followed a policy of overt racial discrimination in a period prior to the Act, such conduct had ceased. The District Court also concluded that Title VII was intended to be prospective only and, consequently, the impact of prior inequities was beyond the reach of corrective action authorized by the Act.

. . . The Court of Appeals concluded there was no violation of the Act.

* * * * *

The objective of Congress in the enactment of Title VII is plain from the language of the statute. It was to achieve equality of employment opportunities and remove barriers that have operated in the past to favor an identifiable group of white employees over other employees. Under the Act, practices, procedures, or tests neutral on their face, and even neutral in terms of intent, cannot be maintained if they operate to "freeze" the status quo of prior discriminatory employment practices.

The Court of Appeals' opinion, and the partial dissent, agreed that, on the record in the present case, "whites register far better on the company's alternative requirements" than Negroes. This consequence would appear to be directly traceable to race. Basic intelligence must have the means of articulation to manifest itself fairly in a testing process. Because they are Negroes, petitioners have long received inferior education in segregated schools.

. . . Congress did not intend by Title VII, however, to guarantee a job to every person regardless of qualifications. In short, the Act does not command that any person be hired simply because he was formerly the subject of discrimination, or because he is a member of a minority group. Discriminatory preference for any group, minority or majority, is precisely and only what Congress has proscribed. . . .

. . . The Act proscribes not only overt discrimination but also practices that are fair in form, but discriminatory in operation. The touchstone is business necessity. If an employment practice which operates to exclude Negroes cannot be shown to be related to job performance, the practice is prohibited.

On the record before us, neither the high school completion requirement nor the general intelligence test is shown to bear a demonstrable relationship to successful performance of the jobs for which it was used. Both were adopted, as the Court of Appeals noted, without meaningful study of their relationship to job-performance ability. Rather, a vice president of the company testified, the requirements were instituted on the company's judgment that they generally would improve the overall quality of the workforce.

The evidence, however, shows that employees who have not completed high school or taken the tests have continued to perform satisfactorily and make progress in departments for which the high school and test criteria are not used. . . .

The Court of Appeals held that the company had adopted the diploma and test requirements without any "intention to discriminate against Negro employees." We do not suggest that either the District Court or the Court of Appeals erred in examining the employer's intent; but good intent or absence of discriminatory intent does not redeem employment procedures or testing mechanisms that operate as "built-in headwinds" for minority groups and are unrelated to measuring job capability.

* * * * *

The facts of this case demonstrate the inadequacy of broad and general testing devices as well as the infirmity of using diplomas or degrees as fixed measures of capability. . . .

The company contends that its general intelligence tests are specifically permitted by Section 703(h) of the Act. That section authorizes the use of "any professionally developed ability test" that is not "designed, intended *or used* to discriminate because of race. . . ." (Emphasis added.)

The Equal Employment Opportunity Commission, having enforcement responsibility, has issued guidelines interpreting Section 703(h) to permit only the use of job-related tests. The administrative interpretation of the Act by the enforcing agency is entitled to great deference. Since the Act and its legislative history support the commission's construction, this affords good reason to treat the guidelines as expressing the will of Congress.

. . . From the sum of the legislative history relevant in this case, the conclusion is inescapable that the EEOC's construction of Section 703(h) to require that employment tests be job related comports with congressional intent.

Nothing in the Act precludes the use of testing or measuring procedures; obviously they are useful. What Congress has forbidden is giving these devices and mechanisms controlling force unless they are demonstrably a reasonable measure of job performance. Congress has not commanded that the less qualified be preferred over the better qualified simply because of minority origins. Far from disparaging job qualifications as such, Congress has made such qualifications the controlling factor, so that race, religion, nationality, and sex become irrelevant. What Congress has commanded is that any tests used must measure the person for the job and not the person in the abstract.

The judgment of the Court of Appeals is . . . reversed.

Questions

1. According to the Supreme Court, what was Congress's objective in enacting Title VII?

2. Had Duke Power been able to establish that its reasons for adopting the diploma and test standards were entirely without discriminatory intent, would the Supreme Court have ruled differently? Explain.

3. What is the central issue in this case?

4. Why was North Carolina's social and educational history relevant to the outcome of the case?

5. Statistical evidence showed that 35 percent of new hires in grocery and produce at Lucky Stores, a retail grocery chain, were women, while 84 percent of new hires in deli, bakery, and general merchandise were women. Statistical evidence also showed that 31 percent of those promoted into apprentice jobs in grocery and produce were women, while women comprised 75 percent of those promoted into apprentice jobs in deli, bakery, and general merchandise. Grocery and produce jobs generally were higher-paying jobs than those in deli, bakery, and general merchandise. Women received significantly fewer overtime hours than men.

    Do these facts regarding Lucky Stores suggest discrimination? Explain. See *Stender v. Lucky Stores, Inc.,* 803 F. Supp. 259 (DC Cal. 1992).

6. To determine whether police officers were using illegal drugs, the Boston Police Department used hair tests. The police department took adverse employment actions against several African American police officers who had failed the test. The officers brought a Title VII action claiming the test created a disparate impact based on race. African American officers had passed the test at rates between 97 and 99 percent, while white officers' pass rate was 99 and 100 percent. However, the officers' expert offered evidence that fail rates of African American police officers were "statistically significant"—between two and four standard deviations. The Boston Police Department asked for summary judgment. Should the disparate impact claim be allowed to proceed? Explain. *See Jones v. City of Boston,* 2012 U.S. Dist. LEXIS 141440 (D. Mass. September 28, 2012).

7. Eighty-one percent of the hires at Consolidated Service Systems, a small Chicago janitorial company, were of Korean origin. The EEOC brought a disparate treatment claim, saying the firm discriminated in favor of Koreans by relying primarily on word-of-mouth recruiting. Hwang, the owner, is Korean. Seventy-three percent of the job applicants were Korean. One percent of the Chicago-area workforce is Korean, and not more than 3 percent of the janitorial workforce for the area is Korean. The court found no persuasive evidence of intentional discrimination, although the government claimed that 99 applicants were denied jobs because they were not Koreans.

    a. Does restricting hiring to members of one ethnic group constitute discrimination where hiring is accomplished by word of mouth? Explain.

    b. What if a firm, using the word-of-mouth approach, hired only white applicants? Explain.

    c. In this case, the EEOC brought but dropped a disparate impact claim. Analyze the case using the disparate impact test. See *Equal Employment Opportunity Commission v. Consolidated Service Systems,* 989 F.2d 233 (7th Cir. 1993).

Statutory Defenses

In addition to the aforementioned defenses against disparate treatment and disparate impact claims, Title VII also affords specific exemptions or defenses, three of which are of particular note: (1) seniority, (2) employee testing, and (3) bona fide occupational qualification. Bona fide occupational qualifications are addressed in the next section as part of the sex discrimination discussion.

Seniority

Differences in wages and conditions of employment are permissible under the Civil Rights Act of 1964 where those differences are the result of a bona fide (good faith) seniority system, as long as the system was not intended to hide or facilitate discrimination. Seniority is important because it often determines who is laid off first and who gets promotions, vacations, and so forth. Because white employees often have greater seniority than blacks, the result is that seniority may perpetuate the effects of historical discrimination. The Supreme Court has made it clear, however, that a bona fide seniority system that perpetuates past wrongs is illegal only if discriminatory intent is proven.[16]

Job-Related Employee Testing

Many employers use testing in making hiring and promotion decisions. The availability of online applications has contributed to an increase in this practice.[17] To avoid a disparate impact created by employee testing, an employer must be able to show that the test in question is job-related and consistent with business necessity; that is, the test must evaluate an individual's skills as they relate to the relevant employment opportunity. To prevent unlawful disparate treatment, an employer's test must be uniformly applied regardless of an applicant's or employee's race, sex, or other protected categories. For example, Title VII would prohibit an employer from testing the reading ability of African American applicants or employees while not requiring the same test of their white counterparts.[18]

The Four-Fifths Rule and Disparate Impact

The Four-Fifths Rule compares results of an employer's selection tool, such as testing for hiring or measuring sales numbers for promotions, to determine whether the tool creates a disproportionately adverse impact on a group in a protected class. Consider this scenario: 150 applicants apply to be gift wrappers for an online retailer. Applicants who pass a "gift wrap test" will be hired. One hundred of the applicants are female and 50 are male. Of the 100 female applicants, 75 pass the test and are hired. Of the 50 male applicants, only 10 pass the test and are rejected. Instead of comparing raw numbers, or even the raw pass rate (selection rate) of male to female applicants, the "four-fifths rule" takes 80 percent—or four-fifths—of the higher selection rate and compares it to the excluded group's selection rate (see Table 13.1).

TABLE 13.1 Four-Fifths Rule—Gift Wrapping Scenario

Applicant	Numbers Passing Test/Hired	Selection Rate
Female	75 out of 100	75%
Male	10 out of 50	20%

75% × .80 = 60% > 20%

Because the selection rate of males is less than 80 percent of the higher selection rate for females, the employment practice in question will be presumed to create a disparate impact against men in violation of Title VII. The online retailer would then have to show the job-relatedness of the employment practice in question and demonstrate that a good-faith effort was made to find a selection procedure that lessened the disparate impact on protected classes.

Questions

1. African American men are six times more likely to be incarcerated than white men, according to a 2013 Pew Center study. If those with criminal convictions are disproportionately African American, do you think criminal background checks in hiring create a disparate impact in violation of Title VII? Should employers "ban the box" on applications that asks about criminal records so that employers can first consider the applicants' qualifications before inquiring about criminal history? Discuss. See *EEOC v. Freeman,* 778 F.3d 463 (4th Cir. 2015); National Employment Law Project, "Ban the Box: U.S. Cities, Counties, and States Adopt Fair Hiring Policies," NELP Toolkit, February 1, 2017 [**www.nelp.org**]; and Bruce Drake, "Incarceration Gap Widens between Whites and Blacks," *Pew Research Center,* September 6, 2013 [**www.pewresearch.org/ fact-tank/2013/09/06/incarceration-gap-between-whites-and-blacks-widens**].

2. Dianne Rawlinson sought employment as a prison guard in Alabama. She was a 22-year-old college graduate with a degree in correctional psychology. She was denied employment because she failed to meet the 120-pound weight requirement for the job. The state also required such employees to be at least 5 feet 2 inches tall. Alabama operated four all-male, maximum-security prisons. The district court characterized the Alabama prison system as one of "rampant violence." Rawlinson sued, claiming employment discrimination. Decide. Explain. See *Dothard v. Rawlinson,* 97 S. Ct. 2720 (1977). See also *Ambat v. City and County of San Francisco,* 757 F.3d 1017 (9th Cir. 2014), in Part Three.

National Origin

Employment discrimination often reflects larger social issues that come to influence workplace relations. In the aftermath of the September 11, 2001, terrorist attacks on the United States, between September 11, 2001, and September 11, 2004, for example, the EEOC processed more than 900 claims of national origin discrimination in a three-year period associated with the September 11 attacks, resulting in approximately $3.2 million in monetary relief.[19] One claim brought by the EEOC, settled in 2005, was against Pesce, an upscale Houston-based restaurant. In his August 2001 review, Karim El-Raheb, then a Pesce general manager, had been told he was doing very well. After business declined following the September 11 terrorist attacks, Pesce's co-owners speculated that customers may be frightened by El-Raheb's appearance and name, suggesting that he could "pass for Hispanic" and should change his name accordingly. In November 2001, El-Raheb was fired because "things weren't working out."[20]

Under its 2017–2021 Strategic Enforcement Plan, the protection of vulnerable workers including immigrants and migrants is one of the EEOC's central enforcement priorities.[21] In November 2016, the EEOC issued new guidance on national origin discrimination, along with a "Questions and Answers" on workplace rights of employees who are, or are perceived to be, Muslim or Middle Eastern.[22] The EEOC cited "heightened concerns" for protecting these employees following the "attacks in Paris and San Bernardino" in late 2015, but the rhetoric of the 2016 presidential campaign also may have contributed to an increased focus on national origin discrimination in employment. The 2016 Enforcement Guidance noted that national origin discrimination may overlap with other forms of discrimination that Title VII protects against, such as religion and race.[23] This is known as ***intersectional discrimination***.

"English Only" and Other Restrictive Language Policies

Reflecting a national debate over whether English should be the official language of the United States, "Speak English Only" rules in the workplace have generated controversy as well as national origin discrimination claims as language is closely related to "cultural or ethnic identity."[24] Similarly, other conceivable restrictive language policies, such as a "Speak Spanish Only" policy, could give rise to national origin discrimination claims.

Employers argue that the rules are necessary when needed to communicate with customers, to maintain job safety, and to encourage congenial worker relations. The 2016 EEOC guidelines reasserted its prohibition of a blanket ban on employees speaking their primary language in the workplace; however, an English-only rule at certain times is permissible if justified by "substantial business reasons."[25] In *Garcia v. Spun Steak Co.,* the employer, a producer of meat products, instituted an English-only rule for its bilingual employees to enhance safety and product quality and to address allegations that some employees were making rude comments in Spanish to English-speaking employees. The English-only rule applied to work but not to lunch, breaks, or employees' own time. The employer's rule was upheld by a federal appellate court on the grounds that it was narrowly defined and did not create a discriminatory atmosphere.[26]

Question

Rodriguez, a FedEx employee of Hispanic origin, informed FedEx's regional human resources manager, Adkinson, that he wanted to obtain a promotion to a supervisory position. After applying and interviewing for an available supervisory position, Rodriguez was rejected. The manager who interviewed Rodriguez found him to be qualified but did not hire him because of Adkinson's expressed concerns that Rodriguez's "accent and speech pattern" would undermine his ability to rise through the corporate ranks. Another FedEx manager stated that when he asked Adkinson why Rodriguez had not received the promotion, Adkinson made derogatory comments about Rodriguez's "language" and "how he speaks." Is FedEx liable for national origin discrimination based on its failure to promote Rodriguez? Decide. Explain. See *Rodriguez v. FedEx Freight East, Inc.,* 487 F.3d 1001 (6th Cir. 2007).

Racial Harassment

| The hangman's noose. |

The hangman's noose, perhaps the most hurtful and disgraceful expression of racism, has sadly appeared in recent racial harassment cases. In 2013, a federal jury awarded $200,000 in compensatory and punitive damages against a North Carolina trucking company on behalf of two former African American truck drivers who were subjected to racial slurs and threats involving nooses.[27] In 2012, an Atlanta manufacturer settled an EEOC lawsuit that alleged that racially charged graffiti and comments were directed at African American employees, one of whom found a hangman's noose at his workstation.[28]

As startling as these claims may seem, whether racially charged workplace conduct rises to the level of unlawful harassment appears to be a subject of conflict among federal courts. In 2012, for example, an Arkansas federal court found that the use of a racial slur in the workplace was not derogatory but "at most coarse jesting."[29] However, a 2015 federal appellate court decision concluded that a racially hostile environment in violation of Title VII was created when an African American cocktail waitress was called "porch monkey" by a Caucasian restaurant manager twice within a 24-hour period.[30]

In addition to overt forms of workplace harassment such as racial slurs and threats, the use of more subtle "code words" such as calling African American male employees "boy" or labeling black employees as "all of you" may constitute racial harassment under Title VII.[31] Legal requirements and the evolving standards for analyzing harassment claims will be explored later in the context of sexual harassment—perhaps the most familiar form of workplace harassment.

Part Three—Sex Discrimination

Gender Equality

In 2016, the U.S. Bureau of Labor Statistics (BLS) reported that the median weekly earnings of American women working full time in 2014 was 83 percent of that earned by men, but this percentage varied by occupation.[32] However, supported by other statistics, a rise in women's power in the workplace has been observed in recent years. For example, childless women in their 20s earn more than their male counterparts.[33] Yet women's perception of gender bias—such as lower pay and other forms of discrimination—have remained high.[34]

A 2015 survey of female congressional staffers revealed an unexpected consequence of employers' policies meant to avoid sexual harassment: the creation of a gender gap in workplace opportunities. For example, an office policy that a congressman was not to be alone with a female staffer made engaging in "sensitive and strategic discussions" difficult for a woman in a senior position.[35] Men allowed to be alone with male leaders under such a policy may be given an unfair advantage.

The power and limits of statutory protections against sex discrimination are also evident in the Title VII class-action lawsuits that have been brought by female employees alleging disparity in pay, work assignments, and promotion, from financial services to retail. However, the class-action approach to discrimination litigation suffered a significant setback in

2011 when class certification was denied to female Walmart employees claiming sex discrimination.[36] The Supreme Court decision did not reach the substantive merits of the discrimination complaint. Rather, the Supreme Court ruled that the case could not go forward as a class action because the plaintiffs did not point to specific, consistent, nationwide employment policies or practices that harmed the class members. In 2012, a class of female Costco employees alleging sex discrimination in promotions to managerial positions was certified, with a settlement later reached that included Costco's commitment to change its promotional practices.[37] (See Chapter 4 for more on the Walmart case and its impact on class actions.)

Glass Ceiling? Does a "glass ceiling" of implicit bias hold women back from roles of power and career advancement? A recent study found a 40 percent disparity between male and female MBAs 10 years after graduation.[38]

Lean In

In her 2013 book entitled *Lean In,* Facebook chief operating officer Sheryl Sandberg observes that too few women are reaching leadership positions in business because of, among other factors, women's choices to curtail their own career ambitions. To support women's professional success and leadership, Sandberg advises women to "lean in" to their careers and make themselves more visible and heard at the workplace.

Questions

1. Do you agree with Sandberg's observations? Explain.

2. What choices might women make that interfere with their career advancement? What other factors may blunt women's career growth? Explain.

3. A recent study involving fictitious chief executive officers (CEOs) revealed that women who are seen as "chatty" or talkative are viewed as less competent, whereas men who dominate workplace conversations are more likely to succeed. A quiet female is viewed far more favorably than her chatty female counterpart: Her competence is assumed to be about equal to that of a talkative male. What might this mean for women who "lean in" at the workplace? Explain.

Sources: David Wessel, "The Positive Economics of 'Leaning In,'" *The Wall Street Journal,* April 3, 2013 [**http://online.wsj.com/news/articles/SB10001424127887323916304578400192414995044?mg=reno64-wsj**]; and Leslie Kwoh, "Talkative Women Lose at Work, Study Says," *The Wall Street Journal,* May 16, 2012, p. B8. [For a video of Sheryl Sandberg discussing "Lean In," visit **http://leanin.org/book/**].

Analysis of Sex Discrimination: Current Issues

Sex discrimination claims that may be brought under Title VII include disparate treatment and disparate impact, as well as sexual harassment. Although employee training and policies targeting sex discrimination have become common in the American workplace, sex discrimination claims remained the basis for approximately 30 percent of the charges filed with the EEOC from 1997 to 2016.[39] Thus, sex discrimination claims remain a critical area of Title VII analysis.

High-Tech Sexism?

Silicon Valley, considered the center of the "high-tech" industry, has been the setting of recent high-profile sex discrimination claims that have brought scrutiny to the workplace culture in such companies as the ride-sharing app pioneer Uber. In a February 2017 blog post, former Uber engineer Susan Fowler described Uber's systemic discrimination against women and her own experience at being sexually harassed by a supervisor. Former Uber CEO Travis Kalanick, who has been criticized for Uber's aggressive business tactics and perceived workplace culture, opened an internal investigation into Fowler's allegations and announced plans to address such concerns.

Questions

1. If you were a consultant for Uber, what steps might you suggest to mitigate the risk of discriminatory treatment of its female workers? Explain.

2. What might contribute to hostile work environments for women in the high-tech industry? How might colleges and universities assist in creating more equal employment opportunities for women in Silicon Valley companies? Explain.

Sources: Mike Isaac, "Inside Uber's Aggressive, Unrestrained Workplace Culture," *The New York Times,* February 22, 2017 [**www.nytimes.com/2017/02/22/technology/uber-workplace-culture.html**]; Resty Woro Yuniar, "Uber Executive: Workplace Culture Needs a Lot of Work," *The Wall Street Journal,* March 2, 2017 [**www.wsj.com/articles/uber-executive-workplace-culture-needs-a-lot-of-work-1488454848**]; and Jessica Guynn and Marco della Cava, "Silicon Valley's Dirty Little Secret: The Way It Treats Women," *USA TODAY,* March 3, 2017 [**www.usatoday.com/story/tech/news/2017/03/03/silicon-valleys-dirty-little-secret-sexual-harassment-discrimination-of-women/98646108/**].

Bona Fide Occupational Qualification

Often in intentional sex discrimination cases, the key inquiry involves the ***bona fide occupational qualification (BFOQ)*** defense provided by Title VII. Discrimination is lawful where sex, religion, or national origin is a BFOQ reasonably necessary to the normal operation of that business. The exclusion of race and color from the list suggests Congress thought those categories always unacceptable as bona fide occupational qualifications. The BFOQ was meant to be a very limited exception applicable to situations where specific inherent characteristics are necessary to the job (for example, wet nurse) or where authenticity (actors), privacy (nurses), or safety (guards) is required. Broadly, the BFOQ defense rests on this question: Is being a female, for example, necessary to perform the *essence* of the job?

Essence

An employer can lawfully insist on a woman to fill a woman's modeling role because being female goes to the essence of the job. Airlines, on the other hand, cannot hire only women as flight attendants even if customers prefer females and even if females perform the supplementary elements of the job (like charming passengers) better than most men. Those duties "are tangential to the essence of the business involved"[40] (the essence being the maintenance of safe, orderly conditions; providing service as needed; etc.). Presumably, gender has little to do with the ability to perform those essential ingredients of the job.

Many employers have simply assumed that women could not perform certain tasks. For example, women were thought to be insufficiently aggressive for sales roles, and women were denied employment because they were assumed to have a higher turnover rate because of the desire to marry and have children. Those stereotypes are at the heart of sex discrimination litigation generally and do not support a BFOQ defense.

LEGAL BRIEFCASE

Ambat v. City & County of San Francisco
757 F.3d 1017 (9th Cir. 2014)

Opinion

MURGUIA, Circuit Judge:

Plaintiffs, . . . deputies of the San Francisco Sheriff's Department ("SFSD"), appeal the district court's order granting summary judgement to the City and County of San Francisco (the "County") on their challenge to SFSD's policy prohibiting male deputies from supervising female inmates in the housing units of SFSD's jails. The district court concluded that SFSD's policy did not violate Title VII's prohibition on sex discrimination because it fell within the statute's "bona fide occupational qualification" exception. We reverse the district court's grant of summary judgment to the County on the sex discrimination claims and vacate the denial of summary judgment to plaintiffs on those claims.

I. Facts and Procedural History

In October 2006, SFSD implemented a new policy prohibiting male deputies from supervising female inmates in the housing units of the jails operated by the County (the "Policy"). . . .

The adoption of the Policy coincided with SFSD's plan to consolidate all of its female inmates within a single facility, County Jail 8 ("CJ8"). CJ8 housing units, or "pods," are composed of cells or sleeping bays arrayed around a central congregation space. Each pod has two tiers and between 56 and 88 beds. At the center of the pod is a podium from which a deputy can see into common areas and into the cells and sleeping bays. Each pod is staffed by two deputies, one of whom remains at the podium while the other makes rounds. Female inmates fill some, but not all, of the available housing pods in CJ8. . . .

Although housing pods are single-sex, CJ8's pod for inmates receiving medical or psychiatric care is not sex-segregated. Male deputies are not permitted under the Policy to work with female inmates in the housing pods; however, male deputies may be assigned to the mixed-sex medical pod or assigned to transport female inmates between CJ8 and other locations. Male deputies may also enter female housing pods in some circumstances, such as to assist with feeding female inmates.

According to San Francisco Sheriff Michael Hennessey (the "Sheriff"), . . . he adopted the Policy for four reasons: (1) to protect the safety of female inmates from sexual misconduct perpetrated by male deputies, (2) to maintain the security of the jail in the face of female inmates' ability to manipulate male deputies and of the deputies' fear of false allegations of sexual misconduct by the inmates, (3) to protect the privacy of female inmates, and (4) to promote the successful rehabilitation of female inmates.

Of the four reasons the Sheriff claims led him to enact the Policy, he identified protecting the safety of inmates from sexual misconduct as the most important. As the County pointed out, between 2001 and 2009, SFSD investigated twelve complaints of sexual misconduct or inappropriate sexual relationships between a male deputy and a female inmate. Ten of those incidents occurred before the Policy was implemented in 2006, and two occurred after. . . .

With this concern for inmate safety in mind, the Sheriff asserts that he considered three responses, apart from enacting the Policy, to the problem of protecting female inmates from sexual misconduct: (1) implementing additional screening of male deputies to determine whether they were likely to engage in sexual misconduct with female inmates, (2) installing additional surveillance cameras to monitor activities in CJ8's housing pods, and (3) providing additional training to deputies. However, he claims to have rejected each of these alternatives as ineffective or unfeasible, so he proceeded to implement the Policy.

In July 2007, 35 deputies—a majority of whom were female—filed suit against the County, alleging that the policy constituted sex discrimination in violation of Title VII of the Civil Rights Act of 1964 ("Title VII"). . . .

. . . Although it did not dispute that the Policy discriminates against deputies on the basis of sex, the County . . . argued that the discrimination that resulted from the Policy was permissible under the "bona fide occupational qualification" ("BFOQ") exception to Title VII. . . .

[T]he district court ruled that the County was entitled to summary judgment on plaintiffs' discrimination claims because it had made out a valid BFOQ defense. . . .

II. Title VII Claim

* * * * *

B. Bona Fide Occupational Qualification Defense
Although Title VII prohibits employment discrimination on the basis of sex in most instances, it permits discrimination where "sex . . . is a bona fide occupational qualification reasonably necessary to the normal operation of [the defendant's] particular business or enterprise." For example, Title VII would not compel a producer to audition men for a female role in a film, because being female could be a BFOQ for playing that role.

Nevertheless, "[t]he BFOQ defense is written narrowly, and [the Supreme Court] has read it narrowly." . . .

* * * * *

To justify discrimination under the BFOQ exception, an employer must "prove by a preponderance of the evidence: 1) that the job qualification justifying the discrimination is reasonably necessary to the essence of its business; and 2) that [sex] is a legitimate proxy for the qualification because (a) it has a substantial basis for believing that all or nearly all [men] lack the qualification, or . . . (b) it is impossible or highly impractical . . . to insure by individual testing that its employees will have the necessary qualifications for the job."

After "surveying . . . decisions applying the BFOQ exception in the prison context," we observed that "even in the unique context of prison employment, administrators seeking to justify a BFOQ must show 'a high correlation between sex and ability to perform job functions.'" We also recognized that it would be impossible to prove a BFOQ defense without "demonstrat[ing] that . . . alternative approaches . . . are not viable."

[W]e must first address the issue of the deference owed to the Sheriff's judgment in implementing the Policy.

1. Deference to the Sheriff's Judgment
"Judgments by prison administrators that 'are the product of a reasoned decision-making process, based on available information and experience,' are entitled to some deference."

* * * * *

Here, the record demonstrates that there are genuine issues of material fact as to whether or not such a process led to the Sheriff's adoption of the Policy. . . .

* * * * *

2. Job Qualifications Reasonably Necessary to the Essence of Operating San Francisco's Jails
Although deference to the Sheriff's judgment cannot play a role in our analysis, it is still necessary for us to consider each rationale that has been offered by the County in order to determine whether the County is able to satisfy our BFOQ inquiry based solely on the evidence in the record. We must consider each of the four rationales offered by the County in order to determine (1) whether any rationale suggests a job qualification reasonably necessary to the essence of operating SFSD's jails, and, if so, (2) whether sex is a legitimate proxy for determining whether a deputy actually has that qualification.

[T]he County easily meets its burden . . . of demonstrating that there are job qualifications derived from the four justifications that are reasonably necessary to the essence of operating SFSD's jails. Each of the four justifications that the Sheriff claims drove his decision to implement the Policy . . . is essential to the operation of a corrections facility. . . .

Based on these important rationales for the Policy, we have no difficulty in identifying four "job qualification[s] . . . reasonably necessary to the essence of" operating SFSD's jails, any of which would satisfy the first prong of our test. These qualifications corresponding to the four rationales are (1) not posing a threat to the safety of female inmates due to a likelihood of perpetrating sexual misconduct against them; (2) not posing a threat to jail security; (3) not posing a threat to female inmates' privacy; and (4) not posing a threat to female inmates' ability to rehabilitate. We now consider each of these four qualifications under the second prong of our test to determine whether there is any genuine dispute of material fact as to whether being male is a "legitimate proxy" for any of them.

3. Whether Sex Is a Legitimate Proxy for Reasonably Necessary Job Qualifications
The County may show that excluding all male deputies is a "legitimate proxy" for excluding deputies who lack one of the four qualifications if there is (a) "a substantial basis for believing that all or nearly all [men] lack the qualification" or (b) "it is impossible or highly impractical . . . to insure by individual testing" whether or not a male deputy has the qualification. . . .

The County asserts that the primary reason for the Sheriff's adoption of the Policy was to protect the safety of female inmates by reducing the possibility of sexual harassment and abuse by male deputies. While . . . this is an extremely important interest, . . . the County has not shown that the Sheriff had "a substantial basis for believing that all or nearly all" male deputies were likely to engage in sexual misconduct with female inmates, nor has it shown that "it is impossible or highly impractical . . . to insure by individual testing" that a male deputy does not pose such a threat.

The statistics on sexual misconduct perpetrated by male deputies against female inmates in SFSD's jails are deeply troubling. . . .

Nevertheless, these statistics by themselves do not prove that "all or substantially all" male deputies are likely to perpetrate sexual misconduct. . . .

[T]he County is also unable to show that . . . it is impossible or highly impractical to insure by individual testing that a male deputy does not have a propensity to perpetrate sexual misconduct. . . . As the County points out, peace officer candidates must also undergo psychological examinations.

While conceding that background checks and psychological testing are used for the purpose of screening for a propensity to perpetrate sexual misconduct, the County suggests that such screening mechanisms are inadequate because they are unable to detect *all* potential perpetrators. Removing every deputy with any potential for engaging in misconduct may be a laudable goal, but that goal is insufficient to justify a policy that discriminates in such broad strokes. Rather, . . . a BFOQ defense cannot be maintained if available testing offers "a practical reliable differentiation of the unqualified from the qualified applicant, [even if it is] not a perfect differentiation." The record before us does not resolve the genuine dispute over whether the tests that are presently used or that could be used by SFSD would permit it to make a practical reliable differentiation between those who are likely to engage in sexual misconduct and those who are not.

The County also argues that employing male deputies in the female housing pods poses a threat to jail security. In so arguing, it points to two specific assertions offered by the Sheriff. First, the Sheriff expressed concern that male deputies were particularly vulnerable to manipulation by female inmates, potentially leading them to overlook conduct in violation of jail regulations, such as smuggling contraband into the jail. Second, he claimed that the consequence of male deputies' fear of being accused of sexual misconduct could be that those deputies would be unwilling to supervise female inmates as closely as necessary, leading to an even greater risk of female inmates being able to violate jail rules.

However, the record on summary judgment is insufficient to demonstrate that there is no genuine dispute as to whether "all or substantially all" male deputies would be vulnerable to manipulation by female inmates or as to whether it would be "impossible or highly impractical" to test for whether a male deputy is manipulable. . . .

The County's third justification for the Policy is protecting the privacy interests of female inmates. However, the record does not demonstrate that there is an actual risk of female inmates' privacy being compromised by male deputies. SFSD has policies in place to prevent male deputies from taking on duties, such as strip searches, that might violate the privacy of female inmates. The inmates are required to remain clothed at all times, except when showering. When showering or using the toilet, inmates' bodies are covered by a privacy screen.

The Sheriff claims that the use of privacy screens compromises jail security, but there is a genuine dispute as to whether privacy screens actually do compromise jail security where, as here, the screens remained in use even after the Policy was adopted.

The County's final justification for the Policy is promoting the rehabilitation of female inmates. The Sheriff asserts that he was concerned that surveillance by male deputies could traumatize female inmates, particularly those who had suffered physical or sexual abuse in the past. The County introduced evidence that a disproportionately high number of female inmates had suffered such abuse. Nevertheless, there is a genuine dispute over whether excluding male deputies is a legitimate proxy for excluding deputies who would interfere with female inmates' rehabilitation.

. . . Further, there is no evidence in the record that the individuals staffing the rehabilitative programs . . . are themselves required to be female. If female inmates were supervised by men in their rehabilitative programs while the Policy was in effect, that fact alone would defeat the County's argument that excluding men from supervisory roles was necessary to promote female inmates' rehabilitation. . . .

C. Conclusion

The justifications offered by the County in support of the Policy each speak to extremely important concerns. . . . However, the fact that the Policy seeks to advance such important goals as inmate safety is not, by itself, sufficient to permit discrimination on the basis of sex. . . .

* * * * *

. . . The district court's grant of summary judgment as to plaintiffs' sex discrimination claims and other claims predicated thereon is REVERSED.

. . . This case is REMANDED for further proceedings on these claims.

Questions

1. What is the two-prong test to justify a BFOQ exception to Title VII's protection against sex discrimination?
   a. Which prong did the County of San Francisco satisfy? Why? Explain.

b. Which prong did the County of San Francisco fail to satisfy? Why? Explain.

2. Should Women's Workout World, a health and exercise club, be able to lawfully decline to accept men as customers and/or employees? Decide the case. Explain. See *U.S. EEOC v. Sedita,* 816 F. Supp. 1291 (N.D. Ill. 1993).

3. Can the Hooters restaurant chain lawfully decline to hire men to be food servers? Scantily clad "Hooters girls" serve food and beverages to Hooters restaurant customers. Explain. See Matthew Heller, "Texas Man Aims to Bust Open Hooters Girl Hiring," *On Point.com* (January 13, 2009) [**www.onpointnews.com/NEWS/texas-man-aims-to-bust-open-hooters-girl-hiring.html**].

Looks Discrimination

Harrah's Reno, Nevada, casino instituted a "Personal Best" appearance policy requiring its female bartenders to wear makeup while prohibiting their male counterparts from wearing any. After a successful 20-year career as a Harrah's bartender, Darlene Jespersen was fired for refusing to wear makeup under the policy.

Brenna Lewis staffed the front desks of Heartland Inn motels near Des Moines, Iowa. Her performance was excellent, earning her compliments from customers and merit raises. A new Heartland executive, Barbara Cullinan, had approved hiring Lewis for a full-time position staffing one motel's front desk during the day, but Cullinan became dissatisfied after seeing Lewis in person. Cullinan was heard saying that Heartland staff should be "pretty," especially those working at the front desk. Lewis was self-described as "slightly more masculine," avoiding makeup and wearing her hair short. The Heartland front desk job description did not mention appearance, stating only that a guest service representative must create "a warm, inviting atmosphere" and perform tasks such as relaying information and receiving reservations. Over protests of her direct manager, Lewis was eventually fired.

Both Jespersen and Lewis brought Title VII claims against their former employers.

Questions

1. What do these cases have in common? How do they differ? Explain. Decide each case.
2. Should the law recognize a separate cause of action for "looks discrimination"? Explain.

Sources: *Jespersen v. Harrah's,* 444 F.3d 1104 (9th Cir. 2006); and *Lewis v. Heartland Inns,* 591 F.3d 1033 (8th Cir. 2010).

Work-Life Balance and Sex Discrimination

Antidiscrimination law has been critical in allowing women to pursue careers and in providing some refuge from the professional disadvantages of pregnancy experienced at some workplaces.

Pregnancy Discrimination

The Pregnancy Discrimination Act (PDA) amended Title VII of the Civil Rights Act of 1964 so that discrimination with regard to pregnancy is treated as a form of sex discrimination. Broadly, the PDA requires that pregnant employees be treated the same as all other employees with temporary disabilities. In general, an employer should not ask job applicants about pregnancy, and applicants have no duty to reveal that pregnancy. Further, a pregnant employee cannot be forced to take time off or be forced to quit due to pregnancy. Additionally, an employer cannot discriminate against female applicants or employees because they might start a family. [For the 2014 EEOC enforcement guidance on pregnancy discrimination, see "EEOC Enforcement Guidance on Pregnancy Discrimination and Related Issues" at **https://www.eeoc.gov/laws/guidance/pregnancy_guidance.cfm**].

Family Responsibilities Discrimination

"Family Responsibilities Discrimination" (FRD) has achieved increased recognition in recent years. While no express antidiscrimination statutory protection is afforded to parents or caregivers, FRD claims may be based on existing statutes such as Title VII. For example, a federal appeals court allowed the mother of six-year-old triplets and an older child to proceed with a Title VII claim alleging that she was rejected for a promotion in favor of a less-qualified woman as a result of a sex-based stereotype that mothers with young children neglect their careers because of child care responsibilities.[41] [For the EEOC enforcement guidance on FRD, see "EEOC Enforcement Guidance: Unlawful Disparate Treatment of Workers with Caregiving Responsibilities" at **www.eeoc.gov/policy/docs/caregiving.html**].

> Stereotype that mothers with young children neglect their careers.

Questions

1. Waitresses at the Rustic Inn were prohibited under a written policy from waiting tables past their fifth month of pregnancy and required either to suspend working or to switch to working as cashiers or hostesses, who are paid less because they do not receive gratuities. The EEOC filed a lawsuit against the employer on behalf of a class of three aggrieved employees, alleging that the policy violated the PDA. Decide. See *EEOC v. W&O Inc.*, 213 F.3d 600 (11th Cir. 2000).

2. Besides avoiding FRD liability, how might an employer benefit from effectively supporting employees' balancing of work and life responsibilities? Should parents and other caregivers be given express statutory protection against employment discrimination? Explain.

Equal Pay

Title VII affords broad protection from discrimination in pay because of sex. The Equal Pay Act of 1963 directly forbids discrimination on the basis of sex by paying wages to employees of one sex at a rate less than the rate paid to employees of the opposite sex for equal work on jobs requiring equal skill, effort, and responsibility and performed under similar working conditions (*equal* has been interpreted to mean "substantially equal"). The act provides for certain exceptions. Unequal wage payments are lawful if paid pursuant to (1) a seniority system, (2) a merit system, (3) a system that measures earnings by quantity or quality of production, or (4) a differential based on "any . . . factor other than sex." The employer seeking to avoid a violation of the Equal Pay Act can adjust its wage structure by raising the pay of the disfavored sex performing equal work. Lowering the pay of the favored sex violates the act.

If a male employee has a greater skill set—such as accounting skills—than his female coworker doing "equal work," the employer may pay the man at a higher rate, as long as the male employee's superior skills are actually considered in making the pay decision.[42]

Salary Negotiating Skills

Dreves was terminated from her $48,500 job as a general manager of Hudson's retail operation at Burlington International Airport and replaced by Dixon, a male, at a salary of $52,500. Dreves filed an Equal Pay Act lawsuit and moved for summary judgment. In defending against the motion for summary judgment, Hudson argued that the salary difference was based on "factors other than sex": Dixon had to relocate his family from another state and had strong negotiating skills. Did the employer violate the Equal Pay Act? Decide. Explain. *Dreves v. Hudson Group,* 2013 U.S. Dist. LEXIS 82636 (D. Vt. June 12, 2013).

Sexual Harassment

If asked, "what is an example of sexual harassment?," a typical and reasonable response might be "a male boss making unwanted sexual advances on a female employee, telling her that such conduct is a job requirement," or "a male employee touching his female coworker in a sexual and unwanted manner." Although these examples offer solid bases for sexual harassment claims, they do not provide a complete picture. As a form of sex discrimination actionable under Title VII, sexual harassment protection covers both men and women and strives to maintain equal opportunity in the workplace.

According to a recent Society for Human Resource Management (SHRM) poll, nearly two-thirds of organizations received sexual harassment complaints from employees in the previous 24 months, and a quarter of organizations noted an increase in such claims during that time. Nearly one-fifth of organizations reported that the sexual harassment complaints were brought by male and female employees equally.[43]

Question

Women in authority seem to be particularly susceptible to sexual harassment. A 2012 study showed that female supervisors were more likely to be harassed than women in subordinate positions.[44] Why might women in powerful positions be more likely to experience sexual harassment? How might an employer address this issue? See Eve Tahmincioglu, "Female Managers Face More Sexual Harassment," *Careers on msnbc.com,* August 24, 2009 [**www.msnbc.msn.com/id/32476564/ns/business-careers**].

The Customer Is Not Always Right

Two female cashiers at Love's truck stop in Buckeye, Arizona, ages 18 and 20, were allegedly subjected to unwanted sexual touching and pressing, crude and obscene remarks, sexual demands and innuendos, and demands for personal information—by customers, sometimes in front of other customers. The EEOC filed a claim asserting that Love's management knew about and tolerated this sexually hostile work environment caused by its customers. Further, at least one manager allegedly laughed about it, and another manager said the harassment was to be expected because it is a truck stop. Managers also told the two cashiers to "deal with it," especially the misconduct of one repeat customer because "he's always like that." Should the employer be held liable for workplace harassment by its customers? Explain.

Source: U.S. Equal Employment Opportunity Commission, "Arizona Truck Stop to Pay $70,000 to Settle EEOC Suit Charging Sex Harassment by Customers," press release, August 3, 2010 [**www.eeoc.gov/eeoc/newsroom/release/8-3-10a.cfm**].

The Law of Sexual Harassment

Sexual harassment, as a form of discrimination, consists of unwelcome sexual advances, requests for sexual favors, and other verbal or physical conduct of a sexual nature that (1) becomes a condition of employment, (2) becomes a basis for employment decisions, or (3) unreasonably interferes with work performance or creates a hostile working environment.

There are two types of sexual harassment: *quid pro quo* ("this for that," such as a sexual favor in exchange for keeping one's job) and *hostile work environment* (a workplace rendered offensive and abusive by such conduct as sexual comments, pictures, jokes, sexual aggression, and the like where no employment benefit is gained or lost). As discussed earlier in this chapter, hostile work environments may be created by offensive or abusive conduct involving protected categories other than sex, including race, religion, national origin, and disability. The law of sexual harassment, particularly in regard to hostile work environments, may apply to these cases.

The Test

LO 13-6

Identify when unlawful sexual harassment has occurred.

LO 13-7

Identify when employers are liable for unlawful sexual harassment.

Once we have some idea of behavior that constitutes sexual harassment, our concern turns to which remedies are available for the victims. Although the question is not settled, most federal courts to date have ruled that victims of sexual harassment seeking recovery under Title VII cannot sue the person who actually committed the harassment. The victim might be able to sue the wrongdoer under a state statute or by using a tort claim such as assault, but under Title VII, *personal liability* appears not to be available. This result, if the current judicial pattern continues, is not as unfair as might at first appear because well-settled principles of justice hold the employer, and not the employer's agents or employees, generally responsible for workplace wrongdoing. The victim, therefore, can seek damages from the employer as the responsible party. A pair of 1998 U.S. Supreme Court decisions in the *Burlington Industries* and *Faragher*[45] cases considerably clarified the circumstances under which an employer is liable for sexual harassment in the workplace. The analysis proceeds as follows:

1. **Proof of sexual harassment**—The plaintiff/employee/victim must prove items a to c:
   a. The harassing conduct is unwelcome.
   b. The harassing conduct is because of sex.
   c. The harassing conduct resulted in a tangible employment action, or was sufficiently severe or pervasive as to unreasonably alter the conditions of employment and create a hostile, abusive work environment.

   If the plaintiff is unable to prove items a to c, the claim fails. If the plaintiff proves items a to c, the inquiry then turns to the question of whether the employer bears responsibility for the harassment, as analyzed in Part 2.

2. **Employer liability and the affirmative defense**
   a. If the wrongdoer is a coworker, the plaintiff/employee can bring a negligence claim seeking to prove that the employer unreasonably failed to prevent or remedy the discriminatory harassment of the plaintiff/employee where management knew or should have known about the harassment.
   b. If the wrongdoer is a supervisor with authority over the plaintiff/employee, and if the employee suffered a *tangible employment action* (job loss, demotion) because of the harassment, the employer is vicariously liable (indirect liability—see Chapter 12) for the employee's losses. That is, the employer is strictly liable for the employee's wrong and cannot offer a defense regardless of lack of knowledge, absence of negligence, or any other factor.
   c. If the wrongdoer is a supervisor with authority over the plaintiff/employee, but the employee suffered no tangible employment action, the employer can avoid liability by proving both elements of the following affirmative defense:

   (1) The employer exercised reasonable care to prevent and correct the harassment promptly (by instituting antiharassment training programs, having a policy for reporting harassment, and so on) and (2) the employee unreasonably failed to take advantage of those opportunities.

In its 2013 decision in a Title VII sexual harassment claim, *Vance v. Ball State University,* the U.S. Supreme Court restricted the definition of *supervisor* to one who could take a tangible employment action against the allegedly harassed employee.[46] The impact of that decision is illustrated in the case that follows.

McCormack v. Safeway

2014 U.S. Dist. LEXIS 17805 (D. Ariz. February 12, 2014)

LEGAL BRIEFCASE

David G. Campbell

I. BACKGROUND

Plaintiffs are two women, Mary McCormack and Samantha Stabenchek, who worked as cashiers for a Safeway store in Scottsdale, Arizona. McCormack is the mother of Stabenchek. Stabenchek was 17 years old when she started work at Safeway and appears to have been a minor during the events at issue in this case.

On March 3, 2011, Jose Lopez, a general clerk at the store, cornered Ms. Stabenchek, grabbed her buttocks, and kissed her.

Plaintiffs allege that the assault was the culmination of months of sexual harassment in which Lopez made inappropriate comments to Stabenchek in the workplace and sent her sexually explicit text messages. After the assault, McCormack reported Lopez's conduct. Stabenchek participated in Safeway's internal investigation of the assault, which led to Lopez's termination on March 26, 2011.

Less than a month after reporting the sexual assault, Plaintiffs were both interviewed about McCormack's alleged violation of Safeway's coupon policy. Safeway alleges that in late December 2010, a Safeway security analyst reported that it appeared as though McCormack was violating the company's coupon policies. The analyst allegedly discovered more evidence of coupon abuse, which she reported to a loss prevention investigator in April 2011. The investigator confronted Stabenchek and McCormack in connection with his investigation. McCormack was suspended pending further investigation. Feeling that their honesty was impugned "on the heels" of their reports about Lopez's misconduct, Plaintiffs resigned on April 13, 2011.

Stabenchek has asserted [a] sexual harassment . . . [claim] against Safeway under Title VII of the Civil Rights Act of 1964 . . . ("Title VII"). . . .

* * * * *

III. HARASSMENT CLAIMS

Title VII provides that an employer may not "discriminate against an individual with respect to [her] compensation, terms, conditions, or privileges of employment because of [her] . . . sex[.]" Sexual harassment constitutes unlawful discrimination under Title VII. *Meritor Sav. Bank v. Vinson*. . . . If the harassing employee is the victim's coworker, the employer may be held liable only if it was negligent in controlling working conditions. *Vance v. Ball State Univ.* . . . "In cases in which the harasser is a 'supervisor,' however, different rules apply," and the employer may be held vicariously liable."

A. Vicarious Liability

Safeway asserts that it cannot be held vicariously liable for Lopez's harassment because Lopez was not Stabenchek's supervisor. "[A]n employee is a 'supervisor' for purposes of vicarious liability under Title VII if he or she is empowered by the employer to take tangible employment actions against the victim." *Vance*. . . . "The ability to direct another employee's tasks is simply not sufficient" to give rise to "supervisor" status. Instead, supervisors are a "*distinct class* of agent [empowered] to make economic decisions affecting other employees under his or her control. . . . Tangible employment actions are the means by which the supervisor brings the official power of the enterprise to bear on subordinates.". . . [internal quotation marks and citation omitted] [emphasis in original].

Lopez was a front end manager when Stabenchek became an employee at Defendant's Scottsdale location, but he had been demoted to general clerk by the time much of the alleged harassment

took place, including the sexual assault. The distinction is not important, however, because neither front end managers nor general clerks qualify as supervisors under *Vance*. Front end managers and general clerks lack authority to make economic decisions affecting other employees under their control. Front end managers and general clerks are not empowered by Safeway to hire, promote, demote, fire, increase pay, decrease pay, or impose any economic change on any employees.

Plaintiffs assert that Lopez was Stabenchek's supervisor under *Vance* because he was in charge of the store during some of Stabenchek's shifts and because he sat in on Stabenchek's initial job interview and assured her that she would get her hired. Plaintiffs have presented evidence that front end managers occasionally directed other employees to sign documents that Safeway "uses to bind their employees." In addition, Plaintiffs assert that front end managers are supervisors because they have significant decision-making power, including telling employees when to clock out and when to take breaks. But Plaintiffs have provided no evidence that Lopez had any ability to influence Stabenchek's employment beyond determining the timing of her breaks and the manner in which she performed her job, and *Vance* states that "the ability to direct employee's tasks is simply not sufficient" to justify a finding that a manager is a supervisor for purposes of Title VII vicarious liability. *Vance* requires Plaintiffs to show that Lopez had power to make economic decisions affecting Stabenchek's employment at Safeway such as the ability to fire, hire, promote, or change Stabenchek's compensation. Plaintiffs have presented no evidence that Lopez possessed such authority.

Plaintiffs' reliance on *Lindquist v. Tanner* . . . is misplaced. . . . [I]n *Tanner* . . . the harasser was able to impact the plaintiff's employment status. The harasser actively recruited the plaintiff . . . [appeared] that he had the ability to determine whether or not plaintiff would become a full-time employee, and the harasser was the most senior employee on-site. . . . Lopez participated in Stabenchek's hiring process. Safeway has shown, however, that while Lopez sat in on Stabenchek's initial 5-minute screening interview, . . . the hiring decision was made by a different Safeway employee after an hour-long interview. . . . In addition, the fact that Lopez was occasionally the person in charge at Safeway's Scottsdale store is a far cry from the authority required by *Vance*.

Undisputed facts show that Lopez was not Stabenchek's supervisor as a matter of law. As a result, Safeway cannot be held vicariously liable for Lopez's harassment.

B. Liability in Negligence

Where harassment by a coworker is alleged, the employer can be held liable only if "its own negligence is a cause of the harassment." . . . Thus, an employer is responsible for its own actions or omissions and not for a coworker's harassment. "If the employer fails to take corrective action after learning of an employee's sexually harassing conduct, or takes inadequate action that emboldens the harasser to continue his misconduct, the employer can be deemed to have 'adopt[ed] the offending conduct and its results, quite as if they have been authorized affirmatively as the employer's policy.'"

An employer cannot be held liable for misconduct of which it is unaware. . . .

Safeway asserts that it cannot be held liable under a negligence theory because, although Stabenchek claims that Lopez had been making hundreds of sexual comments and sending thousands of sexual messages to her for months before the March 3 incident, Stabenchek never told anyone about any alleged harassment until March 5, the day before McCormack reported it to Safeway. Plaintiffs rejoin that Safeway can be liable because one of Safeway's managers observed Lopez harassing Stabenchek and did nothing to stop it.

. . . Stabenchek testified that about one month before the sexual assault, Megan Oxford, a second assistant manager, approached Stabenchek about an incident Oxford had witnessed. Oxford told Stabenchek that she saw an exchange between Lopez and Stabenchek after which Stabenchek looked at Lopez like she was disgusted. Oxford had not heard what Lopez said, but she urged Stabenchek to share anything that Stabenchek thought Oxford needed to know. Stabenchek declined to share any specific information with Oxford because she was uncomfortable and embarrassed. Oxford again asked Stabenchek if she wanted to report anything, but Stabenchek responded that Lopez was just being a "creep" and that she did not want to report anything.

Oxford's observations, and Stabenchek's subsequent responses to Oxford's questions, did not put Safeway on notice of Lopez's sexually harassing conduct toward Stabenchek. . . . Although Stabenchek told Oxford that Lopez was being a "creep," that uninformative comment was not enough to communicate that Lopez was sexually harassing Stabenchek.

* * * * *

Once Safeway actually learned of Lopez's sexually harassing conduct, it took prompt corrective action. Stabenchek told her mother about the Lopez's harassment on Saturday, March 5. McCormack told second assistant manager Ryan on Sunday, March 6. By Monday, March 7, the store manager, Anthony Duran, and a human resources advisor, Joyce Cameron, initiated an investigation of the incident. Lopez was interviewed later that day and was immediately suspended pending the results of the investigation. Lopez never returned to work at Safeway and was fired. . . .

* * * * *

IT IS ORDERED that Defendant's motion for summary judgment is granted.

Questions

1. According to the court, under *Vance,* Lopez was not Stabenchek's supervisor for purposes of Title VII sexual harassment liability. Why?
   a. What was the basis for the plaintiffs' assertion that Lopez was Stabenchek's supervisor? Explain.
   b. Do you think Lopez and others who are, for example, placed in charge of a store during shifts should be considered a supervisor for purposes of Title VII sexual harassment liability? Explain.

2. Truck driver Lesley Parkins claimed she was a victim of hostile environment sexual harassment while employed by Civil Constructors beginning in 1994. Parkins alleged that coworkers subjected her to foul language, sexual stories, and touching. Parkins complained to her dispatcher, Tim Spellman, and to one of her purported harassers, Robert Strong. She saw the job superintendent and the company EEO officer almost daily, but she did not complain to either. In 1996 Parkins filed a grievance with her union—Teamsters Local 325. The union contacted the company EEO officer, who immediately launched an investigation that led to punishment for the employees. Parkins conceded that she was not harassed following the company punishment. Parkins filed suit charging Civil Constructors with sexual harassment. Parkins claimed that two of her harassers, Strong and Charles Boeke, were foremen who supervised her work. Assuming Parkins can prove that she was, in fact, sexually harassed, what must she prove in order to hold Civil Constructors liable? See *Parkins v. Civil Constructors of Illinois,* 163 F.3d 1027 (7th Cir. 1998).

3. Eileen Craig worked for the Mahoney Group as the branch manager in Tucson and reported to Leon Byrd, the interim president. Over the course of several months, Byrd made repeated inappropriate comments to Craig about her legs and how she should wear shorter skirts. Although Craig thought the comments were obnoxious, she was not particularly offended. At Byrd's invitation, Craig met him for drinks after work at a restaurant, as they had done previously to discuss work-related matters. After Byrd made a sexual proposition, Craig laughed and shook her head but did not leave the restaurant. Byrd later followed Craig into the restaurant's restroom, grabbed her, and kissed her. Craig did not report this incident. Byrd made further advances to Craig that she rejected. At some point, Byrd told Craig that he didn't think he could work with her anymore. Craig finally reported Byrd's conduct under the company's sexual harassment policy. The company took immediate action: Byrd was instructed to stay away from Craig and to stop making sexual comments to her, and Craig began reporting to another company executive. The investigator retained by the employer recommended, among other things, that Byrd receive a reprimand

and training. At the end of the investigation, Craig began reporting again to Byrd. Eventually, Craig resigned and filed a complaint asserting a Title VII sexual harassment claim.

    a. Is Mahoney liable for quid pro quo sexual harassment? What questions would you have if you were on the jury? Explain.

    b. Is Mahoney liable for hostile work environment sexual harassment? What other facts might you need to know before deciding? Explain.

4. A female employed as an Installation and Repairs Technician claimed a hostile work environment was created in the garage in which she worked by the routine use of profanity, crude humor, vulgar graffiti depicting sexual acts, and especially by sexually demeaning conversations conveying a profound disrespect for women. While the comments and graffiti demeaned some male employees, the conduct was directed at all the women working in the garage. In deciding whether the conduct constituted hostile environment sexual harassment, should the court evaluate the facts from the point of view of a "reasonable person" or a "reasonable woman"? Explain.

Consider the Context: Sexual Harassment at the Casino

While she was a bartender at Gold Strike Casino Resort in Tunica County, Mississippi, Debra Brockington allegedly was subjected to sexual harassment by her female supervisor, Wanda Haley, as well as her former boyfriend and coworker, Ed Ogden. The alleged harassment included Haley grabbing Brockington's breasts, making sexually suggestive remarks to others about Brockington, and snapping a towel against her buttocks. Brockington admitted to engaging in off-color conversations and conduct with her female coworkers. In her subsequent Title VII claim, a federal trial court, addressing Haley's behavior, held that "within the context of the plaintiff's work environment the alleged harassment in this case was neither severe nor pervasive."

Questions

1. Do you agree with the court's reasoning about the importance of workplace context in determining whether unlawful harassment has occurred? Explain.

2. In its ruling, the court said, "[C]asino bartenders have the same right as other employees to expect that they will not be subjected to unlawful harassment. . . ." What impact might the court's ruling on workplace context have on the sexual harassment protections of casino bartenders and others working in similar environments?

Source: Brockington v. Circus Circus Mississippi, 2008 U.S. Dist. LEXIS 39482 (N.D. Miss. May 15, 2008).

Same Sex?

Joseph Oncale, a heterosexual who worked on an offshore oil rig, charged a supervisor and two male coworkers with sexually harassing him, including repeated taunts and several sexual assaults, one with a bar of soap while Oncale was showering. Oncale complained to superiors, but to no avail. He then quit his job and sued his employer for sexual harassment. The case went to the U.S. Supreme Court, which unanimously ruled that same-sex harassment is actionable under Title VII.[47] Oncale then settled out of court for an undisclosed amount of money. Justice Scalia, who wrote the Supreme Court opinion, explained that the harassment must be "because of sex" (that is, gender); that harassment can be motivated by hostility as well as by desire; and that common sense and social context count. Thus, smacking a football teammate on the rear end, horseplay, roughhousing, or occasional gender-related jokes, teasing, and abusive language normally would not constitute harassment. Ordinarily, plaintiffs in same-sex harassment cases must show that the behavior was motivated by (a) sexual desire, (b) general hostility to one or other gender, or (c) the victim's failure to conform to sexual stereotypes (such as effeminate behavior by a male). [For an analysis of the significance of the *Oncale* case, see **http://reason.com/archives/2003/01/01/man-trouble**].

> **What if the harasser bothers both genders equally?**

Oncale settles the big question of protection against same-sex harassment, but it raises other puzzles. For example, what if the harasser bothers both genders equally?

After *Oncale,* a husband and wife, who were also coworkers, brought a Title VII claim against their employer alleging that their supervisor had harassed both of them by soliciting sex from each of them on separate occasions. The federal appeals court affirmed the district court's dismissal, concluding that the "equal opportunity harasser" does not give rise to a Title VII sex discrimination complaint.[48]

Sexual Harassment in Other Nations

American managers working abroad must deal with international differences in attitudes toward sexual behavior in the workplace, although a general shift in harassment law in the direction of the American model is evident. This shift is significant for the American manager working abroad for a U.S.-based company, or a foreign employer controlled by an American company. The Civil Rights Act of 1991 extends Title VII's protection to American employees working abroad for such employers, but offers a "foreign law defense" under which the employer would not be required to comply with Title VII if doing so would violate the host country's law.[49] The European Union has adopted laws requiring harassment-free workplaces.[50] In Japan, sexual harassment law resembles the U.S. model.[51] In China, a woman who is sexually harassed in her workplace may file a complaint with the police under China's Protection of Rights and Interests of Women law.[52]

Retaliation

LO 13-8
Describe protections against retaliation offered under the federal statutes prohibiting employment discrimination.

The power in an employment relationship often is unbalanced in favor of the employer. In bringing a discrimination claim, an employee is vulnerable to the employer's retaliatory action. In order to protect against an employer's abuse of power and to encourage exercise of employees' rights, Title VII's antiretaliation provision prohibits an employer from discriminating against an employee for engaging in a protected activity. Protected activities include opposing an employment practice that is reasonably believed to violate Title VII or participating in a complaint made under Title VII, such as filing a charge of workplace discrimination. Other civil rights laws, including the Americans with Disabilities Act (ADA), the Age Discrimination in Employment Act (ADEA), and the Civil Rights Act of 1866, offer similar protections against retaliation.

A *prima facie* case of retaliation requires

1. Participation in a protected activity.
2. An employment action disadvantaging the plaintiff.
3. A causal connection between the protected activity and the adverse employment action.

In several recent cases, the U.S. Supreme Court has addressed Title VII's antiretaliation protection. In *Crawford v. Metropolitan Government of Nashville & Davidson County,*[53] the Court held that employees who respond to questions about workplace discrimination during the employer's informal investigation are engaged in protected activity under Title VII's antiretaliation provision, even if they did not make the complaint being investigated. In *Burlington Northern & Santa Fe Railway v. White,*[54] the U.S. Supreme Court, recognizing that a broad range of employer conduct could discourage the reasonable employee from exercising Title VII rights, held that assigning a complainant to less desirable duties is an adverse employment action on which a Title VII retaliation claim may be based. In 2011, the U.S. Supreme Court held in *Thompson v. North American Stainless*[55] that an employee is protected against retaliation resulting when his fiancée and coworker file a Title VII claim, noting that it was "obvious" that a reasonable worker might hesitate to exercise Title VII rights if it would cause the person who he or she intended to marry to be fired.

After these employee-friendly rulings, the U.S. Supreme Court's 2013 decision in *University of Texas Southwestern Medical Center v. Nassar* created a higher standard for retaliation claims than applied to "status discrimination" claims such as, for example, gender or national origin.[56] Dr. Naiel Nassar, a physician of Middle Eastern descent who was both a medical school faculty member and a staff physician at the school's affiliated hospital, complained to his department chair, Dr. Fitz, that one of Dr. Nassar's other supervisors, Dr. Levine, was biased against him based on national origin and religion. Dr. Nassar arranged to continue working as a hospital staff physician without being a member of the medical school's faculty, and sent a resignation letter to Dr. Fitz and several others explaining that he was resigning owing to Dr. Levine's harassment. Upset at the letter's statements regarding Dr. Levine, Dr. Fitz objected to the hospital's arrangement with Dr. Nassar, asserting that it violated the hospital's affiliation agreement with the medical school, under which its staff physicians were exclusively the school's faculty members; the offer was withdrawn. Dr. Nassar's resulting Title VII lawsuit included a retaliation claim based on Dr. Fitz's actions to stop his hospital employment because he had complained. A federal appellate court affirmed the trial court's finding of retaliation, as the evidence supported the conclusion that Dr. Fitz was, at least in part, motivated to retaliate against Dr. Nassar for his complaints. The U.S. Supreme Court reversed, interpreting Title VII's antiretaliation provision as requiring "but for" causation. Here, Dr. Nassar's continued employment with the hospital would have violated the hospital's affiliation agreement with the medical school, which arguably would have caused the medical school's objection to and ultimate withdrawal of Nassar's offer.

Part Four—Affirmative Action

LO 13-9
Discuss the purposes and development of affirmative action.

Some viewed the 2008 election of Barack Obama, the first African American president of the United States, as evidence that the racism staining the country's history was no longer an urgent concern. Therefore, it was argued, ***affirmative action*** efforts on behalf of minorities and women could be reduced or eliminated. However, a 2009 *Washington Post/ABC News* poll revealed that nearly half of African Americans and almost a quarter of white Americans continued to see racism as a significant social problem.[57] A 2015 poll, taken after a series of racially charged events including a hate crime attack on a South Carolina African American church, found that six in 10 Americans believed race relations in the United States were generally bad.[58] Perceptions of race discrimination and the need for affirmative action are deeply divided on racial lines, with a Tufts University study finding that whites are more likely to think antiwhite discrimination is a bigger problem than bias against African Americans.[59]

In following an affirmative action plan, employers consciously take positive steps to seek out minorities and women for hiring and promotion opportunities, and they often employ goals and timetables to measure progress toward a workforce that is representative of the qualified labor pool. Affirmative action is a means of remedying past and present discriminatory wrongs in a more expeditious and thorough manner than the market might achieve on its own.

Affirmative action efforts arise in four ways: (1) Courts may order the implementation of affirmative action after a finding of wrongful discrimination, (2) employers may voluntarily adopt affirmative action plans, (3) some statutes require affirmative action, and (4) employers may adopt affirmative action in order to do business with government agencies. Federal contractors must meet the affirmative action standards of the Office of Federal Contract Compliance Programs. [For criticisms of affirmative action, see the Center for Equal Opportunity at **www.ceousa.org**].

Early Affirmative Action Law

For nearly 20 years, judicial decisions were firmly supportive of affirmative action. A massive system of remedies emerged at all levels of government and in the private sector. In a 1979 case, *United Steelworkers of America v. Weber,*[60] the U.S. Supreme Court set out perhaps its most detailed "recipe" for those qualities that would allow a voluntary affirmative action plan in the private sector to withstand scrutiny. Weber, a white male, challenged the legality of an affirmative action plan that set aside for black employees 50 percent of the openings in a training program until the percentage of black craft workers in the plant equaled the percentage of blacks in the local labor market. The plan was the product of a collective bargaining agreement between the Steelworkers and Kaiser Aluminum and Chemical. In Kaiser's Grammercy, Louisiana, plant, only 5 of 273 skilled craft workers were black, whereas the local workforce was approximately 39 percent black. In the first year of the affirmative action plan, seven blacks and six whites were admitted to the craft training program. The most junior black employee accepted for the program had less seniority than several white employees who were not accepted. Weber was among the white males denied entry to the training program.

Weber filed suit, claiming Title VII forbade an affirmative action plan that granted a racial preference to blacks where whites dramatically exceeded blacks in skilled craft positions but where there was no proof of discrimination. The federal district court and the federal court of appeals held for Weber, but the U.S. Supreme Court reversed. Several qualities of the Steelworkers' plan were instrumental in the Court's favorable ruling:

1. The affirmative action was part of a plan.
2. The plan was designed to "open employment opportunities for Negroes in occupations which have been traditionally closed to them."

3. The plan was temporary.
4. The plan did not unnecessarily harm the rights of white employees. That is,
   a. The plan did not require the discharge of white employees.
   b. The plan did not create an absolute bar to the advancement of white employees.

Then, in an important 1987 public-sector decision, *Johnson v. Transportation Agency,*[61] the Supreme Court approved the extension of affirmative action to women. The political tides were turning, however. The 1980s were politically conservative years. Appointments to the Supreme Court and to the lower federal courts, by President Reagan in particular, reflected that mood. Affirmative action was under attack.

Rethinking Affirmative Action

From the late 1980s to the present, a series of judicial decisions and increasing public and political skepticism have challenged the legality and the wisdom of affirmative action, at least where the government is involved. The 1989 *City of Richmond v. J. A. Croson Co.*[62] case struck down Richmond, Virginia's minority "set-aside" program that required prime contractors who were doing business with the city to subcontract at least 30 percent of the work to minority businesses. The Court said such race-conscious remedial plans were constitutional only if (1) the city or state could provide specific evidence of discrimination against a particular protected class in the past (rather than relying on proof of general societywide discrimination) and (2) its remedy was "narrowly tailored" to the needs of the situation.

Then, in *Adarand Constructors v. Pena,* a landmark 1995 decision, the Supreme Court struck down a federal highway program that extended bidding preferences to "disadvantaged" contractors.[63] The suit was brought by Randy Pech, a white contractor whose low bid on a Colorado guardrail project was rejected in favor of the bid of a minority firm. The Supreme Court ruled that the government's preference program denied Pech his right to equal protection under the law as guaranteed by the Fifth Amendment to the federal Constitution. [For a "Timeline of Affirmative Action Milestones," see **www.infoplease.com/spot/affirmativetimeline1.html**].

In the 2009 *Ricci v. DeStefano* decision that follows, the U.S. Supreme Court addressed the dilemma employers sometimes face in using hiring and promotion tests that may have a disparate impact on some groups of employees.

LEGAL BRIEFCASE

Ricci v. DeStefano
129 S. Ct. 2658 (2009)

Justice Kennedy

* * * * *

In 2003, 118 New Haven [Connecticut] firefighters took examinations to qualify for promotion to the rank of lieutenant or captain. . . . The results would determine which firefighters would be considered for promotions during the next two years, and the order in which they would be considered. Many firefighters studied for months, at considerable personal and financial cost.

When the examination results showed that white candidates had outperformed minority candidates, the mayor and other local politicians opened a public debate that turned rancorous. Some firefighters argued the tests should be discarded because the results showed the tests to be discriminatory. They threatened a discrimination lawsuit if the City made promotions based on the tests. Other firefighters said the exams were neutral and fair. And they, in turn, threatened a discrimination lawsuit if the City, relying on the statistical racial disparity, ignored the test results and denied promotions to the candidates who had performed well. In the end the City took the side of those who protested the test results. It threw out the examinations.

Certain white and Hispanic firefighters who likely would have been promoted based on their good test performance sued the City and some of its officials. Theirs is the suit now before us. The suit alleges that, by discarding the test results, the City and the named officials discriminated against the plaintiffs based on their race, in violation of . . . Title VII of the Civil Rights Act of 1964. . . . The City and the officials defended their actions, arguing that if they had certified the results, they could have faced liability under Title VII for adopting a practice that had a disparate impact on the minority firefighters.

I

* * * * *

A

The [City] charter establishes a merit system. That system requires the City to fill vacancies in the classified civil-service ranks with the most qualified individuals, as determined by job-related examinations. After each examination, the New Haven Civil Service Board (CSB) certifies a ranked list of applicants who passed the test. Under the charter's "rule of three," the relevant hiring authority must fill each vacancy by choosing one candidate from the top three scorers on the list.

* * * * *

Under the [union] contract, applicants for lieutenant and captain positions were to be screened using written and oral examinations, with the written exam accounting for 60 percent and the oral exam 40 percent of an applicant's total score. To sit for the examinations, candidates for lieutenant needed 30 months' experience in the Department, a high-school diploma, and certain vocational training courses. Candidates for captain needed one year's service as a lieutenant in the Department, a high-school diploma, and certain vocational training courses.

* * * * *

The City hired Industrial/Organizational Solutions, Inc. (IOS) to develop and administer the examinations, at a cost to the City of $100,000. IOS is an Illinois company that specializes in designing entry-level and promotional examinations for fire and police departments. In order to fit the examinations to the New Haven Department,

IOS began the test-design process by performing job analyses to identify the tasks, knowledge, skills, and abilities that are essential for the lieutenant and captain positions.

* * * * *

At every stage of the job analyses, IOS, by deliberate choice, oversampled minority firefighters to ensure that the results—which IOS would use to develop the examinations—would not unintentionally favor white candidates. With the job-analysis information in hand, IOS developed the written examinations to measure the candidates' job-related knowledge.

* * * * *

After IOS prepared the tests, the City opened a 3-month study period. It gave candidates a list that identified the source material for the questions, including the specific chapters from which the questions were taken. IOS developed the oral examinations as well. These concentrated on job skills and abilities.

* * * * *

Candidates took the examinations in November and December 2003. Seventy-seven candidates completed the lieutenant examination—43 whites, 19 blacks, and 15 Hispanics. Of those, 34 candidates passed—25 whites, 6 blacks, and 3 Hispanics. Eight lieutenant positions were vacant at the time of the examination. Under the rule of three, this meant that the top 10 candidates were eligible for an immediate promotion to lieutenant. All 10 were white.

* * * * *

Forty-one candidates completed the captain examination—25 whites, 8 blacks, and 8 Hispanics. Of those, 22 candidates passed—16 whites, 3 blacks, and 3 Hispanics. Seven captain positions were vacant at the time of the examination. Under the rule of three, 9 candidates were eligible for an immediate promotion to captain—7 whites and 2 Hispanics.

B

Based on the test results, the City officials expressed concern that the tests had discriminated against minority candidates.

* * * * *

[The City decided] not to certify the results.

C

The [City's] decision not to certify the examination results led to this lawsuit. The plaintiffs—who are the petitioners here—are 17 white firefighters and 1 Hispanic firefighter who passed the examinations but were denied a chance at promotions when the [City] refused to certify the test results. They include the named plaintiff, Frank Ricci. . . .

Petitioners . . . filed timely charges of discrimination with the Equal Employment Opportunity Commission (EEOC); . . . asserting that the City violated the disparate-treatment prohibition contained in Title VII of the Civil Rights Act of 1964. . . .

Respondents [the defendants] asserted they had a good-faith belief that they would have violated the disparate impact prohibition in Title VII . . . had they certified the examination results. It follows, they maintained, that they cannot be held liable under Title VII's disparate-treatment provision for attempting to comply with Title VII's disparate-impact bar. Petitioners countered that respondents' good-faith belief was not a valid defense to allegations of disparate treatment. . . .

The District Court granted summary judgment for respondents. . . . The Court of Appeals affirmed. . . .

II

B [A OMITTED—ED.]

Petitioners allege that when the [City] refused to certify the captain and lieutenant exam results based on the race of the successful candidates, it discriminated against them in violation of Title VII's disparate-treatment provision. The City counters that its decision was permissible because the tests "appear[ed] to violate Title VII's disparate-impact provisions."

Our analysis begins with this premise: The City's actions would violate the disparate-treatment prohibition of Title VII absent some valid defense. All the evidence demonstrates that the City chose not to certify the examination results because of the statistical disparity based on race—i.e., how minority candidates had performed when compared to white candidates. . . .

We consider, therefore, whether the purpose to avoid disparate-impact liability excuses what otherwise would be prohibited disparate-treatment discrimination.

* * * * *

If an employer cannot rescore a test based on the candidates' race, then it follows . . . that it may not take the greater step of discarding the test altogether to achieve a more desirable racial distribution of promotion-eligible candidates—absent a strong basis in evidence that the test was deficient and that discarding the results is necessary to avoid violating the disparate-impact provision. . . .

For the foregoing reasons, we adopt the strong-basis-in-evidence standard as a matter of statutory construction to resolve any conflict between the disparate-treatment and disparate-impact provisions of Title VII.

* * * * *

Title VII does not prohibit an employer from considering, before administering a test or practice, how to design that test or practice in order to provide a fair opportunity for all individuals, regardless of their race. . . . We hold only that, under Title VII, before an employer can engage in intentional discrimination for the asserted purpose of avoiding or remedying an unintentional disparate impact, the employer must have a strong basis in evidence to believe

it will be subject to disparate-impact liability if it fails to take the race-conscious, discriminatory action.

* * * * *

C

The City argues that, even under the strong-basis-in-evidence standard, its decision to discard the examination results was permissible under Title VII. That is incorrect.

* * * * *

. . . [T]here is no evidence—let alone the required strong basis in evidence—the tests were flawed because they were not job-related or because other, equally valid and less discriminatory tests were available to the City. Fear of litigation alone cannot justify an employer's reliance on race to the detriment of individuals who passed the examination and qualified for promotions. The City's discarding the test results was impermissible under Title VII. . . .

Our holding today clarifies how Title VII applies to resolve competing expectations under the disparate-treatment and disparate-impact provisions. If, after it certifies the test results, the City faces a disparate-impact suit, then in light of our holding today it should be clear that the City would avoid disparate-impact liability based on the strong basis in evidence that, had it not certified the results, it would have been subject to disparate-treatment liability.

[Reversed and remanded.]

Questions

1. *a.* Why did the city of New Haven reject the results of the promotion examination?
   b. Why did the court rule that the city had violated Title VII?
   c. Do you agree with the judgment of the court?

2. What could an employer do to avoid the situation New Haven faced in this case?

3. Frederick Claus, a white man with a degree in electrical engineering and 29 years of experience with Duquesne Light Company, was denied a promotion in favor of a black man who had not earned a bachelor's degree and did not have the required seven years of experience. Only 2 of 82 managers in that division of Duquesne Light were black. Claus sued, claiming in effect that he was a victim of "reverse discrimination." At trial, both sides conceded that the black candidate was an outstanding employee and that he was qualified to be a manager. Decide the case. Explain. See *Claus v. Duquesne Light Co.,* 46 F.3d 1115 (1994), *cert. denied,* 115 S. Ct. 1700 (1995).

4. In 1974, Birmingham, Alabama, was accused of unlawfully excluding blacks from management roles in its fire department. After several years of litigation, Birmingham adopted an affirmative action plan that guaranteed black firefighters one of every two available promotions. The city, the Justice Department, and others applauded the arrangement, but a group of 14 white

firefighters claimed they were victims of reverse discrimination. After years of wrangling, the white firefighters' claim reached the 11th Circuit Federal Court of Appeals. Was the affirmative action plan lawful? Explain. See *In re Birmingham Reverse Discrimination Employment Litigation*, 20 F.3d 1525 (11th Cir. 1994), *cert. denied sub nom. Martin v. Wilks*, 115 S. Ct. 1695 (1995).

5. In a later case involving the same promotional examinations at issue in *Ricci*, Michael Briscoe, an African American firefighter for the city of New Haven who applied to be promoted to lieutenant but was rejected, brought a Title VII claim asserting that the city had created a disparate impact against African Americans by weighing the written test more heavily

than the oral examination. The city of New Haven brought a motion to dismiss in federal trial court. Decide. See *Briscoe v. New Haven*, 654 F.3d 200 (2d Cir. 2011), *cert. denied*, 132 S. Ct. 2741 (2012).

6. Shea, a white Foreign Service officer, brought a Title VII suit against the State Department alleging its hiring plan from 1990 to 1992 to increase racial diversity among the Foreign Service's officer corps caused him to enter the Foreign Service at a lower level than he would have had he been a minority. The plan targeted manifest imbalances in senior-level Foreign Service officer positions that had resulted from past discrimination. Does *Ricci* apply to this case? What should be the outcome? Explain. See *Shea v. Kerry*, 796 F.3d 42 (D.C. Cir. 2015).

Affirmative Action: Where Are We?

Some confusion remains after *Ricci*, given differences in analysis between cases based on the Constitution and those brought under Title VII,[64] and whether those cases address employers' screening, set-asides, or other practices. What has been made clear is that both quotas and affirmative action justified broadly by "societal discrimination" are unconstitutional.

Quotas are unconstitutional.

A lawful affirmative action remedy in employment cases apparently will be evaluated, in most cases, by the following considerations:

- The plan addresses a compelling interest such as remedying past or present discrimination or correcting the underutilization of women and minorities.
- The plan is temporary.
- The plan is narrowly tailored to minimize layoffs and other burdens.

In *Ricci*, the U.S. Supreme Court noted that employers could still make "affirmative efforts" to encourage equal opportunity in promotions.[65] While ensuring that screening procedures are not discriminatory or irrelevant,[66] employers may undertake diversity initiatives designed to create an inclusive workplace environment that supports fairness, respect, and equal opportunity. While President Obama supported workplace diversity initiatives through executive orders, at this writing President Trump is expected to rescind these, and corporate diversity officers have looked to expand diversity initiatives to include socioeconomic opportunity.[67] [For information on diversity programs at U.S. companies, see Diversity Inc. at **http://diversityinc.com/**].

Part Five—Additional Discrimination Topics

Religious Discrimination

LO 13-10
Describe the concept of reasonable accommodation as applied to religious- and disability-based discrimination claims.

Kimberly Cloutier was employed as a cashier at Costco in West Springfield, Massachusetts. The store revised its dress code to prohibit all facial jewelry other than earrings. Cloutier, a member of the "Church of Body Modification,"

> A member of the "Church of Body Modification."

was advised to remove her facial piercings. She declined to do so saying that her piercings were part of her religion. The church's approximately 1,000 members engaged in such practices as piercing, tattooing, branding, and cutting. Eventually, Cloutier was fired. She sued Costco claiming she was a victim of religious discrimination in violation of Title VII of the Civil Rights Act of 1964. Costco, however, prevailed when the federal First Circuit Court of Appeals ruled that excusing Cloutier from the dress code would be an undue hardship for Costco because the company had a legitimate interest in presenting to the public a workforce that was reasonably professional in appearance.[68]

The Law

Title VII's protections against religious discrimination and harassment in the workplace include the employer's duty to reasonably accommodate employees' religious beliefs and practices. As was evident in Cloutier's conflict with Costco, reasonably accommodating religious practices often poses challenges for employers. Consider, for example, the employer who must balance an employee's religious practice of proselytizing or discussing religion in the workplace against other employees' right to be free from religious harassment.

Employers need not accommodate an employee's religious practice or belief if it creates an "undue hardship"—an unreasonable burden—on the workplace. The leading religious discrimination case is *Trans World Airlines, Inc. v. Hardison,* in which the plaintiff, who celebrated his religion on Saturdays, was unable to take that day off from his work in a parts warehouse.[69] Efforts to swap shifts or change jobs were unsuccessful. The company rejected Hardison's request for a four-day week because it would have required the use of another employee at premium pay. The Supreme Court's ruling in the case reduced the employer's duty to a very modest standard: "To require TWA to bear more than a *de minimis* cost in order to give Hardison Saturdays off is an *undue hardship*." Saturdays off for Hardison would have imposed extra costs on TWA and would have constituted religious discrimination against other employees who would have sought Saturday off for reasons not grounded in religion. So any accommodation imposing more than a *de minimis* cost on the employer represents an undue hardship and is not required by Title VII. Of course, the lower courts have differed considerably on what constitutes a *de minimis* cost and an undue hardship. For example, an Ohio court ruled that an employee, a Seventh Day Adventist, was discriminated against when he was fired for refusing to work from sundown Friday to sundown Saturday. The employee could have been moved to an earlier shift at no cost.[70]

An employer might be unsure whether employees who request accommodation are sincere in their religious beliefs or merely seeking an advantage such as a longer break or trying to avoid workplace requirements under attendance or grooming policies. The EEOC defines religion broadly as "moral and ethical beliefs of what is right and wrong which are sincerely held with the strength of religious views."[71] This broad view of religious beliefs arguably indicates that employers should err in favor of moving forward to the central issue: Is an accommodation reasonable or would it create an undue hardship?

Questions

1. Resolving job-related religious conflicts can be among the most emotionally demanding management dilemmas. For example, what challenges would you face as a manager if one of your subordinates, as an expression of her religious beliefs, wore to work an antiabortion button displaying a picture of a fetus? How would you address these challenges? See *Wilson v. U.S. West Communications,* 58 F.3d 1337 (8th Cir. 1995).

2. Yisrael worked as a dump truck driver for a North Carolina company providing paving, grading, and utility services for transportation projects. As a member of the Hebrew Israelite faith, Yisrael observed Sabbath on Saturday. After refusing to work three different Saturdays, he was terminated. The EEOC filed a lawsuit on behalf of Yisrael. What further information would you need to decide this case? Explain. See *EEOC v. Thompson Contracting, Grading, Paving, & Utilities, Inc.,* 499 F. App'x 275 (4th Cir. 2012) (unpublished op.).

3. An Oklahoma lighting company, Voss, advertised a vacancy for an "operations supervisor" position at its Tulsa location through the website of a Tulsa-area church attended by a Voss supervisor. Wolfe, who had prior operations management experience, learned about the vacancy and applied for the position although he did not himself attend the church. Most of the job interview concerned Wolfe's religious activities and beliefs and whether he "would have a problem" coming into work early to attend Bible study before clocking in. The branch manager seemed hesitant to accept Wolf's answers as truthful. At the time Wolfe was interviewed, Voss had no viable candidates for the position being filled. Wolfe was not offered the job, and after continuing its search, the company hired an individual whose religious ideology matched that of the company's leadership. Wolfe filed an EEOC religious discrimination complaint.[71] Decide. Explain.

The Americans with Disabilities Act (ADA)

As a child, Edward Carmona was diagnosed with psoriasis, a skin disease causing intermittent but treatable inflammations. As an adult working as a flight attendant for Southwest Airlines, Carmona was diagnosed with psoriatic arthritis, which causes painful joint swelling and stiffness during attacks of psoriasis. Although medication eased some of his discomfort, these attacks left Carmona unable to walk without great pain for one-half to one-third of each month. After his intermittent leave under Family and Medical Leave Act (FMLA—see Chapter 12) expired, he was fired for excessive absenteeism. Carmona brought a disability discrimination claim against Southwest Airlines under the Americans with Disabilities Act (ADA), winning a jury verdict that was vacated by the federal trial court. A federal appeals court overturned the federal trial court's decision to vacate the jury's award, concluding that Southwest Airlines' attendance policy was extremely lenient, and the jury could have reasonably found other nondisabled flight attendants with similar absenteeism not being fired, and that Carmona's supervisors were annoyed by his disability-related absences.[73]

This situation illustrates the general purpose of the ADA, which seeks to remove barriers to a full, productive life for individuals with disabilities. The ADA forbids discrimination in employment, public accommodations, public services, transportation, and telecommunications. Small businesses with fewer than 15 employees are exempted from the employment portions of the ADA. The Rehabilitation Act of 1973 protects public sector workers with disabilities from employment discrimination.

Under the ADA, a qualified individual who (1) has a physical or mental impairment that substantially limits one or more *major life activities,* (2) has a record of such an impairment, or (3) is regarded as having such an impairment may not be discriminated against in employment.

In a series of decisions, the U.S. Supreme Court narrowed the scope of the ADA, prompting a leading disabilities rights advocate to call the ADA "the incredible shrinking law."[74] In response, the Americans with Disabilities Amendments Act (ADAAA) was passed by Congress and signed into law by President George W. Bush in 2008 to overturn those decisions and establish broader definitional guidelines under the ADA.

Defining Disabilities

As amended by the ADAAA, the ADA emphasizes that "disability" should be defined broadly in offering protection from employment discrimination. Examples of such disabilities include epilepsy, hypertension, asthma, diabetes, major depressive disorder, bipolar disorder, and schizophrenia. A nonexhaustive list of major life activities specified by the ADAAA includes eating, sleeping, standing, lifting, bending, concentrating, thinking, communicating, and all major bodily functions, including reproduction.

Alcoholism, drug addiction, and AIDS are disabilities under the ADA. However, the ADA excludes from its protection job applicants and employees who *currently* use illegal drugs. Employees with past drug or alcohol problems are protected by the ADA, as are employees with current alcohol problems who are able to perform the essential functions of the job. An employer may lawfully take an adverse employment action on the basis of, for example, a drug test showing use of illegal controlled substances or alcohol-induced unprofessional conduct at work. Those who are rehabilitated or are currently in rehabilitation are protected from disabilities discrimination. In sum, the ADA treats alcoholism and drug addiction as medical conditions and protects those who are overcoming these impairments.

Taking medication or using a prosthetic device to overcome an impairment does not exclude an individual from the ADA's protection. Episodic conditions such as epilepsy, if creating a "substantial limitation" on an individual's major life activities, ordinarily would be covered by the ADA. In addition, an impairment in remission, such as cancer, is covered if it would substantially limit a major life activity when active.[75]

"Regarded as Having" a Disability

An individual who does not have a disability may still be protected under the ADA. If an employer incorrectly assumes that an applicant or employee has a disability, and then takes discriminatory action on that basis, the employer has violated the ADA. For example, an employer who denies an employee a promotion to a managerial position requiring extensive client contact is likely to have violated the ADA if the promotion was denied because of the employer's mistaken belief that the employee is a recovering alcoholic who would not be able to manage client meetings where alcohol is frequently served.

Accommodating Individuals with Disabilities

An employer may not discriminate in hiring or employment against a *qualified person with a disability*. A qualified person is one who can perform the *essential job functions* with or without *reasonable accommodation*. The ADA requires employers to make reasonable accommodations for disabled employees and applicants. Reasonable accommodations might include structural changes in the workplace, job reassignment, job restructuring, or new equipment. Employers are not required to provide an accommodation that would create an *undue hardship*. For example, the employer need not create a new position to reassign an employee who can no longer perform the essential job functions, but rather should place the employee in an appropriate vacant job. The employer should engage in an interactive dialogue with the employee to explore possible reasonable accommodations. [For EEOC advice about small employers and reasonable accommodation, see **www.eeoc.gov/facts/accommodation.html**].

"Getting to Work" with Reasonable Accommodation

Jeanette Colwell was hired as a part-time retail clerk at a Rite Aid store in Old Forge, Pennsylvania. She worked various shifts, including 5 pm to 9 pm, and she earned supervisors' recognition for good performance. A few months after being hired, Colwell was diagnosed with "retinal vein occlusion and glaucoma in her left eye," and eventually she became blind in that eye. Colwell informed her supervisor, Susan Chapman, that her partial blindness made it dangerous and difficult for her to drive to work at night. She asked to be assigned to day shifts only so that she would be able to get to work. (Bus service stopped at 6 pm, and there were no taxis serving the area where the store was located.) Chapman refused the request because it "wouldn't be fair" to other workers, and she continued to schedule Colwell for a mix of day and evening shifts. Colwell later sent Chapman a doctor's note recommending that Colwell not drive at night, but Chapman was still unwilling to assign Colwell to day shifts only. Colwell resigned and brought an ADA claim against Rite Aid. The federal trial court ruled that Rite Aid had no duty to accommodate Colwell because she was able to perform all her work duties at the store; Colwell appealed.

Questions

1. Is Colwell an "individual with a disability" under the ADA? Explain.
2. How should Chapman have responded to Colwell's request? Explain.
3. A part-time retail clerk who is unable to drive because he is "legally blind" requests a late arrival to his shift due to a long bus commute. The store manager refuses his request and subsequently terminates him for being late to work on a number of occasions. The clerk brings an ADA claim against his former employer. Decide. Explain.

Source: Colwell v. Rite Aid, 602 F.3d 495 (3d Cir. 2010).

The ADA in Practice

In early 2016, the unemployment rate for individuals with a disability was nearly 11 percent, while the general unemployment rate dipped below 5 percent.[76] Some employers may hesitate to hire workers with disabilities out of misconceptions and fear of added costs for accommodations.[77] However, in recent years companies have made efforts to increase the presence of individuals with disabilities in the professional workforce. For example, the National Business & Disability Council runs "Emerging Leaders," a summer internship program offering business placements for college and graduate students with disabilities.[78] [For more information, see Emerging Leaders at **www.emerging-leaders.com/**].

Tax credits to hire and provide access to individuals with disabilities, as well as tax deductions to remove architectural barriers to make its facilities more accessible, also provide incentives for employers to hire and retain employees with disabilities.[79]

Rosa's Law: Changing the Words

Signed by President Obama in 2010, Rosa's Law, named after Rosa Marcellino, a nine-year-old with Down Syndrome, changes the language in all federal health, education, and labor laws to remove the phrase "mentally retarded" and replace it with "intellectual disability." President Obama quoted Rosa's brother Nick as saying: "What you call people is how you treat them. If we change the words, maybe it will be the start of a new attitude towards people with disabilities."

Sources: Rosa's Law, Pub. L. No. 111-256, 124 Stat. 2643 (2010) [**www.govtrack.us/congress/bill. xpd?bill=s111-2781**]; and President Barack Obama, "Remarks by the President at the Signing of the 21st Century Communications and Video Accessibility Act of 2010," White House Press Office, October 8, 2010 [**www.whitehouse. gov/the-press-office/2010/10/08/remarks-president-signing-21st-century-communications-and-video-accessib**].

ADA Questions

1. Core, a social services worker, had difficulty breathing at work when she was exposed to the perfume Japanese Cherry Blossom, worn by coworkers; on one occasion, she sought emergency medical treatment. Core's coworkers allegedly mocked her condition on their Facebook pages. Her employer rejected several of her accommodation requests, including a proposed fragrance-free workplace policy. The employer sent an e-mail message to employees asking that they not enter into Core's cubicle but to communicate with her instead by telephone and e-mail only, and asked Core to hold office discussions in better ventilated areas. After exhausting her FMLA leave entitlements (see Chapter 12), Core was placed on inactive pay status. The employer offered to permit Core to return to work and make such accommodations as instructing staff to refrain from wearing Japanese Cherry Blossom and allowing her to take breaks to get fresh air. Core rejected these offers and was effectively terminated. Core brought an ADA claim against her former employer. Decide. Explain. *Core v. Champaign County Board of Commissioners,* 2012 U.S. Dist. LEXIS 149120 (S.D. Ohio October 17, 2012).

2. Foley was terminated from his job as a financial advisor with Morgan Stanley after he removed and took away the central processing unit (CPU)—including the hard drive—from his office computer without authorization, and was not truthful about his actions for several days after doing so. Morgan Stanley's employment policies and procedures forbid the removal of its "trade secrets," defined as including computer software or hardware used in computers or word processors. Foley admitted he was terminated because of his misconduct but argued that his actions in taking the computer and being untruthful were caused by a manic episode of bipolar disorder. Therefore, in bringing an ADA claim against Morgan Stanley, Foley argued that the resulting termination was "because of" his disability. Decide. Explain. See *Foley v. Morgan Stanley Smith Barney,* 2013 U.S. Dist. LEXIS 28873 (S.D. Fla. March 4, 2013).

Genetic Testing

Title I of the Genetic Information Nondiscrimination Act (GINA) prohibits employers from discriminating because of genetic information. With few exceptions, employers are not allowed to gather genetic information regarding an employee or the employee's family members.[80] For example, using "family medical history" as a basis for an employment decision because of the individual's increased risk of heart disease in the future would be unlawful because it is not relevant to the individual's "current ability to work."[81]

Age Discrimination

Can a clothing store featuring styles designed for the college market lawfully prefer youthful salespersons? May a marketing firm reject older applicants in an effort to bring "new blood" into its workforce? While these questions are not definitively resolved, employers taking such actions might face liability for age discrimination.

ADEA Claims   The Age Discrimination in Employment Act (ADEA) protects those 40 years and older from employment discrimination based on their age. Disparate treatment and harassment claims may be brought under the ADEA, and a 2005 Supreme Court decision extended ADEA protection to disparate impact claims also.[82] In its 2009 *Gross v. FBL* decision, the U.S. Supreme Court made it more difficult to win an ADEA disparate treatment claim.[83] Jack Gross had worked for FBL for over 30 years when at age 54 he was reassigned from Claims Administration Director to Coordinator, while his former duties were transferred to a younger worker whom he had supervised. Gross filed an ADEA claim against FBL claiming the demotion violated the ADEA, and he won a jury verdict after showing that his age played a role in FBL's decision. FBL appealed. The U.S. Supreme Court held that an ADEA disparate treatment claim requires the plaintiff to show that age was not just one factor, but the deciding or "but-for" factor in the employer's decision.[84] The proposed Protecting Older Workers Against Discrimination Act, which would have reversed *Gross,* was introduced in Congress but was not enacted.

Defenses   The employer may defend against an age discrimination claim by showing that the termination was based on a *legitimate, nondiscriminatory reason* (such as poor performance) or that age is a bona fide occupational qualification (BFOQ). For example, if there is no test available to predict when a commercial airline pilot over 60 years of age might experience a medical emergency that could jeopardize aviation safety, then being under 60 years of age is arguably a BFOQ for that job.[85] The ADEA also provides that an employer can defeat an age discrimination claim by demonstrating that a "reasonable factor other than age" (like poor attendance) was the actual reason for terminating or otherwise disfavoring an older worker. In 2008, the U.S. Supreme Court held that an employer using this defense in a disparate impact case carries the burden of proving a "reasonable factor other than age." [86]

Reverse Age Discrimination?

Being young is cool, but younger workers may get cold treatment in the workplace. Younger workers often seem to take the brunt of layoffs. Recently, the unemployment rate for those between the ages of 25 and 34 was 9.6 percent, as compared with 6.5 percent for those 55 or older. Fear of ADEA lawsuits may be one reason companies use seniority to determine who will be retained in a reduction in force.

Question

Should the ADEA protect against age discrimination, regardless of age? Explain.

Source: Dana Mattioli, "With Jobs Scarce, Age Becomes an Issue," *The Wall Street Journal,* May 19, 2009 [**www/ wsj.com**].

Questions

1. Mary, 61 years old, worked as a leasing consultant for a realty company for over two years before she was fired. The primary duty of a leasing consultant is to rent apartments. The company used phone and video evaluations to assess employees' performance. During her employment, Mary's scores allegedly were, with one exception, consistently below expectations. Allegedly, she violated company policies by showing an apartment without getting the prospective tenant's proof of identification, holding an apartment without a deposit, and showing an apartment not to be shown. Mary, who allegedly had been warned and placed on probation, claimed that during the termination meeting, her supervisor made age-related comments, as she had on several prior occasions. Mary sued her former employer for discrimination under the ADEA. Decide. Explain. See *Marsh v. Associated Estates Realty Corp.,* 521 F. App'x 460 (6th Cir. 2013) (unpublished op.).

2. The Insurance Company of North America (ICNA) sought to hire a "loss control representative." The ad called for a B.S. degree, two years of experience, and other qualities. The plaintiff, who had 30 years of loss control experience, applied for the job but was

not interviewed. ICNA hired a 28-year-old woman with no loss control experience. The plaintiff sued claiming age discrimination. ICNA said the plaintiff was overqualified.

a. Explain both the plaintiff's and defendant's arguments.

b. Decide the case. Explain. See *EEOC v. Insurance Co. of North America,* 49 F.3d 1418 (9th Cir. 1995).

Sexual Orientation Discrimination

LO 13-11

Discuss the current status of protections against sexual orientation discrimination in the workplace.

At this writing, sexual orientation is not itself a protected category under Title VII. However, federal courts have interpreted Title VII to allow sexual orientation discrimination claims as a "subset" of sex discrimination claims. For example, a 2017 federal appellate court decision found that an openly lesbian part-time faculty member who had been denied full-time opportunities and then not reappointed in her adjunct position, allegedly because of her sexual orientation, could bring a Title VII sex discrimination claim based on her right to associate with members of the same sex, and her apparent nonconformity with gender norms.[87] In 2013, the Employment Non-Discrimination Act (ENDA), which would prohibit employers from discriminating on the basis of an employee's actual or perceived sexual orientation, was reintroduced after having been proposed but not enacted over the years.[88] It failed to pass Congress, although a 2013 poll showed that a majority of Americans support legal protection against employment discrimination based on sexual orientation.[89] In 2014, President Obama signed Executive Order 13672 that added sexual orientation and gender identity to protection against discrimination in hiring and employment by federal government contractors, and the Fair Pay and Safe Workplaces Executive Order 13673, which required that these contractors demonstrate compliance with antidiscrimination protections.[90] In March 2017, President Trump revoked Executive Order 13673.[91] Given the political climate at this writing, the possible enactment of federal statutory protections against sexual orientation discrimination in the near future seems remote. Nevertheless, as of this writing, 22 states and the District of Columbia prohibit employment discrimination based on sexual orientation.[92]

Sexual Orientation Discrimination or Sex Stereotyping?

Henderson began working for a staffing company that gave preference to employees with transportation. Although Henderson had transportation, he was assigned to projects when it was difficult to find someone else. Henderson filed a lawsuit alleging that he was routinely subjected to derogatory remarks by and in the presence of his supervisors, including that he "looked just like a woman," was not a "real man," and that he was a "woman pretending to be something else. . . ." In denying the company's motion for summary judgment on the Title VII claims, the court noted that Henderson's claim demonstrates the tension between two legal principles. On the one hand, Title VII does not protect against discrimination based on sexual orientation. On the other hand, an employer cannot discriminate against an employee who does not meet gender stereotypes or norms. See *Henderson v. Labor Finders of Virginia,* 2013 U.S. Dist. LEXIS 47753 (E.D. Va. April 2, 2013).

Gender Identity Discrimination

Several states and the District of Columbia prohibit employment discrimination based on gender identity or expression.[93]

> The supervisor saw only a man in a woman's clothing.

In the 2012 case of *Macy v. Holder,* the EEOC decided that it would treat transgender discrimination complaints as sex discrimination claims.[94] Federal courts have also recognized such claims as sex discrimination based on stereotyping men and women.[95]

In 2015, the Equality Act was proposed to add both gender identity and sexual orientation as protected categories under Title VII, but it failed in Congress.[96] Executive Order 13672, signed in 2014 by President Obama and discussed above, added gender identity to the antidiscrimination protections of federal civil service workers and prohibited federal government contractors from discriminating on the basis of both sexual orientation and gender identity in their hiring and employment practices.[97] At this writing, President Trump has not revoked this Executive Order. However, his revocation of President Obama's 2014 Fair Pay and Safe Workplaces Executive Order 13673 has been seen as effectively nullifying Executive Order 13672's protections of federal government contractors' employees because contractors will no longer be required to show their compliance with labor laws as a requisite for obtaining federal contracts.[98]

[For an American Civil Liberties Union video advocating a transgender-inclusive Employment Non-Discrimination Act, see "New Video Shows the Need for a Transgender-Inclusive ENDA" at **[https://youtu.be/UEPsK_axRqo]**.] For an EEOC training seminar on the EEOC's *Macy* decision, see EEOC Federal Training and Outreach Division, "What Does the *Macy* Decision Mean for Title VII?" June 15, 2012 [**www.eeoc.gov/federal/training/brown_bag_macy.cfm**].

Internet Exercise

At this writing, the Healthy Workplace bill addressing workplace bullying has been introduced in a number of state legislatures. Using the Healthy Workplace Campaign's web page [**www.healthyworkplacebill.org/faq.php**], answer the following questions:

1. How is workplace bullying defined?
2. What is the argument supporting legislation addressing workplace bullying?
3. How is the Healthy Workplace bill different from antidiscrimination protections?
4. What arguments might be raised against the Healthy Workplace bill?

Chapter Questions

1. Blockbuster established a grooming policy forbidding long hair for men but allowing it for women. Four men, who were fired for refusing to cut their long hair, sued Blockbuster for sex discrimination. Has Blockbuster violated Title VII? Explain. See *Kenneth Harper et al. v. Blockbuster,* 139 F.3d 1385 (11th Cir.), *cert. denied,* 525 U.S. 1000 (1998).

2. In 2006, the EEOC filed a class action against Lawry's Restaurants, including Lawry's The Prime Rib, Five Crowns, and The Tam O'Shanter Inn, on behalf of all male applicants for server positions who were systematically rejected because of their gender. Since 1938, Lawry's had hired only females as servers and did not update their policy after the passage of Title VII. Servers' uniforms are antiquated women's costumes. What might Lawry's defense be? Will this defense be successful? Explain. See Equal Employment Opportunity Commission, "Lawry's to Pay $1 Billion for Sex Bias Against Men in Hiring," press release, November 2, 2009 [**www.eeoc.gov/eeoc/ newsroom/release/11-2-09.cfm**].

3. Emma, a Chinese American, applies for an available server position in a Mexican restaurant and is rejected. She suspects it is because of her national origin. What might the Mexican restaurant say in defense of a national origin discrimination complaint made by Emma? Will this defense be successful? Explain. See *EEOC Compliance Manual,* Section 13: National Origin, at 13-II-C (2002) [**https://www.eeoc.gov/laws/ guidance/national-origin-guidance.cfm**].

4. Reeves worked as a transportation sales representative at a shipping company. Reeves was the only woman working on the sales floor, an open area structured into a "pod" of cubicles. Six males worked with Reeves. Reeves could often hear the language of her male coworkers as they spoke over the phone or with each other. Reeves could also hear the central office radio located in the "pod" that was used by her coworkers to listen to a crude morning show. On a daily basis at work, Reeves heard vulgar language and discussions of sexual topics, including such derogatory terms as "bitch" and "whore," which her male coworkers used to describe customers. The male branch manager once asked Reeves to speak to "that stupid bitch on line 4." Reeves brings a Title VII sexual harassment claim against her employer. Decide the case. Explain. See *Reeves v. Robinson Worldwide, Inc.,* 594 F.3d 798 (11th Cir. 2010).

5. In *McCormack v. Safeway,* included as a "Legal Briefcase" in this chapter, the plaintiffs brought a retaliation claim along with their sexual harassment claims. Less than a month after reporting the sexual assault, the plaintiffs were both interviewed about McCormack's alleged violation of Safeway's coupon policy. A Safeway loss prevention investigator confronted Stabenchek and McCormack in connection with his investigation. McCormack was suspended pending further investigation. Feeling their honesty was being questioned because of their complaint, plaintiffs resigned. Decide the retaliation claim. Explain. See *McCormack v. Safeway,* 2014 U.S. Dist. LEXIS 17805 (D. Ariz. February 12, 2014).

6. A company runs credit checks on applicants for senior executive and financial positions. Among the "red flags" are bankruptcy filings, delinquent child support payments, and wage garnishments. The EEOC brought a lawsuit alleging that a disproportionate number of African Americans were adversely impacted by this credit check. What would the EEOC need to show to prove its claim, and what evidence would be needed? Explain. See *EEOC v. Kaplan Higher Education Corp.,* 748 F.3d 749 (6th Cir. 2014).

7. Assume a company located near your college has asked you to create an outreach program to increase diversity in its workforce. What challenges would you face? What steps would you take? Explain.

8. Hooters, a restaurant chain mentioned earlier that features scantily clad female waitresses, maintained an "Image Policy" that required waitresses' hair to be "styled and glamorous," and not appear "bizarre, outrageous or extreme," or be colored "more than two-shades in variance" from a natural color. Farryn Johnson, an African American Hooters waitress, decided to put blond highlights in her hair during the summer. She was told by her Hooters manager to take out the highlights because they were not natural to African American women, while white waitresses were allowed to keep similar hairstyles because some white women have that color hair naturally. Has Hooters violated Title VII? Decide. Explain. See Joel Landau, "Hooters Ordered to Pay $250,000 to Black Waitress Who Was Told She Couldn't Have Blonde Streaks in Her Hair," *New York Daily News,* April 8, 2015 [**www.nydailynews.com/news/national/hooters-ordered-pay-250-000-racial-discrimination-article-1.2177919**].

9. Thornton worked as a manager at a Connecticut retail store. In accordance with his religious beliefs, Thornton notified his manager that he could no longer work on Sundays as required by company (Caldor, Inc.) policy. A Connecticut statute provided that: "No person who states that a particular day of the week is observed as his Sabbath may be required by his employer to work on such day. An employee's refusal to work on his Sabbath shall not constitute grounds for his dismissal." Management offered Thornton the options of transferring to a Massachusetts store where Sunday work was not required or transferring to a lower-paying supervisory job in the Connecticut store. Thornton refused both, and he was transferred to a lower-paying clerical job in the Connecticut store. Thornton claimed a violation of the Connecticut statute. The store argued that the statute violated the Establishment Clause (see Chapter 5) of the First Amendment, which forbids establishing an official state religion and giving preference to one religion over another or over none at all. Ultimately the case reached the U.S. Supreme Court.

   a. Decide. Explain.

   b. Do the religious accommodation provisions of Title VII of the Civil Rights Act violate the Establishment Clause? See *Estate of Thornton v. Caldor, Inc.,* 472 U.S. 703 (1985).

10. Sanchez worked as a host and food server at a pair of Azteca restaurants. Throughout his work experience, male coworkers and a supervisor referred to him as "she" and "her." He was mocked for walking and carrying his serving tray "like a woman." He was called a "faggot" and a "female whore." This abuse occurred repeatedly.

   a. Make the argument that Sanchez was not a victim of sexual harassment.

   b. Decide the case. Explain. See *Nichols v. Azteca Restaurant Enterprises,* 256 F.3d 864 (9th Cir. 2001).

11. Jane Doe was employed by C.A.R.S. Protection Plus for nearly a year when she learned she was pregnant. After amniocentesis revealed severe defects, Doe decided to terminate her pregnancy. Doe then took one week of vacation to recuperate from the procedure. The following week, she was fired for unexcused absences and job abandonment. Doe filed a claim under the Pregnancy Discrimination Act (PDA), alleging she was fired because of her choice to undergo a surgical abortion. Decide the case. Explain. See *Doe v. C.A.R.S. Protection Plus,* 527 F.3d 358 (3d Cir. 2008).

12. After settling or litigating sexual harassment claims against its executives, Fox News is at this writing the defendant in a racial discrimination suit brought by two African American employees. The lawsuit focuses on Judy Slater, the former Fox News controller who was fired amid complaints that she regularly made racist and inappropriate comments to her African American employees. The suit asserts that Slater also made similar comments to members of other ethnic groups. If the case goes to trial, what defenses would you expect Fox News to raise? Explain. See Stephen Battaglio, "Two Black Workers Sue Fox News in Bias Case," *Los Angeles Times,* March 30, 2017, p. C3.

13. Michael Cooke, an African American male, worked at Novellus Systems in Silicon Valley where he had to listen on a regular basis to a Vietnamese American coworker playing and rapping aloud to music lyrics that included racial epithets such as the "N-word." Although Cooke complained several times to his supervisors and made it clear that the language was offensive to him, the coworker continued to sing along to offensive lyrics within Cooke's earshot, and to use slang including racial epithets. The EEOC, on behalf of Cooke, brought a Title VII claim against Novellus Systems for racial harassment. Decide. See U.S. Equal Employment Opportunity Commission, "Silicon Valley Manufacturer Novellus . . . Racial Harassment," press release, June 24, 2008 [**www.eeoc.gov/eeoc/newsroom/release/6-24-08.cfm**].

14. Victoria Pietras, a female probationary volunteer firefighter of the Farmingville Fire District, had passed the written and medical exams to become a volunteer firefighter. However, she failed a physical agility test requiring her to perform nine tasks such as dragging a water-filled hose weighing approximately 280 pounds for 150 feet in four minutes or less. The time requirement was based on average times of the mostly male firefighters who participated in a test run. Pietras brought a Title VII sex discrimination claim that the physical test created an unlawful disparate impact against women.

    a. If you were the EEOC investigator, what questions would you have? Explain. See *Pietras v. Farmingville Fire District,* 180 F.3d 468 (2d Cir. 1999).

    b. On a related note, should physical agility or fitness tests be gender-normed so that, for example, female FBI trainees can be required to only do a minimum of 14 push-ups, while male trainees must complete at least 30 pushups? Explain. See *Bauer v. Lynch,* 561 F.3d 38 (4th Cir. 2016).

15. Should American firms abroad adhere to American antidiscrimination policies even if those policies might put the American firms at a competitive disadvantage or offend the values and mores of the host country? Explain.

16. Reeves, who has Down Syndrome, was employed by a supermarket as a bagger for eight years. He received vocational tutoring and individual training from Jewel and a social service agency. Jewel created supervision policies that applied only to Reeves, such as a daily feedback form sent to his parents, his legal guardians, at their request. Reeves was fired after he cursed and insulted a cashier within the earshot of a customer and other employees. Reeves' parents filed an ADA claim on his behalf, alleging that Jewel discriminated against Reeves because of his disability. Decide. Explain. See *Reeves v. Jewel Stores,* 759 F.3d 698 (7th Cir. 2014).

Notes

1. 135 S. Ct. 2028 (2015).
2. See Jenny Strasburg, "Abercrombie to Pay $50 Million in Bias Suits," *San Francisco Chronicle,* November 10, 2004, p. C1; and Julie Tamaki, "Judge Accepts Abercrombie Plan to Settle Hiring Lawsuits," *Los Angeles Times,* November 17, 2004, p. C2.
3. *Abercrombie & Fitch,* 135 S. Ct. 2028, *rev'g* 731 F.3d 1106 (10th Cir. 2015).
4. Michael Lopardi, "Minority Groups Sue Abercrombie for $40 M," *University Wire,* January 27, 2005.
5. Devah Pager, "The Mark of a Criminal Record," *American Journal of Sociology* 105, no. 5 (March 2003), pp. 937–975 [**www.northwestern.edu/ipr/publications/papers/2003/pager-ajs.pdf**].
6. General Accounting Office, "Diversity Management: Expert-Identified Leading Practices and Agency Examples," GAO-05-90 (Washington, DC, January 14, 2005) [**www.gao.gov/htext/d0590.html**].
7. 347 U.S. 483 (1954).
8. A portion of this paragraph is drawn from William P. Murphy, Julius G. Getman, and James E. Jones Jr., *Discrimination in Employment,* 4th ed. (Washington, DC: Bureau of National Affairs, 1979), pp. 1–4.
9. 127 S. Ct. 2162 (2007).
10. Pub. L. No. 111-2, 123 Stat. 5 (2009).
11. *Mach Mining v. EEOC,* 135 S. Ct. 1645 (2015).
12. *EEOC v. Waffle House Inc.,* 534 U.S. 279 (2002).
13. Martha Neil, "Most Job Discrimination Suits Win, at Best, Small Settlements, Study Says," *ABA Journal,* June 9, 2010 [**www.abajournal.com/news/article/most_job_discrimination_suits_win_small_settlements_at_best_study_says**].
14. American Bar Foundation, "ABF Study of Unfairness in Employment Discrimination Lawsuits Published in *Law & Society Review,*" press release, May 8, 2012 [**www.americanbarfoundation.org/news/331**].
15. *Haynes v. W.C. Caye & Co.,* 52 F.3d 926 (11th Cir. 1995).
16. See *International Brotherhood of Teamsters v. United States,* 97 S. Ct. 1843 (1977); *American Tobacco v. Patterson,* 456 U.S. 63 (1982); and *Firefighters Local Union No. 1784 v. Stotts,* 467 U.S. 561 (1984).
17. Tresa Baldas, "Employment Tests May Fail Legal Exam," *National Law Journal,* February 18, 2008, p. 4.
18. Equal Employment Opportunity Commission, Fact Sheet on Employment Tests and Selection Procedures [**www.eeoc.gov/policy/docs/factemployment_procedures.html**].
19. Equal Employment Opportunity Commission, "EEOC to Receive 'Friend in Government' Award from American Arab Anti-Discrimination Committee," press release, October 1, 2004 [**www.eeoc.gov/eeoc/newsroom/release/10-1-04.cfm**].
20. Pamela Babcock, "Sample post-Sept. 11 discrimination cases filed with EEOC," *SHRM HR News,* September 1, 2006 [**https://www.shrm.org/hr-today/news/hr-news/Pages/0906editors2.aspx**].
21. Equal Employment Opportunity Commission, "Strategic Enforcement Plan: Fiscal Years 2017–2021" [**www.eeoc.gov/eeoc/plan/sep-2017.cfm**].
22. Equal Employment Opportunity Commission, "Questions and Answers for Employees: Workplace Rights of Employees Who Are, or Are Perceived to Be, Muslim or Middle Eastern," November 2016 [**www.eeoc.gov/eeoc/publications/muslim_middle_eastern_employees.cfm**].

23. Equal Employment Opportunity Commission, "Enforcement Guidance on National Origin Discrimination," November 18, 2016 [**www.eeoc.gov/eeoc/publications/muslim_middle_eastern_employees.cfm**].

24. Ibid.

25. Ibid.

26. *Garcia v. Spun Steak Co.,* 998 F.2d 1480 (9th Cir. 1993), *cert. denied,* 114 S. Ct. 2726 (1994).

27. Equal Employment Opportunity Commission, "Jury Awards $200,000 in Damages Against A.C. Widenhouse in EEOC Race Harassment Suit," press release, February 1, 2013 [**www.eeoc.gov/eeoc/newsroom/release/2-1-13.cfm**].

28. Equal Employment Opportunity Commission, "RockTenn Services Pays $500,000 to Settle EEOC Race Harassment Suit," press release, December 3, 2012 [**www.eeoc.gov/eeoc/newsroom/release/12-3-12b.cfm**].

29. *Tyrrell v. Oaklawn Jockey Club,* 2012 U.S. Dist. LEXIS 157482 (W.D. Ark. November 2, 2012).

30. *Boyer-Liberto v. Fontainebleau Corp.,* 786 F.3d 264 (4th Cir. 2015).

31. *Ash v. Tyson,* 546 U.S. 454 (2006); and *Aman v. Cort Furniture Rental Corp.,* 85 F.3d 1074 (3d Cir. 1996).

32. "Women's Earnings 83 Percent of Men's, but Vary by Occupation," U.S. Bureau of Labor Statistics, January 15, 2016 [**www.bls.gov/opub/ted/2016/womens-earnings-83-percent-of-mens-but-vary-by-occupation.htm**].

33. Matthew Rousu, "Childless Women in Their Twenties Out-Earn Men. So?" *Forbes,* February 24, 2014 [**www.forbes.com**].

34. Colleen McCain Nelson, "Most Women See Bias in the Workplace," *The Wall Street Journal,* April 11, 2013 [**http://online.wsj.com/news/articles/SB10001424127887324695104578417020376740796**].

35. Kim Elsesser, "Harassment v. the Gender Gap," *Los Angeles Times,* October 9, 2015 [**www.latimes.com**].

36. *Walmart v. Dukes,* 564 U.S. 338 (2011).

37. Impact Fund, "Update: Settlement Approved in the Costco Gender Discrimination Class-Action" [**www.impactfund.org/litigation/impact-fund-cases/ellis-v-costco-wholesale-corp**].

38. Stacy Blackman, "Study Examines Male–Female Wage Gap, Post–MBA," *US News: Education,* August 26, 2011 [**www.usnews.com/education/blogs/mba-admissions-strictly-business/2011/08/26/study-examines-male-female-wage-gap-post-mba**].

39. "Charge Statistics (Charges Filed with the EEOC) FY 1997–2016," U.S. Economic Opportunity Employment Commission [**www.eeoc.gov/eeoc/statistics/enforcement/charges.cfm**].

40. See, generally, *Diaz v. Pan American World Airways Inc.,* 442 F.2d 385 (5th Cir.), *cert. denied,* 404 U.S. 950 (1971).

41. *Chadwick v. Wellpoint Inc.,* 561 F.3d 38 (1st Cir. 2009).

42. *Warren v. Solo Cup,* 516 F.3d 627 (7th Cir. 2008).

43. Society for Human Resource Management, "Is Workplace Harassment on the Rise?" SHRM Poll, April 16, 2010 [**www.shrm.org/Research/SurveyFindings/Articles/Pages/SexualHarassmentontheRise.aspx**].

44. "Study Finds Link between Women in Power, Sexual Harassment," *Phys.org,* August 2, 2012 [**http://phys.org/news/2012-08-link-women-power-sexual.html**].

45. *Burlington Industries v. Ellerth,* 524 U.S. 742 (1998); and *Faragher v. Boca Raton,* 524 U.S. 775 (1998).

46. 133 S. Ct. 2434 (2013).

47. *Oncale* v. *Sundowner Offshore Services,* 523 U.S. 75 (1998).

48. *Holman v. State of Indiana,* 211 F.3d 299 (7th Cir. 2000).

49. Kiren Dosanjh, "Crossing Boundaries: Sexual Harassment Liability of U.S.-Based Multi-National Corporations in Developing Countries," [**www.sba.muohio.edu/abas/2001/brussels/Dosanjh_Crossing_Boundaries.pdf**].

50. Stephen Miller, "Sexual Jokes No Laughing Matter," *Glasgow Herald,* June 7, 2002, p. 4.

51. Gerald L. Maatman Jr., "A Global View of Sexual Harassment," *HR Magazine,* July 2000, p. 151.

52. "Government Laws on Sexual Harassment in Various Countries," *The Economic Times,* August 22, 2010 [**http://articles.economictimes.indiatimes.com/2010-08-22/news/28445217_1_sexual-harassment-title-vii-equal-employment-opportunity-commission**].

53. 555 U.S. 271 (2009).

54. 548 U.S. 53 (2006).

55. 131 S. Ct. 863 (2011).

56. 133 S. Ct. 2517 (2013).

57. Michael A. Fletcher and Jon Cohen, "Far Fewer Consider Racism Big Problem," *The Washington Post,* January 19, 2009 [**www.washingtonpost.com/wp-dyn/content/article/2009/01/18/AR2009011802538.html**].

58. Douglas G. Ware, "Americans Feel Race Relations Are Bad or Worse," *UPI.com,* July 23, 2015 [**www.upi.com/Top_News/US/2015/07/23/Poll-Americans-feel-race-relations-are-bad-or-worse/9421437699774**].

59. Asraa Mustufa, "Study: Whites Think 'Reverse Racism' Is on the Rise," *Colorlines,* May 24, 2011 [**www.colorlines.com/articles/study-whites-think-reverse-racism-rise**].

60. 443 U.S. 193 (1979).

61. 480 U.S. 616 (1987).

62. 488 U.S. 469 (1989).

63. 115 S. Ct. 2097 (1995).

64. Charles A. Sullivan, "Circling Back to the Obvious: The Convergence of Traditional and Reverse Discrimination in Title VII Proof," *William and Mary Law Review* 46 (December 2004), p. 1031.

65. *Ricci v. DeStefano,* 129 S. Ct. 2658, 2677 (2009).

66. Steven Greenhouse, "Supreme Court Ruling Offers Little Guidance on Hiring," *The New York Times,* June 30, 2009 [**www.nytimes.com**].

67. John Simons, "Workplace Diversity Efforts Get a Reboot," *The Wall Street Journal,* February 15, 2017, p. B5.

68. *Cloutier v. Costco,* 390 F.3d 126 (1st Cir. 2004), *cert. denied,* 545 U.S. 1131 (2005).

69. 423 U.S. 63 (1977).

70. *Franks v. National Lime & Stone Co.,* 740 N.E.2d 694 (Ohio Ct. App. 2000).

71. *EEOC Compliance Manual,* Section 12: Religious Discrimination, July 22, 2008 [**www.eeoc.gov/policy/docs/religion.html**].

72. U.S. Equal Employment Opportunity Commission, "Voss Lighting to Pay $82,500 to Settle Religious Discrimination Lawsuit," press release, March 19, 2013 [**www.eeoc.gov/eeoc/newsroom/release/3-19-13a.cfm**].

73. *Carmona v. Southwest Airlines,* 604 F.3d 848 (5th Cir. 2010).

74. Joan Biskupic, "High Court Raises Bar for ADA," *USA TODAY,* January 9, 2002, p. 3A.

75. *Hoffman v. Carefirst of Fort Wayne Inc.,* 2010 U.S. Dist. LEXIS 107493 (N.D. Ind. October 6, 2010).

76. Shaun Heasley, "Hiring Dips for People with Disabilities," *Disability Scoop,* February 5, 2016 [**www.disabilityscoop.com/2016/02/05/jobs-january-16/21873**].

77. Sara Murray, "Disabled Face Sharply Higher Jobless Rate," *The Wall Street Journal,* August 26, 2010, p. A5.

78. Suzanne Robitalle, "Support Grows for Disabled Job Seekers," *The Wall Street Journal,* July 22, 2008, p. D4.

79. "Facts About Disability-Related Tax Provisions," Equal Employment Opportunity Commission [**www.eeoc.gov/facts/fs-disab.html**].

80. Pub. L. No. 110-233, 122 Stat. 881 (2008).

81. "Types of Discrimination: Genetic Information Discrimination," Equal Employment Opportunity Commission [**www.eeoc.gov/laws/types/genetic.cfm**].

82. *Smith v. City of Jackson,* 544 U.S. 228 (2005).

83. 129 S. Ct. 2343 (2009).

84. Ibid.

85. Protecting Older Workers Against Discrimination Act, S. 2189, 112th Cong. (2012) [**www.govtrack.us/congress/bills/112/s2189**].

86. *Meacham v. Knolls Atomic Power Laboratory,* 554 U.S. 84 (2008).

87. *Hively v. Ivy Tech,* 2017 U.S. App. LEXIS 5839 (7th Cir. April 4, 2017); see also *Terveer v. Billington,* 34 F. Supp. 3d 100 (D.D.C. 2014).

88. Employment Non-Discrimination Act, S. 815, 113th Cong. (2013) [**www.govtrack.us/congress/bills/113/s815**].

89. Andrew Gelman, "Poll Says ENDA Has Majority Support in Every Congressional District," *The Washington Post,* November 20, 2013 [**www.washingtonpost.com/blogs/monkey-cage/wp/2013/11/20/polls-say-enda-has-majority-support-in-every-congressional-district**].

90. Exec. Order No. 13672 of July 21, 2014, *Federal Register* 79 (July 23, 2014), pp. 42971–42972; and Exec. Order No. 13673 of July 31, 2014, *Federal Register* 79 (August 5, 2014), pp. 45309–45315.

91. White House Office of the Press Secretary, March 27, 2017 "Presidential Executive Order on the Revocation of Federal Contracting Executive Orders" [**https://www.whitehouse.gov/the-press-office/2017/03/27/presidential-executive-order-revocation-federal-contracting-executive**].

92. "Non-Discrimination Laws: State-by-State Information—Map," American Civil Liberties Union (as of March 31, 2017) [**www.aclu.org/map/non-discrimination-laws-state-state-information-map**].

93. Ibid.

94. "Processing Complaints by LGBT Federal Employees," U.S. Equal Employment Opportunity Commission [**www.eeoc.gov/federal/directives/lgbt_complaint_processing.cfm**].

95. *Schroer v. Billington,* 577 F. Supp. 2d (D.D.C. 2008).

96. The Equality Act, H.R. 3185, 114th Cong. (2015) [**www.congress.gov/bill/114th-congress/house-bill/3185**].

97. Exec. Order No. 13672.

98. Lisa Hardaway, "Trump to Businesses—'Federal Government Doesn't Care How You Treat Your Employees,'" *Lambda Legal,* March 27, 2017 [**www.lambdalegal.org/news/us_20170327_trump-rescinds-federal-business-anti-discrim-eo**].

Video icon credit: ©Comstock Images/Alamy

CHAPTER FOURTEEN

Employment Law III: Labor–Management Relations

After completing this chapter, students will be able to fulfill the following learning objectives:

14-1. Describe both the decline of labor unions and their hopes for renewal.

14-2. Describe the goals of the National Labor Relations Act (NLRA).

14-3. Identify unfair labor practices by management and unions.

14-4. Describe the role of the National Labor Relations Board (NLRB) in enforcing the NLRA.

14-5. Describe the process of union organizing and the related legal issues.

14-6. Describe "bargaining in good faith."

14-7. Distinguish between "unfair labor practice strikes" and "economic strikes."

14-8. Compare and contrast "primary picketing" and "secondary picketing/boycotts."

14-9. Describe employees' rights within or against unions.

14-10. Explain the impact of "right-to-work" laws on union security agreements.

Introduction

Working behind the counter of a fast-food restaurant has been commonly thought of as the domain of teenagers looking for a temporary job to make "pocket money." However, the economic downturn found many older workers seeking to make a living as minimum-wage workers in the fast-food industry. In 2013, protests in New York City and Los Angeles by fast-food workers demanding higher wages highlighted this shift and its impact.[1] In April 2016, New York and California passed legislation to gradually increase the minimum wage to $15.[2] That same month, the Fight for $15 campaign launched by a labor union turned its attention to unionizing fast-food workers as a way to improve job conditions. The National Restaurant Association argued that dramatically raising the minimum wage threatens job opportunities to those looking to gain entry into the industry.[3]

Global economic shifts have split America's private-sector unions in two pieces: one, the old-line manufacturing organizations represented by the United Auto Workers (UAW), for example; the other, the emerging service sector organized most notably by the Service Employees International Union (SEIU), which represents approximately 2 million nurses, security guards, janitors, and others. Traditional union power in manufacturing has been deeply undercut by the outsourcing of jobs abroad to take advantage of cheaper wages. Substantial decreases in private consumption and investment in recent years, leading to declines in manufacturing and construction, also have significantly impacted union membership. In 2015, the union membership rate remained at 11.1 percent as in 2014; since 1983, union membership has fallen nearly 50 percent.[4] The unionization rate among public sector workers is more than five times that of private sector workers.[5]

Auto Industry and Unions   The challenges facing unions in the manufacturing sector were vividly illustrated by the 2007 settlements of new labor agreements between the United Auto Workers (UAW) and the Big Three American automobile manufacturers: General Motors (GM), Ford, and Chrysler. In return for automakers' promises of investments to maintain manufacturing jobs in the United States, UAW members agreed to dramatic contract changes, allowing the Big Three to compete more effectively with their nonunion competitors, Toyota, Honda, and others.[6] After the UAW's attempts to unionize auto workers in foreign-owned auto plants such as Volkswagen in Tennessee were unsuccessful, Volkswagen announced an "engagement policy" under which a union demonstrating 15 percent membership at the plant could engage in constructive dialog with management, but not collectively bargain on behalf of workers. The opportunities for engagement increase with higher levels of membership. UAW created Local 42 for the plant's workers, which met the membership requirement for the highest level of engagement: meeting biweekly with Human Resources and monthly with the plant's Executive Committee.[7]

Union Support   According to a 2015 Gallup poll, nearly 6 out of 10 Americans have a favorable view of labor unions, up from an all-time low favorability rating of 48 percent in 2009.[8] However, laws curtailing the power of unions have been passed in state legislatures. For example, as discussed later in this chapter, a 2011 Wisconsin law restricts public-sector employees' collective-bargaining rights.[9] In 2015, Wisconsin joined other traditionally "union" states such as Michigan in becoming a "right to work" state, also discussed later in this chapter. A shift away from traditional unionized industries along with union corruption has certainly played a big role in union struggles, but union supporters say corporate resistance has made organizing very difficult. To counteract this, some unions have moved beyond traditional organizing to engage nonunion workers in workplace activism.[10] [See Working America, **www.workingamerica.org/**].

Questions

1. What are the arguments both for and against a wage increase for fast-food workers? Cities including Chicago, San Francisco, and Los Angeles have their own minimum wage requirements that are higher than the federal minimum wage. Why might a city set a higher minimum wage? Explain.

2. Andrew Puzder, a fast-food restaurant executive who withdrew as President Trump's first nominee for U.S. Secretary of Labor, has observed that replacing workers with machines is an understandable reaction to raising the minimum wage.[11] Should companies be allowed to replace workers with machines to maximize profit? What might be the economic and social impacts of automating jobs held by workers? Explain.

Does the Union Have a Fight Song?

In 2015, the NLRB rejected Northwestern University football players' petition to unionize, declining to exercise jurisdiction over the issue of whether NCAA athletes could be considered employees and unionize. The NLRB noted the complexities that would result if one NCAA team unionized while others did not, if a union negotiated terms that conflicted with the NCAA's rules. In 2014, an NLRB Chicago regional director had ruled that the Northwestern football players were employees based on the hours they spent each week in practice, the strict rules set by coaches, and the financial aid they received as compensation. The 2015 decision by the NLRB board applies only to the Northwestern players' petition, not student teaching assistants or other student workers, and leaves open the possibility of allowing college athletes to unionize in the future.

Questions

1. Do you support the unionization of college athletes? Explain.
2. Do you think student teaching assistants, student janitors, and other student workers should be allowed to unionize? Explain.

Sources: Douglas Belkin, Melanie Trottman, and Rachel Bachman, "College's Football Team Can Unionize," *The Wall Street Journal,* March 27, 2014, p. A2; and Ben Strauss, "NLRB Rejects Northwestern Football Players' Union Bid," *The New York Times,* August 17, 2015.

Part One—History

LO 14-1

Describe both the decline of labor unions and their hopes for renewal.

As the United States moved from an agrarian to an industrial society in the late 1880s, business competition was fierce. Costs had to be cut. By paying workers as little as possible and making them work 14- to 18-hour days, employers could prosper. Farmers began moving to the city to be near their jobs and thus left their safety net of gardens, chickens, and cows. Similarly, immigrants streamed into the big cities, and competition for jobs became heated. Wages fell, and deplorable working conditions were the norm.[12] Some of those immigrants brought with them ideas and experiences in labor conflict and class struggle that would soon contribute to dramatic changes in the American workplace.

A Grim Picture

To say that working conditions for many people at this time were unpleasant or even dismal would be a vast understatement. The term *desperate* better describes the problem. Children were impressed into service as soon as they were big enough to do a job and

> Children were employed in coal mines because they were small enough to fit in the confined spaces

then made to work 12- and 14-hour days.[13] In fact, small children were employed in coal mines for 10 to 12 hours each day, and at a rate of $1 to $3 per week, because they were small enough to fit in the confined spaces.[14] Textile companies sent men called *slavers* to New England and southern farm communities to gather young women to work in the mills.[15]

The following firsthand report from the early 20th century reveals the grim picture:

When I moved from the North to the South in my search for work, I entered a mill village to work in a cotton mill as a spinner. There I worked 11 hours a day, five and a half days a week, for $7 a week. In a northern mill I had done the same kind of work for $22 a week, and less hours. I worked terribly hard. . . .

The sanitary conditions were ghastly. When I desired a drink of water, I had to dip my cup into a pail of water that had been brought into the mill from a spring in the fields. It tasted horrible to me. Often I saw lint from the cotton in the room floating on top of the lukewarm water. All of the men chewed tobacco, and most of the women used snuff. Little imagination is needed to judge the condition of the water which I had to drink, for working in that close, hot spinning room made me thirsty. Toilet facilities were provided three stories down in the basement of the mill in a room without any ventilation. Nowhere was there any running water. . . .

Everything in the village is company owned. The houses look like barns on stilts, and appear to have been thrown together. When I would go inside one of them, I could see outside through the cracks in the walls. The workers do all of their trading at the company store and bank, and use the company school and library for they have no means of leaving the village.[16]

Compare those working-class conditions with the lifestyle of John D. Rockefeller, the great tycoon of the same era. Although Rockefeller was notoriously frugal, his estate at Pocantico Hills, New York, contained

. . . more than 75 buildings. . . . Within his estate were 75 miles of private roads on which he could take his afternoon drive; private golf links on which he could play his morning game; and anywhere from 1,000 to 1,500 employees, depending on the season.

. . . Rockefeller also owned an estate at Lakewood, [New Jersey] which he occupied in the spring; an estate at Ormond Beach in Florida for his winter use; a townhouse . . . in New York; an estate at Forest Hill, Cleveland which he did not visit; and a house on Euclid Avenue in Cleveland, likewise unused by him.[17]

These circumstances enable us to better understand the sense of injustice felt by many workers. [For a timeline of the labor movement, see **http://75.afscme.org/history**].

Who's the Boss?

In 2014, the NLRB authorized complaints against both McDonald's franchisees and McDonald's USA, LLC, as joint employers alleging that McDonald's workers had faced workplace retaliation for participating in wage protests (see this chapter's Introduction). The following year, the NLRB changed its joint-employer standard to make a business that has "indirect control" over its subcontractor's employees a "joint employer" of those workers, and therefore required to collectively bargain with the workers' union. Critics believe these decisions could destroy the franchise business model and undermine business service contracts.

Question

From an ethical perspective, should McDonald's as a corporate entity be held accountable for its franchisee's labor practices? How about a tech company that contracts with a janitorial services company—should the tech company be treated as a joint employer of the janitors? Discuss.

Sources: National Labor Relations Board, "NLRB Office of the General Counsel Authorizes Complaints Against McDonald's Franchisees and Determines McDonald's, USA, LLC Is a Joint Employer," July 29, 2014 [**www.nlrb. gov**]; and Opinion, "NLRB Joint Employer Attack," *The Wall Street Journal,* August 28, 2015 [**www.nlrb.gov**].

Organizing Labor

The Knights of Labor, the first major labor organization in the United States, had a large following during the 1870s and 1880s.[18] The order admitted any workers to its ranks, regardless of occupation, gender, or nationality; in fact, the only people excluded from the group were gamblers, bankers, stockbrokers, and liquor dealers.[19] The Knights of Labor dedicated itself to principles of social reform, including the protection of wage and hour laws, improved health care systems, and mandatory education.[20] However, the goals of the Knights of Labor were perhaps too broad and far-reaching to bring workers any relief from their immediate problems. Great philosophical divisions within the Knights of Labor brought about its rapid decline.[21]

Skilled Workers

Samuel Gompers, who built and developed the American Federation of Labor (AFL), had more practical, attainable goals in mind for his organization. Gompers, a worker in the cigar industry, saw the need to organize workers along craft lines (such as plumbers, electricians, and machinists) so that each craft group could seek higher wages and better working conditions for its own workers, all of whom had the same type of skills and, presumably, shared the same occupational goals.[22] This approach, a national association of local unions directed to workers' pragmatic needs rather than the more politically motivated activities of the Knights of Labor, proved to be a successful formula for union organization.

Laborers

The Congress of Industrial Organizations (CIO) was organized in response to the needs of ordinary laborers not working in the skilled trades to which the AFL was devoted. The CIO was organized in 1935 and served assembly line workers and others who often performed repetitive, physically demanding tasks. The AFL and CIO were fierce competitors, but after years of bitter conflict, the two groups united forces in 1955. They function together today as the AFL–CIO. [For the AFL–CIO home page, see **www.aflcio.org**].

Unions and the Developing Law

Labor Protection

Responding to mounting public pressure, Congress passed the Norris–LaGuardia Act in 1932 making clear that the terminology "restraint of trade," which was the heart of the 1890 Sherman Antitrust Act (see Chapter 10), was not meant to include labor organizations or activities.

From 1932 to 1935, labor tensions continued to mount. The nation was still caught in the Great Depression. Believing that one element essential to economic recovery was stability in the workforce, Congress addressed the labor question with the Wagner Act of 1935. This legislation gave workers for the first time the unequivocal right to organize and engage in concerted activities for their mutual aid and benefit. To protect this right, Congress identified and made illegal a number of unfair labor practices. Through the Wagner Act, Congress also established the National Labor Relations Board (see below).

Management Protection

Unions grew rapidly with the passage of the Wagner Act, and by 1947 Congress decided management might need a little help in coping with ever-growing labor organizations.[23] Congress enacted the Taft–Hartley Act, identifying as unfair labor practices certain activities unions used to exercise economic leverage over employers as part of the collective bargaining process. The Taft–Hartley Act also ensured employers' right to speak out in opposition to union organizing—in effect, protecting their First Amendment right to freedom of speech. Thus, the Taft–Hartley Act signaled a move by the government away from unconditional support for labor toward a balance of rights between labor and management.[24]

Corrupt Union Leaders

In response to the growing evidence that union leaders were benefiting at the expense of the membership, Congress in 1959 enacted the Landrum–Griffin Act, requiring unions to keep records of their funds. It also prohibits unions from lending money except under specified circumstances and procedures, all of which must be reported annually to the government.

Members' Rights

The Landrum–Griffin Act also contains a set of provisions often referred to as the "Bill of Rights" for individual union members. These provisions are designed to protect union members by requiring that union meetings be held, that members be permitted to speak and vote at these meetings, that every employee covered by a collective-bargaining agreement has the right to see a copy of that agreement, and that a union member be informed of the reasons and given a chance for a hearing if the union wishes to suspend or take disciplinary action against that member, unless he or she is being suspended for nonpayment of dues.[25]

The law has also regulated the manner in which unions represent employees in the collective-bargaining process. Because a union serves as employees' exclusive bargaining representative, the courts have devised a *duty of fair representation*.[26] To fulfill this duty, a union must represent employees, in both negotiating and enforcing the collective-bargaining agreement, "without hostility or discrimination . . . [and] . . . with complete good faith and honesty [so as to] avoid arbitrary conduct."[27]

Part Two—Labor Legislation Today

Today labor–management relations are governed by the National Labor Relations Act (NLRA), as enforced by the National Labor Relations Board (NLRB).[28] This act includes within it the Wagner Act, the Taft–Hartley Act, and portions of the Landrum–Griffin Act. The remaining provisions of the Landrum–Griffin Act make up the Labor–Management Reporting and Disclosure Act and the Bill of Rights of Members of Labor Organizations.

PRACTICING ETHICS)   Reading Your Rights at Work

Posters by the U.S. Department of Labor (see Chapter 12) and the Equal Employment Opportunity Commission (EEOC—see Chapter 13) informing workers of their rights are familiar sights in the workplace. In 2012, the NLRB issued a Notice Posting Rule requiring most private-sector employers— regardless of whether their workers were unionized—to post a notice advising employees of their rights under the NLRA. However, two federal appellate decisions invalidated this rule; the NLRB announced in 2014 that it would not seek review by the U.S. Supreme Court. Under a 2015 Executive Order, federal contractors and subcontractors are still required to inform employees of their NLRA rights, but whether that remains in effect under the Trump administration is unclear at this writing. The workplace poster remains available on the NLRB website [see www.nlrb.gov/poster]. In addition, the NLRB has established a free NLRB mobile app for iPhone and Android

users to provide the public with information about the National Labor Relations Act.

Questions

1. Legal requirements aside, are employers ethically obligated to inform their workers of NLRA rights? Explain.

2. From an ethical perspective, should NLRA posting requirements be different for a nonunionized workplace versus a unionized workplace? Explain.

Sources: NLRB Office of Public Affairs, "The NLRB's Notice Posting Rule," January 6, 2014 [**www.nlrb.gov/news-outreach/news-story/nlrbs-notice-posting-rule**]; and U.S. Department of Labor, Executive Order 13496, Notification of Employee Rights under Federal Labor Laws, January 29, 2015 [**www.dol.gov/olms/regs/compliance/EO13496.htm**].

Right to Organize and Engage in Concerted Activities

LO 14-2

Describe the goals of the National Labor Relations Act (NLRA).

The NLRA gives employees the right to engage in concerted activity, including strikes and collective bargaining. Section 7 of the NLRA states:

> Employees shall have the right to self-organization, to form, join, or assist labor organizations, to bargain collectively through representatives of their own choosing, and to engage in other concerted activities for the purpose of collective bargaining or other mutual aid or protection, and shall also have the right to refrain from any and all of such activities except to the extent that such right may be affected by an agreement requiring membership in a labor organization as a condition of employment.

Signing in Solidarity?

A grocery store cashier wrote a note to her supervisor on the break room's "whiteboard" regarding a training program known as "TIPS." The next day, she noticed that the word "TIPS" had been changed to "TITS" and a "picture of a worm or peanut urinating" on her name had been added. She hand-copied the altered whiteboard message on a piece of paper and asked her team leader and two other employees to sign the paper to confirm the accuracy of its depiction, telling each her intent to file a complaint before they signed. While she did not intend to file a joint complaint, she believed the altered message amounted to sexual harassment of other female workers as well. During the employer's investigation, the cashier was told that while she may ask other employees to be witnesses, she was to refrain from soliciting more signatures.

> **Question**
>
> In seeking her co-workers' signatures, was the cashier engaged in concerted activity for "mutual aid or protection" under Section 7 of the NLRA? If so, did the employer violate that right? Decide. Explain.
>
> *Source: Fresh & Easy Neighborhood Market,* 361 N.L.R.B. No. 12 (2014).

When political issues such as immigration become heated, such as during the 2016 presidential election, employees' political advocacy efforts may affect the workplace. Political advocacy, in some circumstances, may be considered a *concerted activity* for "mutual aid or protection" under Section 7. Under 2008 NLRB guidelines, the first question is whether there is a direct connection between the political issue at stake and a "specifically identified employment concern of the participating employees." Even if that direct connection is found, however, the employer may discipline the employees if the political activity, like attending a rally, for example, violates "neutrally applied" work rules such as restrictions on leaving work without permission.[29] [For a database of federal and state labor law statutes and regulations, see **http://topics.law.cornell.edu/wex/labor**].

Unfair Labor Practices by Management

LO 14-3

Identify unfair labor practices by management and unions.

The NLRA describes and outlaws certain activities by employers that would hamper or discourage employees from exercising the rights granted to them in Section 7. Thus, Section 8(a) of the act makes it an *unfair labor practice* for an employer to

1. Interfere with, restrain, or coerce employees in the exercise of the rights given to them by Section 7;
2. Dominate, interfere, or assist with the formation of any labor organization, including contributing financial support to it;
3. Encourage or discourage membership in any labor organization by discrimination in regard to hiring, tenure of employment, promotion, salary, or any other term of employment;
4. Discharge or take any other action against an employee because he or she has filed charges or given testimony under the act; and
5. Refuse to bargain collectively with a duly certified representative of the employees.

These five provisions are designed to allow employees to organize in an atmosphere free from intimidation by the employer. In addition, if employees have chosen a union as their exclusive collective bargaining representative, Section 8(a) regulates the bargaining between the employer and the union. The provisions also ensure that the employer will not be able to interfere with union activities by either seizing control of the union or rendering it impotent by refusing to bargain collectively.

At-Will Disclaimers

Recently, the employee handbook has been the source of complaints that employers are violating their employees' NLRA rights. For example, the at-will provision, typically signed by new employees, may state: "I agree that the at-will employment relationship cannot be amended, modified, or altered in any way." This provision may be unlawful because it waives the employee's right to act with other employees to change the nature of their employment relationship.[30] However, an at-will provision declaring that managers and supervisors have no authority to alter the employment relationship's at-will status, without restricting the employee's ability to engage in concerted activity to do so as well, has been considered valid by the NLRB.[31]

Dress Codes

Generally, employees have the right to wear to work pro-union hats, T-shirts, and other "message clothing" commonly used in union campaigns. A 2016 federal appellate court underscored this general rule in enforcing the NLRB's decision that a car dealer's dress code prohibiting employees who have contact with the public from wearing pins, insignias, and other message clothing was unlawful.[32] However, under a "special circumstances" exception, employers may limit such attire for a legitimate business interest. For example, AT&T suspended employees for wearing a shirt while visiting customer homes that said "Inmate" on the front and "Prisoner of AT&T" on the back, designed to raise awareness of problematic contract negotiations. Vacating the NLRB's ruling that the suspensions violated the employees' NLRA rights, the D.C. Court of Appeals in 2015 held that a company can lawfully prohibit employees from wearing messages that it reasonably believes could harm its customer relations or public image, citing the "special circumstances" exception and "common sense."[33]

All Because of a Bad Haircut?

Embarrassed over a bad haircut, Nichole Wright-Gore, a supply clerk for White Oak Manor, started wearing a hat to work. After several days, supervisors told her to remove the hat as it violated a company dress code prohibiting hats; she refused and was disciplined. Wright-Gore subsequently began to take photos of her coworkers, some with and without consent, showing them wearing hats and violating the dress code in other ways, which she shared with coworkers while discussing with them the unequal enforcement of the dress code. After employees complained about having their photos taken and shared with others without their consent, Wright-Gore was terminated for violating White Oak's policy prohibiting photos being taken in the facility. Did Wright-Gore's termination violate the NLRA? Explain.

Source: NLRB v. White Oak Manor, 452 F. App'x 374 (4th Cir. 2011) (unpublished op.).

Social Media Policies

Can a Facebook posting or comment be protected activity under the NLRA? Coworkers who are "Facebook friends" or otherwise connected on social media might want to communicate about workplace issues through these venues. Employers, seeking to protect their online reputation and lessen their risk of employment-related liability for, as an example, harassment (see Chapter 13), may have a "social media policy" prohibiting certain conduct on Facebook and similar sites. The NLRB's Advice Memos on social media policies offer that if employees would reasonably read an employer's social media policy to mean, for example, that they are not allowed to discuss wages or ask each other about perceptions of unfair treatment, then the policy would likely violate the NLRA.[34] In 2012, the NLRB found that Costco's social media policy violated the NLRA in prohibiting employees from electronically posting statements that would, for example, "defame the Company" or "damage any person's reputation." Employees could interpret this broad policy as preventing them from engaging in such concerted activity as discussing possible mistreatment of employees.[35] In 2013, the NLRB found that a clothing store wrongfully terminated several employees for posting negative comments on Facebook relating to a dispute with the store manager about closing time, given their concerns with the store's location.[36] In the case that follows, the NLRB considers whether a Facebook "like" of a coworker's post is protected concerted activity under the NLRA.

LEGAL BRIEFCASE

Three D, LLC (Triple Play Sports Bar and Grille) and Jillian Sanzone and Vincent Spinella
361 NLRB No. 31 (2014), *aff'd*, Three D, LLC v. NLRB, 629 F. App'x 33 (2d Cir. 2015)

By Members Miscimarra, Hirozawa, and Schiffer

Decision and Order

The principal issue in this case is whether the Respondent violated Section 8(a)(1) of the [National Labor Relations] Act by discharging two employees for their participation in a Facebook discussion involving claims that employees unexpectedly owed additional State income taxes because of the Respondent's withholding mistakes. We agree with the [administrative law] judge that the discharges were unlawful. . . .

I.

Section 7 of the National Labor Relations Act provides, in pertinent part, that "[e]mployees shall have the right to self-organization, to form, join, or assist labor organizations, to bargain collectively through representatives of their own choosing, and to engage in other concerted activities for the purpose of collective bargaining or other mutual aid or protection . . . ." Under Section 7, employees have a statutory right to act together "to improve terms and conditions of employment or otherwise improve their lot as employees"—including by using social media to communicate with each other and with the public for that purpose. At the same time, online employee communications can implicate legitimate employer interests, including the "right of employers to maintain discipline in their establishments." However, neither of these rights is "unlimited in the sense that [neither] can be exercised without regard to any duty which the existence of rights in others may place upon employer or employee." In this case, there is no dispute that the Facebook communications at issue constituted "concerted activities" and that they were "for the purpose of . . . mutual aid or protection." Rather, mindful of the balance to be struck between employee rights under Section 7 and legitimate employer interests, our focus here is on whether these Facebook activities, which indisputably prompted the Respondent to discharge the two employees, lost the protection of the Act. * * * * * [W]e agree that they did not.

A.

The Respondent, which is owned by Ralph DelBuono and Thomas Daddona, operates a bar and restaurant; DelBuono is responsible for the Respondent's accounting. The Respondent's employees are not represented by a labor organization.

The Respondent employed Jillian Sanzone as a waitress and bartender, and Vincent Spinella as a cook. In approximately January 2011, Sanzone and at least one other employee discovered that they owed more in State income taxes than they had expected. Sanzone discussed this at work with other employees, and some employees complained to the Respondent. In response to the complaints, the Respondent planned a staff meeting for February with its payroll provider to discuss the employees' concerns.

Sanzone, Spinella, and former employee Jamie LaFrance, who left the Respondent's employ in November 2010, have Facebook accounts. On January 31 [2011], LaFrance posted the following "status update" to her Facebook page:

> Maybe someone should do the owners of Triple Play a favor and buy it from them. They can't even do the tax paperwork correctly!!! Now I OWE money...W-- [acronym for expletive]!!!!

The following comments were posted to LaFrance's page in response:

> KEN DESANTIS (a Facebook "friend" of LaFrance's and a customer): "You owe them money...that's f---ed up."

> DANIELLE MARIE PARENT (Triple Play employee): "I F---G OWE MONEY TOO!"

> LAFRANCE: "The state. Not Triple Play. would never give that place a penny of my money. Ralph [DelBuono] f---ed up the paperwork . . . as per usual."

> DESANTIS: "[Y]eah I really [don't] go to that place anymore."

> LAFRANCE: "It's all Ralph's fault. He didn't do the paperwork right. I'm calling the labor board to look into it [because] he still owes me about 2000 in paychecks."

> (At this juncture, employee Spinella selected the "Like" option under LaFrance's initial status update. The discussion continued as follows.)

> LAFRANCE: "We shouldn't have to pay it. It's every employee there that it[']s happening to."

> DESANTIS: "[Y]ou better get that money . . . that[']s b---it if that[']s the case [I']m sure he did it to other people too."

> PARENT: "Let me know what the board says because I owe $323 and [I']ve never owed."

> LAFRANCE: "I'm already getting my 2000 after writing to the labor board and them investigating but now I find out he f--ed up my taxes and I owe the state a bunch. Grrr."

> PARENT: "I mentioned it to him and he said that we should want to owe."

> LAFRANCE: "Hahahaha he's such a shady little man. He [pro[bab] ly pocketed it all from all our paychecks. I've never owed a penny in my life till I worked for him. Thank goodness I got outta there."

> SANZONE: "I owe too. Such an a---le."

> PARENT: "[Y]eah me neither, [I] told him we will be discussing it at the meeting."

> SARAH BAUMBACH (Triple Play employee): "I have never had to owe money at any jobs . . . I hope I won[']t have to at TP . . . probably will have to seeing as everyone else does!"

> LAFRANCE: "Well discuss good [because] I won't be there to hear it. And let me know what his excuse is ;)."

> JONATHAN FEELEY (a Facebook "friend" of LaFrance's and customer): "And the[y're] way to[o] expensive."

Sanzone added her comment from her cell phone on February 1. She testified that her Facebook privacy settings permit only her Facebook friends to view her posts. LaFrance's privacy settings are not in the record.

Co-owner Daddona learned about the Facebook discussion from his sister, who, in addition to being employed by the Respondent, is a Facebook friend of LaFrance. On February 2, when Sanzone reported to work, Daddona told her she was being discharged. When Sanzone asked why, Daddona responded that she was not loyal enough to be working for the Respondent because of her Facebook comment.

When Spinella reported for work on February 3, he was summoned to the Respondent's office, where Daddona and DelBuono were waiting; the Facebook comments from LaFrance's account were displayed on a computer screen in the office. After asking Spinella if he "had a problem with them, or the company," DelBuono and Daddona interrogated him about the Facebook discussion, the meaning of his "Like" selection, the identity of the other people who had participated in the conversation, and whether Spinella had written anything negative about DelBuono or Daddona. DelBuono told Daddona that the "Like" option meant that Spinella stood behind the other commenters [and] because he "liked the disparaging and defamatory comments," it was "apparent" that Spinella wanted to work somewhere else. . . .

B.

The judge found that the Facebook discussion was *concerted* activity because it involved four current employees (Danielle Marie Parent, Sarah Baumbach, Sanzone, Spinella) and was "part of an ongoing sequence" of discussions that began in the workplace about the Respondent's calculation of employees' tax withholding. Noting that the employees, in their Facebook conversation, discussed issues they intended to raise at an upcoming staff meeting as well as possible avenues for complaints to government entities, the judge found that the participants were seeking to initiate, induce, or prepare for group action. . . .

The judge further found that Sanzone and Spinella were engaged in *protected* concerted activity because the discussion concerned workplace complaints about tax liabilities, the Respondent's tax withholding calculations, and LaFrance's assertion that she was owed back wages. The judge found that Spinella's selection of the "Like" button expressed his support for the others who were sharing their concerns and "constituted participation in the discussion that was sufficiently meaningful as to rise to the level of" protected, concerted activity. . . . [T]he judge further found that they did not lose the Act's protection [and] concluded that the Respondent unlawfully discharged Sanzone and Spinella for their protected Facebook posts.

C.

The Respondent . . . contends that, as a result of their Facebook activities, Sanzone and Spinella adopted LaFrance's allegedly defamatory and disparaging comments and lost the protection of the Act. The Respondent asserts that the Facebook posts were made in a "public" forum accessible to both employees and customers and that, as a result, they undermined DelBuono's authority in the workplace and adversely affected the Respondent's public image. . . .

D.

* * * * *

The Board has long recognized that an employer has a legitimate interest in preventing the disparagement of its products or services and, relatedly, in protecting its reputation (and the reputations of its agents as to matters within the scope of their agency) from defamation. Section 7 rights are balanced against these interests, if and when they are implicated. In striking that balance, the Board applies these principles in accordance with the Supreme Court's decisions in *Jefferson Standard* and *Linn.*

In *Jefferson Standard,* the Court upheld the discharge of employees who publicly attacked the quality of their employer's product and its business practices without relating their criticisms to a labor controversy. The Court found that the employees' conduct amounted to disloyal disparagement of their employer and, as a result, fell outside the Act's protection.

In *Linn,* the Court limited the availability of State-law remedies for defamation in the course of a union organizing campaign "to those instances in which the complainant can show that the defamatory statements were circulated with malice and caused him damage." The Court indicated that the meaning of "malice," for these purposes, was that the statement was uttered "with knowledge of its falsity, or with reckless disregard of whether it was true or false."

Applying these precedents, the Board has held that "'employee communications to third parties in an effort to obtain their support are protected where the communication indicated it is related to an ongoing dispute between the employees and the employers and the communication is not so disloyal, reckless, or maliciously untrue as to lose the Act's protection.'"

Turning to the facts of this case, we first adopt the judge's finding that the only employee conduct to be analyzed is Sanzone's comment ("I owe too. Such an a---le.") and Spinella's indication that he "liked" LaFrance's initial status update ("Maybe someone should do the owners of Triple Play a favor and buy it from them. They can't even do the tax paperwork correctly!!! Now I OWE money . . . W-- [acronym for expletive]!!!!"). In agreement with the judge, we find that in the context of the ongoing dialogue among employees about tax withholding, Sanzone's comment effectively endorsed LaFrance's complaint that she owed money on her taxes due to a tax-withholding error on the Respondent's part. While Spinella's "like" is more ambiguous, we treat it for purposes of our analysis as expressing agreement with LaFrance's original complaint.

We reject the Respondent's contention that Sanzone or Spinella can be held responsible for any of the other comments posted in this exchange. Neither Sanzone nor Spinella accused the Respondent of pocketing employees' money or endorsed any comment by LaFrance to that effect. Assuming, arguendo, that such an accusation would have been unprotected, neither Sanzone nor Spinella would have lost the protection of the Act merely by participating in an otherwise protected discussion in which other persons made unprotected statements.

The comments at issue here are qualitatively different from the disparaging communications that lost protection in the *Jefferson Standard* case. First, the Facebook discussion here clearly disclosed the existence of an ongoing labor dispute concerning the Respondent's tax-withholding practices. Second, the evidence does not establish that the discussion in general, or Sanzone's and Spinella's participation in particular, was directed to the general public. The comments at issue were posted on an individual's personal page rather than, for example, a company page providing information about its products or services. Although the record does not establish the privacy settings of LaFrance's page, or of individuals other than Sanzone who commented . . . , we find that such discussions are clearly more comparable to a conversation that could potentially be overheard by a patron or other third party than the communications at issue in *Jefferson Standard,* which were clearly directed at the public.

In any event, we find that Spinella's and Sanzone's comments were not "so disloyal . . . as to lose the Act's protection" . . . . Where, as here, the purpose of employee communications is to seek and provide mutual support looking toward group action to encourage the employer to address problems in terms or conditions of employment, not to disparage its product or services or undermine its reputation, the communications are protected.

The comments at issue likewise were not defamatory. . . . [T]here is no basis for finding that the employees' claims that their withholding was insufficient to cover their tax liability, or that this shortfall was due to an error on the Respondent's part, were maliciously untrue. And Sanzone's characterization of DelBuono as an "a---le" in connection with the asserted tax-withholding errors cannot reasonably be read as a statement of fact; rather, Sanzone was merely (profanely) voicing a negative personal opinion of DelBuono. Accordingly, we find that these statements also did not lose protection under *Linn*.

[W]e adopt the judge's finding that the discharges of Sanzone and Spinella violated Section 8(a)(1). . . .

Questions

1. The NLRB concluded that the Facebook discussion was more like a conversation that could be overheard by a customer rather than communications "clearly directed at the public." Should Facebook discussions on workplace issues be treated the same as workplace conversations? Why or why not?

2. How did the administrative law judge ("the judge") view Spinella's "liking" of LaFrance's post? How did the NLRB view it? For purposes of the NLRA, should "liking" a co-worker's Facebook post on a work condition be treated as supporting others' express comments on the post? Explain.

3. In affirming the NLRB's decision that the Facebook activity at issue did not lose the protection of the NLRA simply because it contained obscenities, the Second Circuit Court of Appeals cited the "reality of modern-day social media use." (See *Three D LLC v. NLRB,* 629 F. App'x 33 (2d Cir. 2015).

a. Do you agree that obscenities are part of the "reality of modern-day social media use"? Should obscene language in otherwise protected, concerted activity *always* receive protection under the NLRA? Discuss.

b. Two days before a union election at a catering company, while working as a server at a fund-raising event, a long-time employee got upset at his supervisor, Bob, for what he believed were Bob's disrespectful tone and comments towards the waitstaff. On break, the employee posted a message to his personal Facebook page: "Bob is such a nasty MO---ER F--ER don't know how to talk to people!!!!!! F--k his mother and his entire f---ng family!!!! What a LOSER!!!! Vote YES for the UNION!!!!!!" The post was visible to the employee's Facebook friends, who included some co-workers. The post was deleted the day after the election, but the employee was fired approximately two weeks later for the posting. Did the catering company violate the NLRA in terminating the employee? Decide. Explain. See *Pier Sixty, LLC,* 362 N.L.R.B. 59 (2015).

4. A school district's after-school center for high-school students that hires employees on an annual basis held a meeting in which staff anonymously identified the pros and cons of working at the center. Two employees who believed that management was not serious about addressing these concerns tried unsuccessfully to meet with their supervisor. These employees engaged in a Facebook conversation that advocated insubordination, such as not following specific school-district rules. Another employee forwarded the conversation to the center's management, and the two employees' reemployment offers were withdrawn. Did the center violate the NLRA in withdrawing those offers? Decide. Explain. See *Richmond District Neighborhood Center,* 361 N.L.R.B. No. 74 (2014).

Unfair Labor Practices by Unions

Section 8(b) lists activities constituting unfair labor practices by a labor organization. Some of these provisions mirror some of the activities prohibited to employers. Moreover, at least since the enactment of the Taft–Hartley Act, the law is not sympathetic to labor organizations that try to use certain coercive tactics, threats of the loss of livelihood, or any other strong-arm methods. Finally, Section 8(b) also regulates the union's collective bargaining practices, including economic action. Thus, a labor organization is not permitted to

1. Restrain or coerce any employee in the exercise of his or her rights as granted by Section 7.

2. Cause or attempt to cause an employer to discriminate against an employee who has chosen not to join a particular labor organization or has been denied membership in such an organization.

3. Refuse to bargain collectively with an employer on behalf of the bargaining unit it is certified to represent.

4. Induce or attempt to induce an employer to engage in secondary boycott activities.

5. Require employees to become union members and then charge them excessive or discriminatory dues.

6. Try to make an employer compensate workers for services not performed.

7. Picket or threaten to picket an employer in an attempt to force the employer to recognize or bargain with a labor organization that is not the duly certified representative of a bargaining unit.

Representation Procedures

Section 9 of the NLRA specifies the election procedures by which employees may choose whether to be represented by a particular union or no union at all.

National Labor Relations Board (NLRB)

LO 14-4
Describe the role of the National Labor Relations Board (NLRB) in enforcing the NLRA.

The NLRB is a federal administrative agency responsible for regulating labor–management relations. Its primary tasks are designating appropriate bargaining units of workers (deciding which workers have a sufficient community of interest so that their needs can best be acknowledged and so that collective bargaining is efficient for the employer and the union); conducting elections for union representation within the chosen bargaining unit; certifying the results of such elections; and investigating, prosecuting, and adjudicating charges of unfair labor practices.[37]

Although the congressional mandate by which the NLRB was formed gives the agency jurisdiction theoretically to the full extent of the interstate commerce powers vested in Congress, the agency has neither the funding nor the staff to administer its duties to all of American industry. Some smaller businesses, government employees, railroad and airline workers covered by the Railway Labor Act, agricultural workers, domestic workers, independent contractors, and supervisors and other managerial employees are not protected by the board.[38]

Over the years, the five-member NLRB has been criticized for sometimes reaching decisions based on political/philosophical considerations rather than legal reasoning and Board precedent. As successive presidential administrations appoint NLRB members, the Board's decisions often "seesaw" according to the changes in Washington political power. [For more on the NLRB, see **www.nlrb.gov**].

Part Three—Elections

Choosing a Bargaining Representative

Representation elections are the process by which the NLRB achieves the first of the two statutory goals under the NLRA—employee freedom of choice. That goal, however, is sometimes in conflict with the other statutory goal—stable collective bargaining.

LO 14-5
Describe the process of union organizing and the related legal issues.

The NLRB has devised rules to resolve such conflicts. As described below, the NLRB in 2014 adopted new election rules that went into effect in April 2015 ("the 2015 rules") that are designed to simplify and modernize procedures for establishing union representation.[39] Critics refer to these as the "'ambush' NLRB election rules"[40] because of the significantly shortened timeline between petition and election that arguably harms employers' ability to mount a defense to unionization, but a federal appellate court in 2016 rejected a challenge to the 2015 rules.[41] At this writing, no other such challenges have been successful; however, whether these new representation procedures will remain in effect under the Trump administration is unknown. [For the AFL–CIO view of why workers should join unions, see **www.workingamerica.org/issues** and for the National Right to Work Legal Defense Foundation's information on employees' rights not to join a union, see **http://nrtw.org/know-your-rights**].

Election Petition

Employees, unions, and, under certain circumstances, employers[42] may file representation petitions asking the NLRB to conduct an election to determine if employees wish to be represented by a union for purposes of collective bargaining with their employer. The 2015 rules allow electronic filing, which also speeds up the process. The petition must be supported by at least 30 percent of the employees in the proposed bargaining unit, and evidence of this substantial showing of interest has to be submitted along with the petition under the 2015 rules; NLRB's General Counsel has offered guidance allowing electronic signatures for this purpose.[43] Additionally, under the 2015 rules, the petitioner must serve the petition on the other party (for example, the union must serve the petition on the employer) so that the party is simultaneously notified with the NLRB, instead of having to wait for the NLRB's notice. The NLRB will investigate these petitions to assess whether an election should be conducted and will direct an election, if appropriate.[44] The employer is free to simply acknowledge its employees' interest in joining a particular union and to engage in bargaining with that union, a decision normally called *voluntary recognition*.

The employer must post a notice of the election petition where other employee notices are posted so that employees are aware of it; if an employer typically communicates with employees through electronic means, then the notice also must be electronically distributed.[45]

Employees' support for a union had often been established by a *card check* method where employees signify their interest in the union simply by signing authorization cards, thus bypassing secret ballot elections and making union organizing easier. However, the NLRB in 2007 overturned 40 years of precedent and made the card check method less useful for union organizing. In *Dana Corporation/Metaldyne,*[46] the NLRB ruled that where an employer voluntarily recognizes a union based on a card check majority, antiunion employees have 45 days to petition the board for a federally supervised, secret ballot election to *decertify* the newly recognized union or to support a petition by a rival union.

Preelection Hearings

If the parties do not agree on an election, the NLRB's regional office holds a preelection hearing. Under the 2015 rules, the nonpetitioning party (e.g., the employer if the union filed the petition) must submit and serve on the petitioning party a Statement of

Position prior to the hearing; this defines what issues will be decided. If an election is determined to be appropriate, the NLRB's regional office sets the election for the earliest date practicable under the 2015 rules; the prior automatic delay of 25–30 days is no longer given.[47]

The crucial issue to be addressed at this point, however, is normally whether the proposed bargaining unit (the designated employee group—for example, all hourly workers at a facility, all welders, all sales clerks) is appropriate for the election.

Appropriate Bargaining Unit

The key consideration in establishing an appropriate employee bargaining unit is the community of interest among the employees because collective bargaining will not be stable and efficient if it involves employees with diverse interests. Therefore, the bargaining unit may range from a portion of a plant to multiple employees in several plants. Similarly, a workplace may have more than one appropriate bargaining unit, depending on the composition of the workforce. In 2013, a federal appellate court upheld the NLRB's 2011 decision in S*pecialty Healthcare,*[48] in which a nursing home challenged the certification of Certified Nursing Assistants (CNAs) as a stand-alone bargaining unit; the employer argued that an appropriate bargaining unit would include all nonprofessional service and maintenance employees. The NLRB rejected the challenge, finding that a bargaining unit of a clearly identifiable group of employees is presumably appropriate. An employer challenging a bargaining unit as inappropriately excluding other employees must show that the excluded workers share an "overwhelming community of interest" with those included in the bargaining unit.[49]

Certain classes of employees, such as supervisors, are excluded from the bargaining unit. Supervisors are excluded because they act on behalf of the employer and, through their power to direct and assign work and to discipline and discharge employees, exert control over their subordinates, who are or may be in the bargaining unit. Often labor and management do not agree about the classification of workers as supervisors. In a 2006 decision outraging union activists, the NLRB substantially expanded the range of employees who might lawfully be considered supervisors (and thus ineligible for union membership) to include those assigned supervisory duties just 10 or 15 percent of the time.[50]

Independent contractors are not protected under the NLRA. In 2009, a federal appeals court set aside the NLRB's decision that FedEx had unlawfully failed to bargain with a union that had been certified to represent drivers at two FedEx home terminals. The appeals court concluded that the drivers were independent contractors who had been *misclassified* as employees by the NLRB.[51]

Question

The Macy's store in Saugus, Massachusetts, is divided into 11 primary sales departments: juniors, ready-to-wear, women's shoes, handbags, furniture, housewares, men's clothing, bridal, fine jewelry, fashion jewelry, and cosmetics and fragrances. Local 1445, United Food and Commercial Workers Union, filed a petition with the NLRB for a representation election among all cosmetics and fragrances employees of the Saugus Macy's store. Is the proposed bargaining unit appropriate? What facts would you want to know before making your decision? See *Macy's v. NLRB,* 824 F.3d 557 (5th Cir. 2016).

Union Solicitation, E-mail, and the Employer

Historically, unions relied on a physical presence on employers' property to organize employees. A 1992 U.S. Supreme Court decision in *Lechmere*[52] limited that presence in allowing employers to bar from their property union organizers who are not employees. This resulted in an increase in *salting,* the practice of union organizers applying for jobs with the intent of unionizing the other employees from the inside. The Supreme Court's 1995 *Town & Country* decision[53] held that salts are employees, thus affording them NLRA protection from discrimination based on union affiliation; an NLRB decision later clarified that only those salts who are "genuinely interested" in obtaining employment are protected.[54]

Both the NLRB's 2015 revised election rules and its 2014 decision in *Purple Communications*[55] support union organizing via e-mail. The 2015 rules require employers to provide, seven days after the union petition is filed, information on employees in the proposed bargaining unit including their personal e-mail addresses if known to the employer. Further, recognizing e-mail's prominent role in workplace communications, *Purple Communications* allows employees who already have access to their employer's e-mail system to use it during nonworking time for union organizing; however, the employer is allowed to ban all nonworking time use of its e-mail system if "special circumstances" show such a ban is needed to "maintain production or discipline."[56]

The case that follows involves a Walmart employee's efforts to interest coworkers in joining a union.

Wal-Mart Stores, Inc. v. National Labor Relations Board

LEGAL BRIEFCASE 400 F.3d 1093 (8th Cir. 2005)

Circuit Judge Melloy

Petitioner appeals the National Labor Relations Board's order finding that it violated the National Labor Relations Act by punishing employee Brian Shieldnight for union solicitation.

I

This case arises from efforts to unionize employees at the Wal-Mart store in Tahlequah, Oklahoma. The store, like all Wal-Mart stores, maintains and enforces a policy that prohibits solicitation during employees' work time, regardless of the cause or organization.

Brian Shieldnight, an employee of the Tahlequah Wal-Mart, contacted the United Food and Commercial Workers Union, Local 1000 ("Union") about possible union representation. He obtained authorization cards from the union to organize employees at the Tahlequah store.

On January 29, 2001, Shieldnight entered the store while off-duty. He wore a T-shirt that read "Union Teamsters" on the front and "Sign a card . . . Ask me how!" on the back. Assistant Store Manager John Lamont and Assistant Night Manager Tammy Flute saw Shieldnight's T-shirt and saw him speak to an associate. Flute told the associate to return to work, and Lamont ordered Shieldnight to leave associates alone. Lamont then consulted a Wal-Mart "union hotline." The hotline representative told Lamont that Shieldnight's shirt constituted solicitation and that Shieldnight should be removed from the store. Lamont and Flute sought out Shieldnight. They found him in the jewelry department talking to two friends who were not associates. Lamont informed Shieldnight that his shirt constituted a form of solicitation and that he would have to leave the store immediately. Lamont escorted Shieldnight to the front door of the store and instructed him to leave the store and Wal-Mart property.

The next incident occurred on January 30, 2001. While on duty at the store, Shieldnight invited Department Manager Debra Starr and associates Patricia Scott and James Parsons, all of whom were also on duty, to a union meeting. Shieldnight asked Starr to come to the meeting and stated that he would like her to consider signing a union authorization card. Shieldnight separately asked Scott and Parsons to attend the meeting to hear "the other side of the story."

Based on these two incidents, Co-Manager Rick Hawkins and Assistant Manager John Lamont held a written "coaching session" with Shieldnight for violating the no-solicitation rule. A "coaching session" is part of Wal-Mart's progressive discipline process. Verbal coaching and written coaching are the first two steps in a four-step process. Hawkins and Lamont explained to Shieldnight that he had violated the solicitation policy on January 29 by soliciting on the sales floor with his T-shirt and on January 30 by verbally soliciting employees while on-duty and on the sales floor. Lamont told Shieldnight that it was wrong to have sent Shieldnight off Wal-Mart property completely. Lamont clarified that while Shieldnight could not solicit on the sales floor, he could do so in the parking lot while not on duty. Hawkins, Lamont, and Shieldnight also discussed Shieldnight's questions and concerns regarding Wal-Mart employment policies, such as health insurance for associates. Lamont suggested Shieldnight should raise the matter in "grassroots" meetings that all Wal-Mart stores hold to identify the top three companywide issues. The three men arranged a time to meet in the future. That meeting never occurred.

The union subsequently filed an unfair labor practice charge against Wal-Mart. . . .

[A] divided Board panel found that Shieldnight had not engaged in solicitation when he (1) wore the T-shirt during his shift; (2) asked on-duty employees to attend a union meeting; or (3) asked a coworker to sign a union card. . . . Wal-Mart appeals. . . .

II

* * * * *

A. The T-Shirt

The union contends that Shieldnight's T-shirt did not constitute solicitation, but rather was a "union insignia." Wal-Mart argues that by encouraging people to approach him, Shieldnight's T-shirt was a form of solicitation. In *NLRB v. W.W. Grainger, Inc.,* the board held,

> "Solicitation" for a union usually means asking someone to join the union by signing his name to an authorization card in the same way that solicitation for a charity would mean asking an employee to contribute to a charitable organization . . . or in the commercial context asking an employee to buy a product or exhibiting the product for him. . . .

Ordinarily, employees may wear union insignia while on their employer's premises. . . .

The board stated that the T-shirt should be treated as union insignia because "it did not 'speak' directly to any specific individual . . . and it did not call for an immediate response, as would an oral person-to-person invitation to accept or sign an authorization card." The board found that there was "no claim or evidence that Shieldnight did anything in furtherance of the T-shirt message. . . . He merely walked around and socialized. . . about nonunion matters." Anyone, including any Wal-Mart employee who saw Shieldnight was free to ignore both Shieldnight and the message on the T-shirt. In contrast, a solicitation to sign an authorization card requires more interaction, likely a direct yes or no answer. Absent further evidence of direct inquiry by Shieldnight, the board's conclusion was supported by substantial evidence.

Wal-Mart alleges that the panel's conclusion is not reasonable because it ignores both Shieldnight's purpose and the long-held rule that an employer may implement rules against solicitation during work time to prevent interference with work productivity.

* * * * *

Wal-Mart failed to demonstrate how the T-shirt interfered in any manner with the operation of the store. Accordingly, substantial evidence supports the board's conclusion that Shieldnight's T-shirt did not constitute solicitation.

B. The Coworker Conversations

* * * * *

Shieldnight invited three coworkers to a union meeting. . . . Shieldnight's statements did not require an immediate response from the three coworkers. Instead of a solicitation that required a response, the record shows that Shieldnight's statements were more akin to a statement of fact that put his coworkers on notice that there was to be a union meeting that night and that they were welcome to attend. Nothing in the record suggests that the environment at Wal-Mart made Shieldnight's actions uniquely disruptive. Accordingly, the panel's conclusion regarding Shieldnight's conversations was supported by substantial evidence. Furthermore, the panel acted reasonably when it concluded that "simply informing another employee of an upcoming meeting or asking a brief, union-related question does not occupy enough time to be treated as a work interruption in most settings."

C. Asking Coworker to Sign a Card

The board concluded that it was not solicitation when Shieldnight asked a coworker to sign a union authorization card. . . .

In light of the totality of the circumstances, Shieldnight's actions constituted solicitation even though he did not actually offer Starr a card at the time he asked her to sign. Shieldnight had contacted the union about obtaining union representation and had obtained cards from the union for the purpose of organizing employees at the Tahlequah store. There is little doubt as to Shieldnight's intent in the words he spoke to Starr. The record indicates that Shieldnight did not have a card in his hand at the time he spoke to Starr. It is silent as to whether he had a card on his person. The fact that he did not place a card directly in front of Starr at the time of his statement makes little difference in regard to the nature of his conversation. Further, Shieldnight's actions in this instance are more analogous to a direct solicitation than when he asked his coworkers to attend the union meeting. Asking someone to sign a union card offers that individual person the choice to be represented by a union. Informing coworkers about a union meeting merely puts fellow employees on notice that a meeting is going to take place.

Accordingly, there is insufficient evidence to support the board's conclusion that Shieldnight's actions were not solicitation, and thus we reverse the board regarding the authorization card issue.

*   *   *   *   *

Questions

1. Why was the T-shirt not a form of solicitation?

2. Why was Shieldnight's invitation to three coworkers to attend a union meeting not a form of solicitation, while asking a coworker to sign a card was considered impermissible solicitation?

3. While U.S. Walmart workers are not unionized, Walmart has negotiated union contracts in other countries such as Brazil and Argentina, where unionization is seen as the "prevailing practice." The international trade union coalition, UNI, has asked Walmart to consider a global agreement similar to other retailers such as Ikea and H&M. Should Walmart engage in such an agreement? Discuss. See Yian Q. Mui, "Wal-Mart Works with Unions Abroad, but Not at Home," *The Washington Post,* June 7, 2011 [**www.washingtonpost.com**].

The Election for Union Representation

The union may be selected only by a majority of the votes cast by the employees. The NLRB oversees the election to ensure the process is carried on under "laboratory conditions."[57] In other words, elections must be held under circumstances that, to the extent possible, are free from undue or unfair influence either by the employer or by unions vying for the right to represent the bargaining unit.

Employers have the right to speak out against unions in the form of ads, speeches, and the like. Section 8(c) of the Taft–Hartley Act is designed to ensure employers' and labor organizations' traditional First Amendment rights as long as they do not overstep certain bounds:

> The expressing of any views, argument, or opinion, or the dissemination thereof, whether in written, printed, graphic, or visual form, shall not constitute or be evidence of an unfair labor practice . . . if such expression contains no threat of reprisal or force or promise of benefit.

A "Punch in the Face" Is Not a Punchline

During a union election campaign for employees of a skilled-nursing facility, two bargaining unit nurses threatened to "punch people in the face," "beat people up and destroy their cars," and "slash their tires" if the union did not win. While these comments were made in a joking manner, other unit employees who were told about them believed the threats were serious. The employer provided additional security for several days after the election as a result, although the union had won by two votes. The employer challenged the election results due to the violent threats. The NLRB found the remarks to be casual jokes that had been distorted in their retelling among other employees, and not proper grounds for overturning an election. However, a federal appellate court agreed with the employer, finding the remarks to have sufficiently disrupted the election, and noting that the speakers' joking intent was not relevant in evaluating the threats objectively. See *ManorCare of Kingston PA LLC v. National Labor Relations Board,* 823 F.3d 81 (D.C. Cir. 2016).

Threats of Reprisal or Force

Employers cannot discriminate in employment to encourage or discourage union membership. Clearly, an employer who tells employees, for example, that they will all be discharged if they engage in union activity has interfered with their rights. Similarly, an employer who interrogates employees about their activities or spies on them while they attend union meetings has engaged in unlawful interference. Problems often arise, however, in determining whether antiunion arguments by an employer are legitimate or whether they contain veiled threats. Suppose, for instance, that a company owner tells her employees that in a unionized workplace, they would have to go through the union representative to make their complaints, who would decide whether to bring these to the company's attention. The NLRB has determined that such a statement is not a threat, but rather an accurate reflection of the nature of unionized workplaces.[58]

Promise of Benefit

Although threats of force or reprisal are clearly unlawful in union campaigns, the rationale behind the prohibition against promises of benefit is not as intuitively obvious.

In a dispute that reached the U.S. Supreme Court, Exchange Parts sent its employees a letter shortly before a representation election that spoke of "the empty promises of the union" and "the fact that it is the company that puts things in your envelope." After mentioning a number of benefits, the letter said,

> The union can't put any of those things in your envelope.

"The union can't put any of those things in your envelope—only the company can do that." Further on, the letter stated, "It didn't take a union to get any of those things and . . . it won't take a union to get additional improvements in the future." Accompanying the letter was a detailed statement of the benefits granted by the company and an estimate of the monetary value of such benefits to the employees.

In the representation election two weeks later, the union lost, but the outcome was challenged in court. Eventually the Supreme Court ruled that the employer's actions constituted an unfair labor practice, reasoning that "well-timed increases in benefits" provide a clear message that those who provide advantages are the same people who can withdraw those benefits should their wishes not be followed.[59]

Buying Votes?

An Atlantic City, New Jersey, limousine service held a union election-day raffle for a TV/VCR. The NLRB ruled, 3–2, that the raffle was an unfair labor practice that might reasonably be interpreted to be a reward that would influence voting. A new election was ordered. The NLRB order banned election-day raffles, but minor "gifts" such as food, drinks, and buttons would be considered case-by-case if an objection were lodged.

Source: Atlantic Limousine, 331 N.L.R.B. No. 134 (2000).

Union Persuasion

Unions, like employers, are restricted in the type of preelection persuasion they employ. In cases involving promises of benefits made by the union, the NLRB has been more reluctant to set aside elections than it has when such promises have been made by management.

The Board's reasoning is that employees realize that union preelection promises are merely expressions of a union platform, so to speak. Employees recognize that these are benefits for which the union intends to fight. Employers, on the other hand, really do hold the power to confer or withdraw benefits. Nonetheless, a union promise to employees to provide "the biggest party in the history of Texas" if the union won the next day's election was an unfair labor practice.[60]

> "The biggest party in the history of Texas."

Remedies for Election Misconduct

Unfair labor practices during a representation election can result in the imposition of penalties and remedies. If the union loses the election and the employer engaged in wrongful behavior, a new election or other remedies may be ordered.

Decertification

After a union has been certified or recognized, an employee or group of employees may continue to resist the union or may lose confidence in it. If so, they can file a decertification petition with the NLRB. The employees must be able to demonstrate at least 30 percent support for their petition. Once a decertification petition is properly filed with the board, the usual election rules are followed to determine whether the union enjoys continuing majority support. If not, the union is decertified, and ordinarily at least one year must pass before a new representation election can be conducted. [For management advice about decertification, see **www.nrtw.org/d/decert.htm**].

Withdrawal of Recognition

An employer may unilaterally withdraw recognition of a union that has lost the support of a majority of its members. Objective evidence such as a petition signed by a majority of unit employees is required. The NLRB will review the petition and its specific language, however, to make sure that it shows employees' desire to decline union representation. For example, a petition entitled "showing of interest for decertification" was found to be insufficient evidence, while a petition's statement of "wish for a vote to remove the Union" is more likely to show whether employees no longer desire the union's representation.[61]

Escape the Union?

If a union clearly is about to win a representation election or already has done so, thus establishing its right to collective bargaining, management sometimes continues to resist. One strategy is to declare bankruptcy. That tactic may be lawful but only after bargaining sincerely with the union and only after convincing the bankruptcy court that fairness requires modification or rejection of the collective-bargaining agreement. Similarly, a company may simply choose to shut down its business rather than engage in collective bargaining. Going out of business is fully lawful unless the reason for doing so was to discourage union efforts at plants in other locations. Likewise, companies sometimes employ the *runaway shop* strategy, in which the about-to-be-unionized plant is simply shut down and replaced by another in a location less responsive to union interests. If that move was made for the purpose of thwarting union interests, it is an unfair labor practice, but if the move reflected legitimate economic goals such as reduced wages or taxes, the move is probably lawful.

> Companies sometimes employ the *runaway shop* strategy.

The Union as Exclusive Bargaining Agent

Once a union has been elected and certified as the representative of a bargaining unit, it becomes the exclusive agent for all of the employees within that bargaining unit, whether they voted for the union or not. The exclusivity of the union's authority has a number of implications, but one is particularly relevant in determining whether an employer has failed to demonstrate good faith at the bargaining table. Specifically, the employer must deal with the certified representative who acts on behalf of all employees in the bargaining unit. The employer commits an unfair labor practice if she or he attempts to deal directly with the employees or recognizes someone other than the workers' chosen representative. In both instances, the issue is fairly straightforward. The employer is undermining the position of the representative by ignoring him or her.

Part Four—Collective Bargaining

Section 8(a)(5) of the NLRA requires an employer to engage in *good-faith* collective bargaining with a representative of the employees, and Section 8(b)(3) imposes the same duty on labor organizations. Failure to bargain by either an employer or a representative of the employees constitutes an unfair labor practice.

What is collective bargaining? What must one do to discharge the duty imposed? According to Section 8(d) of the NRLA,

> [t]o bargain collectively is the performance of the mutual obligation of the employer and the representatives of the employees to meet at reasonable times and confer in good faith with respect to wages, hours, and other terms and conditions of employment . . . but such obligation does not compel either party to agree to a proposal or require the making of a concession.

Note what is *not* included: The parties are not required to reach an agreement. Thus, the NLRA governs only the process, not the result, of collective bargaining.

Bargaining in Good Faith

LO 14-6
Describe "bargaining in good faith."

The duty to bargain in *good faith* obligates the union and employer to participate actively in the deliberations, showing a sincere and honest effort to reach common ground. Whether a party is bargaining in good faith is determined by the totality of the circumstances. Some of the objective criteria used by the NLRB in reviewing complaints asserting that this duty has been violated include whether the party is willing to meet at reasonable times and intervals, and whether the party is represented by someone who has the authority to make decisions at the table.[62]

Mandatory Bargaining Subjects   Although employers and labor representatives are free to discuss whatever lawful subjects they mutually choose, Section 8(d) of the NLRA clearly sets out some mandatory subjects over which the parties must bargain. These are wages, hours, and "other terms and conditions of employment." Although these topics for mandatory bargaining seem simple enough, questions still arise frequently. For example, suppose the union and employer bargain over wages and agree to institute merit increases for employees. Must the employer also bargain over which employees are entitled to receive these increases or who will make the decision at the time they are to be given? What about a decision to close a plant?

Generally, the board and the courts will balance three factors. First, they look at the effect of a particular decision on the workers—how direct is it and to what extent is the effect felt? Second, they consider the degree to which bargaining would constitute an intrusion into entrepreneurial interest or, from the opposite side, an intrusion into union affairs. Third, they examine the practice historically in the industry or the company itself.[63]

Permissive and Prohibited Bargaining Subjects Those matters not directly related to wages, hours, and terms and conditions of employment and not falling within the category of prohibited subjects are considered permissive. Either party may raise permissive subjects during the bargaining process, but neither may pursue them to the point of a bargaining impasse. Refusal to bargain over a permissive subject does not constitute an NLRA violation, and permissive subjects must simply be dropped if the parties do not reach agreement.

> Whether a union has a right to bargain over management's placement of hidden surveillance cameras in the workplace.

Permissive subjects ordinarily would include such items as alteration of a defined bargaining unit, internal union affairs, and strike settlement agreements. Prohibited bargaining subjects are those that are illegal under the NLRA or other laws. In the case that follows, the NLRB had to decide whether a union has a right to bargain over management's placement of hidden surveillance cameras in the workplace.

LEGAL BRIEFCASE

Colgate–Palmolive Co.
323 N.L.R.B. No. 82 (1997)

FACTS

Colgate–Palmolive's Jeffersonville, Indiana, plant employed approximately 750 workers. Colgate and the employees had a collective bargaining arrangement for over 20 years. In 1994 an employee discovered a surveillance camera in a restroom air vent. The union president later discussed the matter with Colgate's human resources officer, who indicated that the camera had been placed in the vent because of theft concerns and that the camera had been removed after employees objected to it. The Union filed a grievance over the matter, and the parties met for discussion where Colgate argued that it had the absolute right to install internal surveillance cameras. Later, the Union sent a letter to Colgate demanding to bargain over the subject of cameras within the plant. Colgate did not respond, and the Union filed an unfair labor practice charge. The case was heard by an administrative law judge. Evidence indicated that Colgate had installed 11 secret cameras over four years to address problems of theft and misconduct, including sleeping on the job. The cameras were placed in several offices, a fitness center, a restroom, and as a monitor for an overhead door that was not a proper exit from the building. The Union

and some employees were aware of various "unhidden" cameras in the workplace and in some instances fortuitously discovered some of the hidden cameras.

The administrative law judge (ALJ) concluded that the use of hidden surveillance cameras is a mandatory subject of bargaining and by failing to do so, Colgate–Palmolive violated the National Labor Relations Act. The ALJ's ruling was then appealed to the National Labor Relations Board. The *NLRB* decision follows.

Chairman Gould and Members Fox and Higgins

In *Ford Motor Co. v. NLRB,* the Supreme Court described mandatory subjects of bargaining as such matters that are "plainly germane to the 'working environment'" and "not among those 'managerial decisions, which lie at the core of entrepreneurial control.'" As the judge found, the installation of surveillance cameras is both germane to the working environment, and outside the scope of managerial decisions lying at the core of entrepreneurial control.

As to the first factor—germane to the working environment—the installation of surveillance cameras is analogous to physical examinations, drug/alcohol testing requirements, and polygraph testing, all of which the Board has found to be mandatory subjects of bargaining. They are all investigatory tools or methods used by an employer to ascertain whether any of its employees has engaged in misconduct.

The Respondent [Colgate–Palmolive] acknowledges that employees caught involved in theft and/or other misconduct are subject to discipline, including discharge. Accordingly, the installation and use of surveillance cameras has the potential to affect the continued employment of employees whose actions are being monitored.

Further, as the judge finds, the use of surveillance cameras in the restroom and fitness center raises privacy concerns which add to the potential effect upon employees. We agree that these areas are part of the work environment and that the use of hidden cameras in these areas raises privacy concerns which impinged upon the employees' working conditions. The use of cameras in these or similar circumstances is unquestionably germane to the working environment.

With regard to the second criterion, we agree with the judge that the decision is not a managerial decision that lies at the core of entrepreneurial control.

* * * * *

The use of surveillance cameras is not entrepreneurial in character, is not fundamental to the basic direction of the enterprise, and impinges directly upon employment security. It is a change in the Respondent's methods used to reduce workplace theft or detect other suspected employee misconduct with serious implications for its employees' job security, which in no way touches on the discretionary "core of entrepreneurial control."

The Respondent urges that bargaining before a hidden camera is actually installed would defeat the very purpose of the camera. The very existence of secret cameras, however, is a term and condition of employment, and is thus a legitimate concern for the employees' bargaining representative. Thus, the placing of cameras, and the extent to which they will be secret or hidden, if at all, is a proper subject of negotiations between the Respondent and the union. Concededly, the Respondent also has a legitimate concern. However, bargaining about hidden cameras can embrace a host of matters other than mere location. And, even as to location, mutual accommodations can and should be negotiated. The vice in the instant case was the respondent's refusal to bargain.

* * * * *

Accordingly, we affirm the judge's finding that the union has the statutory right to engage in collective bargaining over the installation and continued use of surveillance cameras, including the circumstances under which the cameras will be activated, the general areas in which they may be placed, and how affected employees will be disciplined if improper conduct is observed.

ORDER

The National Labor Relations Board adopts the recommended Order of the administrative law judge as modified and set forth in full below and orders that the Respondent, its officers, agents, successors, and assigns, shall

1. Cease and desist from
   a. Failing and refusing to bargain with Local 15, International Chemical Workers Union, AFL–CIO with respect to the installation and use of surveillance cameras and other mandatory subjects of bargaining.
2. Take the following affirmative action necessary to effectuate the policies of the Act.
   a. On request, bargain collectively with the Union as the exclusive bargaining representative of the Respondent's employees with respect to the installation and use of surveillance cameras and other mandatory subjects of bargaining.
   b. Within 14 days after the service by the Region, post at its facility in Jeffersonville, Indiana, copies of the attached notice:

Notice to Employees
Posted by Order of the
National Labor Relations Board
An Agency of the United States Government

The National Labor Relations Board has found that we violated the National Labor Relations Act and has ordered us to post and abide by this notice. Section 7 of the Act gives employees these rights.

To organize
To form, join, or assist any union
To bargain collectively through representatives of their own choice
To act together for other mutual aid or protection

To choose not to engage in any of these protected concerted activities.

We will not fail and refuse to bargain with Local 15, International Chemical Workers Union, AFL–CIO over the installation and use of surveillance cameras within our facility and other mandatory subjects of bargaining.

We will not in any like or related manner interfere with, restrain, or coerce you in the exercise of the rights guaranteed you by Section 7 of the Act.

We will, on request, bargain collectively with the Union as the exclusive bargaining representative of our employees with respect to the installation and use of surveillance cameras within our facility and other mandatory subjects of bargaining.

Colgate–Palmolive Company.

Questions

1. What test did the ALJ and the NLRB employ to determine whether the placement of hidden surveillance cameras was a mandatory subject of bargaining?

2. Why did the union win this case?

3. If you were managing a workplace where theft, sleeping on the job, and other misconduct were at a worrisome level, would you employ hidden, secret cameras to monitor restrooms, fitness areas, and the like? Explain.

4. At an Anheuser-Busch brewing facility, a supervisor discovered a table, four chairs, a number of foam mattress pads, and cardboard in a room where only authorized personnel were to be, but which was next to a break area. Suspecting illicit activities including illegal drug use, the company installed two surveillance cameras pointed at the entrance and stairs leading to the room. The cameras led to the company identifying 16 employees who engaged in misconduct. The company took down the cameras on June 30, 1998, and then informed the union of their existence. The company fired and otherwise disciplined the employees in question. Did Anheuser-Busch violate the NLRA? Explain. *Brewers & Maltsters v. NLRB,* 414 F.3d 36 (D.C. Cir. 2005).

Administering the Agreement

Union–management bargaining does not end with the negotiation of a labor agreement. Rather, bargaining continues daily as the parties work out the disputes and confusions and conflicting interpretations that are bound to arise and that cannot be entirely provided for in the labor agreement. Often this process of contract maintenance takes the form of resolving *grievances,* as in the *Colgate–Palmolive* case. Those problems are addressed through the grievance procedure that is included in collective-bargaining agreements. Often the grievance procedure involves a series of steps beginning with informal discussion mechanisms. Failing there, the dissatisfied employee typically files a written complaint (the grievance). Normally, grievances are presented to management by a union representative, often with the worker also present.

Arbitration

If, after negotiation, the parties cannot resolve their dispute, the collective-bargaining agreement ordinarily provides for *final and binding arbitration*. Many court decisions have vigorously supported the arbitration process as the means of settling labor–management contract maintenance disputes and tend to find disputes arbitrable unless the labor agreement explicitly and unambiguously exempts the subject at issue from the arbitration process. Furthermore, but for rare exceptions, neither the company nor the union can turn to the courts to set aside arbitration decisions. However, in 2010 the U.S. Supreme Court held that a dispute between a union and an employer over the ratification date of a collective-bargaining agreement containing an arbitration clause should be resolved by a court rather than an arbitrator.[64]

Fair Representation

Because grievance processing is part of a union's bargaining responsibility, the union might breach its duty if it declined to represent an employer's grievance. An employee who feels wronged when a union does not process his or her grievance has the option of appealing to the NLRB or to the courts. Nevertheless, as the U.S. Supreme Court ruled in *14 Penn Plaza LLC v. Pyett,* a union may collectively bargain for an agreement providing that individual members' employment discrimination claims must be submitted to arbitration.[65]

Part Five—Labor Conflict

PRACTICING ETHICS   Prisoners on Strike

Putting prisoners to work, for free or for nominal wages, is a common practice. For example, an Alabama prisoner made $2 a day at his last prison job, where he has mopped floors and cut license plates. The U.S. Constitution prohibits "involuntary servitude" but makes an exception for work done as part of criminal punishment. The Florida Department of Corrections declared that prisoners working in jobs that served state agencies saved taxpayers $45 million in taxes in 2014, and performed work valued at over $76 million. Private enterprises also benefit from prison labor, such as a furniture company that operates a factory at a South Carolina correctional facility where prisoners work without pay. In 2016, prisoners in several states staged work stoppages and hunger strikes to protest their wages and work conditions. The Industrial Workers of the World (IWW) helped organize the strikes.

Questions

1. Should prisoners be paid minimum wage for their work for state agencies? How about from the private enterprises using their labor? Why or why not?

2. From an ethical perspective, would it be right for a state to replace public sector workers with prison labor as a cost-cutting measure? Why or why not?

3. Should prisoners be allowed to form a union? If so, what barriers may exist to unionizing prisoners? Explain.

Sources: Jaweed Kaleem, "They're in Prison and on Strike," *Los Angeles Times,* November 2, 2016, pp. A1 & A12; and Mike Elk, "The Next Step for Organized Labor: People in Prisons," *The Nation,* July 11, 2016 [**www.thenation.com**].

Strikes

LO 14-7
Distinguish between "unfair labor practice strikes" and "economic strikes."

For many, the initial image of labor conflict is one of employees on strike, picketing a store or factory. Striking is, however, an extremely drastic measure under which employees must bear an immediate loss of wages and, in many instances, risk job loss. Similarly, employers bear the loss of a disruption to continued operations. Work stoppages have declined dramatically since World War II. However, the six-day sit-in of 240 workers at Chicago's Republic Windows and Doors in 2008—sparked by management's announcement that the plant would be closing in three days—became a national symbol of workers' frustration at the wave of layoffs around the United States. The sit-in succeeded in gaining bank loans for the company to meet the workers' demands for 60 days' severance pay and earned vacation time under the WARN Act (see Chapter 12).[66]

> The six-day sit-in became a national symbol of workers' frustration.

On the other hand, a strike's potential toll was seen in the 2012 strike at the Caterpillar factory in Joliet, Illinois, which lasted over three months. After workers rejected the company's demand for a six-year wage freeze for most of the factory's workers, at a time when the company was reporting record profits, more than 700 union members went on strike. Caterpillar had argued that wages for the higher-paid workers at the plant exceeded market levels. Faced with continuing a grueling strike, the workers ratified a deal with Caterpillar that included the wage freeze.[67]

We will examine two kinds of strikes:

1. *Unfair labor practice strikes* are those instituted by workers in response to the employer's commission of an unfair labor practice such as interfering with legitimate union activities or failure to bargain in good faith. These strikers can be temporarily, but not permanently, replaced.

2. *Economic strikes* are those used purely as economic weapons to persuade employers to provide more favorable benefits or better working conditions. All strikes not involving unfair labor practices fall into this category. With some exceptions, economic strikers cannot be fired, but they can be permanently replaced. In what has been labeled "the most significant change in collective bargaining to occur since the passage of the Wagner Act in 1934," employers are now increasingly willing to permanently replace economic strikers.[68] Employers had enjoyed that right where necessary "in an effort to carry on the business" since a 1938 Supreme Court decision, but for practical reasons they had rarely exercised it.[69] Later decisions imposed some limitations on that right. For example, any striker who is permanently replaced is put on a preferential hiring list and will have priority to be selected to fill subsequent vacancies. However, President Reagan's 1981 dismissal of 11,300 striking air traffic controllers effectively crushed their union (PATCO) and caused private-sector employers to reassess their long-standing reluctance to use replacements during and after strikes.[70] Thus, the use of or threat to use permanent replacements has become a powerful tool for employers facing economic strikes.

The following case examines when employers can legitimately decline to reinstate strikers.

Diamond Walnut Growers, Inc. v. NLRB 113 F.3d 1259 (D.C. Cir. 1997), *cert. denied,* 118 S. Ct. 1299 (1998)

Circuit Judge Silberman

I

Diamond Walnut processes and packages walnuts for national and international distribution. . . . Diamond's employees have for years been represented by Cannery Workers, Processors, Warehousemen, and Helpers Local 601 of the International Brotherhood of Teamsters, AFL–CIO (the union). In September of 1991, following expiration of the most recent collective-bargaining agreement between Diamond and the union, nearly 500 of Diamond's permanent and seasonal employees went on strike. Diamond hired replacement workers to allow it to continue operations.

By all accounts, the strike was, and remains, a bitter affair. The strikers are alleged to have engaged in various acts of violence against the replacement workers. . . . In addition, as part of its effort to exert economic pressure on Diamond, the union undertook an international boycott of its product. The boycott included a well-publicized national bus tour during which union members distributed to the public leaflets which described Diamond's workforce as composed of "scabs" who packaged walnuts contaminated with "mold, dirt, oil, worms, and debris."

Approximately one year into the strike, the Board held a representation election. The union lost the election, but its objections prompted the Board to order a rerun to be held in October of 1993. Just over two weeks prior to the new election, a group of four striking employees, represented by a union official, approached Diamond with an unconditional offer to return to work. According to the letter presented to the company at that time by their representative, the employees were convinced that "a fair election [was] simply impossible." Nonetheless, the employees "fe[lt] that it [was] important that the replacement workers . . . have an opportunity to hear from Union sympathizers." Thus, the group of strikers was "available and willing to return to immediate active employment." The following day, the union notified Diamond that pursuant to the above-quoted letter, two additional strikers were willing to return to work.

It is undisputed that for three of the returning strikers, neither the permanent jobs they held before the strike, nor substantially equivalent ones, were available at the time of their return. Diamond placed these three in various seasonal jobs. Prior to the strike, Willa Miller was a quality control supervisor; she was placed in a seasonal packing position even though a seasonal inspection job was available. Alfonsina Munoz had been employed as a lift truck operator and, despite the availability of a seasonal forklift job, was given a seasonal job cracking and inspecting nuts in the growers' inspection department at the front end of the production process. Mohammed Kussair, formerly an air separator machine operator, was, like Munoz, placed in a seasonal cracking and inspecting position in the growers' inspection department. . . .

The rerun election took place as scheduled, and the union lost. Following that election, the General Counsel filed a complaint alleging that Diamond had violated the National Labor Relations Act by unlawfully discriminating against Miller, Munoz, and Kussair. The General Counsel alleged that because of their protected activity, Diamond declined to put them in certain available seasonal positions for which they were qualified and that were preferable to the positions in which they were actually placed. After a hearing, an administrative law judge recommended that the charges be dismissed. He found that Diamond had "discriminated" insofar as it had placed the employees at least in part because of their protected activity, but he did not think that discrimination "unlawful."

*   *   *   *   *

[The NLRB reversed saying] "although [Diamond] was under no legal obligation . . . to reinstate the strikers . . . , once it voluntarily decided to reinstate them, it was required to act in a nondiscriminatory fashion toward the strikers." Diamond had discriminated against Miller, Munoz, and Kussair, in the Board's view, by declining "to place them in the [seasonal] positions of quality control assistant, lift truck operator, and loader, respectively, because of their union status and/or because of certain protected union activity they engaged in while on strike." . . . The Board rejected the contention that the placements were warranted by the employer's concern that the replacement workers might instigate violence against the three and thus justified placement in well-supervised jobs, since "there [was] no evidence that Miller, Munoz, or Kussair were involved" in the

strike-related violence allegedly causing Diamond's concern. The Board also dismissed the notion that the placements of Miller and Munoz were justified by their participation in the boycott and the circulation of disparaging leaflets: "[T]he strikers' conduct constituted protected . . . activity and there is no evidence indicating that such protection was lost because of threats made by Miller and Munoz to damage or sabotage [Diamond's] equipment or products." Since Diamond had failed to justify its discrimination, the Board found unfair labor practices.

*   *   *   *   *

[Diamond sought judicial review of the NLRB ruling.]

II

Diamond Walnut challenges the Board's determination that it lacked substantial business justification for refusing to place the three employees in the specific jobs they sought—quality control assistant, lift truck operator, and loader. It is undisputed that the *Fleetwood* framework governs this case. The General Counsel under *Fleetwood* must make out a *prima facie* case that the employer discriminated within the meaning of the Act, which means the employer's decision as to how to treat the three returning strikers was attributable to their protected activity. *Rose Printing* establishes that a struck employer faced with an unconditional offer to return to work is obliged to treat the returning employee like any other applicant for work (unless the employee's former job or its substantial equivalent is available, in which case the employee is preferred to any other applicant). But Miller and Munoz were not treated like any other applicant for work. Miller was qualified for a seasonal position in quality control that paid 32 cents per hour more than the packing job to which she was assigned. And Munoz was qualified to fill a forklift operating job, a position that paid between $2.75 and $5.00 per hour more than the walnut cracking and inspecting job she received. Diamond admits that it took into account Miller's and Munoz's protected activity in choosing to place them in jobs that were objectively less desirable than those for which they were qualified. Petitioner [Diamond], although it contended that the discrimination was comparatively slight, does not dispute that its action discriminated against Munoz and Miller within the meaning of the Act.

*   *   *   *   *

Under *Fleetwood,* after discrimination is shown, the burden shifts to the employer to establish that its treatment of the employees has a legitimate and substantial business justification. Petitioner declined to give Munoz the forklift driver job because of its concern that driving that piece of equipment throughout the plant would be unduly risky in two respects. First, because of the bad feeling between strikers and replacements, Munoz would be endangered if confronted by hostile replacement workers in an isolated area. Second, since Munoz had participated in the bus tour during which the union had accused the company of producing tainted walnuts, Munoz would be tempted to engage in sabotage by using the 11,000 pound vehicle to cause unspecified damage. As for Miller, who was also on the bus tour, the company declined to put her in the "sensitive position of quality control assistant" where "the final visual inspection of walnuts is made prior to leaving the plant." In that position, she would have "an easy opportunity to let defective nuts go by undetected . . . or to place a foreign object into the final product, thereby legitimizing the Union's claim of tainted walnuts."

* * * * *

A. Munoz

The Board rejected petitioner's proffered justifications for its placement of Munoz on the same ground as did the ALJ. As to Diamond's purported fear for her safety, no evidence had been produced that Munoz was thought to be responsible for any violence, so there was no reason to believe she would have been a special target. The Board said, "[T]here is no specific evidence that any replacements harbored hostility toward these three strikers, and, if such evidence did exist as [Diamond] claims, we fail to see how placing them in the positions to which they were assigned would lessen the perceived danger of retaliatory acts being committed against them." The Board discounted Diamond Walnut's contention that Munoz would be under greater protection if closely supervised, noting that petitioner had admitted that "Munoz freely roamed the plant unsupervised during her breaks."

* * * * *

As for the possibility that Munoz would engage in forklift sabotage, the Board was more terse, stating only that "the strikers' conduct [referring to the bus tour] constituted protected . . . activity," and there was no evidence indicating that such protection was lost because of threats made by Miller and Munoz. If Munoz had uttered specific threats of sabotage, however, she would have lost her protected status. . . . [T]he Board necessarily concluded that the possibility of Munoz engaging in future sabotage by misuse of her forklift was simply not a sufficient risk to constitute a substantial business justification for her treatment.

* * * * *

Similarly, the Board was reasonable in its determination that the risk of Munoz engaging in sabotage while riding around on her 11,000 pound forklift—the petitioner seems to most fear her crashing the forklift into machinery—is not a substantial business justification for her disadvantageous placement in another job. Strikes tend to be hard struggles, and although this one may have been more bitter than most, there is always a potential danger of returning strikers engaging in some form of

sabotage. There is therefore undeniably some risk in employing returning strikers during a strike. But it could not be seriously argued that an employer cannot be forced to assume *any* risk of sabotage, because that would be equivalent to holding that an employer need not take back strikers during an ongoing strike at all. . . .

* * * * *

B. Miller

The Miller case is another matter. It will be recalled that petitioner declined to assign her to the post of quality control assistant, the job responsible for the final inspection of walnuts leaving the plant (she received a job paying 32 cents an hour less). The Board rejected the employer's justification, which was based on Miller's participation in the product boycott and bus tour leafleting, saying only "the strikers' conduct constituted protected . . . activity and there is no evidence indicating that such protection was lost because of threats made by Miller and Munoz to damage or sabotage . . . equipment or products." With respect to Miller, we think the Board's determination that petitioner's business justification is insubstantial is flatly unreasonable.

All strikes are a form of economic warfare, but when a union claims that a food product produced by a struck company is actually tainted it can be thought to be using the strike equivalent of a nuclear bomb; the unpleasant effects will long survive the battle. . . . The company's ability to sell the product . . . could well be destroyed.

* * * * *

The Board's counsel argues that it is unfair to assume that an employee would behave in a disloyal and improper fashion. It is unnecessary, however, for us to make that assumption to decide the Board was unreasonable. The Board accepted petitioner's contention that Miller would have been placed "in the sensitive position . . . where final visual inspection of walnuts is made prior to leaving the plant." Miller would therefore have been put in a rather acute and unusual conflict of interest in which her job for her employer could be thought to have as a function the rebutting of her union's claim. A similar conflict would be raised if she wished a bargaining unit job in the company's public relations department. This conflict makes all too likely the possibility that Miller would be *at least* inattentive to her product quality duties. . . . To make matters worse, any "mistake" by Miller on the product quality control line would not be easily attributable to her unless petitioner paid someone to stand all day looking over Miller's shoulder. . . . If Munoz ran her forklift into valuable machinery, she would run a risk of being discovered and would therefore be deterred. But Miller, as a quality control assistant, could simply avert her eye and cause the damage with apparently little risk of discovery. . . .

In short, she would have had a special motive, a unique opportunity, and little risk of detection to cause severe harm. Both the risk Diamond faced in its placement of Miller was qualitatively different than a normal risk of sabotage, and the deterrence to Miller's possible misbehavior was peculiarly inadequate.

* * * * *

[W]e are obliged to ask in the last analysis whether the Board's decision, as to whether the employer's action was substantially justified by business reasons, falls within the broad stretch of reasonableness. In this case, at least with respect to one part of the Board's decision, we conclude the Board exceeded the reasonableness limits.

So ordered.

AFTERWORD

After nearly 14 years of bitter struggle, the Diamond Walnut strike was settled in March 2005. The settlement allowed strikers to return to work with full seniority and benefits, although many of them had already returned to Diamond Walnut or had moved to other jobs. [For a time line of the Diamond Walnut strike, see **www.teamster.org/divisions/foodprocessing/diamondwalnut/dwtimeline.htm**].

Questions

1. Set out the two-part test the court employed to determine whether Diamond Walnut violated the National Labor Relations Act by discriminating against its employees because of their participation in protected union activities.

2. Explain why the court found that Munoz had been wronged by Diamond but Miller had not.

3. *a.* How would you vote on federal legislation banning the practice of permanently replacing economic strikers? Explain.

   b. Is there any reason to distinguish between economic strikers and unfair labor practice strikers? Any reason not to do so? Explain.

4. A pilots' union, Airline Professionals Association, had a collective-bargaining agreement (CBA) with freight carrier Airborne Express (ABX). The union and ABX had a dispute about time-off provisions in the CBA. The union applied pressure to ABX by asking all pilots not to bid on open flying time not covered in the regular monthly schedule. ABX says it lost jobs due to the lack of pilots and filed a complaint saying the union was engaging in an illegal strike. A district court agreed with ABX, and the union appealed. Decide the case. Explain. See *ABX Air, Inc. v. Airline Professionals Association,* 266 F.3d 392 (6th Cir. 2001), *cert. denied,* 122 S. Ct. 1459 (2002).

Picketing and Boycotts

LO 14-8

Compare and contrast "primary picketing" and "secondary picketing/boycotts."

Primary Picketing   In addition to striking, unions often picket or boycott to publicize their concerns and pressure employers during the negotiating process. Picketing is the familiar process of union members gathering and sometimes marching, placards in hand, at a place of business. Peaceful, informational picketing for a lawful purpose is protected by the NLRA. Some kinds of picketing, however, are forbidden, and all picketing can be regulated by the government to ensure public safety. Primary picketing is expressed directly to the employer with whom the picketers have a dispute. Primary picketing enjoys broad constitutional and statutory protection, but it may be unlawful if violent or coercive.

Secondary Picketing/Boycotts   Secondary picketing or boycotting is directed to a business other than the primary employer, and ordinarily it is unlawful. That is, unions are engaging in an unfair labor practice if they threaten or coerce a third party with whom they are not engaged in a dispute in order to cause that third party to put pressure on the firm that is the real target of the union's concern. Consider, however, the mock funeral case summarized below.

Mock Funeral

The Sheet Metal Workers' union staged a mock funeral outside a Florida hospital in 2004. One person dressed in a "Grim Reaper" costume carrying a plastic sickle, and four "pall-bearers" carried a prop coffin and handed out leaflets. Various somber tunes played in the background on a portable audio system. The leaflets detailed several malpractice lawsuits against the hospital, with the implication that the malpractice was linked to the hospital's decision to contract with nonunion labor. The demonstration was designed to pressure the hospital, a neutral entity, to stop doing business with the picketers' actual target, the non-union contractors. The "funeral" was conducted about 100 feet from the entrance and was separated from it by a street, a strip of grass, a hedge, and a parking lot. The hospital filed an unfair labor practice charge against the union claiming the funeral constituted illegal secondary picketing in violation of the NLRA. The NLRB issued an order commanding the union to cease and desist. That decision was reviewed by the federal District of Columbia Court of Appeals.

Questions

1. What constitutional law defense would you offer on behalf of the Sheet Metal Workers' union?
2. Decide the case. Explain.

Source: Sheet Metal Workers' International Association, Local 15, AFL–CIO v. National Labor Relations Board, 491 F.3d 429 (D.C. Cir. 2007).

Lockouts

Sometimes management takes the initiative in labor disputes by locking its doors to some or all of its employees. Both the NLRB and the courts allow lockouts as defensive acts to protect businesses against sudden strikes and to prevent sabotage or violence. Some court decisions also have expanded lawful lockouts to include those of an offensive nature designed to improve management's bargaining position. Lockouts, however, are clearly not lawful if designed to interfere with bargaining rights and other legitimate union activity.

> **Sports fans have learned some labor law.**

Sports fans have learned some labor law in recent years. National Hockey League owners locked out players and eventually canceled the entire 2004 to 2005 season. Major league baseball has survived several lockouts and player strikes in the last four decades. At this writing, the National Basketball Association (NBA) and the players' union have reached an agreement in principle on a seven-year collective bargaining agreement, avoiding labor conflict through the 2023 to 2024 season.[71]

Question

George A. Hormel & Co. and the United Food and Commercial Workers Union settled a long labor dispute. Thereafter, an unhappy, long-term employee, Robert Langemeier, drove his car in a parade and attended a rally, both of which were designed to encourage a nation-wide boycott of Hormel Products. The employee did nothing to signal his feelings beyond his presence at the two events.

Employees may lawfully be dismissed for disloyalty to their employer. Supporting a boycott of an employer's products ordinarily constitutes disloyalty except where (1) the boycott is related to an ongoing labor dispute and (2) the support does not amount to disparagement of the employer's product.

Was this Hormel employee, Langemeier, engaged in protected activity such that his dismissal was unlawful? Explain. See *George A. Hormel and Company v. National Labor Relations Board,* 962 F.2d 1061 (D.C. Cir. 1992).

Part Six—Employees' Rights within or Against the Union

LO 14-9

Describe employees' rights within or against unions.

The Union's Duty of Fair Representation

As you have seen in previous sections of this chapter, the union is given statutory authority to be the exclusive bargaining agent for the employees in the designated bargaining unit. This means that even if an individual employee in the bargaining unit does not agree with union policies or is not a member of the union, he or she cannot bargain individually with the employer. Such an employee is bound by the terms of the collective-bargaining agreement, and the union has a duty to fairly represent that employee and all members of the bargaining unit, whether or not they become members of the union.

The Bill of Rights of Labor Organization Members

The Bill of Rights for members of labor organizations is contained in Title 1, Section 101 of the Labor–Management Reporting and Disclosure Act (LMRDA or Landrum–Griffin Act). The Bill of Rights was designed to ensure equal voting rights, the right to sue the union, and the rights of free speech and assembly. These rights of union members are tempered by the union's right to enact and enforce "reasonable rules governing the responsibilities of its members."[72]

Union Security Agreements and Right-to-Work Laws

LO 14-10

Explain the impact of "right-to-work" laws on union security agreements.

To maintain their membership, unions typically seek a collective-bargaining clause requiring all employees to become union members after they have been employed for some period—generally 30 days (*union shop agreements*)—or, at the least, requiring them to pay union dues and fees (*agency shop agreements*). These "union security arrangements" are lawful under the NLRA.

Under the 1988 Supreme Court decision in *Communications Workers of America v. Beck,*[73] nonunion employees can be compelled to pay union dues and fees only for core collective bargaining activities. Thus, nonunion employees' agency shop dues and fees must be reduced by an amount equal to that applied to such noncore purposes as lobbying and political campaigning. Similarly, public-sector unions with agency shop agreements can bill nonmembers for nonpolitical expenses related to collective bargaining but cannot require these members to fund political projects. In its 2012 decision in *Knox v. SEIU,* the U.S. Supreme Court reviewed whether a union's special assessment for a "political fight-back fund," aimed at two ballot initiatives the union opposed, required the union to provide nonunion employees with notice to allow them to opt out of paying into the fund. The Court held that the union must gain the affirmative consent of the nonunion employees before imposing such an assessment on them.[74]

Right to Work   According to a 2014 Gallup survey, while unions enjoy the support of a majority of Americans, over 71 percent also support "right to work" laws that prohibit union security arrangements in collective-bargaining agreements.[75] At this writing, 26 states—including traditionally union strongholds such as Indiana, Michigan, and Wisconsin—have enacted right-to-work laws.[76] In these states, nonmembers do not pay dues or fees, but as members of the bargaining unit, they must be represented by the union. Unions regard those employees as *free riders*, but right-to-work supporters see the matter as one of personal freedom.

In 2014, a federal appellate court held that Indiana's right-to-work law prohibiting employers from making union membership or the payment of union dues or fees a condition of employment was not preempted by the NLRA, and affirmed the lower court's dismissal of a union's challenge to that state statute.[77] Also in 2014, the Indiana Supreme Court in a separate case upheld the state's right-to-work law's constitutionality.[78] [For questions and answers on right-to-work laws, see **http://www.nrtw.org/right-to-work-frequently-asked-questions**].

Closed Shop   At one time, powerful unions insisted on *closed-shop* arrangements wherein employers could hire only individuals who already belonged to unions, but those arrangements are now forbidden by the NLRA.

A "Fresh" Approach to Farm Labor Practices?

A 2014 *Los Angeles Times* investigation of labor abuses at Mexican farms that export produce led to reform pledges from retailers and the Mexican government, and raised consumer awareness about food supply chains. In 2016, the Produce Marketing Association and the United Fresh Produce Association formed a Joint Committee on Responsible Labor Practices that may potentially lead to global, industrywide labor standards. At the same time, the "worker-driven" Fair Food Program has leveraged consumer demand to publicly pressure companies to join its efforts to promote fair and safe working conditions for farmworkers. Will such efforts make unions obsolete, or do unions still play an important role in supporting responsible labor practices? Discuss.

Sources: Richard Marosi, "Produce Industry Giants Team Up to Promote Responsible Labor Practices," *Los Angeles Times,* May 18, 2016, pp. A1 & A7; Brian Kocker and Russ Mounce, "A Letter to Our Members: Joint Committee on Responsible Labor Practices," United Fresh Produce Association, May 13, 2016 [**www.unitedfresh.org/a-letter-to-our-members-joint-committee-on-responsible-labor-practices**]; and Fair Food Standards Council, *Fair Food Program 2015 Annual Report,* p. 2 [**http://fairfoodstandards.org/15SOTP-Web.pdf**].

Part Seven—Other Unions

Public-Sector Unions

In 2015, the union membership rate for public-sector workers remained more than five times higher than the rate for private-sector workers.[79] Public-sector collective bargaining has been the target of legislative limitations in recent years. Wisconsin and Ohio approved legislation dramatically limiting public-sector workers' collective-bargaining rights; both prohibit bargaining over health coverage and pensions. Wisconsin's legislation, "Act 10," has survived federal appellate constitutional challenges.[80] The cutbacks in union authority are defended as necessary controls on public workers' wages and benefits, but critics view these laws as a political assault on unions.

Legal regulation of public-sector labor–management relations begins with state law. Although the specific provisions of those laws vary, many NLRA concepts have been adopted. Some fundamental policies and doctrines are quite different, however. A particular distinction lies in the ability of public-sector employees to strike.

Some states prohibit those strikes and others permit them only under restricted conditions. In either case, the rationale for treating public employees differently than private-sector employees is the role of public employees as servants of the voters. Public servants arguably have a higher duty than private employees. In addition, certain public employees, including police officers and firefighters, work in positions that clearly involve public safety, and to permit them to strike might endanger the citizenry.

Public-Sector Unions and Constitutional Rights

The U.S. Supreme Court in the 1977 *Abood* case considered Detroit public school teachers' constitutional challenge of an agency shop clause in their school district's collective-bargaining agreement requiring nonunion members to pay service fees equal to union dues; the teachers, who did not believe in public-sector collective bargaining and did not support the union's ideological activities, argued that the fees requirement violated their freedom of expression and association.[81] While holding that the teachers could prevent a share of their fees from supporting the union's unrelated ideological views, the Court saw the agency fee's impingement of constitutional rights as justified by the "union shop's" role in labor relations under federal legislation.[82]

Abood has been placed under scrutiny by two recent challenges that reached the U.S. Supreme Court. In 2014, the Supreme Court held that health care workers who provided home care to Medicaid recipients under an Illinois program did not have to pay an agency fee required under state law to support the public union they did not wish to join.[83] The Supreme Court reached the decision on the narrow grounds that the workers were only partial public employees, unlike public school teachers, and did not overturn *Abood,* although the Court's majority was critical of it.[84] In 2013, public school teachers again challenged agency fees as violating their freedom of speech, but a federal appellate court affirmed the lower court's dismissal under *Abood.* In 2016, an "equally divided" Supreme Court (due to the Court's vacancy following Justice Scalia's death) affirmed the federal appellate court ruling.[85] The eight justices later unanimously denied a petition for rehearing.[86]

Internet Exercise

Go to National Labor Relations Board's frequently asked questions [**www.nlrb. gov/faq/nlrb**].

1. Explain what an employee at an unionized workplace who is "unhappy" with the union can do.

2. Explain how to file an unfair labor practice (ULP) claim.

Chapter Questions

1. As an employee of a BMW car dealership, Becker complained on his Facebook page about his employer serving hot dogs and potato chips at the launch of the BMW 5 Series. On the day of the event, at the adjacent Land Rover dealership also owned by Becker's employer, a 13-year-old drove a Land Rover into a pond. Becker took photos of the accident, which he also posted on his Facebook page along with some sarcastic comments. After a meeting with the general manager and other supervisors, in which Becker was confronted about his Facebook postings, Becker was fired. Did his termination violate the NLRA? Explain. See *Karl Knaus Motors, Inc.,* 358 N.L.R.B. No. 164 (2012) [**www.nlrb.gov/case/13-CA-046452**].

2. The Eugene, Oregon, *Register-Guard* newspaper maintained a company policy prohibiting employees from using company communications systems such as e-mail to "solicit or proselytize for commercial ventures, religious or political causes, outside organizations, or other nonjob-related solicitations." Employees, however, had not been disciplined for using the e-mail system to invite coworkers to parties, sell sports tickets, and so on. Suzi Prozanski, an employee and union president, used the employer's e-mail system to send three union-related messages to other employees at their work addresses. She was disciplined under the company policy. Did the *Register-Guard* violate the NLRA in disciplining Prozanski? Explain. See *Register-Guard v. NLRB,* 571 F.3d 53 (D.C. Cir. 2009).

3. You are the human resources manager for a manufacturing firm that is presently the subject of an organizing campaign by a union that has filed an election petition with the NLRB just 30 days ago. Your plant manager has come to you and said that she wishes to discharge one of her employees. She further explains that the employee in question has worked for the company for three years and throughout that time has had a terrible attendance record. She adds that up to this point the employee has not received any discipline for his attendance. Upon inquiry, the plant manager tells you that the employee has been seen on the plant floor wearing a button that says: "Union Yes!" In addition, the plant manager tells you that she knows that the employee is an outspoken union activist. How would you advise the plant manager? Explain.

4. ACE/CO, a Milwaukee automobile parts manufacturer, was accused of a series of unfair labor practices springing from company conduct both before and after a disputed union representation election. Among the charges were the following:

   • ACE/CO declined to grant its usual across-the-board wage increases and told employees that the union was responsible for the failure to grant a raise.

   • ACE/CO distributed a memorandum asking employees to inform supervisors whenever they felt pressured to sign a union authorization card. One employee testified that union representatives had visited his home 13 times and that he did feel "pressured" to support the union.

- ACE/CO included in its employee handbook a statement indicating the company's "intention to do everything possible to maintain our company's union-free status for the benefit of both our employees and [the company]."

    a. Why might ACE/CO legitimately decline to offer a wage increase during an organizing campaign?

    b. Do any of these company behaviors constitute unfair labor practices? See *NLRB v. Aluminum Casting & Engineering Co.,* 230 F.3d 286 (7th Cir. 2000).

5. When assistant manager Diane Gorrell was fired from a Bob Evans restaurant in East Peoria, Illinois, most of the employees walked off the job in protest. They stood outside the restaurant for a time and discouraged customers from entering. The restaurant was left in some disarray and problems persisted for a number of days, clearly harming business. Later, all but one of the employees asked to return to their jobs but were refused. The employees filed an unfair labor practices charge with the NLRB.

    a. Justify, as a matter of law, management's decision not to allow the employees to return to work.

    b. Explain the employees' unfair labor practices charge.

    c. Decide the case. Explain. See *Bob Evans Farms, Inc. v. NLRB,* 163 F.3d 1012 (7th Cir. 1998).

6. The Yuwei Plastics and Hardware Product Company Ltd. in Dongguan, China, manufactures and exports auto parts to Ford. The Institute for Global Labour and Human Rights reported that Yuwei workers earn 80¢ an hour, work 14-hour shifts seven days a week, and are docked three days' wages if they miss one day's work. Managers' instructions to turn off safety mechanisms to increase workers' speed have resulted in serious injuries. Managers and workers stated that Ford accounts for approximately four-fifths of Yuwei's total production. Should American corporations be held responsible for their global suppliers' oppressive working conditions? Explain. See Charles Kernaghan, *Dirty Parts: Where Lost Fingers Come Cheap: Ford in China* (Pittsburgh, PA: International Institute for Global Labour and Human Rights, March 2011), pp. 1, 11.

7. Midwestern Personnel Services provided truck drivers to employers in Indiana, Kentucky, and other locations. Midwestern wanted the drivers to join a union so they would be allowed to enter a unionized workplace, AK Steel, where they were to deliver cement. Midwestern management favored Teamsters Local 836 in Middletown, Ohio, for their drivers, but a majority of the drivers voted to join Teamsters Local 215 in Evansville, Indiana. Midwestern refused to recognize Local 215; management and the drivers could not reach agreement about pension rights and contract length; and the drivers went on strike. The drivers later made an unconditional offer to return to work, but Midwestern would not allow them to return because, in its view, the drivers were economic strikers. The NLRB concluded that the drivers were motivated in part by unfair labor practices, and thus should be reinstated to their jobs. Were the drivers entitled to reinstatement? Explain. See *NLRB v. Midwestern Personnel Services,* 322 F.3d 969 (7th Cir. 2003).

8. Ralphs Grocery and the United Food & Commercial Workers Union Local 135's collective-bargaining agreement contained a union security clause and governed the

Oceanside, California, Ralphs grocery store. The union sent a new employee of the Oceanside store, a teenager who planned to work part-time, a letter stating that union membership was a condition of employment and that all new hires were required to come to one of the union's offices to affiliate with it. The new hire's mother called the union office to ask what his reduced dues would be if he objected to union membership and was told her son would have to visit the office in person to receive this information. Eventually, after further written and phone communication, the union sent the new hire information about the reduced fees. Did the union commit an unfair labor practice? Discuss. (See *United Food & Commercial Workers Union, Local 135,* NLRB Case 21-CB-112391 (February 19, 2015).

9. A crew member of the Havertown, Pennsylvania, Chipotle responded to a customer's tweet: "Free chipotle is the best thanks," by tweeting: "nothing is free, only cheap #labor. Crew members only make $8.50hr how much is that steak bowl really?" In replying to a tweet about Chipotle guacamole posted by another customer, Kennedy wrote, "it's extra not like #Qdoba, enjoy the extra $2." Under the direction of Chipotle's social media strategist, the regional manager told the employee to delete the tweets. Did Chipotle violate the NLRA? Decide. Explain. See *Chipotle Services LLC d/b/a Chipotle Mexican Grill and Pennsylvania Workers Organizing Committee,* 364 N.L.R.B. No. 72 (2016).

10. An employer, Ashley Furniture of Arcadia, Wisconsin, instructed its employees not to discuss such workplace issues as disciplinary infractions, the expiration of an employee's work permit, or the receipt of a "no-match" letter from the Social Security Administration. Did the employer violate the NLRA? Explain. See *Ashley Furniture Industries,* 353 N.L.R.B. 071 (2008).

11. Dick's Sporting Goods used a nonunion contractor to prepare for its opening in a Watertown, New York, shopping mall. The local carpenters' union requested permission of the shopping mall's operator to distribute literature in the mall protesting the use of a nonunion contractor. While the mall had previously allowed such charitable organizations as the American Cancer Society and the Boy Scouts to distribute materials on its property, it rejected the union's request. Did the shopping mall violate the NLRA? Explain. See *Salmon Run Shopping Center v. NLRB,* 534 F.3d 108 (2d Cir. 2008).

12. Jerry Kirby was discharged from his job at Ford Motor Company, allegedly because of "being under the influence of alcohol, absenteeism, and threatening management." The United Auto Workers union (UAW) immediately filed a grievance on Kirby's behalf. Kirby lost through the first three steps of the grievance process, and the UAW declined to appeal to arbitration on Kirby's behalf. The UAW said that Kirby had no right to appeal because he had allowed his union membership to lapse. Kirby then filed an unfair labor practice charge against the union. Decide. Explain. See *International Union v. NLRB,* 168 F.3d 509 (D.C. Cir. 1999).

13. LaDonna, who drove a route for a vending machine company, mentioned to her fellow driver, Steve, that she had seen an employment ad online for a route driver, speculating that it had been posted by their employer, perhaps because one of the route drivers was about to be fired. Steve thought he might be the one about to get fired and inquired about it with the employer. LaDonna was then fired for, among other infractions,

spreading gossip among employees about possible terminations. Did firing LaDonna violate the NLRA? Decide. Explain. See *Sabo, Inc. d/b/a Hoodview Vending Co.,* 362 N.L.R.B. No. 81 (2015).

14. What steps can an employer lawfully take to provide the labor necessary to keep a plant operative during a strike?

15. During a strike resulting from failure to reach a collective-bargaining agreement, Pan American Grain laid off 15 striking workers, citing changing labor needs "due to economic reasons and as a result of a substantial decrease in production and sales." Where labor costs are one of the multiple motives for a layoff, does the employer have a duty to bargain with the union over the decision to impose a layoff? Explain. See *Pan American Grain v. NLRB,* 558 F.3d 22 (1st Cir. 2009).

16. Should faculty at private universities be allowed to unionize, or are faculty members more like "managers" at the university? Discuss. See *Pacific Lutheran University,* 361 N.L.R.B. No. 157 (2014).

Notes

1. Tiffany Hsu and Alana Semuels, "Fast-Food Workers Demand Higher Wages," *Los Angeles Times,* August 30, 2013, pp. B1–B5.

2. Daniel Victor, "California Enacts $15 Minimum Wage," *The New York Times,* April 4, 2016 [**https://www.nytimes.com/2016/04/05/us/california-enacts-15-minimum-wage.html?_r=0**].

3. Samantha Masunaga, "California Fast-Food Workers Shift Focus from Minimum Wage to Unionizing," *Los Angeles Times,* April 14, 2016 [**www.latimes.com**].

4. "Union Members Summary," *Bureau of Labor Statistics News,* January 28, 2016 [**www.bls.gov/news.release/union2.nr0.htm**].

5. Ibid.

6. Joseph Szczesny, "Big Three-UAW Contracts Even the Playing Field—Eventually," *Auto Observer,* November 18, 2007 [**www.autoobserver.com/2007/11/big-three-uaw-c.html**].

7. Alexandra Bradbury, "Employee Engagement No Substitute for a Union at VW," *Labornotes,* December 17, 2014 [**http://labornotes.org**].

8. Lydia Saad, "Americans' Support for Labor Unions Continues to Recover," *Gallup,* August 17, 2015 [**www.gallup.com/poll/184622/americans-support-labor-unions-continues-recover.aspx**].

9. Patrick Marley, "Court Throws Out Suit over Wisconsin 'Right to Work' Law," *Milwaukee-Wisconsin Journal Sentinel,* September 26, 2016 [**www.jsonline.com**].

10. Harold Meyerson, "Labor Wrestles with Its Future," *The Washington Post,* May 8, 2013 [**www.washingtonpost.com/opinions/harold-meyerson-labor-wrestles-with-its-future/2013/05/08/852192d6-b74f-11e2-b94c-b684dda07add_story.html**].

11. Michal Addady, "This Fast-Food CEO Wants to Replace Workers with Machines," *Fortune,* March 17, 2016 [**http://fortune.com/2016/03/17/automate-fast-food**].

12. Isaac A. Hourwich, *Immigration and Labor* (New York: Arno Press, 1969), pp. 125–45.

13. John J. Flagler, *The Labor Movement in the United States* (Minneapolis: Lerner Publications, 1972), pp. 26–28.

14. Alan Glassman, Naomi Berger Davidson, and Thomas Cummings, *Labor Relations: Reports from the Firing Line* (New York: Business Publications, 1988), pp. 5–6.

15. Flagler, *Labor Movement,* pp. 26–28.

16. Andria Taylor Hourwich and Gladys L. Palmer, eds., *I Am a Woman Worker* (Affiliated Schools for Workers, 1936), pp. 17ff, in *The American Worker in the Twentieth Century: A History Through Autobiographies,* by Eli Ginzberg and Hyman Berman (New York: Free Press, 1963), pp. 193–95.

17. Flagler, *Labor Movement,* pp. 33, 36, quoting Frederick Lewis Allen, *The Big Change: America Transforms Itself, 1900–1950* (New York: Harper, 1952).

18. Flagler, *Labor Movement,* p. 47.

19. J. David Greenstone, *Labor in American Politics* (New York: Alfred A. Knopf, 1969), p. 21.

20. Archibald Cox, with Derek Bok and Robert A. Gorman, *Cases and Materials in Labor Law,* 8th ed. (Mineola, NY: Foundation Press, 1977), pp. 7–8.

21. Greenstone, *Labor in American Politics,* p. 22.

22. Ibid., p. 23.

23. Patrick Hardin, *The Developing Labor Law* (Washington, DC: Bureau of National Affairs, 1992), pp. 31–32.

24. Ibid., p. 94.

25. Ibid., pp. 1, 108.

26. *Steele v. Louisville and Nashville Railroad,* 323 U.S. 192 (1944).

27. *Vaca v. Sipes,* 386 U.S. 171 (1967); *Miranda Fuel Co.,* 140 N.L.R.B. 181 (1962).

28. The National Labor Relations Act is found in 29 U.S.C. § 151 et seq.

29. National Labor Relations Board, "Guideline Memorandum Concerning Unfair Labor Practice Charges Involving Political Advocacy," July 22, 2008 [**www.nlrb.gov**].

30. *Red Cross Arizona Blood Services Region,* 2012 N.L.R.B. LEXIS 43 (April 20, 2012).

31. Barry J. Kearney, Associate General Counsel, NLRB Advice Memorandum, *SWH Corporation d/b/a Mimi's Café,* October 31, 2012 [**www.minnesotalaboremploymentlawblog.com/ uploads/file/Mimi%27s%20cafe%20NLRB.pdf**].

32. *Bosch Imports, Inc. v. NLRB,* 826 F.3d 558 (1st Cir. 2016).

33. *Southern New England Telephone Company v. NLRB,* 793 F.3d 93 (D.C. Cir. 2015).

34. National Labor Relations Board, "The NLRB and Social Media," *NLRB Fact Sheets* [**www. nlrb.gov/news-outreach/fact-sheets/nlrb-and-social-media**].

35. *Costco Wholesale Corporation,* 358 N.L.R.B. No. 106 (2012) [**www.nlrb.gov/case/34- CA-012421**].

36. *Design Technology Group, d/b/a Bettie Page Clothing,* 359 N.L.R.B. No. 96 (2013) [**www. nlrb.gov/case/20-CA-035511**].

37. Cox, *Labor Law,* pp. 113–22.

38. Ibid., pp. 99–101.

39. "NLRB Representation Case-Procedures Fact Sheet," National Labor Relations Board [**www. nlrb.gov/news-outreach/fact-sheets/nlrb-representation-case-procedures-fact-sheet**].

40. "NLRB 'Ambush' Election Rules Now in Effect," *The National Law Review,* April 14, 2015 [**www.natlawreview.com**].

41. *Associated Builders and Contractors of Texas, Inc. v. NLRB,* 826 F.3d 215 (5th Cir. 2016).

42. "Employer-Filed Petitions—RM," National Labor Relations Board [**www.nlrb.gov/news-out- reach/graphs-data/petitions-and-elections/employer-filed-petitions-rm**].

43. Richard F. Griffin Jr., Memorandum GC 15-08 (Revised), Guidance Memorandum on Electronic Signatures to Support a Showing of Interest, October 26, 2015.

44. "NLRB Representation Case-Procedures Fact Sheet."

45. "Conduct Elections," National Labor Relations Board [**www.nlrb.gov/what-we-do/conduct-elections**].

46. 351 N.L.R.B. No. 28 (2007).

47. "Frequently Asked Questions—2015 Representation Case Procedures," National Labor Relations Board [**www.nlrb.gov/resources/faq/2015-representation-case-procedures#t147n4524**].

48. 357 N.L.R.B. No. 83 (2011), *enforcement granted, Kindred Nursing Centers East v. NLRB,* 727 F.3d 552 (6th Cir. 2013).

49. *Id.*

50. *Oakwood Healthcare, Inc.,* 348 N.L.R.B. No. 37 (2006).

51. *FedEx Home Delivery v. NLRB,* 563 F.3d 492 (D.C. Cir. 2009).

52. *Lechmere, Inc. v. NLRB,* 502 U.S. 527 (1992).

53. *Town & Country v. NLRB,* 516 U.S. 85 (1995).

54. *Toering Electric Company,* 351 N.L.R.B. No. 18 (2007).

55. 361 N.L.R.B. No. 126 (2014).

56. *Id.*

57. See *Sewell Manufacturing Co.,* 138 N.L.R.B. 66 (1962), which states that the board's goal is to conduct elections "in a laboratory under conditions as nearly ideal as possible to determine the uninhibited desires of employees" and "to provide an atmosphere conducive to the sober and informed exercise of the franchise free from . . . elements which prevent or impede reasonable choice."

58. *Dish Network Corp.,* 359 N.L.R.B. No. 32 (2012) (citing *Tri-Cast, Inc.,* 274 N.L.R.B. 377 (1985)) [**www.nlrb.gov/case/16-CA-027316**].

59. *NLRB v. Exchange Parts Co.,* 375 U.S. 405 (1964).

60. *Trencor, Inc. v. National Labor Relations Board,* 110 F.3d 268 (5th Cir. 1997).

61. Ronald Meisburg, NLRB Office of the General Counsel, Memorandum GC 09-04, Guideline Memorandum Concerning Withdrawal of Recognition Based on Loss of Majority Support, November 26, 2008, p. 4 (citing *Highland Regional Medical Center,* 347 N.L.R.B. 1404, 1406 (2006), and *Wurtland Nursing,* 351 N.L.R.B. No. 50, slip op. at 2).

62. "Employer/Union Rights and Obligations," National Labor Relations Board [**www.nlrb.gov/rights-we-protect/employerunion-rights-and-obligations**].

63. See *First National Maintenance Corporation v. NLRB,* 101 S. Ct. 2573 (1981).

64. *Granite Rock v. International Brotherhood of Teamsters,* 130 S. Ct. 2847 (2010).

65. 129 S. Ct. 1456 (2009).

66. Michael Luo and Karen Ann Cullotta, "Even Workers Surprised by Success of Factory Sit-in," *The New York Times,* December 13, 2008 [**www.nytimes.com**].

67. Steven Greenhouse, "Caterpillar Workers Ratify Deal They Dislike," *The New York Times,* August 17, 2012 [**www.nytimes.com/2012/08/18/business/striking-caterpillar-workers-ratify-contract-offer.html?_r=0**].

68. Littler, Mendelson, Fastiff & Tichy, *The 1990 Employer* (San Francisco: Littler, Mendelson, Fastiff & Tichy, P.C., 1990), p. V6.

69. *NLRB v. Mackay Radio & Telegraph Co.,* 304 U.S. 333 (1938).

70. Littler, Mendelson, Fastiff & Tichy, *The 1990 Employer,* p. V6.

71. Scott Cacciola, "N.B.A. and Players Extend Peace Amid Prosperity," *The New York Times,* December 15, 2016, p. B12.

72. *United Steelworkers of America v. Sadlowski,* 457 U.S. 102 (1982).

73. 487 U.S. 735 (1988).

74. 132 S. Ct. 2277 (2012).

75. Jeffrey M. Jones, "Americans Approve of Unions but Support 'Right to Work,'" *Gallup,* August 28, 2014 [**www.gallup.com/poll/175556/americans-approve-unions-support-right-work.aspx**].

76. National Right to Work Legal Defense Foundation, "RIght to Work States" (updated Feb. 2016) [**http://www.nrtw.org/right-to-work-states**].

77. *Sweeney v. Pence,* 767 F.3d 654 (7th Cir. 2014).

78. *Zoellers v. Sweeney,* 19 N.E.3d 749 (Ind. 2014).

79. "Union Members Summary," *Bureau of Labor Statistics News,* January 28, 2016 [**www.bls.gov/news.release/union2.nr0.htm**].

80. *Wisconsin Education Association Council v. Scott Walker,* 705 F.3d 640 (7th Cir. 2013); and *Laborers Local 236, AFL–CIO v. Scott Walker,* 749 F.3d 628 (7th Cir. 2014).

81. *Abood v. Detroit Board of Education,* 431 U.S. 209 (1977).

82. *Id.*

83. *Harris v. Quinn,* 134 S. Ct. 2618 (2014).

84. *Id.*

85. *Friedrichs v. California Teachers Association,* 136 S. Ct. 1083 (2016).

86. *Friedrichs v. California Teachers Association,* 136 S. Ct. 2545 (2016).

Selected Topics in Government–Business Relations

CHAPTER FIFTEEN

Consumer Protection

After completing this chapter, students will be able to fulfill the following learning objectives:

15-1. Identify various consumer protections offered under common law.

15-2. Describe "lemon laws" as an example of state consumer regulation.

15-3. Explain the purpose, roles, and power of the federal consumer protection agencies including the Consumer Financial Protection Bureau (CFPB), the Federal Trade Commission (FTC), the Consumer Product Safety Commission (CPSC), and the Food and Drug Administration (FDA).

15-4. Identify the circumstances in which the Truth in Lending Act (TILA) applies to a consumer loan.

15-5. Identify protections offered under the Fair Credit Reporting Act (FCRA).

15-6. Describe the protections offered by the Fair Credit Billing Act (FCBA).

15-7. Recognize the purpose of the Electronic Fund Transfer Act (EFTA).

15-8. Explain the purpose of the Equal Credit Opportunity Act (ECOA).

15-9. Identify debt collection practices forbidden by the Fair Debt Collection Practices Act (FDCPA).

15-10. Explain the purpose and effect of filing a Chapter 7 liquidation or "straight" bankruptcy.

Introduction

Costly consumer fraud and other forms of consumer abuse, such as invasion of privacy, dangerous products, identity theft, and false advertising, as some examples, are not unusual in our consumption-driven lives. Historically, we relied on the market to address those problems, but in recent decades, legislatures, courts, and administrative agencies have developed laws and rulings to protect us where the market arguably has failed. This chapter surveys some of those legal interventions.

Higher Education Scams? Trump University, 93 percent owned by Donald Trump, was founded in 2005 but is now defunct. Trump University was not, in fact, a university in the conventional sense but rather a profit-seeking business offering real estate seminars. Trump University did not grant credit and students were not graded. Donald Trump held the title of chairman of the University. He and his reputation were at the center of Trump University ads, and he allegedly made decisions regarding ad campaigns.

Trump University was sued by both former "students" and the State of New York. Broadly, Trump University was accused of *fraud* in offering free, introductory real estate investment classes allegedly for the purpose of luring students into expensive seminars, some priced as high as $35,000. That tactic is often labeled a "*bait and switch*." The University also was accused of misleading advertising for, among other things, allegedly claiming that Donald Trump handpicked instructors when he reportedly did not do so. Donald Trump denied any wrongful behavior and pointed to what he says were high approval ratings by the "students." At this writing, President Trump reportedly has agreed to a $25 million settlement of the lawsuit with no admission of wrongdoing on his part.

For-profit schools like the University of Phoenix and Kaplan enroll over two million students in the United States, but they are under pressure from the federal government for low graduation rates, low job placement performance, and high default rates on student loans. The schools defend themselves, in part, by saying that their students have more "risk factors" than traditional college students. Do you think higher education admissions practices are best left to the market and self-regulation, or is aggressive government oversight needed? As you read this chapter, think about the costs and benefits—the wisdom—of the extensive consumer protection laws and mechanisms protecting us.

Part One—Common-Law Consumer Protection

LO 15-1

Identify various consumer protections offered under common law.

Later in this chapter we will explore legislative and regulatory efforts to protect consumers from deception, dangerous products, unfair lending practices, and the like. Before turning to those rules, we need to appreciate the common law (judge-made law) that often preceded and, in some respects, provided the foundation for the many federal, state, and local government initiatives of recent years. In addition to the product liability claims (negligence, warranties, and strict liability) discussed in Chapter 7, injured consumers can look to several other common-law protections, including actions for misrepresentation and unconscionability. [For an extensive menu of consumer law sites, see **www.lectlaw.com/tcos.html**].

Misrepresentation

Fraud   A 2013 Federal Trade Commission survey estimated that 25.6 million American adults were victims of consumer fraud during 2011.[1] Consumer fraud, occurring all across commercial life, can involve phony products, identity theft, credit card scams, and much more. In brief, fraud is an intentional deception designed to secure an unfair or unlawful gain. A victim of civil consumer fraud ordinarily is entitled to rescind the transaction in question and to seek damages, including penalties, in some cases. Fraud also may constitute a crime. A successful fraud claim requires proof of each of the following elements:

1. False statement of a material fact.
2. Knowledge of the falsity by the wrongdoer.
3. Intent to deceive the victim.

4. Justifiable reliance on the falsehood by the victim.

5. Injury suffered by the victim.

Other Forms of Misrepresentation   In addition to fraud, the law often recognizes claims of *negligent misrepresentation* and *innocent misrepresentation*. The former, in brief, involves a false claim resulting not from an intentional untruth, as with fraud, but from a careless or baseless assertion. The false utterance was made without reasonable care. Innocent misrepresentation involves a false claim made in error. The wrongdoer reasonably believed the statement or conduct in question to be true, but he or she was mistaken.

Silence can constitute misrepresentation when material facts are not disclosed, as in the nondisclosure of a latent (hidden) defect during the sale of a house. Misrepresentation can involve false conduct as well as false expressions. A familiar example is the car seller who rolls back an odometer, with the result that the buyer is misled.

PRACTICING ETHICS   Watery Beer?

Several class-action lawsuits were filed against Anheuser-Busch (AB) in 2013 claiming the brewing giant had intentionally watered down some of its beer products during the brewing process. The plaintiffs alleged that AB intentionally deceived buyers by selling beer such as Budweiser, Bud Ice, and Michelob with less alcohol than was indicated on product labels. Plaintiffs based their claims on AB whistle-blowers, including a former operations director. Nonetheless, a federal district court and a federal court of appeals ruled for AB, saying that federal law allows a 0.3 percent tolerance between the true and the claimed alcohol content, and the plaintiffs had not alleged that AB beer exceeded that tolerance. Independent of the lawsuit, National Public Radio commissioned a laboratory report that concluded that the AB beers in question were "found to be in line with their advertised alcohol content."

Questions

1. If AB intentionally reduced alcohol content in some brands beneath the level advertised on the label but within the legal tolerance, did AB commit an ethical wrong? Explain.

2. Evidence indicates that many buyers do not read beer labels and perhaps do not care about precise alcohol content. Given that evidence, if AB did, in fact, dilute its beer, would that dilution constitute an ethical wrong? Explain.

3. Have you noticed other instances of arguable consumer fraud in your daily life? Explain.

Sources: Dan Bobkoff and Bill Chappell, "Budweiser May Seem Watery, but It Tests at Full Strength, Lab Says," *The Salt, NPR,* February 27, 2013 [www.npr.org]; Ben Bouckley, "Judge Throws Out Watered-Down Budweiser Beer Fraud Claims Against Anheuser-Busch," *BeverageDaily.com,* June 9, 2014 [www.beveragedaily.com]; and *In re Anheuser-Busch Beer Labeling,* 644 F. App'x 515 (6th Cir. 2016).

Puffing   In examining misrepresentation, the law distinguishes between statements of objective, verifiable facts and expressions of opinion. The latter ordinarily are not fraudulent even if erroneous. Thus, normal sales *puffing* ("This baby is the greatest little car you're ever gonna drive") is fully lawful, and consumers are expected to exercise good judgment in evaluating such claims. If a misleading expression of opinion comes from an *expert,* however, and the other party does not share that expertise (such as in the sale of a diamond engagement ring), a court probably would offer a remedy.

Did Apple Deceive Laptop Buyers?

Vitt, an Apple iBook G4 laptop purchaser, sued Apple, claiming that advertising words including "mobile," "durable," "rugged," "reliable," and "high value" allegedly constituted a misrepresentation of the durability, portability, and quality of the laptop. Vitt's laptop failed soon after the expiration of its one-year warranty. Vitt argued that it should be expected to last for "at least a couple of years." In Vitt's view, Apple's ads caused buyers to believe the computer was of better quality than it really is. Was Vitt a victim of a misrepresentation? Explain.

Source: See *Vitt v. Apple Computer, Inc.,* 469 F. App'x 605 (2012).

The following case involves a fraud claim against Harley-Davidson.

LEGAL BRIEFCASE

Tietsworth v. Harley-Davidson
677 N.W.2d 233 (WIS. 2004)

Justice Diane S. Sykes

The circuit court dismissed the entire action for failure to state a claim. [T]he court of appeals reinstated [the claims.]

* * * * *

FACTS AND PROCEDURAL HISTORY

Plaintiff Steven C. Tietsworth and the members of the proposed class own or lease 1999 or early-2000 model year Harley motorcycles equipped with Twin Cam 88 or Twin Cam 88B engines. Harley's marketing and advertising literature contained the following statement about the TC-88 engines:

> Developing [the TC-88s] was a six-year process. . . . The result is a masterpiece. We studied everything from the way oil moves through the inside, to the way a rocker cover does its job of staying oil-tight. Only 21 functional parts carry over into the new design. What does carry over is the power of a Harley-Davidson™ engine, only more so.

Harley also stated that the motorcycles were "premium" quality, and described the TC-88 engine as "eighty-eight cubic inches filled to the brim with torque and ready to take you thundering down the road."

On January 22, 2001, Harley sent a letter to Tietsworth and other owners of Harley motorcycles informing them that "the rear cam bearing in a small number of Harley-Davidson's Twin Cam 88 engines has failed. While it is unlikely that you will ever have to worry about this situation, you have our assurance that Harley-Davidson is committed to your satisfaction." The letter went on to explain that the company was extending the warranty on the cam bearing from the standard one-year/unlimited mileage warranty to a five-year/50,000 mile warranty. Separately, Harley developed a $495 "cam bearing repair kit" and made the kit available to its dealers and service departments "to expedite rear cam bearing repair."

* * * * *

The amended complaint alleges that the cam bearing mechanism in the 1999 and early-2000 model year TC-88 engines is inherently defective, causing an unreasonably dangerous propensity for premature engine failure. [T]he amended complaint alleged that Harley's failure to disclose the cam bearing defect induced the plaintiffs to purchase their motorcycles by causing them to reasonably rely upon Harley's representations regarding the "premium" quality of the motorcycles.

The amended complaint further alleges that if the plaintiffs had known of the engine defect, they either would not have purchased

Critics Of course, the CFPB has many doubters and outright enemies. A primary fear is that increased government regulation is likely to reduce the availability of credit or raise the cost of that credit, thereby potentially damaging consumers and the economy. Philosophically, many critics simply want the government to leave the finance market alone. In 2016, a panel of the U.S. Court of Appeals for the D.C. Circuit ruled that the structure of the CFPB violates Article II of the Constitution by, in essence, vesting too much power—with too little oversight—in the CFPB director.[6] The court's remedy restructures the agency such that the U.S. president can remove the director *at will* rather than *for cause* as had originally been provided. The CFPB has petitioned the entire D.C. Circuit court to rehear the case. The CFPB will continue its work, but President Trump, in his campaign, promised to curb financial regulations.

> Many critics simply want the government to leave the finance market alone.

Arbitration Clauses Critics' concerns about government overreach are well-illustrated by the CFPB's 2016 proposed rule to address the widespread use of mandatory *arbitration clauses* in consumer financial instruments. The arbitration clauses in credit card contracts, checking accounts, student loans, and other financial contracts require consumers to agree in advance that any dispute arising out of the contracts will be resolved by arbitration rather than going to court either individually or as part of a class action. The business community defends the arbitration agreements as efficient, quick, inexpensive vehicles for consumer redress, but the CFPB says consumers often don't even realize they have entered the agreements; they seldom seek arbitration, and when they do, their recoveries are small, and they are denied their right to judicial review.

The CFPB has banned arbitration clauses in most residential mortgage contracts, and at this writing it is considering limitations on arbitration clauses in financial contracts involving credit cards, student loans, auto loans, debt collection, and many other transactions. The proposed new rule would allow arbitration clauses broadly, but it would forbid those clauses that prohibit consumers from joining class actions to litigate their grievances.

Arbitration clauses also appear in many other forms of consumer contracts and elsewhere in life, including employment agreements. Judicial decisions to date have been generally supportive of the legality of arbitration agreements. [For a "one-stop shop for the American people to learn how to protect themselves from fraud and to report it wherever—and however—it occurs," see the Federal Financial Fraud Task Force's website: **www.stopfraud.gov**].

PRACTICING ETHICS | CFPB Fines Wells Fargo

From Chapter 1, you will remember that Wells Fargo's salespeople, in recent years, created about two million new accounts without customer permission or knowledge in order to meet sales goals. Wells Fargo fired some 5,300 of its 94,000 managers and employees; CEO John Stumpf resigned and reportedly forfeited at least $41 million; and Carrie Tolstedt, who headed the division in question, forfeited at least $19 million. Reportedly, Tolstedt will leave with about $125 million in stock and options. The CFPB demonstrated its consumer protection power by fining Wells Fargo $100 million of the $185 million in total fines assessed and by assuring consumer refunds of at least $2.6 million. Wells Fargo's 2015 profits were over $20 billion.

Wells Fargo had both warned its employees against the illegal practices and had deployed additional "risk professionals" to investigate. According to Andrew Ross Sorkin, writing in *The New York Times:* Wells Fargo CEO John Stumpf "has always said, fairly, that it is impossible to do a perfect job policing hundreds of thousands of employees."

Question

While perfect supervision presumably cannot be attained, do you think these facts suggest managerial culpability and/or a failure in Wells Fargo's ethical culture? Explain. [You might do a quick Internet search to update the facts since they are only emerging at this writing.]

Sources: Matt Egan and Jackie Wattles, "Wells Fargo CEO Forfeits $41 Million as Company Launches Probe," *CNN Money,* September 28, 2016 [**http://money.cnn.com**]; Renae Merle, "Wells Fargo Fired 5,300 Workers for Improper Sales Push. The Executive in Charge Is Retiring with $125 Million," *The Washington Post,* September 13, 2016 [**www.washingtonpost.com**]; and Andrew Ross Sorkin, "Pervasive Sham Deals at Wells Fargo, and No One Noticed," *The New York Times,* September 12, 2016 [**www.nytimes.com**].

The Federal Trade Commission

The Federal Trade Commission (FTC) was created in 1914 to prevent "unfair methods of competition and unfair or deceptive acts or practices in and affecting commerce." The FTC operates as a miniature government with powerful quasi-legislative (rule-making) and quasi-judicial (adjudication) roles. [For the FTC's Bureau of Consumer Protection home page, see **www.ftc.gov/bcp/index.shtml**].

Rule Making

The FTC performs legislative responsibilities in issuing trade regulation rules to implement the intent of broadly drawn congressional legislation. That is, the rules specify particular acts or practices that the commission deems deceptive.

The FTC's quasi-legislative (rule-making) power is extensive, as evidenced by the following examples:

- In 2015, the FTC received more than three million complaints about telemarketers. The Federal Trade Commission's Do Not Call Registry forbids telemarketers, with certain exceptions, from placing calls to Americans who have added their phone numbers to the Federal Trade Commission's list. Federal law and FTC rules, strengthened in 2015, ban many types of so-called robocalls and texts (prerecorded telemarketing solicitations). New technology, however, makes bulk calling inexpensive and permits calling from abroad, beyond the reach of federal enforcement. Thus, the government has had difficulty enforcing the rules, and the telephone companies, for the most part, have failed to cooperate in providing easy access to the blocking technology that would spare angry consumers.[7] [Those who want to be added to the Do Not Call list or to file complaints can visit **www.donotcall.gov**].

> "Does a moment pass when Kim Kardashian isn't selling?"

- The *Los Angeles Times* asked: "Does a moment pass when Kim Kardashian isn't selling? If she's not hyping her workout video, she's touting her online shoe club, her new book or her sisters' 'reality' TV spin-off, a gripping look inside their high-end Miami boutique."[8]

Kardashian and all others hyping products and services on the Internet are subject to penalties for false or misleading advertising if they fail to comply with the FTC's "Guides Concerning Use of Endorsements and Testimonials in Advertising" (updated in 2015). Testimonials, including those posted on new media sites (blogs, Twitter, Facebook, etc.), must be truthful and endorsers must disclose any material connection they have to the advertiser of the product.

Adjudication

On its own initiative or as a result of a citizen complaint, the FTC may investigate suspect trade practices. At that point, the FTC may drop the proceeding, settle the matter, or issue a formal complaint.

Where a formal complaint is issued, the matter proceeds essentially as a trial conducted before an administrative law judge. The FTC has no authority to impose criminal sanctions.

Federal Trade Commission—Fraud and Deception

Unfair and deceptive trade practices, including those in advertising, are forbidden under Section 5 of the Federal Trade Commission Act. The FTC test for deception requires that the claim is (1) false or likely to mislead the reasonable consumer and (2) material to the consumer's decision making. Unfairness and deception can take many forms:

Herbalife   The multilevel nutrition supplement company agreed to pay $200 million in 2016 to reimburse consumers who lost money trying to sell and distribute its products. While not labeling Herbalife a pyramid scheme, the FTC did say that the company had deceived consumers about how much money they could make selling Herbalife products. Herbalife must restructure its compensation plan to reward distributors for products sold rather than how many people are recruited.

Lumosity   The "brain training" company agreed in 2016 to pay $2 million to settle FTC charges of false and misleading advertising. The FTC said that Lumosity could not provide scientific evidence to support its claims that its "brain training" games could improve performance in everyday tasks like school and work and that its games could reduce or delay cognitive impairments.

Online Dating Services   The FTC issued a warning in 2015 about romance scammers who fabricate heart-wrenching fake online profiles as a way of stealing money from sympathetic subscribers. Some scammers are even practicing bank fraud, persuading online love interests to set up bank accounts to which the scammers transfer stolen money. The victims are then asked to transfer the money out of the country, never realizing they have become parties to bank fraud.

Federal Trade Commission—Consumer Privacy

Kellie Droste, a Maricopa, Arizona, resident, was shocked in March 2013 when she learned that an identity thief had stolen her personal information and filed a tax return in her name to claim her tax refund. Her $2,700 refund was delayed by months.[9] According to the federal

Justice Department, about 7 percent of Americans age 16 or older were victims of identity theft in 2014.[10] Fraudulent use of credit cards, bank accounts, and other accounts such as telephone and insurance were the most common methods of identity theft. Only about 14 percent of victims reported losses of greater than one dollar, and over half of victims were able to resolve any problems associated with the theft in one day or less, while about 9 percent did so in a month.[11] [For a privacy database, see **www.privacyrights.org**].

Privacy intrusions have become an important focus of Federal Trade Commission activities as risks have arisen across the full range of contemporary life from credit cards to health information to big data to connected cars to data brokers (who collect and sell private consumer information).

Privacy Law   The Federal Trade Commission enforces the privacy provisions in a number of federal laws and pursues privacy abuse under its authority to stop unfair methods of competition along with unfair and deceptive acts and practices. The FTC, for example, enforces its "Red Flags Rule," under which all "financial institutions" and "creditors" must establish a written program to prevent identity theft in their organizations by watching for warning signs (red flags) and then mitigating whatever losses may come from identity theft.

Likewise, a recent federal court of appeals decision has confirmed the FTC's authority to sue firms whose lax security policies result in compromised consumer privacy.[12] The Wyndham hotel chain was hacked three times in two years, exposing credit card data for more than 600,000 customers. Those data were transferred to a website in Russia and millions of dollars in losses resulted. The FTC said that Wyndham's failure to use encryption, firewalls, and other basic security measures were "unfair acts or practices in commerce" toward consumers who were led to believe that Wyndham provided satisfactory security. Wyndham subsequently settled with the FTC.[13]

FTC Chair Edith Ramirez has made it clear, however, that the commission should use its authority "very judiciously."[14] Speaking of the FTC's power to police unfairness in the market, Ramirez said, "I want to just emphasize that that's not a blank check for the FTC in going after privacy violations."[15] The market and self-regulation, from the FTC point of view, must remain the core methods for assuring consumer privacy.

The Consumer Product Safety Commission

Samsung Galaxy Note 7 smartphones along with hoverboards such as the Razor and Swagway were sometimes spontaneously bursting into flames in the summer of 2016. The actual numbers were small. Samsung reported 92 instances of batteries overheating in the United States,[16] and hoverboards were linked to about 60 battery fires in more than 20 states, causing at least $2 million in damages.[17] Both the Galaxy Note 7 and several brands of hoverboards were recalled by the Consumer Product Safety Commission (CPSC) in 2016.

> Hoverboards were linked to about 60 fires.

When recalls are issued, consumers may receive repairs, refunds, or a new, safe model of the product in question. On rare occasions, the CPSC finds products so inherently dangerous that they must be banished from the market, as was the case with a familiar baby crib design.

Cribs   After more than 30 infant and toddler deaths and millions of recalls in the previous decade, the CPSC unanimously voted to ban, effective June 28, 2011, the manufacture, sale, and resale (including yard sales) of the traditional drop-side baby crib that has cradled millions. The new standard requires fixed sides on the cribs.[18]

[For an ABC News visit to the Consumer Product Safety Commission Testing Lab, see **http://abcnews.go.com/GMA/video/consumer-product-safety-commission-test-lab-13827984**].

Reducing Risk   Recalls and banishments are the most visible features of a rather comprehensive Consumer Product Safety Commission regulatory structure. The CPSC, created in 1972, is responsible for reducing the risks in using consumer products such as toys, lawn mowers, washing machines, bicycles, fireworks, pools, portable heaters, and household chemicals. The CPSC pursues product safety, initially, by collecting data and conducting research. Via its rule-making authority, the CPSC promulgates mandatory consumer product safety, performance, and labeling standards.

Manufacturers must certify before distribution that products meet federal safety standards. Manufacturing sites may be inspected, and specific product safety testing procedures can be mandated. Businesses other than retailers are required to keep product safety records. In cases of severe and imminent hazards, the CPSC has the power to enforce its decisions by seeking a court order to remove a product from the market. In less urgent circumstances, the commission may proceed with its own administrative remedy. Preferring voluntary compliance, the commission may negotiate with companies to recall dangerous products. Where voluntary negotiations fail, the commission may proceed with an adjudicative hearing before an administrative law judge or members of the commission. That decision may be appealed to the full commission and thereafter to the federal court of appeals. Civil or criminal penalties may result. Office Depot, for example, agreed to pay $3.4 million in 2015 to settle CPSC charges alleging that the office supply company knowingly failed to report hazards associated with two models of office chairs.[19] [For the federal government recall site, see **www.recalls.gov/**].

NEISS   The CPSC maintains the National Electronic Injury Surveillance System that records, through a national sampling of hospital emergency visits, injuries and deaths related to consumer products. A CPSC public database allows all of us to report dangerous products and to search complaints entered by others. We learn, for example, that 2014 saw nearly a quarter million injuries associated with toys, about 30 thousand with chain saws, and over 61 thousand with televisions and their stands.[20] [See **http://saferproducts.gov/**].

Online Robot   Because businesses often have difficulty in determining which CPSC regulations apply to their products, the agency has developed a regulatory "Robot." Businesses can input information to the online Robot and receive guidance about regulations, reporting obligations, and frequently asked questions.

The Food and Drug Administration

E-cigarettes   "In the absence of science-based regulation of all tobacco products, the marketplace has been the wild, wild West," said Mitch Zeller, the director of the Food and Drug Administration's Center for Tobacco Products.[21] Zeller was talking about the FDA decision to begin regulating e-cigarettes as of August 2016. E-cigarettes appear to be healthier than conventional cigarettes, but more research is needed and they do, of course, contain highly addictive nicotine. Under the new rules, e-cigarette manufacturers must disclose the ingredients in their products and submit those products for government approval. Retailers must not sell to those under 18, health warnings must appear on labels, and sales are forbidden from vending machines accessible to minors.

The number of middle and high school students using e-cigarettes tripled between 2013 and 2014, exacerbating officials' fears that vaping would become a gateway to tobacco smoking. A group of tobacco control experts, however, urged the FDA to be "open-minded" about e-cigarettes, saying they are more helpful than harmful and may lead to a reduction in tobacco smoking.[22] What do you think of the wisdom of regulating vaping products?

Graphic Warnings   Conventional tobacco products, according to a surgeon general report, may be more dangerous and addictive than in the past.[23] The FDA in 2011 proposed a series of large, graphic warning labels for placement on cigarette packages in order to discourage smoking. The graphic labels included images like blackened lungs, a baby in a cloud of smoke, and a man breathing through his neck. The tobacco industry challenged the labels on First Amendment grounds, arguing the graphic ads were designed to provoke rather than merely provide factual information and that they amounted to an expropriation of company advertising space for government advocacy. Two federal appeals courts split on the constitutionality of the graphic warnings, and at this writing the FDA is developing new labels.[24] About 80 countries employ the graphic labels and considerable research supports their effectiveness.[25]

Safety and Effectiveness   The FDA monitors much of America's health landscape with responsibility for assuring the safety, effectiveness, and security of food, drugs (prescription and over-the-counter), medical devices, cosmetics, tobacco products, and more. The FDA is empowered to impose fines and remove dangerous drugs from the market. Over-the-counter antibacterial soaps with certain chemical ingredients, for example, were banned from the market by the FDA in 2016 because manufacturers failed to show the ingredients were both safe and more effective than plain soap and water.

> The FDA approves a drug only if it is safe and effective.

Perhaps the biggest FDA duty is to decide when drugs should be approved for marketing. Companies must subject a new drug to extensive testing before the FDA will consider approval. FDA physicians and scientists review the scientific evidence, and thereafter the FDA approves a drug for marketing only if it is both safe and effective.

Food Safety   The FDA recently needed 165 days and 81 days, respectively, to spur company recalls of tainted peanut butter and a contaminated cheese product, leading to a *Washington Post* headline saying "The FDA Is Actually Terrible at Recalling Dangerous Foods."[26]

The 2011 Food Safety and Modernization Act gave the FDA greatly expanded food safety power. With about one in six Americans eating contaminated food each year, the FDA has developed new rules to implement the 2011 Act. Those rules, which are being phased in at this writing, expect human and animal food producers to maintain written safety plans, analyze hazards, and develop safety procedures. The rules require importers to

> "The FDA is actually terrible at recalling dangerous foods."

assure that food entering this country is produced in a manner consistent with U.S. standards. The FDA stations inspectors around the world to strengthen imported food (and drug) safety.

Trust the Market?   The FDA is one of the most criticized divisions of the federal government. Scandalously high prices for some drugs are beyond FDA authority, but the FDA's drug and medical device approval process has been fiercely criticized. Broadly, FDA critics argue for introducing lifesaving new products to the market much more quickly by relying more on market forces and less on government rules. Indeed, new drugs are more readily reaching the consumer. During the first two-thirds of 2015, the FDA approved 89 percent of the new drugs considered, up from 66 percent seven years previously.[27] New drug approvals are now considered the fastest in the world.[28] The 21st Century Cures Act, approved by Congress and President Obama in late 2016, is expected to permit even quicker drug approvals. The FDA, at least in some cases, will be able to accept clinical observations such as case histories to supplement or perhaps even replace the currently required slower, but more scientifically rigorous, randomized clinical trials.

Reduced regulation, of course, carries its own risks. For example, during a recent five-year study period, more than 70 percent of 113 recalled medical devices (such as defibrillators and insulin pumps) had been approved by the FDA under an expedited system.[29] Beyond safety concerns, experts Tomas Philipson and Andrew von Eschenbach argue that reduced and more efficient regulation could double medical innovation and sharply boost the American GDP.[30] Thus, to some critics, the FDA imposes too many rules; to others, too few.

Indoor Tanning

Heather Champion, a Palm Beach, Florida, beauty salon manager, reported that she had tanned indoors so often in her high school days in upstate New York that her tanning "card" often needed additional pages, like a world traveler's passport. She would sometimes tan twice in one day. Then, at age 26, she learned she had melanoma.

While indoor tanning use has declined a bit, one-third of teenage white girls reportedly continue the practice. Evidence of a link between indoor tanning and cancer is not yet conclusive, but experts have found the use of sun beds before age 30 is associated with a 75 percent increase in melanoma risk. About 40 states have some sort of restraint on tanning salon use by minors, and the FDA imposes some standards, including a requirement for timers with tanning devices.

Question

In your judgment, should the FDA ban indoor tanning by minors, as 12 states have already done? Explain.

Sources: Sabrina Tavernise, "Warning: That Tan Could Be Hazardous," *The New York Times,* January 10, 2015 [www.nytimes.com]; and "Indoor Tanning Restrictions for Minors/A State-by-State Comparison," National Conference of State Legislatures, March 31, 2016 [**www.ncsl.org/research/health/indoor-tanning-restrictions.aspx**].

Part Three—Debtor/Creditor Law

Credit Regulations

According to *The Washington Post,* Jaime and Donald Abbott recently joined America's exploding population of rent-to-own consumers when they bought a new $1,500 sofa set for their home in Alabama. They hoped to complete payments in two years. If paid weekly, the total price would reach $4,158. At the time, Donald was earning a steady $500 per week driving a truck, but eight months later, Donald's pay checks had declined and the Abbotts were left with the choice of returning their leased furniture and losing what they had put in it or continuing their uphill financial struggle until times improved.[31]

> America's exploding population of rent-to-own consumers.

Several million rent-to-own customers annually are able to buy furniture, televisions, jewelry, and the like that they often could not otherwise afford. They can return the items when they choose, or they can make the payments and eventually own them. To do so, however, they will pay effective annual interest rates often exceeding 100 percent. To consumer protection advocates, these rentals are simply disguised predatory loans to people who can afford nothing else. At least three states explicitly treat these rental arrangements as a form of credit, thus applying caps on interest rates in keeping with state usury laws. Most other states have some consumer protection limitations on rent-to-own arrangements.[32] Do rent-to-own deals seem like abusive credit arrangements to you? If so, would you support laws treating those arrangements as a form of credit?

Lending and credit abuse led Congress and the state legislatures to supplement the market's powerful messages with an array of protective legislation. Earlier in this chapter and in Chapter 8, we introduced the Consumer Financial Protection Bureau (CFPB) that is designed, in part, to protect consumers from credit abuse. Now we will turn to several other important pieces of federal credit practices law. [For a debtor/creditor law database, see **www.law.cornell.edu/wex/debtor_and_creditor**].

Truth in Lending Act (TILA)

LO 15-4

Identify the circumstances in which the Truth in Lending Act (TILA) applies to a consumer loan.

Consumers often do not understand the full cost of buying on credit. The TILA is designed primarily to assure full disclosure of credit terms. Having been designed for consumer protection, the TILA does not cover all loans. The following standards determine the TILA's applicability:

1. The debtor must be a "natural person" rather than an organization.
2. The creditor must be regularly engaged in extending credit and must be the person to whom the debt is initially payable. Dodd–Frank expressly amends the definition of creditor to include mortgage originators.
3. The purpose of the credit must be "primarily for personal, family, or household purposes" involving transactions of $54,600 or less in 2016 (adjusted annually for inflation), but loans secured by real property (such as mortgages) are covered by the act regardless of the loan amounts.
4. The credit must be subject to a finance charge or payable in more than four installments.

The TILA, along with Regulation Z interpreting the act, were designed both to protect consumers from credit abuse and to assist them in becoming more informed about credit terms and costs so they could engage in comparison shopping. The heart of the act is the required conspicuous disclosure of the amount financed, the finance charge (the actual dollar sum to be paid for credit), the annual percentage rate (APR—the total cost of the credit expressed at an annual rate), and the number of payments. The finance charge includes not just interest but service charges, points, loan fees, carrying charges, and other costs. TILA covers consumer loans generally, including credit cards and auto purchases. The federal Consumer Leasing Act and Regulation M provide protections similar to TILA for consumer leases of personal property.

TILA amendments in Dodd–Frank give extensive, new attention to residential mortgages, a recognition of the subprime mortgage crisis and its destructive impact on the entire American economy. Creditors, for example, are prohibited from making a residential mortgage loan without a good faith determination that the consumer has a reasonable "ability to repay" the loan. Likewise, mortgage service providers must, for example, respond to error notices within a specified period of time. [For an FTC consumer finance database, see **www.ftc.gov/news-events/media-resources/consumer-finance**].

The case that follows examines the application of TILA to a credit card interest rate dispute.

LEGAL BRIEFCASE

Barrer v. Chase Bank USA
566 F.3d 883 (9th Cir. 2009)

Circuit Judge O'Scannlain

We must decide whether a credit card company violates the Truth in Lending Act when it fails to disclose potential risk factors that allow it to raise a cardholder's Annual Percentage Rate.

I

A

Walter and Cheryl Barrer held a credit card account with Chase. The Barrers received and accepted the Cardmember Agreement ("the Agreement") governing their relationship at the relevant time in late 2004. In February 2005, Chase mailed to the Barrers a Change in Terms Notice ("the Notice"), which purported to amend the terms of the Agreement, in particular to increase the Annual Percentage Rate ("APR") significantly. It also allowed the Barrers to reject the amendments in writing by a certain date. They did not do so, and continued to use the credit card. Within two months, the new, higher, APR became effective.

According to the Barrers' First Amended Complaint, they enjoyed a preferred APR of 8.99% under the Agreement. In a section

entitled "Finance Charges," the Agreement provided a mathematical formula for calculating preferred and non-preferred APRs and variable rates. In the event of default, the Agreement stated that Chase might increase the APR on the balance up to a stated default rate. The Agreement specified the following events of default: failure to pay at least a minimum payment by the due date; a credit card balance in excess of the credit limit on the account; failure to pay another creditor when required; the return, unpaid, of a payment to Chase by the customer's bank; or, should Chase close the account, the consumer's failure to pay the outstanding balance at the time Chase has appointed.

Another section entirely, entitled "Changes to the Agreement," provided that Chase "can change this agreement at any time, . . . by adding, deleting, or modifying any provision. [The] right to add, delete, or modify provisions includes financial terms, such as APRs and fees." The next section, entitled "Credit Information," stated that Chase "may periodically review your credit history by obtaining information from credit bureaus and others." These sections appeared five and six pages, respectively, after the "Finance Charge" section.

Around April 2005, the Barrers' noticed that their APR had "sky-rocketed" from 8.99% to 24.24%, the latter a rate close to a non-preferred or default rate. None of the events of default specified in the Agreement, however, had occurred. When the Barrers contacted Chase to find out why their APR had increased, Chase responded in a letter citing judgments it had made on the basis of information obtained from a consumer credit reporting agency. In particular, Chase wrote that: "outstanding credit loan(s) on revolving accounts . . . [were] too high" and there were "too many recently opened installment/revolving accounts." The Barrers do not dispute the facts underlying Chase's judgments.

Despite the Barrers' surprise, the Notice they had received in February contained some indication of what would be forthcoming. Specifically, it disclosed that Chase would shortly increase the APR to 24.24%, a decision "based in whole or in part on the information obtained in a report from the consumer reporting agency."

The Barrers paid the interest on the credit account at the new rate for three months before they were able to pay off the balance. Then they sued Chase in federal district court.

B

The Barrers filed a class action lawsuit on their own behalf and on behalf of all Chase credit card customers similarly harmed and similarly situated. The complaint asserted one cause of action under the Truth in Lending Act ("the Act"), and Regulation Z. The Barrers claim to have been the victims of a practice they now call "adverse action repricing," which apparently means "raising . . . a preferred rate to an essentially non-preferred rate based upon information in a customer's credit report." Though the Barrers do not claim that the practice itself is illegal, they do claim that it was illegal for Chase not to disclose it fully to them or to the other members of the putative class.

[The federal district court dismissed the Barrers' cause of action. The Barrers appealed.]

II

The Truth in Lending Act is designed "to assure a meaningful disclosure of credit terms so that the consumer will be able to compare more readily the various credit terms available to him and avoid the uninformed use of credit." Rather than substantively regulate the terms creditors can offer or include in their financial products, the Act primarily requires disclosure.

* * * * *

In general, the Act regulates credit card disclosures at numerous points in the commercial arrangement between creditor and consumer: at the point of solicitation and application, at the point the consumer and the creditor consummate the deal, at each billing cycle, and at the point the parties renew their arrangement. Specifically, creditors must disclose "[t]he conditions under which a finance charge may be imposed," "[t]he method of determining the

amount of the finance charge," and, "[w]here one or more periodic rates may be used to compute the finance charge, each such rate . . . and the corresponding nominal annual percentage rate."

Regulation Z, 12 C.F.R. Section 226, provides the precise regulations that the Barrers claim Chase violated. In general, these regulations establish two conditions a creditor must meet. "First, it must have disclosed all of the information required by the statute." That is, disclosures must be complete. "And second, [they] must have been true—i.e., . . . accurate representation[s] of the legal obligations of the parties at [the] time [the agreement was made]."

Section 226.6 lists the initial disclosures required of a creditor under a new credit agreement. The list includes "each periodic rate that may be used to compute the finance charge . . . and the corresponding annual percentage rate."

* * * * *

Just as Section 226.6 states what must be disclosed, so Section 226 describes how to disclose it. Among other things, creditors must make the required disclosures "clearly and conspicuously in writing." . . .

The Board has also recognized that creditors may reserve the general right to change the credit agreement, as Chase did in this case. Should the creditor make changes in these ways, it may have to disclose anew under Section 226.9(c).

III

The Barrers argue that . . . Chase failed to disclose completely under the Act why it would change the APRs of its cardholders, in violation of subsection 226.6(a)(2) of Regulation Z.

The Barrers do not argue that either the Agreement or the Notice failed to disclose the APR, which their complaint puts at 8.99% under the Agreement and 24.24% under the Notice. Rather, . . . the gravamen of the Barrers' complaint is that Chase did not disclose that if a cardholder's credit report revealed certain information, what Chase calls "risk factors," the APR might go up.

* * * * *

Regulation Z requires that creditors disclose any APR "that *may* be used to compute the finance charge," and that they do so "clearly and conspicuously."

* * * * *

We are persuaded that Chase adequately disclosed the APRs that the Agreement permitted it to use simply by means of the change-in-terms provision. That provision reserved Chase's right to change APRs, among other terms, without any limitation on why Chase could make such a change. The provision thus disclosed that, by changing the Agreement, Chase could use any APR, a class of APRs that logically includes APRs adjusted on the basis of adverse credit information. Apart from the gloss of Comment 11, neither the Act nor Regulation Z require[s] Chase to disclose the basis on which it would change or use APRs. Therefore the failure to disclose the reason for the change to the Barrers' APR—adverse credit information—and that Chase would look up their credit history to acquire that information does not undermine the adequacy of Chase's disclosure.

Even so, such disclosure must be clear and conspicuous. Neither the Act nor Regulation Z define[s] clarity and conspicuousness in this context. The Staff Commentary explains only that "[t]he clear and conspicuous standard requires that disclosures be in a reasonably understandable form." . . .

Clear and conspicuous disclosures, therefore, are disclosures that a reasonable cardholder would notice and understand. No particular kind of formatting is magical, but, in this case, the document must have made it clear to a reasonable cardholder that Chase was permitted under the agreement to raise the APR not only for the events of default specified in the "Finance Terms" section, but for any reason at all.

. . . [T]he change-in-terms provision appears on pages 10–11 of the Agreement, five dense pages after the disclosure of the APR. It is neither referenced in nor clearly related to the "Finance Terms" section. This provision, as part of the APRs allowed under the contract, is buried too deeply in the fine print for a reasonable cardholder to realize that, in addition to the specific grounds for increasing the APR listed in the "Finance Charges" section, Chase could raise the APR for other reasons.

Therefore, the Barrers have stated a claim because Chase cannot show that, as a matter of law, the Agreement made clear and conspicuous disclosure of the APRs that Chase was permitted to use.

REVERSED and REMANDED.

[For a further ruling in this matter, see *Barrer v. Chase Bank, USA,* 2013 U.S. Dist. LEXIS 24268 (D. Or. February 21, 2013).]

Questions

1. *a.* How did Chase violate Regulation Z and the TILA?
    b. According to this decision, what is a "clear and conspicuous" disclosure?

2. Green Tree Financial financed Randolph's mobile home purchase. Randolph sued, claiming that Green Tree's financing document contained an arbitration clause that violated TILA because it did not provide the same level of protection as TILA accords. If the arbitration clause provided lesser protection than that provided by TILA, as Randolph claimed, should the arbitration go forward? Explain. See *Randolph v. Green Tree Financial Corp.,* 531 U.S. 79 (2000).

3. Sarah Hamm sued Ameriquest Mortgage Company claiming a violation of TILA. Hamm borrowed money secured by a 30-year mortgage from Ameriquest. She signed a "Disclosure Statement" specifying, among other things, that she was responsible for 359 payments at a specified amount and one payment for the last month of a slightly smaller amount. The Statement did not, however, explicitly specify, as required by TILA, the total payments due (360). Was TILA violated? Explain. See *Hamm v. Ameriquest Mortgage,* 506 F.3d 525 (7th Cir. 2007).

Credit and Charge Cards

> College students are burying themselves in debt.

College students are burying themselves in debt. As of 2016, student loan debt (about $1.2 trillion in total) averaged $37,132 per graduating student, a record amount.[33] Student credit card signups, on the other hand, have declined by about 50 percent in recent years.[34] That decline is at least partially attributable to the 2009 federal Credit Card Accountability, Responsibility, and Disclosure Act (CARD Act). CARD forbids lenders from issuing credit cards to those under age 21 without a parent as cosigner or without proof the applicant can make payments. Student debit card use, however, seems to be rising, and colleges are increasingly entering agreements to promote debit account sales on campus.[35]

CARD Act

Some additional CARD Act provisions:

*   Credit card companies are barred from increasing the annual percentage rate on existing account balances except when the cardholder's minimum payment is 60 days overdue.
*   Issuers cannot charge interest on bills paid on time.

- Without specific agreement by the consumer, banks cannot accept charges where doing so puts creditors over their limits.
- Interest rates, with some exceptions, cannot be raised in the first year.

Beyond the CARD Act, other federal credit card rules provide consumer shelter. Those rules, for example, cap fees for late payments, banish penalties for inactive accounts (although those accounts can still simply be closed), and limit consumer liability to $50 in the event of credit card loss or theft.

Success?   The Consumer Financial Protection Bureau reported in 2015 that the CARD Act has reduced over-limit and late credit card fees by a total of more than $16 billion, reduced the total cost of credit by two percent, and increased credit availability by about 10 percent.[36] The CFPB has engaged in a regulatory "crackdown" on credit card abuse. Citibank, for example, was ordered in 2015 to pay an estimated $700 million in consumer relief and nearly $100 million more in penalties for deceptive credit card marketing affecting about seven million accounts. Among other things, Citibank reportedly told its telemarketers to offer "free" 30-day trials, even though consumers actually were charged for those periods.[37]

Question

How would you argue that government intervention in the credit card market is not in the best interest of consumers generally and college students in particular?

PRACTICING ETHICS   Gray Charges

Suppose you use your credit card to sign up online for a free credit report or perhaps a two-week weight loss trial. Later you notice credit card charges for a credit monitoring service or for an extension of that weight loss plan. These "gray charges" pop up when a subscription or membership is automatically renewed or converted from free to pay (in accord with the "fine print" that you failed to read). American consumers' shift to online purchasing and payment through credit and debit cards allows sellers to readily keep billing information on file, thus offering an opening to lure millions of consumers into commercial relationships that usually can be discovered only by reading fine print.

An Aite Group survey found over $14 billion in gray charges for American consumers in 2012. Ron Shevlin, senior analyst at Aite, said: "These gray charges are not illegal; they're just kind of unethical. . . ."[38]

Question

Shevlin is correct that these charges ordinarily are not illegal. Are they, however, deceptive and unethical? Explain.

Sources: Hadley Malcolm, "Americans Rack Up $14.3B in 'Gray' Charges," *The Des Moines Register,* July 29, 2013, p. 6A; and Chris Taylor, "YOUR MONEY—How to Stop Sneaky 'Grey Charges' on Credit Card Bills," *Reuters,* August 24, 2015 [**www.reuters.com**].

Credit Cards Good for the World?

By 2025 or so, Chinese residents are expected to expand their credit card holdings from at least 455 million in 2015 to 1.1 billion and thereby far outpace the United States (540 to 560 million cards currently) as the world's biggest credit card market by number of cards. (Chinese consumers hold many more debit than credit cards.)

Credit cards are becoming a commonplace shopping tool both in newly industrial-ized nations like China and in developing nations. As a result, those consumers are joining Americans and other Westerners in struggling to repay their credit card debt. Credit card payments overdue by six months or more in China had risen by 42 percent at the end of 2014, and Chinese use of consumer credit was increasing by about 27 per-cent annually.

Question

Is the consumer credit path embraced by Americans a wise course for consumers in newly industrialized and/or developing nations around the world? List some of the competing arguments.

Sources: Bloomberg News, "Credit-Card Companies Battle in China," *Bloomberg Businessweek,* May 2, 2013 [**www.businessweek.com**]; and Hudson Lockett, "China's Consumers Embrace Credit Cards as Regulators Rebuff New Industry Entrants," *China Economic Review,* July 23, 2015 [**www.chinaeconomicreview.com**].

Consumer Credit Reports

LO 15-5
Identify protections offered under the Fair Credit Reporting Act (FCRA).

Do you want to borrow money for a new car or a house? Perhaps you want a better job? Success in each of those efforts may depend to a considerable extent on your credit score. The three national credit information giants, Equifax, Experian, and TransUnion, as well as local credit bureaus, provide retailers, employers, insurance companies, and others with consumers' detailed credit histories. From those credit histories, a credit score is computed and sold to lenders. The federal Fair Credit Reporting Act (FCRA) affords consumers the following credit reporting protections, among others:

- Anyone using information from a credit reporting agency (CRA), such as Equifax, to take "adverse action" against you (denying you credit, a job, insurance) must notify you and tell you where it secured the information.
- At your request, a CRA must give you the information in your file and a list of all those who have recently sought information about you.
- If you claim that your credit file contains inaccurate information, the CRA must inves-tigate your complaint and give you a written report. If you remain unsatisfied, you can include a brief statement in your credit file. Notice of the dispute and a summary of your statement normally must accompany future reports.
- All inaccurate information must be corrected or removed from the file, usually within 30 days.
- In most cases, negative information more than seven years old must not be reported.
- You must provide written consent before a CRA can provide information to your em-ployer or prospective employer.
- You can sue for damages if your rights under the act have been violated.
- Lenders are required to provide a consumer's credit score as well as any factors that af-fected that score if the lender took any adverse action based on that score.[39]

Spokeo and LinkedIn   Our expanding online lives are raising new questions about what constitutes a consumer report while also increasing credit reporting hazards for consumers. Thomas Robins sued Spokeo, a people-search website, claiming it violated the FCRA by displaying inaccurate information about him that hindered his employment opportunities. In reviewing the *Spokeo* case, the U.S. Supreme Court, in its words, "assumed" Spokeo qualified as a consumer reporting agency.[40] The *Spokeo* case remains under litigation at this writing. In a related matter, Spokeo had paid $800,000 in 2012 to settle Federal Trade Commission charges that in marketing individuals' profiles to job recruiters, it had failed to comply with FCRA requirements.[41] On the other hand, a federal district court judge in California ruled in 2015 that results from LinkedIn's Reference Search Function do not constitute a consumer report and LinkedIn does not act as a consumer reporting agency because the material was voluntarily provided for the purpose of information sharing.[42] [For practical questions and answers about the Fair Credit Reporting Act, see **www.creditcards.com/credit-card-news/credit-reports-explained-1265.php**].

Fair Credit Billing Act

LO 15-6
Describe the protections offered by the Fair Credit Billing Act (FCBA).

The Fair Credit Billing Act (FCBA) provides a mechanism to deal with the billing errors that accompany credit card and certain other "open-end" credit transactions. A cardholder who receives an erroneous bill must complain in writing to the creditor within 60 days of the time the bill was mailed. The creditor must acknowledge receipt of the complaint within 30 days. Then, within two billing cycles but not more than 90 days, the creditor must issue a response either by correcting the account or by forwarding a written statement to the consumer explaining why the bill is accurate. The creditor cannot threaten the consumer's credit rating or report the consumer as delinquent while the bill is in dispute, although the creditor can report that the bill is being challenged. Where a "reasonable investigation" determines the bill was correct, but the consumer continues to contest it, the consumer may refuse to pay, and the creditor will then be free to commence collection procedures after giving the consumer 10 days to pay the disputed amount. If the bill is reported to a credit bureau as delinquent, that report also must indicate the consumer's belief that the money is not owed, and the consumer must be told who received the report. Wronged consumers may complain to the CFPB and sue for damages.

Electronic Fund Transfers

LO 15-7
Recognize the purpose of the Electronic Fund Transfer Act (EFTA).

The Electronic Fund Transfer Act (EFTA) provides remedies for lost or stolen debit and ATM cards, billing errors, and other such problems involving ATMs, point-of-sale machines, electronic deposits, and the like. ATM and debit card losses are less well protected than those involving credit cards. Under the EFTA, liability for misuse of missing debit and ATM cards is capped at $50 if the consumer provides notice within two business days after learning of the loss. The loss could reach $500 if notice is provided within 60 days and could be unlimited thereafter. [For consumer information on electronic banking, see **www.ftc.gov/bcp/edu/pubs/consumer/credit/cre14.shtm**].

Equal Credit Opportunity

LO 15-8

Explain the purpose of the Equal Credit Opportunity Act (ECOA).

Honda agreed in 2015 to pay $24 million to affected minority car buyers to resolve allegations of discrimination in interest rates on car loans in violation of the federal Equal Credit Opportunity Act (ECOA). The Consumer Financial Protection Bureau and the federal Justice Department alleged that some Honda local dealers charged higher interest rates to thousands of African American, Hispanic, and Asian and Pacific Islander car buyers than to white buyers. In addition to the payment, Honda agreed to reduce the amount of discretion local dealers have in marking up interest rates on auto loans.

The Equal Credit Opportunity Act is designed to combat bias in lending. Credit must be extended to all creditworthy applicants regardless of sex, marital status, age, race, color, religion, national origin, good-faith exercise of rights under the Consumer Credit Protection Act, and receipt of public assistance (like food stamps). Discrimination in credit against women was a primary stimulus for the ECOA. Creditors often would not lend money to married women in their own names, or to single, divorced, and widowed women.

Does the ECOA provision forbidding sex-based credit discrimination also protect against credit discrimination based on gender identity and sexual orientation? [For the Consumer Financial Protection Bureau's 2016 guidance on that question, see **www.cfpb-monitor.com/wp-content/uploads/sites/5/2016/09/SAGE/Letter.pdf**].

The case that follows applies the ECOA to a "cross-dressing" male in the year 2000.

LEGAL BRIEFCASE

Lucas Rosa v. Park West Bank & Trust Co.   214 F.3d 213 (1st Cir. 2000)

Judge Lynch

I

[O]n July 21, 1998, [Lucas] Rosa came to the [Park West] Bank to apply for a loan. A biological male, he was dressed in traditionally feminine attire. He requested a loan application from Norma Brunelle, a bank employee. Brunelle asked Rosa for identification. Rosa produced three forms of photo identification: (1) a Massachusetts Department of Public Welfare Card; (2) a Massachusetts Identification Card; and (3) a Money Stop Check Cashing ID Card. Brunelle looked at the identification cards and told Rosa that she would not provide him with a loan application until he "went home and changed." She said that he had to be dressed like one of the identification cards in which he appeared in more traditionally male attire before she would provide him with a loan application and process his loan request.

II

Rosa sued the Bank. Rosa charged that "by requiring [him] to conform to sex stereotypes before proceeding with the credit transaction, [the Bank] unlawfully discriminated against [him] with respect to an aspect of a credit transaction on the basis of sex." He claims to have suffered emotional distress.

Without filing an answer to the complaint, the Bank moved to dismiss. . . . The district court granted the Bank's motion. The court stated,

> The issue in this case is not [Rosa's] sex, but rather how he chose to dress when applying for a loan. Because the Act does not prohibit discrimination based on the manner in which someone dresses, Park West's requirement that Rosa change his clothes does not give rise to claims of illegal discrimination. Further, even if Park West's statement or action were based upon Rosa's sexual orientation or perceived sexual orientation, the Act does not prohibit such discrimination.

PriceWaterhouse v. Hopkins, which Rosa relied on, was not to the contrary, according to the district court, because that case "neither holds, nor even suggests, that discrimination based merely on a person's attire is impermissible."

On appeal, Rosa says that the district court "fundamentally misconceived the law as applicable to the Plaintiff's claim by concluding that there may be no relationship, as a matter of law, between telling a bank customer what to wear and sex discrimination."

The Bank says that Rosa loses for two reasons. First, citing cases pertaining to gays and transsexuals, it says that the ECOA does not apply to cross-dressers. Second, the Bank says that its employee genuinely could not identify Rosa, which is why she asked him to go home and change.

III

The ECOA prohibits discrimination, "with respect to any aspect of a credit transaction[,] on the basis of race, color, religion, national origin, sex or marital status, or age." Thus to prevail, the alleged discrimination against Rosa must have been "on the basis of . . . sex."

While the district court was correct in saying that the prohibited bases of discrimination under the ECOA do not include style of dress or sexual orientation, that is not the discrimination alleged. It is alleged that the Bank's actions were taken, in whole or in part, "on the basis of . . . [the appellant's] sex." . . . Whatever facts emerge, and they may turn out to have nothing to do with sex-based discrimination, we cannot say at this point that the plaintiff has no viable theory of sex discrimination consistent with the facts alleged.

The evidence is not yet developed, and thus it is not yet clear why Brunelle told Rosa to go home and change. It may be that this case involves an instance of disparate treatment based on sex in the denial of credit. . . . It is reasonable to infer that Brunelle told Rosa to go home and change because she thought that Rosa's attire did not accord with his male gender: in other words, that Rosa did not receive the loan application because he was a man, whereas a similarly situated woman would have received the loan application. That is, the Bank may treat, for credit purposes, a woman who dresses like a man differently than a man who dresses like a woman. If so, the Bank concedes, Rosa may have a claim. Indeed, under *PriceWaterhouse,* "stereotyped remarks [including statements about dressing more 'femininely'] can certainly be evidence that gender played a part." It is also reasonable to infer, though, that Brunelle refused to give Rosa the loan application because she thought he was gay, confusing sexual orientation with cross-dressing. If so, Rosa concedes, our precedents dictate that he would have no recourse under the federal Act. It is reasonable to infer, as well, that Brunelle simply could not ascertain whether the person shown in the identification card photographs was the same person that appeared before her that day. If this were the case, Rosa again would be out of luck. It is reasonable to infer, finally, that Brunelle may have had mixed motives, some of which fall into the prohibited category.

It is too early to say what the facts will show; it is apparent, however, that, under some set of facts within the bounds of the allegations and nonconclusory facts in the complaint, Rosa may be able to prove a claim under the ECOA.

We reverse and remand.

Questions

1. *a.* Did the court of appeals find that Park West Bank had violated the ECOA? Explain.
   b. At trial, if the facts revealed that the bank employee thought Rosa was gay and demanded that he change clothes for that reason, who would have won this case in 2000? Would that result change today? Explain.
   c. According to the court of appeals, how did the lower court misunderstand this case?
2. *a.* Does federal law protect bank customers based on their style of dress? Explain.
   b. Should it offer that protection? Explain.

Debtor Protection

> *A nightmare often magnified by the debt collection process.*

Millions of Americans are deeply in debt, a nightmare often magnified by the debt collection process. Clifford Cain Jr., a retired Baltimore electrician who lives on Social Security and pension benefits, stopped using and making payments on a Citibank credit card. Midland Funding, at the time an unlicensed debt collection company, then sued Cain and garnished his bank account for $4,500 allegedly owed on the card. Cain says he learned of the lawsuit only after the money was gone. Cain brought a class action against Midland, but the lawsuit was dismissed on appeal in 2016 because Cain had agreed to an arbitration clause in the credit card agreement. Cain's frustration was explained by *The New York Times:*

> [D]ebt buyers are using the courts to sue consumers and collect debt, then preventing those same consumers from using the courts to challenge the companies' tactics. Consumer lawyers said this strategy was the legal equivalent of debt collectors having their cake and eating it, too.[43]

About 35 percent of adult Americans (77 million people) have a debt in collections (those that are more than 180 days past due and have been placed in the debt collection process).[44] All debtors, like Cain, are properly expected to repay what they owe, but critics claim debtors often are wrongly pursued. U.S. Senator Sherrod Brown (D-OH) explained:

> It's hard enough when families aren't able to make enough to pay their bills, but it's tragic that families who are struggling to make ends meet are hounded to make payments on debts that they have already paid off or that they never owed in the first place.[45]

In this troubled debt collection environment, both state and federal governments have developed extensive legal protections for debtors.

Debt Collection Law

LO 15-9

Identify debt collection practices forbidden by the Fair Debt Collection Practices Act (FDCPA).

The federal Fair Debt Collection Practices Act (FDCPA) is designed to shield debtors from unfair debt collection tactics by debt collection agencies and attorneys who routinely operate as debt collectors. Often employing very aggressive tactics, about 6,000 debt collection agencies nationwide pursue those who are delinquent in their debts. (FDCPA does not extend to creditors who are themselves trying to recover money owed to them.)

The FDCPA protects consumers by forbidding, among others, the following practices:

- Use of obscene language.
- Contact with third parties other than for the purpose of locating the debtor. (This provision is an attempt to prevent harm to the debtor's reputation.)
- Use of or threats to use physical force.
- Contact with the debtor during "inconvenient" hours. For debtors who are employed during "normal" working hours, the period from 9 pm to 8 am would probably be considered inconvenient.
- Repeated phone calls with the intent to harass.
- Contact with the debtor in an unfair, abusive, or deceptive manner.

The Federal Trade Commission and the Consumer Financial Protection Bureau jointly enforce the FDCPA. The CFPB says that it receives more complaints about debt collection than any other issue. At this writing, the CFPB is considering new debt collection rules that may, among other things, limit the number of times debt collectors may lawfully contact borrowers, make it easier for borrowers to dispute debts, and require companies to confirm information about debts if requested by borrowers. In addition to federal and state regulatory protection, wronged consumers may sue for damages. [For more details about the FDCPA, see **www.ftc.gov/os/statutes/fdcpajump.shtm**].

The case that follows suggests some of the confusion that can arise in the debt collection process.

Avila v. Riexinger & Associates, LLC   817 F.3d 72 (2d Cir. 2016)

Circuit Judge Pooler

BACKGROUND

Plaintiffs Annmarie Avila and Sara Elrod both received collection notices from defendant Riexinger & Associates, LLC. The notices stated that plaintiffs' accounts had been "placed with [the firm] for collection and such action as necessary." The notices stated each plaintiff's "current balance" but did not disclose that this balance was continuing to accrue interest or that, if plaintiffs failed to pay the debt within a certain amount of time, they would be charged a late fee. . . .

Plaintiffs filed this lawsuit, alleging that the collection notices violated the FDCPA. They claimed, among other things, that the collection notices were misleading because they stated the "current balance," but did not disclose that the balance might increase due to interest and fees. They alleged that they believed from reading the notice that the "current balance" was "static" and that their "payment of that amount would satisfy [the debt] irrespective of when [the] payment was remitted." Avila alleges that in fact interest was accruing daily at a rate equivalent to 500% per year and that defendants have tried to collect this interest from her.

Defendants moved to dismiss the complaint, and the district court granted the motion. . . .

DISCUSSION

. . . Section 1692e of the FDCPA provides that "[a] debt collector may not use any false, deceptive, or misleading representation or means in connection with the collection of any debt." The sixteen subsections of Section 1692e set forth a non-exhaustive list of practices that fall within this ban, including "the false representation of the character, amount, or legal status of any debt." "Because the list . . . is non-exhaustive, a debt collection practice can be a 'false, deceptive, or misleading' practice in violation of Section 1692e even if it does not fall within any of the subsections of Section 1692e."

The question presented is whether the sending of a collection notice that states a consumer's "current balance," but does not disclose that the balance may increase due to interest and fees, is a "false, misleading, or deceptive" practice . . . . In considering this question, we are guided by two principles of statutory construction.

The first principle is that, because the FDCPA is "primarily a consumer protection statute," we must construe its terms "in liberal fashion [to achieve] the underlying Congressional purpose." That purpose is to "eliminate abusive debt collection practices by debt collectors, to insure that those debt collectors who refrain from using abusive debt collection practices are not competitively disadvantaged, and to promote consistent State action to protect consumers against debt collection abuses." . . .

The second principle is that, in considering whether a collection notice violated Section 1692e, we apply the "least sophisticated consumer" standard. In other words, we ask how the least sophisticated consumer—"one not having the astuteness of a 'Philadelphia lawyer' or even the sophistication of the average, everyday, common consumer"—would understand the collection notice. Under this standard, a collection notice can be misleading if it is "open to more than one reasonable interpretation, at least one of which is inaccurate."

Applying these principles, we hold that plaintiffs have stated a claim that the collection notices at issue here are misleading within the meaning of Section 1692e. A reasonable consumer could read the notice and be misled into believing that she could pay her debt in full by paying the amount listed on the notice. In fact, however, if interest is accruing daily, or if there are undisclosed late fees, a consumer who pays the "current balance" stated on the notice will not know whether the debt has been paid in full. The debt collector could still seek the interest and fees that accumulated after the notice was sent but before the balance was paid, or sell the consumer's debt to a third party, which itself could seek the interest and fees from the consumer.

Because the statement of an amount due, without notice that the amount is already increasing due to accruing interest or other charges, can mislead the least sophisticated consumer into believing that payment of the amount stated will clear her account, we hold that the FDCPA requires debt collectors, when they notify consumers of their account balance, to disclose that the balance may increase due to interest and fees. We think that requiring such disclosure best achieves the Congressional purpose of full and fair disclosure to consumers that is embodied in Section 1692e. It also protects consumers such as plaintiffs who may hold the reasonable but mistaken belief that timely payment will satisfy their debts.

* * * * *

The district court . . . expressed a concern that requiring debt collectors to disclose this information might lead to more abusive practices, as debt collectors could use the threat of interest and fees to coerce consumers into paying their debts. This is a legitimate concern. To alleviate it, we adopt the "safe harbor" approach adopted by the Seventh Circuit in *Miller v. McCalla, Raymer, Padrick, Cobb, Nichols, & Clark, L.L.C.,* 214 F.3d 872 (7th Cir. 2000).

* * * * *

. . . The [*Miller*] court held that the following statement would satisfy a debt collector's duty to state the amount of debt in cases where the amount varies from day to day:

As of the date of this letter, you owe $_____ [the exact amount due]. Because of interest, late charges, and other charges that may vary from day to day, the amount due on the day you pay may be greater. Hence, if you pay the amount shown above, an adjustment may be necessary after we receive your check, in which event we will inform you before depositing the check for collection. For further information, write the undersigned or call 1-800-[phone number].

The court held that a debt collector who used this form would not violate the "amount of the debt" provision, "provided, of course, that the information [the debt collector] furnishes is accurate and [the debt collector] does not obscure it by adding confusing other information (or misinformation)." . . .

We hold that a debt collector will not be subject to liability under Section 1692e for failing to disclose that the consumer's balance may increase due to interest and fees if the collection notice either accurately informs the consumer that the amount of the debt stated in the letter will increase over time, or clearly states that the holder of the debt will accept payment of the amount set forth in full satisfaction of the debt if payment is made by a specified date. Like the *Miller* court, we do not hold that a debt collector must use any particular disclaimer. Using the language set forth in *Miller* will qualify for safe harbor treatment. . . .

The collection notices at issue here stated only the "current balance" but did not disclose that the balance might increase due to interest and fees. Thus, Plaintiffs have stated a claim that these notices were "misleading" within the meaning of Section 1692e. The district court's dismissal of this claim is vacated, and we remand for further proceedings consistent with this opinion.

Questions

1. *a.* Why did the *Avila* court rule for the plaintiffs?

   b. Do you agree with the court's decision to employ the "least sophisticated consumer" standard? Explain.

   c. How may debt collectors benefit from this decision?

2. Capital One Bank, in 2012, acquired about $28 billion in credit card accounts from HSBC (another bank). Capital One filed suit against Keith Davidson, whose overdue account was one of those acquired. Davidson filed suit claiming Capital One had violated the FDCPA in various ways. Capital One defended by arguing that it was not subject to the FDCPA.

   a. Why did Capital One claim the FDCPA did not reach its effort to collect the debt owed by Davidson?

   b. Decide the case. Explain. See *Davidson v. Capital One Bank,* 797 F.3d 1309 (11th Cir. 2015).

3. Why shouldn't debt collectors be able to use aggressive tactics to encourage payment of legitimate bills?

Part Four—Bankruptcy

> The average household now pays more than $6,600 per year in interest.

The average American household with debt owes about $131,000 (including mortgages). Among households with credit card debt, the average owed is about $16,000. Student loan debt, among households with those loans, now averages nearly $50,000 per household. The average household now pays more than $6,600 per year in interest.[46] Of course, current interest rates are low and borrowing to buy a home is often a wise strategy, but many consumers are struggling to meet their debt burdens.

Fresh Start? Should we lend a hand to those borrowers who are down on their luck? Bankruptcy law was specifically designed to provide a fresh start for those whose financial problems were insurmountable. We believe that both the debtor and society benefit from the new beginning.

Bankruptcy Rules

Bankruptcy in the United States is governed exclusively by federal law; the states do not have the constitutional authority to enact bankruptcy legislation, but they do set their own rules within the limits provided by Congress. Our attention will be limited to the principal federal statute, the Bankruptcy Reform Act of 1978, as amended.

Bankruptcy is an adjudication relieving a debtor of all or part of his/her/its liabilities. Any person, partnership, or corporation may seek debtor relief. Three forms of bankruptcy action are important to us:

1. *Liquidation* (Chapter 7 of the Bankruptcy Act) is used by both individuals and businesses. Most debts are forgiven, all assets except exemptions are fairly distributed to creditors, and debtors receive a "fresh start."

2. *Reorganization* (Chapter 11), used by both individuals and businesses, keeps creditors from the debtor's assets while the debtor, under the supervision of the court, works out a financial reorganization plan and continues to pay creditors.

3. *Adjustment of debts* of an individual with regular income (Chapter 13) protects individuals with limited debts from creditors while paying their debts in installments. [For a bankruptcy database, see **www.lawtrove.com/bankruptcy**].

Liquidation

LO 15-10

Explain the purpose and effect of filing a Chapter 7 liquidation or "straight" bankruptcy.

A Chapter 7 liquidation petition can be *voluntarily* filed in federal court by the debtor, or creditors can seek an *involuntary* bankruptcy judgment. A Chapter 7 liquidation is commonly called a "straight" bankruptcy.

In a voluntary action, the debtor files a petition with the appropriate federal court. The court then has jurisdiction to proceed with the liquidation, and the petition becomes the *order for relief*. The debtor need not be insolvent to seek bankruptcy.

Creditors often can compel an involuntary bankruptcy. The debtor may challenge that bankruptcy action. The court will enter an order for relief if it finds the debtor has not been paying his or her debts when due or if most of the debtor's property is under the control of a custodian for the purpose of enforcing a lien against that property.

After the order for relief is granted, voluntary and involuntary actions proceed in a similar manner. Creditors are restrained from reaching the debtor's assets. An interim bankruptcy trustee is appointed by the court. The creditors then hold a meeting, and a permanent trustee is elected. The trustee collects the debtor's property and converts it to money, protects the interests of the debtor and creditors, may manage the debtor's business, and ultimately distributes the estate proceeds to the creditors. Debtors are allowed to keep exempt property, which varies from state to state but typically includes a car, a homestead, some household or personal items, life insurance, and other "necessities." Normally a dollar maximum is attached to each.

The debtor's nonexempt property is then divided among the creditors according to the priorities prescribed by statute. Secured creditors are paid first. If funds remain, "priority" claims, such as employees' wages and alimony/child support, are paid. Then, funds permitting, general creditors are paid. Each class must be paid in full before a class of lower priority will be compensated. Any remaining funds will return to the debtor.

When distribution is complete, the bankruptcy judge may issue an order discharging (relieving) the debtor of any remaining debts except for certain statutorily specified claims. Those include, for example, taxes and educational loans. Thus the debtor is granted a "fresh start."

Reorganization

Under Chapter 11, the debtor may voluntarily seek reorganization, or the creditors may petition for an involuntary action. When a reorganization petition is filed with the court and relief is ordered, one or more committees of creditors is appointed to participate in bankruptcy procedures. Typically in the case of a business, the debtor continues operations, although the court may appoint a trustee to replace the debtor if required because of dishonesty, fraud, or extreme mismanagement. The company, its bankers, and its suppliers will meet to work out a method for continuing operations. A plan must be developed that will satisfy the creditors that their interests are being served by the reorganization. Perhaps new capital is secured, or perhaps creditors receive some shares in the company. The plan must be approved by the creditors and confirmed by the court. The company is then required to carry out the plan.

Celebrity Chapter 11   Sex tape scandals led both rapper 50 Cent (Curtis Jackson III) and Gawker Media to seek Chapter 11 bankruptcy protection. 50 Cent, who is also called "Fiddy," was ordered by a jury to pay $5 million to Lastonia Leviston after the rapper posted online a video, without permission, of Leviston having sex with a boyfriend. "Fiddy" then entered Chapter 11 bankruptcy, and in 2016 reached an agreement with his creditors to pay off $23.4 million of his more than $28 million in debts (some from a failed venture in headphones) out of future earnings. Similarly, Gawker Media (owner of Deadspin, Gizmodo, and Jezebel) filed for Chapter 11 bankruptcy protection in 2016 after a jury awarded former wrestler Hulk Hogan (Terry G. Bollea) $140 million in an invasion-of-privacy lawsuit over Gawker's publication in 2012 of a tape showing him having sex with the wife of a friend. A federal bankruptcy judge in 2016 approved the $135 million sale of Gawker Media's assets to Univision. At this writing, Gawker and Bollea reportedly have settled the case, with Bollea to receive $31 million and a share of the proceeds from the bankruptcy sale of the Gawker website.

GM Bankruptcy/Bailout

General Motors, in 2009, was forced to enter Chapter 11 bankruptcy as part of a federal government–directed, prepackaged bailout of the then-failing firm. GM reported $82.29 billion in assets and $172.81 billion in debts. The federal government put $49.5 billion into the bailout and took a 60 percent equity stake in the new General Motors, although the company retained control of its day-to-day affairs.

In December 2013, the U.S. Treasury sold the government's remaining GM holdings. Taxpayer loss on the GM bailout totaled $10 to $11 billion. General Motors, now consistently profitable, faces many pre-bankruptcy ignition-switch lawsuits (see Chapter 2) after a federal appeals court in 2016 overturned a bankruptcy judge's ruling that had protected GM from those lawsuits because of its bankruptcy restructuring.

The rescue of GM, Chrysler, and their financing units saved an estimated one million jobs. According to a study by the Center for Automotive Research, had those jobs been lost, the cost to the government in reduced taxes and other negatives would have been nearly $29 billion. Thus, on balance, the Obama administration viewed the bailout as a significant financial and social welfare success. Critics argue, however, that the deal was a dangerous abandonment of market principles. Some of those arguments include

- The bailout encouraged future risky behavior by conveying the message that the government will always be there as a backup.

- Private investors would have moved in to cut costs and restore a new, trimmer GM.
- The $49.5 billion of taxpayer money could have been better spent elsewhere or not spent at all.

Question

Was the federal government wise to bail out General Motors, or should GM have been left to face the force of the market?

Sources: John Lott, "GM's Bailout Is a Financial Disaster," *FoxNews.com,* November 18, 2010 [**www.foxnews. com**]; Mark Guarino, "With Big GM Stock Offering, Vindication for the Government Bailout?" *Christian Science Monitor,* November 19, 2010 [**www.csmonitor.com/2010**]; Drew Winter, "Dear Taxpayer: Your Auto Bailout Loan Is Repaid, with Interest," *Wards Auto,* June 10, 2013 [**http://wardsauto.com**]; and *In re Motors Liquidation Co.,* 829 F.3d 135 (2d Cir. 2016).

Adjustment of Debts

Under Chapter 13, individuals (not partnerships or corporations) can seek the protection of the court to arrange a debt adjustment plan. Chapter 13 permits only voluntary bankruptcies and is restricted to those with steady incomes and somewhat limited debts. The process can begin only with a voluntary petition from the debtor. Creditors are restrained from reaching the debtor's assets. The debtor develops a repayment plan. If creditors' interests are sufficiently satisfied by the plan, the court may confirm it and appoint a trustee to oversee the plan. The debtor may then have three to five years to make the necessary payments. [For an extensive bankruptcy law database, see **www.law.cornell.edu/wex/Bankruptcy**].

Bankruptcy Critique

The stigma that had historically attached to filing for bankruptcy dissipated somewhat in the "greed is good" 1980s, and bankruptcy became a more acceptable way of dealing with debts.[47] In an effort to benefit all by reducing unjustified and sometimes fraudulent bankruptcy filings, Congress enacted the federal Bankruptcy Abuse Prevention and Consumer Protection Act of 2005. The reform law has forced many debtors to seek bankruptcy through the challenging Chapter 13 process rather than the more forgiving Chapter 7. Debtors found to have some money (according to a means test) for debt payment are required to take the Chapter 13 route with its repayment plan rather than the much more attractive "fresh start" of Chapter 7.

Supporters of the 2005 reform argue that it has reduced the cost of credit for all Americans while curbing bankruptcy abuse and unfairness, but opponents see the changes as a punitive assault on those already down on their luck. For individuals, the reform made the process much more complicated, and the average cost of filing in Chapter 7 rose from $600 to $2,500 soon after passage of the new law.[48]

Following the reform, bankruptcies have fallen substantially, but recent evidence finds the decline is largely attributable to those increased costs and other hurdles in filing. Unable to qualify for bankruptcy protection, many lower-income Americans, according to the study, are driven to insolvency and foreclosure. Those in bankruptcy are shielded from creditors and garnishment, and they can have many of their debts discharged, leading to a "fresh start." Those who are insolvent but not eligible for bankruptcy, however, are unable to pay their bills, their credit scores plummet, their debts remain, and they are not able to secure a new start.[49]

Even those who secure bankruptcy protection often barely stay afloat, according to a recent study. Just one year following a declaration of bankruptcy, one in four debtors continues to struggle to pay routine bills and one in three reports a financial condition much the same or worse than was the case prior to the bankruptcy filing.[50] Without steady, sufficient income, the study finds that "bankruptcy is an incomplete tool to rehabilitate those in financial distress."[51]

PRACTICING ETHICS   Bankruptcy—Who Is to Blame?

Commenting on the 2005 bankruptcy reform law, Todd Zywicki, a George Mason University law professor, said, "This is a matter of morality and personal responsibility." Consumer advocates, on the other hand, say the bankruptcy problem lies with the "enablers"—the credit card companies and mortgage lenders that encourage deeper and deeper indebtedness.

Question

Who bears the moral blame for America's bankruptcy struggles? Explain.

Source: Michael Schroeder and Suein Hwang, "Sweeping New Bankruptcy Law to Make Life Harder for Debtors," *The Wall Street Journal*, April 6, 2005, p. A1.

Internet Exercise

Go to the Center for Auto Safety website [**www.autosafety.org/**], click the lemon laws button, and find your state's lemon law. Read the brief summary of the law of your state. Read the summary for the states of Texas, Virginia, and West Virginia.

a. Explain the differences among the state laws you reviewed.

b. Which of those three or four states, in your view, provides the "fairest" protection considering the viewpoints of both consumers and dealers?

Chapter Questions

1. A group of parents sued Gerber claiming its "Fruit Juice Snacks" product packaging was misleading. The words "Fruit Juice" appeared on the package beside images of fruits such as peaches and cherries. In fact, the only fruit juice in the "Snacks" was white grape from concentrate. A side panel statement said the product was made "with real fruit juice and other all natural ingredients," but the primary ingredients were corn syrup and sugar. The side panel also displayed the statement, "one of a variety of nutritious Gerber Graduates foods and juices that have been specifically designed to help toddlers grow up strong and healthy." The actual ingredients were correctly listed in "small print" on the side of the box. Is a "reasonable consumer" "likely to be deceived" by the Gerber packaging? Explain. See *Williams v. Gerber Products,* 523 F.3d 934 (9th Cir. 2008).

2. San Francisco Bay area consumers Wanda Greenwood, Ladelle Hatfield, and Deborah McCleese each signed up for an Aspire Visa credit card marketed by CompuCredit Corp. of Atlanta, Georgia. The card was advertised as a means of rebuilding

cardholders' credit histories as well as providing $300 in immediate credit, with no down payment. The consumers claimed that fees hidden in the fine print of this "fee harvester" agreement claimed much of the $300, with the result that they were misled about the card agreement's capacity to help restore their credit. The agreement also included language requiring both the consumer and the company to resolve disputes using binding arbitration. The federal Credit Repair Organizations Act (CROA) requires credit repair organizations to provide a disclosure statement to consumers saying: "You have a right to sue a credit repair organization that violates the [Act]." The three consumers brought a class-action lawsuit against CompuCredit alleging a violation of CROA, which, among other things, forbids deceptive practices in credit repair.

a. CompuCredit argued that the lawsuit was barred because of the arbitration provision. As you look at the facts, do you think the consumers can sue CompuCredit, or must they turn to binding arbitration? Explain.

b. Does arbitration provide an effective, efficient substitute for litigation in this CompuCredit case? Explain.

c. How might a ruling favoring arbitration encourage fraud by credit card companies? See *CompuCredit Corp. v. Wanda Greenwood, et al.,* 132 S. Ct. 665 (2012).

3. DeSantis sued a debt collection agency, Computer Credit. DeSantis apparently owed $319.50 to Dr. Jeffrey A. Stahl, who assigned the debt to CC for collection. On April 27, 2000, CC sent the following collection letter to DeSantis:

> This notice will serve to inform you that your overdue balance with Dr. Jeffrey A. Stahl has been referred to Computer Credit, Inc., a debt collector. *[The] doctor insists on payment or a valid reason for your failure to make payment.* The law prohibits us from collecting any amount greater than the obligation stated above. Unless you notify us to the contrary, we will assume the amount due is correct. This communication is sent to you in an attempt to collect this debt. Any information obtained will be used for that purpose. *In the absence of a valid reason for your failure to make payment, pay the above debt or contact the doctor to settle this matter.* Payment can be sent directly to the doctor. [Italics added.]

The Fair Debt Collection Practices Act specifies that the consumer may dispute the alleged debt, in which case the debt collector must desist from collection until the debt collector obtains verification regarding the amount of the debt, if any. Given that statutory requirement, was the FDCPA violated by the italicized sentences in the collection letter? Explain. See *DeSantis v. Computer Credit, Inc.,* 269 F.3d 159 (2d Cir. 2001).

4. A 2013 study finds over 4,400 children per year receive hospital care for injuries suffered at amusement parks and water parks, and 29 deaths from amusement rides were reported from 2010 to 2016. The Consumer Product Safety Commission is responsible for temporary parks such as traveling carnivals, while states are responsible for permanent amusement parks. Six states have no laws requiring inspections. Some states provide extensive inspection by state employees, while others allow amusement parks to hire private, licensed inspectors to check for safety problems.[52] Would you favor a federal law requiring uniform, comprehensive inspection of all amusement parks and water parks? Explain.

5. Phusion Projects was accused by the Federal Trade Commission of mislabeling its flavored malt drink Four Loko. The FTC investigated the company's implied claims that consumers could safely drink one 23.5-ounce can at a sitting and that each can contained the alcoholic equivalent of one to two 12-ounce beers and concluded that those claims were misleading. The FTC found that a single Four Loko can contained as much alcohol as four to five beers and that drinking one can on a single occasion would amount to binge drinking. Several states banned the drink and Phusion removed the caffeine and other stimulants. In 2013, the FTC ordered Phusion to put on the back of Four Loko cans containing more than two servings (a "serving" equals 0.6 ounce of alcohol) an "Alcohol Facts" panel that discloses alcohol content, serving size, and the number of servings per can. Phusion also reached an agreement in 2014 with 20 state attorneys general to restrict such marketing practices as using college names, logos, mascots, and so on in its promotional materials.

   a. Many public comments to the FTC called for banning Four Loko from the market. Should the FTC do so? Explain.

   b. From the FTC point of view, what consumer benefit was achieved by the order?

   c. How would you have handled the Four Loko situation?

6. About 3.2 million Americans are "underwater" on their home mortgages; that is, they owe more than their homes are worth.[53] Many of those families could simply walk away from their mortgage, rent a similar home, and save thousands of dollars per year. Doubtless many decline to abandon their mortgages because they fear the consequences for their credit records and they want to avoid the cost of changing homes, but surely some continue to make payments simply because they believe defaulting would be immoral. While serving as U.S. Treasury Secretary, Henry Paulson said that anyone who walks away from his or her mortgage is "simply a speculator—and one who is not honoring his obligation."[54]

   a. Make the argument that deliberately walking away from an underwater home mortgage situation is immoral.

   b. Make the argument that walking away is not immoral.

   c. What would you do? Explain. See Richard H. Thaler, "Underwater, but Will They Leave the Pool?" *The New York Times*, January 24, 2010 [**www.nytimes.com**]; and Brent T. White, "Buyers Have No Moral Duty to Lenders," *Arizona Republic,* April 25, 2010 [**www.azcentral.com/arizonarepublic/viewpoints/articles/2010/04/25/20100425white25.htm**].

7. William Cohan, writing in *The New York Times,* objected to the federal government's consumer protection efforts in the Dodd–Frank Wall Street Reform and Consumer Protection Act, including the creation of the Consumer Financial Protection Bureau. Explain why Cohan and other critics would object to the government's efforts to protect consumers from "devious credit-card companies" and "dishonest mortgage lenders." See William D. Cohan, "The Elizabeth Warren Fallacy," *The New York Times,* September 30, 2010 [**http://opinionator.blogs.nytimes.com**].

8. Recent studies suggest that consumer bankruptcies are much more common in some states than others. Aside from income levels, what socioeconomic factors would you expect to be closely correlated with high bankruptcy rates?

9. Playtex manufactured the market-leading spill-proof cup for children, which a child uses by sucking on a spout to cause a valve to open. Gerber introduced its own version and ran ads showing an unnamed competitor's product and claiming that "Gerber's patented valve makes our cup more than 50 percent easier to drink from than the leading cup." Gerber's claims for the superiority of its cup were backed by tests from an independent laboratory. Playtex said the unnamed cup obviously was its brand and that the superiority claims were false and misleading. Playtex sought an injunction to block the Gerber ads. Would you grant that injunction? Explain. See *Playtex Products v. Gerber Products,* 981 F. Supp. 827 (S.D.N.Y. 1997).

10. The Telephone Consumer Protection Act prohibits companies from making automated calls to a person's cell phone without that person's "prior express consent." Hill fell behind on his mortgage payments. He claims he received some 482 prohibited calls from his creditor, Homeward, from 2009 to 2013. Hill had given his cell number to Homeward; he listed the number on a loan modification document; and he told Homeward not to call him at work, but rather to use his cell number. He also provided written consent to call his cell phone. Hill had not, however, provided the cell phone number when he initially entered the mortgage contract. Do those facts amount to "prior express consent"? Explain. See *Hill v. Homeward Residential,* 799 F.3d 544 (6th Cir. 2015).

11. Evan Parent sued MillerCoors for deceptively marketing its Blue Moon Belgian-style beer in violation of California consumer protection and false advertising laws. Parent argued that MillerCoors was marketing Blue Moon as a "craft beer" produced by Blue Moon Brewing, when in fact it is mass produced by MillerCoors. Parent pointed to the absence of references to MillerCoors on the Blue Moon website and to MillerCoors' use of its registered trademark, "Artfully Crafted," on the label and in advertising. Parent also noted that Blue Moon is sold at a premium price like other craft brews, is stocked by retailers in their craft beer sections, and is listed in the craft beer section on the MillerCoors website. Do these allegations, if true, amount to deceptive, misleading marketing? See *Parent v. MillerCoors,* 2016 U.S. Dist. LEXIS 78764 (S.D. Cal. June 16, 2016).

12. Roseman resigned from the John Hancock Insurance Company following allegations of misuse of his expense account. He reimbursed the account. Subsequently he was denied employment by another insurance firm after that firm read a Retail Credit Company credit report on him. The credit report included accurate information regarding Roseman's resignation. Was Retail Credit in violation of the Fair Credit Reporting Act in circulating information regarding the resignation? Explain. See *Roseman v. Retail Credit Co., Inc.,* 428 F. Supp. 643 (Pa. 1977).

13. Once the government decided to intervene in the free market on behalf of consumers, two broad product safety options presented themselves: (a) the government could have limited its effort to generating and distributing information to consumers or (b) the government could have set safety standards for all products. Assuming the government was forced to choose one or the other but not elements of both, which option should it have chosen? Explain.

14. Consumers sometimes abuse sellers. One familiar technique is shoplifting. Shoplifting is a crime, of course, but the criminal process is cumbersome and often does not result

in monetary recoveries for sellers. As a result, state laws often permit store owners to impose civil fines, the collection of which is usually turned over to a lawyer or collection agency with a threat to sue in civil court, file criminal charges, or both if payment is not forthcoming. Fines may range from $50 to $5,000 or more, depending on the value of the item(s) stolen.

a. Defense lawyers say this civil fine system is unfair. Why?

b. On balance, is the civil fine approach to shoplifting a good idea? Explain.

c. Cite some other examples of consumers abusing businesspeople.

15. Goswami failed to pay her $900 credit card bill. A collection agency, ACEI, mailed her a collection letter with a blue bar across the envelope saying "Priority Letter." The letter did not, in fact, constitute priority mail. The purpose of the bar was to encourage Goswami to open the envelope. Was the bar a deceptive practice in violation of the Fair Debt Collection Practices Act? Explain. See *Goswami v. American Collections Enterprise, Inc.,* 377 F.3d 488 (5th Cir. 2004), *cert. denied,* 546 U.S. 811 (2005).

Notes

1. Bureau of Economics, Federal Trade Commission, "Consumer Fraud in the United States, 2011: The Third FTC Survey," April 2013 [**www.ftc.gov/sites/default/files/documents/ reports/consumer-fraud-united-states-2011-third-ftc-survey/130419fraudsurvey_0.pdf**].

2. Jessica Silver-Greenburg, "Consumer Protection Agency Seeks Limits on Payday Lenders," *The New York Times,* February 8, 2015 [**www.nytimes.com**].

3. Kevin McCoy, "New CFPB Proposal Takes Aim at Payday Debt Trap Loans," *The Des Moines Register,* June 2, 2016, p. 5B.

4. Paige Marta Skiba, "Limiting Access to Payday Loans May Do More Harm Than Good," *The Conversation,* June 5, 2016 [**www.theconversation.com**].

5. "We're on Your Side," Consumer Financial Protection Bureau, 2016 [**www.consumerfinance. gov**].

6. *PHH Corporation v. Consumer Financial Protection Bureau,* 839 F.3d 1 (D.C. Cir. 2016).

7. Helaine Olen, "Congratulations! You Lost," *Slate,* May 24, 2016 [**www.slate.com**].

8. James Rainey, "Truth in Advertising Meets the Blogosphere," *latimes.com,* October 7, 2009 [**www.latimes.com**].

9. J. Craig Anderson, "Identity Theft Growing, Costly to Victims," *The Arizona Republic,* April 14, 2013 [**www.azcentral.com/business/consumer/articles/20130401identity-theft-growing- costly.html**].

10. Bureau of Justice Statistics, "17.6 Million U.S. Residents Experienced Identity Theft in 2014," press release, September 27, 2015 [**www.bjs.gov/content/pub/press/vit14pr.cfm**].

11. Ibid.

12. *Federal Trade Commission v. Wyndham Worldwide Corp.,* 799 F.3d 236 (3d Cir. 2015).

13. Lesley Fair, "Wyndham's Settlement with the FTC: What It Means for Businesses—and Consumers," Federal Trade Commission *Blog,* December 9, 2015 [**www.ftc.gov/news-events/ blogs/business-blog/2015/12/wyndhams-settlement-ftc-what-it-means-businesses- consumers**].

14. Alex Byers, "Privacy Issues at Top of Edith Ramirez's Federal Trade Commission Agenda," *Politico,* March 11, 2013 [**http://dyn.politico.com**].

15. Ibid.

16. Hayley Tsukayama, "Consumer Product Safety Commission Issues Recall for Galaxy Note 7 Because of Fire Risk," *The Washington Post,* September 15, 2016 [**www.washingtonpost.com**].

17. Rachel Abrams, "Fire Risk Prompts Safety Agency to Recall Some Hoverboards," *The New York Times,* July 6, 2016 [**www.nytimes.com**].

18. Associated Press, "New Crib Rules Toughest in World," *The Des Moines Register,* June 30, 2011, p. 7B.

19. Armstrong Teasdale LLP, "Lessons Learned from Office Depot's $3.4 Million Civil Penalty to Settle CPSC Staff's Charges," *LEXOLOGY,* June 18, 2015 [**www.lexology.com**].

20. Consumer Product Safety Commission, "NEISS Data Highlights—2014," [**www.cpsc.gov//Global/Neiss_prod/2014%20Neiss%20data%20highlights.pdf**].

21. Eric Lipton, "A Lobbyist Wrote the Bill. Will the Tobacco Industry Win Its E-Cigarette Fight?" *The New York Times,* September 2, 2016 [**www.nytimes.com**].

22. Laurie McGinley and Brady Dennis, "The Federal Government Is About to Begin Regulating the Booming E-Cigarette Market," *The Washington Post,* May 5, 2016 [**www.washingtonpost.com**].

23. Editorial Board, "Even More Addictive Cigarettes," *The New York Times,* January 23, 2014 [**www.nytimes.com**].

24. *Discount Tobacco City & Lottery v. United States,* 674 F.3d 509 (6th Cir.), *reh'g denied,* 2012 U.S. App. LEXIS 11820 (6th Cir. May 31, 2012), *cert. denied sub nom. American Snuff Co. v. United States,* 133 S. Ct. 1996 (2013), affirmed the constitutionality of the ads while *R.J. Reynolds Tobacco Co. v. Food and Drug Administration,* 696 F.3d 1205 (D.C. Cir. 2012), struck down the ads.

25. Joanna Cohen, "Let Smokers See the Warning They Need," *The New York Times,* June 3, 2016 [**www.nytimes.com**].

26. Lisa Rein, "The FDA Is Actually Terrible at Recalling Dangerous Foods," *The Washington Post,* June 9, 2016 [**www.washingtonpost.com**].

27. Alec MacGillis, "Would Washington's FDA Fix Cure the Patients or the Drug Industry?" *ProPublica,* October 20, 2015 [**www.propublica.com**].

28. Gregg Gonsalves, Mark Harrington, and David A. Kessler, "Don't Weaken the F.D.A.'s Drug Approval Process," *The New York Times,* June 11, 2015 [**www.nytimes.com**].

29. Andrew Zajac, "Most Recalled Medical Devices Received Speedy FDA Review," *latimes.com,* February 15, 2011 [**http://latimes.com/health/la-na-medical-devices-20110215,0,4206876.story**].

30. Thomas Philipson and Andrew von Eschenbach, "FDA Reform Can Lift U.S. Economy," *Bloomberg,* February 28, 2013 [**www.bloomberg.com**].

31. Chico Harlan, "Rental America: Why the Poor Pay $4,150 for a $1,500 Sofa," *The Washington Post,* October 16, 2014 [**www.washingtonpost.com**].

32. Blake Ellis, "Rent-to-Own Furniture, Jewelry Can Cost You Double," *CNN Money,* November 7, 2013 [**http://money.cnn.com**].

33. Josh Mitchell, "Student Debt Is About to Set Another Record, but the Picture Isn't All Bad," *The Wall Street Journal,* May 2, 2016 [**http://blogs.wsj.com**].

34. Danielle Douglas-Gabriel, "Colleges Are Cutting Deals with Wall Street to Steer Students into Debit Cards," *The Washington Post,* December 16, 2014 [**www.washingtonpost.com**].

35. Ibid.

36. Consumer Financial Protection Bureau, "CFPB Finds CARD Act Helped Consumers Avoid More Than \$16 Billion in Gotcha Credit Card Fees," press release, December 3, 2015 [**www.consumerfinance.gov**].

37. Kevin McCoy, "Citi to Pay \$700 M for Deceptive Credit Card Marketing," *The Des Moines Register,* July 22, 2015, p. 5B.

38. Hadley Malcom, "Americans Rack Up \$14.3B in 'Gray' Charges," *The Des Moines Register,* July 29, 2013, p. 6A.

39. This summary of FCRA requirements was drawn largely from the FTC document "A Summary of Your Rights under the Fair Credit Reporting Act" [**www.ftc.gov/bcp/conline/edcams/fcra/summary.htm**].

40. *Spokeo v. Robins,* 136 S. Ct. 1540 (2016).

41. Federal Trade Commission, "Spokeo to Pay \$800,000 to Settle FTC Charges Company Allegedly Marketed Information to Employers and Recruiters in Violation of FCRA," press release, June 12, 2012 [**www.ftc.gov**].

42. *Sweet v. LinkedIn,* 2015 U.S. Dist. LEXIS 49767 (N.D. Cal. April 14, 2015).

43. Jessica Silver-Greenberg and Michael Corkery, "Sued Over Old Debt, and Blocked from Suing Back," *The New York Times,* December 12, 2015 [**www.nytimes.com**].

44. Caroline Ratcliffe et al., "Delinquent Debt in America: An Opportunity and Ownership Initiative Brief," Urban Institute Research Report, July 30, 2014 [**www.urban.org**].

45. Senator Sherrod Brown, "Brown Calls on CFPB to Enact Rules to Rein in Debt Collection Agencies and End Consumer Abuses," press release, June 5, 2013 [**www.brown.senate.gov**].

46. Matthew Frankel, "The Average American Household Owes \$90,336—How Do You Compare?" *The Motley Fool,* May 8, 2016 [**www.fool.com**].

47. John Greenya, "Bankruptcy Reform's Poor Legacy," *Pacific Standard,* October 2, 2008 [**www.psmag.com**].

48. Martin Merzer, "Study: Law Creates Many Too Broke to File for Bankruptcy," *CreditCards.com,* February 24, 2015 [**www.creditcards.com**].

49. Ibid.

50. Katherine Porter and Deborah Thorne, "The Failure of Bankruptcy's Fresh Start," *Cornell Law Review* 92, no. 1 (November 2006), pp. 67–128.

51. Ibid., p. 67.

52. See Kathleen Foody, Erik Schelzig, and Claire Galofaro, "Thrill-Ride Accidents Spark New Demands for Regulation," *The Des Moines Register,* August 23, 2016, p. 10A; and Rick Jervis, "Thousands of Kids Hurt Each Year on Thrill Rides," *The Des Moines Register,* August 10, 2016, p. 2B.

53. Diana Olick, "How Are Millions Still Underwater as Home Prices Rise?" CNBC *Reality Check,* April 4, 2016 [**www.cnbc.com**].

54. Richard H. Thaler, "Underwater, but Will They Leave the Pool?" *The New York Times,* January 24, 2010 [**www.nytimes.com**].

CHAPTER SIXTEEN

International Ethics and Law

After completing this chapter, students will be able to fulfill the following learning objectives:

16-1. Discuss the role of the World Trade Organization (WTO) in reducing global trade barriers.

16-2. Compare and contrast an American firm's social responsibility to its host country with its social responsibility to its home country.

16-3. Discuss the interrelationship of religion, culture, and legal rules with comparisons to American and Islamic viewpoints.

16-4. Discuss the recent use of the Alien Tort Statute against corporate defendants.

16-5. Describe the basic forms of global business expansion.

16-6. Compare and contrast treaties, custom, and comity and give illustrations of each.

16-7. Describe examples of the law governing international business in sales of goods, trade in-services, and employment.

16-8. Identify and describe the four main forms of intellectual property covered in the text and the international agreements that govern them.

16-9. Describe the purposes and effects of the General Agreement on Tariffs and Trade (GATT) and the General Agreement on Trade in Services (GATS).

16-10. Discuss how and why nations regulate imports and exports.

16-11. Identify and evaluate the means for resolving international disputes.

16-12. Explain the act of state doctrine.

16-13. Describe the doctrine of sovereign immunity and its exceptions as codified under the Foreign Sovereign Immunities Act (FSIA).

16-14. Identify some challenges to the enforcement of foreign judgments.

Introduction

The preceding chapters have addressed law and ethics primarily in an American context. However, ours is undeniably a global economy, as painfully evidenced by the global economic recession triggered in 2008 and its continuing repercussions.

The process of globalization is the breaking down of national boundaries and rules to allow free interchange around the world—the free interchange of people, communications, services, goods, businesses, investments, and ideas. Evidence of the global economy is everywhere. Travel the world and you can readily access automated teller machines (ATMs) for local currency that will be instantaneously debited from your domestic bank account. You will see such American logos as Starbucks, McDonald's, and Deloitte adorning shops and buildings. Back at home, on streets and in malls, you can see branches and outlets for HSBC (formerly the Hongkong and Shanghai Banking Corporation, now one of the world's largest banks, headquartered in London), Godiva Chocolatier (founded in Brussels), Hyundai cars (Korean), and H&M clothing stores (Swedish). As for the interchange of people, in addition to the millions of international temporary business and pleasure travelers, there are some 215 million first-generation migrants, 40 percent more than in 1990.[1]

> Globalization is the breaking down of national boundaries to allow free interchange of people, communications, services, goods, businesses, investments, and ideas.

How is business practice affected by this networked global economy? Which laws govern company behavior? The laws of the "home" country? The laws of the "host" country? The laws where the company's suppliers or customers reside? What happens if the laws of the host country and the home country conflict? And what happens when a corporation changes its home country? When the German corporation Daimler Benz merged with Chrysler, becoming Daimler Chrysler, did the laws to which Chrysler was subject change? Did those changes have to be unwound when Daimler later sold Chrysler to Cerberus Capital Management, an American private equity fund, in 2007? In 2014, Chrysler became a wholly owned subsidiary of the Italian automaker Fiat, now known as Fiat Chrysler Automobiles. What law governs the company now? As firms become companies of the world, rather than of one nation, difficult issues of ethics and law arise.

The International Environment

LO 16-1
Discuss the role of the World Trade Organization (WTO) in reducing global trade barriers.

Ever since Adam Smith wrote *The Wealth of Nations* in 1776, many have argued for the axiom that a decrease in trade barriers between any number of countries will stimulate the total world economy, not simply the economies of the countries involved in the specific trade agreement. Belief in this principle is affirmed each time a new nation joins the World Trade Organization (WTO). With the addition of three new countries in 2015 and 2016, including Kazakhstan and Liberia, the WTO is now comprised of 164 members.

A fundamental principle set forth in the preamble to the 1994 Marrakesh Agreement, which established the WTO effective January 1, 1995, is that a "substantial reduction of tariffs and other barriers to trade" will contribute to the objectives of "raising standards of living, ensuring full employment and a large and steadily growing volume of real income."[2]

Member countries in the WTO represent a diverse array of the world's governments: from communist to socialist to capitalist, from Buddhist to Jewish to Christian to Muslim, and from all points around the globe. Thus, belief in the benefits of decreasing trade barriers has been widely shared in the international community, although a shift in this ideology is becoming more evident in recent years. [The WTO maintains an extensive online presence, including full text documents, through its website at **www.wto.org**].

Trade Agreements

The desire to reach a common legal ground in international business is not a recent development. As early as 1778, U.S. commercial treaties have regulated shipping and trading rights and rules between U.S. citizens and those of other countries. Such agreements can be relatively simple—involving only two countries and only a few commodities—or they can be more complex, multilateral agreements involving three or more countries and governing broad areas of their trading relationships, such as the North American Free Trade Agreement (NAFTA) among Canada, the United States, and Mexico. The more countries involved and the more topics on the table, the more complex the agreement. The WTO is the prototypical multilateral agreement. As previously noted, the vast majority of countries are members, and conceivably any trade-related topic could become a topic for negotiation. In principle, involving the maximum number of state actors and addressing the universe of possible trade issues will result in the greatest economic stimulation. As a practical matter, that ideal may be very difficult to effectuate, as was manifestly illustrated by the WTO negotiations that concluded in December 2013.[3]

Those negotiations, known as the Doha Round after the city in Qatar where the round was initiated, began in 2001 and collapsed in 2008. Sticking points included the continuation of substantial agricultural subsidies for farmers in the United States and Europe, which negatively impact the competitive strength of agricultural products originating in other countries, and the relatively high import tariffs on manufactured goods imposed by some emerging economies, such as China and India. Another impediment to its conclusion was the dramatic change in the global trading environment over the 13 years the negotiations continued. Not only have major industrialized countries suffered substantial recessions, but emerging economies began contributing dramatically to the global growth in gross domestic product (GDP)—accounting for two-thirds of it in 2008.[4] Both realities have contributed to a shift in the economic balance of power. The December 2013 agreement reflects a substantially modified agenda compared to that envisioned in 2001 and focuses primarily on the streamlining of international customs rules and procedures.

In light of the limited recent negotiating successes under the auspices of the WTO, the fear is that there will be a return to less comprehensive regional and bilateral negotiations in which the imbalance of power between rich and poor nations will be more pronounced. This imbalance of power may be further amplified by a recent trend in U.S. immigration policies and trade negotiations that reflect a more nationalistic ideology—a belief that globalization hurts American jobs and threatens the American way of life. This is in sharp contrast to globalism, the belief that globalization is good and that national sovereignty should give way to global governance. Political debate during the 2016 U.S. presidential election was sharply divided on these

> "Globalism is an ideology, and its struggle with nationalism will shape the coming decade."

issues, underscoring the idea that "globalism is an ideology, and its struggle with nationalism will shape the coming decade."[5] Other countries, such as Britain and France, are debating similar issues. "Globalization has gone into reverse gear. . . . In the boom years between 2003 and 2010 it appeared that a new era of openness and global supply chains would help emerging countries to grow at turbocharged rates for decades, closing the gap with the rich world. Today that idea is out of fashion."[6]

While WTO negotiations have proven difficult, regional trade agreements do seem to be on the rise, with more than 10 agreements on average each year since 1994.[7] Until recently, the United States had been attempting to negotiate two major regional compacts: one with the European Union (the Transatlantic Trade and Investment Partnership, or TTIP) and the other with 11 countries circling the Pacific (the Trans-Pacific Partnership, or TPP). These negotiations have not been successful. The U.S. abandoned the TPP following the 2016 presidential election of Donald Trump, and it appears that the "TTIP has failed—but no one is admitting it."[8] Meanwhile, China—which was excluded from the TPP—"is pushing rival trade pacts," and if TPP fails, other countries are expected to fill the void with their own trade deals.[9] Notably, none of the major emerging economies—Brazil, Russia, India, and China (BRIC)—were participants of either of these nascent regional compacts.

European Union

One of the most well-known, and most developed, trade agreements is that of the European Union (EU). It is also quite significant for our purposes because the EU is the United States' largest trading partner, and vice versa. As of this writing, the EU is made up of 28 member countries, with four candidate countries: Montenegro, Serbia, the Republic of Macedonia, and Turkey. The EU population far surpasses the United States' (currently 508.5 million compared with 325 million) and its combined gross domestic product is $16.5 trillion, compared to the United States' GDP of $17.9 trillion. Like the United States, the European Union has a robust domestic regulatory regime that impacts foreign companies seeking to do business there. But their regulatory philosophies differ: Europe tends to take a precautionary approach, disallowing new products and technologies until they are proven safe, whereas the United States tends to weigh costs and benefits, even while recognizing that unknowns exist.[10] These differing approaches were one of the challenges of TTIP negotiations. In fact, they may have proven insurmountable.

Like the WTO, the European Union is currently facing considerable challenges. When the financial crisis that began in 2008 spread around the world through the web of global financial and economic ties, not only were weak banks revealed, but also weak countries. The very success of the EU in increasing trade and other economic ties among its member countries became a liability: the economically weaker countries acted as a further drag on stronger economies. Some of the strongest economic ties in the European Union are those that link the 19 countries that have adopted the euro as their common currency. In the usual course, as a national economy deteriorates, its currency is devalued in relation to other currencies, and the economic hardship remains primarily a domestic problem. However, within the eurozone, for example, Greece's currency cannot fall to reflect the degree of its economic difficulties because the value of the euro is tied to perceptions of all countries in the eurozone as a whole. What happens when the world sees weakness not just in Greece, but also in Spain, Portugal, Ireland, and Italy? Even the economically strong eurozone countries suffer the downward revaluation of their shared currency. If they provide the support to prop up the weaker economies, then the issue is whether the recipient countries can and will make changes domestically to strengthen their economies and prevent future negative impacts on the euro. If the stronger economies do not have faith in future change, and cannot compel such change as a condition of their support, they may determine that the better choice for the long run is to abandon the euro. That step could lead to the disintegration of the European Union itself.[11]

Yet another challenge threatening the European Union is "Brexit," the referendum passed by voters in the United Kingdom to pull out of the EU. Many of the voters believed that Britain was subject to too many rules, paid too much in membership fees, and received too little benefit from the EU. Many in the United Kingdom also wanted to pull back on immigration policies, believing the EU does not afford them enough control over the number of European nationals living and working within the United Kingdom's borders. The United Kingdom is the first nation ever to withdraw from the European Union. [EUROPA is the portal site of the European Union, found at europa.eu/european-union/index_en].

Globalization and Countervailing Forces

Recall our definition of globalization: the breaking down of national boundaries to allow free interchange of people, communications, services, goods, businesses, investments, and ideas. Understanding what globalization is *not* may be as important as knowing what it is: It is not homogenization. The goal is not to make us all the same. But the goals do include increased choice through the sharing of diversity, as well as appropriate protection of historical, social, and cultural identities. It is also not just about free trade. Consider again some of the issues on the table in the TTIP and TPP negotiations, such as standards for food safety, Internet freedom, labor, and acceptable environmental practices. The WTO's own website acknowledges, "[T]he WTO is not just about liberalizing trade, and in some circumstances its rules support maintaining trade barriers—for example, to protect consumers or prevent the spread of disease. . . . The system's overriding purpose is to help trade flow as freely as possible—so long as there are no undesirable side-effects."[12]

Unfortunately, the process of globalization has not been uniformly beneficial. "The real question isn't whether free markets are good or bad. It is why they are producing such wildly different results in different countries."[13] One reason for disparate results may be that not all local governments develop in tandem with their economies and capture an appropriate portion of the wealth created to use on behalf of their populations. Where that is not occurring, it has been argued that "multinationals—which account for the bulk of direct cross-border investment and one-third of trade—have social responsibilities in nations where the rule of law is weak. And this view dispenses with the erroneous notion that open markets will magically produce prosperity in all conditions."[14] The challenge is to find ways to correct the inequities as the world becomes increasingly interconnected. As a result, the global impact of multinationals is an important focus of this chapter.

> Globalization has not been uniformly beneficial.

Questions

1. Now that the Brexit referendum has passed, Britain will have two years after invoking Article 50 of the Lisbon Treaty to negotiate its withdrawal from the EU. While many voters were in favor of leaving the EU, they were not uniformly decided on the laws and regulations that must be adopted in place of the European Union's. Britain must resolve some difficult issues in a relatively short amount of time. For instance, should it remain in the EU's single market but exercise sovereignty over its own immigration policies? Alternatively, as a member of the WTO, should Britain negotiate separate trade deals with the EU and with other members of the WTO? Should it adopt the same labor and consumer safety standards currently enforced by the EU? If not, what effect will this have on compliance costs for multinational companies? What concerns would you have if you were operating a multinational company in Europe?

LO 16-2
Compare and contrast an American firm's social responsibility to its host country with its social responsibility to its home country.

2. If multinational corporations have affirmative social responsibilities in "nations where the rule of law is weak," who should identify and impose those responsibilities? If you believe that it is a matter for corporate management, what forces might cause management to act more responsibly? What forces exist that might impede greater corporate social responsibility on the part of multinationals? On the other hand, if you believe that social responsibilities should be imposed on multinationals, what governing body should do so? How will that governing body obtain the power to legislate and enforce such responsibilities?

The Intercultural Environment: Ethics Across International Borders

LO 16-3
Discuss the interrelationship of religion, culture, and legal rules with comparisons to American and Islamic viewpoints.

The September 11, 2001, World Trade Center attack focused light on ethical and legal tensions between the American and Islamic cultures. America's long presence in Iraq and Afghanistan has kept these cultural divisions in the public eye. Recent polls have indicated that a growing majority of Americans believe the values of Islam are at odds with America's own.[15] Yet, the public protests of the Arab Spring in 2011 may have demonstrated that Islamic cultures are no more homogeneous than America's. Many issues triggering the protests—such as human-rights violations, unemployment, and extreme poverty—are issues about which much of the American public was sympathetic. [For more on the Arab Spring, see **en.wikipedia.org/wiki/Arab_Spring**]. Bridging cultural differences is an essential first step in creating an effective working relationship.

Religion often provides the foundation for a culture's ethical structure. Thus, two countries with different religious heritages are likely to have divergent ethical and legal norms. In addition, cultures differ in their judgments about which rights are so important that they should be protected. For example, separation of church and state is a basic legal precept in the United States. The purpose of this legal separation was to permit individuals to practice their own religious traditions and prohibit the government from imposing a single belief system on everyone. By contrast, in some predominantly Islamic countries, religious law is also the law of the state.

> In Islamic countries, religion is the basis for many legal, as well as ethical, standards.

Laws and Social Norms Regarding Free Speech

Standards for appropriate speech are regulated by both societal norms and, in many cases, local law. The bounds of free speech vary considerably from country to country. The Internet magnifies the issue because its inherent nature allows speech to flow freely, divorced from political boundaries. Although Chapter 18 will cover the Internet and free speech under U.S. law, here we look at the issue from an international perspective, not with regard to the speaker, but rather to the service provider that facilitates transmission of the contested speech.

Because service providers such as Google, Facebook, and Twitter store the speech of others on their servers, one issue is whether such a provider can, should, or must remove content that is offensive to portions of its audience, particularly after the provider has been notified of the specific content found objectionable. For example, in 2015, Google received nearly 8,400 requests from governments for the removal of various content, many of which were honored by blocking access from those countries under Google's policy of complying with lawful requests. The United States alone made 766 requests; Brazil made 680. This is not as surprising as it might seem when one considers that countries less tolerant of free speech block content more directly. China's "Great Firewall" is a case in point. What speech draws a red flag in Brazil? Racial issues, but also some political speech. Brazil "has strict electoral laws that limit criticism of candidates in the runup to elections."[16]

A particularly difficult issue facing online providers is the restriction of hate speech. Lawmakers in Germany have been leading the West on this front, demanding that Facebook enforce more restrictions on what users are posting—no easy task considering that there are now 1.8 billion users worldwide. "The often-heated dispute has raised concerns over maintaining freedom of speech while protecting vulnerable minorities in a country where the legacy of World War II and decades of East German communism still resonate."[17] Facebook has since updated its global community standards to protect minority groups around the world and has agreed to work with the government, charities, and others in Germany to counter online hate speech. For starters, it hired a Berlin-based tech company to manage illegal content and began a public campaign in Germany to address local concerns about how it is dealing with the issue.

Yet another issue is the responsibility, if any, of Internet providers to regulate fake news posted on their news feeds. The issue came to a head following the 2016 U.S. presidential election: Facebook met with sharp criticism when conspiracy theories and falsified stories published on its news feeds were blamed not only for influencing the results of the election but also for motivating a man to fire an assault rifle in a pizza restaurant in Washington, D.C. The restaurant, along with other local businesses, had been attacked on social media and received death threats based on their alleged involvement in fake conspiracy theories involving presidential candidate Hillary Clinton. In order to respond to the criticism, Facebook has developed a process by which users can report a potential hoax. The flagged story will then be fact-checked by a third party. If found to be fake, the story will still appear in the news feed but will be flagged as disputed and linked to an explanation as to why. Facebook is also taking measures to eliminate the financial incentives that motivate fake news. For instance, in order to reduce the prevalence of sites pretending to be legitimate, it has eliminated the ability to spoof domains and is evaluating where policy enforcement actions might be necessary.[18]

Facebook has also, at times, angered a considerable number of its U.S. constituents with regard to content that glorifies violence against women. Groups concerned with women's rights have repeatedly reported offensive content, with mixed results. In 2013, they resorted to using one medium to get the attention of another: they "asked Facebook users to use [a particular] Twitter hashtag . . . to call on companies to stop advertising on Facebook if their ads [had] been placed alongside" pages with names such as "Violently Raping Your Friend Just for Laughs." In a very short time, the effort had garnered 224,000 supporters on a petition at change.org, and Facebook publicly stated that its "systems to identify and remove hate speech have failed to work as effectively as we would like, particularly around issues of gender-based hate."[19] In 2016, Facebook met with sharp criticism once again when it failed for over 36 hours to remove "sickening images" of a murdered woman, stating that although the photos were flagged, they didn't violate its graphic-content policy.[20]

Perhaps even more challenging are requests from governments for service providers to turn over information revealing the identity of the content poster. France has anti-hate laws that proscribe anti-Semitic speech. Twitter had already removed at least some of the content at issue when a French court in a civil suit brought by a citizen's group ordered Twitter to identify the individuals who had posted the content. Although its policy is to provide such information only in response to a valid order of a U.S. court, Twitter ultimately agreed to provide the information to French authorities who were seeking to prosecute the posters under their anti-hate laws. In deciding to cooperate, Twitter may have been concerned that the employees of its Paris offices would also be subject to prosecution.[21]

Questions

1. Acceptable speech varies not just by country but also over time, and sensitive topics might stem from local history, customs, and conditions. Consider, for example, Thailand's prohibitions against insults to its monarchy and India's fears about content that could spark religious violence. Hate speech is widely restricted. Try developing a substantive rule that a global Internet provider could use to determine when a request to remove content should be acted upon, regardless of the country of origin. If your rule references hate speech, it will be important to indicate what speech meets that criterion.

2. It is often difficult to balance the protection of free speech and the need to counteract its potentially negative effects. Take, for instance, the issue of fake news. Should it be restricted? Removed? Flagged? Consider a recent study, which found that students have a "dismaying" inability to distinguish between real and fake news.[22] Does this alter your view? Do you think Facebook's approach to handling fake news is an effective means of protecting free speech while also counterbalancing the potentially negative, and sometimes dangerous, effects of false information?

Social Responsibility to Host Country

When doing business abroad, does a firm have social responsibilities to the host country beyond those required by the market and the law of that country? This issue has arisen in many contexts, including factory labor conditions. Not infrequently, corporations have been chastised for allowing working conditions in their foreign operations or in their suppliers' plants that Western cultures consider substandard. *Sweatshops* pose a host of commercial, economic, ethical, political, and social questions. For example, on April 24, 2013, an eight-story building collapsed in a suburb of Dhaka, the capital of Bangladesh, killing over 1,100 garment industry workers. Their employers insisted they continue working despite the fact that serious structural defects had been discovered in the building just the day before.[23] Under pressure to improve its labor standards, Bangladesh has begun working with the International Labour Office (ILO), a U.N. agency that brings governments, employers, and employee representatives from 187 member states together to set fair labor standards. Worker safety in the Bangladesh garment industry has since improved. Unfortunately, the issue of workers' rights has presented greater challenges due to the slowed growth of labor unions and continuing allegations of anti-union discrimination and unfair labor practices.[24] While sweatshops may increase jobs and contribute to a developing country's national wealth, others argue that this wealth may find its way primarily into the hands of industry heads and government employees, without a meaningful increase in the standard of living of much of the population.[25] [For more about the ILO, see www.ilo.org].

[For journalist John Stossel's 2004 overview of sweatshop protests followed by his defense of low-wage jobs, see **www.youtube.com/watch?v=0VaHmgoB10E**].

Question

If you were the vice president of supply chain management for a large manufacturer or retailer, what type of labor standards, if any, would you impose on suppliers from other countries?

Social Responsibility to Home Country?

LO 16-4
Discuss the recent use of the Alien Tort Statute against corporate defendants.

A firm must consider not only the social responsibilities it owes to its host country, but the social responsibilities it owes to its home country as well. In order to fulfill those responsibilities, a company may need to operate in accord with the values of its home country even when doing business abroad. Microsoft and other U.S. companies, for example, have had difficulties with software piracy in foreign countries. Russia, supported by Microsoft lawyers, has taken some action to crack down on such piracy. However, Russian human rights and environmental organizations have alleged that the government selectively investigates the use of illegal software in order to muzzle opposition voices while government allies are rarely, if ever, investigated. In 2010, Microsoft responded by initiating a new policy, providing blanket software licenses to advocacy groups in Russia in order to limit the government's ability to use software piracy as a pretext for government censorship or harassment.[26] Microsoft's adoption of the policy as a means of combating government censorship and harassment is an example of a U.S.-based company acting in accord with American values.

The United States exports its values structure in a variety of ways, including through the *extraterritorial* application of its laws. When the U.S. Supreme Court declared that antidiscrimination provisions of U.S. statutes such as Title VII of the Civil Rights Act of 1964 did not apply extraterritorially,[27] Congress reversed the decision with its 1991 Amendments to Title VII. Extraterritorial application of U.S. civil rights law is considered essential because over five million Americans work abroad. Accordingly, American firms that do not maintain certain Title VII standards abroad may be subject to liability in the United States.

For instance, if a firm conducts operations in Saudi Arabia, where the circumstances under which women are allowed to work are considerably circumscribed, that firm is still held to Title VII's prohibition against gender discrimination. Compliance with American civil rights laws is not required, however, where doing so would violate the host country's laws.

The Alien Tort Statute is another example of how the United States, at least at one time, exported its values structure through the *extraterritorial* application of its laws. It grants U.S. district courts original jurisdiction over claims brought by foreign citizens for torts "committed in violation of the laws of nations or a treaty of the United States." While the statute lay virtually dormant since its enactment in 1789, courts began to utilize it in the 1980s to grant jurisdiction in human rights and product liability cases arising from the alleged actions of foreign companies overseas. More recently, however, the U.S. Supreme Court has effectively limited access to U.S. courts in such cases.[28] Unless Congress passes legislation that extends the application of these laws extraterritorially, the lack of U.S. jurisdiction essentially protects multinational companies by limiting their exposure in the United States when they do business abroad. Consider, for instance, the Supreme Court case below. Pay careful attention not only to the court's legal analysis but also to the "transnational context" of the dispute and the public policy reasons the court gives in support of its findings.

LEGAL BRIEFCASE

Daimler AG v. Bauman
134 S. Ct. 746 (2014)

Justice Ginsburg

This case concerns the authority of a court in the United States to entertain a claim brought by foreign plaintiffs against a foreign defendant based on events occurring entirely outside the United States. The litigation commenced in 2004, when twenty-two Argentinian residents filed a complaint in the United States District Court for the Northern District of California against DaimlerChrysler Aktiengesellschaft (Daimler), a German public stock company, headquartered in Stuttgart, that manufactures Mercedes–Benz vehicles in Germany. The complaint alleged that during Argentina's 1976–1983 "Dirty War," Daimler's Argentinian subsidiary, Mercedes–Benz Argentina (MB Argentina) collaborated with state security forces to kidnap, detain, torture, and kill certain MB Argentina workers, among them, plaintiffs or persons closely related to plaintiffs. Damages for the alleged human-rights violations were sought from Daimler under the laws of the United States, California, and Argentina. Jurisdiction over the lawsuit was predicated on the California contacts of Mercedes–Benz USA, LLC (MBUSA), a subsidiary of Daimler incorporated in Delaware with its principal place of business in New Jersey. MBUSA distributes

Daimler-manufactured vehicles to independent dealerships throughout the United States, including California.

The question presented is whether the Due Process Clause of the Fourteenth Amendment precludes the District Court from exercising jurisdiction over Daimler in this case, given the absence of any California connection to the atrocities, perpetrators, or victims described in the complaint. Plaintiffs invoked the court's general or all-purpose jurisdiction. California, they urge, is a place where Daimler may be sued on any and all claims against it, wherever in the world the claims may arise. For example, as plaintiffs' counsel affirmed, under the proffered jurisdictional theory, if a Daimler-manufactured vehicle overturned in Poland, injuring a Polish driver and passenger, the injured parties could maintain a design defect suit in California. Exercises of personal jurisdiction so exorbitant, we hold, are barred by due process constraints on the assertion of adjudicatory authority.

In *Goodyear Dunlop Tires Operations, S.A. v. Brown,* 564 U.S. __, 131 S. Ct. 2846, 180 L. Ed. 2d 796 (2011), we addressed the distinction between general or all-purpose jurisdiction, and specific or conduct-linked jurisdiction. As to the former, we held that a court may assert jurisdiction over a foreign corporation "to hear any and all claims against [it]" only when the corporation's affiliations with the State in which suit is brought are so constant and pervasive "as to render [it] essentially at home in the forum State." Instructed by *Goodyear,* we conclude Daimler is not "at home" in California, and cannot be sued there for injuries plaintiffs attribute to MB Argentina's conduct in Argentina.

I

In 2004, plaintiffs (respondents here) filed suit in the United States District Court for the Northern District of California, alleging that MB Argentina collaborated with Argentinian state security forces to kidnap, detain, torture, and kill plaintiffs and their relatives during the military dictatorship in place there from 1976 through 1983, a period known as Argentina's "Dirty War." Based on those allegations, plaintiffs asserted claims under the Alien Tort Statute, 28 U.S.C. § 1350, and the Torture Victim Protection Act of 1991, 106 Stat. 73, . . . as well as claims for wrongful death and intentional infliction of emotional distress under the laws of California and Argentina. The incidents recounted in the complaint center on MB Argentina's plant in Gonzalez Catan, Argentina; no part of MB Argentina's alleged collaboration with Argentinian authorities took place in California or anywhere else in the United States.

Plaintiffs' operative complaint names only one corporate defendant: Daimler, the petitioner here. Plaintiffs seek to hold Daimler vicariously liable for MB Argentina's alleged malfeasance.

* * * * *

MBUSA, an indirect subsidiary of Daimler, is a Delaware limited liability corporation. MBUSA serves as Daimler's exclusive importer and distributor in the United States, purchasing Mercedes–Benz automobiles from Daimler in Germany, then importing those vehicles, and ultimately distributing them to independent dealerships located throughout the Nation. Although MBUSA's principal place of business is in New Jersey, MBUSA has multiple California-based facilities. . . . In particular, over 10% of all sales of new vehicles in the United States take place in California, and MBUSA's California sales account for 2.4% of Daimler's worldwide sales.

* * * * *

We granted certiorari to decide whether, consistent with the Due Process Clause of the Fourteenth Amendment, Daimler is amenable to suit in California courts for claims involving only foreign plaintiffs and conduct occurring entirely abroad.

II

Federal courts ordinarily follow state law in determining the bounds of their jurisdiction over persons. See Fed. Rule Civ. Proc. 4(k)(1)(A). Under California's long-arm statute, California state courts may exercise personal jurisdiction "on any basis not inconsistent with the Constitution of this state or of the United States." . . . We therefore

inquire whether the Ninth Circuit's holding comports with the limits imposed by federal due process.

III

In *Pennoyer v. Neff,* 95 U.S. 714, 24 L. Ed. 565 (1878), decided shortly after the enactment of the Fourteenth Amendment, the Court held that a tribunal's jurisdiction over persons reaches no farther than the geographic bounds of the forum. In time, however, that strict territorial approach yielded to a less rigid understanding, spurred by "changes in the technology of transportation and communication, and the tremendous growth of interstate business activity."

"The canonical opinion in this area remains *International Shoe*..., in which we held that a State may authorize its courts to exercise personal jurisdiction over an out-of-state defendant if the defendant has 'certain minimum contacts with [the State] such that the maintenance of the suit does not offend "traditional notions of fair play and substantial justice."'" Following *International Shoe,* "the relationship among the defendant, the forum, and the litigation, rather than the mutually exclusive sovereignty of the States on which the rules of *Pennoyer* rest, became the central concern of the inquiry into personal jurisdiction."

International Shoe's conception of "fair play and substantial justice" presaged the development of two categories of personal jurisdiction. The first category is represented by *International Shoe* itself, a case in which the in-state activities of the corporate defendant "ha[d] not only been continuous and systematic, but also g[a]ve rise to the liabilities sued on." *International Shoe* recognized, as well, that "the commission of some single or occasional acts of the corporate agent in a state" may sometimes be enough to subject the corporation to jurisdiction in that State's tribunals with respect to suits relating to that in-state activity. . . .

International Shoe distinguished between, on the one hand, exercises of specific jurisdiction, as just described, and on the other, situations where a foreign corporation's "continuous corporate operations within a state [are] so substantial and of such a nature as to justify suit against it on causes of action arising from dealings entirely distinct from those activities." As we have since explained, "[a] court may assert general jurisdiction over foreign (sister-state or foreign-country) corporations to hear any and all claims against them when their affiliations with the State are so 'continuous and systematic' as to render them essentially at home in the forum State."

Since *International Shoe,* "specific jurisdiction has become the centerpiece of modern jurisdiction theory, while general jurisdiction [has played] a reduced role." *International Shoe*'s momentous departure from *Pennoyer*'s rigidly territorial focus, we have noted, unleashed a rapid expansion of tribunals' ability to hear claims against out-of-state defendants when the episode-in-suit occurred in the forum or the defendant purposefully availed itself of the forum.

Our subsequent decisions have continued to bear out the prediction that "specific jurisdiction will come into sharper relief and form a considerably more significant part of the scene."

Our post-*International Shoe* opinions on general jurisdiction, by comparison, are few. "[The Court's] 1952 decision in *Perkins v. Benguet Consol. Mining Co.* remains the textbook case of general jurisdiction appropriately exercised over a foreign corporation that has not consented to suit in the forum." The defendant in *Perkins,* Benguet, was a company incorporated under the laws of the Philippines, where it operated gold and silver mines. Benguet ceased its mining operations during the Japanese occupation of the Philippines in World War II; its president moved to Ohio, where he kept an office, maintained the company's files, and oversaw the company's activities. The plaintiff, an Ohio resident, sued Benguet on a claim that neither arose in Ohio nor related to the corporation's activities in that State. We held that the Ohio courts could exercise general jurisdiction over Benguet without offending due process. That was so, we later noted, because "Ohio was the corporation's principal, if temporary, place of business."

The next case on point, *Helicopteros,* 466 U.S. 408, 104 S. Ct. 1868, 80 L. Ed. 2d 404, arose from a helicopter crash in Peru. Four U.S. citizens perished in that accident; their survivors and representatives brought suit in Texas state court against the helicopter's owner and operator, a Colombian corporation. That company's contacts with Texas were confined to "sending its chief executive officer to Houston for a contract-negotiation session; accepting into its New York bank account checks drawn on a Houston bank; purchasing helicopters, equipment, and training services from [a Texas-based helicopter company] for substantial sums; and sending personnel to [Texas] for training." Notably, those contacts bore no apparent relationship to the accident that gave rise to the suit. We held that the company's Texas connections did not resemble the "continuous and systematic general business contacts . . . found to exist in *Perkins*." "[M]ere purchases, even if occurring at regular intervals," we clarified, "are not enough to warrant a State's assertion of *in personam* jurisdiction over a nonresident corporation in a cause of action not related to those purchase transactions."

Most recently, in *Goodyear,* we answered the question: "Are foreign subsidiaries of a United States parent corporation amenable to suit in state court on claims unrelated to any activity of the subsidiaries in the forum State?" That case arose from a bus accident outside Paris that killed two boys from North Carolina. The boys' parents brought a wrongful-death suit in North Carolina state court alleging that the bus's tire was defectively manufactured. The complaint named as defendants not only The Goodyear Tire and Rubber Company (Goodyear), an Ohio corporation, but also Goodyear's Turkish, French, and Luxembourgian subsidiaries. Those foreign subsidiaries, which manufactured tires for sale in Europe and Asia, lacked any affiliation with North Carolina. A small percentage of tires manufactured by the foreign subsidiaries were distributed in North Carolina, however, and on that ground, the North Carolina Court of Appeals held the subsidiaries amenable to the general jurisdiction of North Carolina courts.

We reversed. . . . Although the placement of a product into the stream of commerce "may bolster an affiliation germane to *specific* jurisdiction," we explained, such contacts "do not warrant a determination that, based on those ties, the forum has *general* jurisdiction over a defendant." As *International Shoe* itself teaches, a corporation's "continuous activity of some sorts within a state is not enough to support the demand that the corporation be amenable to suits unrelated to that activity." Because Goodyear's foreign subsidiaries were "in no sense at home in North Carolina," we held, those subsidiaries could not be required to submit to the general jurisdiction of that State's courts.

* * * * *

IV

With this background, we turn directly to the question whether Daimler's affiliations with California are sufficient to subject it to the general (all-purpose) personal jurisdiction of that State's courts. . . . While plaintiffs ultimately persuaded the Ninth Circuit to impute MBUSA's California contacts to Daimler on an agency theory, at no point have they maintained that MBUSA is an alter ego of Daimler.

* * * * *

A

In sustaining the exercise of general jurisdiction over Daimler, the Ninth Circuit relied on an agency theory, determining that MBUSA acted as Daimler's agent for jurisdictional purposes and then attributing MBUSA's California contacts to Daimler. The Ninth Circuit's agency analysis derived from Circuit precedent considering principally whether the subsidiary "performs services that are sufficiently important to the foreign corporation that if it did not have a representative to perform them, the corporation's own officials would undertake to perform substantially similar services."

This Court has not yet addressed whether a foreign corporation may be subjected to a court's general jurisdiction based on the contacts of its in-state subsidiary. Daimler argues, and several Courts of Appeals have held, that a subsidiary's jurisdictional contacts can be imputed to its parent only when the former is so dominated by the latter as to be its alter ego. . . .

. . . The Ninth Circuit's agency theory thus appears to subject foreign corporations to general jurisdiction whenever they have an in-state subsidiary or affiliate, an outcome that would sweep beyond even the "sprawling view of general jurisdiction" we rejected in *Goodyear.*

B

Even if we were to assume that MBUSA is at home in California, and further to assume MBUSA's contacts are imputable to Daimler, there would still be no basis to subject Daimler to general jurisdiction in California, for Daimler's slim contacts with the State hardly render it at home there.

Goodyear made clear that only a limited set of affiliations with a forum will render a defendant amenable to all-purpose jurisdiction there. "For an individual, the paradigm forum for the exercise of general jurisdiction is the individual's domicile; for a corporation, it is an equivalent place, one in which the corporation is fairly re-garded as at home." . . . These bases afford plaintiffs recourse to at least one clear and certain forum in which a corporate defendant may be sued on any and all claims.

*   *   *   *   *

. . . Accordingly, the inquiry under Goodyear is not whether a for-eign corporation's in-forum contacts can be said to be in some sense "continuous and systematic," it is whether that corporation's "affiliations with the State are so 'continuous and systematic' as to render [it] essentially at home in the forum State."

Here, neither Daimler nor MBUSA is incorporated in California, nor does either entity have its principal place of business there. If Daimler's California activities sufficed to allow adjudication of this Argentina-rooted case in California, the same global reach would presumably be available in every other State in which MBUSA's sales are sizable. Such exorbitant exercises of all-purpose jurisdic-tion would scarcely permit out-of-state defendants "to structure their primary conduct with some minimum assurance as to where that conduct will and will not render them liable to suit."

It was therefore error for the Ninth Circuit to conclude that Daimler, even with MBUSA's contacts attributed to it, was at home in California, and hence subject to suit there on claims by foreign plaintiffs having nothing to do with anything that occurred or had its principal impact in California.

C

Finally, the transnational context of this dispute bears attention. The Court of Appeals emphasized, as supportive of the exercise of general jurisdiction, plaintiffs' assertion of claims under the Alien Tort Statute (ATS), 28 U.S.C. § 1350, and the Torture Victim Protection Act of 1991 (TVPA), 106 Stat. 73, note following 28 U.S.C. § 1350. Recent decisions of this Court, however, have rendered plaintiffs' ATS and TVPA claims infirm.

The Ninth Circuit, moreover, paid little heed to the risks to inter-national comity its expansive view of general jurisdiction posed. Other nations do not share the uninhibited approach to personal jurisdiction advanced by the Court of Appeals in this case. In the European Union, for example, a corporation may generally be sued in the nation in which it is "domiciled," a term defined to refer only to the location of the corporation's "statutory seat," "central admin-istration," or "principal place of business." The Solicitor General in-forms us, in this regard, that "foreign governments' objections to some domestic courts' expansive views of general jurisdiction have in the past impeded negotiations of international agreements on the reciprocal recognition and enforcement of judgments." See also U.S. Brief 2 (expressing concern that unpredictable applications of general jurisdiction based on activities of U.S.-based subsidiaries could discourage foreign investors); Brief for Respondents 35 (ac-knowledging that "doing business" basis for general jurisdiction has led to "international friction"). Considerations of international rapport thus reinforce our determination that subjecting Daimler to the general jurisdiction of courts in California would not accord with the "fair play and substantial justice" due process demands.

*   *   *   *   *

For the reasons stated, the judgment of the United States Court of Appeals for the Ninth Circuit is *Reversed*.

Questions

1. What were the facts in *Perkins,* and why did the court rule that it was appropriate to exercise general jurisdiction over the for-eign corporation in that case?

2. In contrast, what were the facts in *Goodyear,* and why did the court rule that it was *not* appropriate to exercise general juris-diction over the foreign corporation in that case?

3. Applying *Perkins* and *Goodyear,* what were the court's reasons for finding that there was a lack of general jurisdiction over Daimler AG?

4. The court proceeded to give public policy reasons reinforcing its denial of general jurisdiction in *Daimler AG*. What is the transnational context for the dispute, and what did the Solicitor General inform the court?

The Foreign Corrupt Practices Act (FCPA)

Consider the problem of bribery and other forms of corruption. Some nations argue that bribery is acceptable behavior, whereas others criticize it severely. In July 2013, the Chinese minister who had overseen a substantial modernization of China's railways was sentenced to death (although reduction to a life sentence was possible) for accepting $10.5 million in bribes.[29] How would you define bribery? What problems are created by a culture of bribery?

For years, U.S. firms have dealt with bribery issues in America and abroad. Congress has attempted to respond harshly to corruption in other governments and to support U.S. firms that do not participate in foreign corruption. As we saw in Chapter 2, the FCPA prohibits businesses from making certain payments or gifts to government officials for the purpose of influencing business decisions. In recent years, the United States has stepped up its enforcement of the FCPA, both through criminal suits brought by the Department of Justice and through civil cases brought by the Securities Exchange Commission.[30] Recent FCPA investigations have involved the following companies:

- Odebrecht: Latin America's largest construction company, and Brasken, a petrochemical firm with which it is affiliated, pleaded guilty to paying hundreds of millions in bribes to government officials in order to win contracts. They will now pay at least $3.5 billion in fines—the largest penalty ever assessed for a FCPA violation—in a case brought by the United States, Brazil, and Switzerland.[31]

- GlaxoSmithKline: The British company allegedly paid $500 million, through Chinese travel agencies, to doctors and hospital personnel to boost their prescriptions of GSK pharmaceuticals, and to government officials and Chinese GSK executives.[32] In September 2014, a Chinese court found GSK's Chinese subsidiary guilty of bribery and fined the company almost $500 million, the largest corporate fine ever assessed in China.[33] In September 2016, GSK agreed to pay $20 million to settle SEC charges that its Chinese subsidiaries engaged in bribery schemes.[34]

Although well intentioned, some critics argue that the FCPA unduly restricts American companies operating abroad and prevents them from competing effectively. However, the biggest settlements under the FCPA have actually been paid by foreign companies, a consequence of the act's application to any company that has securities listed on a U.S. stock exchange or does business in the United States.[35] Others argue the United States should not use foreign trade to unilaterally impose its sense of morality around the globe. Many other countries, however, are enforcing similar antibribery measures. [For more information on FCPA enforcement actions, see **www.fcpablog.com**].

Questions

1. Is it ethical for the U.S. Congress to impose federal laws on the operations of U.S. corporations abroad? Why or why not?

2. Consider the recent scandal involving FIFA, soccer's international governing body. The DOJ brought charges against FIFA officials under both the RICO Act and the Travel Act (which prohibits the engagement in interstate or foreign travel, or the use of any facility in interstate commerce, to carry out an illegal activity) for the alleged transaction of commercial bribes, estimated at $150 million. (The DOJ did not charge FIFA under the FCPA because the alleged criminal activity did not involve bribes paid to government officials.) Russia's foreign ministry viewed it as "'another case of the illegal extraterritorial application of U.S. laws'" and an attempt "'to set itself up as a judge far outside its borders.'"[36] Is it ethical for the U.S. to extraterritorially impose its values

on foreign organizations? Is the U.S. unilaterally imposing its sense of morality around the globe?

Social Responsibility to Humanity?

Are we evolving toward a set of common international ethical standards that can be supported and implemented globally? Would international ethical standards simply represent a natural progression from national standards? At one time, agreements were achieved only at a city level, but state-level agreements followed, and those, in turn, evolved to agreements among federated states. Is a similar progression to global standards inevitable? Does a framework that divides ethical issues between those of the "host" country and those of the "home" country remain a useful analytical tool?

> If we are moving toward global social responsibility, can we do so without sacrificing the existence of wonderfully diverse and unique cultures?

If we are moving toward global social responsibility, can we do so without sacrificing the existence of wonderfully diverse and unique cultures? Do we have to become ever more uniform in our beliefs and practices? Can we agree on fundamentals, but still appreciate diversity?

Consider the evidence. Not only are businesses interacting with stakeholders of ever more diverse nationalities (investors/owners/shareholders, customers/clients, suppliers, general citizenry impacted by business decisions), but the cultural identity of businesses themselves may be unclear. Consider the example of Chrysler's changing ownership in the chapter introduction.

We have growing evidence of voluntary international cooperation to establish acceptable business practices, such as the establishment of October 14 as World Standards Day to honor the work of many nongovernmental international bodies that have established a wide range of voluntary standards addressing global production and trade. Other evidence includes these:

- As far back as 1948, the U.N. General Assembly adopted its Universal Declaration of Human Rights. Inherent in the structure of the declaration is a recognition of the connection between work (and business, by extension) and the protection of fundamental human values. Article 23 declares that everyone has a right "to just and favourable conditions of work" and "to just and favourable remuneration ensuring for himself and his family an existence worthy of human dignity."[37]

- In 2000, the United Nations launched a voluntary initiative to promote corporate social responsibility globally. The 10 principles of the *Global Compact* address human rights, labor standards, the environment, and corruption. Over 9,000 businesses and 12,000 total signatories from 170 countries have joined the Compact. [For more on the Global Compact, see **www.unglobalcompact.org**].

- Social Accountability International has developed SA8000, a social accountability standard based on international norms (such as the Universal Declaration of Human Rights previously mentioned) that companies can adopt to develop and assure an equitable and safe workplace for their employees and those of their suppliers. A verification system was simultaneously developed so results are auditable. As of this writing, more than 3,900 facilities with 2.15 million employees in 55 industries and 68 countries are certified. [For more on SAI and SA8000, see **www.sa-intl.org** and **www.saasaccreditation.org**].

PRACTICING ETHICS   Individual Social Responsibility to Humanity?

Consider the following excerpt from a speech delivered September 28, 2001, by Jose Ramos-Horta, Nobel Peace Prize Laureate (1996) and Minister for Foreign Affairs and Cooperation for the East Timor Transition Government:

> There is no dispute that abject poverty, child labor, and prostitution are a moral indictment of all humanity.

> However, poverty should not only touch our conscience: It is also a matter of peace and security because it destabilizes entire countries and regions. In turn it threatens the integration of the global economy that is vital if the rich are to stay rich or if the poor are to move up, if only an inch.

Peace will be illusory as long as the rich ignore the clamor of the poor for a better life, as long as hundreds of millions of people live below the poverty line, cannot afford a meal a day, do not have access to clean water and a roof.[38]

Question

Should most of us, not just active international businesses, accept a social responsibility to humanity? If we answer yes to this question, how might our actions as students, educators, employees, employers, and investors change?

Laws Governing Cross-Border Business

All businesses must, of course, follow the laws of the countries in which they are physically present and operating. (Whether a business with no physical presence but that solicits or performs business electronically in a foreign country must follow the laws of that country will be examined in Chapter 18.) Foreign firms often wish to establish operations in the United States, in part because Americans are more inclined to buy goods made in this country. As a requirement of doing business in the United States, the foreign firm must comply with U.S. laws and regulations.

Conversely, when U.S. businesses operate abroad, they are required to follow the law of the host country. In 2006, when Google began operating its search engine in China, it accepted the government's requirement that it filter results to remove material the government deemed unsuitable for its citizens. In March 2010, Google ceased that practice and automatically redirected search requests coming from China to its uncensored site in Hong Kong. China then threatened Google with the loss of its license to provide other online services such as its music, mapping, and translation. The license was renewed when Google proposed to stop automatically redirecting search requests and instead simply presented would-be searchers with a clickable link to **google.com.hk**.[39]

Businesses may also be required, even in their foreign operations, to continue to follow certain laws of their home country, as previously discussed. Interestingly, although there is a presumption against the extraterritorial application of U.S. criminal law, where Congress has clearly indicated an intent to cover actions outside of the United States, U.S. citizens can be held accountable in America for their criminal actions abroad.[40]

Finally, businesses operating across national borders will also be subject to international law. The foundation and some examples of international business law will be discussed soon, but first it will be useful to explore some of the different forms of business available to companies wishing to expand their operations into foreign countries.

Forms of Global Business Expansion

Multinational Enterprise (MNE)

LO 16-5
Describe the basic forms of global business expansion.

The term *multinational enterprise* traditionally refers to a company that conducts business in more than one country. Any of the following operations, except for a direct contract with a foreign purchaser, may qualify a company as an MNE.

Direct Contract

A firm may expand its business across territorial borders using a variety of methods. The simplest, from a contractual perspective, occurs where a firm in one country enters an agreement with a person in another country. For example, a firm may contract to sell its product to a purchaser in another country. This is called a *direct sale* to a foreign purchaser. The parties simply agree on the terms of the sale and record them in a contract.

Where the contract is silent as to a term of the sale, the law that will apply to the missing term will be the law specified in the contract; where none is specified, the applicable law will depend on the country in which the court is located. Some courts will employ the *vesting of rights doctrine,* applying the law of the jurisdiction in which the rights in the contract vested. Other courts may apply the *most significant relationship doctrine,* applying the law of the jurisdiction that has the most significant relationship to the contract and the parties. Finally, some courts will apply the *governmental interest doctrine,* applying the law of the jurisdiction that has the greatest interest in the issue's outcome.

Payment is one of the most complicated issues pertaining to direct sales. The seller should and usually does require an *irrevocable letter of credit,* which the buyer obtains from a bank after paying that amount to the bank (or securing that amount of credit). The bank then promises to pay the seller the contract amount after conforming goods have been shipped. The "irrevocable" component prohibits the bank from revoking the letter of credit without the consent of both the buyer and the seller. The seller is protected because the buyer has already provided adequate funds for the purchase, confirmed by a bank. The buyer is protected because the funds are not turned over to the seller until it has been determined that the goods conform to the contract. It is important to the buyer, however, that the letter of credit be specific as to the conformance of the goods because the bank will only ensure that the goods conform to the letter of credit and not to the contract itself.

> Payment is one of the most complicated issues pertaining to direct sales.

Foreign Representation   A second type of foreign expansion is a sale through a distributor, agent, or other type of representative in the foreign country. A firm may decide to sell through an *agent*—that is, the firm hires an individual who will remain permanently in the foreign country, negotiate contracts, and assist in the performance of the contracts. Agents are generally compensated on a commission basis. On the other hand, the firm may act through a *representative,* who may solicit and take orders but, unlike an agent, may not enter into contracts on behalf of the firm. In some countries, laws may substantially restrict the actions a representative may take. For example, in China a representative may generally only gather information and market research, but no direct business activities may be undertaken.[41]

Distributors purchase goods from the seller, then negotiate sales to foreign buyers on their own behalf. In so doing, a distributor may be more likely to invest resources to develop the foreign market for the goods. *Exclusive dealing agreements* with distributors, where a distributor agrees to sell only the goods of one manufacturer and the manufacturer agrees to sell only to that distributor in a particular geographic area, are generally not allowed abroad, although they often are legal in the United States.

Export trading companies specialize in acting as the intermediary between a domestic business and foreign purchasers. The trading company will take title to the goods being sold and then complete the sale in the foreign country. *Export management companies,* on the other hand, merely manage the sale but do not take title to the goods; consequently, they do not share any of the risk associated with the sale.

Joint Venture   Foreign expansion may also occur through a *joint venture* agreement between two or more parties. This type of agreement usually covers one or several specific projects and is in effect for a specified period. For instance, Toyota operated a joint venture with General Motors at a plant in Fremont, California, from 1984 to 2009, and with Subaru at a plant in Lafayette, Indiana, from 2007 to 2016.

Branch Office or Subsidiary   A *branch office* is simply an extension of a foreign corporation into the host country. A *subsidiary,* however, is a legally separate entity formed under the laws of the host country and substantially owned by the foreign parent company. For example, an Indian paper company may open a branch office in London to market and sell its products. That office would be a mere extension of the offices already established in India. On the other hand, the Indian firm could create a British subsidiary to handle its British business from its London offices. Either a subsidiary or branch office relationship could also be established through acquisition of an existing firm in the host country.

The distinction between a subsidiary, which is a legal entity separate from its foreign parent, and a branch office, which is not, has a number of ramifications. For example, many countries may require a local subsidiary to have in-country directors and/or shareholders. On the other hand, setting up a branch office will likely subject the parent company to taxation in the host country. Indeed, the parent company is legally liable for all obligations of a branch office. In contrast, when a subsidiary is sued, the parent company is not generally liable. For example, in *United States v. Philip Morris, Inc.,*[42] the U.S. district court dismissed British American Tobacco (BAT) from the federal government's suit against various cigarette manufacturers for recovery of health care expenses. BAT was the British parent of the U.S. company, Brown & Williamson. The subsidiary, B&W, remained a part of the suit.

Licensing   Where a company has no interest in commencing operations in a foreign country but instead merely wants to have its product or name in that market, the company may decide to license the rights to the name or to manufacture the product to a company in the target market. The benefit to this type of relationship is that the licensor (holder of the right) has the opportunity to enter the foreign market, but the licensee assumes all of the obligations and risks of running the business.

Franchising   In a franchise agreement the franchisee pays the franchisor for a license to use trademarks, formulas, and other trade secrets. The difference between a franchising agreement and a licensing contract is that a franchise agreement is usually made up of a number of licensing arrangements, as well as other obligations. For instance, in a typical fast-food franchise agreement, the franchisor will license to the franchisee the right to use its trademark, name, logo, recipes, menus, and other recognized resources. Kentucky Fried Chicken has over 18,000 franchises in 118 countries, with more than 800 in the United Kingdom and Ireland, and over 4,500 in China alone.

Question

Assume that you are interested in importing silk blouses from Bangkok, Thailand, to France. What facts might persuade you to enter into an agency agreement with a Thai blouse manufacturer rather than a distributorship or vice versa?

Foundations of International Law

LO 16-6
Compare and contrast treaties, custom, and comity and give illustrations of each.

A firm with manufacturing plants in Argentina and Thailand, and corporate headquarters in Bangkok, enters into a contract with a French firm to distribute its products produced in the Argentinean plant. The French firm is not satisfied with the quality of the products being sent. What law would apply to this situation? Argentinean? Thai? French? Or are there, perhaps, specific provisions of international law that will govern? The answer to this question is not simple, even for seasoned lawyers; yet the firms involved will be greatly affected by the result.

The source of law applicable to an international dispute depends in part on the issue involved. In general, private parties are free to form agreements in whatever manner they wish. The parties to the agreement can determine, for instance, which nation's law will govern the contract, where disagreements in connection with the contract will be settled, and even in which language the transactions will be made. This is referred to as the *private law* of contracts. Whenever the parties to a transaction from different jurisdictions are involved in a lawsuit, the court will start by looking at the agreement of the parties themselves to resolve these issues. Where the contract is silent as to the choice of law, jurisdiction, and other questions, the court must decide. Generally, the law of the jurisdiction in which the transaction occurred is applied. If the transaction is consummated through some form of cross-border communication, as are many international trade negotiations, most often the law of the jurisdiction of the seller's place of business will apply. Remember, however, that the parties may always contract for a different result.

> What law would apply to this situation? Argentinean? Thai? French?

Public law, on the other hand, includes those rules of each nation that regulate the contractual agreement between the parties—for instance, import and export taxes, packaging requirements, and safety standards. In addition, public law regulates the relationships among nations.

Public law derives from a number of sources. The most familiar source of international public law is a *treaty* or *convention* (essentially a contract between nations). For example, the United States, Canada, and Mexico have entered into the North American Free Trade Agreement (NAFTA), a convention regarding trade among those countries. Some treaties and conventions are self-executing, which means that once a country has ratified them, a business can rely on and directly enforce treaty terms in court. The United Nations Convention on Contracts for the International Sale of Goods (CISG), which will be discussed soon, is an example of a self-executing convention. On the other hand, some treaties and conventions apply only to government signatories and not directly to private parties. Such a convention may, for example, require an adopting country such as the United States to amend its domestic law to accomplish the purposes of the convention.

Public law is also found in *international custom* or *generally accepted principles of law*. These terms refer to practices that are commonly accepted as appropriate business or commercial practices among nations. For instance, sovereign immunity, discussed later in this chapter, is an accepted principle of international law. A *custom* is derived from consistent behavior over time that is accepted as binding by the countries that engage in that behavior.

Piracy on the High Seas

In recent years, events off the coast of Somalia have raised public awareness of modern-day piracy. One might think that the international law against piracy would be clear given that piracy has existed as a threat to security since well before Britain's Royal Navy returned to port in 1718 with the severed head of Blackbeard. A 2010 federal case in Virginia, as well as attempts to prosecute raiders in other countries, suggested otherwise. What is clear is that generally accepted principles of international law give any country the right to capture pirates on the high seas. U.S. law merely states that "whoever on the high seas, commits the crime of piracy as defined by the law of nations . . . shall be imprisoned for life."

The Virginia court had before it several Somali men who by skiff had approached a U.S. amphibious dock landing ship in the Gulf of Aden in the early morning hours of July 7, 2010. One man shot an AK-47 rifle at the *USS Ashland,* which returned fire, sank the skiff, and then took the assailants into custody. The U.S. government argued that piracy under the law of nations does not require the active taking of property and that any unauthorized armed assault or direct violent act on the high seas is enough. The defense argued the charge could not stand because the defendants "did not board, take control, or otherwise rob the *USS Ashland*." Relying on an 1820 U.S. Supreme Court decision defining piracy as robbery on the high seas and holding that contemporary international law is unsettled on the definition of piracy, the court dismissed the piracy charge.

The case was appealed, as was a later federal district court opinion that upheld piracy charges against five other men who attacked another U.S. vessel off the coast of Somalia. Those defendants were sentenced to life in prison plus 80 years for piracy. The Fourth Circuit affirmed the latter sentences, vacated the *USS Ashland* decision, and held that the 1820 decision did not foreclose conduct other than robbery, including acts of violence committed for private ends against persons on the high seas, from qualifying as piracy.[43]

The Development of Customs

Historically, merchants followed certain accepted *customs* or principles in connection with the sale of goods. These customs or manners of dealing between merchants were often recognized and applied in court decisions, and later in the United States became codified in the Uniform Commercial Code (UCC) Article 2 that regulates the sale of goods, generally, as well as sales between merchants. In this way, customs or practices traditionally followed by merchants have become accepted principles of law throughout the United States (except Louisiana).

In the international legal arena, customary practices are still evolving. For instance, the practice had been that personal information moved freely between countries to encourage efficient information exchange in the business world. However, the European Union in 1998 established minimum standards for the protection of personal data. Any country receiving information from an EU country must comply with those standards. (See Chapter 18 for more on the European Union's Directive on Data Protection.)

Two factors are used to determine whether an international custom exists: (1) consistency and repetition of the action or decision and (2) recognition by nations that this custom is binding. The first merely holds that the action or decision must be accepted by a number of nations for a time long enough to establish uniformity of application. The second dictates that the custom be accepted as binding by nations observing it. If the custom is accepted as merely persuasive, it does not rise to the level of a generally accepted principle of law. Through persistent objections, any nation may ensure that such custom is not applied to cases in which it is involved.

Generally, once a contract has been created, it is enforceable according to its terms by all parties to the contract. In the following case, read carefully to see what law the judge applied. He considered first the *private* law of the parties (that is, the express terms of the contract); then he looked to *custom;* and finally he applied the concept of *commercial impracticability.*

LEGAL BRIEFCASE

Transatlantic Financing Corporation v. United States
363 F.2d 312 (D.C. Cir. 1966)

Judge J. Skelly Wright

[In 1956, Transatlantic Financing, a steamship operator, contracted with the United States to ship wheat from Texas to Iran. Six days after the ship left port for Iran, the Egyptian government was at war with Israel and blocked the Suez Canal to shipping. The steamer therefore was forced to sail around the Cape of Good Hope. Transatlantic accordingly sued the United States for its added expenses as a result of this change of circumstances. Transatlantic contended that it had contracted only to travel the "usual and customary" route to Iran and that the United States had received a greater benefit than that for which it contracted. The district court held for the United States; Transatlantic appealed.]

Transatlantic's claim is based on the following train of argument. The charter was a contract for a voyage from a Gulf port to Iran. Admiralty principles and practices, especially stemming from the doctrine of deviation, require us to [infer] into the contract the term that the voyage was to be performed by the "usual and customary" route. The usual and customary route from Texas to Iran was, at the time of contract, via Suez, so the contract was for a voyage from Texas to Iran via Suez. When Suez was closed this contract became impossible to perform. Consequently, appellant's argument continues, when Transatlantic delivered the cargo by going around the Cape of Good Hope, in compliance with the Government's demand under claim of right, it conferred a benefit upon the United States for which it should be paid on quantum meruit.

The contract in this case does not expressly condition performance upon availability of the Suez route. Nor does it specify "via Suez" or, on the other hand, "via Suez or Cape of Good Hope." Nor are there provisions in the contract from which we may properly [infer] that the continued availability of Suez was a condition of performance. Nor is there anything in custom or trade usage, or in the surrounding circumstances generally, which would support our constructing a condition of performance. The numerous cases requiring performance around the Cape when Suez was closed indicate that the Cape route is generally regarded as an alternative means of performance. So the implied expectation that the route would be via Suez is hardly adequate proof of an allocation to the promisee of the risk of closure. In some cases, even an express expectation may not amount to a condition of performance. The doctrine of deviation supports our assumption that parties normally expect performance by the usual and customary route, but it adds nothing beyond this that is probative of an allocation of the risk.

If anything, the circumstances surrounding this contract indicate that the risk of the Canal's closure may be deemed to have been allocated to Transatlantic. We know or may safely assume that the parties were aware, as were most commercial men with interest affected by the Suez situation, that the Canal might become a dangerous area. No doubt the tension affected freight rates, and it is arguable that the risk of closure became part of the dickered terms. We do not deem the risk of closure so allocated, however. Foreseeability or even recognition of a risk does not necessarily prove its allocation. Parties to a contract are not always able to provide for all the possibilities of which they are aware, sometimes because they cannot agree, often simply because they are too busy. Moreover, that some abnormal risk was contemplated is probative but does not necessarily establish an allocation of the risk of the contingency which actually occurs. In this case, for example, nationalization by Egypt of the Canal Corporation and formation of the Suez Users Group did not necessarily indicate that the Canal would be blocked even if a confrontation resulted. The surrounding circumstances do indicate, however, a willingness by Transatlantic to assume abnormal risks, and this fact should legitimately cause us to judge the impracticability of performance by an alternative route in stricter terms than we would were the contingency unforeseen.

We turn then to the question whether occurrence of the contingency rendered performance commercially impracticable under the circumstances of this case. The goods shipped were not subject to harm from the longer, less temperate Southern route. The vessel and crew were fit to proceed around the Cape. Transatlantic was no less able than the United States to purchase insurance to cover the contingency's occurrence. If anything, it is more reasonable to expect owner–operators of vessels to insure against the hazards of war. They are in the best position to calculate the cost of performance by alternative routes (and therefore to estimate the amount of insurance required), and are undoubtedly sensitive to international troubles that uniquely affect the demand for and cost of their services. The only factor operating here in appellant's favor is the added expense, allegedly $43,972.00 above and beyond the contract price of $305,842.92, of extending a 10,000-mile voyage by approximately 3,000 miles. While it may be an overstatement to say that increased cost and difficulty of performance never constitute impracticability, to justify relief there must be more of a variation between expected cost and the cost of performing by an available alternative than is present in this case, where the promisor can legitimately be presumed to have accepted some degree of abnormal risk, and where impracticability is urged on the basis of added expense alone.

We conclude, therefore, as have most other courts considering related issues arising out of the Suez closure, that performance of this contract was not rendered legally impossible.

Affirmed.

Questions

1. *a.* What did the court find with respect to the private law of the parties?

   b. What did it find with respect to the application of custom?

2. Would the result in this case be different if the shipment had been tomatoes as opposed to wheat? Explain.

3. Would the result in this case be different if the United States and Transatlantic agreed by contract that shipment was to arrive in Iran within a period of time that was only possible if the shipper used the canal route? Explain.

4. What do you think it would take for a court to render a contract commercially impracticable? In this case, the shipper was forced to spend almost $44,000 more than it had expected to spend in performing the $306,000 contract. What if the added cost had amounted to $100,000? Would you be persuaded that the contract was then commercially impracticable? What if the closing of the canal doubled the price of the contract? Explain.

Comity

The unique aspect of public international law is that countries are generally not subject to law in the international arena unless they consent to such jurisdiction. For instance, a country is not bound by a treaty unless that country has signed the treaty. A country is not bound by international custom unless it has traditionally participated in that custom. Prior judicial decisions are only persuasive if a country is convinced by and accepts these decisions as precedent. Perhaps the most critical element in understanding international law is recognizing that it is not "law" in the way we generally think of that term. Countries are not bound to abide by it except through *comity*. Comity is the concept that countries should abide by international custom, treaties, and other sources of international direction because that is the civil way to engage in relationships. Nations must respect one another and respect some basic principles of dealing in order to have effective relationships. Although some believe that the origins of law are in religion and its commandments, others argue that law derives from a natural tendency to prevent chaos. International law is an attempt to prevent chaos in the international arena through the application of universal or widely held principles. Comity is the means by which those principles are encouraged.

The concept of comity also includes the respect one country gives to the actions another country takes in its own territory. Specifically, as stated by the Second Circuit in *Finanz AG Zurich v. Banco Economico S.A.*,[44] comity includes "the recognition which one nation allows within its territory to the legislative, executive, or judicial acts of another nation." Under this principle, U.S. courts "ordinarily refuse to review acts of foreign governments and defer to proceedings taking place in foreign countries." Thus, the *Finanz* court held that a creditor could not sue in the United States to collect a debt that was subject to the jurisdiction of a bankruptcy proceeding in Brazil.

Regulation of International Trade

LO 16-7
Describe examples of the law governing international business in sales of goods, trade in-services, and employment.

As we have just seen, there is no such thing as one body of international law per se that regulates international contracts and trade. Instead, a contract between firms in different countries may be subject to the laws of one country or the other, depending on (1) whether it is a sales contract subject to the U.N. CISG, discussed below; (2) whether the contract itself stipulates the applicable law and forum in which a dispute will be heard; and (3) the rules regarding conflict of laws in each jurisdiction.

In addition, every country has domestic laws that regulate business conducted within its borders and that sometimes regulate its domestic firms outside of its borders. These laws govern the areas of employment-related activities and discrimination, product liability, intellectual property, antitrust and trade practices, and import taxes, to name a few. Consequently, a business owner may actually decide to market a good in one country over another simply because of that country's laws relating to the particular good or to commercial contracts in general. What follows is a brief look at several specific examples of the law governing international business. [For an extensive international trade law database, see **www.jus.uio.no/lm/**].

U.N. Convention on Contracts for the International Sale of Goods (CISG)

In 1988, 10 nations signed and became bound by the U.N. Convention on Contracts for the International Sale of Goods. At this writing, the CISG is enforceable in 85 nations. The CISG applies to contracts between parties of countries that have signed the convention and provides uniform rules for the sale of goods.

The CISG contains rules regarding the interpretation of contracts and negotiations and the form of contracts. Many obligations of the parties are enunciated by the CISG. For instance, the seller is required to deliver the goods and any documents relating to the goods, as well as to make sure that the goods conform to the contract terms. The buyer, on the other hand, is required to pay the contract price and to accept delivery of the goods. [For the Pace University CISG database, see **iicl.law.pace.edu/cisg/cisg**].

The CISG, however, does not answer all questions that may arise in a transaction. For instance, questions of a contract's validity are left to national law. As we saw in Chapter 6, under American law, an enforceable contract requires five elements:

- *Capacity* to enter the contract.
- *Offer and acceptance* of the terms of the contract.
- *Consideration* for the promises in the contract.
- *Genuineness of assent.*
- *Legality of purpose* of the contract.

Countries with civil law systems do not, however, require consideration for a valid contract.

International Trade in Services

Services, as opposed to goods, are the largest component of the world's gross domestic product, accounting for 62.6 percent in 2015.[45] In the United States, this percentage is even higher—services were 79.5 percent of gross national product (GNP) in 2015.[46] Furthermore, trade in services represents about 33 percent of the total dollar value of U.S. exports.[47] The United States isn't the only country exporting services. The popular press continues to report on the "outsourcing" and "offshoring" of U.S. service-sector jobs. Outsourcing generally refers to the contracting by U.S. companies of such services as call centers, accounting, and customer services to foreign companies located in low-wage markets. Offshoring refers to U.S. companies setting up their own offices in foreign low-wage markets to perform services previously done by U.S. employees. Economists argue about whether the net effect on jobs in the United States is negative (through the direct loss of jobs) or positive (through corporate and consumer cost savings that permit job growth in the United States).[48]

What international agreements exist to regulate trade in services? Although international trade in goods has been the subject of international agreement since shortly after WWII, until 1994 no similar agreement existed covering international trade in services. This was remedied with the creation of the General Agreement on Trade in Services (GATS), which is now one of the foundation agreements along with the General Agreement on Tariffs and Trade (GATT) to which all member countries of the World Trade Organization (WTO) must subscribe. [The foundation agreements can be found at the WTO website, in the document area, at **www.wto.org**].

The GATS agreement, still in its infancy, sets forth the general principles for the future of trade in services across borders, but at this time requires very little of member countries in moving toward the realization of those principles. Rather, it sets the stage for future negotiations to reduce barriers to trade in services. The services covered by GATS, and therefore by such negotiations, are broad: "any service in any sector except services supplied in the exercise of governmental authority."[49]

Two important general principles that govern international services negotiations are

- *Most favored nation (MFN) status.* WTO members get treatment by the host country no less favorable than that given to suppliers from any other country, whether or not the other country is a member of the WTO.
- *National treatment.* The national treatment standard calls for a comparison of the treatment accorded to suppliers from WTO member countries with the treatment accorded to domestic suppliers. As a general rule, the treatment is to be "no less favorable" than that received by domestic suppliers.

Question

The WTO member nations have only recently turned their consideration to the barriers between nations that impede the flow of services across boundaries. In the professions, such as medicine, law, and accounting, substantial barriers currently exist. Some barriers are in the form of domestic licensure requirements, which in turn often require a particular educational background for the applicant. Would establishing a clearinghouse for educational equivalencies around the world and requiring WTO members to honor the educational achievements received by applicants in other member countries be a good idea? Why or why not?

Employment-Related Regulations

Social responsibility principles such as those in the U.N. Universal Declaration of Human Rights set aspirational goals for countries and business managers, but they are not enforceable laws. In the absence of enforceable global labor standards, MNEs are left with the obligation to apply substantially varying laws to their employees in different jurisdictions, as well as perhaps having to adhere to their home country laws that have extraterritorial application, such as Title VII for U.S. companies. That said, globalization has transformed workplace governance worldwide, both for good and for ill. A government seeking to improve domestic labor conditions can look to policies and practices that have been successful in other countries, but a government more focused on developing a competitive advantage may specifically exploit its lower labor standards, such as low wages, to attract direct investment by foreign businesses, as seems to be the case for Bangladeshi garment workers as previously discussed.

Even within countries with protective labor regimes, responsible MNEs may be challenged by legal compliance requirements. Not only do substantive laws differ (for example, Germany requires a company to either hire the disabled or pay for an exclusion), but required procedures governing employer–employee relationships vary tremendously. For example, as a result of the recent global recession, an MNE might reasonably determine that a reduction in force across its operations is prudent. Managing such a decision equitably and effectively could be a daunting task. In many countries, nearly all employees may be covered by a works council or trade union with whom the MNE might be required to negotiate a reduction, whereas in the United States less than 10 percent of employees outside the public sector are covered by collective bargaining agreements.[50] In the Netherlands, the government must approve most layoffs; in Columbia, Venezuela, Japan, and China, a successful reduction in force might require either agency or court approval. In Europe, an employer even considering such a reduction must consult in good faith with employees about avoiding or mitigating such an action, even if the reduction policy was set by the board of directors at its foreign headquarters.[51] Similar issues can face MNEs involved in international mergers or acquisitions.

Compulsory Retirement

In late 2007, the European Court of Justice ruled that the European Framework Directive on Equal Treatment, which prohibits unjustified age discrimination in the workplace, applied to national laws requiring age-based compulsory retirement. The case challenged a Spanish law permitting employers to impose a compulsory retirement age. Although the court held the Directive applied to the Spanish law, it nevertheless ruled that the Spanish legislation was a lawful, appropriate means of achieving a legitimate government aim. The law had been passed during a period of high unemployment in Spain and was intended to further a national policy for a better distribution of work between generations.

As discussed in Chapter 13, in the United States, the Age Discrimination in Employment Act (ADEA) prohibits discrimination on the basis of age against individuals who are 40 or older. It applies to decisions to hire or fire, as well as to discriminatory compensation or other terms or conditions of employment. Interestingly, a narrow exception allows universities to require retirement of tenured faculty who reach the age of 70. The ADEA specifically applies to American citizens employed overseas by American companies.

Questions

1. A U.S. corporation operates a branch in Spain. Consistent with Spanish law, it adopts a compulsory retirement age of 62. Is this a violation of the ADEA?

2. Which policy do you favor—the Spanish or the American approach to compulsory retirement? Why? Is this an issue over which countries should be allowed to differ?

Intellectual Property Regulations

LO 16-8
Identify and describe the four main forms of intellectual property covered in the text and the international agreements that govern them.

Intellectual property, most broadly, refers to creations of the mind. As used here, it refers more specifically to creations of the mind for which legal protection is given, especially trade secrets, trademarks, patents, and copyrights. It is a form of personal property or *personalty,* which is the legal term used to denote all forms of property, both tangible and intangible, other than real property or realty. *Realty* is comprised only of land or real estate and items permanently affixed to the land, such as buildings.

The commercial significance of intellectual property has grown tremendously; by one estimate, "70% of the value of publicly traded corporations is estimated to be in 'intangible assets.'"[52] Theft of intellectual property has also grown tremendously; dollar losses amount to hundreds of billions annually, with China named as the world's largest source of theft.[53] Clearly then, understanding the legal protections available for intellectual property is of significant importance to business managers. The greatest losses are suffered by U.S., European, and Japanese business; the largest threats originate from China, India, and Russia.

Even though cybersecurity issues are often in the news, a lot of theft occurs in other manners, such as when "[hard] drives are either duplicated on site or physically stolen by bribed employees; employees . . . leave and illegally share proprietary information; products are dissected, re-engineered, and sold without permission or payment of royalties; . . . [and] phones are tapped for the purpose of obtaining trade secrets."[54] A *trade secret* can be almost any information that has economic value because it is not generally known what a business makes reasonable efforts to keep secret to secure an advantage over its competition.

[For more information on the theft of intellectual property, see the report of the Commission on the Theft of American Intellectual Property, which can be found at **http://ipcommission.org**].

Trademarks

A *trademark* distinguishes the source of a particular good or service, whether that is accomplished by a trade name, packaging, logo, or other distinguishing mark. When the law protects a trademark, it grants to the holder of the mark a limited monopoly: No one else may use that mark without the holder's permission. Under the Tariff Act of 1930, it is unlawful to import goods bearing a trademark registered with the Patent and Trademark Office that is "owned by a citizen of, or by a corporation or association . . . organized within the United States" without the permission of the mark holder.

This provision safeguards a U.S. trademark holder's rights in the United States from infringement by foreign actors. But what about an American company that wants to obtain trademark protection in other countries? Each country has distinct trademark regulations and offers different levels of protection to marks registered in other countries. For example, a battle that lasted nearly a century ended in early 2013 when the EU General Court in Luxembourg ruled that the Czech brewer Budvar could not assert exclusive use of either "Bud" or "Budweiser" throughout the EU because its use of the names was not sufficiently widespread. Anheuser-Busch InBev had claimed use of the Budweiser name as early as 1876, almost 20 years before Budvar was formed.[55]

As of this writing, 176 countries including the United States are parties to a treaty that provides protection for trademarks, known as the *Paris Convention*.[56] More formally called the International Convention for the Protection of Industrial Property, it was originally signed by 11 countries in 1883. According to the Paris Convention, subject to several exceptions, member countries ensure trademark protection to marks registered in other member countries. The convention also provides for *national treatment,* which requires that any individual claiming infringement must have the same protection as would a national of that country. A member country may not favor its own nationals over foreigners. Another treaty, the Madrid Agreement Concerning the International Registration of Marks, attempts to create an international trademark system. If a holder registers a trademark with the World Intellectual Property Organization (WIPO) in Switzerland, that mark is protected in all member countries requested by the holder. A 1989 Protocol relating to the Madrid agreement aimed to render the Madrid system more flexible and more compatible with the domestic legislations of certain countries which had not been able to accede to the Agreement."[57] The United States is a party to the Protocol but has not acceded to the Agreement. [For extensive information on WIPO, see **www.wipo.int**].

Nevertheless, trademark issues still arise between countries, even when both are parties to the Paris Convention and the Madrid Agreement or Protocol. For example, after two French courts found Google guilty of infringing on the Louis Vuitton trademark, the highest French court sought a ruling under EU trademark law from the European Court of Justice (ECJ). At issue was Google's AdWords service, pursuant to which Google sold ad space to a Vuitton competitor next to the search results returned anytime "Louis Vuitton" was entered as a search phrase. The ECJ determined that Google had not impermissibly "used" the Louis Vuitton trademark if its role proved to be "merely technical, automatic and passive," and it had not been active in "drafting the commercial message" displayed by the competitor.[58]

Patents

A *patent* is a monopoly on a product, process, or device where the item or process claimed is an innovation, unique and inventive, and useful. The Paris Convention covers patents as well as trademarks; however, it does not establish a network of protection, even among member countries. Patents granted in different member countries for the same invention are independent of each other. However, the convention does establish a *right of priority,* which gives a patent applicant filing in one member nation one year from the original filing to file in other member countries and have the subsequent filings treated as if made on the date of the first filing. Nevertheless, because a patent must be original to be registered in any country, many countries hold that patents previously awarded in other countries automatically preclude additional patent registration.

Other issues have made the international enforcement of a patent quite challenging. For example, the United States has long awarded patents on a first-to-create basis, whereas most other nations have used a first-to-file rule in cases of multiple applicants. Following the passage of the America Invents Act in 2011, effective March 16, 2013, the United States adopted the first-to-file rule. Europe also seems on the brink of simplifying the patent process across most of the European Union. In late 2012, the European Parliament voted in favor of the creation of a single patent, recognized automatically in 25 EU countries (Italy and Spain have not joined in) without the need to file separately in each country, accompanied with a translation into that country's national tongue.[59] [For more information on the EU's unitary patent, see **https://ec.europa.eu/growth/industry/intellectual-property/patents_en**].

Copyrights

A *copyright* is a government grant giving the copyright holder exclusive control over the reproduction of a literary, musical, or artistic work. Most developed nations provide copyright protection within their borders, but many also belong to international copyright protection pacts. The Berne Convention of 1886 and the Universal Copyright Convention (UCC) of 1952 both provide a measure of international protection against the unauthorized reproduction of books, photos, drawings, movies, and the like. Copyright protection extends for a period provided by national law. For example, in the United States, a copyright currently spans the author's life plus 70 years. The United States is a party to the UCC and the Berne Convention.

The case below points out that formal accession to an international treaty does not necessarily lead to satisfactory compliance in the view of other signatories.

Golan v. Holder
132 S. Ct. 873 (2012)

Justice Ginsburg

The Berne Convention . . . is the principal accord governing international copyright relations. Latecomer to the international copyright regime launched by Berne, the United States joined the Convention in 1989. To perfect U.S. implementation of Berne, . . . Congress, in 1994 [through enactment of] § 514 of the Uruguay Round Agreements Act (URAA) [, extended] copyright protection to preexisting works of Berne member countries, protected in their country of origin, but lacking protection in the United States for any of three reasons: The United States did not protect works from the country of origin at the time of publication; the United States did not protect sound recordings fixed before 1972; or the author had failed to comply with . . . formalities Congress no longer requires as prerequisites to copyright protection.

The URAA accords no protection to a foreign work after its full copyright term has expired, causing it to fall into the public domain, whether under the laws of the country of origin or of this country. Works encompassed by § 514 are granted the protection they would have enjoyed had the United States maintained copyright relations with the author's country or removed formalities incompatible with Berne. Foreign authors, however, gain no credit for the protection they lacked in years prior to § 514's enactment. They therefore enjoy fewer total years of exclusivity than do their U.S. counterparts. As a consequence of the barriers to U.S. copyright protection prior to the enactment of § 514, foreign works "restored" to protection by the measure had entered the public domain in this country. . . .

Petitioners include orchestra conductors, musicians, publishers, and others who formerly enjoyed free access to works § 514 removed from the public domain. They maintain that the Constitution's Copyright and Patent Clause, Art. I, § 8, cl. 8, and First Amendment both decree the invalidity of § 514. [All further reference to petitioners' First Amendment argument has been omitted.—ed.] Under those prescriptions of our highest law, petitioners assert, a work that has entered the public domain, for whatever reason, must forever remain there.

[W]e conclude that § 514 does not transgress constitutional limitations on Congress' authority. . . .

I

Members of the Berne Union agree to treat authors from other member countries as well as they treat their own. . . . Each country, moreover, must afford at least the minimum level of protection specified by Berne. The copyright term must span the author's lifetime, plus at least 50 additional years, whether or not the author has complied with a member state's legal formalities. And, as relevant here, a work must be protected abroad unless its copyright term has expired in either the country where protection is claimed or the country of origin.

A different system of transnational copyright protection long prevailed in this country. Until 1891, foreign works were categorically excluded from Copyright Act protection. Throughout most of the 20th century, the only eligible foreign authors were those whose countries granted reciprocal rights to U.S. authors and whose works were printed in the United States. For domestic and foreign authors alike, protection hinged on compliance with notice, registration, and renewal formalities.

The United States became party to Berne's multilateral, formality-free copyright regime in 1989. Initially, Congress adopted a "minimalist approach" to compliance with the Convention. The Berne Convention Implementation Act of 1988 (BCIA) . . . accorded no protection for "any work that is in the public domain in the United States." . . . Congress indicated, however, that it had not definitively rejected "retroactive" protection for preexisting foreign works; instead it had punted on this issue of Berne's implementation, deferring consideration until "a more thorough examination of Constitutional, commercial, and consumer considerations is possible."

The minimalist approach essayed by the United States did not sit well with other Berne members. . . . Mexican authorities complained about the United States' refusal to grant protection . . . to Mexican works that remained under copyright domestically. The Register of Copyrights also reported "questions" from Turkey, Egypt, and Austria. Thailand and Russia balked at protecting U.S. works, copyrighted here but in those countries' public domains, until the United States reciprocated with respect to their authors' works.

Berne, however, did not provide a potent enforcement mechanism. . . .

The landscape changed in 1994. The Uruguay round of multilateral trade negotiations produced the World Trade Organization (WTO) and the Agreement on Trade-Related Aspects of Intellectual Property Rights (TRIPS). The United States joined both. TRIPS mandates, on pain of WTO enforcement, implementation of Berne's first 21 articles. The WTO gave teeth to the Convention's requirements: Noncompliance with a WTO ruling could subject member countries to tariffs or cross-sector retaliation. The specter of WTO enforcement proceedings bolstered the credibility of our trading partners' threats to challenge the United States for inadequate compliance with Article 18.

Congress' response to the Uruguay agreements put to rest any questions concerning U.S. compliance with Article 18. Section 514 of the URAA extended copyright to works that garnered protection in their countries of origin, but had no right to exclusivity in the United States for any of [the previously listed] three reasons. . . .

. . . Copyrights "restored" under URAA § 514 "subsist for the remainder of the term of copyright that the work would have otherwise been granted . . . if the work never entered the public domain." Prospectively, restoration places foreign works on an equal footing with their U.S. counterparts; assuming a foreign and domestic author died the same day, their works will enter the public domain simultaneously. . . .

The URAA's disturbance of the public domain hardly escaped Congress' attention. Section 514 imposed no liability for any use of foreign works occurring before restoration. In addition, anyone remained free to copy and use restored works for one year following § 514's enactment. . . .

In 2001, petitioners filed this lawsuit challenging § 514. . . .

II

We first address petitioners' argument that Congress lacked authority, under the Copyright Clause, to enact § 514. The Constitution states that "Congress shall have Power . . . [t]o promote the Progress of Science . . . by securing for limited Times to Authors . . . the exclusive Right to their . . . Writings." Art. I, § 8, cl. 8. Petitioners find in this grant of authority an impenetrable barrier to the extension of copyright protection to authors whose writings, for whatever reason, are in the public domain. We see no such barrier in the text of the Copyright Clause, historical practice, or our precedents.

. . . Petitioners' contrary argument relies primarily on the Constitution's confinement of a copyright's lifespan to a "limited Tim[e]." "Removing works from the public domain," they contend, "violates the 'limited [t]imes' restriction by turning a fixed and predictable period into one that can be reset or resurrected at any time, even after it expires."

Our decision in *Eldred* [*v. Ashcroft*] is largely dispositive of petitioners' limited-time argument. There we addressed the question whether Congress violated the Copyright Clause when it extended, by 20 years, the terms of existing copyrights [in the Copyright Term Extension Act (CTEA)]. Ruling that Congress acted within constitutional bounds, we declined to infer from the text of the Copyright Clause "the command that a time prescription, once set, becomes forever 'fixed' or 'inalterable.'" "The word 'limited,'" we observed, . . . is best understood to mean "confine[d] within certain bounds," "restrain[ed]," or "circumscribed." . . .

The terms afforded works restored by § 514 are no less "limited" than those the CTEA lengthened. In light of *Eldred,* petitioners do not here contend that the term Congress has granted U.S. authors—their lifetimes, plus 70 years—is unlimited. Nor do petitioners explain why terms of the same duration, as applied to foreign works, are not equally "circumscribed" and "confined." . . .

The difference, petitioners say, is that the limited time had already passed for works in the public domain. What was that limited term for foreign works once excluded from U.S. copyright protection? Exactly "zero," petitioners respond. We find scant sense in this argument, for surely a "limited time" of exclusivity must begin before it may end. . . .

Historical practice corroborates our reading of the Copyright Clause to permit full U.S. compliance with Berne. . . .

On occasion . . . Congress has seen fit to protect works once freely available. Notably, the Copyright Act of 1790 granted protection to many works previously in the public domain. Before the Act launched a uniform national system, three States provided no statutory copyright protection at all. Of those that did afford some protection, seven failed to protect maps; eight did not cover previously published books; and all ten denied protection to works that failed to comply with formalities. The First Congress, it thus appears, did not view the public domain as inviolate. . . .

Congress has also passed generally applicable legislation granting patents and copyrights to inventions and works that had lost protection. An 1832 statute authorized a new patent for any inventor whose failure, "by inadvertence, accident, or mistake," to comply with statutory formalities rendered the original patent "invalid or inoperative." An 1893 measure similarly allowed authors who had not timely deposited their work to receive "all the rights and privileges" the Copyright Act affords, if they made the required deposit by March 1, 1893. And in 1919 and 1941, Congress authorized the President to issue proclamations granting protection to foreign works that had fallen into the public domain during World Wars I and II. . . .

Installing a federal copyright system and ameliorating the interruptions of global war, it is true, presented Congress with extraordinary situations. Yet the TRIPS accord, leading the United States to comply in full measure with Berne, was also a signal event. Given the authority we hold Congress has, we will not second-guess the political choice Congress made between leaving the public domain untouched and embracing Berne unstintingly.

Petitioners' ultimate argument as to the Copyright and Patent Clause concerns its initial words. Congress is empowered to "promote the Progress of Science and useful Arts" by enacting systems of copyright and patent protection. . . .

The "Progress of Science," petitioners acknowledge, refers broadly to "the creation and spread of knowledge and learning." They nevertheless argue that federal legislation cannot serve the Clause's aim unless the legislation "spur[s] the creation of . . . new works." . . .

. . . In *Eldred,* . . . we held that the Copyright Clause does not demand that each copyright provision, examined discretely, operate to induce new works. Rather, we explained, the Clause "empowers Congress to determine the intellectual property regimes that, overall, in that body's judgment, will serve the ends of the Clause." . . .

. . . Congress rationally could have concluded that adherence to Berne "promotes the diffusion of knowledge." A well-functioning international copyright system would likely encourage the dissemination of existing and future works. Full compliance with Berne,

Congress had reason to believe, would expand the foreign markets available to U.S. authors and invigorate protection against piracy of U.S. works abroad, thereby benefitting copyright-intensive industries stateside and inducing greater investment in the creative process.

. . . Congress determined that exemplary adherence to Berne would serve the objectives of the Copyright Clause. We have no warrant to reject the rational judgment Congress made.

Affirmed.

Questions

1. What does it mean to say that a work is in the "public domain"?
2. *a.* If you were a Canadian composer in 1950 with a new orchestral piece, fully protected under the copyright laws of Canada (a Berne signatory), what would you have had to do to protect your work in the United States (based on the law as it is presented in *Golan*)?

   b. If you were a Canadian composer in 2005 under similar facts?
3. Before Congress passed § 514 of the URAA, what could petitioners do that, after the legislation, was no longer legal?
4. In the words of the Court, why did "Congress have reason to believe" that full compliance with the Berne Convention "would expand the foreign markets available to U.S. authors and invigorate protection against piracy of U.S. works abroad"? Explain.

Agreement on Trade-Related Aspects of Intellectual Property

It can be said that a solid international system for effective protection of intellectual property does not yet exist. That said, the Agreement on Trade-Related Aspects of Intellectual Property (TRIPS) mentioned by the Court in *Golan v. Holder* is having a positive effect. As one of the foundation agreements to which all WTO member countries must subscribe, the provisions of TRIPS are enforceable through the WTO Dispute Settlement Body, which is discussed later in this chapter. TRIPS establishes certain minimum levels of protection for copyrights, trademarks, and patents, and also requires WTO members to adopt effective enforcement measures. Whether members are effectively enforcing its provisions remains an issue regularly raised in WTO settings.

Regulation of Multinational Enterprises (MNEs)

With globalization, the number of MNEs has vastly expanded. Precisely because MNE operations span the globe, regulating their activities has become quite difficult. For example, the health risks from smoking tobacco have been well established, and there are now 180 signatories to the Framework Convention on Tobacco Control, which was negotiated under the auspices of the World Trade Organization and addresses controls on ingredients, packaging, marketing, cessation programs, and smoke-free spaces, all proven to reduce smoking. Yet, tobacco companies "are aggressively recruiting new customers in developing nations."[60] Philip Morris, whose annual sales were twice Uruguay's gross domestic product, even went as far as suing Uruguay in 2010, claiming that its regulations were excessive. As the head of the Convention's Tobacco Free Initiative stated, "[t]hey're using litigation to threaten low- and middle-income countries."[61] [For more on the Convention, see **www.who.int/fctc/en**].

In the absence of effective international regulatory regimes, which do not currently exist, MNEs also face challenges in trying to comply with many different overlapping, often contradictory, national regulatory schemes. Countries that impose regulatory requirements on MNEs may, in any given circumstance, be viewed with approval, be accused of "regulatory imperialism,"[62] or be charged with domestic protectionism.[63] One of the growing issues impacting the effective regulation of MNEs is the growth of state-owned companies, in both number and size. As of 2011, they made up 19 of the world's 100 largest MNEs and 28 of the top 100 emerging market companies, and were found in almost every industry.[64] Many are effectively monopolies at home; many are very active abroad. How they will and can be effectively regulated outside of their home countries is unknown.

We now consider five additional areas of governmental oversight: securities regulation, imposition of financial accounting and auditing standards, anticompetitive restraints of trade, mergers, and import and export restrictions. The U.S. law covering most of these areas was presented in Chapters 9 through 11. Here we will look at their international dimensions, particularly with regard to overseeing the behavior of MNEs.

Securities Regulation

> The SEC has been "the cop on the beat for the world's securities markets."

Most people in the business world are aware of numerous corporate financial scandals that rocked the world around the turn of the millennium: Enron and WorldCom in the United States, Barings Bank in the United Kingdom, HIH Insurance in Australia, and Parmalat in Italy, to name a few. In the United States, the Securities and Exchange Commission (SEC) has long played a major role in uncovering and pursuing financial corporate wrongdoing. But it also has a reputation outside the United States, as one commentator put it, "as the cop on the beat for the world's securities markets."[65] The SEC has a broad reach because of its jurisdiction to regulate all companies that choose to list their equity or debt securities on any U.S. securities market, such as the New York Stock Exchange. But its reach has long been thought to stretch even farther, through the extraterritorial application of the fraud provisions in U.S. securities laws. The application of those laws to foreign companies that list their securities on a U.S. exchange is not an extraterritorial application because those companies have voluntarily availed themselves of U.S. capital markets. But what about foreign companies not so listed that act wrongfully (in light of U.S. law) such that their conduct has a substantial negative effect in the United States or upon U.S. citizens? In a 2010 case, the Supreme Court held the fraud provisions were only intended to apply within the United States.[66] Within a month, however, Congress passed the Dodd–Frank Act, making clear the extraterritorial enforcement powers of the SEC and the U.S. Department of Justice. From Chapter 9, you know that another powerful tool for the enforcement of our securities laws is the ability of harmed investors to bring private suits against violators. Congress has not counteracted the Supreme Court interpretation in that regard.

Accounting Standards

An important component of securities regulation is the establishment of the financial accounting standards that underlie financial statements provided to the public. In the United States, accounting standards are under the authority of the SEC. Internationally, however, the growth in the number of MNEs and the integration of the world's capital markets have propelled the development of financial accounting standards that could be applied transnationally. In 2001, one set of such standards, International Financial Reporting Standards (IFRS), was offered for adoption by the International Accounting Standards Board (IASB) based in London. Over 100 countries, including the entire European Union, have implemented these standards, although many have adopted local variations. In 2006, the IASB and the SEC initiated a harmonization project, generally referred to as convergence, between U.S. Generally Accepted Accounting Principles (GAAP) and IFRS. The process was intended to eliminate major differences so that investors could more readily make comparative evaluations among companies regardless of their home country. Whether there will be universal adoption of either system seems highly unlikely as of this writing.[67] However, the European Union permits U.S. companies to file GAAP financial statements without requiring reconciliation to IFRS, and the SEC permits foreign corporations to file IFRS financial statements (so long as there are no local variations) without reconciliation to GAAP.

The establishment of accounting standards is only one aspect necessary for reliable disclosure to make it into the hands of current and future investors. Independent audits of companies' books also need to be done and by auditors with appropriate credentials. This is not difficult for American companies with audit firms that practice in the United States. However, when foreign companies are listed on a U.S. stock exchange, U.S. investors need to know that the financial statements of those companies are reliable. Accounting fraud at Chinese companies has been much in the news for several years. The headline of one *Wall Street Journal* article in 2012 began, "Accounting fraud and China have become synonymous for many investors."[68] Accounting firms auditing foreign companies need to be registered with and regularly inspected by the U.S. Public Company Accounting Oversight Board (PCAOB). For Chinese companies listed on U.S. exchanges, this was commonly accomplished by having audits done by Chinese affiliates of the Big Four auditing firms. Then China changed its regulations and required that such affiliates be owned by a majority of Chinese partners, while refusing to allow the PCAOB to inspect the Chinese firms. In May 2013, some progress was made when China agreed to give the PCAOB access to documents from the Chinese firms that are necessary for the board to fulfill its oversight responsibilities. However, the agreement did not allow the PCAOB into China to inspect the Chinese audit firms, nor did it allow the SEC to obtain documents relevant to its fraud investigations.[69] In October 2015, the agreement fell through, and as of this writing, no further agreement has been reached.[70] For the time being, investors in Chinese companies still need to take to heart the adage, "buyer beware." [For more information on the IASB and IFRS, see **www.ifrs.org**].

Choice of Nationality? A Cautionary Tale

In today's world, a corporation is generally free to choose its "nationality"—that is, its home country, the country in which it will establish its legal existence or, using U.S. terminology, the country in which it will incorporate. That nation's laws will govern the relationship between the entity and its owners—that is, the corporate governance rules it must follow—as well as the accounting standards with which it must comply. If incorporated outside of the United States, it will only become subject to U.S. securities laws if it chooses to list its securities on a U.S. exchange. Unlike other countries, the United States taxes U.S. corporations on their worldwide income, not just the income earned in the

United States. Thus, if a business incorporates outside the country, it may avoid significant U.S. taxes, substantial U.S. regulation, and the extraterritorial application of U.S. laws. As a foreign corporation, only its U.S. income is subject to U.S. taxes, and its financial reporting requirements are much less than those discussed in Chapter 9. Financial reporting for foreign corporations has been deliberately lessened, precisely to make listing securities more attractive to foreign businesses.

Consider, too, a company's choice as to the place of incorporation for its subsidiaries. For some businesses, a significant source of profits derives from royalty and licensing fees generated by its intellectual property. Thus, a common tax strategy is to incorporate subsidiaries to hold valuable intellectual properties, like patents, in low-tax jurisdictions. Thus, Apple established subsidiaries in Ireland, the Netherlands, Luxembourg, and the British Virgin Islands. "When customers across Europe, Africa or the Middle East . . . download a song, television show or app, the sale is recorded" in Luxembourg.[71] Quite legally, 70 percent of Apple's profits were allocated to its non-U.S. entities and were subject to little tax.[72] Or so Apple thought. In 2016, the EU assessed Apple $14.6 billion in back taxes, plus interest, finding that Ireland gave tax breaks specific to the company—illegal under EU state aid rules—and artificially lowered Apple's tax bill for over 20 years. In effect, Apple had been paying taxes to Ireland at a rate of 1% or less, well below the 35% top marginal rate in the U.S. and Ireland's normal 12.5% rate.[73]

Questions

1. Many companies are legally and advantageously moving some of their income tax liabilities out of the United States. Is this a good trend? Is it equitable? Consider smaller companies without the resources for such sophisticated tax advice. What about profit-comparable companies that suffer higher taxes because their revenues come from physical sales sourced in the U.S. rather than from sales of intellectual property that can be effectively sourced elsewhere? What about countries that can collect taxes from businesses that have little physical presence within their borders other than an office with a mailing address? If there are inequities, what might bring them back into balance?

2. Ireland insists that it will fight the EU's $14.6 billion tax assessment against Apple. It also insists that it has complete jurisdiction to determine its own tax laws. The EU disagrees. It maintains that the tax break breached EU laws on state aid. Should Apple be subject to over 20 years' worth of back taxes, given that it established a subsidiary in Ireland in exchange for the special tax break? Did Apple do its due diligence to determine whether the tax break was legitimate? Should it have considered the fact that Ireland is part of the EU, and whether the tax break that Ireland offered would be prohibited by the EU?

Anticompetitive Restraints

Many countries regulate anticompetitive behaviors such as collusion among competitors and abuse of monopoly power. Two prominent examples involve Microsoft and Google, both of which have been challenged for anticompetitive behaviors in both the United States and Europe.

Microsoft has repeatedly been charged with abusing its monopoly market power in computer operating systems (Windows) to provide an advantage for its browser (Internet Explorer), media player, and servers. In the United States alone, Microsoft faced three successive bouts of litigation brought by the U.S. Department of Justice, as well as numerous suits by private plaintiffs, resulting in payment of substantial settlement sums and long-term government oversight. Microsoft's actions have also been scrutinized by the European Commission (EC) for violations of the EU's Competition Law, suffering an adverse decision and substantial fines in 2004 in a dispute that began in 1998. Then, in 2008, the EC opened another investigation, which was settled when Microsoft agreed to load a ballot box on all new Windows 7 computers sold in Europe that would allow purchasers to select any one of 12 competing browsers. Four years later, the EC fined the company $732 million for failure to live up to the agreement.

Google may fare much worse. It underwent a two-year investigation by the Federal Trade Commission (FTC) and a hearing before the Senate antitrust panel over whether it had abused its dominant position in Internet search engines, in part by giving more prominent placement to its own services over those of its competitors in returning search results. The investigation was closed in 2013 and no charges were brought. However, it appears that the FTC may be starting another investigation, which may include the company's use of Android.[74] Meanwhile, the investigation by the European Commission covered abuse in both Internet search and advertising markets. As of this writing, the EC has charged Google with using Android to promote its digital services over those of its competitors and with two other antitrust charges. The company could be fined up to $7.5 billion, or 10% of its annual revenue, the statutory limit for an infringement of the anticompetition laws.[75]

Mergers

In May 2016, the European Commission approved the takeover of SABMiller, the world's second largest brewer (whose brands include Miller and Pilsner) by AB InBev, already the world's largest brewer (whose brands include Corona and Budweiser). Globally, the merged entity would sell twice as much beer and earn four times more profit than the third largest brewer, Heineken. In Europe, where Heineken is a market leader, the merger would bring together the third and fourth largest brewers by volume. The EC's approval under the EU's Merger Regulation was conditioned on AB InBev's offer to divest all of SABMiller's business in France, Italy, the Netherlands, and the United Kingdom, which it had already agreed to sell to a Japanese brewer, and to divest all of SABMiller's business in the Czech Republic, Hungary, Poland, Romania, and Slovakia. This, the European Commission agreed, would address concerns about the merger removing an important competitor from some markets and about it creating a substantial link, and the likelihood of tacit coordination, with still another competitor in other markets.[76] It is not uncommon for merger regulators to require accommodations to address antitrust national concerns before providing the required approval. Such national-level reviews and negotiations can be a significant cost for mergers and acquisitions involving MNEs. Although some bilateral agreements among countries are in place, the approximately 70 countries with merger review systems as yet do not have an agreement coordinating their processes—not even at the level of coordinating review thresholds, timetables, and required filings.[77]

Regulation of Trade

Import Tariffs

LO 16-9

Describe the purposes and effects of the General Agreement on Tariffs and Trade (GATT) and the General Agreement on Trade in Services (GATS).

The General Agreement on Tariffs and Trade (GATT), now governed by the WTO, regulates import duties among signatory countries to reduce barriers to trade and to ensure fair treatment. Without GATT, it is argued, countries with stronger markets would be able to secure better deals on imports than would other countries. In addition, countries with strong market economies could use the threat of higher import taxes as a bargaining chip in other negotiations. To limit such discriminatory practices, the concepts of MFN status and national treatment are integral to GATT, just as they are to GATS, as discussed earlier in the context of international trade in services. Thus, under GATT, a reduced tariff offered to one WTO member country must be offered to all WTO members and, once a good has been imported, it must be treated just as domestic goods are treated. That, at any rate, is the ideal. In practice GATT has not actually done away with nonconforming tariffs. Rather, it prohibits countries from moving farther away from the ideal, while providing successive rounds of multilateral trade negotiations to encourage countries to collectively move forward on achieving these goals.

A Closer Look at U.S. Tariffs

Assessing tariffs runs counter to the avowed goal of free trade. In addition, there seems to be little logic behind some of the disparities in tariffs imposed by particular countries. Consider, for example, the United States' assessment of an 8.5 percent import duty on women's wool suits, while no import duties were imposed on men's suits. Furthermore, when one considers all of the tariffs the United States assesses on imports, it is evident that the assessment across countries is neither even nor fair. In 2006, both France and Cambodia paid $367 million in duties to the United States; but for its payment, France was able to import $36.8 billion in goods, whereas Cambodia was able to import only $2.2 billion in goods.[78]

Questions

1. Who in the United States is hurt by the tariffs described above? Who in the United States is advantaged by them?

2. Why might U.S. tariffs be friendlier to French products than Cambodian goods?

Export Restrictions

LO 16-10

Discuss how and why nations regulate imports and exports.

Imports are regulated to protect American businesses. Exports by American businesses, on the other hand, may be regulated for several reasons. Specifically, the U.S. Export Administration Act of 1979 permits restrictions on goods and technology where exportation would harm national security, or where restriction would significantly advance U.S. foreign policy, prevent an excessive drain of scarce materials, or reduce serious inflationary impacts from foreign demand. [To learn more about U.S. import and export practices, see **www.cbp.gov/trade**].

Rare Earth Elements

China controls 93 percent of the production of rare earth elements—metals less scarce than precious metals but still relatively rare. Many of these metals have turned out to be important to a wide range of green technologies, such as those used in wind turbines and in the electric motors for the Toyota Prius and Chevrolet Volt. They are also used in the electric motors in some U.S. missile guidance systems. China has been reducing production and exports of such metals to ensure it has an adequate supply for its own needs and to reduce environmental damage from the mines.[79] In 2011, a WTO panel held China's export control impermissible. It noted that the proffered environmental concerns had not resulted in reduced mine production.[80] The panel's decision was affirmed on appeal in 2012.[81]

Question

If these actions were being taken by the United States instead of China, do you think they would be defensible under the Export Administration Act? Why or why not?

Fair Trade Regulations: Dumping and Subsidies

To promote fair trade, the WTO prohibits the practice of *dumping*. Dumping occurs when a manufacturer sells its goods in a foreign country for less than their normal value. If this practice causes or threatens material injury to a domestic or established foreign manufacturer in the foreign country, the act is prohibited. The price is considered less than normal value if it is less than the price charged in the producer's home country. A firm may want to dump its goods in a foreign market for two reasons. First, its home market may be saturated and cannot support any further supply. For example, the U.S. has recently accused China of dumping cheap steel exports in an effort to keep China's steel mills running; there has been a downturn in China's economy, which cannot support previous levels of production. Alternatively, a firm may wish to establish itself and even drive other firms out of the foreign market. To do so, it might sell its goods in the foreign market at a price below those of its competitors, and then support that price with higher prices in its home country. After its competitors are forced out, the firm might set its prices at or above the normal level. In either case, GATT permits retaliatory duties to be imposed on countries that have dumped goods in other member countries.

The WTO also prohibits the payment of *unfair subsidies* by governments. This occurs when a government, perhaps in an effort to encourage growth in a certain industry, offers subsidies to producers in that industry. The producers are then able to sell their goods at a price that is substantially lower than those of their competitors. Subsidies are considered unfair when governments use them to promote export trade that harms another country. When unfair subsidization is found, the WTO permits the harmed country to impose countervailing duties on those products in an amount sufficient to counteract the effect of the offending subsidy. If a country believes that *countervailing duties* have been illegally imposed, it must either sue in the courts of the country imposing the duties, and under that country's laws, or take the dispute through the adjudication process provided by the WTO, discussed later in this chapter.

An ongoing dispute over solar panels illustrates many of these fair trade regulations. In what has been called "the world's largest antidumping and antisubsidy trade cases,"[82] both the United States and the European Union asserted that China has become the world's dominant producer of solar panels through the provision of subsidies in the form of favorable loans from state-owned banks and incentives provided by local and provincial governments to Chinese manufacturers.[83] They also argued that China was dumping its panels into Western markets at prices below its cost of production, resulting in more than 20 American and European manufacturers cutting back production or going bankrupt. In response, both the United States and the European Union imposed substantial tariffs on the importation of Chinese panels. China responded with a tariff of its own—on the importation of polysilicon, one of the main raw materials in the production of the panels. This was a move that didn't particularly harm Chinese panel producers because of the existence of an abundance of other sources for the polysilicon. As of this writing, the countries are in negotiations to find a solution to trade barriers. In any event, the U.S. Commerce Department lowered import duties in 2015 for most Chinese solar panel manufacturers, perhaps because the tariffs were artificially inflating prices and could slow the growth of the U.S. solar industry.[84]

Question

Why do developed countries such as the United States regulate trade through the mechanisms described in this section? Why might a less developed country do so?

Trade Restrictions—A Tangled Web

> Every country has companies and industries that benefit directly from existing barriers.

International trade has never been free of national barriers in modern times. For that reason, WTO negotiations start with existing historical protections. Member countries agree not to increase barriers, and they commit to participating in multilateral trade negotiations with the goal of lessening restrictions over time. New countries are admitted to the WTO only after sometimes prolonged negotiations with existing members over modifications of existing trade-related barriers. Such negotiations are deemed necessary before new members can be admitted. However, even if everyone agreed that the world, as a whole, would be better off without trade restrictions, it does not follow that all countries or that all persons would be better off, certainly not in the short run. Every country has companies and industries that benefit directly from existing barriers—businesses whose profits rely on, and sometimes depend on, protection. Each of these businesses, in turn, has employees, suppliers, and communities that benefit indirectly from those protections. Thus, any change in a nation's trade policies will have a negative effect on some segment of its economy, even if it can be demonstrated that a change will produce a positive effect on its economy as a whole.

Take a specific example: The United States has had an ongoing dispute with China over its protection of, and trade in, intellectual property. In 2009, a WTO dispute resolution panel ruled that China must permit foreign companies to sell music online in China. The panel said China's prohibition on downloaded music violates a promise China made upon joining the WTO that it would open access to foreign mass-produced art. China responded that it never promised to open markets in the electronic distribution of sound recordings in a non-physical form and that the restriction was necessary to protect China's "public morals."[85] Interestingly, only once has the public morals defense previously been used before the WTO—by the United States when it argued in support of its ban on Internet gambling over the objections of Antigua. The United States lost. To succeed, a proponent must be able to show that the restriction is "necessary" to defend public morals.

Now consider more broadly the trade relationship between the United States and China. What other forces influence the resolution of a particular dispute? Consider, for example, that China exports over $4 of goods to the United States for every $1 of goods that the United States exports to China, which suggests that China is more dependent on trade with the United States than the reverse.[86] Conversely, in significant part because of China's large positive trade balance with the United States, China invests its abundance of U.S. dollars in U.S. Treasury bonds. China's demand for treasuries keeps the interest rates that the United States pays on those bonds significantly lower than they would otherwise be, thus reducing the cost of borrowing for the United States.

The United States also has an ongoing trading dispute with Brazil. Brazil forced the United States into the WTO dispute resolution process arguing that the $3 billion per year the United States has been paying to cotton growers (mostly large agribusinesses in the South) constitutes an unfair subsidy. U.S. companies account for about 40 percent of cotton exports globally. The WTO ruled in favor of Brazil and ultimately authorized the imposition of countervailing duties. In order to avoid the imposition of those duties, the United States negotiated a settlement in 2010 that allowed it to continue paying the $3 billion annual subsidy, at least until Congress passed a new farm bill, so long as the United States also paid Brazil $147.3 million per year. However, the parties negotiated a second agreement in 2014 that permits the United States to continue paying the $3 billion annual subsidy until the passage of a new farm bill, in exchange for a final lump-sum payment to Brazil of $300 million.[87]

Questions

1. How would you challenge China's assertion that prohibiting music downloads is necessary to protect public morals in China? What facts might you look for to support your argument?

2. Is it ethical for the United States to dispute China's protectionist policies while spending years defending an enormous annual subsidy that it pays to a well-developed U.S. industry? Explain.

3. The WTO held that the the U.S.'s $3 billion annual payment to American cotton growers is an unfair subsidy. However, the United States subsequently negotiated a settlement with Brazil, the country that brought the dispute, that allows the United States to continue making the payment. Is the settlement ethical? Should the United States be allowed to continue paying an unfair subsidy? What effect does the subsidy have on the cotton industry in developing nations other than Brazil? See "Why the Deal to Pay Brazil $300 Million Just to Keep Subsidies Is Bad for the WTO, Poor Countries, and U.S. Taxpayers," *The Washington Post,* October 12, 2014.

International Dispute Resolution

LO 16-11

Identify and evaluate the means for resolving international disputes.

As we have seen to this point, international business relationships are highly complex. Disputes are inevitable. International dispute resolutions often face roadblocks. Three significant international dispute resolution bodies presently exist: the International Court of Justice, the European Court of Justice, and the WTO Dispute Settlement Body. Alternatively, parties to an international contract may agree to international arbitration in order to resolve their disputes.

International Dispute Resolution Bodies

International Court of Justice

The only court devoted entirely to hearing cases of international public law is the International Court of Justice (ICJ) in the United Nations. The ICJ is made up of 15 judges from 15 different member countries. It may issue two types of decisions. It has advisory jurisdiction where the United Nations asks the court for an opinion on a matter of international law. These opinions do not bind any party. It has contentious jurisdiction where two or more nations (not individual parties) have consented to its jurisdiction and have requested a binding opinion. Such opinions are not, however, precedent for the ICJ in later cases. [For more information about the ICJ, see **www.icj-cij.org**].

How Binding Are ICJ Decisions?

Just how binding an ICJ contentious case decision actually is on U.S. state and federal courts has been called into question by the 2008 U.S. Supreme Court decision in *Medellin v. Texas*.[88] The Court, in a 6–3 decision, held that a Texas court did not have to give effect to an ICJ ruling in spite of the fact that the case was submitted to the ICJ pursuant to a treaty obligation specifying that the ICJ has "compulsory jurisdiction" for all "disputes arising out of the interpretation or application" of the treaty. In the view of the majority, the "most natural reading" of the "compulsory jurisdiction" language is "as a bare grant of jurisdiction. . . . The [treaty] says nothing about the effect of an ICJ decision and does not itself commit signatories to comply with an ICJ judgment." In his dissent, Justice Breyer observed:

> In the majority's view, the [treaty] simply sends the dispute to the ICJ . . . and the U.N. Charter contains no more than a promise to "undertak[e] to comply" with that judgment. Such a promise, the majority says, does not as a domestic law matter . . . "operat[e] of itself without the aid of any legislative provision." Rather, here (and presumably in any other ICJ judgment rendered pursuant to any of the approximately 70 U.S. treaties in force that contain similar provisions for submitting treaty-based disputes to the ICJ for decisions that bind the parties) Congress must enact specific legislation before ICJ judgments entered pursuant to our consent to compulsory ICJ jurisdiction can become domestic law. . . . In my view . . . we must look instead to our own domestic law, in particular, to the many treaty-related cases interpreting the Supremacy Clause. Those cases . . . lead to the conclusion that the ICJ judgment before us is enforceable as a matter of domestic law without further legislation.[89]

European Court of Justice

The European Court of Justice (ECJ) hears cases involving European Community law. Although not required, one judge from each member nation traditionally sits on the ECJ. At first glance, the ECJ may not seem a particularly important court for American business, but in an age of MNEs, its decisions can be very important. The ECJ ruled on whether, under EU trademark law, Google's AdWord service violated the Louis Vuitton trademark when Google sold an ad to a Vuitton competitor next to search results returned any time "Louis Vuitton" was entered as a search phrase.[90] The court held, with certain caveats, that it was not a violation. [For information on the ECJ, see **curia.europa.eu/jcms/jcms/Jo2_6999/**].

WTO Dispute Settlement Body

Although the WTO Dispute Settlement Body (DSB) is not a true court, it is a significant forum for the resolution of international trade disputes between WTO members. The DSB is made up of all member governments, usually represented by ambassadors or the equivalent. The DSB establishes a panel to hear a particular dispute brought by a member state. The panel then reports back to the DSB, which can either accept or reject the panel's findings. Either side can then appeal to the WTO Appellate Body. Again, the DSB can either accept or reject the appeals report. If a WTO member fails to comply with the final decision of the DSB, the opposing party may seek compensation. If compensation is not agreed on between the parties within 20 days, the complaining party can seek authorization for retaliation—that is, the suspension of favorable trade concessions to the noncompliant party. The reality of this power was demonstrated by the DSB's authorization of import duties against U.S. goods by Brazil as previously discussed. In 2016, 11 cases were brought to the WTO. [For more information on the WTO dispute resolution function and dispute documents, see **www.wto.org/english/tratop_e/dispu_e/dispu_e.htm**].

Other International Fora

In addition to the three institutions just discussed, particular treaties may implement specific dispute resolution processes for disputes arising under that treaty between its signatories. For example, NAFTA provides for special tribunals before which corporations can, and have, brought complaints against governments for actions perceived to be unfair or inequitable to them as foreign investors. Of concern to some commentators is that a tribunal under NAFTA can, as a practical matter, operate as a further review of a decision of a domestic court. Thus, after the U.S. Supreme Court declined to review a Massachusetts case brought by a Canadian real estate company, the company took its dispute to a NAFTA tribunal (which decided that Massachusetts had not violated international law).[91] [For information on proceedings before NAFTA tribunals against the governments of Canada, Mexico, and the United States, see the U.S. State Department site at **www.state.gov/s/l/c3439.htm**, as well as a private site, **www.NaftaClaims.com**].

National courts also rule on matters of international law and on matters involving business in international settings. In fact, because of the absence of any international courts of general jurisdiction, national courts are where most international business disputes are heard. When the underlying dispute seems to have little association with the forum state, but that state's national court agrees to rule on the substantive claim, legal commentators may lay charges of "judicial imperialism."[92] The principle of comity previously discussed also applies to the exercise of a national court's jurisdiction.

The Long Road through Court

In the summer of 2007, 12 banana plantation workers from Nicaragua got their day or, rather, their four months in a California federal district court.

The workers were employed by Dole Food Co. on banana plantations in Nicaragua, where a pesticide known as DBCP, manufactured by Dow Chemical Co., was used to increase the weight of the banana harvest and help with rodent and pest control. In 1977 the U.S. government suspended the use of the chemical after complaints arose of sterility in California workers. When Dow informed Dole that it would no longer be producing the chemical, the two companies agreed that Dow would sell to Dole, for use in Central America, the more than 500,000 gallons that had been returned to it by other purchasers.

The plaintiffs were some of the workers who were exposed to DBCP while working for Dole in Nicaragua, workers who then became sterile.

After a successful suit was brought in the United States in the early 1980s on behalf of affected California workers, U.S. law firms began suing in U.S. courts on behalf of workers from other countries. Nearly every case ended when American courts ruled that the principle of forum non conveniens required the lawsuits to be maintained in the countries where the workers had suffered their injuries. Their view was that Nicaragua was a more appropriate forum for the dispute. So the workers tried again at home. After lengthy delays and, ultimately, a change in Nicaraguan law to facilitate the DBPC lawsuits, in 2002 a Nicaraguan court awarded nearly $490 million in damages, and other judgments followed. But so far Dole and Dow have successfully blocked all enforcement of the judgments in U.S. courts. The new laws in Nicaragua have meant, however, that Dole and Dow have ceased invoking the forum non conveniens argument against new suits in the United States.

After a month of deliberations in the 2007 case in California, the jury awarded six of the Nicaraguan workers a total of $3.3 million. Following a number of post-trial motions, the companies successfully reduced the award to $1.58 million to be shared among four of the plaintiffs. The jury decision as to one plaintiff was overturned and Dole was granted a new trial as to another.[93] In the years following, Dole filed post-trial motions to have the jury verdict thrown out; in 2011, the judgment was vacated. At the same time, each side accused the other of fraud, including fraud instigated by the opposing attorneys, but the California State Bar is no longer pursuing investigations of those attorneys.[94]

Questions

1. Why do you think Dole and Dow did not object to the new suits brought in the United States after the plaintiffs' successful suit in Nicaragua?

2. Do you think the Nicaraguan judgments should be enforceable in the United States? Why or why not?

3. Apart from whether Dole or Dow Chemical or both are liable for health issues associated with exposure to DBCP, was it ethical for Dole to use and Dow to supply DBCP for use in Nicaragua and elsewhere after the chemical was banned in the United States? Explain.

Arbitration

In light of the difficulty of litigation between parties of diverse nationalities and the desire for more certainty and expediency in business transactions, parties to an international contract may prefer to insert a clause that calls for the international arbitration of any dispute. As discussed in Chapter 4, arbitration is a nonjudicial means to settle a conflict where the parties agree to a hearing in front of a neutral third party who will issue a binding award decision. [For more information on international arbitration, see **www.arbitration-adr.org** and **www.i-a-a.ch**].

Government Defenses

"Some evil acts don't violate international law unless they are performed by someone acting with government authority."[95] Even where government action is the source of the wrong, two additional doctrines, accepted as general principles of international law, may pose barriers to the judicial enforcement of a party's rights: the *act of state doctrine* and the *doctrine of sovereign immunity*.

Act of State Doctrine

LO 16-12

Explain the act of state doctrine.

It is generally accepted that a country has absolute rule over what occurs within its borders. Consequently, the act of state doctrine holds that a judge in one country does not have the authority to examine or challenge the acts of another country within that country's borders. For instance, an American court may not declare invalid the acts of the British government taken within its own jurisdiction because it is presumed that the foreign country, Britain, acted legally within its own territory.

One government action that has caused a great deal of dispute in connection with the act of state doctrine is *expropriation*. Expropriation is the taking by a national government, without adequate compensation, of property and/or rights of a foreign person within that government's borders. The United States contends that international law requires compensation for the taking. Not all governments agree with the United States' position. In 2012, Argentina nationalized YPF, an affiliate of a Spanish oil company. Shortly before the government acted, YPF had discovered what may be the world's largest deposits of natural gas. Before its privatization in 1999, YPF had been Argentina's state energy corporation. The reason given for the 2012 nationalization was that YPF's production had fallen, causing Argentina to become a net importer of energy.[96]

Doctrine of Sovereign Immunity

LO 16-13

Describe the doctrine of sovereign immunity and its exceptions as codified under the Foreign Sovereign Immunities Act (FSIA).

The doctrine of sovereign immunity is based on the concept that "the king can do no wrong." In other words, if the king makes the rules, how could the king ever be wrong? As Chief Justice Marshall explained in *The Schooner Exchange v. McFaddon*,[97] "The jurisdiction of the nation within its own territory is necessarily exclusive and absolute. It is susceptible of no limitation not imposed by itself; deriving validity from an external source would imply a diminution of its sovereignty to the extent of the restriction, and an investment of that sovereignty to the same extent in that power which could impose such restriction."

The doctrine has been codified in the United States by the Foreign Sovereign Immunities Act of 1976 (FSIA), which provides that foreign countries may not be sued in American courts, subject to several exceptions. Accordingly, U.S. citizens usually would not be allowed to sue Britain in the U.S. courts, unless the claim falls into one of the following FSIA exceptions:

- The foreign country has waived its immunity (that is, it has consented to be sued in another country's courts).
- The legal action is based on a commercial activity by the foreign country in the United States or outside the United States but having a direct effect in the United States.
- The legal action is based on personal injuries "caused by an act of torture, extrajudicial killing, aircraft sabotage, hostage taking, or the provision of material support or resources" for such acts.[98]

Thus, a country that conducts a commercial activity in a foreign country may not hide behind sovereign immunity if sued. In recent years, however, the Supreme Court has effectively limited the jurisdiction of U.S. courts to preside over such cases, stressing that in order do so, the underlying commercial activity must have a sufficient connection to the United States.[99] For instance, in 2015, the Supreme Court held that a California woman who bought a Eurail pass from a Massachusetts-based travel agency and then lost her legs in an Austrian national railway accident could not sue for damages in a United States federal district court.[100] The court held that it was the accident in Austria—not the sale of the Eurail pass—that was central to the case, and, as such, the United States was not the proper forum. Note that a country acting on its own behalf and not for a commercial purpose may avail itself of sovereign immunity. However, the Supreme Court has held that the FSIA provides immunity only to a foreign state and not to a foreign official, even if that official is acting on behalf of the state.[101]

The "restrictive theory of immunity" recognized and applied by the United States is to be contrasted with the policies of some countries that contend that immunity is absolute—no exceptions exist. The following case examines sovereign immunity.

Butters v. Vance International, Inc.
225 F.3d 462 (4th Cir. 2000)

LEGAL BRIEFCASE

Chief Judge Wilkinson

Appellant Nyla Butters brought suit against her employer, Vance International, claiming that Vance discriminated against her on the basis of gender. The district court held that Vance was entitled to immunity from Butters' suit under the Foreign Sovereign Immunities Act because Vance's client, the Kingdom of Saudi Arabia, was responsible for Butters not being promoted.

I

Vance International, headquartered in Oakton, Virginia, provides security services to corporations and foreign sovereigns. In October 1994, Saudi Arabia hired Vance to augment the security provided to Princess Anud, a wife of Saudi King Fhad, while the Princess was undergoing medical treatments in California. The Saudi military was responsible for protecting Princess Anud. The Princess' residence in Bel Air, California, was referred to as "Gold." Saudi Arabian Colonel Mohammed Al-Ajiji supervised all security at the site—three Saudi military officers and the Vance agents. . . . The Saudi government paid Vance for its services.

In August 1995, Vance hired Nyla Butters as a part-time, at-will security agent. From 1995 until April 14, 1998 . . . [on] several occasions, Butters temporarily worked in Gold's command post.

In early April 1998, Vance supervisors at Gold recommended that Butters serve a full rotation in the command post. . . . Gregg Hall, the Vance detail leader, spoke with Mohammed. Colonel Mohammed denied Hall's request for Butters to serve a rotation in the command post. Colonel Mohammed told Hall that such an assignment was unacceptable under Islamic law, and Saudis would consider it inappropriate for their officers to spend long periods of time in a command post with a woman present. This in turn could have political ramifications at home for the Saudi royal family. Mohammed also informed Hall that the Princess and her contingent wanted to speak only to male officers when they called the command post. In total, three Vance supervisors recommended Butters for the assignment. Saudi military officers denied every request.

* * * * *

On May 28, 1998, Butters filed a charge of gender discrimination with the California Department of Fair Employment and Housing. On October 15, 1998, Butters filed suit . . . for discriminatory constructive termination, retaliatory constructive termination, and wrongful constructive termination in violation of public policy under California's Fair Employment and Housing Act. Vance filed a motion for summary judgment with respect to these counts.

On July 30, 1999, the district court granted Vance's motion, finding Vance immune from Butters' suit under the Foreign Sovereign Immunities Act (FSIA). . . . The district court held that derivative FSIA immunity attached to Vance because it was "acting under the direct military orders of Colonel Mohammed when [it] did not allow the plaintiff to work a full rotation in the command center." Butters appeals.

II

Butters first contends that FSIA immunity does not attach to Vance because the action here was a "commercial activity." . . .

The FSIA defines "commercial activity" as "a regular course of commercial conduct or a particular commercial transaction or act. The commercial character of an activity shall be determined by reference to the nature of the course of conduct or particular transaction or act, rather than by reference to its purpose." . . . The Court elaborated on the distinction: "[A] state engages in commercial activity . . . where it exercises 'only those powers that can also be exercised by private citizens,' as distinct from those 'powers peculiar to sovereigns.'"

The relevant act here—a foreign sovereign's decision as to how best to secure the safety of its leaders—is quintessentially an act "peculiar to sovereigns." . . . Indeed, it is difficult to imagine an act closer to the core of a nation's sovereignty. Providing security for the royal family in this country is not a commercial act in which the state is acting "in the manner of a private player within the market." . . .

* * * * *

III

Butters next argues that Vance is not entitled to immunity since Vance, as opposed to the Saudi officials, was responsible for the decision not to promote Butters.

A

If Vance was following Saudi Arabia's orders not to promote Butters, Vance would be entitled to derivative immunity under the FSIA. . . .

. . . To abrogate immunity would discourage American companies from entering lawful agreements with foreign governments and from respecting their wishes even as to sovereign acts. Under the circumstances here, imposing civil liability on the private agents of Saudi Arabia would significantly impede the Saudi government's sovereign interest in protecting its leaders while they are in the United States.

* * * * *

IV

Any type of governmental immunity reflects a trade-off between the possibility that an official's wrongdoing will remain unpunished and the risk that government functions will be impaired. FSIA immunity presupposes a tolerance for the sovereign decisions of other countries that may reflect legal norms and cultural values quite different from our own. Here Saudi Arabia made a decision to protect a member of its royal family in a manner consistent with Islamic law and custom. The Act requires not that we approve of the diverse cultural or political motivations that may underlie another sovereign's acts, but that we respect them. We thus affirm the judgment.

Questions

1. Why did the court hold that Vance, a U.S. corporation, could avoid Butters's claim of discrimination based on a claim of sovereign immunity? Why did Butters argue that sovereign immunity should not apply?

2. How do you feel about the end result of this decision? Did Butters suffer discrimination? Explain.

Subjecting MNEs to Compliance with the Law of Nations

The largest MNEs have economic strength equaling or exceeding that of some countries. In this chapter, we have seen how challenging it can be to effectively regulate their activities. That makes it worth asking whether MNEs should be held liable if, in furtherance of their economic objectives, they either (1) take advantage of foreign government actors willing to subdue a local population or (2) are complicit in a foreign government's perpetuation of its own dominance where the action of the foreign government violates the law of nations.

Some foreign plaintiffs are attempting to hold MNEs liable under such circumstances in suits brought in U.S. federal courts under the Alien Tort Statute. In one sentence, this statute authorizes foreign nationals to file civil suits in the United States against those who violate "the law of nations or a treaty of the United States." Enacted in 1789, in the 1990s the statute began to be used to sue major corporations for alleged complicity in crimes violating human rights by foreign governments, including torture, extrajudicial killings, and war crimes.

Many such suits have withstood motions to dismiss by corporate defendants. In some cases, juries have found against the plaintiffs; a number of suits have been settled, subject generally to a restriction that the settlement terms not be publicly disclosed. An exception to such nondisclosure was a 2009 settlement for $15.5 million of claims against Royal Dutch Shell for its role in the Nigerian government's execution of local activists who protested the environmental damage caused by oil drilling in the Niger delta.[102]

Other plaintiffs did not settle. On April 17, 2013, the U.S. Supreme Court foreclosed their claims, holding that the Alien Tort Statute was subject to the traditional presumption against extraterritorial application, but suggesting that cases that "touch and concern the territory of the United States" might "displace the presumption."[103] U.S. courts may not hear claims of foreign plaintiffs against foreign companies on foreign soil, but other claims—such as those of foreign plaintiffs against U.S. companies on foreign soil—perhaps are still viable.[104]

Under EU law, a European company can be sued "at home for complicity in human-rights violations committed anywhere in the world."[105]

Enforcement of Decisions

LO 16-14
Identify some challenges to the enforcement of foreign judgments.

As we have seen, even if a harmed party in an international dispute successfully initiates a judicial proceeding, many procedural hurdles are likely to be encountered. Recall the forum non conveniens principle that initially kept the Nicaraguan workers from obtaining substantive hearings in U.S. courts. But what happens after the successful conclusion of such a suit? Do challenges arise in the enforcement of the court's decision?

The answer is yes, particularly in those cases where the losing defendant has insufficient or no assets located in the same jurisdiction as the court awarding the plaintiff monetary relief. In those cases, the plaintiff may need to present the judgment to a court in a country where assets of the defendant are located and seek local enforcement. This is an added cost, in time and money, for successful plaintiffs. Furthermore, enforcement may be difficult or impossible to obtain.

Enforcing Foreign Judgments

When a plaintiff is successful in a California court, but the defendant's assets are in New York, the plaintiff may have to seek enforcement from a New York court. In that situation, the U.S. Constitution requires the New York court to give "full faith and credit" to the decision of the California court. No such broad policy exists in U.S. law with respect to decisions of foreign courts; nor does such a broad policy exist in international law. Instead, the court from which enforcement is being requested is likely to consider whether the original foreign judgment violates local notions of justice and morality, or is otherwise contrary to public policy, so as not to be entitled to enforcement. This is also true of foreign arbitration awards if the losing party has refused to satisfy the award—even if both countries are among the 156 current signatories of the U.N. Convention on the Recognition and Enforcement of Foreign Arbitral Awards (also known as the New York Convention). [Current information on the status of the convention, as well as additional information, can be found at **www.uncitral.org/uncitral/en/uncitral_texts/arbitration/NYConvention.html**].

To illustrate, consider the previously discussed Nicaraguan banana plantation workers. After U.S. courts largely refused to allow substantive hearings in the 1980s based on forum non conveniens, the workers took their claims back to Nicaragua, which was exactly what U.S. courts had told them to do. Although resolution of claims in Nicaragua took a long time, some plaintiffs obtained substantial judgments there. In response to plaintiffs' applications to U.S. courts for recognition and enforcement of these Nicaraguan judgments, however, the defendant U.S. corporations have thus far been successful in avoiding the requested enforcement.

Enforcing U.S. Judgments   Similar problems can arise when a U.S. citizen obtains a judgment from a U.S. court against a foreign national, which judgment is then sent for enforcement to the home courts of the foreign national. Consider the case of an Alabama 15-year-old who died in an accident when the buckle of his motorcycle helmet failed. The helmet was made by an Italian company. His mother sued in an Alabama court and won a $1 million judgment. The Italian company refused to pay and the mother presented the judgment to an Italian court for enforcement. The Italian Supreme Court found the award of punitive damages so offensive to its notion of justice that it refused to enforce any of the award. Many countries share the Italian court's distaste for punitive damages in such situations.[106]

Question

On balance, do you think it would be better for countries to agree mutually to simply enforce judgments in favor of private citizens (nationals or nonnationals) obtained from foreign courts, respecting the effort and delay the plaintiff has already undergone in obtaining the judgment and without applying culturally based notions of justice? Why or why not? If not, try generating a list of principles you think should permit a court to refuse enforcement of a foreign judgment.

Internet Exercise

Identify a multinational firm that conducts business with suppliers in developing countries. Find its code of vendor conduct on its website and evaluate the areas of enforcement that might prove to be the most difficult.

Chapter Questions

1. Thomas Friedman, in his 2005 book *The World Is Flat: A Brief History of the Twenty-First Century,* argues that countries with connected manufacturing supply chains won't go to war with one another. He offers an example of Dell's multicountry supply chain for the manufacture of its laptops. On balance, do you think globalization is a catalyst for bringing world peace or a tinderbox that may set international disputes on fire through the collision of differing ideals and competing interests? Explain.

2. *a.* Why do you think China, one of the most communist of nations, wanted to join the WTO?

   b. Would it surprise you to learn that Iraq, Iran, and Syria, while not currently WTO members, are all formally enrolled as observer countries? This means they are (or are considering) pursuing accession negotiations to become WTO member states. Why might they be interested in joining the WTO?

3. From 2010 through 2012, many state legislatures considered or passed laws outlawing aspects of Islamic or Shariah law. Some of them would have prohibited the enforcement of private contracts in which a "butcher would no longer be able to enforce his contract for halal meat—contracts that, like deals for kosher or other faith-sanctioned foods, are regularly enforced around the country. Nor could a Muslim banker seek damages for violations of a financial instrument certified as 'Sharia compliant' since it pays no interest."[107]

   a. Develop an argument that laws prohibiting enforcement of such contracts would be unconstitutional.

   b. What historical parallels exist in which laws in the United States were seen to deny equal protection to a subgroup of American citizens?

4. Different countries and cultures have different norms for dress. In the United States, for example, some restaurants require men to wear jackets and state law generally prohibits even partial public nudity. Public schools often have enforceable dress codes. In the 1960s, those codes often prohibited female students from wearing pants. Consider the following:

   • In 2010, the French Parliament passed a law forbidding people from concealing their faces in public, punishable by fines. Higher fines and prison sentences up to one year could be imposed on individuals who encouraged others to ignore the ban. Although freedom of religion is constitutionally protected in France, it is generally acknowledged that the purpose of the law was to prohibit Muslim women from wearing traditional head coverings and full-body robes. It has been estimated that fewer than 2,000 women in France, most of whom are French nationals, wear them. Some supporters of the ban have said that such robes are a means of forcing women to be submissive and are a sign of enslavement or debasement. Some of the wearers say that the dress is a method to concentrate on their religious faith.[108]

- Also in 2010, one province in Indonesia, the world's most populous Muslim-majority nation, banned Muslim women from wearing revealing clothes such as tight skirts and pants. After their third violation, women could be subject to two weeks' detention. Shopkeepers violating restrictions on selling inappropriate clothing could lose their business licenses.[109]

   a. Do the laws discussed in the sections above seem logical to you? On what basis should you judge them?

   b. Would conflicts with cultural issues, such as those addressed by the local laws above, impact your decision as a manager about where to conduct your business? *Should* they impact your decisions? Explain.

   c. If your job required you to live in a country that had laws with which you disagreed on moral grounds, would you follow those laws? Explain.

5. *a.* What are the relative advantages and disadvantages of each form of doing business in a foreign country?

   b. Why would a firm choose one form over another?

6. The United States exports its values structure in a variety of ways, including through the extraterritorial application of its laws. For instance, American firms must maintain Title VII standards abroad and are therefore prohibited from discriminating against employees anywhere in the world on the basis of sex, race, color, national origin, and religion. Compare this with the Alien Tort Statute, which was enacted in 1789 and authorizes foreign nationals to file civil suits in the United States against those who violate "the law of nations or a treaty of the United States." In 2013, the U.S. Supreme Court held that the Alien Tort Statute (ATS) is subject to the traditional presumption *against* extraterritorial application, and underscored the danger of judicial interference in foreign policy; it ruled that the ATS is presumed to cover only violations of international law occurring in the United States, unless the conduct overseas affects the United States "with sufficient force." The court thus dismissed the underlying action brought by foreign plaintiffs against Royal Dutch Shell (a foreign MNE) for its alleged complicity in the Nigerian government's execution of local activists.[110] What public policy interests are likely to have motivated the Court's decision? See John B. Bellinger III, "Lawsuits Force Foreign Governments to Navigate U.S. Court System," *The Washington Diplomat,* May 3, 2016 [**www.washdiplomat.com/index.php?option=com_content &view=article&id=13515:lawsuits-force-foreign-governments-to-navigate-us-court-system&catid=1544&Itemid=428**].

7. In *Doe v. Nestle USA, Inc., et al.,*[111] three former child slaves brought claims under the Alien Tort Statute (ATS) against a number of defendants alleging they aided and abetted child slavery by providing assistance to farmers in the Ivory Coast. The defendants argued that the complaint should be dismissed based on the Supreme Court's ruling in *Kiobel v. Royal Dutch Petroleum Co.,*[112] which held that ATS is subject to the traditional presumption *against* extraterritorial application. The Ninth Circuit Court of Appeals, however, allowed the case to proceed on the basis that the defendants acted with the purpose to facilitate slavery, a plan that starkly distinguished the case from other ATS decisions in which the defendants merely profited by doing business with known human rights violators. It also remanded the case to allow the plaintiffs to

amend their complaints to allege that some of the activity underlying their ATS claim, such as planning the promotion of child slavery overseas, took place in the United States. The defendants appealed the decision to the U.S. Supreme Court. The Supreme Court, however, denied certiorari, thus refusing to review the Ninth Circuit's controversial decision. One commentator has concerns that the Ninth Circuit's decision will open the doors to many other ATS claims and that corporations can potentially be held liable under ATS for the tortious acts committed outside the United States by foreign actors with whom they do business, "so long as the company intended to turn a profit."[113] Do you agree with this characterization of Nestle's alleged actions—that it merely did business with foreign actors, who committed tortious acts, in order to turn a profit? Do you think that Nestle should not be subject to an ATS claim in the United States if its alleged actions were limited to aiding and abetting child slavery overseas? What if the corporate defendant allegedly undertook planning in the United States to facilitate child slavery in order to maximize its profits?

8. As discussed in the chapter, enforcing a U.S. judgment against a foreign national in the home courts of the foreign national can be problematic. For example, the foreign court may refuse to enforce the judgment if it finds it contrary to the court's notion of justice. What other issues prevent enforcement of U.S. judgments against Chinese companies in China's courts? What alternative does a U.S. national have to collect damages against a Chinese company? See Dan Harris, "Enforcing U.S. Judgments in China. Not Yet," *China Law Blog,* August 1, 2016 [**www.chinalawblog.com/2016/08/enforcing-us-judgments-in-china-not-yet.html**].

9. In 2016, the WTO ruled that a tax break given by Washington state for the aerospace industry was a prohibited subsidy. The tax cut was agreed to when Boeing was considering where to establish a new assembly base, and it was designed to help Boeing develop its new 777X jetliner. Explain how a tax break might serve as a subsidy and thus be prohibited by the WTO. Would it surprise you to learn that, for over 12 years, Boeing and Airbus have accused one other of receiving tens of billions of illegal subsidies? Is it unethical for either of these two companies to have accepted state aid while attacking the other for doing so? Or is this behavior an acceptable means of maximizing profits and getting ahead of the competition?

10. What may look to one observer like the application of objective standards may appear to another observer as improper protectionism. Originally signed in the mid-1990s, NAFTA calls for an open border for commercial truck traffic among Canada, the United States, and Mexico. But in early 2005, Mexican trucks were still not allowed into the United States, due in part to litigation brought by environmental and labor groups. Their claim was that the United States hadn't appropriately considered the environmental impact of letting Mexican trucks roll on American roads because there are no standardized emissions rules for commercial vehicles. On balance, does this argument sound to you more like a principled objection or like protection for U.S. jobs? Why? See *Department of Transportation v. Public Citizen,* 541 U.S. 752 (2004).

11. Camel Manufacturing imported nylon tents to the United States. The tents held nine people and weighed over 30 pounds. The tents' floors ranged from 8 feet by 10 feet to 10 feet by 14 feet. The tents were to be used as shelter during camping. The importer categorized

the goods as "sports equipment," which carried a 10 percent import duty, whereas the U.S. Customs Service considered the tents "textile articles not specifically provided for," with a duty of $0.25 per pound plus 15 percent import duty. The importer appealed the decision. What should be the result? Explain. See *Camel Manufacturing Co. v. United States,* 686 F. Supp. 912 (C.I.T. 1988), *aff'd,* 861 F.2d 1266 (Fed. Cir. 1988).

12. Should a Mexican citizen who bought a Chrysler vehicle in Mexico be allowed to sue the manufacturer in a U.S. court under U.S. product liability laws when the plaintiff's three-year-old son was killed when the passenger-side air bag deployed during an accident in Mexico? See *Gonzalez v. Chrysler Corp.,* 301 F.3d 377 (5th Cir. 2002), *cert. denied,* 538 U.S. 1012 (2003).

13. Prior to 1941, Kalmich owned a business in Yugoslavia. In 1941, the Nazis confiscated his property as a result of Kalmich's Jewish heritage and faith. Bruno purchased the business from the Nazis in 1942 without knowledge of the potential unlawful conversion. Kalmich contended that because the confiscation was in violation of well-defined principles of international law prior to the German occupation, the transfer to Bruno was ineffective. Kalmich sought to apply a 1946 Yugoslavian law called "Law Concerning the Treatment of Property Taken Away from the Owner." That law provided that where property is taken from its owners, the owner may bring an action against "responsible persons" for recovery.

    a. Did the act of state doctrine apply in this case?

    b. If not, what should be the result in an American court? Explain. See *Kalmich v. Bruno,* 450 F. Supp. 227 (N.D. Ill. 1978).

14. Zedan received a telephone call from a Saudi Arabian organization offering him an engineering position at a construction project in Saudi Arabia. The Ministry of Communications, an agency of the government, guaranteed payment to Zedan for any work he performed there, whether for the government or for a nonsovereign third party. After three years, Zedan left the country without being fully paid. After he returned to the United States, he filed an action in federal court seeking to enforce the ministry's guarantee. The ministry argued that it was protected under the Foreign Sovereign Immunities Act.

    a. Was Zedan's recruitment in the United States a commercial activity as required by the act?

    b. Did this action have a direct effect in the United States as required by the act? Explain. See *Zedan v. Kingdom of Saudi Arabia,* 849 F.2d 1511 (D.C. Cir. 1988).

15. From time to time, courts are called on to determine the enforceability of an arbitration clause contained in a contract. One such case was *DiMercurio v. Sphere Drake Insurance.*[114] DiMercurio was injured in 1994 when the commercial fishing vessel in which he was working sank. The vessel was owned by R&M, which was found by a court to be liable to DiMercurio for his injuries and ordered to pay $350,000 in compensation. However, because R&M had no other assets, it assigned to DiMercurio all the rights it had against Sphere Drake, the London-based insurer of the fishing vessel. When DiMercurio looked to Sphere Drake for payment, it denied the claim and invoked the arbitration clause in its insurance policy with R&M, which required the arbitration to take place in England. Should DiMercurio be required to pursue his claim through arbitration in England? Explain.

Notes

1. "Weaving the World Together," *The Economist,* November 19, 2011.

2. "Marrakesh Agreement Establishing the World Trade Organization" [**https://www.wto.org/ english/docs_e/legal_e/04-wto_e.htm**].

3. "Trade Talks Produce a Deal," *The New York Times,* December 12, 2013.

4. "When Giants Slow Down," *The Economist,* July 27, 2013.

5. Greg Ip, "We Are Not the World," *The Wall Street Journal,* January 7–8, 2017, p. C1.

6. "The Long Road," *The Economist,* June 4, 2016.

7. "Regional Trade Deals Aren't as Good as Global Ones but They Are Still Beneficial," *The Economist,* March 21, 2015.

8. "TTIP Has Failed—But No One Is Admitting It, Says German Vice-Chancellor Sigmar Gabriel," *The Independent,* August 28, 2016 [**www.independent.co.uk/news/world/europe/ttip-trade-deal-agreement-failed-brexit-latest-news-eu-us-germany-vice-chancellor-a7213876.html**].

9. "China Readies to Take Trade Mantle," *The Wall Street Journal,* November 12–13, 2016.

10. "A Transatlantic Tipping Point," *The Economist,* April 27, 2013.

11. "Europe's Choice," *The Economist,* May 26, 2012.

12. World Trade Organization [**www.wto.org/english/thewto_e/whatis_e/tif_e/fact1_e.htm**].

13. Pete Engardio, "Global Capitalism: Can It Be Made to Work Better," *BusinessWeek,* November 6, 2000, p. 72.

14. Ibid.

15. Christopher Ingraham, "What Most Americans Think of Islam Today," Wonkblog, *The Washington Post,* November 17, 2015 [**https://www.washingtonpost.com/news/wonk/ wp/2015/11/17/most-americans-say-islam-is-at-odds-with-american-values/?utm_term= .65df93c6b934**].

16. Craig Timberg and Paula Moura, "In Brazil, Google Is in the Middle of a Battle over Free Speech," *The Washington Post,* October 3, 2012.

17. "Facebook Runs Up Against German Hate-Speech Laws," *The New York Times,* November 28, 2016.

18. Bill Chappell, "Facebook Details Its New Plan to Combat Fake News Stories," *NPR,* December 15, 2016 [**http://www.npr.org/sections/thetwo-way/2016/12/15/505728377/facebook-details-its-new-plan-to-combat-fake-news-stories**].

19. Tanzina Vega, "Facebook Says It Failed to Bar Posts with Hate Speech," *The New York Times,* May 28, 2013.

20. Sophia Rosenbaum, "Man Accused of Killing Girlfriend, Posting Gruesome Photo to Facebook," *New York Post,* May 31, 2016 [**nypost.com/2016/05/31/facebook-took-36-hours-to-remove-photos-of-alleged-murder**].

21. Eric Pfanner and Somini Sengupta, "In a French Case, a Battle to Unmask Twitter Users," *The New York Times,* January 24, 2013; and Somini Sengupta, "Twitter Yields to Pressure in Hate Case in France," *The New York Times,* July 12, 2013.

22. Chappell, "Facebook Details Its New Plan to Combat Fake News."

23. Steven Greenhouse, "U.S. Retailers See Big Risk in Safety Plan for Factories in Bangladesh," *The New York Times,* May 22, 2013; and Julfikar Ali Manik and Jim Yardley, "Building Collapse in Bangladesh Leaves Scores Dead," *The New York Times,* April 24, 2013.

24. April 2016 Report, "Strengthening Workplace Safety and Labour Rights in the Bangladesh Ready-Made Garment Sector," p. 3 [available at **https://ilo.userservices.exlibrisgroup.com/ view/delivery/41ILO-INST/1242729840002676**].

25. Steven Greenhouse, "Under Pressure, Bangladesh Adopts New Labor Law," *The New York Times,* July 16, 2013; and Jim Yardley, "Garment Trade Wields Power in Bangladesh," *The New York Times,* July 24, 2013.

26. Clifford J. Levy, "Microsoft Changes Policy over Russian Crackdown," *The New York Times,* September 13, 2010.

27. *EEOC v. Arabian American Oil Co.,* 499 U.S. 244 (1991).

28. "Supreme Court Extends Protections for Multinational Companies," *The Washington Post,* January 14, 2014.

29. "The World This Week," *The Economist,* July 13, 2013.

30. Dionne Searcey, "Watergate-Era Law Revitalized in Pursuit of Corporate Corruption," *The Wall Street Journal,* October 15, 2010.

31. "Secret Unit Helped Brazilian Company Bribe Government Officials," *The New York Times,* December 21, 2016.

32. David Barboza, "Files Suggest a Graft Case in China May Expand," *The New York Times,* July 21, 2013; "Bitter Pill," *The Economist,* July 20, 2013; and Laurie Burkitt, "China Releases Details of Glaxo Bribery Allegations," *The Wall Street Journal,* July 15, 2013.

33. "GlaxoSmithKline Found Guilty of Bribery in China," *The Wall Street Journal,* September 19, 2014.

34. "GlaxoSmithKline to Pay $20 Million to Settle SEC Bribery Probe," *The Wall Street Journal,* September 30, 2016.

35. Leslie Wayne, "Foreign Firms Most Affected by a U.S. Law Barring Bribes," *The New York Times,* September 3, 2012.

36. "Russia Calls FIFA Probe an 'Illegal' Application of US Laws," *Sports News,* May 27, 2015 [**http://in.reuters.com/article/soccer-fifa-arrests-russia-idINKBN0OC29T20150527**]. See also "The World's Lawyer," *The Economist,* June 6, 2015.

37. A copy of the Declaration can be found in the University of Minnesota's Human Rights Library [**http://hrlibrary.umn.edu/instree/b1udhr.htm**].

38. Jose Ramos-Horta, "Speech to the Northern Medical Foundation Tribute to Military Medicine and Lt-Gen. P. Cosgrove," Sydney, Australia, September 28, 2001. Copy with author's work papers.

39. Amir Efrati and Andrew Batson, "Google to Alter Access to Its China Site," *The Wall Street Journal,* June 30, 2010, p. B3; and "China Renews Google's License," *The Waterloo/Cedar Falls Courier,* July 9, 2010, p. A11.

40. See, for example, *United States v. Kim,* 246 F.3d 186 (2d Cir. 2001), in which a New York resident was convicted of wire fraud while working for the United Nations in Croatia.

41. Mayer Brown JSM, *Guide to Doing Business in the PRC* (2010), p. 9.

42. 116 F. Supp. 2d 116 (D.D.C. 2000).

43. *United States v. Said,* 757 F. Supp. 2d 554 (E.D. Va. 2010) (dismissing the statutory piracy charge), *vacated and remanded,* 680 F.3d 374 (4th Cir. 2012); *United States v. Dire,* 680 F.3d 446 (4th Cir. 2012).

44. 192 F.3d 240 (2d Cir. 1999).

45. From the CIA's *World Factbook* [**https://www.cia.gov/library/publications/the-world-factbook/geos/xx.html**].

46. Ibid.

47. From the U.S. Census Bureau, Foreign Trade Division [**www.census.gov/foreign-trade/ statistics/historical/gands.pdf**].

48. Michael Schroeder, "Outsourcing May Create U.S. Jobs," *The Wall Street Journal,* March 30, 2004, p. A2.

49. GATS, Art. I, para. 3(b).

50. Donald C. Dowling Jr. and Oliver Brettle, "Globally Aligning Collective Bargaining Strategy," *White & Case LLP,* June 1, 2010 [**www.lexology.com/library/detail.aspx?g=3f66a46b-d041-4d66-82d6-ac611b8bbfd6**].

51. Donald C. Dowling Jr., "Reductions-in-Force Outside the US," *White & Case LLP,* December 1, 2008 [**www.lexology.com/library/detail.aspx?g=36c0b923-0d90-4e11-8eac-e524a21314cc**].

52. Commission on the Theft of American Intellectual Property, "The IP Commission Report," May 22, 2013 [**http://ipcommission.org**].

53. Ibid.

54. Ibid.

55. "When You Say 'Bud,'" *ABA Journal,* July 2013, p. 12.

56. "WIPO-Administered Treaties," WIPO [**www.wipo.int/treaties/en/ShowResults.jsp?treaty_id=2** (last visited on January 17, 2017)].

57. "Summary of the Madrid Agreement Concerning the International Registration of Marks (1891) and the Protocol Relating to That Agreement (1989)," WIPO [**www.wipo.int/treaties/en/registration/madrid/summary_madrid_marks.html**].

58. Case C-236/08, *Google Inc. v. Louis Vuitton Malletier SA,* 2010 E.C.R. I-02417.

59. "Yes, Ja, Oui, No, No," *The Economist,* December 15, 2012.

60. Duff Wilson, "Cigarette Giants in Global Fight on Tighter Rules," *The New York Times,* November 13, 2010.

61. Ibid.

62. Michael Schroeder and Silvia Ascarelli, "New Role for SEC: Policing Companies beyond U.S. Borders," *The Wall Street Journal,* July 30, 2004, p. A1.

63. "European Imperialism," *The Wall Street Journal,* October 31, 2007, p. A20.

64. "The Company That Ruled the Waves," *The Economist,* December 17, 2011.

65. Schroeder and Ascarelli, "New Role for SEC," p. A1.

66. *Morrison v. National Australia Bank Ltd.,* 130 S. Ct. 2689 (2010).

67. Floyd Norris, "Accounting Détente Delayed," *The New York Times,* July 19, 2012.

68. David Reilly and Duncan Mavin, "Chinese Accounting Earns Tough Stance," *The Wall Street Journal,* August 7, 2012.

69. Michael Rapoport, "U.S., China Set Pact on Auditor Access," *The Wall Street Journal,* May 24, 2013.

70. Dave Michaels, "U.S. Investors Have Another Reason to Fret over China Firms," *Bloomberg,* November 3, 2015 [**www.bloomberg.com/news/articles/2015-11-03/u-s-investors-have-one-more-reason-to-fret-about-chinese-firms**].

71. Charles Duhigg and David Kocieniewski, "How Apple Sidesteps Billions in Taxes," *The New York Times,* April 28, 2012.

72. Ibid.

73. Ivana Kottasova, "EU Hits Apple with $14.6 Billion Tax Bill," *CNNtech,* August 30, 2016 [**http://money.cnn.com/2016/08/30/technology/apple-tax-eu-us-ireland**].

74. Nancy Scola, "Sources: Feds Taking Second Look at Google Search," *Politico,* May 11, 2016 [**www.politico.com/story/2016/05/federal-trade-commission-google-search-questions-223078**].

75. "EU Files Additional Formal Charges Against Google," *The Wall Street Journal,* July 14, 2016.

76. European Commission, "Mergers: Commission Approves AB InBev's Acquisition of SABMiller, Subject to Conditions," press release, May 24, 2016 [**http://europa.eu/rapid/press-release_IP-16-1900_en.htm**].

77. For a good comparison of U.S. and EU merger analysis and enforcement, see Cento Veljanovski, "EC Merger Policy after GE/Honeywell and Airtours," *Antitrust Bulletin* 49 (Spring 2004), p. 153.

78. Editorial, "The Other Boot," *The New York Times,* May 4, 2007.

79. Keith Bradsher, "China Tightens Grip on Rare Minerals," *The New York Times,* September 1, 2009.

80. "Hands Slapped," *The Economist,* July 9, 2011.

81. Paul Geitner, "U.S., Europe and Japan Escalate Rare-Earth Dispute with China," *The New York Times,* June 27, 2012.

82. Keith Bradsher, "U.S. and Europe Prepare to Settle Chinese Solar Panel Cases," *The New York Times,* May 20, 2013.

83. James Kantor and Keith Bradsher, "Europe and China Agree to Settle Solar Panel Fight," *The New York Times,* July 27, 2013.

84. "U.S. Revises Tariffs and Duties on Chinese Solar Imports," *Bloomberg News,* July 9, 2015 [**www.bloomberg.com/news/articles/2015-07-09/u-s-imposes-dumping-duties-on-imports-of-chinese-solar-goods**].

85. "Hollywood Upstages Beijing," *The Wall Street Journal,* August 13, 2009, p. A1.

86. Keith Bradsher, "China Moves to Retaliate Against U.S. Tire Tariff," *The New York Times,* September 14, 2009. See also "Trade in Goods with China," U.S. Census Bureau [**https://www.census.gov/foreign-trade/balance/c5700.html#2016**].

87. "Why the Deal to Pay Brazil $300 Million Just to Keep Subsidies Is Bad for the WTO, Poor Countries, and U.S. Taxpayers," *The Washington Post,* October 12, 2014.

88. 128 S. Ct. 1346 (2008).

89. *Id.* at 1377 (Breyer, J., dissenting).

90. Case C-236/08, *Google v. Louis Vuitton Malletier SA,* 2010 E.C.R. I-02417.

91. Adam Liptak, "NAFTA Tribunals Stir U.S. Worries," *The New York Times,* April 18, 2004.

92. Klaus-Heiner Lehne, "Hands Off Our Torts," *The Wall Street Journal,* November 18, 2003, p. A20.

93. Based on information from T. Christian Miller, "Plantation Workers Look for Justice in the North," *Los Angeles Times,* May 27, 2007; Justin Rebello, "U.S. District Court in Calif. Rules Against Dow Chemical in Pesticide Exposure Case," *Lawyers USA,* December 2007; and "Dole Food Co. Inc. Wins Court Rulings," *Business Wire,* March 10, 2008.

94. Based on information from Victoria Kim, "Judge Throws Out Verdict Awarding Millions to Dole Workers," *Los Angeles Times,* July 16, 2010; Business Wire, "Dole Food Company Announces That Court Enters Final Order Vacating Judgment, Dismissing Fraudulent Lawsuit Brought by Nicaraguans Claiming to Have Been Banana Workers," press release, March 15, 2011 [**www.thestreet.com/story/11046743/1/dole-food-company-announces-that-court-enters-final-order-vacating-judgment-dismissing-fraudulent-lawsuit-brought-by-nicaraguans-claiming-to-have-been-banana-workers.html**]; Amada Bronstad, "California Bar Drops Complaint

Against Dole's Lawyers," February 28, 2011 [**www.law.com**]; and "Juan Dominguez Cleared of any Wrongdoing by State Bar," March 17, 2011 [**www.bananasthemovie.com**].

95. Steve Garmisa, "U.S. Courts Handle International Law," *Chicago Sun-Times,* September 24, 1997.

96. Juan Forero, "Seizure of Repsol Affiliate in Argentina Stuns Oil Markets," *The Washington Post,* April 26, 2012.

97. 11 U.S. (7 Cranch) 116 (1812).

98. *Sutherland v. Islamic Republic of Iran,* 151 F. Supp. 2d 27 (D.D.C. 2001).

99. "Supreme Court Limits Reach of U.S. Courts," *USA Today—The Des Moines Register-State Edition,* December 2, 2015.

100. *OBB Personenverkehr AG v. Sachs*, 136 S. Ct. 390 (2015).

101. *Samantar v. Yousuf,* 130 S. Ct. 2278 (2010).

102. Based on information from Brent Kendal, "High Court Rejects Pfizer Appeal in Nigeria Drug-Trial Case," *The Wall Street Journal,* June 29, 2010; Nathan Koppel, "Arcane Law Brings Conflicts from Overseas to U.S. Courts," *The Wall Street Journal,* August 27, 2009; Jad Mouawad, "Shell to Pay $15.5 Million to Settle Nigerian Case," *The New York Times,* June 9, 2009; Jad Mouawad, "Oil Industry Braces for Trial on Rights Abuses," *The New York Times,* May 22, 2009; Russell Gold, "Chevron Case Weighs Extent of Overseas Liability," *The Wall Street Journal,* December 1, 2008; and Warren Richey, "U.S. High Court Allows Apartheid Claims Against Multinationals," *The Christian Science Monitor,* May 13, 2008.

103. *Kiobel v. Royal Dutch Petroleum Co.,* 133 S. Ct. 1659 (2013). For a similar ruling by the Supreme Court in 2014 regarding alleged human rights violations against Argentinian workers by the German company Daimler AG, see Jess Bravin and Brent Kendall, "Supreme Court Bars Rights Suits Against Daimler in California," *The Wall Street Journal,* January 14, 2014.

104. Mark Walsh, "Global Warning," *ABA Journal,* July 2013, p. 17.

105. "Law's Long Arm," *The Economist,* October 6, 2012.

106. Adam Liptak, "Foreign Courts Wary of U.S. Punitive Damages," *The New York Times,* March 26, 2008.

107. Aziz Huq, "Defend Muslims, Defend America," *The New York Times,* June 19, 2011. See also Eliyahu Stern, "Don't Fear Islamic Law in America," *The New York Times,* September 2, 2011.

108. David Gauthier-Villars and Charles Forelle, "Burqa Is Banned in France," *The Wall Street Journal,* September 15, 2010.

109. Fakhrurradzie Gade, "Indonesia's Aceh Province Enacted a Strict Muslim Law Thursday: A Tight Pants Ban," *The Christian Science Monitor,* May 27, 2010.

110. *Kiobel v. Royal Dutch Petroleum Co.,* 133 S. Ct. 1659 (2013).

111. 766 F.3d 1013 (9th Cir. 2015).

112. 133 S. Ct. 1659.

113. "SCOTUS Decides Not to Review 9th Circuit's Controversial Doe v. Nestle Decision," Institute for Legal Reform, U.S. Chamber of Commerce, January 12, 2016 [**www.instituteforlegalreform.com/resource/scotus-decides-not-to-review-9th-circuits-controversial-doe-v-nestle-decision**].

114. 202 F.3d 71 (1st Cir. 2000).

CHAPTER SEVENTEEN

Environmental Protection

After completing this chapter, students will be able to fulfill the following learning objectives:

17-1. Identify some of the ways market incentives can be used to prevent and correct environmental problems.

17-2. Evaluate particular environmental problems using the concepts of causation and correlation, cost–benefit analysis, future impacts, and identification of costs imposed.

17-3. Describe the National Environmental Policy Act (NEPA).

17-4. Identify duties of the Environmental Protection Agency (EPA).

17-5. Describe the uses of the Clean Air Act (CAA), including its application to greenhouse gas emissions.

17-6. Describe the uses of the Clean Water Act (CWA).

17-7. Describe the legal issue involving the reach of the CWA.

17-8. Identify some of the major federal laws that address land pollution.

17-9. Discuss the purpose and effect of the Comprehensive Environmental Response, Compensation, and Liability Act of 1980 (CERCLA), commonly known as "the Superfund."

17-10. Identify penalties and other enforcement mechanisms under federal and state regulations.

17-11. Describe some of the challenges to protecting a species under the Endangered Species Act.

17-12. Describe the primary common law remedies for environmental damage.

17-13. Give concrete examples of environmental degradation in the United States and globally.

17-14. Discuss the purpose of the Kyoto Protocol and the Paris Agreement.

Introduction

From local decisions—such as routing a new highway around a wetland or allowing the use of wood stoves—to colossal fears such as global climate change, environmental issues mark our lives in a manner that was unimaginable a few decades ago. From the moment a firm begins to produce, service, manufacture, or create, its operations affect the environment. Imagine all the small decisions made by a company: Does it pack its glassware in plastic bubbles or corrugated wrapping? Does it publish a catalog in paper or only through the Internet? Does it meet with the community before choosing a disposal system? Because of the impact on our physical world, it is critical to understand the legal and ethical dimensions of each of the decisions that are made.

A Global View

Environmental issues are complex for a variety of reasons. Consider the fact that a single action can have variable impacts on the environment—for example, reducing the emission of greenhouse gases (GHG) while at the same time adversely affecting water quality. In addition, the consequences of an action in one location may not manifest themselves for some time—and they may not even be apparent in that same location but may impact another location that is a substantial distance away. This is further complicated by the fact that scientific methodology requires a sufficient amount of time to pass in order to establish causation, with a sufficient coefficient of probability, to offset any countervailing arguments that cessation of the act will cause economic harm. Consider, too, that the Earth is a closed, complex, and unique system; no computer program can model it; no lab can test possibilities under lifelike conditions. Finally, no international body has the jurisdiction or credibility to make enforceable decisions to balance competing national interests and protect against devastating harms to the world's delicate ecosystems and even to life itself.

What observable evidence of this complexity do we have? Consider the following:

- In June 2013, the air pollution in both Singapore and southern Malaysia peaked, with the former issuing face masks and the latter declaring a state of emergency. The cause? The intentional burning of forests and peat wetland across the Strait of Malacca in Indonesia in favor of expanding palm oil plantations. Indonesia is one of the world's largest emitters of carbon, primarily because of its clearing of forests. The fires burned in spite of Indonesia's pledge to cut its carbon emissions by at least 26 percent by 2020 and a $1 billion agreement with Norway in support of a U.N. program to reduce deforestation. Both forest and wetlands are "huge absorbers of carbon," and the forests are home to Indonesia's endangered orangutans.[1]

> For 86 days oil spewed out of British Petroleum's Macondo well.

- For 86 days in 2010, oil spewed out of British Petroleum's Macondo well in the Gulf of Mexico. The long-term impacts on sea life, shorelines, and coastal communities from the roughly 200 million gallons spilled, as well as the effects of the nearly 2 million gallons of chemical dispersants used to combat the spill, are unknown.[2] By volume it was far larger than the 1989 *Exxon Valdez* spill in Prince William Sound, Alaska. Globally, these are not isolated events. For example, in the Niger delta where Royal Dutch Shell, Chevron, and ExxonMobil have significant drilling operations, over the last 50 years as many as 546 million gallons of oil have leaked into the waters,[3] averaging annually the rough equivalent of the *Exxon Valdez* spill. [For a copy of the Oil Spill Commission's final report, see **http://oscaction.org/resource-center/commission-reports-papers**].

- In January 2017, the poor air quality in London set a new modern record and was, at times, worse than the air quality in Beijing—a city notorious for dangerous levels of air pollution. Children in London were told to play indoors because pollution levels were double the legal hourly limit, and it took only five days in 2017 for London to surpass its legal annual limit. A judge recently ordered Britain's ministers to address the issue, stating that they had broken the law by failing to do so. Pollution in the city is responsible for having caused an estimated 9,400 premature deaths.[4]

> Until the issue is resolved, Japan's Fukushima nuclear plant—which was crippled by both an earthquake and a tsunami—will produce 400 tons of contaminated water each day. At least 300 tons of this contaminated water has drained into the sea.

- Two-and-a-half years after the earthquake and tsunami that crippled its Fukushima plant, Japan turned off the last of its 50 nuclear reactors, with no date for returning any of them to service. As of this writing, flow of groundwater into the buildings at Fukushima has not been stopped. The plan was to try to seal off the buildings "behind a mile-long subterranean wall of ground frozen by liquid coolant."[5] Japan has invested $320 million to construct this subterranean "ice wall," and there are serious concerns not only about whether it will work—a section of the wall had yet to fully freeze four months after being switched on in the spring of 2016—but whether the electrical structure may be just as susceptible to natural disasters as the nuclear reactor plant itself.[6] Until the groundwater issue is resolved, the plant will continue to produce 400 tons per day of contaminated water that is used to cool the damaged reactors, all of which is stored on site. In July 2013, 300 tons of this water was discovered to have drained into the sea. Yet another issue is the cleanup of the radioactive contamination that spread through the environment at the start of the disaster. The central government is in charge of cleanup efforts in the most heavily contaminated areas, but the rest is left for local governments to handle.[7]

> By 2025, half of the world's population will be living in water-stressed areas due to global warming.

- According to the World Health Organization, 663 million people rely on unimproved sources of drinking water and in low- and middle-income countries, 38 percent of health care facilities lack an improved water source.[8] It is believed that 10 percent of the world's population consumes food that has been irrigated with wastewater, which contributes to the incidence of disease, malnutrition, and death.[9] By 2025, half of the world's population will be living in water-stressed areas due to global warming.[10]

- In 2010, a report for the academic journal *Science* analyzed the danger level for 25,000 species, classifying 13 percent of birds as threatened with extinction, 25 percent of mammals, and 41 percent of amphibians.[11]

PRACTICING ETHICS   Global Environmental Justice

Environmental justice is "the fair treatment and meaningful involvement of all people regardless of race, color, national origin, or income with respect to the development, implementation and enforcement of environmental laws, regulations and policies. Fair treatment means no group of people should bear a disproportionate share of the negative environmental consequences resulting from industrial, governmental and commercial operations or policies."[12]

Studies in the United States have shown that at least some risks, such as proximity to hazardous waste disposal sites, are not equally distributed.[13] Is the concept of equally distributed environmental risks a useful tool in assessing global environmental hazards? Consider the following:

- In Flint, Michigan, 41.6 percent of the population lives below the poverty line and the median household income is approximately half that of the rest of Michigan. The city is 56.6 percent African American.

- In 2011, the state of Michigan took over Flint's finances because of a projected $25 million deficit. In order to reduce the shortfall, the state switched the city's water supply in 2014 from Lake Huron to the Flint River while a new pipeline to Lake Huron was under construction.

- The Flint River had been severely polluted in the 1970s. In 2001, Michigan ordered the monitoring and cleanup of 134 polluted sites within the Flint River watershed, but the state's Department of Environmental Quality allegedly failed to treat the water with an anticorrosive agent, in violation of federal law. The water was found to be 19 times more corrosive than the water supply from Lake Huron. As a result, lead from aging pipes began to leach into the water supply. The pipes were also more susceptible to a buildup of dangerous bacteria.

- Lead is toxic and when consumed can cause heart, kidney, and neurological damage. In children, exposure can cause impaired cognition, behavioral disorders, hearing problems, and delayed puberty.

- In December 2014, the state's Department of Environmental Quality increased the chlorine in the water to control the level of dangerous bacteria. That same month, the General Motors plant in Flint stopped using the city's water because it was concerned about the high levels of chlorine corroding engine parts. A month later, the city declined an offer from its former supplier to reconnect the city's water supply to Lake Huron and to waive a $4 million fee waiver to restore service. The city cited its concerns that water rates could increase by $12 million each year.

- In December 2015, the water crisis led Flint to declare a state of emergency. A probe of the Flint water crisis began, and various actions were filed, including a federal lawsuit alleging violations of the Safe Water Drinking Act. Failures on the part of numerous government agencies have been cited, and a number of officials have been criminally charged. Four officials were charged with felonies in December 2016.

Question

What factors might make a minority or low-income population more susceptible to environmental injustice? Explain.

Source: "Flint Water Crisis Fast Facts," *CNN Library,* updated February 22, 2017 [**www.cnn.com/2016/03/04/us/flint-water-crisis-fast-facts**].

Part One—A Return to Fundamentals: The Market, Government Regulation, and Self-Regulation

The first three chapters set up the following framework for analyzing the substantive law topics covered in this text: (1) consideration of how well market forces achieve the goals we have for our society; (2) a brief investigation of whether government intervention can bring us closer to those societal goals; and (3) reflection on the role that self-regulation, through ethical decision making and corporate social responsibility, can and does play in realizing our goals. This framework is also useful in evaluating the relationship between business and our natural environment.

Market Failure?

Without regulation, a firm may consider that dumping its garbage into a nearby canal is no big deal. In fact, perhaps the slight amount of garbage the firm dumps is no big deal. However, if every firm were allowed to dump that amount, the canal might become thoroughly polluted. Or consider the possibility that we may all prefer less costly cars that pollute more. Would future generations concur with the decisions we would make today in the absence of regulation?

As discussed in Chapter 8, these examples of water and air pollution would be categorized by economists as *negative externalities*. Wilfred Beckerman, a British economist, described the analysis as follows:

> [T]he costs of pollution are not always borne fully, if at all, by the polluter. . . . Naturally, he has no incentive to economize in the use [of the environment] in the same way that he has for other factors of production that carry a cost, such as labor or capital. . . . This defect of the price mechanism needs to be corrected by governmental action in order to eliminate excessive pollution.[14]

Thus, environmentalists claim the market has failed to protect us from pollution, making regulation necessary. The public and Congress have apparently agreed: A substantial number of environmental laws have been enacted since the early 1970s—laws that address pollution of our air and waterways; that regulate use, disposal, and cleanup of hazardous and toxic wastes; and that protect rare plant and animal species. Many of these laws will be discussed in Part Two.

But as we shall see, our conceptualization of the problems we face may be too simplistic. The bulk of our environmental laws and regulations were drafted to address compartmentalized and discrete issues—clean air or clean water or hazardous waste, as well as particular contaminants, point sources, or individual species. They may be inadequate to address the interrelationships that characterize both our environment and our social and political structures.

Elinor Ostrom, a Nobel laureate in economics, was a leading scholar of common-pool resource management before her death in 2012. She studied how communities develop effective rules for governing depletable resources such as water, fishing grounds, and the atmosphere. Her conclusion? All arrangements—"government-controlled, privatized, or owned by a community—work in some places but not in others. The success or failure of a specific approach hinges on the match of the specific institutional arrangement, local culture, and particular problems involved, as well as how the approach is implemented. . . . [P]olicies for common resources should be considered experiments within complex systems."[15]

Market Incentives

LO 17-1
Identify some of the ways market incentives can be used to prevent and correct environmental problems.

One approach federal regulation has taken is to dictate standards with which businesses must comply. Such legislation has led to steady, and at times even spectacular, strides forward in environmental protection in the United States. But this progress has not dispelled the view, particularly among economists and those in business, that regulating standards may not be the best approach to tackle environmental problems. They believe that pollution control is not so much a matter of law as of economics. It follows that, with proper incentives, the market will in some instances prove superior to traditional regulation in preventing and correcting environmental problems. Some examples of market incentives follow.

Cap-and-Trade Programs

Cap-and-Trade Programs

The concept behind cap-and-trade incentives is that a government sets a cap on the total emissions of a particular pollutant that is lower than the existing level of emissions. It then issues pollution credits to the most significant emitters of that pollutant. Credit recipients can either reduce their discharges to within their credit limit or buy credits from other companies that have reduced their emissions below their own credit amounts. Such programs, therefore, allow the most cost-effective pollution reduction methods to be used to reach the desired environmental goals. The United States was very successful using this approach to reduce sulfur dioxide emissions that were a major factor in the creation of acid rain.[16] In 1995 alone, the year the cap-and-trade program took effect, emissions dropped nationally by 3 million tons, well ahead of the schedule required by law.[17] By 1999, electric utilities produced about 41 percent more electricity than they had in 1980 while emitting 25 percent fewer tons of sulfur dioxide,[18] and in 2007, total sulfur dioxide emissions dropped below the long-term goal, ahead of the 2010 statutory deadline.[19] When the House of Representatives passed a cap-and-trade bill in 2009 to address greenhouse gas (GHG) emissions and the Senate declined to act on it, a coalition of nine Northeast and Mid-Atlantic states acted independently to set up a cap-and-trade program for carbon emissions from power plants within its jurisdiction and, in the first three years, cut average annual emissions by 23 percent.[20] As part of its program to cut GHG emissions to 1990 levels by 2020, California began running its own carbon cap-and-trade program on January 1, 2013, the second-largest such program in the world, following only the European Union's.[21]

Valuing Ecosystem Services

The GHG cap-and-trade programs are more complex than the acid rain program in the United States in that there are many, many different sources of GHG emissions and many varied ways to reduce global GHG. For example, forests and peat wetlands act as carbon sinks—naturally capturing atmospheric carbon and locking it up. Thus, a GHG emitter could cause global GHG emissions to decrease by paying a country such as Indonesia to prevent deforestation that would otherwise occur. Such an approach to controlling global GHG emissions raises complex valuation and verification issues. If country A pays country B to protect its forests, how many GHG credits should country A receive? How much carbon is captured by a square mile of Indonesian forest? How long should country B be required to protect that forest for a particular payment?

Some ecologists and economists are working to establish an analytical framework that would facilitate targeted conservation investments, yielding the highest ecological returns by systematically inventorying and valuing the services nature performs, such as carbon absorption. Others, such as foresters, chemists, and accountants, are developing ways to verify and audit such factors as the amount of carbon stored by a particular stand of trees.

This approach to control of GHG has raised ethical issues. One commentator has argued that "farmers should not be paid to reduce their water pollution any more than I should be paid to stop mugging people." In contrast, another sees the possibility of a hybrid "stoplight" approach. "The red part is: Here's some things you can do to your land that are so bad that we're gonna take you to prison. The yellow light is: Here's . . . some minimal stuff that you really ought to do. Then the green light is: Here's some stuff that's above and beyond the stewardship obligation, and we're going to pay you for doing it, because it's to the benefit of society."

Sources: Matt Jenkins, "Mother Nature's Sum," *Pacific Standard,* October 2008 [**www.psmag.com/business-economics/mother-nature-s-sum-4226**]; and Felicity Barringer, "A Grand Experiment to Rein in Climate Change," *The New York Times,* October 13, 2012.

Question

If burning fossil fuels is a major catalyst of global climate change, then the developed world is the major cause. But citizens of the least developed countries will suffer the most severe consequences. If you already suffer food and water insecurity, any further disruption is catastrophic. "Because hunger and misery cannot afford to make the distinctions of the well-fed—to choose between cutting a tree or saving it—poverty is among the greatest environmental threats in the world."[22] Does this reasoning provide a response to the argument that farmers should not be paid to reduce their water pollution? Explain.

Tax Laws

Tax provisions can also affect behavior, either by encouraging certain behaviors through tax incentives or by discouraging other behaviors through additional taxes. For example, federal income tax credits, which reduce the amount of tax owed, have been granted in various years for solar installations, production of power from wind turbines, and purchasing certain new fuel-efficient cars, such as hybrids. Conversely, many in the United States favor the imposition of a new federal tax on carbon, such as a specified tax per ton of carbon dioxide emitted. Proponents argue that such a tax would promote a reduction in emissions and simultaneously raise revenues, which could be used to reduce the federal deficit, lower corporate tax rates to make U.S. companies more competitive, or compensate lower-income citizens who, indirectly, would bear a heavier burden for the tax through higher gas prices and heating bills. According to one estimate, the poorest 20 percent of Americans spend 21.4 percent of their income on gas and utilities, whereas the richest 20 percent spend only 6.8 percent, and 34 of the richest industrialized countries collect an average of $68.4 in fuel taxes per metric ton of carbon dioxide, while the United States collects federal taxes on energy (including the federal gas tax) amounting to only $6.30 per ton.[23]

Other Incentives

Vehicle Rebates

Other targeted market incentives have also been employed to address environmental issues. For example, direct subsidies in the nature of rebates are not uncommon. One example is the Clean Vehicle Rebate Project administered by The California Environment Protection Agency's Air Resources Board, which offers rebates of up to $7,000 for the purchase or lease of certain new zero-emission vehicles.[24] As of this writing, 171,461 rebates totaling $369,241,801 have been issued.[25] Government agencies have also subsidized particular activities through guaranteed loan programs. For instance, in 2010 and 2011, the Department of Energy's Loan Programs Office financed the launch of five of the world's largest commercial-scale concentrating solar power (CSP) plants with thermal energy storage in the United States, sources of clean energy that are "helping to better integrate renewable energy into the electric grid."[26]

Ethical Business Decision Making

Pay-now-or-pay-later

What level of environmental concern can we expect from managers of publicly held corporations? Can we identify examples of environmental corporate social responsibility? The answer is a resounding yes—all one has to do is review a sample of corporate websites. Why are corporate giants voluntarily doing now what they have not done in the past? In part, the answer may be that the market has changed and market forces are operating to reward corporate responsibility. For example, managers may believe that being "green," or at least being seen as being green by consumers and investors, will improve the corporate bottom line. Or a manager may believe that a proactive approach may lessen the likelihood of future regulation on an issue that is becoming increasingly visible.[27] This is one example of a pay-now-or-pay-later analysis. Managers may take a more environmentally responsible approach now because they think the future cost of not doing so could be enormously larger—in negative publicity, the imposition of fines and penalties, or the cost of more stringent future regulation—than the present actual cost of responsible action.

Green growth

Does the market actually reward sound environmental practices? As a general proposition, that has not been shown, but successful *green growth* examples are multiplying—concrete illustrations that economic growth and environment protection are not mutually exclusive. By 1994, 60-year-old Ray Anderson had grown his 15-person carpet-tile company, Interface Inc., into the world's largest carpet-tile maker, but customers were pushing for the company to develop an environmental strategy. Anderson did. His goal for his company? By 2020, to produce no GHG emissions and no waste and to consume no raw materials that could not be rapidly replenished. As of 2010, GHG emissions were down 35 percent, water usage by 82 percent, fossil fuel consumption by 60 percent, and waste sent to landfills by 82 percent. Company sales increased by 64 percent and, by avoiding over $450 million in costs, its earnings more than doubled. Ray Anderson dedicated the rest of his life to advocating for environmental stewardship and sustainability. He received numerous awards worldwide and, until his death in 2011, was widely sought after as a speaker and adviser on environmental issues.[28] In honor of the "noble qualities" he championed, The Ray C. Anderson Foundation was established to "help create a better world for future generations—tomorrow's child."[29]

[For a video of Ray Anderson's 2009 TED Talk, in which he shares his story, see http://www.raycandersonfoundation.org/butterfly-effect]. [For many other examples of environmentally responsible actions of business, see **www.bsr.org/en/about/in-the-new**].

Questions

1. Consider the implications of two recent headlines: "Fiat Chrysler Shares Crash by a Fifth as It Is Drawn into Emissions Scandal by US Regulators"[30] and "FBI Arrests Volkswagen Executive in Emissions Scandal."[31] It appears that Fiat Chrysler and Volkswagen not only failed to act responsibly to comply with emissions regulations, but

they also committed fraud to make government officials and the public believe they were in compliance. Do you think Fiat Chrysler and Volkswagen are regretting the decisions they made in the past to avoid compliance costs? What costs are they paying now?

2. "The single most important and pervasive moral obligation facing mankind is to ensure survival of a healthy planet for our grandchildren and theirs."[32] Do you agree? Why or why not?

Part Two—Laws and Regulations

LO 17-2

Evaluate particular environmental problems using the concepts of causation and correlation, cost–benefit analysis, future impacts, and identification of costs imposed.

Having reviewed both market forces and ethical business decision making, we turn now to government regulation as an approach for meeting our environmental goals. The United States has developed a wide variety of environmental protection laws and remedies, some of which are covered in this section. In evaluating a particular regulation, it will be helpful to keep in mind the following concepts:

- **Cost–Benefit Analysis.** Environmental protection can be expensive. How much as a society are we willing to pay? Do we want clean air at any cost? We may (or may not) be able to estimate the cost of a particular pro-environment action, but we also need to consider its benefits, including its economic benefits. How do we value human life, represented by a statistical decrease in deaths or illness from exposure to environmental pollutants or by decreased productivity? When does environmental protection cause the sacrifice of short-term economic development? Are there offsetting long-term economic benefits? Can these costs and benefits be measured? These are not easy questions. The answers will necessarily be inexact and require subjective judgments and the use of estimates. More attention, however, is being directed at the effort. The Group of Eight Industrialized (G-8) Nations (Canada, France, Germany, Italy, Japan, Russia, the United Kingdom, and the United States) was formed in 1975 and meets annually so that presidents, prime ministers, finance ministers, and foreign ministers can speak candidly about tough global issues, including energy and the environment.[33] It initiated a project in 2007 to study environmental monetary values and estimated that environmental degradation costs the world economy between $2.5 and $4 trillion annually, or up to 5 percent of global GDP.[34]

> How do we value human life?

- **Impact on Future Generations.** When performing a cost–benefit analysis, how do we evaluate the cost to future generations of our failure to take action? How can we measure the value to those generations if we do take action? In some cases, future generations will bear the brunt, whatever choice we make. For example, how do we measure the impact of climate change on future generations? This is a complex question about which there is no scientific, economic, or political consensus.

- **Proving Causation.** If event A occurs followed by event B, is it necessarily true that event A *caused* event B? It could simply be a coincidence that first A was observed and then B. Or there could, in fact, be a *correlation* between events A and B, but no actual causation. For example, event Z might cause both A and B, but no causal link may exist between A and B. In the environmental area, issues of coincidence, correlation, and causation may be extremely difficult to determine. Does exposure to secondhand smoke cause lung cancer in some nonsmokers? Did the observed increase in greenhouse gases contribute to global warming such that sea levels rose, increasing the intensity of Hurricane Katrina, in turn causing property damage to a degree that would not otherwise have occurred?[35] If, in the example of Z, A, and B, we focus our efforts to stop A in order to prevent B, we will be wasting our time and money. On the other hand, how long can we wait to determine definitively whether a causal link exists between A and B? Our answer may depend on the severity of the arm we believe is associated with B.

- **Who Pays?** If we decide to correct an environmental problem, who should pay for the correction? If we require corporate America to invest in pollution control devices, the cost may be shared by consumers (through increased prices) and investors (through a reduced corporate profit). If habitats of endangered species are to be preserved, current landowners may lose all or a portion of their investment and workers employed on the land may lose their jobs. Sometimes the issue of who will pay is central to the controversy as to where a particular facility, such as a hazardous waste disposal site, should be located. Not surprisingly, a common response of citizens near a proposed location is, "yes, it's necessary, but *not in my backyard!*" This response is so common, that it is now referred to as NIMBY.

> "Yes ... but not in my backyard!"

- **Politics.** Environmental protection in the United States is not just a matter of science, cost assessment, and social policy; it is also a matter of politics. California, for example, has historically received permission from the Environmental Protection Agency (EPA) to impose stricter vehicle emission standards than federal law requires. California sought similar permission in 2005, in part to add greenhouse gases to the emissions regulated. After delaying the decision for two years, the EPA denied California's request on the very same day in 2007 that President Bush signed into law the federal 35-miles-per-gallon standard. California responded by taking the EPA to court. A year later, in his first month in the White House, President Obama directed the EPA to reconsider California's application, signaling a sharp break with the Bush administration's less aggressive stance on climate change. The waiver was approved in June 2009.[36] There are many indications that Trump's administration will resume a less aggressive stance on climate change. As Donald Trump was sworn into office on January 20, 2017, the link to the original White House page dedicated to climate change became broken. Referencing specific administrative rulings that the former administration put in place to address climate change, the website now states, "Lifting these restrictions will greatly help American workers, increasing wages by more than $30 billion over the next 7 years."[37]

Question

What environmental issue do you care about most? Greenhouse gases? Deforestation? Drinkable water for the world's population? Protection of the polar bear? Select an issue you care about. (If it's climate change, select a specific potential response to it, such as sharing environmental technologies with developing countries, increasing mileage requirements, requiring the use of energy-efficient light bulbs, etc.) Do some online research for relevant data and explore your issue in light of the five concepts discussed above. Be careful to use reliable online resources in your research.

The Federal Role

The federal government has long maintained a role in the protection of the environment—some argue too great a role. As early as 1899, Congress enacted a law that required a permit to discharge refuse into navigable waters. When it became apparent that private, state, and local environmental efforts were not adequate to address the burgeoning problems, Congress began taking more aggressive legislative steps in the early 1970s.

National Environmental Policy Act

LO 17-3
Describe the National Environmental Policy Act (NEPA).

The 1970 National Environmental Policy Act (NEPA) established a strong federal presence in the promotion of a clean and healthy environment. NEPA represents a general commitment by the federal government to "use all practicable means" to conduct federal affairs in a fashion that both promotes "the general welfare" and operates in "harmony" with the environment.

NEPA established the Council on Environmental Quality (CEQ), which serves as an adviser to the president. The CEQ is a watchdog of sorts. It is required to conduct studies and collect information regarding the state of the environment. The council then develops policy and legislative proposals for the president and Congress. [For CEQ's homepage, see **www.whitehouse.gov/ceq**].

NEPA's primary influence, however, results from its *environmental impact statement* (EIS) requirements. With few exceptions, "proposals for legislation and other major federal action significantly affecting the quality of the human environment" must be accompanied

> NEPA's primary influence results from its environment impact statement (EIS) requirements.

by an EIS explaining the impact on the environment and detailing reasonable alternatives. Completing an EIS requires undertaking a cost–benefit analysis. It also requires consideration of cause-and-effect links. Major federal construction projects (highways, dams, nuclear reactors) would normally require an EIS, but less visible federal programs (ongoing timber management or the abandonment of a lengthy railway) may also require EIS treatment. Although the focus here is on federal actions, thus exempting solely private acts from this scrutiny, a major private-sector action supported by federal funding or by one of several varieties of federal permission also may require an EIS. Therefore, private companies receiving federal contracts, funding, licenses, and the like may be parties to the completion of an EIS.

Question

Should a state be required to prepare an EIS if it wants to use federal funds to promote statewide tourism? Does it matter which state it is? Consider Iowa and then consider Hawaii. Can you identify factors that make one distinctly different from the other?[38]

Environmental Protection Agency

LO 17-4
Identify duties of the Environmental Protection Agency (EPA).

The private sector was not left without regulation or constraint. The Environmental Protection Agency (EPA) was created in 1970 to mount a coordinated attack on environmental problems. EPA duties include, among other things, (1) gathering information, particularly by surveying pollution problems; (2) conducting research on pollution problems; (3) assisting state and local pollution control efforts; and (4) administering many of the federal laws directed to environmental concerns. [For the EPA home page, see **www.epa.gov**].

Fracking: A Cautionary Tale

As previously mentioned, many of the U.S. environmental laws and regulations were drafted to address compartmentalized and discrete issues. This means that, outside of federal action triggering the requirement of an EIS, there may be no forum in which to evaluate the full environmental impact of an activity that raises multiple issues. Consider hydraulic fracturing, commonly referred to as fracking, in which a mixture of sand, fluids, and chemical additives are pumped under high pressure into wells to fracture shale rock, thereby releasing natural gas for extraction. Substantial reserves of natural gas have been found in North America—enough that the United States could overtake Russia as the world's largest producer of oil and gas, a potential global political game-changer. Approximately 13,000 new wells are drilled each year in the United States. In 2000, there were approximately 23,000 wells, and they accounted for 2 percent of the oil produced in the United States. By 2015, there were approximately 300,000 wells, accounting for 51 percent of the oil produced in the United States. If this newly accessible gas is used to produce electricity, allowing coal-fired plants that emit twice the carbon dioxide as gas to be retired, our total carbon dioxide emissions should decrease.

However, whether GHG emissions are actually reduced and whether other substantial environmental issues are created by the fracking process are questions worth considering. At least one report suggests that such issues may well be economically feasible to remediate, but for the most part companies are not currently required to do so. Specific issues that have been raised, but that remain partly or wholly unaddressed, include the following:

- A report released in 2012 by three members of Congress indicates that between 2005 and 2009, 750 chemicals had been used in the fracking process, some of which were extremely toxic, such as benzene and lead. The only fracking fuel additive required by federal law to be disclosed is diesel fuel, in part owing to a 2005 exemption placed in the Safe Drinking Water Act.

- Numerous concerns have been raised with regard to the impact of fracking on local water resources, including concerns that some of the natural gas released may migrate out of the wells and negatively affect drinking, surface, and groundwater. These water resources may also be endangered by escape of the fracking fluid or by the flowback water. The volume of water necessary for the fracking process may also have a negative impact on local water supplies.

- When not actually in use, both the fracking fluid and flowback waters will require environmentally sound storage and disposal. Approximately 60 percent of the flowback water is recycled by transportation to storage and treatment locations via pipelines or trucks and, after treatment (often only by dilution), discharged into surface water. The rest may be injected back into the ground, raising some concerns that this deep injection process may trigger earthquakes.

- Once extracted, the gas itself requires transportation to refineries by rail or pipeline, raising additional environmental issues. Extensions of existing pipelines require regulatory approvals, but most rail transport does not.

Sources: Joe Nocera, "A Fracking Rorschach Test," *The New York Times,* October 4, 2013; Abbi L. Cohen and John M. Ix, "What's the Deal with Fracking?" *Association of Corporate Counsel,* July 18, 2012 [**www.lexology.com**]; "Natural Gas, by the Book," *The New York Times,* June 9, 2012; John M. Broder, "U.S. Caps Emissions in Drilling for Fuel," *The New York Times,* April 19, 2012, p. A20; "The Need to Be Seen to Be Clean," *The Economist,* May 14, 2011, p. 37; and "Today in Energy: Hydraulic Fracturing Accounts for About Half of Current U.S. Crude Oil Production," U.S. Energy Information Administration, March 15, 2016 [**www.eia.gov/todayinenergy/detail.php?id=25372**].

Regulation of Air Pollution

In the United States, we depend on (and, indeed, we emotionally embrace) the automobile. In doing so, we have opened vistas of opportunity not previously imagined. However, motor vehicles also discharge carbon monoxide, nitrogen oxide, and hydrocarbons as by-products of the combustion of fuel, thus fouling our air. Today we know those vehicles also are significant emitters of greenhouse gases. Industrial production, manufacturing, generation of electricity, and the combustion of fossil fuels in homes and workplaces are also significant contributors to the dilemma of dirty air and greenhouse gases.

Clean Air Act of 1990

LO 17-5

Describe the uses of the Clean Air Act (CAA), including its application to greenhouse gas emissions.

Early clean air legislation in 1963 and 1965 afforded the government limited authority. The Clean Air Act (CAA) amendments of 1970 and 1977 gave the EPA the power to set air quality standards and to ensure that those standards are achieved according to a timetable prescribed by the agency. Politics brought clean air to the fore in 1990 and the Clean Air Act of 1990 followed. It phased in new standards over a period of years, generally requiring tougher auto emission controls, cleaner-burning gasoline, and new equipment to capture industrial and business pollution, all of which worked toward the general goal of reducing airborne pollutants by about 50 percent. Under the CAA, air quality standards are set federally, but the states are required to establish implementation plans to achieve and maintain those standards.

In recent years, there has been considerable high-profile litigation over clean air standards. The Supreme Court's decision in *Massachusetts v. EPA,* presented below, has had the most profound effect. In this case, a number of states, cities, and private organizations joined as petitioners to argue that the EPA had abdicated its responsibility under Section 202(a)(1) of the CAA to "prescribe . . . standards applicable to the emission of any air pollutant" when it refused to regulate greenhouse gas emissions from new motor vehicles.

LEGAL BRIEFCASE

Massachusetts v. Environmental Protection Agency   127 S. Ct. 1438 (2007)

Justice Stevens

A well-documented rise in global temperatures has coincided with a significant increase in the concentration of carbon dioxide in the atmosphere. Respected scientists believe the two trends are related. For when carbon dioxide is released into the atmosphere, it acts like the ceiling of a greenhouse, trapping solar energy and retarding the escape of reflected heat. It is therefore a species—the most important species—of a "greenhouse gas."

Calling global warming "the most pressing environmental challenge of our time," a group of states, local governments, and private organizations, alleged . . . [that the] EPA has abdicated its responsibility under the Clean Air Act to regulate the emissions of four greenhouse gases, including carbon dioxide. Specifically, petitioners asked us to answer two questions concerning . . . the Act: whether EPA has the statutory authority to regulate greenhouse gas emissions from new motor vehicles; and if so, whether its stated reasons for refusing to do so are consistent with the statute.

I

Section 202(a)(1) of the Clean Air Act . . . provides:

The [EPA] Administrator shall by regulation prescribe (and from time to time revise) . . . standards applicable to the emission of any air pollutant from any class or classes of new motor vehicles or new motor vehicle engines, which in his judgment cause, or contribute to, air pollution which may reasonably be anticipated to endanger public health or welfare. . . .

The Act defines "air pollutant" to include "any air pollution agent or combination of such agents, including any physical, chemical, biological, radioactive . . . substance or matter which is emitted into or otherwise enters the ambient air." "Welfare" is also defined broadly: among other things, it includes "effects on . . . weather . . . and climate."

* * * * *

II

On October 20, 1999, a group of 19 private organizations filed a rulemaking petition asking EPA to regulate "greenhouse gas emissions from new motor vehicles under Section 202 of the Clean Air Act." . . . As to EPA's statutory authority, the petition observed that the agency itself had already confirmed that it had the power to regulate carbon dioxide. In 1998, Jonathan Z. Cannon, then EPA's General Counsel, prepared a legal opinion concluding that "CO[2] emissions are within the scope of EPA's authority to regulate," even as he recognized that EPA had so far declined to exercise that authority. Cannon's successor, Gary S. Guzy, reiterated that opinion before a congressional committee just two weeks before the rulemaking petition was filed.

* * * * *

On September 8, 2003, EPA entered an order denying the rulemaking petition. The agency gave two reasons for its decision: (1) that contrary to the opinions of its former general counsels, the Clean Air Act does not authorize EPA to issue mandatory regulations to address global climate change; and (2) that even if the agency had the authority to set greenhouse gas emission standards, it would be unwise to do so at this time.

* * * * *

Having reached that conclusion, EPA believed it followed that greenhouse gases cannot be "air pollutants" within the meaning of the Act. . . . The agency bolstered this conclusion by explaining that if carbon dioxide were an air pollutant, the only feasible method of reducing tailpipe emissions would be to improve fuel economy. But because Congress has already created detailed mandatory fuel economy standards subject to Department of Transportation (DOT) administration, the agency concluded that EPA regulation would either conflict with those standards or be superfluous.

Even assuming that it had authority over greenhouse gases, EPA explained in detail why it would refuse to exercise that authority. The

agency began by recognizing that the concentration of greenhouse gases has dramatically increased as a result of human activities, and acknowledged the attendant increase in global surface air temperatures. EPA nevertheless gave controlling importance to the [National Resource Council] Report's statement that a causal link between the two cannot be unequivocally established. Given that residual uncertainty, EPA concluded that regulating greenhouse gas emissions would be unwise.

The agency furthermore characterized any EPA regulation of motor-vehicle emissions as a "piecemeal approach" to climate change and stated that such regulation would conflict with the president's "comprehensive approach" to the problem. That approach involves additional support for technological innovation, the creation of nonregulatory programs to encourage voluntary private-sector reductions in greenhouse gas emissions, and further research on climate change—not actual regulation. According to EPA, unilateral EPA regulation of motor-vehicle greenhouse gas emissions might also hamper the president's ability to persuade key developing countries to reduce greenhouse gas emissions.

V [III–IV omitted—ed.]

* * * * *

[We] "may reverse any such action found to be . . . arbitrary, capricious, an abuse of discretion, or otherwise not in accordance with law."

VI

On the merits, the first question is whether Section 202(a)(1) of the Clean Air Act authorizes EPA to regulate greenhouse gas emissions from new motor vehicles in the event that it forms a "judgment" that such emissions contribute to climate change. We have little trouble concluding that it does. . . .

The statutory text forecloses EPA's reading. The Clean Air Act's sweeping definition of "air pollutant" includes "*any* air pollution agent or combination of such agents, including *any* physical, chemical . . . substance or matter which is emitted into or otherwise enters the ambient air. . . ." On its face, the definition embraces all airborne compounds of whatever stripe, and underscores that intent through the repeated use of the word "any." Carbon dioxide, methane, nitrous oxide, and hydrofluorocarbons are without a doubt "physical [and] chemical . . . substance[s] which [are] emitted into . . . the ambient air." The statute is unambiguous.

* * * * *

EPA finally argues that it cannot regulate carbon dioxide emissions from motor vehicles because doing so would require it to tighten mileage standards, a job (according to EPA) that Congress has assigned to DOT. But that DOT sets mileage standards in no way licenses EPA to shirk its environmental responsibilities. EPA has been charged with protecting the public's "health" and "welfare," a statutory obligation wholly independent of DOT's mandate to promote energy efficiency. The two obligations may overlap, but there is no reason to think the two agencies cannot both administer their obligations and yet avoid inconsistency.

* * * * *

VII

The alternative basis for EPA's decision—that even if it does have statutory authority to regulate greenhouse gases, it would be unwise to do so at this time—rests on reasoning divorced from the statutory text. While the statute does condition the exercise of EPA's authority on its formation of a "judgment," that judgment must relate to whether an air pollutant "cause[s], or contribute[s] to, air pollution which may reasonably be anticipated to endanger public health or welfare." Put another way, the use of the word "judgment" is not a roving license to ignore the statutory text. It is but a direction to exercise discretion within defined statutory limits.

If EPA makes a finding of endangerment, the Clean Air Act requires the agency to regulate emissions of the deleterious pollutant from new motor vehicles. . . . EPA no doubt has significant latitude as to the manner, timing, content, and coordination of its regulations with those of other agencies. But once EPA has responded to a petition for rulemaking, its reasons for action or inaction must conform to the authorizing statute. Under the clear terms of the Clean Air Act, EPA can avoid taking further action only if it determines that greenhouse gases do not contribute to climate change or if it provides some reasonable explanation as to why it cannot or will not exercise its discretion to determine whether they do. To the extent that this constrains agency discretion to pursue other priorities of the administrator or the president, this is the congressional design.

EPA has refused to comply with this clear statutory command. Instead, it has offered a laundry list of reasons not to regulate. For example, EPA said that a number of voluntary executive branch programs already provide an effective response to the threat of global warming, that regulating greenhouse gases might impair the president's ability to negotiate with "key developing nations" to reduce emissions, and that curtailing motor-vehicle emissions would reflect "an inefficient, piecemeal approach to address the climate change issue."

Although we have neither the expertise nor the authority to evaluate these policy judgments, it is evident they have nothing to do with whether greenhouse gas emissions contribute to climate change. Still less do they amount to a reasoned justification for declining to form a scientific judgment. . . .

Nor can EPA avoid its statutory obligation by noting the uncertainty surrounding various features of climate change and concluding that it would therefore be better not to regulate at this time. If the scientific uncertainty is so profound that it precludes EPA from

making a reasoned judgment as to whether greenhouse gases contribute to global warming, EPA must say so. That EPA would prefer not to regulate greenhouse gases because of some residual uncertainty . . . is irrelevant. The statutory question is whether sufficient information exists to make an endangerment finding.

In short, EPA has offered no reasoned explanation for its refusal to decide whether greenhouse gases cause or contribute to climate change. Its action was therefore "arbitrary, capricious, . . . or otherwise not in accordance with law." . . .

[Reversed and remanded.]

Questions

1. Under what conditions did the Supreme Court say it had the power to reverse the EPA's decision not to regulate the carbon dioxide emissions of new vehicles?

2. What did the petitioners, including the Commonwealth of Massachusetts, want the EPA to do?

3. The EPA said that, even if it had the authority to regulate greenhouse gas emissions from motor vehicles, it would not do so. What reasons did the EPA give for this refusal? What did the Supreme Court say about those reasons?

4. Following this decision of the Supreme Court, what was the EPA required to do? Was the EPA required to set a standard for greenhouse gas emissions from new vehicles?

5. Look back at the discussion about proving causation at the start of Part Two of this chapter. Did the Supreme Court say that greenhouse gas emissions from vehicles caused global warming? What did the Court observe about causation?

AFTERWORD

Despite the Court's 2007 ruling in *Massachusetts v. EPA,* not until President Obama took office did the EPA rule that GHG emissions are pollutants that threaten public health. Built on the foundation of its initial endangerment finding, the EPA then promulgated rules establishing fuel economy and greenhouse gas emission standards for cars and light trucks covering model years 2012–2016, as well as a timetable for controlling GHG emissions from power plants and other stationary sources and targeting those controls to cover only the largest emitters. Quickly, the EPA found itself back in court with various industry groups and 14 states, arguing in part that the EPA had impermissibly relied on scientific findings from the U.N. Intergovernmental Panel on Climate Change, the National Research Council, and the U.S. Global Change Research Program. In a sharply worded opinion, the federal Circuit Court for the District of Columbia ruled on June 26, 2012, that

> [the] EPA had before it substantial record evidence that anthropogenic emissions of greenhouse gases "very likely" caused warming of the climate over the last several decades. . . .

Relying again upon substantial scientific evidence, EPA determined that anthropogenically induced climate change threatens both public health and public welfare. It found that extreme weather events, changes in air quality, increases in food- and water-borne pathogens, and increases in temperatures are likely to have adverse health effects. The record also supports EPA's conclusion that climate change endangers human welfare by creating risk to food production and agriculture, forestry, energy, infrastructure, ecosystems, and wildlife. Substantial evidence further supported EPA's conclusion that the warming resulting from the greenhouse gas emissions could be expected to create risks to water resources and in general to coastal areas as a result of expected increase in sea level.[39]

The Supreme Court granted *certiorari* and on June 23, 2014, held that the EPA could regulate GHG emissions from stationary sources that were already subject to regulation based on their emissions of conventional pollutants.[40]

Greenhouse Gas Regulations

Although many have argued that no amount of GHG regulation will be as effective as a federal climate bill, Congress has thus far chosen not to act. The Obama administration, however, made curbing GHG emissions through administrative rule making a priority for his second term. Among other initiatives, it established national standards for carbon dioxide pollution from U.S. power plants, the largest source of carbon pollution in the country. The goal was a 30 percent reduction by 2030 in the level of carbon dioxide that existed in 2005. Under the Clean Power Plan, states could, but were not required to, include cap-and-trade arrangements in their initiatives to control plant emissions. Such arrangements would permit more efficient plants to sell their excess credits to less efficient plants, thereby allowing mandated reductions to be achieved as cost-effectively as possible for the state as a whole. Between 2008 and 2015, there was a 9.4 percent decrease in carbon emissions.[41] However, the EPA repealed the Clean Power Plan rules in December 2016, one month before President Trump took office, signalling that "the federal government has now formally begun to withdraw from its efforts to curb climate change"[42] in an effort to reduce regulation of American industries.

Non-GHG Air-Quality Regulations

Greenhouse gases are, of course, not the only air pollutant hazardous to health. A 2012 report from the American Lung Association noted that 41 percent of our population lives in counties that exceeded standards set for ozone and particulates from 2008 to 2010.[43] In recent years, the EPA has issued stricter standards governing such pollutants as ozone, which is a substantial contributor to smog; fine particulate matter, also known as soot, which can enter the lungs and bloodstream and cause respiratory and heart ailments; and sulfur dioxide, which contributes to acid rain and smog. The EPA has attempted to address another persistent problem—air pollution traveling into downwind states and impairing their capacity to attain federally mandated air standards—through its issuance of the Cross-State Air Pollution Rule (CSAPR). Implementation of the rule was delayed four years, however, until January 1, 2015, after nearly 40 separate petitioners, including cities, states, power companies, and various trade organizations, challenged the EPA's statutory authority in the design of the rule's provisions. The Supreme Court upheld the EPA's authority in April 2014.[44] CSAPR requires power plants in 28 states to install new pollution controls or buy pollution credits under a limited cap-and-trade system.[45]

In any case, tighter regulation of traditional air pollutants, together with price competition from abundant natural gas, has been reducing the amount of power generation contributed by coal-fired plants. At its peak in 1988, coal provided 60 percent of our electricity, but by 2012 its share had dropped almost in half.[46]

Motor Vehicle Emission Standards

The total gallons of gas consumed has gradually decreased since its peak in 2007 due, in part, to the financial crisis, higher gas prices, and increased vehicle fuel efficiency. Consumption in 2012 was about 6 percent below the 2007 peak and roughly on par with usage in 2003.[47] Continued improvement should result from the steady increase in average fuel economy mandates—29 miles per gallon (MPG) in 2012, increased to 35.5 in 2016, and rising to 54.5 MPG for the 2025 model year, standards that have been supported by most major auto manufacturers. The latest regulations also incorporate for the first time express GHG emission standards, which is particularly significant in that light-duty vehicle emissions have accounted for roughly 17 percent of GHG emissions in the United States.[48] On average, European vehicles are 30 percent more fuel-efficient than American vehicles, except with regard to light-duty vehicles, where U.S. standards are tougher, and heavy-duty vehicles, for which Europe sets no fuel-efficiency requirements.[49] One reason for Europe's higher average fuel efficiency is that, unlike the United States, it provides tax incentives for diesel fuel and thus a significant number of cars there run on diesel.[50]

Regulation of Water Pollution

As with the air, we often treat our water resources as free goods. Rather than paying the full cost of producing goods and services, we have simply dumped a portion of that cost into the nearest body of water. The results range from smelly to dangerous to tragic. The evidence can be found in our local rivers and lakes, but also in our global gulfs, seas, and oceans.

BP's 2010 oil spill in the Gulf of Mexico has done, and will do, untold damage, but the waters of the Gulf before the spill were hardly pristine. Ninety percent of America's offshore drilling occurs there, drilling that has gone on for over 60 years and that provides tens of thousands of jobs. Since 1964, more than 300 spills releasing over a half million barrels of oil have occurred, not to mention the thousands of tons of "produced water"—a by-product of drilling that includes oil, grease, and heavy metals—that are dumped annually. After World War II, the Gulf was even used by the government to dispose of surplus mines, bombs, and ammunition.[51]

The debris of our modern lives—including light bulbs, bottle caps, toothbrushes, and all manner of plastics—also shows up in our oceans.[52] In both the Atlantic and Pacific oceans, "garbage patches" involving millions of square miles exist, composed primarily of microplastics broken down from larger items, but also including larger objects such as those already mentioned. We have ample evidence of the consequences for fish and other aquatic life. As one observer who has worked on the Gulf his whole life noted, "You can fool people, but you can't fool the fish."[53] [For more on the Great Pacific Garbage Patch, see **http://education.nationalgeographic.com/education/encyclopedia/great-pacific-garbage-patch/?ar_a=1**].

> "You can fool people, but you can't fool the fish."

Federal Policy

LO 17-6

Describe the uses of the Clean Water Act (CWA).

The 1972 Clean Water Act (CWA), designed to "restore and maintain the chemical, physical, and biological integrity of the nation's waters," established two national goals: (1) achieving water quality sufficient for the protection and propagation of fish, shellfish, and wildlife and for recreation in and on the water and (2) eliminating the discharge of pollutants into navigable waters. The case below is the first to apply *Massachusetts v. EPA* to the CWA but with, perhaps, a surprisingly different outcome. It underscores the fact that states have primary responsibility for enforcing the CWA and that the EPA may assume enforcement authority at its sole discretion.

LEGAL BRIEFCASE

Gulf Restoration Network v. Jackson   2016 WL 7241473 (E.D. La., December 15, 2016)

Judge Jay C. Zainey

I. Background

Plaintiffs are various not-for-profit environmental organizations that strive to protect the environment. Plaintiffs filed this action to assert alleged violations of the Administrative Procedure Act ("APA") by the EPA. The lawsuit derives from EPA's July 29, 2011 denial of a rule-making petition that Plaintiffs filed with the agency.

* * * * *

A. The Petition

* * * * *

[H]igh levels of nitrogen and phosphorous pollution are devastating the Gulf of Mexico as evidenced by a large "dead zone" or "hypoxic zone" in the northern Gulf. . . . [T]he states in the Mississippi River Basin have no numeric water quality standards for phosphorous in rivers or streams or for nitrogen in any waters. And most states do not attempt to limit nitrogen and phosphorous discharges in [National Pollutant Discharge Elimination System] permits. Because the States do not sufficiently limit levels of nitrogen and phosphorous in their own waters, the Mississippi River is inundated with excess levels of harmful nitrogen and phosphorous, thereby leading to the "dead zone" near the mouth of the river.

The crux of the Petition is Plaintiffs' dissatisfaction with what they characterize as EPA's "hands-off approach" to dealing with the problem of nitrogen and phosphorus pollution in the United States. Acknowledging that the Clean Water Act assigns responsibility for such pollution control to the States in the first instance, Plaintiffs

contend that most states to date have done little or nothing to meaningfully control the levels of nitrogen and phosphorous that pollute their waters, and that they have even less political will to protect downstream waters. Plaintiffs explain that over the years EPA has offered many plans and methods for addressing the nitrogen and phosphorous pollution problem but those plans have failed because they have never been backed by direct action by EPA. Recognizing that Congress gave EPA the authority to step in and address the nitrogen/phosphorus problem in light of the States' clear failure to do so, Plaintiffs requested under section 4 of the APA, 5 U.S.C. § 553(e), that EPA use its rulemaking powers to promulgate federal standards to control nitrogen and phosphorous pollution.

The rulemaking powers referenced in the Petition derive from § 303(c)(4) of the Clean Water Act ("CWA"), 33 U.S.C. § 1251, *et seq.* Section 303(c)(4) provides:

> The Administrator shall promptly prepare and publish proposed regulations setting forth a revised or new water quality standard for the navigable waters involved—
>
> (A) if a revised or new water quality standard submitted by such State under paragraph (3) of this subsection for such waters is determined by the Administrator not to be consistent with the applicable requirements of this chapter, or
>
> **(B) in any case where the Administrator determines that a revised or new standard is necessary to meet the requirements of this chapter.**

* * * * *

33 U.S.C. § 1313(c)(4)(A), (B) (emphasis added).

Specifically, Plaintiffs urged EPA to invoke its rulemaking authority under § 303(c)(4)(B), the emphasized language above, to impose federal numeric water quality standards for the portion of the ocean protected by the CWA but outside the jurisdiction of any state and for all water bodies in all states for which numeric water quality standards controlling nitrogen and phosphorous pollution have not yet been established. Alternatively, Plaintiffs proposed that EPA do this for the Northern Gulf of Mexico and for all waters of the United States within the Mississippi River Basin. At a minimum, Plaintiffs urged EPA to establish water quality standards to control nitrogen and phosphorous pollution in the mainstem of the Mississippi River and the Northern Gulf of Mexico. Additionally, Plaintiffs urged EPA to establish TMDLs [Total Maximum Daily Loads] for nitrogen and phosphorous for the Gulf of Mexico, the Mississippi River, and each Mississippi River tributary that fails to meet the numeric standards set for nitrogen and phosphorous for which a TMDL had not already been prepared. At the least, Plaintiffs suggested that EPA should prepare a TMDL for nitrogen and for phosphorous for the mainstem of the Mississippi River and the Northern Gulf of Mexico.

B. EPA's Denial

* * * * *

EPA issued its formal response ("the Denial") on July 29, 2011. . . . EPA neither determined that a new or revised standard was necessary—a threshold determination which would have triggered EPA's non-discretionary duty under § 303(c)(4)(B) to promulgate federal standards—nor determined that a new or revised standard was not necessary—a conclusion that might have been difficult to reconcile with the undisputed evidence demonstrating the significant and serious water quality problems caused by nitrogen and phosphorous pollution. Instead, EPA declined to make a "necessity determination," essentially deciding not to decide. *See Gulf Restoration Network,* 783 F.3d [227,] 238 n.61 [5th Cir. 2015].

C. The Complaint

. . . Plaintiffs requested that the Court declare that EPA's denial of the Petition was arbitrary, capricious, an abuse of discretion, or otherwise not in accordance with law in violation of the APA, 5 U.S.C. § 706(2)(A), and the CWA, 33 U.S.C. § 1313(c)(4)(B). . . .

D. The Court's Ruling

* * * * *

. . . [T]he Court concluded that the Supreme Court's [2007] decision in *Massachusetts v. Environmental Protection Agency* . . . precluded EPA from refusing to make a § 303(c)(4)(B) necessity determination in response to Plaintiffs' petition for rulemaking. . . . The Court rejected, however, Plaintiffs' contention that . . . EPA could not rely on non-scientific factors when making a necessity

determination under § 303(c)(4)(B). . . . The Court declined to grant Plaintiffs' motion insofar as they sought to have the Court rule as a matter of law that a necessity determination under § 303(c)(4)(B) would be limited solely to scientific data. The Court remanded the matter to EPA. . . .

E. The Appeal

EPA appealed the Court's ruling. . . . As to the second question of whether EPA was required to make a necessity determination, in other words whether EPA had discretion under § 303(c)(4)(B) of the CWA to choose not to make a determination, the Fifth Circuit disagreed with the Court. The appellate court was convinced that *Massachusetts v. EPA* did not deprive EPA of discretion to decline to make a necessity determination so long as it provided a "reasonable explanation" grounded in the statute for why it had elected not to do so. The Fifth Circuit vacated the ruling, and remanded the case to have this Court decide in the first instance whether EPA's explanation for why it declined to make a necessity determination was legally sufficient. In doing so, the appellate court not only explained the proper way to apply the *Massachusetts v. EPA* decision but also provided several legal principles to guide this Court's next course of action.

II. Discussion

This Court's task on remand is a narrow one: To determine whether EPA's explanation for why it refused to make a necessity determination was legally sufficient. Per the Fifth Circuit's application of *Massachusetts v. EPA,* legal sufficiency turns on whether EPA has provided a "reasonable explanation," which must be grounded in the statute, as to why it declined to make a necessity determination. In reviewing EPA's refusal to make a necessity determination, the Court applies the arbitrary and capricious standard of review set out in the APA. This standard will be "at the high end of the range of deference" in this case, which while dealing specifically with a refusal to make a threshold determination, is analogous to a refusal to initiate rulemaking. This Court's review is therefore "extremely limited," and must be "highly deferential." EPA's burden is "slight."

Turning to the Denial, EPA did not take issue with Plaintiffs' contentions regarding the significant and serious water quality problems caused by nitrogen and phosphorous pollution. But EPA disagreed that use of its federal rulemaking authority would be the most effective or practical means of addressing the nitrogen/phosphorous problem at this time. Instead, EPA explained that in its judgment the most effective and sustainable way to address widespread and pervasive nutrient pollution in the Mississippi-Atchafalaya River Basin ("MARB") and elsewhere would be to build on its earlier efforts and to continue to work cooperatively with states and tribes to strengthen nutrient management programs. EPA characterized Plaintiffs' proposed rulemaking solution as "unprecedented and complex" as well as "highly resource and time intensive." EPA explained that efforts to promulgate federal numeric nutrient criteria ("NNC") for 50, 31, or even 10 states at one time would involve EPA staff from across the entire agency, as well as support from technical experts outside the agency. Then after the daunting task of completing a rulemaking process of the magnitude proposed, EPA would be faced with sizable regulatory and oversight burdens. EPA summarized its position by stating that it did not believe that the use of its rulemaking authority, especially in light of the sweeping scope of the Petition, would be a practical or efficient way to address nutrient pollution on a national or regional scale.

* * * * *

T]he Denial was grounded primarily on EPA's assessment that working in partnership with the States to reduce nutrient pollution would be a more effective approach at present. In other words, EPA was not ready to give up on the cooperative states-first model upon which the CWA is based. EPA gave a thorough explanation as to why the agency believed that federal rulemaking would not be the most efficacious approach to the nitrogen/phosphorous problem. EPA also explained the non-rulemaking programs that it was implementing to address the problem with the states. EPA did not deny that rulemaking may become necessary at some point if continued efforts at the cooperative approach either fail to improve current water quality conditions appreciably or conditions worsen. EPA did explain the administrative burdens associated with the rulemaking that Plaintiffs were proposing but this explanation was given in light of the sweeping nature of the rulemaking that Plaintiffs were requesting.

The question then is whether the reasons given in the Denial are sufficiently "grounded in the statute" to pass muster as a "reasonable explanation" for EPA's refusal to render a necessity determination. The parties have opposite views as to what constitutes an explanation "grounded in the statute."

Plaintiffs argue that EPA's reasons for refusing to make a necessity determination—as provided in the Denial—are not "grounded in the statute," and reflect the very type of alternative policy arguments that the Supreme Court found unacceptable in *Massachusetts v. EPA*. Plaintiffs characterize the Denial as a "laundry list of reasons not to regulate," that like the unacceptable reasons at issue in *Massachusetts v. EPA,* reflect EPA's own policy preferences rather than the requirements of the CWA. Plaintiffs contend that the Fifth Circuit's opinion on appeal demonstrates that an explanation "grounded in the statute" must include the specific statutory and regulatory requirements of the CWA, which are incorporated by reference into § 303(c)(4)(B). Plaintiffs posit that the strongest evidence that the Denial is not "grounded in the statute" is that it barely mentions the law at all, and omits any analysis of how the

specific statutory and regulatory "requirements" of the CWA informed EPA's decision.

EPA, on the other hand, argues that Plaintiffs' position reflects a far more demanding standard than what either *Massachusetts v. EPA* or the Fifth Circuit's opinion in this case requires. EPA contends that the type of detailed scientific and technical analysis that Plaintiffs want is more akin to what is required when EPA actually makes a necessity determination one way or the other. EPA argues that Plaintiffs are misreading the Fifth Circuit's opinion when they argue that the appellate court's discussion of the specific statutory requirements of the CWA—a discussion that was held to determine judicial reviewability—dictates the content of what a reasonable explanation "grounded in the statute" must contain.

This Court is convinced that the Denial, which again is grounded primarily on EPA's assessment that working in partnership with the States to reduce nutrient pollution would be a more effective approach at present, is sufficiently "grounded in the statute." Section 303(c)(4)(B) draws upon the entire body of the CWA, which itself is a broadly-worded statutory scheme. And as the Court previously explained, the CWA is by design a states-in-the-first-instance regulatory scheme. *See* 33 U.S.C. § 1251(b) ("It is the policy of Congress to recognize, preserve, and protect **the primary responsibilities and rights of States** to prevent, reduce, and eliminate pollution . . . and to consult with the Administrator in the exercise of his authority under this chapter.") (emphasis added). Under the CWA the States are charged with adopting water quality standards for their territorial waters, and EPA exercises oversight, stepping in only when the states demonstrate that they either cannot or will not comply. With the CWA the federal role is properly characterized as a secondary or backstop role. Focusing more narrowly on § 1313 to Title 33 or § 303 of the Act, the primacy of the States' role permeates the text. As a matter of law, the Denial is not based on reasons divorced from the statutory text of the CWA.

Plaintiffs argue that the Denial is deficient because it does not address the specific statutory considerations that the Fifth Circuit identified in its opinion as those that EPA must consider when it declines to make a necessity determination. *Gulf Restoration,* 783 F.3d at 240. The Court disagrees with this characterization of the Denial. As EPA detailed in its brief, the Denial and in particular the substance of EPA's Framework Memo, which is referenced in the Denial, demonstrates that EPA did consider the text of both § 303 and the CWA as a whole when formulating its partnership strategy with the States. A reasonable explanation grounded in a statute need not necessarily contain a verbatim recitation of a statute or parse its provisions to the letter.

Furthermore, *Massachusetts v. EPA* does not preclude EPA from relying on policy grounds in the Denial, only those without clear textual support in the statute. The "policy" of partnering with the

States and maintaining a states-in-the-first-instance approach is not an alternative policy as was the case in *Massachusetts v. EPA* but rather is an integral part of the CWA as enacted by Congress. And as the Court previously explained, *Massachusetts v. EPA* does not stand for the broad proposition that every discretionary EPA determination that serves as a restraint or hurdle to federal action must be based on scientific data.

Of course, what Plaintiffs really question in this case is whether EPA's *continued* reliance on the CWA's states-first approach is reasonable in light of the undisputed scientific data surrounding the serious nature of the nitrogen and phosphorous pollution in the nation's waters. According to Plaintiffs, the state-driven approach upon which the CWA is built is simply not working and the scientific data proves it. Even if the Court were to disagree with EPA's stance on rulemaking the Court cannot properly substitute its own judgment for that of the agency. EPA's assessment that the best approach at this time is to continue in its comprehensive strategy of bringing the States along without the use of federal rule making is subject to the highly deferential and limited review that the Fifth Circuit described in its opinion. Presumably, there is a point in time at which the agency will have abused its great discretion by refusing to concede that the current approach—albeit the one of first choice under the CWA—is simply not going to work. But for now, Plaintiffs have not demonstrated that EPA's assessment was arbitrary, capricious, or contrary to law. EPA is entitled to judgment as a matter of law in its favor.

Accordingly, and for the foregoing reasons;

IT IS ORDERED that the **Motion for Summary Judgment** filed by Plaintiffs is **DENIED**;

IT IS FURTHER ORDERED that the **Cross Motion for Summary Judgment** filed by defendants Gina McCarthy, Administrator, and the United States Environmental Protection Agency is **GRANTED**. Judgment will be entered in favor of Defendants.

Questions

1. What did the plaintiffs want the EPA to do?

2. Did the EPA disagree with plaintiffs about the "significant and serious water quality problems" in the Mississippi River and the Northern Gulf of Mexico? Did it determine that a new or revised standard was necessary—or not necessary—to control the pollution? What exactly did it decide?

3. What reasons did the EPA give for refusing to use its federal rule making authority under the CWA to address the water quality problems at issue?

4. What narrow determination was the court tasked with making? How was *Massachusetts v. EPA* applied? What standard did the court use to evaluate whether the EPA's explanation was legally sufficient regarding its failure to make a necessity determination under the CWA? Did the court rule that the EPA's explanation was sufficiently grounded in the CWA statute? What was the court's reasoning?

5. What did the court ultimately rule? Is the court's decision consistent with the Supreme Court's ruling in *Massachusetts v. EPA*? Does the EPA's responsibility to regulate greenhouse gas emissions under the Clean Air Act differ from its responsibility to regulate pollution under the CWA? Explain.

There is no doubt the CWA has resulted in enormous improvements, but there are problems as well. The EPA conducts national surveys to evaluate water quality, sediment quality, coastal habitats, and fish-tissue contaminants. Its 2012 report rated the West Coast as fair to good; the Northeast, Southeast, and Gulf coasts as fair; and the Great Lakes as poor.[54] The goals of the CWA are implemented primarily by imposing limits on the amount of pollutants that may lawfully enter U.S. waters from any "point source" (typically a pipe). The National Pollutant Discharge Elimination System (NPDES) requires all dischargers to secure a permit, most often from the EPA, but at times from some other government agency, before pouring effluent into a navigable stream. The permit specifies maximum permissible levels of effluent and typically also mandates the use of a particular pollution control process or device to ensure that level is not exceeded. It also requires the permit holder to monitor its own performance and report the results to the state or the EPA. This allows the EPA to take effective action. For instance, the Justice Department and the EPA reached a settlement in 2017 with the Potomac Electric Power Company, which allegedly violated its CWA permit by exceeding the limit on certain metals and other pollutants allowed to enter its storm water drainage system. The storm drainage system empties into a major tributary to the Potomac River, which ultimately flows to the Chesapeake Bay. The company agreed to pay a civil penalty of $1.6 million, undertake a mitigation project at its plant, and implement "Best Management Practices."[55]

> In the Gulf there is a dead zone larger in size than Connecticut.

But regulation of point sources leaves many pollutants unmonitored. Surface water runoff is polluted with our lawn fertilizer, pet waste, and grease and oil from vehicles. In spite of rules put in place in 1999, surface water is also polluted by runoff from large row crop, hog, cattle, and poultry farms. Nitrogen from fertilizers finds its way into the Mississippi River from sources hundreds of miles from the Gulf—1.5 million tons of it yearly. As a result, in the Gulf there is a dead zone larger in size than Connecticut, in which little life can exist.[56]

Discouragingly, even sources covered by the NPDES nevertheless violate the terms of their permits, often with impunity. *The New York Times* published a series of articles over the fall of 2009 based on records received in response to Freedom of Information Act requests made to every state and the EPA. In them, journalist Charles Duhigg presented an alarming picture of CWA violations rising steadily across the nation. Many violations were relatively minor, but about 60 percent were deemed to be in "significant noncompliance." Fewer than 3 percent resulted in fines or other substantial punishment. Some, but not all, of the rise is attributable to insufficient enforcement resources. The number of regulated facilities more than doubled in a 10-year span, but state enforcement budgets remained essentially flat. The EPA made promises to regulate the discharge of such toxic substances as arsenic, lead, and cadmium, but has never done so. [To read the articles in this series, go to **www.nytimes.com/toxicwaters**].

How Did Your State Respond?

The New York Times website provides the data it received from responding states regarding CWA permits, violations, and enforcement actions. The *Times* also provides information from each state on staffing and budgets related to oversight of water pollution. What information was provided from your state? See **http://projects.nytimes.com/toxic-waters/ polluters /state-data**.

Covered Waters

LO 17-7
Describe the legal issue involving the reach of the CWA.

Decades after CWA enactment, it remains unclear exactly what waters are actually covered by the act and therefore subject to EPA regulation. In the 2001 *Northern Cook County* case that follows, the Supreme Court looked at what qualifies as "navigable waters" for purposes of the CWA. Only a bare majority (five) of the justices agreed with this decision; the remaining four dissented. In 2006, the Supreme Court again looked at the issue. That decision will be discussed following *Northern Cook County*.

Chief Justice Rehnquist

Section 404(a) of the Clean Water Act (CWA or Act) regulates the discharge of dredged or fill material into "navigable waters." The United States Army Corps of Engineers (Corps) has interpreted Section 404(a) to confer federal authority over an abandoned sand and gravel pit in northern Illinois that provides habitat for migratory birds. We are asked to decide whether the provisions of Section 404(a) may be fairly extended to these waters, and, if so, whether Congress could exercise such authority consistent with the Commerce Clause. We answer the first question in the negative and therefore do not reach the second.

Petitioner, the Solid Waste Agency of Northern Cook County (SWANCC), is a consortium of 23 suburban Chicago cities and villages that united in an effort to locate and develop a disposal site for baled nonhazardous solid waste. The Chicago Gravel Company informed the municipalities of the availability of a 533-acre parcel, . . . which had been the site of a sand and gravel pit mining operation for three decades up until about 1960. Long since abandoned, the old mining site eventually gave way to a successional stage forest, with its remnant excavation trenches evolving into a scattering of permanent and seasonal ponds of varying size (from under one-tenth of an acre to several acres) and depth (from several inches to several feet).

The municipalities decided to purchase the site. . . .

Section 404(a) grants the Corps authority to issue permits "for the discharge of dredged or fill material into the navigable waters at specified disposal sites." The term "navigable waters" is defined under the Act as "the waters of the United States, including the territorial seas." The Corps has issued regulations defining the term "waters of the United States" to include

> waters such as intrastate lakes, rivers, streams (including intermittent streams), mudflats, sandflats, wetlands, sloughs, prairie potholes, wet meadows, playa lakes, or natural ponds, the use, degradation or destruction of which could affect interstate or foreign commerce. . . .

In 1986, in an attempt to "clarify" the reach of its jurisdiction, the Corps stated that Section 404(a) extends to intrastate waters:

a. Which are or would be used as habitat by birds protected by Migratory Bird Treaties; or

b. Which are or would be used as habitat by other migratory birds which cross state lines; or

c. Which are or would be used as habitat for endangered species; or

d. Used to irrigate crops sold in interstate commerce.

This last promulgation has been dubbed the "Migratory Bird Rule."

The Corps initially concluded that it had no jurisdiction over the site. . . . However, after the Illinois Nature Preserves Commission informed the Corps that a number of migratory bird species had been observed at the site, the Corps reconsidered and ultimately asserted jurisdiction over the balefill site pursuant to subpart (b) of the "Migratory Bird Rule." The Corps found that approximately 121 bird species had been observed at the site, including several known to depend upon aquatic environments for a significant portion of their life requirements. . . .

* * * * *

[The] Corps refused to issue a Section 404(a) permit. The Corps found that SWANCC had not established that its proposal was the "least environmentally damaging, most practicable alternative" for disposal of nonhazardous solid waste; that SWANCC's failure to set aside sufficient funds to remediate leaks posed an "unacceptable risk to the public's drinkingwater supply"; and that the impact of the project upon area-sensitive species was "unmitigatable since a landfill surface cannot be redeveloped into a forested habitat."

Petitioner filed suit. . . . Petitioner argued that respondents had exceeded their statutory authority in interpreting the CWA to cover nonnavigable, isolated, intrastate waters based upon the presence of migratory birds. . . .

The Court of Appeals [held] that respondents' "Migratory Bird Rule" was a reasonable interpretation of the Act.

We granted certiorari. . . .

Congress passed the CWA for the stated purpose of "restoring and maintaining the chemical, physical, and biological integrity of the Nation's waters." In so doing, Congress chose to "recognize, preserve, and protect the primary responsibilities and rights of States to prevent, reduce, and eliminate pollution, to plan the development and use (including restoration, preservation, and enhancement) of land and water resources, and to consult with the Administrator in the exercise of his authority under this chapter." Relevant here, Section 404(a) authorizes respondents to regulate the discharge of fill material into "navigable waters," which the statute defines as "the waters of the United States, including the territorial seas." Respondents have interpreted these words to cover the abandoned gravel pit at issue here because it is used as habitat for migratory birds. We conclude that the "Migratory Bird Rule" is not fairly supported by the CWA.

This is not the first time we have been called upon to evaluate the meaning of Section 404(a). In *United States v. Riverside Bayview Homes, Inc.,* 474 U.S. 121 (1985), we held that the Corps had Section 404(a) jurisdiction over wetlands that actually abutted on a navigable waterway. In so doing, we noted that the term "navigable" is of "limited import" and that Congress evidenced its intent to "regulate at least some waters that would not be deemed 'navigable' under the classical understanding of that term." But our holding was based in large measure upon Congress' unequivocal acquiescence to, and approval of, the Corps' regulations interpreting the CWA to cover wetlands adjacent to navigable waters. We found that Congress' concern for the protection of water quality and aquatic ecosystems indicated its intent to regulate wetlands "inseparably bound up with the 'waters' of the United States."

It was the significant nexus between the wetlands and "navigable waters" that informed our reading of the CWA in *Riverside Bayview Homes*. . . . In order to rule for respondents here, we would have to hold that the jurisdiction of the Corps extends to ponds that are *not* adjacent to open water. But we conclude that the text of the statute will not allow this.

Indeed, the Corps' *original* interpretation of the CWA, promulgated two years after its enactment, is inconsistent with that which it espouses here. Its 1974 regulations defined Section 404(a)'s "navigable waters" to mean "those waters of the United States which are subject to the ebb and flow of the tide, and/or are presently, or have been in the past, or may be in the future susceptible for use for purposes of interstate or foreign commerce." The Corps emphasized that "it is the water body's capability of use by the public for purposes of transportation or commerce which is the determinative factor." Respondents put forward no persuasive evidence that the Corps mistook Congress' intent in 1974.

* * * * *

We hold that [the regulations], as clarified and applied to petitioner's balefill site pursuant to the "Migratory Bird Rule," [exceed] the authority granted to respondents under Section 404(a) of the CWA. The judgment of the Court of Appeals for the Seventh Circuit is therefore
    Reversed.

Questions

1. Summarize the arguments made by the Army Corps of Engineers for finding that the government had the power to regulate this site under the CWA.

2. Explain the Supreme Court's response to each of the Army Corps of Engineers's arguments previously identified.

3. Did the Supreme Court hold that the government could not regulate this type of site or only that Congress had not in fact sought to extend its regulation to this type of site?

4. In your view, should the federal government be able to regulate bodies of water that are of significant use by migratory birds? Explain.

AFTERWORD

In the *Northern Cook County* case, the Supreme Court evaluated a regulation of the Army Corps of Engineers and determined that the Corps exceeded its scope of authority under the CWA. All nine justices agreed that the term "navigable waters" should be interpreted more broadly than its literal meaning, but only four of the justices would have approved the Corps' expansive reading of the statute.

In the 2006 case *Repanos v. United States,* the Supreme Court once again reviewed the term "navigable waters."[57] The same four justices dissented, arguing that the revised, but still broad authority asserted by the Corps was permissible under the statute. This time, however, the remaining five justices did not agree on the reach of the CWA, but only agreed that the Corps was still asserting an authority broader than allowable. The result was that the case was remanded for "further proceedings" but without a standard on which to base those proceedings. The bottom line was that the government was required once again to define the scope of its regulatory authority.

In the meantime, enforcement under the CWA has been substantially hampered. "In drier states, some polluters say the act no longer applies to them and are therefore refusing to renew or apply for permits, making it impossible to monitor what they are dumping." A case in point—Cannon Air Force Base in New Mexico has informed the EPA that it "no longer considers itself subject to the act." According to *The New York Times,* it "dumps wastewater—containing bacteria and human sewage—into a lake on the base."[58] In May 2015, the Obama administration announced a new administrative rule that expanded the scope of the EPA's reach to waters beyond those that are "navigable." The new Waters of the United States Rule (or "Clean Water Rule") met with opposition from many industry leaders. In October 2015, the U.S. Court of Appeals for the Sixth Circuit stayed the Clean Water Rule nationwide pending further action of the court. In addition, the day that President Trump was sworn into office, the White House website indicated that Trump was committed to "eliminating harmful and unnecessary policies such as . . . the Waters of the US Rule."[59] For now, the EPA is stuck with the navigable waters standard.[60]

> In drier states, some polluters say the act no longer applies to them.

Regulation of Land Pollution

LO 17-8
Identify some of
the major federal
laws that address
land pollution.

Pollution does not fit tidily into separate compartments (air, water, land) as might seem to be suggested by the divisions of this chapter. Acid rain debases air and water as well as the fruits of water and land such as fish and trees. So too, the problems of land pollution addressed in this section can seep into the soil, polluting groundwater, and harming plants and animals directly and indirectly. This section addresses the laws governing how we dispose of waste—solid, hazardous, and toxic.

Toxic Substances Control Act

Because our disposal laws vary based on the classification of the materials being disposed, the primary law governing classification is a good place to start. In 1976, Congress approved the Toxic Substances Control Act (TSCA) to identify toxic chemicals, assess their risks, and control dangerous chemicals. Under the terms of TSCA, the EPA is empowered to review and limit or stop the introduction of new chemicals. Companies must notify the EPA before manufacturing or importing new industrial chemicals, but they need not provide any safety data unless the data they have suggest the substance poses a "substantial risk." The EPA has only 90 days to block the chemical and can only suspend review and request company data if the EPA can show a potential risk from the chemical.

The structure of TSCA results in a "safe until proven dangerous" presumption. Only a small fraction of 85,000 industrial chemicals in use today have been tested for safety.[61] Some that have been tested, such as formaldehyde, are still widely used in a large range of products—from nail polish and hair straighteners to many building materials. The Department of Health and Human Services identified formaldehyde as a known carcinogen in June 2011, but as of this writing the EPA has it listed as a "probable human carcinogen."[62] Perhaps more disconcerting, the names and physical properties of nearly 20 percent of the chemicals in use are secret from all but a handful of EPA employees who are required by law to protect the trade secrets of the manufacturers.[63] That protection prohibits disclosure to other federal officials, state health and environmental regulators, and physicians, as well as the public. Although many of these unknown chemicals are likely harmless, in just one month "more than half of the 65 'substantial risk' reports filed" with the EPA by manufacturers "involved secret chemicals." Essentially, we have been trading knowledge about the potential risks in exchange for "ensuring the long-term competitiveness of the U.S. [chemical] industry."[64]

Congress responded to these concerns by enacting the landmark "Frank R. Lautenberg Chemical Safety for the 21st Century Act," which was signed into law in June 2016 with broad bipartisan support. It reforms the "badly broken" TCSA and is focused on offering greater protection to the public and to the environment from dangerous chemicals.[65] This includes increased transparency with the public about chemical information. In November 2016, the EPA announced ahead of schedule the first 10 chemicals—including asbestos—that it will review for potential risks in accordance with the new law. Although "there is ample evidence linking these chemicals to cancer and other severe health problems, they have been on the market largely unchecked and unregulated for decades."[66] The EPA will have three years to complete a risk evaluation and, if any of the chemicals is found to pose a risk, the agency is required to act within two years to mitigate that risk. The new law also calls on the Centers for Disease Control and Prevention to investigate and respond to cancer clusters and to improve communication among various government agencies. [For more about the TSCA and the new law, see **www.epa.gov/opptintr/index.html**].

Pollution in the Movies

Perhaps surprisingly, toxic pollution has provided the central theme in two major Hollywood movies: *Erin Brockovich* and *A Civil Action*. The 2000 movie *Erin Brockovich* tells the story of a California community's battle against Pacific Gas & Electric for allegedly causing groundwater pollution resulting in extensive illness. [For more information on the pollutant at issue in the movie, the carcinogen hexavalent chromium, see **www.atsdr.cdc.gov/csem/csem.asp?csem=10&po=4**].

In the 1998 Disney movie *A Civil Action,* John Travolta played a plaintiff's lawyer based on a true story about some middle-class families who sued two corporate giants, Beatrice Food and W. R. Grace & Co., for allegedly polluting the groundwater in East Woburn, Massachusetts, where eight children died of leukemia. [For more information on this pollutant, trichloroethylene, see **www.atsdr.cdc.gov/phs/phs.asp?id=171&tid=30**].

Question

Look back at the discussion of proving causation at the start of Part Two. Using that terminology, describe the causation issues that had to be addressed in the real-life counterparts to these movies.

Resource Conservation and Recovery Act

By 1976, the dangers of hazardous substances were becoming apparent to all, and Congress complemented the TSCA with the Resource Conservation and Recovery Act (RCRA). The act addresses both nonhazardous and hazardous solid wastes. Its provisions for nonhazardous wastes are more supportive than punitive in tone and approach. The federal government is authorized, among other strategies, to provide technical and financial assistance to states and localities; to prohibit future open dumping; and to establish cooperative federal, state, local, and private-enterprise programs to recover energy and valuable materials from solid waste.

Subtitle C of the RCRA is designed to ensure the safe movement and disposal of hazardous solid wastes. The generator of the waste must determine if that waste is hazardous under EPA guidelines. If so, the waste generator must then create a manifest to be used in tracking the waste from its creation to its disposal. Along the cradle-to-grave path, all those with responsibility for it must sign the manifest and safely store and transport the waste. Once the waste reaches a licensed disposal facility, the owner or manager of that site signs the manifest and returns a copy of it to the generator. Disposal sites must be operated according to EPA standards, and remedial action must be taken should hazardous wastes escape from the sites. [For more information, see the EPA website at **www.epa.gov/epawaste/hazard/tsd/index.htm**].

A preliminary requirement for cradle-to-grave tracking to apply is the statutory requirement that, to be solid waste, the material must be "discarded." The U.S. Court of Appeals for the District of Columbia has ruled that "discarded" means "disposed of," "abandoned," or "thrown away" and has repeatedly held various versions of the EPA's rules to have been too broad because they improperly covered recycling practices when the materials were not discarded within the meaning of the statute.[67] Thus, *recycled* hazardous materials are not covered by RCRA, although they may be subject to other EPA regulations.[68]

Household Recycling

Our lifestyles result in mountains of waste that grow higher every year. On average, each of us produces 7.1 pounds of garbage everyday.[69] Of course, we pay an immediate price to dispose of all of that waste, but what risk does it pose to public health and safety? To the environment? Even state-of-the-art land-fills can leak, with the result that toxic elements can enter our groundwater. Seventy percent of the toxic waste in our landfills comes from electronics. The United States is the only industrialized country that has not ratified the Basel Convention, a treaty prohibiting export or trafficking in toxic e-waste. The solution, of course, is to "reduce, reuse, recycle."

> Seventy percent of the toxic waste in our landfills comes from electronics.

Recycling turns materials that would otherwise become waste into usable resources, which can reduce dependence on new materials (reducing deforestation, for example). It is now cheaper to recycle an aluminum can than it is to make one from new materials. The same is true of plastic bottles.[70] The EPA reports that 89 million tons of solid waste material was recycled and composted in 2014, equivalent to a 36.6 percent recycling rate.[71] Increasingly, large food and beverage companies in the United States are voluntarily taking on the costs of recycling the consumer packaging of their goods, a process known as "extended producer responsibility." For instance, Coca-Cola has implemented recycling programs around the globe,[72] and it is increasing the use of a first-ever fully recyclable lightweight PET bottle made partially from plants, which cuts down significantly on the use of oil and of carbon dioxide emissions.[73] Customers in Starbucks' Chicago-area stores can deposit their cups for recycling, which are then trucked to a Wisconsin recycling facility where they are turned into paper napkins for the store. The company would like to expand such initiatives more broadly but admits that government policies and limited access to recycling markets in different jurisdictions is a challenge. Stonyfield Farm, which produces organic yogurt, now has bins in Whole Foods stores for the recycling of No. 5 plastic containers—the plastic it uses for its yogurt, which most cities do not recycle.[74] Europe has required packaged goods companies to take financial responsibility for package recycling for many years. Of course, the most cost-effective, environmentally friendly practice of all is to simply *reduce* consumption. [For a fun, interactive lesson in garbology, see **www. naturebridge.org/garbology.php**].

LO 17-9
Discuss the purpose and effect of the Comprehensive Environmental Response, Compensation, and Liability Act of 1980 (CERCLA), commonly known as "the Superfund."

Superfund—Comprehensive Environmental Response, Compensation, and Liability Act of 1980

The Comprehensive Environmental Response, Compensation, and Liability Act of 1980 (CERCLA), more commonly known as the Superfund, was enacted for the purpose of identifying and cleaning up abandoned hazardous waste sites. The process involves the assessment and ranking of proposed sites, followed by the development and implementation of cleanup plans for sites added to the National Priorities List. Cleanups may be carried out by the EPA or private parties, either of which may seek reimbursement of costs from those liable under CERCLA. Potentially responsible parties include present owners of the site as well as past owners who operated the site when the hazardous wastes were deposited;

> Any parties found to be responsible are strictly liable.

parent firms can be liable for actions of subsidiaries; and transferors (successive owners of businesses discharging hazardous wastes) are also liable. Any parties found to be responsible are strictly liable— that is, liability attaches without proof of either intent or negligence. Cleanup tends to be very expensive and generally requires considerable time to accomplish. The first listed Superfund site, Love Canal in Niagara Falls, New York, was finally clean enough to be delisted in 2004.[75] Originally cleanup costs were paid from a trust fund created by taxes on chemicals and petroleum, but that taxing authority lapsed in 1995. The Superfund program has since been running on annual appropriations and reserve funds. According to a recent Government Accountability Office report, that funding was likely to be inadequate for the foreseeable future and, in 2014, the EPA testified at a Senate subcommittee hearing that it did not have sufficient funding to move forward with cleaning up several Superfund sites in New Jersey and elsewhere.[76] The annual estimated remediation costs for the five years ending in 2014 ranged from $335 to $681 million, but from 2000 to 2009 the highest funding received was only $267 million.[77] As of November 29, 2016, there are 53 proposed new Superfund sites, 1,337 sites currently on the national priorities list, and only 392 sites that have been delisted.[78]

How Does Your Community Compare?

Thirty-seven years after the passage of CERCLA, some of the country's most hazardous sites remain toxic. Until the earthquake and tsunami in Japan, the biggest nuclear waste hazard in the Western world was located in southeast Washington—the Hanford nuclear facility, a 586-square-mile site constructed as part of the Manhattan project to produce weapons-grade plutonium in nine nuclear reactors along the banks of the Columbia River. The highly toxic waste is currently stored in underground tanks, where it will continue to wait until at least 2019 when it is projected that a specialized waste-treatment plant will commence transforming the waste into still-radioactive glass logs that will be more suitable for long-term storage.[79] [For maps and some aerial pictures of Hanford, explore the site beginning at its home page, **yosemite.epa.gov/r10/cleanup.nsf/sites/hanford**].

What do you know about the pollution in your community? Find out by logging onto **http://scorecard.goodguide.com/community/index.tcl** and inserting your zip code. Then visit the EPA's site and discover any Superfund sites near you on its maps at **www.epa.gov/ superfund/sites/npl/where.htm.**

Questions
1. Are there any Superfund sites in or near your community?
2. How does your hometown rate with regard to the industrial release of toxic chemicals?
3. How does your air quality stack up with other communities in the United States?
4. How clean are your rivers and lakes?

Small Business Liability Relief and Brownfields Revitalization Act

There has been considerable dissatisfaction over CERCLA for a number of reasons, including the percentage of Superfund dollars that have gone to administration expenses and litigation, as well as the slow remediation process at most sites. Worried about liability risks, developers were often reluctant to buy and improve brownfield sites, but that problem was alleviated with the passage of the 2002 Small Business Liability Relief and Brownfields Revitalization Act (Brownfields Act). This law provides liability protection for prospective purchasers and contiguous property owners and authorizes increased funding for state and local programs that assess and clean up brownfields. [For more on brownfields, see **www.epa.gov/brownfields/index.html**].

PRACTICING ETHICS   Environmentally Aware Decision Making

Imagine you have just been hired as the business manager for a chain of restaurants in your state. During the interview process, you were told that part of your responsibilities would be to develop more environmentally friendly practices to be implemented at all 10 locations, while making sure that the changes overall have either a neutral or a positive impact on the business's bottom line. A local business school professor is interested in having her students do semester-long service learning projects on the feasibility of various green projects for local businesses. Develop a list of possible practices your restaurants could implement to share with the professor for further development by her students.

Part Three—Penalties and Enforcement under Federal Law

LO 17-10

Identify penalties and other enforcement mechanisms under federal and state regulations.

Many environmental statutes require companies to monitor their own environmental performance and report that information, including violations, to the government. As noted above in discussing the Clean Water Act, such disclosure does not necessarily lead to any form of corrective or enforcement action. Government agencies also have broad authority to conduct environmental inspections of both plants and records as necessary, although they must obtain search warrants if criminal prosecutions are anticipated.

A broad array of enforcement actions is available to both state and federal agencies. Often violators initially are simply warned and a compliance schedule may be prescribed. If corrective action is not forthcoming, sterner measures may follow, including an administrative order to comply. Such orders are somewhat less effective in the future, given the Supreme Court's 2012 decision in *Sackett v. EPA*[80] and its 2016 decision in *U.S. Army Corps of Engineers v. Hawkes Co.*[81] In *Sackett,* the Court held the issuance of a compliance order under the Clean Water Act, requiring the plaintiffs to restore the wetlands on their property and subjecting them to a $75,000-per-day penalty for any noncompliance, was a final agency action entitling them to immediate judicial review for declaratory relief. Likewise, the Court held in *Hawkes* that a jurisdictional determination issued by the Army Corp of Engineers under the CWA constitutes a final agency action that a landowner can challenge in court. These rulings will very likely impact the effectiveness of compliance orders under many other environmental programs as well.

Alternatively, the government may resort to litigation. It may seek an injunction to prevent continued or future violations or to require the polluter to remediate the environmental damage that has occurred. Monetary civil penalties and fines may be imposed under most environmental statutes. Governments that have incurred cleanup costs responding to the violation may also seek recovery of those costs. Although many suits are brought, most are settled rather than litigated. Settlement opens the possibility of somewhat more creative solutions, sometimes including Supplemental Environmental Projects (SEPs). Such projects involve the violator undertaking some environmental "good work" or community service project. For example, in two separate settlements, Scotts Miracle-Gro agreed to pay $500 million in contributions to various charities dedicated to the protection of bird populations and $2 million to acquire and protect 300 acres to prevent runoff of agricultural chemicals into nearby waterways.[82] [To find other examples of SEPs, explore the database maintained by the EPA at **www.epa-echo.gov/echo/about_sep.html**].

Many environmental laws also provide for the imposition of criminal penalties, as well as imprisonment. Individual corporate officers can be held criminally liable if they either had actual knowledge of the criminal action or they are held to be a "responsible person" under the appropriate law. So, for example, in December 2016, Princess Cruises pleaded guilty to seven felony charges in federal court and was fined $40 million—the largest criminal penalty ever imposed for intentional vessel dumping. For over eight years, five Princess cruise ships employed several tactics, including a "magic pipe," to circumvent water cleaning mechanisms and devices that monitored oil. When a newly hired engineer observed over 4,000 gallons of contaminated waste being dumped into the ocean off of England's coast, he reported it to officials and then quit as soon as the ship docked on dry land.[83] In January 2017, the FBI arrested a Volkswagen executive for allegedly playing a central role in a conspiracy to keep U.S. officials from discovering that diesel vehicles it made were programmed to cheat on emissions tests.[84]

BP Gulf Oil Spill: A Case Study of Costs

BP has incurred $53.8 billion as a result of the Gulf oil spill. Here is an estimate of some of those costs:

- As of mid-2013, BP had already spent $14 billion to plug the Macondo well and clean up spilled oil.

- In November 2012, BP pleaded guilty to 14 criminal charges and agreed with the Justice Department to pay $4.5 billion over five years in fines and other penalties.

- BP was subject to civil fines under the Clean Water Act, based in part on the volume of oil spilled as well as the level of BP's culpability. In 2015, it agreed to a $20 billion settlement, including $7.1 billion for natural resource damages, $5.5 billion for Clean Water Act fines, and $4.9 billion in payments to various states

- BP set up a $20-billion compensation fund in August 2010 to address damages suffered by individuals and businesses. In 2012, BP reached a settlement with tens of thousands of Gulf Coast businesses and individuals for economic and property loss. That settlement set up standards for establishing claims but did not set a cap on the total payments. By July 2013, BP indicated that $19.7 billion of the total had been committed. It also stated that there could be another $4.5 billion in payments due on claims already submitted and that new claims could be submitted until April 2014.

- BP also incurred legal fees, estimated by one account at $2 billion, including fees of experts necessary to pursue and defend the various legal actions.

Sources: Justin Scheck, Tom Fowler, and Selina Williams, "BP Says Spill Fund Is Running on Fumes," *The Wall Street Journal,* July 30, 2013; "Deepwater, Deep Pockets," *The Economist,* July 13, 2013, p. 59; Clifford Krauss and Stanley Reed, "Leaner BP Blanches at Bill for Cleanup," *The New York Times,* July 11, 2013; Clifford Krauss and Barry Meier, "As Oil Spill Trial Opens, Push for a Deal Continues," *The New York Times,* February 25, 2013; "Gulf of Mexico Oil Spill, 2010," *The New York Times,* April 25, 2011; Associated Press, "Tallying the Spill's Cost," *The Des Moines Register,* December 30, 2010, p. 8B; and Susan Heavey, Patrick Rucker, and Emily Stephenson, "U.S. Says BP to Pay $20 Billion in Fines for 2010 Oil Spill," *Reuters,* October 5, 2015 [**www.reuters.com/article/us-bp-usa-idUSKCN0RZ14A20151005**].

Citizen Suits

In addition to the aforementioned mechanisms, many environmental statutes allow citizen suits, in which individuals may challenge government environmental decisions, such as the granting of a permit, and generally demand both governmental and private-sector compliance with the law. *Massachusetts v. EPA,* the Clean Air Act case above, was brought by a group of states, local governments, and private organizations as a citizen suit.

Citizen suits have often been brought under the Endangered Species Act (ESA), which provides a federal program for the protection of threatened and endangered species and their habitats. Such suits may either seek greater protection for a species or argue that proposed protections exceed that which is necessary. The two cases that follow illustrate both types of concerns. In the first, more protection for the Cook Inlet beluga whale was sought; in the second, plaintiffs argued that too large an area had been designated for the protection of the Mexican spotted owl in the southeastern United States. In both cases petitioners lost. When reading the cases, pay attention to the process required of the government in listing a species as threatened or endangered and in defining its protected habitat.

LEGAL BRIEFCASE

Cook Inlet Beluga Whale v. Daley   156 F. Supp. 2d 16 (D.C.D.C. 2001)

Judge James Robertson

The Cook Inlet Beluga Whale . . . is a genetically distinct, geographically isolated marine mammal with a remnant population that inhabits Cook Inlet from late April or early May until October or November. NMFS [National Marine Fisheries Service] estimates that in the mid-1980s, between 1,000 and 1,300 whales inhabited the inlet. Today, the population is estimated at between 300 and 400 whales. It is not disputed that the single most significant factor in the population decline has been Native American hunting. . . . That is why, in March 1999, the plaintiffs filed a petition to list the Cook Inlet Beluga Whale under the Endangered Species Act (ESA).

The Endangered Species Act delegates to the Secretary of Commerce the authority to determine whether fish, wildlife, or plant species should be listed as endangered or threatened. A species is "endangered" when it is in "danger of extinction throughout all or a significant part of its range," and it is "threatened" when it is "likely to become an endangered species within the foreseeable future." The Secretary's ESA determination is made on the basis of five statutorily prescribed factors, any one of which is sufficient to support a listing determination.

Within 30 days of plaintiffs' request for an ESA listing, the NMFS published formal notice that action under the ESA "may be warranted." That notice triggered a one-year status review period.

On October 19, 1999, the NMFS published a proposed rule, not under the ESA, but under the Marine Mammal Protection Act (MMPA), to list the whale as "depleted." . . . Under the MMPA, the Secretary can designate a species as "depleted" . . . if the Secretary determines that the stock is below its Optimum Sustainable Population. Once a marine mammal has been listed as "depleted," the Secretary is authorized to promulgate regulations limiting takings by Native Americans, but a listing under the MMPA does not have the regulatory, economic, and environmental fallout of a listing as "threatened" or "endangered" under the ESA.

On June 22, 2000, the NMFS determined that an ESA listing was "not warranted." It is that determination which, in plaintiffs' submission, was "arbitrary, capricious, an abuse of discretion, or otherwise not in accordance with law."

ARGUMENT

"In exercising its narrowly defined duty . . . , the Court must consider whether the agency acted within the scope of its legal authority, adequately explained its decision, based its decision on facts in the record, and considered the relevant factors." Plaintiffs argue that the agency decision in this case improperly applied the law and facts to the five-factor determination; failed to apply the best scientific and commercial data available; and improperly considered political and economic factors.

I. Statutory Factors

A decision whether or not to list a species shall be made "solely on the basis of the best scientific and commercial data available . . . after conducting a review of the status of the species and after taking into account those efforts, if any, being made by any State or foreign nation." Applying this standard, the Secretary must list a species as endangered or threatened if "any of Section 1533(a)(1)'s five factors are sufficiently implicated." Each of the five factors is considered below.

(A) The Present or Threatened Destruction, Modification, or Curtailment of the Species' Habitat or Range The agency's conclusion that "no indication exists that the range has been, or is threatened with being modified or curtailed to an extent that appreciably diminishes the value of the habitat for both survival and recovery of the species," was not arbitrary or capricious. There is no dispute that the Cook Inlet, the whale's habitat, has changed over time in response to the increasing demand of municipal, industrial, and recreational activities, but there is no record basis for concluding that these changes have had a deleterious effect on the whale. Plaintiffs can point only to the fact that the whales have increasingly inhabited the upper inlet in recent decades. The agency concedes that this change in whale behavior might be in response to human activities, but no data suggest that the change threatens extinction. The agency is not required to conduct further testing to determine the effect of various environmental factors, such as oil drilling, on

the whale population. "The 'best available data' requirement makes it clear that the Secretary has no obligation to conduct independent studies."

(B) Overutilization All agree that Native American harvesting has been the most significant factor in the declining whale population. The agency has found "that a failure to restrict the subsistence harvest would likely cause CI beluga whales to become in danger of extinction in the foreseeable future." But the agency has also concluded that "overutilization" does not support ESA listing because it has been stopped—by designating the whale as "depleted" under the MMPA. Plaintiffs attack that conclusion as unreasonable.

If the moratorium fails to control Native American harvesting in the future, ESA listing will be warranted. That much is agreed. But plaintiffs have been unable to point to anything in the record indicating that the current whale population is unsustainable if the harvest is indeed restricted successfully. . . .

[There] is no reason to believe that the MMPA's enforcement mechanisms, which are identical to those of the ESA, will be less effective in controlling illegal takings. Plaintiffs' concerns are reasonable, and enforcement should be carefully monitored, but the record contains support for the agency's conclusion that future takings will be minimal and that the current population is sustainable.

(C) Disease or Predation The agency concedes that both disease or predation "occur in the CI beluga population and may affect reproduction and survival," but it has concluded that these factors are not causing the stock to be threatened or endangered. Plaintiff has not shown that conclusion to be arbitrary or capricious. . . .

(D) Inadequacy of Existing Regulatory Mechanisms We have found nothing in the record, and plaintiff has identified nothing, showing that there are inadequacies in existing regulatory mechanisms or, if there were, what the effects of such inadequacies would be. Plaintiffs argue that the MMPA is inadequate to ensure that illegal hunting does not occur . . . , but that argument simply asserts plaintiffs' policy preference for a remedy under the ESA and begs the question of whether ESA listing is required.

(E) Other Natural or Manmade Factors Affecting Its Continued Existence Plaintiffs argue that there are many other factors—strandings, oil spills, takings through commercial fishing, effects of pollutants, ship strikes, noise, urban runoff, etc.—that put the species at risk and that it was arbitrary and capricious for the agency to determine that "the best available information . . . indicates that these activities, alone or cumulatively, have not caused the stock to be in danger of extinction and are not likely to do so in the foreseeable future." . . .

It is true that the absence of "conclusive evidence" of a real threat to a species does not justify an agency's finding that ESA listing is not warranted. But neither is listing required simply because the agency is unable to rule out factors that could contribute to a population decline. It was not arbitrary or capricious for the agency to place its principal reliance on the cessation of Native American hunts and the [study that concluded] that the Cook Inlet Beluga Whale population could sustain itself, even accounting for stochastic events.

[Plaintiffs' remaining arguments have been omitted.]

Ordered that defendant's motion for summary judgment is granted.

Questions

1. Why did the plaintiffs want the Cook Inlet Beluga Whale listed as endangered under the ESA?

2. What was the standard of review that the court applied to the agency's decision?

3. What five factors are to be considered in the listing of a species as endangered under the Endangered Species Act?

LEGAL BRIEFCASE

Arizona Cattle Growers' Association v. Salazar
606 F.3d 1160 (9th Cir. 2010)

Judge Betty B. Fletcher

Litigation History

In 1993 the Mexican Spotted Owl was listed as a threatened species under the Endangered Species Act ("ESA"). The listing decision prompted a series of lawsuits alternately seeking to compel the FWS [U.S. Fish and Wildlife Service] to designate critical habitat for the owl and, following the FWS's designation of habitat, attacking that designation.

The first such lawsuit was in 1995 to compel the FWS to designate critical habitat and resulted in the FWS's issuing a final rule designating 4.6 million acres of critical owl habitat, a designation that was quickly challenged in court and then revoked in 1998. After another lawsuit was filed to compel the FWS to designate habitat, the FWS proposed a rule in 2000 to designate 13.5 million acres of critical habitat and in 2001 the agency promulgated a final rule that again designated 4.6 million acres. That rule was later struck down and . . . the FWS reopened the comment period on the rule it proposed in 2000. In 2004 the FWS designated approximately 8.6 million acres of critical habitat. It is this designation, the 2004 Final Rule, that Arizona Cattle challenges in the current action.

Arizona Cattle moved for summary judgment to set aside the 2004 Final Rule. . . . The District Court rejected Arizona Cattle's arguments. . . .

THE 2004 FINAL RULE

The FWS relied on three types of habitat management areas . . . as a starting point for the 2004 Final Rule: protected areas, restricted areas, and other forest and woodland types. Protected areas are those

areas containing known owl sites, termed Protected Activity Centers ("PACs"); "steep slope" areas meeting certain forest conditions; and legally and administratively reserved lands. "PACs include a minimum of 600 acres . . . that includes the best nesting and roosting (i.e., resting) habitat in the area . . . and the most proximal and highly used foraging areas." However, PACs contain only 75% of necessary foraging areas for the owl. Restricted areas include non-steep slope areas with appropriate forest conditions that are "adjacent to or outside of protected areas." "Areas outside of PACs, including restricted areas, provide additional habitat appropriate for foraging." . . .

* * * * *

THE ESA AND THE DEFINITION OF "OCCUPIED"

The ESA defines a species' critical habitat as . . . "the specific areas within the geographical area occupied by the species, at the time it is listed. . . ."

The statute thus differentiates between "occupied" and "unoccupied" areas. . . . [We] face the preliminary issue of what it means for an area to be "occupied" under the ESA.

It is useful to unpack this inquiry into two components: uncertainty and frequency. Uncertainty is a factor when the FWS has reason to believe that owls are present in a given area, but lacks conclusive proof of their presence. Frequency is a factor when owls are shown to have only an intermittent presence in a given area. Occasionally, both factors will play a part in determining whether an area is "occupied." Because the ESA permits only one of two possible outcomes for this inquiry—occupied or unoccupied- . . . we must determine the scope of the FWS's authority to categorize as "occupied" those areas that may not fit neatly into either pigeonhole.

We have ample guidance on the "uncertainty" issue. The ESA provides that the agency must determine critical habitat using the "best scientific data available." This standard does not require that the FWS act only when it can justify its decision with absolute confidence. . . .

Turning to the "frequency" component, Arizona Cattle asserts that the word "occupied" is unambiguous and must be interpreted narrowly to mean areas that the species "resides in." In the context of the owl, they argue that such areas consist only of the 600-acre PACs. The FWS argues . . . that where a geographic area is used with such frequency that the owl is likely to be present, the agency may permissibly designate it as occupied. FWS contends that, at a minimum, this includes the owl's "home range" and may include other areas used for intermittent activities.

We cannot agree that "occupied" has an unambiguous, plain meaning as Arizona Cattle suggests. The word "occupied," standing alone, does not provide a clear standard for how frequently a species must use an area before the agency can designate it as critical habitat. Merely replacing the word "occupied" with the word "resides" does not resolve this ambiguity. . . . Viewed narrowly, an owl resides only in its nest; viewed more broadly, an owl resides in a PAC; and viewed more broadly still, an owl resides in its territory or home range. Determining whether a species uses an area with sufficient regularity that it is "occupied" is a highly contextual and fact-dependent inquiry. . . . Such factual questions are within the purview of the agency's unique expertise and are entitled to the standard deference afforded such agency determinations.

* * * * *

The FWS has authority to designate as "occupied" areas that the owl uses with sufficient regularity that it is likely to be present during any reasonable span of time. This interpretation is sensible. . . . Arizona Cattle's "reside in" interpretation would make little sense as applied to nonterritorial, mobile, or migratory animals—including the owl—for which it may be impossible to fix a determinate area in which the animal "resides." Such a narrow interpretation also would mesh poorly with the FWS's authority to act in the face of uncertainty.

* * * * *

It is possible for the FWS to go too far. Most obvious is that the agency may not determine that areas unused by owls are occupied merely because those areas are suitable for future occupancy. Such a position would ignore the ESA's distinction between occupied and unoccupied areas. . . . The fact that a member of the species is not present in an area at a given instant does not mean the area is suitable only for future occupancy if the species regularly uses the area.

Having thus framed the inquiry, we turn to the primary issue before the court: whether the FWS included unoccupied areas in its critical habitat designation.

THE FWS DID NOT DESIGNATE UNOCCUPIED AREAS AS CRITICAL HABITAT

* * * * *

. . . PACs are explicitly defined with reference to frequent owl presence, and non-PAC protected areas and restricted areas are "devised around" and "adjacent to" PACs. More to the point, we note significant record support for owl occupancy of these areas in the form of studies correlating the habitat characteristics of protected and restricted areas with owl presence.

The agency did not stop there. [Its] analysis proceeds, unit by unit, through the addition of areas to the critical habitat proposal on the basis of information about known owl locations. . . .

A point of recurring significance to our analysis is that PACs reflect only known owl sites. Although the 2004 Final Rule identified 1,176 PACs, owl populations have been estimated to be significantly greater than the maximum 2,352 owls reflected by this number of PACs. . . . Efforts by the FWS to identify other evidence of owl presence when it is unable to fix the location of a PAC with certainty are, therefore, highly significant.

Even more significant is the fact that the FWS excluded areas with evidence of few or no owls. . . . Finally, we note that . . . the FWS excluded the vast majority of critical habitat units that contained no PACs and refined the boundaries of the critical habitat units to exclude large areas that are distant from PACs.

The FWS's process for designating critical habitat gives us a strong foundation for our conclusion that the agency did not arbitrarily and capriciously treat areas in which owls are not found as "occupied." . . .

THE AMOUNT OF LAND DESIGNATED IS NOT DISPROPORTIONATE TO THE NUMBER OF OWLS

Arizona Cattle also argues that even using the owl's substantially larger home range as the appropriate measure for the territory occupied by the owl, the FWS has designated a grossly disproportionate amount of land compared to the amount the owl occupies. It ties this argument to a seemingly simple calculation: multiplying the 1,176 PACs by the maximum estimated home range size of the owl of 3,831 acres, the resultant area is only approximately 4.5 million acres, in contrast to the 8.6 million acres designated. This calculation, however, rests on a faulty assumption that the PACs represent all extant owls. We have already explained that PACs reflect only known owl sites and that there is record support for the existence of substantially greater numbers of owls and undiscovered sites. . . . Arizona Cattle's argument does not overcome the strong evidence that the FWS was focused on designating areas occupied by owls.

* * * * *

We find no fault with the FWS's designation of habitat for the Mexican Spotted Owl. . . .

Affirmed.

Questions

1. Identify the statutory language the court had to interpret to resolve this case.

2. How did the FWS select the areas included in its designation of 8.6 million acres as critical habitat for the owl?

3. What contrary arguments were made by Arizona Cattle?

4. What was the standard of review that the court applied to the agency's decision?

5. How many years elapsed between the first lawsuit over the designation of the Mexican spotted owl and the decision in this case?

Endangered Species Act

LO 17-11

Describe some of the challenges to protecting a species under the Endangered Species Act.

The combination of the *Cook Inlet Beluga Whale* and *Arizona Cattle Grower's Association* decisions illustrates how complicated and time-consuming the legal process is for the protection of species. It is also costly—for citizen groups on both sides, for the government (and therefore all of us as taxpayers), for those whose lives and livelihoods may be substantially altered by the protections extended, and also for the species and our world in the event necessary protections are not extended or are not effective.

Consider what may be on the horizon. The International Union for the Conservation of Nature has over 4,200 species listed as critically endangered.[85] The U.N. Intergovernmental Panel on Climate Change indicates temperature increases this century could put 20 to 30 percent of the world's plants and animals in danger of extinction.[86] From 2008 through 2011, environmental groups requested more than 1,230 species be listed under the ESA as threatened or endangered, compared with prior annual averages of about 20 species. This forced the FWS, in its 2012 budget request, to point out that it had neither the personnel nor budget to meet the time constraints for final listing decisions required by law.[87] These facts set the context for a 2011 settlement with two environmental groups in which the FWS pledged to make listing determinations on all backlogged species by 2018. When the backlog is addressed, then 550 other potential candidates will be evaluated. The ultimate result may be that the endangered list could increase by as much as 60 percent.[88] From 2010 to the present, 311 species have been newly listed as either threatened or endangered, compared to a total of 27 in the prior four years.[89] This includes the Rusty Patched Bumble Bee, listed as endangered in 2017 and which, 20 years ago, "was a common sight, so ordinary that it went almost unnoticed."[90] It is the first bumble bee in the United States—and the first bee in the contiguous 48 states—to become endangered.

[For photos of some endangered or threatened species in the United States, see **www.nytimes.com/interactive/2013/03/06/science/earth/endangered-species.html?ref=earth#index**].

Part Four—Common Law Remedies

LO 17-12

Describe the primary common law remedies for environmental damage.

Most of the remedies discussed in Part Three are based on *statutory* claims. But long before federal or state governments became actively involved in environmental issues, courts were grappling with the problem and fashioning *common law* remedies. As early as the 1500s, city officials were ordered by a court to keep the streets clean of dung deposited by swine allowed to run loose; the air was said to be "corrupted and infected" by this practice. Legal arguments have typically revolved around the extent of a person's right to use and enjoy private property if such usage causes harm to a neighbor's property or the use of public property. More recently, tort actions of negligence and strict liability have been pursued by injured individuals. Successful plaintiffs may recover monetary damages for the harm suffered or obtain an injunction to prevent similar conduct (and therefore harm) by the defendant in the future, or both.

Nuisance   A private **nuisance** is a substantial and unreasonable invasion of the private use and enjoyment of one's land; a public nuisance is an unreasonable interference with a right common to the public. Harmful conduct may be both a public and private nuisance simultaneously; the case law distinctions between the two are often blurred. A classic nuisance dispute is the 1970 New York case *Boomer v. Atlantic Cement Co.*[91] Neighboring landowners sued the operator of a cement plant for injury to their properties from the plant's dirt, smoke, and vibration. The court recognized the wrong done and ordered the operator to pay damages.

In the last decade, a number of nuisance cases were initiated in federal courts against emitters of significant greenhouse gases. In one, *Connecticut v. American Electric Power Co.*, several states, New York City, and three land trusts sued operators of coal-fired power plants claiming their carbon emissions were a nuisance under federal common law and seeking an order requiring the utilities to cap and then reduce their carbon dioxide emissions. A unanimous Supreme Court ruled against the plaintiffs in 2011 finding that the Clean Air Act and EPA rule-making authority displaced any common law right to sue to curb carbon dioxide emissions from power plants.[92] The decision affirms the power of the EPA under the CAA and encourages a single nationwide standard for addressing carbon emissions rather than multiple court-imposed remedies. According to some commentators, it may also foreclose the use of the common law cause of action of nuisance for many other environmental harms under federal law. Some further believe it may prevent success under state law based on arguments that, where federal law exists, federal environmental laws preempt state law causes of action.

Trespass   A **trespass** occurs and liability is imposed on any intentional invasion of an individual's right to the exclusive use of his or her own property. For example, in a 1959 Oregon case, *Martin v. Reynolds Metals Co.*, the plaintiffs successfully sued in trespass for damages caused by the operation of an aluminum reduction plant, which caused certain fluoride compounds in the form of gases and particulates to become airborne, settle on the plaintiffs' land, contaminate their forage and water, and poison their cattle.[93]

Negligence   The elements of **negligence** have been previously discussed in Chapter 7. In 2010, the Florida Supreme Court held that fishermen were entitled to recover for the damages they suffered when defendants' wastewater storage pond spilled into the Tampa Bay, killing fish, crabs, and other marine life. Defendants' negligence "interfered with the special interest of the commercial fishermen to use the public waters to earn their livelihood."[94] Particularly troubling causation issues can and have arisen in negligence cases based on environmental pollution, such as when a plaintiff claims injury from a toxic substance manufactured or otherwise supplied by a defendant. Recall the discussion of causation at the start of this chapter, as well as the factual basis for the movies *Erin Brockovich* and *A Class Action*. Think of the factual difficulties of proving that a particular substance causes certain medical conditions, that it was the cause of a particular individual's injury, and that the substance is traceable back to a particular defendant. An organic compound, MTBE, is used around the world as an additive to gas. However, at least half of the U.S. states have banned its use, and the EPA has classified it as a possible human carcinogen. Many lawsuits have been brought against oil companies by municipalities and other governmental bodies to recoup the costs of cleaning up water supplies contaminated with MTBE. New Hampshire brought such a suit against 16 oil companies, all of which, except ExxonMobil, settled with the state for a total of $136 million. In April 2013, a jury returned a $236 million verdict for the state, finding Exxon negligent for putting the additive in its gas and without warning the state of its risks. In 2015, the New Hampshire Supreme Court denied Exxon's appeal.[95]

Strict Liability   Certain activities, such as the use of toxic chemicals, may be seen as so abnormally dangerous as to give rise to a **strict liability** claim (previously discussed in Chapter 7). In an environmental law context, strict liability has been considered where crop dusting contaminated adjacent properties,[96] toxic chemicals were improperly disposed of,[97] and oil contaminated a nearby water well.[98]

Several of the above claims can sometimes be triggered by the same set of facts. In a 2007 West Virginia case, a jury found DuPont negligent in its use of a 112-acre site that for 90 years had been a zinc-smelting plant. The jury also found DuPont had created both a public and a private nuisance, had committed trespass, and should be held strictly liable for exposing local residents to various toxic substances. Residents and property owners had sued, claiming that the company had deliberately dumped toxic heavy metals, particularly zinc, on the site. The medical problems caused by such toxins include cancer, damage to internal organs, and decreased fertility.[99]

Part Five—Global Climate Change

LO 17-13
Give concrete examples of environmental degradation in the United States and globally.

Global climate change has been described as "among the handful of most important public policy issues of our time,[100] "one of the greatest challenges the world faces,"[101] and the "greatest market failure the world has ever seen."[102] At issue is the projected overall increase in surface and ocean temperatures around the globe, substantially caused by the release into the atmosphere of man-made carbon dioxide and other greenhouse gases, largely through the burning of fossil fuels, especially in gasoline engines and coal-fired plants.

Both the politics and the science of global climate change have been controversial—a particularly potent and poignant example of the issues of coincidence, correlation, and causation discussed at the beginning of Part Two. The Intergovernmental Panel on Climate Change (IPCC) states that it is "extremely likely that human influence has been the dominant cause of the observed warming since the mid-20th century" and that human influence "has been detected in warming of the atmosphere and the ocean, in changes in the global water cycle, in reductions in snow and ice, in global mean sea level rise, and in changes in some climate extremes."[103] "Extremely likely" refers to a probability of 95 to 100 percent.[104] [The IPCC Fifth Assessment Report and all prior assessment reports can be found at **www.ipcc.ch/ publications_and_data/publications_and_data_reports.shtml#.Um0UOBCJ0nc**].

Because global average surface temperatures did not appreciably rise (despite significant global GHG emissions) between 1998 and 2012, some commentators recommended a hiatus in the implementation of emission reduction policies while we "see if the nonwarming trend continues."[105] Others pointed out, however, that the "current pause is consistent with numerous prior pauses" and that "it is a mistake to interpret a landing as the end of the climb."[106] In fact, 2016 was the third year in a row that average global temperatures set a new record high, and scientists blame the trend, along with an El Niño, on man-made global warming.[107] Scholar and activist Bill McKibben has argued that we no longer live on the same planet on which our parents grew up, and that climate change has passed the tipping point. "The planet we inhabit has a finite number of huge physical features. Virtually all of them seem to be changing rapidly."[108] Consider the following:

- On September 16, 2012, the Arctic ice sheet shrank to a record low—half of what it was in 1979. The sheet is getting thinner as well—a quarter of what it was in 1979.[109] Glaciers in the Alps, the Andes, the Rocky Mountains, and New Zealand are melting. The ice on the Tibetan plateau and its surrounding mountains, including the Himalayas, is the source of 10 major rivers, and 1.5 billion people live in the basins of those rivers. In 2009, scientists in China, the United States, and Germany began a long-term program called the Third Pole Environment to study the area. Its initial findings are that glaciers in the eastern Himalayas and the eastern Tibetan plateau are retreating fast.[110] The danger posed by melting glaciers is what is called the Albedo Affect: while ice and snow reflect 85 percent of solar radiation, dark open water absorbs 93 percent of that radiation, which, in turn, melts more ice.[111]

> On September 16, 2012, the Arctic ice sheet shrank to half of what it was in 1979.

[For an award-winning 2012 Sundance Film Festival documentary recording receding glaciers throughout the world using time-lapse photography, see **www.chasingice.com**].

- "The oceans, which cover three-fourths of the Earth's surface, are distinctly more acid and their level is rising; they are also warmer, which means the greatest storms on our planet, hurricanes and cyclones, have become more powerful."[112] Acidification of the oceans weakens shells, which means fewer shelled organisms. It may also endanger such commercially important species as marlin, mackerel, and tuna.[113] In 2008, the island nation of the Maldives, which is located in the Indian Ocean and is the lowest country in the world, was reportedly creating a reserve fund to allow the population to resettle in Sri Lanka, India, or Australia in the event they lose their homelands to the sea.[114] In early 2012, the island states of Palau and Grenada requested that the U.N. General Assembly seek an advisory opinion from the International Court of Justice "on the responsibilities of States under international law to ensure that activities carried out under their jurisdiction or control that emit greenhouse gases do not damage other States."[115]

- Between 2030 and 2050, climate change is expected to cause approximately 250,000 additional deaths per year from malnutrition, malaria, diarrhea, and heat stress.[116]

- Deliberate burning of forests in the Amazon and Indonesia reduces the world's carbon sink capacity and releases previously captured carbon into the atmosphere. Deforestation in Indonesia is substantially related to its production of palm oil for export—to be used as biodiesel fuel in European vehicles. Forests are natural carbon sinks, but some may be near their carbon saturation point. It may take a binding agreement on forest management for European forests to continue offsetting carbon emissions from other sources. Better forest management may also be necessary to offset the impact worldwide from such natural, but increasing, devastation from beetles (western United States and British Columbia), drought (Colorado's aspens and the Amazon), heat (South Africa's euphorbia trees, Algeria's cedars, and Australia's eucalyptus), and fires (Siberia and southwestern United States).[117]

The Paris Agreement

LO 17-14

Discuss the purpose of the Kyoto Protocol and the Paris Agreement.

In 1997 the governments of the world, realizing that global action would be required to have any significant impact on overall emissions, adopted the Kyoto Protocol. Specifically, the protocol called for a 5 percent reduction from 1990 levels of greenhouse gas emissions to be achieved by 2012. The protocol acknowledged that developed countries were principally responsible for the GHG levels at that time. These countries agreed to legally binding emission reductions; developing countries did not take on binding reductions and were allowed to grow consistent with their development needs. It became binding when ratified by 180 countries, upon Russia's ratification in late 2004. The United States never ratified the protocol.

In achieving its fundamental objective, the protocol has been a complete failure. In 1990, approximately 31 million metric tons of carbon dioxide equivalents were emitted globally; by 2010 that number had risen to roughly 50 million metric tons.[118] As of 2011, China was the largest GHG emitter, followed by the United States, India, and then Russia.[119] The EU, however, has met and surpassed its goal under the protocol and is on track to reach its further goal of a 20 percent reduction of 1990 levels by 2020. In contrast, emissions from the United States were 8 percent higher in 2012 than in 1990. The Obama administration set a national goal, independently of Kyoto, to reduce emissions 17 percent over 2005 by 2020. Achieving that goal would amount to an approximately 3.4 percent reduction over our 1990 emissions.[120]

Formal discussions for a post-Kyoto international framework to reduce global emissions began in Bali, Indonesia, in December 2007, and a new global agreement was reached at the Paris Climate Change Conference in 2015. The so-called Paris Agreement has several key provisions in which governments agreed to keep the increase in global average temperature to well below 2°C above pre-industrial levels and to pursue efforts to limit it to 1.5°C; to report every five years on their progress and ambitious new targets; and for the EU and other developed countries to provide financing to assist developing countries to reduce emissions and to build resilience to climate change impacts. Participating countries also submitted comprehensive national climate action plans.[121] To date, 135 countries, including the United States, have ratified the new agreement, which will take effect in 2020.[122] The United States has agreed to lower its GHG emissions by 17.89 percent.[123]

Giving the last word to science, we go back to the IPCC's Fifth Assessment Report, published in September 2013, which addresses the physical science of climate change. For the first time, the participating scientists endorsed an upper limit of carbon dioxide—no more than 1 trillion metric tons—that can be produced if a 3.6 degree increase in average global temperature is to be avoided. According to one of the report's authors, "Just over a half-trillion tons have already been burned since the beginning of the Industrial Revolution, and at the rate energy consumption is growing, the trillionth ton will be burned sometime around 2040."[124] Perhaps politicians should take notice.

Internet Exercise

One indication of how much global climate change has become a grassroots issue in the United States is the entry of carbon footprint considerations into everyday conversation. A carbon footprint is a measurement of how much carbon dioxide is emitted into the atmosphere as the result of a particular product, activity, or lifestyle. It is a way to measure the carbon "cost" of a particular activity or the carbon "savings" of changing that activity.

What's your carbon footprint? Find out from **http://www.nature.org/greenliving/ carboncalculator/**. Compare that with your ecological footprint—that is, how many Earths we would have to have if everyone lived as you do. Go to **www.earthday.org/ footprint-calculator**.

Chapter Questions

1. In 2016, 21 teenagers sued the federal government, alleging that it allowed, and even encouraged, carbon emissions to increase over the past 50 years and that the government's actions, and its failure to act, have so profoundly damaged the Earth that they threaten the plaintiff's fundamental rights to due process under the Fifth Amendment. A federal district court judge in Oregon denied the government's motion to dismiss the case, finding that the plaintiffs sufficiently alleged that the government's conduct violated their constitutional right to a clean and healthy climate environment. The court's decision is the first of its kind in the environmental law arena. How might the government's actions and its failure to act constitute violations of due process under the Fifth Amendment? Do you agree with the judge's ruling that the plaintiffs should be allowed to proceed with their case? See *Juliana v. United States,* No. 15-1517, 2016 WL 6661146 (D. Or. Nov. 10, 2016).

2. Consider the politics of environmental law. The Obama administration utilized administrative rulings such as the Clean Power Plan rule in order to promote environmental protections in the absence of legislation. The EPA, however, withdrew the rule one month before President Trump took office, and he threatens to cut back further on regulation in order to promote American industry. Dismantling administrative rulings may be relatively easy. Undoing legislation is not, especially given the many moving parts of environmental law. What about market forces? Will the energy sector continue to transform even if regulation is reduced, and move further towards renewable energy? Clean gas-fired plants are already replacing coal-fired plants, and consumers are buying more energy-efficient homes and appliances. After studying this chapter, what are your thoughts about environmental protections? Should regulations be scaled back in favor of U.S. industry? What are the potential costs of deregulation? Will consumers still want environmentally friendlier products and industry practices?

3. The Dakota Access Pipeline controversy highlights the issues of environmental justice that plague Native Americans. Although 99 percent of the pipeline had been constructed, the Standing Rock Sioux protested further construction in the vicinity of the reservation on the basis that the tribe was excluded from preapproval discussions with the Army Corps of Engineers before the necessary federal permits were issued. The pipeline is over 1,000 miles long and would be used to transport a half million barrels of oil each day past the reservation. Consider the devastating hazards posed by oil spills. During the protests, over 176,000 gallons of oil leaked from a pipeline 150 miles away, and 130,000 of those gallons spilled into a nearby creek.[125] There have been

over 3,300 incidents of oil or gas pipeline leaks and ruptures since 2010.[126] Should the pipeline be allowed in such close proximity to the reservation? Should it be allowed given the fact that the Standing Rock Sioux tribe was excluded, in violation of the rules, from preapproval discussions?

4. "The Aral Sea is going, gone. Once the world's fourth largest inland body of water, the Aral has shriveled to half its former area and a third of its volume. As for the region's drinking water, even the local vodka has a salty tang."[127] The Aral is the victim of the former Soviet Union's central planners, who decreed that the area would be the nation's main source of cotton. To achieve that goal, intense irrigation was required, with the result that only a trickle of fresh water was left to feed the Aral. Refilling the Aral would require tremendous dislocations in the agriculture of the vast region. If you were a member of a commission charged with developing a plan for the future of the Aral Sea, what issues would you cover?

5. Professor and business ethics scholar Norman Bowie:

> Environmentalists frequently argue that business has special obligations to protect the environment. Although I agree with the environmentalists on this point, I do not agree with them as to where the obligations lie. Business does not have an obligation to protect the environment over and above what is required by law; however, business does have a moral obligation to avoid intervening in the political arena in order to defeat or weaken environmental legislation.[128]

   a. Explain Professor Bowie's reasoning.

   b. Do you agree with him? Explain.

6. Mexico is quickly running short of water:

> 85 percent of Mexico's economic growth and 75 percent of its 100 million people are in the north, and the water is far to the south. . . . [P]oliticians facing elections are reluctant to ask voters to spend more on any utility, let alone water. Agriculture uses 80 percent of the water and pays nothing, although it only ranks seventh in contribution to the gross national product. . . . Less than half of the capital's wastewater is treated. The rest sinks into underground lakes or flows toward the Gulf of Mexico, turning rivers into sewers. . . . Well over half of irrigation water is lost to evaporation or seepage.[129]

   Brainstorm as many possible contributions to the solution of Mexico's water problem as you can.

7. Because of the spread of the West Nile virus in the state of New York, an insecticide spraying program was implemented to control the mosquitoes responsible for spreading the virus. Several groups sued, arguing that the spray was a pollutant that damaged waters in violation of the Clean Water Act. What criteria should the court use to decide the outcome? See *No Spray Coalition, Inc. v. The City of New York,* 2000 U.S. Dist. LEXIS 13919, 51 ERC (BNA) 1508 (S.D.N.Y. September 25, 2000).

8. Ott Chemical Co. polluted the ground at its Michigan plant. CPC International created a wholly owned subsidiary to buy Ott, which was accomplished in 1965. CPC retained the original Ott managers. Pollution continued through 1972 when CPC sold Ott. In 1981 the U.S. EPA began a cleanup of the site. To recover some of the tens of millions

in cleanup costs, the EPA sued CPC (called Bestfoods) among other potentially responsible parties. The Superfund law places responsibility on anyone who "owned or operated" a property when pollution was deposited. The district court held that CPC was liable because of its active participation in Ott's business and its control of Ott's decisions in that it selected the Ott board of directors and placed some CPC managers as executives at Ott.

   a. Do you think CPC should be held liable? Why or why not?

   b. What test would you employ to determine whether a parent corporation should be liable for a subsidiary's pollution? See *United States v. Bestfoods,* 524 U.S. 51 (1998).

9. William Tucker:

   > [Environmentalism is] essentially aristocratic in its roots and derives from the land and nature-based ethic that has been championed by upper classes throughout history. Large landowners and titled aristocracies . . . have usually held a set of ideals that stresses "stewardship" and the husbanding of existing resources over exploration and discovery. This view favors handicrafts over mass production and the inheritance ethic over the business ethic.[130]

   Tucker went on to argue that environmentalism favors the economic and social interests of the well-off. He said people of the upper middle class see their future in universities and the government bureaucracy, with little economic stake in industrial expansion. Indeed, such expansion might threaten their suburban property values. Comment.

10. Americans' commitment to the car obviously raises serious environmental problems. The vast spaces required to park those cars are themselves a significant environmental hazard. Explain some of the environmental problems created or encouraged by parking lots.

11. The Endangered Species Act provides that all federal agency actions are to be designed so that they do not jeopardize endangered or threatened species. The act had been interpreted to reach federal agency work or funding in foreign countries, but the federal government changed that interpretation in 1986 to limit the act's reach to the United States and the high seas. A group labeled Defenders of Wildlife filed suit, seeking to reinstate the original interpretation. The case reached the U.S. Supreme Court, where Justice Scalia wrote that Defenders of Wildlife would have to submit evidence showing that at least one of its members would be "directly" affected by the interpretation. In response, one member of Defenders of Wildlife wrote that she had visited Egypt and observed the endangered Nile crocodile and hoped to return to do so again but feared that U.S. aid for the Aswan High Dam would harm the crocodiles. Do you think Defenders of Wildlife should have been permitted to sue? Why or why not? See *Lujan v. Defenders of Wildlife,* 112 S. Ct. 2130 (1992).

12. Economist Robert Crandall:

   > [O]ur best chances for regulatory reform in certain environmental areas, particularly in air pollution policy, come from the states. Probably, responsibility for environmental regulation belongs with the states anyway, and most of it ought to be returned there.[131]

    a. What reasoning supports Crandall's notion that responsibility for environmental regulation belongs with the states?

    b. How might one reason to the contrary?

    c. If the power were yours, would environmental regulation rest primarily at the state, federal, or international level? Explain.

13. The United States seems to be quite enamored with sport utility vehicles (SUVs), in spite of the fact that their gas mileage is considerably poorer than that of most sedans. To graphically bring home the environmental irresponsibility of SUV owners, two men in the San Francisco Bay area dreamed up a scheme to address what they perceived to be a market failure. Uninvited, they stuck homemade bumper stickers on hundreds of SUVs. The bumper stickers read, "I'm changing the environment! Ask me how!"[132]

    a. What effect do you think these self-appointed environmental police sought from their actions?

    b. What effect do you think they actually had?

14. Airplanes are a significant contributor to greenhouse gases. Comment on the following proposal: Each person receives an annual allowance for flights, fuel, gas, and electricity. If a person's use exceeds the allowance, he will have to purchase "carbon points" from someone under their limit.[133]

Notes

1. "Unspontaneous Combustion," *The Economist,* June 29, 2013, p. 39; "Logging the Good News," *The Economist,* May 25, 2013, p. 40; and "REDDY at Last," *The Economist,* December 8, 2012, p. 43.

2. "Gulf of Mexico Oil Spill (2010)," *The New York Times,* updated April 25, 2011; and Henry Fountain, "Gulf Spill Sampling Questioned," *The New York Times,* August 19, 2013.

3. Adam Nossiter, "Far from Gulf, a Spill Scourge 5 Decades Old," *The New York Times,* June 16, 2010; and "A Desperate Need for Reform," *The Economist,* October 20, 2012.

4. Lisa Fleisher and Anna Hirtenstein, "London Just Set a New Modern Pollution Record," *Bloomberg,* January 27, 2017 [**www.bloomberg.com/news/articles/2017-01-27/london-just-set-a-new-modern-pollution-record**].

5. Martin Fackler, "Errors Cast Doubt on Japan's Cleanup of Nuclear Accident Site," *The New York Times,* September 3, 2013. See also "Power Struggle," *The Economist,* September 21, 2013, p. 45.

6. Martin Fackler, "Japan's $320 Million Gamble at Fukushima: An Underground Ice Wall," *The New York Times,* August 29, 2016 [**www.nytimes.com/2016/08/30/science/fukushima-daiichi-nuclear-plant-cleanup-ice-wall.html?_r=0**].

7. Fackler, "Errors Cast Doubt on Japan's Cleanup of Nuclear Accident Site." See also "Power Struggle."

8. "Fact Sheet: Drinking-Water," World Health Organization, November 2016 [**www.who.int/mediacentre/factsheets/fs391/en**].

9. "Fact Sheet: Sanitation," World Health Organization, November 2016 [**www.who.int/mediacentre/factsheets/fs392/en**].

10. "Fact Sheet: Climate Change and Health," World Health Organization, June 2016 [**www.who.int/mediacentre/factsheets/fs266/en**].

11. Ariel Zirulnick, "The Extinction Risk for Birds, Mammals, and Amphibians," *The Christian Science Monitor,* October 27, 2010.

12. "Learn About Environmental Justice," U.S. Environmental Protection Agency [**www.epa.gov/ environmentaljustice/learn-about-environmental-justice**].

13. Amy Littlefield, "EPA Looks at Effects of Waste Plants on Minorities, Poor," *Los Angeles Times,* July 27, 2009.

14. Wilfred Beckerman, cited in Robert Solomon, *The New World of Business* (Lanham, MD: Rowman & Littlefield, 1994), p. 319.

15. "The Science of Sharing," *NYU Law Magazine* 2012, p. 106.

16. Susan Lee, "How Much Is the Right to Pollute Worth?" *The Wall Street Journal,* August 1, 2001, p. A15.

17. Richard Conniff, "The Political History of Cap and Trade," *Smithsonian Magazine,* August 2009 [**www.smithsonianmag.com/air/the-political-history-of-cap-and-trade-34711212/?all**].

18. Mark Golden, "Dirty Dealings," *The Wall Street Journal,* September 13, 1999, p. R13.

19. U.S. Environmental Protection Agency, *Acid Rain and Related Programs: 2007 Progress Report* [**www.epa.gov/sites/production/files/2015-08/documents/2007arpreport.pdf** (last visited January 27, 2017)].

20. Peter Shattuck and Daniel L. Sosland, "Northeast Faces Stark Choice on Climate Pollution," *The New York Times,* January 24, 2013.

21. "Gold and Green," *The Economist,* March 16, 2013, p. 29.

22. Jeff Gersh, "Seeds of Change," *Amicus Journal* 21, no. 2 (Summer 1999), p. 36.

23. Eduardo Porter, "In Energy Taxes, Tools to Help Tackle Climate Change," *The New York Times,* January 29, 2013.

24. "About CVRP," California Clean Vehicle Rebate Project [**https://cleanvehiclerebate.org/eng/ about-cvrp**].

25. Center for Sustainable Energy, "California Air Resources Board Clean Vehicle Rebate Project: Rebate Statistics" (data last updated January 3, 2017) [**https://cleanvehiclerebate.org/rebate-statistics**].

26. Loan Programs Office, U.S. Department of Energy, "Powering New Markets: Energy Storage Poised for Growth," Note from the Executive Director, October 2016 [**www.energy.gov/sites/ prod/files/2016/10/f33/DOE-LPO_Report_Energy-Storage-Growth_FINAL_Oct-2016. pdf**].

27. Jon J. Fialka and Jeffrey Ball, "Companies Get Ready for Greenhouse-Gas Limits," *The Wall Street Journal,* October 26, 2004, p. A2.

28. "Ray Anderson," *The Economist,* September 10, 2011, p. 99; and The Ray C. Anderson Foundation [**http://www.raycandersonfoundation.org/biography**].

29. "Why We Exist," Ray C. Anderson Foundation [**www.raycandersonfoundation.org/why-we-exist**].

30. Alan Tovey, "Fiat Chrysler Shares Crash by a Fifth as It Is Drawn into Emissions Scandal by US Regulators," *The Telegraph,* January 12, 2017 [**www.telegraph.co.uk/business/2017/01/12/ fiat-chrysler-shares-crash-fifth-drawn-emissions-scandal-us**].

31. William Boston, Arian Campo-Flores, and Aruna Viswanatha, "FBI Arrests Volkswagen Executive in Emissions Scandal," *The Wall Street Journal,* January 9, 2017 [**www.wsj.com/ articles/fbi-arrests-volkswagen-executive-1483971808**].

32. Bill Leonard, "Someday We'll Regret Damage to Our Planet," *The Des Moines Register,* September 20, 2004, p. 7A.

33. See Zachary Laub, "The Group of Eight (G8) Industrialized Nations," Council on Foreign Relations, March 3, 2014 [**www.cfr.org/international-organizations-and-alliances/group-eight-g8-industrialized-nations/p10647**]; and "Energy and Environment," Council on Foreign Relations [**http://www.cfr.org/issue/energy-and-environment/ri6**].

34. Katy Daigle, "Putting a Price on Clean Environment," *The Des Moines Register,* June 18, 2012, p. 6A.

35. This was the essence of plaintiffs' nuisance suit against various large greenhouse gas emitters in *Comer v. Murphy Oil USA,* 2007 WL 6942285 (S.D. Miss. 2009). The district court dismissed; a three-judge panel for the 5th Circuit reversed. When defendants sought an en banc rehearing, a number of the circuit judges recused themselves, but the remaining quorum granted the request and vacated the panel decision. Another judge then recused herself, leaving the court without a quorum. It determined the rehearing could not proceed, nor could the panel decision be reinstated. Thus, the district court's dismissal is the final decision.

36. John M. Broder and Peter Baker, "Obama's Order Is Likely to Tighten Auto Standards," *The New York Times,* January 26, 2009; and Editorial, "Cleaner Cars," *The New York Times,* October 5, 2010.

37. Rebecca Leber, "Donald Trump Just Replaced the White House Climate Website with . . . This," *Mother Jones,* January 20, 2017 [**www.motherjones.com/environment/2017/01/donald-trump-climate-white-house-website**].

38. Ellen Goodman, "Can Tourists Love a Place to Death?" *The Des Moines Register,* March 31, 2001, p. 7A.

39. *Coalition for Responsible Regulation, Inc. v. Environmental Protection Agency,* 684 F.3d 102, 121 (D.C. Cir. 2012).

40. *Utility Air Regulatory Group v. Environmental Protection Agency,* 134 S. Ct. 2427 (2014), *appealing Coalition for Responsible Regulation,* 684 F.3d 102.

41. "A Historic Commitment to Protecting the Environment and Addressing the Impacts of Climate Change," *The Record* [**https://obamawhitehouse.archives.gov/the-record/climate**]. See also Coral Davenport, "Obama to Take Action to Slash Coal Pollution," *The New York Times,* June 1, 2014.

42. Duane Morris LLP, "Formal Federal Government Withdrawal from Climate Change Regulation Begins," *Lexology,* December 21, 2016 [**www.lexology.com/library/detail.aspx?g=b4aca25a-d7fd-4a29-adaf-228878ce9a71&utm_source=Lexology+Daily+Newsfeed&utm_medium=HTML+email+-+Body+-+General+section&utm_campaign=Lexology+subscriber+daily+feed&utm_content=Lexology+Daily+Newsfeed+2016-12-23&utm_term=**].

43. David Erickson and Mark Anstoetter, "ALA Report Says U.S. Air Quality Improving," *Association of Corporate Counsel,* May 4, 2012 [**www.lexology.com**].

44. *Environmental Protection Agency v. EME Homer City Generation,* 134 S. Ct. 1584 (2014).

45. "Cross-State Air Pollution Rule (SCAPR)—Regulatory Actions and Litigation," U.S. Environmental Protection Agency [**www.epa.gov/csapr/cross-state-air-pollution-rule-csapr-regulatory-actions-and-litigation**].

46. "Coal in the Rich World: The Mixed Fortunes of a Fuel," *The Economist,* January 5, 2013 [**www.economist.com/news/briefing/21569037-why-worlds-most-harmful-fossil-fuel-being-burned-less-america-and-more-europe**].

47. Janet Larsen, "Falling Gasoline Use Means United States Can Just Say No to New Pipelines and Food-to-Fuel," *Earth Policy Institute,* March 28, 2013 [**www.earth-policy.org/data_highlights/2013/highlights38**].

48. Bill Vlasic, "U.S. Sets Higher Fuel Efficiency Standards," *The New York Times,* August 28, 2012; and Juliet Eilperin, "EPA Issues New Fuel-Efficiency Standard," *The Washington Post,* August 28, 2012.

49. Elisabeth Rosenthal, "Life after Oil and Gas," *The New York Times,* March 23, 2013; and Zack Colman, "U.S. Fuel-Efficiency Standards on Trucks Stricter Than Europe, Canada," *The Hill's Energy & Environment Blog,* September 20, 2012 [**http://thehill.com/blogs/e2-wire/e2-wire/250627-reports-us-gets-good-marks-on-fuel-efficiency-policy**].

50. "Why European Diesel Cars Are Not Available in the U.S.," *Scientific American* [**www.scientificamerican.com/article/why-european-diesel-cars**].

51. Campbell Robertson, "Gulf of Mexico Has Long Been Dumping Site," *The New York Times,* July 29, 2010 [**http://www.nytimes.com/2010/07/30/us/30gulf.html**].

52. Lindsey Hoshaw, "Afloat in the Ocean, Expanding Islands of Trash," *The New York Times,* November 9, 2009.

53. Robertson, "Gulf of Mexico Has Long Been Dumping Site."

54. David Erickson and Mark Anstoetter, "EPA Rates U.S. Coastal Waters as 'Fair,'" *Association of Corporate Counsel,* May 4, 2012 [**www.lexology.com**].

55. U.S. Environmental Protection Agency, "The Justice Department and EPA Reach Clean Water Act Settlement with Pepco to Reduce Pollution to Anacostia River," press release, January 13, 2017 [**www.epa.gov/newsreleases/justice-department-and-epa-reach-clean-water-act-settlement-pepco-reduce-pollution**].

56. "Blooming Horrible," *The Economist,* June 23, 2012, p. 36; and Robertson, "Gulf of Mexico Has Long Been Dumping Site."

57. 547 U.S. 715 (2006).

58. Charles Duhigg and Janet Roberts, "Rulings Restrict Clean Water Act, Foiling E.P.A.," *The New York Times,* February 28, 2010.

59. Leber, "Donald Trump Just Replaced the White House Climate Website with . . . This."

60. "Clean Water Rule Litigation Statement," U.S. Environmental Protection Agency [**www.epa.gov/cleanwaterrule/clean-water-rule-litigation-statement**].

61. Ian Urbina, "Think Those Chemicals Have Been Tested?" *The New York Times,* April 13, 2013.

62. National Toxicology Program, U.S. Department of Health and Human Services, "Formaldehyde," June 2011 [**www.niehs.nih.gov/health/materials/formaldehyde_508.pdf**]; and National Center for Environmental Assessment, U.S. Environmental Protection Agency, "Formaldehyde; CASRN 50-00-0," October 1989 [**https://cfpub.epa.gov/ncea/iris/iris_documents/documents/subst/0419_summary.pdf**].

63. Lyndsey Layton, "Use of Potentially Harmful Chemicals Kept Secret under Law," *The Washington Post,* January 4, 2010, p. A01.

64. Ibid.

65. Sen. Ed Markey, "Bipartisan Group of Senators Urge Smooth Transition for Chemical Safety Reform Implementation in New Administration," press release, November 30, 2016 [**www.markey.senate.gov/news/press-releases/bipartisan-group-of-senators-urge-smooth-transition-for-chemical-safety-reform-implementation-in-new-administration**].

66. Sen. Tom Udall, "Udall: With EPA Announcement of First 10 Chemicals for Review Under New Law, Historic Chemical Reform Bill Already Working to Keep Americans Safe," press release, November 29, 2016 [**www.tomudall.senate.gov/?p=press_release&id=2463**].

67. See, for example, *Safe Food and Fertilizer v. EPA,* 350 F.3d 1263 (D.C. Cir. 2003).

68. "Hazardous Waste," U.S. Environmental Protection Agency [**www.epa.gov/epawaste/hazard/recycling/regulations.htm**].

69. Edward Humes, "Grappling with a Garbage Glut," *The Wall Street Journal,* April 14–15, 2012, p. C3.

70. Stephanie Strom, "Companies Pick Up Used Packaging, and Recycling's Cost," *The New York Times,* March 23, 2012 [**www.nytimes.com/2012/03/24/business/companies-pick-up-used-packaging-and-recyclings-cost.html**].

71. "Advancing Sustainable Materials Management Facts and Figures," U.S. Environmental Protection Agency, [**www.epa.gov/smm/advancing-sustainable-materials-management-facts-and-figures**].

72. "Packaging: Recycling," Coca-Cola Journey, [**www.coca-colacompany.com/stories/packaging-recycling**].

73. "Sustainable Packaging, Building Momentum with PlantBottle™ Packaging," *Coca-Cola 2011/2012 Sustainability Report,* [**www.coca-colacompany.com/sustainabilityreport/world/sustainable-packaging.html#section-building-momentum-with-plantbottle-packaging**].

74. Strom, "Companies Pick Up Used Packaging"; and "Recycling and Reducing Waste," Starbucks [**www.starbucks.com/responsibility/environment/recycling**].

75. Anthony DePalma, "Love Canal Declared Clean, Ending Toxic Horror," *The New York Times,* March 18, 2004, p. A1.

76. U.S. Government Accountability Office, *Report to Congressional Requesters: SUPERFUND: Trends in Federal Funding and Cleanup of EPA's Nonfederal National Priorities List Sites,* Report GAO-15-812, September 2015 [**www.gao.gov/products/GAO-15-812**]; and Nicole Gaudiano, "EPA Short on Funds for Superfund Cleanup in NJ," *The Daily Journal,* June 11, 2014 [**www.thedailyjournal.com/story/news/local/new-jersey/2014/06/11/epa-short-funds-superfund-cleanup-nj/10318037**].

77. David Erickson and James Neet, "CERCLA: GAO Report Says Remediation Funds Insufficient," *Association of Corporate Counsel,* July 2, 2010 [**www.lexology.com**].

78. "Superfund: National Priorities List (NPL)," U.S. Environmental Protection Agency [**www.epa.gov/superfund/sites/npl/index.htm**].

79. "From Bombs to $800 Handbags," *The Economist,* March 19, 2011, p. 40.

80. 132 S. Ct. 1367 (2012).

81. 136 S. Ct. 1807 (2016).

82. May Wall and John Fehrenbach, "Scotts Miracle-Gro to Pay $10 Million in Criminal Fines and Civil Penalties, and Spend $2.5 Million on Environmental Projects, for Violations of Federal Pesticide Laws," *Association of Corporate Counsel,* September 10, 2012.

83. Katie Rogers, "Princess Cruise Lines to Pay $40 Million Fine for Illegal Dumping," *The New York Times,* December 2, 2016 [**www.nytimes.com/2016/12/02/business/princess-cruise-lines-fine.html**].

84. Adam Goldman, Hiroko Tabuchi, and Jack Ewing, "F.B.I. Arrests Volkswagen Executive on Conspiracy Charge in Emissions Scandal," *The New York Times,* January 9, 2017 [**www.nytimes.com/2017/01/09/business/volkswagen-diesel-emissions-investigation-settlement.html**].

85. "Hang On," *The Economist,* September 14, 2013, p. 13.

86. Moises Velasquez-Manoff, "Ecosystems Respond Well to Restoration," *The Christian Science Monitor,* July 13, 2009.

87. Todd Woody, "Wildlife at Risk Face Long Line at U.S. Agency," *The New York Times,* April 20, 2011.

88. Michael Wines, "Endangered or Not, but at Least No Longer Waiting," *The New York Times,* March 6, 2013.

89. "U.S. Federal Endangered and Threatened Species by Calendar Year," Environmental Conservation Online System, U.S. Fish & Wildlife Service [**http://ecos.fws.gov/tess_public/pub/speciesCountByYear.jsp**].

90. "Endangered Species: Rusty Patched Bumble Bee (*Bombus affinis*)," U.S. Fish & Wildlife Service [**www.fws.gov/midwest/endangered/insects/rpbb** (last updated February 14, 2017)].

91. 257 N.E.2d 870 (N.Y. 1970).

92. *American Electric Power Co., Inc. v. Connecticut,* 131 S. Ct. 2527 (2011).

93. 342 P.2d 790 (Or. 1959).

94. *Curd v. Mosaic Fertilizer LLC,* 39 So. 3d 1216 (Fla. 2010).

95. Julian Harrell, "Is Gasoline a Defective Product?" *Association of Corporate Counsel,* April 23, 2013 [**www.lexology.com**]; and Office of the Attorney General, N.H. Department of Justice, "MTBE Jury Verdict," press release, April 9, 2013 [**http://doj.nh.gov/media-center/press-releases/2013/20130410-exxon-mtbe.htm**]. See also "Supreme Court Refuses Appeal of $236M Exxon Mobil Groundwater Contamination Case," *RT,* May 16, 2016 [**www.rt.com/usa/343228-exxon-new-hampshire-mtbe**].

96. *Langan v. Valicopters, Inc.,* 567 P.2d 218 (Wash. 1977).

97. *State Department of Environmental Protection v. Ventron,* 468 A.2d 150 (N.J. 1983).

98. *Branch v. Western Petroleum, Inc.,* 657 P.2d 267 (Utah 1982).

99. Associated Press, "DuPont Found Negligent in Waste-Site Lawsuit," *The Wall Street Journal,* October 3, 2007.

100. David Markell and J. B. Ruhl, "An Empirical Survey of Climate Change Litigation in the United States," *Environmental Law Reporter* 40, no. 7 (2010), pp. 10644–55.

101. Intergovernmental Panel on Climate Change, "Summary for Policymakers of the Synthesis Report of the ICC Fourth Assessment Report" (2007), p. 1 [**www.ipcc.ch/publications_and_data/publications_and_data_reports.shtml**].

102. "Carbon Taxes Cut Debt, Cool Planet," *Bloomberg,* August 14, 2012 [**www.bloomberg.com/news/print/2012-08-14/carbon-taxes-cut-debt-cool-planet.html**].

103. Summary for Policymakers, *Climate Change 2013: The Physical Science Basis, IPCC Fifth Assessment Report,* September 2013 [**www.ipcc.ch/report/ar5/wg1/#.Um0UDBCJ0nc**].

104. Ibid.

105. "Climate of Uncertainty," *The Wall Street Journal,* October 1, 2013.

106. Richard A. Muller, "A Pause, Not an End, to Warming," *The New York Times,* September 25, 2013.

107. Justin Gillis, "Earth Sets a Temperature Record for the Third Straight Year," *The New York Times,* January 18, 2017 [**www.nytimes.com/2017/01/18/science/earth-highest-temperature-record.html?_r=0**].

108. Bill McKibben, *Earth* (New York: Henry Holt, 2010), p. 45.

109. "Tequila Sunset," *The Economist,* February 9, 2013, p. 76.

110. "Pole-land," *The Economist,* May 11, 2013, p. 84.

111. "See for Yourself: How Arctic Ice Is Disappearing," *National Geographic,* January 2016 [**http://ngm.nationalgeographic.com/2016/01/arctic-ice-shrinking-graphic-environment-text**].

112. McKibben, *Earth,* p. 45.

113. "A Look Into the Ocean's Future," *The New York Times,* July 15, 2011.

114. Randeep Ramesh, "Paradise Almost Lost: Maldives Seek to Buy a New Homeland," *The Guardian,* November 10, 2008.

115. Department of Public Information, "Press Conference on Request for International Court of Justice Advisory Opinion on Climate Change," United Nations, February 3, 2012 [**www.un.org/News/briefings/docs/2012/120203_ICJ.doc.htm**].

116. "Fact Sheet: Climate Change and Health," World Health Organization, June 2016 [**www.who.int/mediacentre/factsheets/fs266/en**].

117. Mark Kinver, "European Forests Near 'Carbon Saturation Point'," *BBC News,* August 18, 2013; and Justin Gillis, "With Deaths of Forests, a Loss of Key Climate Protectors," *The New York Times,* October 1, 2011.

118. "Climate Change Indicators: Global Greenhouse Gas Emissions," U.S. Environmental Protection Agency [**www.epa.gov/climate-indicators/climate-change-indicators-global-greenhouse-gas-emissions**]; and U.N. Environment Programme, *The Emissions Gap Report,* November 2012, p. 1 [**www.unep.org/pdf/2012gapreport.pdf**].

119. "Global Greenhouse Gas Emissions Data," U.S. Environmental Protection Agency [**www.epa.gov/ghgemissions/global-greenhouse-gas-emissions-data**].

120. Russell Gold, "Rise in U.S. Gas Production Fuels Unexpected Plunge in Emissions," *The Wall Street Journal,* April 18, 2013; U.S. Environmental Protection Agency, *Inventory of U.S. Greenhouse Gas Emissions and Sinks: 1990–2011—Executive Summary,*" April 2013, p. ES-4 [**www.epa.gov/climatechange/ghgemissions/usinventoryreport.html**].

121. "International Agreements on Climate Action," Council of the European Union, June 2016 [**www.consilium.europa.eu/en/policies/climate-change/international-agreements-climate-action**].

122. "Paris Agreement—Status of Ratification," U.N. Framework Convention on Climate Change [**https://unfccc.int/2860.php**].

123. U.N. Framework Convention on Climate Change, *Report of the Conference of the Parties on Its Twenty-First Session, Held in Paris from 30 November to 13 December 2016,* Annex I, p. 33 [**http://unfccc.int/resource/docs/2015/cop21/eng/10.pdf#page=30**].

124. Justin Gillis, "U.N. Climate Panel Endorses Ceiling on Global Emissions," *The New York Times,* September 27, 2013.

125. Chandrika Narayan, "Pipeline 150 Miles from Dakota Access Protests Leaks 176,000 Gallons," *CNN,* December 13, 2016 [**www.cnn.com/2016/12/13/us/pipeline-spill-north-dakota**].

126. Ibid.

127. Hugh Pope, "Uzbeks Manage to Endure Amid Ruins of the Aral Sea," *The Wall Street Journal,* February 5, 1998, p. A18.

128. Norman Bowie and Kenneth Goodpaster, "Corporate Conscience, Money and Motorcars," *Business Ethics Report, Highlights of Bentley College's Eighth National Conference on Business Ethics* (ed. Peter Kent 1989), pp. 4, 6.

129. "Profligate Past, Poor Planning Created Mexican Water Crisis," *Associated Press,* August 22, 2002.

130. "Tucker Contra Sierra," *Regulation,* March–April 1983, pp. 48–49.

131. Robert Crandall, "The Environment," in "Regulation—The First Year," *Regulation,* January–February 1982, pp. 19, 29, 31.

132. "'Mad Taggers' Leave Their Mark on SUV Culture," *The Waterloo/Cedar Falls Courier,* December 26, 2000, p. B5.

133. "Save the Planet: Stop Flying," *Parade,* January 7, 2007, p. 22.

CHAPTER EIGHTEEN

Internet Law and Ethics

After completing this chapter, students will be able to fulfill the following learning objectives:

18-1. Explain the ethical dilemmas referred to as the digital divide and net neutrality.

18-2. Apply the requirements of personal jurisdiction to a dispute arising in cyberspace, both where the parties are residents of different states and where they are residents of different countries.

18-3. Identify free speech issues that arise in the context of the Internet and present the competing interests that make each particular issue difficult to resolve.

18-4. Provide examples of online activities that raise privacy concerns.

18-5. Explain the differences in online privacy protection between the United States and the European Union.

18-6. Describe several Internet-related crimes, including cyberstalking and cybersecurity.

18-7. Explain the impact of the Electronic Signatures in Global and National Commerce Act (E-SIGN).

18-8. Discuss the legal effect of click-wrap agreements.

18-9. Discuss standard-essential patents and give an example.

18-10. Explain the copyright doctrines of fair use and first sale.

18-11. Explain the trademark issues described in the text affecting Google and eBay.

18-12. Identify and discuss the basic tax issue that arises from cyberspace transactions.

Introduction: The Internet and Globalization

> Over 3.5 billion of the world's 7 billion inhabitants have Internet access.

The Internet has changed our lives. Over 3.5 billion of the world's 7 billion inhabitants have Internet access.[1] That number has been made possible, in part, because of the relatively cheap access offered by cell phones in comparison with the cost of computers. The extraordinary power of this nearly instantaneous global communication system has produced remarkable new opportunities and challenges, creating and facilitating relationships (whole new "communities" of interest) among individuals, businesses, and governments that could never have occurred without it. The Internet is itself a catalyst for continuing globalization, breaking down national boundaries and rules to allow free interchange of communications, ideas, goods, and services around the world.

This global communication system raises yet another opportunity to consider some fundamental issues. What substantive law do we want to govern the world's Internet activities? What process should we use to establish standards that apply worldwide to this global medium? Consensus is necessary on everything from the assignment of domain names to when and what cyberattacks are allowable as weapons of war.[2] Can national governments legitimately impose standards and sanctions? Will international fora, such as the U.N. Internet Governance Forum, be necessary to resolve issues that have global ramifications? Will international bodies be able to act fast enough and with enough legitimacy to secure national acquiescence? Will international enforcement tools need to be developed? Will grassroots use of the Internet among individuals, business, and government drive the development of this new medium so vigorously that it will be a driving force in the fundamental restructuring of our global relationships?

Part One—The Market, Law, and Ethics

The roots of the Internet date back to the late 1960s when a small group of researchers sought a way to freely exchange digital information with colleagues at other institutions. By the end of the 1980s, a backbone system of networked computers had been created, and e-mail use reached the general public. In the mid-1990s, the first browser was released and the World Wide Web was born.[3] Since then the cost of both technology and access has dropped sufficiently to make the Internet a truly public, and international, space.

Policy makers, users, and posters are all concerned about the degree to which the force of law can, and should be, imposed on the Internet. Originally, it was an open-access forum only lightly touched by regulation. The growth in users and uses has created arguably the most diverse community imaginable—nearly as diverse as the human race itself. Unfortunately, along with volume and diversity comes conflict, and peaceful and dependable dispute resolution requires the existence of an established dispute resolution mechanism. Some conflict is resolvable by developing norms of conduct—such as e-mail and Internet etiquette—and some is resolvable by the establishment and enforcement of site principles by a site administrator. But some conflicts will end up in court because it remains our traditional mechanism for peaceful dispute resolution.

> The growth in users and uses . . . has created arguably the most diverse community imaginable.

To be accepted by the disputants, judicial decisions need to be based on shared principles. Likewise, we have developed legislative processes for the creation of rules to govern behavior. No existing judicial or legislative body, however, has obvious or natural jurisdiction over the Internet in its entirety. "[T]herein lies the central truth of globalization today: We're all connected and nobody is in charge."[4]

What choices do we have in this difficult situation? On one end of the spectrum, one might argue for the establishment and enforcement of globally applicable principles and processes. On the other end of the spectrum, one might predict complete balkanization with countries enforcing national standards by creating isolated domestic internets. As with most aspects of our globalized world, the more likely result will fall in the middle: global standards where uniformity is critical to the functioning of the whole system, national regulation where fundamental cultural values and political choices vary, and, perhaps, also the establishment of physically separate national internets, as Iran has proposed.[5]

Market Forces and Government Regulation

A discussion of regulating business that is conducted through the Internet must begin with the impact the market has in developing (or, put another way, "regulating") appropriate business behavior. For example, the photo- and video-sharing social network Instagram triggered a public outcry late in 2012 by announcing a change in its terms of use that would allow it to use posted photos for advertising purposes, without specific permission of the poster and without providing a general opt-out mechanism. Within a day, the provision was removed.

In regulating the functioning of the Internet and its component parts, global norms are required. Many norms, such as the assignment of top-level domain names (.com, .org, and so forth) and the system for routing digital traffic, had routinely been set by the United States. However, the European Union, and Brazil in particular, argued that matters of Internet governance should be globalized instead of resting with the United States.[6] The United States conceded. Effective October 1, 2016, it relinquished control of the Internet Corporation for Assigned Names and Numbers (ICANN). Originally established by the U.S. Department of Commerce, ICANN is now an independent organization that will continue to oversee the distribution of Internet addresses. ICANN now also owns the Internet Assigned Numbers Authority (IANA), the database that stores all Internet domain names.[7]

One function of the Internet is that it serves as a mass communications system. Much like the traditional broadcast systems of radio and TV, the Internet can deliver the same content to an infinite number of users. Most, if not all, countries regulate content delivered by traditional broadcast systems. This will likely continue to be true for content delivered through the Internet, as we will further discuss in Part Three.

The Internet also delivers private communications between particular users, much as a phone system. Generally, Western governments do not censor private communications, but they do at times seek information from carriers about the existence of participants in private communications. Governments also may seek access to the content of private communications sent through public networks as, for example, through phone wiretaps. In the digital world, the content of private communications can be stored as data for substantial lengths of time on the equipment of the service provider, which means that a much larger volume of such communications may be subject to government access. Again, market forces have little bearing on government access to such information, although the political maelstrom raised by Edward Snowden's disclosures about U.S. surveillance programs resulted in perhaps more transparency, if not significant change, to some of the government's practices.[8] Government access rules vary significantly among countries, and service providers subject to the jurisdiction of a particular country must comply with those rules. At times, however, a provider may elect not to do business in a particular country rather than subject itself to access demands with which it disagrees.

LO 18-1

Explain the ethical dilemmas referred to as the digital divide and net neutrality.

Internet Access

As we have seen in other areas, market forces and legal regulation will blend in some uncertain, emerging formula to provide the security and confidence necessary for effective e-commerce. But ethics, too, will play a part. The speed, traffic volume, surface anonymity, and global reach of the Internet suggest ethical issues that are both new and complex. They also suggest ethical issues that are seemingly familiar but framed in a new context. That brings us to the the issue of access.

The Digital Divide

The divide in the United States is not just along economic lines, but also along lines of race, age, and geography. As of 2013, 76 percent of white households were connected to the Internet, but only 57 percent of African American households were; 75 percent of those under 65 used the Internet, but only about 50 percent of those 65 and older did; and the lowest Internet usage was in Mississippi, Alabama, and Arkansas. Although nearly 98 percent of American households were located where broadband is available, 20 percent of American adults were not connected—not at home, at work, through public access points such as libraries, or through a smartphone. Availability of service is not the problem; the cost of connecting and digital literacy is. But presumptions about availability exacerbate the disadvantages of the unconnected, as job announcements and applications, public school homework assignments, and government services information and applications, among many other things, migrate to the web.[9]

An even greater disparity in access exists at the global level. For example, in 2016, only 29 percent of Africa's citizens had Internet access, compared with 89 percent in North America. Worldwide, it is estimated that 50 percent of the population is connected.[10] This is a significant improvement over the numbers in 2013, when only 15.6 percent Africa's citizens had access. That year, a group of seven well-known high-tech companies announced the start of an Internet access project to address the two-thirds of the world's population that was on the other side of the divide. As in the United States, one issue of access is availability, another is user cost, and yet another is training. But each of these issues is more intransigent outside of the United States. For example, in 2013, only 24 percent of the population in sub-Saharan Africa had access to electricity and, in most of these countries, the gross domestic product per capita was under $2,000.[11] [For current statistics on world Internet usage, see **www.internetworld-stats.com/stats.htm**].

Questions

1. Can you think of any creative ways to provide widespread Internet access in developing countries? For one approach, watch the TEDx talk available at **www.ted.com/talks/aleph_molinari_let_s_bridge_the_digital_divide.html.**

2. How would you deal with the reality that most Internet content is in English?

Net Neutrality

The Federal Communications Commission (FCC) describes "net neutrality," or an "open internet," as the principle that consumers should be able to go where they want on the Internet, when they want. In other words, if someone in the United States contracts with a commercial Internet service provider (ISP), such as AT&T, Comcast, or Verizon, and pays a fee for the type of service (for example, dial-up or broadband) and level of service (including speed, data volume, and the length of term), that person should then have access to any legal content provider, whether it is Amazon, Craigslist, Google, or YouTube. It implies that ISPs will not discriminate against the traffic of any legal content provider. Some ISPs would like the right to change that—for example, by charging certain content providers for access or for enhanced transmission speeds to the ISP's subscribers. Their argument is that bandwidth is not infinite and they need to be able to manage traffic during periods of congestion to prevent performance degradation over the entire system. Specifically, ISPs want to charge content providers with heavy traffic, such as sites where users download music and videos, for the substantial bandwidth used to access their sites, products, and services. The consequence of nonpayment would be either blocked access at certain times or degraded speed at which access is provided.

Vigorous arguments have been raised against such fees, including

- ISP subscribers already pay for the distribution system (and pay higher fees for various types and levels of service).
- Some ISPs compete with content providers (for example, cable companies provide content as well as access) and might discriminate either in price or speed to favor their own content.
- Variable pricing might make it difficult for new content providers to succeed. (**Amazon.com** had high-volume traffic long before it became profitable.)

In December 2010, the FCC issued new rules on net neutrality to address these issues. These regulations were challenged by Verizon, however, and the federal Court of Appeals for the District of Columbia Circuit held, in January 2014, that the FCC's equal access rules were unsustainable (but that the disclosure requirements were both severable and enforceable). The court determined that the FCC had changed the classification of broadband providers to "information services," which are not subject to common carrier regulation under the Telecommunications Act of 1996.[12] In 2015, however, the FCC reclassified Internet service once again—this time as a utility—and issued Open Internet rules effective June 2015.[13] The rules apply to both fixed and mobile Internet service, "ensuring consumers and businesses have access to a fast, fair, and open Internet."[14]

Specifically, the FCC's rules provide for

- No Blocking: Broadband providers may not block access to legal content, applications, services, or nonharmful devices.
- No Throttling: Broadband providers may not impair or degrade lawful Internet traffic on the basis of content, applications, services, or nonharmful devices.
- No Paid Prioritization: Broadband providers may not favor some lawful Internet traffic over other lawful traffic in exchange for consideration of any kind—in other words, no "fast lanes."

This rule also bans ISPs from prioritizing content and services of their affiliates.[15]

Question

The issue of net neutrality raises the question of whether regulation is either appropriate or necessary to restrict unwanted behavior. Would you prefer to leave it to the market to determine which ISPs will be successful? Explain your response.

Part Two—Jurisdiction to Adjudicate

LO 18-2

Apply the requirements of personal jurisdiction to a dispute arising in cyberspace, both where the parties are residents of different states and where they are residents of different countries.

Business in the cyberworld raises puzzling new legal problems. The Internet, after all, is borderless. We communicate and engage in transactions around the world. When a dispute arises from one of those billions of communications and transactions, where will that dispute be litigated? If an American website provides child pornography viewed by a resident of Germany, which nation will have the authority to prosecute the offense?[16] If a Massachusetts resident posts an arguably libelous article on an Internet bulletin board sited in New York, may the Texas resident who claims harm from the libel sue the author and the bulletin board host in a Texas court?[17] These are *jurisdictional* questions. The party filing suit must take its claim to a court that has both *subject-matter jurisdiction* (the authority to address the particular kind of legal problem raised) and *personal jurisdiction* (the power to compel the defendant to respond). (For a general discussion of jurisdiction, see Chapter 4.)

In the United States, where the plaintiff and defendant are both residents of the forum state, personal jurisdiction ordinarily is not an issue. However, personal jurisdiction over nonresidents depends on the constitutional requirement of *due process*. In practice, the test is one of *minimum contacts*: Did the defendant have sufficient contact with the forum state that being sued there would be fair and just? Put another way, was the defendant's contact with the forum state of such a nature that it should expect to be subject to the state's courts? Thus, the more business a defendant does in a state, the more likely personal jurisdiction will be found. Internet business raises special problems because the "contacts" are often electronic and fleeting.

> Did the defendant have sufficient contact . . . that being sued there would be fair and just?

Several cases have arisen in the United States that begin to answer these personal jurisdiction questions. In one, the Fifth Circuit held in a case of alleged copyright violation that Texas did not have personal jurisdiction over a Vermont corporation merely because the corporation's website was accessible from Texas.[18] It reached this conclusion, in part, because there was no specific connection between the existence of the corporation's website and the harm complained of by the plaintiff. Thus, the Vermont corporation could be sued in Texas only if it had contacts with Texas that were sufficiently "continuous and systematic" as to subject the corporation to suit in Texas generally. A passive website was insufficient to do this. When the defendant has more contact with the forum state than the existence of a passive website reachable by forum state computer users, the due process analysis becomes more complex and hinges on an evaluation of the defendant's specific additional contacts with the state. The existing decisions are often hard to reconcile and many cases have been reversed on appeal, indicating that judgments as to personal jurisdiction are challenging and uncertain.[19]

Question

The operator of the dating service be2.com sued the CEO of the competing dating service be2.net for trademark infringement. The suit was brought in a federal district court in Illinois. Defendant was a New Jersey resident. The only evidence of his contact with Illinois was a list of 20 Illinois members of be2.net. After the court granted a default judgment when the defendant did not respond to the complaint, defendant moved to vacate the judgment for lack of personal jurisdiction.[20] Should Illinois courts have jurisdiction? Explain.

Jurisdiction in International Suits

Similar jurisdictional issues arise across national boundaries. In 2010, an Italian court convicted three U.S.-based Google executives in absentia of violating Italian privacy laws based on a video posted by third parties on Google's system. The video showed three teenage boys harassing an autistic boy. Italian law holds executives responsible for company actions.[21] Google appealed and the decision was overturned. The appellate court found that Google had not performed an editorial function. Under EU law, mere hosting of user-generated content does not make the hosting service responsible for the content.[22]

In international contexts, it may be useful to distinguish among three types of jurisdiction: jurisdiction to prescribe (legislate), jurisdiction to adjudicate (judicial personal jurisdiction), and jurisdiction to enforce.[23] Most countries have long had laws that prohibit or regulate some forms of commerce, such as pornography, gambling, and alcohol. When a country seeks to apply those laws to foreigners, the question is whether the country has jurisdiction to adjudicate. The Restatement (Third) of Foreign Relations Law attempts to identify the circumstances under which countries have exercised their jurisdiction to adjudicate. It enumerates, among other circumstances: (1) when a person is present in the territory, other than transitorily; (2) when a person is domiciled, a resident, or a national of that country; (3) when a person regularly carries on business in that country; (4) when a person has carried on an activity in the country and that activity is the subject of the dispute; and (5) when a person has done something outside the country that has a "substantial, direct, and foreseeable effect within" the country and that effect forms the subject of the suit. Based on those standards, do you think the Italian courts have jurisdiction over Google's American executives?

> Most countries have long had laws that prohibit or regulate some forms of commerce, such as pornography, gambling, and alcohol.

Consider both the French court's approach and the U.S. district court's approach to the issue of jurisdiction to adjudicate in the following dispute.

LEGAL BRIEFCASE

Yahoo! v. La Ligue Contre Le Racisme et L'Antisemitisme
169 F. Supp. 2d 1181 (N.D. Cal. 2001)

Judge Jeremy Fogel

I. PROCEDURAL HISTORY

[Defendant] La Ligue Contre Le Racisme Et L'Antisemitisme ("LICRA") [is a French nonprofit organization] dedicated to eliminating anti-Semitism. Plaintiff Yahoo!, Inc. ("Yahoo!") is a corporation organized under the laws of Delaware with its principal place of business in Santa Clara, California. . . . Yahoo! services ending in the suffix ".com," without an associated country code as a prefix or extension (collectively, "Yahoo!'s U.S. Services"), use the English language and target users who are residents of, utilize servers based in, and operate under the laws of the United States. Yahoo! subsidiary corporations operate regional Yahoo! sites and services in 20 other nations, including, for example, Yahoo! France, Yahoo! India, and Yahoo! Spain. Each of these regional websites contains the host nation's unique two-letter code as either a prefix or a suffix in its URL. Yahoo!'s regional sites use the local region's primary language, target the local citizenry, and operate under local laws.

Yahoo! provides a variety of means by which people from all over the world can communicate and interact with one another over the Internet. . . . As relevant here, Yahoo!'s auction site allows anyone to post an item for sale and solicit bids from any computer user from around the globe. Yahoo! records when a posting is made and after the requisite time period lapses sends an e-mail notification to the highest bidder and seller with their respective contact information. Yahoo! is never a party to a transaction, and the buyer and seller are responsible for arranging privately for payment and shipment of goods. Yahoo! monitors the transaction through limited regulation by prohibiting particular items from being sold (such as stolen goods, body parts, prescription and illegal drugs, weapons, and goods violating U.S. copyright laws or the Iranian and Cuban embargos). . . . Yahoo! informs auction sellers that they must comply with Yahoo!'s policies and may not offer items to buyers in jurisdictions in which the sale of such item violates the jurisdiction's applicable laws. Yahoo! does not actively regulate the content of each posting, and individuals are able to post, and have in fact posted, highly offensive matter, including Nazi-related propaganda and Third Reich memorabilia, on Yahoo!'s auction sites.

On or about April 5, 2000, LICRA sent a "cease and desist" letter to Yahoo!'s Santa Clara headquarters informing Yahoo! that the sale of Nazi and Third Reich–related goods through its auction services violates French law. LICRA threatened to take legal action unless Yahoo! took steps to prevent such sales within eight days. Defendants subsequently utilized the United States Marshal's Office to serve Yahoo! with process in California and filed a civil complaint against Yahoo! in the Tribunal de Grande Instance de Paris (the "French Court").

The French Court found that approximately 1,000 Nazi and Third Reich–related objects, including Adolf Hitler's *Mein Kampf*, *The Protocol of the Elders of Zion* (an infamous anti-Semitic report produced by the Czarist secret police in the early 1900s), and purported "evidence" that the gas chambers of the Holocaust did not exist, were being offered for sale on Yahoo.com's auction site. Because any French citizen is able to access these materials on Yahoo.com directly or through a link on Yahoo.fr, the French Court concluded that the Yahoo.com auction site violates Section R645-1 of the French Criminal Code, which prohibits exhibition of Nazi propaganda and artifacts for sale. On May 20, 2000, the French Court entered an order requiring Yahoo! to (1) eliminate French citizens' access to any material on the Yahoo.com auction site that offers for sale any Nazi objects, relics, insignia, emblems, and flags; (2) eliminate French citizens' access to Web pages on Yahoo.com displaying text, extracts, or quotations from *Mein Kampf* and *Protocol of the Elders of Zion*; (3) post a warning to French citizens on Yahoo.fr that any search through Yahoo.com may lead to sites containing material prohibited by Section R645-1 of the French Criminal Code, and that such viewing of the prohibited material may result in legal action against the Internet user; (4) remove from all browser directories accessible in the French Republic index headings entitled "negationists" and from all hypertext links the equation of "negationists" under the heading "Holocaust." The order subjects Yahoo! to a penalty of 100,000 Euros for each day that it fails to comply with the order. . . .

The French Court also provided that penalties assessed against Yahoo! Inc. may not be collected from Yahoo! France. Defendants again utilized the United States Marshal's Office to serve Yahoo! in California with the French Order.

Yahoo! subsequently posted the required warning and prohibited postings in violation of Section R645-1 of the French Criminal Code from appearing on Yahoo.fr. Yahoo! also amended the auction policy of Yahoo.com to prohibit individuals from auctioning:

> Any item that promotes, glorifies, or is directly associated with groups or individuals known principally for hateful or violent positions or acts, such as Nazis or the Ku Klux Klan. Official government-issue stamps and coins are not prohibited under this policy. Expressive media, such as books and films, may be subject to more permissive standards as determined by Yahoo! in its sole discretion.

Notwithstanding these actions, the Yahoo.com auction site still offers certain items for sale (such as stamps, coins, and a copy of *Mein Kampf*) which appear to violate the French Order. . . .

Yahoo! claims that because it lacks the technology to block French citizens from accessing the Yahoo.com auction site to view materials which violate the French order or from accessing other Nazi-based content of websites on Yahoo.com, it cannot comply with the French order without banning Nazi-related material from Yahoo.com altogether. Yahoo! contends that such a ban would infringe impermissibly upon its rights under the First Amendment to the United States Constitution. Accordingly, Yahoo! filed a complaint in this Court seeking a declaratory judgment that the French Court's orders are neither cognizable nor enforceable under the laws of the United States.

Defendants immediately moved to dismiss on the basis that this Court lacks personal jurisdiction over them. That motion was denied. . . .

II. OVERVIEW

As this Court and others have observed, the instant case presents novel and important issues arising from the global reach of the

Internet. Indeed, the specific facts of this case implicate issues of policy, politics, and culture that are beyond the purview of one nation's judiciary. Thus it is critical that the Court define at the outset what is and is not at stake in the present proceeding.

This case is *not* about the moral acceptability of promoting the symbols or propaganda of Nazism. Most would agree that such acts are profoundly offensive. By any reasonable standard of morality, the Nazis were responsible for one of the worst displays of inhumanity in recorded history. . . .

Nor is this case about the right of France or any other nation to determine its own law and social policies. A basic function of a sovereign state is to determine by law what forms of speech and conduct are acceptable within its borders. . . .

What *is* at issue here is whether it is consistent with the Constitution and laws of the United States for another nation to regulate speech by a United States resident within the United States on the basis that such speech can be accessed by Internet users in that nation. In a world in which ideas and information transcend borders and the Internet in particular renders the physical distance between speaker and audience virtually meaningless, the implications of this question go far beyond the facts of this case. The modern world is home to widely varied cultures with radically divergent value systems. There is little doubt that Internet users in the United States routinely engage in speech that violates, for example, China's laws against religious expression, the laws of various nations against advocacy of gender equality or homosexuality, or even the United Kingdom's restrictions on freedom of the press.

* * * * *

The French order prohibits the sale or display of items based on their association with a particular political organization and bans the display of websites based on the authors' viewpoint with respect to the Holocaust and anti-Semitism. A United States court constitutionally could not make such an order. The First Amendment does not permit the government to engage in viewpoint-based regulation of speech absent a compelling governmental interest, such as averting a clear and present danger of imminent violence.

* * * * *

Comity

No legal judgment has any effect, of its own force, beyond the limits of the sovereignty from which its authority is derived. . . . The extent to which the United States, or any state, honors the judicial decrees of foreign nations is a matter of choice, governed by "the comity of nations." United States courts generally recognize foreign judgments and decrees unless enforcement would be prejudicial or contrary to the country's interests.

As discussed previously, the French order's content and viewpoint-based regulation of the Web pages and auction site on Yahoo.com, while entitled to great deference as an articulation of French law, clearly would be inconsistent with the First Amendment if mandated by a court in the United States. . . . The reason for limiting comity in this area is sound. "The protection to free speech and the press embodied in [the First] amendment would be seriously jeopardized by the entry of foreign judgments granted pursuant to standards deemed appropriate in [another country] but considered antithetical to the protections afforded the press by the U.S. Constitution." Absent a body of law that establishes international standards with respect to speech on the Internet and an appropriate treaty or legislation addressing enforcement of such standards to speech originating within the United States, the principle of comity is outweighed by the Court's obligation to uphold the First Amendment.

* * * * *

CONCLUSION

Yahoo! seeks a declaration from this Court that the First Amendment precludes enforcement within the United States of a French order intended to regulate the content of its speech over the Internet. . . . Accordingly, the motion for summary judgment will be granted.

AFTERWORD

On appeal in 2006, the Ninth Circuit Court of Appeals ruled by a vote of eight to three that the California district court had personal jurisdiction over the French defendants, but six judges also held that Yahoo! could not pursue its declaratory judgment action. Three of those six said the declaratory judgment action was not "ripe" for decision, while the other three were the minority that held that the court had no personal jurisdiction.[24] The Supreme Court declined to review the decision.[25]

Questions

1. We cannot tell from this opinion why the French court believed it had jurisdiction to adjudicate against Yahoo!, as opposed to Yahoo! France. Look back at the discussion of the Restatement (Third) of Foreign Relations Law immediately before this case. Why might the French court have had jurisdiction over Yahoo! France? Over Yahoo!?

2. If you were sitting on the Ninth Circuit, how would you have decided the jurisdiction question? Consider both the U.S. rule of minimum contacts and the Restatement provision.

3. Notice the court's conclusion that the principle of comity is outweighed by its constitutional obligation to uphold the freedom of speech. Is this approach to the requirements of comity consistent with the discussion of comity in Chapter 16?

Part Three—Constitutional Law: Speech and Privacy

Speech

LO 18-3
Identify free
speech issues
that arise in the
context of the In-
ternet and pres-
ent the competing
interests that
make each par-
ticular issue dif-
ficult to resolve.

The district court opinion in *Yahoo! v. La Ligue Contre Le Racisme et L'Antisemitisme* illustrates one of the free speech issues the Internet raises. Internet content has also raised
free speech issues here at home. The Internet's seeming anonymity, ease of use, relatively
low costs, and global reach make it a natural vehicle for transporting speech messages. As
we saw in Chapter 5, the First Amendment protects us from government restraints on the
content of speech, although reasonable restraints on the *context* (time, place, and manner)
of that speech are sometimes constitutionally permissible. Thus, a court will not restrain
free speech by enjoining someone from posting defamatory or copyrighted material, but the
damaged party may, of course, sue for defamation or copyright infringement after the posting.[26] [For articles on cyberlaw free speech, search for "free speech" at **http://repository.
jmls.edu/**].

One of the most troublesome Internet free speech issues is whether and how children
can be protected from online pornography while maintaining adult access to constitutionally protected content. In a 2007 survey, 34 percent of Internet users
aged 10 to 17 experienced "unwanted exposure to online pornography."[27] But Congress has been unsuccessful in its repeated attempts
to enact constitutional legislation that would still effectively eliminate access by minors. In 1997, the Supreme Court held critical
provisions of the Communications Decency Act of 1996 were overbroad and therefore violated the First Amendment.[28] Then, in 2007,
a federal district court found the Child Online Protection Act of
1998 unconstitutional and permanently enjoined its enforcement. In refusing to hear the
government's appeal in 2009, the Supreme Court effectively left the permanent injunction
in place.[29]

> Thirty-four percent of
> Internet users aged 10 to
> 17 experienced "unwanted
> exposure to online
> pornography."

Somewhat more successfully, Congress has also addressed a slightly different
problem—the exploitation of children in the making of child pornography and its online
accessibility to predators of children. Its first attempt was held unconstitutional by the
Supreme Court,[30] but in 2008 the Court upheld the PROTECT Act of 2003. Nevertheless,
child pornography remains one of the Internet's most intractable challenges, "too large for
law enforcement, policy makers and child protection groups to handle on their own."[31] (For
more on child online protection, see Chapter 5.)

Anonymous Speech

"[An] author's decision to remain anonymous, like other decisions concerning omissions
or additions to the content of a publication, is an aspect of the freedom of speech protected
by the First Amendment."[32]

A unique characteristic of the Internet and electronic communication through the Internet is the ease with which a poster or sender can be anonymous and remain so without

"fear of economic or official retaliation . . . [or] social ostracism."[33] Anonymity makes it more likely that individuals will feel free to say things about which they would otherwise keep silent. Thus, it can promote "the robust exchange of ideas."[34] Anonymity may, however, make individuals bolder about asserting untruths—misleading, fraudulent, or otherwise unprotected speech. For example, sites containing "revenge porn" have proliferated; these are sites on which ex-boyfriends, ex-husbands, and ex-lovers can post explicit photos of their former partners, at times along with disparaging remarks, information on where the women work and live, and links to their Facebook pages.

The victim of such a post can request the hosting site remove the material; indeed, hundreds of thousands of content complaints (for many different reasons) are received by Facebook, Google, and Twitter each week.[35] But it is largely up to the hosting site whether the content will actually be removed. Even if the offending material is removed from the originating site, there is a significant chance that it has been copied and could reappear in other locations at any time. The Communications Decency Act makes it very unlikely that the hosting website will be held liable for such postings, particularly if it removes the material when requested to do so. The law rests liability on the "information content provider," and courts have generally held that website owners are not content providers on these facts. Some lower courts seem willing to consider that some actions of a hosting website may result in liability—such as itself supplying responsive comments supportive of the original post or by naming the site in such a way as to encourage offensive, damaging, or defamatory posts.[36]

With regard to the original poster, there is very little state law that would criminalize the posting of such material. Victims occasionally have brought civil suits for damages, depending on the facts based on harassment, invasion of privacy, copyright infringement, or child pornography claims. [For more on the campaign to end revenge porn, see **https://www.cybercivilrights.org/**].

Before a victim of revenge porn or other forms of online harassment, defamation, and invasion of privacy can sue the content provider, the victim has to be able to prove who that is. Seeking the release of that information from the website or the ISP of the poster triggers First Amendment claims to anonymity on behalf of the original poster. In the case that follows, a Yahoo! poster argues the First Amendment prohibits Yahoo! from responding to a subpoena from Immunomedics, a corporation claiming the anonymous poster is or was an employee who violated the company's confidentiality agreement by posting company information on a Yahoo! message board.

LEGAL BRIEFCASE

Immunomedics v. Jean Doe
775 A.2d 773 (N.J. Super. 2001)

Judge Fall

Defendant Jean Doe, a/k/a "moonshine_fr," appeals from an order . . . denying her motion to quash a subpoena issued to Yahoo! by plaintiff, Immunomedics, Inc., seeking all personally identifiable information relating to the person or identity who posted messages on the Yahoo! Finance Message Board under the identifier "moonshine_fr" which may identify or lead to the identification of that person or entity.

Immunomedics is a publicly held biopharmaceutical Delaware corporation . . . focused on the development, manufacture, and commercialization of diagnostic imaging and therapeutic products for the detection and treatment of cancer and infectious diseases.

Yahoo! is an Internet Service Provider (ISP) that maintains a Web site that includes a section called Yahoo! Finance. Yahoo! Finance maintains a message board for every publicly traded company, including Immunomedics. Visitors to the Immunomedics site can obtain up-to-date information on the company, and can post and exchange messages about issues related to the operation or performance of the company.

On October 12, 2000, Immunomedics filed a complaint against Jean Doe, also known by the computer screen name "moonshine_ fr" ("Moonshine"). The complaint alleged that Moonshine had "posted a message on Yahoo! Finance." Immunomedics claimed that message contained information confidential and proprietary to Immunomedics. As a result, Immunomedics asserted it had sustained injury and that Moonshine should be held liable under theories of breach of contract, breach of duty of loyalty, and negligently revealing confidential and proprietary information.

*   *   *   *   *

Of the two messages in question, the first, with Moonshine describing herself as "[a] worried employee," stated that Immunomedics was "out of stock for diagnostic products in Europe" and claimed that there would be "no more sales if [the] situation [did] not change." The second message, allegedly posted by Moonshine after the initial complaint was filed, reported that Chairman of the Company Dr. Goldenberg was going to fire the Immunomedics "european manager." In her certification to the trial court, Immunomedics' Executive Vice President and Chief Operations Officer Cynthia L. Sullivan admitted that the statements were true, but that, as an employee, Moonshine had violated the company's confidentiality agreement and "several provisions" of the company's Employee Handbook.

On or about October 20, 2000, Immunomedics served a subpoena on Yahoo!, seeking discovery of Moonshine's true identity. Yahoo!, in turn, contacted Moonshine. In response, Moonshine filed a motion to quash the subpoena on or about November 15, 2000.

. . . After considering the arguments, the judge denied Moonshine's motion, stating, in pertinent part,

> We have two issues here. We have an issue, she's an employee, she signed a confidential document saying that she was not going to speak freely about information she learned at the company. So she contracted away her right of free speech if she's an employee. Number two, free speech, anonymous, but if it harms another individual, that is another way that we have a little bit of a dent in our rights for free speech.

*   *   *   *   *

Moonshine contends the motion judge erred in denying her motion to quash the subpoena, as anonymous speech is constitutionally

protected and Immunomedics' complaint is insufficient to warrant a breach of that anonymity. Immunomedics argues that, while anonymous speech is constitutionally protected, that protection can be overcome if a defendant uses that freedom in an unlawful manner. . . .

In another case involving an application for expedited discovery to disclose the identity of an anonymous user of an ISP message board, we concluded that courts must decide such applications by striking a balance between the First Amendment right of an individual to speak anonymously and the right of a company to protect its proprietary interest in the pursuit of claims based on actionable conduct by the ISP message board user.

*   *   *   *   *

We hold that . . . the trial court should first require the plaintiff to undertake efforts to notify the anonymous posters that they are the subject of a subpoena or application for an order of disclosure, and withhold action to afford the fictitiously named defendants a reasonable opportunity to file and serve opposition to the application. These notification efforts should include posting a message of notification of the identity discovery request to the anonymous user on the ISP's pertinent message board.

The court shall also require the plaintiff to identify and set forth the exact statements purportedly made by each anonymous poster that plaintiff alleges constitute actionable speech.

The complaint and all information provided to the court should be carefully reviewed to determine whether plaintiff has set forth a prima facie cause of action against the fictitiously named anonymous defendants. In addition to establishing that its action can withstand a motion to dismiss for failure to state a claim upon which relief can be granted, the plaintiff must produce sufficient evidence supporting each element of its cause of action, on a prima facie basis, prior to a court ordering the disclosure of the identity of the unnamed defendant.

Finally, assuming the court concludes that the plaintiff has presented a prima facie cause of action, the court must balance the defendant's First Amendment right of anonymous free speech against the strength of the prima facie case presented and the necessity for the disclosure of the anonymous defendant's identity to allow the plaintiff to properly proceed.

The application of these procedures and standards must be undertaken and analyzed on a case-by-case basis. The guiding principle is a result based on a meaningful analysis and a proper balancing of the equities and rights at issue.

. . . Here, Immunomedics' cause of action is based on Moonshine's status as an employee and her alleged violation of a confidentiality agreement, and Moonshine's alleged breach of her common law duty of loyalty. . . .

Applying the procedure and test outlined, we conclude Judge Zucker-Zarett properly analyzed the disclosure issue, and we affirm substantially for the reasons articulated by the judge in her oral opinion. . . . We add the following. Immunomedics presented sufficient evidence that Moonshine is, or was, an employee of Immunomedics. Ms. Sullivan indicated in her certification that "all employees are bound by several Company policies and a confidentiality agreement." Within its "Confidentiality and Assignment Agreement," Immunomedics includes the following language:

> This Agreement and any disputes arising under or in connection with it shall be governed by the laws of the State of New Jersey and each of the parties hereto hereby submits to the jurisdiction of any Federal or state court sitting in the State of New Jersey over any such dispute.

Accordingly, Immunomedics clearly established a prima facie cause of action for breach of the confidentiality agreement founded on the content of Moonshine's posted messages.

In balancing Moonshine's right of anonymous free speech against the strength of the prima facie case presented and the necessity for disclosure, it is clear that the motion judge struck the proper balance in favor of identity disclosure. With evidence demonstrating Moonshine is an employee of Immunomedics, that employees execute confidentiality agreements, and the content of Moonshine's posted messages providing evidence of the breach thereof, the disclosure of Moonshine's identity, which can be reasonably calculated to be achieved by information obtained from the subpoena, was fully warranted. Although anonymous speech on the Internet is protected, there must be an avenue for redress for those who are wronged. Individuals choosing to harm another or violate an agreement through speech on the Internet cannot hope to shield their identity and avoid punishment through invocation of the First Amendment.

* * * * *

Affirmed.

Questions

1. In your opinion, should employers, victimized individuals, and others who have been damaged by anonymous postings be able to obtain the identity of the poster from the hosting site or the poster's ISP? Explain.

2. An FBI agent monitored an AOL chat room suspected of being a site for exchanging child pornography. The agent did not participate in the chat room conversations. Charbonneau allegedly distributed child pornography to the chat room participants, including the FBI agent. Charbonneau was arrested. Did Charbonneau have a First Amendment free speech right to transmit child pornography online? Explain. See *U.S. v. Kenneth Charbonneau,* 979 F. Supp. 1177 (S.D. Ohio 1997).

3. Having read these materials on freedom of speech and the limits on the right to anonymity, what would you advise a friend who was a regular blogger? A classmate posting comments on **www.ratemyprofessors.com**? Your middle school cousin who is an avid Facebook user? Explain.

Commercial Speech

Remember from Chapter 5 that commercial speech has been accorded reduced but significant First Amendment protection. Thus, online advertising is subject to the same kinds of government oversight as that in print and on television. One form of online commercial message receiving special attention is so-called *spam* (mass e-mails). This electronic junk mail may be a legitimate form of commercial message at times, but it may also be an annoyance or a threat to the efficiency of the Internet because of its volume. It also may be deceptive or fraudulent, or contain objectionable content, such as obscenity or viruses. Globally, about 70 percent of all e-mail is spam.[37]

The federal CAN-SPAM Act of 2003 establishes both civil and criminal penalties for violations of its provisions. The Federal Trade Commission (FTC), charged with enforcing the act, won a substantial victory in 2008 when it obtained a court order freezing the assets of and shutting down a spam network that was capable of sending 10 billion e-mail messages a day and was responsible at one point for one-third of all spam. The group based its websites in China, processed credit card payments through Cyprus and the former Soviet republic of Georgia, and in one month cleared $400,000 in credit card charges from sales of replica watches, as well as pharmaceuticals for weight loss and for the enhancement of the male anatomy.[38] In 2013, a court in Moscow convicted two Russians of designing and controlling a botnet—a network of infected computers that can be harnessed to take coordinated action, such as sending spam. Most hijacked infected computers are located in developing countries where users often cannot afford virus protection software. This particular botnet, known as Festi outside of Russia, for a three-month period in 2012 generated a third of all spam e-mail messages circulating globally.[39] [To file a complaint with the FTC about spam you receive, go to **https://www.ftccomplaintassistant.gov**].

Privacy

LO 18-4
Provide examples of online activities that raise privacy concerns.

Most individuals probably do not fully appreciate the amount of their personal information that is available online, how it may be used, or the degree to which it may be misused. This is likely still the case, even after the 2013 disclosures precipitated by Edward J. Snowden of the extent to which the National Security Administration has routinely collected data on U.S. citizens. Most of the outcry following Snowden's disclosures addressed the legality of the government's actions under the Fourth Amendment's search and seizure restrictions and probable cause warrant requirements. Our focus here is different—this section looks at privacy concerns stemming from the way the Internet facilitates broad availability and accessibility of users' personal data, in ways that are often unintended and sometimes harmful.

The Internet has brought with it an explosion of accessible data, including personal data. Some of the information now available online has in fact been public for decades, but most people were not aware that it was public, did not know how to obtain it, or simply never bothered, a reality sometimes referred to as "practical obscurity."[40] For example, local governments keep property, tax, criminal, and court records, often housed in the local courthouse but not easily searchable. Now local governments are making much of these data available online and accessible to those who are simply curious.[41] Similarly, governmental agencies responsible for professional and occupational licensing may now have websites with membership lists, complaints filed, and disciplinary actions taken. Marketing firms, of course, have long collected all of this information and more, including home and work addresses, phone numbers, profession, income information, credit scores, bankruptcies, home ownership, mortgage amounts, vehicle and boat registrations, hunting licenses, bridal and birth registries, warranty cards, magazine and newspaper subscriptions, and even dog licenses. But maintaining current data was costly and the resulting profiles were not available to the general public. With the advent of the Internet that has changed. At CriminalSearches.com, a site supported by advertising, anyone can look up neighbors, babysitters, teachers, plumbers, or their children's friends for free, which the site encourages one to do. Many other sites will provide similar information for a fee to anyone willing to pay. How long will it be before jurors are tempted to look up the criminal record of the defendant?

A simple browser search can turn up much more information from the public pages of social media sites, both self-disclosed and posted by friends, family, and acquaintances. Consider the following information, which is readily available or which you yourself may be unwittingly providing:

- Satellite and street views of your home, your work, and your children's school. Scouting a location or stalking someone has never been easier.

• Candid pictures and videos of you and your family, while attending your daughter's school Halloween party or at a business lunch or making a quick dash into your local convenience store or sitting at your MacBook surfing the Internet. Digital cameras are cheap, tiny, and potentially anywhere. Most cell phones come with built-in cameras. Several vendors sell miniature, high-definition Wi-Fi cameras for under $200, which one such company promotes "with easy setup in 60 seconds" and "continuous cloud recording." In early 2014, that company was uploading 1,000 hours of video per minute, 10 times the amount uploaded to YouTube.[42] Then there's Google Glass—a small computer worn on a person's face, which connects wirelessly to a smartphone and can do much of what a cell phone can do, including take pictures and videos of persons without their knowledge or consent. Finally, we have learned that laptop webcams are susceptible to hacking. A paper by researchers at Johns Hopkins explains how to reprogram a MacBook webcam to record without triggering the LED indicator that is supposed to alert the user that the camera is on. "There is only really one solution that can guarantee no one is spying on you: a piece of tape stuck over your computer camera."[43]

• Facebook confessions of indiscretions or, worse, crimes that find their way into police reports, school and job application files, and credit evaluations, as well as Instagram pictures that show up in divorce and child custody proceedings. Social media are having a wider impact than most people imagine, and the legal system may be having a hard time keeping up. Lawyers are turning to blog posts and online profiles to evaluate potential jurors; jurors have been "caught tweeting during testimony, polling Facebook friends for input on the verdict," and doing online research related to crimes with which the defendant has been charged. Some judges now require all electronic devices to be left outside the courtroom and, presumably, the jury room.[44]

> Jurors have been caught tweeting during testimony, polling Facebook friends for input on the verdict.

Data Mining

Now consider the amount of information residing in the databases of institutions with whom we regularly deal: credit card companies, online vendors, membership organizations, schools, pharmacies, medical service providers, our ISPs, phone companies, and so forth. Data mining is the process of building profiles of individuals by organizing all the disparate pieces of information collected in the normal course of business. Those profiles can be used to provide better services to repeat customers—from the pizza outlet that knows what you ordered last time (and how often, as well as how much you spend and, possibly, whether you tip) to Netflix that knows all your historical downloads and rentals (and how you rated them), as well as everything listed in your queue, and from that information can give you tailored recommendations for other movies you might like. Significant efficiencies can be achieved from the use of mined data, but there are downsides as well.

Personalized responses can also permit price discrimination. An investigation by *The Wall Street Journal* discovered such "dynamic pricing" used by Staples.com—the same stapler offered for $14.29 and $15.79. From a sampling of visits from more than 42,000 zip codes, "statistically speaking, by far the strongest correlation involved the distance to a rival's store from the center of a zip code."[45] That is, if the query came from a shopper close to a brick-and-mortar Office Depot or Office Max, the online price of the stapler was lower. This can replicate discrimination that mimics offline shopping: higher prices in locations with less competition, including rural and poor areas. Visit a comparison shopping site before going to your chosen vendor and the offered price may drop; "click too quickly from home-page to product page to checkout, and the seller can conclude that you have already decided to buy—so why offer you a discount?"[46]

Visit your favorite news or bookstore or streaming video site and you may get recommendations based on your prior viewing history. A convenience? Perhaps. But it may also steer you away from news stories, books, and movies that don't fit the profile labels the filtering algorithms have decided your online history reveals. If the algorithm concludes a user is likely to be a shopaholic or financially overextended, payday lender ads may start appearing on the screen. Not only are many users not aware of the extent of personalization occurring, but even if they are, there is no process for correcting these hidden profiles that influence one's online experience nor right to delete them.

To achieve this degree of personalization, the data collected on users go significantly beyond an individual site mining the data provided while a user browses its site. Users of a site may also knowingly give the merchant personal information to complete their transaction. Amazon.com identifies the following as examples of information customers provide: "your name, address, and phone numbers; credit card information; people to whom purchases have been shipped, including addresses and phone number; . . . e-mail addresses of your friends and other people; . . . and financial information, including Social Security and driver's license numbers."[47] Profiles built by one online vendor, including both browsing history and user-provided information, also may be provided to or aggregated with information gathered by affiliated businesses or by third-party advertisers. Or the business that compiles the profiles may sell them to marketing firms and others.

Cross-Device Tracking

Instead of one vendor, consider for a moment the source of the user-specific data available to certain iconic Internet businesses, such as Facebook, Google, Apple, and Microsoft. When repeat customers use Staples' website, they are likely to browse the site for desired items and then proceed to checkout, entering their username and password to do so. When they have finished, they leave the site. Users of Facebook, on the other hand, log in and then are likely to have the program running for extended periods of time, using various apps, chatting with friends, and so on. Even when they go elsewhere on the Internet, they may "like" places they visit, connecting them back to their Facebook accounts. If the users also own a smartphone, they may also use it to access Facebook and have it running as they travel through their day. This allows Facebook to collect user-specific information across multiple devices (laptop, work computer, smartphone), from many other websites, over extended periods of time, and from many geographical locations.

Google, Apple, and Microsoft can also do cross-device tracking—Google by connecting its users through Google Plus, whether they are on its Chrome browser, Google search, Gmail, Google maps, or its phones; Apple among its phones, its iPads, and laptops running its Safari browser, and its app stores; and Microsoft through its browsers, MSN, Hotmail, Outlook.com, Xbox, phones, and Bing. These companies are not only tracking across devices, but also across many different platforms.

All four of these companies can both develop extensive user profiles and reap substantial advertising dollars by facilitating targeted third-party ads to users manifesting specific attributes.

Aggregators

In this user-information market, will anyone be able to compete with these Internet giants? So far the answer remains yes—aggregators can and do.

An aggregator in our context is any person who takes data that are discrete at the level of the individual and aggregates them with individual-level data from one or more other sources. By itself, a data file containing the browsing history of 200 discrete individuals (each person's browsing history separately presented but with no information identifying whose history it is) may not seriously threaten the anonymity of those individuals. By combining data from various sources, however, an aggregator creates even more detailed individual profiles, thereby increasing the probability that the data reveal the identity of the person behind it.

Where does an aggregator obtain the data sets that it combines? One major source is to develop profiles of users' web browsing habits by placing cookies, tiny pieces of code, on thousands of websites to track users' online movements. When a visitor to a site logs in, about 25 percent of the time the site passes along the user's name, e-mail address, and other personal information to any third-party company with its own cookie on the page.[48] In a study conducted in 2012, 6,485 cookies were found on the 100 most popular websites—a majority of which were placed by third-party trackers, not the websites themselves.[49]

Although cookies may work on mobile browsers, iPhone's mobile Safari blocks all third-party cookies, and cookies do not attach at all to mobile apps. However, third-party aggregators successfully take advantage of so-called leaky apps that transmit identifiable user data, including locational data, as smartphones surf the web, send e-mails and texts, and make calls. Apparently, both the U.K. and U.S. governments have been able to collect considerable data when smartphone users send posts to such popular services as Facebook, Flickr, LinkedIn, and Twitter.[50]

Of considerable concern is that no state or federal law prohibits the collection or sharing of most data by third parties, and independent aggregators have no privacy agreements with the individuals who are profiled and may have no agreement with the data source to restrict the use of the data. Aggregators generally are in the business of selling these data.

Privacy Policies: Did Someone Say Privacy?

These days an online merchant is likely to have a privacy policy posted on its site that describes, among other things, what data it collects and how they are used. For example, Amazon.com's Privacy Notice states, "Information about our customers is an important part of our business, and we are not in the business of selling it to others."[51] The information it automatically collects includes "login; e-mail address; password; computer and connection information such as browser type, version, and time-zone setting, browser plug-in types and versions, operating system, and platform; purchase history . . . ; the full Uniform Resource Locator (URL) clickstream to, through, and from our website, including date and time; cookie number; [and] products you viewed or searched for." It also receives information such as "account information, purchase or redemption information, and page-view information from some merchants with which we operate co-branded businesses." A partial list of such businesses includes "Starbucks, OfficeMax, American Apparel, Verizon Wireless, Sprint, T-Mobile, AT&T, J&R Electronics, PacSun, Eddie Bauer and Northern Tool + Equipment." The notice further acknowledges that its site includes third-party advertising and links to other websites. It then states, "We do not have access to or control over cookies or other features that advertisers and third party sites may use, and the information practices of these advertisers and third-party websites are not covered by our Privacy Notice."

Having read the materials in this section on data mining, think about the vast amount of personal data you now know is compiled and stored by various entities—Internet vendors, social media sites, and aggregators, as well as phone companies and such traditional institutions such as banks and employers. Now consider the ramifications of the fact that anything stored can likely be stolen. For example, Google is one of the strongest, most technically sophisticated Internet companies in the world, but even it cannot prevent covert cyberattacks on its systems. Neither can Facebook, Apple, Twitter, Yahoo!, LinkedIn, Bloomberg, the International Monetary Fund, the FBI, or the Pentagon, all of which have acknowledged that their systems have suffered successful attacks. Indeed, the opening lines of a recent *New York Times* article were, "The question is no longer who has been hacked. It's who hasn't?"[52]

Question

How would you rate the privacy protections available to individuals who purchase items through Amazon.com? How safe are similar data of individuals who have never purchased an item through Amazon.com?

Privacy of Employees

As discussed in Chapter 12, whether and when employers can legally access e-mails sent from or received on office computers continues to be uncertain. In a 2010 case, the New Jersey Supreme Court held that an employee had an expectation of privacy in an e-mail sent from her office computer but through a personal, password-protected web mail account, an expectation the employer violated when it forensically retrieved her e-mail off of office servers. The result might have been different if the employer's privacy policy had clearly advised employees that their e-mails, even those sent through personal web mail accounts, could be reviewed by the employer.[53] On the other hand, a U.S. Supreme Court case held that a city's review of a police officer's text messages was a reasonable search under the Fourth Amendment when the texts were sent from a wireless pager provided to the officer by the city, even if the officer had had a reasonable expectation of privacy.[54]

In recent years, a number of states have passed laws prohibiting employers from requiring log-on information to employee social media accounts, such as Facebook and Twitter, as a condition for the employee to get or keep a job. Exceptions are provided if an employer has specific information about work-related employee misconduct occurring through the use of such accounts or an employee's unauthorized publication of the employer's proprietary information.

Today's software can be customized to look for such things as company officers' and competitors' names, as well as inappropriate language. Software is also available today that can "track every keystroke, file download, and Internet page that appears on an employee's computer screen."[55] It can also be customized to look for such things as company officers' and competitors' names, as well as inappropriate language in office e-mail traffic. In part, companies may adopt some of these strategies to protect themselves from lawsuits. Employers wishing to implement such monitoring programs should, however, expressly advise their employees of that fact and have all employees sign an acknowledgment so there is no question about whether an employee has any expectation of privacy on company systems.

Question

Explain why employers might want to monitor their employees' computer activities.

Regulation

The United States has no comprehensive privacy law addressing the Internet environment. Instead, the privacy of users has largely been left to the "self-regulation" of service and content providers, buffered primarily only by periodic public outcries over, for example, a company's unilateral change in its stated privacy policy and occasional civil suits based on existing legal principles, such as defamation.

Most online content is and has remained free to users, funded primarily by advertising dollars. To make that advertising more effective, and thus able to generate more revenue, advertisers and content providers have developed behavioral tracking to follow users' paths through the Internet, thereby allowing ads targeted to users' specific interests. In a very real sense, Google and Facebook and other advertising-driven business models sell their users' data to pay for the services they give without charge to their users. "Self-regulation" then puts users' privacy protection into the very hands that derive substantial revenue from the sale of personal information. This is an irreconcilable conflict of interest. Periodically, lawmakers have acted, but the resulting laws have largely addressed privacy issues in discrete areas, such as motor vehicle records, patient billing, or video rental records. California law requires websites and apps to have privacy policies, and the FTC has taken action against companies that violate their stated privacy policies, as it did with Google in 2012. But there are no laws governing the content of company privacy policies. Similarly, there has been substantial discussion over many years on "Do Not Track" rules. Most browsers now have a user-controlled setting to alert advertisers that they do not want their web activities tracked. But engaging that setting is largely symbolic—online advertisers are not required to honor the user's wishes. A working group established by the World Wide Web Consortium has been arguing over Do Not Track standards for over six years, with little evidence that a consensus will be reached anytime soon.[56]

Child Privacy Online

The United States does have a separate law addressing the privacy of children online. The 1998 Children's Online Privacy Protection Act (COPPA) prohibits websites from collecting personal information from children under 13 without parental permission and requires that parents be allowed to review and correct any information collected about their children. The FTC is charged with primary enforcement of COPPA. In 2012, it updated its rules under COPPA in a number of ways: by expanding the definition of "personal information" to include not just names, phone numbers, and home and e-mail addresses, but also mobile phone serial numbers, and extending the rule's application to cover social media sites, interactive gaming sites, and smartphone and tablet apps. It also puts more substantial restrictions on the use of behavior-based online advertising. The information that triggers the need for parental consent now includes photos, video, and the location of the child's mobile device.[57] [For more information about COPPA, go to **https://www.ftc.gov/tips-advice/business-center/guidance/complying-coppa-frequently-asked-questions**].

LO 18-5

Explain the differences in online privacy protection between the United States and the European Union.

Privacy in Europe

The European Union has taken quite a different tack than America's market-driven approach to online privacy. The European Union's 1998 Data Protection Directive first established the right of individual consumers to decide how their collected data could be used. Thus, if a European consumer provides personal information such as an address when buying from an online store, that store cannot legally send an ad to the purchaser without first seeking permission.[58] The directive also prohibited the transfer of data to countries outside the European Union that do not have "adequate" privacy rules.[59] The United States was one of the nations deemed inadequate, but by June 2000, European and U.S. negotiators had reached an agreement shielding U.S. companies from prosecution by EU governments for violation of the Data Protection Directive as long as the companies complied with a list of "safe harbor" privacy principles.[60] Following the revelations in 2013 of the extent of U.S. digital surveillance activities in Europe, however, there were many calls in the European Union to reconsider the terms of the safe harbor.

Two major developments have since taken place. First, in 2016, the European Union adopted the General Data Protection Regulation to strengthen consumer rights under the existing data protection rules and give them greater control over their personal data. Under the new rules, which take effect in May 2018, consumers will be provided more information about how their data is processed, the right to transfer their data between service providers, the right generally to have their data deleted when they no longer want it processed (unless there is a legitimate reason for retaining it), and the right to be notified when their data has been hacked. At the same time, the regulation establishes one set of rules with which business in the European Union must comply. A company's failure to comply with the rules can result in a fine of up to 4 percent of its global annual turnover.

Another major development occurred in October 2015 when the European Court of Justice declared the then existing safe harbor rules shielding U.S. companies from prosecution invalid. The European Commission and the United States subsequently agreed on a new framework for transatlantic data flows called the EU-US Privacy Shield. Under the new agreement, companies are under a stronger obligation to protect the personal data of their European consumers, and both the Department of Commerce and the Federal Trade Commission are obligated to undertake stronger monitoring and enforcement of the rules in cooperation with European Data Protection Authorities.

The philosophical chasm separating U.S. and EU data privacy policies was dramatically illustrated when it became public that Google occasionally collected e-mails and passwords from residential Wi-Fi networks while its cars were driving city streets taking photos for its

Street View mapping service. In the United States, the FTC ended its inquiry when Google pledged to stop gathering that information. In Europe, Google agreed to destroy the data collected in Austria, Britain, Denmark, France, and Ireland, and then in 2012 acknowledged that it had not actually done so. The Czech Republic banned Google from expanding its mapping program; Google was sued by an association of Internet users in Spain; and in 2013 authorities in Germany imposed close to the maximum fine its law allowed, although that was just shy of $190,000.[61]

Part Four—Crime

LO 18-6

Describe several Internet-related crimes, including cyberstalking and cybersecurity.

Crimes facilitated by the Internet include both truly new types and some old, familiar crimes in somewhat new clothing. Some statutes previously discussed, such as the CAN-SPAM and PROTECT acts, provide criminal penalties. Other laws criminalize specific online behavior, such as the Computer Pornography and Child Exploitation Prevention Act of 1999, which makes it unlawful to use a computer to solicit, lure, or entice a child or otherwise engage in sexual offenses with a child. The Computer Fraud and Abuse Act of 1986 bars individuals from accessing networked computers without authorization or obtaining information the individual is not authorized to take. Violation can result in substantial jail time and fines. There is considerable difference among the federal circuits as to the breadth of its reach: The Ninth and Fourth Circuits read the law narrowly, limited to unauthorized access of computer systems,[62] while the First, Fifth, Seventh, and Eleventh Circuits have taken a broader view. For example, the Seventh Circuit found that an employee who had been given access could still violate the law if the employee used that access to take unauthorized actions, such as deleting stored information.[63] Judge Kozinski of the Ninth Circuit, concerned with vast expansion in the reach of the law, queried: "Many employers have adopted policies prohibiting the use of work computers for nonbusiness purposes. Does an employee who violates such a policy commit a federal crime?"

Many of our long-standing, pre-Internet criminal laws can be applied to both online and offline behavior. For example, in February 2013, over just a few hours, digital thieves stole $45 million from thousands of ATM machines in New York City.[64] Fundamentally, this is no different from an old-fashioned bank robbery but using modern-day tools. Likewise, it is a federal crime to transport stolen property across state lines, even if the property is an intangible such as a detailed litigation strategy e-mailed by a law firm's employee to opposing counsel in another state.[65]

So too, fraud can be perpetrated with or without the aid of computers and the Internet. Recently hatched schemes include

- Ransomware, which locks a user's computer and sends a fake police warning charging the user with abusive use of the Internet and imposing a fine to get the computer unlocked.[66]

- Bogus tech support calls, in which a person who receives a call, allegedly from a company such as Microsoft, is told that his or her computer has reported a virus. If given remote access to the computer, the caller will download a program onto the computer and then show the owner a file that displays a warning message. The caller then offers to remove the virus immediately for a specified fee.[67]

- Malware delivered to Apple computers through a security breach in a Java program that co-opts the computer into a botnet controlling thousands of such computers to perpetrate click fraud that, alternatively, can cause the computers to click repeatedly on ads for a particular business, causing its advertising bill to skyrocket, or to click repeatedly on ads appearing on a host website, earning revenue for that site for getting potential customers to the advertiser's site.[68]

- Fake reviews on Yelp, Google, Citysearch, and similar sites posted by reputation enhancement companies on behalf of client restaurants, dentists, lawyers, and others, for the purpose of directing business to them based on fictitious experiences.[69]

Yet some existing criminal laws describe the prohibited behavior in terms that often prevent their application to cyber-versions of what is, at its essence, the same bad act, such as between physical stalking and *cyberstalking*. In a 2005 Illinois case, a former electronics store employee was sentenced to four years in prison for sending lewd photos and threatening e-mail and phone messages to a 22-year-old woman who had taken her computer in for repair.[70] This is *cyberstalking*—the repeated use of electronic media (such as e-mail or chat rooms) to harass or threaten another person. Every state has laws criminalizing traditional physical stalking. Most of these laws require that the perpetrator make a credible threat of violence for the action to be a violation; many do not expressly include cyberstalking, although under appropriate facts it might be covered.

In recent years, the biggest stories in cybercrime have not been crimes targeted at specific individuals or even major crimes such as the New York City bank heist. Instead what has dominated the news is organized, widespread criminal activity directed at major institutions, both commercial and governmental, which raises an issue unique to our newly digital world—cybersecurity.

Cybersecurity

We live in the age of information. With the near complete infiltration of digital technology into the basic fabric of our lives, much of our most valuable information is stored on computers, with vast quantities of information available even on single computer systems, enticing a whole new category of thieves—*hackers*. Thanks to the Internet, hackers can break into our computers from the privacy of their own home, even if that home is a three-room apartment in St. Petersburg, Russia.[71] Hacking can be simply malicious—destroying data or whole computer networks.[72] Or computing power can be the object of the theft, as is true with botnets that were used in conjunction with the spam attacks previously discussed.

On the other hand, the goal of some hacks is the theft of personal data from, at times, millions of individuals simultaneously. In 2012, the tax records of 3.8 million individuals and 850,000 businesses were stolen from the South Carolina Department of Revenue's database, records that contained information ranging from Social Security numbers to bank account information.[73] From late November through mid-December 2013, thieves hacked into the cash registers at Target stores, stealing tens of millions of payment card numbers.[74] By some estimates, 12.6 million people in the United States were victims of identity theft in 2012 alone.[75]

As devastating as identity theft can be for the individual whose identity has been stolen, from a societal point of view it gets worse. Of considerable concern has been the rise of cyberespionage—both industrial and military espionage for the purpose of stealing military and economic secrets and intellectual property. The perpetrators can strike from U.S. soil or from foreign nations; there has been considerable speculation that such attacks have been sourced from governments, including China, Iran, North Korea, and the United States.[76] The United States has expressed concern that its critical infrastructure is being targeted, such as its electricity grids, water supplies, computer and cell phone networks, and banks.[77]

The cost of all this cybercrime, which includes the spending to defend against it, has been estimated at $1 trillion. But more recently, a study undertaken in part by the Center for Strategic and International Studies, a nonprofit based in Washington, D.C., estimated the cost at $100 billion per year.[78] That said, Congress has not addressed the problem with legislation and the Obama administration issued only voluntary cybersecurity guidelines for certain crucial industries, such as banks and utilities.[79]

International Computer-Facilitated Crime

As is obvious from the foregoing, any truly effective response to cybercrime would be substantially aided by an international, coordinated approach. The Council of Europe has proffered the Convention on Cybercrime as an international effort to address computer-facilitated crime. It has been signed by 44 member states and four nonmember states, although only 40 states have ratified it.[80] The convention went into force July 1, 2004, for the original ratifying states. It requires "the criminalization of a long list of computer activities—everything from breaking into a computer to the 'deterioration' of computer data. . . . It also requires countries to make sure they can snoop through Internet data in real time. And it obliges nations to assist each other's investigations by monitoring Net communications."[81]

Each country's decisions to criminalize certain behaviors reflect that country's moral attitudes and historical experiences. Some proscribed behaviors such as murder are fairly universal, but other behaviors are acceptable in some countries while criminalized in others. Where such crimes are facilitated by the Internet, international disputes over the appropriate reach of such laws have arisen. We have already seen one example in the *Yahoo! v. La Ligue Contre Le Racisme et L'Antisemitisme* case in Part Two of this chapter, where France sought to enforce its ban on the sale of Nazi memorabilia to French citizens.

Both the United Kingdom and Germany have enforced criminal laws based on pornographic materials posted on websites outside their geographic boundaries. The United Kingdom convicted one of its citizens operating out of his home in the United Kingdom of "publication" of pornographic materials on websites located in the United States.[82] Germany originally convicted the German head of CompuServe, a U.S. company, for allowing German citizens access to pornographic websites hosted outside Germany, despite the fact that CompuServe had no feasible technological way to block access. (Blocking access would have required the U.S. corporation to block access to all of its customers worldwide.) The conviction was overturned a year later.[83]

Part Five—Commercial Law

Contracts and Uniform Laws

Internet sales have grown significantly, but for the Internet to reach its commercial potential, a routine, well-settled contracts structure is essential. The basic ingredients of a binding contract, as we saw in Chapter 6, also apply to Internet transactions:

- **Capacity** to enter the contract.
- **Offer and acceptance** of the terms of the contract.
- **Consideration** for the promises in the contract.
- **Genuineness of assent**.
- **Legality of purpose** of the contract.

Thus, an e-mail exchange fulfilling the traditional contract requirements should result in an enforceable agreement. But what if acceptance is indicated only by providing an "electronic signature" (a digital code unique to an individual), downloading some information, opening a shrink-wrap package, or clicking an "Accept" button?

LO 18-7
Explain the impact of the Electronic Signatures in Global and National Commerce Act (E-SIGN).

E-Signature   Electronic signatures can take a variety of forms (voice prints, distinctive marks, mathematical codes), but they share a common purpose—to have the same legal effect as a signature affixed by hand. On June 30, 2000, President Clinton signed into law the Electronic Signatures in Global and National Commerce Act (E-SIGN), giving electronic signatures the same legal stature as handwritten ones, at least for most commercial purposes.[84] Consumers, however, cannot be forced to accept electronic signature agreements or to receive records and documents electronically rather than in paper form. [For a look at the digital signature laws of the United Nations, European Union, and the United Kingdom, see **http://law.richmond.edu/jolt/v11i2/article6.pdf**].

UCITA   In 1999, the National Conference of Commissioners on Uniform State Laws (NCCUSL) approved a model law designed to achieve uniformity across the United States in the law governing software and Internet transactions. The proposed law reaches all deals involving computer information or goods and is designed to address the special problems of the electronic market, including software licensure (right to use). The Uniform Computer Information Transactions Act (UCITA) addresses the substance of computer information transactions, rather than procedural aspects such as electronic signatures.

To this point, UCITA has been amended twice (2000 and 2002), but it has been adopted in only Maryland and Virginia.[85] Until it or some other such legislation is widely approved, the Uniform Commercial Code (UCC), other applicable state and federal laws, and the common law of contracts (judge-made law) will govern electronic contractual arrangements. (The UCC, having been approved in 49 of the 50 states, is designed to provide nationwide consistency, predictability, and fairness in contract law where a sale of goods is involved.)

LO 18-8

Discuss the legal effect of click-wrap agreements.

Click-Wrap Agreements   Today, software is typically downloaded with license terms provided onscreen during the installation process. Those terms often say that by using the software the buyer agrees to the terms. Whether all of those terms are enforceable in court is the subject of dispute. The likelihood is that many terms will be enforceable if the buyer has a reasonable opportunity to review those terms and can abort the installation (and the charge) if the terms are unacceptable. The court in *Caspi v. Microsoft Network*,[86] applying a traditional contract law analysis, ruled that the choice of forum provision in just such an online click-wrap agreement was enforceable.

Critics are increasingly concerned, however, about just how voluntary some provisions in such standard-form contracts are. That is, has the purchaser genuinely consented to the contract terms? It can appear that retailers are, perhaps deliberately, obscuring one-sided terms.[87] Who has not viewed with trepidation the presentation of contract terms in a 2-by-4-inch scrollable window with an "Agree" button prominently displayed below?

Intellectual Property

Continued expansion of electronic commerce depends to a significant extent on the business community's success in protecting its technology from theft, copying, infringement, and the like. Intellectual property, broadly, is composed of creative ideas that are the products of the human mind. Songs, computer programs, new medicines, a novel, and so on are forms of intellectual property. Recalling our discussion of market failure in Chapter 8, you may recognize that intellectual property, from an economics point of view, is a public good.

> Intellectual property, from an economics point of view, is a public good.

Intellectual property laws have been developed to provide a measure of protection from theft and exploitation to creators of such properties. The goal is to reward those whose ingenuity and hard work have produced tangible results (recordings, movies, and the like) as an incentive for them and others to continue doing so. At least that is the American and Western view of intellectual property. Some cultures remain reluctant to recognize property rights of this kind, but globalization seems certain to generate relatively consistent intellectual property standards for most of the world. Inclusion of the Agreement on Trade-Related Aspects of Intellectual Property Rights (TRIPS Agreement) as one of the WTO's foundation agreements supports this projection. [For more on intellectual property law, see **http://www.ipmall.info/**].

LO 18-9

Discuss standard-essential patents and give an example.

Patents   Exactly what role patents will play in the future development of the Internet is still somewhat uncertain. The grant of some early patents associated with basic methods of doing business online (such as Amazon.com's "one-click" method for making Internet purchases and Priceline.com's process of "reverse" auctions) raised considerable controversy, resulting in the announcement by the U.S. Patent and Trademark Office in 2000 that it was overhauling the way it processes and awards patents for many online processes.[88] [For more on business methods patents, see **www.uspto.gov/web/menu/pbmethod**].

The Patent Wars

In recent years, the most prominent Internet-related patent issues have arisen in disputes involving the thousands of patents associated with mobile devices such as smartphones and tablets, referred to as "a tsunami of patent-related lawsuits"[89] in courts all over the world, including Australia, Britain, Germany, Japan, South Korea, the Netherlands, and the United States. The disputes have focused on acceptable license fees for standard-essential patents and on patent infringement allegations with regard to design and functionality characteristics.

Standard-essential patents are those that address matters of basic communication and data handling that support and permit industrywide standards. For example, the technology behind wireless communication requires standardization so that smartphones made by any company can interact appropriately with Wi-Fi hotspots. Within the industry, companies that own standard-essential patents have generally agreed to license the technology to other companies and to charge rates that are fair, reasonable, and nondiscriminatory (FRAND). It is in the patent holders' interest for their patents to become industry standards because license fees then produce a continuing income stream. On the other hand, it is equally important that standard-essential patent holders not be allowed to abuse their monopoly power with high fees so as to impair their competitors' financial ability to compete. Complaints of overreaching rates have generated much litigation. In one such case, Microsoft argued Motorola's offered rate could cost Microsoft $4 billion annually; the judge ruled that the interest of the whole market had to be considered in resolving the dispute, not just the interests of the two litigants, and set a rate of just under $1.8 million a year. The court pointed out that at least 92 entities own standard-essential patents related to the operational standard at issue in the suit. "If each of these 92 entities sought royalties similar to Motorola's request of 1.15% to 1.73% of the end-product price, the aggregate royalty to implement [this operational standard] would exceed the total product price."[90]

Apple and Samsung, the industry leaders in the smartphone market, have been involved in an epic patent infringement battle that began in a California federal district court in April 2011 when Apple sued Samsung for copying patented aspects of Apple's iPhones, including their distinct look (a rectangle with rounded corners) and a number of their software and hardware features. Samsung counterclaimed charging Apple with violations of some of Samsung's standard-essential patents. They have pursued this battle, over these and other patents, not just in California, where this first suit was filed, but also in Germany, South Korea, the Netherlands, and the United Kingdom. In August 2012, the jury in the California case found in favor of Apple and awarded $1 billion in damages (which was later somewhat reduced). Apple proceeded to pursue an injunction against Samsung continuing to produce its smartphone models that incorporated the infringed patents. While that issue was proceeding through motions and then appeals, Samsung pursued its fight in front of the U.S. International Trade Commission (ITC), which has the power to ban importation of items that it determines infringe others' patents. The ITC ruled in June 2013 that Apple infringed some of Samsung's patents with regard to wireless connectivity and banned importation of some older models of Apple's iPhones and iPads, which order was vetoed by the Obama administration in early August, on the basis that such bans were inappropriate where the infringement was related to standard-essential patents, such as was the case with the Samsung patents at issue. A mere week later, the ITC issued another order banning importation, this time at Apple's request and against certain Samsung devices. This time no standard-essential patents were involved.

At this writing, there has been no, and likely won't be any, clear winner in these battles between Apple and Samsung. But then, many observers have pointed out that these battles aren't really about patent protection, but rather represent a battle for dominance in the mobile device market, including smartphones and tablets. It is worthy of note that in other contexts, Apple and Samsung work in concert: Apple is the largest customer for components manufactured by Samsung.[91]

Copyrights

LO 18-10

Explain the copyright doctrines of fair use and first sale.

In America and much of the world, anyone who creates "original works of authorship," whether in print or digital form, is in most cases automatically protected by copyright laws if the "works" are original and are "fixed in tangible form" (written down on paper, for example). The author has exclusive rights to commercially exploit those works for a period of years. Virtually all of the information available online is protected by the U.S. Copyright Act and includes such intellectual creations as data, databases, literature, music, software, photos, and multimedia works. Although original works of authorship are automatically copyrighted, the fullest protection of the law can only be achieved by placing a copyright notice on the work (such as "copyright 2017 McGraw-Hill") and registering the copyright with the U.S. Copyright Office. International protection is provided by the principal copyright treaty, the Berne Convention. [Information on the U.S. Copyright Office can be found at **www.copyright.gov**].

The copyright holder possesses the exclusive right to (1) reproduce the copyrighted work, (2) prepare adaptations based on the copyrighted material, (3) distribute the material by sale or otherwise, and (4) perform or display the material. When anyone other than the copyright holder, or one acting with the holder's permission, makes use of one of those rights, the copyright has been infringed, unless the use falls within a series of exceptions. Perhaps the most notable of those exceptions is the *fair use doctrine,* which allows use of copyrighted material without permission under some conditions, such as limited, nonprofit use in a classroom.

Another exception is the *first sale doctrine,* which provides that someone who owns a copy of a copyrighted work is free to resell it without infringing on the author's rights. The court in *Capitol Records v. ReDIGI* held that songs bought from Apple's iTunes and similar retailers cannot be resold by the original purchaser under the first sale doctrine because the doctrine protects only the owner of a particular copy, and no one can own a particular copy of a digital song—all copies are indistinguishable. It was also persuaded by the fact that physical copies degrade, whereas a digital copy could last forever.[92]

One of the most visible Internet copyright disputes has been the ongoing battle of the music recording industry to protect its copyrights. Music file sharing took off in the late 1990s through the use of the Napster website, where users could swap digital music. The recording industry successfully obtained an injunction against Napster's facilitation of such file sharing;[93] but the practice continued, aided by peer-to-peer computer programs such as KaZaA and Grokster, which are installed on users' computers. The recording industry sued Grokster and other file-sharing software distributors. The defendants prevailed at the district and circuit court levels.[94] Then, in the following unanimous Supreme Court decision, the recording industry achieved a major victory.

Metro-Goldwyn-Mayer Studios v. Grokster   125 S. Ct. 2764 (2005)

Justice Souter

I

A

Respondents, Grokster, Ltd., and StreamCast Networks, Inc., defendants in the trial court, distribute free software products that allow computer users to share electronic files through peer-to-peer networks, so called because users' computers communicate directly with each other, not through central servers. . . .

A group of copyright holders (MGM for short, but including motion picture studios, recording companies, songwriters, and music publishers) sued Grokster and StreamCast for their users' copyright infringements, alleging that they knowingly and intentionally distributed their software to enable users to reproduce and distribute the copyrighted works in violation of the Copyright Act.

* * * * *

Although Grokster and StreamCast do not know when particular files are copied, a few searches using their software would show what is available on the networks the software reaches. MGM commissioned a statistician to conduct a systematic search, and his study showed that nearly 90 percent of the files available for download on the FastTrack system were copyrighted works. Grokster and StreamCast dispute this figure. . . . They also argue that potential noninfringing uses of their software are significant in kind, even if infrequent in practice. Some musical performers, for example, have gained new audiences by distributing their copyrighted works for free across peer-to-peer networks, and some distributors of unprotected content have used peer-to-peer networks to disseminate files, Shakespeare being an example. . . .

But MGM's evidence gives reason to think that the vast majority of users' downloads are acts of infringement, and because well over 100 million copies of the software in question are known to have been downloaded, and billions of files are shared across the FastTrack and Gnutella networks each month, the probable scope of copyright infringement is staggering.

Grokster and StreamCast concede the infringement in most downloads, and it is uncontested that they are aware that users employ their software primarily to download copyrighted files, even if the decentralized . . . networks fail to reveal which files are being copied, and when. . . .

Grokster and StreamCast are not, however, merely passive recipients of information about infringing use. The record is replete with evidence that from the moment Grokster and StreamCast began to distribute their free software, each one clearly voiced the objective that recipients use it to download copyrighted works, and each took active steps to encourage infringement.

After the notorious file-sharing service, Napster, was sued by copyright holders for facilitation of copyright infringement, StreamCast gave away a software program of a kind known as OpenNap, designed as compatible with the Napster program and open to Napster users for downloading files from other Napster and OpenNap users' computers. Evidence indicates that "it was always [StreamCast's] intent to use [its OpenNap network] to be able to capture e-mail addresses of [its] initial target market so that [it] could promote [its] StreamCast Morpheus interface to them."

* * * * *

StreamCast developed promotional materials to market its service as the best Napster alternative. One proposed advertisement read, "Napster Inc. has announced that it will soon begin charging you a fee. That's if the courts don't order it shut down first. What will you do to get around it?" Another proposed ad touted StreamCast's software as the "#1 alternative to Napster" and asked "when the lights went off at Napster . . . where did the users go?"

* * * * *

In addition to this evidence of express promotion, marketing, and intent to promote further, the business models employed by Grokster and StreamCast confirm that their principal object was use of their software to download copyrighted works. Grokster and StreamCast receive no revenue from users, who obtain the software itself for nothing. Instead, both companies generate income by selling advertising space, and they stream the advertising to Grokster and Morpheus users while they are employing the programs. As the number of users of each program increases, advertising opportunities become worth more.

Finally, there is no evidence that either company made an effort to filter copyrighted material from users' downloads or otherwise impede the sharing of copyrighted files. . . .

B

The District Court . . . granted summary judgment in favor of Grokster and StreamCast as to any liability arising from distribution of the then current versions of their software. Distributing that software gave rise to no liability in the court's view, because its use did not provide the distributors with actual knowledge of specific acts of infringement.

The Court of Appeals affirmed. In the court's analysis, a defendant was liable as a contributory infringer when it had knowledge of direct infringement and materially contributed to the infringement. But the court read [our decision in] *Sony Corp. of America v. Universal City Studios, Inc.* as holding that distribution of a commercial product capable of substantial noninfringing uses could not give rise to contributory liability for infringement unless the distributor had actual knowledge of specific instances of infringement and failed to act on that knowledge. The fact that the software was capable of substantial noninfringing uses in the Ninth Circuit's view meant that Grokster and StreamCast were not liable, because they had no such actual knowledge, owing to the decentralized architecture of their software. The court also held that Grokster and StreamCast did not materially contribute to their users' infringement because it was the users themselves who searched for, retrieved, and stored the infringing files, with no involvement by the defendants beyond providing the software in the first place.

II

A

* * * * *

The argument for imposing indirect liability in this case is . . . a powerful one, given the number of infringing downloads that occur every day using StreamCast's and Grokster's software. When a widely shared service or product is used to commit infringement, it may be impossible to enforce rights in the protected work effectively against all direct infringers, the only practical alternative being to go against the distributor of the copying device for secondary liability on a theory of contributory or vicarious infringement.

B

* * * * *

In *Sony Corp. v. Universal City Studios* this Court addressed a claim that secondary liability for infringement can arise from the very distribution of a commercial product. There, the product, novel at the time, was what we know today as the videocassette recorder or VCR. Copyright holders sued Sony as the manufacturer, claiming it was contributorily liable for infringement that occurred when VCR owners taped copyrighted programs because it supplied the means used to infringe, and it had constructive knowledge that infringement would occur. At the trial on the merits, the evidence showed that the principal use of the VCR was for "'time-shifting,'" or taping a program for later viewing at a more convenient time, which the Court found to be a fair, not an infringing, use. There was no evidence that Sony had expressed an object of bringing about taping in violation of copyright or had taken active steps to increase its profits from unlawful taping. Although Sony's advertisements urged consumers to buy the VCR to "'record favorite shows'" or "'build a library'" of recorded programs, neither of these uses was necessarily infringing.

On those facts, with no evidence of stated or indicated intent to promote infringing uses, the only conceivable basis for

imposing liability was on a theory of contributory infringement arising from its sale of VCRs to consumers with knowledge that some would use them to infringe. But because the VCR was "capable of commercially significant noninfringing uses," we held the manufacturer could not be faulted solely on the basis of its distribution.

* * * * *

Because the Circuit [Court of Appeals] found the StreamCast and Grokster software capable of substantial lawful use, it concluded on the basis of its reading of *Sony* that neither company could be held liable, since there was no showing that their software, being without any central server, afforded them knowledge of specific unlawful uses.

This view of *Sony,* however, was error. . . .

C

[Nothing] in *Sony* requires courts to ignore evidence of intent if there is such evidence. . . . Thus, where evidence goes beyond a product's characteristics or the knowledge that it may be put to infringing uses, and shows statements or actions directed to promoting infringement, *Sony*'s . . . rule will not preclude liability. The classic case of direct evidence of unlawful purpose occurs when one induces commission of infringement by another, or "entices or persuades another" to infringe, as by advertising.

* * * * *

[The] inducement rule is a sensible one for copyright. We adopt it here, holding that one who distributes a device with the object of promoting its use to infringe copyright, as shown by clear expression or other affirmative steps taken to foster infringement, is liable for the resulting acts of infringement by third parties. We are, of course, mindful of the need to keep from trenching on regular commerce or discouraging the development of technologies with lawful and unlawful potential. Accordingly, just as *Sony* did not find intentional inducement despite the knowledge of the VCR manufacturer that its device could be used to infringe, mere knowledge of infringing potential or of actual infringing uses would not be enough here to subject a distributor to liability. Nor would ordinary acts incident to product distribution, such as offering customers technical support or product updates, support liability in themselves. The inducement rule, instead, premises liability on purposeful, culpable expression and conduct, and thus does nothing to compromise legitimate commerce or discourage innovation having a lawful promise.

III

A

The only apparent question about treating MGM's evidence as sufficient to withstand summary judgment under the theory of inducement goes to the need on MGM's part to adduce evidence that StreamCast and Grokster communicated an inducing message to their software users.

* * * * *

Here, the . . . record is replete with evidence that Grokster and StreamCast, unlike the manufacturer and distributor in *Sony,* acted with a purpose to cause copyright violations by use of software suitable for illegal use.

Three features of this evidence of intent are particularly notable. First, each company showed itself to be aiming to satisfy a known source of demand for copyright infringement, the market comprising former Napster users.

* * * * *

Second, this evidence of unlawful objective is given added significance by MGM's showing that neither company attempted to develop filtering tools or other mechanisms to diminish the infringing activity using their software.

Third, [it] is useful to recall that StreamCast and Grokster make money by selling advertising space, by directing ads to the screens of computers employing their software. . . .

B

In addition to intent to bring about infringement and distribution of a device suitable for infringing use, the inducement theory of course requires evidence of actual infringement by recipients of the device, the software in this case. As the account of the facts indicates, there is evidence of infringement on a gigantic scale, and there is no serious issue of the adequacy of MGM's showing on this point. . . . There is substantial evidence in MGM's favor on all elements of inducement, and summary judgment in favor of Grokster and StreamCast was error.

[Vacated and remanded.]

Questions

1. *a.* Explain how the Court was able to hold software distributors like Grokster liable for the misconduct of others (those who actually used the peer-to-peer networks to download copyrighted materials).

   b. What does the Court mean by "contributory" and "vicarious" copyright infringement?

   c. Why did the Supreme Court overrule the court of appeals decision?

2. Has this decision effectively stopped illegal downloading of copyrighted material? Explain.

3. As a consequence of this decision, is peer-to-peer technology now unlawful? Explain.

4. In your judgment do Grokster and other peer-to-peer software distributors have a moral responsibility regarding the unlawful use of their products by third parties? Explain.

AFTERWORD

Concurrently with suing file-sharing facilitators such as Grokster and StreamCast, the recording industry pursued the file sharers as well—35,000 of them between 2003 and 2008 including many university students.[95] According to one source, in 2006 "college students illegally obtained two-thirds of their music and accounted for 1.3 billion illegal downloads."[96] Under the Digital Millennium Copyright Act (DMCA), copyright holders can subpoena ISPs, including universities, to obtain the identity of those believed to be infringing. Of the 35,000 identified file sharers mentioned above, 12,000 lawsuits were filed, with two ultimately proceeding to trial. In one, a jury set damages against a former graduate student of $22,500 per song. The $675,000 award became final after the Supreme Court declined to hear the student's petition in 2012.[97] Just one month later, the Eighth Circuit reinstated a jury verdict of $220,000 in the second case.[98]

Market Response

While record labels were pursuing copyright infringers, some of the largest online music stores changed policies to remove usage restrictions from downloaded files. In mid-2007, both Apple and Amazon.com announced that their music would no longer be locked to certain players or programs. Both have the support of EMI, one of the largest record labels. The restrictions against putting their downloads on multiple computers and mobile devices (restrictions that aren't imposed when a CD is purchased) had long annoyed consumers. It had also drawn the unfavorable attention of EU regulators, who saw it as a form of unfair competition.[99]

In 2013, Amazon and Apple once more seemed to be positioning themselves to lead the market. In January 2013, Amazon received a patent "to set up an exchange for all sorts of digital material."[100] And in March 2013, the U.S. Patent and Trademark Office published an application from Apple for a patent of its own for a digital marketplace for users to sell or give away various digital copyrighted material. Thus, both companies seem to be exploring the possibility of having the first sale doctrine apply to digital copies or perhaps lobbying for a statutory change to the DMCA.

Grokster Redux?

In 2007, Viacom sued Google's YouTube video-sharing service alleging willful facilitation of infringement on a massive scale of Viacom's copyrights from shows on Comedy Central, MTV, and Nickelodeon. Viacom claimed over $1 billion in damages.[101] The trial court granted YouTube's motion for summary judgment. The DMCA provides a safe harbor against copyright infringement claims for ISPs and host websites if the host site responds expeditiously to remove, or disable access to, the copyrighted material when notified of violations. The court pointed out that Viacom had invoked the DMCA safe harbor when it notified YouTube of 100,000 offending videos and, by the next business day, YouTube had removed virtually all of them.[102] The Second Circuit vacated the decision, stating that, at least with respect to "a handful of the offending clips," "a reasonable jury could conclude that YouTube had knowledge or awareness" of infringement. It also directed the lower court to consider whether YouTube had been "willfully blind" to the presence of infringing material on its site. On remand, the lower court was to "allow the parties to brief [the specified] issues, with a view to permitting renewed motions for summary judgment as soon as practicable."[103] A year later, the lower court once again granted YouTube's motion for summary judgment, in a two-sentence opinion presenting summary conclusions on the issues remanded by the Second Circuit without analysis.[104]

What should be clear at this point is that copyright infringement is rampant, and the Internet has caused its exponential growth. What is not at all clear is what can or should be done about it. On the one side, content owners individually have very little ability to stop infringement of their copyrights. On the other side, seeking to impose the cost of protection on payment processors, advertising services, and domain name registries, as the Stop Online Piracy Act (SOPA) and the PROTECT IP Act (both introduced in Congress in 2012) would have done, may be costly to those middlemen and, in the end, not much more effective—costly because reviewing and removing all the potentially infringing material would be a herculean task; likely ineffective because offending content could be posted from and in any part of the world and still be accessible in nearly any other part.[105] This problem lets us reconsider an issue we have seen repeatedly in this text—who has the power and the right to assert jurisdiction over what is a worldwide problem? At the moment, there really is no answer to that question.

LO 18-11

Explain the trademark issues described in the text affecting Google and eBay.

Trademarks and Domain Names

Trademarks

Words, names, symbols, devices, or combinations thereof that are used to distinguish one seller's products from those of another are called *trademarks* when associated with products (like IBM, Coke, and Pepsi) and *service marks* when associated with service businesses (United Airlines). Having established a trademark (or service mark), the holder can prohibit any unauthorized use of the mark, thus ensuring consumers can trust the source of goods they are buying. The mark also protects mark owners by preventing loss of reputation and value, for example, when the unauthorized product is of poor quality. Mark owners are also protected from an increase in supply that dilutes the product's value. Infringement cannot occur unless, however, the marks are sufficiently similar that consumers could be confused.

The Internet has created new opportunities for confusion and, therefore, potential infringement. Recall the discussion of the dispute between Google and Louis Vuitton from Chapter 16. The issue was whether Google was infringing on Vuitton's trademarks by selling ad space to Vuitton's competitors at the top of Google's search results when individuals used Google's search engine looking for Vuitton products. The European Court of Justice said no. Another company that has had to defend repeated trademark infringement suits is eBay. Individuals sometimes try to sell counterfeit goods on eBay. At times, for some luxury goods manufacturers, the percentage of counterfeits available on the site had been quite high. The issue raised is the extent to which eBay has a duty to weed out counterfeit goods. After being sued, eBay improved its processes to greatly lessen the quantity of counterfeits sold, but it is also protected from liability by quickly removing any items when advised by the trademark holder that the goods are counterfeit.

Domain Names

The Internet address for a web page is called its domain name. The Domain Name System (DNS) for the whole of the Internet is overseen by the Internet Corporation for Assigned Names and Numbers (ICANN), a nonprofit organization with its headquarters in California. Ordinarily, a business engaging in electronic commerce will want to use the simplest form of its name as its domain name. Rights to a domain name are secured simply by being the first to request a name and pay the registration fee. The 1999 Anticybersquatting Consumer Protection Act creates a cause of action if a trademark is infringed by another's registration of a domain name that web searchers may confuse with that trademark. The Third Circuit has also held that registration of deliberate misspellings of famous marks is a violation of the act.[106]

In 1999, ICANN set up an arbitration process for the resolution of domain name disputes. Since then, more than 20,000 cases have been filed; as of 2013, 91 percent had been decided for the complainant.[107] Carmen Electra, Michael Crichton, Kevin Spacey, Pamela Anderson, Celine Dion, and Bruce Springsteen have all used the process to have domain name versions of their names transferred to them, all of which were previously registered by the same Canadian company.[108] [For information on the arbitration services available from the United Nations' World Intellectual Property Organization pursuant to ICANN's domain name arbitration policy, see **www.wipo.int/amc/en/domains**].

PRACTICING ETHICS · Top-Level Domain Name Sale

At this writing, more than a thousand new top-level domain names (TLDs) are just starting to go live. TLDs are the descriptors that follow the period in a web address, such as .com, .org, and .gov. Up until 2014, there were 22 general TLDs and 280 country-specific ones.[109] Some of the new TLDs will be written in Arabic, Chinese, and Russian scripts; others are likely to be company names, such as .google or .amazon; still others will be generic terms, such as .blog or .pizza. Successful registrants will have the right to sell second-level domains (the portion of the address that precedes the TLD). Thus, popular TLDs could also be very lucrative to their holders. Verisign, which currently manages the .com and .net TLDs, reported $874 million in 2012 revenues. ICANN accepted proposals from applicants for both open-use TLDs and restricted TLDs, the use of which the successful applicant might reserve solely for itself. L'Oreal is seeking the TLD .beauty and has stated that it would reserve some second-level domains, such as personal.beauty, for itself. Amazon indicated that all of the TLDs for which it applied will be closed, for its use only. ICANN has indicated, however, that it has not yet determined whether to allow "closed generic domains."[110] [For more on the new TLDs, see **http://newgtlds.icann.org/en**].

Questions

1. If you were a member of ICANN, who would you vote to give the TLD of .amazon to—Amazon.com or the consortium of Latin American countries through which the Amazon River runs?[111] Would you agree to the creation of such TLDs as .Jew, .Christian, .Muslim, .Baha'i, .Moses, .Jesus, and .Mohamad? Explain. Should community, cultural, or historical interests—such as the use of a name—be in control of commercial interests and individual companies? Discuss.

2. Applicants were charged $185,000 for each TLD application they filed. They will incur another $25,000 annually for each TLD they retain.[112] Do these fees raise ethical issues in terms of who might have wanted to control a particular TLD but were financially unable to pay these fees? Explain.

3. Donuts Inc. filed the most applications, 307, and paid $57 million for the privilege to do so.[113] It was the only applicant for 149 of them. Some have expressed concern with Donuts Inc. as an appropriate registrant because of its alleged ties to Demand Media, "a company with a well-documented history of providing services to spammers and other perpetrators of Internet abuses."[114] Demand Media has been a "host to sites that commit 'cybersquatting.'"[115] Would you vote to allow Donuts Inc. to control over a hundred new TLDs? Discuss.

4. As stated above, Donuts Inc. applied for 307 TLDs. Google applied for 101 TLDs; Amazon, for 76.[116] Should one entity be permitted to control that many TLDs? Is it anticompetitive to give control over generic TLDs to private companies? Discuss.

Taxes

LO 18-12
Identify and discuss the basic tax issue that arises from cyberspace transactions.

We close this chapter with an interesting public policy question raised by the remarkable confusion (and profusion) of the Internet. It is a policy issue, like many discussed in this chapter, that crosses traditional jurisdictional lines—both state boundaries in the United States and national boundaries around the world. Its resolution, either at the national level or at the international level, will require substantial negotiation, compromise, and, ultimately, consensus building.

What is the issue? We start with a national example: If you buy a CD on the Internet, your neighborhood retailer will not receive your business and your state and local governments often will not receive sales taxes as they would have if you had made the purchase at a local store. In pre-Internet days, the Supreme Court had ruled that an out-of-state vendor cannot be required to collect sales taxes for any state in which that vendor does not have some significant presence, including a physical presence.[117] The Court held that it would be an undue burden on interstate commerce for states to be able to require out-of-state vendors to comply with each unique set of state and local sales tax rules. Thus, many states joined an effort to streamline, simplify, and coordinate their sales tax laws. The idea is that, if state sales taxes are more uniform, the burden on interstate commerce from requiring the compliance of out-of-state vendors will be materially reduced.

As of this writing, a majority of states have been involved in the project, and 37 states and the District of Columbia have conformed their laws to the requirements of the negotiated agreement, which became operational in 2005.[118] Participation on the part of vendors is voluntary, but many have registered and are now remitting taxes to member states. The primary incentive for voluntary participation is a grant of amnesty for any prior unpaid taxes that might have been owed.[119] [For more on the Multistate Tax Compact, see **www.mtc.gov**].

That said, many online businesses have not agreed to submit voluntarily to collection of state taxes in states where they have no physical presence. Seven states are attempting to push the point through state legislation that defines nexus more broadly than determined by the Supreme Court in 1992. New York has passed such a law and sought to enforce it by suing noncomplying Internet vendors. The highest state court ruled that the state could require Internet retailers to collect sales taxes "if a vendor is paying New York residents to actively solicit business in this state" and denied appeals from both Amazon.com and Overstock.com. With regard to the law's constitutionality under the prior Supreme Court decision, the New York judge wrote, "The world has changed dramatically in the last two decades and it may be that the physical presence test is outdated. An entity may now have a profound impact upon a foreign jurisdiction solely through its virtual projection via the Internet. That question, however, would be for the United States Supreme Court to consider."[120] That may be, but in December 2013 the Supreme Court declined to do so when it declined the companies' petitions for *certiorari,* leaving New York's ruling to stand, thus requiring collection of state sales taxes.[121]

The problem is just as complex, if not more so, on an international scale. Here the issue spans the whole range of taxes, paralleling both our income tax laws and our sales tax laws. In a nutshell, what nation is entitled to tax cross-border transactions? In the international arena, certain key principles were adopted in 1998 by the countries that comprise the Organization for Economic Cooperation and Development (OECD), including the principle that consumption taxes (like our sales taxes) should be collected by the jurisdiction where consumption takes place. But finding workable arrangements to effectuate the general principles has proven elusive. [For more on the OECD, see **www.oecd.org**].

Reprise: Who Governs Cyberspace?

We near the end of this chapter examining the same kinds of questions we have raised throughout this book: How much government do we need in our lives? To what extent should government restrain the explosive and stupendously successful cyberspace industry? Is the Internet a bit too much of a "Wild West" environment for the general good? Consider the story that follows:

Bitcoin: The Rise and Fall of a Virtual Currency

A paper published anonymously in 2008 outlined a method for creating a digital currency that could be exchanged on a peer-to-peer basis, but which would not be susceptible to unauthorized duplication. A year later, the first Bitcoins were "mined" using an open-source program, which by design constrains how many digital coins can be created and at what intervals (currently 25 every 10 minutes, but dropping in half every four years, with a total cap of 21 million). Digital currencies, of which Bitcoin is just one example, although the one with the largest circulation thus far, are creatures of the Internet. They may have no issuing or governing body, can be self-authenticating, and are usable worldwide by members of the general public to engage in the same types of direct, one-to-one transactions that daily occur using government-issued currencies.

As a currency, a digital currency may have some advantages over other mediums of exchange. For example, merchants may prefer payment in Bitcoins because there is little or no transaction cost, in contrast to the 2 to 3 percent charged on most credit card transactions. Fees are charged on exchanges of Bitcoins into or out of a specific national currency, which is also true for any foreign-exchange transaction. But the global nature of Bitcoin makes such exchanges less necessary—or at least will make them less necessary if its fluctuation in value ultimately settles down. At present, however, its value can fluctuate tremendously. For example, as of early March 2014, one exchange showed its historical high closing at $1,147 on December 4, 2013, but on February 25, 2014, the closing was $535, following the announcement that the world's largest Bitcoin exchange, Mt. Gox in Japan, was likely to file for bankruptcy following its discovery of a large theft from its exchange. Just a week later, however, the price was hovering around $660.[122]

Another cause of its fluctuating price is that the currency has largely gone unregulated by the world's governments. The United States has exerted some authority over the regulation of exchanges that deal in Bitcoin, but the currency itself is largely free of governmental interference. If the currency is going to survive, that likely will change at least to some degree.

Question

The questions for digital currencies are, of course, should they be regulated and, if so, by whom? Based on Bitcoin's short history, what could regulation achieve? What might it impede?

Internet Exercise

Review the materials on privacy issues in this chapter and then log on to the website for an Internet vendor that you, or someone you know, has used. Can you find the vendor's privacy policy? Is it easy to find? Is it easy to access, read, and understand? How long is it? How complicated? Do any of its provisions surprise you? What control do you have over the use of your personal information by that vendor? Is that information easy to find? Can you tell when the policy was last updated and what changes were made in it? Has the policy received approval from truste.com (indicated by a seal displayed on the policy page)? Would you purchase again from this vendor?

Chapter Questions

1. The United Nations has warned that the worldwide growth of e-commerce may constitute a threat to the well-being of the world's developing nations as well as parts of Europe. Explain the U.N. concerns.

2. Psychologists are worried that the Internet will make shopping too easy. Explain their concern.

3. In March 1992, Danish police seized the business records of BAMSE, a computer bulletin board system based in Denmark that sold child pornography over the Internet. The records included information that Mohrbacher, who lived in Paradise, California, had downloaded two graphic interface format (GIF) images from BAMSE in January 1992.

   In March 1993, police executed a search warrant at Mohrbacher's workplace and found, among other images, two files that had been downloaded from BAMSE, one of a nude girl and one of a girl engaged in a sex act with an adult; both girls were under 12. During the execution of the warrant, Mohrbacher was cooperative, confessing that he had downloaded the two images from BAMSE. Mohrbacher was charged with transporting or shipping images by computer as prohibited by 18 U.S.C. § 2252(a)(1). Mohrbacher argued that downloading is properly characterized as receiving images by computer, which is proscribed by section 2252(a)(2). He was not charged under section 2252(a)(2).

   Should downloading from a computer bulletin board constitute shipping or transporting within the meaning of 18 U.S.C. § 2252(a)(1)? Explain. See *U.S. v. Mohrbacher*, 182 F.3d 1041 (9th Cir. 1999).

4. *a.* Should online bloggers be entitled to protection as journalists under the First Amendment with regard to the confidentiality of their sources?
   b. What if those sources have illegally revealed corporate trade secrets?[123]

5. America Online (AOL), an ISP, sued TSF Marketing and Joseph Melle, who founded TSF. AOL claimed that Melle and TSF sent spam to AOL subscribers. The e-mail contained the letters "aol.com" in the headers. AOL claimed that the e-mail totaled some 60 million messages over a 10-month period. Melle allegedly continued the mailings after he was notified in writing by AOL to stop. AOL received over 50,000 complaints from subscribers. AOL claimed, among other things, that Melle had diluted its trademark.[124] The case arose before the passage of the CAN-SPAM Act. Would Melle have been liable under that act? Explain.

6. McLaren was an employee of Microsoft Corporation. In December 1996, Microsoft suspended McLaren's employment pending an investigation into accusations of sexual harassment and "inventory questions." McLaren requested access to his electronic mail to disprove the allegations against him. According to McLaren, he was told he could access his e-mail only by requesting it through company officials and telling them the location of a particular message. By memorandum, McLaren requested that no one tamper with his Microsoft office workstation or his e-mail. McLaren's employment was terminated on December 11, 1996.

   Following the termination of his employment, McLaren filed suit against the company alleging as his sole cause of action a claim for invasion of privacy. In support of his claim, McLaren alleged that, on information and belief, Microsoft had invaded his privacy by "breaking into" some or all of the personal folders maintained on his office computer and releasing the contents of the folders to third parties. According to

McLaren, the personal folders were part of a computer application created by Microsoft in which e-mail messages could be stored. Access to the e-mail system was obtained through a network password. Access to personal folders could be additionally restricted by a "personal store" password created by the individual user. McLaren created and used a personal store password to restrict access to his personal folders.

McLaren concedes in his petition that it was possible for Microsoft to "decrypt" his personal store password. McLaren alleges, however, that "[b]y allowing [him] to have a personal store password for his personal folders, [McLaren] manifested and [Microsoft] recognized an expectation that the personal folders would be free from intrusion and interference." McLaren characterizes Microsoft's decrypting or otherwise "breaking in" to his personal folders as an intentional, unjustified, and unlawful invasion of privacy.

Did Microsoft unlawfully invade McLaren's privacy? Explain. See *McLaren v. Microsoft,* 1999 Texas App. LEXIS 4103 (Tex. Ct. App. May 28, 1999).

7. Bensusan Restaurant Corporation owns the famous New York City jazz club "The Blue Note," and in 1985 it registered the name as a federal trademark. Since 1980, King has operated a small club in Columbia, Missouri, also named "The Blue Note." Around 1993, Bensusan wrote to King demanding that he discontinue use of "The Blue Note" name. King's attorney responded by saying that Bensusan had no legal right to make the demand. In 1996, King created, in Missouri, a website for "The Blue Note," which also contained a hyperlink to the New York club's website. Bensusan then sued in the Southern District of New York, alleging Lanham Act and trademark violations, among other things. The New York court dismissed the case for lack of personal jurisdiction. Bensusan appealed. Decide. Explain. See *Bensusan Restaurant Corp. v. King,* 126 F.3d 25 (2d Cir. 1997).

8. Plaintiff Marobie-FL, Inc., released software of copyrighted clip art for use in the fire service industry. Robisheaux administered the National Association of Fire Equipment Distributors (NAFED) web page. He received the clip art from a source that he could not remember. He placed the clip art on NAFED's web page. At that point, the clip art could be readily accessed and downloaded by any web user. Marobie claimed copyright infringement. Among other arguments, NAFED claimed that its display of the clip art constituted a fair use, within the meaning of federal copyright law. Decide. Explain. See *Marobie-FL v. National Association of Fire Equipment Distributors,* 983 F. Supp. 1167 (N.D. Ill. 1997).

9. Journalist John Snell remarked, "Not long ago you couldn't turn around in cyberspace without bumping into a tech geek. Now you're no more than a mouse click away from a lawyer. Attorneys are everywhere."[125] What factors account for the dramatic increase in lawyers addressing Internet issues?

Notes

1. "Internet Users," *internet live stats* [**www.internetlivestats.com/internet-users**].
2. Duncan B. Hollis, "E-War Rules of Engagement," *Los Angeles Times,* October 8, 2007.
3. Anick Jesdanun, "As Internet Turns 40, Barriers Run Contrary to Creators' Aims," *The Des Moines Register,* August 31, 2009, p. 1A.

4. Thomas L. Friedman, "The Great Iceland Meltdown," *The New York Times,* October 19, 2008. Although this statement was offered in a somewhat different context—the financial crisis of 2008—it is equally applicable to this discussion of the Internet.

5. "The World Is What You Make It," *The Economist,* October 27, 2012, p. 20.

6. "Doing the ICANN-can," *The Economist,* March 22, 2014, p. 62.

7. Klint Finley, "The Internet Finally Belongs to Everyone," *Wired,* October 3, 2016 [**www.wired.com/2016/10/internet-finally-belongs-everyone**].

8. Sarah Childress, "United States of Secrets: How the NSA Spying Programs Have Changed Since Snowden," *Frontline,* February 9, 2015 [**www.pbs.org/wgbh/frontline/article/how-the-nsa-spying-programs-have-changed-since-snowden**].

9. Edward Wyatt, "Most of U.S. Is Wired, but Millions Aren't Plugged In," *The New York Times,* August 18, 2013.

10. "Usage and Population Statistics," *Internet World Stats* [**www.internetworldstats.com/stats.htm**].

11. Evelyn M. Rusli and Don Clark, "Facebook CEO Announces Internet Access Project," *The Wall Street Journal,* August 21, 2013.

12. *Verizon v. F.C.C.,* 740 F.3d 623 (D.C. Cir. 2014); Gautham Nagesh and Brent Kendall, "Appeals Court Strikes Down FCC's Net Neutrality Rules," *The Wall Street Journal,* January 14, 2014; and Edward Wyatt, "Industry and Congress Await the F.C.C. Chairman's Next Moves on Internet Rules," *The New York Times,* February 9, 2014.

13. Cecilia Kang, "Court Backs Rules Treating Internet as Utility, Not Luxury," *The New York Times,* June 14, 2016 [**www.nytimes.com/2016/06/15/technology/net-neutrality-fcc-appeals-court-ruling.html?_r=0**].

14. "Open Internet," Federal Communications Commission [**www.fcc.gov/general/open-internet**].

15. Ibid.

16. "Ex-CompuServe Chief's Conviction Overturned; German Case Involved Child Porn Sites," *Houston Chronicle,* November 18, 1999, p. 3. The head of CompuServe Germany was convicted in 1998 of violating German law by failing to block CompuServe's customers' access to child pornography websites. At the time, the only technical way for CompuServe to comply was to block all of its worldwide users from access. The conviction was reversed in 1999.

17. See *Revell v. Lidov,* 317 F.3d 467 (5th Cir. 2002). Lidov posted an article he wrote on the "bombing of Pan Am Flight 103, which exploded over Lockerbie, Scotland, in 1988. The article alleges that a broad politically motivated conspiracy among senior members of the Reagan administration lay behind their willful failure to stop the bombing despite clear advance warnings. Furthermore, Lidov charged that the government proceeded to cover up its receipt of advance warning. . . . Specifically, the article singles out Oliver 'Buck' Revell, then Associate Deputy Director of the FBI, for severe criticism, accusing him of complicity in the conspiracy and cover-up." The article was posted on an Internet bulletin board maintained by Columbia University's School of Journalism. "At the time he wrote the article, Lidov had never been to Texas, except possibly to change planes, or conducted business there, and was apparently unaware that Revell then resided in Texas." "Columbia, since it began keeping records, never received more than 20 Internet subscriptions to the *Columbia Journalism Review* from Texas residents." The Fifth Circuit found that neither general nor specific jurisdiction existed in the Texas courts.

18. *Mink v. AAAA Development,* 190 F.3d 333 (5th Cir. 1999).

19. See, for example, *Pavlovich v. DVD Copy Control Association.* A California appeals court held that a Texas resident was subject to California's jurisdiction for the knowing posting of trade

secrets of a California company on an Indiana website. 91 Cal. App. 4th 409, 109 Cal. Rptr. 2d 909 (Cal. Ct. App. 2001). But the California Supreme Court reversed. 58 P.3d 2 (Cal. 2002). See also *Gator.com Corp. v. L. L. Bean, Inc.,* where the district court held that L. L. Bean could not be sued in California where it had no stores or agents, although it did sell merchandise to California residents through its website. 2001 U.S. Dist. LEXIS 19737 (N.D. Cal. November 21, 2001). A three-judge panel of the Ninth Circuit reversed, finding in part that the volume of Internet business done by L. L. Bean with California residents made it subject to California's jurisdiction. 341 F.3d 1072 (9th Cir. 2003). That decision was vacated, however, when the Ninth Circuit decided to rehear the case en banc. 366 F.3d 789 (9th Cir. 2004). After oral argument on the rehearing, however, Gator.com and L. L. Bean settled their substantive dispute, and thus the Ninth Circuit dismissed the appeal because of the lack of a continuing case or controversy. 398 F.3d 1125 (9th Cir. 2005).

20. Ryan Davis, "7th Circ. Lets Bulgarian Dating Site Off Hook in IP Row," *Law 360,* April 27, 2011 [**www.law360.com**].

21. Rachel Donadio, "Larger Threat Is Seen in Google Case," *The New York Times,* February 25, 2010.

22. Eric Pfanner, "Italian Appeals Court Acquits 3 Google Executives in Privacy Case," *The New York Times,* December 21, 2012.

23. Stephan Wilske and Teresa Schiller, "International Jurisdiction in Cyberspace: Which States May Regulate the Internet?" *Federal Communications Law Journal* 50 (December 1997), p. 117.

24. *Yahoo! Inc. v. La Ligue Contre Le Racisme et L'Antisemitisme,* 433 F.3d 1199 (9th Cir. 2006).

25. *La Ligue Contre Le Racisme v. Yahoo!,* 126 S. Ct. 2332 (2006).

26. *Obsidian Finance Group v. Cox,* 740 F.3d 1284 (9th Cir. 2014). At trial, a federal jury found a Montana-based blogger had defamed both an Oregon attorney and the finance firm of which he was a principal, awarding damages to both plaintiffs. In her blog, defendant had asserted the attorney, a court-appointed trustee in a bankruptcy proceeding, had committed tax fraud. The Ninth Circuit held that unlawful acts of a person in such a position was a matter of public concern. Thus, plaintiffs could not prevail simply by proving the assertion to be false, but were also required to prove negligence on plaintiff's part. In addition, any damage award would require proof of actual damages. The case was remanded for a new trial.

27. "42% of Youths Report Exposure to Porn on Web," *The Des Moines Register,* February 5, 2007, p. 5A.

28. *Reno v. ACLU,* 521 U.S. 844 (1997).

29. *ACLU v. Gonzales,* 478 F. Supp. 2d 775 (E.D. Pa. 2007); *Mukasey v. ACLU,* 139 S. Ct. 1032 (2009).

30. *Ashcroft v. Free Speech Coalition,* 122 S. Ct. 1389 (2002).

31. Christine Arena, "Child Porn Too Big for Law Enforcement? Microsoft Steps In," *The Christian Science Monitor,* June 13, 2010.

32. *McIntyre v. Ohio Elections Commission,* 514 U.S. 334, 342 (1995).

33. Ibid.

34. *In re Anonymous Online Speakers v. U.S. Dist. Ct. for the Dist. of Nevada, Reno,* 661 F.3d 1168 (9th Cir. 2011).

35. Somini Sengupta, "Free Speech in the Age of YouTube," *The New York Times,* September 22, 2012.

36. Robert L. Rogers III, "Two Federal Cases Hold Website 'Responsible' for Postings on *thedirty. com*," *Association of Corporate Counsel,* January 31, 2013 [**www.lexology.com**].

37. Andrew E. Kramer, "Online Attack Leads to Peek into Spam Den," *The New York Times,* September 2, 2013.

38. Brad Stone, "Authorities Shut Down Spam Ring," *The New York Times,* October 15, 2008.

39. Andrew E. Kramer, "Online Attack Leads to Peek into Spam Den," *The New York Times,* September 2, 2013 [**www.nytimes.com/2013/09/03/business/global/online-attack-leads-to-peek-into-spam-den.html**].

40. Brad Stone, "If You Run a Red Light, Will Everyone Know?" *The New York Times,* August 3, 2008.

41. Jim Stanton, "From Where Your House Is to How Much You Paid for It—It's All on the Internet for Anyone to See," *The Waterloo/Cedar Falls Courier,* August 27, 2000, p. A1.

42. Quentin Hardy, "Webcams See All (Tortoise, Watch Your Back)," *The New York Times,* January 7, 2014.

43. Nick Bilton, "Researchers Hack Webcam While Disabling Warning Lights," *The New York Times,* December 19, 2013.

44. Ian Urbina, "Social Media, a Trove of Clues and Confessions," *The New York Times,* February 15, 2014.

45. Jennifer Valentino-Devries, Jeremy Singer-Vine, and Ashkan Soltani, "Websites Vary Prices, Deals Based on Users' Information," *The Wall Street Journal,* December 24, 2012.

46. "Caveat emptor.com," *The Economist,* June 30, 2012, p. 12.

47. Amazon.com Privacy Notice, February 22, 2014 (accessed through the Privacy Notice link at the bottom of its web pages) [**www.amazon.com**].

48. Jennifer Valentino-Devries and Jeremy Singer-Vine, "They Know What You're Shopping For," *The Wall Street Journal,* December 7, 2012.

49. Natasha Singer, "More Companies Are Tracking Online Data, Study Finds," *The New York Times,* November 12, 2012.

50. James Glanz, Jeff Larson, and Andrew W. Lehren, "Spy Agencies Tap Data Streaming from Phone Apps," *The New York Times,* January 27, 2014.

51. These statements from Amazon come from pages reached through the Privacy Notice link at the bottom of its web pages. It was accessed on February 22, 2014.

52. Nicole Perlroth, "*Washington Post* Joins List of News Media Hacked by the Chinese," *The New York Times,* February 1, 2013.

53. *Stengart v. Loving Care Agency,* 990 A.2d 650 (N.J. 2010).

54. *City of Ontario v. Quon,* 130 S. Ct. 2619 (2010).

55. Pui-Wing Tam, Erin White, Nick Wingfield, and Kris Maher, "Snooping E-Mail by Software Is Now a Workplace Norm," *The Wall Street Journal,* March 9, 2005, p. B1.

56. **https://www.eff.org/issues/do-not-track**.

57. Natasha Singer, "New Online Privacy Rules for Children," *The New York Times,* December 19, 2012.

58. Glenn Simpson, "U.S., EU Negotiators Reach Agreement on Electronic-Commerce Privacy Rules," *The Wall Street Journal,* March 15, 2000, p. B4.

59. Carter Manny, "Privacy Controls on Trans-Border Flows of Personal Data from Europe," *Business Law Review,* Spring 2001, pp. 101–120.

60. "U.S., Europe Move to Net Privacy Pact," *The Waterloo/Cedar Falls Courier,* June 5, 2000, p. B5.

61. Claire Cain Miller, "Stern Words, and a Pea-Size Punishment, for Google," *The New York Times,* April 2, 2013; Eric Pfanner, "Google Failed to Delete Street View Data in France," *The*

New York Times, July 31, 2012; Cecilia Kang, "Satisfied with Google's Promise to Restrain Street View, FTC Drops Privacy-Breach Probe," *The Washington Post,* October 27, 2010; and Raphael Minder, "Google Sued in Spain over Data Collection," *The New York Times,* August 17, 2010.

62. *WEC Carolina Energy Solutions LLC v. Miller,* 687 F.3d 199 (4th Cir. 2012); *U.S. v. Nosal,* 676 F.3d 854 (9th Cir. 2012).

63. *International Airport Centers, LLC v. Citrin,* 440 F.3d 418 (7th Cir. 2006).

64. Nicole Perlroth, "Robbing a Gas Station: The Hacker Way," *The New York Times,* June 6, 2013.

65. *U.S. v. Farraj,* 142 F. Supp. 2d 484 (S.D.N.Y. 2001).

66. Raphael Minder, "Cybercrime Network Based in Spain Is Broken Up," *The New York Times,* February 13, 2013.

67. Edward Wyatt, "Multinational Crackdown on Computer Con Artists," *The New York Times,* October 3, 2012.

68. Nicole Perlroth, "A New Variant of Malware Takes Aim at Mac Users," *The New York Times,* April 23, 2012.

69. David Streitfeld, "Give Yourself 5 Stars? Online, It Might Cost You," *The New York Times,* September 22, 2013.

70. "Former Worker Gets 4 Years for Cyberstalking," *Chicago Tribune,* March 18, 2005, p. 13.

71. Kramer, "Online Attack Leads to Peek into Spam Den."

72. Spencer E. Ante and Brian Grow, "Meet the Hackers," *BusinessWeek,* May 29, 2006, p. 58.

73. "Let's Stay Together," *The Economist,* December 1, 2012, p. 34.

74. Nicole Perlroth, "Reporting from the Web's Underbelly," *The New York Times,* February 16, 2014.

75. "SIRF's Up," *The Economist,* November 30, 2013, p. 27.

76. Thom Shanker and David E. Sanger, "U.S. Helps Allies Trying to Battle Iranian Hackers," *The New York Times,* June 8, 2013; and Jackie Calmes and Steven Lee Myers, "U.S. and China Move Closer on North Korea, but Not on Cyberespionage," *The New York Times,* June 8, 2013.

77. "War on Terabytes," *The Economist,* February 2, 2013, p. 63; David E. Sanger and Eric Schmitt, "Rise Is Seen in Cyberattacks Targeting U.S. Infrastructure," *The New York Times,* July 26, 2012; and "The War on Terabytes," *The Economist,* December 31, 2011, p. 57.

78. Siobhan Gorman, "Annual U.S. Cybercrime Costs Estimated at $100 Billion," *The Wall Street Journal,* July 22, 2013.

79. Gautham Nagesh and Danny Yadron, "White House Releases Voluntary Cybersecurity Rules for Critical Infrastructure," *The Wall Street Journal,* February 12, 2014.

80. "Chart of Signatures and Ratifications of Treaty 185," Council of Europe [**http://conventions. coe.int/Treaty/Commun/ChercheSig.asp?NT=185&CM=&DF=&CL=ENG**].

81. Thomas Weber, "Treaty on Cybercrime Flew under the Radar Despite Potential Risks," *The Wall Street Journal,* December 3, 2001, p. B1.

82. Alan S. Reid and Nic Ryder, "The Case of Richard Tomlinson: The Spy Who E-Mailed Me," *Information & Communications Technology Law* 9 (March 2000), p. 61.

83. "Ex-CompuServe Chief's Conviction Overturned," p. 3.

84. P. Liddell, M. Moore, and R. Moore, "Just Sign on the Electronic Line," *Journal of the Academy of Marketing Science,* Winter 2001, p. 110.

85. "Computer Information Transactions Act," Uniform Law Commission [**www.uniformlaws. org/Act.aspx?title=Computer%20Information%20Transactions%20Act**].

86. 732 A.2d 528 (N.J. Super. 1999).

87. Ronald J. Mann and Travis Siebeneicher, "Just One Click: The Reality of Internet Retail Contracting," *University of Texas Law, Law and Econ Research Paper* No. 104, May 2007 [**http://ssrn.com/abstract=988788**].

88. Anna Mathews, "U.S. Will Give Web Patents More Scrutiny," *The Wall Street Journal,* March 29, 2000, p. B1.

89. "Swipe, Pinch and Zoom to the Courtroom," *The Economist,* September 1, 2012.

90. *Microsoft Corp. v. Motorola Inc.,* 2013 WL 2111217 (W.D. Wash. September 24, 2013); and Steve Lohr, "Court Ruling Takes a Stand on Essential High-Tech Patents," *The New York Times,* April 28, 2013.

91. In addition to the previously cited sources, the discussion of the patent wars also relies on the following: Daisuke Wakabayashi and Ian Sherr, "Jury Orders Samsung to Pay $119 Million to Apple in Patent Case," *The Wall Street Journal,* May 2, 2014; Brent Kendall and Don Clark, "U.S. Panel Orders Import Ban on Some Samsung Devices," *The Wall Street Journal,* August 10, 2013; Brian X. Chen, "Trade Commission Orders Ban on Some Samsung Products," *The New York Times,* August 9, 2013; Nick Wingfield and Brian X. Chen, "Patent Case Has Potential to Give Apple the Upper Hand," *The New York Times,* August 8, 2013; Ian Sherr and Jessica E. Lessin, "Ruling Blocks iPhone Sales," *The Wall Street Journal,* June 4, 2013; Jessica E. Vascellaro, "Apple Wins Big in Patent Case," *The Wall Street Journal,* August 25, 2012; and Kevin J. O'Brien, "German Courts at Epicenter of Global Patent Battles Among Tech Rivals," April 8, 2012.

92. *Capitol Records v. ReDIGI,* 934 F. Supp. 2d 640 (S.D.N.Y. 2013); and Ben Sisario, "A Setback for Resellers of Digital Products," *The New York Times,* April 1, 2013.

93. *A & M Records, Inc. v. Napster, Inc.,* 284 F.3d 1091 (9th Cir. 2002); and *A & M Records, Inc. v. Napster, Inc.,* 239 F.3d 1004 (9th Cir. 2001).

94. *Metro-Goldwyn-Mayer Studios, Inc. v. Grokster, Ltd.,* 380 F.3d 1154 (9th Cir. 2004).

95. Sarah McBride and Ethan Smith, "Music Industry to Abandon Mass Suits," *The Wall Street Journal,* December 19, 2008.

96. Amy Brittain, "Universities Strike Back in Battle over Illegal Downloads," *The Christian Science Monitor,* June 18, 2007.

97. Susan Neuberger Weller, "Are You Willing to Pay $22,500 to Download a Song?" *Association of Corporate Counsel,* August 28, 2012 [**www.lexology.com**]; and Ben Sisario, "Supreme Court Passes on File-Sharing Case, but Still No End Is in Sight," *The New York Times,* May 21, 2012.

98. *Capitol Records v. Thomas-Rasset,* 692 F.3d 899 (8th Cir. 2012).

99. Rob Peoraro, "The Sound of Copy Restrictions Crashing," *The Washington Post,* May 17, 2007, p. D1; and Michelle Quinn, Alana Semuels, and Dawn C. Chmielewski, "Apple Seeks to Unchain Melodies," *Los Angeles Times,* February 7, 2007.

100. David Streitfeld, "Imagining a Swap Meet for E-Books and Music," *The New York Times,* March 7, 2013.

101. Miguel Helft, "Judge Sides with Google in Viacom Video Suit," *The New York Times,* June 23, 2010.

102. *Viacom International Inc. v. YouTube, Inc.,* 718 F. Supp. 2d 514 (S.D.N.Y. 2010).

103. *Viacom International Inc. v. YouTube, Inc.,* 676 F.3d 19 (2d Cir. 2012).

104. *Viacom International Inc. v. YouTube, Inc.,* 940 F. Supp. 2d 110 (S.D.N.Y. 2013).

105. Michael Davis-Wilson, "The Burden of Online Misdeeds: Who Should Be Responsible?" *Association of Corporate Counsel,* March 19, 2012 [**www.lexology.com**]; and "Stopping SOPA," *The Economist,* January 21, 2012.

106. *Shields v. Zuccarini,* 254 F.3d 476 (3d Cir. 2001).

107. Christy Roth, Marianne Dunham, and Jason Watson, "Cybersquatting; Typosquatting— Facebook's $2.8 Million in Damages and Domain Names," *Association of Corporate Counsel,* May 10, 2013.

108. "People: News/Gossip/Scoops," *St. Louis Post–Dispatch,* January 17, 2004, p. 41.

109. "The Name Game," *The Economist,* February 8, 2014, p. 59.

110. Natasha Singer, "When You Can't Tell Web Suffixes Without a Scorecard," *The New York Times,* August 17, 2013.

111. Eric Pfanner, "Amazon Rejected as Domain Name After South American Objections," *The New York Times,* July 18, 2013.

112. "The Name Game."

113. Singer, "When You Can't Tell Web Suffixes Without a Scorecard."

114. Craig Timberg and James Ball, "Donuts Inc.'s Major Play for New Web Domain Names Raises Fears of Fraud," *The Washington Post,* September 24, 2012.

115. Ibid.

116. John McKeown, "What Brand Owners Need to Do to Cope with the New Domain Names after Reveal Day," *Association of Corporate Counsel,* October 15, 2012.

117. *Quill Corporation v. North Dakota,* 504 U.S. 298 (1992).

118. "Member States: About the National Nexus Program," Multistate Tax Commission [**http://www.mtc.gov/Nexus-Program/Member-States**].

119. Michelle Blackson, "Closing the Online Tax Loophole," *State Legislatures* 34, no. 4 (April 2008), p. 24.

120. Adam Liptak, "Justices Pass on Tax Case from Online Merchants," *The New York Times,* December 2, 2013.

121. *Amazon.com v. New York State Department of Taxation and Finance,* 134 S. Ct. 682 (2013); *Overstock.com v. New York State Department of Taxation and Finance,* 134 S. Ct. 682 (2013).

122. See the historical price information at CoinDesk [**www.coindesk.com/price**].

123. Compare *Apple Computer v. Doe,* 2005 WL 578641 (Cal. Super. Ct. Mar. 11, 2005) (requiring disclosure), with *O'Grady v. Superior Ct.,* 44 Cal. Rptr. 3d 72 (Cal. App. 2006) (reversing on appeal).

124. See *America Online, Inc. v. IMS,* 24 F. Supp. 2d 548 (E.D. Va. 1998).

125. John Snell, "Lawyers Drawn to Unsettled Internet; Lots of Legal Issues, Large and Small, Must Be Sorted Out," *Minneapolis Star Tribune,* November 29, 1999, p. 6D.

The Constitution of the United States of America

Preamble

We the People of the United States, in Order to form a more perfect Union, establish Justice, insure domestic Tranquility, provide for the common defence, promote the general Welfare, and secure the Blessings of Liberty to ourselves and our Posterity, do ordain and establish this Constitution for the United States of America.

Article I

Section 1. All legislative Powers herein granted shall be vested in a Congress of the United States, which shall consist of a Senate and House of Representatives.

Section 2. (1) The House of Representatives shall be composed of Members chosen every second Year by the People of the several States, and the Electors in each State shall have the Qualifications requisite for Electors of the most numerous Branch of the State Legislature.

(2) No Person shall be a Representative who shall not have attained to the Age of twenty-five Years, and been seven Years a Citizen of the United States, and who shall not, when elected, be an Inhabitant of that State in which he shall be chosen.

(3) Representatives and direct Taxes shall be apportioned among the several States which may be included within this Union, according to their respective Numbers, which shall be determined by adding to the whole Number of free Persons, including those bound to Service for a Term of Years, and excluding Indians not taxed, three fifths of all other Persons.[1] The actual Enumeration shall be made within three Years after the first Meeting of the Congress of the United States, and within every subsequent Term of ten Years, in such Manner as they shall by Law direct. The Number of Representatives shall not exceed one for every thirty Thousand, but each State shall have at Least one Representative; and until such enumeration shall be made, the State of New Hampshire shall be entitled to chuse three, Massachusetts eight, Rhode Island and Providence Plantations one, Connecticut five, New York six, New Jersey four, Pennsylvania eight, Delaware one, Maryland six, Virginia ten, North Carolina five, South Carolina five, and Georgia three.

[1]Refer to the Fourteenth Amendment.

(4) When vacancies happen in the Representation from any State, the Executive Authority thereof shall issue Writs of Election to fill such Vacancies.

(5) The House of Representatives shall chuse their Speaker and other Officers; and shall have the sole Power of Impeachment.

Section 3. (1) The Senate of the United States shall be composed of two Senators from each State, chosen by the Legislature thereof,[2] for six Years; and each Senator shall have one Vote.

(2) Immediately after they shall be assembled in Consequence of the first Election, they shall be divided as equally as may be into three Classes. The Seats of the Senators of the first Class shall be vacated at the Expiration of the Second Year, of the second Class at the Expiration of the fourth Year, and of the third Class at the Expiration of the sixth Year, so that one third may be chosen every second Year; and if Vacancies happen by Resignation, or otherwise, during the Recess of the Legislature of any State, the Executive thereof may make temporary Appointments until the next Meeting of the Legislature, which shall then fill such Vacancies.[3]

(3) No Person shall be a Senator who shall not have attained to the Age of thirty Years, and been nine Years a Citizen of the United States, and who shall not, when elected, be an Inhabitant of that State for which he shall be chosen.

(4) The Vice President of the United States shall be President of the Senate, but shall have no Vote, unless they be equally divided.

(5) The Senate shall chuse their other Officers, and also a President pro tempore, in the Absence of the Vice President, or when he shall exercise the Office of President of the United States.

(6) The Senate shall have the sole Power to try all Impeachments. When sitting for that Purpose, they shall be on Oath or Affirmation. When the President of the United States is tried, the Chief Justice shall preside: And no Person shall be convicted without the Concurrence of two thirds of the Members present.

(7) Judgment in Cases of Impeachment shall not extend further than to removal from Office, and disqualification to hold and enjoy any Office of honor, Trust, or Profit under the United States: but the Party convicted shall nevertheless be liable and subject to Indictment, Trial, Judgment, and Punishment, according to Law.

Section 4. (1) The Times, Places and Manner of holding Elections for Senators and Representatives, shall be prescribed in each State by the Legislature thereof; but the Congress may at any time by Law make or alter such Regulations, except as to the Places of chusing Senators.

(2) The Congress shall assemble at least once in every year, and such Meeting shall be on the first Monday in December, unless they shall by Law appoint a different Day.[4]

Section 5. (1) Each House shall be the Judge of the Elections, Returns, and Qualifications of its own Members, and a Majority of each shall constitute a Quorum to do Business; but a smaller Number may adjourn from day to day, and may be authorized to compel the Attendance of absent Members, in such Manner, and under such Penalties as each House may provide.

---

[2]Refer to the Seventeenth Amendment.

[3]Ibid.

[4]Refer to the Twentieth Amendment.

(2) Each House may determine the Rules of its Proceedings, punish its Members for disorderly Behavior, and, with the Concurrence of two thirds, expel a Member.

(3) Each House shall keep a Journal of its Proceedings, and from time to time publish the same, excepting such Parts as may in their Judgment require Secrecy; and the Yeas and Nays of the Members of either House on any question shall, at the Desire of one fifth of those Present, be entered on the Journal.

(4) Neither House, during the Session of Congress, shall, without the Consent of the other, adjourn for more than three days, nor to any other Place than that in which the two Houses shall be sitting.

Section 6. (1) The Senators and Representatives shall receive a Compensation for their Services, to be ascertained by Law, and paid out of the Treasury of the United States. They shall in all Cases, except Treason, Felony and Breach of the Peace, be privileged from Arrest during their Attendance at the Session of their respective Houses, and in going to and returning from the same; and for any Speech or Debate in either House, they shall not be questioned in any other Place.

(2) No Senator or Representative shall, during the Time for which he was elected, be appointed to any civil Office under the Authority of the United States, which shall have been created, or the Emoluments whereof shall have been encreased during such time; and no Person holding any Office under the United States, shall be a Member of either House during his Continuance in Office.

Section 7. (1) All Bills for raising Revenue shall originate in the House of Representatives; but the Senate may propose or concur with Amendments as on other Bills.

(2) Every Bill which shall have passed the House of Representatives and the Senate, shall, before it becomes a Law, be presented to the President of the United States; If he approve he shall sign it, but if not he shall return it, with his Objections to the House in which it shall have originated, who shall enter the Objections at large on their Journal, and proceed to reconsider it. If after such Reconsideration two thirds of that House shall agree to pass the Bill, it shall be sent together with the Objections, to the other House, by which it shall likewise be reconsidered, and if approved by two thirds of that House, it shall become a Law. But in all such Cases the Votes of both Houses shall be determined by yeas and Nays, and the Names of the Persons voting for and against the Bill shall be entered on the Journal of each House respectively. If any Bill shall not be returned by the President within ten Days (Sundays excepted) after it shall have been presented to him, the Same shall be a Law, in like Manner as if he had signed it, unless the Congress by their Adjournment prevent its Return in which Case it shall not be a Law.

(3) Every Order, Resolution, or Vote, to Which the Concurrence of the Senate and House of Representatives may be necessary (except on a question of Adjournment) shall be presented to the President of the United States; and before the same shall take Effect, shall be approved by him, or being disapproved by him, shall be repassed by two thirds of the Senate and House of Representatives, according to the Rules and Limitations prescribed in the Case of a Bill.

Section 8. (1) The Congress shall have Power To lay and collect Taxes, Duties, Imposts and Excises, to pay the Debts and provide for the common Defence and general Welfare of the United States; but all Duties, Imposts and Excises shall be uniform throughout the United States;

(2) To borrow money on the credit of the United States;

(3) To regulate Commerce with foreign Nations, and among the several States, and with the Indian Tribes;

(4) To establish a uniform Rule of Naturalization, and uniform Laws on the subject of Bankruptcies throughout the United States;

(5) To coin Money, regulate the Value thereof, and of foreign Coin, and fix the Standard of Weights and Measures;

(6) To provide for the Punishment of counterfeiting the Securities and current Coin of the United States;

(7) To Establish Post Offices and Post Roads;

(8) To promote the Progress of Science and useful Arts, by securing for limited Times to Authors and Inventors the exclusive Right to their respective Writings and Discoveries;

(9) To constitute Tribunals inferior to the Supreme Court;

(10) To define and punish Piracies and Felonies committed on the high Seas, and Offenses against the Law of Nations;

(11) To declare War, grant Letters of Marque and Reprisal, and make Rules concerning Captures on Land and Water;

(12) To raise and support Armies, but no Appropriation of Money to that Use shall be for a longer Term than two Years;

(13) To provide and maintain a Navy;

(14) To make Rules for the Government and Regulation of the land and naval Forces;

(15) To provide for calling forth the Militia to execute the Laws of the Union, suppress Insurrections and repel Invasions;

(16) To provide for organizing, arming, and disciplining, the Militia, and for governing such Part of them as may be employed in the Service of the United States, reserving to the States respectively, the Appointment of the Officers, and the Authority of training the Militia according to the discipline prescribed by Congress;

(17) To exercise exclusive Legislation in all Cases whatsoever, over such District (not exceeding ten Miles square) as may, by Cession of particular States, and the Acceptance of Congress, become the Seat of the Government of the United States, and to exercise like Authority over all Places purchased by the Consent of the Legislature of the State in which the Same shall be, for the Erection of Forts, Magazines, Arsenals, dock-Yards, and other needful Buildings;—And

(18) To make all Laws which shall be necessary and proper for carrying into Execution the foregoing Powers, and all other Powers vested by this Constitution in the Government of the United States, or in any Department or Officer thereof.

Section 9. (1) The Migration or Importation of Such Persons as any of the States now existing shall think proper to admit, shall not be prohibited by the Congress prior to the Year one thousand eight hundred and eight, but a Tax or duty may be imposed on such Importation, not exceeding ten dollars for each Person.

(2) The privilege of the Writ of Habeas Corpus shall not be suspended, unless when in Cases of Rebellion or Invasion the public Safety may require it.

(3) No Bill of Attainder or ex post facto Law shall be passed.

(4) No Capitation, or other direct, Tax shall be laid, unless in proportion to the Census or Enumeration herein before directed to the taken.[5]

---

[5]Refer to the Sixteenth Amendment.

(5) No Tax or Duty shall be laid on Articles exported from any state.

(6) No Preference shall be given by any Regulation of Commerce or Revenue to the Ports of one State over those of another; nor shall Vessels bound to, or from, one State be obliged to enter, clear, or pay Duties in another.

(7) No money shall be drawn from the Treasury, but in Consequence of Appropriations made by Law; and a regular Statement and Account of the Receipts and Expenditures of all public Money shall be published from time to time.

(8) No Title of Nobility shall be granted by the United States; And no person holding any Office of Profit or Trust under them, shall, without the Consent of the Congress, accept of any present, Emolument, Office or Title, of any kind whatever, from any King, Prince, or foreign State.

Section 10. (1) No State shall enter into any Treaty, Alliance, or Confederation; grant Letters of Marque and Reprisal; coin Money; emit Bills of Credit; make any Thing but gold and silver Coin a Tender in Payment of Debts; pass any Bill of Attainder, ex post facto Law, or Law impairing the Obligation of Contracts, or grant any Title of Nobility.

(2) No State shall, without the Consent of the Congress, lay any Imposts or Duties on Imports or Exports, except what may be absolutely necessary for executing its inspection Laws: and the net Produce of all Duties and Imposts, laid by any State on Imports or Exports, shall be for the Use of the Treasury of the United States; and all such Laws shall be subject to the Revision and Controul of the Congress.

(3) No State shall, without the Consent of Congress, lay any Duty of Tonnage, keep Troops, or Ships of War in time of Peace, enter into any Agreement or Compact with another State, or with a foreign Power, or engage in War, unless actually invaded, or in such imminent Danger as will not admit of delay.

Article II

Section 1. (1) The executive Power shall be vested in a President of the United States of America. He shall hold his Office during the Term of four Years, and, together with the Vice President, chosen for the same Term, be elected as follows:

(2) Each State shall appoint, in such Manner as the Legislature thereof may direct, a Number of Electors, equal to the whole Number of Senators and Representatives to which the State may be entitled in the Congress; but no Senator or Representative, or Person holding an Office of Trust or Profit under the United States, shall be appointed an Elector.

(3) The Electors shall meet in their respective States, and vote by Ballot for two Persons, of whom one at least shall not be an Inhabitant of the same State with themselves. And they shall make a list of all the Persons voted for, and of the Number of Votes for each; which List they shall sign and certify, and transmit sealed to the Seat of the Government of the United States, directed to the President of the Senate. The President of the Senate shall, in the Presence of the Senate and House of Representatives, open all the Certificates, and the Votes shall then be counted. The Person having the greatest Number of Votes shall be the President, if such Number be a Majority of the whole Number of Electors appointed; and if there be more than one who have such Majority, and have an equal Number of Votes, then the House of Representatives shall immediately chuse by Ballot one of them for President; and if no Person have a Majority, then from the five highest on the List the said

House shall in like Manner chuse the President. But in chusing the President, the Votes shall be taken by States, the Representation from each State have one Vote; A quorum for this Purpose shall consist of a Member or Members from two thirds of the States, and a Majority of all the States shall be necessary to a Choice. In every Case, after the Choice of the President, the Person having the greater Number of Votes of the Electors shall be the Vice President. But if there should remain two or more who have equal Votes, the Senate shall chuse from them by Ballot the Vice President.[6]

(4) The Congress may determine the Time of chusing the Electors, and the Day on which they shall give their Votes; which Day shall be the same throughout the United States.

(5) No person except a natural born Citizen, or a Citizen of the United States, at the time of the Adoption of this Constitution, shall be eligible to the Office of President; neither shall any Person be eligible to that Office who shall not have attained to the Age of thirty-five Years, and been fourteen Years a Resident within the United States.

(6) In case of the removal of the President from Office, or of his Death, Resignation or Inability to discharge the Powers and Duties of the said Office, the Same shall devolve on the Vice President, and the Congress may by Law provide for the Case of Removal, Death, Resignation or Inability, both of the President and Vice President, declaring what Officer shall then act as President, and such Officer shall act accordingly, until the Disability be removed, or a President shall be elected.[7]

(7) The President shall, at stated Times, receive for his Services, a Compensation, which shall neither be encreased nor diminished during the Period for which he shall have been elected, and he shall not receive within that Period any other Emolument from the United States, or any of them.

(8) Before he enter on the Execution of his Office, he shall take the following Oath or Affirmation: "I do solemnly swear (or affirm) that I will faithfully execute the Office of President of the United States, and will to the best of my Ability, preserve, protect, and defend the Constitution of the United States."

Section 2. (1) The President shall be Commander in Chief of the Army and Navy of the United States, and of the militia of the several States, when called into the actual Service of the United States; he may require the Opinion, in writing, of the principal Officer in each of the executive Departments, upon any Subject relating to the Duties of their respective Offices, and he shall have Power to grant Reprieves and Pardons for Offenses against the United States, except in Cases of Impeachment.

(2) He shall have Power, by and with the Advice and Consent of the Senate, to make Treaties, provided two thirds of the Senators present concur; and he shall nominate, and by and with the Advice and Consent of the Senate, shall appoint Ambassadors, other public Ministers and Consuls, Judges of the supreme Court, and all other Officers of the United States, whose Appointments are not herein otherwise provided for, and which shall be established by Law; but the Congress may by Law vest the Appointment of such inferior Officers, as they think proper, in the President alone, in the Courts of Law, or in the Heads of Departments.

---

[6]Refer to the Twelfth Amendment.

[7]Refer to the Twenty-Fifth Amendment.

(3) The President shall have Power to fill up all Vacancies that may happen during the Recess of the Senate, by granting Commissions which shall expire at the End of their next Session.

Section 3. He shall from time to time give to the Congress Information of the State of the Union, and recommend to their Consideration such Measures as he shall judge necessary and expedient; he may, on extraordinary Occasions, convene both Houses, or either of them, and in Case of Disagreement between them, with Respect to the Time of Adjournment, he may adjourn them to such Time as he shall think proper; he shall receive Ambassadors and other public Ministers; he shall take Care that the Laws be faithfully executed, and shall Commission all the Officers of the United States.

Section 4. The President, Vice President and all civil Officers of the United States, shall be removed from Office on Impeachment for, and Conviction of, Treason, Bribery, or other high Crimes and Misdemeanors.

Article III

Section 1. The judicial Power of the United States, shall be vested in one supreme Court, and in such inferior Courts as the Congress may from time to time ordain and establish. The Judges, both of the supreme and inferior Courts, shall hold their Offices during good Behaviour, and shall, at stated Times, receive for their Services a Compensation, which shall not be diminished during their Continuance in Office.

Section 2. (1) The judicial Power shall extend to all Cases, in Law and Equity, arising under this Constitution, the Laws of the United States, and Treaties made, or which shall be made, under their Authority;—to all Cases affecting Ambassadors, other public Ministers and Consuls;—to all Cases of admiralty and maritime Jurisdiction;—to Controversies to which the United States shall be a Party;—to Controversies between two or more States;—between a State and Citizens of another State,[8]—between Citizens of different states;—between Citizens of the same State claiming Lands under the Grants of different States, and between a State, or the Citizens thereof, and foreign States, Citizens or Subjects.

(2) In all Cases affecting Ambassadors, other public Ministers and Consuls, and those in which a State shall be a Party, the supreme Court shall have original Jurisdiction. In all the other Cases before mentioned, the supreme Court shall have appellate Jurisdiction, both as to Law and Fact, with such Exceptions, and under such Regulations as the Congress shall make.

(3) The trial of all Crimes, except in Cases of Impeachment, shall be by Jury; and such Trial shall be held in the State where the said Crimes shall have been committed; but when not committed within any State, the Trial shall be at such Place or Places as the Congress may by Law have directed.

Section 3. (1) Treason against the United States, shall consist only in levying War against them, or, in adhering to their enemies, giving them Aid and Comfort. No Person shall be convicted of Treason unless on the Testimony of two Witnesses to the same overt Act, or on Confession in open Court.

[8]Refer to the Eleventh Amendment.

(2) The Congress shall have Power to declare the Punishment of Treason, but no Attainder of Treason shall work Corruption of Blood, or Forfeiture except during the Life of the Person attainted.

Article IV

Section 1. Full Faith and Credit shall be given in each State to the public Acts, Records, and judicial Proceedings of every other State. And the Congress may by general Laws prescribe the Manner in which such Acts, Records and Proceedings shall be proved, and the Effect thereof.

Section 2. (1) The Citizens of each State shall be entitled to all Privileges and Immunities of Citizens in the several States.

(2) A Person charged in any State with Treason, Felony, or other Crime, who shall flee from Justice, and be found in another State, shall on demand of the executive Authority of the State from which he fled, be delivered up, to be removed to the State having Jurisdiction of the Crime.

(3) No Person held to Service or Labour in one State, under the Laws thereof, escaping into another, shall, in Consequence of any Law or Regulation therein, be discharged from such Service or Labour, but shall be delivered up on Claim of the Party to whom such Service or Labour may be due.[9]

Section 3. (1) New States may be admitted by the Congress into this Union; but no new State shall be formed or erected within the Jurisdiction of any other State; nor any State be formed by the Junction of two or more States, or Parts of States without the Consent of the Legislatures of the States concerned as well as of the Congress.

(2) The Congress shall have Power to dispose of and make all needful Rules and Regulations respecting the Territory or other Property belonging to the United States; and nothing in this Constitution shall be so construed as to Prejudice any Claims of the United States, or of any particular State.

Section 4. The United States shall guarantee to every State in this Union a Republican Form of Government, and shall protect each of them against Invasion; and on Application of the Legislature, or of the Executive (when the Legislature cannot be convened) against domestic Violence.

Article V

The Congress, whenever two thirds of both Houses shall deem it necessary, shall propose Amendments to this Constitution, or, on the Application of the Legislatures of two thirds of the several States, shall call a Convention for proposing Amendments, which, in either Case, shall be valid to all Intents and Purposes, as part of this Constitution, when ratified by the Legislatures of three fourths of the several States, or by Conventions in three fourths thereof, as the one or the other Mode of Ratification may be proposed by the Congress; Provided that no Amendment which may be made prior to the Year One thousand eight hundred and eight shall in any Manner affect the first and fourth Clauses in the Ninth Section

[9]Refer to the Thirteenth Amendment.

of the first Article; and that no State, without its Consent, shall be deprived of its equal Suffrage in the Senate.

Article VI

(1) All Debts contracted and Engagements entered into, before the Adoption of this Constitution shall be as valid against the United States under this Constitution, as under the Confederation.

(2) This Constitution, and the Laws of the United States which shall be made in Pursuance thereof; and all Treaties made, or which shall be made, under the Authority of the United States, shall be the supreme Law of the Land; and the Judges in every State shall be bound thereby, any Thing in the Constitution or Laws of any State to the Contrary notwithstanding.

(3) The Senators and Representatives before mentioned, and the Members of the several State Legislatures, and all executive and judicial Officers, both of the United States and of the several States, shall be bound by Oath or Affirmation, to support this Constitution, but no religious Test shall ever be required as a Qualification to any Office or public Trust under the United States.

Article VII

The Ratification of the Conventions of nine States shall be sufficient for the Establishment of this Constitution between the States so ratifying the Same.
[Amendments 1 to 10, the Bill of Rights, were ratified in 1791.]

Amendment I

Congress shall make no law respecting an establishment of religion, or prohibiting the free exercise thereof; or abridging the freedom of speech, or of the press; or the right of the people peaceably to assemble, and to petition the Government for a redress of grievances.

Amendment II

A well regulated Militia, being necessary to the security of a free State, the right of the people to keep and bear Arms, shall not be infringed.

Amendment III

No Soldier shall, in time of peace be quartered in any house, without the consent of the Owner, nor in time of war, but in a manner to be prescribed by law.

Amendment IV

The right of the people to be secure in their persons, houses, papers, and effects, against unreasonable searches and seizures, shall not be violated, and no Warrants shall issue, but upon probable cause, supported by Oath or affirmation, and particularly describing the place to be searched, and the persons or things to be seized.

Amendment V

No person shall be held to answer for a capital, or otherwise infamous crime, unless on a presentment or indictment of a Grand Jury, except in cases arising in the land or naval forces, or in the Militia, when in actual service in time of War or public danger; nor shall any person be subject for the same offence to be twice put in jeopardy of life or limb; nor shall be compelled in any criminal case to be a witness against himself, nor be deprived of life, liberty, or property, without due process of law; nor shall private property be taken for public use, without just compensation.

Amendment VI

In all criminal prosecutions, the accused shall enjoy the right to a speedy and public trial, by an impartial jury of the State and district wherein the crime shall have been committed, which district shall have been previously ascertained by law, and to be informed of the nature and cause of the accusation; to be confronted with the witness against him; to have compulsory process for obtaining witnesses in his favor, and to have the Assistance of Counsel for his defence.

Amendment VII

In Suits at common law, where the value in controversy shall exceed twenty dollars, the right of trial by jury shall be preserved, and no fact tried by jury, shall be otherwise reexamined in any Court of the United States, than according to the rules of the common law.

Amendment VIII

Excessive bail shall not be required, nor excessive fines imposed, nor cruel and unusual punishments inflicted.

Amendment IX

The enumeration in the Constitution, of certain rights, shall not be construed to deny or disparage others retained by the people.

Amendment X

The powers not delegated to the United States by the Constitution, nor prohibited by it to the States, are reserved to the States respectively, or to the people.

Amendment XI [1798]

The Judicial power of the United States shall not be construed to extend to any suit in law or equity, commenced or prosecuted against one of the United States by Citizens of another State, or by Citizens or Subjects of any Foreign State.

Amendment XII [1804]

The Electors shall meet in their respective states and vote by ballot for President and Vice-President, one of whom, at least, shall not be an inhabitant of the same state with themselves; they shall name in their ballots the person voted for as President, and in distinct ballots the person voted for as Vice-President, and they shall make distinct lists of all persons voted for as President, and of all persons voted for as Vice-President, and of the number of votes for each, which lists they shall sign and certify, and transmit sealed to the seat of the government of the United States, directed to the President of the Senate;—The President of the Senate shall, in the presence of the Senate and House of Representatives, open all the certificates and the votes shall then be counted;—The person having the greatest number of votes for President, shall be the President, if such number be a majority of the whole number of Electors appointed; and if no person have such majority, then from the persons having the highest numbers not exceeding three on the list of those voted for as President, the House of Representatives shall choose immediately, by ballot, the President. But in choosing the President, the votes shall be taken by states, the representation from each state having one vote; a quorum for this purpose shall consist of a member or members from two-thirds of the states, and a majority of all the states shall be necessary to a choice. And if the House of Representatives shall not choose a President whenever the right of choice shall devolve upon them before the fourth day of March next following, then the Vice-President shall act as President, as in the case of the death or other constitutional disability of the President.[10]—The person having the greatest number of votes as Vice-President, shall be the Vice-President, if such number be a majority of the whole number of Electors appointed, and if no person have a majority, then from the two highest numbers on the list, the Senate shall choose the Vice-President; a quorum for the purpose shall consist of two-thirds of the whole number of Senators, and a majority of the whole number shall be necessary to a choice. But no person constitutionally ineligible to the office of President shall be eligible to that of Vice-President of the United States.

Amendment XIII [1865]

Section 1. Neither slavery nor involuntary servitude, except as a punishment for crime whereof the party shall have been duly convicted, shall exist within the United States, or any place subject to their jurisdiction.

Section 2. Congress shall have power to enforce this article by appropriate legislation.

[10]Refer to the Twentieth Amendment.

Amendment XIV [1868]

Section 1. All persons born or naturalized in the United States, and subject to the jurisdiction thereof, are citizens of the United States and of the State wherein they reside. No State shall make or enforce any law which shall abridge the privileges or immunities of citizens of the United States; nor shall any State deprive any person of life, liberty, or property, without due process of law; nor deny to any person within its jurisdiction the equal protection of the laws.

Section 2. Representatives shall be apportioned among the several States according to their respective numbers, counting the whole number of persons in each State, excluding Indians not taxed. But when the right to vote at any election for the choice of electors for President and Vice President of the United States, Representatives in Congress, the Executive and Judicial officers of a State, or the members of the Legislature thereof, is denied to any of the male inhabitants of such State, being twenty-one years of age,[11] and citizens of the United States, or in any way abridged, except for participation in rebellion, or other crime, the basis of representation therein shall be reduced in the proportion which the number of such male citizens shall bear to the whole number of male citizens twenty-one years of age in such State.

Section 3. No person shall be a Senator or Representative in Congress, or elector of President and Vice President, or hold any office, civil or military, under the United States, or under any State, who having previously taken an oath, as a member of Congress, or as an officer of the United States, or as a member of any State legislature, or as an executive or judicial officer of any State, to support the Constitution of the United States, shall have engaged in insurrection or rebellion against the same, or given aid or comfort to the enemies thereof. But Congress may by a vote of two thirds of each House, remove such disability.

Section 4. The validity of the public debt of the United States, authorized by law, including debts incurred for payment of pensions and bounties for services in suppressing insurrection or rebellion, shall not be questioned. But neither the United States nor any State shall assume or pay any debt or obligation incurred in aid of insurrection or rebellion against the United States, or any claim for the loss or emancipation of any slave; but all such debts, obligations and claims shall be held illegal and void.

Section 5. The Congress shall have power to enforce, by appropriate legislation, the provisions of this article.

Amendment XV [1870]

Section 1. The right of citizens of the United States to vote shall not be denied or abridged by the United States or by any State on account of race, color, or previous condition of servitude.

Section 2. The Congress shall have power to enforce this article by appropriate legislation.

[11]Refer to the Twenty-Sixth Amendment.

Amendment XVI [1913]

The Congress shall have power to lay and collect taxes on incomes, from whatever source derived, without apportionment among the several States, and without regard to any census or enumeration.

Amendment XVII [1913]

(1) The Senate of the United States shall be composed of two Senators from each State, elected by the people thereof, for six years; and each Senator shall have one vote. The electors in each State shall have the qualifications requisite for electors of the most numerous branch of the State legislatures.

(2) When vacancies happen in the representation of any State in the Senate, the executive authority of such State shall issue writs of election to fill such vacancies: *Provided,* That the legislature of any State may empower the executive thereof to make temporary appointments until the people fill the vacancies by election as the legislature may direct.

(3) This amendment shall not be so construed as to affect the election or term of any Senator chosen before it becomes valid as part of the Constitution.

Amendment XVIII [1919]

Section 1. After one year from the ratification of this article the manufacture, sale, or transportation of intoxicating liquors within, the importation thereof into, or the exportation thereof from the United States and all territory subject to the jurisdiction thereof for beverage purposes is hereby prohibited.

Section 2. The Congress and the several States shall have concurrent power to enforce this article by appropriate legislation.

Section 3. This article shall be inoperative unless it shall have been ratified as an amendment to the Constitution by the legislatures of the several States, as provided in the Constitution, within seven years from the date of the submission hereof to the States by the Congress.[12]

Amendment XIX [1920]

(1) The right of citizens of the United States to vote shall not be denied or abridged by the United States or by any State on account of sex.

(2) Congress shall have power to enforce this article by appropriate legislation.

Amendment XX [1933]

Section 1. The terms of the President and Vice President shall end at noon on the 20th day of January, and the terms of Senators and Representatives at noon on the 3rd day of

[12]Refer to the Twenty-First Amendment.

January, of the years in which such terms would have ended if this article had not been ratified; and the terms of their successors shall then begin.

Section 2. The Congress shall assemble at least once in every year, and such meeting shall begin at noon on the 3rd day of January, unless they shall by law appoint a different day.

Section 3. If, at the time fixed for the beginning of the term of the President, the President elect shall have died, the Vice President elect shall become President. If the President shall not have been chosen before the time fixed for the beginning of his term or if the President elect shall have failed to qualify, then the Vice President elect shall act as President until a President shall have qualified; and the Congress may by law provide for the case wherein neither a President elect nor a Vice President elect shall have qualified, declaring who shall then act as President, or the manner in which one is to act shall be selected, and such person shall act accordingly until a President or Vice President shall have qualified.

Section 4. The Congress may by law provide for the case of the death of any of the persons from whom the House of Representatives may choose a President whenever the right of choice shall have devolved upon them, and for the case of the death of any of the persons from whom the Senate may choose a Vice President whenever the right of choice shall have devolved upon them.

Section 5. Sections 1 and 2 shall take effect on the 15th day of October following the ratification of this article.

Section 6. This article shall be inoperative unless it shall have been ratified as an amendment to the Constitution by the legislatures of three-fourths of the several States within seven years from the date of its submission.

Amendment XXI [1933]

Section 1. The eighteenth article of amendment to the Constitution of the United States is hereby repealed.

Section 2. The transportation or importation into any State, Territory, or possession of the United States for delivery or use therein of intoxicating liquors, in violation of the laws thereof, is hereby prohibited.

Section 3. This article shall be inoperative unless it shall have been ratified as an amendment to the Constitution by conventions in the several States, as provided in the Constitution, within seven years from the date of the submission hereof to the States by the Congress.

Amendment XXII [1951]

Section 1. No person shall be elected to the office of the President more than twice, and no person who has held the office of President, or acted as President, for more than two years of a term to which some other person was elected President shall be elected to the office of President more than once. But this Article shall not apply to any person holding the office of President when this Article was proposed by the Congress, and shall not prevent any person who may be holding the office of President, or acting as President, during the term within which this Article becomes operative from holding the office of President or acting as president during the remainder of such term.

Section 2. This article shall be inoperative unless it shall have been ratified as an amendment to the Constitution by the legislatures of three-fourths of the several States within seven years from the date of its submission to the States by the Congress.

Amendment XXIII [1961]

Section 1. The District constituting the seat of Government of the United States shall appoint in such manner as the Congress may direct:

A number of electors of President and Vice President equal to the whole number of Senators and Representatives in Congress to which the District would be entitled if it were a State, but in no event more than the least populous state; they shall be in addition to those appointed by the states, but they shall be considered, for the purposes of the election of President and Vice Prisident, to be electors appointed by a state; and they shall meet in the District and perform such duties as provided by the twelfth article of amendment.

Section 2. The Congress shall have power to enforce this article by appropriate legislation.

Amendment XXIV [1964]

Section 1. The right of citizens of the United States to vote in any primary or other election for President or Vice President, for electors for President or Vice President, or for Senator or Representative in Congress, shall not be denied or abridged by the United States or any State by reason of failure to pay any poll tax or other tax.

Section 2. The Congress shall have power to enforce this article by appropriate legislation.

Amendment XXV [1967]

Section 1. In case of the removal of the President from office or of his death or resignation, the Vice President shall become President.

Section 2. Whenever there is a vacancy in the office of the Vice President, the President shall nominate a Vice President who shall take office upon confirmation by a majority vote of both Houses of Congress.

Section 3. Whenever the President transmits to the President pro tempore of the Senate and the Speaker of the House of Representatives his written declaration that he is unable to discharge the powers and duties of his office, and until he transmits to them a written declaration to the contrary, such powers and duties shall be discharged by the Vice President as Acting President.

Section 4. Whenever the Vice President and a majority of either the principal officers of the executive departments or of such other body as Congress may by law provide, transmit to the President pro tempore of the Senate and the Speaker of the House of Representatives their written declaration that the President is unable to discharge the powers and duties of his office, the Vice President shall immediately assume the powers and duties of the office as Acting President.

Thereafter, when the President transmits to the President pro tempore of the Senate and the Speaker of the House of Representatives his written declaration that no inability exists, he shall resume the powers and duties of his office unless the Vice President and a majority of either the principal officers of the executive departments or of such other body as Congress may by law provide, transmit within four days to the President pro tempore of the Senate and the Speaker of the House of Representatives their written declaration that the President is unable to discharge the powers and duties of his office. Thereupon Congress shall decide the issue, assembling within forty-eight hours for that purpose if not in session. If the Congress, within twenty-one days after receipt of the latter written declaration, or, if Congress is not in session, within twenty-one days after Congress is required to assemble, determines by two-thirds vote of both Houses that the President is unable to discharge the powers and duties of his office, the Vice President shall continue to discharge the same as Acting President; otherwise, the President shall resume the powers and duties of his office.

Amendment XXVI [1971]

Section 1. The right of citizens of the United States, who are eighteen years of age or older, to vote shall not be denied or abridged by the United States or by any State on account of age.

Section 2. The Congress shall have power to enforce this article by appropriate legislation.

Amendment XXVII [1992]

No law, varying the compensation for the services of the Senators and Representatives, shall take effect, until an election of Representatives shall have intervened.

The Uniform Commercial Code

The Uniform Commercial Code, or UCC, was developed by the American Law Institute (ALI) and the National Conference of Commissioners on Uniform State Laws (NCCUSL) as a body of rules intended to make the application of law to commercial transactions consistent across fifty states. The UCC has been adopted in whole by all but one state legislature, Louisiana, which adopts only certain sections. Such widespread use of the UCC, even with the minor deviations some jurisdictions make from the official code, makes possible more efficient and more confident transactions across state lines.

We reference UCC Articles 2 and 2(A) when discussing sales and leases of goods, respectively. These Articles, along with the rest of the UCC, can be accessed here: https://www.law.cornell.edu/ucc.

A

absolute privilege   In libel and slander law, situations where a defendant is entirely excused from liability for defamatory statements because of the circumstances under which the statements were made.

acceptance   The actual or implied receipt and retention of that which is tendered or offered.

accord and satisfaction   A legally binding agreement to settle a disputed claim for a definite amount.

accounting   The legal determination of a partnership interest's value.

accredited investor   Financial institutions, charities, directors and officers of the issuer, and individuals with annual net income of at least $200,000 and/or net worth of at least $1,000,000 (excluding their personal residence). Such persons are presumed to understand, and be able to withstand the risk associated with, securities investments.

actus reus   Wrongful act or omission.

adjustment of debts   Individuals with limited debts are protected from creditors while paying their debts in installments (Chapter 13 bankruptcy).

affidavit   A written statement sworn to by a person officially empowered to administer an oath.

affirmative action   A government or private-sector program, springing from the civil rights movement, designed to actively promote the employment or educational opportunities of protected classes rather than merely forbidding discrimination.

affirmative defense   A portion of a defendant's answer to a complaint in which defendant presents contentions that, if proved true, will relieve the defendant of liability even if the assertions in the complaint are correct.

agreement   A meeting of the minds based on an offer by one party and acceptance by another.

answer   The defendant's first pleading in a lawsuit, in which the defendant responds to the allegations raised in the plaintiff's complaint.

appellant   The party filing an appeal.

appellee   The party against whom an appeal is filed.

arbitration   An extrajudicial process in which a dispute is submitted to a mutually agreeable third party for a decision.

arraignment   A criminal law proceeding in which a defendant is brought before a judge to be informed of the charges and to file a plea.

articles of dissolution   The document filed with the state to dissolve a corporation.

articles of incorporation   The document filed with a state to create a corporation.

articles of organization   The document filed with a state to create a limited liability company.

assault   A show of force that would cause reasonable persons to believe that they are about to receive an intentional, unwanted, harmful physical touching.

assignee   The person to whom an assignment is made.

assignment   A transfer of property, or some right or interest therein, from one person to another.

assignor   The maker of an assignment.

assumption of risk   An affirmative defense in a negligence case in which the defendant seeks to bar recovery by the plaintiff by showing that the plaintiff knowingly exposed himself or herself to the danger that resulted in injury.

audited financial statements   Income statement, balance sheet, statement of cash flows, and other items prepared by management and audited by an independent certified public accountant to ensure the disclosures are made in accordance with generally accepted accounting principles.

B

balance sheet   Financial statement showing a business's assets, liabilities, and equity at a point in time.

battery   An intentional, unwanted, harmful physical touching.

beneficiary   In the context of fiduciary duties, the person on whose behalf the fiduciary is acting.

beyond a reasonable doubt   The level of proof required for conviction in a criminal case.

bilateral contract   A contract formed by an offer requiring a reciprocal promise.

blue laws   Laws forbidding certain kinds of business on Sundays.

blue sky laws   State laws regulating the purchase and sale of securities in a manner similar to federal securities regulation. Unlike federal securities law, however, some states engage in a substantive review intended to evaluate the economic merits of the investment.

board of directors   The body elected by the shareholders to govern the corporation.

bona fide occupational qualification (BFOQ)   A defense in a discrimination claim where the employer argues that a particular religion, sex, or national origin is a necessary qualification for a particular job.

bonds   A long-term debt security issued to raise capital for a venture.

breach of contract   Failure, without legal excuse, to perform any promise that forms the whole or part of a contract.

bribe   Anything of value given or taken with the corrupt intent to influence an official in the performance of her or his duties.

broker   A person who acts as a sales agent in the purchase or sale of a security.

business judgment rule   A rule protecting business managers from liability for making bad decisions when they have acted in accordance with the fiduciary duties of loyalty and due care.

buy-sell agreement   A contract under which a shareholder is required to sell (or offer to sell) its stock to the corporation or another shareholder upon the occurrence of a specified event, such as leaving the corporation's employment or death.

bylaws   The document that governs the management and operation of an organization.

C

C corporation   All corporations that have not elected to be taxed as an S corporation. All corporations are C corporations by default.

capacity   The ability to incur legal obligations and acquire legal rights.

capital   In the finance context, the resources required by a venture to acquire its assets and operate. It is comprised of debt capital and equity capital.

capital structure   The relative use of debt and equity capital in financing a venture.

cease and desist order   A directive from an agency ordering a party to refrain from engaging in specified conduct.

certificate of limited partnership   The document filed with a state to create a limited partnership.

certified public accountant   An accounting professional licensed by a state to perform auditing and high-level tax services.

churning   Excessive purchasing and selling of securities by a broker to generate unwarranted fees resulting in financial harm to the investor.

civil law   The branch of law dealing with private rights. Contrast with **criminal law**.

closely held corporation   A corporation with relatively few shareholders, the stock of which is not traded on a public market. Also referred to as a *close corporation*.

commercial impracticability   The standard used by the Uniform Commercial Code (UCC) to relieve a party of his or her contract obligations because of the occurrence of unforeseeable, external events beyond his or her control.

common law   Judge-made law. To be distinguished from statutory law as created by legislative bodies.

common stock   The residual ownership interest in a corporation. It carries the rights to participate in control, earnings, and assets upon liquidation.

compensatory damages   Damages that will compensate a party for actual losses due to an injury suffered.

complaint   The first pleading filed by the plaintiff in a civil lawsuit.

concurrent conditions   When each party's obligation to perform under a contract is dependent on the other party's performance.

conditions precedent   Conditions that operate to give rise to a contracting party's duty to perform.

conditions subsequent   Conditions that operate to discharge one from an obligation under a contract.

consequential damages   Damages that do not flow directly and immediately from an act but rather flow from the results of the act.

consideration   A required element in an enforceable contract. The thing of value passing between the parties that results in a benefit to the one making the promise or a detriment to the one receiving the promise.

conversion   Wrongfully exercising control over the personal property of another.

corporate governance   The system of rules and processes by which the board of directors governs a corporation.

corporation   A form of business created under state law that is owned by shareholders who have no inherent right to manage the business. Corporations are governed by a board of directors elected by the shareholders and managed by a cadre of executives appointed by the board.

counterclaim   A cause of action filed by the defendant in a lawsuit against the plaintiff in the same suit.

counteroffer   Response by the offeree that, in its legal effect, constitutes a rejection of the original offer and proposes a new offer to the offeror.

creditor beneficiary   Person who has given consideration, who is an intended beneficiary of a contract though not a party, and thus is entitled to enforce the contract.

crime   A public wrong; an act punishable by the state.

criminal law   Wrongs against society that the state has seen fit to label as crimes and that may result in penalties against the perpetrator(s). Contrast with **civil law**.

crown jewel defense   A hostile takeover defense in which the target corporation prearranges to sell critical assets to a friendly third party, which will make them available should management successfully resist the takeover.

D

day trading   Purchasing and selling securities in rapid succession to exploit small, highly time-sensitive changes in market price.

dealer   In the securities context, a person who purchases securities hoping to profit from their resale.

debt capital   Resources obtained from lenders to acquire assets and conduct operations.

debt covenant   Promises made by a borrower in a lending agreement for the protection of the creditors.

deceit   A tort involving intentional misrepresentation to deceive or trick another.

defamation   A false and intentional verbal or written expression that damages the reputation of another.

default judgment   A judgment entered by the court in favor of the plaintiff because the defendant failed to respond to the plaintiff's complaint.

deposition   A discovery procedure wherein a witness's sworn testimony is taken out of court, prior to trial, for subsequent use at trial.

directed verdict   A party to a lawsuit makes a motion asking the judge to instruct the jury to reach a particular decision because reasonable minds could not differ about the correct outcome of the case.

director   A person elected by the shareholders to govern, along with the other members of the board, the corporation. Individual directors have no authority; only when they act as a board do directors have the power to govern.

discovery   Legal procedures by which one party to a litigation may obtain information from the other party. Depositions and interrogatories are examples of discovery procedures.

disgorgement   The forfeiture of ill-gotten gains.

dissociation   The cessation of a person's status as a partner without causing the partnership's dissolution.

dissolution   The termination of an entity's existence.

dividend   A distribution by a corporation to a shareholder, typically out of earnings.

donee beneficiary   Person who has not given consideration but is an intended beneficiary of a contract, though not a party, and is entitled to enforce the contract.

double jeopardy   The U.S. Constitution provides that the same individual may not be tried twice in the same tribunal for the same criminal offense.

double taxation   The fact that a corporation is first taxed on its income, after which the shareholders are taxed again on that income when it is distributed to them as dividends.

due diligence   A defense in a securities action involving a materially misleading statement or omission in a registration statement. The defendant must demonstrate that a reasonable investigation was undertaken to provide a plausible basis for believing the accuracy of the registration statement. Proving due diligence depends on whether the defendant is an expert; experts are held to a significantly higher standard.

duress   Overpowering of the will of a person by force or fear.

duty of due care   The standard of conduct expected of a reasonable, prudent person under the circumstances.

duty of loyalty   The standard of conduct that requires a person to act in the best interests of another.

E

equity   Fairness; a system of courts that developed in England. A chancellor presided to mete out fairness in cases that were not traditionally assigned to the law courts headed by the king.

equity capital   Resources obtained from owners to acquire assets and conduct operations.

exculpatory clause   Portion of a contract that seeks to relieve one of the parties to the contract from any liability for breach of duty under that contract.

executed   In contract law, full performance of the terms of the bargain.

executed contract   Performances are complete.

executory contract   Not yet fully performed or completed.

exempt security   A security that is not required to satisfy the full registration requirements under the 1933 Securities Act because of the nature of the issuer; for example, a government or financial institution.

exempt transaction   A form of security issuance that is not required to satisfy the full registration requirements under the 1933 Securities Act; for example, a private placement restricted to accredited investors.

express authorization   In contract law, offeror specifies a means of communication by which the offeree can accept.

express conditions   Conditions within contracts that are clear from the language.

F

false imprisonment   Tort of intentionally restricting the freedom of movement of another.

false light   Falsely and publicly attributing certain characteristics, conduct, or beliefs to another such that a reasonable person would be highly offended.

felony   A crime of a serious nature ordinarily involving punishment by death or imprisonment in a penitentiary.

fiduciary   One who holds a relationship of trust with another and has an obligation to act in the other's best interests. For example, the executor is the fiduciary of the estate's beneficiaries.

fiduciary duty   The responsibility of one in a position of trust with another to act in the best interests of the other.

firm offer   Under the Uniform Commercial Code (UCC), a signed, written offer by a merchant containing assurances that it will be held open, and which is not revocable for the time stated in the offer, or for a reasonable time if no such time is stated.

Form 8-K   The required filing with the SEC anytime an entity whose securities are publicly traded has a major event, such as the resignation of a director, a change in certified public accountants, or the breach of a bond covenant.

Form 10-K   The principal annual required filing with the SEC by entities whose securities are publicly traded. Contents include audited financial statements and management commentary on past performance and future prospects.

Form 10-Q   The required quarterly filing with the SEC by corporations whose securities are publicly traded. Unaudited interim financial statements are presented along with limited management commentary.

franchise   An arrangement in which the franchisor permits the franchisee to produce, distribute, and/or sell the franchisor's products or services using the franchisor's name, trademark, and other intangibles, including the rights to participate in the franchisor's supply chain and marketing programs, and to obtain consultation in franchise operation.

franchisee   The holder of a franchise.

franchisor   The party granting a franchise.

fraud   An intentional misrepresentation of a material fact with intent to deceive where the misrepresentation is justifiably relied on by another and damages result.

fraud-on-the-market theory   Misleading statements distort the market and thus defraud a securities buyer or seller regardless of whether that party relied on the actual misstatement. The theory is based on the assumption that a stock's price reflects all available information (a core tenet of the efficient markets hypothesis).

G

general jurisdiction   A court's authority to hear cases that arise within the geographical region over which the court has power. For example, California state courts have general jurisdiction over cases that arise in California.

general partner   A partner who participates in management and has unlimited liability for partnership obligations.

general partnership   A partnership in which all partners are general partners.

generally accepted accounting principles   Legally mandated rules for measuring and disclosing the amounts shown on financial statements.

generally accepted auditing standards   Legally mandated rules for performing audits.

genuineness of assent   In contract law, the parties knowingly agreed to the same thing.

going private   A transaction in which private investors buy all of the equity securities of a publicly held corporation.

going public   A reference to the first time an entity, typically a corporation, sells its equity interests (for example, corporate stock) in the public market.

golden parachute   An employment contract clause granting a generous severance package to an executive ousted in a hostile takeover.

greenmail   A hostile takeover defense involving the target corporation's repurchase of a takeover raider's stock at a premium not offered to other shareholders.

H

hostile takeover   The acquisition of control of a corporation by outsiders over the strong opposition of management.

hybrid form   A form of business that combines the characteristics of corporations and general partnerships.

I

implied authorization   In contract law, where the offeror's behavior or previous dealings with the offeree suggest an agreeable means of communicating an acceptance.

implied-in-fact conditions   Conditions derived from the parties' conduct and the circumstances of the bargain.

implied-in-fact contract   Contract whose terms are implicitly understood based on the behavior of the parties.

implied-in-law conditions or constructive conditions Conditions imposed by the court to avoid unfairness.

in personam jurisdiction   The power of the court over a person.

incidental beneficiary   Person who is not a party to a contract, who benefits indirectly from the contract, who was not contemplated by the parties, and who may not enforce the contract.

incidental damages   Collateral damages that are incurred because of a breach; damages that compensate a person injured by a breach of contract for reasonable costs incurred in an attempt to avoid further loss.

income statement   Financial statement showing revenues, expenses, gains, and losses, ultimately displaying net income or net loss.

incorporator   The person who files the articles of incorporation with a state to create a corporation.

indemnification   A corporate policy to compensate officers and directors for losses and costs sustained in defending themselves against litigation associated with their professional duties where those duties were performed in accordance with their fiduciary duties.

independent director   An outside director who has no relationship with the corporation that would improperly align the director's interests with those of management.

indictment   A grand jury's formal accusation of a crime.

information   A prosecutor's formal accusation of a crime.

initial public offering   A security offered for sale to the public for the first time.

injunction   A court order commanding a person to do or not do a specified action.

injurious falsehood   Intentional tort based on a false statement made with malice that disparages the property of another.

inside director   Director who is an officer or employee of the corporation.

insider   In the securities law context, anyone under a fiduciary duty who has knowledge of material facts not available to the general public.

insider trading   Trading securities while in possession of material nonpublic information in violation of a fiduciary duty.

intent   A conscious and purposeful state of mind.

intentional tort   Voluntary civil wrong causing harm to a protected interest.

interrogatories   An ingredient in the discovery process wherein one party in a lawsuit directs written questions to another party in the lawsuit.

Intersectional Discrimination   Occurs when an individual is discriminated against on combined protected bases such as national origin and religion.

interstate offering   Offering to sell a security to persons residing in states other than that in which the issuer is incorporated.

intrastate offerings   Offering to sell a security only to persons residing in the same state as that in which the issuer is incorporated.

intrusion   Wrongfully entering on or prying into the solitude or property of another.

invasion of privacy   Violation of the right to be left alone.

inversion   Reincorporating a corporation in a tax haven without any change in the location of the corporation's actual economic activities in order to reduce taxation in the United States.

investment contract   A form of security that is comprised of a contract, transaction, or scheme whereby a person invests money in a common enterprise and is led to expect profits solely from the efforts of someone else.

issuer   An entity, typically a corporation, that is offering to sell, or has already sold, a security to the public.

J

joint and several liability   The nature of a liability of a group of persons such that the plaintiff has the choice of suing all members of the group collectively, or only one member or a subset of members, for the entire amount.

judgment notwithstanding the verdict (judgment n.o.v.)
A judge's decision overruling the finding of the jury.

jurisdiction   The power of a judicial body to adjudicate a dispute. Also, the geographical area within which that judicial body has authority to operate.

L

lease   A contract for the possession and use of land or other property, including goods, on one side, and a recompense of rent or other income on the other.

legal detriment   Any act or forbearance by a promisee.

legal impossibility   A party to a contract is relieved of his or her duty to perform when that performance has become objectively impossible because of the occurrence of an event unforeseen at the time of contracting.

legality of purpose   The object of the contract does not violate law or public policy.

libel   Tort of defaming or injuring another's reputation by a published writing.

limited liability   The circumstance in which the investor's loss is limited to the amount invested in the venture.

limited liability company   A hybrid form of business combining the economic flexibility and tax advantages of a general partnership with the limited liability and other operating advantages of a corporation.

limited liability partnership   A partnership form providing enhanced limited liability.

limited partner   A partner in a limited partnership who does not participate in management and enjoys limited liability.

limited partnership   A partnership with at least one general partner who manages the business and has unlimited liability for partnership obligations, and with at least one limited partner who has no role in management but who enjoys limited liability.

liquidated damages   Damages made certain by the prior agreement of the parties.

liquidation   In the bankruptcy context, an action in which all assets (except those that are exempt) are distributed to creditors (Chapter 7 bankruptcy). In the business form context, the distribution of all assets, first to creditors and then to owners, followed by the termination of existence.

M

mailbox rule   Rule holding that a mailed acceptance is effective upon dispatch when the offeror has used the mail to invite acceptance; the rule has been expanded to include the use of any reasonable manner of acceptance.

malice   A required element of proof in a libel or slander claim by a public figure. Proof of a defamatory statement expressed with actual knowledge of its falsity or with reckless disregard for the truth would establish malice.

managing partner   A partner to whom the other partners have delegated most or all of their rights to participate in control.

market share liability   Product liability action by which plaintiffs may be able to recover against manufacturers of defective products based on those manufacturers' market shares even though proof of causation cannot be established.

materially misleading   A statement or omission of information by an issuer that has a high likelihood of leading a reasonable investor to form an incorrect judgment about a security.

mediation   An extrajudicial proceeding in which a third party (the mediator) attempts to assist disputing parties to reach an agreeable, voluntary resolution of their differences.

member   An owner of a limited liability company.

member's interest   The ownership interest of a limited liability company member.

mens rea   Evil intent.

misappropriation   In the securities law context, taking material, nonpublic information and engaging in insider trading in violation of a fiduciary duty. In the context of torts, wrongfully using an individual's name or image without permission for commercial purposes.

misdemeanor   A criminal offense less serious than a felony normally requiring a fine or less than a year in a jail other than a penitentiary.

mitigation   Obligation of a person who has been injured by a breach of a contract to attempt to reduce the damages.

mutual agency   The power of a general partner to bind the partnership in business matters.

mutual mistake   Where both parties to the contract are in error about a material fact.

N

necessaries   That which is reasonably necessary for a minor's proper and suitable maintenance.

negligence   Failure to do something that a reasonable person would do under the circumstances, or an action that a reasonable and prudent person would not take under the circumstances.

nominal damages   Small damages, oftentimes $1, awarded to show that there was a legal wrong even though the damages were very slight or nonexistent.

nuisance   A class of wrongs that arise from the unreasonable, unwarrantable, or unlawful use by a person of his or her property that produces material annoyance, inconvenience, discomfort, or hurt.

O

offer   A proposal by one person to another that is intended to create legal relations on acceptance by the person to whom it is made.

offeree   In the contract law context, one to whom an offer is made. In the securities law context, a person to whom a security is offered for sale.

officer   A person holding executive authority in an organization.

oligopoly   An economic condition in which the market for a particular good or service is controlled by a small number of producers or distributors.

operating agreement   The governing instrument of a limited liability company.

option contract   A separate contract in which an offeror agrees not to revoke her or his offer for a stated period in exchange for some valuable consideration.

ordinance   A law, rule, or regulation enacted by a local unit of government (such as a town or city).

outside director   Director who is neither an officer nor an employee of the corporation.

over-the-counter market   A computer network linking dealers to effectuate the purchase and sale of securities.

P

partner   An owner of a partnership.

partnership   An association of two or more persons who carry on a business a co-owners.

partnership agreement   The governing instrument of a partnership.

partnership interest   The ownership interest of a partner.

past consideration   Performance that is not bargained for and was not given in exchange for the promise.

peremptory challenge   An attorney's authority to dismiss prospective members of the jury without offering any justification for that dismissal.

personal property   Movable property. All property other than real estate.

physical exchange   A physical location at which agents of buyers and sellers deal directly with each other to effectuate the purchases and sales of securities.

piercing the corporate veil   Holding a shareholder responsible for acts of a corporation because of the shareholder's domination and improper use thereof.

pleadings   The formal entry of written statements by which the parties to a lawsuit set out their contentions and thereby formulate the issues on which the litigation will be based.

poison pill defense   A tactic to resist a hostile takeover, one version of which involves the target corporation prearranging a new issuance of a significant amount of common stock to existing shareholders at a discounted price.

post-effective period   In the securities law context, the period beginning after the SEC has approved the issuer's registration statement during which securities sales can be solicited and consummated.

preferred stock   Corporate ownership interests that enjoy a priority over common stock with respect to the rights to participate in earnings and assets upon liquidation, but that typically lack the right to participate in control.

prefiling period   In the securities law context, the time before the registration statement has been filed with the SEC during which securities sales can be neither solicited nor consummated.

private law   Individually determined agreement of the parties relating to choice of laws, where disagreements shall be settled, and the language of the transactions.

private placements   Securities sold without a public offering, thus eliminating most of the registration requirements of the Securities Act of 1933.

procedural rules   In administrative law, an agency's internal operating structure and methods.

promisee   The person to whom a promise is made.

promisor   A person who makes a promise to another.

promissory estoppel   An equitable doctrine that protects those who foreseeably and reasonably rely on the promises of others by enforcing such promises when enforcement is necessary to avoid injustice.

prospectus   A communication, usually in the form of a pamphlet, offering a security for sale and summarizing the information needed for a prospective buyer to evaluate it.

proximate cause   Occurrences that in a natural sequence, unbroken by potent intervening forces, produce an injury that would not have resulted in the absence of those occurrences.

proxy   Written permission from a shareholder to another to vote the share at a stockholders' meeting.

proxy fight   An attempt to oust corporate management by securing a sufficient number of proxies to take control of the board of directors.

public disclosure of private facts   Public disclosure of private facts where disclosure of the matter in question would be highly offensive to a reasonable person.

public law   Rules of national law that regulate transactions between parties, as well as the relationships between nations.

public policy   That which is good for the general public, as gleaned from a state's constitution, statutes, and case law.

publicly held corporation   A corporation with publicly traded shares. Also referred to as a **public corporation**.

punitive damages   Damages designed to punish flagrant wrongdoers and to deter them and others from engaging in similar conduct in the future.

Q

qualified privilege   In libel and slander law, situations where a defendant is excused from liability for defamatory statements except where the statements were motivated by malice.

quasi-contract   The doctrine by which courts imply, as a matter of law, a promise to pay the reasonable value of goods or services when the party receiving such goods or services has knowingly done so under circumstances that make it unfair to retain them without paying for them.

R

ratify   Adopting or affirming a prior, nonbinding act.

real property   Land, buildings, and things permanently attached to land or buildings.

reasonable person   Fictitious being the law constructs to determine whether a person's behavior falls short of what a "reasonable person" would do under the circumstances.

red herring prospectus   The draft securities prospectus included in the registration statement filed with the SEC. It does not constitute an offer to sell the security.

reformation   An equitable remedy in which a court effectively rewrites the terms of a contract.

registration statement   The document filed with the SEC with respect to a proposed issuance detailing the information needed to evaluate the security.

Regulation A+   The term used to describe the greatly expanded Regulation A pursuant to the Dodd–Frank Act amendments. For example, the $5 million annual cap was raised to $50 million.

release   Agreement to relinquish a right or a claim. Sometimes labeled a *waiver* or a *hold harmless clause*.

remand   To send back. For example, a higher court sends a case back to the lower court from which it came.

reorganization   A bankruptcy action in which creditors are kept from the debtor's assets while the debtor, under court supervision, works out a repayment plan and continues operations (Chapter 11 bankruptcy).

res ipsa loquitur   The thing speaks for itself. Rule of evidence establishing a presumption of negligence if the instrumentality causing the injury was in the exclusive control of the defendant, the injury would not ordinarily occur unless someone was negligent, and there is no evidence of other causes.

rescission   Canceling a contract; its effect is to restore the parties to their original position.

respondeat superior   "Let the master answer." The doctrine holding employers liable for acts (especially negligent acts) committed by employees when acting for the employer.

restitution   A remedy whereby one is able to obtain the return of that which she has given the other party, or an equivalent amount of money.

reverse   Overturn the decision of a court.

right of contribution   The right of a partner to be reimbursed by the other partners for its payment of a disproportionate amount of a partnership obligation.

risk–utility test   Measure of negligence holding that a product is negligently designed if the benefits of that product's design are outweighed by the risks that accompany that design.

S

S corporation   A closely held corporation whose shareholders have elected to be taxed in a manner similar to the way partners are taxed. Also referred to as a **subchapter S corporation**.

say-on-pay   The nonbinding shareholder resolution required by the SEC to be put to a vote before board approval of an executive compensation arrangement.

secrecy jurisdiction   A country that allows entities to be owned anonymously and that refuses to cooperate with other countries' investigations.

Securities and Exchange Commission   The federal regulatory agency, created in 1934, that is responsible for overseeing the securities markets.

securities crowdfunding   Raising equity and interest-paying debt capital from a large number of investors in relatively small amounts using the Internet and SEC-approved intermediaries to solicit and consummate the issuance of the security.

security   In the securities law context, stock, bonds, and investment contracts. In the debtor–creditor context, it refers to liens, promises, mortgages, or the like, given by a debtor to assure payment or performance on a debt.

shareholder   An owner of a corporation. Also referred to as a **stockholder**.

shareholder derivative suit   An action brought on behalf of a harmed corporation by a shareholder, usually for wrongs done to the corporation by directors or officers. All relief obtained inures to the benefit of the corporation, not to the shareholder bringing the action.

shelf registration   A registration that permits the issuer to hold the securities for sale until favorable market conditions emerge or the issuer needs the proceeds.

short-swing profits   Any profits made by an insider through the sale of a security within six months of acquisition. Insider trading is conclusively presumed.

slander   A defamatory statement orally communicated to at least one third party.

slander per se   Category of oral defamation not requiring proof of actual harm to recover.

small claims courts   Courts of limited powers designed to hear cases involving modest sums of money (typically limited to $2,000–$7,500, but some states permit recoveries of $15,000 or more) in hearings free of many of the formalities and burdens associated with the more conventional judicial process.

social business   A business form that is unique compared with for-profit to not-for-profit entities. Unlike a for-profit business, it is formed primarily to further a social objective, rather than to seek profit maximization. It is distinct from a not-for-profit enterprise because (1) it is intended to be economically self-sustaining and (2) its start-up capital is to be returned without interest.

sole proprietorship   A form of business in which one person owns and controls the business. The business is legally indistinguishable from the owner.

solicitation   Offering to sell a security.

sophisticated investor   A person with sufficient knowledge and experience in financial matters to need less protection under the securities laws (or a person advised by such a person).

specific performance   A contract remedy whereby the defendant is ordered to perform precisely according to the terms of her contract.

stare decisis   Let the decision stand. A doctrine of judicial procedure expecting a court to follow precedent in all cases involving substantially similar issues unless extremely compelling circumstances dictate a change in judicial direction.

stateless income   Income purportedly subject to taxation nowhere in the world.

statement of cash flows   Financial statement that identifies the reasons the cash balance changed over a period of time.

statement of qualification   The document filed with a state that creates a limited liability partnership.

Statute of Frauds   A statute specifying that certain contracts must be in writing to be enforceable.

statute of limitations   A statute requiring that certain classes of lawsuits must be brought within defined limits of time after the right to begin them accrued or the right is lost.

stock   The ownership interest of a shareholder.

stockholder   An owner of a corporation. Also referred to as a **shareholder**.

strict liability   Civil wrong springing from defective and "unreasonably dangerous" products where responsibility automatically attaches without proof of blame or fault.

subchapter S corporation A closely held corporation whose shareholders have elected to be taxed in a manner similar to the way partners are taxed. Also referred to as an *S corporation*.

subject-matter jurisdiction The authority of a particular court to judge a particular kind of dispute.

supplemental information All information in the registration statement other than the prospectus.

T

tax avoidance Minimizing taxes by lawful means.

tax evasion Minimizing taxes by unlawful means.

tax haven A country that offers exceptionally low tax rates on income, typically viewed as abetting tax evasion or highly aggressive tax avoidance.

tender offer A public offer to buy common stock at a specified price for a specified period of time.

tippee One who receives inside information about a security from another.

tipper One who conveys inside information about a security to another.

tombstone ad A securities advertisement that does not constitute an offer to sell, but rather informs the public that the security might be offered for sale in the future.

tort A civil wrong, not arising from a contract, for which a court will provide a remedy.

trading suspension The SEC-mandated suspension of trading in a security when serious misconduct or material misrepresentation is suspected.

trespass Entering the property of another without any right, lawful authority, or invitation.

tying arrangement Dealer agrees to sell or lease a product (the tying product) only on the condition that the buyer also purchases or leases another product (the tied product).

U

underwriter A finance professional who acts as the issuer's sales agent in a securities offering (best-efforts underwriter) or who buys the securities from the issuer hoping to profit from their resale to the public (firm-commitment underwriter).

unenforceable contract Meets basic requirements, but remains faulty.

unilateral contract A contract wherein the only acceptance of the offer that is necessary is the performance of the act.

unilateral mistake Where one party to a contract is in error about a material fact.

unjust enrichment An unearned benefit knowingly accepted.

usury Charging an interest rate exceeding the legally permissible maximum.

V

valid contract Effective; sufficient in law.

venture capitalists Those who invest in new, risky business ventures.

venue The specific geographic location in which a court holding jurisdiction should properly hear a case, given the convenience of the parties and other relevant considerations.

void contract Entirely null; no contract at all.

voidable contract Capable of being made void; enforceable but can be canceled.

voir dire The portion of a trial in which prospective jurors are questioned to determine their qualifications, including absence of bias, to sit in judgment in the case.

W

waiting period The time between filing the registration statement and SEC approval during which securities sales may not be consummated, but limited solicitation of interest may be undertaken.

CASE INDEX